ADVANCES IN NEURAL INFORMATION PROCESSING SYSTEMS 10

ADVANCES IN NEURAL INFORMATION PROCESSING SYSTEMS

Published by Morgan-Kaufmann

NIPS-1

Advances in Neural Information Processing Systems 1: Proceedings of the 1988 Conference,
David S. Touretzky, ed., 1989.

NIPS-2

Advances in Neural Information Processing Systems 2: Proceedings of the 1989 Conference,
David S. Touretzky, ed., 1990.

NIPS-3

Advances in Neural Information Processing Systems 3: Proceedings of the 1990 Conference,
Richard Lippmann, John E. Moody and David S. Touretzky, eds., 1991.

NIPS-4

Advances in Neural Information Processing Systems 4: Proceedings of the 1991 Conference,
John E. Moody, Stephen J. Hanson and Richard P. Lippmann, eds., 1992.

NIPS-5

Advances in Neural Information Processing Systems 5: Proceedings of the 1992 Conference,
Stephen J. Hanson, Jack D. Cowan and C. Lee Giles, eds., 1993.

NIPS-6

Advances in Neural Information Processing Systems 6: Proceedings of the 1993 Conference,
Jack D. Cowan, Gerald Tesauro and Joshua Alspector, eds., 1994.

Published by The MIT Press

NIPS-7

Advances in Neural Information Processing Systems 7: Proceedings of the 1994 Conference,
Gerald Tesauro, David S. Touretzky and Todd K. Leen, eds., 1995.

NIPS-8

Advances in Neural Information Processing Systems 8: Proceedings of the 1995 Conference,
David S. Touretzky, Michael C. Mozer and Michael E. Hasselmo, eds., 1996.

NIPS-9

Advances in Neural Information Processing Systems 9: Proceedings of the 1996 Conference,
Michael C. Mozer, Michael I. Jordan and Thomas Petsche, eds., 1997.

NIPS-10

Advances in Neural Information Processing Systems 10: Proceedings of the 1997 Conference,
Michael I. Jordan, Michael J. Kearns and Sara A. Solla, eds., 1998.

ADVANCES IN NEURAL INFORMATION PROCESSING SYSTEMS 10

Proceedings of the 1997 Conference

edited by
Michael I. Jordan, Michael J. Kearns and Sara A. Solla

A Bradford Book
The MIT Press
Cambridge, Massachusetts
London, England

This book was printed and bound in the United States of America.

ISSN: 1049-5258
ISBN: 0-262-10076-2

Contents

Part I Cognitive Science

Part II Neuroscience

Part III Theory

Part V   Implementation

Part VI   Speech, Handwriting and Signal Processing

Part VII   Visual Processing

Part VIII Applications

Part IX Control, Navigation and Planning

Preface

The papers in this volume describe the work presented at the Eleventh Annual Conference on Neural Information Processing (NIPS), held in Denver, Colorado from December 1 to December 6, 1997. The usual competitive standards for acceptance held again, with the 150 papers presented having been selected from 491 submissions.

NIPS is arguably one of the strongest and most ambitious interdisciplinary conferences, consistently bringing together top researchers in computer science, neuroscience, physics, statistics, and many related areas. The unifying topics are broad, such as the study of the brain, or interest in biological or computational mechanisms for learning. With such diverse participants and such large themes, it is natural to ask what holds NIPS together, and how it became the central technical gathering for so many of its participants. One way of expressing the answer is to say that the "relatedness graph" of the work presented at NIPS is not a clique, but is strongly connected. Thus, while it is an easy task to find two papers in these proceedings and ask how in the world they came to lie in the same volume, that same challenge can be met by a list of other papers that fill in the scientific "distance" between the initial pair. Thus the entry "Spectrotemporal Receptive Fields for Neurons in the Primary Auditory Cortex of the Awake Primate" (DeCharms and Merzenich), which describes the application of a clever reverse correlation technique to identify receptive fields for auditory neurons, is related in statistical spirit to "Using Helmholtz Machines to Analyze Multi-Channel Neuronal Recordings" (De Sa, DeCharms, and Merzenich), which models spike train data with multilayer generative models. This latter paper, in turn, shares an interest in hidden-variable representations of probability distributions with "A Revolution: Belief Propagation in Graphs with Cycles" (Frey and MacKay); which then has a common interest in information theory with "The Canonical Distortion Measure in Feature Space and 1-NN Classification" (Baxter and Bartlett). The point is not that the bonds between adjacent papers in this sequence are inherent and unbreakable; rather, it is that although the first and last papers are on rather different topics and from rather different communities, one can see how the interests of a single researcher might easily straddle any one of the links. We leave it as exercises for the ambitious reader to construct similar paths between "A Neural Network Model of Naive Preference and Filial Imprinting in the Domestic Chick" (Hadden) and "Phase Transitions and Perceptual Organization of Video Sequences" (Weiss), and between "Modeling Seasonality and Trends in Daily Rainfall Data" (Williams) and "Extended ICA Removes Artifacts in White Blood Cell Identification" (Song et al.). While we have not worked these particular examples out, we are confident that reasonably short solutions exist.

In addition to the strong program of submitted papers, the conference also featured a lively schedule of invited speakers. Ken Nakayama of Harvard gave the banquet talk on "Psychological Studies of Visual Perception", and invited talks were given by Yoav Freund of AT&T Labs ("Boosting: A New Method for Combining Classifiers"), John Hopfield of Princeton University ("Computing with Action Potentials"), John Kauer of Tufts University ("Odor Encoding by the Olfactory System — from Biology to a Receptorless Artificial Nose"), Stuart Russell of U.C. Berkeley ("Learning in Rational Agents"), and Manfred Warmuth of U.C. Santa Cruz ("Relative Loss Bounds, the Minimum Relative Entropy Principle, and EM"). As is traditional, the main conference was again preceded by a day of tutorials introducing current topics of interest to the uninitiated, and followed by two days of intensive workshops on a collection of topics that again reflects the focused diversity that is the strength of NIPS.

The continued success of NIPS is the result of many hours of hard work by a large and distributed group of devoted individuals. We extend many thanks to the members of the organizing committee, the program committee, the publicity committee and the NIPS Foundation board. Special gratitude is due to the referees, whose efforts are clearly shown in the quality of the papers gathered here. Thanks to the workshop chairs Steven Nowlan and Richard Zemel, tutorials chair Satinder Singh, publicity chair Tony Bell, treasurer Bartlett Mel, and local arrangements chair Arun Jagota. A special thanks to Thomas Petsche, who in his role of Publication Chair for NIPS*96 developed an excellent and comprehensive set of formatting tools for the production of both the Conference Program and the NIPS Proceedings. Finally, many thanks to Denise Prull of Conference Consulting Associates for her excellent and professional work, and to the many student volunteers who helped with conference logistics. We are also grateful to the Office of Naval Research for providing financial support to allow many graduate students and young investigators to attend the meeting.

Michael I. Jordan, Massachusetts Institute of Technology
Michael J. Kearns, AT&T Labs – Research
Sara A. Solla, Northwestern University

January 24, 1998

NIPS Committees

Organizing Committee

General Chair	*Michael Jordan*, MIT
Program Chair	*Michael Kearns*, AT&T Labs – Research
Workshop Co-Chairs	*Steven Nowlan*, Lexicus Division, Motorola
	Richard Zemel, University of Arizona
Tutorials Chair	*Satinder Singh*, University of Colorado
Publicity Chair	*Tony Bell*, Salk Institute
Publications Chair	*Sara Solla*, Northwestern University
Treasurer	*Bartlett Mel*, University of Southern California
Local Arrangements Chair	*Arun Jagota*, UC Santa Cruz

Program Committee

Program Chair	*Michael Kearns*, AT&T Labs – Research
Algorithms and Architectures	*Joachim Buhmann*, University of Bonn
	Tom Dietterich, Oregon State University
	Lawrence Saul, AT&T Labs – Research
	Jude Shavlik, University of Wisconsin
Theory	*Naftali Tishby*, Hebrew University
	Michael Turmon, Jet Propulsion Lab
Vision	*Paul Viola*, MIT
Speech and Signal Processing	*Richard Lippmann*, MIT Lincoln Lab
Control and Navigation	*Rich Sutton*, University of Massachusetts
Artificial Intelligence & Cognitive Science	*Sue Becker*, McMaster University
Neuroscience	*Tony Zador*, Salk Institute
Applications	*John Wawrzynek*, UC Berkeley
Implementations	*John Wawrzynek*, UC Berkeley

Publicity Committee

Publicity Chair	*Tony Bell*, Salk Institute
Liason for Australia, Singapore and India	*Marwan Jabri*, University of Sydney
Liason for Europe	*Joachim Buhmann*, University of Bonn
Liason for Hong Kong, China and Taiwan	*Lei Xu*, Chinese University of Hong Kong
Liason for Israel	*Hava Siegelmann*, Technion
Liason for Japan	*Kenji Doya*, ATR Research Laboratories
Liason for Turkey	*Ethem Alpaydin*, Bogazici University
Liason for United Kingdom	*Alan Murray*, Edinburgh Univesity
Liason for South America	*Andreas Meier*, Simon Bolivar University
Web Master	*Doug Baker*, Carnegie Mellon University

NIPS Foundation Board Members

Reviewers

Joshua Alspector
Charles Anderson
James Anderson
Timothy Anderson
Krste Asanovic
Chris Atkeson
Leemon Baird
Pierre Baldi
Shumeet Baluja
Naama Barkai
Marian Bartlett
Peter Bartlett
Hans-Ulrich Bauer
Jon Baxter
Francoise Beaufays
Yoshua Bengio
Michael Berry
Bill Bialek
Michael Biehl
Kwabena Boahen
Leon Bottou
Herve Bourlard
Matthew Brand
Emanuela Bricolo
Timothy Brown
Nader Bshouty
Neil Burgess
Paul Bush
Rich Caruana
Gert Cauwenberghs
Eric Chang
Gerald Cheang
Corinna Cortes
Gary Cottrell
Mark Craven
Peter Dayan
Joachim Diederich
Charles Elkan
Terry Fine
Gary Flake
Paolo Frasconi
Yoav Freund

Brendan Frey
Nir Friedman
Juergen Fritsch
Patrick Gallinari
Davi Geiger
Zoubin Ghahramani
Lee Giles
Federico Girosi
Moises Goldszmidt
Marco Gori
Michael Gray
Rod Grupen
Isabelle Guyon
David Hansel
Lars Hansen
John Harris
Trevor Hastie
Simon Haykin
David Heckerman
John Hertz
Andreas Herz
Geoffrey Hinton
Thomas Hofmann
Sean Holden
David Horn
Nathan Intrator
Tommi Jaakkola
Marwan Jabri
Robert Jacobs
Charles Jankowski
Mike Jones
Michael Jordan
Leslie Kaelbling
Bert Kappen
Mitsuo Kawato
Hiroaki Kitano
Adam Kowalczyk
John Lazzaro
Yvan Leclerc
Yann LeCun
Tai Sing Lee
Todd Leen

Zhaoping Li
Jennifer Linden
Christiane Linster
Michael Littman
David Lowe
Gabor Lugosi
Wolfgang Maass
David Madigan
Sridhar Mahadevan
Zach Mainen
Andrew McCallum
Marina Meila
Ron Meir
Bartlett Mel
Risto Miikkulainen
David Miller
Kenneth Miller
Tom Mitchell
Eric Mjolsness
John Moody
Andrew Moore
Javier Movellan
Michael Mozer
Klaus Mueller
Sayandev Mukherjee
Paul Munro
Alan Murray
Venkatesh Murthy
Radford Neal
Kenney Ng
Anna Nobre
Bruno Olshausen
David Opitz
Manfred Opper
Michael Oren
Art Owen
Klaus Pawelzik
Barak Pearlmutter
John Pearson
Fernando Pereira
Thomas Petsche
James Pittman

John Platt
Alexandre Pouget
Jose Principe
Rajesh Rao
Anand Rangarajan
Steve Renals
Martin Riedmiller
Brian Ripley
Raphael Ritz
Tony Robinson
David Saad
Maneesh Sahani
Stefan Schaal
Dale Schuurmans
Sebastian Seung
Patrice Simard

Eero Simoncelli
Yoram Singer
Satinder Singh
Diana Smetters
Padhraic Smyth
Haim Sompolinsky
Eduardo Sontag
Paul Stolorz
Gene Stoner
Josh Tenenbaum
Gerald Tesauro
Geoffrey Towell
Volker Tresp
Todd Troyer
John Tsitsiklis
Ian Underwood

Lyle Ungar
Joachim Utans
Benjamin VanRoy
Rita Venturini
Grace Wahba
Eric Wan
Manfred Warmuth
Daphna Weinshall
Yair Weiss
Janet Wiles
Christopher Williams
Ronald Williams
Laurenz Wiskott
David Wolpert
George Zavaliagkos
Richard Zemel

PART I
COGNITIVE SCIENCE

Synchronized Auditory and Cognitive 40 Hz Attentional Streams, and the Impact of Rhythmic Expectation on Auditory Scene Analysis

Bill Baird
Dept Mathematics, U.C.Berkeley, Berkeley, Ca. 94720.
baird@math.berkeley.edu

Abstract

We have developed a neural network architecture that implements a theory of attention, learning, and trans-cortical communication based on adaptive synchronization of 5-15 Hz and 30-80 Hz oscillations between cortical areas. Here we present a specific higher order cortical model of attentional networks, rhythmic expectancy, and the interaction of higher-order and primary cortical levels of processing. It accounts for the "mismatch negativity" of the auditory ERP and the results of psychological experiments of Jones showing that auditory stream segregation depends on the rhythmic structure of inputs. The timing mechanisms of the model allow us to explain how relative timing information such as the relative order of events between streams is lost when streams are formed. The model suggests how the theories of auditory perception and attention of Jones and Bregman may be reconciled.

1 Introduction

Amplitude patterns of synchronized "gamma band" (30 to 80 Hz) oscillation have been observed in the ensemble activity (local field potentials) of vertebrate olfactory, visual, auditory, motor, and somatosensory cortex, and in the retina, thalamus, hippocampus, reticular formation, and EMG. Such activity has not only been found in primates, cats, rabbits and rats, but also insects, slugs, fish, amphibians, reptiles, and birds. This suggests that gamma oscillation may be as fundamental to neural processing at the network level as action potentials are at the cellular level.

We have shown how oscillatory associative memories may be coupled to recognize and generate sequential behavior, and how a set of novel mechanisms utilizing these complex dynamics can be configured to solve attentional and perceptual processing problems. For pointers to full treatment with mathematics and complete references see [Baird et al., 1994]. An important element of intra-cortical communication in the brain, and between modules in this architecture, is the ability of a module to detect and respond to the proper input signal from a particular module, when inputs from other modules which are irrelevant to the present computation are contributing crosstalk noise. We have demonstrated that selective control of synchronization, which we hypothesize to be a model of "attention", can be used to solve this coding problem and control program flow in an architecture with dynamic attractors [Baird et al., 1994].

Using dynamical systems theory, the architecture is constructed from recurrently interconnected oscillatory associative memory modules that model higher order sensory and motor areas of cortex. The modules learn connection weights between themselves which cause the system to evolve under a 5-20 Hz clocked sensory-motor processing cycle by a sequence of transitions of synchronized 30-80 Hz oscillatory attractors within the modules. The architecture employs selective"attentional" control of the synchronization of the 30-80 Hz gamma band oscillations between modules to direct the flow of computation to recognize and generate sequences. The 30-80 Hz attractor amplitude patterns code the information content of a cortical area, whereas phase and frequency are used to "softwire" the network, since only the synchronized areas communicate by exchanging amplitude information. The system works like a broadcast network where the unavoidable crosstalk to all areas from previous learned connections is overcome by frequency coding to allow the moment to moment operation of attentional communication only between selected task-relevant areas.

The behavior of the time traces in different modules of the architecture models the temporary appearance and switching of the synchronization of 5-20 and 30-80 Hz oscillations between cortical areas that is observed during sensorimotor tasks in monkeys and humans. The architecture models the 5-20 Hz evoked potentials seen in the EEG as the control signals which determine the sensory-motor processing cycle. The 5-20 Hz clocks which drive these control signals in the architecture model thalamic pacemakers which are thought to control the excitability of neocortical tissue through similar nonspecific biasing currents that cause the cognitive and sensory evoked potentials of the EEG. The 5-20 Hz cycles "quantize time" and form the basis of derived somato-motor rhythms with periods up to seconds that entrain to each other in motor coordination and to external rhythms in speech perception [Jones et al., 1981].

1.1   Attentional Streams of Synchronized 40 Hz Activity

There is extensive evidence for the claim of the model that the 30-80 Hz gamma band activity in the brain accomplishes attentional processing, since 40 Hz appears in cortex when and where attention is required. For example, it is found in somatosensory, motor and premotor cortex of monkeys when they must pick a rasin out of a small box, but not when a habitual lever press delivers the reward. In human attention experiments, 30-80 Hz activity goes up in the contralateral auditory areas when subjects are instructed to pay attention to one ear and not the other. Gamma activity declines in the dominant hemisphere along with errors in a learnable target and distractors task, but not when the distractors and target vary at random on each trial. Anesthesiologists use the absence of 40 Hz activity as a reliable indicator of unconsciousness. Recent work has shown that cats with convergent and divergent strabismus who fail on tasks where perceptual binding is required also do not exhibit cortical synchrony. This is evidence that gamma synchronization is perceptually functional and not epiphenomenal.

The architecture illustrates the notion that synchronization of gamma band activity not only"binds" the features of inputs in primary sensory cortex into "objects", but further binds the activity of an attended object to oscillatory activity in associational and higher-order sensory and motor cortical areas to create an evolving attentional network of intercommunicating cortical areas that directs behavior. The binding of sequences of attractor transitions between modules of the architecture by synchronization of their activity models the physiological mechanism for the formation of perceptual and cognitive "streams" investigated by Bregman [Bregman, 1990], Jones [Jones et al., 1981], and others. In audition, according to Bregman's work, successive events of a sound source are bound together into a distinct sequence or "stream" and segregated from other sequences so that one pays attention to only one sound source at a time (the cocktail party problem). Higher order cortical or "cognitive" streams are in evidence when subjects are unable to recall the relative order of the telling of events between two stories told in alternating segments.

MEG tomographic observations show large scale rostral to caudal motor-sensory sweeps of coherent thalamo-cortical 40Hz activity accross the entire brain, the phase of which is reset by sensory input in waking, but not in dream states [Llinas and Ribary, 1993]. This suggests an inner higher order "attentional stream" is constantly cycling between motor (rostral) and sensory (caudal) areas in the absence of input. It may be interrupted by input "pop out" from primary areas or it may reach down as a "searchlight" to synchronize with particular ensembles of primary activity to be attended.

2   Jones Theory of Dynamic Attention

Jones [Jones et al., 1981] has developed a psychological theory of attention, perception, and motor timing based on the hypothesis that these processes are organized by neural rhythms in the range of 10 to .5 Hz – the range within which subjects perceive periodic events as a rhythm. These rhythms provide a multiscale representation of time and selectively synchronize with the prominant periodicities of an input to provide a temporal expectation mechanism for attention to target particular points in time.

For example, some work suggests that the accented parts of speech create a rhythm to which listeners entrain. Attention can then be focused on these expected locations as recognition anchor points for inference of less prominant parts of the speech stream. This is the temporal analog of the body centered spatial coordinate frame and multiscale covert attention window system in vision. Here the body centered temporal coordinates of the internal time base orient by entrainment to the external rhythm, and the window of covert temporal attention can then select a level of the multiscale temporal coordinates.

In this view, just as two cortical areas must synchronize to communicate, so must two nervous systems. Work using frame by frame film analysis of human verbal interaction, shows evidence of "interactional synchrony" of gesture and body movement changes and EEG of both speaker and listener with the onsets of phonemes in speech at the level of a 10 Hz "microrhythm" – the base clock rate of our models. Normal infants synchronize their spontaneous body flailings at this 10 Hz level to the mothers voice accents, while autistic and schitzophrenic children fail to show interactional synchrony. Autistics are unable to tap in time to a metronome.

Neural expectation rhythms that support Jones' theory have been found in the auditory EEG. In experiments where the arrival time of a target stimulus is regular enough to be learned by an experimental subject, it has been shown that the 10 Hz activity *in advance of the stimulus* becomes phase locked to that expected arrival time. This fits our model of rhythmic expectation where the 10 Hz rhythm is a fast base clock that is shifted in phase and frequency to produce a match in timing between the stimulus arrival and the output of longer period cycles derived from this base clock.

2.1 Mismatch Negativity

The "mismatch negativity" (MNN) [Naatanen, 1992] of the auditory evoked potential appears to be an important physiological indicator of the action of a neural expectancy system like that proposed by Jones. It has been localized to areas within primary auditory cortex by MEG studies [Naatanen, 1992] and it appears as an increased negativity of the ERP in the region of the N200 peak whenever a psychologically discriminable deviation of a repetitive auditory stimulus occurs. Mismatch is caused by deviations in onset or offset time, rise time, frequency, loudness, timbre, phonetic structure, or spatial location of a tone in the sequence. The mismatch is abolished by blockers of the action of NMDA channels [Naatanen, 1992] which are important for the synaptic changes underlying the kind of Hebbian learning which is used in the model.

MNN is not a direct function of echoic memory because it takes several repetitions for the expectancy to begin to develop, and it decays in 2 - 4 seconds. It appears only for repetition periods greater that 50-100 msec and less than 2-4 seconds. Thus the time scale of its operation is in the appropriate range for Jones' expectancy system. Stream formation also takes several cycles of stimulus repetition to build up over 2-4 seconds and decays away within 2-4 seconds in the absence of stimulation. Those auditory stimulus features which cause streaming are also features which cause mismatch. This supports the hypothesis in the model that these phenomena are functionally related.

Finally, MNN can occur independent of attention – while a subject is reading or doing a visual discrimination task. This implies that the auditory system at least must have its own timing system that can generate timing and expectancies independent of other behavior. We can talk or do internal verbal thinking while doing other tasks. A further component of this negativity appears in prefrontal cortex and is thought by Nataanen to initiate attentional switching toward the deviant event causing perceptual "pop out" [Naatanen, 1992].

Stream formation is known to affect rhythm perception. The galloping rhythm of high H and low L tones – HLH-HLH-HLH, for example becomes two separate isochronous rhythmic streams of H-H-H-H and L—L—L—L when the H and L tones are spread far enough apart [Bregman, 1990]. Evidence for the effect of input rhythms on stream formation, however, is more sparse, and we focus here on the simulation of a particular set of experiments by Jones [Jones et al., 1981] and Bregman [Bregman, 1990] where this effect has been demonstrated.

2.2 Jones-Bregman Experiment

Jones [Jones et al., 1981] replicated and altered a classic streaming experiment of Bregman and Rudnicky [Bregman, 1990], and found that their result depended on a specific choice of the rhythm of presentation. The experiment required human subjects to determine the order of presentation of a pair of high target tones AB or BA of slightly different frequencies. Also presented before and after the target tones were a series of identical much lower frequency tones called the capture tones CCC and two identical tones of intermediate frequency before and after the target tones called the flanking tones F - CCCFABFCCC. Bregman and Rudnicky found that target order determination performance was best when the capture tones were near to the flanking tones in frequency, and deteriorated as the captor tones were moved away. Their explanation was that the flanking tones were captured by the background capture tone stream when close in frequency, leaving the target tones to stand out by themselves in the attended stream. When the captor tones were absent or far away in frequency, the flanking tones were included in the attended stream and obscured the target tones.

Jones noted that the flanking tones and the capture stream were presented at a stimulus onset rate of one per 240 ms and the targets appeared at 80 ms intervals. In her experiments, when the captor and flanking tones were given a rhythm in common with the targets, no effect of the distance of captor and flanking tones appeared. This suggested that rhythmic distinction of targets and distractors was necessary in addition to the frequency distinction to allow selective attention to segregate out the target stream. Because performance in the single rhythm case was worse than that for the control condition without captors, it appeared that no stream segregation of targets and captors and flanking tones was occurring until the rhythmic difference was added. *From this evidence we make the assumption in the model that the distance of a stimulus in time from a rhythmic expectancy acts like the distance between stimuli in pitch, loudness, timbre, or spatial location as factor for the formation of separate streams.*

3   Architecture and Simulation

To implement Jones's theory in the model and account for her data, subsets of the oscillatory modules are dedicated to form a rhythmic temporal coordinate frame or time base by dividing down a thalamic 10 Hz base clock rate in steps from 10 to .5 Hz. Each derived clock is created by an associative memory module that has been specialized to act stereotypically as a counter or shift register by repeatedly cycling through all its attractors at the rate of one for each time step of its clock. Its overall cycle time is therefore determined by the number of attractors. Each cycle is guaranteed to be identical, as required for clocklike function, because of the strong attractors that correct the perturbing effect of noise. Only one step of the cycle can send output back to primary cortex - the one with the largest weight from receiving the most match to incoming stimuli. Each clock derived in this manner from a thalamic base clock will therefore phase reset itself to get the best match to incoming rhythms. The match can be further refined by frequency and phase entrainment of the base clock itself.

Three such counters are sufficient to model the rhythms in Jones' experiment as shown in the architecture of figure 1. The three counters divide the 12.5 Hz clock down to 6.25 and 4.16 Hz. The first contains one attractor at the base clock rate which has adapted to entrain to the 80 msec period of target stimulation (12.5 Hz). The second cycles at $12.5/2 = 6.25$ Hz, alternating between two attractors, and the third steps through three attractors, to cycle at $12.5/3 = 4.16$ Hz, which is the slow rhythm of the captor tones.

The modules of the time base send their internal 30-80 Hz activity to primary auditory cortex in 100msec bursts at these different rhythmic rates through fast adapting connections (which would use NMDA channels in the brain) that continually attempt to match incoming stimulus patterns using an incremental Hebbian learning rule. The weights decay to zero over 2-4 sec to simulate the data on the rise and fall of the mismatch negativity. These weights effectively compute a low frequency discrete Fourier transform over a sliding window of several seconds, and the basic periodic structure of rhythmic patterns is quickly matched. This serves to establish a quantized temporal grid of expectations against which expressive timing deviations in speech and music can be experienced.

Following Jones [Jones et al., 1981], we hypothesize that this happens automatically as a constant adaptation to environmental rhythms, as suggested by the mismatch negativity. Retained in these weights of the timebase is a special kind of short term memory of the activity which includes temporal information since the timebase will partially regenerate the previous activity in primary cortex *at the expected recurrence time*. This top-down input causes enchanced sensitivity in target units by increasing their gain. Those patterns which meet these established rhythmic expectancy signals in time are thereby boosted in amplitude and pulled into synchrony with the 30-80 Hz attentional searchlight stream to become part of the attentional network sending input to higher areas. In accordance with Jones' theory, voluntary top-down attention can probe input at different hierarchical levels of periodicity by selectively synchronizing a particular cortical column in the time base set to the 40 Hz frequency of the inner attention stream. Then the searchlight into primary cortex is synchro-

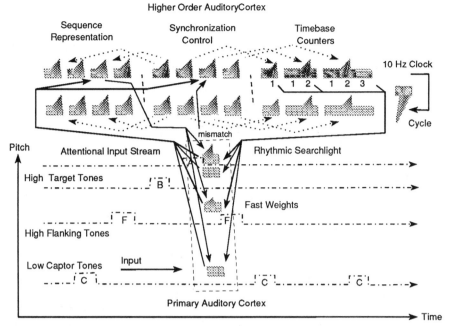

Figure 1: Horizontally arrayed units at the top model higher order auditory and motor cortical columns which are sequentially clocked by the (thalamic) base clock on the right to alternate attractor transitions between upper hidden (motor) and lower context (sensory) layers to act as an Elman net. Three cortical regions are shown – sequence representation memory, attentional synchronization control, and a rhythmic timebase of three counters. The hidden and context layers consist of binary "units" composed of two oscillatory attractors. Activity levels oscillate up and down through the plane of the paper. Dotted lines show frequency shifting outputs from the synchronization (attention) control modules. The lower vertical set of units is a sample of primary auditory cortex frequency channels at the values used in the Jones-Bregman experiment. The dashed lines show the rhythmic pattern of the target, flanking, and captor tones moving in time from left to right to impact on auditory cortex.

nizing and reading in activity occuring at the peaks of that particular time base rhythm.

3.1   Cochlear and Primary Cortex Model

At present, we have modeled only the minimal aspects of primary auditory cortex sufficient to qualitatively simulate the Jones-Bregman experiment, but the principles at work allow expansion to larger scale models with more stimulus features. We simulate four sites in auditory cortex corresponding to the four frequencies of stimuli used in the experiment, as shown in figure 1. There are two close high frequency target tones, one high flanking frequency location, and the low frequency location of the captor stream. These cortical locations are modeled as oscillators with the same equations used for associative memory modules [Baird et al., 1994], with full linear cross coupling weights. This lateral connectivity is sufficient to promote synchrony among simultaneously activated oscillators, but insufficient to activate them strongly in the absence of external input. This makes full synchrony of activated units the default condition in the model cortex, as in Brown's model [Brown and Cooke, 1996], so that the background activation is coherent, and can be read into higher order cortical levels which synchronize with it. The system assumes that all input is due to the same environmental source in the absence of evidence for segregation [Bregman, 1990].

Brown and Cooke [Brown and Cooke, 1996] model the cochlear and brainstem nuclear output as a set of overlapping bandpass ("gammatone") filters consistent with auditory nerve responses and psychophysical "critical bands". A tone can excite several filter outputs at once. We approximate this effect of the gammatone filters as a lateral fan out of input activations with weights that spread the activation in the same way as the overlapping gammatone filters do.

Experiments show that the intrinsic resonant or "natural" frequencies or "eigenfrequencies" of cortical tissue within the 30-80 Hz gamma band vary within individuals on different trials of a task, and that neurotransmitters can quickly alter these resonant frequencies of neural clocks. Following the evidence that the oscillation frequency of binding in vision goes up with the speed of motion of an object, we assume that unattended activity in auditory cortex synchronizes at a default background frequency of 35 Hz, while the higher order attentional stream is at a higher frequency of 40 Hz. Just as fast motion in vision can cause stimulus driven capture of attention, we hypothesize that expectancy mismatch in audition causes the deviant activity to be boosted above the default background frequency to facilitate synchronization with the attentional stream at 40 Hz. This models the mechanism of involuntary stimulus driven attentional "pop out". Multiple streams of primary cortex activity synchronized at different eigenfrequencies can be selectively attended by uniformly sweeping the eigenfrequencies of all primary ensembles through the passband of the 40 Hz higher order attentional stream to "tune in" each in turn as a radio reciever does.

Following, but modifing the approach of Brown and Cooke [Brown and Cooke, 1996], the core of our primary cortex stream forming model is a fast learning rule that reduces the lateral coupling and (in our model) spreads apart the intrinsic cortical frequencies of sound frequency channels that do not exhibit the same amplitude of activity at the same time. This coupling and eigenfrequency difference recovers between onsets. In the absence of lateral synchronizing connections or coherent top down driving, synchrony between cortical streams is rapidly lost because of their distant resonant frequencies. Activity not satisfying the Gestalt principle of "common fate" [Bregman, 1990] is thus decorrelated.

The trade off of the effect of temporal and sound frequency proximity on stream segregation follows because close stimulus frequencies excite each other's channel filters. Each produces a similar output in the other, and their activitites are not decorrelated by coupling reduction and resonant frequency shifts. On the other hand, to the extent that they are distant enough in sound frequency, each tone onset weakens the weights and shifts the eigenfrequencies of the other channels that are not simultaneously active. This effect is greater, the faster the presentation rate, because the weight recovery rate is overcome. This recovery rate can then be adjusted to yield stream segregation at the rates reported by van Noorden [Bregman, 1990] for given sound frequency separations.

3.2   Sequential Grouping by Coupling and Resonant Frequency Labels

In the absence of rhythmic structure in the input, the temporary weights and resonant frequency "labels" serve as a short term "stream memory" to bridge time (up to 4 seconds) so that the next nearby input is "captured" or "sequentially bound" into the same ensemble of synchronized activity. This pattern of synchrony in primary cortex has been made into a temporary attractor by the temporary weight and eigenfrequency changes from the previous stimulation. This explains the single tone capture experiments where a series of identical tones captures later nearby tones. For two points in time to be sequentially grouped by this mechanism, there is no need for activity to continue between onsets as in Browns model [Brown and Cooke, 1996], or to be held in multiple spatial locations as Wang [Wang, 1995] does. Since the gamma band response to a single auditory input onset lasts only 100 - 150 ms, there is no 40 Hz activity available in primary cortex (at most stimulus rates) for succesive inputs to synchronize with for sequential binding by these mechanisms.

Furthermore, the decorrelation rule, when added to the mechanism of timing expectancies, explains the loss of relative timing (order) between streams, since the lateral connections that normally broadcast actual and expected onsets accross auditory cortex, are cut between two streams by the decorrelating weight reduction. Expected and actual onset events in different streams can no longer be directly (locally) compared. Experimental evidence for the broadcast of expectancies comes from the fast generalization to other frequencies of a learned expectancy for the onset time of a tone of a particular frequency (Schreiner lab - personal communication).

When rhythmic structure is present, the expectancy system becomes engaged, and this becomes an additional feature dimension along which stimuli can be segregated. Distance from expected *timing* as well as sound quality is now an added factor causing stream formation by decoupling and eigenfrequency shift. Feedback of expected input can also partially"fill in" missing input for a cycle or two so that the expectancy protects the binding of features of a stimulus and stabilizes a perceptual stream accross seconds of time.

3.3   Simulation of the Jones-Bregman Experiment

Figure 2 shows the architecture used to simulate the Jones-Bregman experiment. The case shown is where the flanking tones are in the same stream as the targets because the captor stream is at the lower sound frequency channel. At the particular point in time shown here, the first flanking tone has just finished, and the first target tone has arrived. Both channels are therfore active, and synchronized with the attentional stream into the higher order sequence recognizer.

Our mechanistic explanation of the Bregman result is that the early standard target tones arriving at the 80 msec rate first **prime** the dynamic attention system by setting the 80 msec clock to oscillate at 40 Hz and depressing the oscillation frequency of other auditory cortex background activity. Then the slow captor tones at the 240 msec period establish a background stream at 30 Hz with a rhythmic expectancy that is later violated by the appearance of the fast target tones. These now fall outside the correlation attractor basin of the background stream because the mismatch increases their cortical oscillation frequency. They are explicitly brought into the 40 Hz foreground frequency by the mismatch pop out mechanism. This allows the attentional stream into the Elman sequence recognition units to synchronize and read in activity due to the target tones for order determination. It is assisted by the timebase searchlight at the 80 msec period which synchronizes and enhances activity arriving at that rhythm. In the absence of a rhythmic distinction for the target tones, their sound frequency difference alone is insufficient to separate them from the background stream, and the targets cannot be reliably discriminated.

In this simulation, the connections to the first two Elman associative memory units are hand wired to the A and B primary cortex oscillators to act as a latching, order determining switch. If synchronized to the memory unit at the attentional stream frequency, the A target tone oscillator will drive the first memory unit into the 1 attractor which then inhibits the second unit from being driven to 1 by the B target tone. The second unit has similar wiring from the B tone oscillator, so that the particular higher order (intermediate term) memory unit which is left in the 1 state after a trial indicates to the rest of the brain which tone came first. The flanking and high captor tone oscillator is connected equally to both memory units, so that a random attractor transition occurs before the targets arrive, when it is interfering at the 40 Hz attentional frequency, and poor order determination results. If the flanking tone oscillator is in a separate stream along with the captor tones at the background eigenfrequency of 35 Hz, it is outside the recieving passband of the memory units and cannot cause a spurious attractor transition.

This architecture demonstrates mechanisms that integrate the theories of Jones and Bregman about auditory perception. Stream formation is a preattentive process that works well on non-rhythmic inputs as Bregman asserts, but an equally primary and preattentive rhythmic expectancy process is also at work as Jones asserts and the mismatch negativity indicates. This becomes a factor in stream formation when rhythmic structure is present in stimuli as demonstrated by Jones.

References

[Baird et al., 1994] Baird, B., Troyer, T., and Eeckman, F. H. (1994). Gramatical inference by attentional control of synchronization in an oscillating elman network. In Hanson, S., Cowan, J., and Giles, C., editors, *Advances in Neural Information Processing Systems 6*, pages 67–75. Morgan Kaufman.

[Bregman, 1990] Bregman, A. S. (1990). *Auditory Scene Analysis*. MIT Press, Cambridge.

[Brown and Cooke, 1996] Brown, G. and Cooke, M. (1996). A neural oscillator model of auditory stream segregation. In *IJCAI Workshop on Computational Auditory Scene Analysis*. to appear.

[Jones et al., 1981] Jones, M., Kidd, G., and Wetzel, R. (1981). Evidence for rhythmic attention. *Journal of Experimental Psychology: Human Perception and Performance*, 7:1059–1073.

[Llinas and Ribary, 1993] Llinas, R. and Ribary, U. (1993). Coherent 40-hz oscillation characterizes dream state in humans. *Proc. Natl. Acad. Sci. USA*, 90:2078–2081.

[Naatanen, 1992] Naatanen, R. (1992). *Attention and Brain Function*. Erlbaum, New Jersey.

[Wang, 1995] Wang, D. (1995). An oscillatory correlation theory of temporal pattern segmentation. In Covey, E., Hawkins, H., McMullen, T., and Port, R., editors, *Neural Representations of Temporal Patterns*. Plenum. to appear.

On Parallel Versus Serial Processing: A Computational Study of Visual Search

Eyal Cohen
Department of Psychology
Tel-Aviv University Tel Aviv 69978, Israel
eyalc@devil.tau.ac.il
Eytan Ruppin
Departments of Computer Science & Physiology
Tel-Aviv University Tel Aviv 69978, Israel
ruppin@math.tau.ac.il

Abstract

A novel neural network model of pre-attention processing in visual-search tasks is presented. Using displays of line orientations taken from Wolfe's experiments [1992], we study the hypothesis that the distinction between parallel versus serial processes arises from the availability of global information in the internal representations of the visual scene. The model operates in two phases. First, the visual displays are compressed via principal-component-analysis. Second, the compressed data is processed by a target detector module in order to identify the existence of a target in the display. Our main finding is that targets in displays which were found experimentally to be processed in parallel can be detected by the system, while targets in experimentally-serial displays cannot. This fundamental difference is explained via variance analysis of the compressed representations, providing a numerical criterion distinguishing parallel from serial displays. Our model yields a mapping of response-time slopes that is similar to Duncan and Humphreys's "search surface" [1989], providing an explicit formulation of their intuitive notion of feature similarity. It presents a neural realization of the processing that may underlie the classical metaphorical explanations of visual search.

1   Introduction

This paper presents a neural-model of pre-attentive visual processing. The model explains why certain displays can be processed very fast, "in parallel", while others require slower, "serial" processing, in subsequent attentional systems. Our approach stems from the observation that the visual environment is overflowing with diverse information, but the biological information-processing systems analyzing it have a limited capacity [1]. This apparent mismatch suggests that *data compression* should be performed at an early stage of perception, and that via an accompanying process of *dimension reduction*, only a few essential features of the visual display should be retained. We propose that only parallel displays incorporate global features that enable fast target detection, and hence they can be processed pre-attentively, with all items (target and distractors) examined at once. On the other hand, in serial displays' representations, global information is obscure and target detection requires a serial, attentional scan of local features across the display. Using principal-component-analysis (PCA), our main goal is to demonstrate that neural systems employing compressed, dimensionally reduced representations of the visual information can successfully process only parallel displays and not serial ones. The source of this difference will be explained via variance analysis of the displays' projections on the principal axes.

The modeling of visual attention in cognitive psychology involves the use of metaphors, e.g., Posner's beam of attention [2]. A visual attention system of a surviving organism must supply fast answers to burning issues such as detecting a target in the visual field and characterizing its primary features. An attentional system employing a constant-speed beam of attention [3] probably cannot perform such tasks fast enough and a pre-attentive system is required. Treisman's feature integration theory (FIT) describes such a system [4]. According to FIT, features of separate dimensions (shape, color, orientation) are first coded pre-attentively in a locations map and in separate feature maps, each map representing the values of a particular dimension. Then, in the second stage, attention "glues" the features together conjoining them into objects at their specified locations. This hypothesis was supported using the *visual-search* paradigm [4], in which subjects are asked to detect a target within an array of distractors, which differ on given physical dimensions such as color, shape or orientation. As long as the target is significantly different from the distractors in one dimension, the reaction time (RT) is short and shows almost no dependence on the number of distractors (low RT slope). This result suggests that in this case the target is detected pre-attentively, in parallel. However, if the target and distractors are similar, or the target specifications are more complex, reaction time grows considerably as a function of the number of distractors [5, 6], suggesting that the displays' items are scanned serially using an attentional process.

FIT and other related cognitive models of visual search are formulated on the conceptual level and do not offer a detailed description of the processes involved in transforming the visual scene from an ordered set of data points into given values in specified feature maps. This paper presents a novel computational explanation of the source of the distinction between parallel and serial processing, progressing from general metaphorical terms to a neural network realization. Interestingly, we also come out with a computational interpretation of some of these metaphorical terms, such as feature similarity.

2   The Model

We focus our study on visual-search experiments of line orientations performed by
Wolfe et. al. [7], using three set-sizes composed of 4, 8 and 12 items. The number of
items equals the number of distractors + target in target displays, and in non-target
displays the target was replaced by another distractor, keeping a constant set-size.
Five experimental conditions were simulated: (A) - a 20 degrees tilted target among
vertical distractors (homogeneous background). (B) - a vertical target among 20
degrees tilted distractors (homogeneous background). (C) - a vertical target among
heterogeneous background (a mixture of lines with ±20, ±40 , ±60 , ±80 degrees
orientations). (E) - a vertical target among two flanking distractor orientations (at
±20 degrees), and (G) - a vertical target among two flanking distractor orientations
(±40 degrees). The response times (RT) as a function of the set-size measured by
Wolfe et. al. [7] show that type A, B and G displays are scanned in a parallel
manner (1.2, 1.8, 4.8 msec/item for the RT slopes), while type C and E displays are
scanned serially (19.7, 17.5 msec/item). The input displays of our system were prepared following Wolfe's prescription: Nine images of the basic line orientations were
produced as nine matrices of gray-level values. Displays for the various conditions
of Wolfe's experiments were produced by randomly assigning these matrices into
a 4x4 array, yielding 128x100 display-matrices that were transformed into 12800
display-vectors. A total number of 2400 displays were produced in 30 groups (80
displays in each group): 5 conditions (A, B, C, E, G) × target/non-target × 3
set-sizes (4, 8, 12).

Our model is composed of two neural network modules connected in sequence as
illustrated in Figure 1: a PCA module which compresses the visual data into a set
of principal axes, and a Target Detector (TD) module. The latter module uses the
compressed data obtained by the former module to detect a target within an array
of distractors. The system is presented with line-orientation displays as described
above.

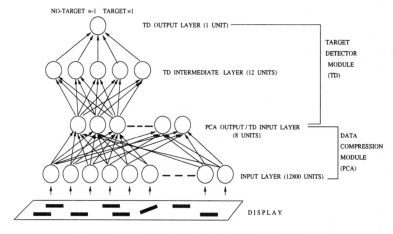

Figure 1: General architecture of the model

For the PCA module we use the neural network proposed by Sanger, with the
connections' values updated in accordance with his Generalized Hebbian Algorithm
(GHA) [8]. The outputs of the trained system are the projections of the display-
vectors along the first few principal axes, ordered with respect to their eigenvalue
magnitudes. Compressing the data is achieved by choosing outputs from the first

few neurons (maximal variance and minimal information loss). Target detection in our system is performed by a feed-forward (FF) 3-layered network, trained via a standard back-propagation algorithm in a supervised-learning manner. The input layer of the FF network is composed of the first eight output neurons of the PCA module. The transfer function used in the intermediate and output layers is the hyperbolic tangent function.

3   Results

3.1   Target Detection

The performance of the system was examined in two simulation experiments. In the first, the PCA module was trained only with "parallel" task displays, and in the second, only with "serial" task displays. There is an inherent difference in the ability of the model to detect targets in parallel versus serial displays. In parallel task conditions (A, B, G) the target detector module learns the task after a comparatively small number (800 to 2000) of epochs, reaching performance level of almost 100%. However, the target detector module is not capable of learning to detect a target in serial displays (C, E conditions). Interestingly, these results hold (1) whether the preceding PCA module was trained to perform data compression using parallel task displays or serial ones, (2) whether the target detector was a linear simple perceptron, or the more powerful, non-linear network depicted in Figure 1, and (3) whether the full set of 144 principal axes (with non-zero eigenvalues) was used.

3.2   Information Span

To analyze the differences between parallel and serial tasks we examined the eigenvalues obtained from the PCA of the training-set displays. The eigenvalues of condition B (parallel) displays in 4 and 12 set-sizes and of condition C (serial-task) displays are presented in Figure 2. Each training set contains a mixture of target and non-target displays.

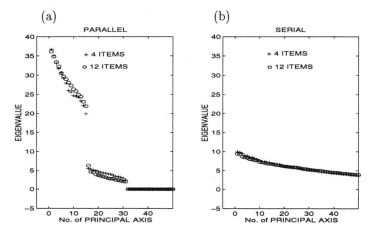

Figure 2: Eigenvalues spectrum of displays with different set-sizes, for parallel and serial tasks. Due to the sparseness of the displays (a few black lines on white background), it takes only 31 principal axes to describe the parallel training-set in full (see fig 2a. Note that the remaining axes have zero eigenvalues, indicating that they contain no additional information.), and 144 axes for the serial set (only the first 50 axes are shown in fig 2b).

As evident, the eigenvalues distributions of the two display types are fundamentally different: in the parallel task, most of the eigenvalues "mass" is concentrated in the first few (15) principal axes, testifying that indeed, the dimension of the parallel displays space is quite confined. But for the serial task, the eigenvalues are distributed almost uniformly over 144 axes. This inherent difference is independent of set-size: 4 and 12-item displays have practically the same eigenvalue spectra.

3.3 Variance Analysis

The target detector inputs are the projections of the display-vectors along the first few principal axes. Thus, some insight to the source of the difference between parallel and serial tasks can be gained performing a variance analysis on these projections. The five different task conditions were analyzed separately, taking a group of 85 target displays and a group of 85 non-target displays for each set-size. Two types of variances were calculated for the projections on the 5th principal axis: The "within groups" variance, which is a measure of the statistical noise within each group of 85 displays, and the "between groups" variance, which measures the separation between target and non-target groups of displays for each set-size. These variances were averaged for each task (condition), over all set-sizes. The resulting ratios Q of within-groups to between-groups standard deviations are: $Q_A = 0.0259$, $Q_B = 0.0587$, and $Q_G = 0.0114$ for parallel displays (A, B, G), and $Q_E = 0.2125$ $Q_C = 0.771$ for serial ones (E, C).

As evident, for parallel task displays the Q values are smaller by an order of magnitude compared with the serial displays, indicating a better separation between target and non-target displays in parallel tasks. Moreover, using Q as a criterion for parallel/serial distinction one can predict that displays with $Q << 1$ will be processed in parallel, and serially otherwise, in accordance with the experimental response time (RT) slopes measured by Wolfe et. al. [7]. This differences are further demonstrated in Figure 3, depicting projections of display-vectors on the sub-space spanned by the 5, 6 and 7th principal axes. Clearly, for the parallel task (condition B), the PCA representations of the target-displays (plus signs) are separated from non-target representations (circles), while for serial displays (condition C) there is no such separation. It should be emphasized that there is no other principal axis along which such a separation is manifested for serial displays.

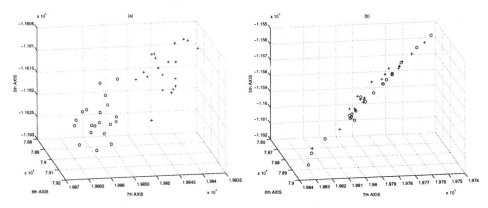

Figure 3: Projections of display-vectors on the sub-space spanned by the 5, 6 and 7th principal axes. Plus signs and circles denote target and non-target display-vectors respectively, (a) for a parallel task (condition B), and (b) for a serial task (condition C). Set-size is 8 items.

While Treisman and her co-workers view the distinction between parallel and serial tasks as a fundamental one, Duncan and Humphreys [5] claim that there is
no sharp distinction between them, and that search efficiency varies continuously
across tasks and conditions. The determining factors according to Duncan and
Humphreys are the similarities between the target and the non-targets (T-N similarities) and the similarities between the non-targets themselves (N-N similarity).
Displays with homogeneous background (high N-N similarity) and a target which is
significantly different from the distractors (low T-N similarity) will exhibit parallel,
low RT slopes, and vice versa. This claim was illustrated by them using a qualitative
"search surface" description as shown in figure 4a. Based on results from our variance analysis, we can now examine this claim quantitatively: We have constructed
a "search surface", using actual numerical data of RT slopes from Wolfe's experiments, replacing the N-N similarity axis by its mathematical manifestation, the
within-groups standard deviation, and N-T similarity by between-groups standard
deviation [1]. The resulting surface (Figure 4b) is qualitatively similar to Duncan and
Humphreys's. This interesting result testifies that the PCA representation succeeds
in producing a viable realization of such intuitive terms as inputs similarity, and is
compatible with the way we perceive the world in visual search tasks.

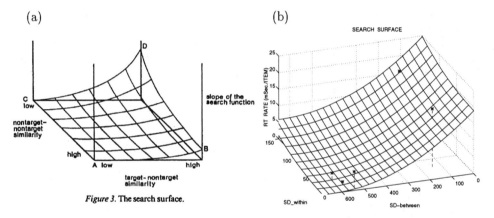

Figure 4: RT rates versus: (a) Input similarities (the search surface, reprinted from
Duncan and Humphreys, 1989). (b) Standard deviations (within and between) of
the PCA variance analysis. The asterisks denote Wolfe's experimental data.

4   Summary

In this work we present a two-component neural network model of pre-attentional
visual processing. The model has been applied to the visual search paradigm performed by Wolfe et. al. Our main finding is that when global-feature compression
is applied to visual displays, there is an inherent difference between the representations of serial and parallel-task displays: The neural network studied in this paper
has succeeded in detecting a target among distractors only for displays that were
experimentally found to be processed in parallel. Based on the outcome of the

---

[1] In general, each principal axis contains information from different features, which may
mask the information concerning the existence of a target. Hence, the first principal axis
may not be the best choice for a discrimination task. In our simulations, the 5th axis
for example, was primarily dedicated to target information, and was hence used for the
variance analysis (obviously, the neural network uses information from all the first eight
principal axes).

variance analysis performed on the PCA representations of the visual displays, we present a quantitative criterion enabling one to distinguish between serial and parallel displays. Furthermore, the resulting 'search-surface' generated by the PCA components is in close correspondence with the metaphorical description of Duncan and Humphreys.

The network demonstrates an interesting generalization ability: Naturally, it can learn to detect a target in parallel displays from examples of such displays. However, it can also learn to perform this task from examples of serial displays only! On the other hand, we find that it is impossible to learn serial tasks, irrespective of the combination of parallel and serial displays that are presented to the network during the training phase. This generalization ability is manifested not only during the learning phase, but also during the performance phase; displays belonging to the same task have a similar eigenvalue spectrum, irrespective of the actual set-size of the displays, and this result holds true for parallel as well as for serial displays.

The role of PCA in perception was previously investigated by Cottrell [9], designing a neural network which performed tasks as face identification and gender discrimination. One might argue that PCA, being a global component analysis is not compatible with the existence of local feature detectors (e.g. orientation detectors) in the cortex. Our work is in line with recent proposals [10] that there exist two pathways for sensory input processing: A fast sub-cortical pathway that contains limited information, and a slow cortical pathway which is capable of providing richer representations of the stimuli. Given this assumption this paper has presented the first neural realization of the processing that may underline the classical metaphorical explanations involved in visual search.

References

[1] J. K. Tsotsos. Analyzing vision at the complexity level. *Behavioral and Brain Sciences*, 13:423–469, 1990.

[2] M. I. Posner, C. R. Snyder, and B. J. Davidson. Attention and the detection of signals. *Journal of Experimental Psychology: General*, 109:160–174, 1980.

[3] Y. Tsal. Movement of attention across the visual field. *Journal of Experimental Psychology: Human Perception and Performance*, 9:523–530, 1983.

[4] A. Treisman and G. Gelade. A feature integration theory of attention. *Cognitive Psychology*, 12:97–136, 1980.

[5] J. Duncan and G. Humphreys. Visual search and stimulus similarity. *Psychological Review*, 96:433–458, 1989.

[6] A. Treisman and S. Gormican. Feature analysis in early vision: Evidence from search assymetries. *Psychological Review*, 95:15–48, 1988.

[7] J. M. Wolfe, S. R. Friedman-Hill, M. I. Stewart, and K. M. O'Connell. The role of categorization in visual search for orientation. *Journal of Experimental Psychology: Human Perception and Performance*, 18:34–49, 1992.

[8] T. D. Sanger. Optimal unsupervised learning in a single-layer linear feedforward neural network. *Neural Network*, 2:459–473, 1989.

[9] G. W. Cottrell. Extracting features from faces using compression networks: Face, identity, emotion and gender recognition using holons. *Proceedings of the 1990 Connectionist Models Summer School*, pages 328–337, 1990.

[10] J. L. Armony, D. Servan-Schreiber, J. D. Cohen, and J. E. LeDoux. Computational modeling of emotion: exploration through the anatomy and physiology of fear conditioning. *Trends in Cognitive Sciences*, 1(1):28–34, 1997.

Task and Spatial Frequency Effects on Face Specialization

Matthew N. Dailey   **Garrison W. Cottrell**
Department of Computer Science and Engineering
U.C. San Diego
La Jolla, CA 92093-0114
{mdailey,gary}@cs.ucsd.edu

Abstract

There is strong evidence that face processing is localized in the brain. The double dissociation between prosopagnosia, a face recognition deficit occurring after brain damage, and visual object agnosia, difficulty recognizing other kinds of complex objects, indicates that face and non-face object recognition may be served by partially independent mechanisms in the brain. Is neural specialization innate or learned? We suggest that this specialization could be the result of a competitive learning mechanism that, during development, devotes neural resources to the tasks they are best at performing. Further, we suggest that the specialization arises as an interaction between task requirements and developmental constraints. In this paper, we present a feed-forward computational model of visual processing, in which two modules compete to classify input stimuli. When one module receives low spatial frequency information and the other receives high spatial frequency information, and the task is to identify the faces while simply classifying the objects, the low frequency network shows a strong specialization for faces. No other combination of tasks and inputs shows this strong specialization. We take these results as support for the idea that an innately-specified face processing module is unnecessary.

1   Background

Studies of the preserved and impaired abilities in brain damaged patients provide important clues on how the brain is organized. Cases of prosopagnosia, a face recognition deficit often sparing recognition of non-face objects, and visual object agnosia, an object recognition deficit that can occur without appreciable impairment of face recognition, provide evidence that face recognition is served by a "special" mechanism. (For a recent review of this evidence, see Moscovitch, Winocur, and Behrmann (1997)). In this study, we begin to provide a computational account of the double dissociation.

Evidence indicates that face recognition is based primarily on holistic, configural information, whereas non-face object recognition relies more heavily on local features and analysis of the parts of an object (Farah, 1991; Tanaka and Sengco, 1997). For instance, the distance between the tip of the nose and an eye in a face is an important factor in face recognition, but such subtle measurements are rarely as critical for distinguishing, say, two buildings. There is also evidence that configural information is highly relevant when a human becomes an "expert" at identifying individuals within other visually homogeneous object classes (Gauthier and Tarr, 1997).

What role might configural information play in the development of a specialization for face recognition? de Schonen and Mancini (1995) have proposed that several factors, including different rates of maturation in different areas of cortex, an infant's tendency to track the faces in its environment, and the gradual increase in visual acuity as an infant develops, all combine to force an early specialization for face recognition. If this scenario is correct, the infant begins to form configural face representations very soon after birth, based primarily on the low spatial frequency information present in face stimuli. Indeed, Costen, Parker, and Craw (1996) showed that although both high-pass and low-pass image filtering decrease face recognition accuracy, high-pass filtering degrades identification accuracy more quickly than low-pass filtering. Furthermore, Schyns and Oliva (1997) have shown that when asked to recognize the identity of the "face" in a briefly-presented hybrid image containing a low-pass filtered image of one individual's face and a high-pass filtered image of another individual's face, subjects consistently use the low-frequency component of the image for the task. This work indicates that low spatial frequency information may be more important for face identification than high spatial frequency information.

Jacobs and Kosslyn (1994) showed how differential availability of large and small receptive field sizes in a mixture of experts network (Jacobs, Jordan, Nowlan, and Hinton, 1991) can lead to experts that specialize for "what" and "where" tasks. In previous work, we proposed that a neural mechanism allocating resources according to their ability to perform a given task could explain the apparent specialization for face recognition evidenced by prosopagnosia (Dailey, Cottrell, and Padgett, 1997). We showed that a model based on the mixture of experts architecture, in which a gating network implements competitive learning between two simple homogeneous modules, could develop a specialization such that damage to one module disproportionately impaired face recognition compared to non-face object recognition.

In the current study, we consider how the availability of spatial frequency information affects face recognition specialization given this hypothesis of neural resource allocation by competitive learning. We find that when high and low frequency information is "split" between the two modules in our system, and the task is to identify the faces while simply classifying the objects, the low-frequency module consistently specializes for face recognition. After describing the study, we discuss its results and their implications.

2   Experimental Methods

We presented a modular feed-forward neural network preprocessed images of 12 different faces, 12 different books, 12 different cups, and 12 different soda cans. We gave the network two types of tasks:

1. Learning to recognize the superordinate classes of all four object types (hereafter referred to as *classification*).

2. Learning to distinguish the individual members of one class (hereafter referred to

as *identification*) while simply classifying objects of the other three types.

For each task, we investigated the effects of high and low spatial frequency information on identification and classification in a visual processing system with two competing modules. We observed how splitting the range of spatial frequency information between the two modules affected the specializations developed by the network.

2.1 Image Data

We acquired face images from the Cottrell and Metcalfe facial expression database (1991) and captured multiple images of several books, cups, and soda cans with a CCD camera and video frame grabber. For the face images, we chose five grayscale images of each of 12 individuals. The images were photographed under controlled lighting and pose conditions; the subjects portrayed a different facial expression in each image. For each of the non-face object classes, we captured five different grayscale images of each of 12 books, 12 cups, and 12 cans. These images were also captured under controlled lighting conditions, with small variations in position and orientation between photos. The entire image set contained 240 images, each of which we cropped and scaled to a size of 64x64 pixels.

2.2 Image Preprocessing

To convert the raw grayscale images to a biologically plausible representation more suitable for network learning and generalization, and to experiment with the effect of high and low spatial frequency information available in a stimulus, we extracted Gabor jet features from the images at multiple spatial frequency scales then performed a separate principal components analysis on the data from each filter scale separately to reduce input pattern dimensionality.

2.2.1 Gabor jet features

The basic two-dimensional Gabor wavelet resembles a sinusoid grating restricted by a two-dimensional Gaussian, and may be tuned to a particular orientation and sinusoidal frequency scale. The wavelet can be used to model simple cell receptive fields in cat primary visual cortex (Jones and Palmer, 1987). Buhmann, Lades, and von der Malsburg (1990) describe the Gabor "jet," a vector consisting of filter responses at multiple orientations and scales.

We convolved each of the 240 images in the input data set with two-dimensional Gabor filters at five scales in eight orientations $(0, \frac{\pi}{8}, \frac{\pi}{4}, \frac{3\pi}{8}, \frac{\pi}{2}, \frac{5\pi}{8}, \frac{3\pi}{4}, \frac{7\pi}{8})$ and subsampled an 8x8 grid of the responses to each filter. The process resulted in 2560 complex numbers describing each image.

2.2.2 Principal components analysis

To reduce the dimensionality of the Gabor jet representation while maintaining a segregation of the responses from each filter scale, we performed a separate PCA on each spatial frequency component of the pattern vector described above. For each of the 5 filter scales in the jet, we extracted the subvectors corresponding to that scale from each pattern in the training set, computed the eigenvectors of their covariance matrix, projected the subvectors from each of the patterns onto these eigenvectors, and retained the eight most significant coefficients. Reassembling the pattern set resulted in 240 40-dimensional vectors.

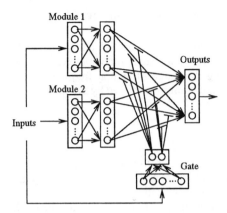

Figure 1: Modular network architecture. The gating network units mix the outputs of the hidden layers multiplicatively.

2.3 The Model

The model is a simple modular feed-forward network inspired by the mixture of experts architecture (Jordan and Jacobs, 1995); however, it contains hidden layers and is trained by backpropagation of error rather than maximum likelihood estimation or expectation maximization. The connections to the output units come from two separate input/hidden layer pairs; these connections are gated multiplicatively by a simple linear network with softmax outputs. Figure 1 illustrates the model's architecture. During training, the network's weights are adjusted by backpropagation of error. The connections from the softmax units in the gating network to the connections between the hidden layers and output layer can be thought of as multiplicative connections with a constant weight of 1. The resulting learning rules gate the amount of error feedback received by a module according to the gating network's current estimate of its ability to process the current training pattern. Thus the model implements a form of competitive learning in which the gating network learns which module is better able to process a given pattern and rewards the "winner" with more error feedback.

2.4 Training Procedure

Preprocessing the images resulted in 240 40-dimensional vectors; four examples of each face and object composed a 192-element training set, and one example of each face and object composed a 48-element test set. We held out one example of each individual in the training set for use in determining when to stop network training. We set the learning rate for all network weights to 0.1 and their momentum to 0.5. Both of the hidden layers contained 15 units in all experiments. For the identification tasks, we determined that a mean squared error (MSE) threshold of 0.02 provided adequate classification performance on the hold out set without overtraining and allowed the gate network to settle to stable values. For the four-way classification task, we found that an MSE threshold of 0.002 was necessary to give the gate network time to stabilize and did not result in overtraining. On all runs reported in the results section, we simply trained the network until it reached the relevant MSE threshold.

For each of the tasks reported in the results section (four-way classification, book identification, and face identification), we performed two experiments. In the first, as a control, both modules and the gating network were trained and tested with the full 40-dimensional pattern vector. In the second, the gating network received the full 40-dimensional vector, but module 1 received a vector in which the elements corresponding to the largest two Gabor filter scales were set to 0, and the elements corresponding to the middle filter scale were reduced by 0.5. Module 2, on the other hand, received a vector in which the elements corresponding to the smallest two filter scales were set to 0 and the elements corresponding to the middle filter were reduced by 0.5. Thus module 1 received mostly high-frequency information, whereas module 2 received mostly low-frequency information, with deemphasized overlap in the middle range.

For each of these six experiments, we trained the network using 20 different initial random weight sets and recorded the softmax outputs learned by the gating network on each training pattern.

3   Results

Figure 2 displays the resulting degree of specialization of each module on each stimulus class. Each chart plots the average weight the gating network assigns to each module for the training patterns from each stimulus class, averaged over 20 training runs with different initial random weights. The error bars denote standard error. For each of the three reported tasks (four-way classification, book identification, and face identification), one chart shows division of labor between the two modules in the control situation, in which both modules receive the same patterns, and the other chart shows division of labor between the two modules when one module receives low-frequency information and the other receives high-frequency information.

When required to identify faces on the basis of high- or low-frequency information, compared with the four-way-classification and same-pattern controls, the low-frequency module wins the competition for face patterns extremely consistently (lower right graph). Book identification specialization, however, shows considerably less sensitivity to spatial frequency.

We have also performed the equivalent experiments with a cup discrimination and a can discrimination task. Both of these tasks show a low-frequency sensitivity lower than that for face identification but higher than that for book identification. Due to space limitations, these results are not presented here.

The specialized face identification networks also provide good models of prosopagnosia and visual object agnosia: when the face-specialized module's output is "damaged" by removing connections from its hidden layer to the output layer, the overall network's generalization performance on face identification drops dramatically, while its generalization performance on object recognition drops much more slowly. When the non-face-specialized (high frequency) module's outputs are damaged, the opposite effect occurs: the overall network's performance on each of the object recognition tasks drops, whereas its performance on face identification remains high.

4   Discussion

The results in Figure 2 show a strong preference for low-frequency information in the face identification task, empirically demonstrating that, given a choice, a competitive mechanism will choose a module receiving low-frequency, large receptive field information for this task. This result concurs with the psychological evidence for configural face representations based upon low spatial frequency information, and suggests how the developing brain could be biased toward a specialization for face recognition by the infant's initially low visual acuity.

On the basis of these results, we predict that human subjects performing face and object

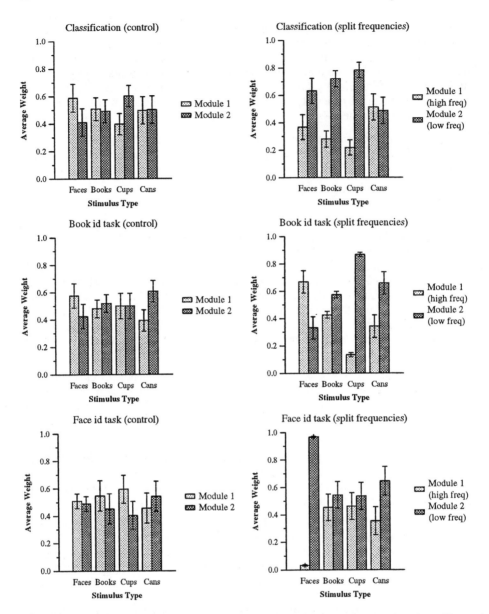

Figure 2: Average weight assigned to each module broken down by stimulus class. For each task, in the control experiment, each module receives the same pattern; the split-frequency charts summarize the specialization resulting when module 1 receives high-frequency Gabor filter information and module 2 receives low-frequency Gabor filter information.

identification tasks will show more degradation of performance in high-pass filtered images of faces than in high-pass filtered images of other objects. To our knowledge, this has not been empirically tested, although Costen et al. (1996) have investigated the effect of high-pass and low-pass filtering on face images in isolation, and Parker, Lishman, and Hughes (1996) have investigated the effect of high-pass and low-pass filtering of face and object images used as 100 ms cues for a same/different task. Their results indicate that relevant high-pass filtered images cue object processing better than low-pass filtered images, but the two types of filtering cue face processing equally well. Similarly, Schyns & Oliva's (1997) results described earlier suggest that the human face identification network preferentially responds to low spatial frequency inputs.

Our results suggest that simple data-driven competitive learning combined with constraints and biases known or thought to exist during visual system development can account for some of the effects observed in normal and brain-damaged humans. The study lends support to the claim that there is no need for an innately-specified face processing module — face recognition is only "special" insofar as faces form a remarkably homogeneous category of stimuli for which within-category discrimination is ecologically beneficial.

References

Buhmann, J., Lades, M., and von der Malsburg, C. (1990). Size and distortion invariant object recognition by hierarchical graph matching. In *Proceedings of the IJCNN International Joint Conference on Neural Networks*, volume II, pages 411–416.

Costen, N., Parker, D., and Craw, I. (1996). Effects of high-pass and low-pass spatial filtering on face identification. *Perception & Psychophysics*, 38(4):602–612.

Cottrell, G. and Metcalfe, J. (1991). Empath: Face, gender and emotion recognition using holons. In Lippman, R., Moody, J., and Touretzky, D., editors, *Advances in Neural Information Processing Systems 3*, pages 564–571.

Dailey, M., Cottrell, G., and Padgett, C. (1997). A mixture of experts model exhibiting prosopagnosia. In *Proceedings of the Nineteenth Annual Conference of the Cognitive Science Society*, pp. 155-160. Stanford, CA, Mahwah: Lawrence Erlbaum.

de Schonen, S. and Mancini, J. (1995). About functional brain specialization: The development of face recognition. TR 95.1, MRC Cognitive Development Unit, London, UK.

Farah, M. (1991). Patterns of co-occurrence among the associative agnosias: Implications for visual object representation. *Cognitive Neuropsychology*, 8:1–19.

Gauthier, I. and Tarr, M. (1997). Becoming a "greeble" expert: Exploring mechanisms for face recognition. *Vision Research*. In press.

Jacobs, R. and Kosslyn, S. (1994). Encoding shape and spatial relations — The role of receptive field size in coordinating complementary representations. *Cognitive Science*, 18(3):361–386.

Jacobs, R., Jordan, M., Nowlan, S., and Hinton, G. (1991). Adaptive mixtures of local experts. *Neural Computation*, 3:79–87.

Jones, J. and Palmer, L. (1987). An evaluation of the two-dimensional Gabor filter model of simple receptive fields in cat striate cortex. *J. Neurophys.*, 58(6):1233–1258.

Moscovitch, M., Winocur, G., and Behrmann, M. (1997). What is special about face recognition? Nineteen experiments on a person with visual object agnosia and dyslexia but normal face recognition. *Journal of Cognitive Neuroscience*, 9(5):555–604.

Parker, D., Lishman, J., and Hughes, J. (1996). Role of coarse and fine spatial information in face and object processing. *Journal of Experimental Psychology: Human Perception and Performance*, 22(6):1445–1466.

Schyns, P. and Oliva, A. (1997). Dr. Angry and Mr. Smile: The multiple faces of perceptual categorizations. Submitted for publication.

Tanaka, J. and Sengco, J. (1997). Features and their configuration in face recognition. *Memory and Cognition*. In press.

Neural Basis of Object-Centered Representations

Sophie Deneve and Alexandre Pouget
Georgetown Institute for Computational and Cognitive Sciences
Georgetown University
Washington, DC 20007-2197
sophie, alex@giccs.georgetown.edu

Abstract

We present a neural model that can perform eye movements to a particular side of an object regardless of the position and orientation of the object in space, a generalization of a task which has been recently used by Olson and Gettner [4] to investigate the neural structure of object-centered representations. Our model uses an intermediate representation in which units have oculocentric receptive fields– just like collicular neurons— whose gain is modulated by the side of the object to which the movement is directed, as well as the orientation of the object. We show that these gain modulations are consistent with Olson and Gettner's single cell recordings in the supplementary eye field. This demonstrates that it is possible to perform an object-centered task without a representation involving an object-centered map, viz., without neurons whose receptive fields are defined in object-centered coordinates. We also show that the same approach can account for object-centered neglect, a situation in which patients with a right parietal lesion neglect the left side of objects regardless of the orientation of the objects.

Several authors have argued that tasks such as object recognition [3] and manipulation [4] are easier to perform if the object is represented in object-centered coordinates, a representation in which the subparts of the object are encoded with respect to a frame of reference centered on the object. Compelling evidence for the existence of such representations in the cortex comes from experiments on hemineglect— a neurological syndrome resulting from unilateral lesions of the parietal cortex such that a right lesion, for example, leads patients to ignore stimuli located on the left side of their egocentric space. Recently, Driver et al. (1994) showed that the deficit can also be object-centered. Hence, hemineglect patients can detect a gap in the upper edge of a triangle when this gap is associated with the right side of the object

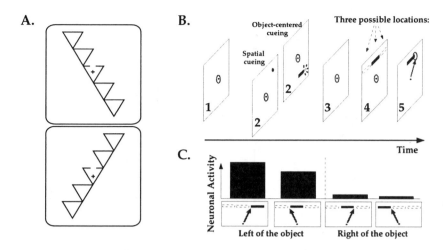

Figure 1: A- Driver et al. (1994) experiment demonstrating object-centered neglect. Subjects were asked to detect a gap in the upper part of the middle triangle, while fixating at the cross, when the overall figure is tilted clockwise (top) or counterclockwise (bottom). Patients perform worse for the clockwise condition, when the gap is perceived to be on the left of the overall figure. B- Sequence of screens presented on each trial in Olson and Gettner experiment (1995). 1- Fixation, 2- apparition of a cue indicating where the saccade should go, either in object-centered coordinates (object-centered cueing), or in screen coordinates (spatial cueing), 3- delay period, 4- apparition of the bar in one of three possible locations (dotted lines), and 5- saccade to the cued location. C- Schematic response of an SEF neuron for 4 different conditions. Adapted from [4].

but not when it belongs to the left side (figure 1-A).

What could be the neural basis of these object-centered representations? The simplest scheme would involve neurons with receptive fields defined in object-centered coordinates, i.e., the cells respond to a particular side of an object regardless of the position and orientation of the object. A recent experiment by Olson and Gettner (1995) supports this possibility. They recorded the activity of neurons in the supplementary eye field (SEF) while the monkey was performing object-directed saccades. The task consisted of making a saccade to the right or left side of a bar, independently of the position of the bar on the screen and according to the instruction provided by a visual cue. For instance, the cue corresponding to the instruction 'Go to the right side of the bar' was provided by highlighting the right side of a small bar briefly flashed at the beginning of the trial (step 2 in figure 1-B).

By changing the position of the object on the screen, it is possible to compare the activity of a neuron for movements involving different saccade directions but directed to the same side of the object, and vice-versa, for movements involving the same saccade direction but directed to opposite sides of the object. Olson and Gettner found that many neurons responded more prior to saccades directed to a particular side of the bar, independently of the direction of the saccades. For example, some neurons responded more for an upward right saccade directed to the *left* side of the bar but not at all for the same upward right saccade directed to the *right* side of the bar (column 1 and 3, figure 1-C). This would suggest that these neurons have bar-centered receptive[1] fields, i.e., their receptive fields are centered

---

[1]we use the term receptive field in a general sense, meaning either receptive or motor

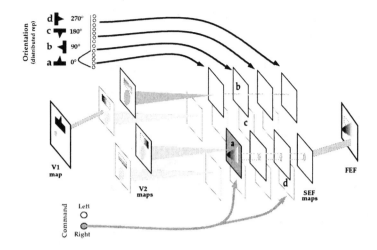

Figure 2: Schematic structure of the network with activity patterns in response to the horizontal bar shown in the V1 map and the command 'Go to the right'. Only one SEF map is active in this case, the one selective to the right edge of the bar (where right is defined in retinal coordinates), object orientation of 0° and the command 'Go to the right'. The letter a, b, c and d indicate which map would be active for the same command but for various orientations of the object, respectively, 0°, 90°, 180°, 270°. The dotted lines on the maps indicate the outline of the bar. Only a few representative connections are shown.

on the bar and not on the retina. This would correspond to what we will call an *explicit* object-centered representation.

We argue in this paper that these data are compatible with a different type of representation which is more suitable for the task performed by the monkey. We describe a neural network which can perform a saccade to the right, or left, boundary of an object, regardless of its orientation, position or size— a generalization of the task used by Olson and Gettner. This network uses units with receptive fields defined in oculocentric coordinates, i.e., they are selective for the direction and amplitude of saccades with respect to the fixation point, just like collicular neurons. These tuning curves, however, are also modulated by two types of signals, the orientation of the object, and the command indicating the side of the object to which the saccade should be directed. We show that these response properties are compatible with the Olson and Gettner data and provide predictions for future experiments. We also show that a simulated lesion leads to object-centered neglect as observed by Driver et al. (1994).

1 Network Architecture

The network performs a mapping from the image of the bar and the command (indicating the side of the object to which the saccade must be directed) to the appropriate motor command in oculocentric coordinates (the kind of command observed in the frontal eye field, FEF). We use a bar whose left and right sides are defined with respect to a a triangle appearing on the top of the bar (see figure 2).

The network is composed of four parts. The first two parts of the network models the

---

field.

lower areas in visual cortex, where visual features are segmented within retinotopic maps. In the first layer, the image is projected on a very simple V1-like map (10 by 10 neurons with activity equal to one if a visual feature appears within their receptive field, and zero otherwise). The second part on the network contains 4 different V2 retinotopic maps, responding respectively to the right, left, top and bottom boundary of the bar.

This model of V2 is intended to reproduce the response properties of a subset of cells recently discovered by Zhou et al. (1996). These cells respond to oriented edges, like V1 cells, but when the edge belongs to a closed figure, they also show a selectivity for the side on which the figure appears with respect to the edge. For example, a cell might respond to a vertical edge only if this edge is on the right side of the figure but not on the left (where right and left are defined with respect to the viewer, not the object itself). This was observed for any orientation of the edge, but we limit ourselves in this model to horizontal and vertical ones.

The third part of the network models the SEF and is divided into 4 groups of 4 maps, each group receiving connections from the corresponding map in V2 (figure 2). Within each group of maps, visual activity is modulated by signals related to the orientation of the object (assumed to be computed in temporal cortex) such that each of the 4 maps respond best for one particular orientation (respectively 0°, 90°, 180° and 270°). For example, a neuron in the second map of the top group responds maximally if: 1- there is an edge in its receptive field and the figure is below, and 2- the object has an orientation of 90° counterclockwise. Note that this situation arises *only* if the left side of the object appears in the cell's receptive field; it will never occur for the right side. However, the cell is only partially selective to the left side of the object, e.g., it does not respond when the left side is in the retinal receptive field and the orientation of the object is 270° counterclockwise.

These collection of responses can be used to generate an object-centered saccade by selecting the maps which are partially selective for the side of the object specified by the command. This is implemented in our network by modulating the SEF maps by signals related to the command. For example, the unit encoding 'go to the right' send a positive weight to any map compatible with the right side of the object while inhibiting the other maps (figure 2).

Therefore, the activity, B_{ij}^k, of a neuron at position ij on the map k in the SEF is the product of three functions:

$$B_{ij}^k = V_{ij} f_k(\theta) g_k(C)$$

where V_{ij} is the visual receptive field from the V2 map, $f_k(\theta)$ is a gaussian function of orientation centered on the cell preferred orientation, θ_k, and $g_k(C)$ is the modulation by the command unit.

Olson and Gettner also used a condition with spatial cueing, viz., the command was provided by a spatial cue indicating where the saccade should go, as opposed to an object-centered instruction (see figure 1-B). We modeled this condition by simply multiplying the activity of neurons coding for this location in all the SEF maps by a fixed constant (10 in the simulations presented here). We also assume that there is no modulation by orientation of the object since this information is irrelevant in this experimental condition.

Finally, the fourth part of the network consists of an oculocentric map similar to the one found in the frontal eye field (FEF) or superior colliculus (SC) in which the command for the saccade is generated in oculocentric coordinates. The activity in the output map, $\{O_{ij}\}$, is obtained by simply summing the activities of all the

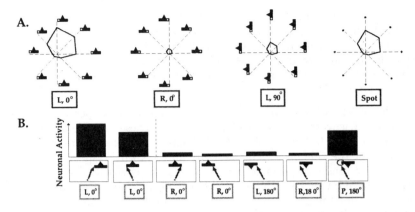

Figure 3: A- Polar plots showing the selectivity for saccade direction of a representative SEF units. The first three plots are for various combinations of command (L: left, R: right, P: spatial cueing) and object orientation. The left plot corresponds to saccades to a single dot. B- Data for the same unit but for a subset of the conditions. The first four columns can be directly compared to the experimental data plotted in figure 1-C from Olson and Gettner. The 5th and 6th columns show responses when the object is inverted. The seventh columns corresponds to spatial cueing.

SEF maps. The result is typically a broad two dimensional bell-shaped pattern of activity from which one can read out the horizontal and vertical components, x_s and y_s, of the intended saccade by applying a center-of-mass operator.

$$x_s = \frac{\sum_i x_i O_{ij}}{\sum_{ij} O_{ij}}, \quad y_s = \frac{\sum_j y_j O_{ij}}{\sum_{ij} O_{ij}} \tag{1}$$

2   Results

This network is able to generate a saccade to the right or to left of a bar, whatever its position, size and orientation. This architecture is basically like a radial basis function network, i.e., a look-up table with broad tuning curves allowing for interpolation. Consequently, one or two of the SEF maps light up at the appropriate location for any combination of the command and, position and orientation of the bar.

Neurons in the SEF maps have the following property: 1- they have an invariant tuning curve for the direction (and amplitude) of saccadic eye movements in oculocentric coordinates, just like neurons in the FEF or the SC, and 2- the gain of this tuning curve is modulated by the orientation of the object as well as the command. Figure 3-A shows how the tuning curve for saccade direction of one particular unit varies as a function of these two variables. In this particular case, the cell responds best to a right-upward saccade directed to the left side of the object when the object is horizontal. Therefore, the SEF units in our model do not have an invariant receptive field in object-centered coordinates but, nevertheless, the gain modulation is sufficient to perform the object-centered saccade. We predict that similar response properties should be found in the SEF, and perhaps parietal cortex, of a monkey trained on a task analogous to the one described here.

Since Olson and Gettner (1995) tested only three positions of the bar and held its orientation constant, we cannot determine from their data whether SEF neurons are gain modulated in the way we just described. However, they found that all the SEF neurons had oculocentric receptive fields when tested on saccades to a single dot (personal communication), an observation which is consistent with our hypothesis (see fourth plot in figure 3-A) while being difficult to reconcile with an explicit object-centered representation. Second, if we sample our data for the conditions used by Olson and Gettner, we find that our units behave like real SEF cells. The first four columns of figure 3-B shows a unit with the same response properties as the cell represented in figure 1-C. Figure 3-B also shows the response of the same unit when the object is upside down and when we use a spatial cue. Note that this unit responds to the left side of the bar when the object is upright (1st column), but not when it is rotated by 180° (5th column), unless we used a spatial cue (7th column). The absence of response for the inverted object is due to the selectivity of the cell to orientation. The cell nevertheless responds in the spatial cueing conditions because we have assumed that orientation does not modulate the activity of the units in this case, since it is irrelevant to the task.

Therefore, the gain modulation observed in our units is consistent with available experimental data and makes predictions for future experiments.

3 Simulation of Neglect

Our representational scheme can account for neglect if the parietal cortex contains gain modulated cells like the ones we have described and if each cortical hemisphere contains more units selective for the contralateral side of space. This is known to be the case for the retinal input; hence most cells in the left hemisphere have their receptive field on the right hemiretina. We propose that the left hemisphere also over-represents the right side of objects and vice-versa (where right is defined in object-centered coordinates).

Recall that the SEF maps in our model are partially selective for the side of objects. A hemispheric preference for the contralateral side of objects could therefore be achieved by having all the maps responding to the left side of objects in the right hemisphere. Clearly, in this case, a right lesion would lead to left object-centered neglect; our network would no longer be able to perform a saccade to the left side of an object.

If we add the retinal gradient and make the previous gradient not quite as binary, then we predict that a left lesion leads to a syndrome in which the network has difficulty with saccades to the left side of an object but more so if the object is shown in the left hemiretina. Preliminary data from Olson and Gettner (personal communication) are compatible with this prediction.

The same model can also account for Driver et al. (1994) experiment depicted in figure 1-A. If the hemispheric gradients are as we propose, a right parietal lesion would lead to a situation in which the overall activity associated with the gap, i.e., the summed activity of all the neurons responding to this retinal location, is greater when the object is rotated counterclockwise— the condition in which the gap is perceived as belonging to the right side of the object— than in the clockwise condition. This activity difference, which can be thought as being a difference in the saliency of the upper edge of the triangle, may be sufficient to account for patients' performance.

Note that object-centered neglect should be observed only if the orientation of the object is taken into consideration by the SEF units. If the experimental conditions are such that the orientation of the object can be ignored by the subject —a situation similar to the spatial cueing condition modeled here— we do not expect to observe neglect. This may explain why several groups (such as Farah et al., 1990) have failed to find object-centered neglect even though they used a paradigm similar to Driver et al. (1994).

4   Discussion

We have demonstrated how object-centered saccades can be performed using neurons with oculocentric receptive fields, gain modulated by the orientation of the object and the command. The same representational scheme can also account for object-centered neglect without invoking an explicit object-centered representation, i.e., representation in which neurons' receptive fields are defined in object-centered coordinates. The gain modulation by the command is consistent with the single cell data available [4], but the modulation by the orientation of the object is a prediction for future experiments.

Whether explicit object-centered representations exist, remains an empirical issue. In some cases, such representations would be computationally inefficient. In the Olson and Gettner experiment, for instance, having a stage in which motor commands are specified in object-centered coordinates does not simplify the task. Encoding the motor command in object-centered coordinates in the intermediate stage of processing requires (i) recoding the sensory input into object-centered coordinates, (ii) decoding the object-centered command into an oculocentric command, which is ultimately what the oculomotor system needs to generate the appropriate saccade. Each of these steps are computationally as complex as performing the overall transformation directly as we have done in this paper.

Therefore, gain modulation provides a simple algorithm for performing object-centered saccades. Interestingly, the same basic mechanism underlies spatial representations in other frames of reference, such as head-centered and body-centered. We have shown previously that these responses can be formalized as being basis functions of their sensory and postures inputs, a set of function which is particularly useful for sensory-motor transformations [5]. The same result applies to the SEF neurons considered in this paper, suggesting that basis functions may provide a unified theory of spatial representations in any spatial frame of reference.

References

[1] J. Driver, G. Baylis, S. Goodrich, and R. Rafal. Axis-based neglect of visual shapes. *Neuropsychologia*, 32(11):1353–1365, 1994.

[2] M. Farah, J. Brunn, A. Wong, M. Wallace, and P. Carpenter. Frames of reference for allocating attention to space: evidence from the neglect syndrome. *Neuropsychologia*, 28(4):335–47, 1990.

[3] G. Hinton. Mapping part-whole hierarchies into connectionist networks. *Artificial Intelligence*, 46(1):47–76, 1990.

[4] C. Olson and S. Gettner. Object-centered direction selectivity in the macaque supplementary eye. *Science*, 269:985–988, 1995.

[5] A. Pouget and T. Sejnowski. Spatial transformations in the parietal cortex using basis functions. *Journal of Cognitive Neuroscience*, 9(2):222–237, 1997.

[6] H. Zhou, H. Friedman, and R. von der Heydt. Edge selective cells code for figure-ground in area V2 of monkey visual cortex. In *Society For Neuroscience Abstracts*, volume 22, page 160.1, 1996.

A Neural Network Model of Naive Preference and Filial Imprinting in the Domestic Chick

Lucy E. Hadden
Department of Cognitive Science
University of California, San Diego
La Jolla, CA 92093
hadden@cogsci.ucsd.edu

Abstract

Filial imprinting in domestic chicks is of interest in psychology, biology, and computational modeling because it exemplifies simple, rapid, innately programmed learning which is biased toward learning about some objects. Horn et al. have recently discovered a naive visual preference for heads and necks which develops over the course of the first three days of life. The neurological basis of this predisposition is almost entirely unknown; that of imprinting-related learning is fairly clear. This project is the first model of the predisposition consistent with what is known about learning in imprinting. The model develops the predisposition appropriately, learns to "approach" a training object, and replicates one interaction between the two processes. Future work will replicate more interactions between imprinting and the predisposition in chicks, and analyze why the system works.

1 Background

Filial imprinting in domestic chicks is of interest in psychology, biology, and computational modeling (O'Reilly and Johnson, 1994; Bateson and Horn, 1994) because it exemplifies simple, rapid, innately programmed learning which is biased toward learning about some particular objects, and because it has a sensitive period in which learning is most efficient. Domestic chicks will imprint on almost anything (including boxes, chickens, and humans) which they see for enough time (Horn, 1985). Horn and his colleagues (Horn, 1985) have recently found a naive visual preference (predisposition) for heads and necks which develops over the course of the first three days of life. In particular, the birds prefer to approach objects shaped like heads and necks, even if they are the heads and necks of other species, including ducks and polecats (Horn, 1985). This preference interacts interestingly with filial imprinting, or learning to recognize a parent. Chicks can still learn about (and imprint on) other objects even in the presence of this predisposition, and the predisposition can override previously learned preferences (Johnson et al., 1985), which is usually hard with imprinted chicks. These interactions are like other systems which rely on naive preferences and learning.

While the neurological basis of imprinting is understood to some extent, that of the predisposition for heads and necks is only beginning to be investigated. Imprinting learning is known to take place in IMHV (intermediate and medial portions of the hyperstriatum ventrale) (Horn, 1985), and to rely on noradrenaline (Davies et al., 1992). The predisposition's location is currently unknown, but its strength correlates with plasma testosterone levels (Horn, 1985).

1.1   Previous Models

No previous models of imprinting have incorporated the predisposition in any meaningful way. O'Reilly & Johnson's (1994) model focussed on accounting for the sensitive period via an interaction between hysteresis (slow decay of activation) and a Hebbian learning rule, and ignored the predisposition. The only model which did try to include a predisposition (Bateson and Horn, 1994) was a 3-layer Hebbian network with real-valued input vectors, and outputs which represented the strength of an "approach" behavior. Bateson and Horn (1994) found a "predisposition" in their model by comparing networks trained on input vectors of 0s and 1s (High) to vectors where non-zero entries were 0.6 (Low). Untrained networks preferred (produced a higher output value for) the high-valued input ("hen"), and trained networks preferred the stimulus they were trained on ("box"). Of course, in a network with identical weights, an input with higher input values will naturally excite an output unit more than one with lower input values. Thus, this model's predisposition is implicit in the input values, and is therefore hard to apply to chicks.

In this project, I develop a model which incorporates both the predisposition and imprinting, and which is as consistent as possible with the known neurobiology. The overall goals of the project are to clarify how this predisposition might be implemented, and to examine more generally the kinds of representations that underlie naive preferences that interact with and facilitate, rather than replace, learning. These particular simulations show that the model exhibits the same qualitative behavior as chicks under three important sets of conditions.

The rest of the paper first describes the architecture of the current model (in general terms and then in more detail). It goes on to describe the particular simulations, and then compares the results of those simulations with the data gathered from chicks.

2   Architecture

The neural network model's architecture is shown in Figure 1. The input layer is a 6x6 pixel "retina" to which binary pictures are presented. The next layer is a feature detector. The predisposition serves as the home of the network's naive preference, while the IMLL (intermediate learning layer) is intended to correspond to a chick's IMHV, and is where the network stores its learned representations. The output layer consists of two units which are taken to represent different action patterns (following Bateson and Horn (1994)): an "approach" unit and a "withdraw" unit. These are the two chick behaviors which researchers use to assess a chick's degree of preference for a particular stimulus. The feature detector provides input to the predisposition and IMLL layers; they in turn provide input to the output layer. Where there are connections, layers (and subparts) are fully interconnected.

The feature detector uses a linear activation function; the rest of the network has a hyperbolic tangent activation function. All activations and all connections can be either positive

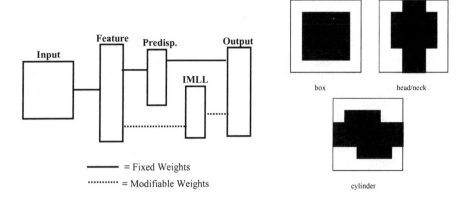

Figure 1: The network architecture sketched. All connections are feedforward (from input toward output) only.

Figure 2: The three input patterns used by the network. They have between 16 and 18 pixels each, and the central moment of each image is the same.

or negative; the connections are limited to ±0.9. Most of the learning takes place via a covariant Hebb rule, because it is considered to be plausible neurally.

The lowest level of the network is a feature-detecting preprocessor. The current implementation of this network takes crude 6x6 binary pictures (examples of which can be seen in Fig. 2), and produces a 15-place floating-point vector. The output units of the feature detector are clustered into five groups of three units each; each group of three units operates under a winner-take-all rule, in order to increase the difference between preprocessed patterns for the relevant pictures. The feature detector was trained on random inputs for 400 cycles with a learning rate of .01, and its weights were then frozen. Training on random input was motivated by the finding that the lower levels of the visual system require some kind of input in order to organize; Miller et al. (1989) suggest that, at least in cats, the random firing of retinal neurons is sufficient.

The predisposition layer was trained via backprop using the outputs of the feature detector as its inputs. The pattern produced by the "head-neck" picture in the feature detector was trained to excite the "approach" output unit and inhibit the "withdraw" unit; other patterns were trained to a neutral value on both output units. These weights were stored, and treated as fixed in the larger network. (In fact, these weights were scaled down by a constant factor (.8) before being used in the larger network.) Since this is a naive preference, or predisposition, these weights are assumed to be fixed evolutionarily. Thus, the method of setting them is irrelevant; they could also have been found by a genetic algorithm.

The IMLL layer is a winner-take-all network of three units. Its connections with the feature detector's outputs are learned by a Hebb rule with learning rate .01 and a weight decay (to 0) term of .0005. For these simulations, its initial weights were fixed by hand, in a pattern which insured that each IMLL unit received a substantially different value for the same input pattern. This pattern of initial weights also increased the likelihood that the three patterns of interest in the simulations maximally affected different IMLL units.

As previously mentioned, the output layer consists of an "approach" and a "withdraw" unit. It also learns via a Hebb rule, with the same learning rate and decay term as IMLL. Its connections with IMLL are learned; those with the predisposition layer are fixed. Initial weights between IMLL and the output layer are random, and vary from -0.3 to 0.3. The bias to the approach unit is 0; that to the withdraw unit is 0.05.

2.1 Training

In the animal experiments on which this model is based, chicks are kept in the dark (and in isolation) except for training and testing periods. Training periods involve visual exposure to an object (usually a red box); testing involves allowing the chick to choose between approaching the training object and some other object (usually either a stuffed hen or a blue cylinder) (Horn, 1985). The percentage of time the chick approaches the training object (or other object of interest) is its preference score for that object (Horn, 1985). A preference score of 50% indicates indifference; scores above 50% indicate a preference for the target object, and those below indicate a preference for the other object. For the purposes of modeling, the most relevant information is the change (particularly the direction of change) in the preference score between two conditions.

Following this approach, the simulations use three preset pictures. One, a box, is the only one for which weights are changed; it is the training pattern. The other two pictures are test patterns; when they are shown, the network's weights are not altered. One of these test patterns is the head/neck picture on which the predisposition network was trained; the other is a cylinder. As with chicks, the behavioral measure is the preference score. For the network, this is calculated as pref. score $= 100 \times a_t/(a_t + a_c)$, where a_t is the activation of the approach unit when the network is presented with the training (or target) picture, and a_c is the activation of the approach unit given the comparison picture. It is assumed that both values are positive; otherwise, the approach unit is taken to be off.

In these simulations, the network gets the training pattern (a "box") during training periods, and random input patterns (simulating the random firing of retinal neurons) otherwise. The onset of the predisposition is modeled by allowing the predisposition layer to help activate the outputs only after the network receives an "experience" signal. This signal models the sharp rise in plasma testosterone levels in dark-reared chicks following any sort of handling (Horn, 1985). Once the network has received the "experience" signal, the weights are modified for random input as well as for the box picture. Until then, weights are modified only for the box picture. Real chicks can be tested only once because of the danger of one-trial learning, so all chick data compares the behavior of groups of chicks under different conditions. The network's weights can be kept constant during testing, and the same network's responses can be measured before and after it is exposed to the relevant condition. All simulations were 100 iterations long.

3 Simulations

The simulations using this model currently address three phenomena which have been studied in chicks. First, in simple imprinting chicks learn to recognize a training object, and usually withdraw from other objects once they have imprinted on the training object. This simulation requires simply exposing the network to the training object and measuring its responses. The model "imprints" on the box if its preference for the box relative to both the head/neck and cylinder pictures increases during training. Ideally, the value of the approach unit for the cylinder and box will also decrease, to indicate the network's tendency to withdraw from "unfamiliar" stimuli.

Second, chicks with only the most minimal experience (such as being placed in a dark running wheel) develop a preference for a stuffed fowl over other stimuli. That is, they will approach the fowl significantly more than another object (Horn, 1985). This is modeled by turning on the "predisposition" and allowing the network to develop with no training whatsoever. The network mimics chick behavior if the preference score for the head/neck picture increases relative to the box and the cylinder pictures.

Third, after the predisposition has been allowed to develop, training on a red box decreases

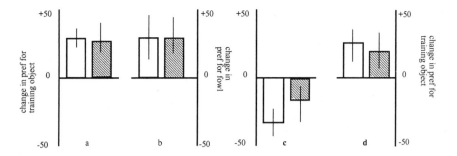

Figure 3: A summary of the results of the model. All bars are differences in preference scores between conditions for chicks (open bars) and the model (striped bars). a: Imprinting (change in preference for training object): trained − untrained. b: Predisposition (change in preference for fowl): experience − no experience (predisposition − no predisposition). c: Change in preference for fowl vs. box: trained − predisposition only. d: Change in preference for box vs. cylinder: trained − predisposition only. (Chick data adapted from (Horn, 1985; Bolhuis et al., 1989).)

a chick's preference for the fowl relative to the box. It also increases the chick's preference for the box relative to a blue cylinder or other unfamiliar object (Bolhuis et al., 1989). In the model, the predisposition layer is allowed to activate the output layer for 20 iterations before training starts. Then the model is exposed to the network for 25 iterations. If its preference score for the fowl decreases after training, the network has shown the same pattern as chicks.

4   Results and Discussion

A summary of the results is shown in Figure 3. Since these simulations try to capture the qualitative behavior of chicks, all results are shown as the change in preference scores between two conditions. For the chick data, the changes are approximate, and calculated from the means only. The network data is the average of the results for 10 networks, each with a different random seed (and therefore initial weight patterns). For the three conditions tested, the model's preference scores moved in the same direction as the chicks.

The interaction between imprinting and the predisposition cannot be investigated computationally unless the model displays both behaviors. These baseline behaviors are shown in Fig. 3-a and b. Trained chicks prefer the training object more after training than before (Horn, 1985); so does the model (Fig. 3-a). In the case of the predisposition (Fig. 3-b), the bird data is a difference between preferences for a stuffed fowl in chicks which had developed the predisposition (and therefore preferred the fowl) and those which had not (and therefore did not). Similarly, the network preferred the head/neck picture more after the predisposition had been allowed to develop than at the beginning of the simulation.

The interactions between imprinting and the predisposition are the real measures of the model's success. In Fig. 3-c, the predisposition has been allowed to develop before training begins. Trained birds with the predisposition were compared with untrained birds also with the predisposition (trained − untrained). Trained birds preferred the stuffed fowl less than their untrained counterparts (Bolhuis et al., 1989). The network's preference score just before training is subtracted from its score after training. As with the real chicks, the network prefers the head/neck picture less after training than it did before. Fig. 3-d shows that, as with chicks, the network's preference for the box increased relative to that for the cylinder during the course of training. For these three conditions, then, the model is qualitatively a success.

4.1   Discussion of Basic Results

The point of network models is that their behavior can be analyzed and understood more easily than animals'. The predisposition's behavior is quite simple: to the extent that a random input pattern is similar to the head/neck picture, it activates the predisposition layer, and through it the approach unit. Thus the winning unit in IMLL is correlated with the approach unit, and the connections are strengthened by the Hebb rule. Imprinting is similar, but only goes through the IMLL layer, so the approach unit may not be on. In both cases, the weights from the other units decay slowly during training, so that usually the other input patterns fail to excite the approach unit, and even excite the withdraw unit slightly because of its small positive bias. Only one process is required to obtain both the predisposition and imprinting, since both build representations in IMLL.

The interaction between imprinting and the predisposition first increases the preference for the predisposition, and then alters the weights affecting the reaction to the box picture. The training phase acts just like the ordinary imprinting phase, so that preference for both the head/neck and the cylinder decrease during training.

Some exploration of the relevant parameters suggests that the predisposition's behavior does not depend simply on its strength. Because IMLL is a winner-take-all layer, changing the predisposition's strength can, by moving the winning node around during training, cause previous learning to be lost. Such motion obviously has a large effect on the outcome of the simulation.

4.2   Temporal aspects of imprinting

The primary weakness of the model is its failure to account for some critical temporal aspects of imprinting. It is premature to draw many conclusions about chicks from this model, because it fails to account for either long-term sensitive periods or the short-term time course of the predisposition.

Neither the predisposition nor imprinting in the model have yet been shown to have sensitive periods, though both do in real birds (Horn, 1985; Johnson et al., 1985). Preliminary results, however, suggest that imprinting in the networks does have a sensitive period, presumably because of weight saturation during learning. It is not yet clear whether the predisposition's sensitive period will require an exogenous process.

Second, the model does not yet show the appropriate time course for the development of the predisposition. In chicks, the predisposition develops fairly slowly over the course of five or so hours (Johnson et al., 1985). In chicks for which the first experience is training, the predisposition's effect is to increase the bird's preference for the fowl regardless of training object, over the course of the hours following training (Johnson et al., 1985). In the model, the predisposition appears quickly and, because of weight decay and other factors, the strength of the predisposition slowly decreases over the iterations following training, rather than increasing. Increasing the learning rate of IMLL over time could solve this problem. Once it exhibits time course behaviors, especially if no further processes need to be postulated, the model will facilitate interesting analyses of how a simple set of processes and assumptions can interact to produce highly complicated behavior.

5   Conclusion

This model displays some important interactions between learning and a predisposition in filial imprinting. It is the first which accounts for the predisposition at all. Other models of imprinting have either ignored the issue or built in the predisposition by hand. In this model, the interaction between two simple systems, a fixed predisposition and a learned approach system, gives rise to one important more complex behavior. In addition, the two representations of the head/neck predisposition can account for lesion studies in which lesioning IMLL removes a chick's memory of its training object or prevents it from learning anything new about specific objects, but leaves the preference for heads and necks intact (Horn, 1985). Clearly, if the IMLL layer is missing, the network loses any information it might have learned about training objects, and is unable to learn anything new from future training. The predisposition, however, is still intact and able to influence the network's behavior.

The nature of predispositions like chicks' naive preference for heads and necks, and how they interact with learning, are interesting in a number of fields. Morton and Johnson (1991) have already explored the similarities between chicks' preferences for heads and necks and human infants' preferences for human faces. Such naive preferences are also important in any discussion of innate information, and the number of processes needed to handle innate and learned information. Although this model and its successors cannot directly address these issues, I hope that their explication of how fairly general predispositions can influence learning will improve understanding of some of the mechanisms underlying them.

Acknowledgements

This work was supported by a fellowship from the National Physical Sciences Consortium.

References

P. Bateson and G. Horn. Imprinting and recognition memory: A neural net model. *Animal Behaviour*, 48(3):695–715, 1994.

J. J. Bolhuis, M. H. Johnson, and G. Horn. Interacting mechanisms during the formation of filial preferences: The development of a predisposition does not prevent learning. *Journal of Experimental Psychology: Animal Behavior Processes*, 15(4):376–382, 1989.

D. C. Davies, M. H. Johnson, and G. Horn. The effect of the neurotoxin dsp4 on the development of a predisposition in the domestic chick. *Developmental Psychobiology*, 25(2):251–259, 1992.

G. Horn. *Memory, Imprinting, and the Brain: An inquiry into mechanisms*. Clarendon Press, Oxford, 1985.

M. H. Johnson, J. J. Bolhuis, and G. Horn. Interaction between acquired preferences and developing predispositions during imprinting. *Animal Behaviour*, 33(3):1000–1006, 1985.

K. Miller, J. Keller, and M. Stryker. Ocular dominance column development: analysis and simulation. *Science*, 245:605–615, 1989.

J. Morton and M. H. Johnson. Conspec and conlern: a two-process theory of infant face recognition. *Psychological Review*, 98(2):164–181, 1991.

R. C. O'Reilly and M. H. Johnson. Object recognition and sensitive periods: A computational analysis of visual imprinting. *Neural Computation*, 6(3):357–389, 1994.

Adaptation in Speech Motor Control

John F. Houde*
UCSF Keck Center
Box 0732
San Francisco, CA 94143
houde@phy.ucsf.edu

Michael I. Jordan
MIT Dept. of Brain and Cognitive Sci.
E10-034D
Cambridge, MA 02139
jordan@psyche.mit.edu

Abstract

Human subjects are known to adapt their motor behavior to a shift of the visual field brought about by wearing prism glasses over their eyes. We have studied the analog of this effect in speech. Using a device that can feed back transformed speech signals in real time, we exposed subjects to alterations of their own speech feedback. We found that speakers learn to adjust their production of a vowel to compensate for feedback alterations that change the vowel's perceived phonetic identity; moreover, the effect generalizes across consonant contexts and to different vowels.

1   INTRODUCTION

For more than a century, it has been know that humans will adapt their reaches to altered visual feedback [8]. One of the most studied examples of this adaptation is prism adaptation, which is seen when a subject reaches to targets while wearing image-shifting prism glasses [2]. Initially, the subject misses the targets, but he soon learns to compensate and reach accurately. This compensation is retained beyond the time that the glasses are worn: when the glasses are removed, the subject's reaches now overshoot targets in the direction that he compensated. This retained compensation is called adaptation, and its generation from exposure to altered sensory feedback is called *sensorimotor adaptation* (SA).

In the study reported here, we investigated whether SA could be observed in a motor task that is quite different from reaching – speech production. Specifically, we examined whether the control of phonetically relevant speech features would respond adaptively to altered auditory feedback. By itself, this is an important theoretical question because various aspects of speech production have already been shown to be sensitive to auditory feedback [5, 1, 4]. Moreover, we were particularly

---
*To whom correspondence should be addressed.

interested in whether speech SA would also exhibit generalization. If so, speech SA could be used to examine the organization of speech motor control. For example, suppose we observed adaptation of [ε] in "get". We could then examine whether we also see adaptation of [ε] in "peg". If so, then producing [ε] in the two different words must access a common, adapted representation – evidence for a hierarchical speech production system in which word productions are composed from smaller units such as phonemes. We could also examine whether adapting [ε] in "get" causes adaptation of [æ] in "gat". If so, then the production representations of [ε] and [æ] could not be independent, supporting the idea that vowels are produced by controlling a common set of features. Such theories about the organization of the speech production system have been postulated in phonology and phonetics, but the empirical evidence supporting these theories has generally been observational and hence not entirely conclusive [7, 6].

2 METHODS

To study speech SA, we focused on vowel production because the phonetically relevant features of vowel sounds are formant frequencies, which are feasible to alter in real time.[1]

To alter the formants of a subject's speech feedback, we built the apparatus shown in Figure 1. The subject wears earphones and a microphone and sits in front of a PC video monitor that presents words to be spoken aloud. The signal from the microphone is sent to a Digital Signal Processing board, which collects a 64ms time interval from which a magnitude spectrum is calculated. From this spectrum, formant frequencies and amplitudes are estimated. To alter the speech, the first three formant frequencies are shifted, and the shifted formants drive a formant synthesizer that creates the output speech sent to the subject's earphones. This analysis-synthesis process was accomplished with only 16ms of feedback delay. To minimize how much the subject directly heard of his own voice via bone conduction, the subject produced only whispered speech, masked with mild noise.

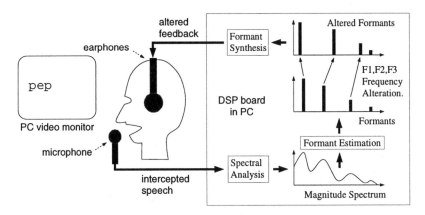

Figure 1: The apparatus used in the study.

For each subject in our experiment, we shifted formants along the path defined by the (F1,F2,F3) frequencies of a subject's productions of the vowels [i], [ɩ], [ε], [æ],

---

[1]See [3] for detailed discussion of the methods used in this study.

and [a].[2] Figure 2 shows examples of this shifting process in (F1,F2) space for the feedback transformations that were used in the study. To shift formants along the subject's [i]-[a] path, we extend the path at both ends and we number the endpoints and vowels to make a path position measure that normalizes the distances between vowels. The formants of each speech sound F produced by the subject were then re-represented in terms of path projection – the path position of nearest path point P, and path deviation – the distance D to this point P. Feedback transformations were constructed to alter path projections while preserving path deviations. Two different transformations were used. The +2.0 transformation added 2.0 to path projections: under this transform, if the subject produced speech sound F (a sound near [ε]), he heard instead sound F+ (a sound near [a]). The subject could compensate for this transform and hear sound F only by shifting his production of F to F- (a sound near [i]). The -2.0 transformation subtracted 2.0 from path projections: under this transformation, if the subject produced F, he heard F-. Thus, in this case, the subject could compensate by shifting production to F+.

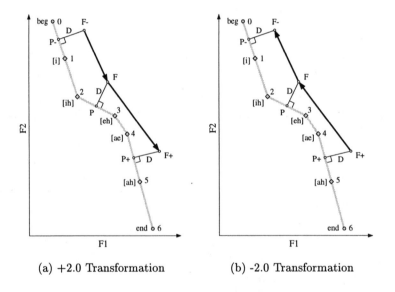

(a) +2.0 Transformation   (b) -2.0 Transformation

Figure 2: Feedback transformations used in the study.

These feedback transformations were used in an experiment in which a subject was visually prompted to whisper words with a 300ms target duration. Word promptings occurred in groups of ten called *epochs*. Within each epoch, the first six words came from a set of training words and the last four came from a set of testing words. The subject heard feedback of his first five word productions in each epoch, while masking noise blocked his hearing for his remaining five word productions in the epoch. Thus, the subject only heard feedback of his production of the first five training words and never heard his productions of the testing words.

---

[2]Where possible, we use standard phonetic symbols for vowel sounds: [i] as in "seat", [ɪ] as in "hit", [ε] as in "get", [æ] as in "hat", and [a] as in "pop". Where font limitations prevent us from using these symbols, we use the alternate notation of [i], [ih], [eh], [ae], and [ah], respectively, for the same vowel sounds.

The experiment lasted 2 hours and consisted of 422 epochs divided over five phases:

1. A 10 minute *warmup phase* used to acclimate the subject to the experimental setup.

2. A 17 minute *baseline phase* used to measure formants of the subject's normal vowel productions.

3. A 20 minute *ramp phase* in which the subject's feedback was increasingly altered up to a maximum value.

4. A 1 hour *training phase* in which the subject produced words while the feedback was maximally altered.

5. A 17 minute *test phase* used to measure formants of the subject's post-exposure vowel productions while his feedback was maximally altered.

By the end of the ramp phase, feedback alteration reached its maximum strength, which was +2.0 for half the subjects and -2.0 for the other subjects. In addition, all subjects were run in a control experiment in which feedback was never altered.

The two word sets from which prompted words were selected were both sets of CVC words. Training words (in which adaptation was induced) were all bilabials with [ε] as the vowel ("pep", "peb", "bep", and "beb"). Testing words (in which generalization of the training word adaptation was measured) were divided into two subsets, each designed to measure a different type of generalization: (1) context generalization words, which had the same vowel [ε] as the training words but varied the consonant context ("peg", "gep", and "teg"); (2) vowel target generalization words, which had the same consonant context as the training words but varied the vowel ("pip,", "peep,","pap", and "pop").

Eight male MIT students participated in the study. All were native speakers of North American English and all were naive to the purpose of the study.

3 RESULTS

To illustrate how we measured compensation and adaptation in the experiments, we first show the results for an individual subject. Figure 3 shows (F1,F2) plots of response of subject OB in both the adaptation experiment (in which he was exposed to the -2.0 feedback transformation) and the control experiment. In each figure, the dotted line is OB's [i]-[a] path.

Figure 3(a) shows OB's compensation responses, which were measured from his productions of the training words made when he heard feedback of his whispering. The solid arrow labeled "-2.0 xform" shows how much his mean vowel formants changed (testing phase - baseline phase) after being exposed to the -2.0 feedback transformation. It shows he shifted his production of [ε] to something a bit past [æ], which corresponds to a path projection change of slightly more than one vowel interval towards [a]. Thus, since the path projection shift of the transform was -2.0 (2.0 vowel intervals towards [i]), the figure shows that OB compensates for over half the action of the transformation. The hollow arrow in Figure 3(a) shows how OB heard his compensation. It shows he heard his actual production shift from [ε] towards [a] as a shift from [i] back towards [ε].

Figure 3(b) shows how much of OB's compensation was retained when he whispered the training words with feedback blocked by noise. This retained compensation is called adaptation, and it was measured from path projection changes by the same method used to measure compensation. In the figure, we see OB's adaptation response (the solid "-2.0 xform" arrow) is a path projection shift of slightly less than one vowel interval, so his adaptation is slightly less than half. Thus, the figure shows that OB retains an appreciable amount of his compensation in the absence of feedback.

Finally, in both plots of Figure 3, the almost non-existent "control" arrows show that OB exhibited almost no formant change in the control experiment – as we would expect since feedback was never altered in this experiment.

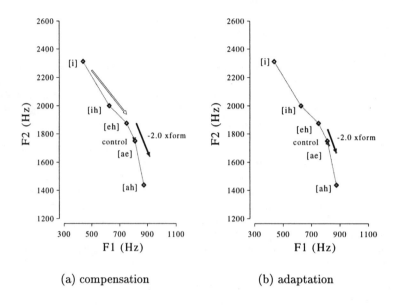

(a) compensation   (b) adaptation

Figure 3: Subject OB compensation and adaptation.

The plots in Figure 4 show that there was significant compensation and adaptation across all subjects. In these plots, the vertical scale indicates how much the changes in mean vowel formants (testing phase - baseline phase) in each subject's productions of the training words compensated for the action of the feedback transformation he was exposed to. The filled circles linked by the solid line show compensation (Figure 4(a)) and retained compensation, or adaptation (Figure 4(b)) across subjects in the adaptation experiment in which feedback was altered; the open circles linked by the dotted line show the same measures from the control experiment in which feedback was not altered. (The solid and dotted lines facilitate comparison of results across subjects but do not signify any relationship between subjects.) In the control experiment, for each subject, compensation and adaptation were measured with respect to the feedback transformation used in the adaptation experiment.

The plots show that there are large variations in compensation and adaptation across subjects, but overall there was significantly more compensation ($p < 0.006$) and adaptation ($p < 0.023$) in the adaptation experiments that in the control experiments.

Figure 5 shows plots of how much of the adaptation observed in the training words carried over the the testing words. For each testing word shown, a measure of this carryover called mean generalization is plotted, which was calculated as a ratio of adaptations: the adaptation seen in the testing word divided by the adaptation seen in the training words (adaptation values observed in the control experiment were

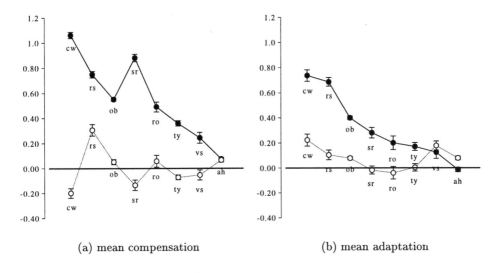

(a) mean compensation   (b) mean adaptation

Figure 4: Mean compensation and adaptation across all subjects.

subtracted out to remove any effects not arising from exposure to altered feedback).

Figure 5(a) shows mean generalization for the context generalization words except for "pep" (since "pep" was also a training word). The plot shows large variance in mean generalization for each of the three words, but overall there was significant ($p < 0.040$) mean generalization. Thus, there was significant carryover of the adaptation of [ε] in the training words to different consonant contexts.

Figure 5(b) shows mean generalization for the vowel target generalization words. Not all of these words are shown: unfortunately, we weren't able to accurately estimate the formants of [i] and [a], so "peep" and "pop" were dropped from our generalization analysis. For the remaining two vowel target generalization words, the plot shows large variance in mean generalization for each of the words, but overall there was significant ($p < 0.013$) mean generalization. Thus, there was significant generalization of the adaptation of [ε] to the vowels [ɪ] and [æ].

4   DISCUSSION

Several conclusions can be drawn from the experiment described above. First, comparison of the adaptation and control experiment results seen in Figure 4 shows a clear effect of exposure to the altered feedback: this exposure caused compensation responses in most subjects. Furthermore, the adaptation results show that this compensation was retained in absence of acoustic feedback. Next, the context generalization results seen in Figure 5(a) show that some adapted representation of [ε] is shared across the training and testing words. These results provide evidence for a hierarchical speech production system in which words are composed from smaller phoneme-like units. Finally, the vowel target generalization results seen in Figure 5(b) show that the production representations of [ɪ], [ε], and [æ] are not independent, suggesting that these vowels are produced by controlling a common set of features.

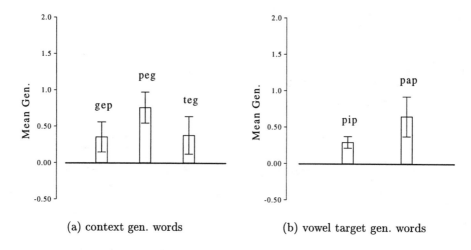

Figure 5: Mean generalization for the testing words, averaged across subjects.

Thus, in summary, our study has shown (1) that speech production, like reaching, can be made to exhibit sensorimotor adaptation, and (2) that this adaptation effect exhibits generalization that can be used to make inferences about the structure of the speech production system.

Acknowledgments

We thank J. Perkell, K. Stevens, R. Held and P. Sabes for helpful discussions.

References

[1] V. L. Gracco et al., (1994) *J. Acoust. Soc. Am.* 95:2821

[2] H. V. Helmholtz, (1867) *Treatise on physiological optics, Vol. 3* (Eng. Trans. by Optical Soc. of America, Rochester, NY, 1925)

[3] J. F. Houde (1997), *Sensorimotor Adaptation in Speech Production*, Doctoral Dissertation, M. I. T., Cambridge, MA.

[4] H. Kawahara (1993) *J. Acoust. Soc. Am.* 94:1883.

[5] B. S. Lee (1950) *J. Acoust. Soc. Am.* 22:639.

[6] W. J. M. Levelt (1989), *Speaking: from intention to articulation*, MIT Press, Cambridge, MA.

[7] A. S. Meyer (1992), *Cognition* 42:181.

[8] R. B. Welch (1986), *Handbook of Perception and Human Performance*, K. R. Boff, L. Kaufman, J. P. Thomas Eds., John Wiley and Sons, New York.

Learning Human-like Knowledge by Singular Value Decomposition: A Progress Report

Thomas K. Landauer   **Darrell Laham**
Department of Psychology & Institute of Cognitive Science
University of Colorado at Boulder   Boulder, CO 80309-0345
{landauer, dlaham}@psych.colorado.edu

Peter Foltz
Department of Psychology
New Mexico State University   Las Cruces, NM 88003-8001
pfoltz@crl.nmsu.edu

Abstract

Singular value decomposition (SVD) can be viewed as a method for unsupervised training of a network that associates two classes of events reciprocally by linear connections through a single hidden layer. SVD was used to learn and represent relations among very large numbers of words (20k-60k) and very large numbers of natural text passages (1k-70k) in which they occurred. The result was 100-350 dimensional "semantic spaces" in which any trained or newly added word or passage could be represented as a vector, and similarities were measured by the cosine of the contained angle between vectors. Good accuracy in simulating human judgments and behaviors has been demonstrated by performance on multiple-choice vocabulary and domain knowledge tests, emulation of expert essay evaluations, and in several other ways. Examples are also given of how the kind of knowledge extracted by this method can be applied.

1 INTRODUCTION

Traditionally, imbuing machines with human-like knowledge has relied primarily on explicit coding of symbolic facts into computer data structures and algorithms. A serious limitation of this approach is people's inability to access and express the vast reaches of unconscious knowledge on which they rely, knowledge based on masses of implicit inference and irreversibly melded data. A more important deficiency of this state of affairs is that by coding the knowledge ourselves, (as we also do when we assign subjectively hypothesized rather than objectively identified features to input or output nodes in a neural net) we beg important questions of how humans acquire and represent the coded knowledge in the first place.

Thus, from both engineering and scientific perspectives, there are reasons to try to design learning machines that can acquire human-like quantities of human-like knowledge from the same sources as humans. The success of such techniques would not prove that the same mechanisms are used by humans, but because we presently do not know how the problem can be solved in principle, successful simulation may offer theoretical insights as well as practical applications. In the work reported here we have found a way to induce significant amounts of knowledge about the meanings of passages and of their constituent vocabularies of words by training on large bodies of natural text. In general terms, the method simultaneously extracts the similarity between words (the likelihood of being used in passages that convey similar ideas) and the similarity of passages (the likelihood of containing words of similar meaning). The conjoint estimation of similarity is accomplished by a fundamentally simple representational technique that exploits mutual constraints implicit in the occurrences of very many words in very many contexts. We view the resultant system both as a means for automatically learning much of the semantic content of words and passages, and as a potential computational model for the process that underlies the corresponding human ability.

While the method starts with data about the natural contextual co-occurrences of words, it uses them in a different manner than has previously been applied. A long-standing objection to co-occurrence statistics as a source of linguistic knowledge (Chomsky's 1957) is that many grammatically acceptable expressions, for example sentences with potentially unlimited embedding structures, cannot be produced by a finite Markov process whose elements are transition probabilities from word to word. If word-word probabilities are insufficient to generate language, then, it is argued, acquiring estimates of such probabilities cannot be a way that language can be learned. However, our approach to statistical knowledge learning differs from those considered in the past in two ways. First, the basic associational data from which knowledge is induced are not transition frequencies between successive individual words or phrases, but rather the frequencies with which particular words appear as components of relatively large natural passages, utterances of the kind that humans use to convey complete ideas. The result of this move is that the statistical regularities reflected are relations among unitary expressions of meaning, rather than syntactic constraints on word order that may serve additional purposes such as output and input processing efficiencies, error protection, or esthetic style. Second, the mutual constraints inherent in a multitude of such local co-occurrence relations are jointly satisfied by being forced into a global representation of lower dimensionality. This constraint satisfaction, a form of induction, was accomplished by singular value decomposition, a linear factorization technique that produces a representational structure equivalent to a three layer neural network model with linear activation functions.

2 THE TEXT ANALYSIS MODEL AND METHOD

The text analysis process that we have explored is called Latent Semantic Analysis (LSA) (Deerwester et al., 1990; Landauer and Dumais, 1997). It comprises four steps:

(1) A large body of text is represented as a matrix [ij], in which rows stand for individual word types, columns for meaning-bearing passages such as sentences or paragraphs, and cells contain the frequency with which a word occurs in a passage.

(2) Cell entries $(freq_{ij})$ are transformed to:

$$\frac{\log\left(freq_{ij}+1\right)}{-\sum_{1-j}\left(\left(\frac{freq_{ij}}{\sum_{1-j}freq_{ij}}\right)*\log\left(\frac{freq_{ij}}{\sum_{1-j}freq_{ij}}\right)\right)}$$

a measure of the first order association of a word and its context.

(3) The matrix is then subjected to singular value decomposition (Berry, 1992):

$$[ij] = [ik] [kk] [jk]'$$

in which [ik] and [jk] have orthonormal columns, [kk] is a diagonal matrix of singular values, and $k <= max (i,j)$.

(4) Finally, all but the d largest singular values are set to zero. Pre-multiplication of the right-hand matrices produces a least-squares best approximation to the original matrix given the number of dimensions, d, (hidden units in a corresponding neural net model representation) that are retained. The SVD with dimension reduction constitutes a constraint-satisfaction induction process in that it predicts the original observations on the basis of linear relations among the abstracted representations of the data that it has retained. By hypothesis, the analysis induces human-like relationships among passages and words because humans also make inferences about semantic relationships from abstracted representations based on limited data, and do so by an analogous process.

In the result, each word and passage is represented as a vector of length d. Performance depends strongly on the choice of number of dimensions. The optimal number is typically around 300. The similarity of any two words, any two text passages, or any word and any text passage, are computed by measures on their vectors. We have most often used the cosine (of the contained angle between the vectors in semantic d-space) — which we interpret as the degree of qualitative similarity of meaning. The length of vectors is also useful and interpretable.

3 TESTS OF LSA'S PERFORMANCE

LSA's ability to simulate human knowledge and meaning relations has been tested in a variety of ways. Here we describe two relatively direct sources of evidence and briefly list several others.

3.1 VOCABULARY & DOMAIN KNOWLEDGE TESTS

In all cases, LSA was first trained on a large text corpus intended to be representative of the text from which humans gain most of the semantic knowledge to be simulated. In a previously reported test (Landauer and Dumais, 1997), LSA was trained on approximately five million words of text sampled from a high-school level encyclopedia, then tested on multiple choice items from the Educational Testing Service Test of English as a Foreign Language (TOEFL). These test questions present a target word or short phrase and ask the student to choose the one of four alternative words or phrases that is most similar in meaning. LSA's answer was determined by computing the cosine between the derived vector for the target word or phrase and each of the alternatives and choosing the largest. LSA was correct on 64% of the 80 items, identical to the average of a large sample of students from non-English speaking countries who had applied for admission to U. S. colleges. When in error, LSA made choices positively correlated (product-moment $r = .44$) with those preferred by students. We have recently replicated this result with training on a similar sized sample from the Associated Press newswire

In a new set of tests, LSA was trained on a popular introductory psychology textbook (Myers, 1995) and tested with the same four-alternative multiple choice tests used for students in two large classes. In these experiments, LSA's score was about 60%—lower than the class averages but above passing level, and far above guessing probability. Its errors again resembled those of students; it got right about half as many of questions rated difficult by the test constructors as ones rated easy (Landauer, Foltz and Laham, 1997).

3.2 ESSAY TESTS

Word-word meaning similarities are a good test of knowledge—indeed, vocabulary tests are the best single measure of human intelligence. However, they are not sufficient to assess the correspondence of LSA and human knowledge because people usually express knowledge via larger verbal strings, such as sentences, paragraphs and articles. Thus, just as multiple choice tests of student knowledge are often supplemented by essay tests whose content is then judged by humans, we wished to evaluate the adequacy of LSA's representation of knowledge in complete passages of text. We could not have LSA write essays because it has no means for producing sentences. However, we were able to assess the accuracy with which LSA could extract and represent the knowledge expressed in essays written by students by simulating judgments about their content that were made by human readers (Landauer, Laham, Rehder, & Schreiner, in press).

In these tests, students were asked to write short essays to cover an assigned topic or to answer a posed question. In various experiments, the topics included anatomy and function of the heart, phenomena from introductory psychology, the history of the Panama Canal, and tolerance of diversity in America. In each case, LSA was first trained either on a large sample of instructional text from the same domain or, in the latter case, on combined text from the very large number of essays themselves, to produce a high-dimensional (100-350 dimensions in the various tests) semantic space. We then represented each essay simply as the vector average of the vectors for the words it contained. Two properties of these average vectors were then used to measure the quality and quantity of knowledge conveyed by an essay: (1) the similarity (measured as the cosine of the angle between vectors) of the student essay and one or more standard essays, and (2) the total amount of domain specific content, measured as the vector length.

In each case, two human experts independently rated the overall quality of each essay on a five or ten point scale. The judges were either university course instructors or professional exam readers from Educational Testing Service. The LSA measures were calibrated with respect to the judges' rating scale in several different ways, but because they gave nearly the same results only one will be described here. In this method, each student essay was compared to a large (90-200) set of essays previously scored by experts, and the ten most similar (by cosine) identified. The target essay was then assigned a "quality" score component consisting of the cosine-weighted average of the ten. A second, "relevant quantity", score component was the vector length of the student essay. Finally, regression on expert scores was used to weight the quality and quantity scores (However, the weights in all cases were so close to equal that merely adding them would have given comparable results). Calibration was performed on data independent of that used to evaluate the relation between LSA and expert ratings.

The correlation between the LSA score for an essay and that assigned by the average of the human readers was .80, .64, .XX and .84 for the four sets of exams. The comparable correlation between one reader and the other was .83, .65, .XX and .82, respectively. In the heart topic case, each student had also taken a carefully constructed "objective" test over the same material (a short answer test with near perfect scoring agreement). The correlation between the LSA essay score and the objective test was .81, the average correlation for the two expert readers .74.

A striking aspect of these results is that the LSA representations were based on analyses of the essays that took no account of word order, each essay was treated as a "bag of words". In extracting meaning from a text, human readers presumably rely on syntax as well as the mere combination of words it contains, yet they were no better at agreeing on an essay's quality or in assigning a score that predicted a performance on a separate test of knowledge. Apparently, either the relevant information conveyed by word order in sentences is redundant with the information that can be inferred from the combination of words in the essay, or the processes used by LSA and humans extract different but compensatingly useful information.

3.3   OTHER EVIDENCE

LSA has been compared with human knowledge in several additional ways, some confirming the correspondence, others indicating limitations. Here are some examples, all based on encyclopedia corpus training.

(1) Overall LSA similarity between antonyms (mean cos = .18) was equivalent to that between synonyms (mean cos = .17) in triplets sampled from an antonym/synonym dictionary (W & R Chambers, 1989), both of which significantly exceeded that for unrelated pairs (mean cos = .01; *ps* < .0001). However for antonym (but not for synonym) pairs a dominant dimension of difference could easily be extracted by computing a one dimensional unfolding using the LSA cosines from a set of words listed in Roget's (1992) thesaurus as related respectively to the two members of the pair.

(2) Anglin (1970) asked children and adults to sort words varying in concept relations and parts of speech. LSA word-word similarity correlates .50 with children and .32 with adults for the number of times they sorted two words together. Conceptual structure is reflected, but grammatical classification, strong in the adult data, is not.

(3) When people are asked to decide that a letter string is a word, they do so faster if they have just read a sentence that does not contain the word but implies a related concept (e.g. Till, Mross & Kintsch, 1988). LSA mirrors this result with high similarities between the same sentences and words. (Landauer & Dumais, 1997).

(4) People frequently make a logical error, called the conjunction error by Tversky and Kahneman (1974), in which they estimate that the probability that an object is a member of a class is greater than that it is a member of a superset class when the description of the object is "similar" to the description of the subset. For example, when told that "Linda is a young woman who is single, outspoken...deeply concerned with issues of discrimination and social justice," over 80% of even statistically sophisticated subjects rate it more likely that Linda is a feminist bank teller than that Linda is a bank teller (Tversky & Kahneman, 1980). LSA similarities between descriptions of people and occupations of this kind taken from Shafir, Smith and Osherson (1990) were computed as the cosine between the vector averages of words in the paired person-occupation descriptions. Conjunction error statements were more similar to the subset than superset statement in 12 out of 14 cases (*p*<.01), showing that LSA's representation of sentential meaning reflected similarity relations of the sort that have been hypothesized to underlie the conjunction fallacy in human judgment.

(5) A semantic subspace was constructed for words from natural kind and artifact categories whose differential preservation is characteristic of agnosias due to local damage from herpes simplex encephalitis (Warrington & Shallice, 1984). Principal components analysis of the similarities among these words as represented by LSA revealed that categories that tend to be lost contain words that are more highly inter-related than those in preserved categories (Laham, in press).

Of course, LSA does not capture all of the human knowledge conveyed by text. Some of the shortfall is probably due merely to the use of training corpora that are still imperfectly representative of the language experience of a typical person, and to lack of knowledge from non-textual sources. For example, in all these studies, less total text was used for LSA training than even a single educated adult would have read. However, a more fundamental restriction is that the analysis does not reflect order relations between words, and therefore cannot extract information that depends on syntax. Because the analysis discovers and represents only unsigned continuous similarities, it can be used to induce only certain classes of structural relations, not including ones that express Boolean, causal or other non-commutative logical relations. As we have seen, this lack does not prevent accurate simulation of human cognition in many cases, possibly because humans also frequently rely on similarity rather than syntax-based, discrete logic (Tversky and Kahneman, 1983); however, it does limit the utility of the results for populating the symbolic data structures commonly used to represent knowledge in traditional AI. On the other hand, as examples in the next section show, continuous-valued similarity relations can be fruitfully applied if appropriate computational use is made of them.

4 SAMPLE APPLICATIONS

LSA has been used successfully in a variety of experimental applications, including the essay scoring techniques described earlier. Here are some additional examples:

(1) The technique has been used to improve automatic information retrieval by 20-30% over otherwise identical methods by allowing users' queries to match documents with the desired conceptual meaning but expressed in different words (Dumais, 1991, 1994).

(2) By training on corpora of translated text in which the words of corresponding paragraphs in the two languages are combined in the "bags of words", LSA has been able to provide at least as good retrieval when queries and documents are in a different language as when in the same language (Landauer and Littman, 1990).

(3) LSA-based measures of the similarity of student essays on a topic to instructional texts can predict how much an individual student will learn from a particular text (Wolfe et al., in press; Rehder et al., in press). To do this, the full set of student essays and the texts in question are aligned along a single dimension that best accommodates the LSA similarities among them. Estimates from one such experiment showed that using LSA to choose the optimal one of four texts for each student (a text that is slightly more sophisticated than the student) rather than assigning all students the overall best text (which LSA also picked correctly) increased the average amount learned by over 40%.

(4) LSA-based measures of conceptual similarity between successive sentences accurately predict differences in judged coherence and measured comprehensibility of text (Foltz, Kintsch and Landauer, in press).

5 SUMMARY

SVD-based learning of the structure underlying the use of words in meaningful contexts has been found capable of deriving and representing the similarity of meaning of words and text passages in a manner that accurately simulates corresponding similarity relations as reflected in several sorts of human judgments and behavior. The validity of the resulting representation of meaning similarities has been established in a variety of ways, and the utility of its knowledge representation illustrated by several educational and cognitive psychological research applications. It is obviously too early to assess whether the particular computational model is a true analog of the process used by the human brain to accomplish the same things. However, the basic process, the representation of myriad local associative relations between components and larger contexts of experience in a joint space of lower dimensionality, offers, for the first time, a candidate for such a mechanism that has been shown sufficient to approximate human knowledge acquisition from natural sources at natural scale.

Acknowledgments

We thank members of the LSA research group at the University of Colorado for valuable collaboration and advice: Walter Kintsch, Bob Rehder, Mike Wolfe, & M. E. Shreiner. We especially acknowledge two participants from the Spring 1997 LSA seminar at CU whose unpublished work is described: Alan Sanfey (3.3.4) and Michael Emerson (3.3.1). Thanks also to Susan T. Dumais of Bellcore.

References

Anglin, J. M. (1970). *The growth of word meaning.* Cambridge, MA: MIT.

Berry, M. W. (1992). Large scale singular value computations. *International Journal of Supercomputer Applications,* **6**, 13-49.

Deerwester, S., Dumais, S. T., Furnas, G. W., Landauer, T. K., & Harshman, R. (1990). Indexing By Latent Semantic Analysis. *Journal of the American Society For Information Science,* **41**, 391-407.

Dumais, S. T. (1991). Improving the retrieval of information from external sources. *Behavior Research Methods, Instruments and Computers,* **23**, 229-236.

Dumais, S. T. (1994). Latent semantic indexing (LSI) and TREC-2. In D. Harman (Ed.), *National Institute of Standards and Technology Text Retrieval Conference.* NIST special publication.

Foltz, P. W., Kintsch, W., & Landauer, T. K. (in press). Analysis of text coherence using Latent Semantic Analysis. *Discourse Processes.*

Laham, D. (in press). Latent Semantic Analysis approaches to categorization. *Proceedings of the Cognitive Science Society,* 1997.

Landauer, T. K., & Dumais, S. T. (1997). A solution to Plato's problem: The Latent Semantic Analysis theory of the acquisition, induction, and representation of knowledge. *Psychological Review,* **104**, 211-240.

Landauer, T. K., Foltz, P. W., & Laham, D. (1997). *Latent Semantic Analysis passes the test: knowledge representation and multiple-choice testing.* Manuscript in preparation.

Landauer, T. K., Laham, D., Rehder, B. & Schreiner, M .E. (in press). How well can passage meaning be derived without using word order: A comparison of Latent Semantic Analysis and humans. *Proceedings of the Cognitive Science Society,* 1997.

Landauer, T. K., & Littman, M. L. (1990). Fully automatic cross-language document retrieval using latent semantic indexing. In *Proceedings of the Sixth Annual Conference of the UW Centre for the New Oxford English Dictionary and Text Research* (pp. 31-38). Waterloo, Ontario: UW Centre for the New OED.

Myers, D. G. (1995). *Psychology, Fourth Edition.* NY, NY: Worth.

Rehder, B., Schreiner, M. E., Wolfe, B. W., Laham, D., Landauer, T. K., & Kintsch, W. (in press). Using Latent Semantic Analysis to assess knowledge: Some technical considerations. *Discourse Processes.*

Shafir, E., Smith, E. E., & Osherson, D. N. (1990). Typicality and reasoning judgments. *Memory & Cognition,* **3**, 229-239.

Till, R. E., Mross, E. F., & Kintsch. W. (1988). Time course of priming for associate and inference words in discourse context. *Memory and Cognition,* **16**, 283-299.

Tversky, A., & Kahneman, D. (1974). Judgment under uncertainty: Heuristics and biases. *Science,* **185**, 1124-1131.

Tversky, A., & Kahneman, D. (1980). Judgments of and by representativeness. In D. Kahneman, P. Slovic, & A. Tversky (Eds.), *Judgment under uncertainty: Heuristics and biases.* New York: Cambridge University Press.

Tversky, A., & Kahneman, D. (1983). Extensional versus intuitive reasoning: The conjunction fallacy in probability judgment. *Psychological Review,* **90**, 293-315.

Warrington, E. K., & Shallice, T. (1984). Category-specific semantic impairments. *Brain,* **107**, 829-853.

Wolfe, M. B., Schreiner, M. E., Rehder, B., Laham, D., Foltz, P. W., Kintsch, W., & Landauer, T. K. (in press). Learning from text: Matching readers and text by Latent Semantic Analysis. *Discourse Processes.*

Multi-modular Associative Memory

Nir Levy   David Horn
School of Physics and Astronomy
Tel-Aviv University Tel Aviv 69978, Israel

Eytan Ruppin
Departments of Computer Science & Physiology
Tel-Aviv University Tel Aviv 69978, Israel

Abstract

Motivated by the findings of modular structure in the association
cortex, we study a multi-modular model of associative memory that
can successfully store memory patterns with different levels of activity. We show that the segregation of synaptic conductances into
intra-modular linear and inter-modular nonlinear ones considerably
enhances the network's memory retrieval performance. Compared
with the conventional, single-module associative memory network,
the multi-modular network has two main advantages: It is less susceptible to damage to columnar input, and its response is consistent
with the cognitive data pertaining to category specific impairment.

1   Introduction

Cortical modules were observed in the somatosensory and visual cortices a few
decades ago. These modules differ in their structure and functioning but are likely to
be an elementary unit of processing in the mammalian cortex. Within each module
the neurons are interconnected. Input and output fibers from and to other cortical
modules and subcortical areas connect to these neurons. More recently, modules
were also found in the association cortex [1] where memory processes supposedly
take place. Ignoring the modular structure of the cortex, most theoretical models
of associative memory have treated single module networks. This paper develops
a novel multi-modular network that mimics the modular structure of the cortex.
In this framework we investigate the computational rational behind cortical multi-
modular organization, in the realm of memory processing.

Does multi-modular structure lead to computational advantages? Naturally one may think that modules are necessary in order to accommodate memories of different coding levels. We show in the next section that this is not the case, since one may accommodate such memories in a standard sparse coding network . In fact, when trying to capture the same results in a modular network we run into problems, as shown in the third section: If both inter and intra modular synapses have linear characteristics, the network can sustain memory patterns with only a limited range of activity levels. The solution proposed here is to distinguish between intra-modular and inter-modular couplings, endowing the inter-modular ones with nonlinear characteristics. From a computational point of view, this leads to a modular network that has a large capacity for memories with different coding levels. The resulting network is particularly stable with regard to damage to modular inputs. From a cognitive perspective it is consistent with the data concerning category specific impairment.

2 Homogeneous Network

We study an excitatory-inhibitory associative memory network [2], having N excitatory neurons. We assume that the network stores M_1 memory patterns η^μ of sparse coding level p and M_2 patterns ξ^ν with coding level f such that $p < f << 1$. The synaptic efficacy J_{ij} between the jth (presynaptic) neuron and the ith (postsynaptic) neuron is chosen in the Hebbian manner

$$J_{ij} = \frac{1}{Np} \sum_{\mu=1}^{M_1} \eta^\mu{}_i \eta^\mu{}_j + \frac{1}{Np} \sum_{\mu=1}^{M_2} \xi^\nu{}_i \xi^\nu{}_j \ , \tag{1}$$

The updating rule for the activity state V_i of the ith binary neuron is given by

$$V_i(t+1) = \Theta\left(h_i(t) - \theta\right) \tag{2}$$

where Θ is the step function and θ is the threshold.

$$h_i(t) = h_i^e(t) - \frac{\gamma}{p} Q(t) \tag{3}$$

is the local field, or membrane potential. It includes the excitatory Hebbian coupling of all other excitatory neurons,

$$h_i^e(t) = \sum_{j \neq i}^{N} J_{ij} V_j(t) \ , \tag{4}$$

and global inhibition that is proportional to the total activity of the excitatory neurons

$$Q(t) = \frac{1}{N} \sum_{j}^{N} V_j(t) \ . \tag{5}$$

The overlap $m(t)$ between the network activity and the memory patterns is defined for the two memory populations as

$$m_\xi{}^\nu(t) = \frac{1}{Nf} \sum_{j}^{N} \xi^\nu{}_j V_j(t) \ , \qquad m_\eta{}^\mu(t) = \frac{1}{Np} \sum_{j}^{N} \eta^\mu{}_j V_j(t) \ . \tag{6}$$

The storage capacity $\alpha = M/N$ of this network has two critical capacities. $\alpha_{c\xi}$ above which the population of ξ^ν patterns is unstable and $\alpha_{c\eta}$ above which the population of η^μ patterns is unstable. We derived equations for the overlap and total activity of the two populations using mean field analysis. Here we give the fixed-point equations for the case of $M_1 = M_2 = \frac{M}{2}$ and $\gamma = M_1 f^2 + M_2 p^2$. The resulting equations are

$$m_\eta = \Phi\left(\frac{\theta - m_\eta}{\phi}\right) , \qquad\qquad \mathcal{Q} = pm_\eta + \Phi\left(\frac{\theta}{\phi}\right) , \qquad (7)$$

and

$$m_\xi = \Phi\left(\frac{\theta - \frac{f}{p}m_\xi}{\phi}\right) , \qquad\qquad \mathcal{Q} = fm_\xi + \Phi\left(\frac{\theta}{\phi}\right) , \qquad (8)$$

where

$$\phi^2 = \frac{1}{2}\alpha\mathcal{Q}\left(1 + \frac{f^2}{p^2}\right) + \frac{1}{2}\alpha Np\mathcal{Q}^2\left(1 + \frac{f^3}{p^3}\right) , \qquad (9)$$

and

$$\Phi(x) = \int_x^\infty \exp\left(-\frac{z^2}{2}\right)\frac{dz}{\sqrt{2\pi}} . \qquad (10)$$

(a)   (b)

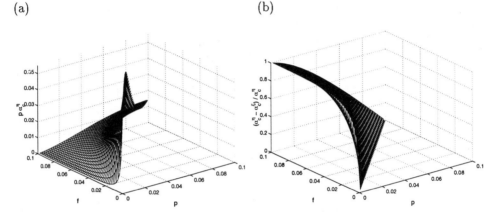

Figure 1: (a) The critical capacity $\alpha_{c\eta}$ vs. f and p for $f \geq p$, $\theta = 0.8$ and $N = 1000$. (b) $(\alpha_{c\eta} - \alpha_{c\xi})/\alpha_{c\eta}$ versus f and p for the same parameters as in (a). The validity of these analytical results was tested and verified in simulations.

Next, we look for the critical capacities, $\alpha_{c\eta}$ and $\alpha_{c\xi}$ at which the fixed-point equations become marginally stable. The results are shown in Figure 1. Figure 1(a) shows $\alpha_{c\eta}$ vs. the coding levels f and p ($f \geq p$). Similar results were obtained for $\alpha_{c\xi}$. As evident the critical capacities of both populations are smaller than the one observed in a homogeneous network in which $f = p$. One hence necessarily pays a price for the ability to store patterns with different levels of activity.

Figure 1(b) plots the relative capacity difference $(\alpha_{c\eta} - \alpha_{c\xi})/\alpha_{c\eta}$ vs. f and p. The function is non negative, i.e., $\alpha_{c\eta} \geq \alpha_{c\xi}$ for all f and p. Thus, low activity memories are more stable than high activity ones.

Assuming that high activity codes more features [3], these results seem to be at odds with the view [3, 4] that memories that contain more semantic features, and therefore correspond to larger Hebbian cell assemblies, are more stable, such as concrete versus abstract words. The homogeneous network, in which the memories with high activity are more susceptible to damage, cannot account for these observations. In the next section we show how a modular network can store memories with different activity levels and account for this cognitive phenomenon.

3 Modular Network

We study a multi modular excitatory-inhibitory associative memory network, storing M memory patterns in L modules of N neurons each. The memories are coded such that in every memory a variable number Ω of 1 to L modules is active. This number will be denoted as *modular coding*. The coding level inside the modules is sparse and fixed, i.e., each modular Hebbian cell assembly consists of pN active neurons with $p \ll 1$. The synaptic efficacy $J_{ij}{}^{lk}$ between the jth (presynaptic) neuron from the kth module and the ith (postsynaptic) neuron from the lth module is chosen in a Hebbian manner

$$J_{ij}{}^{lk} = \frac{1}{Np} \sum_{\mu=1}^{M} \eta^{\mu}{}_{il} \eta^{\mu}{}_{jk} , \tag{11}$$

where $\eta^{\mu}{}_{il}$ are the stored memory patterns. The updating rule for the activity state V_i^l of the ith binary neuron in the lth module is given by

$$V_i^l(t+1) = \mathcal{S}\left(h_i^l(t) - \theta_s\right) , \tag{12}$$

where θ_s is the threshold, and $\mathcal{S}(x)$ is a stochastic sigmoid function, getting the value 1 with probability $(1 + e^{-x})^{-1}$ and 0 otherwise. The neuron's local field, or membrane potential has two components,

$$h_i^l(t) = h_i^l{}_{internal}(t) + h_i^l{}_{external}(t) . \tag{13}$$

The internal field, $h_i^l{}_{internal}(t)$, includes the contributions from all other excitatory neurons that are situated in the lth module, and inhibition that is proportional to the total modular activity of the excitatory neurons, i.e.,

$$h_i^l{}_{internal}(t) = \sum_{j \neq i}^{N} J_{ij}{}^{ll} V_j^l(t) - \gamma_s \mathcal{Q}^l(t) , \tag{14}$$

where

$$\mathcal{Q}^l(t) = \frac{1}{Np} \sum_{j}^{N} V_j^l(t) . \tag{15}$$

The external field component, $h_i^l{}_{external}(t)$, includes the contributions from all other excitatory neurons that are situated outside the lth module, and inhibition that is proportional to the total network activity.

$$h_i^l{}_{external}(t) = \mathcal{G}\left(\sum_{k \neq l}^{L} \sum_{j}^{N} J_{ij}{}^{lk} V_j^k(t) - \gamma_d \sum_{k}^{L} \mathcal{Q}^k(t) - \theta_d \right) . \tag{16}$$

We allow here for the freedom of using more complicated behavior than the standard $\mathcal{G}(x) = x$ one. In fact, as we will see, the linear case is problematic, since only memory storage with limited modular coding is possible.

The retrieval quality at each trial is measured by the overlap function, defined by

$$m^{\mu}(t) = \frac{1}{pN\Omega^{\mu}} \sum_{k=1}^{L} \sum_{i=1}^{N} \eta^{\mu}{}_{ik} V_i^k(t) , \tag{17}$$

where Ω^{μ} is the modular coding of η^{μ}.

In the simulations we constructed a network of $L = 10$ modules, where each module contains $N = 500$ neurons. The network stores $M = 50$ memory patterns randomly distributed over the modules. Five sets of ten memories each are defined. In each set the modular coding is distributed homogeneously between one to ten active modules. The sparse coding level within each module was set to be $p = 0.05$. Every simulation experiment is composed of many trials. In each trial we use as initial condition a corrupted version of a stored memory pattern with error rate of 5%, and check the network's retrieval after it converges to a stable state.

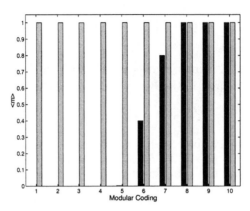

Figure 2: Quality of retrieval *vs.* memory modular coding. The dark shading represents the mean overlap achieved by a network with linear intra-modular and inter-modular synaptic couplings. The light shading represents the mean overlap of a network with sigmoidal inter-modular connections, which is perfect for all memory patterns. The simulation parameters were: $L = 10$, $N = 500$, $M = 50$, $p = 0.05$, $\lambda = 0.7$, $\theta_d = 2$ and $\theta_s = 0.6$.

We start with the standard choice of $\mathcal{G}(x) = x$, i.e. treating similarly the intra-modular and inter-modular synaptic couplings. The performance of this network is shown in Figure 2. As evident, the network can store only a relatively narrow span of memories with high modular coding levels, and completely fails to retrieve memories with low modular coding levels (see also [5]). If, however, $\mathcal{G}$ is chosen to be a sigmoid function, a completely stable system is obtained, with all possible coding levels allowed. A sigmoid function on the external connections is hence very effective in enhancing the span of modular coding of memories that the network can sustain. The segregation of the synaptic inputs to internal and external connections has been motivated by observed patterns of cortical connectivity: Axons forming excitatory intra-modular connections make synapses more proximal to the cell body than do inter-modular connections [6]. Dendrites, having active conductances, embody a rich repertoire of nonlinear electrical and chemical dynamics (see [7] for a review). In our model, the setting of $\mathcal{G}$ to be a sigmoid function crudely mimics these active conductance properties.

We may go on and envisage the use of a nested set of sigmoidal dendritic transmission functions. This turns out to be useful when we test the effects of pathologic alterations on the retrieval of memories with different modular codings. The amazing result is that if the damage is done to modular inputs, the highly nonlinear transmission functions are very resistible to it. An example is shown in Fig. 3.

Here we compare two nonlinear functions:

$$\mathcal{G}_1 = \lambda\Theta\left[\sum_{k\neq l}^{L}\sum_{j}^{N}J_{ij}{}^{lk}V_j{}^k(t) - \gamma_d\sum_{k\neq l}^{L}\mathcal{Q}_k(t) - \theta_d\right],$$

$$\mathcal{G}_2 = \lambda\Theta\left[\sum_{k\neq l}^{L}\Theta\left[\sum_{j}^{N}J_{ij}{}^{lk}V_j{}^k(t) - \gamma_d\mathcal{Q}_k(t) - \theta_k\right] - \theta_d\right].$$

The second one is the nested sigmoidal function mentioned above. Two types of input cues are compared: correct $\eta^\mu{}_{il}$ to one of the modules and no input to the rest, or partial input to all modules.

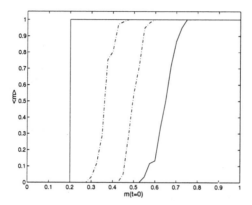

Figure 3: The performance of modular networks with different types of non-linear inter-connections when partial input cues are given. The mean overlap is plotted *vs.* the overlap of the input cue. The solid line represents the performance of the network with $\mathcal{G}_2$ and the dash-dot line represents $\mathcal{G}_1$. The left curve of $\mathcal{G}_2$ corresponds to the case when full input is presented to only one module (out of the 5 that comprise a memory), while the right solid curve corresponds to partial input to all modules. The two $\mathcal{G}_1$ curves describe partial input to all modules, but correspond to two different choices of the threshold parameter θ_d, 1.5 (left) and 2 (right). Parameters are $L = 5$, $N = 1000$, $p = 0.05$, $\lambda = 0.8$, $\Omega = 5$, $\theta_s = 0.7$ and $\theta_k = 0.7$.

As we can see, the nested nonlinearities enable retrieval even if only the input to a single module survives. One may therefore conclude that, under such conditions, patterns of high modular coding have a grater chance to be retrieved from an input to a single module and thus are more resilient to afferent damage. Adopting the assumption that different modules code for distinct semantic features, we now find that a multi-modular network with nonlinear dendritic transmission can account for the view of [3], that memories with more features are more robust.

4   Summary

We have studied the ability of homogeneous (single-module) and modular networks to store memory patterns with variable activity levels. Although homogeneous networks can store such memory patterns, the critical capacity of low activity memories was shown to be larger than that of high activity ones. This result seems to be inconsistent with the pertaining cognitive data concerning category specific semantic impairment, which seem to imply that high activity memories should be the more stable ones.

Motivated by the findings of modular structure in associative cortex, we developed a multi-modular model of associative memory. Adding the assumption that dendritic non-linear processing operates on the signals of inter-modular synaptic connections, we obtained a network that has two important features: coexistence of memories with different modular codings and retrieval of memories from cues presented to a small fraction of all modules. The latter implies that memories encoded in many modules should be more resilient to damage in afferent connections, hence it is consistent with the conventional interpretation of the data on category specific impairment.

References

[1] R. F. Hevner. More modules. *TINS*, 16(5):178, 1993.

[2] M. V. Tsodyks. Associative memory in neural networks with the hebbian learning rule. *Modern Physics Letters B*, 3(7):555–560, 1989.

[3] G. E. Hinton and T. Shallice. Lesioning at attractor network: investigations of acquired dyslexia. *Psychological Review*, 98(1):74–95, 1991.

[4] G. V. Jones. Deep dyslexia, imageability, and ease of predication. *Brain and Language*, 24:1–19, 1985.

[5] R. Lauro Grotto, S. Reich, and M. A. Virasoro. The computational role of conscious processing in a model of semantic memory. In *Proceedings of the IIAS Symposium on Cognition Computation and Consciousness*, 1994.

[6] P. A. Hetherington and L. M. Shapiro. Simulating hebb cell assemblies: the necessity for partitioned dendritic trees and a post-not-pre ltd rule. *Network*, 4:135–153, 1993.

[7] R. Yuste and D. W. Tank. Dendritic integration in mammalian neurons a century after cajal. *Neuron*, 16:701–716, 1996.

Serial Order in Reading Aloud: Connectionist Models and Neighborhood Structure

Jeanne C. Milostan
Computer Science & Engineering 0114
University of California San Diego
La Jolla, CA 92093-0114

Garrison W. Cottrell
Computer Science & Engineering 0114
University of California San Diego
La Jolla, CA 92093-0114

Abstract

Dual-Route and Connectionist Single-Route models of reading have been at odds over claims as to the correct explanation of the reading process. Recent Dual-Route models predict that subjects should show an increased naming latency for irregular words when the irregularity is earlier in the word (e.g. **chef** is slower than **glow**) - a prediction that has been confirmed in human experiments. Since this would appear to be an effect of the left-to-right reading process, Coltheart & Rastle (1994) claim that Single-Route parallel connectionist models cannot account for it. A refutation of this claim is presented here, consisting of network models which do show the interaction, along with orthographic neighborhood statistics that explain the effect.

1   Introduction

A major component of the task of learning to read is the development of a mapping from orthography to phonology. In a complete model of reading, message understanding must play a role, but many psycholinguistic phenomena can be explained in the context of this simple mapping task. A difficulty in learning this mapping is that in a language such as English, the mapping is *quasiregular* (Plaut et al., 1996); there are a wide range of exceptions to the general rules. As with nearly all psychological phenomena, more frequent stimuli are processed faster, leading to shorter naming latencies. The regularity of mapping interacts with this variable, a robust finding that is well-explained by connectionist accounts (Seidenberg and McClelland, 1989; Taraban and McClelland, 1987).

In this paper we consider a recent effect that seems difficult to account for in terms of the standard parallel network models. Coltheart & Rastle (1994) have shown

Filler		Position 1	of 2	Irregular 3	Phoneme 4	5
Nonword						
	Irregular	554	542	530	529	537
	Regular Control	502	516	518	523	525
	Difference	52	26	12	6	12
Exception						
	Irregular	545	524	528	526	528
	Regular Control	500	503	503	515	524
	Difference	45	21	25	11	4
	Avg. Diff.	48.5	23.5	18.5	8.5	8

Table 1: Naming Latency vs. Irregularity Position

that the amount of delay experienced in naming an exception word is related to the phonemic position of the irregularity in pronunciation. Specifically, the earlier the exception occurs in the word, the longer the latency to the onset of pronouncing the word. Table 1, adapted from (Coltheart and Rastle, 1994) shows the response latencies to two-syllable words by normal subjects. There is a clear left-to-right ranking of the latencies compared to controls in the last row of the Table. Coltheart *et al.* claim this delay ranking cannot be achieved by standard connectionist models. This paper shows this claim to be false, and shows that the origin of the effect lies in a statistical regularity of English, related to the number of "friends" and "enemies" of the pronunciation within the word's neighborhood [1].

2   Background

Computational modeling of the reading task has been approached from a number of different perspectives. Advocates of a dual-route model of oral reading claim that two separate routes, one lexical (a lexicon, often hypothesized to be an associative network) and one rule-based, are *required* to account for certain phenomena in reaction times and nonword pronunciation seen in human subjects (Coltheart et al., 1993). Connectionist modelers claim that the same phenomena can be captured in a single-route model which learns simply by exposure to a representative dataset (Seidenberg and McClelland, 1989).

In the Dual-Route Cascade model (DRC) (Coltheart et al., 1993), the lexical route is implemented as an Interactive Activation (McClelland and Rumelhart, 1981) system, while the non-lexical route is implemented by a set of grapheme-phoneme correspondence (GPC) rules learned from a dataset. Input at the letter identification layer is activated in a left-to-right sequential fashion to simulate the reading direction of English, and fed simultaneously to the two pathways in the model. Activation from both the GPC route and the lexicon route then begins to interact at the output (phoneme) level, starting with the phonemes at the beginning of the word. If the GPC and the lexicon agree on pronunciation, the correct phonemes will be activated quickly. For words with irregular pronunciation, the lexicon and GPC routes will activate different phonemes: the GPC route will try to activate the regular pronunciation while the lexical route will activate the irregular (correct)

[1]Friends are words with the same pronunciations for the ambiguous letter-to-sound correspondence; enemies are words with different pronunciations.

pronunciation. Inhibitory links between alternate phoneme pronunciations will slow down the rise in activation, causing words with inconsistencies to be pronounced more slowly than regular words. This slowing will not occur, however, when an irregularity appears late in a word. This is because in the model the lexical node spreads activation to *all* of a word's phonemes as soon as it becomes active. If an irregularity is late in a word, the correct pronunciation will begin to be activated before the GPC route is able to vote against it. Hence late irregularities will not be as affected by conflicting information. This result is validated by simulations with the one-syllable DRC model (Coltheart and Rastle, 1994).

Several connectionist systems have been developed to model the orthography to phonology process (Seidenberg and McClelland, 1989; Plaut et al., 1996). These connectionist models provide evidence that the task, with accompanying phenomena, can be learned through a single mechanism. In particular, Plaut *et al.* (henceforth PMSP) develop a recurrent network which duplicates the naming latencies appropriate to their data set, consisting of approximately 3000 one-syllable English words (monosyllabic words with frequency greater than 1 in the Kucera & Francis corpus (Kucera and Francis, 1967)). Naming latencies are computed based on time-to-settle for the recurrent network, and based on MSE for a feed-forward model used in some simulations. In addition to duplicating frequency and regularity interactions displayed in previous human studies, this model also performs appropriately in providing pronunciation of pronounceable nonwords. This provides an improvement over, and a validation of, previous work with a strictly feed-forward network (Seidenberg and McClelland, 1989). However, to date, no one has shown that Coltheart's naming latency by irregularity of position interaction can be accounted for by such a model. Indeed, it is difficult to see how such a model *could* account for such a phenomenon, as its explanation (at least in the DRC model) seems to require the serial, left-to-right nature of processing in the model, whereas networks such as PMSP present the word orthography all at once. In the following, we fill this gap in the literature, and explain why a parallel, feed-forward model *can* account for this result.

3 Experiments & Results

3.1 The Data

Pronunciations for approximately 100,000 English words were obtained through an electronic dictionary developed by CMU [2]. The provided format was not amenable to an automated method for distinguishing the number of syllables in the word. To obtain syllable counts, English two-syllable words were gathered from the Medical Research Council (MRC) Psycholinguistic Database (Coltheart and Rastle, 1994), which is conveniently annotated with syllable counts and frequency (only those with Kucera-Francis written frequency of one or greater were selected). Intersecting the two databases resulted in 5,924 two-syllable words. There is some noise in the data; ZONED and AERIAL, for example, are in this database of purported two-syllable words. Due to the size of the database and time limitations, we did not prune the data of these errors, nor did we eliminate proper nouns or foreign words. Single-syllable words with the same frequency criterion were also selected for comparison with previous work. 3,284 unique single-syllable words were obtained, in contrast to 2,998 words used by PMSP. Similar noisy data as in the two-syllable set exists in this database. Each word was represented using the orthography and phonology representation scheme outlined by PMSP.

---

[2] Available via ftp://ftp.cs.cmu.edu/project/fgdata/dict/

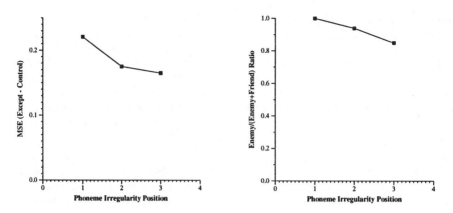

Figure 1: 1-syllable network latency differences & neighborhood statistics

3.2   Methods

For the single syllable words, we used an identical network to the feed-forward network used by PMSP, i.e., a 105-100-61 network, and for the two syllable words, we simply used the same architecture with the each layer size doubled. We trained each network for 300 epochs, using batch training with a cross entropy objective function, an initial learning rate of 0.001, momentum of 0.9 after the first 10 epochs, weight decay of 0.0001, and delta-bar-delta learning rate adjustment. Training exemplars were weighted by the log of frequency as found in the Kucera-Francis corpus. After this training, the single syllable feed-forward networks averaged 98.6% correct outputs, using the same evaluation technique outlined in PMSP. Two syllable networks were trained for 1700 epochs using online training, a learning rate of 0.05, momentum of 0.9 after the first 10 epochs, and raw frequency weighting. The two syllable network achieved 85% correct. Naming latency was equated with network output MSE; for successful results, the error difference between the irregular words and associated control words should decrease with irregularity position.

3.3   Results

Single Syllable Words   First, Coltheart's challenge that a single-route model cannot produce the latency effects was explored. The single-syllable network described above was tested on the collection of single-syllable words identified as irregular by (Taraban and McClelland, 1987). In (Coltheart and Rastle, 1994), control words are selected based on equal number of letters, same beginning phoneme, and Kucera-Francis frequency between 1 and 20 (controls were not frequency matched). For single syllable words used here, the control condition was modified to allow frequency from 1 to 70, which is the range of the "low frequency" exception words in the Taraban & McClelland set. Controls were chosen by drawing randomly from the words meeting the control criteria.

Each test and control word input vector was presented to the network, and the MSE at the output layer (compared to the expected correct target) was calculated. From these values, the differences in MSE for target and matched control words were calculated and are shown in Figure 1. Note that words with an irregularity in the first phoneme position have the largest difference from their control words, with this (exception - regular control) difference decreasing as phoneme position increases. Contrary to the claims of the Dual-Route model, this network does show the desired rank-ordering of MSE/latency.

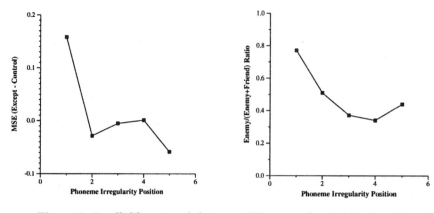

Figure 2: 2-syllable network latency differences & neighborhood statistics

Two Syllable Words Testing of the two-syllable network is identical to that of the one-syllable network. The difference in MSE for each test word and its corresponding control is calculated, averaging across all test pairs in the position set. Both test words and their controls are those found in (Coltheart and Rastle, 1994). The 2-syllable network appears to produce approximately the correct linear trend in the naming MSE/latency (Figure 2), although the results displayed are not monotonically decreasing with position. Note, however, that the results presented by Coltheart, when taken separately, also fail to exhibit this trend (Table 1). For correct analysis, several "subject" networks should be trained, with formal linear trend analysis then performed with the resulting data. These further simulations are currently being undertaken.

4 Why the network works: Neighborhood effects

A possible explanation for these results relies on the fact that connectionist networks tend to extract statistical regularities in the data, and are affected by regularity by frequency interactions. In this case, we decided to explore the hypothesis that the results could be explained by a *neighborhood effect*: Perhaps the number of "friends" and "enemies" in the neighborhood (in a sense to be defined below) of the exception word varies in English in a position-dependent way. If there are more enemies (different pronunciations) than friends (identical pronunciations) when the exception occurs at the beginning of a word than at the end, then one would expect a network to reflect this statistical regularity in its output errors. In particular, one would expect higher errors (and therefore longer latencies in naming) if the word has a higher proportion of enemies in the neighborhood.

To test this hypothesis, we created some data search engines to collect word neighborhoods based on various criteria. There is no consensus on the exact definition of the "neighborhood" of a word. There are some common measures, however, so we explored several of these. Taraban & McClelland (1987) neighborhoods (T&M) are defined as words containing the same vowel grouping and final consonant cluster. These neighborhoods therefore tend to consist of words that rhyme (MUST, DUST, TRUST). There is independent evidence that these word-body neighbors are psychologically relevant for word naming tasks (i.e., pronunciation) (Treiman and Chafetz, 1987). The neighborhood measure given by Coltheart (Coltheart and Rastle, 1994), N, counts same-length words which differ by only one letter, taking string position into account. Finally, edit-distance-1 (ED1) neighborhoods are those words which can be generated from the target word by making one change

(Peereman, 1995): either a letter substitution, insertion or deletion. This differs from the Coltheart N definition in that "TRUST" is in the ED1 neighborhood (but not the N neighborhood) of "RUST", and provides a neighborhood measure which considers both pronunciation and spelling similarity. However, the N and the ED-1 measure have not been shown to be psychologically real in terms of affecting naming latency (Treiman and Chafetz, 1987).

We therefore extended T&M neighborhoods to multi-syllable words. Each vowel group is considered within the context of its rime, with each syllable considered separately. Consonant neighborhoods consist of orthographic clusters which correspond to the same location in the word. This results in 4 consonant cluster locations: first syllable onset, first syllable coda, second syllable onset, and second syllable coda. Consonant cluster neighborhoods include the preceeding vowel for coda consonants, and the following vowel for onset consonants.

The notion of exception words is also not universally agreed upon. Precisely which words are exceptions is a function of the working definition of pronunciation and regularity for the experiment at hand. Given a definition of neighborhood, then, exception words can be defined as those words which do not agree with the phonological mapping favored by the majority of items in that particular neighborhood. Alternatively, in cases assuming a set of rules for grapheme-phoneme correspondence, exception words are those which violate the rules which define the majority of pronunciations. For this investigation, single syllable exception words are those defined as exception by the T&M neighborhood definition. For instance, PINT would be considered an exception word compared to its neighbors MINT, TINT, HINT, etc. Coltheart, on the other hand, defines exception words to be those for which his GPC rules produce incorrect pronunciation. Since we are concerned with addressing Coltheart's claims, these 2-syllable exception words will also be used here.

4.1 Results

Single syllable words For each phoneme position, we compare each word with irregularity at that position with its neighbors, counting the number of enemies (words with alternate pronunciation at the supposed irregularity) and friends (words with pronunciation in agreement) that it has. The T&M neighborhood numbers (words containing the same vowel grouping and final consonant cluster) used in Figure 1 are found in (Taraban and McClelland, 1987). For each word, we calculate its (enemy) / (friend+enemy) ratio; these ratios are then averaged over all the words in the position set. The results using neighborhoods as defined in Taraban & McClelland clearly show the desired rank ordering of effect. First-position-irregularity words have more "enemies" and fewer "friends" than third-position-irregularity words, with the second-position words falling in the middle as desired. We suggest that this statistical regularity in the data is what the above networks capture.

However convincing these results may be, they do not fully address Coltheart's data, which is for two syllable words of five phonemes or phoneme clusters, with irregularities at each of five possible positions. Also, due to the size of the T&M data set, there are only 2 members in the position 1 set, and the single-syllable data only goes up to phoneme position 3. The neighborhoods for the two-syllable data set were thus examined.

Two syllable results Recall that the two-syllable test words are those used in the (Coltheart and Rastle, 1994) subject study, for which naming latency differences are shown in Table 1. Coltheart's 1-letter-different neighborhood definition is not very informative in this case, since by this criterion most of the target words provided in (Coltheart and Rastle, 1994) are loners (i.e., have no neighbors at all). However, using a neighborhood based on T&M-2 recreates the desired ranking (Figure 2) as indicated by the ratio of hindering pronunciations to the total of the helping and hindering pronunciations. As with the single syllable words, each test word is compared with its neighbor words and the (enemy)/(friend+enemy) ratio is calculated. Averaging over the words in each position set, we again see that words with early irregularities are at a support disadvantage compared to words with late irregularities.

5 Summary

Dual-Route models claim the irregularity position effect can only be accounted for by two-route models with left-to-right activation of phonemes, and interaction between GPC rules and the lexicon. The work presented in this paper refutes this claim by presenting results from feed-forward connectionist networks which show the same rank ordering of latency. Further, an analysis of orthographic neighborhoods shows *why* the networks can do this: the effect is based on a statistical interaction between friend/enemy support and position. Words with irregular orthographic-phonemic correspondence at word beginning have less support from their neighbors than words with later irregularities; it is this difference which explains the latency results. The resulting statistical regularity is then easily captured by connectionist networks exposed to representative data sets.

References

Coltheart, M., Curitis, B., Atkins, P., and Haller, M. (1993). Models of reading aloud: Dual-route and parallel-distributed-processing approaches. *Psychological Review*, 100(4):589–608.

Coltheart, M. and Rastle, K. (1994). Serial processing in reading aloud: Evidence for dual route models of reading. *Journal of Experimental Psychology: Human Perception and Performance*, 20(6):1197–1211.

Kucera, H. and Francis, W. (1967). *Computational Analysis of Present-Day American English*. Brown University Press, Providence, RI.

McClelland, J. and Rumelhart, D. (1981). An interactive activation model of context effects in letter perception: Part 1. an account of basic findings. *Psychological Review*, 88:375–407.

Peereman, R. (1995). Naming regular and exception words: Further examination of the effect of phonological dissension among lexical neighbours. *European Journal of Cognitive Psychology*, 7(3):307–330.

Plaut, D., McClelland, J., Seidenberg, M., and Patterson, K. (1996). Understanding normal and impaired word reading: Computational principles in quasi-regular domains. *Psychological Review*, 103(1):56–115.

Seidenberg, M. and McClelland, J. (1989). A distributed, developmental model of word recognition and naming. *Psychological Review*, 96:523–568.

Taraban, R. and McClelland, J. (1987). Conspiracy effects in word pronunciation. *Journal of Memory and Language*, 26:608–631.

Treiman, R. and Chafetz, J. (1987). Are there onset- and rime-like units in printed words? In Coltheart, M., editor, *Attention and Performance XII: The Psychology of Reading*. Erlbaum, Hillsdale, NJ.

A Superadditive-Impairment Theory
of Optic Aphasia

Michael C. Mozer
Dept. of Computer Science
University of Colorado
Boulder, CO 80309–0430

Mark Sitton
Dept. of Computer Science
University of Colorado
Boulder, CO 80309–0430

Martha Farah
Dept. of Psychology
University of Pennsylvania
Phila., PA 19104–6196

Abstract

Accounts of neurological disorders often posit damage to a specific functional pathway of the brain. Farah (1990) has proposed an alternative class of explanations involving partial damage to multiple pathways. We explore this explanation for *optic aphasia*, a disorder in which severe performance deficits are observed when patients are asked to name visually presented objects, but surprisingly, performance is relatively normal on naming objects from auditory cues and on gesturing the appropriate use of visually presented objects. We model this highly specific deficit through partial damage to two pathways—one that maps visual input to semantics, and the other that maps semantics to naming responses. The effect of this damage is *superadditive,* meaning that tasks which require one pathway or the other show little or no performance deficit, but the damage is manifested when a task requires both pathways (i.e., naming visually presented objects). Our model explains other phenomena associated with optic aphasia, and makes testable experimental predictions.

Neuropsychology is the study of disrupted cognition resulting from damage to functional systems in the brain. Generally, accounts of neuropsychological disorders posit damage to a particular functional system or a disconnection between systems. Farah (1990) suggested an alternative class of explanations for neuropsychological disorders: partial damage to multiple systems, which is manifested through interactions among the loci of damage. We explore this explanation for the neuropsychological disorder of *optic aphasia*.

Optic aphasia, arising from unilateral left posterior lesions, including occipital cortex and the splenium of the corpus callosum (Schnider, Benson, & Scharre, 1994), is marked by a deficit in naming visually presented objects, hereafter referred to as *visual naming* (Farah, 1990). However, patients can demonstrate recognition of visually presented objects nonverbally, for example, by gesturing the appropriate use of an object or sorting visual items into their proper superordinate categories (hereafter, *visual gesturing*). Patients can also name objects by nonvisual cues such as a verbal definition or typical sounds made by the objects (hereafter, *auditory naming*). The highly specific nature of the deficit rules out an explanation in terms of damage to a single pathway in a standard model of visual naming (Figure 1), suggesting that a more complex model is required, involving

FIGURE 1. A standard box-and-arrow model of visual naming. The boxes denote levels of representation, and the arrows denote pathways mapping from one level of representation to another. Although optic aphasia cannot be explained by damage to the vision-to-semantics pathway or the semantics-to-naming pathway, Farah (1990) proposed an explanation in terms of partial damage to both pathways (the X's).

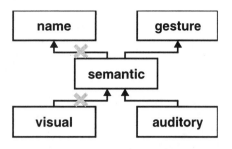

multiple semantic systems or multiple pathways to visual naming. However, a more parsimonious account is suggested by Farah (1990): Optic aphasia might arise from *partial* lesions to two pathways in the standard model—those connecting visual input to semantics, and semantics to naming—and the effect of damage to these pathways is *superadditive*, meaning that tasks which require only one of these pathways (e.g., visual gesturing, or auditory naming) will be relatively unimpaired, whereas tasks requiring both pathways (e.g., visual naming) will show a significant deficit.

1 A MODEL OF SUPERADDITIVE IMPAIRMENTS

We present a computational model of the superadditive-impairment theory of optic aphasia by elaborating the architecture of Figure 1. The architecture has four pathways: visual input to semantics (V→S), auditory input to semantics (A→S), semantics to naming (S→N), and semantics to gesturing (S→G). Each pathway acts as an associative memory. The critical property of a pathway that is required to explain optic aphasia is a *speed-accuracy trade off*: The initial output of a pathway appears rapidly, but it may be inaccurate. This "quick and dirty" guess is refined over time, and the pathway output asymptotically converges on the best interpretation of the input.

We implement a pathway using the architecture suggested by Mathis and Mozer (1996). In this architecture, inputs are mapped to their best interpretations by means of a two-stage process (Figure 2). First, a quick, one-shot *mapping* is performed by a multilayer feedforward connectionist network to transform the input directly to its corresponding output. This is followed by a slower iterative *clean-up* process carried out by a recurrent attractor network. This architecture shows a speed-accuracy trade off by virtue of the assumption that the feedforward mapping network does not have the capacity to produce exactly the right output to every input, especially when the inputs are corrupted by noise or are otherwise incomplete. Consequently, the clean up stage is required to produce a sensible interpretation of the noisy output of the mapping network.

Fully distributed attractor networks have been used for similar purposes (e.g., Plaut & Shallice, 1993). For simplicity, we adopt a localist-attractor network with a layer of *state* units and a layer of radial basis function (RBF) units, one RBF unit per attractor. Each RBF or *attractor* unit measures the distance of the current state to the attractor that it represents. The activity of attractor unit i, a_i, is:

FIGURE 2. Connectionist implementation of a processing pathway. The pathway consists of feedforward *mapping* network followed by a recurrent *clean-up* or attractor network. Circles denote connectionist processing units and arrows denote connections between units or between layers of units.

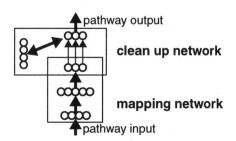

$$\hat{a}_i(t) = \exp(-\|s(t) - \mu_i\|^2 / \beta_i) \tag{1}$$

$$a_i(t) = \frac{\hat{a}_i(t)}{\sum_j \hat{a}_j(t)} \tag{2}$$

where $s(t)$ is the state unit activity vector at time t, μ_i is the vector denoting the location of attractor i, and β_i is the *strength* of the attractor. The strength determines the region of the state space over which an attractor will exert its pull, and also the rate at which the state will converge to the attractor. The state units receive input from the mapping network and from the attractor units and are updated as follows:

$$s_i(t) = d_i(t)e_i(t) + (1 - d_i(t))\sum_j a_j(t-1)\mu_{ji} \tag{3}$$

where $s_i(t)$ is the activity of state unit i at time t, e_i is the ith output of the mapping net, μ_{ji} is the ith element of attractor j, and d_i is given by

$$d_i(t) = h\left[1 - \frac{\bar{e}_i(t-1)}{e_i(t)}\right] \tag{4}$$

where $h[.]$ is a linear threshold function that bounds activity between -1 and $+1$, $\bar{e}_i$ is a weighted time average of the ith output of the mapping net,

$$\bar{e}_i(t) = \alpha e_i(t) + (1 - \alpha)\bar{e}_i(t-1) \tag{5}$$

In all simulations, $\alpha = .02$.

The activity of the state units are governed by two forces—the external input from the feedforward net (first term in Equation 3) and the attractor unit activities (second term). The parameter d_i acts as a kind of attentional mechanism that modulates the relative influence of these two forces. The basic idea is that when the input coming from the mapping net is changing, the system should be responsive to the input and should not yet be concerned with interpreting the input. In this case, the input is copied straight through to the state units and hence d_i should have a value close to 1. When the input begins to stabilize, however, the focus shifts to interpreting the input and following the dynamics of the attractor network. This shift corresponds to d_i being lowered to zero. The weighted time average in the update rule for d_i is what allows for the smooth transition of the function to its new value. For certain constructions of the function d, Zemel and Mozer (in preparation) have proven convergence of the algorithm to an attractor.

Apart from speed-accuracy trade off, these dynamics have another important consequence for the present model, particularly with respect to cascading pathways. If pathway A feeds into pathway B, such as V→S feeding into S→N, then the state unit activities of A act as the input to B. Because these activities change over time as the state approaches a well-formed state, the dynamics of pathway B can be quite complex as it is forced to deal with an unstable input. This property is important in explaining several phenomena associated with optic aphasia.

1.1 PATTERN GENERATION

Patterns were constructed for each of the five representational spaces: *visual* and *auditory* input, *semantic*, *name* and *gesture* responses. Each representational space was arbitrarily made to be 200 dimensional. We generated 200 binary-valued $(-1,+1)$ patterns in each space, which were meant to correspond to known entities of that representational domain.

For the visual, auditory, and semantic spaces, patterns were partitioned into 50 similarity *clusters* with 4 *siblings* per cluster. Patterns were chosen randomly subject to two constraints: patterns in different clusters had to be at least 80° apart, and siblings had to be between 25° and 50° apart. Because similarity of patterns in the name and gesture spaces was irrelevant to our modeling, we did not impose a similarity structure on these spaces.

Instead, we generated patterns in these spaces at random subject to the constraint that every pattern had to be at least 60° from every other.

After generating patterns in each of the representational spaces, we established arbitrary correspondences among the patterns such that visual pattern *n*, auditory pattern *n*, semantic pattern *n*, name pattern *n*, and gesture pattern *n* all represented the same concept. That is, the appropriate response in a visual-naming task to visual pattern *n* would be semantic pattern *n* and name pattern *n*.

1.2 TRAINING PROCEDURE

The feedforward networks in the four pathways (V→S, A→S, S→N, and S→G) were independently trained on all 200 associations using back propagation. Each of these networks contained a single hidden layer of 150 units, and all units in the network used the symmetric activation function to give activities in the range [−1,+1]. The amount of training was chosen such that performance on the training examples was not perfect; usually several elements in the output would be erroneous—i.e., have the wrong sign—and others would not be exactly correct—i.e., −1 or +1. This was done to embody the architectural assumption that the feedforward net does not have the capacity to map every input to exactly the right output, and hence, the clean-up process is required.

Training was not required for the clean-up network. Due to the localist representation of attractors in the clean-up network, it was trivial to hand wire each clean-up net with the 200 attractors for its domain, along with one *rest-state* attractor. All attractor strengths were initialized to the same value, $\beta=15$, except the rest-state attractor, for which $\beta=5$. The rest-state attractor required a lower strength so that even a weak external input would be sufficient to kick the attractor network out of the rest state.

1.3 SIMULATION METHODOLOGY

After each pathway had been trained, the model was damaged by "lesioning" or removing a fraction γ of the connections in the V→S and S→N mapping networks. The lesioned connections were chosen at random and an equal fraction was removed from the two pathways. The clean-up nets were not damaged. The architecture was damaged a total of 30 different times, creating 30 simulated patients who were tested on each of the four tasks and on all 200 input patterns for a task. The results we report come from averaging across simulated patients and input patterns. Responses were determined after the system had been given sufficient time to relax into a name or gesture attractor, which was taken to be the response. Each response was classified as one of the following mutually exclusive response types: *correct*, *perseveration* (response is the same as that produced on any of the three immediately preceding trials), *visual error* (the visual pattern corresponding to the incorrect response is a sibling of the visual pattern corresponding to the correct response), *semantic error*, *visual+semantic error*, or *other error*.

1.4 PRIMING MECHANISM

Priming—the increased availability of recently experienced stimuli—has been found across a wide variety of tasks in normal subjects. We included priming in our model as a strengthening (increasing the β_i parameter) of recently visited attractors (see Mathis & Mozer 1996, for details, and Becker, Behrmann, & Moscovitch, 1993, for a related approach). In the damaged model, this mechanism often gave rise to perseverations.

2 RESULTS

We have examined the model's behavior as we varied the amount of damage, quantified by the parameter γ. However, we report on the performance of simulated patients with $\gamma = .30$. This intermediate amount of damage yielded no floor or ceiling effects, and also produced error rates for the visual-naming task in the range of 30-40%, roughly the median performance of patients in the literature.

TABLE 1. Error rate of the damaged model on various tasks.

task	error rate
auditory gesturing	0.0%
auditory naming	0.5%
visual gesturing	8.7%
visual naming	36.8%

Table 1 presents the error rates of the model on four tasks. The pattern of errors shows a qualitative fit to human patient data. The model produced no errors on the auditory gesturing task because the two component pathways (A→S and S→G) were undamaged. Relatively few errors were made on the auditory-naming and visual-gesturing tasks, each of which involved one damaged pathway, because the clean-up nets were able to compensate for the damage. However, the error rate for the visual-naming task was quite large, due to damage on both of its component pathways (V→S and S→N). The error rate for visual naming cannot be accounted for by summing the effects of the damage to the two component pathways because the sum of the error rates for auditory naming and visual gesturing, each of which involves one of the two partially damaged pathways, is nearly four times smaller. Rather, the effects of damage on these pathways interact, and their interaction leads to superadditive impairments.

When a visual pattern is presented to the model, it is mapped by the damaged V→S pathway into a corrupted semantic representation which is then cleaned up. While the corruption is sufficiently minor that clean up will eventually succeed, the clean up process is slowed considerably by the corruption. During the period of time in which the semantic clean-up network is searching for the correct attractor, the corrupted semantic representation is nonetheless fed into the damaged S→N pathway. The combined effect of the (initially) noisy semantic representation serving as input to a damaged pathway leads to corruption of the naming representation past the point where it can be cleaned-up properly.

Interactions in the architecture are inevitable, and are not merely a consequence of some arbitrary assumption that is built into our model. To argue this point, we consider two modifications to the architecture that might eliminate the interaction in the damaged model. First, if we allowed the V→S pathway to relax into a well-formed state before feeding its output into the S→N pathway, there would be little interaction—the effects of the damage would be additive. However, cortical pathways do not operate sequentially, one stage finishing its computation and then turning on the next stage. Moreover, in the undamaged brain, such a processing strategy is unadaptive, as cascading partial results from one pathway to the next can speed processing without the introduction of errors (McClelland, 1979). Second, the interaction might be eliminated by making the S→N pathway continually responsive to changes in the output of the V→S pathway. Then, the rate of convergence of the V→S pathway would be irrelevant to determining the eventual output of the S→N pathway. However, because the output of the S→N pathway depends not only on its input but its internal state (the state of the clean-up net), one cannot design a pathway that is continually responsive to changes in the input and is also able to clean up noisy responses. Thus, the two modifications one might consider to eliminate the interactions in the damaged model seriously weaken the computational power of the undamaged model. We therefore conclude that the framework of our model makes it difficult to avoid an interaction of damage in two pathways.

A subtle yet significant aspect of the model's performance is that the error rate on the visual-gesturing task was reliably higher than the error rate on the auditory-naming task, despite the fact that each task made use of one damaged pathway, and the pathways were damaged to the same degree. The difference in performance is due to the fact that the damaged pathway for the visual-gesturing task is the first in a cascade of two, while the damaged pathway for the auditory-naming task is the second. The initially noisy response from a damaged pathway early in the system propagates to subsequent pathways, and although the damaged pathway will eventually produce the correct response, this is not sufficient to ensure that subsequent pathways will do so as well.

2.1 DISTRIBUTION OF ERRORS FOR VISUAL OBJECT NAMING

Figure 2 presents the model's error distribution for the visual-naming task. Consistent with the patient data (Farah, 1990), the model produces many more semantic and perseveration errors than by chance. The chance error proportions were computed by assuming that if the correct response was not made, then all other responses had an equal probability of being chosen.

To understand the predominance of semantic errors, consider the effect of damage to the V→S pathway. For relatively small amounts of damage, the mapping produced will be close to the correct mapping. "Close" here means that the Euclidean distance in the semantic output space between the correct and perturbed mapping is small. Most of the time, minor perturbation of the mapping will be compensated for by the clean-up net. Occasionally, the perturbation will land the model in a different attractor basin, and a different response will be made. However, when the wrong attractor is selected, it will be one "close" to the correct attractor, i.e., it will likely be a sibling in the same pattern cluster as the correct attractor. In the case of the V→S pathway, the siblings of the correct attractor are by definition semantically related. A semantic error will be produced by the model when a sibling semantic attractor is chosen, and then this pattern is correctly mapped to a naming response in the S→N pathway.

In addition to semantic errors, the other frequent error type in visual naming is perseverations. The priming mechanism is responsible for the significant number of perseverations, although in the unlesioned model, it facilitates processing of repeated stimuli without producing perseverations.

Just as important as the presence of perseverative and semantic errors is the absence of visual errors, a feature of optic aphasia that contrasts sharply with visual agnosia (Farah, 1990). The same mechanisms explain why the rate of visual errors is close to its chance value and why visual+semantic errors are above chance. Visual-naming errors occur because there is an error either in the V→S or S→N mappings, or both. Since the erroneous outputs of these pathways show a strong tendency to be similar to the correct output, and because semantic and name similarity does not imply visual similarity (the patterns were paired randomly), visual errors should only occur by chance. When a visual error does occur, though, there is a high probability that the error is also semantic because of the strong bias that already exists toward producing semantic errors. This is the reason why more visual+semantic errors occur than by chance and why the proportion of these

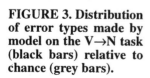

FIGURE 3. Distribution of error types made by model on the V→N task (black bars) relative to chance (grey bars).

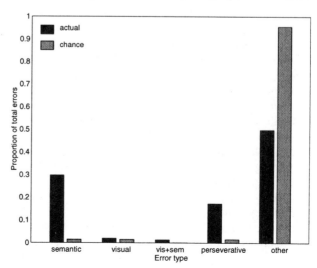

errors is only slightly less than the proportion of visual errors.

Plaut and Shallice (1993) have proposed a connectionist model to account for the distribution of errors made by optic aphasics. Although their model was not designed to account for any of the other phenomena associated with the disorder, it has much in common with the model we are proposing. Unlike our model, however, theirs requires the assumption that visually similar objects also share semantic similarity. This assumption might be questioned, especially because our model does not require this assumption to produce the correct distribution of error responses.

3 DISCUSSION

In demonstrating superadditive effects of damage, we have offered an account of optic aphasia that explains the primary phenomenon: severe impairments in visual naming in conjunction with relatively spared performance on naming from verbal description or gesturing the appropriate use of a visually presented object. The model also explains the distribution of errors on visual naming. Although we did not have the space in this brief report to elaborate, the model accounts for several other distinct characteristics of optic aphasia, including the tendency of patients to "home in" on the correct name for a visually presented object when given sufficient time, and a positive correlation between the error rates on naming and gesturing responses to a visual object (Sitton, Mozer, & Farah, 1998). Further, the model makes several strong predictions which have yet to be tested experimentally. One such prediction, which was apparent in the results presented earlier, is that a higher error rate should be observed on visual gesturing than on auditory naming when the tasks are equated for difficulty, as our simulation does.

More generally, we have strengthened the plausibility of Farah's (1990) hypothesis that partial damage to two processing pathways may result in close-to-normal performance on tasks involving one pathway or the other while yielding a severe performance deficit on tasks involving both damaged pathways. The superadditive-impairment theory thus may provide a more parsimonious account of various disorders that were previously believed to require more complex architectures or explanations.

4 ACKNOWLEDGMENTS

This research was supported by grant 97-18 from the McDonnell-Pew Program in Cognitive Neuroscience.

5 REFERENCES

Becker, S., Behrmann, M., & Moscovitch, K. (1993). Word priming in attractor networks. *Proceedings of the Fifteenth Annual Conference of the Cognitive Science Society* (pp. 231–236). Hillsdale, NJ: Erlbaum.

Farah, M. J. (1990). *Visual agnosia*. Cambridge, MA: MIT Press/Bradford Books.

Mathis, D. W., & Mozer, M. C. (1996). Conscious and unconscious perception: A computational theory. In G. Cottrell (Ed.), *Proceedings of the Eighteenth Annual Conference of the Cognitive Science Society* (pp. 324–328). Hillsdale, NJ: Erlbaum.

McClelland, J. L. (1979). On the time relations of mental processes: An examination of systems of processes in cascade. *Psychological Review, 86,* 287–330.

Plaut, D., & Shallice, T. (1993). Perseverative and semantic influences on visual object naming errors in optic aphasia: A connectionist approach. *Journal of Cognitive Neuroscience, 5,* 89-112.

Schnider, A., Benson, D. F., and Scharre, D. W. (1994). Visual agnosia and optic aphasia: Are they anatomically distinct? *Cortex, 30,* 445-457.

Sitton, M., Mozer, M. C., & Farah, M. (1998). *Diffuse lesions in a modular connectionist architecture: An account of optic aphasia*. Manuscript submitted for publication.

A Hippocampal Model of Recognition Memory

Randall C. O'Reilly
Department of Psychology
University of Colorado at Boulder
Campus Box 345
Boulder, CO 80309-0345
oreilly@psych.colorado.edu

Kenneth A. Norman
Department of Psychology
Harvard University
33 Kirkland Street
Cambridge, MA 02138
norman@wjh.harvard.edu

James L. McClelland
Department of Psychology and
Center for the Neural Basis of Cognition
Carnegie Mellon University
Pittsburgh, PA 15213
jlm@cnbc.cmu.edu

Abstract

A rich body of data exists showing that recollection of specific information makes an important contribution to recognition memory, which is distinct from the contribution of familiarity, and is not adequately captured by existing unitary memory models. Furthermore, neuropsychological evidence indicates that recollection is subserved by the hippocampus. We present a model, based largely on known features of hippocampal anatomy and physiology, that accounts for the following key characteristics of recollection: 1) false recollection is rare (i.e., participants rarely claim to recollect having studied nonstudied items), and 2) increasing interference leads to less recollection but apparently does not compromise the *quality* of recollection (i.e., the extent to which recollected information veridically reflects events that occurred at study).

1   Introduction

For nearly 50 years, memory researchers have known that our ability to remember specific past episodes depends critically on the hippocampus. In this paper, we describe our initial attempt to use a mechanistically explicit model of hippocampal function to explain a wide range of human memory data.

Our understanding of hippocampal function from a computational and biological perspective is based on our prior work (McClelland, McNaughton, & O'Reilly, 1995; O'Reilly & McClelland, 1994). At the broadest level, we think that the hippocampus exists in part to provide a memory system which can learn arbitrary information rapidly without suffering undue amounts of interference. This memory system sits on top of, and works in conjunction with, the neocortex, which learns slowly over many experiences, producing integrative representations of the relevant statistical features of the environment. The hippocampus accomplishes rapid, relatively interference-free learning by using relatively non-overlapping (*pattern separated*) representations. Pattern separation occurs as a result of 1) the *sparseness* of hippocampal representations (relative to cortical representations), and 2) the fact that hippocampal units are sensitive to *conjunctions* of cortical features — given two cortical patterns with 50% feature overlap, the probability that a particular conjunction of features will be present in both patterns is much less than 50%.

We propose that the hippocampus produces a relatively high-threshold, high-quality recollective response to test items. The response is "high-threshold" in the sense that studied items sometimes trigger rich recollection (defined as "retrieval of most or all of the test probe's features from memory") but lures never trigger rich recollection. The response is "high-quality" in the sense that, most of the time, the recollection signal consists of part or all of a single studied pattern, as opposed to a blend of studied patterns. The high-threshold, high-quality nature of recollection can be explained in terms of the conjunctivity of hippocampal representations: Insofar as recollection is a function of whether the features of the test probe were encountered *together* at study, lures (which contain many novel feature conjunctions, even if their constituent features are familiar) are unlikely to trigger rich recollection; also, insofar as the hippocampus stores feature conjunctions (as opposed to individual features), features which appeared together at study are likely to appear together at test. Importantly, in accordance with dual-process accounts of recognition memory (Yonelinas, 1994; Jacoby, Yonelinas, & Jennings, 1996), we believe that hippocampally-driven recollection is not the sole contributor to recognition memory performance. Rather, extensive evidence exists that recollection is complemented by a "fallback" familiarity signal which participants consult when rich recollection does not occur. The familiarity signal is mediated by as-yet unspecified areas (likely including the parahippocampal temporal cortex: Aggleton & Shaw, 1996; Miller & Desimone, 1994).

Our account differs substantially from most other computational and mathematical models of recognition memory. Most of these models compute the "global match" between the test probe and stored memories (e.g., Hintzman, 1988; Gillund & Shiffrin, 1984); recollection in these models involves computing a similarity-weighted average of stored memory patterns. In other memory models, recollection of an item depends critically on the extent to which the components of the item's representation were linked with that of the study context (e.g., Chappell & Humphreys, 1994). Critically, recollection in all of these models lacks the high-threshold, high-quality character of recollection in our model. This is most evident when we consider the effects of manipulations which increase interference (e.g., increasing the length of the study list, or increasing inter-item similarity). As interference increases, global matching models predict increasingly "blurry" recollection (reflecting the contribution of more items to the composite output vector), while the other models predict that false recollection of lures will increase. In contrast, our model predicts that increasing interference should lead to decreased correct recollection of studied test probes, but there should be no concomitant increase in "erroneous" types of recollection (i.e., recollection of details which mismatch studied test probes, or rich recollection of lures). This prediction is consistent with the recent finding that correct recollection of studied items decreases with increasing list length (Yonelinas, 1994). Lastly, although extant data certainly do not contradict the claim that the veridicality of recollection is robust to interference, we acknowledge that additional, focused experimentation is needed to definitively resolve this issue.

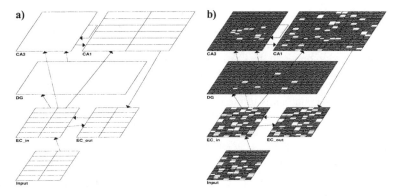

Figure 1: The model. **a)** Shows the areas and connectivity, and the corresponding columns within the Input, EC, and CA1 (see text). **b)** Shows an example activity pattern. Note the sparse activity in the DG and CA3, and intermediate sparseness of the CA1.

2 Architecture and Overall Behavior

Figure 1 shows a diagram of our model, which contains the basic anatomical regions of the hippocampal formation, as well as the entorhinal cortex (EC), which serves as the primary cortical input/output pathway for the hippocampus. The model as described below instantiates a series of hypotheses about the structure and function of the hippocampus and associated cortical areas, which are based on anatomical and physiological data and other models as described in O'Reilly and McClelland (1994) and McClelland et al. (1995), but not elaborated upon significantly here.

The *Input* layer activity pattern represents the state of the EC resulting from the presentation of a given item. We assume that the hippocampus stores and retrieves memories by way of reduced representations in the EC, which have a correspondence with more elaborated representations in other areas of cortex that is developed via long-term cortical learning. We further assume that there is a rough topology to the organization of EC, with different cortical areas and/or sub-areas represented by different *slots*, which can be thought of as representing different feature dimensions of the input (e.g., color, font, semantic features, etc.). Our EC has 36 slots with four units per slot; one unit per slot was active (with each unit representing a particular "feature value"). Input patterns were constructed from prototypes by randomly selecting different feature values for a random subset of slots. There are two functionally distinct layers of the EC, one which receives input from cortical areas and projects into the hippocampus (superficial or EC_{in}), and another which receives projections from the CA1 and projects back out to the cortex (deep or EC_{out}). While the representations in these layers are probably different in their details, we assume that they are functionally equivalent, and use the same representations across both for convenience. EC_{in} projects to three areas of the hippocampus: the dentate gyrus (DG), area CA3, and area CA1. The storage of the input pattern occurs through weight changes in the feedforward and recurrent projections into the CA3, and the CA3 to CA1 connections. The CA3 and CA1 contain the two primary representations of the input pattern, while the DG plays an important but secondary role as a pattern-separation enhancer for the CA3.

The CA3 provides the primary sparse, pattern-separated, conjunctive representation described above. This is achieved by random, partial connectivity between the EC and CA3, and a high threshold for activation (i.e., sparseness), such that the few units which are activated in the CA3 (5% in our model) are those which have the most inputs from active EC units. The odds of a unit having such a high proportion of inputs from even two relatively similar EC patterns is low, resulting in pattern separation (see O'Reilly & McClelland,

1994 for a much more detailed and precise treatment of this issue, and the role of the DG in facilitating pattern separation). While these CA3 representations are useful for allowing rapid learning without undue interference, the pattern-separation process eliminates any systematic relationship between the CA3 pattern and the original EC pattern that gave rise to it. Thus, there must be some means of translating the CA3 pattern back into the language of the EC. The simple solution of directly associating the CA3 pattern with the corresponding EC pattern is problematic due to the interference caused by the relatively high activity levels in the EC (around 15%, and 25% in our model). For this reason, we think that the translation is formed via the CA1, which (as a result of long-term learning) is capable of expanding EC representations into sparser patterns that are more easily linked to CA3, and then mapping these sparser patterns back onto the EC.

Our CA1 has separate representations of small combinations of slots (labeled *columns*); columns can be arbitrarily combined to reproduce any valid EC representation. Thus, representations in CA1 are intermediate between the fully conjunctive CA3, and the fully combinatorial EC. This is achieved in our model by training a single CA1 column of 32 units with slightly less than 10% activity levels to be able to reproduce any combination of patterns over 3 EC_{in} slots (64 different combinations) in a corresponding set of 3 EC_{out} slots. The resulting weights are replicated across columns covering the entire EC (see Figure 1a). The cost of this scheme is that more CA1 units are required (32 *vs* 12 per column in the EC), which is nonetheless consistent with the relatively greater expansion of this area relative to other hippocampal areas as a function of cortical size.

After learning, our model recollects studied items by simply reactivating the original CA3, CA1 and EC_{out} patterns via facilitated weights. With partial or noisy input patterns (and with interference), these weights and two forms of recurrence (the "short loop" within CA3, and the "big loop" out to the EC and back through the entire hippocampus) allow the hippocampus to bootstrap its way into recalling the complete original pattern (*pattern completion*). If the EC input pattern corresponds to a nonstudied pattern, then the weights will not have been facilitated for this particular activity pattern, and the CA1 will not be strongly driven by the CA3. Even if the EC_{in} activity pattern corresponds to two components that were previously studied, but not together (see below), the conjunctive nature of the CA3 representations will minimize the extent to which recall occurs.

Recollection is operationalized as successful recall of the test probe. This raises the basic problem that the system needs to be able to distinguish between the EC_{out} activation due to the item input on EC_{in} (either directly or via the CA1), and that which is due to activation coming from recall in the CA3-CA1 pathway. One solution to this problem, which is suggested by autocorrelation histograms during reversible CA3 lesions (Mizumori et al., 1989), is that the CA3 and CA1 are 180° out of phase with respect to the theta rhythm. Thus, when the CA3 drives the CA1, it does so at a point when the CA1 units would otherwise be silent, providing a means for distinguishing between EC and CA3 driven CA1 activation. We approximate something like this mechanism by simply turning off the EC_{in} inputs to CA1 during testing. We assess the quality of hippocampal recall by comparing the resulting EC_{out} pattern with the EC_{in} cue. The number of active units that match between EC_{in} and EC_{out} (labeled C) indicates how much of the test probe was recollected. The number of units that are active in EC_{out} but not in EC_{in} (labeled E) indicates the extent to which the model recollected an item other than the test probe.

3   Activation and Learning Dynamics

Our model is implemented using the Leabra framework, which provides a robust mechanism for producing controlled levels of sparse activation in the presence of recurrent activation dynamics, and a simple, effective Hebbian learning rule (O'Reilly, 1996)[1]. The activation function is a simple thresholded single-compartment neuron model with continuous-valued spike rate output. Membrane potential is updated by $\frac{dV_m(t)}{dt} = \tau \sum_c g_c(t)\overline{g_c}(E_c - V_m(t))$, with 3 channels ($c$) corresponding to: e excitatory input; l leak current; and i inhibitory input. Activation communicated to other cells is a simple thresholded function of the membrane potential: $y_j(t) = 1/\left(1 + \frac{1}{\gamma[V_m(t)-\Theta]_+}\right)$. As in the hippocampus (and cortex), all principal weights (synaptic efficacies) are excitatory, while the local-circuit inhibition controls positive feedback loops (i.e., preventing epileptiform activity) and produces sparse representations. Leabra assumes that the inhibitory feedback has an approximate set-point (i.e., strong activity creates compensatorially stronger inhibition, and vice-versa), resulting in roughly constant overall activity levels, with a firm upper bound. Inhibitory current is given by $g_i = g^\Theta_{k+1} + q(g^\Theta_k - g^\Theta_{k+1})$, where $0 < q < 1$ is typically .25, and $g^\Theta = \frac{\sum_{c \neq i} g_c \overline{g_c}(E_c - \Theta)}{\Theta - E_i}$ for the units with the k th and $k + 1$ th highest excitatory inputs. A simple, appropriately normalized Hebbian rule is used in Leabra: $\Delta w_{ij} = x_i y_j - y_j w_{ij}$, which can be seen as computing the expected value of the sending unit's activity conditional on the receiver's activity (if treated like a binary variable active with probability y_j): $w_{ij} \approx \langle x_i | y_j \rangle_p$. This is essentially the same rule used in standard competitive learning or mixtures-of-Gaussians.

4   Interference and List-Length, Item Similarity

Here, we demonstrate that the hippocampal recollection system degrades with increasing interference in a way that preserves its essential high-threshold, high-quality nature. Figure 2 shows the effects of list length and item similarity on our C and E measures. Only studied items appear in the high C, low E corner representing rich recollection. As length and similarity increase, interference results in decreased C for studied items (without increased E), but critically there is no change in responding to new items. Interference in our model arises from the reduced but nevertheless extant overlap between representations in the hippocampal system as a function of item similarity and number of items stored. To the extent that increasing numbers of individual CA3 units are linked to multiple contradictory CA1 representations, their contribution is reduced, and eventually recollection fails. As for the frequently obtained finding that decreased recollection of studied items is accompanied by an increase in overall false alarms, we think this results from subjects being forced to rely more on the (less reliable) fallback familiarity mechanism.

5   Conjunctivity and Associative Recognition

Now, we consider what happens when lures are constructed by recombining elements of studied patterns (e.g., study "window-reason" and "car-oyster", and test with "window-oyster"). One recent study found that participants are much more likely to claim to recollect studied pairs than re-paired lures (Yonelinas, 1997). Furthermore, data from this study is consistent with the idea that re-paired lures sometimes trigger recollection of the studied word pairs that were re-combined to generate the lure; when this happens (assuming that each word occurred in only one pair), the participant can confidently reject the lure. Our simulation data is consistent with these findings: For studied word pairs, the model (richly) recollected both pair components 86% of the time. As for re-paired lures, both pair components were never recalled together, but 16% of the time the model recollected one of the pair components, along with the component that it was paired with at study. The

---

[1]Note that the version of Leabra described here is an update to the cited version, which is currently being prepared for publication.

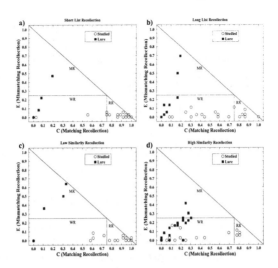

Figure 2: Effects of list length and similarity on recollection performance. Responses can be categorized according to the thresholds shown, producing three regions: rich recollection (*RR*), weak recollection (*WR*), and misrecollection (*MR*). Increasing list length and similarity lead to less rich recollection of studied items (without increasing misrecollection for these items), and do not significantly affect the model's responding to lures.

model responded in a similar fashion to pairs consisting of one studied word and a new word (never recollecting both pair components together, but recollecting the old item and the item it was paired with at study 13% of the time). Word pairs consisting of two new items failed to trigger recollection of even a single pair component. Similar findings were obtained in our simulation of the (Hintzman, Curran, & Oppy, 1992) experiment involving recombinations of word and plurality cues.

6   Discussion

While the results presented above have dealt with the presentation of complete probe stimuli for recognition memory tests, our model is obviously capable of explaining cued recall and related phenomena such as source or context memory by virtue of its pattern completion abilities. There are a number of interesting issues that this raises. For example, we predict that successful item recollection will be highly correlated with the ability to recall additional information from the study episode, since both rely on the same underlying memory. Further, to the extent that elderly adults form less distinct encodings of stimuli (Rabinowitz & Ackerman, 1982), this explains both their impaired recollection on recognition tests (Parkin & Walter, 1992) and their impaired memory for contextual ("source") details (Schacter et al., 1991).

In summary, existing mathematical models of recognition memory are most likely incorrect in assuming that recognition is performed with one memory system. Global matching models may provide a good account of familiarity-based recognition, but they fail to account for the contributions of recollection to recognition, as discussed above. For example, global matching models predict that lures which are similar to studied items will always trigger a stronger signal than dissimilar lures; as such, these models can not account for the fact that sometimes subjects can reject similar lures with high levels of confidence (due, in our model, to recollection of a similar studied item; Brainerd, Reyna, & Kneer, 1995; Hintzman et al., 1992). Further, global matching models confound the signal for the extent to which individual components of the test probe were present at all during study, and signal for the extent to which they occurred together. We believe that these signals may be separable, with recollection (implemented by the hippocampus) showing sensitivity to conjunctions of features, but not the occurrence of individual features, and familiarity (implemented by cortical regions) showing sensitivity to component occurrence but not co-occurence. This division of labor is consistent with recent data showing that familiarity does not discriminate well between studied item pairs and lures constructed by conjoining items from two different studied pairs (so long as the pairings are truly novel) (Yonelinas, 1997), and with the point, set forth by (McClelland et al., 1995), that catastrophic interference would occur if rapid learning (required to learn feature co-occurrences) took place in the neocortical structures which generate the familiarity signal.

7 References

Aggleton, J. P., & Shaw, C. (1996). Amnesia and recognition memory: a re-analysis of psychometric data. *Neuropsychologia, 34*, 51.

Brainerd, C. J., Reyna, V. F., & Kneer, R. (1995). False-recognition reversal: When similarity is distinctive. *Journal of Memory and Language, 34*, 157–185.

Chappell, M., & Humphreys, M. S. (1994). An auto-associative neural network for sparse representations: Analysis and application to models of recognition and cued recall. *Psychological Review, 101*, 103–128.

Gillund, G., & Shiffrin, R. M. (1984). A retrieval model for both recognition and recall. *Psychological Review, 91*, 1–67.

Hintzman, D. L. (1988). Judgments of frequency and recognition memory in a multiple-trace memory model. *Psychological Review, 95*, 528–551.

Hintzman, D. L., Curran, T., & Oppy, B. (1992). Effects of similarity and repetition on memory: Registration without learning. *Journal of Experimental Psychology: Learning, Memory, and Cognition, 18*, 667–680.

Jacoby, L. L., Yonelinas, A. P., & Jennings, J. M. (1996). The relation between conscious and unconscious (automatic) influences: A declaration of independence. In J. D. Cohen, & J. W. Schooler (Eds.), *Scientific approaches to the question of consciousness* (pp. 13–47). Hillsdale, NJ: Lawrence Erbaum Associates.

McClelland, J. L., McNaughton, B. L., & O'Reilly, R. C. (1995). Why there are complementary learning systems in the hippocampus and neocortex: Insights from the successes and failures of connectionst models of learning and memory. *Psychological Review, 102*, 419–457.

Miller, E. K., & Desimone, R. (1994). Parallel neuronal mechanisms for short-term memory. *Science, 263*, 520–522.

Mizumori, S. J. Y., McNaughton, B. L., Barnes, C. A., & Fox, K. B. (1989). Preserved spatial coding in hippocampal CA1 pyramidal cells during reversible suppression of CA3c output: Evidence for pattern completion in hippocampus. *Journal of Neuroscience, 9*(11), 3915–3928.

O'Reilly, R. C. (1996). *The leabra model of neural interactions and learning in the neocortex.* PhD thesis, Carnegie Mellon University, Pittsburgh, PA, USA.

O'Reilly, R. C., & McClelland, J. L. (1994). Hippocampal conjunctive encoding, storage, and recall: Avoiding a tradeoff. *Hippocampus, 4*(6), 661–682.

Parkin, A. J., & Walter, B. M. (1992). Recollective experience, normal aging, and frontal dysfunction. *Psychology and Aging, 7*, 290–298.

Rabinowitz, J. C., & Ackerman, B. P. (1982). General encoding of episodic events by elderly adults. In F. I. M. C. S. Trehub (Ed.), *Aging and cognitive processes*. Plenum Publishing Corporation.

Schacter, D. L., Kaszniak, A. W., Kihlstrom, J. F., & Valdiserri, M. (1991). The relation between source memory and aging. *Psychology and Aging, 6*, 559–568.

Yonelinas, A. P. (1994). Receiver-operating characteristics in recognition memory: Evidence for a dual-process model. *Journal of Experimental Psychology: Learning, Memory, and Cognition, 20*, 1341–1354.

Yonelinas, A. P. (1997). Recognition memory ROCs for item and associative information: The contribution of recollection and familiarity. *Memory and Cognition, 25*, 747–763.

Correlates of Attention in a Model of Dynamic Visual Recognition*

Rajesh P. N. Rao
Department of Computer Science
University of Rochester
Rochester, NY 14627
rao@cs.rochester.edu

Abstract

Given a set of objects in the visual field, how does the the visual system learn
to attend to a particular object of interest while ignoring the rest? How are
occlusions and background clutter so effortlessly discounted for when recognizing a familiar object? In this paper, we attempt to answer these questions in the context of a Kalman filter-based model of visual recognition that
has previously proved useful in explaining certain neurophysiological phenomena such as endstopping and related extra-classical receptive field effects in the visual cortex. By using results from the field of robust statistics,
we describe an extension of the Kalman filter model that can handle multiple
objects in the visual field. The resulting robust Kalman filter model demonstrates how certain forms of attention can be viewed as an emergent property of the interaction between top-down expectations and bottom-up signals. The model also suggests functional interpretations of certain attention-
related effects that have been observed in visual cortical neurons. Experimental results are provided to help demonstrate the ability of the model
to perform robust segmentation and recognition of objects and image sequences in the presence of varying degrees of occlusions and clutter.

1 INTRODUCTION

The human visual system possesses the remarkable ability to recognize objects despite the
presence of distractors and occluders in the field of view. A popular suggestion is that an "attentional spotlight" mediates this ability to preferentially process a relevant object in a given
scene (see [5, 9] for reviews). Numerous models have been proposed to simulate the control of
this "focus of attention" [10, 11, 15]. Unfortunately, there is inconclusive evidence for the existence of an explicit neural mechanism for implementing an attentional spotlight in the visual

---
*This research was supported by NIH/PHS research grant 1-P41-RR09283. I am grateful to Dana
Ballard for many useful discussions and suggestions. Author's current address: The Salk Institute, CNL,
10010 N. Torrey Pines Road, La Jolla, CA 92037. E-mail: rao@salk.edu.

cortex. Thus, an important question is whether there are alternate neural mechanisms which don't explicitly use a spotlight but whose effects can nevertheless be interpreted as attention. In other words, can attention be viewed as an emergent property of a distributed network of neurons whose primary goal is visual recognition?

In this paper, we extend a previously proposed Kalman filter-based model of visual recognition [13, 12] to handle the case of multiple objects, occlusions, and clutter in the visual field. We provide simulation results suggesting that certain forms of attention can be viewed as an emergent property of the interaction between bottom-up signals and top-down expectations during visual recognition. The simulation results demonstrate how "attention" can be switched between different objects in a visual scene without using an explicit spotlight of attention.

2 A KALMAN FILTER MODEL OF VISUAL RECOGNITION

We have previously introduced a hierarchical Kalman filter-based model of visual recognition and have shown how this model can be used to explain neurophysiological effects such as end-stopping and neural response suppression during free-viewing of natural images [12, 13]. The Kalman filter [7] is essentially a linear dynamical system that attempts to mimic the behavior of an observed natural process. At any time instant t, the filter assumes that the internal state of the given natural process can be represented as a $k \times 1$ vector $\mathbf{r}(t)$. Although not directly accessible, this internal state vector is assumed to generate an $n \times 1$ measurable and observable output vector $\mathbf{I}(t)$ (for example, an image) according to:

$$\mathbf{I}(t) = U\mathbf{r}(t) + \mathbf{n}(t) \tag{1}$$

where U is an $n \times k$ *generative (or measurement) matrix*, and $\mathbf{n}(t)$ is a Gaussian stochastic noise process with mean zero and a covariance matrix given by $\Sigma = E[\mathbf{n}\mathbf{n}^T]$ (E denotes the expectation operator and T denotes transpose).

In order to specify how the internal state $\mathbf{r}$ changes with time, the Kalman filter assumes that the process of interest can be modeled as a *Gauss-Markov random process* [1]. Thus, given the state $\mathbf{r}(t-1)$ at time instant $t-1$, the next state $\mathbf{r}(t)$ is given by:

$$\mathbf{r}(t) = V\mathbf{r}(t-1) + \mathbf{m}(t-1) \tag{2}$$

where V is the *state transition (or prediction) matrix* and $\mathbf{m}$ is white Gaussian noise with mean $\overline{\mathbf{m}} = E[\mathbf{m}]$ and covariance $\Pi = E[(\mathbf{m} - \overline{\mathbf{m}})(\mathbf{m} - \overline{\mathbf{m}})^T]$.

Given the generative model in Equation 1 and the dynamics in Equation 2, the goal is to optimally estimate the current internal state $\mathbf{r}(t)$ using only the measurable inputs $\mathbf{I}(t)$. An optimization function whose minimization yields an estimate of $\mathbf{r}$ is the *weighted least-squares criterion*:

$$J = (\mathbf{I} - U\mathbf{r})^T \Sigma^{-1}(\mathbf{I} - U\mathbf{r}) + (\mathbf{r} - \overline{\mathbf{r}})^T M^{-1}(\mathbf{r} - \overline{\mathbf{r}}) \tag{3}$$

where $\overline{\mathbf{r}}(t)$ is the mean of the state vector *before* measurement of the input data $\mathbf{I}(t)$ and $M = E[(\mathbf{r} - \overline{\mathbf{r}})(\mathbf{r} - \overline{\mathbf{r}})^T]$ is the corresponding covariance matrix. It is easy to show [1] that J is simply the sum of the negative log-likelihood of generating the data $\mathbf{I}$ given the state $\mathbf{r}$, and the negative log of the prior probability of the state $\mathbf{r}$. Thus, minimizing J is equivalent to maximizing the posterior probability $p(\mathbf{r}|\mathbf{I})$ of the state $\mathbf{r}$ given the input data.

The optimization function J can be minimized by setting $\frac{\partial J}{\partial \mathbf{r}} = 0$ and solving for the minimum value $\widehat{\mathbf{r}}$ of the state $\mathbf{r}$ (note that $\widehat{\mathbf{r}}$ equals the mean of $\mathbf{r}$ after measurement of $\mathbf{I}$). The resultant *Kalman filter* equation is given by:

$$\widehat{\mathbf{r}}(t) = \overline{\mathbf{r}}(t) + N(t)U^T \Sigma(t)^{-1}(\mathbf{I}(t) - U\overline{\mathbf{r}}(t)) \tag{4}$$

$$\overline{\mathbf{r}}(t) = V\widehat{\mathbf{r}}(t-1) + \overline{\mathbf{m}}(t-1) \tag{5}$$

where $N(t) = (U^T \Sigma(t)^{-1}U + M(t)^{-1})^{-1}$ is a "normalization" matrix that maintains the covariance of the state $\mathbf{r}$ after measurement of $\mathbf{I}$. The matrix M, which is the covariance before measurement of $\mathbf{I}$, is updated as $M(t) = VN(t-1)V^T + \Pi(t-1)$. Thus, the Kalman filter predicts one step into the future using Equation 5, obtains the next sensory input $\mathbf{I}(t)$, and then corrects its prediction $\bar{\mathbf{r}}(t)$ using the sensory residual error $(\mathbf{I}(t) - U\bar{\mathbf{r}}(t))$ and the Kalman gain $N(t)U^T\Sigma(t)^{-1}$. This yields the corrected estimate $\hat{\mathbf{r}}(t)$ (Equation 4), which is then used to make the next state prediction $\bar{\mathbf{r}}(t+1)$.

The measurement (or generative) matrix U and the state transition (or prediction) matrix V used by the Kalman filter together encode an *internal model* of the observed dynamic process. As suggested in [13], it is possible to *learn* an internal model of the input dynamics from observed data. Let $\mathbf{u}$ and $\mathbf{v}$ denote the vectorized forms of the matrices U and V respectively. For example, the $n \times k$ generative matrix U can be collapsed into an $nk \times 1$ vector $\mathbf{u} = [U^1 U^2 \dots U^n]^T$ where U^i denotes the ith row of U. Note that $(\mathbf{I} - U\mathbf{r}) = (\mathbf{I} - R\mathbf{u})$ where R is the $n \times nk$ matrix given by:

$$R = \begin{bmatrix} \mathbf{r}^T & \mathbf{0} & \dots & \mathbf{0} \\ \mathbf{0} & \mathbf{r}^T & \dots & \mathbf{0} \\ \vdots & \vdots & \vdots & \vdots \\ \mathbf{0} & \dots & \mathbf{0} & \mathbf{r}^T \end{bmatrix} \tag{6}$$

By minimizing an optimization function similar to J [13], one can derive a Kalman filter-like "learning rule" for the generative matrix U:

$$\hat{\mathbf{u}}(t) \quad = \quad \bar{\mathbf{u}}(t) + N_u(t)R(t)^T\Sigma(t)^{-1}(\mathbf{I}(t) - R(t)\bar{\mathbf{u}}(t)) - \alpha N_u(t)\bar{\mathbf{u}}(t) \tag{7}$$

where $\bar{\mathbf{u}}(t) = \hat{\mathbf{u}}(t-1)$, $N_u(t) = (N_u(t-1)^{-1} + R(t)^T\Sigma(t)^{-1}R(t) + \alpha I)^{-1}$, and I is the $nk \times nk$ identity matrix. The constant α determines the decay rate of $\bar{\mathbf{u}}$.

As in the case of U, an estimate of the prediction matrix V can be obtained via the following learning rule for $\mathbf{v}$ [13]:

$$\hat{\mathbf{v}}(t) \quad = \quad \bar{\mathbf{v}}(t) + N_v(t)\hat{R}(t)^T M(t)^{-1}[\mathbf{r}(t+1) - \bar{\mathbf{r}}(t+1)] - \beta N_v(t)\bar{\mathbf{v}}(t) \tag{8}$$

where $\bar{\mathbf{v}}(t) = \hat{\mathbf{v}}(t-1)$, $N_v(t) = (N_v(t-1)^{-1} + \hat{R}(t)^T M(t)^{-1}\hat{R}(t) + \beta I)^{-1}$ and $\hat{R}$ is a $k \times k^2$ matrix analogous to R (Equation 6) but with $\mathbf{r}^T = \hat{\mathbf{r}}^T$. The constant β determines the decay rate for $\mathbf{v}$ while I denotes the $k^2 \times k^2$ identity matrix. Note that in this case, the estimate of V is corrected using the prediction residual error $(\mathbf{r}(t+1) - \bar{\mathbf{r}}(t+1))$, which denotes the difference between the actual state and the predicted state. One unresolved issue is the specification of values for $\mathbf{r}(t)$ (comprising R(t)) in Equation 7 and $\mathbf{r}(t+1)$ in Equation 8. The Expectation-Maximization (EM) algorithm [4] suggests that in the case of static stimuli ($\bar{\mathbf{r}}(t) = \hat{\mathbf{r}}(t-1)$), one may use $\mathbf{r}(t) = \hat{\mathbf{r}}$ which is the converged optimal state estimate for the given static input. In the case of dynamic stimuli, the EM algorithm prescribes $\mathbf{r}(t) = \hat{\mathbf{r}}(t|N)$, which is the optimal temporally *smoothed* state estimate [1] for time t ($\leq N$), given input data for each of the time instants $1, \dots, N$. Unfortunately, the smoothed estimate requires knowledge of future inputs and is computationally quite expensive. For the experimental results, we used the on-line estimates $\hat{\mathbf{r}}(t)$ when updating the matrices U and V during training.

3   ROBUST KALMAN FILTERING

The standard derivation of the Kalman filter minimizes Equation 3 but unfortunately does not specify how the covariance Σ is to be obtained. A common choice is to use a constant matrix or even a constant scalar. Making Σ constant however reduces the Kalman filter estimates to standard least-squares estimates, which are highly susceptible to outliers or gross errors i.e. data points that lie far away from the bulk of the observed or predicted data [6]. For example, in the case where $\mathbf{I}$ represents an input image, occlusions and clutter will cause many pixels in $\mathbf{I}$ to deviate significantly from corresponding pixels in the predicted image $U\mathbf{r}$. The problem

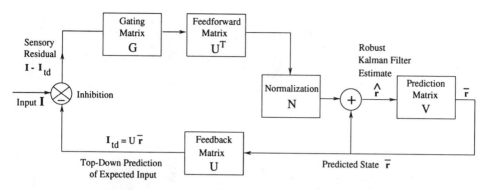

Figure 1: **Recurrent Network Implementation of the Robust Kalman Filter**. The gating matrix G is a non-linear function of the current residual error between the input $\mathbf{I}$ and its top-down prediction $U\bar{\mathbf{r}}$. G effectively filters out any high residuals, thereby preventing outliers in input data $\mathbf{I}$ from influencing the robust Kalman filter estimate $\hat{\mathbf{r}}$. Note that the entire filter can be implemented in a recurrent neural network, with U, U^T, and V represented by the synaptic weights of neurons with linear activation functions and G being implemented by a set of threshold non-linear neurons with binary outputs.

of outliers can be tackled using *robust estimation procedures* [6] such as M-estimation, which involves minimizing a function of the form:

$$J' = \sum_{i=1}^{n} \rho \left(\mathbf{I}^i - U^i \mathbf{r} \right) \tag{9}$$

where $\mathbf{I}^i$ and U^i are the ith pixel and ith row of $\mathbf{I}$ and U respectively, and ρ is a function that increases less rapidly than the square. This reduces the influence of large residual errors (which correspond to outliers) on the optimization of J', thereby "rejecting" the outliers. A special case of the above function is the following weighted least squares criterion:

$$J' = (\mathbf{I} - U\mathbf{r})^T S (\mathbf{I} - U\mathbf{r}) \tag{10}$$

where S is a diagonal matrix whose diagonal entries $S^{i,i}$ determine the weight accorded to the corresponding pixel error $(\mathbf{I}^i - U^i \mathbf{r})$. A simple but attractive choice for these weights is the non-linear function given by $S^{i,i} = \min \left\{ 1, c/(\mathbf{I}^i - U^i \mathbf{r})^2 \right\}$, where c is a threshold parameter. To understand the behavior of this function, note that S effectively clips the ith summand in J' (Equation 10 above) to a constant value c whenever the ith squared residual $(\mathbf{I}^i - U^i \mathbf{r})^2$ exceeds the threshold c; otherwise, the summand is set equal to the squared residual.

By substituting $\Sigma^{-1} = S$ in the optimization function J (Equation 3), we can rederive the following *robust Kalman filter* equation:

$$\hat{\mathbf{r}}(t) = \bar{\mathbf{r}}(t) + N(t)U^T G(t)(\mathbf{I} - U\bar{\mathbf{r}}(t)) \tag{11}$$

where $\bar{\mathbf{r}}(t) = V\hat{\mathbf{r}}(t-1)) + \bar{\mathbf{m}}(t-1)$, $N(t) = (U^T G(t)U + M(t)^{-1})^{-1}$, $M(t) = VN(t-1)V^T + \Pi(t-1)$, and $G(t)$ is an $n \times n$ diagonal matrix whose diagonal entries at time instant t are given by:

$$G^{i,i} = \begin{cases} 0 & \text{if } (\mathbf{I}^i(t) - U^i \bar{\mathbf{r}}(t))^2 > c(t) \\ 1 & \text{otherwise} \end{cases}$$

G can be regarded as the sensory residual gain or "gating" matrix, which determines the (binary) gain on the various components of the incoming sensory residual error vector. By effectively filtering out any high residuals, G allows the Kalman filter to ignore the corresponding outliers in the input $\mathbf{I}$, thereby enabling it to robustly estimate the state $\mathbf{r}$. Figure 1 depicts an implementation of the robust Kalman filter in the form of a recurrent network of linear and threshold non-linear neurons. In particular, the feedforward, feedback and prediction neurons possess linear activation functions while the gating neurons implementing G compute binary outputs based on a threshold non-linearity.

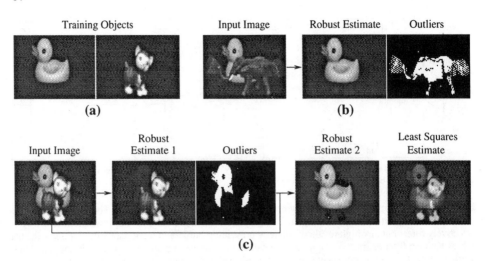

Figure 2: **Correlates of Attention during Static Recognition.** (a) Images of size 105×65 used to train a robust Kalman filter network. The generative matrix U was 6825×5. (b) Occlusions and background clutter are treated as outliers (white regions in the third image, depicting the diagonal of the gating matrix G). This allows the network to "attend to" and recognize the training object, as indicated by the accurate reconstruction (middle image) of the training image based on the final robust state estimate. (c) In the more interesting case of the training objects occluding each other, the network converges to one of the objects (the "dominant" one in the image - in this case, the object in the foreground). Having recognized one object, the second object is attended to and recognized by taking the complement of the outliers (diagonal of G) and repeating the robust filtering process (third and fourth images). The fifth image is the image reconstruction obtained from the standard (least squares derived) Kalman filter estimate, showing an inability to resolve or recognize either of the two objects.

4 VISUAL ATTENTION IN A SIMULATED NETWORK

The gating matrix G allows the Kalman filter network to "selectively attend" to an object while treating the remaining components of the sensory input as outliers. We demonstrate this capability of the network using three different examples. In the first example, a network was trained on static grayscale images of a pair of $3D$ objects (Figure 2 (a)). For learning static inputs, the prediction matrix V is unnecessary since we may use $\bar{\mathbf{r}}(t) = \hat{\mathbf{r}}(t-1)$ and $M(t) = N(t-1)$. After training, the network was tested on images containing the training objects with varying degrees of occlusion and clutter (Figure 2 (b) and (c)). The outlier threshold c was initialized to the sum of the mean plus k standard deviations of the current distribution of squared residual errors $(\mathbf{I}^i - U^i\mathbf{r})^2$. The value of k was gradually decreased during each iteration in order to allow the network to refine its robust estimate by gradually pruning away the outliers as it converges to a single object estimate. After convergence, the diagonal of the matrix G contains zeros in the image locations containing the outliers and ones in the remaining locations. As shown in Figure 2 (b), the network was successful in recognizing the training object despite occlusion and background clutter.

More interestingly, the outliers (white) produce a crude *segmentation* of the occluder and background clutter, which can subsequently be used to focus "attention" on these previously ignored objects and recover their identity. In particular, an *outlier mask* $\mathbf{m}$ can be defined by taking the complement of the diagonal of G (i.e. $\mathbf{m}^i = 1 - G^{i,i}$). By replacing the diagonal of G with $\mathbf{m}$ in Equation 11[1] and repeating the estimation process, the network can "attend to"

---

[1] Although not implemented here, this "shifting of attentional focus" can be automated using a model of neuronal fatigue and active decay (see, for example, [3]).

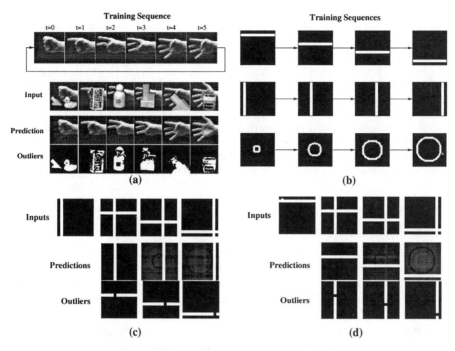

Figure 3: Correlates of Attention during Dynamic Recognition. (a) A network was trained on a cyclic image sequence of gestures (top), each image of size 75×75, with U and V of size 5625×15 and 15×15 respectively. The panels below show how the network can ignore various forms of occlusion and clutter (outliers), "attending to" the sequence of gestures that it has been trained on. The outlier threshold c was computed as the mean plus 0.3 standard deviations of the current distribution of squared residual errors. Results shown are those obtained after 5 cycles of exposure to the occluded images. (b) Three image sequences used to train a network. (c) and (d) show the response of the network to ambiguous stimuli comprised of images containing both a horizontal *and* a vertical bar. Note that the network was trained on a horizontal bar moving downwards and a vertical bar moving rightwards (see (b)) but not both simultaneously. Given ambiguous stimuli containing both these stimuli, the network interprets the input differently depending on the initial "priming" input. When the initial input is a vertical bar as in (c), the network interprets the sequence as a vertical bar moving rightwards (with some minor artifacts due to the other training sequences). On the other hand, when the initial input is a horizontal bar as in (d), the sequence is interpreted as a horizontal bar moving downwards, not paying "attention" to the extraneous vertical bars, which are now treated as outliers.

the image region(s) that were previously ignored as outliers. Such a two-step serial recognition process is depicted in Figure 2 (c). The network first recognizes the "dominant" object, which was generally observed to be the object occupying a larger area of the input image or possessing regions with higher contrast. The outlier mask **m** is subsequently used for "switching attention" and extracting the identity of the second object (lower arrow). Figure 3 shows examples of attention during recognition of dynamic stimuli. In particular, Figure 3 (c) and (d) show how the same image sequence can be interpreted in two different ways depending on which part of the stimulus is "attended to," which in turn depends on the initial priming input.

5   CONCLUSIONS

The simulation results indicate that certain experimental observations that have previously been interpreted using the metaphor of an attentional spotlight can also arise as a result of competition and cooperation during visual recognition within networks of linear and non-linear neurons. Although not explicitly designed to simulate attention, the robust Kalman filter networks nevertheless display some of the essential characteristics of visual attention, such as the preferential processing of a subset of the input signals and the consequent "switching" of attention to previously ignored stimuli. Given multiple objects or conflicting stimuli in their receptive fields (Figures 2 and 3), the responses of the feedforward, feedback, and prediction neurons in the simulated network were modulated according to the current object being "attended to." The modulation in responses was mediated by the non-linear gating neurons G, taking into account both bottom-up signals as well top-down feedback signals. This suggests a network-level interpretation of similar forms of attentional response modulation in the primate visual cortex [2, 8, 14], with the consequent prediction that the genesis of attentional modulation in such cases may not necessarily lie within the recorded neurons themselves but within the distributed circuitry that these neurons are an integral part of.

References

[1] A.E. Bryson and Y.-C. Ho. *Applied Optimal Control*. New York: John Wiley, 1975.

[2] L. Chelazzi, E.K. Miller, J. Duncan, and R. Desimone. A neural basis for visual search in inferior temporal cortex. *Nature*, 363:345–347, 1993.

[3] P. Dayan.   An hierarchical model of visual rivalry.   In M. Mozer, M. Jordan, and T. Petsche, editors, *Advances in Neural Information Processing Systems 9*, pages 48–54. Cambridge, MA: MIT Press, 1997.

[4] A.P. Dempster, N.M. Laird, and D.B. Rubin. Maximum likelihood from incomplete data via the EM algorithm. *J. Royal Statistical Society Series B*, 39:1–38, 1977.

[5] R. Desimone and J. Duncan. Neural mechanisms of selective visual attention. *Annual Review of Neuroscience*, 18:193–222, 1995.

[6] P.J. Huber. *Robust Statistics*. New York: John Wiley, 1981.

[7] R.E. Kalman. A new approach to linear filtering and prediction theory. *Trans. ASME J. Basic Eng.*, 82:35–45, 1960.

[8] J. Moran and R. Desimone. Selective attention gates visual processing in the extrastriate cortex. *Science*, 229:782–784, 1985.

[9] W.T. Newsome. Spotlights, highlights and visual awareness. *Current Biology*, 6(4):357–360, 1996.

[10] E. Niebur and C. Koch. Control of selective visual attention: Modeling the "where" pathway. In D. Touretzky, M. Mozer, and M. Hasselmo, editors, *Advances in Neural Information Processing Systems 8*, pages 802–808. Cambridge, MA: MIT Press, 1996.

[11] B.A. Olshausen, D.C. Van Essen, and C.H. Anderson. A neurobiological model of visual attention and invariant pattern recognition based on dynamic routing of information. *Journal of Neuroscience*, 13:4700–4719, 1993.

[12] R.P.N. Rao and D.H. Ballard. The visual cortex as a hierarchical predictor. Technical Report 96.4, National Resource Laboratory for the Study of Brain and Behavior, Department of Computer Science, University of Rochester, September 1996.

[13] R.P.N. Rao and D.H. Ballard. Dynamic model of visual recognition predicts neural response properties in the visual cortex. *Neural Computation*, 9(4):721–763, 1997.

[14] S. Treue and J.H.R. Maunsell. Attentional modulation of visual motion processing in cortical areas MT and MST. *Nature*, 382:539–541, 1996.

[15] J.K. Tsotsos, S.M. Culhane, W.Y.K. Wai, Y. Lai, N. Davis, and F. Nuflo. Modeling visual attention via selective tuning. *Artificial Intelligence*, 78:507–545, 1995.

Recurrent Neural Networks Can Learn to Implement Symbol-Sensitive Counting

Paul Rodriguez
Department of Cognitive Science
University of California, San Diego
La Jolla, CA. 92093
prodrigu@cogsci.ucsd.edu

Janet Wiles
School of Information Technology and
Department of Psychology
University of Queensland
Brisbane, Queensland 4072 Australia
janetw@it.uq.edu.au

Abstract

Recently researchers have derived formal complexity analysis of analog computation in the setting of discrete-time dynamical systems. As an empirical constrast, training recurrent neural networks (RNNs) produces self-organized systems that are realizations of analog mechanisms. Previous work showed that a RNN can learn to process a simple context-free language (CFL) by counting. Herein, we extend that work to show that a RNN can learn a harder CFL, a simple palindrome, by organizing its resources into a symbol-sensitive counting solution, and we provide a dynamical systems analysis which demonstrates how the network can not only count, but also copy and store counting information.

1 INTRODUCTION

Several researchers have recently derived results in analog computation theory in the setting of discrete-time dynamical systems(Siegelmann, 1994; Maass & Opren, 1997; Moore, 1996; Casey, 1996). For example, a dynamical recognizer (DR) is a discrete-time continuous dynamical system with a given initial starting point and a finite set of Boolean output decision functions(Pollack, 1991; Moore, 1996; see also Siegelmann, 1993). The dynamical system is composed of a space,$\Re^n$, an alphabet A, a set of functions (1 per element of A) that each maps $\Re^n \rightarrow \Re^n$ and an accepting region H_{yes} in $\Re^n$. With enough precision and appropriate differential equations, DRs can use real-valued variables to encode contents of a stack or counter (for details see Siegelmann, 1994; Moore, 1996).

As an empirical contrast, training recurrent neural networks (RNNs) produces self-organized implementations of analog mechanisms. In previous work we showed that an RNN can learn to process a simple context-free language, $a^n b^n$, by organizing its resources into a counter which is similar to hand-coded dynamical recognizers but also exhibits some novelties (Wiles & Elman, 1995). In particular, similar to hand-coded counters, the network developed proportional contracting and expanding rates and precision matters - but unexpectedly the network distributed the contraction/expansion axis among hidden units, developed a saddle point to transition between the first half and second half of a string, and used oscillating dynamics as a way to visit regions of the phase space around the fixed points. In this work we show that an RNN can implement a solution for a harder CFL, a simple palindrome language(described below), which requires a symbol-sensitive counting solution. We provide a dynamical systems analysis which demonstrates how the network can not only count, but also copy and store counting information implicitly in space around a fixed point.

2   TRAINING an RNN TO PROCESS CFLs

We use a discrete-time RNN that has 1 hidden layer with recurrent connections, and 1 output layer without recurrent connections so that the accepting regions are determined by the output units. The RNN processes output in Time(n), where n is the length of the input, and it can recognize languages that are a proper subset of context-sensitive languages and a proper superset of regular languages(Moore, 1996). Consequently, the RNN we investigate can in principle embody the computational power needed to process self-recursion.

Furthermore, many connectionist models of language processing have used a prediction task(e.g. Elman, 1990). Hence, we trained an RNN to be a real-time transducer version of a dynamical recognizer that predicts the next input in a sequence. Although the network does not explicitly accept or reject strings, if our network makes all the right predictions possible then performing the prediction task subsumes the accept task, and in principle one could simply reject unmatched predictions. We used a threshhold criterion of .5 such that if an ouput node has a value greater than .5 then the network is considered to be making that prediction. If the network makes all the right predictions possible for some input string, then it is correctly processing that string. Although a finite dimensional RNN cannot process CFLs robustly with a margin for error (e.g.Casey, 1996;Maass and Orponen,1997), we will show that it can acquire the right kind of trajectory to process the language in a way that generalizes to longer strings.

2.1   A SIMPLE PALINDROME LANGUAGE

A *palindrome* language (mirror language) consists of a set of strings, S, such that each string, $s \in S$, $s = ww^r$, is a concatenation of a substring, w, and its reverse, w^r. The relevant aspect of this language is that a mechanism cannot use a simple counter to process the string but must use the functional equivalent of a stack that enables it to match the symbols in second half of the string with the first half.

We investigated a palindrome language that uses only two symbols for w, two other symbols for w^r, such that the second half of the string is fully predictable once the change in symbols occurs. The language we used is a simple version restricted such that one symbol is always present and precedes the other, for example: $w = a^n b^m, w^r = B^m A^n$, e.g. $aaaabbbBBBAAAA$, (where $n > 0$, $m >= 0$). Note that the embedded subsequence $b^m B^m$ is just the simple-CFL used in Wiles & Elman (1995) as mentioned above, hence, one can reasonably expect that a solution to this task has an embedded counter for the subsequence $b...B$.

2.2   LINEAR SYSTEM COUNTERS

A basic counter in analog computation theory uses real-valued precision (e.g. Siegelman 1994; Moore 1996). For example, a 1-dimensional up/down counter for two symbols $\{a, b\}$

is the system $f(x) = .5x + .5a$, $f(x) = 2x - .5b$ where x is the state variable, a is the input variable to count up(push), and b is the variable to count down(pop). A sequence of input $aaabbb$ has state values(starting at 0): .5,.75,.875, .75,.5,0.

Similarly, for our transducer version one can develop piecewise linear system equations in which counting takes place along different dimensions so that different predictions can be made at appropriate time steps[1]. The linear system serves as a hypothesis before running any simulations to understand the implementation issues for an RNN. For example, using the function $f(x) = x$ for $x \in [0, 1]$, 0 for $x < 0$, 1 for $x > 1$, then for the simple palindrome task one can explicitly encode a mechanism to copy and store the count for a across the $b...B$ subsequences. If we assign dimension-1 to a, dimension-2 to b, dimension-3 to A, dimension-4 to B, and dimension-5 to store the a value, we can build a system so that for a sequence $aaabbBBAAA$ we get state variables values: initial, $(0,0,0,0,0)$, $(.5,0,0,0,0)$, $(.75,0,0,0,0)$, $(.875,0,0,0,0)$, $(0,.5,0,0,.875)$, $(0,.75,0,0,.875)$, $(0,0,0,.5,.875)$, $(0,0,0,0,.875)$, $(0,0,.75,0,0)$, $(0,0,.5,0,0)$, $(0,0,0,0,0)$. The matrix equations for such a system could be:

$$X_t = f(\begin{bmatrix} .5 & 0 & 0 & 0 & 0 \\ 0 & .5 & 0 & 0 & 0 \\ 0 & 0 & 2 & 0 & 2 \\ 0 & 2 & 0 & 2 & 0 \\ 1 & 0 & 0 & 0 & 1 \end{bmatrix} * X_{t-1} + \begin{bmatrix} .5 & -5 & 0 & 0 \\ 0 & .5 & 0 & -5 \\ 0 & 0 & -1 & -5 \\ 0 & -5 & 0 & -1 \\ -5 & 0 & -5 & 0 \end{bmatrix} * I_t)$$

where t is time, X_t is the 5-dimensional state vector, I_t is the 4-dimensional input vector using 1-hot encoding of $a = [1, 0, 0, 0]$; $b = [0, 1, 0, 0]$; $A = [0, 0, 1, 0]$, $B = [0, 0, 0, 1]$. The simple trick is to use the input weights to turn on or off the counting. For example, the dimension-5 state variable is turned off when input is a or A, but then turned on when b is input, at which time it copies the last a value and holds on to it. It is then easy to add Boolean output decision functions that keep predictions linearly separable.

However, other solutions are possible. Rather than store the a count one could keep counting up in dimension-1 for b input and then cancel it by counting down for B input. The questions that arise are: Can an RNN implement a solution that generalizes? What kind of store and copy mechanism does an RNN discover?

2.3 TRAINING DATA & RESULTS

The training set consists of 68 possible strings of total length ≤ 25, which means a maximum of $n + m = 12$, or 12 symbols in the first half, 12 symbols in the second half, and 1 end symbol [2]. The complete training set has more short strings so that the network does not disregard the transitions at the end of the string or at the end of the $b...B$ subsequence. The network consists of 5 input, 5 hidden, 5 output units, with a bias node. The hidden and recurrent units are updated in the same time step as the input is presented. The recurrent layer activations are input on the next time step. The weight updates are performed using back-propagation thru time training with error injected at each time step backward for 24 time steps for each input.

We found that about half our simulations learn to make predictions for transitions, and most will have few generalizations on longer strings not seen in the training set. However, no network learned the complete training set perfectly. The best network was trained for 250K sweeps (1 per character) with a learning parameter of .001, and 136K more sweeps with .0001, for a total of about 51K strings. The network made 28 total prediction errors on 28

---

[1]These can be expanded relatively easily to include more symbols, different symbol representations, harder palindrome sequences, or different kind of decision planes.

[2]We removed training strings $w = a^n b$, for $n > 1$; it turns out that the network interpolates on the B-to-A transition for these. Also, we added an end symbol to help reset the system to a consistent starting value.

different strings in the test set of 68 possible strings seen in training. All of these errors were isolated to 3 situations: when the number of a input $= 2 or 4$ the error occurred at the B-to-A transition, when the number of a input $= 1$, for $m > 2$, the error occurred as an early A-to-end transition.

Importantly, the network made correct predictions on many strings longer than seen in training, e.g. strings that have total length > 25 (or $n + m > 12$). It counted longer strings of $a..A$s with or without embedded $b..B$s; such as: $w = a^{13}$; $w = a^{13}b^2$; $w = a^n b^7$, $n = 6, 7 or 8$ (recall that w is the first half of the string). It also generalized to count longer subsequences of $b..B$s with or without more $a..A$s; such as $w = a^5 b^n$, where $n = 8, 9, 10, 11, 12$. The longest string it processed correctly was $w = a^9 b^9$, which is 12 more characters than seen during training. The network learned to store the count for a^9 for up to $9bs$, even though the longest example it had seen in training had only $3bs$ - clearly it's doing something right.

2.4   NETWORK EVALUATION

Our evaluation will focus on how the best network counts, copies, and stores information. We use a mix of graphical analysis and linear system analysis, to piece together a global picture of how phase space trajectories hold informational states. The linear system analysis consists of investigating the local behaviour of the Jacobian at fixed points under each input condition separately. We refer to F_a as the autonomous system under a input condition and similarly for F_b, F_A, and F_B.

The most salient aspect to the solution is that the network divides up the processing along different dimensions in space. By inspection we note that hidden unit1 (HU1) takes on low values for the first half of the string and high values for the second half, which helps keep the processing linearly separable. Therefore in the graphical analysis of the RNN we can set HU1 to a constant.

First, we can evaluate how the network counts the $b..B$ subsequences. Again, by inspection the network uses dimensions HU3,HU4. The graphical analysis in Figure 1a and Figure 1b plots the activity of HU3xHU4. It shows how the network counts the right number of Bs and then makes a transition to predict the first A. The dominant eigenvalues at the F_b attracting point and F_B saddle point are inversely proportional, which indicates that the contraction rate to and expansion rate away from the fixed points are inversely matched. The F_B system expands out to a periodic-2 fixed point in HU3xHU4 subspace, and the unstable eigenvector corresponding to the one unstable eigenvalue has components only in HU3,HU4. In Figure 2 we plot the vector field that describes the flow in phase space for the composite F_B^2, which shows the direction where the system contracts along the stable manifold, and expands on the unstable manifold. One can see that the nature of the transition after the last b to the first B is to place the state vector close to saddle point for F_B so that the number of expansion steps matches the number of the F_b contraction steps. In this way the b count is copied over to a different region of phase space.

Now we evaluate how the network counts $a...A$, first without any $b...B$ embedding. Since the output unit for the end symbol has very high weight values for HU2, and the F_a system has little activity in HU4, we note that a is processed in HU2xHU3xHU5. The trajectories in Figure 3 show a plot of $a^{13}A^{13}$ that properly predicts all As as well as the transition at the end. Furthermore, the dominant eigenvalues for the F_a attracting point and the F_A saddle point are nearly inversely proportional and the F_A system expands to a periodic-2 fixed point in 4-dimensions (HU1 is constant, whereas the other HU values are periodic). The F_a eigenvectors have strong-moderate components in dimensions HU2, HU3, HU5; and likewise in HU2, HU3, HU4, HU5 for F_A.

The much harder question is: How does the network maintain the information about the count of as that were input while it is processing the $b..B$ subsequence? Inspection shows that after processing a^n the activation values are not directly copied over any HU values, nor do they latch any HU values that indicate how many as were processed. Instead, the last state value after the last a affects the dynamics for $b...B$ in such a way that clusters the last state value after the last B, but only in HU3xHU4 space (since the other HU dimensions were unchanging throughout $b...B$ processing).

We show in Figure 4 the clusters for state variables in HU3xHU4 space after processing $a^n b^m B^m$, where $n = 2, 3, 4, 5 or 6; m = 1..10$. The graph shows that the information about how many a's occurred is "stored" in the HU3xHU4 region where points are clustered. Figure 4 includes the dividing line from Figure 1b for the predict A region. The network does not predict the B-to-A transition after a^4 or a^2 because it ends up on the wrong side of the dividing line of Figure 1b, but the network in these cases still predicts the A-to-end transition. We see that if the network did not oscillate around the F_B saddle point while exanding then the trajectory would end up correctly on one side of the decision plane.

It is important to see that the clusters themselves in Figure 4 are on a contracting trajectory toward a fixed point, which stores information about increasing number of as when matched by an expansion of the F_A system. For example, the state values after $a^5 AA$ and $a^5 b^m B^m AA, m = 2..10$ have a total hamming distance for all 5 dimensions that ranged from .070 to .079. Also, the fixed point for the F_a system, the estimated fixed point for the composite $F_B^m \circ F_b^m \circ F_a^n$, and the saddle point of the F_A system are colinear [3]. in all the relevant counting dimensions: 2,3,4, and 5. In other words, the F_A system contracts the different coordinate points, one for a^n and one for $a^n b^m B^m$, towards the saddle point to nearly the same location in phase space, treating those points as having the same information. Unfortunately, this is a contraction occuring through a 4 dimensional subspace which we cannot easily show graphically.

3 CONCLUSION

In conclusion, we have shown that an RNN can develop a symbol-sensitive counting solution for a simple palindrome. In fact, this solution is not a stack but consists of non-independent counters that use dynamics to visit different regions at appropriate times. Furthermore, an RNN can implement counting solutions for a prediction task that are functionally similar to that prescribed by analog computation theory, but the store and copy functions rely on distance in phase space to implicitly affect other trajectories.

Acknowledgements

This research was funded by the UCSD, Center for Research in Language Training Grant to Paul Rodriguez, and a grant from the Australian Research Council to Janet Wiles.

References

Casey, M. (1996) The Dynamics of Discrete-Time Computation, With Application to Recurrent Neural Networks and Finite State Machine Extraction. Neural Computation, 8.

Elman, J.L. (1990) Finding Structure in Time. Cognitive Science, 14, 179-211.

Maass, W. , Orponen, P. (1997) On the Effect of Analog Noise in Discrete-Time Analog Computations. Proceedings Neural Information Processing Systems, 1996.

Moore, C. (1996) Dynamical Recognizers: Real-Time Language Recognition by Analog Computation. Santa Fe InstituteWorking Paper 96-05-023.

---

[3]Relative to the saddle point, the vector for one fixed point, multiplied by a constant had the same value(to within .05) in each of 4 dimensions as the vector for the other fixed point

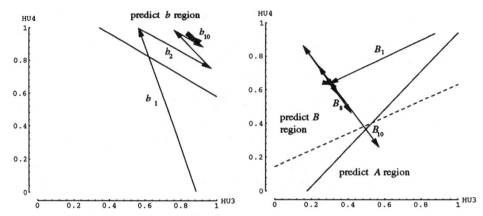

Figure 1: 1a)Trajectory of b^{10} (after a^5) in HU3xHU4. Each arrow represents a trajectory step:the base is a state vector at time t, the head is a state at time $t+1$. The first b trajectory step has a base near (.9,.05), which is the previous state from the last a. The output node b is $> .5$ above the dividing line. 1b) Trajectory of B^{10} (after $a^5 b^{10}$) in HU3xHU4. The output node B is $> .5$ above the dashed dividing line, and the output node A is $> .5$ below the solid dividing line. The system crosses the line on the last B step, hence it predicts the B-to-A transition.

Pollack, J.B. (1991) The Induction of Dynamical Recognizers. Machine Learning, 7, 227-252.

Siegelmann, H.(1993) Foundations of Recurrent Neural Networks. Ph.D. dissertation, unpublished. New Brunswick Rutgers, The State University of New Jersey.

Wiles, J., Elman, J. (1995) Counting Without a Counter: A Case Study in Activation Dynamics. Proceedings of the Seventeenth Annual Conference of the Cognitive Science Society. Hillsdale, N.J.: Lawrence Erlbaum Associates.

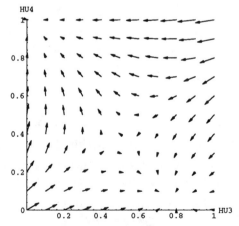

Figure 2: Vector field that describes the flow of F_B^2 projected onto HU3xHU4. The graph shows a saddle point near (.5,.5)and a periodic-2 attracting point.

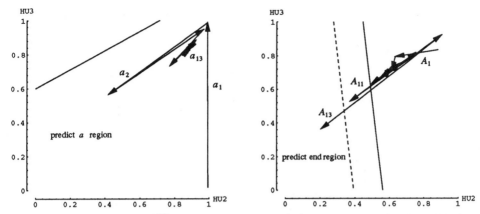

Figure 3: 3a) Trajectory of a^{13} projected onto HU2xHU3. The output node a is > .5 below and right of dividing line. The projection for HU2xHU5 is very similar. 3b) Trajectory of A^{13}(after a^{13}) projected onto HU2xHU3. The output node for the end symbol is > .5 on the 13th trajectory step left of the solid dividing line, and it is > .5 on the 11th step left of the dashed dividing line (the hyperplane projection must use values at the appropriate time steps), hence the system predicts the A-to-end transition. The graph for HU2xHU5 and HU2xHU4 is very similar.

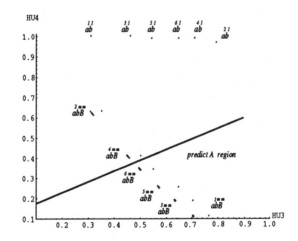

Figure 4: Clusters of last state values $a^n b^m B^m$, $m > 1$, projected onto HU3xHU4. Notice that for increasing n the system oscillates toward an attracting point of the system $F_B^m \circ F_b^m \circ F_a^n$.

Comparison of Human and Machine Word Recognition

M. Schenkel
Dept of Electrical Eng.
University of Sydney
Sydney, NSW 2006, Australia
schenkel@sedal.usyd.edu.au

C. Latimer
Dept of Psychology
University of Sydney
Sydney, NSW 2006, Australia

M. Jabri
Dept of Electrical Eng.
University of Sydney
Sydney, NSW 2006, Australia
marwan@sedal.usyd.edu.au

Abstract

We present a study which is concerned with word recognition rates for heavily degraded documents. We compare human with machine reading capabilities in a series of experiments, which explores the interaction of word/non-word recognition, word frequency and legality of non-words with degradation level. We also study the influence of character segmentation, and compare human performance with that of our artificial neural network model for reading. We found that the proposed computer model uses word context as efficiently as humans, but performs slightly worse on the pure character recognition task.

1 Introduction

Optical Character Recognition (OCR) of machine-print document images has matured considerably during the last decade. Recognition rates as high as 99.5% have been reported on good quality documents. However, for lower image resolutions (200 DpI and below), noisy images, images with blur or skew, the recognition rate declines considerably. In bad quality documents, character segmentation is as big a problem as the actual character recognition. In many cases, characters tend either to merge with neighbouring characters (dark documents) or to break into several pieces (light documents) or both. We have developed a reading system based on a combination of neural networks and **hidden Markov models** (HMM), specifically for low resolution and degraded documents.

To assess the limits of the system and to see where possible improvements are still to be expected, an obvious comparison is between its performance and that of the best reading system known, the human reader. It has been argued, that humans use an extremely wide range of context information, such as current topics, syntax and semantic analysis in addition to simple lexical knowledge during reading. Such higher level context is very hard to model and we decided to run a first comparison on a word recognition task, excluding any context beyond word knowledge.

The main questions asked for this study are: how does human performance compare with our system when it comes to pure character recognition (no context at all) of bad quality' documents? How do they compare when word context can be used? Does character segmentation information help in reading?

2   Data Preparation

We created as stimuli 36 data sets, each containing 144 character strings, 72 words and 72 non-words, all lower case. The data sets were generated from 6 original sets, each containing 144 unique words/non-words. For each original set we used three ways to divide the words into the different degradation levels such that each word appears once in each degradation level. We also had two ways to pick segmented/non-segmented so that each word is presented once segmented and once non-segmented. This counterbalancing creates the 36 sets out of the six original ones. The order of presentation within a test set was randomized with respect to degradation, segmentation and lexical status.

All character strings were printed in 'times roman 10 pt' font. Degradation was achieved by photocopying and faxing the printed document before scanning it at 200DpI. Care was taken to randomize the print position of the words such that as few systematic degradation differences as possible were introduced.

Words were picked from a dictionary of the 44,000 most frequent words in the 'Sydney Morning Herald'. The length of the words was restricted to be between 5 and 9 characters. They were divided in a 3x3x2 mixed factorial model containing 3 word-frequency groups, 3 stimulus degradation levels and visually segmented/non-segmented words. The three word-frequency groups were: 1 to 10 occurences/million (o/m) as low frequency, 11 to 40 o/m as medium frequency and 41 or more o/m as high frequency. Each participant was presented with four examples per stimulus class (e.g. four high frequency words in medium degradation level, not segmented).

The non-words conformed to a 2x3x2 model containing legal/illegal non-words, 3 stimulus degradation levels and visually segmented/non-segmented strings. The illegal non-words (e.g. 'ptvca') were generated by randomly selecting a word length between 5 and 9 characters (using the same word length frequencies as the dictionary has) and then randomly picking characters (using the same character frequencies as the dictionary has) and keeping the unpronounceable sequences. The legal non-words (e.g. 'slunk') were generated by using trigrams (using the dictionary to compute the trigram probabilities) and keeping pronounceable sequences. Six examples per non-word stimulus class were used in each test set. (e.g. six illegal non-words in high degradaton level, segmented).

3   Human Reading

There were 36 participants in the study. Participants were students and staff of the University of Sydney, recruited by advertisement and paid for their service. They were all native English speakers, aged between 19 and 52 with no reported uncorrected visual deficits.

The participants viewed the images, one at a time, on a computer monitor and were asked to type in the character string they thought would best fit the image. They had been instructed that half of the character strings were English words and half non-words, and they were informed about the degradation levels and the segmentation hints. Participants were asked to be as fast and as accurate as possible. After an initial training session of 30 randomly picked character strings not from an independent training set, the participants had a short break and were then presented with the test set, one string at a time. After a Carriage Return was typed, time was recorded and the next word was displayed. Training and testing took about one hour. The words were about 1-1.5cm large on the screen and viewed at a distance of 60cm, which corresponds to a viewing angle of 1°.

4 Machine Reading

For the machine reading tests, we used our integrated segmentation/recognition system, using a sliding window technique with a combination of a neural network and an HMM [6]. In the following we describe the basic workings without going into too much detail on the specific algorithms. For more detailed description see [6].

A sliding window approach to word recognition performs no segmentation on the input data of the recognizer. It consists basically of sweeping a window over the input word in small steps. At each step the window is taken to be a tentative character and corresponding character class scores are produced. Segmentation and recognition decisions are then made on the basis of the sequence of character scores produced, possibly taking contextual information into account.

In the **preprocessing** stage we normalize the word to a fixed height. The result is a grey-normalized pixel map of the word. This pixel map is the input to a **neural network** which estimates a *posteriori* probabilities of occurrence for each character given the input in the sliding window whose length corresponds approximately to two characters. We use a space displacement neural network (SDNN) which is a multi-layer feed-forward network with local connections and shared weights, the layers of which perform successively higher-level feature extraction. SDNN's are derived from Time Delay Neural Networks which have been successfully used in speech recognition [2] and handwriting recognition [4, 1]. Thanks to its convolutional structure the computational complexity of the sliding window approach is kept tractable. Only about one eighth of the network connections are reevaluated for each new input window. The outputs of the SDNN are processed by an HMM. In our case the HMM implements character duration models. It tries to align the best scores of the SDNN with the corresponding expected character durations. The Viterbi algorithm is used for this alignment, determining simultaneously the segmentation and the recognition of the word. Finding this state sequence is equivalent to finding the most probable path through the graph which represents the HMM. Normally additive costs are used instead of multiplicative probabilities. The HMM then selects the word causing the smallest costs.

Our best architecture contains 4 convolutional layers with a total of 50,000 parameters [6]. The training set consisted of a subset of 180,000 characters from the SEDAL database, a low resuloution degraded document database which was collected earlier and is independent of any data used in this experiment.

4.1 The Dictionary Model

A natural way of including a **dictionary** in this process, is to restrict the solution space of the HMM to words given by the dictionary. Unfortunately this means calculating the cost for each word in the dictionary, which becomes prohibitively slow with increasing dictionary size (we use a combination of available dictionaries with a total size of 98,000 words). We thus chose a two step process for the dictionary search: in a first step a list of the most probable words is generated, using a fast-matcher technique. In the second step the HMM costs are calculated for the words in the proposed list.

To generate the word list, we take the character string as found by the HMM *without* the dictionary and calculate the edit-distance between that string and all the words in the dictionary. The edit-distance measues how many edit operations (insertion, deletion and substitution) are necessary to convert a given input string into a target word [3, 5]. We now select all dictionary words that have the smallest edit-distance to the string recognized without using the dictionary. The composed word list contains on average 10 words, and its length varies considerably depending on the quality of the initial string.

For all words in the word list the HMM cost is now calculated and the word with the smallest cost is the proposed dictionary word. As the calculation of the edit-distance is much faster than the calculation of the HMM costs, the recognition speed is increased substantially.

In a last step the difference in cost between the proposed dictionary word and the initial string is calculated. If this difference is smaller than a threshold, the system will return the dictionary word, otherwise the original string is returned. This allows for the recognition of non-dictionary words. The value for the threshold determines the amount of reliance on the dictionary. A high value will correct most words but will also force non-words to be recognized as words. A low value, on the other hand, leaves the non-words unchanged but doesn't help for words either. Thus the value of the threshold influences the difference between word and non-word recognition. We chose the value such that the over-all error rate is optimized.

4.2 The Case of Segmented data

When character segmentation is given, we know how many characters we have and where to look for them. There is no need for an HMM and we just sum up the character probabilities over the x-coordinate in the region corresponding to a segment. This leaves a vector of 26 scores (the whole alphabet) for each character in the input string. With no dictionary constraints, we simply pick the label corresponding to the highest probability for each character. The dictionary is used in the same way, replacing the HMM scores by calculating the word scores directly from the corresponding character probabilities.

5 Results

Recognition Performance

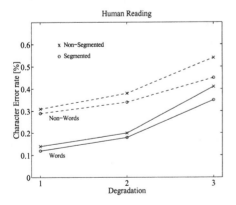

Figure 1: **Human Reading Performance.**

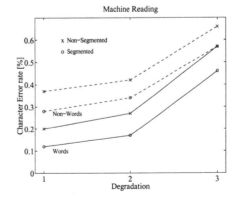

Figure 2: **Machine Reading Performance.**

Figure 1 depicts the recognition results for human readers. All results are per character error rates counted by the edit-distance. All results reported as significant pass an F-test with $p < .01$. As expected there was a significant interaction between error rate and degradation and clearly non-words have higher error rates than words. Also character segmentation has also an influence on the error rate. Segmentation seems to help slightly more for higher degradations.

Figure 2 shows performance of the machine algorithm. Again greater degradation leads to higher error rates and non-words have higher error rates than words. Segmentation hints lead to significantly better recognition for all degradation levels; in fact there is no interaction between degradation and segmentation for the machine algorithm. In general the machine benefited more from segmentation than humans.

One would expect a smaller gain from lexical knowledge for higher error rates (i.e. higher degradation) as in the limit of complete degradation *all* error rates will be 100%. Both humans and machine show this 'closing of the gap'.

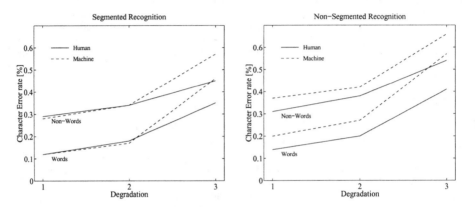

Figure 3: **Segmented Data.**   Figure 4: **Non-Segmented Data.**

More interesting is the direct comparison between the error rates for humans and machine as shown in figure 3 and figure 4. The difference for non-words reflects the difference in ability to recognize the geometrical shape of characters without context. For degradation levels 1 and 2, the machine has the same reading abilities as humans for segmented data and looses only about 7% in the non-segmented case. For degradation level 3, the machine clearly performs worse than human readers.

The difference between word and non-word error rates reflects the ability of the participant to use lexical knowledge. Note that the task contains word/non-word discrimination as well as recognition. It is striking how similar the behaviour for humans and machine is for degradation levels 1 and 2.

Timing Results

Figure 5 shows the word entry times for humans. As the main goal was to compare recognition rates, we did not emphasize entry speed when instructing the participants. However, we recorded the word entry time for each word (which includes inspection time and typing). When analysing the timimg data the only interest was in relative difference between word groups. Times were therefore converted for each participant into a z-score (zero mean with a standard deviation of one) and statistics were made over the z-scores of all participants.

Non-words generally took longer to recognize than words and segmented data took longer

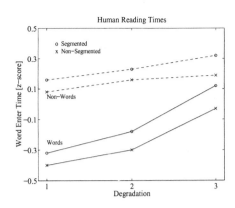

Figure 5: **Human Reading Times**.

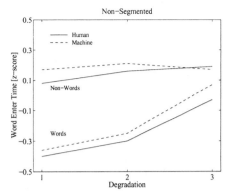

Figure 6: **Non-Segmented Reading Times**.

to recognize than non-segmented for humans which we believe stems from participants not being used to reading segmented data. When asked, participants reported difficulties in using the segmentation lines. Interestingly this segmentation effect is significant only for words but not for non-words.

As predicted there is also an interaction between time and degradation. Greater degradations take longer to recognize. Again, the degradation effect for time is only significant for words but barely for non-words.

Our machine reading algorithm behaves differently in segmented and non-segmented mode with respect to time consumption. In segmented mode, the time for evaluating the word list in our system is very short compared to the base recognition time, as there is no HMM involved. Accordingly we found no or very little effects on timing for our system for segmented data. All the timing information for the machine refer to the non-segmented case (see Figure 6).

Frequency and Legality

Table 5 shows word frequencies, legality of non-words and entry-time. Our experiment confirmed the well known frequency and legality effect for humans in recognition rate as well as time and respectively for frequency. The only exception is that there is no difference in error rate for middle and low frequency words.

The machine shows (understandably) no frequency effect in *error rate* or time, as all lexical words had the same prior probability. Interestingly even when using the correct prior probabilities we could not produce a strong word frequency effect for the machine. Also no legality effect was observed for the *error rate*. One way to incorporate legality effects would be the use of Markov chains such as n-grams.

Note however, how the recognition time for non-words is higher than for words and the legality effect for the recognition time. Recognition times for our system in non-segmented mode depend mainly on the time it takes to evaluate the word list. Non-words generally produce longer word lists than words, because there are no good quality matches for a non-word in the dictionary (on average a word list length of 8.6 words was found for words and of 14.5 for non-words). Also illegal non-words produce longer word lists than legal ones, again because the match quality for illegal non-words is worse than for legal ones (average length for illegal non-words 15.9 and for legal non-words 13.2). The z-scores for the word list length parallel nicely the recognition time scores.

In segmented mode, the time for evaluating the word list is very short compared to the base recognition time, as there is no HMM involved. Accordingly we found no or very little effects on timing for our system in the segmented case.

Error [%]	Humans		Machine	
	Error	z-Time	Error	z-Time
Words 41+	0.22	-0.37	0.36	-0.14
Words 11-40	0.27	-0.13	0.34	-0.19
Words 1-10	0.26	-0.06	0.33	-0.22
Legal Non-W.	0.36	0.07	0.47	0.09
Illegal Non-W.	0.46	0.31	0.49	0.28

Table 1: **Human and Machine Error rates for the different word and non-word classes.** The z-times for the machine are for the non-segmented data only.

6 Discussion

The ability to recognize the geometrical shape of characters without the possibility to use any sort of context information is reflected in the error rate of illegal non-words. The difference between the error rate for illegal non-words and the one for words reflects the ability to use lexical knowledge. To our surprise the behavior of humans and machine is very similar for both tasks, indicating a near to optimal machine recognition system. Clearly this does not mean our system is a good model for human reading. Many effects such as semantic and repetition priming are not reproduced and call for a system which is able to build semantic classes and memorize the stimuli presented. Nevertheless, we believe that our experiment validates empirically the verification model we implemented, using real world data.

Acknowledgments

This research is supported by a grant from the Australian Research Council (grant No A49530190).

References

[1] I. Guyon, P. Albrecht, Y. Le Cun, J. Denker, and W. Hubbard. Design of a neural network character recognizer for a touch terminal. *Pattern Recognition*, 24(2):105–119, 1991.

[2] K. J. Lang and G. E. Hinton. A Time Delay Neural Network architecture for speech recognition. Technical Report CMU-cs-88-152, Carnegie-Mellon University, Pittsburgh PA, 1988.

[3] V. I. Levenshtein. Binary codes capable of correcting deletions, insertions and reversals. *Soviet Physics-Doklady*, 10(8):707–710, 1966.

[4] O. Matan, C. J. C. Burges, Y. Le Cun, and J. Denker. Multi-digit recognition using a Space Dispacement Neural Network. In J. E. Moody, editor, *Advances in Neural Information Processing Systems 4*, pages 488–495, Denver, 1992. Morgan Kaufmann.

[5] T. Okuda, E. Tanaka, and K. Tamotsu. A method for the correction of garbled words based on the Levenshtein metric. *IEEE Transactions on Computers*, c-25(2):172–177, 1976.

[6] M. Schenkel and M. Jabri. Degraded printed document recognition using convolutional neural networks and hidden markov models. In *Proceedings of the ACNN*, Melbourne, 1997.

PART II
NEUROSCIENCE

Coding of Naturalistic Stimuli by Auditory Midbrain Neurons

H. Attias* and C.E. Schreiner[†]
Sloan Center for Theoretical Neurobiology and
W.M. Keck Foundation Center for Integrative Neuroscience
University of California at San Francisco
San Francisco, CA 94143-0444

Abstract

It is known that humans can make finer discriminations between familiar sounds (e.g. syllables) than between unfamiliar ones (e.g. different noise segments). Here we show that a corresponding enhancement is present in early auditory processing stages. Based on previous work which demonstrated that natural sounds had robust statistical properties that could be quantified, we hypothesize that the auditory system exploits those properties to construct efficient neural codes. To test this hypothesis, we measure the information rate carried by auditory spike trains on narrow-band stimuli whose amplitude modulation has naturalistic characteristics, and compare it to the information rate on stimuli with non-naturalistic modulation. We find that naturalistic inputs significantly enhance the rate of transmitted information, indicating that auditiory neural responses are matched to characteristics of natural auditory scenes.

1 Natural Scene Statistics and the Neural Code

A primary goal of hearing research is to understand how complex sounds that occur in natural scenes are processed by the auditory system. However, natural sounds are difficult to describe quantitatively and the complexity of auditory responses they evoke makes it hard to gain insight into their processing. Hence, most studies of auditory physiology are restricted to pure tones and noise stimuli, resulting in a limited understanding of auditory encoding. In this paper we pursue a novel approach to the study of natural sound encoding in auditory spike trains. Our

---

* Corresponding author. E-mail: hagai@phy.ucsf.edu.
[†] E-mail: chris@phy.ucsf.edu.

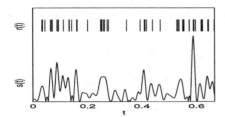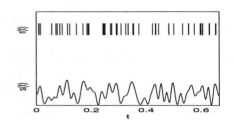

Figure 1: Left: amplitude modulation stimulus drawn from a naturalistic stimulus set, and the evoked spike train of an inferior colliculus neuron. Right: amplitude modulation from a non-naturalistic set and the evoked spike train of the same neuron.

method consists of measuring statistical characteristics of natural auditory scenes, and incorporating them into simple stimuli in a systematic manner, thus creating 'naturalistic' stimuli which enable us to study the encoding of natural sounds in a controlled fashion. The first stage of this program has been described in (Attias and Schreiner 1997); the second is reported below.

Fig. 1 shows two segments of long stimuli and the corresponding spike trains of the same neuron, elicited by pure tones that were amplitude-modulated by these stimuli. While both stimuli appear to be random and to have the same mean and both spike trains have the same firing rate, one may observe that high and low amplitudes are more likely to occur in the stimulus on the left; indeed, these stimuli are drawn from two stimulus sets with different statistical properties. Our present study of auditory coding focuses on assessing the efficiency of this neural code: for a given stimulus set, how well can the animal reconstruct the input sound and discriminate between similar sound segments, based on the evoked spike train, and how those abilities are affected by changing the stimulus statistics. We quantify the discrimination capability of auditory neurons in the inferior colliculus of the cat using concepts from information theory (Bialek et al. 1991; Rieke et al. 1997).

This leads to the issue of optimal coding (Atick 1992). Theoretically, given an auditory scene with particular statistical properties, it is possible to design an encoding scheme that would exploit those properties, resulting in a neural code that is optimal for that scene but is consequently less efficient for other scenes. Here we investigate the hypothesis that the auditory system uses a code that is adapted to natural auditory scenes. This question is addressed by comparing the discrimination capability of auditory neurons between sound segments drawn from a naturalistic stimulus set, to the one for a non-naturalistic set.

2   Statistics of Natural Sounds

As a first step in investigating the relation between neural responses and auditory inputs, we studied and quantified temporal statistics of natural auditory scenes (Attias and Schreiner 1997). It is well-known that different locations on the basal membrane respond selectively to different frequency components of the incoming sound $x(t)$ (e.g., Pickles 1988), hence the frequency ν corresponds to a spatial coordinate, in analogy with retinal location in vision. We therefore analyzed a large database of sounds, including speech, music, animal vocalizations, and background sounds, using various filter banks comprising $0 - 10$kHz. In each frequency band ν, the amplitude $a(t) \geq 0$ and phase $\phi(t)$ of the band-limited signal $x_\nu(t) = a(t)\cos(\nu t + \phi(t))$ were extracted, and the amplitude probability distribution $p(a)$ and auto-correlation

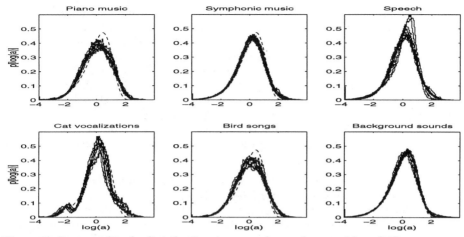

Figure 2: Log-amplitude distribution in several sound ensembles. Different curves for a given ensemble correspond to different frequency bands. The low amplitude peak in the cat plot reflect abundance of silent segments. The theoretical curve $p(\bar{a})$ (1) is plotted for comparison (dashed line).

function $c(\tau) = \langle a(t)a(t+\tau) \rangle$ were computed, as well as those of the instantaneous frequency $d\phi(t)/dt$.

Those statistics were found to be nearly identical in all bands and across all examined sounds. In particular, the distribution of the log-amplitude $\bar{a} = \log a$, normalized to have zero mean and unit variance, could be well-fitted to the form

$$p(\bar{a}) = \beta \exp\left(\beta\bar{a} + \alpha - e^{\beta\bar{a}+\alpha}\right) \qquad (1)$$

(with normalization constants $\alpha = -.578$ and $\beta = 1.29$), which should, however, be corrected at large amplitude ($> 5\sigma$). Several examples are displayed in Fig. 1. The log-amplitude distribution (1) corresponds mathematically to the *amplitude* distribution of musical instruments and vocalizations, found to be $p(a) = e^{-a}$ (known as the Laplace distribution in speech signal processing), as well as that of background sounds, where $p(a) \propto ae^{-a^2}$ (which can be shown to be the band amplitude distribution for a Gaussian signal). The power spectra of $a(t)$ (Fourier transform of $c(\tau)$) were found to have a modified $1/f$ form.

Together with the results for $\phi(t)$, those findings show that natural sounds are distinguished from arbitrary ones by robust characteristics. In the present paper we explore to what extent the auditory system exploits them in constructing efficient neural codes. Another important point made by (Attias and Schreiner 1997), as well as by (Ruderman and Bialek 1994) regarding visual signals, is that natural inputs are very often not Gaussian (e.g. (1)), unlike the signals used by conventional system-identification methods often applied to the nervous system. In this paper we use non-Gaussian stimuli to study auditory coding.

3 Measuring the Rate of Information Transfer

3.1 Experiment

Based on our results for temporal statistics of natural auditory scenes, we can construct 'naturalistic' stimuli by starting with a simple signal and systematically incorporate successively more complicated characteristics of natural sounds into it.

We chose to use narrow-band stimuli consisting of amplitude-modulated carriers $a(t)\cos(\nu t)$ at sound frequencies $\nu = 2 - 9\text{kHz}$ with no phase modulation. Focusing on one-point amplitude statistics, we constructed a white naturalistic amplitude by choosing $a(t)$ from an exponential distribution with a cutoff, $p(0 \le a \le a_c) \propto e^{-a}$, $p(a > a_c) = 0$ at each time point t independently, using a cutoff modulation frequency of $f_c = 100\text{Hz}$ (i.e., $\mid \tilde{a}(f \le f_c) \mid = const.$, $\mid \tilde{a}(f > f_c) \mid = 0$, where $\tilde{a}(f)$ is the Fourier transform of $a(t)$). We also used a non-naturalistic stimulus set where $a(t)$ was chosen from a uniform distribution $p(0 \le a \le b_c) = 1/b_c$, $p(a > b_c) = 0$, with b_c adjusted so that both stimulus sets had the same mean. A short segment from each set is shown in Fig. 1, and the two distributions are plotted in Figs. 3,4 (right).

Stimuli of $15 - 20\text{min}$ duration were played to ketamine-anesthetized cats. To minimize adaptation effects we alternated between the two sets using 10sec long segments. Single-unit recordings were made from the inferior colliculus (IC), a sub-thalamic auditory processing stage (e.g., Pickles 1988). Each IC unit responds best to a narrow range of sound frequencies, the center of which is called its 'best frequency' (BF). Neighboring units have similar BF's, in accord with the topographic frequency organization of the auditory system. For each unit, stimuli with carrier frequency ν at most 500Hz away from the unit's BF were used. Firing rates in response to those stimuli were between $60 - 100\text{Hz}$. The stimulus and the electrode signal were recorded simultaeneously at a sampling rate of 24kHz. After detecting and sotring the spikes and extracting the stimulus amplitude, both amplitude and spike train were down-sampled to 3kHz.

3.2 Analysis

In order to assess the ability to discriminate between different inputs based on the observed spike train, we computed the mutual information $I_{r,s}$ between the spike train response $r(t) = \sum_i \delta(t - t_i)$, where t_i are the spike times, and the stimulus amplitude $s(t)$. I consists of two terms, $I_{r,s} = H_s - H_{s\mid r}$, where H_s is the stimulus entropy (the log-number of different stimuli) and $H_{s\mid r}$ is the entropy of the stimulus conditioned on the response (the log-number of different stimuli that could elicit a given response, and thus could not be discriminated based on that response, averaged over all responses). Our approach generally follows the ideas of (Bialek et al. 1991; Rieke et al. 1997).

To simplify the calculation, we first modified the stimuli $s(t)$ to get $s'(t) = f(s(t))$, where the function $f(s)$ was chosen so that s' was Gaussian. Hence for exponential stimuli $f(s) = \sqrt{(2)}\text{erfi}(1 - 2e^{-s})$ and for uniform stimuli $f(s) = \sqrt{(2)}\text{erfi}(2s/b_c - 1)$, where erfi is the inverse error function. This Gaussianization has two advantages: first, the expression for the mutual information $I_{r,s'}$ $(= I_{r,s})$ is now simpler, being given by the frequency-dependent signal-to-noise ratio $\text{SNR}(f)$ (see below), since $H_{s'}$ depends only on the power spectrum of $s'(t)$; second and more importantly, the noise distribution was observed to become closer to Gaussian following this transformation.

To compute $H_{s'\mid r}$ we bound it from above by $\int_0^{f_c} df\, H[\tilde{s}'(f) \mid \tilde{r}(f)]$, the calculation of which requires the conditional distribution $p[\tilde{s}'(f) \mid \tilde{r}(f)]$ (note that these variables are complex, hence this is the joint ditribution of the real and imaginary parts). The latter is approximated by a Gaussian with mean $\tilde{s}'_r(f)$ and variance $N_r(f)$. This variance is, in fact, the power spectrum of the noise, $N_r(f) = \langle \mid \tilde{n}_r(f) \mid^2 \rangle$, which we define by $n_r(t) = s'(t) - s'_r(t)$. Computing the mutual information for those Gaussian distributions is straightforward and provides a lower bound on the

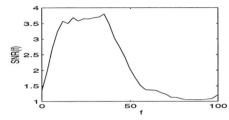 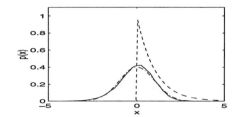

Figure 3: Left: signal-to-noise ratio SNR(f) vs. modulation frequency f for naturalistic stimuli. Right: normalized noise distribution (solid line), amplitude distribution of stimuli (dashed line) and of Gaussianized stimuli (dashed-dotted line).

true $I_{r,s}$,

$$I_{r,s} = I_{r,s'} \geq \int_0^{f_c} df \log_2 \mathrm{SNR}(f) \ . \tag{2}$$

The signal-to-noise ratio is given by $\mathrm{SNR}(f) = S'(f)/\langle N_r(f)\rangle_r$, where $S'(f) = \langle| \tilde{s}'(f) |^2\rangle$ is the spectrum of the Gaussianized stimulus and the averaging $\langle\cdot\rangle_r$ is performed over all responses.

The main object here is $\tilde{s}'_r(f)$, which is an estimate of the stimulus from the elicited spike train, and would optimally be given by the conditional mean $\int d\tilde{s}' \tilde{s}' p(\tilde{s}' \mid \tilde{r})$ at each f (Kay 1993). For Gaussian $p(\tilde{s}', \tilde{r})$ this estimator, which is generally non-linear, becomes linear in $\tilde{r}(f)$ and is given by $\tilde{h}(f)\tilde{r}(f)$, where $\tilde{h}(f) = \langle \tilde{s}'(f)\tilde{r}^\star(f)\rangle/\langle\tilde{r}(f)\tilde{r}^\star(f)\rangle$ is the Wiener filter. However, since our distributions were only approximately Gaussians we used the conditional mean, obtained by the kernel estimate

$$\tilde{s}'_r(f) = \sqrt{S'(f)}\sum_i \int df' \frac{\tilde{s}'_i(f')}{\sqrt{S'(f')}} k_i(f,f')/\sum_j \int df'' k_j(f,f'') \ ,$$

$$k_i(f,f') = k\left[\frac{\tilde{r}(f)}{\sqrt{R(f)}} - \frac{\tilde{r}_i(f')}{\sqrt{R(f')}}\right] \tag{3}$$

where k is a Gaussian kernel, $R(f)$ is the spectrum of the spike train, and i indexes the data points obtained by computing FFT using a sliding window. The scaling by $\sqrt{S'}, \sqrt{R}$ reflects the assumption that the distributions at all f differ only by their variance, which enables us to use the data points at all frequencies to estimate $\tilde{s}'_r$ at a given f. Our estimate produced a slightly higher SNR(f) than the Wiener estimate used by (Bialek et al. 1991;Rieke et al. 1997) and others.

4   Information on Naturalistic Stimuli

The SNR(f) for exponential stimuli is shown in Fig. 3 (left) for one of our units. IC neurons have a preferred modulation frequency f_m (e.g., Pickles 1988), which is about 40Hz for this unit; notice that generally SNR(f) ≥ 1, with equality when the stimulus and response are completely independent. Thus, stimulus components at frequencies higher than 60Hz effectively cannot be estimated from the spike train. The stimulus amplitude distribution is shown in Fig. 3 (right, dashed line), together with the noise distribution (normalized to have unit variance; solid line) which is nearly Gaussian.

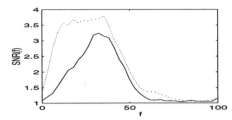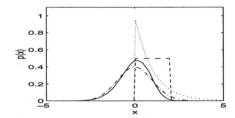

Figure 4: Left: signal-to-noise ratio SNR(f) vs. modulation frequency f for non-naturalistic stimuli (solid line) compared with naturalistic stimuli (dotted line). Right: normalized noise distribution (solid line), amplitude distribution of stimuli (dashed line) compared with that of naturalistic stimuli (dotted line), and of Gaussianized stimuli (dashed-dotted line).

Using (2) we obtain an information rate of $I_{r,s} \geq 114$bit/sec. For the spike rate of 82spike/sec measured in this unit, this translates into 1.4bit/spike. Averaging across units, we have 1.3 ± 0.2bit/spike for naturalistic stimuli.

Although this information rate was computed using the conditional mean estimator (3), it is interesting to examine the Wiener filter $h(t)$ which provides the optimal linear estimator of the stimulus, as discussed in the previous section. This filter is displayed in Fig. 5 (solid line) and has a temporal width of several tens of milliseconds.

5   Information on Non-Naturalistic Stimuli

The SNR(f) for uniform stimuli is shown in Fig. 4 (left, solid line) for the same unit as in Fig. 3, and is significantly lower than the corresponding SNR(f) for exponential stimuli plotted for comparison (dashed line). For the mutual information rate we obtain $I_{r,s} \geq 77$bit/sec, which amounts to 0.94bit/spike. Averaging across units, we have 0.8 ± 0.2bit/spike for non-naturalistic stimuli.

The stimulus amplitude distribution is shown in Fig. 4 (right, dashed line), together with the exponential distribution (dotted line) plotted for comparison, as well as the noise distribution (normalized to have unit variance). The noise in this case is less Gaussian than for exponential stimuli, suggesting that our calculated bound on $I_{r,s}$ may be lower for uniform stimuli.

Fig. 5 shows the stimulus reconstruction filter (dashed line). It has a similar time course as the filter for exponential stimuli, but the decay is significantly slower and its temporal width is more than 100msec.

6   Conclusion

We measured the rate at which auditory neurons carry information on simple stimuli with naturalistic amplitude modulation, and found that it was higher than for stimuli with non-naturalistic modulation. A result along the same lines for the frog was obtained by (Rieke et al. 1995) using Gaussian signals whose spectrum was shaped according to the frog call spectrum. Similarly, work in vision (Laughlin 1981; Field 1987; Atick and Redlich 1990; Ruderman and Bialek 1994; Dong and Atick 1995) suggests that visual receptive field properties are consistent with optimal coding predictions based on characteristics of natural images. Future work will explore coding of stimuli with more complex natural statistical characteristics and

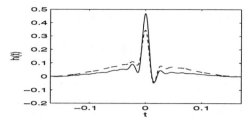

Figure 5: Impulse response of Wiener reconstruction filter for naturalistic stimuli (solid line) and non-naturalistic stimuli (dashed line).

will extend to higher processing stages.

Acknowledgements

We thank W. Bialek, K. Miller, S. Nagarajan, and F. Theunissen for useful discussions and B. Bonham, M. Escabi, M. Kvale, L. Miller, and H. Read for experimental support. Supported by The Office of Naval Research (N00014-94-1-0547), NIDCD (R01-02260), and the Sloan Foundation.

References

J.J. Atick and N. Redlich (1990). Towards a theory of early visual processing. Neural Comput. **2**, 308-320.

J.J. Atick (1992). Could information theory provide an ecological theory of sensory processing. Network **3**, 213-251.

H. Attias and C.E. Schreiner (1997). Temporal low-order statistics of natural sounds. In *Advances in Neural Information Processing Systems 9*, MIT Press.

W. Bialek, F. Rieke, R. de Ruyter van Steveninck, and D. Warland (1991). Reading the neural code. *Science* **252**, 1854-1857.

D.W. Dong and J.J. Atick (1995). Temporal decorrelation: a theory of lagged and non-lagged responses in the lateral geniculate nucleus. Network **6**, 159-178.

D.J. Field (1987). Relations between the statistics of natural images and the response properties of cortical cells. J. Opt. Soc. Am. **4**, 2379-2394.

S.M. Kay (1993). *Fundamentals of Statistical Signal Processing: Estimation Theory.* Prentice-Hall, New Jersey.

S.B. Laughlin (1981). A simple coding procedure enhances a neuron's information capacity. Z. Naturforsch. **36c**, 910-912.

J.O. Pickles (1988). *An introduction to the physiology of hearing* (2nd Ed.). San Diego, CA: Academic Press.

F. Rieke, D. Bodnar, and W. Bialek (1995). Naturalistic stimuli increase the rate and efficiency of information transmission by primary auditory neurons. *Proc. R. Soc. Lond. B*, **262**, 259-265.

F. Rieke, D. Warland, R. de Ruyter van Steveninck, and W. Bialek (1997). *Spikes: Exploring the Neural Code.* MIT Press, Cambridge, MA.

D.L. Ruderman and W. Bialek (1994). Statistics of natural images: scaling in the woods. Phys. Rev. Lett. **73**, 814-817.

Refractoriness and Neural Precision

Michael J. Berry II and Markus Meister
Molecular and Cellular Biology Department
Harvard University
Cambridge, MA 02138

Abstract

The relationship between a neuron's refractory period and the precision of its response to identical stimuli was investigated. We constructed a model of a spiking neuron that combines probabilistic firing with a refractory period. For realistic refractoriness, the model closely reproduced both the average firing rate and the response precision of a retinal ganglion cell. The model is based on a "free" firing rate, which exists in the absence of refractoriness. This function may be a better description of a spiking neuron's response than the peri-stimulus time histogram.

1 INTRODUCTION

The response of neurons to repeated stimuli is intrinsically noisy. In order to take this trial-to-trial variability into account, the response of a spiking neuron is often described by an instantaneous probability for generating an action potential. The response variability of such a model is determined by Poisson counting statistics; in particular, the variance in the spike count is equal to the mean spike count for any time bin (Rieke, 1997). However, recent experiments have found far greater precision in the vertebrate retina (Berry, 1997) and the H1 interneuron in the fly visual system (de Ruyter, 1997). In both cases, the neurons exhibited sharp transitions between silence and nearly maximal firing. When a neuron is firing near its maximum rate, refractoriness causes spikes to become more regularly spaced than for a Poisson process with the same firing rate. Thus, we asked the question: does the refractory period play an important role in a neuron's response precision under these stimulus conditions?

2 FIRING EVENTS IN RETINAL GANGLION CELLS

We addressed the role of refractoriness in the precision of light responses for retinal ganglion cells.

2.1 RECORDING AND STIMULATION

Experiments were performed on the larval tiger salamander. The retina was isolated from the eye and superfused with oxygenated Ringer's solution. Action potentials from retinal ganglion cells were recorded extracellularly with a multi-electrode array, and their spike times measured relative to the beginning of each stimulus repeat (Meister, 1994). Spatially uniform white light was projected from a computer monitor onto the photoreceptor layer. The intensity was flickered by choosing a new value at random from a Gaussian distribution (mean I, standard deviation δI) every 30 ms. The mean light level ($I = 4 \cdot 10^{-3}$ W/m^2) corresponded to photopic (daylight) vision. Contrast C is defined here as the temporal standard deviation of the light intensity divided by the mean, $C = \delta I / I$. Recordings extended over 60 repeats of a 60-sec segment of random flicker.

The qualitative features of ganglion cell responses to random flicker stimulation at 35 % contrast are seen in Fig. 1. First, spike trains had extensive periods in which no spikes were seen in 60 repeated trials. Many spike trains were sparse, in that the silent periods covered a large fraction of the total stimulus time. Second, during periods of firing, the peri-stimulus time histogram (PSTH) rose from zero to the maximum firing rate (~200 Hz) on a time scale comparable to the time interval between spikes (~10 ms). We have argued that these responses are better viewed as a set of discrete firing "events" than as a continuously varying firing rate (Berry, 1997). In general, the firing events were bursts containing more than one spike (Fig. 1B). Identifiable firing events were seen across cell types; similar results were also found in the rabbit retina (Berry, 1997).

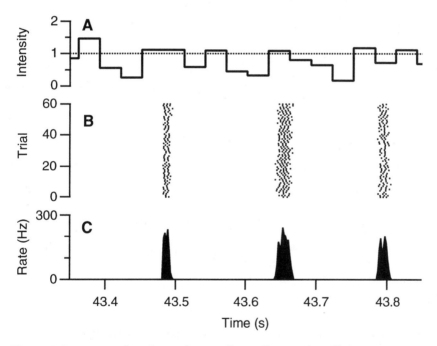

Figure 1: Response of a salamander ganglion cell to random flicker stimulation. (A) Stimulus intensity in units of the mean for a 0.5-s segment, (B) spike rasters from 60 trials, and (C) the firing rate $r(t)$.

2.2 FIRING EVENT PRECISION

Discrete episodes of ganglion cell firing were recognized from the PSTH as a contiguous period of firing bounded by periods of complete silence. To provide a consistent demarcation of firing events, we drew the boundaries of a firing event at minima v in the PSTH that were significantly lower than neighboring maxima p_1 and p_2, such that $\sqrt{p_1 p_2}/v \geq \phi$ with 95 % confidence (Berry, 1997). With these boundaries defined, every spike in each trial was assigned to exactly one firing event.

Measurements of both timing and number precision can be obtained if the spike train is parsed into such firing events. For each firing event i, we accumulated the distribution of spike times across trials and calculated several statistics: the average time T_i of the first spike in the event and its standard deviation δT_i across trials, which quantified the temporal jitter of the first spike; similarly, the average number N_i of spikes in the event and its variance δN_i^2 across trials, which quantified the precision of spike number. In trials that contained zero spikes for event i, no contribution was made to T_i or δT_i, while a value of zero was included in the calculation of N_i and δN_i^2.

For the ganglion cell shown in Fig. 1, the temporal jitter δT of the first spike in an event was very small (1 to 10 ms). Thus, repeated trials of the same stimulus typically elicit action potentials with a timing uncertainty of a few milliseconds. The temporal jitter of all firing events was distilled into a single number τ by taking the median over all events. The variance δN^2 in the spike count was remarkably low as well: it often approached the lower bound imposed by the fact that individual trials necessarily produce integer spike counts. Because $\delta N^2 \ll N$ for all events, ganglion cell spike trains cannot be completely characterized by their firing rate (Berry, 1997). The spike number precision of a cell was assessed by computing the average variance over events and dividing by the average spike count: $F = \langle \delta N^2 \rangle / \langle N \rangle$. This quantity, also known as the Fano factor, has a value of one for a Poisson process with no refractoriness.

3 PROBABILISTIC MODELS OF A SPIKE TRAIN

We start by reviewing one of the simplest probabilistic models of a spike train, the inhomogeneous Poisson model. Here, the measured spike times $\{t_i\}$ are used to estimate the instantaneous rate $r(t)$ of spike generation during a time Δt. This can be written formally as

$$r(t) = \frac{1}{M\,\Delta t} \Sigma_i\, \Theta(t_i - t)\, \Theta(t + \Delta t - t_i)$$

where M is the number of repeated stimulus trials and $\Theta(x)$ is the Heaviside function

$$\Theta(x) = \left. \begin{array}{cc} 1 & x \geq 0 \\ 0 & x < 0 \end{array} \right\} \quad .$$

We can randomly generate a sequence of spike trains from a set of random numbers between zero and one: $\{\alpha_i\}$ with $\alpha_i \in (0,1]$. If there is a spike at time t_i, then the next spike time t_{i+1} is found by numerically solving the equation

$$-\ln \alpha_{i+1} = \int_{t_i}^{t_{i+1}} r(t)\, dt \quad .$$

3.1 INCLUDING AN ABSOLUTE REFRACTORY PERIOD

In order to add refractoriness to the Poisson spike-generator, we expressed the firing rate as the product of a "free" firing rate $q(t)$, which obtains when the neuron is not refractory, and a recovery function $w(t)$, which describes how the neuron recovers from refractoriness (Johnson, 1983; Miller, 1985). When the recovery function is zero, spiking is not possible; and when it is one, spiking is not affected. The modified rule for selecting spikes then becomes

$$-\ln \alpha_{i+1} = \int_{t_i}^{t_{i+1}} q(t)\, w(t - t_i)\, dt \quad .$$

For an absolute refractory period of time μ, the weight function is zero for times between 0 and μ and one otherwise

$$w(t;\mu) = 1 - \Theta(t)\Theta(\mu - t) \quad .$$

Because the refractory period may exclude spiking in a given time bin, the probability of firing a spike when not prevented by the refractory period is higher than predicted by $r(t)$. This free firing rate $q(t;\mu)$ can be estimated by excluding trials where the neuron is unable to fire due to refractoriness

$$q(t;\mu) = \frac{r(t)}{1 - \frac{1}{M}\sum_i \left[1 - w(t - t_i;\mu)\right]} \quad .$$

The sum is restricted to spike times t_i nearest to the time bin on a given trial. This restriction follows from the assumption that the recovery function only depends on the time since the last action potential. Notice that this new probability obeys the inequality $q(t) \geq p(t)$ and also that it depends upon the refractory period μ.

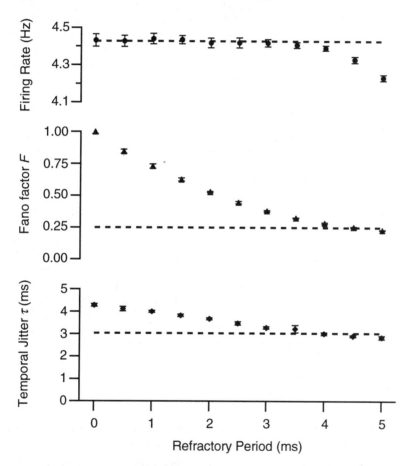

Figure 2: Results for model spike trains with an absolute refractory period. (A) Mean firing rate averaged over a 60-s segment (circles), (B) Fano factor F, a measure of spike number precision in an event (triangles), and (C) temporal jitter τ (diamonds) plotted versus the absolute refractory period μ. Shown in dotted in each panel is the value for the real data.

With this definition of the free firing rate, we can now generate spike trains with the same first order statistics (i.e., the average firing rate) for a range of values of the refractory period μ. For each value of μ, we can then compare the second order statistics (i.e., the precision) of the model spike trains to the real data. To this end, the free rate $q(t)$ was calculated for a 60-s segment of the response to random flicker of the salamander ganglion cell shown in Fig. 1. Then, $q(t)$ was used to generate 60 spike trains. Firing events were identified in the set of model spike trains, and their precision was calculated. Finally, this procedure was repeated 10 times for each value of the refractory period.

Figure 2A plots the firing rate (circles) generated by the model, averaged over the entire 60-s segment of random flicker with error bars equal to the standard deviation of the rate among the 10 repeated sets. The firing rate of the model matches the actual firing rate for the real ganglion cell (dashed) up to refractory periods of $\mu \approx 4$ ms, although the deviation for larger refractory periods is still quite small. For large enough values of the absolute refractory period, there will be inter-spike intervals in the real data that are shorter than μ. In this case, the free firing rate $q(t)$ cannot be enhanced enough to match the observed firing rate.

While the mean firing rate is approximately constant for refractory periods up to 5 ms, the precision changes dramatically. Figure 2B shows that the Fano factor F (triangles) has the expected value of 1 for no refractory period, but drops to ~ 0.2 for the largest refractory period. In Fig. 2C, the temporal jitter τ (diamonds) also decreases as refractoriness is added, although the effect is not as large as for the precision of spike number. The sharpening of temporal precision is due to the fact that the probability $q(t)$ rises more steeply than $r(t)$ (see Fig. 4), so that the first spike occurs over a narrower range of times. The number precision of the model matches the real data for $\mu = 4$ to 4.5 ms and the timing precision matches for $\mu \approx 4$ ms. Therefore, a probabilistic spike generator with an absolute refractory period can match both the average firing rate and the precision of a retinal ganglion cell's spike train with roughly the same value of one free parameter.

3.2 USING A RELATIVE REFRACTORY PERIOD

Salamander ganglion cells typically have a relative refractory period that lasts beyond their absolute refractory period. This can be seen in Fig. 3A from the distribution of inter-spike intervals $P(\Delta)$ for the ganglion cell shown above – the absolute refractory period lasts for only 2 ms, while relative refractoriness extends to ~ 5 ms. We can include the effects of relative refractoriness by using weight values in $w(t)$ that are between zero and one. Figure 3 illustrates a parameter-free method for determining this weight function. If there were no refractoriness and a neuron had a constant firing rate q, then the inter-spike interval distribution would drop exponentially. This behavior is seen from the curve fit in Fig. 3A for intervals in the range 5 to 10 ms. The recovery function $w(t)$ can then be found from the inter-spike interval distribution (Berry, 1998)

$$w(t) = \frac{1}{q} \frac{P(t)}{1 - \int_o^t P(\Delta)\, d\Delta} \quad .$$

Notice in Fig. 3B, that the recovery function $w(t)$ is zero out to 3 ms, rises almost linearly between 3 and 5 ms, and then reaches unity beyond 5 ms.

Using the weight function shown in Fig. 3B, the free firing rate $q(t)$ was calculated and 10 sets of 60 spike trains were generated. The results, summarized in Table 1, give very close agreement with the real data:

Table 1: Results for a Relative Refractory Period

QUANTITY	REAL DATA	MODEL	STD. DEV.
Firing Rate	4.43 Hz	4.44 Hz	0.017 Hz
Timing Precision τ	3.20 ms	2.95 ms	0.09 ms
Number Precision F	0.250	0.266	0.004

Thus, a Poisson spike generator with a relative refractory period reproduces the measured precision. A similar test, performed over a population of ganglion cells, also yielded close agreement (Berry, 1998).

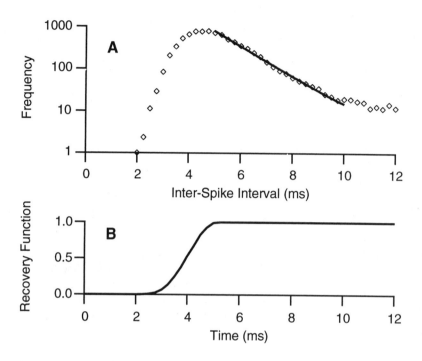

Figure 3: Determination of the relative refractory period. (A) The inter-spike interval distribution (diamonds) is fit by an exponential curve (solid), resulting in (B) the recovery function.

Not only is the average firing rate well-matched by the model, but the firing rate in each time bin is also very similar. Figure 4A compares the firing rate for the real neuron to that generated by the model. The mean-squared error between the two is 4 %, while the counting noise, estimated as the variance of the standard error divided by the variance of $r(t)$, is also 4 %. Thus, the agreement is limited by the finite number of repeated trials. Figure 4B compares the free firing rate $q(t)$ to the observed rate firing $r(t)$. $q(t)$ is equal to $r(t)$ at the beginning of a firing event, but becomes much larger after several spikes have occurred. In addition, $q(t)$ is generally smoother than $r(t)$, because there is a greater enhancement in $q(t)$ at times following a peak in $r(t)$.

In summary, the free firing rate $q(t)$ can be calculated from the raw spike train with no more computational difficulty than $r(t)$, and thus can be used for any spiking neuron. Furthermore, $q(t)$ has some advantages over $r(t)$: 1) in conjunction with a refractory spike-generator, it produces the correct response precision; 2) it does not saturate at high firing rates, so that it can continue to distinguish gradations in the neuron's response. Thus, $q(t)$ may prove useful for constructing models of the input-output relationship of a spiking neuron (Berry, 1998).

Acknowledgments

We would like to thank Mike DeWeese for many useful conversations. One of us, MJB, acknowledges the support of the National Eye Institute. The other, MM, acknowledges the support of the National Science Foundation.

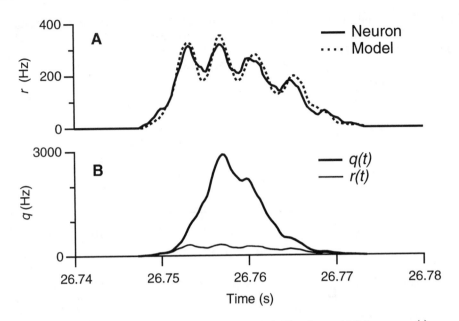

Figure 4: Illustration of the free firing rate. (A) The observed firing rate $r(t)$ for real data (solid) is compared to that from the model (dotted). (B) The free rate $q(t)$ (thick) is shown on the same scale as $r(t)$ (thin). All rates used a time bin of 0.25 ms and boxcar smoothing over 9 bins.

References

Berry, M. J., D. K. Warland, and M. Meister, *The Structure and Precision of Retinal Spike Trains.* PNAS, USA, 1997. **94**: pp. 5411-5416.

Berry II, M. J. and Markus Meister, *Refractoriness and Neural Precision.* J. Neurosci., 1998. in press.

De Ruyter van Steveninck, R. R., G. D. Lewen, S. P. Strong, R. Koberle, and W. Bialek, *Reliability and Variability in Neural Spike Trains.* Science, 1997. **275**: pp. 1805-1808.

Johnson, D. H. and A. Swami, *The Transmission of Signals by Auditory-Nerve Fiber Discharge Patterns.* J. Acoust. Soc. Am., 1983. **74**: pp. 493-501.

Meister, M., J. Pine, and D. A. Baylor, *Multi-Neuronal Signals from the Retina: Acquisition and Analysis.* J. Neurosci. Methods, 1994. **51**: pp. 95-106.

Miller, M. I. *Algorithms for Removing Recovery-Related Distortion gtom Auditory-Nerve Discharge Patterns.* J. Acoust. Soc. Am., 1985. **77**: pp. 1452-1464.

Rieke, F., D. K. Warland, R. R. de Ruyter van Steveninck, and W. Bialek, *Spikes: Exploring the Neural Code.* 1997, Cambridge, MA: MIT Press.

Statistical Models of Conditioning

Peter Dayan*
Brain & Cognitive Sciences
E25-210 MIT
Cambridge, MA 02139

Theresa Long
123 Hunting Cove
Williamsburg, VA 23185

Abstract

Conditioning experiments probe the ways that animals make predictions about rewards and punishments and use those predictions to control their behavior. One standard model of conditioning paradigms which involve many conditioned stimuli suggests that individual predictions should be added together. Various key results show that this model fails in some circumstances, and motivate an alternative model, in which there is attentional selection between different available stimuli. The new model is a form of mixture of experts, has a close relationship with some other existing psychological suggestions, and is statistically well-founded.

1 Introduction

Classical and instrumental conditioning experiments study the way that animals learn about the causal texture of the world (Dickinson, 1980) and use this information to their advantage. Although it reached a high level of behavioral sophistication, conditioning has long since gone out of fashion as a paradigm for studying learning in animals, partly because of the philosophical stance of many practitioners, that the neurobiological implementation of learning is essentially irrelevant. However, more recently it has become possible to study how conditioning phenomena are affected by particular lesions or pharmacological treatments to the brain (*eg* Gallagher & Holland, 1994), and how particular systems, during simple learning tasks, report information that is consistent with models of conditioning (Gluck & Thompson, 1987; Gabriel & Moore, 1989).

In particular, we have studied the involvement of the dopamine (DA) system in the ventral tegmental area of vertebrates in reward based learning (Montague *et al*, 1996; Schultz *et al*, 1997). The activity of these cells is consistent with a model in which they report a temporal difference (TD) based prediction error for reward

---

*This work was funded by the Surdna Foundation.

(Sutton & Barto, 1981; 1989). This prediction error signal can be used to learn correct predictions and also to learn appropriate actions (Barto, Sutton & Anderson, 1983). The DA system is important since it is crucially involved in normal reward learning, and also in the effects of drugs of addiction, self stimulation, and various neural diseases.

The TD model is consistent with a whole body of experiments, and has even correctly anticipated new experimental findings. However, like the Rescorla-Wagner (RW; 1972) or delta rule, it embodies a particular additive model for the net prediction made when there are multiple stimuli. Various sophisticated conditioning experiments have challenged this model and found it wanting. The results support competitive rather than additive models. Although *ad hoc* suggestions have been made to repair the model, none has a sound basis in appropriate prediction. There is a well established statistical theory for competitive models, and it is this that we adopt.

In this paper we review existing evidence and theories, show what constraints a new theory must satisfy, and suggest and demonstrate a credible candidate. Although it is based on behavioral data, it also has direct implications for our neural theory.

2   Data and Existing Models

Table 1 describes some of the key paradigms in conditioning (Dickinson, 1980; Mackintosh, 1983). Although the collection of experiments may seem rather arcane (the standard notation is even more so), in fact it shows exactly the basis behind the key capacity of animals in the world to predict events of consequence. We will extract further biological constraints implied by these and other experiments in the discussion.

In the table, l (light) and s (tone) are potential predictors (called *conditioned stimuli* or CSs), of a consequence, r, such as the delivery of a reward (called an *unconditioned stimulus* or US). Even though we use TD rules in practice, we discuss some of the abstract learning rules without much reference to the detailed time course of trials. The same considerations apply to TD.

In Pavlovian conditioning, the light acquires a positive association with the reward in a way that can be reasonably well modeled by:

$$\Delta w_l(t) = \alpha_l(t)(r(t) - w_l(t))l(t), \tag{1}$$

where $l(t) \in \{0, 1\}$ represents the presence of the light in trial t ($s(t)$ will similarly represent the presence of a tone), $w_l(t)$ (we will often drop the index t) represents the strength of the expectation about the delivery of reward $r(t)$ in trial t if the light is also delivered, and $\alpha_l(t)$ is the learning rate. This is just the delta rule. It also captures well the probabilistic contingent nature of conditioning – for binary $r(t) \in \{0, 1\}$, animals seem to assess $\epsilon_l = \mathcal{P}[r(t)|l(t) = 1] - \mathcal{P}[r(t)|l(t) = 0]$, and then only expect reward following the light (in the model, have $w_l > 0$) if $\epsilon_l > 0$.

Pavlovian conditioning is easy to explain under a whole wealth of rules. The trouble comes in extending equation 1 to the case of multiple predictors (in this paper we consider just two). The other paradigms in table 1 probe different aspects of this. The one that is most puzzling is (perversely) called *downwards unblocking* (Holland, 1988). In a first set of trials, an association is established between the light and two presentations of reward separated by a few (u) seconds. In a second set, a tone is included with the light, but the second reward is dropped. The animal amasses *less* reward in conjunction with the tone. However, when presented with the tone

	Name	Set 1	Set 2	Test
1	Pavlovian		$l \to r$	$l \looparrowright r$
2	Overshadowing		$l + s \to r$	$\left\{ \begin{array}{l} l \looparrowright r^{\frac{1}{2}} \\ s \looparrowright r^{\frac{1}{2}} \end{array} \right\}$
3	Inhibitory		$\left\{ \begin{array}{l} l \to r \\ l + s \to \cdot \end{array} \right\}$	$s \looparrowright \bar{r}$
4	Blocking	$l \to r$	$l + s \to r$	$s \looparrowright \cdot$
5	Upwards unblocking	$l \to r$	$l + s \to r\Delta_u r$	$s \looparrowright r$
.6	Downwards unblocking	$l \to r\Delta_u r$	$l + s \to r$	$s \looparrowright \pm r$

Table 1: Paradigms. Sets 1 and 2 are separate sets of learning trials, which are continued until convergence. Symbols l and s indicate presentation of lights and tones as potential predictors. The $\looparrowright$ in the test set indicates that the associations of the predictors are tested, producing the listed results. In overshadowing, association with the reward can be divided between the light and the sound, indicated by $r^{\frac{1}{2}}$. In some cases overshadowing favours one stimulus at the complete expense of the other; and at the end of very prolonged training, all effects of overshadowing can disappear. In blocking, the tone makes no prediction of r. In set 2 of inhibitory conditioning, the two types of trials are interleaved and the outcome is that the tone predicts the absence of reward. In upwards and downwards unblocking, the Δ_u indicates that the delivery of two rewards is separated by time u. For downwards unblocking, if u is small, then s is associated with the *absence* of r; if u is large, then s is associated with the *presence* of r.

---

alone, the animal expects the *presence* rather than the absence of reward. On the face of it, this seems an insurmountable challenge to prediction-based theories. First we describe the existing theories, then we formalise some potential replacements.

One theory (called a US-processing theory) is due to Rescorla & Wagner (RW; 1972), and, as pointed out by Sutton & Barto (1981), is just the delta rule. For RW, the animal constructs a net prediction:

$$V(t) = w_l(t)l(t) + w_s(t)s(t) \tag{2}$$

for $r(t)$, and then changes $\Delta w_l(t) = \alpha_l(t)(r(t) - V(t))l(t)$ (and similarly for $w_s(t)$) using the prediction error $r(t) - V(t)$. Its foundation in the delta rule makes it computationally appropriate (Marr, 1982) as a method of making predictions. TD uses the same additive model in equation 2, but uses $r(t) + V(t+1) - V(t)$ as the prediction error.

RW explains overshadowing, inhibitory conditioning, blocking, and upwards unblocking, but *not* downwards unblocking. In overshadowing, the terminal association between l and r is weaker if l and s are simultaneously trained – this is expected under RW since learning stops when $V(t) = r(t)$, and w_l and w_s will share the prediction. In inhibitory conditioning, the sound comes to predict the absence of r. The explanation of inhibitory conditioning is actually quite complicated (Konorski, 1967; Mackintosh, 1983); however RW provides the simple account that $w_l = r$ for the $l \to r$ trials, forcing $w_s = -r$ for the $l+s \to \cdot$ trials. In blocking, the prior association between l and r means that $w_l = r$ in the second set of trials, leading to no learning for the tone (since $V(t) - r(t) = 0$). In upwards unblocking, $w_l = r$ at the start of set 2. Therefore, $r(t) - w_l = r > 0$, allowing w_s to share in the prediction.

As described above, downwards unblocking is the key thorn in the side of RW. Since the TD rule combines the predictions from different stimuli in a similar way, it also fails to account properly for downwards unblocking. This is one reason why it is *incorrect* as a model of reward learning.

The class of theories (called CS-processing theories) that is alternative to RW does not construct a net prediction $V(t)$, but instead uses equation 1 for all the stimuli, only changing the learning rates $\alpha_l(t)$ and $\alpha_s(t)$ as a function of the conditioning history of the stimuli (*eg* Mackintosh, 1975; Pearce & Hall, 1980; Grossberg, 1982). A standard notion is that there is a competition between different stimuli for a limited capacity learning processor (Broadbent, 1958; Mackintosh, 1975; Pearce & Hall, 1980), translating into competition between the learning rates. In blocking, nothing unexpected happens in the second set of trials and equally, the tone does not predict anything novel. In either case α_s is set to ~ 0 and so no learning happens. In these models, downwards unblocking now makes qualitative sense: the surprising consequences in set 2 can be enough to set $\alpha_s \gg 0$, but then learning according to equation 1 can make $w_s > 0$. Whereas Mackintosh's (1975) and Pearce and Hall's (1980) models only consider competition between the stimuli for *learning*, Grossberg's (1982) model incorporates competition during *representation*, so the net prediction on a trial is affected by competitive interactions between the stimuli. In essence, our model provides a statistical formalisation of this insight.

3   New Models

From the previous section, it would seem that we have to abandon the computational basis of the RW and TD models in terms of making collective predictions about the reward. The CS-processing models do not construct a net prediction of the reward, or say anything about how possibly conflicting information based on different stimuli should be integrated. This is a key flaw – doing anything other than well-founded prediction is likely to be maladaptive. Even quite successful pre-synaptic models, such as Grossberg (1982), do not justify their predictions.

We now show that we can take a different, but still statistically-minded approach to combination in which we specify a parameterised probability distribution $\mathcal{P}[r(t)|s(t), l(t)]$ and perform a form of maximum likelihood (ML) inference, updating the parameters to maximise this probability over the samples. Consider three natural models of $\mathcal{P}[r(t)|s(t), l(t)]$:

$$\mathcal{P}_G[r(t)|s(t), l(t)] \;=\; \mathcal{N}[w_l l(t) + w_s s(t), \sigma^2] \tag{3}$$

$$\mathcal{P}_M[r(t)|s(t), l(t)] \;=\; \pi_l(t)\mathcal{N}[w_l, \sigma^2] + \pi_s(t)\mathcal{N}[w_s, \sigma^2] + \bar{\pi}(t)\mathcal{N}[\bar{w}, \tau^2] \tag{4}$$

$$\mathcal{P}_J[r(t)|s(t), l(t)] \;=\; \mathcal{N}[w_l \pi_l(t)l(t) + w_s \pi_s(t)s(t), \sigma^2] \tag{5}$$

where $\mathcal{N}[\mu, \sigma^2]$ is a normal distribution, with mean μ and variance σ^2. In the latter two cases, $0 \leq \pi_l(t) + \pi_s(t) \leq 1$, implementing a form of competition between the stimuli, and $\pi_*(t) = 0$ if stimulus $*$ is not presented. In equation 4, $\mathcal{N}[\bar{w}, \tau^2]$ captures the background expectation if neither the light nor the tone wins, and $\bar{\pi}(t) = 1 - \pi_l(t) - \pi_s(t)$. We will show that the data argue against the first two and support the third of these models.

Rescorla-Wagner: $\mathcal{P}_G[r(t)|s(t), l(t)]$

The RW rule is derived as ML inference based on equation 3. The only difference is the presence of the variance, σ^2. This is useful for capturing the partial reinforcement effect (see Mackintosh, 1983), in which if $r(t)$ is corrupted by substantial noise (*ie* $\sigma^2 \gg 0$), then learning to r is demonstrably slower. As we discussed above, downwards unblocking suggests that animals are not using $\mathcal{P}_G[r(t)|s(t),l(t)]$ as the basis for their predictions.

Competitive mixture of experts: $\mathcal{P}_M[r(t)|s(t),l(t)]$

$\mathcal{P}_M[r(t)|s(t),l(t)]$ is recognisable as the generative distribution in a mixture of Gaussians model (Nowlan, 1991; Jacobs *et al*, 1991b). Key in this model are the mixing proportions $\pi_l(t)$ and $\pi_s(t)$. Online variants of the E phase of the EM algorithm (Dempster *et al*, 1977) compute posterior responsibilities as $q_l(t) + q_s(t) + \bar{q}(t) = 1$, where $q_l(t) \propto \pi_l(t)e^{-(r(t)-w_l l(t))^2/2\sigma^2}$ (and similarly for the others), and then perform a partial M phase as

$$\Delta w_l(t) \propto (r(t) - w_l(t))q_l(t) \qquad \Delta w_s(t) \propto (r(t) - w_s(t))q_s(t) \qquad (6)$$

which has just the same character as the presynaptic rules (depending on how $\pi_l(t)$ is calculated). As in the mixture of experts model, each expert (each *stimulus* here) that seeks to predict $r(t)$ (*ie* each stimulus $*$ for which $q_*(t) \neq 0$) has to predict the whole of $r(t)$ by itself. This means that the model can capture downwards unblocking in the following way. The absence of the second r in the second set of trials forces $\pi_s(t) > 0$, and, through equation 6, this in turn means that the tone will come to predict the presence of the first r. The time u between the rewards can be important because of temporal discounting. This means that there are sufficiently large values of u for which the inhibitory effect of the absence of the second reward will be dominated. Note also that the *expected* reward based on $l(t)$ and $s(t)$ is the sum

$$\pi_l(t)w_l l(t) + \pi_s(t)w_s s(t) + \bar{\pi}(t)\bar{w} \qquad (7)$$

Although the net prediction given in equation 7 is indeed based on all the stimuli, it does not directly affect the course of learning. This means that the model has difficulty with inhibitory conditioning. The trouble with inhibitory conditioning is that the model cannot use $w_s < 0$ to counterbalance $w_l > 0$ – it can at best set $w_s = 0$, which is experimentally inaccurate. Note, however, this form of competition bears some interesting similarities with comparator models of conditioning (see Miller & Matzel, 1989). It also has some problems in explaining overshadowing, for similar reasons.

Cooperative mixture of experts: $\mathcal{P}_J[r(t)|s(t),l(t)]$

The final model $\mathcal{P}_J[r(t)|s(t),l(t)]$ is just like the mixture model that Jacobs *et al* (1991a) suggested (see also Bordley, 1982). One statistical formulation of this model considers that, independently,

$$P[w_l(t)|r] = \mathcal{N}[r, \rho_l^{-1}(t)] \qquad P[w_s(t)|r] = \mathcal{N}[r, \rho_s^{-1}(t)]$$

where $\rho_l(t)$ and $\rho_s(t)$ are inverse variances. This makes

$$\sigma^2 = (\rho_l(t) + \rho_s(t))^{-1} \quad \pi_l(t) = \rho_l(t)\sigma^2 \quad \pi_s(t) = \rho_s(t)\sigma^2.$$

Normative learning rules should emerge from a statistical model of uncertainty in the world. Short of such a model, we used:

$$\Delta w_l = \alpha_w \frac{\pi_l(t)}{\rho_l(t)}\delta(t) \qquad \Delta \rho_l = \alpha_\rho \rho_l \left(\frac{1}{\delta(t)^2 + 0.1} - \frac{1}{\sigma^2} \right)$$

where $\delta(t) = r(t) - \pi_l(t)w_l(t) - \pi_s(t)w_s(t)$ is the prediction error; the $1/\rho_l(t)$ term in changing w_l makes learning *slower* if w_l is more certainly related to r (*ie* if $\rho_l(t)$ is greater); the 0.1 substitutes for background noise; if $\delta^2(t)$ is too large, then $\rho_l + \rho_s$

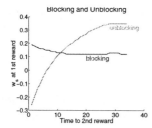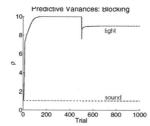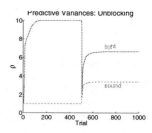

Figure 1: Blocking and downwards unblocking with 5 steps to the first reward; and a variable number to the second. Here, the discount factor $\gamma = 0.9$, and $\alpha_w = 0.5$, $\alpha_\rho = 0.02$, $\mu = 0.75$. For blocking, the second reward remains; for unblocking it is removed after 500 trials. a) The terminal weight for the sound after learning – for blocking it is always small and positive; for downwards unblocking, it changes from negative at small Δ_u to positive at large Δ_u. b,c) Predictive variances $\rho_l(t)$ and $\rho_s(t)$. In blocking, although there is a small change when the sound is introduced because of additivity of the variances, learning to the sound is substantially prevented. In downwards unblocking, the surprise omission of the second reward makes the sound associable and unblocks learning to it.

is shared out in proportion of ρ_l^μ to capture the insight that there can be dramatic changes to variabilities; and the variabilities are bottom-limited.

Figure 1 shows the end point and course of learning in blocking and downwards unblocking. Figure 1a confirms that the model captures downwards unblocking, making the terminal value of w_s negative for short separations between the rewards and positive for long separations. By comparison, in the blocking condition, for which both rewards are always presented, w_s is always small and positive. Figures 1b,c show the basis behind this behaviour in terms of $\rho_l(t)$ and $\rho_s(t)$. In particular, the heightened associability of the sound in unblocking following the prediction error when the second reward is removed accounts for the behavior.

As for the mixture of experts model (and also for comparator models), the presence of $\pi_l(t)$ and $\pi_s(t)$ makes the explanation of inhibitory conditioning and overshadowing a little complicated. For instance, if the sound is associable ($\rho_s(t) \gg 0$), then it can seem to act as a conditioned inhibitor even if $w_s = 0$. Nevertheless, unlike the mixture of experts model, the fact that learning is based on the joint prediction makes true inhibitory conditioning possible.

4   Discussion

Downwards unblocking may seem like an extremely abstruse paradigm with which to refute an otherwise successful and computationally sound model. However, it is just the tip of a conditioning iceberg that would otherwise sink TD. Even in other reinforcement learning applications of TD, there is no *a priori* reason why predictions should be made according to equation 2 – the other statistical models in equations 4 and 5 could also be used. Indeed, it is easy to generate circumstances in which these more competitive models will perform better. For the neurobiology, experiments on the behavior of the DA system in these conditioning tasks will help specify the models further.

The model is incomplete in various important ways. First, it makes no distinction between preparatory and consumatory conditioning (Konorski, 1967). There is evidence that the predictions a CS makes about the *affective* value of USs fall in a different class from the predictions it makes about the actual USs that appear.

For instance, an inhibitory stimulus reporting the absence of expected delivery of food can block learning to the delivery of shock, implying that aversive events form a single class. The affective value forms the preparatory aspect, is likely what is reported by the DA cells, and perhaps controls orienting behavior, the characteristic reaction of animals to the conditioned stimuli that may provide an experimental handle on the attention they are paid. Second, the model does not use opponency (Konorski, 1967; Solomon & Corbit, 1974; Grossberg, 1982) to handle inhibitory conditioning. This is particularly important, since the dynamics of the interaction between the opponent systems may well be responsible for the importance of the delay u in downwards unblocking. Serotonin is an obvious candidate as an opponent system to DA (Montague *et al* 1996). We also have not specified a substrate for the associabilities or the attentional competition – the DA system itself may well be involved. Finally, we have not specified an overall model of how the animal might expect the contingency of the world to change over time – which is key to the statistical justification of appropriate learning rules.

References

[1] Barto, AG, Sutton, RS & Anderson, CW (1983). *IEEE Transactions on Systems, Man, and Cybernetics*, **13**, pp 834-846.

[2] Bordley, RF (1982). *Journal of the Operational Research Society*, **33**, 171-174.

[3] Broadbent, DE (1958). *Perception and Communication*. London: Pergamon.

[4] Buhusi, CV & Schmajuk, NA. *Hippocampus*, **6**, 621-642.

[5] Dempster, AP, Laird, NM & Rubin, DB (1977). *Proceedings of the Royal Statistical Society*, **B-39**, 1–38.

[6] Dickinson, A (1980). *Contemporary Animal Learning Theory*. Cambridge, England: Cambridge University Press.

[7] Gabriel, M & Moore, J, editors (1989). *Learning and Computational Neuroscience*. Cambridge, MA: MIT Press.

[8] Gallagher, M & Holland, PC (1994). *PNAS*, **91**, 11771-6.

[9] Gluck, MA & Thompson, RF (1987). *Psychological Reviews*, **94**, 176-191.

[10] Grossberg, S (1982). *Psychological Review*, **89**, 529-572.

[11] Holland, PC (1988). *Journal of Experimental Psychology: Animal Behavior Processes*, **14**, 261-279.

[12] Jacobs, RA, Jordan, MI & Barto, AG (1991). *Cognitive Science*, **15**, 219-250.

[13] Jacobs, RA, Jordan, MI, Nowlan, SJ & Hinton, GE (1991). *Neural Computation*, **3**, 79-87.

[14] Konorski, J (1967). *Integrative Activity of the Brain*. Chicago, Il: Chicago University Press.

[15] Mackintosh, NJ (1975). *Psychological Review*, **82**, 276-298.

[16] Mackintosh, NJ (1983). *Conditioning and Associative Learning*. Oxford, UK: Oxford University Press.

[17] Marr, D (1982). *Vision*. New York, NY: Freeman.

[18] Miller, RR & Matzel, LD (1989). In SB Klein & RR Mowrer, editors, *Contemporary Learning Theories: Pavlovian Conditioning and the Status of Traditional Theory*. Hillsdale, NJ: Lawrence Erlbaum.

[19] Montague, PR, Dayan, P & Sejnowski, TK (1996). *Journal of Neuroscience*, **16**, 1936-1947.

[20] Nowlan, SJ (1991). *Soft Competitive Adaptation: Neural Network Learning Algorithms Based on Fitting Statistical Mixtures*. PhD Thesis, Department of Computer Science, Carnegie-Mellon University.

[21] Pearce, JM & Hall, G (1980). *Psychological Review*, **87**, 532-552.

[22] Rescorla, RA & Wagner, AR (1972). In AH Black & WF Prokasy, editors, *Classical Conditioning II: Current Research and Theory*, pp 64-69. New York, NY: Appleton-Century-Crofts.

[23] Schultz, W, Dayan, P & Montague, PR (1997). *Science*, **275**, 1593-1599.

[24] Solomon, RL & Corbit, JD (1974). *Psychological Review*, **81**, 119-145.

[25] Sutton, RS & Barto, AG (1981). *Psychological Review*, **88** 2, pp 135-170.

[26] Sutton, RS & Barto, AG (1989). In Gabriel & Moore (1989).

Characterizing Neurons in the Primary Auditory Cortex of the Awake Primate Using Reverse Correlation

R. Christopher deCharms
decharms@phy.ucsf.edu

Michael M. Merzenich
merz@phy.ucsf.edu

W. M. Keck Center for Integrative Neuroscience
University of California, San Francisco CA 94143

Abstract

While the understanding of the functional role of different classes of neurons in the awake primary visual cortex has been extensively studied since the time of Hubel and Wiesel (Hubel and Wiesel, 1962), our understanding of the feature selectivity and functional role of neurons in the primary auditory cortex is much farther from complete. Moving bars have long been recognized as an optimal stimulus for many visual cortical neurons, and this finding has recently been confirmed and extended in detail using reverse correlation methods (Jones and Palmer, 1987; Reid and Alonso, 1995; Reid et al., 1991; Ringach et al., 1997). In this study, we recorded from neurons in the primary auditory cortex of the awake primate, and used a novel reverse correlation technique to compute receptive fields (or preferred stimuli), encompassing both multiple frequency components and ongoing time. These spectrotemporal receptive fields make clear that neurons in the primary auditory cortex, as in the primary visual cortex, typically show considerable structure in their feature processing properties, often including multiple excitatory and inhibitory regions in their receptive fields. These neurons can be sensitive to stimulus edges in frequency composition or in time, and sensitive to stimulus transitions such as changes in frequency. These neurons also show strong responses and selectivity to continuous frequency modulated stimuli analogous to visual drifting gratings.

1 Introduction

It is known that auditory neurons are tuned for a number of independent feature parameters of simple stimuli including frequency (Merzenich et al., 1973), intensity (Sutter and Schreiner, 1995), amplitude modulation (Schreiner and Urbas, 1988), and others. In addition, auditory cortical responses to multiple stimuli can enhance or suppress one another in a time dependent fashion (Brosch and Schreiner, 1997; Phillips and Cynader, 1985; Shamma and Symmes, 1985), and auditory cortical neurons can be highly selective for species-specific vocalizations (Wang et al., 1995; Wollberg and Newman, 1972), suggesting complex acoustic processing by these cells. It is not yet known if these many independent selectivities of auditory cortical neurons reflect a discernible underlying pattern of feature decomposition, as has often been suggested (Merzenich et al., 1985; Schreiner and Mendelson, 1990; Wang et al., 1995). Further, since sustained firing rate responses in the auditory cortex to tonal stimuli are typically much lower than visual responses to drifting bars (deCharms and Merzenich, 1996b), it has been suggested that the preferred type of auditory stimulus may still not be known (Nelken et al., 1994). We sought to develop an unbiased method for determining the full feature selectivity of auditory cortical neurons, whatever it might be, in frequency and time based upon reverse correlation.

2 Methods

Recordings were made from a chronic array of up to 49 individually placed ultra-fine extracellular Iridium microelectrodes, placed in the primary auditory cortex of the adult owl monkey. The electrodes had tip lengths of 10-25microns, which yield impedance values of .5-5MOhm and good isolation of signals from individual neurons or clusters of nearby neurons. We electrochemically activated these tips to add an ultramicroscopic coating of Iridium Oxide, which leaves the tip geometry unchanged, but decreases the tip impedance by more than an order of magnitude, resulting in substantially improved recording signals. These signals are filtered from .3-8kHz, sampled at 20kHz, digitized, and sorted. The stimuli used were a variant of random

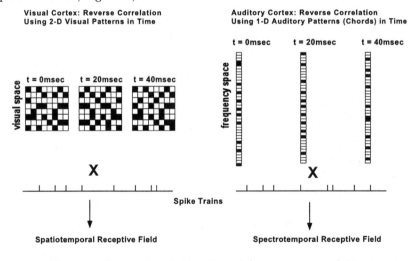

Figure 1: Schematic of stimuli used for reverse correlation.

white noise which was designed to allow us to characterize the responses of neurons in time and in frequency. As shown in figure 1, these stimuli are directly analogous to stimuli that have been used previously to characterize the response properties of neurons in the primary visual cortex (Jones and Palmer, 1987; Reid and Alonso, 1995; Reid et al., 1991). In the visual case, stimuli consist of spatial checkerboards that span some portion of the two-dimensional visual field and change pattern with a short sampling interval. In the auditory case, which we have studied here, the stimuli chosen were randomly selected chords, which approximately evenly span a portion of the one-dimensional receptor surface of the cochlea. These stimuli consist of combinations of pure tones, all with identical phase and all with 5 msec cosine-shaped ramps in amplitude when they individually turn on or off. Each chord was created by randomly selecting frequency values from 84 possible values which span 7 octaves from 110Hz to 14080Hz in even semitone steps. The density of tones in each stimulus was 1 tone per octave on average, or 7 tones per chord, but the stimuli were selected stochastically so a given chord could be composed of a variable number of tones of randomly selected frequencies. We have used sampling rates of 10-100 chords/second, and the data here are from stimuli with 50 chords/second. Stimuli with random, asynchronous onset times of each tone produce similar results. These stimuli were presented in the open sound field within an acoustical isolation chamber at 44.1kHz sampling rate directly from audio compact disk, while the animal sat passively in the sound field or actively performed an auditory discrimination task, receiving occasional juice rewards. The complete characterization set lasted for ten minutes, thereby including 30,000 individual chords.

Spike trains were collected from multiple sites in the cortex simultaneously during the presentation of our characterization stimulus set, and individually reverse correlated with the times of onset of each of the tonal stimuli. The reverse correlation method computes the number of spikes from a neuron that were detected, on average, during a given time preceding, during, or following a particular tonal stimulus component from our set of chords. These values are presented in spikes/s for all of the tones in the stimulus set, and for some range of time shifts. This method is somewhat analogous in intention to a method developed earlier for deriving spectrotemporal receptive fields for auditory midbrain neurons (Eggermont et al., 1983), but previous methods have not been effective in the auditory cortex.

3   Results

Figure 2 shows the spectrotemporal responses of neurons from four locations in the primary auditory cortex. In each panel, the time in milliseconds between the onset of a particular stimulus component and a neuronal spike is shown along the horizontal axis. Progressively greater negative time shifts indicate progressively longer latencies from the onset of a stimulus component until the neuronal spikes. The frequency of the stimulus component is shown along the vertical axis, in octave spacing from a 110Hz standard, with twelve steps per octave. The brightness corresponds to the average rate of the neuron, in spk/s, driven by a particular stimulus component. The reverse-correlogram is thus presented as a stimulus triggered spike rate average, analogous to a standard peristimulus time histogram but reversed in time, and is identical to the spectrogram of the estimated optimal stimulus for the cell (a spike triggered stimulus average which would be in units of mean stimulus density).

A minority of neurons in the primary auditory cortex have spectrotemporal receptive fields that show only a single region of increased rate, which corresponds to the traditional characteristic frequency of the neuron, and no inhibitory region. We have found that cells of this type (less than 10%, not shown) are less common than cells with multimodal receptive field structure. More commonly, neurons have regions of both increased and decreased firing rate relative to their mean rate within their receptive fields. For terminological convenience, these will be referred to as excitatory and inhibitory regions, though these changes in rate are not diagnostic of an underlying mechanism. Neurons with receptive fields of this type can serve as detectors of stimulus edges in both frequency space, and in time. The neuron shown in figure 2a has a receptive field structure indicative of lateral inhibition in frequency space. This cell prefers a very narrow range of frequencies, and decreases its firing rate for nearby frequencies, giving the characteristic of a sharply-tuned bandpass filter. This

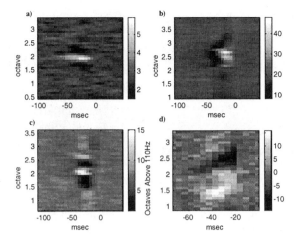

Figure 2: Spectrotemporal receptive fields of neurons in the primary auditory cortex of the awake primate. These receptive fields are computed as described in methods. Receptive field structures read from left to right correspond to a preferred stimulus for the neuron, with light shading indicating more probable stimulus components to evoke a spike, and dark shading indicating less probable components. Receptive fields read from right to left indicate the response of the neuron in time to a particular stimulus component. The colorbars correspond to the average firing rates of the neurons in Hz at a given time preceding, during, or following a particular stimulus component.

type of response is the auditory analog of a visual or tactile edge detector with lateral inhibition. Simple cells in the primary visual cortex typically show similar patterns of center excitation along a short linear segment, surrounded by inhibition (Jones and Palmer, 1987; Reid and Alonso, 1995; Reid et al., 1991). The neuron shown in figure 2b shows a decrease in firing rate caused by a stimulus frequency which at a later time causes an increase in rate. This receptive field structure is ideally suited to detect stimulus transients, and can be thought of as a detector of temporal edges. Neurons in the auditory cortex typically prefer this type of stimulus, which is initially soft or silent and later loud. This corresponds to a neuronal response which shows an increase followed by a decrease in firing rate. This is again analogous to neuronal responses in the primary visual cortex, which also typically show a firing rate pattern to an optimal stimulus of excitation followed by inhibition, and preference for stimulus transients such as when a stimulus is first off and then comes on.

The neuron shown in figures 2c shows an example which has complex receptive field structure, with multiple regions. Cells of this type would be indicative of selectivity for feature conjunctions or quite complex stimuli, perhaps related to sounds in the animal's learned environment. Cells with complex receptive field structures are common in the awake auditory cortex, and we are in the process of quantifying the percentages of cells that fit within these different categories.

Neurons were observed which respond with increased rate to one frequency range at one time, and a different frequency range at a later time, indicative of selectivity for frequency modulations(Suga, 1965). Regions of decreased firing rate can show similar patterns. The neuron shown in figure 2d is an example of this type. This pattern is strongly analogous to motion energy detectors in the visual system (Adelson and Bergen, 1985), which detect stimuli moving in space, and these cells are selective for changes in frequency.

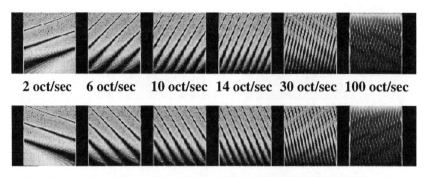

Figure 3: Parametric stimulus set used to explore neuronal responses to continuously changing stimulus frequency. Images are spectrograms of stimuli from left to right in time, and spanning seven octaves of frequency from bottom to top. Each stimulus is one second. Numbers indicate the sweep rate of the stimuli in octaves per second.

Based on the responses shown, we wondered whether we could find a more optimal class of stimuli for these neuron, analogous to the use of drifting bars or gratings in the primary visual cortex. We have created auditory stimuli which correspond exactly to the preferred stimulus computed for a particular cell from the cell's spectrotemporal receptive field (manuscript in preparation), and we have also designed a parametric class of stimuli which are designed to be particularly effective for neurons selective for stimuli of changing amplitude or frequency, which are presented here. The stimuli shown in figure 3 are auditory analogous of visual drifting grating stimuli. The stimuli are shown as spectrograms, where time is along the horizontal axis, frequency content on an octave scale is along the vertical axis, and brightness corresponds to the intensity of the signal. These stimuli contain frequencies that change in time along an octave frequency scale so that they repeatedly pass approximately linearly through a neurons receptive field, just as a drifting grating would pass repeatedly through the receptive field of a visual neuron. These stimuli are somewhat analogous to drifting ripple stimuli which have recently been used by Kowalski, et.al. to characterize the linearity of responses of neurons in the anesthetized ferret auditory cortex (Kowalski et al., 1996a; Kowalski et al., 1996b).

Neurons in the auditory cortex typically respond to tonal stimuli with a brisk onset response at the stimulus transient, but show sustained rates that are far smaller than found in the visual or somatosensory systems (deCharms and Merzenich, 1996a). We have found neurons in the awake animal that respond with high firing rates and significant selectivity to the class of moving stimuli shown in figure 3. An outstanding example of this is shown in figure 4. The neuron in this example showed a very high sustained firing rate to the optimal drifting stimulus, as high as 60 Hz for one second. The neuron shown in this example also showed considerable selectivity for stimulus velocity, as well as some selectivity for stimulus direction.

4   Conclusions

These stimuli enable us to efficiently quantify the response characteristics of neurons in the awake primary auditory cortex, as well as producing optimal stimuli for particular neurons. The data that we have gathered thus far extend our knowledge about the complex receptive field structure of cells in the primary auditory cortex,

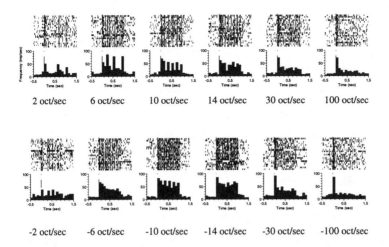

Figure 4: Responses of a neuron in the primary auditory cortex of the awake primate to example stimuli take form our characterization set, as shown in figure 3. In each panel, the average response rate histogram in spikes per second is shown below rastergrams showing the individual action potentials elicited on each of twenty trials.

and show some considerable analogy with neurons in the primary visual cortex. In addition, they indicate that it is possible to drive auditory cortical cells to high rates of sustained firing, as in the visual cortex. This method will allow a number of future questions to be addressed. Since we have recorded many neurons simultaneously, we are interested in the interactions among large populations of neurons and how these relate to stimuli. We are also recording responses to these stimuli while monkeys are performing cognitive tasks involving attention and learning, and we hope that this will give us insight into the effects on cell selectivity of the context provided by other stimuli, the animal's behavioral state or awareness of the stimuli, and the animal's prior learning of stimulus sets.

5 References

Adelson EH, Bergen JR (1985) Spatiotemporal energy models for the perception of motion. J. Opt. Soc. Am. A, 2, 284-299.

Brosch M, Schreiner CE (1997) Time course of forward masking tuning curves in cat primary auditory cortex. J Neurophysiol, 77, 923-43.

deCharms RC, Merzenich MM (1996a) Primary cortical representation of sounds by the coordination of action-potential timing. Nature, 381, 610-3.

deCharms RC, Merzenich MM (1996b) Primary cortical representation of sounds by the coordination of action-potential timing. Nature, 381, 610-613.

Eggermont JJ, Aertsen AM, Johannesma PI (1983) Quantitative characterisation procedure for auditory neurons based on the spectro-temporal receptive field. Hear Res, 10, 167-90.

Hubel DH, Wiesel TN (1962) Receptive fields, binocular interaction and functional archtecture in the cat's visual cortex. J. Physiol., 160, 106-154.

Jones JP, Palmer LA (1987) The two-dimensional spatial structure of simple receptive fields in cat striate cortex. J Neurophysiol, 58, 1187-211.

Kowalski N, Depireux DA, Shamma SA (1996a) Analysis of dynamic spectra in ferret primary auditory cortex. I. Characteristics of single-unit responses to moving ripple spectra. J Neurophysiol, 76, 3503-23.

Kowalski N, Depireux DA, Shamma SA (1996b) Analysis of dynamic spectra in ferret primary auditory cortex. II. Prediction of unit responses to arbitrary dynamic spectra. J Neurophysiol, 76, 3524-34.

Merzenich MM, Jenkins WM, Middlebrooks JC (1985) Observations and hypotheses on special organizational features of the central auditory nervous system. In: Dynamic Aspects of Neocortical Function. Edited by E. G. a. W. M. C. G. Edelman. New York: Wiley, pp. 397-423.

Merzenich MM, Knight PL, Roth GL (1973) Cochleotopic organization of primary auditory cortex in the cat. Brain Res, 63, 343-6.

Nelken I, Prut Y, Vaadia E, Abeles M (1994) In search of the best stimulus: an optimization procedure for finding efficient stimuli in the cat auditory cortex. Hear Res, 72, 237-53.

Phillips DP, Cynader MS (1985) Some neural mechanisms in the cat's auditory cortex underlying sensitivity to combined tone and wide-spectrum noise stimuli. Hear Res, 18, 87-102.

Reid RC, Alonso JM (1995) Specificity of monosynaptic connections from thalamus to visual cortex. Nature, 378, 281-4.

Reid RC, Soodak RE, Shapley RM (1991) Directional selectivity and spatiotemporal structure of receptive fields of simple cells in cat striate cortex. J Neurophysiol, 66, 505-29.

Ringach DL, Hawken MJ, Shapley R (1997) Dynamics of orientation tuning in macaque primary visual cortex. Nature, 387, 281-4.

Schreiner CE, Mendelson JR (1990) Functional topography of cat primary auditory cortex: distribution of integrated excitation. J Neurophysiol, 64, 1442-59.

Schreiner CE, Urbas JV (1988) Representation of amplitude in the auditory cortex of the cat. II. Comparison between cortical fields. Hear. Res., 32, 49-64.

Shamma SA, Symmes D (1985) Patterns of inhibition in auditory cortical cells in awake squirrel monkeys. Hear Res, 19, 1-13.

Suga N (1965) Responses of cortical auditory neurones to frequency modulated sounds in echo-locating bats. Nature, 206, 890-1.

Sutter ML, Schreiner CE (1995) Topography of intensity tuning in cat primary auditory cortex: single-neuron versus multiple-neuron recordings. J Neurophysiol, 73, 190-204.

Wang X, Merzenich MM, Beitel R, Schreiner CE (1995) Representation of a species-specific vocalization in the primary auditory cortex of the common marmoset: temporal and spectral characteristics. J Neurophysiol, 74, 2685-706.

Wollberg Z, Newman JD (1972) Auditory cortex of squirrel monkey: response patterns of single cells to species-specific vocalizations. Science, 175, 212-214.

Using Helmholtz Machines to analyze multi-channel neuronal recordings

Virginia R. de Sa
desa@phy.ucsf.edu

R. Christopher deCharms
decharms@phy.ucsf.edu

Michael M. Merzenich
merz@phy.ucsf.edu

Sloan Center for Theoretical Neurobiology and
W. M. Keck Center for Integrative Neuroscience
University of California, San Francisco CA 94143

Abstract

One of the current challenges to understanding neural information processing in biological systems is to decipher the "code" carried by large populations of neurons acting in parallel. We present an algorithm for automated discovery of stochastic firing patterns in large ensembles of neurons. The algorithm, from the "Helmholtz Machine" family, attempts to predict the observed spike patterns in the data. The model consists of an observable layer which is directly activated by the input spike patterns, and hidden units that are activated through ascending connections from the input layer. The hidden unit activity can be propagated down to the observable layer to create a prediction of the data pattern that produced it. Hidden units are added incrementally and their weights are adjusted to improve the fit between the predictions and data, that is, to increase a bound on the probability of the data given the model. This greedy strategy is not globally optimal but is computationally tractable for large populations of neurons. We show benchmark data on artificially constructed spike trains and promising early results on neurophysiological data collected from our chronic multi-electrode cortical implant.

1 Introduction

Understanding neural processing will ultimately require observing the response patterns and interactions of large populations of neurons. While many studies have demonstrated that neurons can show significant pairwise interactions, and that these pairwise interactions can code stimulus information [Gray et al., 1989, Meister et al., 1995, deCharms and Merzenich, 1996, Vaadia et al., 1995], there is currently little understanding of how large ensembles of neurons might function together to represent stimuli. This situation has arisen partly out of the historical difficulty of recording from large numbers of neurons simultaneously. Now that this is becoming technically feasible, the remaining analytical challenge is to understand how to decipher the information carried in distributed neuronal responses.

Extracting information from the firing patterns in large neuronal populations is difficult largely due to the combinatorial complexity of the problem, and the uncertainty about how information may be encoded. There have been several attempts to look for higher order correlations [Martignon et al., 1997] or decipher the activity from multiple neurons, but existing methods are limited in the type of patterns they can extract assuming absolute reliability of spikes within temporal patterns of small numbers of neurons [Abeles, 1982, Abeles and Gerstein, 1988, Abeles et al., 1993, Schnitzer and Meister,] or considering only rate codes [Gat and Tishby, 1993, Abeles et al., 1995]. Given the large numbers of neurons involved in coding sensory events and the high variability of cortical action potentials, we suspect that meaningful ensemble coding events may be statistically similar from instance to instance while not being identical. Searching for these type of stochastic patterns is a more challenging task.

One way to extract the structure in a pattern dataset is to construct a generative model that produces representative data from hidden stochastic variables. Helmholtz machines [Hinton et al., 1995, Dayan et al., 1995] efficiently [Frey et al., 1996] produce generative models of datasets by maximizing a lower bound on the log likelihood of the data. Cascaded Redundancy Reduction [de Sa and Hinton, 1998] is a particularly simple form of Helmholtz machine in which hidden units are incrementally added. As each unit is added, it greedily attempts to best model the data using all the previous units. In this paper we describe how to apply the Cascaded Redundancy Reduction algorithm to the problem of finding patterns in neuronal ensemble data, test the performance of this method on artificial data, and apply the method to example neuronal spike trains.

1.1 Cascaded Redundancy Reduction

The simplest form of generative model is to model each observed (or input) unit as a stochastic binary random variable with generative bias b_i. This generative input is passed through a transfer function to give a probability of firing.

$$p_i = \sigma(b_i) = \frac{1}{1 + e^{-b_i}} \tag{1}$$

While this can model the individual firing rates of binary units, it cannot account for correlations in firing between units. Correlations can be modeled by introducing hidden units with generative weights to the correlated observed units. By cascading hidden units as in Figure 1, we can represent higher order correlations. Lower units sum up their total generative input from higher units and their generative bias.

$$x_i = b_i + \sum_{j>i} s_j g_{j,i} \qquad\qquad p_i = \sigma(x_i) \tag{2}$$

Finding the optimal generative weights $(g_{j,i}, b_i)$ for a given dataset involves an intractable search through an exponential number of possible states of the hidden units. Helmholtz machines approximate this problem by using forward recognition connections to compute an approximate distribution over hidden states for each data pattern. Cascaded Redundancy Reduction takes this approximation one step further by approximating the distribution by a single state. This makes the search for recognition and generative weights much simpler. Given a data vector, d, considering the state produced by the recognition connections as s^d gives a lower bound on the log

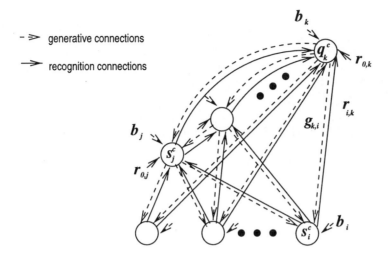

Figure 1: The Cascaded Redundancy Reduction Network. Hidden units are added incrementally to help better model the data.

likelihood of the data. Units are added incrementally with the goal of maximizing this lower bound, C,

$$C = \cdot \sum_d [(s_k^d \log \sigma(b_k) + (1-s_k^d)\log(1-\sigma(b_k)) + \sum_i s_i^d \log \sigma(x_i^d) + (1-s_i^d)\log(1-\sigma(x_i^d))]$$

$$(3)$$

Before a unit is added it is considered as a temporary addition. Once its weights have been learned, it is added to the permanent network only if adding it reduces the cost on an independent validation set from the same data distribution. This is to prevent overtraining. While a unit is considered for addition, all weights other than those to and from the new unit and the generative bias weights are fixed. The learning of the weights to and from the new unit is then a fairly simple optimization problem involving treating the unit as stochastic, and performing gradient descent on the resulting modified lower bound.

2 Method

This generic pattern finding algorithm can be applied to multi-unit spike trains by treating time as another spatial dimension as is often done for time series data. The spikes are binned on the order of a few to tens of milliseconds and the algorithm looks for patterns in finite time length windows by sliding a window centered on each spike from a chosen *trigger channel*. An example extracted window using channel 4 as the trigger channel is shown in Figure 2.

Because the number of spikes can be larger than one, the observed units (bins) are modeled as discrete Poisson random variables rather than binary random variables (the hidden units are still kept as binary units). To reflect the constraint that the expected number of spikes cannot be negative but may be larger than one, the transfer function for these observed bins was chosen to be exponential. Thus if x_i is the total summed generative input, λ_i, the expected mean number of spikes in bin i, is calculated as e^{x_i} and the probability of finding s spikes in that bin is given by

$$p_i = \frac{e^{-\lambda_i}\lambda^s}{s!} = \frac{e^{-e^{x_i}}e^{x_i s}}{s!} \qquad (4)$$

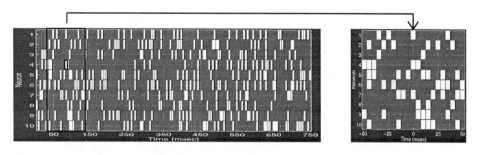

Figure 2: The input patterns for the algorithm are windows from the full spatio-temporal firing patterns. The full dataset is windows centered about every spike in the trigger channel.

The terms in the lower bound objective function due to the observed bins are modified accordingly.

3   Experimental Results

Before applying the algorithm to real neural spike trains we have characterized its properties under controlled conditions. We constructed sample data containing two random patterns across 10 units spanning 100 msec. The patterns were stochastic such that each neuron had a probability of firing in each time bin of the pattern. Sample patterns were drawn from the stochastic pattern templates and embedded in other "noise" spikes. The sample pattern templates are shown in the first column of Figure 3. 300 seconds of independent training, validation and test data were generated. All results are reported on the test data .

After training the network, performance was assessed by stepping through the test data and observing the pattern of activation across the hidden units obtained from propagating activity through the forward (recognition) connections and their corresponding generative pattern $\{\lambda_i\}$ obtained from the generative connections from the binary hidden unit pattern. Typically, many of the theoretically possible 2^n hidden unit patterns do not occur. Of the ones that do, several may code for the noise background. A crucial issue for interpreting patterns in real neural data is to discover which of the hidden unit activity patterns correspond to actual meaningful patterns. We use a measure that calculates the quality of the match of the observed pattern and the generative pattern it invokes. As the algorithm was not trained on the test data, close matches between the generative pattern and the observed pattern imply real structure that is common to the training and test dataset. With real neural data, this question can also be addressed by correlating the occurrence of patterns to stimuli or behavioural states of the animal.

One match measure we have used to pick out temporally modulated structure is the cost of coding the observed units using the hidden unit pattern compared to the cost of using the optimal rate code for that pattern (derived by calculating the firing rate for each channel in the window excluding the trigger bin). Match values were calculated for each hidden unit pattern by averaging the results across all its contributing observed patterns. Typical generative patterns of the added template patterns (in noise) are shown in the second column of Figure 3. The third column in the figure shows example matches from the test set, (i.e. patterns that activated the hidden unit pattern corresponding to the generative pattern in column 2). Note that the instances of the patterns are missing some spikes present in the template, and are surrounded by many additional spikes.

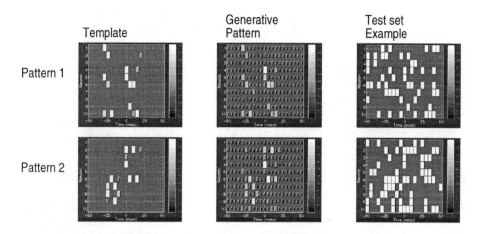

Figure 3: Pattern templates, resulting generative patterns after training (showing the expected number of spikes the algorithm predicts for each bin), and example test set occurrences. The size and shade of the squares represents the probability of activation of that bin (or 0/1 for the actual occurrences), the colorbars go from 0 to 1.

We varied both the frequency of the pattern occurrences and that of the added background spikes. Performance as a function of the frequency of the background spikes is shown on the left in Figure 4 for a pattern frequency of .4 Hz. Performance as a function of the pattern frequency for a noise spike frequency of 15Hz is shown on the right of the Figure. False alarm rates were extremely low ranging from 0-4% across all the tested conditions. Also, importantly, when we ran three trials with no added patterns, no patterns were detected by the algorithm.

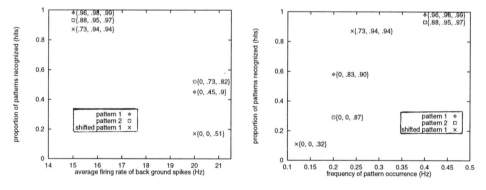

Figure 4: Graphs showing the effect of adding more background spikes (left) and decreasing the number of pattern occurrences in the dataset (right) on the percentage of patterns correctly detected. The detection of shifted pattern is due to the presence of a second spike in channel 4 in the pattern (hits for this case are only calculated for the times when this spike was present – the others would all be missed). In fact in some cases the presence of the only slightly probable 3rd bin in channel 4 was enough to detect another shifted pattern 1. Means over 3 trials are plotted with the individual trial values given in braces

The algorithm was then applied to recordings made from a chronic array of extracellular microelectrodes placed in the primary auditory cortex of one adult marmoset monkey and one adult owl monkey [deCharms and Merzenich, 1998]. On some elec-

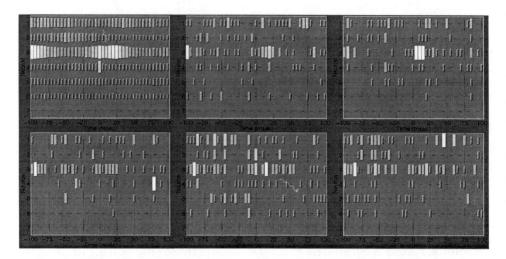

Figure 5: Data examples (all but top left) from neural recordings in an awake marmoset monkey that invoke the same generative pattern (top left). The instances are patterns from the test data that activated the same hidden unit activity pattern resulting in the generative pattern in the top left. The data windows were centered around all the spikes in channel 4. The brightest bins in the generative pattern represent an expected number of spikes of 1.7. In the actual patterns, The darkest and smallest bins represent a bin with 1 spike; each discrete grayscale/size jump represents an additional spike. Each subfigure is individually normalized to the bin with the most spikes.

trodes spikes were isolated from individual neurons; others were derived from small clusters of nearby neurons. Figure 5 shows an example generative pattern (accounting for 2.8% of the test data) that had a high match value together with example occurrences in the test data. The data were responses recorded to vocalizations played to the marmoset monkey, channel 4 was used as the trigger channel and 7 hidden units were added.

4   Discussion

We have introduced a procedure for searching for structure in multineuron spike trains, and particularly for searching for statistically reproducible stochastic temporal events among ensembles of neurons. We believe this method has great promise for exploring the important question of ensemble coding in many neuronal systems, a crucial part of the problem of understanding neural information coding. The strengths of this method include the ability to deal with stochastic patterns, the search for any type of reproducible structure including the extraction of patterns of unsuspected nature, and its efficient, greedy, search mechanism that allows it to be applied to large numbers of neurons.

Acknowledgements

We would like to acknowledge Geoff Hinton for useful suggestions in the early stages of this work, David MacKay for helpful comments on an earlier version of the manuscript, and the Sloan Foundation for financial support.

References

[Abeles, 1982] Abeles, M. (1982). *Local Cortical Circuits An Electrophysiological Study*, volume 6 of *Studies of Brain Function*. Springer-Verlag.

[Abeles et al., 1995] Abeles, M., Bergman, H., Gat, I., Meilijson, I., Seidemann, E., Tishby, N., and Vaadia, E. (1995). Cortical activity flips among quasi-stationary states. *Proceedings of the National Academy of Science*, 92:8616–8620.

[Abeles et al., 1993] Abeles, M., Bergman, H., Margalit, E., and Vaadia, E. (1993). Spatiotemporal firing patterns in the frontal cortex of behaving monkeys. *Journal of Neurophysiology*, 70(4):1629–1638.

[Abeles and Gerstein, 1988] Abeles, M. and Gerstein, G. L. (1988). Detecting spatiotemporal firing patterns among simultaneously recorded single neurons. *Journal of Neurophysiology*, 60(3).

[Dayan et al., 1995] Dayan, P., Hinton, G. E., Neal, R. M., and Zemel, R. S. (1995). The helmholtz machine. *Neural Computation*, 7:889–904.

[de Sa and Hinton, 1998] de Sa, V. R. and Hinton, G. E. (1998). Cascaded redundancy reduction. to appear in *Network*(February).

[deCharms and Merzenich, 1996] deCharms, R. C. and Merzenich, M. M. (1996). Primary cortical representation of sounds by the coordination of action-potential timing. *Nature*, 381:610–613.

[deCharms and Merzenich, 1998] deCharms, R. C. and Merzenich, M. M. (1998). Characterizing neurons in the primary auditory cortex of the awake primate using reverse correlation. this volume.

[Frey et al., 1996] Frey, B. J., Hinton, G. E., and Dayan, P. (1996). Does the wake-sleep algorithm produce good density estimators? In Touretzky, D., Mozer, M., and Hasselmo, M., editors, *Advances in Neural Information Processing Systems 8*, pages 661–667. MIT Press.

[Gat and Tishby, 1993] Gat, I. and Tishby, N. (1993). Statistical modeling of cell-assemblies activities in associative cortex of behaving monkeys. In Hanson, S., Cowan, J., and Giles, C., editors, *Advances in Neural Information Processing Systems 5*, pages 945–952. Morgan Kaufmann.

[Gray et al., 1989] Gray, C. M., Konig, P., Engel, A. K., and Singer, W. (1989). Oscillatory responses in cat visual cortex exhibit inter-columnar synchronization which reflects global stimulus properties. *Nature*, 338:334–337.

[Hinton et al., 1995] Hinton, G. E., Dayan, P., Frey, B. J., and Neal, R. M. (1995). The wake-sleep algorithm for unsupervised neural networks. *Science*, 268:1158–1161.

[Martignon et al., 1997] Martignon, L., Laskey, K., Deco, G., and Vaadia, E. (1997). Learning exact patterns of quasi-synchronization among spiking neurons from data on multi-unit recordings. In Mozer, M., Jordan, M., and Petsche, T., editors, *Advances in Neural Information Processing Systems 9*, pages 76–82. MIT Press.

[Meister et al., 1995] Meister, M., Lagnado, L., and Baylor, D. (1995). Concerted signaling by retinal ganglion cells. *Science*, 270:95–106.

[Schnitzer and Meister,] Schnitzer, M. J. and Meister, M. Information theoretic identification of neural firing patterns from multi-electrode recordings. in preparation.

[Vaadia et al., 1995] Vaadia, E., Haalman, I., Abeles, M., Bergman, H., Prut, Y., Slovin, H., and Aertsen, A. (1995). Dynamics of neuronal interactions in monkey cortex in relation to behavioural events. *Nature*, 373:515–518.

Instabilities in Eye Movement Control: A Model of Periodic Alternating Nystagmus

Ernst R. Dow
Center for Biophysics and
Computational Biology,
Beckman Institute
University of Illinois at Urbana-
Champaign,Urbana, IL 61801.
edow@uiuc.edu

Thomas J. Anastasio
Department of Molecular and Integra-
tive Physiology, Center for Biophysics
and Computational Biology,
Beckman Institute
University of Illinois at Urbana-
Champaign, Urbana, IL 61801.
tstasio@uiuc.edu

Abstract

Nystagmus is a pattern of eye movement characterized by smooth rotations of the eye in one direction and rapid rotations in the opposite direction that reset eye position. Periodic alternating nystagmus (PAN) is
a form of uncontrollable nystagmus that has been described as an unstable but amplitude-limited oscillation. PAN has been observed previously only in subjects with vestibulo-cerebellar damage. We describe
results in which PAN can be produced in normal subjects by prolonged
rotation in darkness. We propose a new model in which the neural circuits that control eye movement are inherently unstable, but this instability is kept in check under normal circumstances by the cerebellum.
Circumstances which alter this cerebellar restraint, such as vestibulo-
cerebellar damage or plasticity due to rotation in darkness, can lead to
PAN.

1 INTRODUCTION

Visual perception involves not only an operating visual sensory system, but also the ability to control eye movements. The oculomotor subsystems provide eye movement control. For example, the vestibulo-ocular reflex (VOR) maintains retinal image stability by
making slow-phase eye rotations that counterbalance head rotations, making it possible to
move and see at the same time (Wilson and Melvill Jones, 1979). The VOR makes slow-
phase eye rotations that are directed opposite to head rotations. When these ongoing
slow-phase eye rotations are interrupted by fast-phase eye rotations that reset eye position, the resulting eye movement pattern is called nystagmus. Periodic alternating nys-

tagmus (PAN) is a congenital or acquired eye movement disorder characterized by uncontrollable nystagmus that alternates direction roughly sinusoidally with a period of 200 s to 400 s (Baloh et al., 1976; Leigh et al., 1981; Furman et al., 1990). Furman and colleagues (1990) have determined that PAN in humans is caused by lesions of parts of the vestibulo-cerebellum known as the nodulus and uvula (NU). Lesions to the NU cause PAN in the dark (Waespe et al., 1985; Angelaki and Hess, 1995). NU lesions also prevent habituation (Singleton, 1967; Waespe et al, 1985; Torte et al., 1994), which is a semi-permanent decrease in the gain (eye velocity / head velocity) of the VOR response that can be brought about by prolonged low-frequency rotational stimulation in the dark. Vestibulo-cerebellectomy in habituated goldfish causes VOR dishabituation (Dow and Anastasio, 1996). Temporary inactivation of the vestibulo-cerebellum in habituated goldfish causes temporary dishabituation and can result in a temporary PAN (Dow and Anastasio, in press). Stimulation of the NU temporarily abolish the VOR response (Fernández and Fredrickson, 1964). Cerebellar influence on the VOR may be mediated by connections between the NU and vestibular nucleus neurons, which have been demonstrated in many species (Dow, 1936; 1938).

We have previously shown that intact goldfish habituate to prolonged low-frequency (0.01 Hz) rotation (Dow and Anastasio, 1996) and that rotation at higher frequencies (0.05-0.1 Hz) causes PAN (Dow and Anastasio, 1997). We also proposed a limit-cycle model of PAN in which habituation or PAN result from an increase or decrease, respectively, of the inhibition of the vestibular nuclei by the NU. This model suggested that velocity storage, which functions to increase low-frequency VOR gain above the biophysical limits of the semicircular canals (Robinson, 1977;1981), is mediated by a potentially unstable low-frequency resonance. This instability is normally kept in check by constant suppression by the NU.

2 METHODS

PAN was studied in intact, experimentally naïve, comet goldfish (*carassius auratus*). Each goldfish was restrained horizontally underwater with the head at the center of a cylindrical tank. Eye movements were measured using the magnetic search coil technique (Robinson, 1963). For technical details see Dow and Anastasio (1996). The tank was centered on a horizontal rotating platform. Goldfish were rotated continuously for various durations (30 min to 2 h) in darkness at various single frequencies (0.03 - 0.17 Hz). Some data have been previously reported (Dow and Anastasio, 1997). All stimuli had peak rotational velocities of 60 deg/s. Eye position and rotator (i.e. head) velocity signals were digitized for analysis. Eye position data were digitally differentiated to compute eye velocity and fast-phases were removed. Data were analyzed and simulated using MATLAB and SIMULINK (The Mathworks, Inc.).

3 RESULTS

Prolonged rotation in darkness at frequencies which produced some habituation in naïve goldfish (0.03-0.17 Hz) could produce a lower-frequency oscillation in slow-phase eye velocity that was superimposed on the normal VOR response (fig 1). This lower-frequency oscillation produced a periodic alternating nystagmus (PAN). When PAN occurred, it was roughly sinusoidal and varied in period, amplitude, and onset-time. Habituation could occur simultaneously with PAN (fig 1B) or habituation could completely

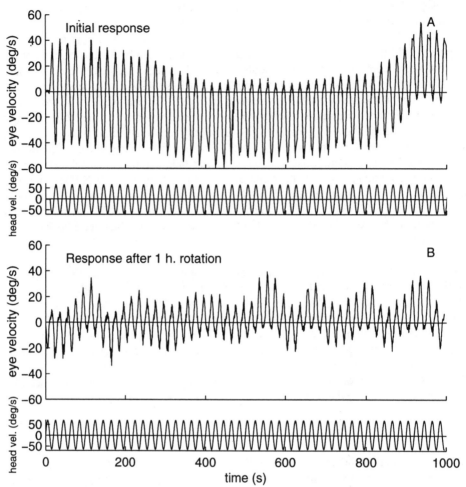

Figure 1: Initial 1000 s 0.05 Hz rotation showing PAN (**A**). Slow-phase
eye velocity shows that PAN starts almost immediately and there is a
slight reduction in VOR gain after 1000 s. Following 1 h continuous rotation in the same goldfish (**B**), VOR gain has decreased.

suppress PAN (fig 4). PAN observed at lower frequencies (0.03 and 0.05 Hz) typically
decreased in amplitude as rotation continued.

Previous work has shown that PAN was most likely to occur during prolonged rotations at
frequencies between 0.05 and 0.1 Hz (Dow and Anastasio, 1997). At these frequencies,
habituation also caused a slight decrease in VOR gain (1.3 to 1.8 times, initial gain / final
gain) following 1 h of rotation. At higher frequencies, neither habituation nor PAN were
observed. At lower frequencies (0.03 Hz) PAN could occur before habituation substantially reduced VOR gain (fig 4). PAN, was not observed in naïve goldfish rotated a lower
frequency (0.01 Hz) where VOR gain fell by 22 times due to habituation (Dow and Anastasio, 1997).

4 MODEL

Previously, a non-linear limit cycle model was constructed by Leigh, Robinson, and Zee (1981; see also Furman, 1989) to simulate PAN in humans. This model included a velocity storage loop with saturation, and a central adaptation loop. This second order system would spontaneously oscillate, producing PAN, if the gain of the velocity storage loop was greater than 1.

We adjusted Robinson's model to simulate rotation inducible PAN and habituation in the goldfish. Input to and output from the model (fig 2) represent head and slow-phase eye velocity, respectively. The time constants of the canal ($s\tau_c/(s\tau_c+1)$) and velocity-storage ($g_s/(s\tau_s+1)$) elements were set to the value of the canal time constant as determined experimentally in goldfish ($\tau_c = \tau_s = 3$ s) (Hartman and Klinke, 1980). The time constant of the central adaptation element ($1/s\tau_a$) was 10 times longer ($\tau_a = 30$ s). The Laplace variable (s) is complex frequency ($s = j\omega$ where j^2 is –1 and ω is frequency in rad/s). The gain of the velocity-storage loop (g_s) is 1.05 while that of the central adaptation loop (g_a) is 1. The central adaptation loop represents in part a negative feedback loop onto vestibular nucleus neurons through inhibitory Purkinje cells of the NU. The vestibulo-cerebellum is known to modulate the gain of the VOR (Wilson and Melvill Jones, 1979). The static nonlinearity in the velocity storage loop consists of a threshold (± 0.0225) and a saturation (± 1.25). The threshold was added to model the decay in PAN following termination of rotation (Dow and Anastasio, 1997), which is not modeled here.

Increases or decreases in the absolute value of g_a will cause VOR habituation or PAN, respectively. However, it was more common for VOR habituation and PAN to occur simultaneously (fig 1B). This behavior could not be reproduced with the lumped model (fig 2). It would be necessary on one hand to increase g_a to decrease overall VOR gain while, on the other hand, decrease g_a to produce PAN. A distributed system would address this problem, with multiple parallel pathways, each having velocity-storage and adaptive control through the NU. The idea can be illustrated using the simplest distributed system which has 2 lumped models in parallel (not shown), each having an independently adjustable g_a. The results from such a two parallel pathway model are shown in fig 3. In one pathway, g_a(h) was increased to model habituation, and g_a(o) was decreased to start oscillations. Paradoxically, although the ultimate effect of increasing g_a(h) is to decrease VOR gain, the initial effect as g_a(h) is increased is to increase gain. This is due to the resonant frequency of the system continuously shifting to higher frequencies and temporarily matching the frequency of rotation (see DISCUSSION). Conversely, when g_a(o) is decreased, there is a temporary decrease in gain as the resonant frequency moves away from the frequency of rotation. The two results are combined after the gain is reduced by half (fig 3B).

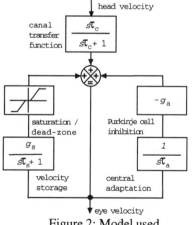

Figure 2: Model used to simulation PAN (Dow and Anastasio 1997). Used with permission.

The combined result shows a continual decrease in VOR gain with the oscillations superimposed.

5 DISCUSSION

If the nonlinearities (i.e. threshold and saturation) in the model are ignored, linear analysis shows that the model will be unstable when $[(1-g_s)/\tau_s + g_a/\tau_a]$ is negative, and will oscillate with a period of $[2\pi\sqrt{(\tau_s\tau_a/g_a)}]$. With the initial parameters, the model is stable because the central adaptation loop can compensate for the unstable gain of the velocity storage loop. The natural frequency of the system, calculated from the above equation, is 0.017 Hz. This resonance, which peaks at the resonant frequency but is still pronounced at nearby frequencies, produces an enhancement of the VOR response. The hypothesis that low frequency VOR gain enhancement is produced by a potentially unstable resonance is a novel feature of our model. The natural frequency increases with increases in g_a and can alter the frequency specific enhancement.

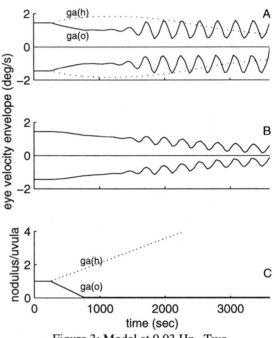

Figure 3: Model at 0.03 Hz. Two simulations with differing values of g_a (A) are combined in (B) with the values of g_a in (C).

Decreases in g_a, in addition to decreasing the natural frequency, also cause the model to become unstable. (If g_a is reduced to zero, the model becomes first order and the equations are no longer valid). The ability to get either habituation or PAN by varying only one parameter suggests that habituation and PAN are a related phenomena

Through the process of habituation, prolonged low frequency rotation (0.01 Hz) in goldfish severely decreased VOR gain, often abruptly and unilaterally (Dow and Anastasio, in press). The decrease in gain due to habituation can effectively eliminate PAN at the lowest frequency at which PAN was observed (0.03 Hz) as shown in fig 4. In this example the naïve VOR responds symmetrically for the first cycle of rotation. It then becomes markedly asymmetrical, with a strong, unilateral response in one direction for ~10 cycles followed by another in the opposite direction for ~17 cycles. The VOR response abruptly habituates after that with no PAN. Complete habituation can be simulated by further increases in the value of g_a in the limit-cycle model (fig 2). Unilateral habituation has been simulated previously with a bilateral network model of the VOR in which the cerebellum inhibits the vestibular nuclei unilaterally (Dow and Anastasio, in press).

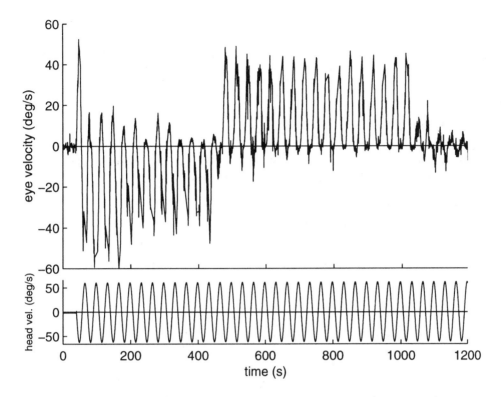

Figure 4: PAN superimposed on the VOR response to continuous rotation
at 0.03 Hz. Upper trace, slow-phase eye velocity (fast phases removed);
lower trace, head velocity (not to scale).

The cerebellum has several circuits which could provide an increase in firing rate of some
Purkinje cells with a concurrent decrease in the firing rate of other Purkinje cells sug-
gested by the model. There are many lateral inhibitory pathways including inhibition of
Purkinje cells to neighboring Purkinje cells (Llinás and Walton, 1990). Therefore, if one
Purkinje cell were to increase its firing rate, this circuitry suggests that neighboring
Purkinje cells would decrease their firing rates. Also, experimental evidence shows that
during habituation, not all vestibular nuclei gradually decrease their firing rate as might be
expected. Kileny and colleagues (1980) recorded from vestibular nucleus neurons during
habituation. They could divide the neurons into 3 roughly equal groups based on response over time: continual decrease, constant followed by a decrease, and increase followed by decrease. The cerebellar circuitry and the single-unit recording data support
multiple, variable levels of inhibition from the NU. How this mechanism may work is
being explored with a more biologically realistic distributed model.

6 CONCLUSION

Our experimental results are consistent with a multi-parallel pathway model of the VOR.
In each pathway an unstable, positive velocity-storage loop is stabilized by an inhibitory,
central adaptation loop, and their interaction produces a low-frequency resonance that
enhances the low-frequency response of the VOR. Prolonged rotation at specific frequencies could produce a decrease in central adaptation VOR gain in some pathways resulting in an unstable, low-frequency oscillation resembling PAN in these pathways. An

increase in adaptation loop gain in the other pathways would result in a decrease in VOR gain resembling habituation. The sum over the VOR pathways would show PAN and habituation occurring together. We suggest that resonance enhancement and multiple parallel (i.e. distributed) pathways are necessary to model the interrelationship between PAN and habituation.

Acknowledgments

The work was supported by grant MH50577 from the National Institutes of Health. We thank M. Zelaya and X. Feng for experimental assistance.

References

Angelaki DE and Hess BJM. *J Neurophysl* **73** 1729-1751 (1995).

Baloh RW, Honrubia V and Konrad HR. *Brain* **99** 11-26 (1976).

Dow ER and Anastasio TJ. *NeuroReport* **7** 1305-1309 (1996).

Dow ER and Anastasio TJ. NeuroReport **8** 2755-2759 (1997).

Dow ER and Anastasio TJ. *J. Computat. Neuro.* in press.

Dow RS. *J Comp Neurol* **63** 527-548 (1936).

Dow RS. *J Comp Neurol* **68** 297-305 (1938).

Fernández C and Fredrickson JM. *Acta Otolaryngol Suppl* **192** 52-62 (1964).

Furman JMR, Wall C and Pang D. *Brain* **113** 1425-1439 (1990).

Furman JMR, Hain TC and Paige GD. *Biol Cybern* **61** 255-264 (1989).

Hartmann R and Klinke R. *Pflugers Archiv* **388** 111-121 (1980).

Kileny P, Ryu JH, McCabe BF and Abbas PJ. *Acta Otolaryngol* **90** 175-183 (1980).

Leigh RJ, Robinson DA and Zee DS. *Ann NY Acad Sci* **374** 619-635 (1981).

Llinás RR and Walton KD. Cerebellum. In: Shepherd GM ed. *The Synaptic Organization of the Brain.* Oxford: Oxford University Press, 1990: 214-245.

Remmel RS. *IEEE Trans Biomed Eng* **31** 388-390 (1984).

Robinson DA. *IEEE Trans Biomed Eng* **10** 137-145 (1963).

Robinson DA. *Exp Brain Res* **30** 447-450 (1977).

Robinson DA. *Ann Rev Neurosci* **4** 463-503 (1981).

Singleton GT. *Laryngoscope* **77** 1579-1620 (1967).

Torte MP, Courjon JH, Flandrin JM, et al. *Exp Brain Res* **99** 441-454 (1994).

Waespe W, Cohen B and Raphan T. *Science* **228** 199-202 (1985).

Wilson V and Melvill Jones G. *Mammalian Vestibular Physiology,* New York: Plenum Press, 1979.

Hippocampal Model of Rat Spatial Abilities Using Temporal Difference Learning

David J Foster*
Centre for Neuroscience
Edinburgh University

Richard GM Morris
Centre for Neuroscience
Edinburgh University

Peter Dayan
E25-210, MIT
Cambridge, MA 02139

Abstract

We provide a model of the standard watermaze task, and of a more challenging task involving novel platform locations, in which rats exhibit one-trial learning after a few days of training. The model uses hippocampal place cells to support reinforcement learning, and also, in an integrated manner, to build and use allocentric *coordinates*.

1 INTRODUCTION

Whilst it has long been known both that the hippocampus of the rat is needed for normal performance on spatial tasks[13, 11] and that certain cells in the hippocampus exhibit place-related firing,[12] it has not been clear how place cells are actually used for navigation. One of the principal conceptual problems has been understanding how the hippocampus could specify or learn paths to goals when spatially tuned cells in the hippocampus respond only on the basis of the rat's current location. This work uses recent ideas from reinforcement learning to solve this problem in the context of two rodent spatial learning results.

Reference memory in the watermaze[11] (RMW) has been a key task demonstrating the importance of the hippocampus for spatial learning. On each trial, the rat is placed in a circular pool of cloudy water, the only escape from which is a platform which is hidden (below the water surface) but which remains in a constant position. A random choice of starting position is used for each trial. Rats take asymptotically short paths after approximately 10 trials (see figure 1 a). Delayed match-to-place (DMP) learning is a refined version in which the platform's location is changed on each day. Figure 1b shows escape latencies for rats given four trials per day for nine days, with the platform in a novel position on each day. On early days, acquisition

---

*Crichton Street, Edinburgh EH8 9LE, United Kingdom. Funded by Edin. Univ. Holdsworth Scholarship, the McDonnell-Pew foundation and NSF grant IBN-9634339. Email: djf@cfn.ed.ac.uk

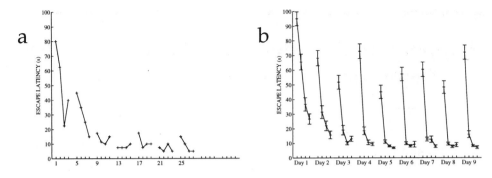

Figure 1: a) Latencies for rats on the reference memory in the watermaze (RMW) task (N=8). b) Latencies for rats on the Delayed Match-to-Place (DMP) task (N=62).

is gradual but on later days, rats show one-trial learning, that is, near asymptotic performance on the second trial to a novel platform position.

The RMW task has been extensively modelled.[6, 4, 5, 20] By contrast, the DMP task is new and computationally more challenging. It is solved here by integrating a standard actor-critic reinforcement learning system[2, 7] which guarantees that the rat will be competent to perform well in arbitrary mazes, with a system that learns spatial *coordinates* in the maze. Temporal difference learning[17] (TD) is used for actor, critic *and* coordinate learning. TD learning is attractive because of its generality for arbitrary Markov decision problems and the fact that reward systems in vertebrates appear to instantiate it.[14]

2 THE MODEL

The model comprises two distinct networks (figure 2): the actor-critic network and a coordinate learning network. The contribution of the hippocampus, for both networks, is to provide a state-space representation in the form of place cell basis functions. Note that only the activities of place cells are required, by contrast with decoding schemes which require detailed information about each place cell.[4]

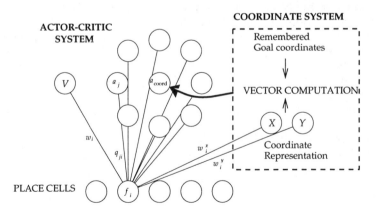

Figure 2: Model diagram showing the interaction between actor-critic and coordinate system components.

2.1 Actor-Critic Learning

Place cells are modelled as being tuned to location. At position $\mathbf{p}$, place cell i has an output given by $f_i(\mathbf{p}) = \exp\{-||\mathbf{p} - \mathbf{s}_i||^2/2\sigma^2\}$, where $\mathbf{s}_i$ is the place field centre, and $\sigma = 0.1$ for all place fields. The critic learns a value function $\hat{V}(\mathbf{p}) = \sum_i w_i f_i(\mathbf{p})$ which comes to represent the distance of $\mathbf{p}$ from the goal, using the TD rule $\Delta w_i^t \propto \delta^t f_i(\mathbf{p}^t)$, where

$$\delta^t = r(\mathbf{p}^t, \mathbf{p}^{t+1}) + \gamma \hat{V}(\mathbf{p}^{t+1}) - \hat{V}(\mathbf{p}^t) \tag{1}$$

is the TD error, $\mathbf{p}^t$ is position at time t, and the reward $r(\mathbf{p}^t, \mathbf{p}^{t+1})$ is 1 for any move onto the platform, and 0 otherwise. In a slight alteration of the original rule, the value $V(\mathbf{p})$ is set to zero when $\mathbf{p}$ is *at* the goal, thus ensuring that the total future rewards for moving onto the goal will be exactly 1. Such a modification improves stability in the case of TD learning with overlapping basis functions. The discount factor, γ, was set to 0.99. Simultaneously the rat refines a policy, which is represented by eight action cells. Each action cell (a_j in figure 2) receives a parameterised input at any position $\mathbf{p}$: $a_j(\mathbf{p}) = \sum_i q_{ji} f_i(\mathbf{p})$. An action is chosen stochastically with probabilities given by $P(a_j) = \exp\{2a_j\}/\sum_k \exp\{2a_k\}$. Action weights are reinforced according to:[2]

$$\Delta q_{ji}^t \propto \delta^t f_i(\mathbf{p}^t) g_j(\theta^t) \tag{2}$$

where $g_j(\theta^t)$ is a gaussian function of the difference between the head direction θ^t at time t and the preferred direction of the jth action cell. Figure 3 shows the development of a policy over a few trials.

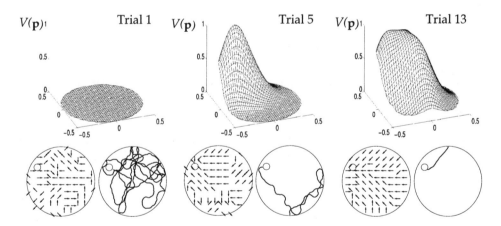

Figure 3: The RMW task: the value function gradually disseminates information about reward proximity to all regions of the environment. Policies and paths are also shown.

There is no analytical guarantee for the convergence of TD learning with policy adaptation. However our simulations show that the algorithm always converges for the RMW task. In a simulated arena of diameter 1m and with swimming speeds of 20cm/s, the simulation matched the performance of the real rats very closely (see figure 5). This demonstrates that TD-based reinforcement learning is adequately fast to account for the learning performance of real animals.

2.2 Coordinate Learning

Although the learning of a value function and policy is appropriate for finding a fixed platform, the actor-critic model does not allow the transfer of knowledge from the task defined by one goal position to that defined by any other; thus it could not generate the sort of one-trial learning that is shown by rats on the DMP task (see figure 1b). This requires acquisition of some goal-independent knowledge about space. A natural mechanism for this is the path integration or self-motion system.[20, 10] However, path integration presents two problems. First, since the rat is put into the maze in a different position for each trial, how can it learn *consistent* coordinates across the whole maze? Second, how can a general, powerful, but slow, behavioral learning mechanism such as TD be integrated with a specific, limited, but fast learning mechanism involving spatial coordinates?

Since TD critic learning is based on enforcing consistency in estimates of future reward, we can also use it to learn spatially consistent coordinates on the basis of samples of self-motion. It is assumed that the rat has an allocentric frame of reference.[18] The model learns parameterised estimates of the x and y coordinates of all positions $\mathbf{p}$: $x(\mathbf{p}) = \sum_i w_i^x f_i(\mathbf{p})$ and $y(\mathbf{p}) = \sum_i w_i^y f_i(\mathbf{p})$. Importantly, while place cells were again critical in supporting spatial representation, *they do not embody a map of space*. The coordinate functions, like the value function previously, have to be learned.

As the simulated rat moves around, the coordinate weights $\{w_i^x\}$ are adjusted according to:

$$\Delta w_i^x \propto \left(\Delta \hat{x}^t + \hat{X}(\mathbf{p}^{t+1}) - \hat{X}(\mathbf{p}^t)\right) \sum_{k=1}^{t} \lambda^{t-k} f_i(\mathbf{p}^k) \tag{3}$$

where $\Delta \hat{x}_t$ is the self-motion estimate in the x direction. A similar update is applied to $\{w_i^y\}$. In this case, the full TD(λ) algorithm was used (with $\lambda = 0.9$); however TD(0) could also have been used, taking slightly longer. Figure 4a shows the x and y coordinates at early and late phases of learning. It is apparent that they rapidly become quite accurate – this is an extremely easy task in an open field maze.

An important issue in the learning of coordinates is *drift*, since the coordinate system receives no direct information about the location of the origin. It turns out that the three controlling factors over the implicit origin are: the boundary of the arena, the prior setting of the coordinate weights (in this case all were zero) and the position and prior value of any absorbing area (in this case the platform). If the coordinate system as a whole were to drift once coordinates have been established, this would invalidate coordinates that have been remembered by the rat over long periods. However, since the expected value of the prediction error at time steps should be zero for any self-consistent coordinate mapping, such a mapping should remain stable. This is demonstrated for a single run: figure 4b shows the mean value of coordinates x evolving over trials, with little drift after the first few trials.

We modeled the coordinate system as influencing the choice of swimming direction in the manner of an abstract action.[15] The (internally specified) coordinates of the most recent goal position are stored in short term memory and used, along with the current coordinates, to calculate a vector heading. This vector heading is thrown into the stochastic competition with the other possible actions, governed by a single weight which changes in a similar manner to the other action weights (as in equation 2, see also fig 4d), depending on the TD error, and on the angular proximity of the current head direction to the coordinate direction. Thus, whether the the coordinate-based direction is likely to be used depends upon its past performance.

One simplification in the model is the treatment of extinction. In the DMP task,

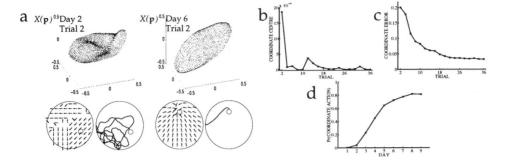

Figure 4: The evolution of the coordinate system for a typical simulation run: a.) coordinate outputs at early and late phases of learning, b.) the extent of drift in the coordinates, as shown by the mean coordinate value for a single run, c.) a measure of coordinate error for the same run $\hat{\sigma}_E^2 = \dfrac{\sum_r \sum_k \{\hat{X}_r(\mathbf{p}_k) - \bar{X}_r - X(\mathbf{p}_k)\}^2}{(N_p - 1)N_r}$, where k indexes measurement points (max N_p) and r indexes runs (max N_r), $X_r(\mathbf{p}_k)$ is the model estimate of X at position $\mathbf{p}_k$, $X(\mathbf{p}_k)$ is the ideal estimate for a coordinate system centred on zero, and $\bar{X}_r$ is the mean value over all the model coordinates, d.) the increase during training of the probability of choosing the abstract action. This demonstrates the integration of the coordinates into the control system.

real rats extinguish to a platform that has moved fairly quickly whereas the actor-critic model extinguishes far more slowly. To get around this, when a simulated rat reaches a goal that has just been moved, the value and action weights are reinitialised, but the coordinate weights w_i^x and w_i^y, and the weights for the abstract action, are not.

3   RESULTS

The main results of this paper are the replication by simulation of rat performance on the RMW and DMP tasks. Figures 1a and b show the course of learning for the rats; figures 5a and b for the model. For the DMP task, one-shot acquisition is apparent by the end of training.

4   DISCUSSION

We have built a model for one-trial spatial learning in the watermaze which uses a single TD learning algorithm in two separate systems. One system is based on a reinforcement learning that can solve general Markovian decision problems, and the other is based on coordinate learning and is specialised for an open-field water maze. Place cells in the hippocampus offer an excellent substrate for learning the actor, the critic and the coordinates.

The model is explicit about the relationship between the general and specific learning systems, and the learning behavior shows that they integrate seamlessly. As currently constituted, the coordinate system would fail if there were a barrier in the maze. We plan to extend the model to allow the coordinate system to specify abstract targets other than the most recent platform position – this could allow it fast navigation around a larger class of environments. It is also important to improve the model of learning 'set' behavior – the information about the nature of

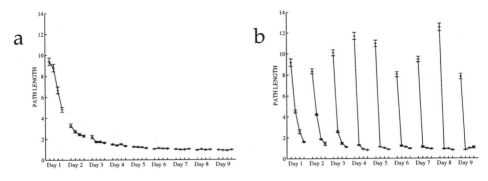

Figure 5: a.) Performance of the actor-critic model on the RMW task, and b.) performance of the full model on the DMP task. The data for comparison is shown in figures 1a and b.

the DMP task that the rats acquire over the course of the first few days of training. Interestingly, learning set is incomplete – on the first trial of each day, the rats still aim for the platform position on the previous day, even though this is never correct.[16] The significant differences in the path lengths on the first trial of each day (evidence in figure 1b and figure 5b) come from the relative placements of the platforms. However, the model did not use the same positions as the empirical data, and, in any case, the model of exploration behavior is rather simplistic.

The model demonstrates that reinforcement learning methods are perfectly fast enough to match empirical learning curves. This is fortunate, since, unlike most models specifically designed for open-field navigation,[6, 4, 5, 20] RL methods can provably cope with substantially more complicated tasks with arbitrary barriers, *etc*, since they solve the temporal credit assignment problem in its full generality. The model also addresses the problem that coordinates in different parts of the same environment need to be mutually consistent, even if the animal only experiences some parts on separate trials. An important property of the model is that there is no requirement for the animal to have any explicit knowledge of the relationship between different place cells or place field position, size or shape. Such a requirement is imposed in various models.[9, 4, 6, 20]

Experiments that are suggested by this model (as well as by certain others) concern the relationship between hippocampally dependent and independent spatial learning. First, once the coordinate system has been acquired, we predict that merely placing the rat at a new location would be enough to let it find the platform in one shot, though it might be necessary to reinforce the placement e.g. by first placing the rat in a bucket of cold water. Second, we know that the establishment of place fields in an environment happens substantially faster than establishment of one-shot or even ordinary learning to a platform.[23] We predict that blocking plasticity in the hippocampus *following* the establishment of place cells (possibly achieved without a platform) would *not* block learning of a platform. In fact, new experiments show that after extensive pre-training, rats can perform one-trial learning in the same environment to new platform positions on the DMP task without hippocampal synaptic plasticity.[16] This is in contrast to the effects of hippocampal lesion, which completely disrupts performance. According to the model, coordinates will have been learned during pre-training. The full prediction remains untested: that once place fields have been established, coordinates could be learned in the absence of hippocampal synaptic plasticity. A third prediction follows from evidence that rats with restricted hippocampal lesions can learn the fixed platform task, but much more slowly, based on a gradual "shaping" procedure.[22] In our model, they may also be able to learn coordinates. However, a lengthy training procedure could be required, and testing might be complicated if expressing the knowledge required the use of hippocampus dependent short-term memory for the last platform location.[16]

One way of expressing the contribution of the hippocampus in the model is to say that its function is to provide a behavioural state space for the solution of complex tasks. Hence the contribution of the hippocampus to navigation is to provide place cells whose firing properties remain consistent in a given environment. It follows that in different behavioural situations, hippocampal cells should provide a representation based on something other than locations — and, indeed, there is evidence for this.[8] With regard to the role of the hippocampus in spatial tasks, the model demonstrates that the hippocampus may be fundamentally necessary without embodying a map.

References

[1] Barto, AG & Sutton, RS (1981) *Biol. Cyber.*, **43**:1-8.

[2] Barto, AG, Sutton, RS & Anderson, CW (1983) *IEEE Trans. on Systems, Man and Cybernetics* **13**:834-846.

[3] Barto, AG, Sutton, RS & Watkins, CJCH (1989) *Tech Report 89-95*, CAIS, Univ. Mass., Amherst, MA.

[4] Blum, KI & Abbott, LF (1996) *Neural Computation*, **8**:85-93.

[5] Brown, MA & Sharp, PE (1995) *Hippocampus* **5**:171-188.

[6] Burgess, N, Recce, M & O'Keefe, J (1994) *Neural Networks*, **7**:1065-1081.

[7] Dayan, P (1991) *NIPS 3*, RP Lippmann et al, eds., 464-470.

[8] Eichenbaum, HB (1996) *Curr. Opin. Neurobiol.*, **6**:187-195.

[9] Gerstner, W & Abbott, LF (1996) *J. Computational Neurosci.* **4**:79-94.

[10] McNaughton, BL et al (1996) *J. Exp. Biol.*, **199**:173-185.

[11] Morris, RGM et al (1982) *Nature*, **297**:681-683.

[12] O'Keefe, J & Dostrovsky, J (1971) *Brain Res.*, **34**(171).

[13] Olton, DS & Samuelson, RJ (1976) *J. Exp. Psych: A.B.P.*, **2**:97-116.
Rudy, JW & Sutherland, RW (1995) *Hippocampus*, **5**:375-389.

[14] Schultz, W, Dayan, P & Montague, PR (1997) *Science*, **275**, 1593-1599.

[15] Singh, SP Reinforcement learning with a hierarchy of abstract models.

[16] Steele, RJ & Morris, RGM *in preparation*.

[17] Sutton, RS (1988) *Machine Learning*, **3**:9-44.

[18] Taube, JS (1995) *J. Neurosci.* **15**(1):70-86.

[19] Tsitsiklis, JN & Van Roy, B (1996) *Tech Report LIDS-P-2322*, M.I.T.

[20] Wan, HS, Touretzky, DS & Redish, AD (1993) *Proc. 1993 Connectionist Models Summer School*, Lawrence Erlbaum, 11-19.

[21] Watkins, CJCH (1989) PhD Thesis, Cambridge.

[22] Whishaw, IQ & Jarrard, LF (1996) *Hippocampus*

[23] Wilson, MA & McNaughton, BL (1993) *Science* **261**:1055-1058.

Gradients for retinotectal mapping

Geoffrey J. Goodhill
Georgetown Institute for Cognitive and Computational Sciences
Georgetown University Medical Center
3970 Reservoir Road
Washington DC 20007
geoff@giccs.georgetown.edu

Abstract

The initial activity-independent formation of a topographic map in the retinotectal system has long been thought to rely on the matching of molecular cues expressed in gradients in the retina and the tectum. However, direct experimental evidence for the existence of such gradients has only emerged since 1995. The new data has provoked the discussion of a new set of models in the experimental literature. Here, the capabilities of these models are analyzed, and the gradient shapes they predict in vivo are derived.

1   Introduction

During the early development of the visual system in for instance rats, fish and chickens, retinal axons grow across the surface of the optic tectum and establish connections so as to form an ordered map. Although later neural activity refines the map, it is not required to set up the initial topography (for reviews see Udin & Fawcett (1988); Goodhill (1992)). A long-standing idea is that the initial topography is formed by matching gradients of receptor expression in the retina with gradients of ligand expression in the tectum (Sperry, 1963). Particular versions of this idea have been formalized in theoretical models such as those of Prestige & Willshaw (1975), Willshaw & von der Malsburg (1979), Whitelaw & Cowan (1981), and Gierer (1983;1987). However, these models were developed in the absence of any direct experimental evidence for the existence of the necessary gradients. Since 1995, major breakthroughs have occurred in this regard in the experimental literature. These center around the Eph (Erythropoetin-producing hepatocellular) subfamily of receptor tyrosine kinases. Eph receptors and their ligands have been shown to be expressed in gradients in the developing retina and tectum respectively, and to play a role in guiding axons to appropriate positions. These exciting new developments have led experimentalists to discuss theoretical models different from those previously proposed (e.g. Tessier-Lavigne (1995); Tessier-Lavigne & Goodman (1996); Nakamoto et al, (1996)). However, the mathematical consequences of these new models, for instance the precise gradient shapes they require, have not been analyzed. In this paper, it is shown that only certain combinations of gradients produce appropriate maps in these models, and that the validity of these models is therefore experimentally testable.

2 Recent experimental data

Receptor tyrosine kinases are a diverse class of membrane-spanning proteins. The Eph subfamily is the largest, with over a dozen members. Since 1990, many of the genes encoding Eph receptors and their ligands have been shown to be expressed in the developing brain (reviewed in Friedman & O'Leary, 1996). Ephrins, the ligands for Eph receptors, are all membrane anchored. This is unlike the majority of receptor tyrosine kinase ligands, which are usually soluble. The ephrins can be separated into two distinct groups A and B, based on the type of membrane anchor. These two groups bind to distinct sets of Eph receptors, which are thus also called A and B, though receptor-ligand interaction is promiscuous within each subgroup. Since many research groups discovered members of the Eph family independently, each member originally had several names. However a new standardized notation was recently introduced (Eph Nomenclature Committee, 1997), which is used in this paper.

With regard to the mapping from the nasal-temporal axis of the retina to the anterior-posterior axis of the tectum (figure 1), recent studies have shown the following (see Friedman & O'Leary (1996) and Tessier-Lavigne & Goodman (1996) for reviews).

- EphA3 is expressed in an increasing nasal to temporal gradient in the retina (Cheng et al, 1995).

- EphA4 is expressed uniformly in the retina (Holash & Pasquale, 1995).

- Ephrin-A2, a ligand of both EphA3 and EphA4, is expressed in an increasing rostral to caudal gradient in the tectum (Cheng et al, 1995).

- Ephrin-A5, another ligand of EphA3 and EphA4, is also expressed in an increasing rostral to caudal gradient in the tectum, but at very low levels in the rostral half of the tectum (Drescher et al, 1995).

All of these interactions are *repulsive*. With regard to mapping along the complementary dimensions, EphB2 is expressed in a high ventral to low dorsal gradient in the retina, while its ligand ephrin-B1 is expressed in a high dorsal to low ventral gradient in the tectum (Braisted et al, 1997). Members of the Eph family are also beginning to be implicated in the formation of topographic projections between many other pairs of structures in the brain (Renping Zhou, personal communication). For instance, EphA5 has been found in an increasing lateral to medial gradient in the hippocampus, and ephrin-A2 in an increasing dorsal to ventral gradient in the septum, consistent with a role in establishing the topography of the map between hippocampus and septum (Gao et al, 1996).

The current paper focusses just on the paradigm case of the nasal-temporal to anterior-posterior axis of the retinotectal mapping. Actual gradient shapes in this system have not yet been quantified. The analysis below will assume that certain gradients are linear, and derive the consequences for the other gradients.

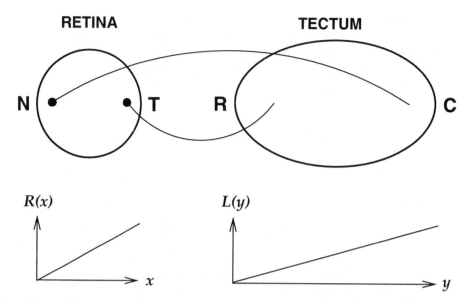

Figure 1: This shows the mapping that is normally set up from the retina to the tectum. Distance along the nasal-temporal axis of the retina is referred to as x and receptor concentration as $R(x)$. Distance along the rostral-caudal axis of the tectum is referred to as y and ligand concentration as $L(y)$.

3 Mathematical models

Let R be the concentration of a receptor expressed on a growth cone or axon, and L the concentration of a ligand present in the tectum. Refer to position along the nasal-temporal axis of the retina as x, and position along the rostral-caudal axis of the tectum as y, so that $R = R(x)$ and $L = L(y)$ (see figure 1). Gierer (1983; 1987) discusses how topographic information could be signaled by interactions between ligands and receptors. A particular type of interaction, proposed by Nakamoto et al (1996), is that the concentration of a "topographic signal", the signal that tells axons where to stop, is related to the concentration of receptor and ligand by the law of mass action:

$$G(x, y) = kR(x)L(y) \tag{1}$$

where $G(x, y)$ is the concentration of topographic signal produced within an axon originating from position x in the retina when it is at position y in the tectum, and k is a constant. In the general case of multiple receptors and ligands, with promiscuous interactions between them, this equation becomes

$$G(x, y) = \sum_{i,j} k_{ij} R_i(x) L_j(y) \tag{2}$$

Whether each receptor-ligand interaction is attractive or repulsive is taken care of by the sign of the relevant k_{ij}.

Two possibilities for how $G(x, y)$ might produce a stop (or branch) signal in the growth cone (or axon) are that this occurs when (1) a "set point" is reached (discussed in, for example, Tessier-Lavigne & Goodman (1996); Nakamoto et al (1996)) , i.e. $G(x, y) = c$ where c is a constant, or (2) attraction (or repulsion) reaches a local maximum (or minimum), i.e. $\frac{\partial G(x,y)}{\partial y} = 0$ (Gierer, 1983; 1987). For a smooth, uniform mapping, one of these conditions must hold along a line $y \propto x$. For simplicity assume the constant of proportionality is unity.

3.1 Set point rule

For one gradient in the retina and one gradient in the tectum (i.e. equation 1), this requires that the ligand gradient be inversely proportional to the receptor gradient:

$$L(x) = \frac{c}{R(x)}$$

If $R(x)$ is linear (c.f. the gradient of EphA3 in the retina), the ligand concentration is required to go to infinity at one end of the tectum (see figure 2). One way round this is to assume $R(x)$ does not go to zero at $x = 0$: the experimental data is not precise enough to decide on this point. However, the addition of a second receptor gradient gives

$$L(x) = \frac{c}{k_1 R_1(x) + k_2 R_2(x)}$$

If $R_1(x)$ is linear and $R_2(x)$ is flat (c.f. the gradient of EphA4 in the retina), then $L(y)$ is no longer required to go to infinity (see figure 2). For two receptor and two ligand gradients many combinations of gradient shapes are possible. As a special case, consider $R_1(x)$ linear, $R_2(x)$ flat, and $L_1(y)$ linear (c.f. the gradient of Elf1 in the tectum). Then L_2 is required to have the shape

$$L_2(y) = \frac{ay^2 + by}{dy + e}$$

where a, b, d, e are constants. This shape depends on the values of the constants, which depend on the relative strengths of binding between the different receptor and ligand combinations. An interesting case is where R_1 binds only to L_1 and R_2 binds only to L_2, i.e. there is no promiscuity. In this case we have

$$L_2(y) \propto y^2$$

(see figure 2). This function somewhat resembles the shape of the gradient that has been reported for ephrin-A5 in the tectum. However, this model requires one gradient to be attractive, whereas both are repulsive.

3.2 Local optimum rule

For one retinal and one tectal gradient we have the requirement

$$R(x) \frac{\partial L(y)}{\partial y} = 0$$

This is not generally true along the line $y = x$, therefore there is no map. The same problem arises with two receptor gradients, whatever their shapes. For two receptor and two ligand gradients many combinations of gradient shapes are possible. (Gierer (1983; 1987) investigated this case, but for a more complicated reaction law for generating the topographic signal than mass action.) For the special case introduced above, $L_2(y)$ is required to have the shape

$$L_2(y) = ay + b\log(dy + e) + f$$

where a, b, d, e, and f are constants as before. Considering the case of no promiscuity, we again obtain

$$L_2(y) \propto y^2$$

i.e. the same shape for $L_2(y)$ as that specified by the set point rule.

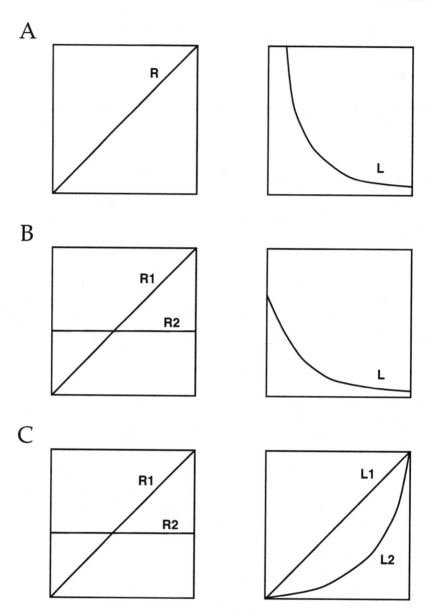

Figure 2: Three combinations of gradient shapes that are sufficient to produce a smooth mapping with the mass action rule. In the left column the horizontal axis is position in the retina while the vertical axis is the concentration of receptor. In the right column the horizontal axis is position in the tectum while the vertical axis is the concentration of ligand. Models A and B work with the set point but not the local optimum rule, while model C works with both rules. For models B and C, one gradient is negative and the other positive.

4 Discussion

For both rules, there is a set of gradient shapes for the mass-action model that is consistent with the experimental data, except for the fact that they require one gradient in the tectum to be attractive. Both ephrin-A2 and ephrin-A5 have repulsive effects on their receptors expressed in the retina, which is clearly a problem for these models. The local optimum rule is more restrictive than the set point rule, since it requires at least two ligand gradients in the tectum. However, unlike the set point rule, it supplies directional information (in terms of an appropriate gradient for the topographic signal) when the axon is not at the optimal location.

In conclusion, models based on the mass action assumption in conjunction with either a "set point" or "local optimum" rule can be true only if the relevant gradients satisfy the quantitative relationships described above. A different theoretical approach, which analyzes gradients in terms of their ability to guide axons over the maximum possible distance, also makes predictions about gradient shapes in the retinotectal system (Goodhill & Baier, 1998). Advances in experimental technique should enable a more quantitative analysis of the gradients in situ to be performed shortly, allowing these predictions to be tested. In addition, analysis of particular Eph and ephrin knockout mice (for instance ephrin-A5 (Yates et al, 1997)) is now being performed, which should shed light on the role of these gradients in normal map development.

Bibliography

Braisted, J.E., McLaughlin, T., Wang, H.U., Friedman, G.C., Anderson, D.J. & O'Leary, D.D.M. (1997). Graded and lamina-specific distributions of ligands of EphB receptor tyrosine kinases in the developing retinotectal system. *Developmental Biology*, **191** 14-28.

Cheng, H.J., Nakamoto, M., Bergemann, A.D & Flanagan, J.G. (1995). Complementary gradients in expression and binding of Elf-1 and Mek4 in development of the topographic retinotectal projection map. *Cell*, **82**, 371-381.

Drescher, U., Kremoser, C., Handwerker, C., Loschinger, J., Noda, M. & Bonhoeffer, F. (1995). In-vitro guidance of retinal ganglion-cell axons by RAGS, a 25 KDa tectal protein related to ligands for Eph receptor tyrosine kinases. *Cell*, **82**, 359-370.

Eph Nomenclature Committee (1997). Unified nomenclature for Eph family receptors and their ligands, the ephrins. *Cell*, **90**, 403-404.

Friedman, G.C. & O'Leary, D.D.M. (1996). Eph receptor tyrosine kinases and their ligands in neural development. *Curr. Opin. Neurobiol.*, **6**, 127-133.

Gierer, A. (1983). Model for the retinotectal projection. *Proc. Roy. Soc. Lond. B*, **218**, 77-93.

Gierer, A. (1987). Directional cues for growing axons forming the retinotectal projection. *Development*, **101**, 479-489.

Gao, P.-P., Zhang, J.-H., Yokoyama, M., Racey, B., Dreyfus, C.F., Black, I.B. & Zhou, R. (1996). Regulation of topographic projection in the brain: Elf-1 in the hippocampalseptal system. *Proc. Nat. Acad. Sci. USA*, **93**, 11161-11166.

Goodhill, G.J. (1992). *Correlations, Competition and Optimality: Modelling the Development of Topography and Ocular Dominance*. Cognitive Science Research Paper CSRP 226, University of Sussex. Available from www.giccs.georgetown.edu/~geoff

Goodhill, G.J. & Baier, H. (1998). Axon guidance: stretching gradients to the limit. *Neural Computation*, in press.

Holash, J.A. & Pasquale, E.B. (1995). Polarized expression of the receptor protein-tyrosine kinase Cek5 in the developing avian visual system. *Developmental Biology*, **172**, 683-693.

Nakamoto, M., Cheng H.J., Friedman, G.C., Mclaughlin, T., Hansen, M.J., Yoon, C.H., O'Leary, D.D.M. & Flanagan, J.G. (1996). Topographically specific effects of ELF-1 on retinal axon guidance in-vitro and retinal axon mapping in-vivo. *Cell*, **86**, 755-766.

Prestige, M.C. & Willshaw, D.J. (1975). On a role for competition in the formation of patterned neural connexions. *Proc. R. Soc. Lond. B*, **190**, 77-98.

Sperry, R.W. (1963). Chemoaffinity in the orderly growth of nerve fiber patterns and connections. *Proc. Nat. Acad. Sci., U.S.A.*, **50**, 703-710.

Tessier-Lavigne, M. (1995). Eph receptor tyrosine kinases, axon repulsion, and the development of topographic maps. *Cell*, **82**, 345-348.

Tessier-Lavigne, M. and Goodman, C.S. (1996). The molecular biology of axon guidance. *Science*, **274**, 1123-1133.

Udin, S.B. & Fawcett, J.W. (1988). Formation of topographic maps. *Ann. Rev. Neurosci.*, **11**, 289-327.

Whitelaw, V.A. & Cowan, J.D. (1981). Specificity and plasticity of retinotectal connections: a computational model. *Jou. Neurosci.*, **1**, 1369-1387.

Willshaw, D.J. & Malsburg, C. von der (1979). A marker induction mechanism for the establishment of ordered neural mappings: its application to the retinotectal problem. *Phil. Trans. Roy. Soc. B*, **287**, 203-243.

Yates, P.A., McLaughlin, T., Friedman, G.C., Frisen, J., Barbacid, M. & O'Leary, D.D.M. (1997). Retinal axon guidance defects in mice lacking ephrin-A5 (AL-1/RAGS). *Soc. Neurosci. Abstracts*, **23**, 324.

A mathematical model of axon guidance by diffusible factors

Geoffrey J. Goodhill
Georgetown Institute for Cognitive and Computational Sciences
Georgetown University Medical Center
3970 Reservoir Road
Washington DC 20007
`geoff@giccs.georgetown.edu`

Abstract

In the developing nervous system, gradients of target-derived diffusible factors play an important role in guiding axons to appropriate targets. In this paper, the shape that such a gradient might have is calculated as a function of distance from the target and the time since the start of factor production. Using estimates of the relevant parameter values from the experimental literature, the spatiotemporal domain in which a growth cone could detect such a gradient is derived. For large times, a value for the maximum guidance range of about 1 mm is obtained. This value fits well with experimental data. For smaller times, the analysis predicts that guidance over longer ranges may be possible. This prediction remains to be tested.

1 Introduction

In the developing nervous system, growing axons are guided to targets that may be some distance away. Several mechanisms contribute to this (reviewed in Tessier-Lavigne & Goodman (1996)). One such mechanism is the diffusion of a factor from the target through the extracellular space, creating a gradient of increasing concentration that axons can sense and follow. In the central nervous system, such a process seems to occur in at least three cases: the guidance of axons from the trigeminal ganglion to the maxillary process in the mouse (Lumsden & Davies, 1983, 1986), of commissural axons in the spinal cord to the floor plate (Tessier-Lavigne et al., 1988), and of axons and axonal branches from the corticospinal tract to the basilar pons (Heffner et al., 1990). The evidence for this comes from both in vivo and in vitro experiments. For the latter, a piece of target tissue is embedded in a three dimensional collagen gel near to a piece of tissue containing the appropriate population of neurons. Axon growth is then observed directed towards the target, implicating a target-derived diffusible signal. In vivo, for the systems described, the target is always less than 500 μm from the population of axons. In vitro, where the distance between axons and target can readily be varied, guidance is generally not seen for distances greater than $500 - 1000$ μm. Can such a limit be explained in terms of the mathematics of diffusion?

There are two related constraints that the distribution of a diffusible factor must satisfy to provide an effective guidance cue at a point. Firstly, the *absolute concentration* of factor must not be too small or too large. Secondly, the *fractional change in concentration* of factor across the width of the gradient-sensing apparatus, generally assumed to be the growth cone, must be sufficiently large. These constraints are related because in both cases the problem is to overcome statistical noise. At very low concentrations, noise exists due to thermal fluctuations in the number of molecules of factor in the vicinity of the growth cone (analyzed in Berg & Purcell (1977)). At higher concentrations, the limiting source of noise is stochastic variation in the amount of binding of the factor to receptors distributed over the growth cone. At very high concentrations, all receptors will be saturated and no gradient will be apparent. The closer the concentration is to the upper or lower limits, the higher the gradient that is needed to ensure detection (Devreotes & Zigmond, 1988; Tessier-Lavigne & Placzek, 1991). The limitations these constraints impose on the guidance range of a diffusible factor are now investigated. For further discussion see Goodhill (1997; 1998).

2   Mathematical model

Consider a source releasing factor with diffusion constant D cm^2/sec, at rate q moles/sec, into an infinite, spatially uniform three-dimensional volume. Initially, zero decay of the factor is assumed. For radially symmetric Fickian diffusion in three dimensions, the concentration $C(r,t)$ at distance r from the source at time t is given by

$$C(r,t) = \frac{q}{4\pi Dr}\,\mathrm{erfc}\frac{r}{\sqrt{4Dt}} \tag{1}$$

(see e.g. Crank (1975)), where erfc is the complementary error function. The percentage change in concentration p across a small distance Δr (the width of the growth cone) is given by

$$p = -\frac{\Delta r}{r}\left[1 + \frac{r}{\sqrt{\pi Dt}}\frac{e^{-r^2/4Dt}}{\mathrm{erfc}(r/\sqrt{4Dt})}\right] \tag{2}$$

This function has two perhaps surprising characteristics. Firstly, for fixed r, $|p|$ *decreases* with t. That is, the largest gradient at any distance occurs immediately after the source starts releasing factor. For large t, $|p|$ asymptotes at $\Delta r/r$. Secondly, for fixed $t < \infty$, numerical results show that p is *nonmonotonic* with r. In particular it decreases with distance, reaches a minimum, then increases again. The position of this minimum moves to larger distances as t increases.

The general characteristics of the above constraints can be summarized as follows. (1) At small times after the start of production the factor is very unevenly distributed. The concentration C falls quickly to almost zero moving away from the source, the gradient is steep, and the percentage change across the growth cone p is everywhere large. (2) As time proceeds the factor becomes more evenly distributed. C everywhere increases, but p everywhere decreases. (3) For large times, C tends to an inverse variation with the distance from the source r, while $|p|$ tends to $\Delta r / r$ independent of all other parameters. This means that, for large times, the maximum distance over which guidance by diffusible factors is possible scales linearly with growth cone diameter Δr.

3 Parameter values

Diffusion constant, D. Crick (1970) estimated the diffusion constant in cytoplasm for a molecule of mass 0.3 - 0.5 kDa to be about 10^{-6} cm^2/sec. Subsequently, a direct determination of the diffusion constant for a molecule of mass 0.17 kDa in the aqueous cytoplasm of mammalian cells yielded a value of about 3.3×10^{-6} cm^2/sec (Mastro et al., 1984). By fitting a particular solution of the diffusion equation to their data on limb bud determination by gradients of a morphogenetically active retinoid, Eichele & Thaller (1987) calculated a value of 10^{-7} cm^2/sec for this molecule (mass 348.5 kDa) in embryonic limb tissue. One chemically identified diffusible factor known to be involved in axon guidance is the protein netrin-1, which has a molecular mass of about 75 kDa (Kennedy et al., 1994). D should scale roughly inversely with the radius of a molecule, i.e. with the cube root of its mass. Taking the value of 3.3×10^{-6} cm^2/sec and scaling it by $(170/75,000)^{1/3}$ yields 4.0×10^{-7} cm^2/sec. This paper therefore considers $D = 10^{-6}$ cm^2/sec and $D = 10^{-7}$ cm^2/sec.

Rate of production of factor q. This is hard to estimate in vivo: some insight can be gained by considering in vitro experiments. Gundersen & Barrett (1979) found a turning response in chick spinal sensory axons towards a nearby pipette filled with a solution of NGF. They estimated the rate of outflow from their pipette to be 1 μl/hour, and found an effect when the concentration in the pipette was as low as 0.1 nM NGF (Tessier-Lavigne & Placzek, 1991). This corresponds to a q of 3×10^{-11} nM/sec. Lohof et al. (1992) studied growth cone turning induced by a gradient of cell-membrane permeant cAMP from a pipette containing a 20 mM solution and a release rate of the order of 0.5 pl/sec: $q = 10^{-5}$ nM/sec. Below a further calculation for q is performed, which suggests an appropriate value may be $q = 10^{-7}$ nM/sec.

Growth cone diameter, Δr. For the three systems mentioned above, the diameter of the main body of the growth cone is less than 10 μm. However, this ignores filopodia, which can increase the effective width for gradient sensing purposes. The values of 10 μm and 20 μm are considered below.

Minimum concentration for gradient detection. Studies of leukocyte chemotaxis suggest that when gradient detection is limited by the dynamics of receptor binding rather than physical limits due to a lack of molecules of factor, optimal detection occurs when the concentration at the growth cone is equal to the dissociation constant for the receptor (Zigmond, 1981; Devreotes & Zigmond, 1988). Such studies also suggest that the low concentration limit is about 1% of the dissociation constant (Zigmond, 1981). The transmembrane protein Deleted in Colorectal Cancer (DCC) has recently been shown to possess netrin-1 binding activity, with an order of magnitude estimate for the dissociation constant of 10 nM (Keino-Masu et al, 1996). For comparison, the dissociation constant of the low-affinity NGF receptor P75 is about 1 nM (Meakin & Shooter, 1992). Therefore, low concentration limits of both 10^{-1} nM and 10^{-2} nM will be considered.

Maximum concentration for gradient detection. Theoretical considerations suggest that, for leukocyte chemotaxis, sensitivity to a fixed gradient should fall off symmetrically in a plot against the log of background concentration, with the peak at the dissociation constant for the receptor (Zigmond, 1981). Raising the concentration to several hundred times the dissociation constant appears to prevent axon guidance (discussed in Tessier-Lavigne & Placzek (1991)). At concentrations very much greater than the dissociation constant, the number of receptors may be downregulated, reducing sensitivity (Zigmond, 1981). Given the dissociation constants above, 100 nM thus constitutes a reasonable upper bound on concentration.

Minimum percentage change detectable by a growth cone, p. By establishing gradients of a repellent, membrane-bound factor directly on a substrate and measuring the response of chick retinal axons, Baier & Bonhoeffer (1992) estimated p to be about 1%. Studies of cell chemotaxis in various systems have suggested optimal values of 2%: for concentrations far from the dissociation constant for the receptor, p is expected to be larger (Devreotes & Zigmond, 1988). Both $p = 1\%$ and $p = 2\%$ are considered below.

4 Results

In order to estimate bounds for the rate of production of factor q for biological tissue, the empirical observation is used that, for collagen gel assays lasting of the order of one day, guidance is generally seen over distances of at most 500 μm (Lumsden & Davies, 1983, 1986; Tessier-Lavigne et al., 1988). Assume first that this is constrained by the low concentration limit. Substituting the above parameters (with $D = 10^{-7}$ cm^2/sec) into equation 1 and specifying that $C(500\mu\text{m}, 1 \text{ day}) = 0.01$ nM gives $q \approx 10^{-9}$ nM/sec. On the other hand, assuming constraint by the high concentration limit, i.e. $C(500\mu\text{m}, 1 \text{ day}) = 100$ nM, gives $q \approx 10^{-5}$ nM/sec. Thus it is reasonable to assume that, roughly, 10^{-9} nM/sec $< q < 10^{-5}$ nM/sec. The results discussed below use a value in between, namely $q = 10^{-7}$ nM/sec.

The constraints arising from equations 1 and 2 are plotted in figure 1. The cases of $D = 10^{-6}$ cm^2/sec and $D = 10^{-7}$ cm^2/sec are shown in (A,C) and (B,D) respectively. In all four pictures the constraints $C = 0.01$ nM and $C = 0.1$ nM are plotted. In (A,B) the gradient constraint $p = 1\%$ is shown, whereas in (C,D) $p = 2\%$ is shown. These are for a growth cone diameter of 10 μm. The graph for a 2% change and a growth cone diameter of 20 μm is identical to that for a 1% change and a diameter of 10 μm. Each constraint is satisfied for regions to the left of the relevant line. The line $C = 100$ nM is approximately coincident with the vertical axis in all cases. For these parameters, the high concentration limit does not therefore prevent gradient detection until the axons are within a few microns of the source, and it is thus assumed that it is not an important constraint.

As expected, for large t the gradient constraint asymptotes at $\Delta r/r = p$, i.e. $r = 1000$ μm for $p = 1\%$ and $r = 500$ μm for $p = 2\%$ and a 10 μm growth cone. That is, the gradient constraint is satisfied at all times when the distance from the source is less than 500 μm for $p = 2\%$ and $\Delta r = 10$ μm. The gradient constraint lines end to the right because at earlier times p exceeds the critical value over all distances (since the formula for p is non-monotonic with r, there is sometimes another branch of each p curve (not shown) off the graph to the right). As t increases from zero, guidance is initially limited only by the concentration constraint. The maximum distance over which guidance can occur increases smoothly with t, reaching for instance 1500 μm (assuming a concentration limit of 0.01 nM) after about 2 hours for $D = 10^{-6}$ cm^2/sec and about 6 hours for $D = 10^{-7}$ cm^2/sec. However at a particular time, the gradient constraint starts to take effect and rapidly reduces the maximum range of guidance towards the asymptotic value as t increases. This time (for $p = 2\%$) is about 2 hours for $D = 10^{-6}$ cm^2/sec, and about one day for $D = 10^{-7}$ cm^2/sec. It is clear from these pictures that although the exact size of

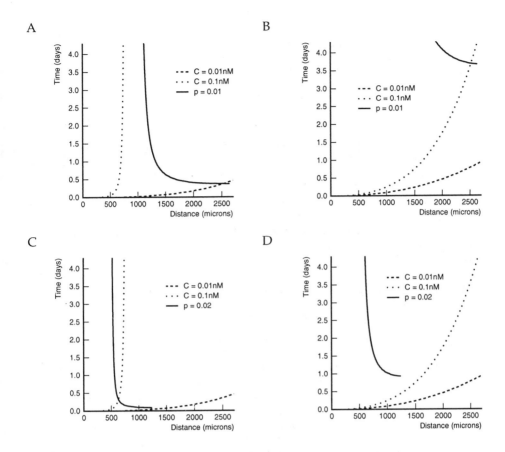

Figure 1: Graphs showing how the gradient constraint (solid line) interacts with the minimum concentration constraint (dashed/dotted lines) to limit guidance range, and how these constraints evolve over time. The top row (A,B) is for $p = 1\%$, the bottom row (C,D) for $p = 2\%$. The left column (A,C) is for $D = 10^{-6}$ cm^2/sec, the right column (B,D) for $D = 10^{-7}$ cm^2/sec. Each constraint is satisfied to the left of the appropriate curve. It can be seen that for $D = 10^{-6}$cm^2/sec the gradient limit quickly becomes the dominant constraint on maximum guidance range. In contrast for $D = 10^{-7}$ cm^2/sec, the concentration limit is the dominant constraint at times up to several days. However after this the gradient constraint starts to take effect and rapidly reduces the maximum guidance range.

the diffusion constant does not affect the position of the asymptote for the gradient constraint, it does play an important role in the interplay of constraints while the gradient is evolving. The effect is however subtle: reducing D from 10^{-6} cm^2/sec to 10^{-7} cm^2/sec increases the time for the $C = 0.01$ nM limit to reach 2000 μm, but *decreases* the time for the $C = 0.1$ nM limit to reach 2000 μm.

5 Discussion

Taking the gradient constraint to be a fractional change of at least 2% across a growth cone of width of 10 μm or 20 μm yields asymptotic values for the maximum distance over which guidance can occur once the gradient has stabilized of 500 μm and 1000 μm respectively. This fits well with both in vitro data, and the fact that for the systems mentioned in the introduction, the growing axons are always less than 500 μm from the target in vivo. The concentration limits seem to provide a weaker constraint than the gradient limit on the maximum distances possible. However, this is very dependent on the value of q, which has only been very roughly estimated: if q is significantly less than 10^{-7} nM/sec, the low concentration limits will provide more restrictive constraints (q may well have different values in different target tissues). The gradient constraint curves are independent of q. The gradient constraint therefore provides the most robust explanation for the observed guidance limit.

The model makes the prediction that guidance over longer distances than have hitherto been observed may be possible before the gradient has stabilized. In the early stages following the start of factor production the concentration falls off more steeply, providing more effective guidance. The time at which guidance range is a maximum depends on the diffusion constant D. For a rapidly diffusing molecule ($D \approx 10^{-6}$ cm^2/sec) this occurs after only a few hours. For a more slowly diffusing molecule however ($D \approx 10^{-7}$ cm^2/sec) this occurs after a few days, which would be easier to investigate in vitro. In vivo, molecules such as netrin-1 may thus be large because, during times immediately following the start of production by the source, there could be a definite benefit (i.e. steep gradient) to a slowly-diffusing molecule. Also, it is conceivable that Nature has optimized the start of production of factor relative to the time that guidance is required in order to exploit an evolving gradient for extended range. This could be especially important in larger animals, where axons may need to be guided over longer distances in the developing embryo.

Bibliography

Baier, H. & Bonhoeffer, F. (1992). Axon guidance by gradients of a target-derived component. *Science*, **255**, 472-475.

Berg, H.C. and Purcell, E.M. (1977). Physics of chemoreception. *Biophysical Journal*, **20**, 193-219.

Crick, F. (1970). Diffusion in embryogenesis. *Nature*, **255**, 420-422.

Crank, J. (1975). The mathematics of diffusion, Second edition. Oxford, Clarendon.

Devreotes, P.N. & Zigmond, S.H. (1988). Chemotaxis in eukaryotic cells: a focus on leukocytes and *Dictyostelium*. *Ann. Rev. Cell. Biol.*, **4**, 649-686.

Eichele, G. & Thaller, C. (1987). Characterization of concentration gradients of a morphogenetically active retinoid in the chick limb bud. *J. Cell. Biol.*, **105**, 1917-1923.

Goodhill, G.J. (1997). Diffusion in axon guidance. *Eur. J. Neurosci.*, **9**, 1414-1421.

Goodhill, G.J. (1998). Mathematical guidance for axons. *Trends. Neurosci.*, in press.

Gundersen, R.W. & Barrett, J.N. (1979). Neuronal chemotaxis: chick dorsal-root axons turn toward high concentrations of nerve growth factor. *Science*, **206**, 1079-1080.

Heffner, C.D., Lumsden, A.G.S. & O'Leary, D.D.M. (1990). Target control of collateral extension and directional growth in the mammalian brain. *Science*, **247**, 217-220.

Keino-Masu, K., Masu, M., Hinck, L., Leonardo, E.D., Chan, S.S.-Y., Culotti, J.G. & Tessier-Lavigne, M. (1996). *Deleted in Colorectal Cancer (DCC)* encodes a netrin receptor. *Cell*, **87**, 175-185.

Kennedy, T.E., Serafini, T., de al Torre, J.R. & Tessier-Lavigne, M. (1994). Netrins are diffusible chemotropic factors for commissural axons in the embryonic spinal cord. *Cell*, **78**, 425-435.

Lohof, A.M., Quillan, M., Dan, Y, & Poo, M-m. (1992). Asymmetric modulation of cytosolic cAMP activity induces growth cone turning. *J. Neurosci.*, **12**, 1253-1261.

Lumsden, A.G.S. & Davies, A.M. (1983). Earliest sensory nerve fibres are guided to peripheral targets by attractants other than nerve growth factor. *Nature*, **306**, 786-788.

Lumsden, A.G.S. & Davies, A.M. (1986). Chemotropic effect of specific target epithelium in the developing mammalian nervous system. *Nature*, **323**, 538-539.

Mastro, A.M., Babich, M.A., Taylor, W.D. & Keith, A.D. (1984). Diffusion of a small molecule in the cytoplasm of mammalian cells. *Proc. Nat. Acad. Sci. USA*, **81**, 3414-3418.

Meakin, S.O. & Shooter, E.M. (1992). The nerve growth family of receptors. *Trends. Neurosci.*, **15**, 323-331.

Tessier-Lavigne, M. & Placzek, M. (1991). Target attraction: are developing axons guided by chemotropism? *Trends Neurosci.*, **14**, 303-310.

Tessier-Lavigne, M. & Goodman, C.S. (1996). The molecular biology of axon guidance. *Science*, **274**, 1123-1133.

Tessier-Lavigne, M., Placzek, M., Lumsden, A.G.S., Dodd, J. & Jessell, T.M. (1988). Chemotropic guidance of developing axons in the mammalian central nervous system. *Nature*, **336**, 775-778.

Tranquillo, R.T. & Lauffenburger, D.A. (1987). Stochastic model of leukocyte chemosensory movement. *J. Math. Biol.*, **25**, 229-262.

Zigmond, S.H. (1981). Consequences of chemotactic peptide receptor modulation for leukocyte orientation. *J. Cell. Biol.*, **88**, 644-647.

Computing with Action Potentials

John J. Hopfield*   Carlos D. Brody [†]   Sam Roweis [†]

Abstract

Most computational engineering based loosely on biology uses continuous variables to represent neural activity. Yet most neurons communicate with action potentials. The engineering view is equivalent to using a rate-code for representing information and for computing. An increasing number of examples are being discovered in which biology may not be using rate codes. Information can be represented using the *timing* of action potentials, and efficiently computed with in this representation. The "analog match" problem of odour identification is a simple problem which can be efficiently solved using action potential timing and an underlying rhythm. By using adapting units to effect a fundamental change of representation of a problem, we map the recognition of words (having uniform time-warp) in connected speech into the same analog match problem. We describe the architecture and preliminary results of such a recognition system. Using the fast events of biology in conjunction with an underlying rhythm is one way to overcome the limits of an event-driven view of computation. When the intrinsic hardware is much faster than the time scale of change of inputs, this approach can greatly increase the effective computation per unit time on a given quantity of hardware.

1   Spike timing

Most neurons communicate using action potentials – stereotyped pulses of activity that are propagated along axons without change of shape over long distances by active regenerative processes. They provide a pulse-coded way of sending information. Individual action potentials last about 2 ms. Typical active nerve cells generate 5–100 action potentials/sec.

Most biologically inspired engineering of neural networks represent the activity of a nerve cell by a continuous variable which can be interpreted as the short-time average rate of generating action potentials. Most traditional discussions by neurobiologists concerning how information is represented and processed in the brain have similarly relied on using "short term mean firing rate" as the carrier of information and the basis for computation. But this is often an ineffective way to compute and represent information in neurobiology.

*Dept. of Molecular Biology, Princeton University. jhopfield@watson.princeton.edu
[†] Computation & Neural Systems, California Institute of Technology.

To define "short term mean firing rate" with reasonable accuracy, it is necessary to either wait for several action potentials to arrive from a single neuron, or to average over many roughly equivalent cells. One of these necessitates slow processing; the other requires redundant "wetware".

Since action potentials are short events with sharp rise times, action potential timing is another way that information can be represented and computed with ([Hopfield, 1995]). Action potential timing seems to be the basis for some neural computations, such as the determination of a sharp response time to an ultrasonic pulse generated by the moustache bat. In this system, the bat generates a 10 ms pulse during which the frequency changes monotonically with time (a "chirp"). In the cochlea and cochlear nucleus, cells which are responsive to different frequencies will be sequentially driven, each producing zero or one action potentials during the time when the frequency is in their responsive band. These action potentials converge onto a target cell. However, while the times of initiation of the action potentials from the different frequency bands are different, the length and propagation speed of the various axons have been coordinated to result in all the action potentials arriving at the target cell at the same time, thus recognizing the "chirped" pulse as a whole, while discriminating against random sounds of the same overall duration.

Taking this hint from biology, we next investigate the use of action potential timing to represent information and compute with in one of the fundamental computational problems relevant to olfaction, noting why the elementary "neural net" engineering solution is poor, and showing why computing with action potentials lacks the deficiencies of the conventional elementary solution.

2 Analog match

The simplest computational problem of odors is merely to identify a known odor when a single odor dominates the olfactory scene. Most natural odors consist of mixtures of several molecular species. At some particular strength a complex odor b can be described by the concentrations N_i^b of its constitutive molecular of species i. If the stimulus intensity changes, each component increases (or decreases) by the same multiplicative factor. It is convenient to describe the stimulus as a product of two factors, an intensity λ and normalized components n_i^b as:

$$\lambda = \Sigma_j N_j^b \quad \Rightarrow \quad n_i^b = N_i^b/\lambda \quad \text{or} \quad N_i^b = \lambda n_i^b \qquad (1)$$

The n_i^b are normalized, or relative concentrations of different molecules, and λ describes the overall odor intensity. Ideally, a given odor quality is described by the pattern of n_i^b, which does not change when the odor intensity λ changes. When a stimulus s described by a set $\{N_j^s\}$ is presented, an ideal odor quality detector answers "yes" to the question "is odor b present?" if and only if for some value of λ:

$$N_j^s \approx \lambda n_j^b \quad \forall j \qquad (2)$$

This general computation has been called *analog match*.[1]

The elementary "neural net" way to solve analog match and recognize a single odor independent of intensity would be to use a single "grandmother unit" of the following type.

---

[1]The analog match problem of olfaction is actually viewed through olfactory receptor cells. Studies of vertebrate sensory cells have shown that each molecular species stimulates many different sensory cells, and each cell is excited by many different molecular species. The pattern of relative excitation across the population of sensory cell classes determines the odor quality in the generalist olfactory system. There are about 1000 broadly responsive cell types; thus, the olfactory systems of higher animals apparently solve an analog match problem of the type described by (2), except that the indices refer to cell types, and the actual dimension is no more than 1000.

Call the unknown odor vector I, and the weight vector W. The input to the unit will then be $I \cdot W$. If $W = n/\|n\|$ and I is pre-normalized by dividing by the Euclidean magnitude $\|I\|$, recognition can be identified by $I \cdot W > .95$, or whatever threshold describes the degree of precision in identification which the task requires.

This solution has four major weaknesses.

1. Euclidean normalization is used; not a trivial calculation for real neural hardware.

2. The size of input components I_k and their importance is confounded. If a weak component has particular importance, or a strong one is not reliable, there is no way to represent this. W describes only the size of the target odor components.

3. There is no natural composition if the problem is to be broken into a hierarchy by breaking the inputs into several parts, solving independently, and feeding these results on to a higher level unit for a final recognition. This is best seen by analogy to vision. If I recognize in a picture grandmother's nose at one scale, her mouth at another, and her right eye at a third scale, then it is assuredly *not* grandmother. Separate normalization is a disaster for creating hierarchies.

4. A substantial number of inputs may be missing or giving grossly wrong information. The "dot-product-and-threshold" solution cannot contend with this problem. For example, in olfaction, two of the common sources of noise are the adaptation of a subset of sensors due to previous strong odors, and receptors stuck "on" due to the retention of strongly bound molecules from previous odors.

All four problems are removed when the information is encoded and computed with in an action potential representation, as illustrated below. The three channels of analog input I_a, I_b, I_c are illustrated on the left. They are converted to a spike timing representation by the position of action potentials with respect to a fiducial time T. The interval between T and the time of an action potential in a channel j is equal to $\log I_j$. Each channel is connected to an output unit through a delay line of length $\Delta_j = \log n_j^b$, where n^b is the target vector to be identified. When the analog match criterion is satisfied, the pulses on all three channels will arrive at the target unit at the same time, driving it strongly. If all inputs are scaled by α, then the times of the action potentials will all be changed by $\log \alpha$. The three action potentials will arrive at the recognition unit simultaneously, but a a time shifted by $\log \alpha$. Thus a pattern can be recognized (or not) on the basis of its relative components. Scale information is retained in the *time* at which the recognition unit is driven. The system clearly "composes", and difficulty (3) is surmounted. No normalization is required, eliminating difficulty (1). Each pathway has two parameters describing it, a delay (which contains the information about the pattern to be recognized) and a synaptic strength (which describes the weight of the action potential at the recognition unit). Scale and importance are separately represented. The central computational motif is very similar to that used in bat sonar, using relative timing to represent information and time delays to represent target patterns.

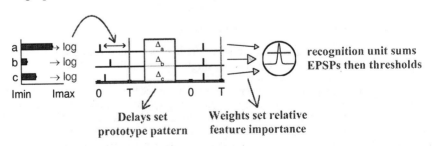

This system also tolerates errors due to missing or grossly inaccurate information. The figure below illustrates this fact for the case of three inputs, and contrasts the receptive fields of a system computing with action potentials with those of a conventional grandmother cell. (The only relevant variables are the projections of the input vector on the surface of the unit sphere, as illustrated.) When the thresholds are set high, both schemes recognize a small, roughly circular region around the target pattern (here chosen as 111). Lowering the recognition threshold in the action-potential based scheme results in a star-shaped region being recognized; this region can be characterized as "recognize if any two components are in the correct ratio, independent of the size of the third component." Pattern 110 is thus recognized as being similar to 111 while still rejecting most of the space as not resembling the target. In contrast, to recognize 110 with the conventional unit requires such threshold lowering that almost any vector would be recognized.

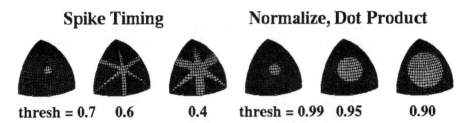

Spike Timing			**Normalize, Dot Product**		
thresh = 0.7	0.6	0.4	thresh = 0.99	0.95	0.90

This method of representation and computation using action potential timing requires a fiducial time available to all neurons *participating in stimulus encoding*. Fiducial times might be externally generated by salient events, as they are in the case of moustache bat sonar. Or they could be internally generated, sporadically or periodically. In the case of the olfactory system, the first processing area of all animals has an oscillatory behavior. A large piece of the biophysics of neurons can be represented by the idea that neurons are leaky integrators, and that when their internal potential is pushed above a critical value, they produce an action potential, and their internal potential is reset a fixed distance below threshold. When a sub-threshold input having a frequency f is combined with a steady analog current I, the system generates action potentials at frequency f, but whose phase with respect to the underlying oscillation is a monotone function of I. Thus the system encodes I into a phase (or time) of an action potential with respect to the underlying rhythm. Interestingly, in mammals, the second stage of the olfactory system, the prepiriform cortex, has slow axons propagating signals across it. The propagation time delays are comparable to $1/f$. The system has the capability of encoding and analyzing information in action potential timing.

3 Time warp and speech

Recognizing syllables or words independent of a uniform stretch ("uniform time warp") can in principle be cast as an analog match problem and transformed into neural variables [Hopfield, 1996]. We next describe this approach in relationship to a previous "neural network" way of recognizing words in connected speech [Hopfield and Tank, 1987, Unnikrishnan et al., 1991, Unnikrishnan et al., 1992] (UHT for short).

A block diagram below shows the UHT neural network for recognizing a small vocabulary of words in connected speech. The speech signal is passed through a bank of band-pass filters, and an elementary neural feature detector then examines whether each frequency is a local maximum of the short-term power spectrum. If so, it propagates a "1" down a delay line from that feature detector, thus converting the pattern of features in time into a pattern in space. The recognition unit for a particular word is then connected to these delay lines by a pattern of weights which are trained on a large data base.

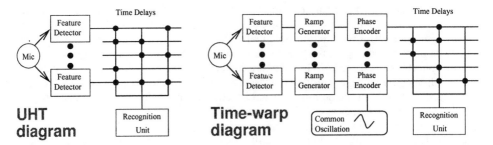

UHT diagram   **Time-warp diagram**

The conceptual strength of this circuit is that it requires no indication of the boundaries between words. Indeed, there is no such concept in the circuit. The conceptual weakness of this "neural network" is that the recognition process for a particular word is equivalent to sliding a rigid template across the feature pattern. Unfortunately, even a single speaker has great variation in the duration of a given word under different circumstances, as illustrated in the two spectrograms below. Clearly no single template will fit these both of these utterances of "one" very well. This general problem is known as *time-warp*. A time-warp invariant recognizer would have considerable advantage.

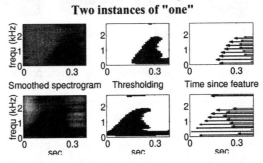

Two instances of "one"

The UHT approach represents a sequence by the presence of a signal on feature signal lines A, B, C, as shown on the left of the figure below. Suppose the end of the word occurs at some particular time as indicated. Then the feature starts and stops can be described as an analog vector of times, whose components are shown by the arrows as indicated. In this representation, a word which is spoken more slowly simply has all its vector components multiplied by a common factor. The problem of recognizing words within a uniform time warp is thus isomorphic with the analog match problem, and can be readily solved by using action potential timing and an underlying rhythm, as described above. In our present modeling, the rhythm has a frequency of 50 Hz, significantly faster than the rate at which new features appear in speech. This frequency corresponds to the clock rate at which speech features are effectively "sampled". In the UHT circuit this rate was set by the response timescale of the recognition units. But where each template in the UHT circuit attempted only a single match with the feature vector per sample, this circuit allows the attempted match of many possible time-warps with the feature vector per sample. (The range of time-warps allowed is determined by the oscillation frequency and the temporal resolution of the spike timing system.)

The block diagram of the neural circuit necessary to recognize words in connected speech with uniform time warp is sketched above. It looks superficially similar to the UHT circuit beside it, except for the insertion of a ramp generator and a phase encoder between the feature detectors and the delay system. Recognizing a feature activates a ramp generator whose output decays. This becomes the input to a "neuron" which has an additional oscillatory input at frequency f. If the ramp decay and oscillation shapes are properly matched, the logarithm of the time since the occurrence of a feature is encoded in action potential timing as above. Following this encoding system there is a set of tapped delay lines of the same style which would have been necessary to solve the olfactory decoding problem. The total the amount of hardware is similar to the UHT approach because the connections and delay lines dominate the resource requirements.

The operation of the present circuit is, however, entirely different. What the present circuit does is to "remember" recent features by using ramp generators, encode the logarithms of times since features into action potential timing, and recognize the pattern with a time-delay circuit. The time delays in the present circuit have an entirely different meaning from those of the UHT circuit, since they are dimensionally not physical time, but instead are a representation of the logarithm of feature times. The time delays are only on the scale of $1/f$ rather than the duration of a word. There are simple biological implementations of these ideas. For example, when a neuron responds, as many do, to a step in its input by generating a train of action potentials with gradually falling firing frequency (adaptation), the temporal spacing between the action potentials is an implicit representation of the time since the "step" occurred (see [Hopfield, 1996]).

For our initial engineering investigations, we used very simple features. The power within each frequency band is merely thresholded. An upward crossing of that threshold represents a "start" feature for that band, and a downward crossing a "end" feature. A pattern of such features is identified above beside the spectrograms. Although the pattern of feature vectors for the two examples of "one" do not match well because of time warp, when the logarithms of the patterns are taken, the difference between the two patterns is chiefly a shift, i.e. the dominant difference between the patterns is merely uniform time warp.

To recognize the spoken digit "one", for example, the appropriate delay for each channel was chosen so as to minimize the variance of the post-delay spike times (thus aligning the spikes produced by all features), averaged over the different exemplars which contained that feature. All channels with a feature present were given a unity weight connection at that delay value; inactive channels were given weight zero. The figure below shows, on the left, the spike input to the recognition unit (top) and the sum of the EPSPs caused by these inputs (bottom). The examples of "one" produced maximum outputs in different cycles of the oscillation, corresponding to the actual "end times" at which the words should be viewed as recognized. Only the maximum cycle for each utterance is shown here. Within their maximum cycle, different examples of the utterances produced maximal outputs at different phases of the cycle, corresponding to the fact that the different utterances were recognized as having different time warp factors. The panels on the right show the result of playing spoken "four"s into the same recognition unit.

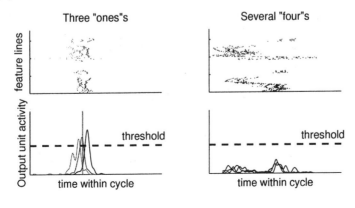

There is no difficulty in distinguishing "ones" from other digits. When, however, the possibility of adjusting the time-warp is turned off, resulting in a "rigid" template it was not possible to discriminate between "one" and other digits. (Disabling time-warp effectively forces recognition to take place at the same "time" during each oscillation. Imagine drawing a vertical line in the figure and notice that it cannot pass through all the peaks of output unit activities.)

We have described the beginning of a research project to use action potentials and timing to solve a real speech problem in a "neural" fashion. Very unsophisticated features were used, and no competitive learning was employed in setting the connection weights. Even so, the system appears to function in a word-spotting mode, and displays a facility of matching patterns with time warp. Its intrinsic design makes it insensitive to burst noise and to frequency-band noise.

How is computation being done? After features are detected, rates of change are slow, and little additional information is accumulated during say a 50 ms. interval. If we let "time be its own representation", as Carver Mead used to say, we let the information source be the effective clock, and the effective clock rate is only about 20 Hz. Instead, by adding a rhythm, we can interleave many calculations (in this particular case about the possibility of different time warps) while the basic inputs are changing very little. Using an oscillation frequency of 50 Hz and a resolving time of 1 ms in the speech example we describe increases the effective clock rate by more than a factor of 10 compared to the effective clock rate of the UHT computation.

We believe that "time as its own representation" is a loser for processing information when the computation desired is complex but the data is slowly changing. No computer scientist would use a computer with a 24 Hz clock to analyze a movie because the movie is viewed at 24 frames a second. Biology will surely have found its way out of this "paced by the environment" dilemma. Finally, because problems are easy or hard according to how algorithms fit on hardware and according to the representation of information, the differences in operation between the system we have described and conventional ANN suggest the utility of thinking about other problems in a timing representation.

Acknowledgements

The authors thank Sanjoy Mahajan and Erik Winfree for comments and help with preparation of the manuscript. This work was supported in part by the Center for Neuromorphic Systems Engineering as a part of the National Science Foundation Engineering Research Center Program under grant EEC-9402726. Roweis is supported by the Natural Sciences and Engineering Research Council of Canada under an NSERC 1967 Award.

References

[Hopfield, 1995] Hopfield, J. (1995). Pattern recognition computation using action potential timing for stimulus representation. *Nature*, 376:33–36.

[Hopfield, 1996] Hopfield, J. (1996). Transforming neural computations and representing time. *Proceedings of the National Academy of Sciences*, 93:15440–15444.

[Hopfield and Tank, 1987] Hopfield, J. and Tank, D. (1987). Neural computation by concentrating information in time. *Proceedings of the National Academy of Sciences*, 84:1896–1900.

[Unnikrishnan et al., 1991] Unnikrishnan, K., Hopfield, J., and Tank, D. (1991). Connected digit speaker-dependent speech recognition using a neural network with time-delayed connections. *IEEE Transactions on Signal Processing*, 39:698–713.

[Unnikrishnan et al., 1992] Unnikrishnan, K., Hopfield, J., and Tank, D. (1992). Speaker-independent digit recognition using a neural network with time-delayed connections. *Neural Computation*, 4:108–119.

A Model of Early Visual Processing

Laurent Itti, Jochen Braun, Dale K. Lee and Christof Koch
{itti, achim, jjwen, koch}@klab.caltech.edu
Computation & Neural Systems, MSC 139-74
California Institute of Technology, Pasadena, CA 91125, U.S.A.

Abstract

We propose a model for early visual processing in primates. The model consists of a population of linear spatial filters which interact through non-linear excitatory and inhibitory pooling. Statistical estimation theory is then used to derive human psychophysical thresholds from the responses of the entire population of units. The model is able to reproduce human thresholds for contrast and orientation discrimination tasks, and to predict contrast thresholds in the presence of masks of varying orientation and spatial frequency.

1 INTRODUCTION

A remarkably wide range of human visual thresholds for spatial patterns appears to be determined by the earliest stages of visual processing, namely, orientation- and spatial frequency-tuned visual filters and their interactions [18, 19, 3, 22, 9]. Here we consider the possibility of quantitatively relating arbitrary spatial vision thresholds to a single computational model. The success of such a unified account should reveal the extent to which human spatial vision indeed reflects one particular stage of processing. Another motivation for this work is the controversy over the neural circuits that generate orientation and spatial frequency tuning in striate cortical neurons [13, 8, 2]. We think it is likely that behaviorally defined visual filters and their interactions reveal at least some of the characteristics of the underlying neural circuitry. Two specific problems are addressed: (i) what is the minimal set of model components necessary to account for human spatial vision, (ii) is there a general decision strategy which relates model responses to behavioral thresholds and which obviates case-by-case assumptions about the decision strategy in different behavioral situations. To investigate these questions, we propose a computational model articulated around three main stages: first, a population of bandpass linear filters extracts visual features from a stimulus; second, linear filters interact through non-linear excitatory and inhibitory pooling; third, a noise model and decision strategy are assumed in order to relate the model's output to psychophysical data.

2   MODEL

We assume spatial visual filters tuned for a variety of orientations $\theta \in \Theta$ and spatial periods $\lambda \in \Lambda$. The filters have overlapping receptive fields in visual space. Quadrature filter pairs, $F_{\lambda,\theta}^{even}$ and $F_{\lambda,\theta}^{odd}$, are used to compute a phase-independent linear energy response, $E_{\lambda,\theta}$, to a visual stimulus S. A small constant background activity, ϵ, is added to the linear energy responses:

$$E_{\lambda,\theta} = \sqrt{(F_{\lambda,\theta}^{even} * S)^2 + (F_{\lambda,\theta}^{odd} * S)^2} + \epsilon$$

Filters have separable Gaussian tuning curves in orientation and spatial frequency. Their corresponding shape in visual space is close to that of Gabor filters, although not separable along spatial dimensions.

2.1   Pooling: self excitation and divisive inhibition

A model based on linear filters alone would not correctly account for the non-linear response characteristics to stimulus contrast which have been observed psychophysically [19]. Several models have consequently introduced a non-linear transducer stage following each linear unit [19]. A more appealing possibility is to assume a non-linear pooling stage [6, 21, 3, 22]. In this study, we propose a pooling strategy inspired by Heeger's model for gain control in cat area V1 [5, 6]. The pooled response $R_{\lambda,\theta}$ of a unit tuned for (λ, θ) is computed from the linear energy responses of the entire population:

$$R_{\lambda,\theta} = \frac{E_{\lambda,\theta}^{\gamma}}{S^{\delta} + \sum_{\lambda',\theta'} W_{\lambda,\theta}(\lambda', \theta') E_{\lambda',\theta'}^{\delta}} + \eta \qquad (1)$$

where the sum is taken over the entire population and $W_{\lambda,\theta}$ is a two-dimensional Gaussian weighting function centered around (λ, θ), and η a background activity. The numerator in **Eq. 1** represents a non-linear self-excitation term. The denominator represents a divisive inhibitory term which depends not only on the activity of the unit (λ, θ) of interest, but also on the responses of other units. We shall see in **Section 3** that, in contrast to Heeger's model for electrophysiological data in which all units contribute equally to the pool, it is necessary to assume that only a subpopulation of units with tuning close to (λ, θ) contribute to the pool in order to account for psychophysical data. Also, we assume $\gamma > \delta$ to obtain a power law for high contrasts [7], as opposed to Heeger's physiological model in which $\gamma = \delta = 2$ to account for neuronal response saturation at high contrasts.

Several interesting properties result from this pooling model. First, a sigmoidal transducer function – in agreement with contrast discrimination psychophysics – is naturally obtained through pooling and thus need not be introduced *post-hoc*. The transducer slope for high contrasts is determined by $\gamma - \delta$, the location of its inflexion point by S, and the slope at this point by the absolute value of γ (and δ). Second, the tuning curves of the pooled units for orientation and spatial period do not depend of stimulus contrast, in agreement with physiological and psychophysical evidence [14]. In comparison, a model which assumes a non-linear transducer but no pooling exhibits sharper tuning curves for lower contrasts. Full contrast independence of the tuning is achieved only when all units participate in the inhibitory pool; when only sub-populations participate in the pool, some contrast dependence remains.

2.2   Noise model: Poisson$^{\alpha}$

It is necessary to assume the presence of noise in the system in order to be able to derive psychophysical performance from the responses of the population of pooled units. The deterministic response of each unit then represents the mean of a randomly distributed "neuronal" response which varies from trial to trial in a simulated psychophysical experiment.

Existing models usually assume constant noise variance in order to simplify the subsequent decision stage [18]. Using the decision strategy presented below, it is however possible to derive psychophysical performance with a noise model whose variance increases with mean activity, in agreement with electrophysiology [16]. In what follows, Poisson$^\alpha$ noise will be assumed and approximated by a Gaussian random variable with *variance = mean$^\alpha$* (α is a constant close to unity).

2.3 Decision strategy

We use tools from statistical estimation theory to compute the system's behavioral response based on the responses of the population of pooled units. Similar tools have been used by Seung and Sompolinsky [12] under the simplifying assumption of purely Poisson noise and for the particular task of orientation discrimination in the limit of an infinite population of oriented units. Here, we extend this framework to the more general case in which any stimulus attribute may differ between the two stimulus presentations to be discriminated by the model. Let's assume that we want to estimate psychophysical performance at discriminating between two stimuli which differ by the value of a stimulus parameter ζ (e.g. contrast, orientation, spatial period).

The central assumption of our decision strategy is that the brain implements an *unbiased efficient statistic* $T(\mathcal{R};\zeta)$, which is an estimator of the parameter ζ based on the population response $\mathcal{R} = \{R_{\lambda,\theta}; \lambda \in \Lambda, \theta \in \Theta\}$. The efficient statistic is the one which, among all possible estimators of ζ, has the property of minimum variance in the estimated value of ζ. Although we are not suggesting any putative neuronal correlate for T, it is important to note that the assumption of efficient statistic does not require T to be prohibitively complex; for instance, a maximum likelihood estimator proposed in the decision stage of several existing models is asymptotically (with respect to the number of observations) a efficient statistic.

Because T is efficient, it achieves the Cramér-Rao bound [1]. Consequently, when the number of observations (i.e. simulated psychophysical trials) is large,

$$E[T] = \zeta \qquad \text{and} \qquad var[T] = 1/\mathcal{J}(\zeta)$$

where $E[.]$ is the mean over all observations, $var[.]$ the variance, and $\mathcal{J}(\zeta)$ is the Fisher information. The Fisher information can be computed using the noise model assumption and tuning properties of the pooled units: for a random variable X with probability density $f(x;\zeta)$, it is given by [1]:

$$J(\zeta) = E\left[\frac{\partial}{\partial\zeta}\ln f(x;\zeta)\right]^2$$

For our Poisson$^\alpha$ noise model and assuming that different pooled units are independent [15], this translates into:

One unit $R_{\lambda,\theta}$: $\quad J_{\lambda,\theta}(\zeta) = \left(\frac{\partial R_{\lambda,\theta}}{\partial\zeta}\right)^2 \left[\frac{1}{R_{\lambda,\theta}^\alpha} + \frac{\alpha^2}{2R_{\lambda,\theta}^2}\right]$

All independent units: $\quad \mathcal{J}(\zeta) = \sum_{\lambda,\theta} J_{\lambda,\theta}(\zeta)$

The Fisher information computed for each pooled unit and three types of stimulus parameters ζ is shown in **Figure 1**. This figure demonstrates the importance of using information from all units in the population rather than from only one unit optimally tuned for the stimulus: although the unit carrying the most information about contrast is the one optimally tuned to the stimulus pattern, more information about orientation or spatial frequency is carried by units which are tuned to flanking orientations and spatial periods and whose tuning curves have maximum slope for the stimulus rather than maximum absolute sensitivity. In our implementation, the derivatives of pooled responses used in the expression of Fisher information are computed numerically.

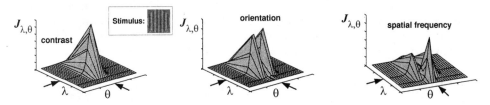

Figure 1: Fisher information computed for contrast, orientation and spatial frequency. Each node in the tridimensional meshes represents the Fisher information for the corresponding pooled unit (λ, θ) in a model with 30 orientations and 4 scales. Arrows indicate the unit (λ, θ) optimally tuned to the stimulus. The total Fisher information in the population is the sum of the information for all units.

Using the estimate of ζ and its variance from the Fisher information, it is possible to derive psychophysical performance for a discrimination task between two stimuli with parameters $\zeta_1 \leq \zeta_2$ using standard ideal observer signal discrimination techniques [4]. For such discrimination, we use the Central Limit Theorem (in the limit of large number of trials) to model the noisy responses of the system as two Gaussians with means ζ_1 and ζ_2, and variances $\sigma_1^2 = 1/\mathcal{J}(\zeta_1)$ and $\sigma_2^2 = 1/\mathcal{J}(\zeta_2)$ respectively. A decision criterion D is chosen to minimize the overall probability of error; since in our case $\sigma_1 \neq \sigma_2$ in general, we derive a slightly more complicated expression for performance P at a Yes/No (one alternative forced choice) task than what is commonly used with models assuming constant noise [18]:

$$D = \frac{\zeta_2 \sigma_1^2 - \zeta_1 \sigma_2^2 - \sigma_1 \sigma_2 \sqrt{(\zeta_1 - \zeta_2)^2 + 2(\sigma_1^2 - \sigma_2^2)\log(\sigma_1/\sigma_2)}}{\sigma_1^2 - \sigma_2^2}$$

$$P = \frac{1}{2} + \frac{1}{4}\mathrm{erf}\left(\frac{\zeta_2 - D}{\sigma_2 \sqrt{2}}\right) + \frac{1}{4}\mathrm{erf}\left(\frac{D - \zeta_1}{\sigma_1 \sqrt{2}}\right)$$

where erf is the Normal error function. The expression for D extends by continuity to $D = (\zeta_2 - \zeta_1)/2$ when $\sigma_1 = \sigma_2$. This decision strategy provides a unified, task-independent framework for the computation of psychophysical performance from the deterministic responses of the pooled units. This strategy can easily be extended to allow the model to perform discrimination tasks with respect to additional stimulus parameters, under exactly the same theoretical assumptions.

3   RESULTS

3.1   Model calibration

The parameters of the model were automatically adjusted to fit human psychophysical thresholds measured in our laboratory [17] for contrast and orientation discrimination tasks (**Figure 2**). The model used in this experiment consisted of 60 orientations evenly distributed between 0 and 180deg. One spatial scale at 4 cycles per degree (cpd) was sufficient to account for the data. A multidimensional simplex method with simulated annealing overhead was used to determine the best fit of the model to the data [10]. The free parameters adjusted during the automatic fits were: the noise level α, the pooling exponents γ and δ, the inhibitory pooling constant S, and the background firing rates, ϵ and η.

The error function minimized by the fitting algorithm was a weighted average of three constraints: 1) least-square error with the contrast discrimination data in **Figure 2.a**; 2) least-square error with the orientation discrimination data in **Figure 2.b**; 3) because the data was sparse in the "dip-shaped" region of the curve in **Figure 2.a**, and unreliable due to the limited contrast resolution of the display used for the psychophysics, we added an additional constraint favoring a more pronounced "dip", as has been observed by several other groups [11, 19, 22].

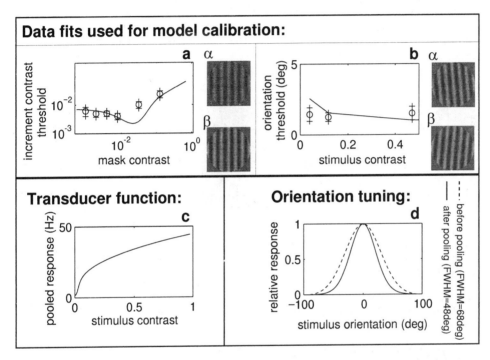

Figure 2: The model (solid lines) was calibrated using data from two psychophysical experiments: (**a**) discrimination between a pedestal contrast (**a.**α) and the same pedestal plus an increment contrast (**a.**β); (**b**) discrimination between two orientations near vertical (**b.**α and **b.**β). After calibration, the transducer function of each pooled unit (**c**) correctly exhibits an accelerating non-linearity near threshold (contrast $\approx 1\%$) and compressive non-linearity for high contrasts (Weber's law). We can see in (**d**) that pooling among units with similar tuning properties sharpens their tuning curves. Model parameters were: $\alpha \approx 0.75, \gamma \approx 4, \delta \approx 3.5, \epsilon \approx 1\%, \eta \approx 1.7Hz, S$ such that transducer inflexion point is at $4\times$ detection threshold contrast, orientation tuning FWHM=68deg (full width at half maximum), orientation pooling FWHM=40deg.

Two remaining parameters are the orientation tuning width, σ_θ, of the filters and the width, σ_{W_θ}, of the pool. It was not possible from the data in **Figure 2** alone to unambiguously determine these parameters. However, for any given σ_θ, σ_{W_θ} is uniquely determined by the following two qualitative constraints: first, a small pool size is not desirable because it yields contrast-dependent orientation tuning; it however appears from the data in **Figure 2.b** that this tuning should not vary much over a wide range of contrasts. The second constraint is qualitatively derived from **Figure 3.a**: for large pool sizes, the model predicted significant interference between mask and test patterns even for large orientation differences. Such interference was not observed in the data for orientation differences larger than 45deg. It consequently seems that a partial inhibitory pool, composed only of a fraction of the population of oriented filters with tuning similar to the central excitatory unit, accounts best for the psychophysical data. Finally, σ_θ was fixed so as to yield a correct qualitative curve shape for **Figure 3.a**.

3.2 Predictions

We used complex stimuli from masking experiments to test the predictive value of the model **(Figure 3)**. Although it was necessary to use some of the qualitative properties of the data seen in **Figure 3.a** to calibrate the model as detailed above, the calibrated model correctly produced a quantitative fit of this data. The calibrated model also correctly predicted the complex data of **Figure 3.b**.

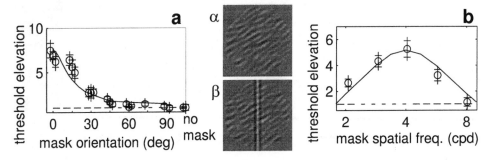

Figure 3: Prediction of psychophysical contrast thresholds in the presence of an oblique mask. The mask was a 50%-contrast stochastic oriented pattern (α), and the superimposed test pattern was a sixth-derivative of Gaussian bar (β). In (a), threshold elevation (i.e. ratio of threshold in the presence of mask to threshold in the absence of mask) was measured for varying mask orientation, for mask and test patterns at 4 cycles per degree (cpd). In (b), orientation difference between test and mask was fixed to 15deg, and threshold elevation was measured as a function of mask spatial frequency. Solid lines represent model predictions, and dashed lines represent unity threshold elevation.

4   DISCUSSION AND CONCLUSION

We have developed a model of early visual processing in humans which accounts for a wide range of measured spatial vision thresholds and which predicts behavioral thresholds for a potentially unlimited number of spatial discriminations. In addition to orientation- and spatial-frequency-tuned units, we have found it necessary to assume two types of interactions between such units: (i) non-linear self-excitation of each unit and (ii) divisive normalization of each unit response relative to the responses of similarly tuned units. All model parameters are constrained by psychophysical data and an automatic fitting procedure consistently converged to the same parameter set regardless of the initial position in parameter space.

Our two main contributions are the small number of model components and the unified, task-independent decision strategy. Rather than making different assumptions about the decision strategy in different behavioral tasks, we combine the information contained in the responses of all model units in a manner that is optimal for any behavioral task. We suggest that human observers adopt a similarly optimal decision procedure as they become familiar with a particular task ("task set"). Although here we apply this decision strategy only to the discrimination of stimulus contrast, orientation, and spatial frequency, it can readily be generalized to arbitrary discriminations such as, for example, the discrimination of vernier targets.

So far we have considered only situations in which the same decision strategy is optimal for every stimulus presentation. We are now studying situations in which the optimal decision strategy varies unpredictably from trial to trial ("decision uncertainty"). For example, situations in which the observer attempts to detect an increase in either the spatial frequency or the contrast of stimulus. In this way, we hope to learn the extent to which our model reflects the decision strategy adopted by human observers in an even wider range of situations. We have also assumed that the model's units were independent, which is not strictly true in biological systems (although the main source of correlation between neurons is the overlap between their respective tuning curves, which is accounted for in the model). The mathematical developments necessary to account for fixed or variable covariance between units are currently under study.

In contrast to other models of early visual processing [5, 6], we find that the psychophysical data is consistent only with interactions between similarly tuned units (e.g., "near-orientation inhibition"), not with interactions between units of very different tuning (e.g., "cross-orientation inhibition"). Although such partial pooling does not render tuning functions completely contrast-independent, an additional degree of contrast-independence could be provided by pooling across different spatial locations. This issue is currently under investigation.

In conclusion, we have developed a model based on self-excitation of each unit, divisive normalization [5, 6] between similarly tuned units, and an ideal observer decision strategy. It was able to reproduce a wide range of human visual thresholds. The fact that such a simple and idealized model can account quantitatively for a wide range of psychophysical observations greatly strengthens the notion that spatial vision thresholds reflect processing at one particular neuroanatomical level.

Acknowledgments: This work was supported by NSF-Engineering Research Center (ERC), NIMH, ONR, and the Sloan Center for Theoretical Neurobiology.

References

[1] Cover TM, Thomas JA. Elem Info Theo, Wiley & Sons, 1991

[2] Ferster D, Chung S, Wheat H. *Nature* 1996;380(6571):249-52

[3] Foley JM. *J Opt Soc A* 1994;11(6):1710-9

[4] Green DM, Swets JA. Signal Detectability and Psychophys. Wiley & Sons, 1966.

[5] Heeger DJ. Comput Models of Vis Processing, MIT Press, 1991

[6] Heeger DJ. *Vis Neurosci* 1992;9:181-97

[7] Nachmias J, Sansbury RV. *Vis Res* 1974;14:1039-42

[8] Nelson S, Toth L, Sheth B, Sur M. *Science* 1994;265(5173):774-77

[9] Perona P, Malik J. *J Opt Soc A* 1990;7(5):923-32

[10] Press WH, Teukolsky SA, *et al.* Num Rec in C. Cambridge University Press, 1992

[11] Ross J, Speed HD. *Proc R Soc B* 1991;246:61-9

[12] Seung HS, Sompolinksy H. *Proc Natl Acad Sci USA* 1993;90:10749-53.

[13] Sillito AM. *Progr Brain Res* 1992;90:349-84

[14] Skottun BC, Bradley A, Sclar G *et al.* J Neurophys 1987;57(3):773-86

[15] Snippe HP, Koenderink JJ. *Biol Cybern* 1992;67:183-90

[16] Teich MC, Turcott RG, Siegel RM. *IEEE Eng Med Biol* 1996;Sept-Oct,79-87

[17] Wen J, Koch C, Braun J. *Proc ARVO* 1997;5457

[18] Wilson HR, Bergen JR. *Vis Res* 1979;19:19-32

[19] Wilson HR. *Biol Cybern* 1980;38:171-8

[20] Wilson HR, McFarlane DK, Phillips GC. *Vis Res* 1983;23;873-82.

[21] Wilson HR, Humanski R. *Vis Res* 1993;33(8):1133-50

[22] Zenger B, Sagi D. *Vis Res* 1996;36(16):2497-2513.

Perturbative M-Sequences for Auditory Systems Identification

Mark Kvale and Christoph E. Schreiner[*]
Sloan Center for Theoretical Neurobiology, Box 0444
University of California, San Francisco
513 Parnassus Ave, San Francisco, CA 94143

Abstract

In this paper we present a new method for studying auditory systems based on m-sequences. The method allows us to perturbatively study the linear response of the system in the presence of various other stimuli, such as speech or sinusoidal modulations. This allows one to construct linear kernels (receptive fields) at the same time that other stimuli are being presented. Using the method we calculate the modulation transfer function of single units in the inferior colliculus of the cat at different operating points and discuss nonlinearities in the response.

1 Introduction

A popular approach to systems identification, i.e., identifying an accurate analytical model for the system behavior, is to use Volterra or Wiener expansions to model behavior via functional Taylor or orthogonal polynomial series, respectively [Marmarelis and Marmarelis1978]. Both approaches model the response $r(t)$ as a linear combination of small powers of the stimulus $s(t)$. Although effective for mild nonlinearities, deriving the linear combinations becomes numerically unstable for highly nonlinear systems. A more serious problem is that many biological systems are adaptive, i.e., the system behavior is dependent on the stimulus ensemble. For instance, [Rieke *et al.*1995] found that in the auditory nerve of the bullfrog linearity and information rates depended sensitively on whether a white noise or naturalistic ensemble is used.

One approach to handling these difficulties is to forgo the full expansion, and simply compute the linear response to small (perturbative) stimuli in the presence of various different ensembles, or operating points. By collecting linear responses

---

[*]Email: kvale@phy.ucsf.edu and chris@phy.ucsf.edu

from different operating points, one may fit nonlinear responses as one fits a non-linear function with a piecewise linear approximation. For adaptive systems the same procedure would be applied, with different operating points corresponding to different points along the time axis. Perturbative stimuli have wide application in condensed-matter physics, where they are used to characterize linear responses such as resistance, elasticity and viscosity, and in engineering, perturbative analyses are used in circuit analysis (small signal models) and structural diagnostics (vibration analysis). In neurophysiology, however, perturbative stimuli are unknown.

An effective stimulus for calculating the perturbative linear response of a system is the m-sequence. M-sequences have a long history of use in engineering and the physical sciences, with applications ranging from systems identification to cryptography and cellular communication. In physiology, m-sequences have been used primarily to compute system kernels [Marmarelis and Marmarelis1978], especially in the visual system [Pinter and Nabet1987]. In this work, we use perturbative m-sequences to study the linear response of single units in the inferior colliculus of a cat to amplitude-modulated (AM) stimuli. We add a small m-sequence signal to an AM carrier, which allows us to study the linear behavior of the system near a particular operating point in a non-destructive manner, i.e., without changing the operating point. Perturbative m-sequences allow one to calculate linear responses near the particular stimuli under study with only a little extra effort, and allow us to characterize the system over a wide range of stimuli, such as sinusoidal AM and naturalistic stimuli.

The auditory system we selected to study was the response of single units in the central nucleus of the inferior colliculus (IC) of an anaesthetised cat. Single unit responses were recorded extracellularly. Action potentials were amplified and stored on DAT tape, and were discriminated offline using a commercial computer-based spike sorter (Brainwave). 20 units were recorded, of which 10 yielded sufficiently stable responses to be analyzed.

2 M-Sequences and Linear Systems

A binary m-sequence is a two-level pseudo-random sequence of $+1$'s and -1's. The sequence length is $L = 2^n - 1$, where n is the order of the sequence. Typically, a binary m-sequence can be generated by a shift register with n bits and feedback connections derived from an irreducible polynomial over the multiplicative group Z_2 [Golomb1982]. For linear systems identification, m-sequences have two important properties. The first is that m-sequences have nearly zero mean: $\sum_{t=0}^{L-1} m[t] = -1$. The second is that the autocorrelation function takes on the impulse-like form

$$S_{mm}(\tau) = \sum_{t=0}^{L-1} m[t]m[t+\tau] = \begin{cases} L & \text{if } \tau = 0 \\ -1 & \text{otherwise} \end{cases} \tag{1}$$

Impulse stimuli also have a δ-function autocorrelation function. In the context of perturbative stimuli, the advantage of an m-sequence stimulus over an impulse stimulus is that for a given signal to noise ratio, an m-sequence perturbation stays much closer to the original signal (in the least squares sense) than an impulse perturbation. Thus the perturbed signal does not stray as far from the operating point and measurement of linear response about that operating point is more accurate.

We model the IC response with a system F through which a scalar stimulus $s(t)$ is passed to give a response $r(t)$:

$$r(t) = F[s(t)]. \tag{2}$$

For the purposes of this section, the functional F is taken to be a linear functional plus a DC component. In real experiments, the input and output signal are sampled into discrete sequences with t becoming an integer indexing the sequence. Then the system can be written as the discrete convolution

$$r[t] = h_0 + \sum_{t_1=0}^{L-1} h[t_1]s[t - t_1] \tag{3}$$

with kernels h_0 and $h[t_1]$ to be determined. We assume that the system has a finite memory of M time steps (with perhaps a delay) so that at most M of the $h[t]$ coefficients are nonzero. To determine the kernels perturbatively, we add a small amount of m-sequence to a base stimulus s_0:

$$s[t] = s_0[t] + \alpha m[t]. \tag{4}$$

Cross-correlating the response with the original m-sequence yields

$$R_{rm}(\tau) = \sum_{t=0}^{L-1} m[t]r[t+\tau] = \sum_{t=0}^{L-1} m[t]h_0 + \sum_{t=0}^{L-1}\sum_{t_1=0}^{L-1} h[t_1]m[t]s_0[t + \tau - t_1]$$

$$+ \sum_{t=0}^{L-1}\sum_{t_1=0}^{L-1} \alpha h[t_1]m[t]m[t + \tau - t_1]. \tag{5}$$

Using the sum formula for am -sequence above, the first sum in Eq. (5) can be simplified to $-h_0$. Using the autocorrelation Eq. (1), the third sum in Eq. (5) simplifies, and we find

$$R_{rm}(\tau) = \alpha(L+1)h[\tau] - h_0 - \alpha \sum_{t_1=0}^{L-1} h[t_1] + \sum_{t=0}^{L-1}\sum_{t_1=0}^{L-1} h[t_1]m[t]s_0[t + \tau - t_1] \tag{6}$$

Although the values for the kernels $h(t)$ are set implicitly by this equation, the terms on the right hand side of Eq. (6) are widely different in size for large L and the equation can be simplified. As is customary in auditory systems, we assume the DC response h_0 is small. To estimate the size of the other terms, we compute statistical estimates of their sizes and look at their scaling with the parameters. The term $\alpha \sum_{t_1=0}^{L-1} h[t_1]$ is a sum of M kernel elements; they may be correlated or uncorrelated, so a conservative estimate of their size is on the order of $O(\alpha M)$.

The last term in (6) is more subtle. We rewrite it as

$$\sum_{t_1=0}^{L-1}\sum_{t=0}^{L-1} h[t_1]m[t]s_0[t + \tau - t_1] = \sum_{t_1=0}^{L-1} h[t_1]p[\tau, t_1]$$

$$p[\tau, t_1] = \sum_{t=0}^{L-1} m[t]s_0[t + \tau - t_1] \tag{7}$$

The time series of the ambient stimulus $s_0[t]$ and m-sequence $m[t]$ are assumed to be uncorrelated. By the central limit theorem, the sum $p[\tau, t_1]$ will then have an average of zero with a standard deviation of $O(L^{1/2})$. If in turn, the terms $p[\tau, t_1]$ are uncorrelated with the kernels $h[t_1]$, we have that

$$\sum_{t_1=0}^{L-1}\sum_{t=0}^{L-1} h[t_1]m[t]s_0[t + \tau - t_1] \sim O(M^{1/2}L^{1/2}) \tag{8}$$

If N cycles of the m-sequence are performed, in which $s_0[t]$ is different for each cycle, all the terms in Eq. (6) scale with N as $O(N)$, except for the double sum. By the same central limits arguments above, the double sum scales as $O(N^{1/2})$.

Putting all these results together into Eq. (6) and solving for the kernels yields

$$
\begin{aligned}
h(\tau) &= \frac{1}{\alpha(L+1)}R_{rm}(\tau) - O\left(\frac{M}{L}\right) + O\left(\frac{M^{1/2}}{\alpha N^{1/2}L^{1/2}}\right). \\
&\approx \frac{1}{\alpha(L+1)}R_{rm}(\tau) - C_1\frac{M}{L} + C_2\frac{M^{1/2}}{\alpha N^{1/2}L^{1/2}},
\end{aligned}
\tag{9}
$$

with the constants $C_1, C_2 \sim O(h[\tau])$ depending neural firing rate, statistics, etc., determined from experiment. If we take the kernel element $h(\tau)$ to be the first term in Eq. 9, then the last two terms in Eq. (9) contribute errors in determining the kernel and can be thought of as noise. Both error terms vanish as $L \to \infty$ and the procedure is asymptotically exact for arbitrary uncorrelated stimuli $s_0[t]$. In order for the cross-correlation $R_{sm}(\tau)$ to yield a good estimate, the inequalities

$$
C_1 M \ll L \quad \text{and} \quad \alpha \gg C_2 M^{1/2}(NL)^{-1/2}
\tag{10}
$$

must hold. In practice, the kernel memory is much smaller than the sequence length, and the second inequality is the stricter bound. The second inequality represents a tradeoff among sequence length, number of trials and the size of the perturbation for a given level of systematic noise in the kernel estimate. For instance, if $L = 2^{15} - 1$, $N = 10$, $M = 30$, and noise floor at 10%, the perturbation should be larger than $\alpha = 0.095$. If no signal $s_0[t]$ is present, then the $O(M^{1/2}\alpha^{-1}(NL)^{-1/2})$ term drops out and the usual m-sequence cross-correlation result is recovered.

3 M-Sequences for Modulation Response

Previous work, e.g., [Møller and Rees1986, Langner and Schreiner1988] has shown that many of the cells in the inferior colliculus are tuned not only to a characteristic frequency, but are also tuned to a best frequency of modulation of the carrier. A highly simplified model of the IC unit response to sound stimuli is the $L1 - N - L2$ cascade filter, with $L1$ a linear tank circuit with a transfer function matching that of the frequency tuning curve, N a nonlinear rectifying unit, and $L2$ a linear circuit with a transfer function matching that of the modulation transfer function. Detecting this modulation is an inherently nonlinear operation and N is not well approximated by a linear kernel. Thus IC modulation responses will not be well characterized by ordinary m-sequence stimuli using the methods described in Section 2.

A better approach is to bypass the $L1 - N$ demodulation step entirely and concentrate on measuring $L2$. This can be accomplished by creating a *modulation m-sequence*:

$$
s[t] = a\,(s_0[t] + b\,m[t])\sin[\omega_c t],
\tag{11}
$$

where $|s_0[t]| \leq 1$ is the ambient signal, i.e., the operating point, $m[t] \in [-1, 1]$ is an m-sequence added with amplitude b, and ω_c is the carrier frequency. Demodulation gives the effective input stimulus

$$
s_m[t] = a\,(s_0[t] + b\,m[t]).
\tag{12}
$$

Note that there is little physiological evidence for a purely linear rectifier N. In fact, both the work of [Møller and Rees1986, Rees and Møller1987] and ours below show that there is a nonlinear modulation response. Taking a modulation transfer function seriously, however, implies that one assumes that modulation response is linear, which implies that the static nonlinearity used is something like a half-wave rectifier. Linearity is used here as a convenient assumption for organizing the stimulus and asking whether nonlinearities exist.

For full m-sequence modulation ($s_0[t] = 1$ and $b = 1$) the stimulus s_m and the neural response can be used to compute, via the Lee-Schetzen cross-correlation, the modulation transfer function for the $L2$ system. Alternatively, for $b \ll 1$, the m-sequence is a perturbation on the underlying modulation envelope $s_0[t]$. The derivation above shows that the linear modulation kernel can also be calculated using a Lee-Schetzen cross-correlation. M-sequences at full modulation depth were first used by [Møller and Rees1986, Rees and Møller1987] to calculate white-noise kernels. Here, we are using m-sequence in a different way—we are calculating the small-signal properties around the stimulus $s_0[t]$.

The m-sequences used in this experiment were of length $2^{15} - 1 = 32,767$. For each unit, 10 cycles of the m-sequence were presented back-to-back. After determining the characteristic frequency of a unit, stimuli were presented which never differed from the characteristic frequency by more than 500 Hz. Figure 1 depicts the sinusoidal and m-sequence components and their combined result. The stimuli were presented in random order so as to mitigate adaptation effects.

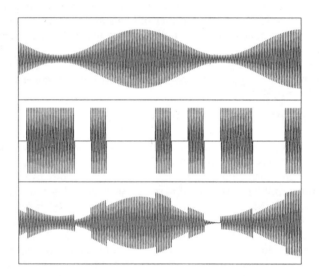

Figure 1: A depiction of stimuli used in the experiment. The top graph shows a pure sine wave modulation at modulation depth 0.8. The middle graph shows an m-sequence modulation at depth 1.0. The bottom graph shows a perturbative m-sequence modulation at depth 0.2 added to a sinusoidal modulation at depth 0.8.

4   Results

Figure 2 shows the spike rates for both the pure sinusoid and the combined sinusoid and m-sequence stimuli. Note that the rates are nearly the same, indicating that the perturbation did not have a large effect on the average response of the unit. The unit shows an adaptation in firing rate over the 10 trials, but we did not find a statistically significant change in the kernels of different trials in any of the units.

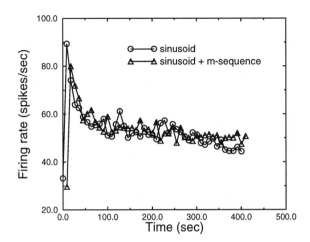

Figure 2: A plot of the unit firing rates for both the pure sinusoid and the sinusoid + m-sequence stimuli. The carrier frequency is 9 kHz and is close to the characteristic frequency of the neuron. The sinusoidal modulation has a frequency of 20 Hz and the m-sequence modulation has a frequency of 800 sec^{-1}.

Figure 3 shows modulation response kernels at several different values of the modulation depth. Note that if the system was a linear, superposition would cause all the kernels to be equivalent; in fact it is seen that the nonlinearities are of the same magnitude as the linear response. In this particular unit, the triphasic behavior at small modulation depths gives way to monophasic behavior at high modulation depths and an FFT of the kernel shows that the bandwidth of the modulation transfer function also broadens with increasing depth.

5   Discussion

In this paper, we have introduced a new type of stimulus, perturbative m-sequences, for the study of auditory systems and derived their properties. We then applied perturbative m-sequences to the analysis of the modulation response of units in the IC, and found the linear response at a few different operation point. We demonstrated that the nonlinear response in the presence of sinusoidal modulations are nearly as large as the linear response and thus a description of unit response with only an MTF is incomplete. We believe that perturbative stimuli can be an effective tool for the analysis of many systems whose units phase lock to a stimulus.

The main limiting factor is the systematic noise discussed in section 2, but it is possible to trade off duration of measurement and size of the perturbation to achieve good results. The m-sequence stimuli also make it possible to derive higher order information [Sutter1987] and with a suitable noise floor, it may be possible to derive second-order kernels as well.

This work was supported by The Sloan foundation and ONR grant number N00014-94-1-0547.

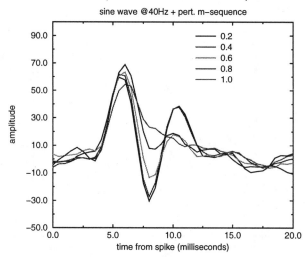

Figure 3: A plot of the temporal kernels derived from perturbative m-sequence stimuli in conjunction with sinusoidal modulations at various modulation depth. The y-axis units are amplitude per spike and the x-axis is in milliseconds *before* the spike.

References

[Golomb1982] S. W. Golomb. *Shift Register Sequences*. Aegean Park Press, Laguna Hills, CA, 1982.

[Langner and Schreiner1988] G. Langner and C. E. Schreiner. Periodicity coding in the inferior colliculus of the cat: I. neuronal mechanisms. *Journal of Neurophysiology*, 60:1799–1822, 1988.

[Marmarelis and Marmarelis1978] Panos Z. Marmarelis and Vasilis Z. Marmarelis. *Analysis of Physiological Systems*. Plenum Press, New York, NY, 10011, 1978.

[Møller and Rees1986] Aage R. Møller and Adrian Rees. Dynamic properties of single neurons in the inferior colliculus of the rat. *Hearing Research*, 24:203–215, 1986.

[Pinter and Nabet1987] Robert B. Pinter and Bahram Nabet. *Nonlinear Vision*. CRC Press, Boca Raton, FL, 1987.

[Rees and Møller1987] Adrian Rees and Aage R. Møller. Stimulus properties influencing the responses of inferior colliculus neurons to amplitude-modulated sounds. *Hearing Research*, 27:129–143, 1987.

[Rieke *et al.*1995] F. Rieke, D. A. Bodnar, and W. Bialek. Naturalistic stimuli increase the rate and efficiency of information transmission by primary auditory afferents. *Proceedings of the Royal Society of London. Series B*, 262:259–265, 1995.

[Sutter1987] E. E. Sutter. A practical non-stochastic approach to nonlinear time-domain analysis. In Vasilis Z. Marmarelis, editor, *Advanced Methods of Physiological Modeling, Vol. 1*, pages 303–315. Biomedical Simulations Resource, University of Southern California, Los Angeles, CA 90089-1451, 1987.

Effects of Spike Timing Underlying Binocular Integration and Rivalry in a Neural Model of Early Visual Cortex

Erik D. Lumer
Wellcome department of Cognitive Neurology
Institute of Neurology, University College of London
12 Queen Square, London, WC1N 3BG, UK

Abstract

In normal vision, the inputs from the two eyes are integrated into a single percept. When dissimilar images are presented to the two eyes, however, perceptual integration gives way to alternation between monocular inputs, a phenomenon called binocular rivalry. Although recent evidence indicates that binocular rivalry involves a modulation of neuronal responses in extrastriate cortex, the basic mechanisms responsible for differential processing of conflicting and congruent stimuli remain unclear. Using a neural network that models the mammalian early visual system, I demonstrate here that the desynchronized firing of cortical-like neurons that first receive inputs from the two eyes results in rivalrous activity patterns at later stages in the visual pathway. By contrast, synchronization of firing among these cells prevents such competition. The temporal coordination of cortical activity and its effects on neural competition emerge naturally from the network connectivity and from its dynamics. These results suggest that input-related differences in relative spike timing at an early stage of visual processing may give rise to the phenomena both of perceptual integration and rivalry in binocular vision.

1 Introduction

The neural determinants of visual perception can be probed by subjecting the visual system to ambiguous viewing conditions - stimulus configurations that admit more than one perceptual interpretation. For example, when a left-tilted grating is shown to the left eye and a right-tilted grating to the right eye, the two stimuli are momentarily perceived together as a plaid pattern, but soon only one line grating becomes visible, while the other is suppressed. This phenomenon, known as binocular rivalry, has long been thought to involve competition between monocular neurons within the primary visual cortex (V1), leading to the suppression of information from one eye (Lehky, 1988; Blake, 1989). It has recently been shown, however, that neurons whose activity covaries with perception during rivalry are found mainly in higher cortical areas and respond to inputs from both eyes, thus suggesting that rivalry arises instead through competition between alternative stimulus interpretations in extrastriate cortex (Leopold and Logothetis, 1996). Because eye-specific information appears to be lost at this stage, it remains unclear how the stimulus conditions (i.e. conflicting monocular stimuli) yielding binocular rivalry are distinguished from the conditions (i.e. matched monocular inputs) that produce stable single vision.

I propose here that the degree of similarity between the images presented to the two eyes is registered by the temporal coordination of neuronal activity in V1, and that changes in relative spike timing within this area can instigate the differential responses in higher cortical areas to conflicting or congruent visual stimuli. Stimulus and eye-specific synchronous activity has been described previously both in the lateral geniculate nucleus (LGN) and in the striate cortex (Gray et al., 1989; Sillito et al., 1994; Neuenschwander and Singer, 1996). It has been suggested that such synchrony may serve to bind together spatially distributed neural events into coherent representations (Milner, 1974; von der Malsburg, 1981; Singer, 1993). In addition, reduced synchronization of striate cortical responses in strabismic cats has been correlated with their perceptual inability to combine signals from the two eyes or to incorporate signals from an amblyopic eye (König et al., 1993; Roelfsema et al., 1994). However, the specific influences of interocular input-similarity on spike coordination in the striate cortex, and of spike coordination on competition in other cortical areas, remain unclear.

To examine these influences, a simplified neural model of an early visual pathway is simulated. In what follows, I first describe the anatomical and physiological constraints incorporated in the model, and then show that a temporal patterning of neuronal activity in its primary cortical area emerges naturally. By manipulating the relative spike timing of neuronal discharges in this area, I demonstrate its role in inducing differential responses in higher visual areas to conflicting or congruent visual stimulation. Finally, I discuss possible implications of these results for understanding the neural basis of normal and ambiguous perception in vivo.

2   Model overview

The model has four stages based on the organization of the mammalian visual pathway (Gilbert, 1993). These stages represent: (i) sectors of an ipsilateral ('left eye') and a contralateral ('right eye') lamina of the LGN, which relay visual inputs to the cortex; (ii) two corresponding monocular regions in layer 4 of V1 with different ocular dominance; (iii) a primary cortical sector in which the monocular inputs are first combined (called Vp in the model); and (iv) a secondary visual area of cortex in which higher-order features are extracted (Vs in the model; Fig. 1). Each stage consists of 'standard' integrate-and-fire neurons that are incorporated in synaptic networks. At the cortical stages, these units are grouped in local recurrent circuits that are similar to those used in previous modeling studies (Douglas et al., 1995; Somers et al., 1995). Synaptic interactions in these circuits are both excitatory and inhibitory between cells with similar orientation selectivity, but are restricted to in-

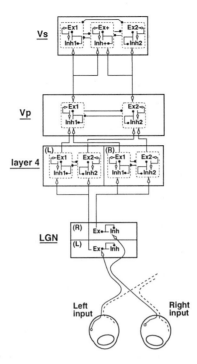

Figure 1: Architecture of the model. Excitatory and inhibitory connections are represented by lines with arrowheads and round terminals, respectively. Each lamina in the LGN consists of 100 excitatory units (Ex) and 100 inhibitory units (Inh), coupled via local inhibition. Cortical units are grouped into local recurrent circuits (stippled boxes), each comprising 200 Ex units and 100 Inh units. In each monocular patch of layer 4, one cell group (Ex1 and Inh1) responds to left-tilted lines (orientation 1), whereas a second group (Ex2 and Inh2) is selective for right-tilted lines (orientation 2). The same orientation selectivities are remapped onto Vp and Vs, although cells in these areas respond to inputs from both eyes. In addition, convergent inputs from Vp to Vs establish a third selectivity in Vs, namely for line crossings (Ex+ and Inh+).

hibition only between cell groups with orthogonal orientation preference (Kisvárday and Eysel, 1993). Two orthogonal orientations (orientation 1 and 2) are mapped in each monocular sector of layer 4, and in Vp. To account for the emergence of more complex response properties at higher levels in the visual system (Van Essen and Gallant, 1994), forward connectivity patterns from Vp to Vs are organized to support three feature selectivities in Vs, one for orientation 1, one for orientation 2, and one for the conjunction of these two orientations, i.e. for line crossings. These forward projections are reciprocated by weaker backward projections from Vs to Vp. As a general rule, connections are established at random within and between interconnected populations of cells, with connection probabilities between pairs of cells ranging from 1 to 10 %, consistent with experimental estimates (Thomson et al., 1988; Mason et al., 1991). Visual stimulation is achieved by applying a stochastic synaptic excitation independently to activated cells in the LGN. A quantitative description of the model parameters will be reported elsewhere.

3   Results

In a first series of simulations, the responses of the model to conflicting and congruent visual stimuli are compared. When the left input consists of left-tilted lines (orientation 1) and the right input of right-tilted lines (orientation 2), rivalrous response suppression occurs in the secondary visual area. At any moment, only one of the three feature-selective cell groups in Vs can maintain elevated firing rates (Fig. 2a). By contrast, when congruent plaid patterns are used to stimulate the two monocular channels, these cell groups are forced in a regime in which they all sustain elevated firing rates (Fig. 2b). This concurrent activation of cells selective for orthogonal orientations and for line crossings can be interpreted as a distributed representation of the plaid pattern in Vs [1]. A quantitative assessment of the degree of competition in Vs is shown in Figure 2c. The rivalry index of two groups of neurons is defined as the mean absolute value of the difference between their instantaneous group-averaged firing rates divided by the highest instantaneous firing rate among the two cell groups. This index varies between 0 for nonrivalrous groups of neurons and 1 for groups of neurons with mutually exclusive patterns of activity. Groups of cells with different selectivity in Vs have a significantly higher rivalry index when stimulated by conflicting rather than by congruent visual inputs ($p < 0.0001$) (Fig. 2c).

Note that, in the example shown in Figure 2a, the differential responses to conflicting inputs develop from about 200 ms after stimulus onset and are maintained over the remainder of the stimulation epoch. In other simulations, alternation between dominant and suppressed responses was also observed over the same epoch as a result of fluctuations in the overall network dynamics. A detailed analysis of the dynamics of perceptual alternation during rivalry, however, is beyond the scope of this report.

Although Vp exhibits a similar distribution of firing rates during rivalrous and nonrivalrous stimulation, synchronization between the two cell groups in Vp is more pronounced in the nonrivalrous than in the rivalrous case (Fig. 2d, upper plots). Subtraction of the shift predictor demonstrates that the units are not phase-locked to the stimuli. The changes in spike coordination among Vp units reflects the temporal patterning of their layer 4 inputs. During rivalry, Vp cells with different orientation selectivity are driven by layer 4 units that belong to separate monocular pathways, and hence, are uncorrelated (Fig. 2d, lower left). By contrast, cells in Vp receive convergent inputs from both eyes during nonrivalrous stimulation. Because of the synchronization of discharges among cells responsive to the same eye within layer 4 (Fig. 2d, lower right), the paired activities from the two monocular channels are also synchronized, and provide synchronous inputs to cells with different orientation selectivity in Vp.

To establish unequivocally that changes in spike coordination within Vp are sufficient to trigger differential responses in Vs to conflicting and congruent stimuli, the model can be modified as follows. A single group of cells in layer 4 is used to drive with equal strength both orientation-selective populations of neurons in Vp. The outputs from layer 4, however, is relayed to these two target populations with average transmission delays that differ by either 10 ms or by 0 ms. In the first case, competition prevails among cells in the secondary visual area. This contrasts with the nonrivalrous activity in this area when similar transmission delays are used at an earlier stage (data not shown). This test confirms that changes in relative spike

---

[1]To discount possible effects of binocular summmation, synaptic strengths from layer 4 to Vp are reduced during congruent stimulation so as to produce a feedforward activation of Vp comparable to that elicited by conflicting monocular inputs.

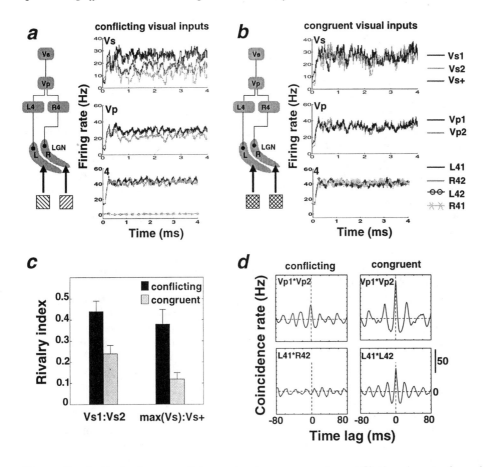

Figure 2: **A**, Instantaneous firing rates in response to conflicting inputs for cell groups in layer 4, in Vp, and in Vs (stimulus onset at $t = 250ms$). Discharge rates of layer 4 cells driven by different 'eyes' are similar (lower plot). By contrast, Vs exhibits competitive firing patterns soon after stimulus onset (upper plot). Feedback influence from Vs to Vp results in comparatively weaker competition in Vp (middle plot). **B**, Responses to congruent inputs. All cell groups in layer 4 are activated by visual inputs. Nonrivalrous firing patterns ensue in Vp and Vs. **C**, Rivalry indices during conflicting and congruent stimulation, are calculated for the two orientation-selective cell groups and for the dominant and cross-selective cell group in Vs. **D**, Interocular responses are uncorrelated in layer 4 (lower left), whereas intraocular activities are synchronous at this stage (lower right). Enhanced synchronization of discharges ensues between cell groups in Vp during congruent stimulation (upper right), relative to the degree of coherence during conflicting stimulation (upper left).

timing are sufficient to switch the outcome of neural network interactions involving strong mutual inhibition from competitive to cooperative.

4 Conclusion

In the present study, a simplified model of a visual pathway was used to gain insight into the neural mechanisms operating during binocular vision. Simulations of neuronal responses to visual inputs revealed a stimulus-related patterning of relative spike timing at an early stage of cortical processing. This patterning reflected the degree of similarity between the images presented to the two 'eyes', and, in turn, it altered the outcome of competitive interactions at later stages along the visual pathway. These effects can help explaining how the same cortical networks can exhibit both rivalrous and nonrivalrous activity, depending on the temporal coordination of their synaptic inputs.

These results bear on the interpretation of recent empirical findings about the neuronal correlates of rivalrous perception. In experiments with awake monkeys, Logothetis and colleagues (Sheinberg et al., 1995; Leopold and Logothetis, 1996) have shown that neurons whose firing rate correlates with perception during rivalry are distributed at several levels along the primate visual pathways, including V1/V2, V4, and IT. Importantly, the fraction of modulated responses is lower in V1 than in extrastriate areas, and it increases with the level in the visual hierarchy. Simulations of the present model exhibit a behavior that is consistent with these observations. However, these simulations also predict that both rivalrous and nonrivalrous perception may have a clear neurophysiological correlate in V1, i.e. at the earliest stage of visual cortical processing. Accordingly, congruent stimulation of both eyes will synchronize the firing of binocular cells with overlapping receptive fields in V1. By contrast, conflicting inputs to the two eyes will cause a desynchronization between their corresponding neural events in V1. Because this temporal registration of stimulus dissimilarity instigates competition among binocular cells in higher visual areas and not between monocular pathways, the ensuing pattern of response suppression and dominance is independent of the eyes through which the stimuli are presented. Thus, the model can in principle account for the psychophysical finding that a single phase of perceptual dominance during rivalry can span multiple interocular exchanges of the rival stimuli (Logothetis et al., 1996).

The present results also reveal a novel property of canonical cortical-like circuits interacting through mutual inhibition, i.e. the degree of competition among such circuits exhibits a remarkable sensitivity to the relative timing of neuronal action potentials. This suggests that the temporal patterning of cortical activity may be a fundamental mechanism for selecting among stimuli competing for the control of attention and motor action.

Acknowledgements

This work was supported in part by an IRSIA visiting fellowship at the Center for Nonlinear Phenomena and Complex Systems, Université Libre de Bruxelles. I thank Professor Grégoire Nicolis for his hospitality during my stay in Brussels; and David Leopold and Daniele Piomelli for helpful discussions and comments on an earlier version of the manuscript.

References

Blake R (1989) A neural theory of binocular vision. Psychol Rev 96:145-167.

Douglas RJ, Koch C, Mahowald M, Martin K, Suarez H (1995) Recurrent excitation in neocortical circuits. Science 269:981-985.

Gilbert C (1993) Circuitry, architecture, and functional dynamics of visual cortex. Cereb Cortex 3:373-386.

Gray CM, König P, Engel AK, Singer, W (1989) Oscillatory responses in cat visual cortex exhibit inter-columnar synchronization which reflects global stimulus properties. Nature 338:334-337.

Kisvárday ZF, Eysel UT (1993) Functional and structural topography of horizontal inhibitory connections in cat visual cortex. Europ J Neurosci 5:1558-1572.

König P, Engel AK, Löwel S, Singer, W (1993) Squint affects synchronization of oscillatory responses in cat visual cortex. Eur J Neurosci 5:501-508.

Lehky SR (1988) An astable multivibrator model of binocular rivalry. Perception 17: 215- 228.

Leopold DA, Logothetis NK (1996) Activity changes in early visual cortex reflect monkeys percepts during binocular rivalry. Nature 379:549-553.

Logothetis NK, Leopold DA, Sheinberg DL (1996) What is rivalling during rivalry? Nature 380:621-624.

Neuenschwander S, Singer W (1996) Long-range synchronization of oscillatory light responses in the cat retina and lateral geniculate nucleus. Nature 379:728-733.

Milner PM (1974) A model of visual shape recognition. Psychol Rev 81:521-535.

Roelfsema PR, König P, Engel AK, Sireteanu R, Singer W (1994) Reduced synchronization in the visual cortex of cats with strabismic amblyopia. Eur J Neurosci 6:1645-1655.

Sheinberg DL, Leopold DA, Logothetis NK (1995) Effects of binocular rivalry on face cell activity in monkey temporal cortex. Soc Neurosci Abstr 21:15.12.

Sillito AM, Jones HE, Gerstein GL, West DC (1994) Feature-linked synchronization of thalamic relay cell firing induced by feedback from the visual cortex. Nature 369:479-482.

Singer W (1993) Synchronization of cortical activity and its putative role in information processing. Annu Rev Physiol 55:349-374.

Somers D, Nelson S, Sur M (1995) An emergent model of orientation selectivity in cat visual cortical simple cells. J Neurosci 15:5448-5465.

Van Essen DC, Gallant JL (1994) Neural mechanisms of form and motion processing in the primate visual system. Neuron 13:1-10.

von der Malsburg C (1981) The correlation theory of the brain. Internal Report 81-2, Max Planck Institute for Biophysical Chemistry, Göttingen.

Dynamic Stochastic Synapses as Computational Units

Wolfgang Maass
Institute for Theoretical Computer Science
Technische Universität Graz,
A–8010 Graz, Austria.
email: maass@igi.tu-graz.ac.at

Anthony M. Zador
The Salk Institute
La Jolla, CA 92037, USA
email: zador@salk.edu

Abstract

In most neural network models, synapses are treated as static weights that change only on the slow time scales of learning. In fact, however, synapses are highly dynamic, and show use-dependent plasticity over a wide range of time scales. Moreover, synaptic transmission is an inherently stochastic process: a spike arriving at a presynaptic terminal triggers release of a vesicle of neurotransmitter from a release site with a probability that can be much less than one. Changes in release probability represent one of the main mechanisms by which synaptic efficacy is modulated in neural circuits.

We propose and investigate a simple model for dynamic stochastic synapses that can easily be integrated into common models for neural computation. We show through computer simulations and rigorous theoretical analysis that this model for a dynamic stochastic synapse increases computational power in a nontrivial way. Our results may have implications for the processing of time-varying signals by both biological and artificial neural networks.

A synapse S carries out computations on spike trains, more precisely on trains of spikes from the presynaptic neuron. Each spike from the presynaptic neuron may or may not trigger the release of a neurotransmitter-filled vesicle at the synapse. The probability of a vesicle release ranges from about 0.01 to almost 1. Furthermore this release probability is known to be strongly "history dependent" [Dobrunz and Stevens, 1997]. A spike causes an excitatory or inhibitory potential (EPSP or IPSP, respectively) in the postsynaptic neuron only when a vesicle is released.

A spike train is represented as a sequence $\underline{t}$ of firing times, i.e. as increasing sequences of numbers $t_1 < t_2 < \ldots$ from $\mathbf{R}^+ := \{z \in \mathbf{R} : z \geq 0\}$. For each spike train $\underline{t}$ the output of synapse S consists of the sequence $S(\underline{t})$ of those $t_i \in \underline{t}$ on which vesicles are "released" by S , i.e. of those $t_i \in \underline{t}$ which cause an excitatory or inhibitory postsynaptic potential (EPSP or IPSP, respectively). The map $\underline{t} \rightarrow S(\underline{t})$ may be viewed as a stochastic function that is *computed* by synapse S . Alternatively one can characterize the output $S(\underline{t})$ of a synapse S through its *release pattern* $\underline{q} = q_1 q_2 \ldots \in \{R, F\}^*$, where R stands for release and F for failure of release. For each $t_i \in \underline{t}$ one sets $q_i = R$ if $t_i \in S(\underline{t})$, and $q_i = F$ if $t_i \notin S(\underline{t})$.

1 Basic model

The central equation in our dynamic synapse model gives the probability $p_S(t_i)$ that the ith spike in a presynaptic spike train $\underline{t} = (t_1, \dots, t_k)$ triggers the release of a vesicle at time t_i at synapse S,

$$p_S(t_i) = 1 - e^{-C(t_i) \cdot V(t_i)} . \tag{1}$$

The release probability is assumed to be nonzero only for $t \in \underline{t}$, so that releases occur only when a spike invades the presynaptic terminal (*i.e.* the spontaneous release probability is assumed to be zero). The functions $C(t) \geq 0$ and $V(t) \geq 0$ describe, respectively, the states of facilitation and depletion at the synapse at time t .

The dynamics of facilitation are given by

$$C(t) = C_0 + \sum_{t_i < t} c(t - t_i) , \tag{2}$$

where C_0 is some parameter ≥ 0 that can for example be related to the resting concentration of calcium in the synapse. The exponential response function $c(s)$ models the response of $C(t)$ to a presynaptic spike that had reached the synapse at time $t - s$: $c(s) = \alpha \cdot e^{-s/\tau_C}$, where the positive parameters τ_C and α give the decay constant and magnitude, respectively, of the response. The function C models in an abstract way internal synaptic processes underlying presynaptic facilitation, such as the concentration of calcium in the presynaptic terminal. The particular exponential form used for $c(s)$ could arise for example if presynaptic calcium dynamics were governed by a simple first order process.

The dynamics of depletion are given by

$$V(t) = \max(0, V_0 - \sum_{t_i: \, t_i < t \text{ and } t_i \in S(\underline{t})} v(t - t_i)) , \tag{3}$$

for some parameter $V_0 > 0$. $V(t)$ depends on the subset of those $t_i \in \underline{t}$ with $t_i < t$ on which vesicles were actually released by the synapse, i.e. $t_i \in S(\underline{t})$. The function $v(s)$ models the response of $V(t)$ to a preceding release of the same synapse at time $t - s \leq t$. Analogously as for $c(s)$ one may choose for $v(s)$ a function with exponential decay $v(s) = e^{-s/\tau_V}$, where $\tau_V > 0$ is the decay constant. The function V models in an abstract way internal synaptic processes that support presynaptic depression, such as depletion of the pool of readily releasable vesicles. In a more specific synapse model one could interpret V_0 as the maximal number of vesicles that can be stored in the readily releasable pool, and $V(t)$ as the expected number of vesicles in the readily releasable pool at time t.

In summary, the model of synaptic dynamics presented here is described by five parameters: C_0, V_0, τ_C, τ_V and α. The dynamics of a synaptic computation and its internal variables $C(t)$ and $V(t)$ are indicated in Fig. 1.

For low release probabilities, Eq. 1 can be expanded to first order around $r(t) := C(t) \cdot V(t) = 0$ to give

$$p_S(t_i) = C(t_i) \cdot V(t_i) + O([C(t_i) \cdot V(t_i)]^2). \tag{4}$$

Similar expressions have been widely used to describe synaptic dynamics for multiple synapses [Magleby, 1987, Markram and Tsodyks, 1996, Varela et al., 1997].

In our synapse model, we have assumed a standard exponential form for the decay of facilitation and depression (see e.g. [Magleby, 1987, Markram and Tsodyks, 1996, Varela et al., 1997, Dobrunz and Stevens, 1997]). We have further assumed a multiplicative interaction between facilitation and depletion. While this form has not been validated

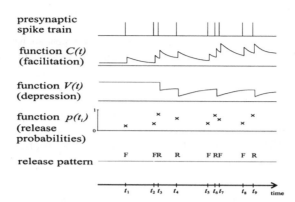

Figure 1: *Synaptic computation on a spike train* $\underline{t}$, *together with the temporal dynamics of the internal variables C and V of our model. Note that $V(t)$ changes its value only when a presynaptic spike causes release.*

at single synapses, in the limit of low release probability (see Eq. 4), it agrees with the multiplicative term employed in [Varela et al., 1997] to describe the dynamics of multiple synapses.

The assumption that release at individual release sites of a synapse is binary, *i.e.* that each release site releases 0 or 1—but not more than 1—vesicle when invaded by a spike, leads to the exponential form of Eq. 1 [Dobrunz and Stevens, 1997]. We emphasize the formal distinction between *release site* and *synapse*. A synapse might consist of several release sites in parallel, each of which has a dynamics similar to that of the stochastic "synapse model" we consider.

2   Results

2.1   Different "Weights" for the First and Second Spike in a Train

We start by investigating the range of different release probabilities $p_S(t_1), p_S(t_2)$ that a synapse S can assume for the first two spikes in a given spike train. These release probabilities depend on $t_2 - t_1$ as well as on the values of the internal parameters $C_0, V_0, \tau_C, \tau_V, \alpha$ of the synapse S. Here we analyze the potential freedom of a synapse to choose values for $p_S(t_1)$ and $p_S(t_2)$. We show in Theorem 2.1 that the range of values for the release probabilities for the first two spikes is quite large, and that the entire attainable range can be reached through through suitable choices of C_0 and V_0.

Theorem 2.1 *Let* $\langle t_1, t_2 \rangle$ *be some arbitrary spike train consisting of two spikes, and let* $p_1, p_2 \in (0, 1)$ *be some arbitrary given numbers with* $p_2 > p_1 \cdot (1 - p_1)$. *Furthermore assume that arbitrary positive values are given for the parameters* α, τ_C, τ_V *of a synapse S. Then one can always find values for the two parameters C_0 and V_0 of the synapse S so that* $p_S(t_1) = p_1$ *and* $p_S(t_2) = p_2$.

Furthermore the condition $p_2 > p_1 \cdot (1 - p_1)$ *is necessary in a strong sense. If* $p_2 \leq p_1 \cdot (1 - p_1)$ *then no synapse S can achieve* $p_S(t_1) = p_1$ *and* $p_S(t_2) = p_2$ *for any spike train* $\langle t_1, t_2 \rangle$ *and for any values of its parameters* $C_0, V_0, \tau_C, \tau_V, \alpha$.

If one associates the current sum of release probabilities of multiple synapses or release sites between two neurons u and v with the current value of the "connection strength" $w_{u,v}$ between two neurons in a formal neural network model, then the preceding result points

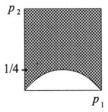

Figure 2: *The dotted area indicates the range of pairs $\langle p_1, p_2 \rangle$ of release probabilities for the first and second spike through which a synapse can move (for any given interspike interval) by varying its parameters C_0 and V_0.*

to a significant difference between the dynamics of computations in biological circuits and formal neural network models. Whereas in formal neural network models it is commonly assumed that the value of a synaptic weight stays fixed during a computation, the release probabilities of synapses in biological neural circuits may change on a fast time scale within a single computation.

2.2 Release Patterns for the First Three Spikes

In this section we examine the variety of release patterns that a synapse can produce for spike trains $t_1, t_2, t_3, \ldots$ with at least three spikes. We show not only that a synapse can make use of different parameter settings to produce different release patterns, but also that a synapse with a *fixed* parameter setting can respond quite differently to spike trains with different interspike intervals. Hence a synapse can serve as *pattern detector* for temporal patterns in spike trains.

It turns out that the structure of the triples of release probabilities $\langle p_S(t_1), p_S(t_2), p_S(t_3) \rangle$ that a synapse can assume is substantially more complicated than for the first two spikes considered in the previous section. Therefore we focus here on the dependence of the *most likely release pattern* $\underline{q} \in \{R, F\}^3$ on the internal synaptic parameters and on the interspike intervals $I_1 := t_2 - t_1$ and $I_2 := t_3 - t_2$. This dependence is in fact quite complex, as indicated in Fig. 3.

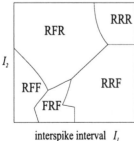

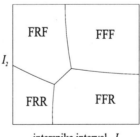

Figure 3: **(A, left)** *Most likely release pattern of a synapse in dependence of the interspike intervals I_1 and I_2. The synaptic parameters are $C_0 = 1.5$, $V_0 = 0.5$, $\tau_C = 5$, $\tau_V = 9$, $\alpha = 0.7$.* **(B, right)** *Release patterns for a synapse with other values of its parameters ($C_0 = 0.1$, $V_0 = 1.8$, $\tau_C = 15$, $\tau_V = 30$, $\alpha = 1$).*

Fig. 3A shows the most likely release pattern for each given pair of interspike intervals $\langle I_1, I_2 \rangle$, given a particular *fixed* set of synaptic parameters. One can see that a synapse with fixed parameter values is likely to respond quite differently to spike trains with different interspike intervals. For example even if one just considers spike trains with $I_1 = I_2$ one moves in Fig. 3A through 3 different release patterns that take their turn in becoming the most likely release pattern when I_1 varies. Similarly, if one only considers spike trains with a fixed time interval $t_3 - t_1 = I_1 + I_2 = \Delta$, but with different positions of the second spike within this time interval of length Δ, one sees that the most likely release pattern is quite sensitive to the position of the second spike within this time interval Δ. Fig. 3B shows that a different set of synaptic parameters gives rise to a completely different assignment of release patterns.

We show in the next Theorem that the boundaries between the zones in these figures are "plastic": by changing the values of C_0, V_0, α the synapse can move the zone for most of the release patterns $\underline{q}$ to any given point $\langle I_1, I_2 \rangle$. This result provides another example for a new type of synaptic plasticity that can no longer be described in terms of a decrease or increase of the synaptic "weight".

Theorem 2.2 *Assume that an arbitrary number $p \in (0,1)$ and an arbitrary pattern $\langle I_1, I_2 \rangle$ of interspike intervals is given. Furthermore assume that arbitrary fixed positive values are given for the parameters τ_C and τ_V of a synapse S. Then for any pattern $\underline{q} \in \{R, F\}^3$ except RRF, FFR one can assign values to the other parameters α, C_0, V_0 of this synapse S so that the probability of release pattern $\underline{q}$ for a spike train with interspike intervals I_1, I_2 becomes larger than p.*

It is shown in the full version of this paper [Maass and Zador, 1997] that it is not possible to make the release patterns RRF and FFR arbitrarily likely for any given spike train with interspike intervals $\langle I_1, I_2 \rangle$.

2.3 Computing with Firing Rates

So far we have considered the effect of short trains of two or three presynaptic spikes on synaptic release probability. Our next result (cf. Fig.5) shows that also two longer Poisson spike trains that represent the *same* firing rate can produce quite different numers of synaptic releases, depending on the synaptic parameters. To emphasize that this is due to the pattern of interspike intervals, and not simply to the number of spikes, we compared the outputs in response to two Poisson spike trains A and B with the same number (10) of spikes. These examples indicate that even in the context of rate coding, synaptic efficacy may not be well described in terms of a single scalar parameter w.

2.4 Burst Detection

Here we show that the computational power of a spiking (e.g. integrate-and-fire) neuron with stochastic dynamic synapses is strictly larger than that of a spiking neuron with traditional "static" synapses (cf Lisman, 1997). Let T be a some given time window, and consider the computational task of detecting whether at least one of n presynaptic neurons $a_1, \ldots, a_n$ fire at least twice during T ("burst detection"). To make this task computationally feasible we assume that none of the neurons $a_1, \ldots, a_n$ fires outside of this time window.

Theorem 2.3 *A spiking neuron v with dynamic stochastic synapses can solve this burst detection task (with arbitrarily high reliability). On the other hand no spiking neuron with static synapses can solve this task (for any assignment of "weights" to its synapses).* [1]

---

[1]We assume here that neuronal transmission delays differ by less than $(n - 1) \cdot T)$, where by *transmission delay* we refer to the temporal delay between the firing of the presynaptic neuron and its effect on the postsynaptic target.

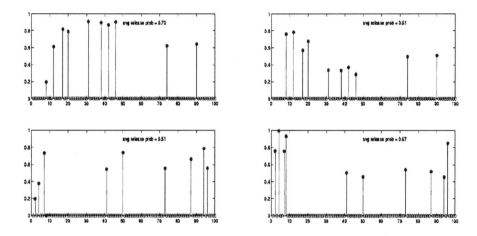

Figure 4: *Release probabilities of two synapses for two Poisson spike trains A and B with 10 spikes each. The release probabilities for the first synapse are shown on the left hand side, and for the second synapse on the right hand side. For both synapses the release probabilities for spike train A are shown at the top, and for spike train B at the bottom. The first synapse has for spike train A a 22 % higher average release probability, whereas the second synapse has for spike train B a 16 % higher average release probability. Note that the fourth spike in spike train B has for the first synapse a release probability of nearly zero and so is not visible.*

2.5 Translating Interval Coding into Population Coding

Assume that information is encoded in the length I of the interspike interval between the times t_1 and t_2 when a certain neuron v fires, and that different motor responses need to be initiated depending on whether $I < a$ or $I > a$, where a is some given parameter (c.f. [Hopfield, 1995]). For that purpose it would be useful to translate the information encoded in the interspike interval I into the firing activity of populations of neurons ("population coding"). Fig. 5 illustrates a simple mechanism for that task based on dynamic synapses. The synaptic parameters are chosen so that facilitation dominates (i.e., C_0 should be small and α large) at synapses between neuron v and the postsynaptic population of neurons. The release probability for the first spike is then close to 0, whereas the release probability for the second spike is fairly large if $I < a$ and significantly smaller if I is substantially larger than a. If the resulting firing activity of the postsynaptic neurons is positively correlated with the total number of releases of these synapses, then their population response is also positively correlated with the length of the interspike interval I.

$$\xleftarrow{\quad I \quad}\rightarrow \qquad \begin{cases} FR & , \text{ if } I < a \\ FF & , \text{ if } I > a \end{cases} \qquad \begin{cases} 1 & , \text{ if } I < a \\ 0 & , \text{ if } I > a \end{cases}$$

presynaptic spikes   synaptic response   resulting activation of
postsynaptic neurons

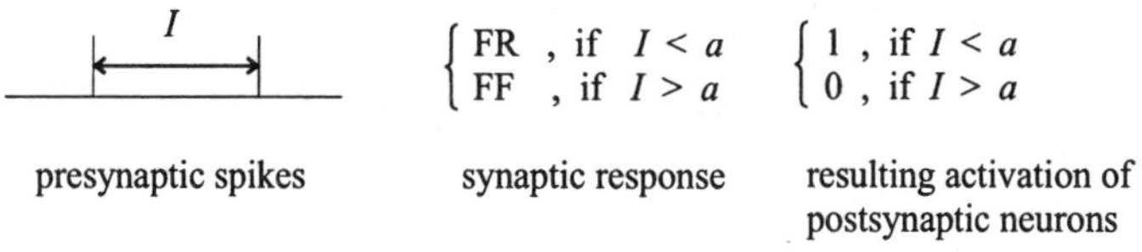

Figure 5: *A mechanism for translating temporal coding into population coding.*

3   Discussion

We have explored computational implications of a dynamic stochastic synapse model. Our model incorporates several features of biological synapses usually omitted in the connections or weights conventionally used in artificial neural network models. Our main result is that a neural circuit in which connections are dynamic has fundamentally greater power than one in which connections are static. We refer to [Maass and Zador, 1997] for details. Our results may have implications for computation in both biological and artificial neural networks, and particularly for the processing of signals with interesting temporal structure.

Several groups have recently proposed a computational role for one form of use-dependent short term synaptic plasticity [Abbott et al., 1997, Tsodyks and Markram, 1997]. They showed that, under the experimental conditions tested, synaptic depression (of a form analogous to $V(t)$ in our Eq. (3) can implement a form of gain control in which the steady-state synaptic output is independent of the input firing rate over a wide range of firing rates. We have adopted a more general approach in which, rather than focussing on a particular role for short term plasticity, we allow the dynamic synapse parameters to vary. This approach is analogous to that adopted in the study of artificial neural networks, in which few if any constraints are placed on the connections between units. In our more general framework, standard neural network tasks such as supervised and unsupervised learning can be formulated (*see also* [Liaw and Berger, 1996]). Indeed, a backpropagation-like gradient descent algorithm can be used to adjust the parameters of a network connected by dynamic synapses (Zador and Maass, *in preparation*). The advantages of dynamic synapses may become most apparent in the processing of time-varying signals.

References

[Abbott et al., 1997] Abbott, L., Varela, J., Sen, K., and S.B., N. (1997). Synaptic depression and cortical gain control. *Science*, 275:220–4.

[Dobrunz and Stevens, 1997] Dobrunz, L. and Stevens, C. (1997). Heterogeneity of release probability, facilitation and depletion at central synapses. *Neuron*, 18:995–1008.

[Hopfield, 1995] Hopfield, J. (1995). Pattern recognition computation using action potential timing for stimulus representation. *Nature*, 376:33–36.

[Liaw and Berger, 1996] Liaw, J.-S. and Berger, T. (1996). Dynamic synapse: A new concept of neural representation and computation. *Hippocampus*, 6:591–600.

[Lisman, 1997] Lisman, J. (1997). Bursts as a unit of neural information: making unreliable synapses reliable. *TINS*, 20:38–43.

[Maass and Zador, 1997] Maass, W. and Zador, A. (1997). Dynamic stochastic synapses as computational units. *http://www.sloan.salk.edu/~zador/publications.html* .

[Magleby, 1987] Magleby, K. (1987). Short term synaptic plasticity. In Edelman, G. M., Gall, W. E., and Cowan, W. M., editors, *Synaptic function*. Wiley, New York.

[Markram and Tsodyks, 1996] Markram, H. and Tsodyks, M. (1996). Redistribution of synaptic efficacy between neocortical pyramidal neurons. *Nature*, 382:807–10.

[Stevens and Wang, 1995] Stevens, C. and Wang, Y. (1995). Facilitation and depression at single central synapses. *Neuron*, 14:795–802.

[Tsodyks and Markram, 1997] Tsodyks, M. and Markram, H. (1997). The neural code between neocortical pyramidal neurons depends on neurotransmitter release probability. *Proc. Natl. Acad. Sci.*, 94:719–23.

[Varela et al., 1997] Varela, J. A., Sen, K., Gibson, J., Fost, J., Abbott, L. F., and Nelson, S. B. (1997). A quantitative description of short-term plasticity at excitatory synapses in layer 2/3 of rat primary visual cortex. *J. Neurosci*, 17:7926–7940.

Synaptic Transmission: An Information-Theoretic Perspective

Amit Manwani and Christof Koch
Computation and Neural Systems Program
California Institute of Technology
Pasadena, CA 91125
email: quixote@klab.caltech.edu
koch@klab.caltech.edu

Abstract

Here we analyze synaptic transmission from an information-theoretic perspective. We derive closed-form expressions for the lower-bounds on the capacity of a simple model of a cortical synapse under two explicit coding paradigms. Under the "signal estimation" paradigm, we assume the signal to be encoded in the mean firing rate of a Poisson neuron. The performance of an optimal linear estimator of the signal then provides a lower bound on the capacity for signal estimation. Under the "signal detection" paradigm, the presence or absence of the signal has to be detected. Performance of the optimal spike detector allows us to compute a lower bound on the capacity for signal detection. We find that single synapses (for empirically measured parameter values) transmit information poorly but significant improvement can be achieved with a small amount of redundancy.

1 Introduction

Tools from estimation and information theory have recently been applied by researchers (Bialek *et. al*, 1991) to quantify how well neurons transmit information about their random inputs in their spike outputs. In these approaches, the neuron is treated like a black-box, characterized empirically by a set of input-output records. This ignores the specific nature of neuronal processing in terms of its known biophysical properties. However, a systematic study of processing at various stages in a biophysically faithful model of a single neuron should be able to identify the role of each stage in information transfer in terms of the parameters relating to the neuron's dendritic structure, its spiking mechanism, *etc*. Employing this reductionist approach, we focus on a important component of neural processing, the synapse, and analyze a simple model of a cortical synapse under two different representational paradigms. Under the "signal estimation" paradigm, we assume that the input signal is linearly encoded in the mean firing rate of a Poisson neuron and the mean-square error in the reconstruction of the signal from the post-synaptic voltage quantifies system performance. From the performance of the optimal linear estimator of the signal, a lower bound on the capacity for signal estimation can be computed. Under the "signal detection" paradigm, we assume that information is encoded in an all-or-none format and the error in deciding whether or not a presynaptic spike occurred by observing the post-synaptic voltage quantifies system performance. This is similar to the conventional absent/present(Yes-No) decision paradigm used in psychophysics. Performance of the optimal spike detector in this case allows us to compute a lower bound on the capacity for signal detection.

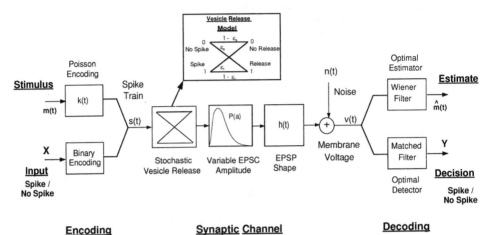

Figure 1: Schematic block diagram for the signal detection and estimation tasks. The synapse is modeled as a binary channel followed by a filter $h(t) = a\, t\, exp(-t/t_s)$. where a is a random variable with probability density, $P(a) = \alpha\, (\alpha a)^{k-1} exp(-\alpha a)/(k-1)!$. The binary channel, (inset, $\epsilon_0 = $ Pr[spontaneous release], $\epsilon_1 = $ Pr [release failure]) models probabilistic vesicle release and $h(t)$ models the variable epsp size observed for cortical synapses. $n(t)$ denotes additive post-synaptic voltage noise and is assumed to be Gaussian and white over a bandwidth B_n. Performance of the optimal linear estimator (*Wiener Filter*) and the optimal spike detector (*Matched Filter*) quantify synaptic efficacy for signal estimation and detection respectively.

2   The Synaptic Channel

Synaptic transmission in cortical neurons is known to be highly random though the role of this variability in neural computation and coding is still unclear. In central synapses, each synaptic bouton contains only a single active release zone, as opposed to the hundreds or thousands found at the much more reliable neuromuscular junction. Thus, in response to an action potential in the presynaptic terminal at most one vesicle is released (Korn and Faber, 1991). Moreover, the probability of vesicle release p is known to be generally low (0.1 to 0.4) from *in vitro* studies in some vertebrate and invertebrate systems (Stevens, 1994). This unreliability is further compounded by the trial-to-trial variability in the amplitude of the post-synaptic response to a vesicular release (Bekkers *et. al*, 1990). In some cases, the variance in the size of EPSP is as large as the mean. The empirically measured distribution of amplitudes is usually skewed to the right (possibly biased due the inability of measuring very small events) and can be modeled by a Gamma distribution.

In light of the above, we model the synapse as a binary channel cascaded by a random amplitude filter (Fig. 1). The binary channel accounts for the probabilistic vesicle release. ϵ_0

and ϵ_1 denote the probabilities of spontaneous vesicle release and failure respectively. We follow the binary channel convention used in digital communications ($\epsilon_1 = 1-p$), whereas, p is more commonly used in neurobiology. The filter $h(t)$ is chosen to correspond to the epsp profile of a fast AMPA-like synapse. The amplitude of the filter a is modeled as random variable with density $P(a)$, mean μ_a and standard deviation σ_a. The CV (standard deviation/mean) of the distribution is denoted by CV_a. We also assume that additive Gaussian voltage noise $n(t)$ at the post-synaptic site further corrupts the epsp response. $n(t)$ is assumed to white with variance σ_n^2 and a bandwidth B_n corresponding to the membrane time constant τ. One can define an effective signal-to-noise ratio, $SNR = E_a/N_o$, given by the ratio of the energy in the epsp pulse, $E_h = \int_0^\infty h^2(t)\,dt$ to the noise power spectral density, $N_o = \sigma_n^2/B_n$. The performance of the synapse depends on the SNR and not on the absolute values of E_h or σ_n. In the above model, by regarding synaptic parameters as constants, we have tacitly ignored history dependent effects like paired-pulse facilitation, vesicle depletion, calcium buffering, etc., which endow the synapse with the nature of a sophisticated nonlinear filter (Markram and Tsodyks, 1997).

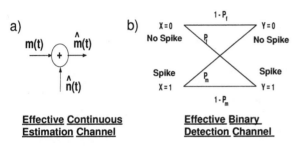

Figure 2: (a) Effective channel model for signal estimation. $m(t)$, $\hat{m}(t)$, $\hat{n}(t)$ denote the stimulus, the best linear estimate, and the reconstruction noise respectively. (b) Effective channel model for signal detection. X and Y denote the binary variables corresponding to the input and the decision respectively. P_f and P_m are the effective error probabilities.

3 Signal Estimation

Let us assume that the spike train of the presynaptic neuron can be modeled as a doubly stochastic Poisson process with a rate $\lambda(t) = k(t) * m(t)$ given as a convolution between the stimulus $m(t)$ and a filter $k(t)$. The stimulus is drawn from a probability distribution which we assume to be Gaussian. $k(t) = exp(-t/\tau)$ is a low-pass filter which models the phenomenological relationship between a neuron's firing rate and its input current. τ is chosen to correspond to the membrane time constant. The exact form of $k(t)$ is not crucial and the above form is assumed primarily for analytical tractability. The objective is to find the optimal estimator of $m(t)$ from the post-synaptic voltage $v(t)$, where optimality is in a least-mean square sense. The optimal mean-square estimator is, in general, nonlinear and reduces to a linear filter only when all the signals and noises are Gaussian. However, instead of making this assumption, we restrict ourselves to the analysis of the optimal linear estimator, $\hat{m}(t) = g(t) * v(t)$, i.e. the filter $g(t)$ which minimizes the mean-square error $E = \langle (m(t) - \hat{m}(t))^2 \rangle$ where $\langle . \rangle$ denotes an ensemble average. The overall estimation system shown in Fig. 1 can be characterized by an effective continuous channel (Fig. 2a) where $\hat{n}(t) = \hat{m}(t) - m(t)$ denotes the effective reconstruction noise. System performance can be quantified by E, the lower E, the better the synapse at signal transmission. The expression for the optimal filter (*Wiener filter*) in the frequency domain is $g(\omega) = S_{mv}(-\omega)/S_{vv}(\omega)$ where $S_{mv}(\omega)$ is the cross-spectral density (Fourier transform of the cross-correlation R_{mv}) of $m(t)$ and $s(t)$ and $S_{vv}(\omega)$ is the power spectral density of $v(t)$. The minimum mean-square error is given by, $E = \sigma_m^2 - \int_S |S_{mv}(\omega)|^2 / S_{vv}(\omega)\,d\omega$. The set $S = \{\omega \mid S_{vv}(\omega) \neq 0\}$ is called the *support* of $S_{vv}(\omega)$.

Another measure of system performance is the mutual information rate $I(m; v)$ between $m(t)$ and $v(t)$, defined as the rate of information transmitted by $v(t)$ about $s(t)$. By the Data Processing inequality (Cover 1991), $I(m, v) \geq I(m, \hat{m})$. A lower bound of $I(m, \hat{m})$ and thus of $I(m; v)$ is given by the simple expression $I_{lb} = \frac{1}{2} \int_{S} \log_2 [\frac{S_{mm}(\omega)}{S_{\hat{n}\hat{n}}(\omega)}] \, d\omega$ (units of bits/sec). The lower bound is achieved when $\hat{n}(t)$ is Gaussian and is independent of $m(t)$. Since the spike train $s(t) = \sum \delta(t - t_i)$ is a Poisson process with rate $k(t) * m(t)$, its power spectrum is given by the expression, $S_{ss}(\omega) = \bar{\lambda} + | K(\omega) |^2 S_{mm}(\omega)$ where $\bar{\lambda}$ is the mean firing rate. We assume that the mean (μ_m) and variance (σ_m^2) of $m(t)$ are chosen such that the probability that $\lambda(t) < 0$ is negligible[1] The vesicle release process is the spike train gated by the binary channel and so it is also a Poisson process with rate $(1 - \epsilon_1)\lambda(t)$. Since $v(t) = \sum a_i h(t - t_i) + n(t)$ is a filtered Poisson process, its power spectral density is given by $S_{vv}(\omega) = | H(\omega) |^2 \{(\mu_a^2 + \sigma_a^2)(1 - \epsilon_1)\bar{\lambda} + \mu_a^2(1 - \epsilon_1)^2 | K(\omega) |^2 S_{mm}(\omega)\} + S_{nn}(\omega)$. The cross-spectral density is given by the expression $S_{vm}(\omega) = (1 - \epsilon_1)\mu_a S_{mm}(\omega)H(\omega)K(\omega)$. This allows us to write the mean-square error as,

$$E = \sigma_m^2 - \int_{S} \frac{S_{mm}^2(\omega)}{\lambda_{eff}(\omega) + S_{mm}(\omega) + S_{eff}(\omega)} \, d\omega$$

$$\lambda_{eff}(\omega) = \frac{\bar{\lambda}(1 + CV_a^2)}{(1 - \epsilon_1) | K(\omega) |^2}, \quad S_{eff}(\omega) = \frac{S_{nn}(\omega)}{(1 - \epsilon_1)^2 \mu_a^2 | H(\omega) |^2 | K(\omega) |^2}$$

Thus, the power spectral density of $\hat{n}(t)$ is given by $S_{\hat{n}\hat{n}} = \lambda_{eff}(\omega) + S_{eff}(\omega)$. Notice that if $K(\omega) \to \infty$, $E \to 0$ *i.e.* perfect reconstruction takes place in the limit of high firing rates. For the parameter values chosen, $S_{eff}(\omega) \ll \lambda_{eff}(\omega)$, and can be ignored. Consequently, signal estimation is *shot noise* limited and synaptic variability increases shot noise by a factor $N_{syn} = (1 + CV_a^2)/(1 - \epsilon_1)$. For $CV_a = 0.6$ and $\epsilon_1 = 0.6$, $N_{syn} = 3.4$, and for $CV_a = 1$ and $\epsilon_1 = 0.6$, $N_{syn} = 5$. If $m(t)$ is chosen to be white, band-limited to B_m Hz, closed-form expressions for E and I_{lb} can be obtained. The expression for I_{lb} is tedious and provides little insight and so we present only the expression for E below.

$$E(\gamma, B_T) = \sigma_m^2 [1 - \frac{\gamma}{\sqrt{1 + \gamma}} \frac{1}{B_T} tan^{-1}(\frac{B_T}{\sqrt{1 + \gamma}})]$$

$$\gamma = \frac{\sigma_m^2 \bar{\lambda}}{2\mu_m^2 N_{syn} B_m}, \quad B_T = 2\pi B_m \tau$$

E is a monotonic function of γ (decreasing) and B_T (increasing). γ can be considered as the effective number of spikes available per unit signal bandwidth and B_T is the ratio of the signal bandwidth and the neuron bandwidth. Plots of normalized reconstruction error $E_r = E/\sigma_m^2$ and I_{lb} versus mean firing rate $(\bar{\lambda})$ for different values of signal bandwidth B_m are shown in Fig. 3a and Fig. 3b respectively. Observe that I_{lb} (bits/sec) is insensitive to B_m for firing rates upto 200Hz because the decrease in quality of estimation (E increases with B_m) is compensated by an increase in the number of independent samples ($2B_m$) available per second. This phenomenon is characteristic of systems operating in the low SNR regime. I_{lb} has the generic form, $I_{lb} = B \log(1 + S/(NB))$, where B, S and N denote signal bandwidth, signal power and noise power respectively. For low SNR, $I \approx B S/(NB) = S/N$, is independent of B. So one can argue that, for our choice of parameters, a single synapse is a low SNR system. The analysis generalizes very easily to the case of multiple synapses where all are driven by the same signal $s(t)$. (Manwani and Koch, in preparation). However, instead of presenting the rigorous analysis, we appeal to the intuition gained from the single synapse case. Since a single synapse can be regarded as a shot noise source, n parallel synapses can be treated as n parallel noise sources. Let us make the plausible

---

[1] We choose μ_m and σ_m so that $\bar{\lambda} = 3\sigma_\lambda$ (std of λ) so that Prob$[\lambda(t) \leq 0] < 0.01$.

assumption that these noises are uncorrelated. If optimal estimation is carried out separately for each synapse and the estimates are combined optimally, the effective noise variance is given by the harmonic mean of the individual variances *i.e.* $1/\sigma^2_{neff} = \sum_i 1/\sigma^2_{ni}$. However, if the noises are added first and optimal estimation is carried out with respect to the sum, the effective noise variance is given by the arithmetic mean of the individual variances, *i.e.* $\sigma^2_{neff} = \sum_i \sigma^2_{ni}/n^2$. If we assume that all synapses are similar so that $\sigma^2_{ni} = \sigma^2$, $\sigma^2_{neff} = \sigma^2/n$. Plots of E_r and I_{lb} for the case of 5 identical synapses are shown in Fig. 3c and Fig. 3d respectively. Notice that I_{lb} increases with B_m suggesting that the system is no longer in the low SNR regime. Thus, though a single synapse has very low capacity, a small amount of redundancy causes a considerable increase in performance. This is consistent with the fact the in the low SNR regime, I increases linearly with SNR, consequently, linearly with n, the number of synapses.

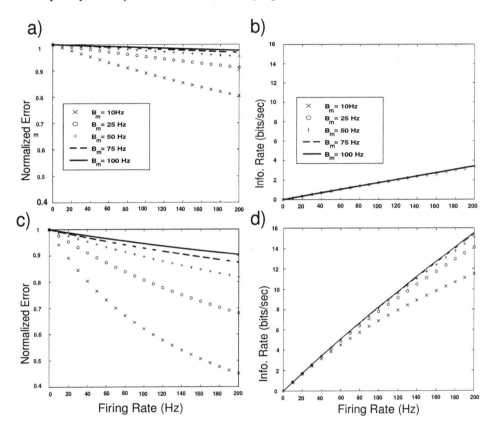

Figure 3: E_r and I_{lb} vs. mean firing rate ($\bar{\lambda}$) for n = 1 [(a) and (b)] and n = 5 [(c) and (d)] identical synapses respectively (different values of B_m) for signal estimation. Parameter values are $\epsilon_1 = 0.6$, $\epsilon_0 = 0$, $CV_a = 0.6$, $t_s = 0.5$ msec, $\tau = 10$msec, $\sigma_n = 0.1$ mV, $B_n = 100$ Hz.

4 Signal Detection

The goal in signal detection is to decide which member from a finite set of signals was generated by a source, on the basis of measurements related to the output only in a statistical sense. Our example corresponds to its simplest case, that of *binary detection*. The objective is to derive an optimal spike detector based on the post-synaptic voltage in a given time interval. The criterion of optimality is minimum probability of error (P_e). A false alarm

(FA) error occurs when a spike is falsely detected even when no presynaptic spike occurs and a miss error (M) occurs when a spike fails to be detected. The probabilities of the errors are denoted by P_f and P_m respectively. Thus, $P_e = (1-p_o) P_f + p_o P_m$ where p_o denotes the a priori probability of a spike occurrence. Let X and Y be binary variables denoting spike occurrence and the decision respectively. Thus, $X = 1$ if a spike occurred else $X = 0$. Similarly, $Y = 1$ expresses the decision that a spike occurred. The *posterior likelihood* ratio is defined as $\mathcal{L}(v) = Pr(v \mid X = 1)/Pr(v \mid X = 0)$ and the prior likelihood as $\mathcal{L}_o = (1 - p_o)/p_o$. The optimal spike detector employs the well-known *likelihood ratio test*, "If $\mathcal{L}(v) \geq \mathcal{L}_o$ **Y = 1** else **Y = 0**". When $X = 1$, $v(t) = a\, h(t) + n(t)$ else $v(t) = n(t)$. Since a is a random variable, $\mathcal{L}(v) = (\int Pr(v \mid X = 1; a) P(a)\, da)/Pr(v \mid X = 0)$. If the noise $n(t)$ is Gaussian and white, it can be shown that the optimal decision rule reduces to a *matched filter*[2], *i.e.* if the correlation, r between $v(t)$ and $h(t)$ exceeds a particular threshold (denoted by η), $Y = 1$ else $Y = 0$. The overall decision system shown in Fig. 1 can be treated as effective binary channel (Fig. 2b). The system performance can be quantified either by P_e or $I(X;Y)$, the mutual information between the binary random variables, X and Y. Note that even when $n(t) = 0$ ($SNR = \infty$), $P_e \neq 0$ due to the unreliability of vesicular release. Let P_e^* denote the probability of error when $SNR = \infty$. If $\epsilon_0 = 0$, $P_e^* = p_o \epsilon_1$ is the minimum possible detection error. Let P_f^o and P_m^o denote FA and M errors when the release is ideal ($\epsilon_1 = 0$, $\epsilon_0 = 0$). It can be shown that

$$P_e = P_e^* + P_m^o[p_o(1 - \epsilon_1) - (1 - p_o)\epsilon_0] + P_f^o[(1 - p_o)(1 - \epsilon_0) - p_o\epsilon_1]$$

$$P_f = P_f^o \,, \ P_m = P_m^o + \epsilon_1(1 - P_m^o + P_f^o)$$

Both P_f^o and P_m^o depend on η. The optimal value of η is chosen such that P_e is minimized. In general, P_f^o and P_m^o can not be expressed in closed-form and the optimal η is found using the graphical *ROC analysis* procedure. If we normalize a such that $\mu_a = 1$, P_f^o and P_m^o can be parametrically expressed in terms of a normalized threshold η^*, $P_f^o = 0.5[1 - Erf(\eta^*)]$, $P_m^o = 0.5[1 + \int_0^\infty Erf(\eta^* - \sqrt{SNR}\, a)\, P(a)\, da]$. $I(X;Y)$ can be computed using the formula for the mutual information for a binary channel, $I = \mathcal{H}(p_o (1 - P_m) + (1 - p_o) P_f) - p_o\mathcal{H}(P_m) - (1 - p_o)\mathcal{H}(P_f)$ where $\mathcal{H}(x) = -x \log_2(x) - (1 - x) \log_2(1 - x)$ is the binary entropy function. The analysis can be generalized to the case of n synapses but the expressions involve n-dimensional integrals which need to be evaluated numerically. The Central Limit Theorem can be used to simplify the case of very large n. Plots of P_e and $I(X;Y)$ versus n for different values of SNR (1,10,∞) for the case of identical synapses are shown in Fig. 4a and Fig. 4b respectively. Yet again, we observe the poor performance of a single synapse and the substantial improvement due to redundancy. The linear increase of I with n is similar to the result obtained for signal estimation.

5 Conclusions

We find that a single synapse is rather ineffective as a communication device but with a little redundancy neuronal communication can be made much more robust. Infact, a single synapse can be considered as a low SNR device, while 5 independent synapses in parallel approach a high SNR system. This is consistently echoed in the results for signal estimation and signal detection. The values of information rates we obtain are very small compared to numbers obtained from some peripheral sensory neurons (Rieke *et. al*, 1996). This could be due to an over-conservative choice of parameter values on our part or could argue for the preponderance of redundancy in neural systems. What we have presented above are preliminary results of work in progress and so the path ahead is much

---

[2]For deterministic a, the result is well-known, but even if a is a one-sided random variable, the matched filter can be shown to be optimal.

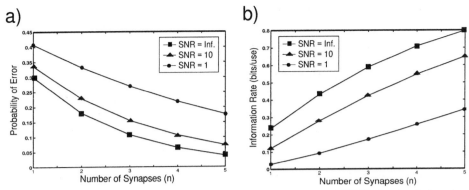

P_e (a) and I_{lb} (b) vs. the number of synapses, n, (different values of SNR) for signal detection. $SNR =$ Inf. corresponds to no post-synaptic voltage noise. All the synapses are assumed to be identical. Parameter values are $p_o = 0.5$, $\epsilon_1 = 0.6$, $\epsilon_0 = 0$, $CV_a = 0.6$, $t_s = 0.5$ msec, $\tau = 10$ msec, $\sigma_n = 0.1$ mV, $B_n = 100$ Hz.

longer than the distance we have covered so far. To the best of our knowledge, analysis of distinct individual components of a neuron from an communications standpoint has not been carried out before.

Acknowledgements

This research was supported by NSF, NIMH and the Sloan Center for Theoretical Neuroscience. We thank Fabrizio Gabbiani for illuminating discussions.

References

Bekkers, J.M., Richerson, G.B. and Stevens, C.F. (1990) "Origin of variability in quantal size in cultured hippocampal neurons and hippocampal slices," *Proc. Natl. Acad. Sci. USA* **87:** 5359-5362.

Bialek, W. Rieke, F. van Steveninck, R.D.R. and Warland, D. (1991) "Reading a neural code," *Science* **252:** 1854-1857.

Cover, T.M., and Thomas, J.A. (1991) *Elements of Information Theory.* New York: Wiley.

Korn, H. and Faber, D.S. (1991) "Quantal analysis and synaptic efficacy in the CNS," *Trends Neurosci.* **14:** 439-445.

Markram, H. and Tsodyks, T. (1996) "Redistibution of synaptic efficacy between neocortical pyramidal neurons," *Nature* **382:** 807-810.

Rieke, F. Warland, D. van Steveninck, R.D.R. and Bialek, W. (1996) *Spikes: Exploring the Neural Code.* Cambridge: MIT Press.

Stevens, C.F. (1994) "What form should a cortical theory take," In: *Large-Scale Neuronal Theories of the Brain,* Koch, C. and Davis, J.L., eds., pp. 239-256. Cambridge: MIT Press.

Toward a Single-Cell Account for Binocular Disparity Tuning: An Energy Model May be Hiding in Your Dendrites

Bartlett W. Mel
Department of Biomedical Engineering
University of Southern California, MC 1451
Los Angeles, CA 90089
mel@quake.usc.edu

Daniel L. Ruderman
The Salk Institute
10010 N. Torrey Pines Road
La Jolla, CA 92037
ruderman@salk.edu

Kevin A. Archie
Neuroscience Program
University of Southern California
Los Angeles, CA 90089
karchie@quake.usc.edu

Abstract

Hubel and Wiesel (1962) proposed that complex cells in visual cortex are driven by a pool of simple cells with the same preferred orientation but different spatial phases. However, a wide variety of experimental results over the past two decades have challenged the pure hierarchical model, primarily by demonstrating that many complex cells receive monosynaptic input from unoriented LGN cells, or do not depend on simple cell input. We recently showed using a detailed biophysical model that nonlinear interactions among synaptic inputs to an excitable dendritic tree could provide the nonlinear subunit computations that underlie complex cell responses (Mel, Ruderman, & Archie, 1997). This work extends the result to the case of complex cell binocular disparity tuning, by demonstrating in an isolated model pyramidal cell (1) disparity tuning at a resolution much finer than the the overall dimensions of the cell's receptive field, and (2) systematically shifted optimal disparity values for rivalrous pairs of light and dark bars—both in good agreement with published reports (Ohzawa, DeAngelis, & Freeman, 1997). Our results reemphasize the potential importance of intradendritic computation for binocular visual processing in particular, and for cortical neurophysiology in general.

1 Introduction

Binocular disparity is a powerful cue for depth in vision. The neurophysiological basis for binocular disparity processing has been of interest for decades, spawned by the early studies of Hubel and Wiesel (1962) showing neurons in primary visual cortex which could be driven by both eyes. Early qualitative models for disparity tuning held that a binocularly driven neuron could represent a particular disparity (zero, near, or far) via a relative shift of receptive field (RF) centers in the right and left eyes. According to this model, a binocular cell fires maximally when an optimal stimulus, e.g. an edge of a particular orientation, is simultaneously centered in the left and right eye receptive fields, corresponding to a stimulus at a specific depth relative to the fixation point. An account of this kind is most relevant to the case of a cortical "simple" cell, whose phase-sensitivity enforces a preference for a particular absolute location and contrast polarity of a stimulus within its monocular receptive fields.

This global receptive field shift account leads to a conceptual puzzle, however, when binocular *complex* cell receptive fields are considered instead, since a complex cell can respond to an oriented feature nearly independent of position within its monocular receptive field. Since complex cell receptive field diameters in the cat lie in the range of 1-3 degrees, the excessive "play" in their monocular receptive fields would seem to render complex cells incapable of signaling disparity on the much finer scale needed for depth perception (measured in minutes).

Intriguingly, various authors have reported that a substantial fraction of complex cells in cat visual cortex are in fact tuned to left-right disparities much finer than that suggested by the size of the monocular RF's. For such cells, a stimulus delivered at the proper disparity, regardless of absolute position in either eye, produces a neural response in excess of that predicted by the sum of the monocular responses (Pettigrew, Nikara, & Bishop, 1968; Ohzawa, DeAngelis, & Freeman, 1990; Ohzawa et al., 1997). Binocular responses of this type suggest that for these cells, the left and right RF's are combined via a correlation operation rather than a simple sum (Nishihara & Poggio, 1984; Koch & Poggio, 1987). This computation has also been formalized in terms of an "energy" model (Ohzawa et al., 1990, 1997), building on the earlier use of energy models to account for complex cell orientation tuning (Pollen & Ronner, 1983) and direction selectivity (Adelson & Bergen, 1985). In an energy model for binocular disparity tuning, sums of linear Gabor filter outputs representing left and right receptive fields are squared to produce the crucial multiplicative cross terms (Ohzawa et al., 1990, 1997).

Our previous biophysical modeling work has shown that the dendritic tree of a cortical pyramidal cells is well suited to support an approximative high-dimensional quadratic input-output relation, where the second-order multiplicative cross terms arise from local interactions among synaptic inputs carried out in quasi-isolated dendritic "subunits" (Mel, 1992b, 1992a, 1993). We recently applied these ideas to show that the position-invariant orientation tuning of a monocular complex cell could be computed within the dendrites of a single cortical cell, based exclusively upon excitatory inputs from a uniform, overlapping population of unoriented ON and OFF cells (Mel et al., 1997). Given the similarity of the "energy" formulations previously proposed to account for orientation tuning and binocular disparity tuning, we hypothesized that a similar type of dendritic subunit computation could underlie disparity tuning in a binocularly driven complex cell.

Parameter	Value
R_m	$10\mathrm{k\Omega cm}^2$
R_a	$200\Omega\mathrm{cm}$
C_m	$1.0\mu\mathrm{F/cm}^2$
V_{rest}	-70 mV
Compartments	615
Somatic $\bar{g}_{\mathrm{Na}}, \bar{g}_{\mathrm{DR}}$	$0.20, 0.12 \mathrm{\ S/cm}^2$
Dendritic $\bar{g}_{\mathrm{Na}}, \bar{g}_{\mathrm{DR}}$	$0.05, 0.03 \mathrm{\ S/cm}^2$
Input frequency	$0 - 100$ Hz
$\bar{g}_{\mathrm{AMPA}}$	0.027 nS – 0.295 nS
$\tau_{\mathrm{AMPA}}(on, off)$	0.5 ms, 3 ms
$\bar{g}_{\mathrm{NMDA}}$	0.27 nS – 2.95 nS
$\tau_{\mathrm{NMDA}}(on, off)$	0.5 ms, 50 ms
E_{syn}	0 mV

Table 1: Biophysical simulation parameters. Details of HH channel implementation are given elsewhere (Mel, 1993); original HH channel implementation courtesy Ojvind Bernander and Rodney Douglas. In order that local EPSP size be held approximately constant across the dendritic arbor, peak synaptic conductance at dendritic location x was approximately scaled to the local input resistance (inversely), given by $\bar{g}_{\mathrm{syn}}(x) = c/\tilde{R}_{in}(x)$, where c was a constant, and $\tilde{R}_{in}(x) = \max(R_{in}(x), 200M\Omega)$. Input resistance $R_{in}(x)$ was measured for a passive cell. Thus $\bar{g}_{\mathrm{syn}}$ was identical for all dendritic sites with input resistance below $200M\Omega$, and was given by the larger conductance value shown; roughly 50% of the tree fell within a factor of 2 of this value. Peak conductances at the finest distal tips were smaller by roughly a factor of 10 (smaller number shown). Somatic input resistance was near $24M\Omega$. The peak synaptic conductance values used were such that the ratio of steady state current injection through NMDA vs. AMPA channels was 1.2 ± 0.4. Both AMPA and NMDA-type synaptic conductances were modeled using the kinetic scheme of Destexhe et al. (1994); synaptic activation and inactivation time constants are shown for each.

2   Methods

Compartmental simulations of a pyramidal cell from cat visual cortex (morphology courtesy of Rodney Douglas and Kevan Martin) were carried out in NEURON (Hines, 1989); simulation parameters are summarized in Table 1. The soma and dendritic membrane contained Hodgkin-Huxley-type (HH) voltage-dependent sodium and potassium channels. Following evidence for higher spike thresholds and decremental propagation in dendrites (Stuart & Sakmann, 1994), HH channel density was set to a uniform, 4-fold lower value in the dendritic membrane relative to that of the cell body. Excitatory synapses from LGN cells included both NMDA and AMPA-type synaptic conductances. Since the cell was considered to be isolated from the cortical network, inhibitory input was not modeled. Cortical cell responses were reported as average spike rate recorded at the cell body over the 500 ms stimulus period, excluding the 50 ms initial transient.

The binocular LGN consisted of two copies of the monocular LGN model used previously (Mel et al., 1997), each consisting of a superimposed pair of 64x64 ON and OFF subfields. LGN cells were modeled as linear, half-rectified center-surround filters with centers 7 pixels in width. We randomly subsampled the left and right LGN arrays by a factor of 16 to yield 1,024 total LGN inputs to the pyramidal cell.

A developmental principle was used to determine the spatial arrangement of these 1,024 synaptic contacts onto the dendritic branches of the cortical cell, as follows. A virtual stimulus ensemble was defined for the cell, consisting of the complete set of single vertical light or dark bars presented binocularly at zero-disparity within the cell's receptive field. Within this ensemble, strong pairwise correlations existed among cells falling into vertically aligned groups of the same (ON or OFF) type, and cells in the vertical column at zero horizontal disparity in the other eye. These binocular cohorts of highly correlated LGN cells were labeled mutual "friends". Progressing through the dendritic tree in depth first order, a randomly chosen LGN cell was assigned to the first dendritic site. A randomly chosen "friend" of hers was assigned to the second site, the third site was assigned to a friend of the site 2 input, etc., until all friends in the available subsample were assigned (4 from each eye, on average). If the friends of the connection at site i were exhausted, a new LGN cell was chosen at random for site $i + 1$. In earlier work, this type of synaptic arrangement was shown to be the outcome of a Hebb-type correlational learning rule, in which random, activity independent formation of synaptic contacts acted to slowly randomize the axo-dendritic interface, shaped by Hebbian stabilization of synaptic contacts based on their short-range correlations with other synapses.

3 Results

Model pyramidal cells configured in this way exhibited prominent phase-invariant orientation tuning, the hallmark response property of the visual complex cell. Multiple orientation tuning curves are shown, for example, for a monocular complex cell, giving rise to strong tuning for light and dark bars across the receptive field (fig. 1). The bold curve shows the average of all tuning curves for this cell; the half-width at half max is 25°, in the normal range for complex cells in cat visual cortex (Orban, 1984). When the spatial arrangement of LGN synaptic contacts onto the pyramidal cell dendrites was randomly scrambled, leaving all other model parameters unchanged, orientation tuning was abolished in this cell (right frame), confirming the crucial role of spatially-mediated nonlinear synaptic interactions (average curve from left frame is reproduced for comparison).

Disparity-tuning in an orientation-tuned binocular model cell is shown in fig. 2, compared to data from a complex cell in cat visual cortex (adapted from Ohzawa et al. (1997)). Responses to contrast matched (light-light) and contrast non-matched (light-dark) bar pairs were subtracted to produce these plots. The strong diagonal structure indicates that both the model and real cells responded most vigorously when contrast-matched bars were presented at the same horizontal position in the left and right-eye RF's (i.e. at zero-disparity), whereas peak responses to contrast-non-matched bars occured at symmetric near and far, non-zero disparities.

4 Discussion

The response pattern illustrated in fig. 2A is highly similar to the response generated by an analytical binocular energy model for a complex cell (Ohzawa et al., 1997):

$$
\begin{aligned}
R_C(X_L, X_R) = \ & \{\exp\left(-kX_L^2\right)\cos\left(2\pi f X_L\right) + \exp\left(-kX_R^2\right)\cos\left(2\pi f X_R\right)\}^2 + \\
& \{\exp\left(-kX_L^2\right)\sin\left(2\pi f X_L\right) + \exp\left(-kX_R^2\right)\sin\left(2\pi f X_R\right)\}^2,
\end{aligned}
\tag{1}
$$

where X_L and X_R are the horizontal bar positions to the two eyes, k is the factor

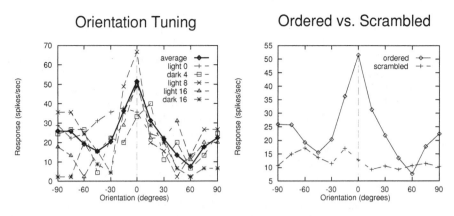

Figure 1: Orientation tuning curves are shown in the left frame for light and dark bars at 3 arbitrary positions. Essentially similar responses were seen at other receptive field positions, and for other complex cells. Bold trace indicates average of tuning curves at positions 0, 1, 2, 4, 8, and 16 for light and dark bars. Similar form of 6 curves shown reflects the translation-invariance of the cell's response to oriented stimuli, and symmetry with respect to ON and OFF input. Orientation tuning is eliminated when the spatial arrangement of LGN synapses onto the model cell dendrites is randomly scrambled (right frame).

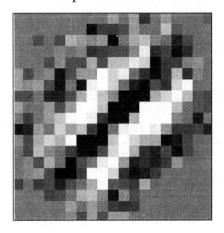

Complex Cell Model

Complex Cell in Cat V1
Ohzawa, Deangelis, & Freeman, 1997

Left eye position

Right eye position

Right eye position

Figure 2: Comparison of disparity tuning in model complex cell to that of a binocular complex cell from cat visual cortex. Light or dark bars were presented simultaneously to the left and right eyes. Bars could be of same polarity in both eyes (light, light) or different polarity (light, dark); cell responses for these two cases were subtracted to produce plot shown in left frame. Right frame shows data similarly displayed for a binocular complex cell in cat visual cortex (adapted from Ohzawa et al. (1997)).

that determines the width of the subunit RF's, and f is the spatial frequency.

In lieu of literal simple cell "subunits", the present results indicate that the subunit computations associated with the terms of an energy model could derive largely from synaptic interactions within the dendrites of the individual cortical cell, driven exclusively by excitatory inputs from unoriented, monocular ON and OFF cells drawn from a uniform overlapping spatial distribution. While lateral inhibition and excitation play numerous important roles in cortical computation, the present results suggest they are not essential for the basic features of the nonlinear disparity tuned responses of cortical complex cells. Further, these results address the paradox as to how inputs from both unoriented LGN cells and oriented simple cells can coexist without conflict within the dendrites of a single complex cell.

A number of controls from previous work suggest that this type of subunit processing is very robustly computed in the dendrites of an individual neuron, with little sensitivity to biophysical parameters and modeling assumptions, including details of the algorithm used to spatially organize the geniculo-cortical projection, specifics of cell morphology, synaptic activation density across the dendritic tree, passive membrane and cytoplasmic parameters, and details of the kinetics, voltage-dependence, or spatial distribution of the voltage-dependent dendritic channels.

One important difference between a standard energy model and the intradendritic responses generated in the present simulation experiments is that the energy model has oriented RF structure at the linear (simple-cell-like) stage, giving rise to oriented, antagonistic ON-OFF subregions (Movshon, Thompson, & Tolhurst, 1978), whereas the linear stage in our model gives rise to center-surround antagonism only within individual LGN receptive fields. Put another way, the LGN-derived subunits in the present model cannot provide all the negative cross-terms that appear in the energy model equations, specifically for pairs of pixels that fall outside the range of a single LGN receptive field.

While the present simulations involve numerous simplifications relative to the full complexity of the cortical microcircuit, the results nonetheless emphasize the potential importance of intradendritic computation in visual cortex.

Acknowledgements

Thanks to Ken Miller, Allan Dobbins, and Christof Koch for many helpful comments on this work. This work was funded by the National Science Foundation and the Office of Naval Research, and by a Sloan Foundation Fellowship (D.R.).

References

Adelson, E., & Bergen, J. (1985). Spatiotemporal energy models for the perception of motion. *J. Opt. Soc. Amer.*, A *2*, 284–299.

Hines, M. (1989). A program for simulation of nerve equations with branching geometries. *Int. J. Biomed. Comput.*, *24*, 55–68.

Hubel, D., & Wiesel, T. (1962). Receptive fields, binocular interaction and functional architecture in the cat's visual cortex. *J. Physiol.*, *160*, 106–154.

Koch, C., & Poggio, T. (1987). Biophysics of computation: Neurons, synapses, and membranes. In Edelman, G., Gall, W., & Cowan, W. (Eds.), *Synaptic function*, pp. 637–697. Wiley, New York.

Mel, B. (1992a). The clusteron: Toward a simple abstraction for a complex neuron. In Moody, J., Hanson, S., & Lippmann, R. (Eds.), *Advances in Neural*

Information Processing Systems, vol. *4*, pp. 35–42. Morgan Kaufmann, San Mateo, CA.

Mel, B. (1992b). NMDA-based pattern discrimination in a modeled cortical neuron. *Neural Computation*, *4*, 502–516.

Mel, B. (1993). Synaptic integration in an excitable dendritic tree. *J. Neurophysiol.*, *70*(3), 1086–1101.

Mel, B., Ruderman, D., & Archie, K. (1997). Complex-cell responses derived from center-surround inputs: the surprising power of intradendritic computation. In Mozer, M., Jordan, M., & Petsche, T. (Eds.), *Advances in Neural Information Processing Systems*, Vol. 9, pp. 83–89. MIT Press, Cambridge, MA.

Movshon, J., Thompson, I., & Tolhurst, D. (1978). Receptive field organization of complex cells in the cat's striate cortex. *J. Physiol.*, *283*, 79–99.

Nishihara, H., & Poggio, T. (1984). Stereo vision for robotics. In Brady, & Paul (Eds.), *Proceedings of the First International Symposium of Robotics Research*, pp. 489–505. MIT Press, Cambridge, MA.

Ohzawa, I., DeAngelis, G., & Freeman, R. (1990). Stereoscopic depth discrimination in the visual cortex: Neurons ideally suited as disparity detectors. *Science*, *249*, 1037–1041.

Ohzawa, I., DeAngelis, G., & Freeman, R. (1997). Encoding of binocular disparity by complex cells in the cat's visual cortex. *J. Neurophysiol.*, *June*.

Orban, G. (1984). *Neuronal operations in the visual cortex*. Springer Verlag, New York.

Pettigrew, J., Nikara, T., & Bishop, P. (1968). Responses to moving slits by single units in cat striate cortex. *Exp. Brain Res.*, *6*, 373–390.

Pollen, D., & Ronner, S. (1983). Visual cortical neurons as localized spatial frequency filters. *IEEE Trans. Sys. Man Cybern.*, *13*, 907–916.

Stuart, G., & Sakmann, B. (1994). Active propagation of somatic action potentials into neocortical pyramidal cell dendrites. *Nature*, *367*, 69–72.

Just One View:
Invariances in Inferotemporal Cell Tuning

Maximilian Riesenhuber   **Tomaso Poggio**
Center for Biological and Computational Learning and
Department of Brain and Cognitive Sciences
Massachusetts Institute of Technology, E25-201
Cambridge, MA 02139
{max,tp}@ai.mit.edu

Abstract

In macaque inferotemporal cortex (IT), neurons have been found to respond selectively to complex shapes while showing broad tuning ("invariance") with respect to stimulus transformations such as translation and scale changes and a limited tuning to rotation in depth. Training monkeys with novel, paperclip-like objects, Logothetis *et al.*[9] could investigate whether these invariance properties are due to experience with exhaustively many transformed instances of an object or if there are mechanisms that allow the cells to show response invariance also to previously unseen instances of that object. They found object-selective cells in anterior IT which exhibited limited invariance to various transformations after training with single object views. While previous models accounted for the tuning of the cells for rotations in depth and for their selectivity to a specific object relative to a population of distractor objects,[14, 1] the model described here attempts to explain in a biologically plausible way the additional properties of translation and size invariance. Using the same stimuli as in the experiment, we find that model IT neurons exhibit invariance properties which closely parallel those of real neurons. Simulations show that the model is capable of unsupervised learning of view-tuned neurons.

We thank Peter Dayan, Marcus Dill, Shimon Edelman, Nikos Logothetis, Jonathan Murnick and Randy O'Reilly for useful discussions and comments.

1   Introduction

Neurons in macaque inferotemporal cortex (IT) have been shown to respond to views of complex objects,[8] such as faces or body parts, even when the retinal image undergoes size changes over several octaves, is translated by several degrees of visual angle[7] or rotated in depth by a certain amount[9] (see [13] for a review).

These findings have prompted researchers to investigate the physiological mechanisms underlying these tuning properties. The original model[14] that led to the physiological experiments of Logothetis et al.[9] explains the behavioral view invariance for rotation in depth through the learning and memory of a few example views, each represented by a neuron tuned to that view. Invariant recognition for translation and scale transformations have been explained either as a result of object-specific learning[4] or as a result of a normalization procedure ("shifter") that is applied to any image and hence requires only one object-view for recognition.[12]

A problem with previous experiments has been that they did not illuminate the mechanism underlying invariance since they employed objects (*e.g.,* faces) with which the monkey was quite familiar, having seen them numerous times under various transformations. Recent experiments by Logothetis et al.[9] addressed this question by training monkeys to recognize *novel* objects ("paperclips" and amoeba-like objects) with which the monkey had no previous visual experience. After training, responses of IT cells to transformed versions of the training stimuli and to distractors of the same type were collected. Since the views the monkeys were exposed to during training were tightly controlled, the paradigm allowed to estimate the degree of invariance that can be extracted from just one object view.

In particular, Logothetis et al.[9] tested the cells' responses to rotations in depth, translation and size changes. Defining "invariance" as yielding a higher response to test views than to distractor objects, they report[9,10] an average rotation invariance over 30°, translation invariance over ±2°, and size invariance of up to ±1 octave around the training view.

These results establish that there are cells showing some degree of invariance even after training with just one object view, thereby arguing against a completely learning-dependent mechanisms that requires visual experience with each transformed instance that is to be recognized. On the other hand, invariance is far from perfect but rather centered around the object views seen during training.

2   The Model

Studies of the visual areas in the ventral stream of the macaque visual system[8] show a tendency for cells higher up in the pathway (from V1 over V2 and V4 to anterior and posterior IT) to respond to increasingly complex objects and to show increasing invariance to transformations such as translations, size changes or rotation in depth.[13]

We tried to construct a model that explains the receptive field properties found in the experiment based on a simple feedforward model. Figure 1 shows a cartoon of the model: A retinal input pattern leads to excitation of a set of "V1" cells, in the figure abstracted as having derivative-of-Gaussian receptive field profiles. These "V1" cells are tuned to simple features and have relatively small receptive fields. While they could be cells from a variety of areas, *e.g.,* V1 or V2 (cf. Discussion), for simplicity, we label them as "V1" cells (see figure). Different cells differ in preferred feature, *e.g.,* orientation, preferred spatial frequency (scale), and receptive field location. "V1" cells of the same type (*i.e.,* having the same preferred stimulus, but of different preferred scale and receptive field location) feed into the same neuron in an intermediate layer. These intermediate neurons could be complex cells in V1 or V2 or V4 or even posterior IT: we label them as "V4" cells, in the same spirit in which we labeled the neurons feeding into them as "V1" units. Thus, a "V4" cell receives inputs from "V1" cells over a large area and different spatial scales ([8] reports an average receptive field size in V4 of 4.4° of visual angle, as opposed to about 1° in V1; for spatial frequency tuning, [3] report an average FWHM of 2.2 octaves, compared to 1.4 (foveally) to 1.8 octaves (parafoveally) in V1[5]). These "V4" cells in turn feed into a layer of "IT" neurons, whose invariance properties are to be compared with the experimentally observed ones.

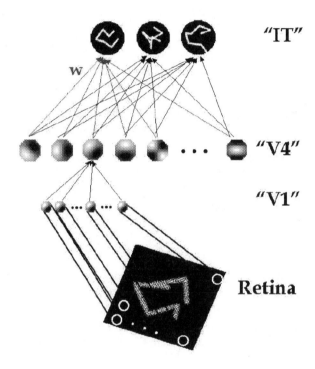

Figure 1: Cartoon of the model. See text for explanation.

A crucial element of the model is the mechanism an intermediate neuron uses to pool the activities of its afferents. From the computational point of view, the intermediate neurons should be robust feature detectors, *i.e.*, measure the presence of specific features without being confused by clutter and context in the receptive field. More detailed considerations (Riesenhuber and Poggio, in preparation) show that this cannot be achieved with a response function that just summates over all the afferents (cf. Results). Instead, intermediate neurons in our model perform a "max" operation (akin to a "Winner-Take-All") over all their afferents, *i.e., the response of an intermediate neuron is determined by its most strongly excited afferent.* This hypothesis appears to be compatible with recent data,[15] that show that when two stimuli (gratings of different contrast and orientation) are brought into the receptive field of a V4 cell, the cell's response tends to be close to the stronger of the two individual responses (instead of *e.g.,* the sum as in a linear model).

Thus, the response function o_i of an intermediate neuron i to stimulation with an image $\mathbf{v}$ is

$$o_i = \max_{j \in \mathcal{A}_i}\{\mathbf{v}_{\alpha(j)} \cdot \xi_j\}, \tag{1}$$

with $\mathcal{A}_i$ the set of afferents to neuron i, $\alpha(j)$ the receptive field center of afferent j, $\mathbf{v}_{\alpha(j)}$ the (square-normalized) image patch centered at $\alpha(j)$ that corresponds in size to the receptive field, ξ_j (also square-normalized) of afferent j and "$\cdot$" the dot product operation.

Studies have shown that V4 neurons respond to features of "intermediate" complexity such as gratings, corners and crosses.[8] In V4 the receptive fields are comparatively large (4.4° of visual angle on average[8]), while the preferred stimuli are usually much smaller.[3] Interestingly, cells respond independently of the location of the stimulus within the receptive field. Moreover, average V4 receptive field size is comparable to the range of translation invariance of IT cells ($\leq \pm 2°$) observed in the experiment.[9] For afferent receptive fields ξ_j, we chose features similar to the ones found for V4 cells in the visual system:[8] bars (modeled as second derivatives of Gaussians) in two orientations, and "corners" of four different orientations and two different degrees of obtuseness. This yielded a total of 10 intermediate neurons. This set of features was chosen to give a compact and biologically plausible representation. Each intermediate cell received input from cells with the same type of preferred stimulus densely covering the visual field of 256×256 pixels (which thus would correspond to about 4.4° of visual angle, the average receptive field size in V4[8]), with receptive field sizes of afferent cells ranging from 7 to 19 pixels in steps of 2 pixels. The features used in this paper represent the first set of features tried, optimizing feature shapes might further improve the model's performance.

The response t_j of top layer neuron j with connecting weights $\mathbf{w}_j$ to the intermediate layer was set to be a Gaussian, centered on $\mathbf{w}_j$,

$$t_j = \frac{1}{\sqrt{2\pi\sigma^2}} \exp\left(-\frac{||\mathbf{o} - \mathbf{w}_j||^2}{2\sigma^2}\right) \tag{2}$$

where $\mathbf{o}$ is the excitation of the intermediate layer and σ the variance of the Gaussian, which was chosen based on the distribution of responses (for section 3.1) or learned (for section 3.2).

The stimulus images were views of 21 randomly generated "paperclips" of the type used in the physiology experiment.[9] Distractors were 60 other paperclip images generated by the same method. Training size was 128×128 pixels.

3 Results

3.1 Invariance of Representation

In a first set of simulations we investigated whether the proposed model could indeed account for the observed invariance properties. Here we assumed that connection strengths from the intermediate layer cells to the top layer had already been learned by a separate process, allowing us to focus on the tolerance of the representation to the above-mentioned transformations and on the selectivity of the top layer cells.

To establish the tuning properties of view-tuned model neurons, the connections $\mathbf{w}_j$ between the intermediate layer and top layer unit j were set to be equal to the excitation o_{training} in the intermediate layer caused by the training view. Figure 2 shows the "tuning curve" for rotation in depth and Fig. 3 the response to changes in stimulus size of one such neuron. The neuron shows rotation invariance (*i.e.*, producing a higher response than to any distractor) over about 44° and invariance to scale changes over the whole range tested. For translation

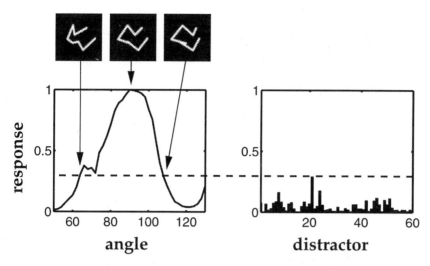

Figure 2: Responses of a sample top layer neuron to different views of the training stimulus and to distractors. The left plot shows the rotation tuning curve, with the training view (90° view) shown in the middle image over the plot. The neighboring images show the views of the paperclip at the borders of the rotation tuning curve, which are located where the response to the rotated clip falls below the response to the best distractor (shown in the plot on the right). The neuron exhibits broad rotation tuning over more than 40°.

(not shown), the neuron showed invariance over translations of ±96 pixels around the center in any direction, corresponding to ±1.7° of visual angle.

The average invariance ranges for the 21 tested paperclips were 35° of rotation angle, 2.9 octaves of scale invariance and ±1.8° of translation invariance. Comparing this to the experimentally observed[10] 30°, 2 octaves and ±2°, resp., shows a very good agreement of the invariance properties of model and experimental neurons.

3.2 Learning

In the previous section we assumed that the connections from the intermediate layer to a view-tuned neuron in the top layer were pre-set to appropriate values. In this section, we investigate whether the system allows unsupervised learning of view-tuned neurons.

Since biological plausibility of the learning algorithm was not our primary focus here, we chose a general, rather abstract learning algorithm, *viz.* a mixture of Gaussians model trained with the EM algorithm. Our model had four neurons in the top level, the stimuli were views of four paperclips, randomly selected from the 21 paperclips used in the previous experiments. For each clip, the stimulus set contained views from 17 different viewpoints, spanning 34° of viewpoint change. Also, each clip was included at 11 different scales in the stimulus set, covering a range of two octaves of scale change.

Connections $\mathbf{w}_i$ and variances σ_i, $i = 1, \ldots, 4$, were initialized to random values at the beginning of training. After a few iterations of the EM algorithm (usually less than 30), a stationary state was reached, in which each model neuron had become tuned to views of one paperclip: For each paperclip, all rotated and scaled views were mapped to (*i.e.,* activated most strongly) the same model neuron and views of different paperclips were mapped to different neurons. Hence, when the system is presented with multiple views of different objects, receptive fields of top level neurons self-organize in such a way that different neurons become tuned to different objects.

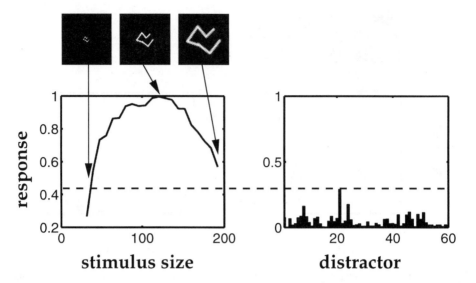

Figure 3: Responses of the same top layer neuron as in Fig. 2 to scale changes of the training stimulus and to distractors. The left plot shows the size tuning curve, with the training size (128 × 128 pixels) shown in the middle image over the plot. The neighboring images show scaled versions of the paperclip. Other elements as in Fig. 2. The neuron exhibits scale invariance over more than 2 octaves.

4   Discussion

Object recognition is a difficult problem because objects must be recognized irrespective of position, size, viewpoint and illumination. Computational models and engineering implementations have shown that most of the required invariances can be obtained by a relatively simple learning scheme, based on a small set of example views.[14, 17] Quite sensibly, the visual system can also achieve some significant degree of scale and translation invariance from just one view. Our simulations show that the maximum response function is a key component in the performance of the model. Without it — *i.e.,* implementing a direct convolution of the filters with the input images and a subsequent summation — invariance to rotation in depth and translation both decrease significantly. Most dramatically, however, invariance to scale changes is abolished completely, due to the strong changes in afferent cell activity with changing stimulus size. Taking the maximum over the afferents, as in our model, always picks the best matching filter and hence produces a more stable response. We expect a maximum mechanism to be essential for recognition-in-context, a more difficult task and much more common than the recognition of isolated objects studied here and in the related psychophysical and physiological experiments.

The recognition of a specific paperclip object is a difficult, subordinate level classification task. It is interesting that our model solves it well and with a performance closely resembling the physiological data on the same task. The model is a more biologically plausible and complete model than previous ones[14, 1] but it is still at the level of a plausibility proof rather than a detailed physiological model. It suggests a maximum-like response of intermediate cells as a key mechanism for explaining the properties of view-tuned IT cells, in addition to view-based representations (already described in [1, 9]).

Neurons in the intermediate layer currently use a very simple set of features. While this appears to be adequate for the class of paperclip objects, more complex filters might be necessary for more complex stimulus classes like faces. Consequently, future work will aim to improve the filtering step of the model and to test it on more real world stimuli. One can imagine a hierarchy of cell layers, similar to the "S" and "C" layers in Fukushima's

Neocognitron,[6] in which progressively more complex features are synthesized from simple ones. The corner detectors in our model are likely candidates for such a scheme. We are currently investigating the feasibility of such a hierarchy of feature detectors.

The demonstration that unsupervised learning of view-tuned neurons is possible in this representation (which is not clear for related view-based models[14, 1]) shows that different views of one object tend to form distinct clusters in the response space of intermediate neurons. The current learning algorithm, however, is not very plausible, and more realistic learning schemes have to be explored, as, for instance, in the attention-based model of Riesenhuber and Dayan[16] which incorporated a learning mechanism using bottom-up and top-down pathways. Combining the two approaches could also demonstrate how invariance over a wide range of transformations can be learned from several example views, as in the case of familiar stimuli. We also plan to simulate detailed physiological implementations of several aspects of the model such as the maximum operation (for instance comparing nonlinear dendritic interactions[11] with recurrent excitation and inhibition). As it is, the model can already be tested in additional physiological experiments, for instance involving partial occlusions.

References

[1] Bricolo, E, Poggio, T & Logothetis, N (1997). 3D object recognition: A model of view-tuned neurons. In *Advances In Neural Information Processing* 9, 41-47. MIT Press.

[2] Bülthoff, H & Edelman, S (1992). Psychophysical support for a two-dimensional view interpolation theory of object recognition. *Proc. Nat. Acad. Sci. USA* **89**, 60-64.

[3] Desimone, R & Schein, S (1987). Visual properties of neurons in area V4 of the macaque: Sensitivity to stimulus form. *J. Neurophys.* **57**, 835-868.

[4] Földiák, P (1991). Learning invariance from transformation sequences. *Neural Computation* **3**, 194-200.

[5] Foster, KH, Gaska, JP, Nagler, M & Pollen, DA (1985). Spatial and temporal selectivity of neurones in visual cortical areas V1 and V2 of the macaque monkey. *J. Phy.* **365**, 331-363.

[6] Fukushima, K (1980). Neocognitron: A self-organizing neural network model for a mechanism of pattern recognition unaffected by shift in position. *Biological Cybernetics* **36**, 193-202.

[7] Ito, M, Tamura, H, Fujita, I & Tanaka, K (1995). Size and position invariance of neuronal responses in monkey inferotemporal cortex. *J. Neurophys.* **73**, 218-226.

[8] Kobatake, E & Tanaka, K (1995). Neuronal selectivities to complex object features in the ventral visual pathway of the macaque cerebral cortex *J. Neurophys.,* **71**, 856-867.

[9] Logothetis, NK, Pauls, J & Poggio, T (1995). Shape representation in the inferior temporal cortex of monkeys. *Current Biology,* **5**, 552-563.

[10] Nikos Logothetis, personal communication.

[11] Mel, BW, Ruderman, DL & Archie, KA (1997). Translation-invariant orientation tuning in visual 'complex' cells could derive from intradendritic computations. Manuscript in preparation.

[12] Olshausen, BA, Anderson, CH & Van Essen, DC (1993). A neurobiological model of visual attention and invariant pattern recognition based on dynamic routing of information. *J. Neurosci.* **13**, 4700-4719.

[13] Perret, D & Oram, M (1993). Neurophysiology of shape processing. *Image Vision Comput.* **11**, 317-333.

[14] Poggio, T & Edelman, S (1990). A Network that learns to recognize 3D objects. *Nature* **343**, 263-266.

[15] Reynolds, JH & Desimone, R (1997). Attention and contrast have similar effects on competitive interactions in macaque area V4. *Soc. Neurosc. Abstr.* **23**, 302.

[16] Riesenhuber, M & Dayan, P (1997). Neural models for part-whole hierarchies. In *Advances In Neural Information Processing* **9**, 17-23. MIT Press.

[17] Ullman, S (1996). *High-level vision: Object recognition and visual cognition.* MIT Press.

On the Separation of Signals from Neighboring Cells in Tetrode Recordings

Maneesh Sahani, John S. Pezaris and Richard A. Andersen
maneesh@caltech.edu, pz@caltech.edu, andersen@vis.caltech.edu
Computation and Neural Systems
California Institute of Technology
216-76 Caltech, Pasadena, CA 91125 USA

Abstract

We discuss a solution to the problem of separating waveforms produced by multiple cells in an extracellular neural recording. We take an explicitly probabilistic approach, using latent-variable models of varying sophistication to describe the distribution of waveforms produced by a single cell. The models range from a single Gaussian distribution of waveforms for each cell to a mixture of hidden Markov models. We stress the overall statistical structure of the approach, allowing the details of the generative model chosen to depend on the specific neural preparation.

1 INTRODUCTION

Much of our empirical understanding of the systems-level functioning of the brain has come from a procedure called extracellular recording. The electrophysiologist inserts an insulated electrode with exposed tip into the extracellular space near one or more neuron cell bodies. Transient currents due to action potentials across nearby cell membranes are then recorded as deflections in potential, *spikes*, at the electrode tip. At an arbitrary location in gray matter, an extracellular probe is likely to see pertubations due to firing in many nearby cells, each cell exhibiting a distinct waveform due to the differences in current path between the cells and the electrode tip. Commonly, the electrode is maneuvered until all the recorded deflections have almost the same shape; the spikes are then all presumed to have arisen from a single *isolated* cell. This process of cell isolation is time-consuming, and it permits recording from only one cell at a time. If differences in spike waveform can be exploited to *sort* recorded events by cell, the experimental cost of extracellular recording can be reduced, and data on interactions between simultaneously recorded cells can be obtained.

Many *ad hoc* solutions to spike sorting have been proposed and implemented, but thus far an explicit statistical foundation, with its accompanying benefits, has mostly been lacking. Lewicki (1994) is the exception to this rule and provides a well-founded probabilistic approach, but uses assumptions (such as isotropic Gaussian variability) that are not well supported in many data sets (see Fee *et al* (1996)).

A first step in the construction of a solution to the spike-sorting problem is the specification of a model by which the data are taken to be generated. The model has to be powerful enough to account for most of the variability observed in the data, while being simple enough to allow tractable and robust inference. In this paper we will discuss a number of models, of varying sophistication, that fall into a general framework. We will focus on the assumptions and inferential components that are common to these models and consider the specific models only briefly. In particular, we will state the inference algorithms for each model without derivation or proof; the derivations, as well as measures of performance, will appear elsewhere.

2 DATA COLLECTION

The algorithms that appear in this paper are likely to be of general applicability. They have been developed, however, with reference to data collected from the parietal cortex of adult rhesus macaques using tetrodes (Pezaris *et al* 1997).

The tetrode is a bundle of four individually insulated 13μm-diameter wires twisted together and cut so that the exposed ends lie close together. The potential on each wire is amplified (custom electronics), low-pass filtered (9-pole Bessel filter, $f_c = 6.4$ kHz) to prevent aliasing, and digitized (f_s between 12.8 and 20 kHz) (filters and A/D converter from Tucker Davis Technologies). This data stream is recorded to digital media; subsequent operations are currently performed off-line.

In preparation for inference, candidate events (where at least one cell fired) are identified in the data stream. The signal is digitally high-pass filtered ($f_c = 0.05f_s$) and the root-mean-square (RMS) amplitude on each channel is calculated. This value is an upper bound on the noise power, and approaches the actual value when the firing rates of resolvable cells are low. Epochs where the signal rises above three times the RMS amplitude for two consecutive signals are taken to be spike events. The signal is upsampled in the region of each such threshold crossing, and the time of the maximal subsequent peak across all channels is determined to within one-tenth of a sample. A short section is then extracted at the original f_s such that this *peak time* falls at a fixed position in the extracted segment. One such waveform is extracted for each threshold crossing.

3 GENERATIVE FRAMEWORK

Our basic model is as follows. The recorded potential trace $V(t)$ is the sum of influences that are due to resolvable *foreground* cells (which have a relatively large effect) and a *background* noise process. We write

$$V(t) = \sum_{\tau} (c_1^\tau S_1^\tau (t - \tau) + c_2^\tau S_2^\tau (t - \tau) + \cdots) + \eta(t) \qquad (1)$$

Here, c_m^τ is an indicator variable that takes the value 1 if the mth cell fires at time τ and 0 otherwise. If cell m fires at τ it adds a deflection of shape $S_m^\tau (t - \tau)$ to the recorded potential. The effect of all background neural sources, and any electrical noise, is gathered into a single term $\eta(t)$. For a multichannel probe, such as a tetrode, all of $V(t)$, $\eta(t)$ and $S_m^\tau(t)$ are vector-valued. Note that we have indexed

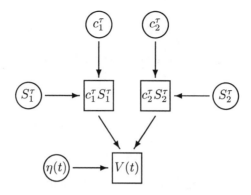

Figure 1: Schematic graph of the general framework.

the spike shapes from the mth cell by time; this allows us to model changes in the spike waveform due to intrinsic biophysical processes (such as sodium inactivation during a burst of spikes) as separate to the additive background process. We will discuss models where the choice of S_m^τ is purely stochastic, as well as models in which both the probability of firing and the shape of the action potential depend on the recent history of the cell.

It will be useful to rewrite (1) in terms of the event waveforms described in section 2. At times τ when no foreground cell fires all the c_m^τ are zero. We index the remaining times (when at least one cell fired) by i and write c_m^i for c_m^τ at τ^i (similarly for S_m^i) to obtain

$$V(t) = \sum_i \left(c_1^i S_1^i(t - \tau^i) + c_2^i S_2^i(t - \tau^i) + \cdots \right) + \eta(t) \qquad (2)$$

This basic model is sketched, for the case of two cells, in figure 1. Circles represent stochastic variables and squares deterministic functions, while arrows indicate conditional or functional dependence. We have not drawn nodes for $\boldsymbol{\theta}_\eta$ and $\boldsymbol{\theta}$. The representation chosen is similar to, and motivated by, a directed acyclic graph (DAG) model of the generative distribution. For clarity, we have not drawn edges that represent dependencies across time steps; the measurement $V(t)$ depends on many nearby values of S_m^τ and c_m^τ, and $\eta(t)$ may be autocorrelated. We will continue to omit these edges, even when we later show connections in time between c_m^τ and S_m^τ.

4   INFERENCE

We have two statistical objectives. The first is model selection, which includes the choice of the number of cells in the foreground. The second is inference: finding good estimates for the c_m^τ given the measured $V(t)$. We will have little to say on the subject of model selection in this paper, besides making the observation that standard techniques such as cross-validation, penalized likelihood or approximation of the marginal likelihood (or "evidence") are all plausible approaches. We will instead focus on the inference of the spike times.

Rather than calculating the marginalized posterior for the c_m^τ we will find the distribution conditioned on the most probable values of the other variables. This is a common approximation to the true posterior (compare Lewicki (1994)).

A simple property of the data allows us to estimate the most probable values of the parameters in stages; times at which at least one foreground cell fires can be identified by a threshold, as described in section 2. We can then estimate the noise parameters θ_η by looking at segments of the signal with no foreground spikes, the waveform distribution and firing time parameters θ from the collection of spike events, and finally the spike times c_m^τ and the waveforms S_m^τ by a filtering process applied to the complete data $V(t)$ given these model parameters.

4.1   NOISE

We study the noise distribution as follows. We extract 1ms segments from a band-passed recording sampled at 16 kHz from a four-channel electrode, avoiding the foreground spikes identified as in section 2. Each segment is thus a 64-dimensional object. We find the principal components of the ensemble of such vectors, and construct histograms of the projections of the vectors in these directions. A few of these histograms are shown on a log-scale in figure 2 (points), as well as a zero-mean Gaussian fit to the distribution projected along the same axes (lines). It is clear that the Gaussian is a reasonable description, although a slight excess in kurtosis is visible in the higher principal components.

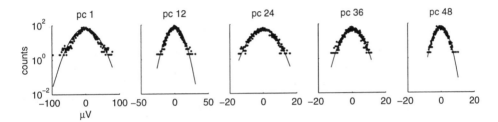

Figure 2: Distribution of background noise.

The noise parameters are now seen to be the covariance of the noise, Σ_η (we represent it as a covariance *matrix* taken over the length of a spike). In general, we can fit an autoregressive process description to the background and apply a filter that will whiten the noise. This will prove to be quite useful during the filtering stages.

4.2   WAVEFORM PARAMETERS

We can make some general remarks about the process of inferring the parameters of the models for S_m^τ and c_m^τ. Specific models and their inference algorithms will appear in section 5.

The models will, in general, be fit to the collection of segments extracted and aligned as described in section 2. At other times they have no influence on the waveform recorded. We will represent these segments by V^i, implying a connection to the firing events τ^i used in (2). It should be borne in mind that the threshold-based trigger scheme will not exactly identify all of the true τ^i correctly.

We will assume that each segment represents a single S_m, that is, that no two cells fire at times close enough for their spike waveforms to overlap. This is an unreasonable assumption; we can shore it up partially by eliminating from our collection of V^i segments that appear heuristically to contain overlaps (for example, double-peaked waveforms). Ultimately, however, we will need to make our inference procedure robust enough that the parameters describing the model are well estimated despite the errors in the data.

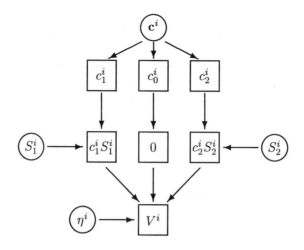

Figure 3: The mixture model for V^i.

The advantage to making this assumption is that the overall model for the distribution of the V^i becomes a mixture: a single control variable $\mathbf{c}^i$ sets exactly one of the c_m^i to 1. V^i is then drawn from the distribution of waveforms for the selected cell, convolved with the noise. This is a formal statement of the "clustering" approach to spike-sorting. Mixture models such as these are easy to fit using the Expectation-Maximization (EM) algorithm (Dempster *et al* 1977). We will also consider models with additional latent state variables, which are used to describe the distributions of the S_m and c_m, where again EM will be of considerable utility.

The measured ensemble V^i will be incorrect on a number of counts. The threshold may make either false positive or false negative errors in selecting τ^i, and some of the identified V^i will represent overlaps. We can use heuristics to minimize such errors, but need to account for any remaining outliers in our models. We do so by introducing additional mixture components. Segments of noise that are incorrectly identified as foreground events are handled by an explicit zero mixture component whose variability is entirely due to the background noise. Overlaps are handled by providing very broad low-probability components spanning large areas in waveform space; clusters of overlap waveforms are likely to be diffuse and sparse.

The mixture model is sketched in figure 3. In the basic model the variables are chosen independently for each cross-threshold event. The dynamic models discussed below will introduce dependencies in time.

4.3 SPIKE TIMES

In our final stage of inference, we make estimates of the c_m^τ given the $V(t)$ and the most-probable parameters fit in the previous two stages. This is exactly the signal detection problem of identifying pulses (perhaps with random or else adapting parameters) in Gaussian noise of known covariance. Solutions to this are well known (McDonough and Whalen 1995) and easily adapted to the problem at hand (Sahani *et al* 1998).

5 SPECIFIC MODELS

Finally, we describe examples of models that may be used within this framework. As stated before, in this brief catalog we summarize the motivation for each, and state without derivation or proof the algorithms for inference. The details of these algorithms, as well as tests of performance, will appear elsewhere.

5.1 CONSTANT WAVEFORM

The simplest model is one in which we take the waveform of the mth cell to remain unchanged and the firing probability of each cell to be constant. In this case we drop the index τ or i on the waveform shape and just write $S_m(t - \tau^i)$. We write p_m for the probability that a given event is due to the mth cell firing. The mixture model is then a mixture of multivariate Gaussian distributions, each with covariance Σ_η, mean S_m and mixture fraction p_m. The EM algorithm for such a mixture is well known (Nowlan 1990).

Given parameters $\boldsymbol{\theta}^{(n)} = \{S_m^{(n)}, p_m^{(n)}\}$ from the nth iteration, we find the expected values of the c_m^i (called the *responsibilities*),

$$r_m^i = \mathcal{E}[c_m^i \mid \{V^i\}, \boldsymbol{\theta}^{(n)}] = \frac{p_m^{(n)} N(V^i; S_m^{(n)}, \Sigma_\eta)}{\sum_{\tilde{m}} p_{\tilde{m}}^{(n)} N(V^i; S_{\tilde{m}}^{(n)}, \Sigma_\eta)}, \tag{3}$$

and then reestimate the parameters from the data weighted by the responsibilities.

$$p_m^{(n+1)} = \frac{\sum_i r_m^i}{N} \; ; \; S_m^{(n+1)} = \frac{\sum_i r_m^i V^i}{\sum_i r_m^i}. \tag{4}$$

5.2 REFRACTORY FIRING

A simple modification to this scheme can be used to account for the refractory period between spikes from the same cell (Sahani *et al* 1998). The model is similar to the Gaussian mixture above, except that the choice of mixture component is no longer independent for each waveform. If the waveforms arrive within a refractory period they cannot have come from the same cell. This leads to the altered responsibilities:

$$s_m^i = \frac{r_m^i}{Z^i} \prod_{j:(i,j) \text{ refractory}} (1 - r_m^j) \tag{5}$$

where Z is a normalizing constant.

The M step here is identical to (4), with the responsibilities s_m^i replacing the r_m^i.

5.3 STATIC MIXTURE

As we have suggested above, the waveform of the mth cell is not, in fact, unchanged each time the cell fires. Variability in excess of the additive background noise is introduced by changes in the biophysical properties of the cell (due to recent firing patterns, or external modulators) as well as by background activity that may be correlated with foreground events. We can attempt to model this variability as giving rise to a discrete set of distinct waveforms, which are then convolved with the previously measured noise covariance to obtain the distribution of measurements. In effect, we are tiling an irregularly shaped distribution with a mixture of Gaussians of fixed shape, Σ_η. We obtain a hierarchical mixture distribution in which each component corresponding to a cell is itself is a mixture of Gaussians. Given a particular hierarchical arrangement the parameters can be fit exactly as above.

While this approach seems attractive, it suffers from the flaw that model selection is not well defined. In particular, the hierarchical mixture is equivalent in terms of likelihood and parameters to a single-layer, flat, mixture. To avoid this problem we may introduce a prior requiring that the Gaussian components from a single cell overlap, or otherwise lie close together. It is, however, difficult to avoid excessive sensitivity to such a prior.

5.4 DYNAMICAL MIXTURE

An alternative approach is to replace the independent transitions between the components of the mixture distribution of a single cell with a dynamical process that reflects the manner in which both firing probability and waveform shape depend on the recent history of the cell. In this view we may construct a mixture of hidden Markov models (HMMs), one for each cell. Our earlier mixture assumption now means that the models must be coupled so that on any one time step at most one makes a transition to a state corresponding to firing. This structure may be thought of as a special case of the factorial HMM discussed by Gharamani and Jordan (1997).

The general model is known to be intractable. In this special case, however, the standard forward-backward procedure for a single HMM can be modified to operate on reponsibility-weighted data, where the reponsibilities are themselves calculated during the forward phase. This is empirically found to provide an effective E step. The M step is then straightforward.

Acknowledgements

This work has benefited considerably from important discussions with both Bill Bialek and Sam Roweis. John Hopfield has provided invaluable advice and mentoring to MS. We thank Jennifer Linden and Philip Sabes for useful comments on an earlier version of the manuscript. Funding for various components of the work has been provided by the Keck Foundation, the Sloan Center for Theoretical Neuroscience at Caltech, the Center for Neuromorphic Systems Engineering at Caltech, and the National Institutes of Health.

References

Dempster, A. P., N. M. Laird, and D. B. Rubin (1977). *J. Royal Stat. Soc. B 39*, 1–38.

Fee, M. S., P. P. Mitra, and D. Kleinfeld (1996). *J. Neurophys. 76*(3), 3823–3833.

Gharamani, Z. and M. I. Jordan (1997). *Machine Learning 29*, 245–275.

Lewicki, M. S. (1994). *Neural Comp. 6*(5), 1005–1030.

McDonough, R. N. and A. D. Whalen (1995). *Detection of Signals in Noise* (2nd ed.). San Diego: Academic Press.

Nowlan, S. J. (1990). In D. S. Touretzky (Ed.), *Advances in Neural Information Processing Systems 2*, San Mateo, CA. Morgan Kaufmann.

Pezaris, J. S., M. Sahani, and R. A. Andersen (1997). In J. M. Bower (Ed.), *Computational Neuroscience: Trends in Research, 1997*.

Sahani, M., J. S. Pezaris, and R. A. Andersen (1998). In J. M. Bower (Ed.), *Computational Neuroscience: Trends in Research, 1998*.

Independent Component Analysis for identification of artifacts in Magnetoencephalographic recordings

Ricardo Vigário[1][*] **Veikko Jousmäki**[2],
Matti Hämäläinen[2]**, Riitta Hari**[2]**, and Erkki Oja**[1]

[1]Lab. of Computer & Info. Science
Helsinki University of Technology
P.O. Box 2200, FIN-02015 HUT, Finland
{Ricardo.Vigario, Erkki.Oja}@hut.fi

[2]Brain Research Unit, Low Temperature Lab.
Helsinki University of Technology
P.O. Box 2200, FIN-02015 HUT, Finland
{veikko, msh, hari}@neuro.hut.fi

Abstract

We have studied the application of an independent component analysis (ICA) approach to the identification and possible removal of artifacts from a magnetoencephalographic (MEG) recording. This statistical technique separates components according to the kurtosis of their amplitude distributions over time, thus distinguishing between strictly periodical signals, and regularly and irregularly occurring signals. Many artifacts belong to the last category. In order to assess the effectiveness of the method, controlled artifacts were produced, which included saccadic eye movements and blinks, increased muscular tension due to biting and the presence of a digital watch inside the magnetically shielded room. The results demonstrate the capability of the method to identify and clearly isolate the produced artifacts.

1   Introduction

When using a magnetoencephalographic (MEG) record, as a research or clinical tool, the investigator may face a problem of extracting the essential features of the neuromagnetic

---

[*]Corresponding author

signals in the presence of artifacts. The amplitude of the disturbance may be higher than that of the brain signals, and the artifacts may resemble pathological signals in shape. For example, the heart's electrical activity, captured by the lowest sensors of a whole-scalp magnetometer array, may resemble epileptic spikes and slow waves (Jousmäki and Hari 1996).

The identification and eventual removal of artifacts is a common problem in electroencephalography (EEG), but has been very infrequently discussed in context to MEG (Hari 1993; Berg and Scherg 1994).

The simplest and eventually most commonly used artifact correction method is *rejection*, based on discarding portions of MEG that coincide with those artifacts. Other methods tend to restrict the subject from producing the artifacts (e.g. by asking the subject to fix the eyes on a target to avoid eye-related artifacts, or to relax to avoid muscular artifacts). The effectiveness of those methods can be questionable in studies of neurological patients, or other non-co-operative subjects. In eye artifact canceling, other methods are available and have recently been reviewed by Vigário (1997b) whose method is close to the one presented here, and in Jung et al. (1998).

This paper introduces a new method to separate brain activity from artifacts, based on the assumption that the brain activity and the artifacts are anatomically and physiologically separate processes, and that their independence is reflected in the statistical relation between the magnetic signals generated by those processes.

The remaining of the paper will include an introduction to the independent component analysis, with a presentation of the algorithm employed and some justification of this approach. Experimental data are used to illustrate the feasibility of the technique, followed by a discussion on the results.

2 Independent Component Analysis

Independent component analysis is a useful extension of the principal component analysis (PCA). It has been developed some years ago in context with blind source separation applications (Jutten and Herault 1991; Comon 1994). In PCA, the eigenvectors of the signal covariance matrix $\mathbf{C} = E\{\mathbf{x}\mathbf{x}^T\}$ give the directions of largest variance on the input data $\mathbf{x}$. The principal components found by projecting $\mathbf{x}$ onto those perpendicular basis vectors are uncorrelated, and their directions orthogonal.

However, standard PCA is not suited for dealing with non-Gaussian data. Several authors, from the signal processing to the artificial neural network communities, have shown that information obtained from a second-order method such as PCA is not enough and higher-order statistics are needed when dealing with the more demanding restriction of independence (Jutten and Herault 1991; Comon 1994). A good tutorial on neural ICA implementations is available by Karhunen et al. (1997). The particular algorithm used in this study was presented and derived by Hyvärinen and Oja (1997a, 1997b).

2.1 The model

In blind source separation, the original independent sources are assumed to be unknown, and we only have access to their weighted sum. In this model, the signals recorded in an MEG study are noted as $x_k(i)$ (i ranging from 1 to L, the number of sensors used, and k denoting discrete time); see Fig. 1. Each $x_k(i)$ is expressed as the weighted sum of M

independent signals $s_k(j)$, following the vector expression:

$$\mathbf{x}_k = \sum_{j=1}^{M} \mathbf{a}(j)s_k(j) = \mathbf{A}\mathbf{s}_k, \tag{1}$$

where $\mathbf{x}_k = [x_k(1),\ldots,x_k(L)]^T$ is an L-dimensional data vector, made up of the L mixtures at discrete time k. The $s_k(1),\ldots,s_k(M)$ are the M zero mean independent source signals, and $\mathbf{A} = [\mathbf{a}(1),\ldots,\mathbf{a}(M)]$ is a mixing matrix independent of time whose elements a_{ij} are the unknown coefficients of the mixtures. In order to perform ICA, it is necessary to have at least as many mixtures as there are independent sources ($L \geq M$). When this relation is not fully guaranteed, and the dimensionality of the problem is high enough, we should expect the first independent components to present clearly the most strongly independent signals, while the last components still consist of mixtures of the remaining signals. In our study, we did expect that the artifacts, being clearly independent from the brain activity, should come out in the first independent components. The remaining of the brain activity (e.g. α and μ rhythms) may need some further processing.

The mixing matrix $\mathbf{A}$ is a function of the geometry of the sources and the electrical conductivities of the brain, cerebrospinal fluid, skull and scalp. Although this matrix is unknown, we assume it to be constant, or slowly changing (to preserve some local constancy).

The problem is now to estimate the independent signals $s_k(j)$ from their mixtures, or the equivalent problem of finding the separating matrix $\mathbf{B}$ that satisfies (see Eq. 1)

$$\hat{\mathbf{s}}_k = \mathbf{B}\mathbf{x}_k. \tag{2}$$

In our algorithm, the solution uses the statistical definition of fourth-order cumulant or kurtosis that, for the ith source signal, is defined as

$$kurt(s(i)) = E\{s(i)^4\} - 3[E\{s(i)^2\}]^2,$$

where $E(s)$ denotes the mathematical expectation of s.

2.2 The algorithm

The initial step in source separation, using the method described in this article, is whitening, or sphering. This projection of the data is used to achieve the uncorrelation between the solutions found, which is a prerequisite of statistical independence (Hyvärinen and Oja 1997a). The whitening can as well be seen to ease the separation of the independent signals (Karhunen et al. 1997). It may be accomplished by PCA projection: $\mathbf{v} = \mathbf{V}\mathbf{x}$, with $E\{\mathbf{v}\mathbf{v}^T\} = I$. The whitening matrix $\mathbf{V}$ is given by

$$\mathbf{V} = \Lambda^{-1/2}\Xi^T,$$

where $\Lambda = \text{diag}[\lambda(1),\ldots,\lambda(M)]$ is a diagonal matrix with the eigenvalues of the data covariance matrix $E\{\mathbf{x}\mathbf{x}^T\}$, and Ξ a matrix with the corresponding eigenvectors as its columns.

Consider a linear combination $y = \mathbf{w}^T\mathbf{v}$ of a sphered data vector $\mathbf{v}$, with $\|\mathbf{w}\| = 1$. Then $E\{y^2\} = 1$ and $kurt(y) = E\{y^4\}-3$, whose gradient with respect to $\mathbf{w}$ is $4E\{\mathbf{v}(\mathbf{w}^T\mathbf{v})^3\}$.

Based on this, Hyvärinen and Oja (1997a) introduced a simple and efficient fixed-point algorithm for computing ICA, calculated over sphered zero-mean vectors $\mathbf{v}$, that is able to find one of the rows of the separating matrix $\mathbf{B}$ (noted $\mathbf{w}$) and so identify one independent source at a time — the corresponding independent source can then be found using Eq. 2. This algorithm, a gradient descent over the kurtosis, is defined for a particular k as

   1. Take a random initial vector $\mathbf{w}_0$ of unit norm. Let $l = 1$.

2. Let $\mathbf{w}_l = E\{\mathbf{v}(\mathbf{w}_{l-1}^T\mathbf{v})^3\} - 3\mathbf{w}_{l-1}$. The expectation can be estimated using a large sample of $\mathbf{v}_k$ vectors (say, 1,000 vectors).

3. Divide $\mathbf{w}_l$ by its norm (e.g. the Euclidean norm $\|\mathbf{w}\| = \sqrt{\sum_i \mathbf{w}_i^2}$).

4. If $|\mathbf{w}_l^T\mathbf{w}_{l-1}|$ is not close enough to 1, let $l = l+1$ and go back to step 2. Otherwise, output the vector $\mathbf{w}_l$.

In order to estimate more than one solution, and up to a maximum of M, the algorithm may be run as many times as required. It is, nevertheless, necessary to remove the information contained in the solutions already found, to estimate each time a different independent component. This can be achieved, after the fourth step of the algorithm, by simply subtracting the estimated solution $\hat{s} = \mathbf{w}^T\mathbf{v}$ from the unsphered data $\mathbf{x}_k$. As the solution is defined up to a multiplying constant, the subtracted vector must be multiplied by a vector containing the regression coefficients over each vector component of $\mathbf{x}_k$.

3 Methods

The MEG signals were recorded in a magnetically shielded room with a 122-channel whole-scalp Neuromag-122 neuromagnetometer. This device collects data at 61 locations over the scalp, using orthogonal double-loop pick-up coils that couple strongly to a local source just underneath, thus making the measurement "near-sighted" (Hämäläinen et al. 1993).

One of the authors served as the subject and was seated under the magnetometer. He kept his head immobile during the measurement. He was asked to blink and make horizontal saccades, in order to produce typical ocular artifacts. Moreover, to produce myographic artifacts, the subject was asked to bite his teeth for as long as 20 seconds. Yet another artifact was created by placing a digital watch one meter away from the helmet into the shieded room. Finally, to produce breathing artifacts, a piece of metal was placed next to the navel. Vertical and horizontal electro-oculograms (VEOG and HEOG) and electro-cardiogram (ECG) between both wrists were recorded simultaneously with the MEG, in order to guide and ease the identification of the independent components. The bandpass-filtered MEG (0.03–90 Hz), VEOG, HEOG, and ECG (0.1–100 Hz) signals were digitized at 297 Hz, and further digitally low-pass filtered, with a cutoff frequency of 45 Hz and downsampled by a factor of 2. The total length of the recording was 2 minutes. A second set of recordings was performed, to assess the reproducibility of the results.

Figure 1 presents a subset of 12 spontaneous MEG signals from the frontal, temporal and occipital areas. Due to the dimension of the data (122 magnetic signals were recorded), it is impractical to plot all MEG signals (the complete set is available on the internet — see reference list for the adress (Vigário 1997a)). Also both EOG channels and the electrocardiogram are presented.

4 Results

Figure 2 shows sections of 9 independent components (IC's) found from the recorded data, corresponding to a 1 min period, starting 1 min after the beginning of the measurements. The first two IC's, with a broad band spectrum, are clearly due to the musclular activity originated from the biting. Their separation into two components seems to correspond, on the basis of the field patterns, to two different sets of muscles that were activated during the process. IC3 and IC5 are, respectively showing the horizontal eye movements and the eye blinks, respectively. IC4 represents cardiac artifact that is very clearly extracted. In agreement with Jousmäki and Hari (1996), the magnetic field pattern of IC4 shows some predominance on the left.

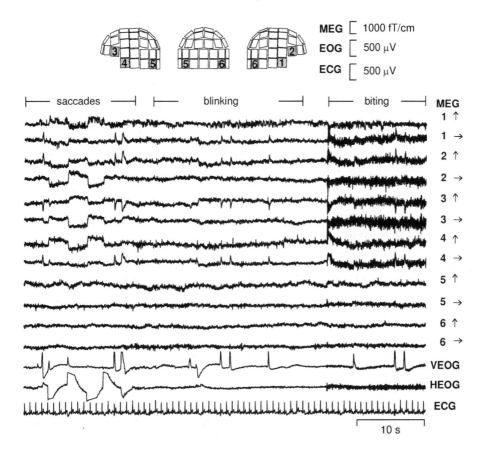

Figure 1: *Samples of MEG signals, showing artifacts produced by blinking, saccades, biting and cardiac cycle. For each of the 6 positions shown, the two orthogonal directions of the sensors are plotted.*

The breathing artifact was visible in several independent components, e.g. IC6 and IC7. It is possible that, in each breathing the relative position and orientation of the metallic piece with respect to the magnetometer has changed. Therefore, the breathing artifact would be associated with more than one column of the mixing matrix $\mathbf{A}$, or to a time varying mixing vector.

To make the analysis less sensible to the breathing artifact, and to find the remaining artifacts, the data were high-pass filtered, with cutoff frequency at 1 Hz. Next, the independent component IC8 was found. It shows clearly the artifact originated at the digital watch, located to the right side of the magnetometer.

The last independent component shown, relating to the first minute of the measurement, shows an independent component that is related to a sensor presenting higher RMS (root mean squared) noise than the others.

5 Discussion

The present paper introduces a new approach to artifact identification from MEG recordings, based on the statistical technique of Independent Component Analysis. Using this method, we were able to isolate both eye movement and eye blinking artifacts, as well as cardiac, myographic, and respiratory artifacts.

The basic assumption made upon the data used in the study is that of independence between brain and artifact waveforms. In most cases this independence can be verified by the known differences in physiological origins of those signals. Nevertheless, in some event-related potential (ERP) studies (e.g. when using infrequent or painful stimuli), both the cerebral and ocular signals can be similarly time-locked to the stimulus. This local time dependence could in principle affect these particular ICA studies. However, as the independence between two signals is a measure of the similarity between their joint amplitude distribution and the product of each signal's distribution (calculated throughout the entire signal, and not only close to the stimulus applied), it can be expected that the very local relation between those two signals, during stimulation, will not affect their global statistical relation.

6 Acknowledgment

Supported by a grant from Junta Nacional de Investigação Científica e Tecnológica, under its 'Programa PRAXIS XXI' (R.V.) and the Academy of Finland (R.H.).

References

Berg, P. and M. Scherg (1994). A multiple source approach to the correction of eye artifacts. *Electroenceph. clin. Neurophysiol. 90*, 229–241.

Comon, P. (1994). Independent component analysis - a new concept? *Signal Processing 36*, 287–314.

Hämäläinen, M., R. Hari, R. Ilmoniemi, J. Knuutila, and O. V. Lounasmaa (1993, April). Magnetoencephalography—theory, instrumentation, and applications to noninvasive studies of the working human brain. *Reviews of Modern Physics 65*(2), 413–497.

Hari, R. (1993). Magnetoencephalography as a tool of clinical neurophysiology. In E. Niedermeyer and F. L. da Silva (Eds.), *Electroencephalography. Basic principles, clinical applications, and related fields*, pp. 1035–1061. Baltimore: Williams & Wilkins.

Hyvärinen, A. and E. Oja (1997a). A fast fixed-point algorithm for independent component analysis. *Neural Computation* (9), 1483–1492.

Hyvärinen, A. and E. Oja (1997b). One-unit learning rules for independent component analysis. In *Neural Information Processing Systems 9 (Proc. NIPS'96)*. MIT Press.

Jousmäki, V. and R. Hari (1996). Cardiac artifacts in magnetoencephalogram. *Journal of Clinical Neurophysiology 13*(2), 172–176.

Jung, T.-P., C. Humphries, T.-W. Lee, S. Makeig, M. J. McKeown, V. Iragui, and T. Sejnowski (1998). Extended ica removes artifacts from electroencephalographic recordings. In *Neural Information Processing Systems 10 (Proc. NIPS'97)*. MIT Press.

Jutten, C. and J. Herault (1991). Blind separation of sources, part i: an adaptive algorithm based on neuromimetic architecture. *Signal Processing 24*, 1–10.

Karhunen, J., E. Oja, L. Wang, R. Vigário, and J. Joutsensalo (1997). A class of neural networks for independent component analysis. *IEEE Trans. Neural Networks 8*(3), 1–19.

Vigário, R. (1997a). WWW adress for the MEG data: http://nucleus.hut.fi/˜rvigario/NIPS97_data.html.

Vigário, R. (1997b). Extraction of ocular artifacts from eeg using independent component analysis. To appear in *Electroenceph. clin. Neurophysiol.*

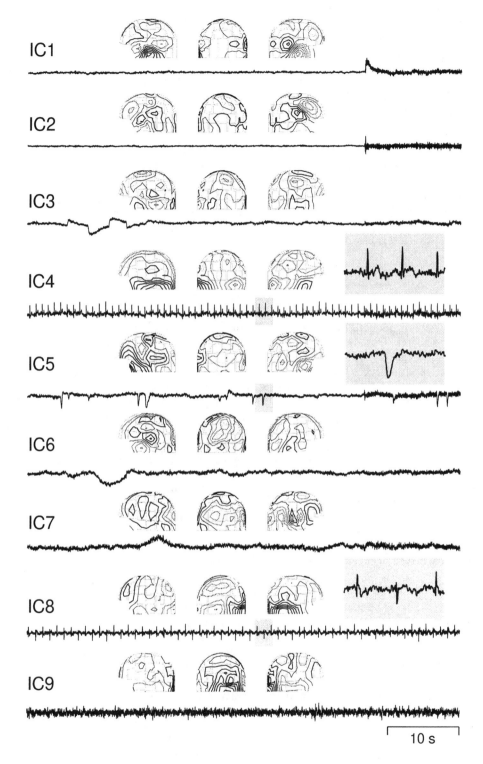

Figure 2: *Nine independent components found from the MEG data. For each component the left, back and right views of the field patterns generated by these components are shown — full line stands for magnetic flux coming out from the head, and dotted line the flux inwards.*

Modeling Complex Cells in an Awake Macaque During Natural Image Viewing

William E. Vinje
vinje@socrates.berkeley.edu

Department of Molecular and
Cellular Biology, Neurobiology Division
University of California, Berkeley
Berkeley, CA, 94720

Jack L. Gallant
gallant@socrates.berkeley.edu

Department of Psychology
University of California, Berkeley
Berkeley, CA, 94720

Abstract

We model the responses of cells in visual area V1 during natural
vision. Our model consists of a classical energy mechanism whose
output is divided by nonclassical gain control and texture contrast
mechanisms. We apply this model to *review movies*, a stimulus
sequence that replicates the stimulation a cell receives during free
viewing of natural images. Data were collected from three cells
using five different review movies, and the model was fit separately
to the data from each movie. For the energy mechanism alone we
find modest but significant correlations (r_E = **0.41, 0.43, 0.59,
0.35**) between model and data. These correlations are improved
somewhat when we allow for suppressive surround effects (r_{E+G} =
0.42, 0.56, 0.60, 0.37). In one case the inclusion of a delayed
suppressive surround dramatically improves the fit to the data by
modifying the time course of the model's response.

1 INTRODUCTION

Complex cells in the primary visual cortex (area V1 in primates) are tuned to
localized visual patterns of a given spatial frequency, orientation, color, and drift
direction (De Valois & De Valois, 1990). These cells have been modeled as linear
spatio-temporal filters whose output is rectified by a static nonlinearity (Adelson
& Bergen, 1985); more recent models have also included a divisive contrast gain
control mechanism (Heeger, 1992; Wilson & Humanski, 1993; Geisler & Albrecht,
1997). We apply a modified form of these models to a stimulus that simulates
natural vision. Our model uses relatively few parameters yet incorporates the cells'
temporal response properties and suppressive influences from beyond the classical
receptive field (CRF).

2 METHODS

Data Collection: Data were collected from one awake behaving Macaque monkey, using single unit recording techniques described elsewhere (Connor *et al.*, 1997).[1] First, the cell's receptive field size and location were estimated manually, and tuning curves were objectively characterized using two-dimensional sinusoidal gratings. Next a static color image of a natural scene was presented to the animal and his eye position was recorded continuously as he freely scanned the image for 9 seconds (Gallant *et al.*, 1998).[2] Image patches centered on the position of the cell's CRF (and 2-4 times the CRF diameter) were then extracted using an automated procedure. The sequence of image patches formed a continuous 9 second *review movie* that simulated all of the stimulation that had occurred in and around the CRF during free viewing.[3] Although the original image was static, the review movies contain the temporal dynamics of the saccadic eye movements made by the animal during free viewing. Finally, the review movies were played in and around the CRF while the animal performed a fixation task.

During free viewing each eye position is unique, so each image patch is likely to enter the CRF only once. The review movies were therefore replayed several times and the cell's average response with respect to the movie timestream was computed from the peri-stimulus time histogram (PSTH). These review movies also form the model's stimulus input, while its output is relative spike probability versus time (the model cell's PSTH).

Before applying the model each review movie was preprocessed by converting to gray scale (since the model does not consider color tuning), setting the average luminance level to zero (on a frame by frame basis) and prefiltering with the human contrast sensitivity function to more accurately reflect the information reaching cells in V1.

Divisive Normalization Model: The model consists of a classical receptive field energy mechanism, E_{CRF}, whose output is divided by two nonclassical suppressive mechanisms, a gain control field, G, and a texture contrast field, T.

$$PSTH_{model}(t) \propto \frac{E_{CRF}(t)}{1 + \alpha\,G(t - \delta) + \beta\,T(t - \delta)} \qquad (1)$$

We include a delay parameter for suppressive effects, consistent with the hypothesis that these effects may be mediated by local cortical interactions (Heeger, 1992; Wilson & Humanski, 1993). Any latency difference between the central energy mechanism and the suppressive surround will be reflected as a positive delay offset ($\delta > 0$ in Equation 1).

Classical Receptive Field Energy Mechanism: The energy mechanism, E_{CRF}, is composed of four phase-dependent subunits, U^ϕ. Each subunit computes an inner product in space and a convolution in time between the model cell's space-time classical receptive field, $CRF^\phi(x, y, \tau)$, and the image, $I(x, y, t)$.

$$U^\phi(t) = \iiint CRF^\phi(x, y, \tau) \cdot I(x, y, t - \tau)\, dx\, dy\, d\tau \qquad (2)$$

---

[1] Recording was performed under a university-approved protocol and conformed to all relevant NIH and USDA guidelines.

[2] Images were taken from a Corel Corporation photo-CD library at 1280x1024 resolution.

[3] Eye position data were collected at 1 KHz, whereas the monitor display rate was 72.5 Hz (14 ms per frame). Therefore each review movie frame was composed of the average stimulation occurring during the corresponding 13.8 ms of free viewing.

The model presented here incorporates the simplifying assumption of a space-time separable receptive field structure, $CRF^\phi(x, y, \tau) = CRF^\phi(x, y) \, CRF(\tau)$.

$$U^\phi(t) = \sum_\tau CRF(\tau) \left(\sum_x \sum_y CRF^\phi(x, y) \cdot I(x, y, t - \tau) \right) \qquad (3)$$

Time is discretized into frames and space is discretized into pixels that match the review movie input. $CRF^\phi(x, y)$ is modeled as a sinusoidal grating that is spatially weighted by a Gaussian envelope (i.e. a Gabor function). In this paper $CRF(\tau)$ is approximated as a delta function following a constant latency. This minimizes model parameters and highlights the model's responses to the stimulus present at each fixation. The latency, orientation and spatial frequency of the grating, and the size of the CRF envelope, are all determined empirically by maximizing the fit between model and data.[4]

A static non-linearity ensures that the model PSTH does not become negative. We have examined both half-wave rectification, $\tilde{U}^\phi(t) = \max[U^\phi(t), 0]$, and half-squaring, $\bar{U}^\phi(t) = (\max[U^\phi(t), 0])^2$; here we present the results from half-wave rectification. Half-squaring produces small changes in the model PSTH but does not improve the fit to the data.

The energy mechanism is made phase invariant by averaging over the rectified phase-dependent subunits:

$$E_{CRF}(t) = \frac{1}{4} \left(\tilde{U}^0(t) + \tilde{U}^{90}(t) + \tilde{U}^{180}(t) + \tilde{U}^{270}(t) \right) \qquad (4)$$

Gain Control Field: Cells in V1 incorporate a contrast gain control mechanism that compensates for changes in local luminance. The gain control field, G, models this effect as the total image power in a region encompassing the CRF and surround.

$$G(t - \delta) = \sum_\tau CRF(\tau) \left(\sum_{k_x} \sum_{k_y} \sqrt{P(k_x, k_y, \tau)} \right) \qquad (5)$$

$$P(k_x, k_y, \tau) = FFT[\mu_G(x, y, \tau)] \, FFT^*[\mu_G(x, y, \tau)] \qquad (6)$$

$$\mu_G(x, y, \tau) = \nu_G(x, y) \, I(x, y, (t - \delta) - \tau) \qquad (7)$$

$P(k_x, k_y, \tau)$ is the spatial Fourier power of $\mu_G(x, y, \tau)$ and ν_G is a two dimensional Gaussian weighting function whose width sets the size of the gain control field.

Heeger's (1992) divisive gain control term sums over many discrete energy mechanisms that tile space in and around the area of the CRF. Equation 5 approximates Heeger's approach in the limiting case of dense tiling.

Texture Contrast Field: Cells in area V1 can be affected by the image surrounding the region of the CRF (Knierim & Van Essen, 1992). The responses of many V1 cells are highest when the optimal stimulus is presented alone within the CRF, and lowest when that stimulus is surrounded with a texture of similar orientation and frequency. The texture contrast field, T, models this effect as the image power

---

[4]As a fit statistic we use the linear correlation coefficient (Pearson's r) between model and data. Fitting is done with a gradient ascent algorithm. Our choice of correlation as a statistic eliminates the need to explicitly consider model normalization as a variable, and is very sensitive to latency mismatches between model and data. However, linear correlation is more prone to noise contamination than is χ^2.

in the spatial region surrounding the CRF that matches the CRF's orientation and spatial frequency.

$$T(t-\delta) = \frac{1}{4} \sum_{\phi=0}^{90,180,270} \left[\sum_{\tau} CRF(\tau) \left(\sum_{k_x} \sum_{k_y} \sqrt{P^\phi(k_x, k_y, \tau)} \right) \right] \tag{8}$$

$$P^\phi(k_x, k_y, \tau) = FFT[\mu_T^\phi(x, y, \tau)] \, FFT^*[\mu_T^\phi(x, y, \tau)] \tag{9}$$

$$\mu_T^\phi(x, y, \tau) = \xi_T^\phi(x, y) \, (1 - \nu_{CRF}(x, y)) \, I(x, y, (t-\delta) - \tau) \tag{10}$$

ξ_T^ϕ is a Gabor function whose orientation and spatial frequency match those of the best fit $CRF^\phi(x, y)$. The envelope of ξ_T^ϕ defines the size of the texture contrast field. ν_{CRF} is a two dimensional Gaussian weighting function whose width matches the CRF envelope, and which suppresses the image center. Thus the texture contrast term picks up oriented power from an annular region of the image surrounding the CRF envelope. T is made phase invariant by averaging over phase.

3   RESULTS

Thus far our model has been evaluated on a small data set collected as part of a different study (Gallant *et al.*, 1998). Two cells, 87A and 98C, were examined with one review movie each, while cell 97A was examined with three review movies. Using this data set we compare the model's response in two interesting situations: cell 97A, which had high orientation-selectivity, versus cell 87A, which had poor orientation-selectivity; and cell 98C, which was directionally-selective, versus cell 97A, which was not directionally-selective.

CRF Energy Mechanism: We separately fit the energy mechanism parameters to each of the three different cells. For cell 97A the three review movies were fit independently to test for consistency of the best fit parameters.

Table 1 shows the correlation between model and data using only the CRF energy mechanism ($\alpha = \beta = 0$ in Equation 1). The significance of the correlations was assessed via a permutation test. The correlation values for cells 97A and 98C, though modest, are significant ($p < 0.01$). For these cells the 95% confidence intervals on the best fit parameter values are consistent with estimates from the flashed grating tests. The best fit parameter values for cell 97A are also consistent across the three independently fit review movies.

The model best accounts for the data from cell 97A. This cell was highly selective for vertical gratings and was not directionally-selective. Figure 1 compares the PSTH obtained from cell 97A with movie B to the model PSTH. The model generally responds to the same features that drive the real cell, though the match is imperfect. Much of the discrepancy between the model and data arises from our approximation of $CRF(t)$ as a delta function. The model's response is roughly constant during

Cell	87A	97A	97A	97A	98C
Movie	A	A	B	C	A
Oriented	No	Yes	Yes	Yes	Yes
Directional	No	No	No	No	Yes
r_E	NA	0.41	0.43	0.59	0.35

Table 1: Correlations between model and data PSTHs. *Oriented* cells showed orientation-selectivity in the flashed grating test while *Directional* cells showed directional-selectivity during manual characterization. r_E is the correlation between E_{CRF} and the data. No fit was obtained for cell 87A.

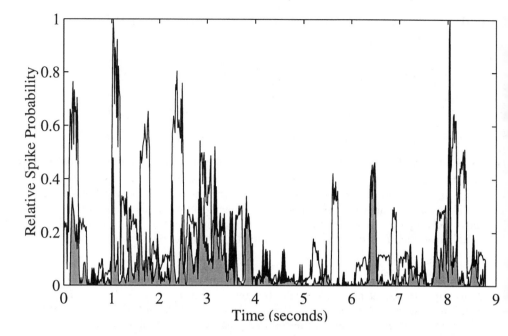

Figure 1: CRF energy mechanism versus data (Cell 97A, Movie B). White indicates that the model response is greater than the data, while black indicates the data is greater than the model and gray indicates regions of overlap. A perfect match between model and data would result in the entire area under the curve being gray. Our approximation of $CRF(t)$ leads to a relatively constant model PSTH during each fixation. In contrast the real cell generally gives a phasic response as each saccade brings a new stimulus into the CRF. In general the same movie features drive both model and cell.

each fixation, which causes the model PSTH to appear stepped. In contrast the data PSTH shows a strong phasic response at the beginning of each fixation when a new stimulus patch enters the cell's CRF.

The model is less successful at accounting for the responses of the directionally-selective cell, 98C. This is probably because the model's space-time separable receptive field misses motion energy cues that drive the cell. The model completely failed to fit the data from cell 87A. This cell was not orientation-selective, so the fitting procedure was unable to find an appropriate orientation for the $CRF^\phi(x,y)$ Gabor function.[5]

CRF Energy Mechanism with Suppressive Surround: Table 2 lists the improvements in correlation obtained by adding the gain control term ($\alpha > 0, \beta = 0$ in Equation 1). For cell 97A (all three movies) the best correlations are obtained when the surround effects are delayed by 56 ms relative to the center. The best correlation for cell 98C is obtained when the surround is not delayed.

In three out of four cases the correlation values are barely improved when the surround effects are included, suggesting that the cells were not strongly surround-inhibited by these review movies. However, the improvement is quite striking in the

---

[5]For cell 87A the correlation values in the orientation and spatial frequency parameter subspace contained three roughly equivalent maxima. Contamination by multiple cells was unlikely due to this cell's excellent isolation.

Cell	97A	97A	97A	98C
Movie	A	B	C	A
r_{E+G}	0.42	0.56	0.60	0.37
Δr	+0.01	+0.13	+0.01	+0.02

Table 2: Correlation improvements due to surround gain control mechanism. r_{E+G} gives the correlation value between the best fit model and the data. Δr gives the improvement over r_E. Including G in Equation 1 leads to a dramatic correlation increase for cell 97A, movie B, but not for the other review movies.

case of cell 97A, movie B. Figure 2 compares the data with a model using both E_{crf} and G in Equation 1. Here the delayed surround suppresses the sustained responses seen in Figure 1 and results in a more phasic model PSTH that closely matches the data.

We consider G and T fields both independently and in combination. For each we independently fit for α, β, δ, and the size of the suppressive fields. However, the oriented Fourier power correlates with the total Fourier power for our sample of natural images, so that G and T are highly correlated. Combined fitting of G and T terms leads to competition and dominance by G (i.e. $\beta \to 0$). In this paper we only report the effects of the gain control mechanism; the texture contrast mechanism results in similar (though slightly degraded) results.

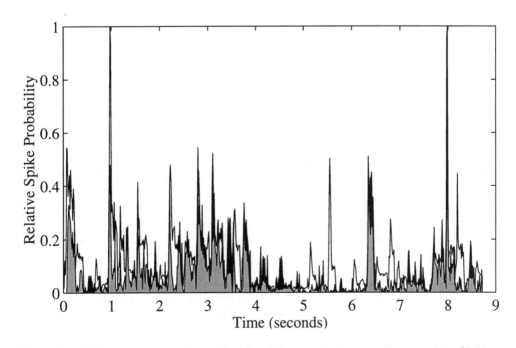

Figure 2: CRF energy mechanism with delayed surround gain control versus data (Cell 97A, Movie B). Color scheme as in Figure 1. The inclusion of the delayed G term results in a more phasic model response which greatly improves the match between model and data.

4 DISCUSSION

This preliminary study suggests that models of the form outlined here show great promise for describing the responses of area V1 cells during natural vision. For comparison consider the correlation values obtained from an earlier neural network model that attempted to reproduce V1 cells' responses to a variety of spatial patterns (Lehky et al. 1992). They report a median correlation value of 0.65 for complex stimuli, whereas the average correlation score from Table 2 is 0.49. This is remarkable considering that our model has only 7 free parameters, a very limited data set for fitting, doesn't yet consider color tuning or directional-selectivity *and* considers response across time.

Future implementations of the model will use a more sophisticated energy mechanism that allows for nonseparable space time receptive field structure and more realistic temporal response dynamics. We will also incorporate more detail into the surround mechanisms, such as asymmetric surround structure and a broadband texture contrast term.

By abstracting physiological observation into approximate functional forms our model balances explanatory power against parametric complexity. A cascaded series of these models may form the foundation for future modeling of cells in extra-striate areas V2 and V4. Natural image stimuli may provide an appropriate stimulus set for development and validation of these extrastriate models.

Acknowledgements

We thank Joseph Rogers for assistance in this study, Maneesh Sahani for the extremely useful suggestion of fitting the CRF parameters, Charles Connor for help with data collection and David Van Essen for support of data collection.

References

Adelson, E. H. & Bergen, J. R. (1985) Spatiotemporal energy models for the perception of motion. *Journal of the Optical Society of America, A,* **2**, 284-299.

Connor, C. C., Preddie, D. C., Gallant, J. L. & Van Essen, D. C. (1997) Spatial attention effects in macaque area V4. *Journal of Neuroscience,* **77**, 3201-3214.

De Valois, R. L. & De Valois, K. K. (1990) *Spatial Vision.* New York: Oxford University Press.

Gallant, J. L., Connor, C. E., & Van Essen, D. C. (1998) Neural Activity in Areas V1, V2 and V4 During Free Viewing of Natural Scenes Compared to Controlled Viewing. *NeuroReport,* **9**.

Geisler, W. S., Albrecht, D. G. (1997) Visual cortex neurons in monkeys and cats: Detection, discrimination, and identification. *Visual Neuroscience,* **14**, 897-919.

Heeger, D. J. (1992) Normalization of cell responses in cat striate cortex. *Visual Neuroscience,* **9**, 181-198.

Knierim, J. J. & Van Essen, D. C. (1992) Neuronal responses to static texture patterns in area V1 of the alert macaque monkey. *Journal of Neurophysiology,* **67**, 961-980.

Lehky, S. R., Sejnowski, T. J. & Desimone, R. (1992) Predicting Responses of Nonlinear Neurons in Monkey Striate Cortex to Complex Patterns. *Journal of Neuroscience,* **12**, 3568-3581.

Wilson, H. R. & Humanski, R. (1993) Spatial frequency adaptation and contrast gain control. *Vision Research,* **33**, 1133-1149.

PART III
THEORY

The Canonical Distortion Measure in Feature Space and 1-NN Classification

Jonathan Baxter*and Peter Bartlett
Department of Systems Engineering
Australian National University
Canberra 0200, Australia
{jon,bartlett}@syseng.anu.edu.au

Abstract

We prove that the Canonical Distortion Measure (CDM) [2, 3] is the optimal distance measure to use for 1 nearest-neighbour (1-NN) classification, and show that it reduces to squared Euclidean distance in feature space for function classes that can be expressed as linear combinations of a fixed set of features. PAC-like bounds are given on the sample-complexity required to learn the CDM. An experiment is presented in which a neural network CDM was learnt for a Japanese OCR environment and then used to do 1-NN classification.

1 INTRODUCTION

Let X be an input space, P a distribution on X, $\mathcal{F}$ a class of functions mapping X into Y (called the "environment"), Q a distribution on $\mathcal{F}$ and σ a function $\sigma: Y \times Y \to [0, M]$. The *Canonical Distortion Measure* (CDM) between two inputs x, x' is defined to be:

$$\rho(x, x') = \int_{\mathcal{F}} \sigma(f(x), f(x')) \, dQ(f). \tag{1}$$

Throughout this paper we will be considering real-valued functions and squared loss, so $Y = \mathbb{R}$ and $\sigma(y, y') := (y - y')^2$. The CDM was introduced in [2, 3], where it was analysed primarily from a vector quantization perspective. In particular, the CDM was proved to be the optimal distortion measure to use in vector quantization, in the sense of producing the best approximations to the functions in the environment $\mathcal{F}$. In [3] some experimental results were also presented (in a toy domain) showing how the CDM may be learnt.

The purpose of this paper is to investigate the utility of the CDM as a classification tool. In Section 2 we show how the CDM for a class of functions possessing a common feature

---

*The first author was supported in part by EPSRC grants #K70366 and #K70373

set reduces, via a change of variables, to squared Euclidean distance in feature space. A lemma is then given showing that the CDM is the optimal distance measure to use for 1-nearest-neighbour (1-NN) classification. Thus, for functions possessing a common feature set, optimal 1-NN classification is achieved by using squared Euclidean distance in feature space.

In general the CDM will be unknown, so in Section 4 we present a technique for learning the CDM by minimizing squared loss, and give PAC-like bounds on the sample-size required for good generalisation. In Section 5 we present some experimental results in which a set of features was learnt for a machine-printed Japanese OCR environment, and then squared Euclidean distance was used to do 1-NN classification in feature space. The experiments provide strong empirical support for the theoretical results in a difficult real-world application.

2   THE CDM IN FEATURE SPACE

Suppose each $f \in \mathcal{F}$ can be expressed as a linear combination of a fixed set of features $\Phi := (\phi_1, \ldots, \phi_k)$. That is, for all $f \in \mathcal{F}$, there exists $\mathbf{w} := (w_1, \ldots, w_k)$ such that $f = \mathbf{w} \cdot \Phi = \sum_{i=1}^{k} w_i \phi_i$. In this case the distribution Q over the environment $\mathcal{F}$ is a distribution over the weight vectors $\mathbf{w}$. Measuring the distance between function values by $\sigma(y, y') := (y - y')^2$, the CDM (1) becomes:

$$\rho(x, x') = \int_{\mathbb{R}^k} \left[\mathbf{w} \cdot \Phi(x) - \mathbf{w} \cdot \Phi(x') \right]^2 dQ(\mathbf{w}) = (\Phi(x) - \Phi(x'))W(\Phi(x) - \Phi(x'))'$$
(2)

where $W = \int_{\mathbf{w}} \mathbf{w}' \mathbf{w} \, dQ(\mathbf{w})$. is a $k \times k$ matrix. Making the change of variable $\Phi \to \Phi\sqrt{W}$, we have $\rho(x, x') = \|\Phi(x) - \Phi(x')\|^2$. Thus, the assumption that the functions in the environment can be expressed as linear combinations of a fixed set of features means that the CDM is simply squared Euclidean distance in a feature space related to the original by a linear transformation.

3   1-NN CLASSIFICATION AND THE CDM

Suppose the environment $\mathcal{F}$ consists of classifiers, i.e. $\{0, 1\}$-valued functions. Let f be some function in $\mathcal{F}$ and $\mathbf{z} := (x_1, f(x_1)), \ldots, (x_n, f(x_n))$ a training set of examples of f. In 1-NN classification the classification of a novel x is computed by $f(x^*)$ where $x^* = \operatorname{argmin}_{x_i} d(x, x_i))$, i.e. the classification of x is the classification of the nearest training point to x under some distance measure d. If both f and x are chosen at random, the expected misclassification error of the 1-NN scheme using d and the training points $\mathbf{x} := (x_1, \ldots, x_n)$ is

$$\operatorname{er}(\mathbf{x}, d) := \mathbf{E}_{\mathcal{F}} \mathbf{E}_X \left[f(x) - f(x^*) \right]^2,$$
(3)

where x^* is the nearest neighbour to x from $\{x_1, \ldots, x_n\}$. The following lemma is now immediate from the definitions.

Lemma 1. *For all sequences* $\mathbf{x} = (x_1, \ldots, x_n)$, $\operatorname{er}(\mathbf{x}, d)$ *is minimized if d is the CDM ρ.*

Remarks. Lemma 1 combined with the results of the last section shows that for function classes possessing a common feature set, optimal 1-NN classification is achieved by using squared Euclidean distance in feature space. In Section 5 some experimental results on Japanese OCR are presented supporting this conclusion.

The property of optimality of the CDM for 1-NN classification may not be stable to small perturbations. That is, if we learn an approximation g to ρ, then even if $\mathbf{E}_{X \times X}(g(x, x') -$

$\rho(x, x'))^2$ is small it may not be the case that 1-NN classification using g is also small. However, one can show that stability is maintained for classifier environments in which positive examples of different functions do not overlap significantly (as is the case for the Japanese OCR environment of Section 5, face recognition environments, speech recognition environments and so on). We are currently investigating the general conditions under which stability is maintained.

4   LEARNING THE CDM

For most environments encountered in practice (e.g speech recognition or image recognition), ρ will be unknown. In this section it is shown how ρ may be estimated or *learnt* using function approximation techniques (*e.g.* feedforward neural networks).

4.1   SAMPLING THE ENVIRONMENT

To learn the CDM ρ, the learner is provided with a class of functions (*e.g.* neural networks) $\mathcal{G}$ where each $g \in \mathcal{G}$ maps $X \times X \to [0, M]$. The goal of the learner is to find a g such that the error between g and the CDM ρ is small. For the sake of argument this error will be measured by the expected squared loss:

$$\mathrm{er}_P(g) := \mathbf{E}_{X \times X} \left[g(x, x') - \rho(x, x') \right]^2, \tag{4}$$

where the expectation is with respect to P^2.

Ordinarily the learner would be provided with training data in the form $(x, x', \rho(x, x'))$ and would use this data to minimize an empirical version of (4). However, ρ is unknown so to generate data of this form ρ must be estimated for each training pair x, x'. Hence to generate training sets for learning the CDM, both the distribution Q over the environment $\mathcal{F}$ and the distribution P over the input space X must be sampled. So let $\mathbf{f} := (f_1, \ldots, f_m)$ be m i.i.d. samples from $\mathcal{F}$ according to Q and let $\mathbf{x} := (x_1, \ldots, x_n)$ be n i.i.d. samples from X according to P. For any pair x_i, x_j an estimate of $\rho(x_i, x_j)$ is given by

$$\hat{\rho}(x_i, x_j) := \frac{1}{m} \sum_{k=1}^{m} \sigma(f_k(x_i), f_k(x_j)). \tag{5}$$

This gives $n(n-1)/2$ training *triples*,

$$\{(x_i, x_j, \hat{\rho}(x_i, x_j)), 1 \le i < j \le n\},$$

which can be used as data to generate an empirical estimate of $\mathrm{er}_P(g)$:

$$\hat{\mathrm{er}}_{\mathbf{x}, \mathbf{f}}(g) := \frac{2}{n(n-1)} \sum_{1 \le i < j \le n} \left[g(x_i, x_j) - \hat{\rho}(x_i, x_j) \right]^2. \tag{6}$$

Only $n(n-1)/2$ of the possible n^2 training triples are used because the functions $g \in \mathcal{G}$ are assumed to already be symmetric and to satisfy $g(x, x) = 0$ for all x (if this is not the case then set $g'(x, x') := (g(x, x') + g(x', x))/2$ if $x \ne x'$ and $g'(x, x) = 0$ and use $\mathcal{G}' := \{g' : g \in \mathcal{G}\}$ instead).

In [3] an experiment was presented in which $\mathcal{G}$ was a neural network class and (6) was minimized directly by gradient descent. In Section 5 we present an alternative technique in which a set of features is first learnt for the environment and then an estimate of ρ in feature space is constructed explicitly.

4.2   UNIFORM CONVERGENCE

We wish to ensure good generalisation from a g minimizing $\hat{\text{er}}_{\mathbf{x},\mathbf{f}}$, in the sense that (for small ε, δ),

$$\Pr\left\{\mathbf{x},\mathbf{f}: \sup_{g\in\mathcal{G}}\left|\hat{\text{er}}_{\mathbf{x},\mathbf{f}}(g) - \text{er}_P(g)\right| > \varepsilon\right\} < \delta,$$

The following theorem shows that this occurs if both the number of functions m and the number of input samples n are sufficiently large. Some exotic (but nonetheless benign) measurability restrictions have been ignored in the statement of the theorem. In the statement of the theorem, $\mathcal{N}(\varepsilon,\mathcal{G})$ denotes the smallest ε-cover of $\mathcal{G}$ under the $L_1(P^2)$ norm, where $\{g_1,\ldots,g_N\}$ is an ε-cover of $\mathcal{G}$ if for all $g\in\mathcal{G}$ there exists g_i such that $\|g_i - g\| \leq \varepsilon$.

Theorem 2. *Assume the range of the functions in the environment $\mathcal{F}$ is no more than $[-\sqrt{B/2}, \sqrt{B/2}]$ and in the class $\mathcal{G}$ (used to approximate the CDM) is no more than $[0, \sqrt{B}]$. For all $\varepsilon > 0$ and $0 < \delta \leq 1$, if*

$$m \geq \frac{32B^4}{\varepsilon^2}\log\frac{4}{\delta} \tag{7}$$

and

$$n \geq \frac{512B^2}{\varepsilon^2}\left(\log\mathcal{N}(\varepsilon,\mathcal{G}) + \log\frac{512B^2}{\varepsilon^2} + \log\frac{8}{\delta}\right) \tag{8}$$

then

$$\Pr\left\{\mathbf{x},\mathbf{f}: \sup_{g\in\mathcal{G}}\left|\hat{\text{er}}_{\mathbf{x},\mathbf{f}}(g) - \text{er}_P(g)\right| > \varepsilon\right\} < \delta. \tag{9}$$

Proof. For each $g\in\mathcal{G}$, define

$$\hat{\text{er}}_{\mathbf{x}}(g) := \frac{2}{n(n-1)}\sum_{1\leq i<j\leq n}[g(x_i,x_j) - \rho(x_i,x_j)]^2. \tag{10}$$

If for any $\mathbf{x} = (x_1,\ldots,x_n)$,

$$\Pr\left\{\mathbf{f}: \sup_{g\in\mathcal{G}}|\hat{\text{er}}_{\mathbf{x},\mathbf{f}}(g) - \hat{\text{er}}_{\mathbf{x}}(g)| > \frac{\varepsilon}{2}\right\} \leq \frac{\delta}{2}, \tag{11}$$

and

$$\Pr\left\{\mathbf{x}: \sup_{g\in\mathcal{G}}|\hat{\text{er}}_{\mathbf{x}}(g) - \text{er}_P(g)| > \frac{\varepsilon}{2}\right\} \leq \frac{\delta}{2}, \tag{12}$$

then by the triangle inequality (9) will hold. We treat (11) and (12) separately.

Equation (11). To simplify the notation let $g_{ij}, \hat{\rho}_{ij}$ and ρ_{ij} denote $g(x_i,x_j), \hat{\rho}(x_i,x_j)$ and $\rho(x_i,x_j)$ respectively. Now,

$$\begin{aligned}
|\hat{\text{er}}_{\mathbf{x},\mathbf{f}}(g) - \hat{\text{er}}_{\mathbf{x}}(g)| &= \frac{2}{n(n-1)}\left|\sum_{1\leq i<j\leq n}(g_{ij} - \hat{\rho}_{ij})^2 - \sum_{1\leq i<j\leq n}(g_{ij} - \rho_{ij})^2\right| \\
&= \frac{2}{n(n-1)}\left|\sum_{1\leq i<j\leq n}(\rho_{ij} - \hat{\rho}_{ij})(2g_{ij} - \hat{\rho}_{ij} - \rho_{ij})\right| \\
&\leq \frac{4B}{n(n-1)}\left|\sum_{1\leq i<j\leq n}(\rho_{ij} - \hat{\rho}_{ij})\right| \\
&= \left|\mathbf{E}_{\mathcal{F}}\mathbf{x}(f) - \frac{1}{m}\sum_{k=1}^{m}\mathbf{x}(f_k)\right|,
\end{aligned}$$

where $\mathbf{x}: \mathcal{F} \to [0, 4B^2]$ is defined by

$$\mathbf{x}(f) := \frac{4B}{n(n-1)} \sum_{1 \le i < j \le n} (f(x_i) - f(x_j))^2.$$

Thus,

$$\Pr\left\{f: \sup_{g \in \mathcal{G}} |\hat{\mathrm{er}}_{\mathbf{x}, \mathbf{f}}(g) - \hat{\mathrm{er}}_{\mathbf{x}}(g)| > \frac{\varepsilon}{2}\right\} \le \Pr\left\{f: \left|\mathbf{E}_{\mathcal{F}}\mathbf{x}(f) - \frac{1}{m}\sum_{k=1}^{m}\mathbf{x}(f_k)\right| > \frac{\varepsilon}{2}\right\}$$

which is $\le 2\exp\left(-m\varepsilon^2/(32B^4)\right)$ by Hoeffding's inequality. Setting this less than $\delta/2$ gives the bound on m in theorem 2.

Equation (12). Without loss of generality, suppose that n is even. The trick here is to split the sum over all pairs (x_i, x_j) (with $i < j$) appearing in the definition of $\hat{\mathrm{er}}_{\mathbf{x}}(g)$ into a double sum:

$$\hat{\mathrm{er}}_{\mathbf{x}}(g) = \frac{2}{n(n-1)} \sum_{1 \le i < j \le n} [g(x_i, x_j) - \rho(x_i, x_j)]^2$$

$$= \frac{1}{n-1} \sum_{i=1}^{n-1} \frac{2}{n} \sum_{j=1}^{n/2} \left[g(x_{\sigma_i(j)}, x_{\sigma'_i(j)}) - \rho(x_{\sigma_i(j)}, x_{\sigma'_i(j)})\right]^2,$$

where for each $i = 1, \ldots, n-1$, σ_i and σ'_i are permutations on $\{1, \ldots, n\}$ such that $\{\sigma_i(1), \ldots, \sigma_i(n/2)\} \cap \{\sigma'_i(1), \ldots, \sigma'_i(n/2)\}$ is empty. That there exist permutations with this property such that the sum can be broken up in this way can be proven easily by induction. Now, conditional on each σ_i, the $n/2$ pairs $\mathbf{x}_i := \{(x_{\sigma_i(j)}, x_{\sigma'_i(j)}), j = 1, \ldots, n/2\}$ are an i.i.d. sample from $X \times X$ according to P^2. So by standard results from real-valued function learning with squared loss [4]:

$$\Pr\left\{\mathbf{x}_i: \sup_{g \in \mathcal{G}} \left|\frac{2}{n}\sum_{j=1}^{n/2} \left[g(x_{\sigma_i(j)}, x_{\sigma'_i(j)}) - \rho(x_{\sigma_i(j)}, x_{\sigma'_i(j)})\right]^2 - \mathrm{er}_P(g)\right| > \frac{\varepsilon}{2}\right\}$$

$$\le 4\mathcal{N}\left(\frac{\varepsilon}{48B^2}, \mathcal{G}\right) \exp\left(-\frac{n\varepsilon^2}{256B^2}\right).$$

Hence, by the union bound,

$$\Pr\left\{\mathbf{x}: \sup_{g \in \mathcal{G}} |\hat{\mathrm{er}}_{\mathbf{x}}(g) - \mathrm{er}_P(g)| > \frac{\varepsilon}{2}\right\} \le 4(n-1)\mathcal{N}\left(\frac{\varepsilon}{48B^2}, \mathcal{G}\right) \exp\left(-\frac{n\varepsilon^2}{256B^2}\right).$$

Setting n as in the statement of the theorem ensures this is less than $\delta/2$. $\qquad \square$

Remark. The bound on m (the number of functions that need to be sampled from the environment) is independent of the complexity of the class $\mathcal{G}$. This should be contrasted with related bias learning (or equivalently, learning to learn) results [1] in which the number of functions does depend on the complexity. The heuristic explanation for this is that here we are only learning a distance function on the input space (the CDM), whereas in bias learning we are learning an entire hypothesis space that is appropriate for the environment. However, we shall see in the next section how for certain classes of problems the CDM can also be used to learn the functions in the environment. Hence in these cases learning the CDM is a more effective method of learning to learn.

5 EXPERIMENT: JAPANESE OCR

To verify the optimality of the CDM for 1-NN classification, and also to show how it can be learnt in a non-trivial domain (only a toy example was given in [3]), the

CDM was learnt for a Japanese OCR environment. Specifically, there were 3018 functions f in the environment $\mathcal{F}$, each one a classifier for a different Kanji character. A database containing 90,918 segmented, machine-printed Kanji characters scanned from various sources was purchased from the CEDAR group at the State University of New York, Buffalo The quality of the images ranged from clean to very degraded (see http://www.cedar.buffalo.edu/Databases/JOCR/).

The main reason for choosing Japanese OCR rather than English OCR as a test-bed was the large number of distinct characters in Japanese. Recall from Theorem 2 that to get good generalisation from a learnt CDM, sufficiently many functions must be sampled from the environment. If the environment just consisted of English characters then it is likely that "sufficiently many" characters would mean *all* characters, and so it would be impossible to test the learnt CDM on novel characters not seen in training.

Instead of learning the CDM directly by minimizing (6), it was learnt implicitly by first learning a set of neural network features for the functions in the environment. The features were learnt using the method outlined in [1], which essentially involves learning a set of classifiers with a common final hidden layer. The features were learnt on 400 out of the 3000 classifiers in the environment, using 90% of the data in training and 10% in testing. Each resulting classifier was a linear combination of the neural network features. The average error of the classifiers was 2.85% on the test set (which is an accurate estimate as there were 9092 test examples).

Recall from Section 2 that if all $f \in \mathcal{F}$ can be expressed as $f = \mathbf{w} \cdot \Phi$ for a fixed feature set Φ, then the CDM reduces to $\rho(x, x') = (\Phi(x) - \Phi(x'))W(\Phi(x) - \Phi(x'))'$ where $W = \int_{\mathbf{w}} \mathbf{w}' \mathbf{w} \, dQ(\mathbf{w})$. The result of the learning procedure above is a set of features $\hat{\Phi}$ and 400 weight vectors $\mathbf{w}_1, \ldots, \mathbf{w}_{400}$, such that for each of the character classifiers f_i used in training, $f_i \simeq \mathbf{w}_i \cdot \hat{\Phi}$. Thus, $g(x, x') := (\hat{\Phi}(x) - \hat{\Phi}(x'))W(\hat{\Phi}(x) - \hat{\Phi}(x'))'$ is an empirical estimate of the true CDM, where $W := \sum_{i=1}^{400} \mathbf{w}_i' \mathbf{w}_i$. With a linear change of variable $\hat{\Phi} \to \hat{\Phi}\sqrt{W}$, g becomes $g(x, x') = \|\hat{\Phi}(x) - \hat{\Phi}(x')\|^2$. This g was used to do 1-NN classification on the test examples in two different experiments.

In the first experiment, all testing and training examples that were not an example of one of the 400 training characters were lumped into an extra category for the purpose of classification. All test examples were then given the label of their nearest neighbour in the training set under g (*i.e.*, initially all training examples were mapped into feature space to give $\{\hat{\Phi}(x_1), \ldots, \hat{\Phi}(x_n)\}$. Then each test example was mapped into feature space and assigned the same label as $\text{argmin}_{x_i} \|\hat{\Phi}(x) - \hat{\Phi}(x_i)\|^2$). The total misclassification error was 2.2%, which can be directly compared with the misclassification error of the original classifiers of 2.85%. The CDM does better because it uses the training data explicitly *and* the information stored in the network to make a comparison, whereas the classifiers only use the information in the network. The learnt CDM was also used to do k-NN classification with $k > 1$. However this afforded no improvement. For example, the error of the 3-NN classifier was 2.54% and the error of the 20-NN classifier was 3.99%. This provides an indication that the CDM may not be the optimal distortion measure to use if k-NN classification ($k > 1$) is the aim.

In the second experiment g was again used to do 1-NN classification on the test set, but this time all 3018 characters were distinguished. So in this case the learnt CDM was being asked to distinguish between 2618 characters that were treated as a single character when it was being trained. The misclassification error was a surprisingly low 7.5%. The 7.5% error compares favourably with the 4.8% error achieved on the same data by the CEDAR group, using a carefully selected feature set and a hand-tailored nearest-neighbour routine [5]. In our case the distance measure was *learnt* from raw-data input, and has not been the subject of any optimization or tweaking.

開 間 関 閑 問
案 業 素 実 常
普 群 勝 費 難
先 火 比 佐 死
暗 階 降 路 結
科 料 時 移 務

Figure 1: Six Kanji characters (first character in each row) and examples of their four nearest neighbours (remaining four characters in each row).

As a final, more qualitative assessment, the learnt CDM was used to compute the distance between every pair of testing examples, and then the distance between each pair of characters (an individual character being represented by a number of testing examples) was computed by averaging the distances between their constituent examples. The nearest neighbours of each character were then calculated. With this measure, every character turned out to be its own nearest neighbour, and in many cases the next-nearest neighbours bore a strong subjective similarity to the original. Some representative examples are shown in Figure 1.

6 CONCLUSION

We have shown how the Canonical Distortion Measure (CDM) is the optimal distortion measure for 1-NN classification, and that for environments in which all the functions can be expressed as a linear combination of a fixed set of features, the Canonical Distortion Measure is squared Euclidean distance in feature space. A technique for learning the CDM was presented and PAC-like bounds on the sample complexity required for good generalisation were proved.

Experimental results were presented in which the CDM for a Japanese OCR environment was learnt by first learning a common set of features for a subset of the character classifiers in the environment. The learnt CDM was then used as a distance measure in 1-NN neighbour classification, and performed remarkably well, both on the characters used to train it and on entirely novel characters.

References

[1] Jonathan Baxter. Learning Internal Representations. In *Proceedings of the Eighth International Conference on Computational Learning Theory*, pages 311–320. ACM Press, 1995.

[2] Jonathan Baxter. The Canonical Metric for Vector Quantisation. Technical Report NeuroColt Technical Report 047, Royal Holloway College, University of London, July 1995.

[3] Jonathan Baxter. The Canonical Distortion Measure for Vector Quantization and Function Approximation. In *Proceedings of the Fourteenth International Conference on Machine Learning*, July 1997. To Appear.

[4] W S Lee, P L Bartlett, and R C Williamson. Efficient agnostic learning of neural networks with bounded fan-in. *IEEE Transactions on Information Theory*, 1997.

[5] S.N. Srihari, T. Hong, and Z. Shi. Cherry Blossom: A System for Reading Unconstrained Handwritten Page Images. In *Symposium on Document Image Understanding Technology (SDIUT)*, 1997.

Multiple Threshold Neural Logic

Vasken Bohossian   **Jehoshua Bruck**

California Institute of Technology
Mail Code 136-93
Pasadena, CA 91125
E-mail: {vincent, bruck}@paradise.caltech.edu

Abstract

We introduce a new Boolean computing element related to the Linear Threshold element, which is the Boolean version of the neuron. Instead of the sign function, it computes an arbitrary (with polynomialy many transitions) Boolean function of the weighted sum of its inputs. We call the new computing element an LTM element, which stands for Linear Threshold with Multiple transitions.

The paper consists of the following main contributions related to our study of LTM circuits: (i) the creation of efficient designs of LTM circuits for the addition of a multiple number of integers and the product of two integers. In particular, we show how to compute the addition of m integers with a single layer of LTM elements. (ii) a proof that the area of the VLSI layout is reduced from $O(n^2)$ in LT circuits to $O(n)$ in LTM circuits, for n inputs symmetric Boolean functions, and (iii) the characterization of the computing power of LTM relative to LT circuits.

1 Introduction

Human brains are by far superior to computers in solving hard problems like combinatorial optimization and image and speech recognition, although their basic building blocks are several orders of magnitude slower. This observation has boosted interest in the field of artificial neural networks [Hopfield 82], [Rumelhart 82]. The latter are built by interconnecting artificial neurons whose behavior is inspired by that of biological neurons. In this paper we consider the Boolean version of an artificial neuron, namely, a Linear Threshold (LT) element, which computes a neural-like

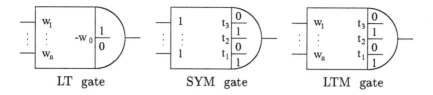

Figure 1: Schematic representation of *LT*, *SYM* and *LTM* computing elements.

Boolean function of n binary inputs [Muroga 71]. An *LT* element outputs the sign of a weighted sum of its Boolean inputs. The main issues in the study of networks (circuits) consisting of *LT* elements, called *LT* circuits, include the estimation of their computational capabilities and limitations and the comparison of their properties with those of traditional Boolean logic circuits based on AND, OR and NOT gates (called *AON* circuits). For example, there is a strong evidence that *LT* circuits are more efficient than *AON* circuits in implementing a number of important functions including the addition, product and division of integers [Siu 94], [Siu 93].

Motivated by our recent work on the VLSI implementation of LT elements [Bohossian 95b], we introduce in this paper a more powerful computing element, a multiple threshold neuron, which we call *LTM*, which stands for Linear Threshold with Multiple transitions, see [Haring 66] and [Olafsson 88]. Instead of the sign function in the LT element it computes an arbitrary (with polynomialy many transitions) Boolean function of the weighted sum of its inputs.

The main issues in the study of *LTM* circuits (circuits consisting of *LTM* elements) include the estimation of their computational capabilities and limitations and the comparison of their properties to those of *AON* circuits. A natural approach in this study is first to understand the relation between *LT* circuits and *LTM* circuits. Our main contributions in this paper are:

- We demonstrate the power of *LTM* by deriving efficient designs of *LTM* circuits for the addition of m integers and the product of two integers.

- We show that *LTM* circuits are more amenable in implementation than *LT* circuits. In particular, the area of the VLSI layout is reduced from $O(n^2)$ in *LT* circuits to $O(n)$ in *LTM* circuits, for n input symmetric Boolean functions.

- We characterize the computing power of *LTM* relative to *LT* circuits.

Next we describe the formal definitions of *LT* and *LTM* elements.

1.1 Definitions and Examples

Definition 1 *(Linear Threshold Gate – LT)*
A linear threshold gate computes a Boolean function of its binary inputs :

$$f(X) = sgn(w_0 + \sum_{i=1}^{n} w_i x_i)$$

where the w_i are integers and $sgn(.)$ outputs 1 if its argument is greater or equal to 0, and 0 otherwise.

Figure 1 shows a n-input LT element; if $\sum_1^n w_i x_i \geq -w_0$ the element outputs 1, otherwise it outputs 0. A single LT gate is unable to compute parity. The latter belongs to the general class of symmetric functions – SYM.

Definition 2 *(Symmetric Functions – SYM)*
A Boolean function f is symmetric if its value depends only on the number of ones in the input denoted by $|X|$.

Figure 1 shows an example of a symmetric function; it has three transitions, it outputs 1 for $|X| < t_1$ and for $t_2 \leq |X| < t_3$, and 0 otherwise. *AND*, *OR* and parity are examples of symmetric functions. A single LT element can implement only a limited subset of symmetric functions. We define LTM as a generalization of SYM. That is, we allow the weights to be arbitrary as in the case of LT, rather than fixed to 1 (see Figure 1).

Definition 3 *(Linear Threshold Gate with Multiple Transitions – LTM)*
A function f is in LTM if there exists a set of weights $w_i \in Z$, $1 \leq i \leq n$ and a function $h : Z \longrightarrow \{0,1\}$ such that

$$f(X) = h(\sum_{i=1}^n w_i x_i) \text{ for all } X \in \{0,1\}^n$$

The only constraint on h is that it undergoes polynomialy many transitions as its input scans $[-\sum_{i=1}^n |w_i|, \sum_{i=1}^n |w_i|]$.

Notice that without the constraint on the number of transitions, an LTM gate is capable of computing any Boolean function. Indeed, given an arbitrary function f, let $w_i = 2^{i-1}$ and $h(\sum_1^n 2^{i-1} x_i) = f(x_1, ..., x_n)$.

Example 1 $(XOR \in LTM)$
$XOR(X)$ outputs 1 if $|X|$, the number of 1's in X, is odd. Otherwise it outputs 0. To implement it choose $w_i = 1$ and $h(k) = \frac{1}{2}(1 - (-1)^k)$ for $0 \leq k \leq n$. Note that $h(k)$ needs not be defined for $k < 0$ and $k > n$, and has polynomialy many transitions.

Another useful function that LTM can compute is $ADD(X, Y)$, the sum of two n-bit integers X and Y.

Example 2 $(ADD \in LTM)$
To implement addition we set $f_l(X, Y) = h_l(\sum_{i=1}^l 2^i (x_i + y_i))$ where $h_l(k) = 1$ for $k \in [2^l, 2 \times 2^l - 1] \cup [3 \times 2^l, +\infty)$. Defined thus, f_l computes the m-th bit of $X + Y$.

1.2   Organization

The paper is organized as follows. In Section 2, we study a number of applications as well as the VLSI implementations of LTM circuits. In particular, we show how to compute the addition of m integers with a single layer of LTM elements. In Section 3, we prove the characterization results of LTM – inclusion relations, in particular $LTM \subseteq \widehat{LT}_2$. In addition, we indicate which inclusions are proper and exhibit functions to demonstrate the separations.

2 *LTM* Constructions

The theoretical results about *LTM* can be applied to the VLSI implementation of Boolean functions. The idea of a gate with multiple thresholds came to us as we were looking for an efficient VLSI implementation of symmetric Boolean functions. Even though a single *LT* gate is not powerful enough to implement any symmetric function, a 2-layer *LT* circuit is. Furthermore, it is well known that such a circuit performs much better than the traditional logic circuit based on *AND*, *OR* and *NOT* gates. The latter has exponential size (or unbounded depth) [Wegener 91].

Proposition 4 *(LT$_2$ versus LTM for symmetric function implementation)*
The LT$_2$ layout of a symmetric function requires area of $O(n^2)$, while using LTM one needs only area of $O(n)$.

PROOF:
Implementing a generalized symmetric function in LT_2 requires up to n LT gates in the first layer. Those have the same weights w_i except for the threshold w_0. Instead of laying out n times the same linear sum $\sum_1^n w_i x_i$ we do it once and compare the result to n different thresholds. The resulting circuit corresponds to a single LTM gate. □

The LT_2 layout is redundant, it has n copies of each weight, requiring area of at least $O(n^2)$. On the other hand, LTM performs a single weighted sum, its area requirement is $O(n)$.

A single LTM gate can compute the addition of m n-bit integers $MADD$. The only constraint is that m be polynomial in n.

Theorem 5 *(MADD $\in$ LTM)*
A single layer of LTM gates can compute the sum of m n-bit integers, provided that m is at most polynomial in n.

PROOF:
$MADD$ returns an integer of at most $n + \log m$ bits. We need one LTM gate per bit. The least significant bit is computed by a simple m-bit XOR. For all other bits we use $f_l(X^{(1)}, .., X^{(m)}) = h_l(\sum_{i=1}^l 2^i \sum_{j=1}^m x_i^{(j)})$ to compute the l-th bit of the sum. □

Corollary 6 *(PRODUCT $\in$ PTM)* *A single layer of PTM (which is defined below) gates, can compute the product of m n-bit integers, provided that m is at most polynomial in n.*

PROOF:
By analogy with PT_1, defined in [Bruck 90], in PTM_1 (or simply PTM) we allow a polynomial rather than a linear sum : $f(X) = h(w_1 x_1 + ... + w_n x_n + w_{(1,2)} x_1 x_2 + ...)$ However we restrict the sum to have polynomialy many terms (else, any Boolean function could be realized with a single gate). The product of two n-bit integers X and Y can be written as $PRODUCT(X, Y) = \sum_{i=1}^n x_i Y$. We use the construction of $MADD$ in order to implement $PRODUCT$. $PRODUCT(X, Y) = MADD(x_1 Y, x_2 Y, ..., x_n Y)$. $f_l(X, Y) = h_l(\sum_{j=1}^n \sum_{i=1}^l 2^i x_j y_i)$ f_l outputs the l-th bit of the product. □

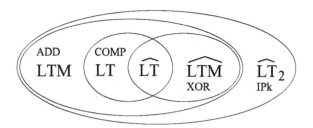

Figure 2: Relationship between Classes

3   Classification of LTM

We use a hat to indicate small (polynomialy growing) weights, e.g. $\widehat{LT}$, $\widehat{LTM}$ [Bohossian 95a], [Siu 91], and a subscript to indicate the depth (number of layers) of the circuit of more than a single layer. All the circuits we consider in this paper are of polynomial size (number of elements) in n (number of inputs). For example, the class $\widehat{LT}_2$ consists of those Boolean functions that can be implemented by a depth-2 polynomial size circuit of $\widehat{LT}$ elements.

Figure 2 depicts the membership relations between five classes of Boolean functions, including, LT, $\widehat{LT}$, LTM, $\widehat{LTM}$ and $\widehat{LT}_2$, along with the functions used to establish the separations.

In this section we will prove the relations illustrated by Figure 2 .

Theorem 7 (*Classification of LTM*)
The inclusions and separations shown in Figure 2 hold. That is,

1. $\widehat{LT} \subseteq LT \subseteq LTM$

2. $\widehat{LT} \subseteq \widehat{LTM} \subseteq LTM$

3. $LTM \subseteq \widehat{LT}_2$

4. $XOR \in \widehat{LTM}$ *but* $XOR \notin LT$

5. $COMP \in LT$ *but* $COMP \notin \widehat{LTM}$

6. $ADD \in LTM$ *but* $ADD \notin LT \cup \widehat{LTM}$

7. $IP_k \in \widehat{LT}_2$ *but* $IP_k \notin LTM$

PROOF:
We show only the outline of the proof. The complete version can be found in [Bohossian 96]. Claims 1 and 2 follow from the definition. The first part of Claim 4 was shown in Example 1 and the second is well known. In Claim 5, $COMP$ stands for the Comparison function, the proof uses the pigeonhole principle and is related to the proof of $COMP \notin \widehat{LT}$ which can be found in [Siu 91]. In Claim 6 to show that $ADD \notin \widehat{LTM}$ we use the same idea as for $COMP$. Claim 3 is proved using a result from [Goldman 93]: a single LT gate with arbitrary weights can be realized by an $\widehat{LT}_2$ circuit. Claim 7 introduces the function $IP_k(X, Y) = 1$ iff $\sum_1^n x_i y_i \geq k$,

0 otherwise. If $IP_k \in LTM$, using the result from [Goldman 93], we can construct a $\widehat{LT}_2$ circuit that computes $IP2$ (Inner Product mod 2) which is known to be false [Hajnal 94]. □

What remains to be shown in order to complete the classification picture is $\widehat{LT} = LT \cap \widehat{LTM}$. We conjecture that this is true.

4 Conclusions

Our original goal was to use theoretical results in order to efficiently lay out a generalized symmetric function. During that process we came to the conclusion that the LT_2 implementation is partially redundant, which lead to the definition of LTM, a new, more powerful computing element. We characterized the power of LTM relative to LT. We showed how it can be used to reduce the area of VLSI layouts from $O(n^2)$ to $O(n)$ and derive efficient designs for multiple addition and product. Interesting directions for future investigation are (i) to prove the conjecture : $\widehat{LT} = LT \cap \widehat{LTM}$, (ii) to apply spectral techniques ([Bruck 90]) to the analysis of LTM, in particular show how PTM fits into the classification picture (Figure 2).

Another direction for future research consists in introducing the ideas described above in the domain of VLSI. We have fabricated a programmable generalized symmetric function on a 2μ, analog chip using the model described above. Floating gate technology is used to program the weights. We store a weight on a single transistor by injecting and tunneling electrons on the floating gate [Hasler 95].

Acknowledgments

This work was supported in part by the NSF Young Investigator Award CCR-9457811 and by the Sloan Research Fellowship.

References

[Bohossian 95a] V. Bohossian and J. Bruck. On Neural Networks with Minimal Weights. In *Advances in Neural Information Processing Systems 8*, MIT Press, Cambridge, MA, 1996, pp.246-252.

[Bohossian 95b] V. Bohossian, P. Hasler and J. Bruck. Programmable Neural Logic. *Proceedings of the second annual IEEE International Conference on Innovative Systems in Silicon*, pp. 13-21, October 1997.

[Bohossian 96] V. Bohossian and J. Bruck. Multiple Threshold Neural Logic. *Technical Report*, ETR010, June 1996. (available at http://paradise.caltech.edu/ETR.html)

[Bruck 90] J. Bruck. Harmonic Analysis of Polynomial Threshold Functions. *SIAM J. Disc. Math*, Vol. 3(No. 2)pp. 168–177, May 1990.

[Goldman 93] M. Goldmann and M. Karpinski. Simulating threshold circuits by majority circuits. In *Proc. 25th ACM STOC*, pages pp. 551–560, 1993.

[Hajnal 94] A. Hajnal, W. Maass, P. Pudlak, M. Szegedy, G. Turan. Threshold Circuits of Bounded Depth. *Journal of Computer and System Sciences*, Vol. 46(No. 2):pp. 129–154, April 1993.

[Haring 66] D.R. Haring. Multi-Threshold Threshold Elements. *IEEE Transactions on Electronic Computers*, Vol. EC-15, No. 1, February 1966.

[Hasler 95] P. Hasler, C. Diorio, B.A. Minch and C.A. Mead. Single Transistor Learning Synapses. *Advances in Neural Information Processing Systems 7*, MIT Press, Cambridge, MA, 1995, pp.817-824.

[Hastad 94] J. Hastad. On the size of weights for threshold gates. *SIAM. J. Disc. Math.*, 7:484–492, 1994.

[Hofmeister 96] T. Hofmeister. A Note on the Simulation of Exponential Threshold Weights. *1996 CONCOON conference.*

[Hopfield 82] J. Hopfield. Neural networks and physical systems with emergent collective computational abilities. *Proc. of the USA National Academy of Sciences*, 79:2554–2558, 1982.

[Muroga 71] M. Muroga. *Threshold Logic and its Applications.* Wiley-Interscience, 1971.

[Olafsson 88] S. Olafsson and Y.S. Abu-Mostafa. The Capacity of Multilevel Threshold Functions. *IEEE Transactions on Pattern Analysis and Machine Intelligence*, Vol.10, No. 2, March 1988.

[Rumelhart 82] D. Rumelhart and J. McClelland. Parallel distributed processing: Explorations in the microstructure of cognition. *MIT Press*, 1982.

[Siu 91] K. Siu and J. Bruck. On the power of threshold circuits with small weights. *SIAM J. Disc. Math.*, Vol. 4(No. 3):pp. 423–435, August 1991.

[Siu 93] K. Siu, J. Bruck, T. Kailath, and T. Hofmeister. Depth Efficient Neural Networks for Division and Related Problems. *IEEE Trans. on Information Theory*, Vol. 39(No. 3), May 1993.

[Siu 94] K. Siu and V.P. Roychowdhury. On Optimal Depth Threshold Circuits for Multiplication and Related Problems. *SIAM J. Disc. Math.*, Vol. 7(No. 2):pp. 284–292, May 94.

[Szegedy 89] M. Szegedy. Algebraic Methods in Lower Bounds for Computational Models with Limited Communication. *PhD Thesis*, Dep. Computer Science, Chicago Univ., December 1989.

[Wegener 91] I. Wegener. The complexity of the parity function in unbounded fan-in unbounded depth circuits. In *Theoretical Computer Science*, Vol. 85, pp. 155–170, 1991.

Generalization in decision trees and DNF: Does size matter?

Mostefa Golea[1], Peter L. Bartlett[1]*, Wee Sun Lee[2] and Llew Mason[1]

[1] Department of Systems Engineering
Research School of Information
Sciences and Engineering
Australian National University
Canberra, ACT, 0200, Australia

[2] School of Electrical Engineering
University College UNSW
Australian Defence Force Academy
Canberra, ACT, 2600, Australia

Abstract

Recent theoretical results for pattern classification with thresh-olded real-valued functions (such as support vector machines, sigmoid networks, and boosting) give bounds on misclassification probability that do not depend on the size of the classifier, and hence can be considerably smaller than the bounds that follow from the VC theory. In this paper, we show that these techniques can be more widely applied, by representing other boolean functions as two-layer neural networks (thresholded convex combinations of boolean functions). For example, we show that with high probability any decision tree of depth no more than d that is consistent with m training examples has misclassification probability no more than $O\left(\left(\frac{1}{m}\left(N_{\mathrm{eff}} \mathrm{VCdim}(\mathcal{U}) \log^2 m \log d\right)\right)^{1/2}\right)$, where $\mathcal{U}$ is the class of node decision functions, and $N_{\mathrm{eff}} \leq N$ can be thought of as the effective number of leaves (it becomes small as the distribution on the leaves induced by the training data gets far from uniform). This bound is qualitatively different from the VC bound and can be considerably smaller.

We use the same technique to give similar results for DNF formulae.

* Author to whom correspondence should be addressed

1   INTRODUCTION

Decision trees are widely used for pattern classification [2, 7]. For these problems, results from the VC theory suggest that the amount of training data should grow at least linearly with the size of the tree[4, 3]. However, empirical results suggest that this is not necessary (see [6, 10]). For example, it has been observed that the error rate is not always a monotonically increasing function of the tree size[6].

To see why the size of a tree is not always a good measure of its complexity, consider two trees, A with N_A leaves and B with N_B leaves, where $N_B \ll N_A$. Although A is larger than B, if most of the classification in A is carried out by very few leaves and the classification in B is equally distributed over the leaves, intuition suggests that A is actually much simpler than B, since tree A can be approximated well by a small tree with few leaves. In this paper, we formalize this intuition.

We give misclassification probability bounds for decision trees in terms of a new complexity measure that depends on the distribution on the leaves that is induced by the training data, and can be considerably smaller than the size of the tree. These results build on recent theoretical results that give misclassification probability bounds for thresholded real-valued functions, including support vector machines, sigmoid networks, and boosting (see [1, 8, 9]), that do not depend on the size of the classifier. We extend these results to decision trees by considering a decision tree as a thresholded convex combination of the *leaf functions* (the boolean functions that specify, for a given leaf, which patterns reach that leaf). We can then apply the misclassification probability bounds for such classifiers. In fact, we derive and use a refinement of the previous bounds for convex combinations of base hypotheses, in which the base hypotheses can come from several classes of different complexity, and the VC-dimension of the base hypothesis class is replaced by the average (under the convex coefficients) of the VC-dimension of these classes. For decision trees, the bounds we obtain depend on the effective number of leaves, a data dependent quantity that reflects how uniformly the training data covers the tree's leaves. This bound is qualitatively different from the VC bound, which depends on the total number of leaves in the tree.

In the next section, we give some definitions and describe the techniques used. We present bounds on the misclassification probability of a thresholded convex combination of boolean functions from base hypothesis classes, in terms of a misclassification margin and the average VC-dimension of the base hypotheses. In Sections 3 and 4, we use this result to give error bounds for decision trees and disjunctive normal form (DNF) formulae.

2   GENERALIZATION ERROR IN TERMS OF MARGIN AND AVERAGE COMPLEXITY

We begin with some definitions. For a class $\mathcal{H}$ of $\{-1, 1\}$-valued functions defined on the input space X, the convex hull $\mathrm{co}(\mathcal{H})$ of $\mathcal{H}$ is the set of $[-1, 1]$-valued functions of the form $\sum_i a_i h_i$, where $a_i \geq 0$, $\sum_i a_i = 1$, and $h_i \in \mathcal{H}$. A function in $\mathrm{co}(\mathcal{H})$ is used for classification by composing it with the threshold function, $\mathrm{sgn} : \mathbb{R} \to \{-1, 1\}$, which satisfies $\mathrm{sgn}(\alpha) = 1$ iff $\alpha \geq 0$. So $f \in \mathrm{co}(\mathcal{H})$ makes a mistake on the pair $(x, y) \in X \times \{-1, 1\}$ iff $\mathrm{sgn}(f(x)) \neq y$. We assume that labelled examples (x, y) are generated according to some probability distribution $\mathcal{D}$ on $X \times \{-1, 1\}$, and we let $\mathbf{P}_{\mathcal{D}}[E]$ denote the probability under $\mathcal{D}$ of an event E. If S is a finite subset of Z, we let $\mathbf{P}_S[E]$ denote the empirical probability of E (that is, the proportion of points in S that lie in E). We use $\mathbf{E}_{\mathcal{D}}[\cdot]$ and $\mathbf{E}_S[\cdot]$ to denote expectation in a similar way. For a function class H of $\{-1, 1\}$-valued functions defined on the input space X, the growth function and VC dimension of H will be denoted by $\Pi_H(m)$ and VCdim(H) respectively.

In [8], Schapire *et al* give the following bound on the misclassification probability of a thresholded convex combination of functions, in terms of the proportion of training data that is labelled to the correct side of the threshold by some margin. (Notice that $\mathbf{P}_D\left[\mathrm{sgn}(f(x)) \neq y\right] \leq \mathbf{P}_D\left[yf(x) \leq 0\right]$.)

Theorem 1 ([8]) *Let D be a distribution on $X \times \{-1,1\}$, $\mathcal{H}$ a hypothesis class with VCdim(H) $= d < \infty$, and $\delta > 0$. With probability at least $1-\delta$ over a training set S of m examples chosen according to D, every function $f \in \mathrm{co}(\mathcal{H})$ and every $\theta > 0$ satisfy*

$$\mathbf{P}_D\left[yf(x) \leq 0\right] \leq \mathbf{P}_S\left[yf(x) \leq \theta\right] + O\left(\frac{1}{\sqrt{m}}\left(\frac{d\log^2(m/d)}{\theta^2} + \log(1/\delta)\right)^{1/2}\right).$$

In Theorem 1, all of the base hypotheses in the convex combination f are elements of a single class $\mathcal{H}$ with bounded VC-dimension. The following theorem generalizes this result to the case in which these base hypotheses may be chosen from any of k classes, $\mathcal{H}_1, \ldots, \mathcal{H}_k$, which can have different VC-dimensions. It also gives a related result that shows the error decreases to twice the error estimate at a faster rate.

Theorem 2 *Let D be a distribution on $X \times \{-1,1\}$, $\mathcal{H}_1, \ldots, \mathcal{H}_k$ hypothesis classes with VCdim(H_i) $= d_i$, and $\delta > 0$. With probability at least $1 - \delta$ over a training set S of m examples chosen according to D, every function $f \in \mathrm{co}\left(\bigcup_{i=1}^k \mathcal{H}_i\right)$ and every $\theta > 0$ satisfy both*

$$\mathbf{P}_D\left[yf(x) \leq 0\right] \leq \mathbf{P}_S\left[yf(x) \leq \theta\right] +$$
$$O\left(\frac{1}{\sqrt{m}}\left(\frac{1}{\theta^2}\left(d\log m + \log k\right)\log\left(m\theta^2/d\right) + \log(1/\delta)\right)^{1/2}\right),$$

$$\mathbf{P}_D\left[yf(x) \leq 0\right] \leq 2\mathbf{P}_S\left[yf(x) \leq \theta\right] +$$
$$O\left(\frac{1}{m}\left(\frac{1}{\theta^2}\left(d\log m + \log k\right)\log\left(m\theta^2/d\right) + \log(1/\delta)\right)\right),$$

where $d = \sum_i a_i d_{j_i}$ and the a_i and j_i are defined by $f = \sum_i a_i h_i$ and $h_i \in \mathcal{H}_{j_i}$ for $j_i \in \{1, \ldots, k\}$.

Proof sketch: We shall sketch only the proof of the first inequality of the theorem. The proof closely follows the proof of Theorem 1 (see [8]). We consider a number of approximating sets of the form $\mathcal{C}_{N,l} = \left\{(1/N)\sum_{i=1}^N \hat{h}_i : \hat{h}_i \in \mathcal{H}_{l_i}\right\}$, where $l = (l_1, \ldots, l_N) \in \{1, \ldots, k\}^N$ and $N \in \mathbb{N}$. Define $\mathcal{C}_N = \bigcup_l \mathcal{C}_{N,l}$. For a given $f = \sum_i a_i h_i$ from $\mathrm{co}\left(\bigcup_{i=1}^k \mathcal{H}_i\right)$, we shall choose an approximation $g \in \mathcal{C}_N$ by choosing $\hat{h}_1, \ldots, \hat{h}_N$ independently from $\{h_1, h_2, \ldots, \}$, according to the distribution defined by the coefficients a_i. Let Q denote this distribution on $\mathcal{C}_N$. As in [8], we can take the expectation under this random choice of $g \in \mathcal{C}_N$ to show that, for any $\theta > 0$, $\mathbf{P}_D\left[yf(x) \leq 0\right] \leq \mathbf{E}_{g \sim Q}\left[\mathbf{P}_D\left[yg(x) \leq \theta/2\right]\right] + \exp(-N\theta^2/8)$. Now, for a given $l \in \{1, \ldots, k\}^N$, the probability that there is a g in $\mathcal{C}_{N,l}$ and a $\theta > 0$ for which $\mathbf{P}_D\left[yg(x) \leq \theta/2\right] > \mathbf{P}_S\left[yg(x) \leq \theta/2\right] + \epsilon_{N,l}$ is at most $8(N+1)\prod_{i=1}^N \left(\frac{2em}{d_{l_i}}\right)^{d_{l_i}} \exp(-m\epsilon_{N,l}^2/32)$. Applying the union bound (over the values of l), taking expectation over $g \sim Q$, and setting $\epsilon_{N,l} = \left(\frac{32}{m} \ln \left(8(N+1) \prod_{i=1}^{N} \left(\frac{2em}{d_{l_i}} \right)^{d_{l_i}} k^N/\delta_N \right) \right)^{1/2}$ shows that, with probability at least $1 - \delta_N$, every f and $\theta > 0$ satisfy $\mathbf{P}_{\mathcal{D}}[yf(x) \leq 0] \leq \mathbf{E}_g[\mathbf{P}_S[yg(x) \leq \theta/2]] + \mathbf{E}_g[\epsilon_{N,l}]$. As above, we can bound the probability inside the first expectation in terms of $\mathbf{P}_S[yf(x) \leq \theta]$. Also, Jensen's inequality implies that $\mathbf{E}_g[\epsilon_{N,l}] \leq \left(\frac{32}{m}(\ln(8(N+1)/\delta_N) + N \ln k + N \sum_i a_i d_{j_i} \ln(2em)) \right)^{1/2}$. Setting $\delta_N = \delta/(N(N+1))$ and $N = \left\lceil \frac{8}{\theta^2} \ln \left(\frac{m\theta^2}{d} \right) \right\rceil$ gives the result. ■

Theorem 2 gives misclassification probability bounds only for thresholded convex combinations of boolean functions. The key technique we use in the remainder of the paper is to find representations in this form (that is, as two-layer neural networks) of more arbitrary boolean functions. We have some freedom in choosing the convex coefficients, and this choice affects both the error estimate $\mathbf{P}_S[yf(x) \leq \theta]$ and the average VC-dimension d. We attempt to choose the coefficients and the margin θ so as to optimize the resulting bound on misclassification probability. In the next two sections, we use this approach to find misclassification probability bounds for decision trees and DNF formulae.

3 DECISION TREES

A two-class decision tree T is a tree whose internal decision nodes are labeled with boolean functions from some class $\mathcal{U}$ and whose leaves are labeled with class labels σ from $\{-1, +1\}$. For a tree with N leaves, define the leaf functions, $h_i : X \to \{-1, 1\}$ by $h_i(x) = 1$ iff x reaches leaf i, for $i = 1, \dots, N$. Note that h_i is the conjunction of all tests on the path from the root to leaf i.

For a sample S and a tree T, let $P_i = \mathbf{P}_S[h_i(x) = 1]$. Clearly, $P = (P_1, \dots, P_N)$ is a probability vector. Let $\sigma_i \in \{-1, +1\}$ denote the class assigned to leaf i. Define the class of leaf functions for leaves up to depth j as

$$\mathcal{H}_j = \{h : \quad h = u_1 \wedge u_2 \wedge \cdots \wedge u_r \mid r \leq j, \ u_i \in \mathcal{U}\}.$$

It is easy to show that $\text{VCdim}(\mathcal{H}_j) \leq 2j\text{VCdim}(\mathcal{U}) \ln(2ej)$. Let d_i denote the depth of leaf i, so $h_i \in \mathcal{H}_{d_i}$, and let $d = \max_i d_i$.

The boolean function implemented by a decision tree T can be written as a thresholded convex combination of the form $T(x) = \text{sgn}(f(x))$, where $f(x) = \sum_{i=1}^{N} w_i \sigma_i ((h_i(x) + 1)/2) = \sum_{i=1}^{N} w_i \sigma_i h_i(x)/2 + \sum_{i=1}^{N} w_i \sigma_i/2$, with $w_i > 0$ and $\sum_{i=1}^{N} w_i = 1$. (To be precise, we need to enlarge the classes $\mathcal{H}_j$ slightly to be closed under negation. This does not affect the results by more than a constant.) We first assume that the tree is consistent with the training sample. We will show later how the results extend to the inconsistent case.

The second inequality of Theorem 2 shows that, for fixed $\delta > 0$ there is a constant c such that, for any distribution $\mathcal{D}$, with probability at least $1 - \delta$ over the sample S we have $\mathbf{P}_{\mathcal{D}}[T(x) \neq y] \leq 2\mathbf{P}_S[yf(x) \leq \theta] + \frac{1}{\theta^2} \sum_{i=1}^{N} w_i d_i B$, where $B = \frac{c}{m}\text{VCdim}(\mathcal{U}) \log^2 m \log d$. Different choices of the w_is and the θ will yield different estimates of the error rate of T. We can assume (wlog) that $P_1 \geq \cdots \geq P_N$. A natural choice is $w_i = P_i$ and $P_{j+1} \leq \theta < P_j$ for some $j \in \{1, \dots, N\}$ which gives

$$\mathbf{P}_{\mathcal{D}}[T(x) \neq y] \leq 2 \sum_{i=j+1}^{N} P_i + \frac{\overline{d}B}{\theta^2}, \tag{1}$$

where $\bar{d} = \sum_{i=1}^{N} P_i d_i$. We can optimize this expression over the choices of $j \in \{1\ldots,N\}$ and θ to give a bound on the misclassification probability of the tree.

Let $\rho(P,U) = \sum_{i=1}^{N}(P_i - 1/N)^2$ be the quadratic distance between the probability vector $P = (P_1,\ldots,P_N)$ and the uniform probability vector $U = (1/N, 1/N, \ldots, 1/N)$. Define $N_{\text{eff}} \equiv N(1 - \rho(P,U))$. The parameter N_{eff} is a measure of the *effective number of leaves* in the tree.

Theorem 3 *For a fixed $\delta > 0$, there is a constant c that satisfies the following. Let $\mathcal{D}$ be a distribution on $X \times \{-1, 1\}$. Consider the class of decision trees of depth up to d, with decision functions in $\mathcal{U}$. With probability at least $1 - \delta$ over the training set S (of size m), every decision tree T that is consistent with S has*

$$\mathbf{P}_{\mathcal{D}}[T(x) \neq y] \leq c \left(\frac{N_{\text{eff}} \, \text{VCdim}(\mathcal{U}) \log^2 m \log d}{m} \right)^{1/2},$$

where N_{eff} is the effective number of leaves of T.

Proof: Supposing that $\theta \geq (\bar{d}/N)^{1/2}$ we optimize (1) by choice of θ. If the chosen θ is actually smaller than $(\bar{d}/N)^{1/2}$ then we show that the optimized bound still holds by a standard VC result. If $\theta \geq (\bar{d}/N)^{1/2}$ then $\sum_{i=j+1}^{N} P_i \leq \theta^2 N_{\text{eff}}/\bar{d}$. So (1) implies that $\mathbf{P}_{\mathcal{D}}[T(x) \neq y] \leq 2\theta^2 N_{\text{eff}}/\bar{d} + \bar{d}B/\theta^2$. The optimal choice of θ is then $(\frac{1}{2}\bar{d}^2 B/N_{\text{eff}})^{1/4}$. So if $(\frac{1}{2}\bar{d}^2 B/N_{\text{eff}})^{1/4} \geq (\bar{d}/N)^{1/2}$, we have the result. Otherwise, the upper bound we need to prove satisfies $2(2N_{\text{eff}}B)^{1/2} > 2NB$, and this result is implied by standard VC results using a simple upper bound for the growth function of the class of decision trees with N leaves. ∎

Thus the parameters that quantify the complexity of a tree are: a) the complexity of the test function class $\mathcal{U}$, and b) the effective number of leaves N_{eff}. The effective number of leaves can potentially be much smaller than the total number of leaves in the tree [5]. Since this parameter is data-dependent, the same tree can be simple for one set of P_is and complex for another set of P_is.

For trees that are not consistent with the training data, the procedure to estimate the error rate is similar. By defining $Q_i = \mathbf{P}_S[y\sigma_i = -1 \mid h_i(x) = 1]$ and $P_i' = P_i(1 - Q_i)/(1 - \mathbf{P}_S[T(x) \neq y])$ we obtain the following result.

Theorem 4 *For a fixed $\delta > 0$, there is a constant c that satisfies the following. Let $\mathcal{D}$ be a distribution on $X \times \{-1, 1\}$. Consider the class of decision trees of depth up to d, with decision functions in $\mathcal{U}$. With probability at least $1 - \delta$ over the training set S (of size m), every decision tree T has*

$$\mathbf{P}_{\mathcal{D}}[T(x) \neq y] \leq \mathbf{P}_S[T(x) \neq y] + c \left(\frac{N_{\text{eff}} \, \text{VCdim}(\mathcal{U}) \log^2 m \log d}{m} \right)^{1/3},$$

where c is a universal constant, and $N_{\text{eff}} = N(1 - \rho(P', U))$ is the effective number of leaves of T.

Notice that this definition of N_{eff} generalizes the definition given before Theorem 3.

4 DNF AS THRESHOLDED CONVEX COMBINATIONS

A DNF formula defined on $\{-1, 1\}^n$ is a disjunction of terms, where each term is a conjunction of literals and a literal is either a variable or its negation. For a given DNF formula g, we use N to denote the number of terms in g, t_i to represent the ith term in f, L_i to represent the set of literals in t_i, and N_i the size of L_i. Each term t_i can be thought of as a member of the class $\mathcal{H}_{N_i}$, the set of monomials with N_i literals. Clearly, $|\mathcal{H}_j| = \binom{2n}{j}$. The DNF g can be written as a thresholded convex combination of the form $g(x) = -\text{sgn}(-f(x)) = -\text{sgn}\left(-\sum_{i=1}^{N} w_i \left((t_i + 1)/2\right)\right)$. (Recall that $\text{sgn}(\alpha) = 1$ iff $\alpha \geq 0$.) Further, each term t_i can be written as a thresholded convex combination of the form $t_i(x) = \text{sgn}(f_i(x)) = \text{sgn}\left(\sum_{l_k \in L_i} v_{ik} \left((l_k(x) - 1)/2\right)\right)$. Assume for simplicity that the DNF is consistent (the results extend easily to the inconsistent case). Let γ^+ (γ^-) denote the fraction of positive (negative) examples under distribution $\mathcal{D}$. Let $\mathbf{P}_{\mathcal{D}+}[\cdot]$ ($\mathbf{P}_{\mathcal{D}-}[\cdot]$) denote probability with respect to the distribution over the positive (negative) examples, and let $\mathbf{P}_{S+}[\cdot]$ ($\mathbf{P}_{S-}[\cdot]$) be defined similarly, with respect to the sample S. Notice that $\mathbf{P}_{\mathcal{D}}[g(x) \neq y] = \gamma^+ \mathbf{P}_{\mathcal{D}+}[g(x) = -1] + \gamma^- \mathbf{P}_{\mathcal{D}-}[(\exists i)\, t_i(x) = 1]$, so the second inequality of Theorem 2 shows that, with probability at least $1 - \delta$, for any θ and any θ_is,

$$\mathbf{P}_{\mathcal{D}}[g(x) \neq y] \leq \gamma^+ \left(2\mathbf{P}_{S+}[f(x) \leq \theta] + \frac{\overline{d}B}{\theta^2}\right) + \gamma^- \sum_{i=1}^{N}\left(2\mathbf{P}_{S-}[-f_i(x) \leq \theta_i] + \frac{B}{\theta_i^2}\right)$$

where $\overline{d} = \sum_{i=1}^{N} w_i N_i$ and $B = c\left(\log n \log^2 m + \log(N/\delta)\right)/m$. As in the case of decision trees, different choices of θ, the θ_is, and the weights yield different estimates of the error. For an arbitrary order of the terms, let P_i be the fraction of positive examples covered by term t_i but not by terms $t_{i-1}, \ldots, t_1$. We order the terms such that for each i, with $t_{i-1}, \ldots, t_1$ fixed, P_i is maximized, so that $P_1 \geq \cdots \geq P_N$, and we choose $w_i = P_i$. Likewise, for a given term t_i with literals $l_1, \ldots, l_{N_i}$ in an arbitrary order, let $P_k^{(i)}$ be the fraction of negative examples uncovered by literal l_k but not uncovered by $l_{k-1}, \ldots, l_1$. We order the literals of term t_i in the same greedy way as above so that $P_1^{(i)} \geq \cdots \geq P_{N_i}^{(i)}$, and we choose $v_{ik} = P_k^{(i)}$. For $P_{j+1} \leq \theta < P_j$ and $P_{j_i+1}^{(i)} \leq \theta_i < P_{j_i+1}^{(i)}$, where $1 \leq j \leq N$ and $1 \leq j_i \leq N_i$, we get

$$\mathbf{P}_{\mathcal{D}}[g(x) \neq y] \leq \gamma^+\left(2\sum_{i=j+1}^{N} P_i + \frac{\overline{d}B}{\theta^2}\right) + \gamma^- \sum_{i=1}^{N}\left(2\sum_{k=j_i+1}^{N_i} P_k^{(i)} + \frac{B}{\theta_i^2}\right)$$

Now, let $P = (P_1, \ldots, P_N)$ and for each term i let $P^{(i)} = (P_1^{(i)}, \ldots, P_{N_i}^{(i)})$. Define $N_{\text{eff}} = N(1 - \rho(P, U))$ and $N_{\text{eff}}^{(i)} = N_i(1 - \rho(P^{(i)}, U))$, where U is the relevant uniform distribution in each case. The parameter N_{eff} is a measure of the effective number of terms in the DNF formula. It can be much smaller than N; this would be the case if few terms cover a large fraction of the positive examples. The parameter $N_{\text{eff}}^{(i)}$ is a measure of the effective number of literals in term t_i. Again, it can be much smaller than the actual number of literals in t_i: this would be the case if few literals of the term uncover a large fraction of the negative examples.

Optimizing over θ and the θ_is as in the proof of Theorem 3 gives the following result.

Theorem 5 *For a fixed $\delta > 0$, there is a constant c that satisfies the following. Let $\mathcal{D}$ be a distribution on $X \times \{-1, 1\}$. Consider the class of DNF formulae with up to N terms. With probability at least $1 - \delta$ over the training set S (of size m), every DNF formulae g that is consistent with S has*

$$\mathbf{P}_{\mathcal{D}}[g(x) \neq y] \leq \gamma^+(N_{\text{eff}}\, dB)^{1/2} + \gamma^- \sum_{i=1}^{N} (N_{\text{eff}}^{(i)} B)^{1/2}$$

where $d = \max_{i=1}^{N} N_i$, $\gamma^{\pm} = \mathbf{P}_{\mathcal{D}}[y = \pm 1]$ and $B = c(\log n \log^2 m + \log(N/\delta))/m$.

5 CONCLUSIONS

The results in this paper show that structural complexity measures (such as size) of decision trees and DNF formulae are not always the most appropriate in determining their generalization behaviour, and that measures of complexity that depend on the training data may give a more accurate description. Our analysis can be extended to multi-class classification problems. A similar analysis implies similar bounds on misclassification probability for decision lists, and it seems likely that these techniques will also be applicable to other pattern classification methods.

The complexity parameter, N_{eff} described here does not always give the best possible error bounds. For example, the effective number of leaves N_{eff} in a decision tree can be thought of as a single number that summarizes the probability distribution over the leaves induced by the training data. It seems unlikely that such a number will give optimal bounds for all distributions. In those cases, better bounds could be obtained by using numerical techniques to optimize over the choice of θ and w_is. It would be interesting to see how the bounds we obtain and those given by numerical techniques reflect the generalization performance of classifiers used in practice.

Acknowledgements

Thanks to Yoav Freund and Rob Schapire for helpful comments.

References

[1] P. L. Bartlett. For valid generalization, the size of the weights is more important than the size of the network. In *Neural Information Processing Systems 9*, pages 134–140. Morgan Kaufmann, San Mateo, CA, 1997.

[2] L. Breiman, J.H. Friedman, R.A. Olshen, and C.J. Stone. *Classification and Regression Trees*. Wadsworth, Belmont, 1984.

[3] A. Ehrenfeucht and D. Haussler. Learning decision trees from random examples. *Information and Computation*, 82:231–246, 1989.

[4] U.M. Fayyad and K.B. Irani. What should be minimized in a decision tree? In *AAAI-90*, pages 249–754, 1990.

[5] R. C. Holte. Very simple rules perform well on most commonly used databases. *Machine learning*, 11:63–91, 1993.

[6] P.M. Murphy and M.J. Pazzani. Exploring the decision forest: An empirical investigation of Occam's razor in decision tree induction. *Journal of Artificial Intelligence Research*, 1:257–275, 1994.

[7] J.R. Quinlan. *C4.5: Programs for Machine Learning*. Morgan Kaufmann, 1992.

[8] R. E. Schapire, Y. Freund, P. L. Bartlett, and W. S. Lee. Boosting the margin: a new explanation for the effectiveness of voting methods. In *Machine Learning: Proceedings of the Fourteenth International Conference*, pages 322–330, 1997.

[9] J. Shawe-Taylor, P. L. Bartlett, R. C. Williamson, and M. Anthony. A framework for structural risk minimisation. In *Proc. 9th COLT*, pages 68–76. ACM Press, New York, NY, 1996.

[10] G.L. Webb. Further experimental evidence against the utility of Occam's razor. *Journal of Artificial Intelligence Research*, 4:397–417, 1996.

Selecting weighting factors in logarithmic opinion pools

Tom Heskes

Foundation for Neural Networks, University of Nijmegen
Geert Grooteplein 21, 6525 EZ Nijmegen, The Netherlands
tom@mbfys.kun.nl

Abstract

A simple linear averaging of the outputs of several networks as e.g. in bagging [3], seems to follow naturally from a bias/variance decomposition of the sum-squared error. The sum-squared error of the average model is a quadratic function of the weighting factors assigned to the networks in the ensemble [7], suggesting a quadratic programming algorithm for finding the "optimal" weighting factors.

If we interpret the output of a network as a probability statement, the sum-squared error corresponds to minus the loglikelihood or the Kullback-Leibler divergence, and linear averaging of the outputs to logarithmic averaging of the probability statements: the logarithmic opinion pool.

The crux of this paper is that this whole story about model averaging, bias/variance decompositions, and quadratic programming to find the optimal weighting factors, is not specific for the sum-squared error, but applies to the combination of probability statements of any kind in a logarithmic opinion pool, as long as the Kullback-Leibler divergence plays the role of the error measure. As examples we treat model averaging for classification models under a cross-entropy error measure and models for estimating variances.

1 INTRODUCTION

In many simulation studies it has been shown that combining the outputs of several trained neural networks yields better results than relying on a single model. For regression problems, the most obvious combination seems to be a simple linear averaging of the network outputs. From a bias/variance decomposition of the sum-squared error it follows that the error of the so obtained average model is always smaller or equal than the average error of the individual models. In [7] simple linear averaging is generalized to weighted linear averaging, with different weighting factors for the different networks in the ensemble. A slightly more involved bias/variance decomposition suggests a rather straightforward procedure for finding "optimal" weighting factors.

Minimizing the sum-squared error is equivalent to maximizing the loglikelihood of the training data under the assumption that a network output can be interpreted as an estimate of the mean of a Gaussian distribution with fixed variance. In these probabilistic terms, a linear averaging of network outputs corresponds to a logarithmic rather than linear averaging of probability statements.

In this paper, we generalize the regression case to the combination of probability statements of any kind. Using the Kullback-Leibler divergence as the error measure, we naturally arrive at the so-called logarithmic opinion pool. A bias/variance decomposition similar to the one for sum-squared error then leads to an objective method for selecting weighting factors.

Selecting weighting factors in any combination of probability statements is known to be a difficult problem for which several suggestions have been made. These suggestions range from rather involved supra-Bayesian methods to simple heuristics (see e.g. [1, 6] and references therein). The method that follows from our analysis is probably somewhere in the middle: easier to compute than the supra-Bayesian methods and more elegant than simple heuristics.

To stress the generality of our results, the presentation in the next section will be rather formal. Some examples will be given in Section 3. Section 4 discusses how the theory can be transformed into a practical procedure.

2 LOGARITHMIC OPINION POOLS

Let us consider the general problem of building a probability model of a variable y given a particular input x. The "output" y may be continuous, as for example in regression analysis, or discrete, as for example in classification. In the latter case integrals over y should be replaced by summations over all possible values of y. Both x and y may be vectors of several elements; the one-dimensional notation is chosen for convenience. We suppose that there is a "true" conditional probability model $q(y|x)$ and have a whole ensemble (also called pool or committee) of experts, each supplying a probability model $p_\alpha(y|x)$. $\rho(x)$ is the unconditional probability distribution of inputs. An unsupervised scenario, as for example treated in [8], is obtained if we simply neglect the inputs x or consider them constant.

We define the distance between the true probability $q(y|x)$ and an estimate $p(y|x)$ to be the Kullback-Leibler divergence

$$K(q, p) \equiv -\int dx\, \rho(x) \int dy\, q(y|x) \log\left[\frac{p(y|x)}{q(y|x)}\right] .$$

If the densities $\rho(x)$ and $q(y|x)$ correspond to a data set containing a finite number P of combinations $\{x^\mu, y^\mu\}$, minus the Kullback divergence is, up to an irrelevant constant, equivalent to the loglikelihood defined as

$$L(p, \{\vec{x}, \vec{y}\}) \equiv \frac{1}{P} \sum_{\mu} \log p(y^{\mu}|x^{\mu}) .$$

The more formal use of the Kullback-Leibler divergence instead of the loglikelihood is convenient in the derivations that follow.

Weighting factors w_{α} are introduced to indicate the reliability of each of the experts α. In the following we will work with the constraints $\sum_{\alpha} w_{\alpha} = 1$, which is used in some of the proofs, and $w_{\alpha} \geq 0$ for all experts α, which is not strictly necessary, but makes it easier to interpret the weighting factors and helps to prevent overfitting when weighting factors are optimized (see details below).

We define the average model $\bar{p}(y|x)$ to be the one that is closest to the given set of models:

$$\bar{p}(y|x) \equiv \underset{p(y|x)}{\text{argmin}} \sum_{\alpha} w_{\alpha} K(p, p_{\alpha}) .$$

Introducing a Lagrange multiplier for the constraint $\int dx p(y|x) = 1$, we immediately find the solution

$$\bar{p}(y|x) = \frac{1}{Z(x)} \prod_{\alpha} [p_{\alpha}(y|x)]^{w_{\alpha}} , \tag{1}$$

with normalization constant

$$Z(x) = \int dy \prod_{\alpha} [p_{\alpha}(y|x)]^{w_{\alpha}} . \tag{2}$$

This is the logarithmic opinion pool, to be contrasted with the linear opinion pool, which is a linear average of the probabilities. In fact, logarithmic opinion pools have been proposed to overcome some of the weaknesses of the linear opinion pool. For example, the logarithmic opinion pool is "externally Bayesian", i.e., can be derived from joint probabilities using Bayes' rule [2]. A drawback of the logarithmic opinion pool is that if any of the experts assigns probability zero to a particular outcome, the complete pool assigns probability zero, no matter what the other experts claim. This property of the logarithmic opinion pool, however, is only a drawback if the individual density functions are not carefully estimated. The main problem for both linear and logarithmic opinion pools is how to choose the weighting factors w_{α}.

The Kullback-Leibler divergence of the opinion pool $\bar{p}(y|x)$ can be decomposed into a term containing the Kullback-Leibler divergences of individual models and an "ambiguity" term:

$$K(q, \bar{p}) = \sum_{\alpha} w_{\alpha} K(q, p_{\alpha}) - \sum_{\alpha} w_{\alpha} K(\bar{p}, p_{\alpha}) \equiv E - A . \tag{3}$$

Proof: The first term in (3) follows immediately from the numerator in (1), the second term is minus the logarithm of the normalization constant $Z(x)$ in (2) which can, using (1), be rewritten as

$$A = \int dx\, \rho(x) \log[Z(x)] = \int dx \rho(x) \log \left[\frac{\prod_{\alpha} [p_{\alpha}(y'|x)]^{w_{\alpha}}}{\bar{p}(y'|x)} \right] ,$$

for any choice of y' for which $\bar{p}(y'|x)$ is nonzero. Integration over y' with probability measure $\bar{p}(y'|x)$ then yields (3).

Since the ambiguity A is always larger than or equal to zero, we conclude that the Kullback-Leibler divergence of the logarithmic opinion pool is never larger than the average Kullback-Leibler divergences of individual experts. The larger the ambiguity, the larger the benefit of combining the experts' probability assessments. Note that by using Jensen's inequality, it is also possible to show that the Kullback-Leibler divergence of the linear opinion pool is smaller or equal to the average Kullback-Leibler divergences of individual experts. The expression for the ambiguity, defined as the difference between these two, is much more involved and more difficult to interpret (see e.g. [10]).

The ambiguity of the logarithmic opinion pool depends on the weighting factors w_α, not only directly as expressed in (3), but also through $\bar{p}(y|x)$. We can make this dependency somewhat more explicit by writing

$$A = \frac{1}{2} \sum_{\alpha\beta} w_\alpha w_\beta K(p_\alpha, p_\beta) + \frac{1}{2} \sum_\alpha w_\alpha \left[K(\bar{p}, p_\alpha) - K(p_\alpha, \bar{p}) \right] . \tag{4}$$

Proof: Equation (3) is valid for any choice of $q(y|x)$. Substitute $q(y|x) = p_\beta(y|x)$, multiply left- and righthand side by w_β, and sum over β. Simple manipulation of terms than yields the result.

Alas, the Kullback-Leibler divergence is not necessarily symmetric, i.e., in general $K(p_1, p_2) \neq K(p_2, p_1)$. However, the difference $K(p_1, p_2) - K(p_2, p_1)$ is an order of magnitude smaller than the divergence $K(p_1, p_2)$ itself. More formally, writing $p_1(y|x) = [1+\epsilon(y|x)]p_2(y|x)$ with $\epsilon(y|x)$ small, we can easily show that $K(p_1, p_2)$ is of order (some integral over) $\epsilon^2(y|x)$ whereas $K(p_1, p_2) - K(p_2, p_1)$ is of order $\epsilon^3(y|x)$. Therefore, if we have reason to assume that the different models are reasonably close together, we can, in a first approximation, and will, to make things tractable, neglect the second term in (4) to arrive at

$$K(q, \bar{p}) \approx \sum_\alpha w_\alpha K(q, p_\alpha) - \frac{1}{4} \sum_{\alpha,\beta} w_\alpha w_\beta \left[K(p_\alpha, p_\beta) + K(p_\beta, p_\alpha) \right] . \tag{5}$$

The righthand side of this expression is quadratic in the weighting factors w_α, a property which will be very convenient later on.

3 EXAMPLES

Regression. The usual assumption in regression analysis is that the output functionally depends on the input x, but is blurred by Gaussian noise with standard deviation σ. In other words, the probability model of an expert α can be written

$$p_\alpha(y|x) = \sqrt{\frac{1}{2\pi\sigma^2}} \exp\left[\frac{-(y - f_\alpha(x))^2}{2\sigma^2} \right] . \tag{6}$$

The function $f_\alpha(x)$ corresponds to the network's estimate of the "true" regression given input x. The logarithmic opinion pool (1) also leads to a normal distribution with the same standard deviation σ and with regression estimate

$$\bar{f}(x) = \sum_\alpha w_\alpha f_\alpha(x) .$$

In this case the Kullback-Leibler divergence

$$K(p_\alpha, p_\beta) = \frac{1}{2\sigma^2} \int dx \, \rho(x) \left[f_\alpha(x) - f_\beta(x) \right]^2$$

is symmetric, which makes (5) exact instead of an approximation. In [7], this has all been derived starting from a sum-squared error measure.

Variance estimation. There has been some recent interest in using neural networks not only to estimate the mean of the target distribution, but also its variance (see e.g. [9] and references therein). In fact, one can use the probability density (6) with input-dependent $\sigma(x)$. We will consider the simpler situation in which an input-dependent model is fitted to residuals y, *after* a regression model has been fitted to estimate the mean (see also [5]). The probability model of expert α can be written

$$p_\alpha(y|x) = \sqrt{\frac{z_\alpha(x)}{2\pi}} \exp\left[-\frac{z_\alpha(x)y^2}{2} \right] ,$$

where $1/z_\alpha(x)$ is the experts' estimate of the residual variance given input x. The logarithmic opinion pool is of the same form with $z_\alpha(x)$ replaced by

$$\bar{z}(x) = \sum_\alpha w_\alpha z_\alpha(x) .$$

Here the Kullback-Leibler divergence

$$K(\bar{p}, p_\alpha) = \frac{1}{2} \int dx \, \rho(x) \left[\frac{\bar{z}(x)}{z_\alpha(x)} - \log \frac{\bar{z}(x)}{z_\alpha(x)} - 1 \right]$$

is asymmetric. We can use (3) to write the Kullback-Leibler divergence of the opinion pool explicitly in terms of the weighting factors w_α. The approximation (5), with

$$K(p_\alpha, p_\beta) + K(p_\beta, p_\alpha) = \frac{1}{2} \int dx \, \rho(x) \frac{[z_\alpha(x) - z_\beta(x)]^2}{z_\alpha(x) z_\beta(x)} ,$$

is much more appealing and easier to handle.

Classification. In a two-class classification problem, we can treat y as a discrete variable having two possible realizations, e.g., $y \in \{-1, 1\}$. A convenient representation for a properly normalized probability distribution is

$$p_\alpha(y|x) = \frac{1}{1 + \exp[-2h_\alpha(x)y]} .$$

In this logistic representation, the logarithmic opinion pool has the same form with

$$\bar{h}(x) = \sum_\alpha w_\alpha h_\alpha(x) .$$

The Kullback-Leibler divergence is asymmetric, but yields the simpler form

$$K(p_\alpha, p_\beta) + K(p_\beta, p_\alpha) = \int dx \, \rho(x) \left[\tanh(h_\alpha(x)) - \tanh(h_\beta(x)) \right] [h_\alpha(x) - h_\beta(x)] ,$$

to be used in the approximation (5). For a finite set of patterns, minus the loglikelihood yields the well-known cross-entropy error.

The probability models in these three examples are part of the exponential family. The mean f_α, inverse variance z_α, and logit h_α are the canonical parameters. It is straightforward to show that, with constant dispersion across the various experts, the canonical parameter of the logarithmic opinion pool is always a weighted average of the canonical parameters of the individual experts. Slightly more complicated expressions arise when the experts are allowed to have different estimates for the dispersion or for probability models that do not belong to the exponential family.

4   SELECTING WEIGHTING FACTORS

The decomposition (3) and approximation (5) suggest an objective method for selecting weighting factors in logarithmic opinion pools. We will sketch this method for an ensemble of models belonging to the same class, say feedforward neural networks with a fixed number of hidden units, where each model is optimized on a different bootstrap replicate of the available data set.

Suppose that we have available a data set consisting of P combinations $\{x^\mu, y^\mu\}$. As suggested in [3], we construct different models by training them on different bootstrap replicates of the available data set. Optimizing nonlinear models is often an unstable process: small differences in initial parameter settings or two almost equivalent bootstrap replicates can result in completely different models. Neural networks, for example, are notorious for local minima and plateaus in weight space where models might get stuck. Therefore, the incorporation of weighting factors, even when models are constructed using the same procedure, can yield a better generalizing opinion pool. In [4] good results have been reported on several regression problems. Balancing clearly outperformed bagging, which corresponds to $w_\alpha = 1/n$ with n the number of experts, and bumping, which proposes to keep a single expert.

Each example in the available data set can be viewed as a realization of an unknown probability density characterized by $\rho(x)$ and $q(y|x)$. We would like to choose the weighting factors w_α such as to minimize the Kullback-Leibler divergence $K(q, \bar{p})$ of the opinion pool. If we accept the approximation (5), we can compute the optimal weighting factors once we know the individual Kullbacks $K(q, p_\alpha)$ and the Kullbacks between different models $K(p_\alpha, p_\beta)$. Of course, both $q(y|x)$ and $\rho(x)$ are unknown, and thus we have to settle for estimates.

In an estimate for $K(p_\alpha, p_\beta)$ we can simply replace the average over $\rho(x)$ by an average over all inputs x^μ observed in the data set:

$$K(p_\alpha, p_\beta) + K(p_\beta, p_\alpha) \approx \frac{1}{P} \sum_\mu \int dy \, [p_\alpha(y|x^\mu) - p_\beta(y|x^\mu)] \log \left[\frac{p_\alpha(y|x^\mu)}{p_\beta(y|x^\mu)} \right] .$$

A similar straightforward replacement for $q(y|x)$ in an estimate for $K(q, p_\alpha)$ is biased, since each expert has, at least to some extent, been overfitted on the data set. In [4] we suggest how to remove this bias for regression models minimizing sum-squared errors. Similar compensations can be found for other probability models.

Having estimates for both the individual Kullback-Leibler divergences $K(q, p_\alpha)$ and the cross terms $K(p_\alpha, p_\beta)$, we can optimize for the weighting factors w_α. Under the constraints $\sum_\alpha w_\alpha = 1$ and $w_\alpha \geq 0$ the approximation (5) leads to a quadratic programming problem. Without this approximation, optimizing the weighting factors becomes a nasty exercise in nonlinear programming.

The solution of the quadratic programming problem usually ends up at the edge of the unit cube with many weighting factors equal to zero. On the one hand, this is a beneficial property, since it implies that we only have to keep a relatively small number of models for later processing. On the other hand, the obtained weighting factors may depend too strongly on our estimates of the individual Kullbacks $K(q, p_\alpha)$. The following version prohibits this type of overfitting. Using simple statistics, we obtain a rough indication for the accuracy of our estimates $K(q, p_\alpha)$. This we use to generate several, say on the order of 20, different samples with estimates $\{K(q, p_1), \ldots, K(q, p_n)\}$. For each of these samples we solve the corresponding quadratic programming problem and obtain a set of weighting factors. The final weighting factors are obtained by averaging. In the end, there are less experts with zero weighting factors, at the advantage of a more robust procedure.

Acknowledgements

I would like to thank David Tax, Bert Kappen, Piërre van de Laar, Wim Wiegerinck, and the anonymous referees for helpful suggestions. This research was supported by the Technology Foundation STW, applied science division of NWO and the technology programme of the Ministry of Economic Affairs.

References

[1] J. Benediktsson and P. Swain. Consensus theoretic classification methods. *IEEE Transactions on Systems, Man, and Cybernetics*, 22:688–704, 1992.

[2] R. Bordley. A multiplicative formula for aggregating probability assessments. *Management Science*, 28:1137–1148, 1982.

[3] L. Breiman. Bagging predictors. *Machine Learning*, 24:123–140, 1996.

[4] T. Heskes. Balancing between bagging and bumping. In M. Mozer, M. Jordan, and T. Petsche, editors, *Advances in Neural Information Processing Systems 9*, pages 466–472, Cambridge, 1997. MIT Press.

[5] T. Heskes. Practical confidence and prediction intervals. In M. Mozer, M. Jordan, and T. Petsche, editors, *Advances in Neural Information Processing Systems 9*, pages 176–182, Cambridge, 1997. MIT Press.

[6] R. Jacobs. Methods for combining experts' probability assessments. *Neural Computation*, 7:867–888, 1995.

[7] A. Krogh and J. Vedelsby. Neural network ensembles, cross validation, and active learning. In G. Tesauro, D. Touretzky, and T. Leen, editors, *Advances in Neural Information Processing Systems 7*, pages 231–238, Cambridge, 1995. MIT Press.

[8] P. Smyth and D. Wolpert. Stacked density estimation. *These proceedings*, 1998.

[9] P. Williams. Using neural networks to model conditional multivariate densities. *Neural Computation*, 8:843–854, 1996.

[10] D. Wolpert. On bias plus variance. *Neural Computation*, 9:1211–1243, 1997.

New Approximations of Differential Entropy for Independent Component Analysis and Projection Pursuit

Aapo Hyvärinen
Helsinki University of Technology
Laboratory of Computer and Information Science
P.O. Box 2200, FIN-02015 HUT, Finland
Email: aapo.hyvarinen@hut.fi

Abstract

We derive a first-order approximation of the density of maximum entropy for a continuous 1-D random variable, given a number of simple constraints. This results in a density expansion which is somewhat similar to the classical polynomial density expansions by Gram-Charlier and Edgeworth. Using this approximation of density, an approximation of 1-D differential entropy is derived. The approximation of entropy is both more exact and more robust against outliers than the classical approximation based on the polynomial density expansions, without being computationally more expensive. The approximation has applications, for example, in independent component analysis and projection pursuit.

1   Introduction

The basic information-theoretic quantity for continuous one-dimensional random variables is differential entropy. The differential entropy H of a scalar random variable X with density $f(x)$ is defined as

$$H(X) = - \int f(x) \log f(x) dx. \tag{1}$$

The 1-D differential entropy, henceforth called simply entropy, has important applications such areas as independent component analysis [2, 10] and projection pursuit [5, 6]. Indeed, both of these methods can be considered as a search for directions in which entropy is minimal, for constant variance.

Unfortunately, the estimation of entropy is quite difficult in practice. Using definition (1) requires estimation of the density of X, which is recognized to be both theoretically difficult and computationally demanding. Simpler approximations of entropy have been proposed both in the context of projection pursuit [9] and independent component analysis [1, 2]. These approximations are usually based on approximating the density $f(x)$ using the polynomial expansions of Gram-Charlier or Edgeworth [11]. This construction leads to the use of higher-order cumulants, like kurtosis. However, such cumulant-based methods often provide a rather poor approximation of entropy. There are two main reasons for this. Firstly, finite-sample estimators of higher-order cumulants are highly sensitive to outliers: their values may depend on only a few, possibly erroneous, observations with large values [6]. This means that outliers may completely determine the estimates of cumulants, thus making them useless. Secondly, even if the cumulants were estimated perfectly, they measure mainly the tails of the distribution, and are largely unaffected by structure near the centre of the distribution [5].

Therefore, better approximations of entropy are needed. To this end, we introduce in this paper approximations of entropy that are both more exact in the expectation and have better finite-sample statistical properties, when compared to the cumulant-based approximations. Nevertheless, they retain the computational and conceptual simplicity of the cumulant-based approach. Our approximations are based on an approximative maximum entropy method. This means that we approximate the *maximum* entropy that is compatible with our measurements of the random variable X. This maximum entropy, or further approximations thereof, can then be used as a meaningful approximation of the entropy of X. To accomplish this, we derive a first-order approximation of the density that has the maximum entropy given a set of constraints, and then use it to derive approximations of the differential entropy of X.

2   Applications of Differential Entropy

First, we discuss some applications of the approximations introduced in this paper. Two important applications of differential entropy are independent component analysis (ICA) and projection pursuit. In the general formulation of ICA [2], the purpose is to transform an observed random vector $\mathbf{x} = (x_1, ..., x_m)^T$ linearly into a random vector $\mathbf{s} = (s_1, ..., s_m)^T$ whose components are statistically as independent from each other as possible. The mutual dependence of the s_i is classically measured by mutual information. Assuming that the linear transformation is invertible, the mutual information $I(s_1, ..., s_m)$ can be expressed as $I(s_1, ..., s_m) = \sum_i H(s_i) - H(x_1, ..., x_m) - \log |\det \mathbf{M}|$ where $\mathbf{M}$ is the matrix defining the transformation $\mathbf{s} = \mathbf{M}\mathbf{x}$. The second term on the right-hand side does not depend on $\mathbf{M}$, and the minimization of the last term is a simple matter of differential calculus. Therefore, the critical part is the estimation of the 1-D entropies $H(s_i)$: finding an efficient and reliable estimator or approximation of entropy enables an efficient and reliable estimation of the ICA decomposition.

In projection pursuit, the purpose is to search for projections of multivariate data which have 'interesting' distributions [5, 6, 9]. Typically, interestingness is considered equivalent with non-Gaussianity. A natural criterion of non-Gaussianity is entropy [6, 9], which attains its maximum (for constant variance) when the distribution is Gaussian, and all other distributions have smaller entropies. Because of the difficulties encountered in the estimation of entropy, many authors have considered other measures of non-Gaussianity (see [3]) but entropy remains, in our view, the best choice of a projection pursuit index, especially because it provides a simple connection to ICA. Indeed, it can be shown [2] that in ICA as well as in projection pursuit, the basic problem is to find directions in which entropy is minimized for constant variance.

3 Why maximum entropy?

Assume that the information available on the density $f(x)$ of the scalar random variable X is of the form

$$\int f(x)G_i(x)dx = c_i, \text{ for } i = 1, ..., n, \tag{2}$$

which means in practice that we have estimated the expectations $E\{G_i(X)\}$ of n different functions of X. Since we are not assuming any model for the random variable X, the estimation of the entropy of X using this information is not a well-defined problem: there exist an infinite number of distributions for which the constraints in (2) are fulfilled, but whose entropies are very different from each other. In particular, the differential entropy reaches $-\infty$ in the limit where X takes only a finite number of values.

A simple solution to this dilemma is the maximum entropy method. This means that we compute the *maximum* entropy that is compatible with our constraints or measurements in (2), which is a well-defined problem. This maximum entropy, or further approximations thereof, can then be used as an approximation of the entropy of X.

Our approach thus is very different from the asymptotic approach often used in projection pursuit [3, 5]. In the asymptotic approach, one establishes a sequence of functions G_i so that when n goes to infinity, the information in (2) gives an asymptotically convergent approximation of some theoretical projection pursuit index. We avoid in this paper any asymptotic considerations, and consider directly the case of finite information, i.e., finite n. This non-asymptotic approach is justified by the fact that often in practice, only a small number of measurements of the form (2) are used, for computational or other reasons.

4 Approximating the maximum entropy density

In this section, we shall derive an approximation of the density of maximum entropy compatible with the measurements in (2). The basic results of the maximum entropy method tell us [4] that under some regularity conditions, the density $f_0(x)$ which satisfies the constraints (2) and has maximum entropy among all such densities, is of the form

$$f_0(x) = A\exp(\sum_i a_iG_i(x)), \tag{3}$$

where A and a_i are constants that are determined from the c_i, using the constraints in (2) (i.e., by substituting the right-hand side of (3) for f in (2)), and the constraint $\int f_0(x)dx = 1$. This leads in general to a system of $n+1$ non-linear equations which is difficult to solve. Therefore, we decide to make a simple approximation of f_0. This is based on the assumption that the density $f(x)$ is *not very far from a Gaussian distribution* of the same mean and variance. Such an assumption, though perhaps counterintuitive, is justified because we shall construct a density expansion (not unlike a Taylor expansion) in the vicinity of the Gaussian density. In addition, we can make the technical assumption that $f(x)$ is near the standardized Gaussian density $\varphi(x) = \exp(-x^2/2)/\sqrt{2\pi}$, since this amounts simply to making X zero-mean and of unit variance. Therefore we put two additional constraints in (2), defined by $G_{n+1}(x) = x, c_{n+1} = 0$ and $G_{n+2}(x) = x^2, c_{n+2} = 1$. To further simplify the calculations, let us make another, purely technical assumption: The functions $G_i, i = 1, ..., n$, form an orthonormal system according to the metric defined by φ, and are orthogonal to all polynomials of second degree. In other words, for all $i, j = 1, ..., n$

$$\int \varphi(x)G_i(x)G_j(x)dx = \left\{ \begin{array}{l} 1, \text{ if } i = j \\ 0, \text{ if } i \neq j \end{array} \right. , \quad \int \varphi(x)G_i(x)x^k dx = 0, k = 0, 1, 2. \quad (4)$$

For any linearly independent functions G_i, this assumption can always be made true by ordinary Gram-Schmidt orthonormalization.

Now, note that the assumption of near-Gaussianity implies that all the other a_i in (3) are very small compared to $a_{n+2} \approx -1/2$, since the exponential in (3) is not far from $\exp(-x^2/2)$. Thus we can make a first-order approximation of the exponential function (detailed derivations can be found in [8]). This allows for simple solutions for the constants in (3), and we obtain the *approximative maximum entropy density*, which we denote by $\hat{f}(x)$:

$$\hat{f}(x) = \varphi(x)(1 + \sum_{i=1}^{n} c_i G_i(x)) \quad (5)$$

where $c_i = E\{G_i(X)\}$. To estimate this density in practice, the c_i are estimated, for example, as the corresponding sample averages of the $G_i(X)$. The density expansion in (5) is somewhat similar to the Gram-Charlier and Edgeworth expansions [11].

5 Approximating the differential entropy

An important application of the approximation of density shown in (5) is in approximation of entropy. A simple approximation of entropy can be found by approximating both occurences of f in the definition (1) by $\hat{f}$ as defined in Eq. (5), and using a Taylor approximation of the logarithmic function, which yields $(1 + \epsilon) \log(1 + \epsilon) \approx \epsilon + \epsilon^2/2$. Thus one obtains after some algebraic manipulations [8]

$$H(X) \approx - \int \hat{f}(x) \log \hat{f}(x)dx \approx H(\nu) - \frac{1}{2} \sum_{i=1}^{n} c_i^2 \quad (6)$$

where $H(\nu) = \frac{1}{2}(1 + \log(2\pi))$ means the entropy of a standardized Gaussian variable, and $c_i = E\{G_i(X)\}$ as above. Note that even in cases where this approximation is not very accurate, (6) can be used to construct a projection pursuit index (or a measure of non-Gaussianity) that is consistent in the sense that (6) obtains its maximum value, $H(\nu)$, when X has a Gaussian distribution.

6 Choosing the measuring functions

Now it remains to choose the 'measuring' functions G_i that define the information given in (2). As noted in Section 4, one can take practically any set of linearly independent functions, say $\bar{G}_i, i = 1, ..., n$, and then apply Gram-Schmidt orthonormalization on the set containing those functions and the monomials $x^k, k = 0, 1, 2$, so as to obtain the set G_i that fulfills the orthogonality assumptions in (4). This can be done, in general, by numerical integration. In the practical choice of the functions $\bar{G}_i$, the following criteria must be emphasized: First, the practical estimation of $E\{\bar{G}_i(x)\}$ should not be statistically difficult. In particular, this estimation should not be too sensitive to outliers. Second, the maximum entropy method assumes that the function f_0 in (3) is integrable. Therefore, to ensure that the maximum entropy distribution exists in the first place, the $\bar{G}_i(x)$ must not grow faster than quadratically as a function of $|x|$, because a function growing faster might lead to non-integrability of f_0 [4]. Finally, the $\bar{G}_i$ must capture aspects of the distribution of X that are pertinent in the computation of entropy. In particular, if the density $f(x)$ were known, the optimal function $\bar{G}_{opt}$ would clearly be $-\log f(x)$, because $-E\{\log f(X)\}$ gives directly the entropy. Thus, one might use the log-densities of some known important densities as $\bar{G}_i$.

The first two criteria are met if the $\bar{G}_i(x)$ are functions that do not grow too fast (not faster than quadratically) when $|x|$ grows. This excludes, for example, the use of higher-order polynomials, as are used in the Gram-Charlier and Edgeworth expansions. One might then search, according to the last criterion above, for log-densities of some well-known distributions that also fulfill the first two conditions. Examples will be given in the next section. It should be noted, however, that the criteria above only delimit the space of function that can be used. Our framework enables the use of very different functions (or just one) as $\bar{G}_i$. The choice is not restricted to some well-known basis of a functional space, as in most approaches [1, 2, 9]. However, if prior knowledge is available on the distributions whose entropy is to estimated, the above consideration shows how to choose the optimal function.

7 A simple special case

A simple special case of (5) is obtained if one uses two functions $\bar{G}_1$ and $\bar{G}_2$, which are chosen so that $\bar{G}_1$ is *odd* and $\bar{G}_2$ is *even*. Such a system of two functions can measure the two most important features of non-Gaussian 1-D distributions. The odd function measures the asymmetry, and the even function measures the bimodality/sparsity dimension (called central hole/central mass concentration in [3]). After extensive experiments, Cook et al [3] also came to the conclusion that two such measures (or two terms in their projection pursuit index) are enough for projection pursuit in most cases. Classically, these features have been measured by skewness and kurtosis, which correspond to $\bar{G}_1(x) = x^3$ and $\bar{G}_2(x) = x^4$, but we do not use these functions for the reasons explained in Section 6.

In this special case, the approximation in (6) simplifies to

$$H(X) \approx H(\nu) - [k_1 (E\{\bar{G}_1(X)\})^2 + k_2 (E\{\bar{G}_2(X)\} - E\{\bar{G}_2(\nu)\})^2] \qquad (7)$$

where k_1 and k_2 are positive constants (see [8]), and ν is a Gaussian random variable of zero mean and unit variance. Practical examples of choices of $\bar{G}_i$ that are consistent with the requirements in Section 6 are the following.

First, for measuring bimodality/sparsity, one might use, according to the recommendations of Section 6, the log-density of the double exponential (or Laplace) distribution: $\bar{G}_{2a}(x) = |x|$. For computational reasons, a smoother version of $\bar{G}_{2a}$ might also be used. Another choice would be the Gaussian function, which may be considered as the log-density of a distribution with infinitely heavy tails: $\bar{G}_{2b}(x) = \exp(-x^2/2)$. For measuring asymmetry, one might use, on more heuristic grounds, the following function: $\bar{G}_1(x) = x \exp(-x^2/2)$. which corresponds to the second term in the projection pursuit index proposed in [3].

Using the above examples one obtains two practical examples of (7):

$$H_a(X) = H(\nu) - [k_1 (E\{X \exp(-X^2/2)\})^2 + k_2^a (E\{|X|\} - \sqrt{2/\pi})^2], \qquad (8)$$

$$H_b(X) = H(\nu) - [k_1 (E\{X \exp(-X^2/2)\})^2 + k_2^b (E\{\exp(-X^2/2)\} - \sqrt{1/2})^2], \qquad (9)$$

with $k_1 = 36/(8\sqrt{3} - 9)$, $k_2^a = 1/(2 - 6/\pi)$, and $k_2^b = 24/(16\sqrt{3} - 27)$. As above, $H(\nu) = \frac{1}{2}(1 + \log(2\pi))$ means the entropy of a standardized Gaussian variable. These approximations $H_a(X)$ and $H_b(X)$ can be considered more robust and accurate generalizations of the approximation derived using the Gram-Charlier expansion in [9]. Indeed, using the polynomials $\bar{G}_1(x) = x^3$ and $\bar{G}_2(x) = x^4$ one obtains the approximation of entropy in [9], which is in practice almost identical to those proposed in [1, 2]. Finally, note that the approximation in (9) is very similar to the first two terms of the projection pursuit index in [3]. Algorithms for independent component analysis and projection pursuit can be derived from these approximations, see [7].

8 Simulation results

To show the validity of our approximations of differential entropy we compared the approximations H_a and H_b in Eqs (8) and (9) in Section 7, with the one offered by higher-order cumulants as given in [9]. The expectations were here evaluated exactly, ignoring finite-sample effects.

First, we used a family of Gaussian mixture densities, defined by

$$f(x) = \mu\varphi(x) + (1 - \mu)2\varphi(2(x - 1)) \tag{10}$$

where μ is a parameter that takes all the values in the interval $0 \leq \mu \leq 1$. This family includes asymmetric densities of both negative and positive kurtosis. The results are depicted in Fig. 1. Note that the plots show approximations of negentropies: the negentropy of X equals $H(\nu) - H(X)$, where ν is again a standardized Gaussian variable. One can see that both of the approximations H_a and H_b introduced in Section 7 were considerably more accurate than the cumulant-based approximation.

Second, we considered the following family of density functions:

$$f_\alpha(x) = C_1 \exp(C_2|x|^\alpha) \tag{11}$$

where α is a positive constant, and C_1, C_2 are normalization constants that make f_α a probability density of unit variance. For different values of α, the densities in this family exhibit different shapes. For $\alpha < 2$, one obtains (sparse) densities of positive kurtosis. For $\alpha = 2$, one obtains the Gaussian density, and for $\alpha > 2$, a density of negative kurtosis. Thus the densities in this family can be used as examples of different symmetric non-Gaussian densities. In Figure 2, the different approximations are plotted for this family, using parameter values $.5 \leq \alpha \leq 3$. Since the densities used are all symmetric, the first terms in the approximations were neglected. Again, it is clear that both of the approximations H_a and H_b introduced in Section 7 were much more accurate than the cumulant-based approximation in [2, 9]. (In the case of symmetric densities, these two cumulant-based approximations are identical). Especially in the case of sparse densities (or densities of positive kurtosis), the cumulant-based approximations performed very poorly; this is probably because it gives too much weight to the tails of the distribution.

References

[1] S. Amari, A. Cichocki, and H.H. Yang. A new learning algorithm for blind source separation. In D. S. Touretzky, M. C. Mozer, and M. E. Hasselmo, editors, *Advances in Neural Information Processing 8 (Proc. NIPS'95)*, pages 757–763. MIT Press, Cambridge, MA, 1996.

[2] P. Comon. Independent component analysis – a new concept? *Signal Processing*, 36:287–314, 1994.

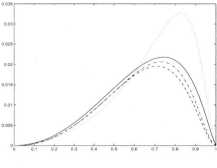

Figure 1: Comparison of different approximations of negentropy, for the family of mixture densities in (10) parametrized by μ ranging from 0 to 1. Solid curve: true negentropy. Dotted curve: cumulant-based approximation. Dashed curve: approximation H_a in (8). Dot-dashed curve: approximation H_b in (9). Our two approximations were clearly better than the cumulant-based one.

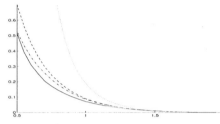
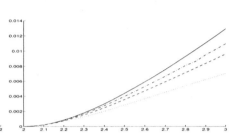

Figure 2: Comparison of different approximations of negentropy, for the family of densities (11) parametrized by α. On the left, approximations for densities of positive kurtosis ($.5 \leq \alpha < 2$) are depicted, and on the right, approximations for densities of negative kurtosis ($2 < \alpha \leq 3$). Solid curve: true negentropy. Dotted curve: cumulant-based approximation. Dashed curve: approximation H_a in (8). Dot-dashed curve: approximation H_b in (9). Clearly, our two approximations were much better than the cumulant-based one, especially in the case of densities of positive kurtosis.

[3] D. Cook, A. Buja, and J. Cabrera. Projection pursuit indexes based on orthonormal function expansions. *J. of Computational and Graphical Statistics*, 2(3):225–250, 1993.

[4] T. M. Cover and J. A. Thomas. *Elements of Information Theory*. John Wiley & Sons, 1991.

[5] J.H. Friedman. Exploratory projection pursuit. *J. of the American Statistical Association*, 82(397):249–266, 1987.

[6] P.J. Huber. Projection pursuit. *The Annals of Statistics*, 13(2):435–475, 1985.

[7] A. Hyvärinen. Independent component analysis by minimization of mutual information. Technical Report A46, Helsinki University of Technology, Laboratory of Computer and Information Science, 1997.

[8] A. Hyvärinen. New approximations of differential entropy for independent component analysis and projection pursuit. Technical Report A47, Helsinki University of Technology, Laboratory of Computer and Information Science, 1997. Available at http://www.cis.hut.fi/~aapo.

[9] M.C. Jones and R. Sibson. What is projection pursuit ? *J. of the Royal Statistical Society, ser. A*, 150:1–36, 1987.

[10] C. Jutten and J. Herault. Blind separation of sources, part I: An adaptive algorithm based on neuromimetic architecture. *Signal Processing*, 24:1–10, 1991.

[11] M. Kendall and A. Stuart. *The Advanced Theory of Statistics*. Charles Griffin & Company, 1958.

Boltzmann Machine learning using mean field theory and linear response correction

H.J. Kappen
Department of Biophysics
University of Nijmegen, Geert Grooteplein 21
NL 6525 EZ Nijmegen, The Netherlands

F. B. Rodríguez
Instituto de Ingeniería del Conocimiento & Departamento de Ingeniería Informática,
Universidad Autónoma de Madrid, Canto Blanco,28049 Madrid, Spain

Abstract

We present a new approximate learning algorithm for Boltzmann
Machines, using a systematic expansion of the Gibbs free energy to
second order in the weights. The linear response correction to the
correlations is given by the Hessian of the Gibbs free energy. The
computational complexity of the algorithm is cubic in the number
of neurons. We compare the performance of the exact BM learning
algorithm with first order (Weiss) mean field theory and second
order (TAP) mean field theory. The learning task consists of a fully
connected Ising spin glass model on 10 neurons. We conclude that
1) the method works well for paramagnetic problems 2) the TAP
correction gives a significant improvement over the Weiss mean field
theory, both for paramagnetic and spin glass problems and 3) that
the inclusion of diagonal weights improves the Weiss approximation
for paramagnetic problems, but not for spin glass problems.

1 Introduction

Boltzmann Machines (BMs) [1], are networks of binary neurons with a stochastic
neuron dynamics, known as Glauber dynamics. Assuming symmetric connections
between neurons, the probability distribution over neuron states $\vec{s}$ will become
stationary and is given by the Boltzmann-Gibbs distribution $P(\vec{s})$. The Boltzmann
distribution is a known function of the weights and thresholds of the network.
However, computation of $P(\vec{s})$ or any statistics involving $P(\vec{s})$, such as mean firing
rates or correlations, requires exponential time in the number of neurons. This is

due to the fact that $P(\vec{s})$ contains a normalization term Z, which involves a sum over all states in the network, of which there are exponentially many. This problem is particularly important for BM learning.

Using statistical sampling techiques [2], learning can be significantly improved [1]. However, the method has rather poor convergence and can only be applied to small networks.

In [3, 4], an acceleration method for learning in BMs is proposed using mean field theory by replacing $\langle s_i s_j \rangle$ by $m_i m_j$ in the learning rule. It can be shown [5] that such a naive mean field approximation of the learning rules does not converge in general. Furthermore, we argue that the correlations can be computed using the linear response theorem [6].

In [7, 5] the mean field approximation is derived by making use of the properties of convex functions (Jensen's inequality and tangential bounds). In this paper we present an alternative derivation which uses a Legendre transformation and a small coupling expansion [8]. It has the advantage that higher order contributions (TAP and higher) can be computed in a systematic manner and that it may be applicable to arbitrary graphical models.

2 Boltzmann Machine learning

The Boltzmann Machine is defined as follows. The possible configurations of the network can be characterized by a vector $\vec{s} = (s_1, .., s_i, .., s_n)$, where $s_i = \pm 1$ is the state of the neuron i, and n the total number of the neurons. Neurons are updated using Glauber dynamics.

Let us define the energy of a configuration $\vec{s}$ as

$$-E(\vec{s}) = \frac{1}{2} \sum_{i,j} w_{ij} s_i s_j + \sum_i s_i \theta_i.$$

After long times, the probability to find the network in a state $\vec{s}$ becomes independent of time (thermal equilibrium) and is given by the Boltzmann distribution

$$p(\vec{s}) = \frac{1}{Z} \exp\{-E(\vec{s})\}. \tag{1}$$

$Z = \sum_{\vec{s}} \exp\{-E(\vec{s})\}$ is the partition function which normalizes the probability distribution.

Learning [1] consists of adjusting the weights and thresholds in such a way that the Boltzmann distribution approximates a target distribution $q(\vec{s})$ as closely as possible.

A suitable measure of the difference between the distributions $p(\vec{s})$ and $q(\vec{s})$ is the Kullback divergence [9]

$$K = \sum_{\vec{s}} q(\vec{s}) \log \frac{q(\vec{s})}{p(\vec{s})}. \tag{2}$$

Learning consists of minimizing K using gradient descent [1]

$$\Delta w_{ij} = \eta \Big(\langle s_i s_j \rangle_c - \langle s_i s_j \rangle \Big), \quad \Delta \theta_i = \eta \Big(\langle s_i \rangle_c - \langle s_i \rangle \Big).$$

The parameter η is the learning rate. The brackets $\langle \cdot \rangle$ and $\langle \cdot \rangle_c$ denote the 'free' and 'clamped' expectation values, respectively.

The computation of both the free and the clamped expectation values is intractible, because it consists of a sum over all unclamped states. As a result, the BM learning algorithm can not be applied to practical problems.

3   The mean field approximation

We derive the mean field free energy using the small γ expansion as introduced by Plefka [8]. The energy of the network is given by

$$E(s, w, h, \gamma) = \gamma E_{\text{int}} - \sum_i \theta_i s_i$$

$$E_{\text{int}} = -\frac{1}{2} \sum_{ij} w_{ij} s_i s_j$$

for $\gamma = 1$. The free energy is given by

$$F(w, \theta, \gamma) = -\log \text{Tr}_s e^{-E(s, w, \theta, \gamma)}$$

and is a function of the independent variables w_{ij}, θ_i and γ. We perform a Legendre transformation on the variables θ_i by introducing $m_i = -\frac{\partial F}{\partial \theta_i}$. The Gibbs free energy

$$G(w, m, \gamma) = F(w, \theta, \gamma) + \sum_i \theta_i m_i$$

is now a function of the independent variables m_i and w_{ij}, and θ_i is implicitly given by $\langle s_i \rangle_\gamma = m_i$. The expectation $\langle \cdot \rangle_\gamma$ is with respect to the full model with interaction γ.

We expand

$$G(\gamma) = G(0) + \gamma G'(0) + \frac{1}{2}\gamma^2 G''(0) + \mathcal{O}(\gamma^3)$$

We directly obtain from [8]

$$G'(\gamma) = \langle E_{\text{int}} \rangle_\gamma$$

$$G''(\gamma) = \langle E_{\text{int}} \rangle_\gamma^2 - \langle E_{\text{int}}^2 \rangle_\gamma + \left\langle E_{\text{int}} \sum_i \frac{\partial \theta_i}{\partial \gamma}(s_i - m_i) \right\rangle_\gamma$$

For $\gamma = 0$ the expectation values $\langle \cdot \rangle_\gamma$ become the mean field expectations which we can directly compute:

$$G(0) = \frac{1}{2} \sum_i \left((1 + m_i) \log \frac{1}{2}(1 + m_i) + (1 - m_i) \log \frac{1}{2}(1 - m_i) \right)$$

$$G'(0) = -\frac{1}{2} \sum_{ij} w_{ij} m_i m_j$$

$$G''(0) = -\frac{1}{4} \sum_{ij} w_{ij}^2 (1 - m_i^2)(1 - m_j^2)$$

Thus

$$G(1) = \frac{1}{2} \sum_i \left((1 + m_i) \log \frac{1}{2}(1 + m_i) + (1 - m_i) \log \frac{1}{2}(1 - m_i) \right)$$

$$- \frac{1}{2} \sum_{ij} w_{ij} m_i m_j$$

$$- \frac{1}{2} \sum_{ij} w_{ij}^2 (1 - m_i^2)(1 - m_j^2) + \mathcal{O}(w^3 f(m)) \tag{3}$$

where $f(m)$ is some unknown function of m.

The mean field equations are given by the inverse Legendre transformation

$$\theta_i = \frac{\partial G}{\partial m_i} = \tanh^{-1}(m_i) - \sum_j w_{ij}m_j + \sum_j w_{ij}^2 m_i(1 - m_j^2), \tag{4}$$

which we recognize as the mean field equations.

The correlations are given by

$$\langle s_i s_j \rangle - \langle s_i \rangle \langle s_j \rangle = -\frac{\partial^2 F}{\partial \theta_i \partial \theta_j} = \frac{\partial m_i}{\partial \theta_j} = \left(\frac{\partial \theta}{\partial m} \right)_{ij}^{-1} = \left(\frac{\partial^2 G}{\partial m^2} \right)_{ij}^{-1}.$$

We therefore obtain from Eq. 3

$$\langle s_i s_j \rangle - \langle s_i \rangle \langle s_j \rangle = A_{ij}$$

with

$$(A^{-1})_{ij} = \delta_{ij} \left(\frac{1}{1 - m_i^2} + \sum_k w_{ik}^2 (1 - m_k^2) \right) - w_{ij} - 2m_i m_j w_{ij}^2 \tag{5}$$

Thus, for given w_{ij} and θ_i, we obtain the approximate mean firing rates m_i by solving Eqs. 4 and the correlations by their linear response approximations Eqs. 5. The inclusion of hidden units is straigthforward. One applies the above approximations in the free and the clamped phase separately [5]. The complexity of the method is $O(n^3)$, due to the matrix inversion.

4 Learning without hidden units

We will assess the accuracy of the above method for networks without hidden units. Let us define $C_{ij} = \langle s_i s_j \rangle_c - \langle s_i \rangle_c \langle s_j \rangle_c$, which can be directly computed from the data. The fixed point equation for $\Delta\theta_i$ gives

$$\Delta\theta_i = 0 \Leftrightarrow m_i = \langle s_i \rangle_c. \tag{6}$$

The fixed point equation for Δw_{ij}, using Eq. 6, gives

$$\Delta w_{ij} = 0 \Leftrightarrow A_{ij} = C_{ij}, i \neq j. \tag{7}$$

From Eq. 7 and Eq. 5 we can solve for w_{ij}, using a standard least squares method. In our case, we used **fsolve** from Matlab. Subsequently, we obtain θ_i from Eq. 4. We refer to this method as the TAP approximation.

In order to assess the effect of the TAP term, we also computed the weights and thresholds in the same way as described above, but without the terms of order w^2 in Eqs. 5 and 4. Since this is the standard Weiss mean field expression, we refer to this method as the Weiss approximation.

The fixed point equations are only imposed for the off-diagonal elements of Δw_{ij} because the Boltzmann distribution Eq. 1 does not depend on the diagonal elements w_{ii}. In [5], we explored a variant of the Weiss approximation, where we included diagonal weight terms. As is discussed there, if we were to impose Eq. 7 for $i = j$ as well, we have $A = C$. If C is invertible, we therefore have $A^{-1} = C^{-1}$. However, we now have more constraints than variables. Therefore, we introduce diagonal weights w_{ii} by adding the term $w_{ii}m_i$ to the righthandside of Eq. 4 in the Weiss approximation. Thus,

$$w_{ij} = \frac{\delta_{ij}}{1 - m_i^2} - (C^{-1})_{ij}$$

and θ_i is given by Eq. 4 in the Weiss approximation. Clearly, this method is computationally simpler because it gives an explicit expression for the solution of the weights involving only one matrix inversion.

5 Numerical results

For the target distribution $q(s)$ in Eq. 2 we chose a fully connected Ising spin glass model with equilibrium distribution

$$q(s) = \frac{1}{Z} \exp\{-\frac{1}{2} \sum_{ij} J_{ij} s_i s_j\}$$

with J_{ij} i.i.d. Gaussian variables with mean $\frac{J_0}{n-1}$ and variance $\frac{J^2}{n-1}$. This model is known as the Sherrington-Kirkpatrick (SK) model [10]. Depending on the values of J and J_0, the model displays a para-magnetic (unordered), ferro-magnetic (ordered) and a spin-glass (frustrated) phase. For $J_0 = 0$, the para-magnetic (spin-glass) phase is obtained for $J < 1$ ($J > 1$). We will assess the effectiveness of our approximations for finite n, for $J_0 = 0$ and for various values of J. Since this is a realizable task, the optimal KL divergence is zero, which is indeed observed in our simulations.

We measure the quality of the solutions by means of the Kullback divergence. Therefore, this comparison is only feasible for small networks. The reason is that the computation of the Kullback divergence requires the computation of the Boltzmann distribution, Eq. 1, which requires exponential time due to the partition function Z.

We present results for a network of $n = 10$ neurons. For $J_0 = 0$, we generated for each value of $0.1 < J < 3$, 10 random weight matrices J_{ij}. For each weight matrix, we computed the $q(\vec{s})$ on all 2^n states. For each of the 10 problems, we applied the TAP method, the Weiss method and the Weiss method with diagonal weights. In addition, we applied the exact Boltzmann Machine learning algorithm using conjugate gradient descent and verified that it gives KL divergence equal to zero, as it should. We also applied a factorized model $p(\vec{s}) = \prod_i \frac{1}{2}(1 + m_i s_i)$ with $m_i = \langle s_i \rangle_c$ to assess the importance of correlations in the target distribution. In Fig. 1a, we show for each J the average KL divergence over the 10 problem instances as a function of J for the TAP method, the Weiss method, the Weiss method with diagonal weights and the factorized model. We observe that the TAP method gives the best results, but that its performance deteriorates in the spin-glass phase ($J > 1$).

The behaviour of all approximate methods is highly dependent on the individual problem instance. In Fig. 1b, we show the mean value of the KL divergence of the TAP solution, together with the minimum and maximum values obtained on the 10 problem instances.

Despite these large fluctuations, the quality of the TAP solution is consistently better than the Weiss solution. In Fig. 1c, we plot the difference between the TAP and Weiss solution, averaged over the 10 problem instances.

In [5] we concluded that the Weiss solution with diagonal weights is better than the standard Weiss solution when learning a finite number of randomly generated patterns. In Fig. 1d we plot the difference between the Weiss solution with and without diagonal weights. We observe again that the inclusion of diagonal weights leads to better results in the paramagnetic phase ($J < 1$), but leads to worse results in the spin-glass phase. For $J > 2$, we encountered problem instances for which either the matrix C is not invertible or the KL divergence is infinite. This problem becomes more and more severe for increasing J. We therefore have not presented results for the Weiss approximation with diagonal weigths for $J > 2$.

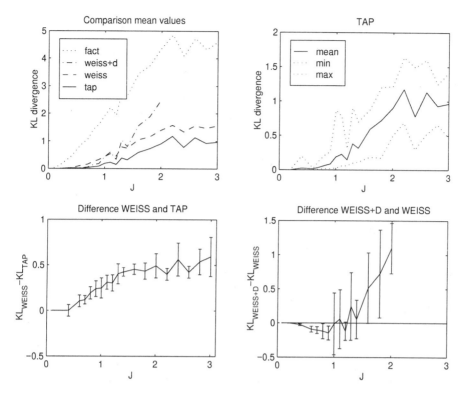

Figure 1: Mean field learning of paramagnetic ($J < 1$) and spin glass ($J > 1$) problems for a network of 10 neurons. a) Comparison of mean KL divergences for the factorized model (fact), the Weiss mean field approximation with and without diagonal weights (weiss+d and weiss), and the TAP approximation, as a function of J. The exact method yields zero KL divergence for all J. b) The mean, minimum and maximum KL divergence of the TAP approximation for the 10 problem instances, as a function of J. c) The mean difference between the KL divergence for the Weiss approximation and the TAP approximation, as a function of J. d) The mean difference between the KL divergence for the Weiss approximation with and without diagonal weights, as a function of J.

6 Discussion

We have presented a derivation of mean field theory and the linear response correction based on a small coupling expansion of the Gibbs free energy. This expansion can in principle be computed to arbitrary order. However, one should expect that the solution of the resulting mean field and linear response equations will become more and more difficult to solve numerically. The small coupling expansion should be applicable to other network models such as the sigmoid belief network, Potts networks and higher order Boltzmann Machines.

The numerical results show that the method is applicable to paramagnetic problems. This is intuitively clear, since paramagnetic problems have a unimodal probability distribution, which can be approximated by a mean and correlations around the mean. The method performs worse for spin glass problems. However, it still gives a useful approximation of the correlations when compared to the factorized model which ignores all correlations. In this regime, the TAP approximation improves significantly on the Weiss approximation. One may therefore hope that higher order approximation may further improve the method for spin glass problems. Therefore, we cannot conclude at this point whether mean field methods are restricted to unimodal distributions. In order to further investigate this issue, one should also study the ferromagnetic case $(J_0 > 1, J > 1)$, which is multimodal as well but less challenging than the spin glass case.

It is interesting to note that the performance of the exact method is absolutely insensitive to the value of J. Naively, one might have thought that for highly multi-modal target distributions, any gradient based learning method will suffer from local minima. Apparently, this is not the case: the exact KL divergence has just one minimum, but the mean field approximations of the gradients may have multiple solutions.

Acknowledgement

This research is supported by the Technology Foundation STW, applied science division of NWO and the techology programme of the Ministry of Economic Affairs.

References

[1] D. Ackley, G. Hinton, and T. Sejnowski. A learning algorithm for Boltzmann Machines. *Cognitive Science*, 9:147–169, 1985.

[2] C. Itzykson and J-M. Drouffe. *Statistical Field Theory*. Cambridge monographs on mathematical physics. Cambridge University Press, Cambridge, UK, 1989.

[3] C. Peterson and J.R. Anderson. A mean field theory learning algorithm for neural networks. *Complex Systems*, 1:995–1019, 1987.

[4] G.E. Hinton. Deterministic Boltzmann learning performs steepest descent in weight-space. *Neural Computation*, 1:143–150, 1989.

[5] H.J. Kappen and F.B. Rodríguez. Efficient learning in Boltzmann Machines using linear response theory. *Neural Computation*, 1997. In press.

[6] G. Parisi. *Statistical Field Theory*. Frontiers in Physics. Addison-Wesley, 1988.

[7] L.K. Saul, T. Jaakkola, and M.I. Jordan. Mean field theory for sigmoid belief networks. *Journal of artificial intelligence research*, 4:61–76, 1996.

[8] T. Plefka. Convergence condition of the TAP equation for the infinite-range Ising spin glass model. *Journal of Physics A*, 15:1971–1978, 1982.

[9] S. Kullback. *Information Theory and Statistics*. Wiley, New York, 1959.

[10] D. Sherrington and S. Kirkpatrick. Solvable model of Spin-Glass. *Physical review letters*, 35:1792–1796, 1975.

Relative Loss Bounds for Multidimensional Regression Problems

Jyrki Kivinen
Department of Computer Science
P.O. Box 26 (Teollisuuskatu 23)
FIN-00014 University of Helsinki, Finland

Manfred K. Warmuth
Department of Computer Science
University of California, Santa Cruz
Santa Cruz, CA 95064, USA

Abstract

We study on-line generalized linear regression with multidimensional outputs, i.e., neural networks with multiple output nodes but no hidden nodes. We allow at the final layer transfer functions such as the softmax function that need to consider the linear activations to all the output neurons. We use distance functions of a certain kind in two completely independent roles in deriving and analyzing on-line learning algorithms for such tasks. We use one distance function to define a matching loss function for the (possibly multidimensional) transfer function, which allows us to generalize earlier results from one-dimensional to multidimensional outputs. We use another distance function as a tool for measuring progress made by the on-line updates. This shows how previously studied algorithms such as gradient descent and exponentiated gradient fit into a common framework. We evaluate the performance of the algorithms using relative loss bounds that compare the loss of the on-line algoritm to the best off-line predictor from the relevant model class, thus completely eliminating probabilistic assumptions about the data.

1 INTRODUCTION

In a regression problem, we have a sequence of n-dimensional real valued *inputs* $x_t \in \mathbf{R}^n$, $t = 1, \ldots, \ell$, and for each input x_t a k-dimensional real-valued *desired output* $y_t \in \mathbf{R}^k$. Our goal is to find a mapping that at least approximately models the dependency between x_t and y_t. Here we consider the parametric case $\widehat{y}_t = f(\omega; x_t)$ where the *actual output* $\widehat{y}_t$ corresponding to the input x_t is determined by a parameter vector $\omega \in \mathbf{R}^m$ (e.g., weights in a neural network) through a given fixed model f (e.g., a neural network architecture).

Thus, we wish to obtain parameters ω such that, in some sense, $f(\omega; x_t) \approx y_t$ for all t. The most basic model f to consider is the linear one, which in the one-dimensional case $k = 1$ means that $f(\omega; x_t) = \omega \cdot x_t$ for $\omega \in \mathbf{R}^n$. In the multidimensional case we actually have a whole matrix $\Omega \in \mathbf{R}^{k \times n}$ of parameters and $f(\Omega; x_t) = \Omega x_t$. The goodness of the fit is quantitatively measured in terms of a *loss function*; the *square loss* given by $\sum_{t,j} (y_{t,j} - \hat{y}_{t,j})^2 / 2$ is a popular choice.

In *generalized linear regression* [MN89] we fix a *transfer function* ϕ and apply it on top of a linear model. Thus, in the one-dimensional case we would have $f(\omega; x_t) = \phi(\omega \cdot x_t)$. Here ϕ is usually a continuous increasing function from $\mathbf{R}$ to $\mathbf{R}$, such as the logistic function that maps z to $1/(1 + e^{-z})$. It is still possible to use the square loss, but this can lead to problems. In particular, when we apply the logistic transfer function and try to find a weight vector ω that minimizes the total square loss over ℓ examples (x_t, y_t), we may have up to ℓ^n local minima [AHW95, Bud93]. Hence, some other choice of loss function might be more convenient. In the one-dimensional case it can be shown that any continuous strictly increasing transfer function ϕ has a specific *matching loss function* L_ϕ such that, among other useful properties, $\sum_t L_\phi(y_t, \phi(\omega \cdot x_t))$ is always convex in ω, so local minima are not a problem [AHW95]. For example, the matching loss function for the logistic transfer function is the *relative entropy* (a generalization of the logarithmic loss for continuous-valued outcomes). The square loss is the matching loss function for the identity transfer function (i.e., linear regression).

The main theme of the present paper is the application of a particular kind of *distance functions* to analyzing learning algorithms in (possibly multidimensional) generalized linear regression problems. We consider a particular manner in which a mapping $\phi \colon \mathbf{R}^k \to \mathbf{R}^k$ can be used to define a distance function $\Delta_\phi : \mathbf{R}^k \times \mathbf{R}^k \to \mathbf{R}$; the assumption we must make here is that ϕ has a convex potential function. The matching loss function L_ϕ mentioned above for a transfer function ϕ in the one-dimensional case is given in terms of the distance function Δ_ϕ as $L_\phi(\phi(a), \phi(\hat{a})) = \Delta_\phi(\hat{a}, a)$. Here, as whenever we use the matching loss $L_\phi(y, \hat{y})$, we assume that y and $\hat{y}$ are in the range of ϕ, so we can write $y = \phi(a)$ and $\hat{y} = \phi(\hat{a})$ for some a and $\hat{a}$. Notice that for $k = 1$, any strictly increasing continuous function has a convex potential (i.e., integral) function. In the more interesting case $k > 1$, we can consider transfer functions such as the softmax function, which is commonly used to transfer arbitrary vectors $a \in \mathbf{R}^k$ into probability vectors $\hat{y}$ (i.e., vectors such that $\hat{y}_i \geq 0$ for all i and $\sum_i \hat{y}_i = 1$). The matching loss function for the softmax function defined analogously with the one-dimensional case turns out to be the relative entropy (or Kullback-Leibler divergence), which indeed is a commonly used measure of distance between probability vectors. For the identity transfer function, the matching loss function is the squared Euclidean distance.

The first result we get from this observation connecting matching losses to a general notion of distance is that certain previous results on generalized linear regression with matching loss on one-dimensional outputs [HKW95] directly generalize to multidimensional outputs. From a more general point of view, a much more interesting feature of these distance functions is how they allow us to view certain previously known learning algorithms, and introduce new ones, in a simple unified framework. To briefly explain this framework without unnecessary complications, we restrict the following discussion to the case $k = 1$, i.e., $f(\omega; x) = \phi(\omega \cdot x) \in \mathbf{R}$ with $\omega \in \mathbf{R}^n$.

We consider on-line learning algorithms, by which we here mean an algorithm that processes the training examples one by one, the pair (x_t, y_t) being processed at time t. Based on the training examples the algorithm produces a whole sequence of weight vectors ω_t, $t = 1, \ldots, \ell$. At each time t the old weight vector ω_t is *updated* into ω_{t+1} based on x_t and y_t. The best-known such algorithm is on-line gradient descent. To see some alternatives, consider first a distance function Δ_ψ defined on $\mathbf{R}^n$ by some function $\psi \colon \mathbf{R}^n \to \mathbf{R}^n$. (Thus, we assume that ψ has a convex potential.) We represent the update somewhat indirectly by introducing a new parameter vector $\theta_t \in \mathbf{R}^n$ from which the actual weights ω_t are obtained by the mapping $\omega_t = \psi(\theta_t)$. The new parameters are updated by

$$\theta_{t+1} = \theta_t - \eta \nabla_\omega \left(L_\phi(y_t, \phi(\omega \cdot x_t)) \right)_{\omega = \psi(\theta_t)} \tag{1}$$

where $\eta > 0$ is a learning rate. We call this algorithm the *general additive algorithm* with *parameterization function* ψ. Notice that here θ is updated by the gradient with respect to ω, so this is not just a gradient descent with reparameterization [JW98]. However, we obtain the usual on-line gradient descent when ψ is the identity function. When ψ is the softmax function, we get the so-called exponentiated gradient (EG) algorithm [KW97, HKW95].

The connection of the distance function Δ_ψ to the update (1) is two-fold. First, (1) can be motivated as an approximate solution to a minimization problem in which the distance $\Delta_\psi(\theta_t, \theta_{t+1})$ is used as a kind of penalty term to prevent too drastic an update based on a single example. Second, the distance function Δ_ψ can be used as a potential function in analyzing the performance of the resulting algorithm. The same distance functions have been used previously for exactly the same purposes [KW97, HKW95] in important special cases (the gradient descent and EG algorithms) but without realizing the full generality of the method.

It should be noted that the choice of the parameterization function ψ is left completely free, as long as ψ has a convex potential function. (In contrast, the choice of the transfer function ϕ depends on what kind of a regression problem we wish to solve.) Earlier work suggests that the softmax parameterization function (i.e., the EG algorithm) is particularly suited for situations in which some sparse weight vector ω gives a good match to the data [HKW95, KW97]. (Because softmax normalizes the weight vector and makes the components positive, a simple transformation of the input data is typically added to realize positive and negative weights with arbitrary norm.)

In work parallel to this, the analogue of the general additive update (1) in the context of linear classification, i.e., with a threshold transfer function, has recently been developed and analyzed by Grove et al. [GLS97] with methods and results very similar to ours. Cesa-Bianchi [CB97] has used somewhat different methods to obtain bounds also in cases in which the loss function does not match the transfer function. Jagota and Warmuth [JW98] view (1) as an Euler discretization of a system of partial differential equations and investigate the performance of the algorithm as the discretization parameter approaches zero.

The distance functions we use here have previously been applied in the context of exponential families by Amari [Ama85] and others. Here we only need some basic technical properties of the distance functions that can easily be derived from the definitions. For a discussion of our line of work in a statistical context see Azoury and Warmuth [AW97].

In Section 2 we review the definition of a matching loss function and give examples. Section 3 discusses the general additive algorithm in more detail. The actual relative on-line loss bounds we have for the general additive algorithm are explained in Section 4.

2 DISTANCE FUNCTIONS AND MATCHING LOSSES

Let $\phi: \mathbf{R}^k \to \mathbf{R}^k$ be a function that has a convex potential function P_ϕ (i.e., $\phi = \nabla P_\phi$ for some convex $P_\phi: \mathbf{R}^k \to \mathbf{R}$). We first define a *distance function* Δ_ϕ for ϕ by

$$\Delta_\phi(\widehat{a}, a) = P_\phi(\widehat{a}) - P_\phi(a) + \phi(a) \cdot (a - \widehat{a}) . \tag{2}$$

Thus, the distance $\Delta_\phi(\widehat{a}, a)$ is the error we make if we approximate $P_\phi(\widehat{a})$ by its first-order Taylor polynomial around a. Convexity of P_ϕ implies that Δ_ϕ is convex in its first argument. Further, $\Delta_\phi(\widehat{a}, a)$ is nonnegative, and zero if and only if $\phi(\widehat{a}) = \phi(a)$.

We can alternatively write (2) as $\Delta_\phi(\widehat{a}, a) = \int_a^{\widehat{a}} (\phi(r) - \phi(a)) \cdot dr$ where the integral is a path integral the value of which must be independent of the actual path chosen between a and $\widehat{a}$. In the one-dimensional case, the integral is a simple definite integral, and ϕ has a convex potential (i.e., integral) function if it is strictly increasing and continuous [AHW95, HKW95].

Let now ϕ have range $V_\phi \subseteq \mathbf{R}^k$ and distance function Δ_ϕ. Assuming that there is a function $L_\phi: V_\phi \times V_\phi \to \mathbf{R}$ such that $L_\phi(\phi(a), \phi(\widehat{a})) = \Delta_\phi(\widehat{a}, a)$ holds for all $\widehat{a}$ and a, we say that L_ϕ is the *matching loss function* for ϕ.

Example 1 Let ϕ be a linear function given by $\phi(a) = Aa$ where $A \in \mathbf{R}^{k \times k}$ is symmetrical and positive definite. Then ϕ has the convex potential function $P_\phi(a) = a^{\mathrm{T}} A a / 2$, and (2) gives $\Delta_\phi(\widehat{a}, a) = \frac{1}{2}(a - \widehat{a})^{\mathrm{T}} A (a - \widehat{a})$. Hence, $L_\phi(y, \widehat{y}) = \frac{1}{2}(y - \widehat{y})^{\mathrm{T}} A^{-1}(y - \widehat{y})$ for all $y, \widehat{y} \in \mathbf{R}^k$. □

Example 2 Let $\sigma: \mathbf{R}^k \to \mathbf{R}^k$, $\sigma_i(a) = \exp(a_i) / \sum_{j=1}^k \exp(a_j)$, be the softmax function. It has a potential function given by $P_\sigma(a) = \ln \sum_{j=1}^k \exp(a_j)$. To see that P_σ is convex, notice that the Hessian $\mathrm{D}^2 P_\sigma$ is given by $\mathrm{D}^2 P_\sigma(a)_{ij} = \delta_{ij} \sigma_i(a) - \sigma_i(a)\sigma_j(a)$. Given a vector $x \in \mathbf{R}^k$, let now X be a random variable that has probability $\sigma_i(a)$ of taking the value x_i. We have $x^{\mathrm{T}} \mathrm{D}\sigma(a) x = \sum_{i=1}^k \sigma_i(a) x_i^2 - \sum_{i=1}^k \sum_{j=1}^k \sigma_i(a) x_i \sigma_j(a) x_j = EX^2 - (EX)^2 = \mathrm{Var} X \geq 0$. Straightforward algebra now gives the relative entropy $L_\sigma(y, \widehat{y}) = \sum_{j=1}^k y_j \ln(y_j / \widehat{y}_j)$ as the matching loss function. (To allow $y_j = 0$ or $\widehat{y}_j = 0$, we adopt the standard convention that $0 \ln 0 = 0 \ln(0/0) = 0$ and $y \ln(y/0) = \infty$ for $y > 0$.) □

In the relative loss bound proofs we use the basic property [JW98, Ama85]

$$\Delta_\phi(\widehat{a}', a) = \Delta_\phi(\widehat{a}', \widehat{a}) + \Delta_\phi(\widehat{a}, a) + (\phi(\widehat{a}) - \phi(a)) \cdot (\widehat{a}' - \widehat{a}) . \tag{3}$$

This shows that our distances do not satisfy the triangle inequality. Usually they are not symmetrical, either.

3 THE GENERAL ADDITIVE ALGORITHM

We consider on-line learning algorithms that at time t first receive an input $x_t \in \mathbf{R}^n$, then produce an output $\widehat{y}_t \in \mathbf{R}^k$, and finally receive as feedback the desired output $y_t \in \mathbf{R}^k$. To define the *general additive algorithm*, assume we are given a transfer function

$\phi: \mathbf{R}^k \to \mathbf{R}^k$ that has a convex potential function. (We will later use the matching loss as a performance measure.) We also require that all the desired outputs y_t are in the range of ϕ. The algorithm's predictions are now given by $\hat{y}_t = \phi(\Omega_t x_t)$ where $\Omega_t \in \mathbf{R}^{k \times n}$ is the algorithm's *weight matrix* at time t. To see how the weight matrix is updated, assume further we have a parameterization function $\psi: \mathbf{R}^n \to \mathbf{R}^n$ with a distance Δ_ψ. The algorithm maintains kn real-valued parameters. We denote by Θ_t the $k \times n$ matrix of the values of these parameters immediately before trial t. Futher, we denote by $\theta_{t,j}$ the jth row of Θ_t, and by $\psi(\Theta_t)$ the matrix with $\psi(\theta_{t,j})$ as its jth row. Given initial parameter values Θ_1 and a learning rate $\eta > 0$, we now define the *general additive* (GA) *algorithm* as the algorithm that repeats at each trial t the following prediction and update steps.

Prediction: Upon recieving the instance x_t, give the prediction $\hat{y}_t = \phi(\psi(\Theta_t)x_t)$.

Update: For $j = 1, \ldots, k$, set $\theta_{t+1,j} = \theta_{t,j} - \eta(\hat{y}_{t,j} - y_{t,j})x_t$.

Note that (2) implies $\nabla_{\hat{a}}\Delta_\phi(\hat{a}, a)) = \phi(\hat{a}) - \phi(a)$, so this update indeed turns out to be the same as (1) when we recall that $L_\phi(y_t, \hat{y}_t) = \Delta_\phi(\Omega_t x_t, a_t)$ where $y_t = \phi(a_t)$.

The update can be motivated by an optimization problem given in terms of the loss and distance. Consider updating an old parameter matrix Θ into a new matrix $\widetilde{\Theta}$ based on a single input x and desired output y. A natural goal would be to minimize the loss $L_\phi(y, \phi(\psi(\widetilde{\Theta})x))$. However, the algorithm must avoid losing too much of the information it has gained during the previous trials and stored in the form of the old parameter matrix Θ. We thus set as the algorithm's goal to minimize the sum $\Delta_\psi(\Theta, \widetilde{\Theta}) + \eta L_\phi(y, \phi(\psi(\widetilde{\Theta})x))$ where $\eta > 0$ is a parameter regulating how fast the algorithm is willing to move its parameters. Under certain regularity assumptions, the update rule of the GA algorithm can be shown to approximately solve this minimization problem. For more discussion and examples in the special case of linear regression, see [KW97]. An interesting related idea is using all the previous examples in the update instead of just the last one. For work along these lines in the linear case see Vovk [Vov97] and Foster [Fos91].

4   RELATIVE LOSS BOUNDS

Consider a sequence $S = ((x_1, y_1), \ldots, (x_\ell, y_\ell))$ of training examples, and let $\mathrm{Loss}_\phi(\mathrm{GA}, S) = \sum_{t=1}^\ell L_\phi(y_t, \hat{y}_t)$ be the loss incurred by the general additive algorithm on this sequence when it always uses its current weights Ω_t for making the tth prediction $\hat{y}_t$. Similarly, let $\mathrm{Loss}_\phi(\Omega, S) = \sum_{t=1}^\ell L_\phi(y_t, \phi(\Omega x_t))$ be the loss of a fixed predictor Ω. Basically, our goal is to show that if some Ω achieves a small loss, then the algorithm is not doing much worse, regardless of how the sequence S was generated. Making additional probabilistic assumptions allows such on-line loss bounds to be converted into more traditional results about generalization errors [KW97]. To give the bounds for $\mathrm{Loss}_\phi(\mathrm{GA}, S)$ in terms of $\mathrm{Loss}_\phi(\Omega, S)$ we need some additional parameters. The first one is the distance $\Delta_\psi(\Theta_1, \Theta)$ where $\Omega = \psi(\Theta)$ and Θ_1 is the initial parameter matrix of the GA algorithm (which can be arbitrary). The second one is defined by

$$b_{\mathcal{X},\psi} = \sup\{x^\mathrm{T}\mathrm{D}\psi(\theta)x \mid \theta \in \mathbf{R}^n, x \in \mathcal{X}\}$$

where $\mathcal{X} = \{x_1, \ldots, x_\ell\}$ is the set of input vectors and $\mathrm{D}\psi(\theta)$ is the Jacobian with $(\mathrm{D}\psi(\theta))_{ij} = \partial\psi_i(\theta)/\partial\theta_j$. The value $b_{\mathcal{X},\psi}$ can be interpreted as the maximum norm of any input vector in a norm defined by the parameterization function ψ. In Example 3 below we show how $b_{\chi,\psi}$ can easily be evaluated when ψ is a linear function or the softmax function. The third parameter c_ϕ, defined as

$$c_\phi = \sup \left\{ \frac{(\boldsymbol{y} - \widehat{\boldsymbol{y}})^2}{2L_\phi(\boldsymbol{y}, \widehat{\boldsymbol{y}})} \mid \boldsymbol{y}, \widehat{\boldsymbol{y}} \in \overline{V_\phi} \right\} \; ,$$

relates the matching loss function for the transfer function ϕ to the square loss. In Example 4 we evaluate this constant for linear functions, the softmax function, and the one-dimensional case.

Example 3 Consider bounding the value $\boldsymbol{x}^{\mathrm{T}} \mathrm{D}\sigma(\theta)\boldsymbol{x}$ where σ is the softmax function. As we saw in Example 2, this value is a variance of a random variable with the range $\{x_1, \ldots, x_n\}$. Hence, we have $b_{\chi,\sigma} \leq \max_{\boldsymbol{x} \in \chi}(\max_i x_i - \min_i x_i)^2/4 \leq \max_{\boldsymbol{x} \in \chi} \|\boldsymbol{x}\|_\infty^2$ where $\|\boldsymbol{x}\|_\infty = \max_i |x_i|$.

If ψ is a linear function with $\psi(\theta) = A\theta$ for a symmetrical positive definite A, we clearly have $b_{\chi,\psi} \leq \lambda_{\max} \max_{\boldsymbol{x} \in \chi} \boldsymbol{x}^2$ where $\lambda_{\max}$ is the largest eigenvalue of A. $\qquad\square$

Example 4 For the softmax function σ the matching loss function L_σ is the relative entropy (see Example 2), for which it is well known that $L_\sigma(\boldsymbol{y}, \widehat{\boldsymbol{y}}) \geq 2(\boldsymbol{y} - \widehat{\boldsymbol{y}})^2$. Hence, we have $c_\phi \leq 1/4$.

If ϕ is a linear function given by a symmetrical positive semidefinite matrix A, we see from Example 1 that c_ϕ is the largest eigenvalue of A.

Finally, in the special case $k = 1$, with $\phi \colon \mathbf{R} \to \mathbf{R}$ differentiable and strictly increasing, we can show $c_\phi \leq Z$ if Z is a bound such that $0 < \phi'(z) \leq Z$ holds for all z. $\qquad\square$

Assume now we are given constants $b \geq b_{\chi,\psi}$ and $c \geq c_\phi$. Our first loss bound states that for any parameter matrix Θ we have

$$\mathrm{Loss}_\phi(\mathrm{GA}, S) \leq 2\mathrm{Loss}_\phi(\psi(\Theta), S) + 4bc\Delta_\psi(\Theta_1, \Theta)$$

when the learning rate is chosen as $\eta = 1/(2bc)$. (Proofs are omitted from this extended abstract.) The advantage of this bound is that with a fixed learning rate it holds for any Θ, so we need no advance knowledge about a good Θ. The drawback is the factor 2 in front of $\mathrm{Loss}_\phi(\psi(\Theta), S)$, which suggests that asymptotically the algorithm might not ever achieve the performance of the best fixed predictor. A tighter bound can be achieved by more careful tuning. Thus, given constants $K \geq 0$ and $R > 0$, if we choose the learning rate as $\eta = (\sqrt{(bcR)^2 + KbcR} - bcR)/(Kbc)$ (with $\eta = 1/(2bc)$ if $K = 0$) we obtain

$$\mathrm{Loss}_\phi(\mathrm{GA}, S) \leq \mathrm{Loss}_\phi(\psi(\Theta), S) + 2\sqrt{KbcR} + 4bcR$$

for any Θ that satisfies $\mathrm{Loss}_\phi(\psi(\Theta), S) \leq K$ and $\Delta_\psi(\Theta_1, \Theta) \leq R$. This shows that if we restrict our comparison to parameter matrices within a given distance R of the initial matrix of the algorithm, and we have a reasonably good guess K as to the loss of the best fixed predictor within this distance, this knowledge allows the algorithm to asymptotically match the performance of this best fixed predictor.

Acknowledgments

The authors thank Katy Azoury, Chris Bishop, Nicolò Cesa-Bianchi, David Helmbold, and Nick Littlestone for helpful discussions. Jyrki Kivinen was supported by the Academy of Finland and the ESPRIT project NeuroCOLT. Manfred Warmuth was supported by the NSF grant CCR 9700201.

References

[Ama85]   S. Amari. *Differential Geometrical Methods in Statistics.* Springer Verlag, Berlin, 1985.

[AHW95] P. Auer, M. Herbster, and M. K. Warmuth. Exponentially many local minima for single neurons. In *Proc. 1995 Neural Information Processing Conference*, pages 316–317. MIT Press, Cambridge, MA, November 1995.

[AW97]   K. Azoury and M. K. Warmuth. Relative loss bounds and the exponential family of distributions. Unpublished manuscript, 1997.

[Bud93]   M. Budinich. Some notes on perceptron learning. *J. Phys. A.: Math. Gen.*, 26:4237–4247, 1993.

[CB97]   N. Cesa-Bianchi. Analysis of two gradient-based algorithms for on-line regression. In *Proc. 10th Annu. Conf. on Comput. Learning Theory*, pages 163–170. ACM, 1997.

[Fos91]   D. P. Foster. Prediction in the worst case. *The Annals of Statistics*, 19(2):1084–1090, 1991.

[GLS97]   A. J. Grove, N. Littlestone, and D. Schuurmans. General convergence results for linear discriminant updates. In *Proc. 10th Annu. Conf. on Comput. Learning Theory*, pages 171–183. ACM, 1997.

[HKW95] D. P. Helmbold, J. Kivinen, and M. K. Warmuth. Worst-case loss bounds for sigmoided linear neurons. In *Proc. Neural Information Processing Systems 1995*, pages 309–315. MIT Press, Cambridge, MA, November 1995.

[JW98]   A. K. Jagota and M. K. Warmuth. Continuous versus discrete-time nonlinear gradient descent: Relative loss bounds and convergence. Presented at *Fifth Symposium on Artificial Intelligence and Mathematics*, Ft. Lauderdale, FL, 1998.

[KW97]   J. Kivinen and M. K. Warmuth. Additive versus exponentiated gradient updates for linear prediction. *Information and Computation*, 132(1):1–64, January 1997.

[MN89]   P. McCullagh and J. A. Nelder. *Generalized Linear Models.* Chapman & Hall, New York, 1989.

[Vov97]   V. Vovk. Competitive on-line linear regression. In *Proc. Neural Information Processing Systems 1997*. MIT Press, Cambridge, MA, 1998.

Asymptotic Theory for Regularization: One-Dimensional Linear Case

Petri Koistinen
Rolf Nevanlinna Institute, P.O. Box 4, FIN-00014 University of Helsinki,
Finland. Email: Petri.Koistinen@rni.helsinki.fi

Abstract

The generalization ability of a neural network can sometimes be improved dramatically by regularization. To analyze the improvement one needs more refined results than the asymptotic distribution of the weight vector. Here we study the simple case of one-dimensional linear regression under quadratic regularization, i.e., ridge regression. We study the random design, misspecified case, where we derive expansions for the optimal regularization parameter and the ensuing improvement. It is possible to construct examples where it is best to use no regularization.

1 INTRODUCTION

Suppose that we have available training data $(X_1, Y_1), \ldots, (X_n, Y_n)$ consisting of pairs of vectors, and we try to predict Y_i on the basis of X_i with a neural network with weight vector w. One popular way of selecting w is by the criterion

$$(1) \qquad \frac{1}{n} \sum_1^n \ell(X_i, Y_i, w) + \lambda Q(w) = \min!,$$

where the loss $\ell(x, y, w)$ is, e.g., the squared error $\|y - g(x, w)\|^2$, the function $g(\cdot, w)$ is the input/output function of the neural network, the penalty $Q(w)$ is a real function which takes on small values when the mapping $g(\cdot, w)$ is smooth and high values when it changes rapidly, and the regularization parameter λ is a nonnegative scalar (which might depend on the training sample). We refer to the setup (1) as (training with) regularization, and to the same setup with the choice $\lambda = 0$ as training without regularization. Regularization has been found to be very effective for improving the generalization ability of a neural network especially when the sample size n is of the same order of magnitude as the dimensionality of the parameter vector w, see, e.g., the textbooks (Bishop, 1995; Ripley, 1996).

In this paper we deal with asymptotics in the case where the architecture of the network is fixed but the sample size grows. To fix ideas, let us assume that the training data is part of an i.i.d. (independent, identically distributed) sequence $(X, Y); (X_1, Y_1), (X_2, Y_2), \ldots$ of pairs of random vectors, i.e., for each i the pair (X_i, Y_i) has the same distribution as the pair (X, Y) and the collection of pairs is independent (X and Y can be dependent). Then we can define the (prediction) risk of a network with weights w as the expected value

$$(2) \qquad r(w) := \mathbb{E}\,\ell(X, Y, w).$$

Let us denote the minimizer of (1) by $\hat{w}_n(\lambda)$, and a minimizer of the risk r by w^*. The quantity $r(\hat{w}_n(\lambda))$ is the average prediction error for data independent of the training sample. This quantity $r(\hat{w}_n(\lambda))$ is a random variable which describes the generalization performance of the network: it is bounded below by $r(w^*)$ and the more concentrated it is about $r(w^*)$, the better the performance. We will quantify this concentration by a single number, the expected value $\mathbb{E}\,r(\hat{w}_n(\lambda))$. We are interested in quantifying the gain (if any) in generalization for training with versus training without regularization defined by

$$(3) \qquad \mathbb{E}\,r(\hat{w}_n(0)) - \mathbb{E}\,r(\hat{w}_n(\lambda)).$$

When regularization helps, this is positive.

However, relatively little can be said about the quantity (3) without specifying in detail how the regularization parameter is determined. We show in the next section that provided λ converges to zero sufficiently quickly (at the rate $o_p(n^{-1/2})$), then $\mathbb{E}\,r(\hat{w}_n(0))$ and $\mathbb{E}\,r(\hat{w}_n(\lambda))$ are equal to leading order. It turns out, that the optimal regularization parameter resides in this asymptotic regime. For this reason, delicate analysis is required in order to get an asymptotic approximation for (3). In this article we derive the needed asymptotic expansions only for the simplest possible case: one-dimensional linear regression where the regularization parameter is chosen independently of the training sample.

2 REGULARIZATION IN LINEAR REGRESSION

We now specialize the setup (1) to the case of linear regression and a quadratic smoothness penalty, i.e., we take $\ell(x, y, w) = [y - x^T w]^2$ and $Q(w) = w^T R w$, where now y is scalar, x and w are vectors, and R is a symmetric, positive definite matrix. It is well known (and easy to show) that then the minimizer of (1) is

$$(4) \qquad \hat{w}_n(\lambda) = \left[\frac{1}{n}\sum_1^n X_i X_i^T + \lambda R\right]^{-1} \frac{1}{n}\sum_1^n X_i Y_i.$$

This is called the *generalized ridge regression estimator*, see, e.g., (Titterington, 1985); ridge regression corresponds to the choice $R = I$, see (Hoerl and Kennard, 1988) for a survey. Notice that (generalized) ridge regression is usually studied in the *fixed design* case, where X_i:s are nonrandom. Further, it is usually assumed that the model is *correctly specified*, i.e., that there exists a parameter such that $Y_i = X_i^T w^* + \epsilon_i$, and such that the distribution of the noise term ϵ_i does not depend on X_i. In contrast, we study the *random design, misspecified* case.

Assuming that $\mathbb{E}\,\|X\|^2 < \infty$ and that $\mathbb{E}\,[X X^T]$ is invertible, the minimizer of the risk (2) and the risk itself can be written as

$$(5) \qquad w^* = A^{-1}\mathbb{E}\,[XY], \quad \text{with} \quad A := \mathbb{E}\,[X X^T]$$

$$(6) \qquad r(w) = r(w^*) + (w - w^*)^T A (w - w^*).$$

If Z_n is a sequence of random variables, then the notation $Z_n = o_p(n^{-\alpha})$ means that $n^{\alpha} Z_n$ converges to zero in probability as $n \to \infty$. For this notation and the mathematical tools needed for the following proposition see, e.g., (Serfling, 1980, Ch. 1) or (Brockwell and Davis, 1987, Ch. 6).

Proposition 1 *Suppose that* $\mathbb{E}\, Y^4 < \infty$, $\mathbb{E}\, \|X\|^4 < \infty$ *and that* $A = \mathbb{E}[XX^T]$ *is invertible. If* $\lambda = o_p(n^{-1/2})$, *then both* $\sqrt{n}(\hat{w}_n(0) - w^*)$ *and* $\sqrt{n}(\hat{w}_n(\lambda) - w^*)$ *converge in distribution to* $N(0, C)$, *a normal distribution with mean zero and covariance matrix* C.

The previous proposition also generalizes to the nonlinear case (under more complicated conditions). Given this proposition, it follows (under certain additional conditions) by Taylor expansion that both $\mathbb{E}\, r(\hat{w}_n(\lambda)) - r(w^*)$ and $\mathbb{E}\, r(\hat{w}_n(0)) - r(w^*)$ admit the expansion $\beta_1 n^{-1} + o(n^{-1})$ with the same constant β_1. Hence, in the regime $\lambda = o_p(n^{-1/2})$ we need to consider higher order expansions in order to compare the performance of $\hat{w}_n(\lambda)$ and $\hat{w}_n(0)$.

3   ONE-DIMENSIONAL LINEAR REGRESSION

We now specialize the setting of the previous section to the case where x is scalar. Also, from now on, we only consider the case where the regularization parameter for given sample size n is deterministic; especially λ is not allowed to depend on the training sample. This is necessary, since coefficients in the following type of asymptotic expansions depend on the details of how the regularization parameter is determined. The deterministic case is the easiest one to analyze.

We develop asymptotic expansions for the criterion

$$(7) \qquad J_n(k) := \mathbb{E}\left(r(\hat{w}_n(k))\right) - r(w^*),$$

where now the regularization parameter k is deterministic and nonnegative. The expansions we get turn out to be valid uniformly for $k \geq 0$. We then develop asymptotic formulas for the minimizer of J_n, and also for $\bar{J}_n(0) - \inf J_n$. The last quantity can be interpreted as the average improvement in generalization performance gained by optimal level of regularization, when the regularization constant is allowed to depend on n but not on the training sample.

From now on we take $Q(w) = w^2$ and assume that $A = \mathbb{E}\, X^2 = 1$ (which could be arranged by a linear change of variables). Referring back to formulas in the previous section, we see that

$$(8) \qquad r(\hat{w}_n(k)) - r(w^*) = (\bar{V}_n - kw^*)^2 / (\bar{U}_n + 1 + k)^2 =: h(\bar{U}_n, \bar{V}_n, k),$$

whence $J_n(k) = \mathbb{E}\, h(\bar{U}_n, \bar{V}_n, k)$, where we have introduced the function h (used heavily in what follows) as well as the arithmetic means $\bar{U}_n$ and $\bar{V}_n$

$$(9) \qquad \bar{U}_n := \frac{1}{n} \sum_1^n U_i, \quad \bar{V}_n := \frac{1}{n} \sum_1^n V_i, \quad \text{with}$$

$$(10) \qquad U_i := X_i^2 - 1, \quad V_i := X_i Y_i - w^* X_i^2$$

For convenience, also define $U := X^2 - 1$ and $V := XY - w^* X^2$. Notice that $U; U_1, U_2, \ldots$ are zero mean i.i.d. random variables, and that $V; V_1, V_2, \ldots$ satisfy the same conditions. Hence $\bar{U}_n$ and $\bar{V}_n$ converge to zero, and this leads to the idea of using the Taylor expansion of $h(u, v, k)$ about the point $(u, v) = (0, 0)$ in order to get an expansion for $J_n(k)$.

To outline the ideas, let $T_j(u, v, k)$ be the degree j Taylor polynomial of $(u, v) \mapsto h(u, v, k)$ about $(0, 0)$, i.e., $T_j(u, v, k)$ is a polynomial in u and v whose coefficients are functions of k and whose degree with respect to u and v is j. Then $\mathbb{E}\, T_j(\bar{U}_n, \bar{V}_n, k)$ depends on n and moments of U and V. By deriving an upper bound for the quantity $\mathbb{E}\, |h(\bar{U}_n, \bar{V}_n, k) - T_j(\bar{U}_n, \bar{V}_n, k)|$ we get an upper bound for the error committed in approximating $J_n(k)$ by $\mathbb{E}\, T_j(\bar{U}_n, \bar{V}_n, k)$. It turns out that for odd degrees j the error is of the same order of magnitude in n as for degree $j - 1$. Therefore we only consider even degrees j. It also turns out that the error bounds are uniform in $k \geq 0$ whenever $j \geq 2$. To proceed, we need to introduce assumptions.

Assumption 1 $\mathbb{E}\, |X|^r < \infty$ and $\mathbb{E}\, |Y|^s < \infty$ for high enough r and s.

Assumption 2 Either (a) for some constant $\beta > 0$ almost surely $|X| \geq \beta$ or (b) X has a density which is bounded in some neighborhood of zero.

Assumption 1 guarantees the existence of high enough moments; the values $r = 20$ and $s = .8$ are sufficient for the following proofs. E.g., if the pair (X, Y) has a normal distribution or a distribution with compact support, then moments of all orders exist and hence in this case assumption 1 would be satisfied. Without some condition such as assumption 2, $J_n(0)$ might fail to be meaningful or finite. The following technical result is stated without proof.

Proposition 2 Let $p > 0$ and let $0 < \mathbb{E}\, X^2 < \infty$. If assumption 2 holds, then

$$\mathbb{E}\left\{ \left[\frac{1}{n}(X_1^2 + \cdots + X_n^2) \right]^{-p} \right\} \to \left[\mathbb{E}\,(X^2) \right]^{-p}, \quad as \quad n \to \infty,$$

where the expectation on the left is finite (a) for $n \geq 1$ (b) for $n > 2p$ provided that assumption 2 (a), respectively 2 (b) holds.

Proposition 3 Let assumptions 1 and 2 hold. Then there exist constants n_0 and M such that

$$J_n(k) = \mathbb{E}\, T_2(\bar{U}_n, \bar{V}_n, k) + R(n, k) \quad where$$
$$\mathbb{E}\, T_2(\bar{U}_n, \bar{V}_n, k) = \frac{(w^*)^2 k^2}{(1 + k)^2} + n^{-1}\left[\frac{\mathbb{E}\, V^2}{(1 + k)^2} + 3\frac{(w^*)^2 k^2 \mathbb{E}\, U^2}{(1 + k)^4} + 4\frac{w^* k \mathbb{E}\, UV}{(1 + k)^3} \right]$$
$$|R(n, k)| \leq Mn^{-3/2}(k + 1)^{-1}, \quad \forall n \geq n_0, k \geq 0.$$

PROOF SKETCH The formula for $\mathbb{E}\, T_2(\bar{U}_n, \bar{V}_n, k)$ follows easily by integrating the degree two Taylor polynomial term by term. To get the upper bound for $R(n, k)$, consider the residual

$$h(u, v, k) - T_2(u, v, k) = \frac{-2(k + 1)^3 uv^2 + -4(w^*)^2 k^2(k + 1)u^3 + \cdots}{(u + 1 + k)^2(k + 1)^4},$$

where we have omitted four similar terms. Using the bound

$$(\bar{U}_n + 1 + k)^2 = \left(\frac{1}{n}\sum_1^n X_i^2 + k \right)^2 \geq \left(\frac{1}{n}\sum_1^n X_i^2 \right)^2, \quad \forall k \geq 0,$$

the L_1 triangle inequality, and the Cauchy-Schwartz inequality, we get

$$|R(n,k)| = |\mathbb{E}\left[h(\bar{U}_n, \bar{V}_n, k) - T_2(\bar{U}_n, \bar{V}_n, k)\right]|$$

$$\leq (k+1)^{-4} \left\{\mathbb{E}\left[\left(\frac{1}{n}\sum_1^n X_i^2\right)^{-4}\right]\right\}^{1/2}$$

$$\left\{2(k+1)^3[\mathbb{E}\left(|\bar{U}_n|^2|\bar{V}_n|^4\right)]^{1/2} + 4(w^*)^2 k^2(k+1)[\mathbb{E}\,|\bar{U}_n|^6]^{1/2}\ldots\right\}$$

By proposition 2, here $\mathbb{E}\left[(\frac{1}{n}\sum_1^n X_i^2)^{-4}\right] = O(1)$. Next we use the following fact, cf. (Serfling, 1980, Lemma B, p. 68).

Fact 1 *Let $\{Z_i\}$ be i.i.d. with $\mathbb{E}[Z_1] = 0$ and with $\mathbb{E}|Z_1|^\nu < \infty$ for some $\nu \geq 2$. Then*

$$\mathbb{E}\left|\frac{1}{n}\sum_1^n Z_i\right|^\nu = O(n^{-\nu/2})$$

Applying the Cauchy-Schwartz inequality and this fact, we get, e.g., that

$$[\mathbb{E}\left(|\bar{U}_n|^2|\bar{V}_n|^4\right)]^{1/2} \leq [(\mathbb{E}\,|\bar{U}_n|^4)^{1/2}(\mathbb{E}\,|\bar{V}_n|^8)^{1/2}]^{1/2} = O(n^{-3/2}).$$

Going through all the terms carefully, we see that the bound holds.   □

Proposition 4 *Let assumptions 1 and 2 hold, assume that $w^* \neq 0$, and set*

$$\alpha_1 := (\mathbb{E}\,V^2 - 2w^*\mathbb{E}\,[UV])/(w^*)^2.$$

If $\alpha_1 > 0$, then there exists a constant n_1 such that for all $n \geq n_1$ the function $k \mapsto \mathbb{E}\,T_2(\bar{U}_n, \bar{V}_n, k)$ has a unique minimum on $[0, \infty)$ at the point k_n^* admitting the expansion

$$k_n^* = \alpha_1 n^{-1} + O(n^{-2}); \quad further,$$

$$J_n(0) - \inf\{J_n(k) : k \geq 0\} = J_n(0) - J_n(\alpha_1 n^{-1}) = \alpha_1^2(w^*)^2 n^{-2} + O(n^{-5/2}).$$

If $\alpha \leq 0$, then

$$\inf\{J_n(k) : k \geq 0\} = J_n(0) + O(n^{-5/2}).$$

PROOF SKETCH The proof is based on perturbation expansion considering $1/n$ a small parameter. By the previous proposition, $S_n(k) := \mathbb{E}\,T_2(\bar{U}_n, \bar{V}_n, k)$ is the sum of $(w^*)^2 k^2/(1+k)^2$ and a term whose supremum over $k \geq k_0 > -1$ goes to zero as $n \to \infty$. Here the first term has a unique minimum on $(-1, \infty)$ at $k = 0$. Differentiating S_n we get

$$S_n'(k) = [2(w^*)^2 k(k+1)^2 + n^{-1}p_2(k)]/(k+1)^5,$$

where $p_2(k)$ is a second degree polynomial in k. The numerator polynomial has three roots, one of which converges to zero as $n \to \infty$. A regular perturbation expansion for this root, $k_n^* = \alpha_1 n^{-1} + \alpha_2 n^{-2} + \ldots$, yields the stated formula for α_1. This point is a minimum for all sufficiently large n; further, it is greater than zero for all sufficiently large n if and only if $\alpha_1 > 0$.

The estimate for $J_n(0) - \inf\{J_n(k) : k \geq 0\}$ in the case $\alpha_1 > 0$ follows by noticing that

$$J_n(0) - J_n(k) = \mathbb{E}\,[h(\bar{U}_n, \bar{V}_n, 0) - h(\bar{U}_n, \bar{V}_n, k)],$$

where we now use a third degree Taylor expansion about $(u, v, k) = (0, 0, 0)$

$$h(u, v, 0) - h(u, v, k) =$$

$$2w^* kv - (w^*)^2 k^2 - 4w^* kuv + 2(w^*)^2 k^2 u + 2kv^2 - 4w^* k^2 v + 2(w^*)^2 k^3 + r(u, v, k).$$

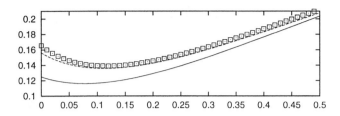

Figure 1: Illustration of the asymptotic approximations in the situation of equation (11). Horizontal axis k; vertical axis $J_n(k)$ and its asymptotic approximations. Legend: markers $J_n(k)$; solid line $\mathbb{E}\,T_2(\bar{U}_n, \bar{V}_n, k)$; dashed line $\mathbb{E}\,T_4(\bar{U}_n, \bar{V}_n, k)$.

Using the techniques of the previous proposition, it can be shown that $\mathbb{E}\,|r(\bar{U}_n, \bar{V}_n, k_n^*)| = O(n^{-5/2})$. Integrating the Taylor polynomial and using this estimate gives

$$J_n(0) - J_n(\alpha_1/n) = \alpha_1^2(w^*)^2 n^{-2} + O(n^{-5/2}).$$

Finally, by the mean value theorem,

$$J_n(0) - \inf\{J_n(k) : k \geq 0\} = J_n(0) - J_n(\alpha_1/n) + \frac{d}{dk}[J_n(0) - J_n(k)]_{|k=\theta}(k_n^* - \alpha_1/n)$$

$$= J_n(0) - J_n(\alpha_1/n) + O(n^{-1})O(n^{-2})$$

where θ lies between k_n^* and α_1/n, and where we have used the fact that the indicated derivative evaluated at θ is of order $O(n^{-1})$, as can be shown with moderate effort. $\square$

Remark In the preceding we assumed that $A = \mathbb{E}\,X^2$ equals 1. If this is not the case, then the formula for α_1 has to be divided by A; again, if $\alpha_1 > 0$, then $k_n^* = \alpha_1 n^{-1} + O(n^{-2})$.

If the model is correctly specified in the sense that $Y = w^* X + \epsilon$, where ϵ is independent of X and $\mathbb{E}\,\epsilon = 0$, then $V = X\epsilon$ and $\mathbb{E}\,[UV] = 0$. Hence we have $\alpha_1 = \mathbb{E}\,[\epsilon^2]/(w^*)^2$, and this is strictly positive expect in the degenerate case where $\epsilon = 0$ with probability one. This means that here regularization helps provided the regularization parameter is chosen around the value α_1/n and n is large enough. See Figure 1 for an illustration in the case

$$(11) \qquad X \sim N(0,1), \quad Y = w^* X + \epsilon, \quad \epsilon \sim N(0,1), \quad w^* = 1,$$

where ϵ and X are independent. $J_n(k)$ is estimated on the basis of 1000 repetitions of the task for $n = 8$. In addition to $\mathbb{E}\,T_2(\bar{U}_n, \bar{V}_n, k)$ the function $\mathbb{E}\,T_4(\bar{U}_n, \bar{V}_n, k)$ is also plotted. The latter can be shown to give $J_n(k)$ correctly up to order $O(n^{-5/2}(k+1)^{-3})$. Notice that although $\mathbb{E}\,T_2(\bar{U}_n, \bar{V}_n, k)$ does not give that good an approximation for $J_n(k)$, its minimizer is near the minimizer of $J_n(k)$, and both of these minimizers lie near the point $\alpha_1/n = 0.125$ as predicted by the theory. In the situation (11) it can actually be shown by lengthy calculations that the minimizer of $J_n(k)$ is exactly α_1/n for each sample size $n \geq 1$.

It is possible to construct cases where $\alpha_1 < 0$. For instance, take

$$X \sim \text{Uniform}(a, b), \quad a = \frac{1}{2}, b = \frac{1}{4}(3\sqrt{5} - 1)$$

$$Y = c/X + d + Z, \quad c = -5, d = 8,$$

and $Z \sim N(0, \sigma^2)$ with Z and X independent and $0 \leq \sigma < 1.1$. In such a case regularization using a positive regularization parameter only makes matters worse; using a properly chosen *negative* regularization parameter would, however, help in this particular case. This would, however, amount to rewarding rapidly changing functions. In the case (11) regularization using a negative value for the regularization parameter would be catastrophic.

4   DISCUSSION

We have obtained asymptotic approximations for the optimal regularization parameter in (1) and the amount of improvement (3) in the simple case of one-dimensional linear regression when the regularization parameter is chosen independently of the training sample. It turned out that the optimal regularization parameter is, to leading order, given by $\alpha_1 n^{-1}$ and the resulting improvement is of order $O(n^{-2})$. We have also seen that if $\alpha_1 < 0$ then regularization only makes matters worse.

Also (Larsen and Hansen, 1994) have obtained asymptotic results for the optimal regularization parameter in (1). They consider the case of a nonlinear network; however, they assume that the neural network model is correctly specified.

The generalization of the present results to the nonlinear, misspecified case might be possible using, e.g., techniques from (Bhattacharya and Ghosh, 1978). Generalization to the case where the regularization parameter is chosen on the basis of the sample (say, by cross validation) would be desirable.

Acknowledgements

This paper was prepared while the author was visiting the Department for Statistics and Probability Theory at the Vienna University of Technology with financial support from the Academy of Finland. I thank F. Leisch for useful discussions.

References

Bhattacharya, R. N. and Ghosh, J. K. (1978). On the validity of the formal Edgeworth expansion. *The Annals of Statistics*, 6(2):434–451.

Bishop, C. M. (1995). *Neural Networks for Pattern Recognition*. Oxford University Press.

Brockwell, P. J. and Davis, R. A. (1987). *Time Series: Theory and Methods*. Springer series in statistics. Springer-Verlag.

Hoerl, A. E. and Kennard, R. W. (1988). Ridge regression. In Kotz, S., Johnson, N. L., and Read, C. B., editors, *Encyclopedia of Statistical Sciences*. John Wiley & Sons, Inc.

Larsen, J. and Hansen, L. K. (1994). Generalization performance of regularized neural network models. In Vlontos, J., Whang, J.-N., and Wilson, E., editors, *Proc. of the 4th IEEE Workshop on Neural Networks for Signal Processing*, pages 42–51. IEEE Press.

Ripley, B. D. (1996). *Pattern Recognition and Neural Networks*. Cambridge University Press.

Serfling, R. J. (1980). *Approximation Theorems of Mathematical Statistics*. John Wiley & Sons, Inc.

Titterington, D. M. (1985). Common structure of smoothing techniques in statistics. *International Statistical Review*, 53:141–170.

Two Approaches to Optimal Annealing

Todd K. Leen
Dept of Comp. Sci. & Engineering
Oregon Graduate Institute of
Science and Technology
P.O.Box 91000, Portland,
Oregon 97291-1000
tleen@cse.ogi.edu

Bernhard Schottky and David Saad
Neural Computing Research Group
Dept of Comp. Sci. & Appl. Math.
Aston University
Birmingham, B4 7ET, UK
schottba{saadd}@aston.ac.uk

Abstract

We employ both master equation and order parameter approaches
to analyze the asymptotic dynamics of on-line learning with different learning rate annealing schedules. We examine the relations
between the results obtained by the two approaches and obtain new
results on the optimal decay coefficients and their dependence on
the number of hidden nodes in a two layer architecture.

1 Introduction

The asymptotic dynamics of stochastic on-line learning and it's dependence on the
annealing schedule adopted for the learning coefficients have been studied for some
time in the stochastic approximation literature [1, 2] and more recently in the neural
network literature [3, 4, 5]. The latter studies are based on examining the Kramers-
Moyal expansion of the master equation for the weight space probability densities.
A different approach, based on the deterministic dynamics of macroscopic quantities
called order parameters, has been recently presented [6, 7]. This approach enables
one to monitor the evolution of the order parameters and the system performance
at all times.

In this paper we examine the relation between the two approaches and contrast the
results obtained for different learning rate annealing schedules in the asymptotic
regime. We employ the order parameter approach to examine the dependence of
the dynamics on the number of hidden nodes in a multilayer system. In addition,
we report some lesser-known results on non-standard annealing schedules

2   Master Equation

Most on-line learning algorithms assume the form $w_{t+1} = w_t + \eta_0/t^p \, H(w_t, x_t)$ where w_t is the weight at time t, x_t is the training example, and $H(w, x)$ is the weight update. The description of the algorithm's dynamics in terms of weight space probability densities starts from the master equation

$$P(w', t+1) = \int dw \left\langle \delta\left(w' - w - \frac{\eta_0}{t^p} H(w, x)\right) \right\rangle_x P(w, t) \tag{1}$$

where $\langle \ldots \rangle_x$ indicates averaging with respect to the measure on x, $P(w, t)$ is the probability density on weights at time t, and $\delta(\ldots)$ is the Dirac function. One may use the Kramers-Moyal expansion of Eq.(1) to derive a partial differential equation for the weight probability density (here in one dimension for simplicity) [3, 4]

$$\partial_t P(w, t) = \sum_{i=1}^{\infty} \frac{(-1)^i}{i!} \left(\frac{\eta_0}{t^p}\right)^i \partial_w^i \left[\langle H^i(w, x) \rangle_x P(w, t)\right] . \tag{2}$$

Following [3], we make a small noise expansion for (2) by decomposing the weight trajectory into a deterministic and stochastic pieces

$$w \equiv \phi(t) + \left(\frac{\eta_0}{t^p}\right)^\gamma \xi \quad \text{or} \quad \xi = \left(\frac{\eta_0}{t^p}\right)^{-\gamma} (w - \phi(t)) \tag{3}$$

where $\phi(t)$ is the deterministic trajectory, and ξ are the fluctuations. Apart from the factor $(\eta_0/t^p)^\gamma$ that scales the fluctuations, this is identical to the formulation for constant learning in [3]. The proper value for the unspecified exponent γ will emerge from homogeneity requirements. Next, the dependence of the jump moments $\langle H^i(w, x) \rangle_x$ on η_0 is explicated by a Taylor series expansion about the deterministic path ϕ. The coefficients in this series expansion are denoted

$$\alpha_i^{(j)} \equiv \partial^j \langle H^i(w, x) \rangle_x / \partial w^j \big|_{w=\phi}$$

Finally one rewrites (2) in terms of ϕ and ξ and the expansion of the jump moments, taking care to transform the differential operators in accordance with (3).

These transformations leave equations of motion for ϕ and the density $\Pi(\xi, t)$ on the fluctuations

$$\frac{d\phi}{dt} = \left(\frac{\eta_0}{t^p}\right) \alpha_1^{(0)}(\phi) = \left(\frac{\eta_0}{t^p}\right) \langle H(\phi, x) \rangle_x \tag{4}$$

$$\partial_t \Pi = -\frac{\gamma p}{t} \partial_\xi(\xi \Pi) + \sum_{m=2}^{\infty} \sum_{i=1}^{m} \frac{(-1)^i}{i!(m-i)!} \alpha_i^{(m-i)} \left(\frac{\eta_0}{t^p}\right)^{i(1-2\gamma)+m\gamma} \partial_\xi^i(\xi^{(m-i)} \Pi) . \tag{5}$$

For stochastic descent $H(w, x) = -\nabla_w E(w, x)$ and (4) describes the evolution of ϕ as descent on the average cost. The fluctuation equation (5) requires further manipulation whose form depends on the context. For the usual case of descent in a quadratic minimum ($\alpha_1^{(1)} = -G$, minus the cost function curvature), we take $\gamma = 1/2$ to insure that for any m, terms in the sum are homogeneous in η_0/t^p

For *constant* learning rate ($p = 0$), rescaling time as $t \to \eta_0 t$ allows (5) to be written in a form convenient for perturbative analysis in η_0 Typically, the limit $\eta_0 \to 0$ is invoked and only the lowest order terms in η_0 retained (e.g. [3]). These comprise a diffusion operator, which results in a Gaussian approximation for equilibrium densities. Higher order terms have been successfully used to calculate corrections to the equilibrium moments in powers of η_0 [8].

Of primary interest here is the case of annealed learning, as required for convergence of the parameter estimates. Again assuming a quadratic bowl and $\gamma = 1/2$, the first few terms of (5) are

$$\partial_t \Pi = -\frac{p}{2t}\,\partial_\xi(\xi\,\Pi) - \alpha_1^{(1)}\,\frac{\eta_0}{t^p}\,\partial_\xi(\xi\,\Pi) + \frac{1}{2}\alpha_2^{(0)}\,\frac{\eta_0}{t^p}\,\partial_\xi^2\,\Pi + \mathcal{O}\left(\frac{\eta_0}{t^p}\right)^{3/2} . \qquad (6)$$

As $t \to \infty$ the right hand side of (6) is dominated by the first three terms (since $0 < p \le 1$). Precisely which terms dominate depends on p.

We will first review the classical case $p = 1$. Asymptotically $\phi \to w^*$, a local optimum. The first three leading terms on the right hand side of (6) are all of order $1/t$. For $t \to \infty$, we discard the remaining terms. From the resulting equation we recover a Gaussian equilibrium distribution for ξ, or equivalently for $\sqrt{t}\,(w - w^*) \equiv \sqrt{t}v$ where v is called the *weight error*. The asymptotically normal distribution for $\sqrt{t}v$ has variance $\sigma^2_{\sqrt{t}v}$ from which the asymptotic expected squared weight error can be derived

$$\lim_{t \to \infty} E[|v|^2] = \sigma^2_{\sqrt{t}v}\,\frac{1}{t} = \frac{\eta_0^2\,\alpha_2^{(0)}}{2\eta_0\,G^* - 1}\,\frac{1}{t} \qquad (7)$$

where $G^* \equiv G(w^*)$ is the curvature at the local optimum.

Positive $\sigma_{\sqrt{t}v}$ requires $\eta_0 > 1/(2G^*)$. If this condition is *not* met the expected squared weight offset converges as $(1/t)^{1-2\eta_0 G^*}$, *slower* than $1/t$ [5, for example, and references therein]. The above confirms the classical results [1] on asymptotic normality and convergence rate for $1/t$ annealing.

For the case $0 < p < 1$, the second and third terms on the right hand side of (6) will dominate as $t \to \infty$. Again, we have a Gaussian equilibrium density for ξ. Consequently $\sqrt{t^p}\,v$ is asymptotically normal with variance $\sigma^2_{\sqrt{t^p}v}$ leading to the expected squared weight error

$$E[|v|^2] = \sigma^2_{\sqrt{t^p}v}\,\frac{1}{t^p} = \frac{\eta_0\,\alpha_2^{(0)}}{2G}\,\frac{1}{t^p} \qquad (8)$$

Notice that the convergence is *slower* than $1/t$ and that there is *no* critical value of the learning rate to obtain a sensible equilibrium distribution. (See [9] for earlier results on $1/t^p$ annealing.)

The generalization error follows the same decay rate as the expected weight offset. In one dimension, the expected squared weight offset is directly related to excess generalization error (the generalization error minus the least generalization error achievable) $\epsilon_g = G\,E[v^2]$. In multiple dimensions, the expected squared weight offset, together with the maximum and minimum eigenvalues of G^* provide upper and lower bounds on the excess generalization error proportional to $E[|v|^2]$, with the criticality condition on G^* (for $p = 1$)replaced with an analogous condition on its eigenvalues.

3 Order parameters

In the Master equation approach, one focuses attention on the weight space distribution $P(w,t)$ and calculates quantities of interested by averaging over this density. An alternative approach is to choose a smaller set of *macroscopic* variables that are sufficient for describing principal properties of the system such as the generalization error (in contrast to the evolution of the weights w which are *microscopic*).

Formally, one can replace the parameter dynamics presented in Eq.(1) by the corresponding equation for macroscopic observables which can be easily derived from the corresponding expressions for w. By choosing an appropriate set of macroscopic variables and invoking the thermodynamic limit (i.e., looking at systems where the number of parameters is infinite), one obtains point distributions for the order parameters, rendering the dynamics deterministic.

Several researchers [6, 7] have employed this approach for calculating the training dynamics of a soft committee machine (SCM) . The SCM maps inputs $x \in \Re^N$ to a scalar, through a model $\rho(\mathbf{w}, \boldsymbol{x}) = \sum_{i=1}^{K} g(\mathbf{w}_i \cdot \boldsymbol{x})$. The activation function of the hidden units is $g(u) \equiv \mathrm{erf}(u/\sqrt{2})$ and $\mathbf{w}_i$ is the set of input-to-hidden adaptive weights for the $i = 1 \ldots K$ hidden nodes. The hidden-to-output weights are set to 1. This architecture preserves most of the properties of the learning dynamics and the evolution of the generalization error as a general two-layer network, and the formalism can be easily extended to accommodate adaptive hidden-to-output weights [10].

Input vectors x are independently drawn with zero mean and unit variance, and the corresponding targets y are generated by deterministic teacher network corrupted by additive Gaussian output noise of zero mean and variance σ_ν^2. The teacher network is also a SCM, with input-to-hidden weights $\mathbf{w}_i^*$. The order parameters sufficient to close the dynamics, and to describe the network generalization error are overlaps between various input-to-hidden vectors $\mathbf{w}_i \cdot \mathbf{w}_k \equiv Q_{ik}$, $\mathbf{w}_i \cdot \mathbf{w}_n^* \equiv R_{in}$, and $\mathbf{w}_n^* \cdot \mathbf{w}_m^* \equiv T_{nm}$.

Network performance is measured in terms of the generalization error $\epsilon_g(\mathbf{w}) \equiv \langle 1/2\,[\,\rho(\mathbf{w}, \boldsymbol{x}) - y\,]^2 \rangle_x$. The generalization error can be expressed in closed form in terms of the order parameters in the thermodynamic limit ($N \to \infty$). The dynamics of the latter are also obtained in closed form [7]. These dynamics are coupled nonlinear ordinary differential equations whose solution can only be obtained through numerical integration. However, the *asymptotic* behavior in the case of annealed learning *is* amenable to analysis, and this is one of the primary results of the paper.

We assume an isotropic teacher $T_{nm} = \delta_{nm}$ and use this symmetry to reduce the system to a vector of four order parameters $u^T = (r, q, s, c)$ related to the overlaps by $R_{in} = \delta_{in}(1 + r) + (1 - \delta_{in})s$ and $Q_{ik} = \delta_{ik}(1 + q) + (1 - \delta_{ik})c$.

With learning rate annealing and $\lim_{t\to\infty} u = 0$ we describe the dynamics in this vicinity by a linearization of the equations of motion in [7]. The linearization is

$$\frac{d}{dt}\mathbf{u} = \eta M\mathbf{u} + \eta^2 \sigma_\nu^2 \mathbf{b}, \qquad (9)$$

where σ_ν^2 is the noise variance, $\mathbf{b}^T = \frac{2}{\pi}\left(0, 1/\sqrt{3}, 0, 1/2\right)$, $\eta = \eta_0/t^p$, and M is

$$M = \frac{2}{3\sqrt{3}\pi} \begin{pmatrix} -4 & \frac{3}{2} & -\frac{9}{4}(K-1)\sqrt{(3)} & \frac{3}{4}(K-1)\sqrt{3} \\ 4 & -3 & \frac{3}{2}(K-1)\sqrt{3} & -\frac{3}{2}(K-1)\sqrt{3} \\ -\frac{3}{2}\sqrt{3} & \frac{3}{8}\sqrt{3} & -\frac{3}{2}(K-2)+\frac{2}{\sqrt{3}} & 0 \\ 3\sqrt{3} & -\frac{9}{4}\sqrt{3} & 3\sqrt{3}(K-2)+\frac{2}{\sqrt{3}} & -3\sqrt{3}(K-2)+\frac{2}{\sqrt{3}} \end{pmatrix}, \qquad (10)$$

The asymptotic equations of motion (9) were derived by dropping terms of order $\mathcal{O}(\eta\|\mathbf{u}\|^2)$ and higher, *and* terms of order $\mathcal{O}(\eta^2\,\mathbf{u})$. While the latter are linear in the order parameters, they are dominated by the $\eta\,\mathbf{u}$ and $\eta^2\sigma_\nu^2\mathbf{b}$ terms in (9) as $t \to \infty$.

This choice of truncations sheds light on the approach to equilibrium that is not implicit in the master equation approach. In the latter, the dominant terms for the asymptotics of (6) were identified by time scale of the coefficients, there was no identification of system observables that signal when the asymptotic regime is entered. For the order parameter approach, the conditions for validity of the asymptotic approximations are cast in terms of system observables $\eta \mathbf{u}$ vs $\eta^2 \mathbf{u}$ vs $\eta^2 \sigma_\nu^2$.

The solution to (9) is

$$\mathbf{u}(t) = \gamma(t, t_0)\, \mathbf{u}_0 + \sigma_\nu^2\, \beta(t, t_0)\, \mathbf{b} \tag{11}$$

where $\mathbf{u}_0 \equiv \mathbf{u}(t_0)$ and

$$\gamma(t, t_0) = \exp\left\{ M \int_{t_0}^{t} d\tau\, \eta(\tau) \right\} \quad \text{and} \quad \beta(t, t_0) = \int_{t_0}^{t} d\tau\, \gamma(t, \tau)\, \eta^2(\tau). \tag{12}$$

The asymptotic order parameter dynamics allow us to compute the generalization error (to first order in $\mathbf{u}$)

$$\epsilon_l = \frac{K}{\pi} \left(\frac{1}{\sqrt{3}} (q - 2r) + \frac{K-1}{2} (c - 2s) \right). \tag{13}$$

Using the solution of Eq.(11), the generalization error consists of two pieces: a contribution depending on the actual initial conditions $\mathbf{u}_0$ and a contribution due to the second term on the r.h.s. of Eq.(11), independent of $\mathbf{u}_0$. The former decays more rapidly than the latter, and we ignore it in what follows. Asymptotically, the generalization error is of the form $\epsilon_l = \sigma_\nu^2(c_1\theta_1(t) + c_2\theta_2(t))$, where c_i are K dependent coefficients, and θ_i are eigenmodes that evolve as

$$\theta_i = -\frac{\eta_0^2}{1 + \alpha_i \eta_0} \left[\frac{1}{t} - t^{\alpha_i \eta_0} t_0^{-(\alpha_i \eta_0 + 1)} \right]. \tag{14}$$

with eigenvalues (Fig. 1(a))

$$\alpha_1 = -\frac{1}{\pi} \left(\frac{4}{\sqrt{3}} - 2 \right) \quad \text{and} \quad \alpha_2 = -\frac{1}{\pi} \left(\frac{4}{\sqrt{3}} + 2(K - 1) \right) \tag{15}$$

The critical learning rate η_0^{crit}, above which the generalization decays as $1/t$ is, for $K \geq 2$,

$$\eta_0^{\text{crit}} = \max\left(-\frac{1}{\alpha_1}, -\frac{1}{\alpha_2} \right) = \frac{\pi}{4/\sqrt{3} - 2}. \tag{16}$$

For $\eta_0 > \eta_0^{\text{crit}}$ both modes $\theta_i, i = 1, 2$ decay as $1/t$, and so

$$\epsilon_l = -\sigma_\nu^2 \eta_0^2 \left(\frac{c_1}{1 + \alpha_1 \eta_0} + \frac{c_2}{1 + \alpha_2 \eta_0} \right) \frac{1}{t} \equiv \sigma_\nu^2 f(\eta_0, K) \frac{1}{t}. \tag{17}$$

Minimizing the prefactor $f(\eta_0, K)$ in (17) minimizes the asymptotic error. The values $\eta_0^{\text{opt}}(K)$ are shown in Fig. 1(b), where the special case of $K = 1$ (see below) is also included: There is a significant difference between the values for $K = 1$ and $K = 2$ and a rather weak dependence on K for $K \geq 2$. The sensitivity of the generalization error decay factor on the choice of η_0 is shown in Fig. 1(c).

The influence of the noise strength on the generalization error can be seen directly from (17): the noise variance σ_ν^2 is just a prefactor scaling the $1/t$ decay. Neither the value for the critical nor for the optimal η_0 is influenced by it.

The calculation above holds for the case $K = 1$ (where c and s and the mode θ_1 are absent). In this case

$$\eta_0^{\mathrm{opt}}(K = 1) = 2\eta_0^{\mathrm{crit}}(K = 1) = -\frac{2}{\alpha_2} = \frac{\sqrt{3}\pi}{2}. \tag{18}$$

Finally, for the general annealing schedule of the form $\eta = \eta_0/t^p$ with $0 < p < 1$ the equations of motion (11) can be investigated, and one again finds $1/t^p$ decay.

4 Discussion and summary

We employed master equation and order parameter approaches to study the convergence of on-line learning under different annealing schedules. For the $1/t$ annealing schedule, the small noise expansion provides a critical value of η_0 (7) in terms of the curvature, above which $\sqrt{t}\,v$ is asymptotically normal, and the generalization decays as $1/t$. The approach is general, but requires knowledge of the first two jump moments in the asymptotic regime for calculating the relevant properties.

By restricting the order parameters approach to a symmetric task characterized by a set of isotropic teacher vectors, one can explicitly solve the dynamics in the asymptotic regime for any number of hidden nodes, and provide explicit expressions for the decaying generalization error and for the critical (16) and optimal learning rate prefactors for any number of hidden nodes K. Moreover, one can study the sensitivity of the generalization error decay to the choice of this prefactor. Similar results have been obtained for the critical learning rate prefactors using both methods, and both methods have been used to study general $1/t^p$ annealing. However, the order parameters approach enables one to gain a complete description of the dynamics and additional insight by restricting the task examined. Finally the order parameters approach expresses the dynamics in terms of ordinary differential equations, rather than partial differential equations; a clear advantage for numerical investigations.

The order parameter approach provides a potentially helpful insight on the passage into the asymptotic regime. Unlike the truncation of the small noise expansion, the truncation of the order parameter equations to obtain the asymptotic dynamics is couched in terms of system observables (c.f. the discussion following (10)). That is, one knows exactly which observables must be dominant for the system to be in the asymptotic regime. Equivalently, starting from the full equations, the order parameters approach can tell us when the system is close to the equilibrium distribution.

Although we obtained a full description of the asymptotic dynamics, it is still unclear how relevant it is in the larger picture which includes *all* stages of the training process, as in many cases it takes a prohibitively long time for the system to reach the asymptotic regime. It would be interesting to find a way of extending this framework to gain insight into earlier stages of the learning process.

Acknowledgements: DS and BS would like to thank the Leverhulme Trust for their support (F/250/K). TL thanks the International Human Frontier Science Program (SF 473-96), and the NSF (ECS-9704094) for their support.

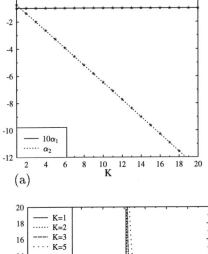

(a)

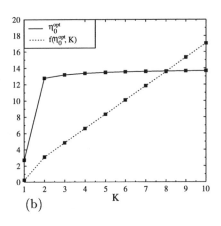

(b)

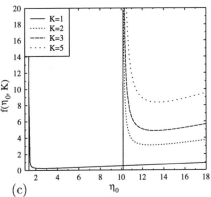

(c)

Figure 1: (a) The dependence of the eigenvalues of M on the the number of hidden units K. Note that the constant eigenvalue α_1 dominates the convergence for $K \geq 2$. (b) η_0^{opt} and the resulting generalization prefactor $f(\eta_0^{opt}, K)$ of (17) as a function of K. (c) The dependence of the generalization error decay prefactor $f(\eta_0, K)$ on the choice of η_0.

References

[1] V. Fabian. *Ann. Math. Statist.*, **39**, 1327 1968.

[2] L. Goldstein. Technical Report DRB-306, Dept. of Mathematics, University of Southern California, LA, 1987.

[3] T. M. Heskes and B. Kappen, *Phys. Rev. A* **44**, 2718 (1991).

[4] T. K. Leen and J. E. Moody. In Giles, Hanson, and Cowan, editors, *Advances in Neural Information Processing Systems, 5*, 451, San Mateo, CA, 1993. Morgan Kaufmann.

[5] T. K. Leen and G. B. Orr. In J.D. Cowan, G. Tesauro, and J. Alspector, editors, *Advances in Neural Information Processing Systems 6*, 477 ,San Francisco, CA., 1994. Morgan Kaufmann Publishers.

[6] M. Biehl and H. Schwarze, *J. Phys. A* **28**, 643 (1995).

[7] D. Saad and S.A. Solla *Phys. Rev. Lett.* **74**, 4337 (1995) and *Phys. Rev. E* **52** 4225 (1995).

[8] G. B. Orr. *Dynamics and Algorithms for Stochastic Search.* PhD thesis, Oregon Graduate Institute, October 1996.

[9] Naama Barkai. *Statistical Mechanics of Learning.* PhD thesis, Hebrew University of Jerusalem, August 1995.

[10] P. Riegler and M. Biehl *J. Phys. A* **28**, L507 (1995).

Structural Risk Minimization for Nonparametric Time Series Prediction

Ron Meir*
Department of Electrical Engineering
Technion, Haifa 32000, Israel
rmeir@dumbo.technion.ac.il

Abstract

The problem of time series prediction is studied within the uniform convergence framework of Vapnik and Chervonenkis. The dependence inherent in the temporal structure is incorporated into the analysis, thereby generalizing the available theory for memoryless processes. Finite sample bounds are calculated in terms of covering numbers of the approximating class, and the tradeoff between approximation and estimation is discussed. A complexity regularization approach is outlined, based on Vapnik's method of Structural Risk Minimization, and shown to be applicable in the context of mixing stochastic processes.

1 Time Series Prediction and Mixing Processes

A great deal of effort has been expended in recent years on the problem of deriving robust distribution-free error bounds for learning, mainly in the context of memoryless processes (e.g. [9]). On the other hand, an extensive amount of work has been devoted by statisticians and econometricians to the study of parametric (often linear) models of time series, where the dependence inherent in the sample, precludes straightforward application of many of the standard results form the theory of memoryless processes. In this work we propose an extension of the framework pioneered by Vapnik and Chervonenkis to the problem of time series prediction. Some of the more elementary proofs are sketched, while the main technical results will be proved in detail in the full version of the paper.

Consider a stationary stochastic process $\bar{X} = \{\cdots, X_{-1}, X_0, X_1, \ldots\}$, where X_i is a random variable defined over a compact domain in $\mathbf{R}$ and such that $|X_i| \leq B$ with probability 1, for some positive constant B. The problem of one-step prediction, in the mean square sense, can then be phrased as that of finding a function $f(\cdot)$ of the infinite past, such that $\mathrm{E}\left|X_0 - f(X_{-\infty}^{-1})\right|^2$ is minimal, where we use the notation $X_i^j = (X_i, X_{i+1}, \ldots, X_j)$,

---

*This work was supported in part by the a grant from the Israel Science Foundation

$j \geq i$. It is well known that the optimal predictor in this case is given by the conditional mean, $\mathrm{E}[X_0|X_{-\infty}^{-1}]$. While this solution, in principle, settles the issue of optimal prediction, it does not settle the issue of actually computing the optimal predictor. First of all, note that to compute the conditional mean, the probabilistic law generating the stochastic process $\bar{X}$ must be known. Furthermore, the requirement of knowing the full past, $X_{-\infty}^{-1}$, is of course rather stringent. In this work we consider the more practical situation, where a *finite* sub-sequence $X_1^N = (X_1, X_2, \cdots, X_N)$ is observed, and an optimal prediction is needed, conditioned on this data. Moreover, for each finite sample size N we allow the predictors to be based only on a finite *lag* vector of size d. Ultimately, in order to achieve full generality one may let $d \to \infty$ when $N \to \infty$ in order to obtain the optimal predictor.

We first consider the problem of selecting an empirical estimator from a class of functions $\mathcal{F}_{d,n} : \mathbf{R}^d \to \mathbf{R}$, where n is a complexity index of the class (for example, the number of computational nodes in a feedforward neural network with a single hidden layer), and $|f| \leq B$ for $f \in \mathcal{F}_{d,n}$. Consider then an empirical predictor $f_{d,n,N}(X_{i-d}^{i-1})$, $i > N$, for X_i based on the finite data set X_1^N and depending on the d-dimensional lag vector X_{i-d}^{i-1}, where $f_{d,n,N} \in \mathcal{F}_{d,n}$. It is possible to split the error incurred by this predictor into three terms, each possessing a rather intuitive meaning. It is the competition between these terms which determines the optimal solution, for a *fixed* amount of data. First, define the loss of a functional predictor $f : \mathbf{R}^d \to \mathbf{R}$ as $L(f) = \mathrm{E}\left|X_i - f(X_{i-d}^{i-1})\right|^2$, and let $f_{d,n}^*$ be the optimal function in $\mathcal{F}_{d,n}$ minimizing this loss. Furthermore, denote the optimal lag d predictor by f_d^*, and its associated loss by L_d^*. We are then able to split the loss of the empirical predictor $f_{d,n,N}$ into three basic components,

$$L(f_{d,n,N}) = \left(L_{d,n,N} - L_{d,n}^*\right) + \left(L_{d,n}^* - L_d^*\right) + L_d^*, \tag{1}$$

where $L_{d,n,N} = L(f_{d,n,N})$. The third term, L_d^*, is related to the error incurred in using a finite memory model (of lag size d) to predict a process with potentially infinite memory. We do not at present have any useful upper bounds for this term, which is related to the rate of convergence in the martingale convergence theorem, which to the best of our knowledge is unknown for the type of mixing processes we study in this work. The second term in (1), is related to the so-called *approximation error*, given by $\mathrm{E}|f_d^*(X_{i-d}^{i-1}) - f_{d,n}^*(X_{i-d}^{i-1})|^2$ to which it can be immediately related through the inequality $||a|^p - |b|^p| \leq p|a-b||\max(a,b)|^{p-1}$. This term measures the excess error incurred by selecting a function f from a class of limited complexity $\mathcal{F}_{d,n}$, while the optimal lag d predictor f_d^* may be arbitrarily complex. Of course, in order to bound this term we will have to make some regularity assumptions about the latter function. Finally, the first term in (1) represents the so called *estimation error*, and is the only term which depends on the data X_1^N. Similarly to the problem of regression for i.i.d. data, we expect that the approximation and estimation terms lead to conflicting demands on the choice of the the complexity, n, of the functional class $\mathcal{F}_{d,n}$. Clearly, in order to minimize the approximation error the complexity should be made as large as possible. However, doing this will cause the estimation error to increase, because of the larger freedom in choosing a specific function in $\mathcal{F}_{d,n}$ to fit the data. However, in the case of time series there is an additional complication resulting from the fact that the misspecification error L_d^* is minimized by choosing d to be as large as possible, while this has the effect of increasing both the approximation as well as the estimation errors. We thus expect that some optimal values of d and n exist for each sample size N.

Up to this point we have not specified how to select the empirical estimator $f_{d,n,N}$. In this work we follow the ideas of Vapnik [8], which have been studied extensively in the context of i.i.d observations, and restrict our selection to that hypothesis which minimizes the empirical error, given by $L_N(f) = \frac{1}{N-d} \sum_{i=d+1}^N \left|X_i - f(X_{i-d}^{i-1})\right|^2$. For this function it is easy to establish (see for example [8]) that $(L_{d,n,N} - L_{d,n}^*) \leq 2 \sup_{f \in \mathcal{F}_{d,n}} |L(f) - L_N(f)|$. The main distinction from the i.i.d case, of course, is that random variables appearing in the empirical error, $L_N(f)$, are no longer independent. It is clear at this point that some assumptions are needed regarding the stochastic process $\bar{X}$, in order that a law of large numbers may be established. In any event, it is obvious that the standard approach of using randomization and symmetrization as in the i.i.d case [3] will not work here. To circumvent this problem, two approaches have been proposed. The first makes use of the so-called method of sieves together with extensions of the Bernstein inequality to dependent data [6]. The second approach, to be pursued here, is based on mapping the problem onto one characterized by an i.i.d process [10], and the utilization of the standard results for the latter case.

In order to have some control of the estimation error discussed above, we will restrict ourselves in this work to the class of so-called *mixing* processes. These are processes for which the 'future' depends only weakly on the 'past', in a sense that will now be made precise. Following the definitions and notation of Yu [10], which will be utilized in the sequel, let $\sigma_l = \sigma(X_1^l)$ and $\sigma_{l+m}' = \sigma(X_{l+m}^\infty)$, be the sigma-algebras of events generated by the random variables $X_1^l = (X_1, X_2, \ldots, X_l)$ and $X_{l+m}^\infty = (X_{l+m}, X_{l+m+1}, \ldots)$, respectively. We then define β_m, the coefficient of absolute regularity, as $\beta_m = \sup_{l \geq 1} \operatorname{E} \sup \{|P(B|\sigma_l) - P(B)| : B \in \sigma_{l+m}'\}$, where the expectation is taken with respect to $\sigma_l = \sigma(X_1^l)$. A stochastic process is said to be β-*mixing* if $\beta_m \to 0$ as $m \to \infty$. We note that there exist many other definitions of mixing (see [2] for details). The motivation for using the β-mixing coefficient is that it is the weakest form of mixing for which uniform laws of large numbers can be established. In this work we consider two type of processes for which this coefficient decays to zero, namely *algebraically* decaying processes for which $\beta_m \leq \bar{\beta} m^{-r}$, $\bar{\beta}, r > 0$, and *exponentially* mixing processes for which $\beta_m \leq \bar{\beta} \exp\{-bm^\kappa\}$, $\bar{\beta}, b, \kappa > 0$. Note that for Markov processes mixing implies exponential mixing, so that at least in this case, there is no loss of generality in assuming that the process is exponentially mixing. Note also that the usual i.i.d process may be obtained from either the exponentially or algebraically mixing process, by taking the limit $\kappa \to \infty$ or $r \to \infty$, respectively.

In this section we follow the approach taken by Yu [10] in deriving uniform laws of large numbers for mixing processes, extending her mainly asymptotic results to finite sample behavior, and somewhat broadening the class of processes considered by her. The basic idea in [10], as in many related approaches, involves the construction of an *independent-block* sequence, which is shown to be 'close' to the original process in a well-defined probabilistic sense. We briefly recapitulate the construction, slightly modifying the notation in [10] to fit in with the present paper. Divide the sequence X_1^N into $2\mu_N$ blocks, each of size a_N; we assume for simplicity that $N = 2\mu_N a_N$. The blocks are then numbered according to their order in the block-sequence. For $1 \leq j \leq \mu_N$ define $H_j = \{i : 2(j-1)a_N + 1 \leq i \leq (2j-1)a_N\}$ and $T_j = \{i : (2j-1)a_N + 1 \leq i \leq (2j)a_N\}$. Denote the random variables corresponding to the H_j and T_j indices as $X^{(j)} = \{X_i : i \in H_j\}$ and $X'^{(j)} = \{X_i : i \in T_j\}$. The sequence of H-blocks is then denoted by $X_{a_N} = \{X^{(j)}\}_{j=1}^{\mu_N}$. Now, construct a sequence of independent and identically distributed (i.i.d.) blocks $\{\Xi^{(j)}\}_{j=1}^{\mu_N}$, where $\Xi^{(j)} = \{\xi_i : i \in H_j\}$, such that the sequence is independent of X_1^N and each block has the same distribution as the block $X^{(j)}$ from the original sequence. Because the process is stationary, the blocks $\Xi^{(j)}$ are not only independent but also identically distributed. The basic idea in the construction of the independent block sequence is that it is 'close', in a well-defined sense to the original blocked sequence X_{a_N}. Moreover, by appropriately selecting the number of blocks, μ_N, depending on the mixing nature of the sequence, one may relate properties of the original sequence X_1^N, to those of the independent block sequence Ξ_{a_N} (see Lemma 4.1 in [10]).

Let $\mathcal{F}$ be a class of bounded functions, such that $0 \leq f \leq B$ for any $f \in \mathcal{F}$. In order to relate the uniform deviations (with respect to $\mathcal{F}$) of the original sequence X_1^N to those of the independent-block sequence Ξ_{a_N}, use is made of Lemma 4.1 from [10]. We also utilize Lemma 4.2 from [10] and modify it so that it holds for finite sample size. Consider the block-independent sequence Ξ_{a_N} and define $\tilde{\mathrm{E}}_{\mu_N}\tilde{f} = \frac{1}{\mu_N}\sum_{j=1}^{\mu_N} \tilde{f}(\Xi^{(j)})$ where $\tilde{f}(\Xi^{(j)}) = \sum_{i \in H_j} f(\xi_i)$, $j = 1, 2, \ldots, \mu_N$, is a sequence of independent random variables such that $|\tilde{f}| \le a_N B$. In the remainder of the paper we use variables with a tilde above them to denote quantities related to the transformed block sequence. Finally, we use the symbol E_N to denote the empirical average with respect to the original sequence, namely $\mathrm{E}_N f = (N - d)^{-1}\sum_{i=d+1}^{N} f(X_i)$. The following result can be proved by a simple extension of Lemma 4.2 in [10].

Lemma 1.1 *Suppose $\mathcal{F}$ is a permissible class of bounded functions, $|f| \le B$ for $f \in \mathcal{F}$. Then*

$$\mathbf{P}\left\{\sup_{f \in \mathcal{F}}|\mathrm{E}_N f - \mathrm{E}f| > \varepsilon\right\} \le 2\tilde{P}\left\{\sup_{f \in \mathcal{F}}|\tilde{\mathrm{E}}_{\mu_N}\tilde{f} - \tilde{\mathrm{E}}\tilde{f}| > a_N\varepsilon\right\} + 2\mu_N\beta_{a_N}. \qquad (2)$$

The main merit of Lemma 1.1 is in the transformation of the problem from the domain of dependent processes, implicit in the quantity $|\mathrm{E}_N f - \mathrm{E}f|$, to one characterized by independent processes, implicit in the term $\tilde{\mathrm{E}}_{\mu_N}\tilde{f} - \tilde{\mathrm{E}}\tilde{f}$, corresponding to the independent blocks. The price paid for this transformation is the extra term $2\mu_N\beta_{a_N}$ which appears on the r.h.s of the inequality appearing in Lemma 1.1.

2   Error Bounds

The development in Section 1 was concerned with a scalar stochastic process $\bar{X}$. In order to use the results in the context of time series, we first define a new vector-valued process $\bar{X}' = \{\cdots, \vec{X}_{-1}, \vec{X}_0, \vec{X}_1, \ldots\}$ where $\vec{X}_i = (X_i, X_{i-1}, \ldots, X_{i-d}) \in \mathbf{R}^{d+1}$. For this sequence the β-mixing coefficients obey the inequality $\beta_m(\bar{X}') \le \beta_{m-d}(\bar{X})$. Let $\mathcal{F}$ be a space of functions mapping $\mathbf{R}^d \to \mathbf{R}$, and for each $f \in \mathcal{F}$ let the loss function be given by $\ell_f(X_{i-d}^i) = |X_i - f(X_{i-d}^{i-1})|^2$. The loss space is given by $\mathcal{L}_{\mathcal{F}} = \{\ell_f : f \in \mathcal{F}\}$. It is well known in the theory of empirical processes (see [7] for example), that in order to obtain upper bounds on uniform deviations of i.i.d sequences, use must be made of the so-called covering number of the function class $\mathcal{F}$, with respect to the empirical $l_{1,N}$ norm, given by $l_{1,N}(f, g) = N^{-1}\sum_{i=1}^{N}|f(X_i) - g(X_i)|$. Similarly, we denote the empirical norm with respect to the independent block sequence by $\tilde{l}_{1,\mu_N}$, where $\tilde{l}_{1,\mu_N}(f, g) = \mu_N^{-1}\sum_{j=1}^{\mu_N}|\tilde{f}(X^{(j)}) - \tilde{g}(X^{(j)}|$, and where $\tilde{f}(X^{(j)}) = \sum_{i \in H_j} X_i$ and similarly for $\tilde{g}$. Following common practice we denote the ε-covering number of the functional space $\mathcal{F}$ using the metric ρ by $\mathcal{N}(\varepsilon, \mathcal{F}, \rho)$.

Definition 1 *Let $\mathcal{L}_{\mathcal{F}}$ be a class of real-valued functions from $\mathbf{R}^D \to \mathbf{R}$, $D = d + 1$. For each $\ell_f \in \mathcal{L}_{\mathcal{F}}$ and $\mathbf{\vec{x}} = (\vec{x}_1, \vec{x}_2, \ldots, \vec{x}_{a_N})$, $\vec{x}_i \in \mathbf{R}^D$, let $\tilde{\ell}_f(\mathbf{\vec{x}}) = \sum_{i=1}^{a_N} \ell_f(\vec{x}_i)$. Then define $\tilde{\mathcal{L}}_{\mathcal{F}} = \left\{\tilde{\ell}_f : \ell_f \in \mathcal{L}_{\mathcal{F}}\right\}$, where $\tilde{\ell}_f : \mathbf{R}^{a_N D} \to \mathbf{R}^+$.*

In order to obtain results in terms of the covering numbers of the space $\mathcal{L}_{\mathcal{F}}$ rather than $\tilde{\mathcal{L}}_{\mathcal{F}}$, which corresponds to the transformed sequence, we need the following lemma, which is not hard to prove.

Lemma 2.1 *For any $\varepsilon > 0$*

$$\mathcal{N}\left(\varepsilon, \tilde{\mathcal{L}}_{\mathcal{F}}, \tilde{l}_{1,\mu_N}\right) \le \mathcal{N}\left(\varepsilon/a_N, \mathcal{L}_{\mathcal{F}}, l_{1,N}\right).$$

PROOF The result follows by sequence of simple inequalities, showing that $\tilde{l}_{1,\mu_N}(\tilde{f}, \tilde{g}) \leq a_N l_{1,N}(f, g)$. ∎

We now present the main result of this section, namely an upper bound for the uniform deviations of mixing processes, which in turn yield upper bounds on the error incurred by the empirically optimal predictor $f_{d,n,N}$.

Theorem 2.1 Let $\bar{X} = \{\ldots, X_1, X_0, X_1, \ldots\}$ be a bounded stationary β-mixing stochastic process, with $|X_i| \leq B$, and let $\mathcal{F}$ be a class of bounded functions, $f : \mathbf{R}^d \to [0, B]$. For each sample size N, let $\hat{f}_N$ be the function in $\mathcal{F}$ which minimizes the empirical error, and f^* is the function in $\mathcal{F}$ minimizing the true error $L(f)$. Then,

$$\mathbf{P}\left\{L(\hat{f}_N) - L(f^*) > \varepsilon\right\} \leq 8E\mathcal{N}(\varepsilon', \mathcal{F}, l_{1,N}) \exp\left\{-\frac{\mu_N \varepsilon^2}{64(2B)^4}\right\} + 2\mu_N \beta_{a_N - d}. \tag{3}$$

where $\varepsilon' = \varepsilon/128B$.

PROOF The theorem is established by making use of Lemma 1.1, and the basic results from the theory of uniform convergence for i.i.d. processes, together with Lemma 2.1 relating the covering numbers of the spaces $\tilde{\mathcal{L}}_{\mathcal{F}}$ and $\mathcal{L}_{\mathcal{F}}$. The covering numbers of $\mathcal{L}_{\mathcal{F}}$ and $\mathcal{F}$ are easily related using $\mathcal{N}(\varepsilon, \mathcal{L}_{\mathcal{F}}, L_1(P)) \leq \mathcal{N}(\varepsilon/2B, \mathcal{F}, L_1(P))$. ∎

Up to this point we have not specified μ_N and a_N, and the result is therefore quite general. In order to obtain weak consistency we require that that the r.h.s. of (3) converge to zero for each $\varepsilon > 0$. This immediately yields the following conditions on μ_N (and thus also on a_N through the condition $2a_N \mu_N = N$).

Corollary 2.1 Under the conditions of Theorem 2.1, and the added requirements that $d = o(a_N)$ and $\mathcal{N}(\varepsilon, \mathcal{F}, l_{1,N}) < \infty$, the following choices of μ_N are sufficient to guarantee the weak consistency of the empirical predictor $\hat{f}_N$:

$$\mu_N \sim N^{\kappa/(1+\kappa)} \qquad \text{(exponential mixing)}, \tag{4}$$

$$\mu_N \sim N^{s/(1+s)}, \ 0 < s < r \qquad \text{(algebraic mixing)}, \tag{5}$$

where the notation $a_N \sim b_N$ implies that $\Omega(b_N) \leq a_N \leq O(b_N)$.

PROOF Consider first the case of exponential mixing. In this case the r.h.s. of (3) clearly converges to zero because of the finiteness of the covering number. The fastest rate of convergence is achieved by balancing the two terms in the equation, leading to the choice $\mu_N \sim N^{\kappa/(1+\kappa)}$. In the case of algebraic mixing, the second term on the r.h.s. of (3) is of the order $O(\mu_N a_N^{-r})$ where we have used $d = o(a_N)$. Since $\mu_N a_N \sim N$, a sufficient condition to guarantee that this term converge to zero is that $\mu_N \sim N^{s/(1+s)}$, $0 < s < r$, as was claimed. ∎

In order to derive bounds on the expected error, we need to make an assumption concerning the covering number of the space $\mathcal{F}$. In particular, we know from the work Haussler [4] that the covering number is upper bounded as follows

$$\mathcal{N}(\varepsilon, \mathcal{F}, L_1(P)) \leq e(\text{Pdim}(\mathcal{F}) + 1)\left(\frac{2eB}{\varepsilon}\right)^{\text{Pdim}(\mathcal{F})},$$

for any measure P. Thus, assuming the finiteness of the pseudo-dimension of $\mathcal{F}$ guarantees a finite covering number.

3 Structural Risk Minimization

The results in Section 2 provide error bounds for estimators formed by minimizing the empirical error over a fixed class of d-dimensional functions. It is clear that the complexity of the class of functions plays a crucial role in the procedure. If the class is too rich, manifested by very large covering numbers, clearly the estimation error term will be very large. On the other hand, biasing the class of functions by restricting its complexity, leads to poor approximation rates. A well-known strategy for overcoming this dilemma is obtained by considering a hierarchy of functional classes with increasing complexity. For any given sample size, the optimal trade-off between estimation and approximation can then be determined by balancing the two terms. Such a procedure was developed in the late seventies by Vapnik [8], and termed by him *structural risk minimization* (SRM). Other more recent approaches, collectively termed complexity regularization, have been extensively studied in recent years (e.g. [1]). It should be borne in mind, however, that in the context of time series there is an added complexity, that does not exist in the case of regression. Recall that the results derived in Section 2 assumed some fixed lag vector d. In general the optimal value of d is unknown, and could in fact be infinite. In order to achieve optimal performance in a nonparametric setting, it is crucial that the size of the lag be chosen adaptively as well. This added complexity needs to be incorporated into the SRM framework, if optimal performance in the face of unknown memory size is to be achieved.

Let $\mathcal{F}_{d,n}$, $d, n \in \mathbf{N}$ be a sequence of functions, and define $\mathcal{F} = \bigcup_{d=1}^{\infty} \bigcup_{n=1}^{\infty} \mathcal{F}_{d,n}$. For any $\mathcal{F}_{d,n}$ let

$$\mathcal{N}_1(\varepsilon, \mathcal{F}_{d,n}) = \sup_{x^N} \mathcal{N}(\varepsilon, \mathcal{F}_{d,n}, l_{1,N}),$$

which from [4] is upper bounded by $c\varepsilon^{-\mathrm{Pdim}(\mathcal{F}_{d,n})}$. We observe in passing that Lugosi and Nobel [5] have recently considered situations where the pseudo-dimension $\mathrm{Pdim}(\mathcal{F}_{d,n})$ is unknown, and the covering number is estimated empirically from the data. Although this line of thought is potentially very useful, we do not pursue it here, but rather assume that upper bounds on the pseudo-dimensions of $\mathcal{F}_{d,n}$ are known, as is the case for many classes of functions used in practice (see for example [9]).

In line with the standard approach in [8] we introduce a new empirical function, which takes into account both the empirical error as well as the complexity costs penalizing overly complex models (large complexity index n and lag size d). Let

$$\tilde{L}_{d,n,N}(f) = L_N(f) + \Delta_{d,n,N}(\varepsilon) + \Delta_{d,N}, \tag{6}$$

where $L_N(f)$ is the empirical error of the predictor f and the complexity penalties Δ are given by

$$\Delta_{d,n,N}(\varepsilon) = \sqrt{\frac{\log \mathcal{N}_1(\varepsilon, \mathcal{F}_{d,n}) + c_n}{\mu_N / 64(2B)^4}} \tag{7}$$

$$\Delta_{d,N} = \sqrt{\frac{c_d}{\mu_N / 64(2B)^4}}. \tag{8}$$

The specific form and constants in these definitions are chosen with hindsight, so as to achieve the optimal rates of convergence in Theorem 3.1 below. The constants c_n and c_d are positive constants obeying $\sum_{n=1}^{\infty} e^{-c_n} \leq 1$ and similarly for c_d. A possible choice is $c_n = 2 \log n + 1$ and $c_d = 2 \log d + 1$. The value of μ_N can be chosen in accordance with Corollary 2.1.

Let $\hat{f}_{d,n,N}$ minimize the empirical error $L_N(f)$ within the class of functions $\mathcal{F}_{d,n}$. We assume that the classes $\mathcal{F}_{d,n}$ are compact, so that such a minimizer exists. Further, let $\hat{f}_N$

be the function in $\mathcal{F}$ minimizing the complexity penalized loss (6), namely

$$\tilde{L}_{d,n,N}(\hat{f}_N) = \min_{d \geq 1} \min_{n \geq 1} \tilde{L}_{d,n,N}(\hat{f}_{d,n,N}) \tag{9}$$

The following basic result establishes the consistency of the structural risk minimization approach, and yields upper bounds on its performance.

Theorem 3.1 *Let $\mathcal{F}_{d,n}$, $d, n \in \mathbf{N}$ be sequence of functional classes, where $f \in \mathcal{F}_{d,n}$ is a mapping from $\mathbf{R}^d$ to $\mathbf{R}$. The expected loss of the function $\hat{f}_N$, selected according to the SRM principle, is upper bounded by*

$$\mathrm{E}L(\hat{f}_N) \leq \min_{d,n} \left\{ \inf_{d,n} L(f) + c_1 \sqrt{\frac{\gamma_{d,n} \log \mu_N + c_n}{\mu_N}} + \sqrt{\frac{c_2}{\mu_N}} \right\} + 4(2B)^2 \mu_N \beta_{a_N/2}. \tag{10}$$

The main merit of Theorem 3.1 is the demonstration that the SRM procedure achieves an optimal balance between approximation and estimation, while retaining its nonparametric attributes. In particular, if the optimal lag d predictor f_d^* belongs to $\mathcal{F}_{d,n_0}$ for some n_0, the SRM predictor would converge to it at the same rate as if n_0 were known in advance. The same type of adaptivity is obtained with respect to the lag size d. The nonparametric rates of convergence of the SRM predictor will be discussed in the full paper.

References

[1] A. Barron. Complexity Regularization with Application to Artificial Neural Networks. In G. Roussas, editor, *Nonparametric Functional Estimation and Related Topics*, pages 561–576. Kluwer Academic Press, 1991.

[2] L. Györfi, W. Härdle, P. Sarda, and P. Vieu. *Nonparametric Curve Estimation from Time Series*. Springer Verlag, New York, 1989.

[3] D. Haussler. Decision Theoretic Generalizations of the PAC Model for Neural Net and Other Learning Applications. *Information and Computation*, 100:78–150, 1992.

[4] D. Haussler. Sphere Packing Numbers for Subsets of the Boolean n-Cube with Bounded Vapnik-Chervonenkis Dimesnion. *J. Combinatorial Theory*, Series A 69:217–232, 1995.

[5] G. Lugosi and A. Nobel. Adaptive Model Selection Using Empirical Complexities. Submitted to *Annals Statis.*, 1996.

[6] D . Modha and E. Masry. Memory Universal Prediction of Stationary Random Processes. *IEEE Trans. Inf. Th.*, January, 1998.

[7] D. Pollard. *Convergence of Empirical Processes*. Springer Verlag, New York, 1984.

[8] V. N. Vapnik. *Estimation of Dependences Based on Empirical Data*. Springer Verlag, New York, 1992.

[9] M. Vidyasagar. *A Theory of Learning and Generalization*. Springer Verlag, New York, 1996.

[10] B. Yu. Rates of convergence for empirical processes of stationary mixing sequences. *Annals of Probability*, 22:94–116, 1984.

Analytical study of the interplay between architecture and predictability

Avner Priel, Ido Kanter, David A. Kessler
Minerva Center and Department of Physics, Bar Ilan University,
Ramat-Gan 52900, Israel.

e-mail: priel@mail.cc.biu.ac.il (web-page: http://faculty.biu.ac.il/~priel)

Abstract

We study model feed forward networks as time series predictors
in the stationary limit. The focus is on complex, yet non-chaotic,
behavior. The main question we address is whether the asymptotic
behavior is governed by the architecture, regardless the details of
the weights. We find hierarchies among classes of architectures
with respect to the attractor dimension of the long term sequence
they are capable of generating; larger number of hidden units can
generate higher dimensional attractors. In the case of a perceptron,
we develop the stationary solution for general weights, and show
that the flow is typically one dimensional. The relaxation time
from an arbitrary initial condition to the stationary solution is
found to scale linearly with the size of the network. In multilayer
networks, the number of hidden units gives bounds on the number
and dimension of the possible attractors. We conclude that long
term prediction (in the non-chaotic regime) with such models is
governed by attractor dynamics related to the architecture.

Neural networks provide an important tool as model free estimators for the solution
of problems when the real model is unknown, or weakly known. In the last decade
there has been a growing interest in the application of such tools in the area of time
series prediction (see Weigand and Gershenfeld, 1994). In this paper we analyse a
typical class of architectures used in this field, i.e. a feed forward network governed
by the following dynamic rule:

$$S_1^{t+1} = S_{out} ; \qquad S_j^{t+1} = S_{j-1}^t \quad j = 2, \ldots, N \qquad (1)$$

where S_{out} is the network's output at time step t and S_j^t are the inputs at that time;
N is the size of the delayed input vector. The rational behind using time delayed
vectors as inputs is the theory of state space reconstruction of a dynamic system

using delay coordinates (Takens 1981, Sauer Yorke and Casdagli 1991). This theory address the problem of reproducing a set of states associated with the dynamic system using vectors obtained from the measured time series, and is widely used for time series analysis. A similar architecture incorporating time delays is the TDNN - time-delay neural network with a recurrent loop (Waibel et. al. 1989). This type of networks is known to be appropriate for learning temporal sequences, e.g. speech signal. In the context of time series, it is mostly used for short term predictions. Our analysis focuses on the various long-time properties of the sequence generated by a given architecture and the interplay between them. The aim of such an investigation is the understanding and characterization of the long term sequences generated by such architectures, and the time scale to reach this asymptotic behavior. Such knowledge is necessary to define adequate measures for the transition between a locally dependent prediction and the long term behavior. Though some work has been done on characterization of a dynamic system from its time series using neural networks, not much analytical results that connect architecture and long-time prediction are available (see M. Mozer in Weigand and Gershenfeld, 1994). Nevertheless, practical considerations for choosing the architecture were investigated extensively (Weigand and Gershenfeld, 1994 and references therein). It has been shown that such networks are capable of generating chaotic like sequences. While it is possible to reconstruct approximately the phase space of chaotic attractors (at least in low dimension), it is clear that prediction of chaotic sequences is limited by the very nature of such systems, namely the divergence of the distance between nearby trajectories. Therefore one can only speak about short time predictions with respect to such systems. Our focus is the ability to generate **complex** sequences, and the relation between architecture and the dimension of such sequences.

1   Perceptron

We begin with a study of the simplest feed forward network, the perceptron. We analyse a perceptron whose output S_{out} at time step t is given by:

$$S_{out} = \tanh\left[\beta\left(\sum_{j=1}^{N}(W_j + W_0)S_j^t\right)\right] \tag{2}$$

where β is a gain parameter, N is the input size. The bias term $,W_0$, plays the same role as the common 'external field' used in the literature, while preserving the same qualitative asymptotic solution. In a previous work (Eisenstein et. al. , 1995) it was found that the stationary state (of a similar architecture but with a "sign" activation function instead of the "tanh", equivalently $\beta \to \infty$) is influenced primarily by one of the larger Fourier components in the power spectrum of the weights vector W of the perceptron. This observation motivates the following representation of the vector W. Let us start with the case of a vector that consists of a single biased Fourier component of the form:

$$W_j = a\cos(2\pi Kj/N) \quad j = 1,\ldots,N ; \qquad W_0 = b \tag{3}$$

where a, b are constants and K is a positive integer. This case is generalized later on, however for clarity we treat first the simple case. Note that the vector W can always be represented as a Fourier decomposition of its values. The stationary solution for the sequence (S^l) produced by the output of the perceptron, when inserting this choice of the weights into equation (2), can be shown to be of the form:

$$S^l = \tanh\left[A(\beta)\cos(2\pi Kl/N) + B(\beta)\right] \tag{4}$$

There are two non-zero solutions possible for the variables (A, B):

$$A = \tfrac{1}{2}\beta Na \sum_{\rho=1}^{\infty} D(\rho)(A/2)^{2\rho-1}(\rho!)^{-2} \quad ; \quad B = 0$$

$$B = \beta Nb \sum_{\rho=1}^{\infty} D(\rho)B^{2\rho-1}((2\rho)!)^{-1} \quad ; \quad A = 0 \tag{5}$$

where $D(\rho) = 2^{2\rho}(2^{2\rho} - 1)\mathcal{B}_{2\rho}$ and $\mathcal{B}_{2\rho}$ are the Bernoulli numbers. Analysis of equations (5) reveals the following behavior as a function of the parameter β. Each of the variables is the amplitude of an attractor. The attractor represented by $(A \neq 0, B = 0)$ is a limit cycle while the attractor represented by $(B \neq 0, A = 0)$ is a fixed point of the dynamics. The onset of each of the attractors $A(B)$ is at $\beta_{c1} = 2(aN)^{-1}$ $(\beta_{c2} = (bN)^{-1})$ respectively. One can identify three regimes: (1) $\beta < \beta_{c1,c2}$ - the stable solution is $S^l = 0$. (2) $min(\beta_{c1}, \beta_{c2}) < \beta < max(\beta_{c1}, \beta_{c2})$ - the system flows for all initial conditions into the attractor whose β_c is smaller. (3) $\beta > \beta_{c1,c2}$ - depending on the initial condition of the input vector, the system flows into one of the attractors, namely, the stationary state is either a fixed point or a periodic flow. β_{c1} is known as a Hopf bifurcation point. Naturally, the attractor whose β_c is smaller has a larger basin of attraction, hence it is more probable to attract the flow (in the third regime).

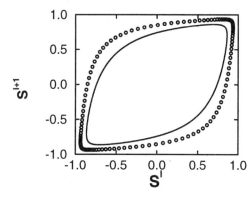

Figure 1: Embedding of a sequence generated by a perceptron whose weights follow eq. 3 (6). Periodic sequence (outer curve) $N = 128$, $k = 17$, $b = 0.3$, $\beta = 1/40$ and quasi periodic (inner) $k = 17$, $\phi = 0.123$, $\beta = 1/45$ respectively.

Next we discuss the more general case where the weights of eq. (3) includes an arbitrary phase shift of the form:

$$W_j = a \cos(2\pi Kj/N - \pi\phi) \quad \phi \in (-1,1) \tag{6}$$

The leading term of the stationary solution in the limit $N \gg 1$ is of the form:

$$S^l = \tanh\left[A(\beta)\cos(2\pi(K - \phi)l/N) + B(\beta)\right] \tag{7}$$

where the higher harmonic corrections are of $\mathcal{O}(1/K)$. A note should be made here that the phase shift in the weights is manifested as a frequency shift in the solution. In addition, the attractor associated with $A \neq 0$ is now a quasi-periodic flow in the generic case when ϕ is irrational. The onset value of the fixed point (β_{c2}) is the same as before, however the onset of the quasi-periodic orbit is $\beta_{c1} = \frac{\pi\phi}{\sin(\pi\phi)}2(aN)^{-1}$. The variables A, B follow similar equations to (5):

$$A = \beta Na\frac{\sin(\pi\phi)}{\pi\phi}\sum_{\rho=1}^{\infty} D(\rho)(A/2)^{2\rho-1}(\rho!)^{-2} \quad ; \quad B = 0$$

$$B = \beta Nb \sum_{\rho=1}^{\infty} D(\rho)B^{2\rho-1}((2\rho)!)^{-1} \quad ; \quad A = 0 \tag{8}$$

The three regimes discussed above appear in this case as well. Figure 1 shows the attractor associated with $(A \neq 0, B = 0)$ for the two cases where the series generated by the output is embedded as a sequence of two dimensional vectors (S^{l+1}, S^l).

The general weights can be written as a combination of their Fourier components with different K's and ϕ's:

$$W_j = \sum_{i=1}^{m} a_i \cos(2\pi K_i j/N - \pi\phi_i) \quad \phi_i \in (-1, 1) \tag{9}$$

When the different K's are not integer divisors of each other, the general solution is similar to that described above:

$$S^l = \tanh \left[\sum_{i=1}^{m} A_i(\beta) \cos(2\pi(K_i - \phi_i)l/N) + B(\beta) \right] \tag{10}$$

where m is the number of relevant Fourier components. As above, the variables A_i, B are coupled via self consistent equations. Nevertheless, the generic stationary flow is one of the possible attractors, depending on β and the initial condition; i.e. ($A_q \neq 0, A_i = 0 \ \forall i \neq q$, $B = 0$) or ($B \neq 0, A_i = 0$). By now we can conclude that the generic flow for the perceptron is one of three: a fixed point, periodic cycle or quasi-periodic flow. The first two have a zero dimension while the last describes a one dimensional flow. we stress that more complex flows are possible even in our solution (eq. 10), however they require special relation between the frequencies and a very high value of β, typically more than an order of magnitude greater than bifurcation value.

2   Relaxation time

At this stage the reader might wonder about the relation between the asymptotic results presented above and the ability of such a model to predict. In fact, the practical use of feed forward networks in time series prediction is divided into two phases. In the first phase, the network is trained in an open loop using a given time series. In the second phase, the network operates in a closed loop and the sequence it generates is also used for the future predictions. Hence, it is clear from our analysis that eventually the network will be driven to one of the attractors. The relevant question is *how long does it takes to arrive at such asymptotic behavior ?* We shall see that the characteristic time is governed by the gap between the largest and the second largest eigenvalues of the linearized map. Let us start by reformulating eqs. (1, 2) in a matrix form, i.e. we linearize the map. Denote $\overline{S}^t = (S_1^t, S_2^t, \ldots, S_N^t)$ and $(\overline{S}^t)'$ is the transposed vector. The map is then $\mathcal{T}(\overline{S}^t)' = (\overline{S}^{t+1})'$ where

$$\mathcal{T} = \begin{bmatrix} c_1 & c_2 & \cdots & c_{N-1} & c_N \\ 1 & 0 & \cdots & 0 & 0 \\ 0 & 1 & \cdots & 0 & 0 \\ \vdots & \vdots & \vdots & \vdots & \vdots \\ 0 & 0 & \cdots & 1 & 0 \end{bmatrix} \qquad c_i = \beta(W_i + W_0) \tag{11}$$

The first row of $\mathcal{T}$ gives the next output value $= S_1^{t+1}$ while the rest of the matrix is just the shift defined by eq. (1) . This matrix is known as the "companion matrix" (e.g. Ralston and Rabinowitz, 1978). The characteristic function of $\mathcal{T}$ can be written as follows:

$$\beta \sum_{n=1}^{N} \frac{c_n}{\lambda^n} = 1 \tag{12}$$

from which it is possible to extract the eigenvalues. At $\beta = \beta_c$ the largest eigenvalue of $\mathcal{T}$ is $|\lambda_1| = 1$. Denote the second largest eigenvalue λ_2 such that $|\lambda_2| = 1 - \Delta$.

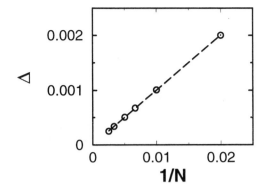

Figure 2: Scaling of Δ for a perceptron with two Fourier components, (eq. 9), with $a_i = 1$, $K_1 = 3$, $\phi_1 = 0.121$, $K_2 = 7$, $\phi_2 = 0$, $W_0 = 0.3$. The dashed line is a linear fit of $0.1/N$, $N = 50, \ldots, 400$.

Applying $\mathcal{T}$ τ - times to an initial state vector results in a vector whose second largest component is of order:

$$|\lambda_2|^\tau = (1 - \Delta)^\tau = \exp\{\tau \log(1 - \Delta)\} \overset{\Delta \ll 1}{\approx} \exp\{-\tau\Delta\} \tag{13}$$

therefore we can define the characteristic relaxation time in the vicinity of an attractor to be $\tau = \Delta^{-1}$. [1]

We have analysed eq. (12) numerically for various cases of c_i, e.g. W_i composed of one or two Fourier components. In all the cases β was chosen to be the minimal β_c to ensure that the linearized form is valid. We found that $\Delta \sim 1/N$. Figure 2 depicts one example of two Fourier components. Next, we have simulated the network and measured the average time ($\overline{\tau^s}$) it takes to flow into an attractor starting from an arbitrary initial condition. The following simulations support the analytical result ($\tau \sim N$) for general (random) weights and high gain (β) value as well. The threshold we apply for the decision whether the flow is already close enough to the attractor is the ratio between the component with the largest power in the spectrum and the total power spectrum of the current state ($\overline{S}^t$), which should exceed 0.95. The results presented in Figure 3 are an average over 100 samples started from random initial condition. The weights are taken at random, however we add a dominant Fourier component with no phase to control the bifurcation point more easily. This component has an amplitude which is about twice the other components to make sure that its bifurcation point is the smallest. We observe a clear linear relation between this time and N ($\overline{\tau^s} \sim N$). The slope depends on the actual values of the weights, however the power law scaling does not change.

On general principles, we expect the analytically derived scaling law for Δ to be valid even beyond the linear regime. Indeed the numerical simulations (Figure 3) support this conjecture.

3   Multilayer networks

For simplicity, we restrict the present analysis to a multilayer network (MLN) with N inputs, H hidden units and a single linear output, however this restriction can be removed, e.g. nonlinear output and more hidden layers. The units in the hidden layer are the perceptrons discussed above and the output is given by:

$$S_{out} = \sum_{m=1}^{H} \tanh\left[\beta\left(\sum_{j=1}^{N}(W_j^m + W_0^m)S_j^t\right)\right] \tag{14}$$

---

[1]Note that if one demand the L.H.S. of eq. (13) to be of $\mathcal{O}(\Delta)$, then $\tau \sim \Delta^{-1}\log(\Delta^{-1})$.

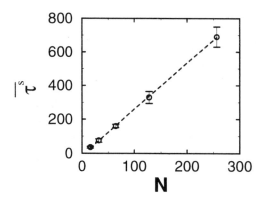

Figure 3: Scaling of $\overline{\tau^s}$ for random weights with a dominant component at $K = 7$, $\phi = 0$, $a = 1$; All other amplitudes are randomly taken between $(0, 0.5)$ and the phases are random as well. $\beta = 3.2/N$. The dashed line is a linear fit of cN, $c = 2.73 \pm 0.03$. $N = 16, \ldots, 256$.

The dynamic rule is defined by eq. (1). First consider the case where the weights of each hidden unit are of the form described by eq. (6), i.e. each hidden unit has only one (possibly biased) Fourier component:

$$W_j^m = a_m \cos(2\pi K_m j/N - \pi\phi_m) ; \quad W_0^m = b_m \qquad m = 1, \ldots, H. \qquad (15)$$

Following a similar treatment as for the perceptron, the stationary solution is a combination of the perceptron-like solution:

$$S^l = \sum_{m=1}^{H} \tanh\left[A_m(\beta) \cos(2\pi(K_m - \phi_m)l/N) + B_m(\beta)\right] \qquad (16)$$

The variables A_m, B_m are the solution of the self consistent coupled equations, however by contrast with the single perceptron, each hidden unit operates independently and can potentially develop an attractor of the type described in section 1. The number of attractors depends on β with a maximum of H attractors. The number of non-zero A_m's defines the attractor's dimension in the generic case of irrational ϕ's associated with them. If different units do not share Fourier components with a common divisor or harmonics of one another, it is easy to define the quantitative result, otherwise, one has to analyse the coupled equations more carefully to find the exact value of the variables. Nevertheless, each hidden unit exhibits only a single highly dominant component ($A \neq 0$ or $B \neq 0$).

Generalization of this result to more than a single biased Fourier component is straightforward. Each vector is of the form described in eq. (9) plus an index for the hidden unit. The solution is a combination of the general perceptron solution, eq. (10). This solution is much more involved and the coupled equations are complicated but careful study of them reveals the same conclusion, namely each hidden unit possess a single dominant Fourier component (possibly with several other much smaller due to the other components in the vector). As the gain parameter β becomes larger, more components becomes available and the number of possible attractors increases. For a very large value it is possible that higher harmonics from different hidden units might interfere and complicate considerably the solution. Still, one can trace the origin of this behavior by close inspection of the fields in each hidden unit.

We have also measured the relaxation time associated with MLN's in simulations. The preliminary results are similar to the perceptron, i.e. $\overline{\tau^s} \sim N$ but the constant prefactor is larger when the weights consist of more Fourier components.

4 Discussion

Neural networks were proved to be universal approximators (e.g. Hornik, 1991), hence they are capable of approximating the prediction function of the delay coordinate vector. The conclusion should be that prediction is indeed possible. This observation holds only for short times in general. As we have shown, long time predictions are governed by the attractor dynamics described above. The results point out the conclusion that the asymptotic behavior for this networks is dictated by the architecture and not by the details of the weights. Moreover, the attractor dimension of the asymptotic sequence is typically bounded by the number of hidden units in the first layer (assuming the network does not contain internal delays). To prevent any misunderstanding we note again that this result refers to the asymptotic behavior although the short term sequence can approximate a very complicated attractor.

The main result can be interpreted as follows. Since the network is able to approximate the prediction function, the initial condition is followed by reasonable predictions which are the mappings from the vicinity of the original manifold created by the network. As the trajectory evolves, it flows to one of the attractors described above and the predictions are no longer valid. In other words, the initial combination of solutions described in eq. (10) or its extension to MLN (with an arbitrary number of non-zero variables, A's or B's) serves as the approximate mapping. Evolution of this approximation is manifested in the variables of the solution, which eventually are attracted to a stable attractor (in the non-chaotic regime). The time scale for the transition is given by the relaxation time developed above.

The formal study can be applied for practical purposes in two ways. First, taking into account this behavior by probing the generated sequence and looking for its indications. One such indication is stationarity of the power spectrum. Second, one can incorporate ideas from local linear models in the reconstructed space to restrict the inputs in such a way that they always remain in the vicinity of the original manifold (Sauer, in Weigand and Gershenfeld, 1994).

Acknowledgments

This research has been supported by the Israel Science Foundation.

References

Weigand A. S. and Gershenfeld N. A. ; *Time Series Prediction*, Addison-Wesley, Reading, MA, 1994.

E. Eisenstein, I. Kanter, D. A. Kessler and W. Kinzel ; Generation and prediction of time series by a neural network, Phys. Rev. Lett. **74**, 6 (1995).

Waibel A., Hanazawa T., Hinton G., Shikano K. and Lang K.; Phoneme recognition using TDNN, IEEE Trans. Acoust., Speech & Signal Proc. **37(3)**, (1989).

Takens F., Detecting strange attractors in turbulence, in Lecture notes in mathematics vol. 898, Springer-Verlag, 1981.

T. Sauer, J. A. Yorke and M. Casdagli; Embedology, J. Stat. Phys. **65(3)**, (1991).

Ralston A. and Rabinowitz P. ; *A first course in numerical analysis*, McGraw-Hill, 1978.

K. Hornik; Approximation capabilities of multilayer feed forward networks, Neural Networks 4, (1991).

Globally Optimal On-line Learning Rules

Magnus Rattray*and David Saad†
Department of Computer Science & Applied Mathematics,
Aston University, Birmingham B4 7ET, UK.

Abstract

We present a method for determining the globally optimal on-line learning rule for a soft committee machine under a statistical mechanics framework. This work complements previous results on locally optimal rules, where only the rate of change in generalization error was considered. We maximize the total reduction in generalization error over the whole learning process and show how the resulting rule can significantly outperform the locally optimal rule.

1 Introduction

We consider a learning scenario in which a feed-forward neural network model (the student) emulates an unknown mapping (the teacher), given a set of training examples produced by the teacher. The performance of the student network is typically measured by its generalization error, which is the expected error on an unseen example. The aim of training is to reduce the generalization error by adapting the student network's parameters appropriately.

A common form of training is on-line learning, where training patterns are presented sequentially and independently to the network at each learning step. This form of training can be beneficial in terms of both storage and computation time, especially for large systems. A frequently used on-line training method for networks with continuous nodes is that of stochastic gradient descent, since a differentiable error measure can be defined in this case. The stochasticity is a consequence of the training error being determined according to only the latest, randomly chosen, training example. This is to be contrasted with batch learning, where all the training examples would be used to determine the training error leading to a deterministic algorithm. Finding an effective algorithm for discrete networks is less straightforward as the error measure is not differentiable.

* rattraym@aston.ac.uk
† saadd@aston.ac.uk

Often, it is possible to improve on the basic stochastic gradient descent algorithm and a number of modifications have been suggested in the literature. At late times one can use on-line estimates of second order information (the Hessian or its eigenvalues) to ensure asymptotically optimal performance (e.g., [1, 2]). A number of heuristics also exist which attempt to improve performance during the transient phase of learning (for a review, see [3]). However, these heuristics all require the careful setting of parameters which can be critical to their performance. Moreover, it would be desirable to have principled and theoretically well motivated algorithms which do not rely on heuristic arguments.

Statistical mechanics allows a compact description for a number of on-line learning scenarios in the limit of large input dimension, which we have recently employed to propose a method for determining globally optimal learning rates for on-line gradient descent [4]. This method will be generalized here to determine globally optimal on-line learning rules for both discrete and continuous machines. That is, rules which provide the maximum reduction in generalization error over the whole learning process. This provides a natural extension to work on locally optimal learning rules [5, 6], where only the rate of change in generalization error is optimized. In fact, for simple systems we sometimes find that the locally optimal rule is also globally optimal. However, global optimization seems to be rather important in more complex systems which are characterized by more degrees of freedom and often require broken permutation symmetries to learn perfectly. We will outline our general formalism and consider two simple and tractable learning scenarios to demonstrate the method.

It should be pointed out that the optimal rules derived here will often require knowledge of macroscopic properties related to the teacher's structure which would not be known in general. In this sense these rules do not provide practical algorithms as they stand, although some of the required macroscopic properties may be evaluated or estimated on the basis of data gathered as the learning progresses. In any case these rules provide an upper bound on the performance one could expect from a real algorithm and may be instrumental in designing practical training algorithms.

2 The statistical mechanics framework

For calculating the optimal on-line learning rule we employ the statistical mechanics description of the learning process. Under this framework, which may be employed for both smooth [7, 8] and discrete systems (e.g. [9]), the learning process is captured by a small number of self-averaging statistics whose trajectory is deterministic in the limit of large input dimension. In this analysis the relevant statistics are overlaps between weight vectors associated with different nodes of the student and teacher networks. The equations of motion for the evolution of these overlaps can be written in closed form and can be integrated numerically to describe the dynamics.

We will consider a general two-layer soft committee machine[1]. The desired teacher mapping is from an N-dimensional input space $\boldsymbol{\xi} \in \Re^N$ onto a scalar $\zeta \in \Re$, which the student models through a map $\sigma(\mathbf{J}, \boldsymbol{\xi}) = \sum_{i=1}^{K} g(\mathbf{J}_i \cdot \boldsymbol{\xi})$, where $g(x)$ is the activation function for the hidden layer, $\mathbf{J} \equiv \{\mathbf{J}_i\}_{1 \le i \le K}$ is the set of input-to-hidden adaptive weights for the K hidden nodes and the hidden-to-output weights are set to 1. The activation of hidden node i under presentation of the input pattern $\boldsymbol{\xi}^{\mu}$ is denoted $x_i^{\mu} = \mathbf{J}_i \cdot \boldsymbol{\xi}^{\mu}$.

---

[1]The general result presented here also applies to the discrete committee machine, but we will limit our discussion to the soft-committee machine.

Training examples are of the form $(\boldsymbol{\xi}^{\mu}, \zeta^{\mu})$ where $\mu = 1, 2, \ldots, P$. The components of the independently drawn input vectors $\boldsymbol{\xi}^{\mu}$ are uncorrelated random variables with zero mean and unit variance. The corresponding output ζ^{μ} is given by a deterministic teacher of a similar configuration to the student except for a possible difference in the number M of hidden units and is of the form $\zeta^{\mu} = \sum_{n=1}^{M} g(\mathbf{B}_n \cdot \boldsymbol{\xi}^{\mu})$, where $\mathbf{B} \equiv \{\mathbf{B}_n\}_{1 \leq n \leq M}$ is the set of input-to-hidden adaptive weights. The activation of hidden node n under presentation of the input pattern $\boldsymbol{\xi}^{\mu}$ is denoted $y_n^{\mu} = \mathbf{B}_n \cdot \boldsymbol{\xi}^{\mu}$. We will use indices $i, j, k, l \ldots$ to refer to units in the student network and $n, m, \ldots$ for units in the teacher network. We will use the commonly used quadratic deviation $\epsilon(\mathbf{J}, \boldsymbol{\xi}) \equiv \frac{1}{2}[\sigma(\mathbf{J}, \boldsymbol{\xi}) - \zeta]^2$, as the measure of disagreement between teacher and student. The most basic learning rule is to perform gradient descent on this quantity. Performance on a typical input defines the generalization error $\epsilon_g(\mathbf{J}) \equiv \langle \epsilon(\mathbf{J}, \boldsymbol{\xi}) \rangle_{\{\xi\}}$ through an average over all possible input vectors $\boldsymbol{\xi}$.

The general form of learning rule we will consider is,

$$\mathbf{J}_i^{\mu+1} = \mathbf{J}_i^{\mu} + \frac{1}{N} F_i^{\mu}(x^{\mu}, \zeta^{\mu})\, \boldsymbol{\xi}^{\mu} \tag{1}$$

where $\mathbf{F} \equiv \{F_i\}$ depends only on the student activations and the teacher's output, and not on the teacher activations which are unobservable. Note that gradient descent on the error takes this general form, as does Hebbian learning and other training algorithms commonly used in discrete machines. The optimal $\mathbf{F}$ can also depend on the self-averaging statistics which describe the dynamics, since we know how they evolve in time. Some of these would not be available in a practical application, although for some simple cases the unobservable statistics can be deduced from observable quantities. This is therefore an idealization rather than a practical algorithm and provides a bound on the performance of a real algorithm.

The activations are distributed according to a multivariate Gaussian with covariances: $\langle x_i x_k \rangle = \mathbf{J}_i \cdot \mathbf{J}_k \equiv Q_{ik}$, $\langle x_i y_n \rangle = \mathbf{J}_i \cdot \mathbf{B}_n \equiv R_{in}$, and $\langle y_n y_m \rangle = \mathbf{B}_n \cdot \mathbf{B}_m \equiv T_{nm}$, measuring overlaps between student and teacher vectors. Angled brackets denote averages over input patterns. The covariance matrix completely describes the state of the system and in the limit of large N we can write equations of motion for each macroscopic (the T_{nm} are fixed and define the teacher):

$$\frac{dR_{in}}{d\alpha} = \langle F_i y_n \rangle \qquad \frac{dQ_{ik}}{d\alpha} = \langle F_i x_k + F_k x_i + F_i F_k \rangle, \tag{2}$$

where angled brackets now denote the averages over activations, replacing the averages over inputs, and $\alpha = \mu/N$ plays the role of a continuous time variable.

3   The globally optimal rule

Carrying out the averaging over input patterns one obtains an expression for the generalization error which depends exclusively on the overlaps R, Q and T. Using the dependence of their dynamics (Eq. 2) on $\mathbf{F}$ one can easily calculate the locally optimal learning rule [5] by taking the functional derivative of $d\epsilon_g(\mathbf{F})/d\alpha$ to zero, looking for the rule that will maximize the reduction in generalization error at the present time step. This approach has been shown to be successful in some training scenarios but is likely to fail where the learning process is characterized by several phases of a different natures (e.g., multilayer networks).

The *globally optimal* learning rule is found by minimizing the total change in generalization error over a fixed time window,

$$\Delta \epsilon_g(\mathbf{F}) = \int_{\alpha_0}^{\alpha_1} \frac{d\epsilon_g}{d\alpha}\, d\alpha = \int_{\alpha_0}^{\alpha_1} \mathcal{L}(\mathbf{F}, \alpha)\, d\alpha. \tag{3}$$

This is a functional of the learning rule which we minimize by a variational approach.

First we can rewrite the integrand by expanding in terms of the equations of motion, each constrained by a Lagrange multiplier,

$$\mathcal{L}(\mathbf{F}, \alpha) = \sum_{in} \frac{\partial \epsilon_g}{\partial R_{in}} \frac{dR_{in}}{d\alpha} + \sum_{ik} \frac{\partial \epsilon_g}{\partial Q_{ik}} \frac{dQ_{ik}}{d\alpha} + \sum_{in} \lambda_{in} \left(\frac{dR_{in}}{d\alpha} - \langle F_i y_n \rangle \right)$$

$$+ \sum_{ik} \nu_{ik} \left(\frac{dQ_{ik}}{d\alpha} - \langle F_i x_k + F_k x_i + F_i F_k \rangle \right) . \qquad (4)$$

The expression for $\mathcal{L}$ still involve two multidimensional integrations over $\mathbf{x}$ and $\mathbf{y}$, so taking variations in $\mathbf{F}$, which may depend on $\mathbf{x}$ and ζ but not on $\mathbf{y}$, we find an expression for the optimal rule in terms of the Lagrange multipliers:

$$\mathbf{F} = -\mathbf{x} - \frac{1}{2} \nu^{-1} \lambda \overline{\mathbf{y}} \qquad (5)$$

where $\nu = [\nu_{ij}]$ and $\lambda = [\lambda_{in}]$. We define $\overline{\mathbf{y}}$ to be the teacher's expected field given the teacher's output and the student activations, which are observable quantities:

$$\overline{\mathbf{y}} = \int \mathbf{dy} \, \mathbf{y} \, p(\mathbf{y}|\mathbf{x}, \zeta) . \qquad (6)$$

Now taking variations in the overlaps w.r.t. the integral in Eq. (3) we find a set of differential equations for the Lagrange multipliers,

$$\frac{d\lambda_{km}}{d\alpha} = -\sum_{in} \lambda_{in} \frac{\partial \langle F_i y_n \rangle}{\partial R_{km}} - \sum_{ij} \nu_{ij} \frac{\partial \langle F_i x_j + F_j x_i + F_i F_j \rangle}{\partial R_{km}}$$

$$\frac{d\nu_{kl}}{d\alpha} = -\sum_{in} \lambda_{in} \frac{\partial \langle F_i y_n \rangle}{\partial Q_{kl}} - \sum_{ij} \nu_{ij} \frac{\partial \langle F_i x_j + F_j x_i + F_i F_j \rangle}{\partial Q_{kl}} , \qquad (7)$$

where $\mathbf{F}$ takes its optimal value defined in Eq. (5). The boundary conditions for the Lagrange multipliers are,

$$\lambda_{in}(\alpha_1) = \left. \frac{\partial \epsilon_g}{\partial R_{in}} \right|_{\alpha_1} \quad \text{and} \quad \nu_{ik}(\alpha_1) = \left. \frac{\partial \epsilon_g}{\partial Q_{ik}} \right|_{\alpha_1} , \qquad (8)$$

which are found by minimizing the rate of change in generalization error at α_1, so that the globally optimal solution reduces to the locally optimal solution at this point, reflecting the fact that changes at α_1 have no affect at other times.

If the above expressions do not yield an explicit formula for the optimal rule then the rule can be determined iteratively by gradient descent on the functional $\Delta \epsilon_g(\mathbf{F})$. To determine all the quantities necessary for this procedure requires that we first integrate the equations for the overlaps forward and then integrate the equations for the Lagrange multipliers backwards from the boundary conditions in Eq. (8).

4   Two tractable examples

In order to apply the above results we must be able to carry out the average in Eq. (6) and then in Eq. (7). These averages are also required to determine the locally optimal learning rule, so that the present method can be extended to any of the problems which have already been considered under the criteria of local optimality. Here we present two examples where the averages can be computed in closed form. The first problem we consider is a boolean perceptron learning a linearly separable task where we retrieve the locally optimal rule [5]. The second problem is an over-realizable task, where a soft committee machine student learns a perceptron with a sigmoidal response. In this example the globally optimal rule significantly outperforms the locally optimal rule and exhibits a faster asymptotic decay.

Boolean perceptron: For the boolean perceptron we choose the activation function $g(x) = \text{sgn}(x)$ and both teacher and student have a single hidden node ($M = K = 1$). The locally optimal rule was determined by Kinouchi and Caticha [5] and they supply the expected teacher field given the teacher output $\zeta = \text{sgn}(y)$ and the student field x (we take the teacher length $T = 1$ without loss of generality),

$$\bar{y} = \frac{R}{Q} \left(x + \frac{\zeta \sqrt{\frac{2}{\pi}} \exp(-\frac{\gamma^2 x^2}{2})}{\gamma \, \text{erfc}\left(\frac{-\zeta x \gamma}{\sqrt{2}}\right)} \right) \quad \text{where} \quad \gamma = \frac{R}{\sqrt{Q^2 - R^2 Q}} \ . \tag{9}$$

Substituting this expression into the Lagrange multiplier dynamics in Eq. (7) shows that the ratio of λ to ν is given by $\lambda/\nu = -2Q/R$, and Eq. (5) then returns the locally optimal value for the optimal rule:

$$F = \frac{\zeta \sqrt{\frac{2}{\pi}} \exp(-\frac{\gamma^2 x^2}{2})}{\gamma \, \text{erfc}\left(\frac{-\zeta x \gamma}{\sqrt{2}}\right)} \ . \tag{10}$$

This rule leads to modulated Hebbian learning and the resulting dynamics are discussed in [5]. We also find that the locally optimal rule is retrieved when the teacher is corrupted by output or weight noise [9].

Soft committee machine learning a continuous perceptron: In this example the teacher is an invertible perceptron ($M = 1$) while the student is a soft committee machine with an arbitrary number (K) of hidden nodes. We choose the activation function $g(x) = \text{erf}(x/\sqrt{2})$ for both the student and teacher since this allows the generalization error to be determined in closed form [7]. This is an example of an over-realizable task, since the student has greater complexity than is required to learn the teacher's mapping. The locally optimal rule for this scenario was determined recently [6].

Since the teacher is invertible, the expected teacher activation $\bar{y}$ is trivially equal to the true activation y. This leads to a particularly simple form for the dynamics (the n suffix is dropped since there is only one teacher node),

$$\frac{dR_i}{d\alpha} = b_i T - R_i \qquad \frac{dQ_{ik}}{d\alpha} = b_i b_k T - Q_{ik} \ , \tag{11}$$

where we have defined $b_i = -\sum_j \nu_{ij}^{-1} \lambda_j / 2$ and the optimal rule is given by $F_i = b_i y - x_i$. The Lagrange multiplier dynamics in Eq. (7) then show that the relative ratios of each Lagrange multiplier remain fixed over time, so that b_i is determined by its boundary value (see Eq. (8)). It is straightforward to find solutions for long times, since the b_i approach limiting values for very small generalization error (there are a number of possible solutions because of symmetries in the problem but any such solution will have the same performance for long times). For example, one possible solution is to have $b_1 = 1$ and $b_i = 0$ for all $i \neq 1$, which leads to an exponential decay of weights associated with all but a single node. This shows how the optimal performance is achieved when the complexity of the student matches that of the teacher.

Figure 1 shows results for a three node student learning a continuous perceptron. Clearly, the locally optimal rule performs poorly in comparison to the globally

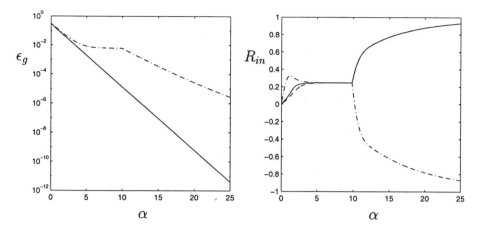

Figure 1: A three node soft committee machine student learns from an continuous perceptron teacher. The figure on the left shows a log plot of the generalization error for the globally optimal (solid line) and locally optimal (dashed line) algorithms. The figure on the right shows the student-teacher overlaps for the locally optimal rule, which exhibit a symmetric plateau before specialization occurs. The overlaps where initialized randomly and uniformly with $Q_{ii} \in [0, 0.5]$ and $R_i, Q_{i \neq j} \in [0, 10^{-6}]$.

optimal rule. In this example the globally optimal rule arrived at was one in which two nodes became correlated with the teacher while a third became anti-correlated, showing another possible variation on the optimal rule (we determined this rule iteratively by gradient descent in order to justify our general approach, although the observations above show how one can predict the final result for long times). The locally optimal rule gets caught in a symmetric plateau, characterized by a lack of differentiation between student vectors associated with different nodes, and also displays a slower asymptotic decay.

5   Conclusion and future work

We have presented a method for determining the optimal on-line learning rule for a soft committee machine under a statistical mechanics framework. This result complements previous work on locally optimal rules which sought only to optimize the rate of change in generalization error. In this work we considered the global optimization problem of minimizing the total change in generalization error over the whole learning process. We gave two simple examples for which the rule could be determined in closed form, for one of which, an over-realizable learning scenario, it was shown how the locally optimal rule performed poorly in comparison to the globally optimal rule. It is expected that more involved systems will show even greater difference in performance between local and global optimization and we are currently applying the method to more general teacher mappings. The main technical difficulty is in computing the expected teacher activation in Eq. (6) and this may require the use of approximate methods in some cases.

It would be interesting to compare the training dynamics obtained by the globally optimal rules to other approaches, heuristic and principled, aimed at incorporating information about the curvature of the error surface into the parameter modification rule. In particular we would like to examine rules which are known to be optimal *asymptotically* (e.g. [10]). Another important issue is whether one can apply these results to facilitate the design of a practical learning algorithm.

Acknowledgement This work was supported by the EPSRC grant GR/L19232.

References

[1] G. B. Orr and T. K. Leen in *Advances in Neural Information Processing Systems, vol 9,* eds M. C. Mozer, M. I. Jordan and T. Petsche (MIT Press, Cambridge MA, 1997) p 606.

[2] Y. LeCun, P. Y. Simard and B. Pearlmutter in *Advances in Neural Information Processing Systems, vol 5,* eds S. J. Hanson, J. D. Cowan and C. L. Giles (Morgan Kaufman, San Mateo, CA, 1993) p 156.

[3] C. M. Bishop, *Neural networks for pattern recognition,* (Oxford University Press, Oxford, 1995).

[4] D. Saad and M. Rattray, *Phys. Rev. Lett.* **79**, 2578 (1997).

[5] O. Kinouchi and N. Caticha *J. Phys. A* **25**, 6243 (1992).

[6] R. Vicente and N. Caticha *J. Phys. A* **30**, L599 (1997).

[7] D. Saad and S. A. Solla, *Phys. Rev. Lett.* **74**, 4337 (1995) and *Phys. Rev. E* **52** 4225 (1995).

[8] M. Biehl and H. Schwarze, *J. Phys. A* **28**, 643 (1995).

[9] M. Biehl, P. Riegler and M. Stechert, *Phys. Rev. E* **52**, R4624 (1995).

[10] S. Amari in *Advances in Neural Information Processing Systems, vol 9,* eds M. C. Mozer, M. I. Jordan and T. Petsche (MIT Press, Cambridge MA, 1997).

Minimax and Hamiltonian Dynamics of Excitatory-Inhibitory Networks

H. S. Seung, T. J. Richardson
Bell Labs, Lucent Technologies
Murray Hill, NJ 07974
{seung|tjr}@bell-labs.com

J. C. Lagarias
AT&T Labs–Research
180 Park Ave. D-130
Florham Park, NJ 07932
jcl@research.att.com

J. J. Hopfield
Dept. of Molecular Biology
Princeton University
Princeton, NJ 08544
jhopfield@watson.princeton.edu

Abstract

A Lyapunov function for excitatory-inhibitory networks is constructed. The construction assumes symmetric interactions within excitatory and inhibitory populations of neurons, and antisymmetric interactions between populations. The Lyapunov function yields sufficient conditions for the global asymptotic stability of fixed points. If these conditions are violated, limit cycles may be stable. The relations of the Lyapunov function to optimization theory and classical mechanics are revealed by minimax and dissipative Hamiltonian forms of the network dynamics.

The dynamics of a neural network with symmetric interactions provably converges to fixed points under very general assumptions[1, 2]. This mathematical result helped to establish the paradigm of neural computation with fixed point attractors[3]. But in reality, interactions between neurons in the brain are asymmetric. Furthermore, the dynamical behaviors seen in the brain are not confined to fixed point attractors, but also include oscillations and complex nonperiodic behavior. These other types of dynamics can be realized by asymmetric networks, and may be useful for neural computation. For these reasons, it is important to understand the global behavior of asymmetric neural networks.

The interaction between an excitatory neuron and an inhibitory neuron is clearly asymmetric. Here we consider a class of networks that incorporates this fundamental asymmetry of the brain's microcircuitry. Networks of this class have distinct populations of excitatory and inhibitory neurons, with antisymmetric interactions between populations and symmetric interactions within each population. Such networks display a rich repertoire of dynamical behaviors including fixed points, limit cycles[4, 5] and traveling waves[6].

After defining the class of excitatory-inhibitory networks, we introduce a Lyapunov function that establishes sufficient conditions for the global asymptotic stability of fixed points. The generality of these conditions contrasts with the restricted nature of previous convergence results, which applied only to linear networks[5], or to nonlinear networks with infinitely fast inhibition[7].

The use of the Lyapunov function is illustrated with a competitive or winner-take-all network, which consists of an excitatory population of neurons with recurrent inhibition from a single neuron[8]. For this network, the sufficient conditions for global stability of fixed points also happen to be necessary conditions. In other words, we have proved global stability over the largest possible parameter regime in which it holds, demonstrating the power of the Lyapunov function. There exists another parameter regime in which numerical simulations display limit cycle oscillations[7].

Similar convergence proofs for other excitatory-inhibitory networks may be obtained by tedious but straightforward calculations. All the necessary tools are given in the first half of the paper. But the rest of the paper explains what makes the Lyapunov function especially interesting, beyond the convergence results it yields: its role in a conceptual framework that relates excitatory-inhibitory networks to optimization theory and classical mechanics.

The connection between neural networks and optimization[3] was established by proofs that symmetric networks could find *minima* of objective functions[1, 2]. Later it was discovered that excitatory-inhibitory networks could perform the minimax computation of finding *saddle points*[9, 10, 11], though no general proof of this was given at the time. Our Lyapunov function finally supplies such a proof, and one of its components is the objective function of the network's minimax computation.

Our Lyapunov function can also be obtained by writing the dynamics of excitatory-inhibitory networks in Hamiltonian form, with extra velocity-dependent terms. If these extra terms are dissipative, then the energy of the system is nonincreasing, and is a Lyapunov function. If the extra terms are not purely dissipative, limit cycles are possible. Previous Hamiltonian formalisms for neural networks made the more restrictive assumption of purely antisymmetric interactions, and did not include the effect of dissipation[12].

This paper establishes sufficient conditions for global asymptotic stability of fixed points. The problem of finding sufficient conditions for oscillatory and chaotic behavior remains open. The perspectives of minimax and Hamiltonian dynamics may help in this task.

1   EXCITATORY-INHIBITORY NETWORKS

The dynamics of an excitatory-inhibitory network is defined by

$$\tau_x \dot{x} + x = f(u + Ax - By) , \tag{1}$$
$$\tau_y \dot{y} + y = g(v + B^T x - Cy) . \tag{2}$$

The state variables are contained in two vectors $x \in R^m$ and $y \in R^n$, which represent the activities of the excitatory and inhibitory neurons, respectively.

The symbol f is used in both scalar and vector contexts. The scalar function $f : R \to R$ is monotonic nondecreasing. The vector function $f : R^m \to R^m$ is defined by applying the scalar function f to each component of a vector argument, i.e., $f(x) = (f(x_1), \ldots, f(x_m))$. The symbol g is used similarly.

The symmetry of interaction within each population is imposed by the constraints $A = A^T$ and $C = C^T$. The antisymmetry of interaction between populations is manifest in the occurrence of $-B$ and B^T in the equations. The terms "excitatory" and "inhibitory" are appropriate with the additional constraint that the entries of matrices A, B, and C are nonnegative. Though this assumption makes sense in a neurobiological context the mathematics does not depends on it. The constant vectors u and v represent tonic input from external sources, or alternatively bias intrinsic to the neurons.

The time constants τ_x and τ_y set the speed of excitatory and inhibitory synapses, respectively. In the limit of infinitely fast inhibition, $\tau_y = 0$, the convergence theorems for symmetric networks are applicable[1, 2], though some effort is required in applying them to the case $C \neq 0$. If the dynamics converges for $\tau_y = 0$, then there exists some neighborhood of zero in which it still converges[7]. Our Lyapunov function goes further, as it is valid for more general τ_y.

The potential for oscillatory behavior in excitatory-inhibitory networks like (1) has long been known[4, 7]. The origin of oscillations can be understood from a simple two neuron model. Suppose that neuron 1 excites neuron 2, and receives inhibition back from neuron 2. Then the effect is that neuron 1 suppresses its own activity with an effective delay that depends on the time constant of inhibition. If this delay is long enough, oscillations result. However, these oscillations will die down to a fixed point, as the inhibition tends to dampen activity in the circuit. Only if neuron 1 also excites itself can the oscillations become sustained.

Therefore, whether oscillations are damped or sustained depends on the choice of parameters. In this paper we establish sufficient conditions for the global stability of fixed points in (1). The violation of these sufficient conditions indicates parameter regimes in which there may be other types of asymptotic behavior, such as limit cycles.

2 LYAPUNOV FUNCTION

We will assume that f and g are smooth and that their inverses f^{-1} and g^{-1} exist. If the function f is bounded above and/or below, then its inverse f^{-1} is defined on the appropriate subinterval of R. Note that the set of (x, y) lying in the range of (f, g) is a positive invariant set under (1) and that its closure is a global attractor for the system.

The scalar function F is defined as the antiderivative of f, and $\bar{F}$ as the Legendre transform $\bar{F}(x) = \max_p \{px - F(p)\}$. The derivatives of these conjugate convex functions are,

$$F'(x) = f(x) , \qquad \bar{F}'(x) = f^{-1}(x) . \tag{3}$$

The vector versions of these functions are defined componentwise, as in the definition of the vector version of f. The conjugate convex pair $G, \bar{G}$ is defined similarly.

The Lyapunov function requires generalizations of the standard kinetic energies $\tau_x \dot{x}^2/2$ and $\tau_y \dot{y}^2/2$. These are constructed using the functions $\Phi : R^m \times R^m \to R$ and $\Gamma : R^n \times R^n \to R$, defined by

$$\Phi(p, x) = 1^T F(p) - x^T p + 1^T \bar{F}(x) , \tag{4}$$

$$\Gamma(q, y) = 1^T G(q) - y^T q + 1^T \bar{G}(y) . \tag{5}$$

The components of the vector $\mathbf{1}$ are all ones; its dimensionality should be clear from context. The function $\Phi(p, x)$ is lower bounded by zero, and vanishes on the manifold $f(p) = x$, by the definition of the Legendre transform. Setting $p = u + Ax - By$, we obtain the generalized kinetic energy $\tau_x^{-1}\Phi(u + Ax - By, x)$, which vanishes when $\dot{x} = 0$ and is positive otherwise. It reduces to $\tau_x \dot{x}^2/2$ in the special case where f is the identity function.

To construct the Lyapunov function, a multiple of the saddle function

$$S = -u^T x - \frac{1}{2}x^T Ax + v^T y - \frac{1}{2}y^T Cy + \mathbf{1}^T \bar{F}(x) + y^T B^T x - \mathbf{1}^T \bar{G}(y) \qquad (6)$$

is added to the kinetic energy. The reason for the name "saddle function" will be explained later. Then

$$L = \tau_x^{-1}\Phi(u + Ax - By, x) + \tau_y^{-1}\Gamma(v + B^T x - Cy, y) + rS \qquad (7)$$

is a Lyapunov function provided that it is lower bounded, nonincreasing, and $\dot{L}$ only vanishes at fixed points of the dynamics. Roughly speaking, this is enough to prove the global asymptotic stability of fixed points, although some additional technical details may be involved.

In the next section, the Lyapunov function will be applied to an example network, yielding sufficient conditions for the global asymptotic stability of fixed points. In this particular network, the sufficient conditions also happen to be necessary conditions. Therefore the Lyapunov function succeeds in delineating the largest possible parameter regime in which point attractors are globally stable. Of course, there is no guarantee of this in general, but the power of the Lyapunov function is manifest in this instance.

Before proceeding to the example network, we pause to state some general conditions for L to be nonincreasing. A lengthy but straightforward calculation shows that the time derivative of L is given by

$$\begin{aligned}
\dot{L} &= \dot{x}^T A\dot{x} - \dot{y}^T C\dot{y} \qquad (8)\\
&\quad -(\tau_x^{-1} + r)\dot{x}^T[f^{-1}(\tau_x\dot{x} + x) - f^{-1}(x)]\\
&\quad -(\tau_y^{-1} - r)\dot{y}^T[g^{-1}(\tau_y\dot{y} + y) - g^{-1}(y)] \ .
\end{aligned}$$

Therefore, L is nonincreasing provided that

$$\max_{a,b} \frac{(a - b)^T A(a - b)}{(a - b)^T[f^{-1}(a) - f^{-1}(b)]} \leq 1 + r\tau_x \ , \qquad (9)$$

$$\min_{a,b} \frac{(a - b)^T C(a - b)}{(a - b)^T[g^{-1}(a) - g^{-1}(b)]} \geq 1 - r\tau_y \ . \qquad (10)$$

The quotients in these inequalities are generalizations of the Rayleigh-Ritz ratios of A and C. If f and g were linear, the left hand sides of these inequalities would be equal to the maximum eigenvalue of A and the minimum eigenvalue of C.

3   AN EXAMPLE: COMPETITIVE NETWORK

The competitive or winner-take-all network is a classic example of an excitatory-inhibitory network[8, 7]. Its population of excitatory neurons x_i receives self-feedback of strength α and recurrent feedback from a single inhibitory neuron y,

$$\tau_x \dot{x}_i + x_i = f(u_i + \alpha x_i - y) \ , \qquad (11)$$

$$\tau_y \dot{y} + y = g\left(\sum_i x_i\right) \ . \qquad (12)$$

This is a special case of (1), with $A = \alpha I$, $B = \mathbf{1}$, and $C = 0$.

The global inhibitory neuron mediates a competitive interaction between the excitatory neurons. If the competition is very strong, a single excitatory neuron "wins," shutting off all the rest. If the competition is weak, more than one excitatory neuron can win, usually those corresponding to the larger u_i. Depending on the choice of f and g, self-feedback α, and time scales τ_x and τ_y, this network exhibits a variety of dynamical behaviors, including a single point attractor, multiple point attractors, and limit cycles[5, 7].

We will consider the specific case where f and g are the rectification nonlinearity $[x]^+ = \max\{x, 0\}$. The behavior of this network will be described in detail elsewhere; only a brief summary is given here. With either of two convenient choices for r, $r = \tau_y^{-1}$ or $r = \alpha - \tau_x^{-1}$, it can be shown that the resulting L is bounded below for $\alpha < 2$ and nonincreasing for $\alpha < \tau_x^{-1} + \tau_y^{-1}$. These are sufficient conditions for the global stability of fixed points. They also turn out to be necessary conditions, as it can be verified that the fixed points are locally unstable if the conditions are violated. The behaviors in the parameter regime defined by these conditions can be divided into two rough categories. For $\alpha < 1$, there is a unique point attractor, at which more than one excitatory neuron can be active, in a soft form of winner-take-all. For $\alpha > 1$, more than one point attractor may exist. Only one excitatory neuron is active at each of these fixed points, a hard form of winner-take-all.

4 MINIMAX DYNAMICS

In the field of optimization, gradient descent-ascent is a standard method for finding saddle points of an objective function. This section of the paper explains the close relationship between gradient descent-ascent and excitatory-inhibitory networks[9, 10]. Furthermore, it reviews existing results on the convergence of gradient descent-ascent to saddle points[13, 10], which are the precedents of the convergence proofs of this paper.

The similarity of excitatory-inhibitory networks to gradient descent-ascent can be seen by comparing the partial derivatives of the saddle function (6) to the velocities $\dot{x}$ and $\dot{y}$,

$$-\frac{\partial S}{\partial x} = f^{-1}(\tau_x \dot{x} + x) - f^{-1}(x) \sim \tau_x \dot{x} , \tag{13}$$

$$\frac{\partial S}{\partial y} = g^{-1}(\tau_y \dot{y} + y) - g^{-1}(y) \sim \tau_y \dot{y} . \tag{14}$$

The notation $a \sim b$ means that the vectors a and b have the same signs, component by component. Because f and g are monotonic nondecreasing functions, $\dot{x}$ has the same signs as $-\partial S/\partial x$, while $\dot{y}$ has the same signs as $\partial S/\partial y$. In other words, the dynamics of the excitatory neurons tends to minimize S, while that of the inhibitory neurons tends to maximize S.

If the sign relation $\sim$ is replaced by equality in (13), we obtain a true gradient descent-ascent dynamics,

$$\tau_x \dot{x} = -\frac{\partial S}{\partial x} , \qquad \tau_y \dot{y} = \frac{\partial S}{\partial y} . \tag{15}$$

Sufficient conditions for convergence of gradient descent-ascent to saddle points are known[13, 10]. The conditions can be derived using a Lyapunov function constructed from the kinetic energy and the saddle function,

$$L = \frac{1}{2}\tau_x |\dot{x}|^2 + \frac{1}{2}\tau_y |\dot{y}|^2 + rS . \tag{16}$$

The time derivative of L is given by

$$\dot{L} = -\dot{x}^T \frac{\partial^2 S}{\partial x^2} \dot{x} + \dot{y}^T \frac{\partial^2 S}{\partial y^2} \dot{y} - r\tau_x \dot{x}^2 + r\tau_y \dot{y}^2 \ . \tag{17}$$

Weak sufficient conditions can be derived with the choice $r = 0$, so that L includes only kinetic energy terms. Then L is obviously lower bounded by zero. Furthermore, L is nonincreasing if $\partial^2 S/\partial x^2$ is positive definite for all y and $\partial^2 S/\partial y^2$ is negative definite for all x. In this case, the existence of a unique saddle point is guaranteed, as S is convex in x for all y, and concave in y for all x[13, 10].

If there is more than one saddle point, the kinetic energy by itself is generally not a Lyapunov function. This is because the dynamics may pass through the vicinity of more than one saddle point before it finally converges, so that the kinetic energy behaves nonmonotonically as a function of time. In this situation, some appropriate nonzero r must be found.

The Lyapunov function (7) for excitatory-inhibitory networks is a generalization of the Lyapunov function (16) for gradient descent-ascent. This is analogous to the way in which the Lyapunov function for symmetric networks generalizes the potential function of gradient descent.

It should be noted that gradient descent-ascent is an unreliable way of finding a saddle point. It is easy to construct situations in which it leads to a limit cycle. The unreliability of gradient descent-ascent contrasts with the reliability of gradient descent at finding local minimum of a potential function. Similarly, symmetric networks converge to fixed points, but excitatory-inhibitory networks can converge to limit cycles as well.

5   HAMILTONIAN DYNAMICS

The dynamics of an excitatory-inhibitory network can be written in a dissipative Hamiltonian form. To do this, we define a phase space that is double the dimension of the state space, adding momenta (p_x, p_y) that are canonically conjugate to (x, y). The phase space dynamics

$$\tau_x \dot{x} + x = f(p_x) \ , \tag{18}$$

$$\tau_y \dot{y} + y = g(p_y) \ , \tag{19}$$

$$\left(r + \frac{d}{dt} \right) (u + Ax - By - p_x) = 0 \ , \tag{20}$$

$$\left(r + \frac{d}{dt} \right) (v + B^T x - Cy - p_y) = 0 \ , \tag{21}$$

reduces to the state space dynamics (1) on the affine space $A = \{(p_x, p_y, x, y) : p_x = u + Ax - By, p_y = v + B^T x - Cy\}$. Provided that $r > 0$, the affine space A is an attractive invariant manifold.

Defining the Hamiltonian

$$H(p_x, x, p_y, y) = \tau_x^{-1} \Phi(p_x, x) + \tau_y^{-1} \Gamma(p_y, y) + rS(x, y) \ , \tag{22}$$

the phase space dynamics (18) can be written as

$$\dot{x} = \frac{\partial H}{\partial p_x} \ , \tag{23}$$

$$\dot{y} = \frac{\partial H}{\partial p_y} \ , \tag{24}$$

$$\dot{p}_x = -\frac{\partial H}{\partial x} + A\dot{x} - B\dot{y} - (\tau_x^{-1} + r)[p_x - f^{-1}(x)] , \tag{25}$$

$$\dot{p}_y = -\frac{\partial H}{\partial y} + B^T\dot{x} - C\dot{y} - (\tau_y^{-1} - r)[p_y - g^{-1}(y)] \tag{26}$$

$$+2r(v + B^Tx - Cy - p_y) . \tag{27}$$

On the invariant manifold A, the Hamiltonian is identical to the Lyapunov function (7) defined previously.

The rate of change of the energy is given by

$$\begin{aligned} \dot{H} = \ & \dot{x}^T A\dot{x} - (\tau_x^{-1} + r)\dot{x}^T[p_x - f^{-1}(x)] \tag{28}\\ & -\dot{y}^T C\dot{y} - (\tau_y^{-1} - r)\dot{y}^T[p_y - g^{-1}(y)] \\ & +2r\dot{y}^T(v + B^Tx - Cy - p_y) . \end{aligned}$$

The last term vanishes on the invariant manifold, leaving a result identical to (8). Therefore, if the noncanonical terms in the phase space dynamics (18) dissipate energy, then the Hamiltonian is nonincreasing. It is also possible that the velocity-dependent terms may pump energy into the system, rather than dissipate it, in which case oscillations or chaotic behavior may arise.

Acknowledgments This work was supported by Bell Laboratories. We would like to thank Eric Mjolsness for useful discussions.

References

[1] M. A. Cohen and S. Grossberg. Absolute stability of global pattern formation and parallel memory storage by competitive neural networks. *IEEE*, 13:815–826, 1983.

[2] J. J. Hopfield. Neurons with graded response have collective computational properties like those of two-state neurons. *Proc. Natl. Acad. Sci. USA*, 81:3088–3092, 1984.

[3] J. J. Hopfield and D. W. Tank. Computing with neural circuits: a model. *Science*, 233:625–633, 1986.

[4] H. R. Wilson and J. D. Cowan. A mathematical theory of the functional dynamics of cortical and thalamic nervous tissue. *Kybernetik*, 13:55–80, 1973.

[5] Z. Li and J. J. Hopfield. Modeling the olfactory bulb and its neural oscillatory processings. *Biol. Cybern.*, 61:379–392, 1989.

[6] S. Amari. Dynamics of pattern formation in lateral-inhibition type neural fields. *Biol. Cybern.*, 27:77–87, 1977.

[7] B. Ermentrout. Complex dynamics in winner-take-all neural nets with slow inhibition. *Neural Networks*, 5:415–431, 1992.

[8] S. Amari and M. A. Arbib. Competition and cooperation in neural nets. In J. Metzler, editor, *Systems Neuroscience*, pages 119–165. Academic Press, New York, 1977.

[9] E. Mjolsness and C. Garrett. Algebraic transformations of objective functions. *Neural Networks*, 3:651–669, 1990.

[10] J. C. Platt and A. H. Barr. Constrained differential optimization. In D. Z. Anderson, editor, *Neural Information Processing Systems*, page 55, New York, 1987. American Institute of Physics.

[11] I. M. Elfadel. Convex potentials and their conjugates in analog mean-field optimization. *Neural Computation*, 7(5):1079–1104, 1995.

[12] J. D. Cowan. A statistical mechanics of nervous activity. In *Some mathematical questions in biology*, volume III. AMS, 1972.

[13] K. J. Arrow, L. Hurwicz, and H. Uzawa. *Studies in linear and non-linear programming*. Stanford University, Stanford, 1958.

Data-Dependent Structural Risk Minimisation for Perceptron Decision Trees

John Shawe-Taylor
Dept of Computer Science
Royal Holloway, University of London
Egham, Surrey TW20 0EX, UK
Email: jst@dcs.rhbnc.ac.uk

Nello Cristianini
Dept of Engineering Mathematics
University of Bristol
Bristol BS8 1TR, UK
Email: nello.cristianini@bristol.ac.uk

Abstract

Perceptron Decision Trees (also known as Linear Machine DTs, etc.) are analysed in order that data-dependent Structural Risk Minimization can be applied. Data-dependent analysis is performed which indicates that choosing the maximal margin hyperplanes at the decision nodes will improve the generalization. The analysis uses a novel technique to bound the generalization error in terms of the margins at individual nodes. Experiments performed on real data sets confirm the validity of the approach.

1 Introduction

Neural network researchers have traditionally tackled classification problems by assembling perceptron or sigmoid nodes into feedforward neural networks. In this paper we consider a less common approach where the perceptrons are used as decision nodes in a decision tree structure. The approach has the advantage that more efficient heuristic algorithms exist for these structures, while the advantages of inherent parallelism are if anything greater as all the perceptrons can be evaluated in parallel, with the path through the tree determined in a very fast post-processing phase.

Classical Decision Trees (DTs), like the ones produced by popular packages as CART [5] or C4.5 [9], partition the input space by means of axis-parallel hyperplanes (one at each internal node), hence inducing categories which are represented by (axis-parallel) hyperrectangles in such a space.

A natural extension of that hypothesis space is obtained by associating to each internal node hyperplanes in general position, hence partitioning the input space by means of polygonal (polyhedral) categories.

This approach has been pursued by many researchers, often with different motivations, and hence the resulting hypothesis space has been given a number of different names: multivariate DTs [6], oblique DTs [8], or DTs using linear combinations of the attributes [5], Linear Machine DTs, Neural Decision Trees [12], Perceptron Trees [13], etc.

We will call them Perceptron Decision Trees (PDTs), as they can be regarded as binary trees having a simple perceptron associated to each decision node.

Different algorithms for Top-Down induction of PDTs from data have been proposed, based on different principles, [10], [5], [8],

Experimental study of learning by means of PDTs indicates that their performances are sometimes better than those of traditional decision trees in terms of generalization error, and usually much better in terms of tree-size [8], [6], but on some data set PDTs can be outperformed by normal DTs.

We investigate an alternative strategy for improving the generalization of these structures, namely placing maximal margin hyperplanes at the decision nodes. By use of a novel analysis we are able to demonstrate that improved generalization bounds can be obtained for this approach. Experiments confirm that such a method delivers more accurate trees in all tested databases.

2 Generalized Decision Trees

Definition 2.1 *Generalized Decision Trees (GDT).*

Given a space X and a set of boolean functions

$\mathcal{F} = \{f : X \rightarrow \{0, 1\}\}$, the class GDT$(\mathcal{F})$ of Generalized Decision Trees over $\mathcal{F}$ are functions which can be implemented using a binary tree where each internal node is labeled with an element of $\mathcal{F}$, and each leaf is labeled with either 1 or 0.

To evaluate a particular tree T on input $x \in X$, All the boolean functions associated to the nodes are assigned the same argument $x \in X$, which is the argument of $T(x)$. The values assumed by them determine a unique path from the root to a leaf: at each internal node the left (respectively right) edge to a child is taken if the output of the function associated to that internal node is 0 (respectively 1). The value of the function at the assignment of a $x \in X$ is the value associated to the leaf reached. We say that input x reaches a node of the tree, if that node is on the evaluation path for x.

In the following, the *nodes* are the internal nodes of the binary tree, and the *leaves* are its external ones.

Examples.

- Given $X = \{0, 1\}^n$, a *Boolean Decision Tree (BDT)* is a GDT over
$$\mathcal{F}_{\mathrm{BDT}} = \{f_i : f_i(\mathbf{x}) = \mathbf{x}_i, \forall \mathbf{x} \in X\}$$
- Given $X = \mathbb{R}^n$, a *C4.5-like Decision Tree (CDT)* is a GDT over
$$\mathcal{F}_{\mathrm{CDT}} = \{f_{i,\theta} : f_{i,\theta}(\mathbf{x}) = 1 \Leftrightarrow x_i > \theta\}$$
  This kind of decision trees defined on a continuous space are the output of common algorithms like C4.5 and CART, and we will call them - for short - CDTs.
- Given $X = \mathbb{R}^n$, a *Perceptron Decision Tree (PDT)* is a GDT over
$$\mathcal{F}_{\mathrm{PDT}} = \{w^T \mathbf{x} : w \in \mathbb{R}^{n+1}\},$$
  where we have assumed that the inputs have been augmented with a coordinate of constant value, hence implementing a thresholded perceptron.

3 Data-dependent SRM

We begin with the definition of the fat-shattering dimension, which was first introduced in [7], and has been used for several problems in learning since [1, 4, 2, 3].

Definition 3.1 *Let $\mathcal{F}$ be a set of real valued functions. We say that a set of points X is γ-shattered by $\mathcal{F}$ relative to $r = (r_x)_{x \in X}$ if there are real numbers r_x indexed by $x \in X$ such that for all binary vectors b indexed by X, there is a function $f_b \in \mathcal{F}$ satisfying*

$$f_b(x) \begin{cases} \geq r_x + \gamma & \text{if } b_x = 1 \\ \leq r_x - \gamma & \text{otherwise.} \end{cases}$$

The fat shattering dimension $\mathrm{fat}_{\mathcal{F}}$ of the set $\mathcal{F}$ is a function from the positive real numbers to the integers which maps a value γ to the size of the largest γ-shattered set, if this is finite, or infinity otherwise.

As an example which will be relevant to the subsequent analysis consider the class:

$$\mathcal{F}_{\mathrm{lin}} = \{x \to \langle w, x \rangle + \theta : \|w\| = 1\}.$$

We quote the following result from [11].

Corollary 3.2 *[11] Let $\mathcal{F}_{\mathrm{lin}}$ be restricted to points in a ball of n dimensions of radius R about the origin and with thresholds $|\theta| \leq R$. Then*

$$\mathrm{fat}_{\mathcal{F}_{\mathrm{lin}}}(\gamma) \leq \min\{9R^2/\gamma^2, n+1\} + 1.$$

The following theorem bounds the generalization of a classifier in terms of the fat shattering dimension rather than the usual Vapnik-Chervonenkis or Pseudo dimension.

Let T_θ denote the threshold function at θ: $T_\theta: \mathbb{R} \to \{0, 1\}$, $T_\theta(\alpha) = 1$ iff $\alpha > \theta$. For a class of functions $\mathcal{F}$, $T_\theta(\mathcal{F}) = \{T_\theta(f): f \in \mathcal{F}\}$.

Theorem 3.3 *[11] Consider a real valued function class $\mathcal{F}$ having fat shattering function bounded above by the function afat : $\mathbb{R} \to \mathbb{N}$ which is continuous from the right. Fix $\theta \in \mathbb{R}$. If a learner correctly classifies m independently generated examples z with $h = T_\theta(f) \in T_\theta(\mathcal{F})$ such that $\mathrm{er}_z(h) = 0$ and $\gamma = \min|f(x_i) - \theta|$, then with confidence $1 - \delta$ the expected error of h is bounded from above by*

$$\epsilon(m, k, \delta) = \frac{2}{m}\left(k \log\left(\frac{8em}{k}\right) \log(32m) + \log\left(\frac{8m}{\delta}\right)\right),$$

where $k = \mathrm{afat}(\gamma/8)$.

The importance of this theorem is that it can be used to explain how a classifier can give better generalization than would be predicted by a classical analysis of its VC dimension. Essentially expanding the margin performs an automatic capacity control for function classes with small fat shattering dimensions. The theorem shows that when a large margin is achieved it is as if we were working in a lower VC class.

We should stress that in general the bounds obtained should be better for cases where a large margin is observed, but that a priori there is no guarantee that such a margin will occur. Therefore a priori only the classical VC bound can be used. In view of corresponding lower bounds on the generalization error in terms of the VC dimension, the a posteriori bounds depend on a favourable probability distribution making the actual learning task easier. Hence, the result will only be useful if the distribution is favourable or at least not adversarial. In this sense the result is a distribution dependent result, despite not being distribution dependent in the traditional sense that assumptions about the distribution have had to be made in its derivation. The benign behaviour of the distribution is automatically estimated in the learning process.

In order to perform a similar analysis for perceptron decision trees we will consider the set of margins obtained at each of the nodes, bounding the generalization as a function of these values.

4   Generalisation analysis of the Tree Class

It turns out that bounding the fat shattering dimension of PDT's viewed as real function classifiers is difficult. We will therefore do a direct generalization analysis mimicking the proof of Theorem 3.3 but taking into account the margins at each of the decision nodes in the tree.

Definition 4.1 *Let (X, d) be a (pseudo-) metric space, let A be a subset of X and $\epsilon > 0$. A set $B \subseteq X$ is an ϵ-cover for A if, for every $a \in A$, there exists $b \in B$ such that $d(a, b) < \epsilon$. The ϵ-covering number of A, $\mathcal{N}_d(\epsilon, A)$, is the minimal cardinality of an ϵ-cover for A (if there is no such finite cover then it is defined to be ∞).*

We write $\mathcal{N}(\epsilon, \mathcal{F}, \mathbf{x})$ for the ϵ-covering number of $\mathcal{F}$ with respect to the ℓ_∞ pseudometric measuring the maximum discrepancy on the sample $\mathbf{x}$. These numbers are bounded in the following Lemma.

Lemma 4.2 (Alon *et al.* **[1])** *Let $\mathcal{F}$ be a class of functions $X \to [0,1]$ and P a distribution over X. Choose $0 < \epsilon < 1$ and let $d = \mathrm{fat}_{\mathcal{F}}(\epsilon/4)$. Then*

$$E\left(\mathcal{N}(\epsilon, \mathcal{F}, \mathbf{x})\right) \leq 2 \left(\frac{4m}{\epsilon^2}\right)^{d \log(2em/(d\epsilon))},$$

where the expectation E is taken w.r.t. a sample $\mathbf{x} \in X^m$ drawn according to P^m.

Corollary 4.3 *[11] Let $\mathcal{F}$ be a class of functions $X \to [a, b]$ and P a distribution over X. Choose $0 < \epsilon < 1$ and let $d = \mathrm{fat}_{\mathcal{F}}(\epsilon/4)$. Then*

$$E\left(\mathcal{N}(\epsilon, \mathcal{F}, \mathbf{x})\right) \leq 2 \left(\frac{4m(b-a)^2}{\epsilon^2}\right)^{d \log(2em(b-a)/(d\epsilon))},$$

where the expectation E is over samples $\mathbf{x} \in X^m$ drawn according to P^m.

We are now in a position to tackle the main lemma which bounds the probability over a double sample that the first half has zero error and the second error greater than an appropriate ϵ. Here, error is interpreted as being differently classified at the output of tree. In order to simplify the notation in the following lemma we assume that the decision tree has K nodes. We also denote $\mathrm{fat}_{\mathcal{F}_{\mathrm{lin}}}(\gamma)$ by $\mathrm{fat}(\gamma)$ to simplify the notation.

Lemma 4.4 *Let T be a perceptron decision tree with K decision nodes with margins $\gamma^1, \gamma^2, \ldots, \gamma^K$ at the decision nodes. If it has correctly classified m labelled examples generated independently according to the unknown (but fixed) distribution P, then we can bound the following probability to be less than δ,*

$$P^{2m}\left\{\mathbf{xy} \colon \exists \text{ a tree } T : T \text{ correctly classifies } \mathbf{x},\right.$$

$$\left. \text{fraction of } \mathbf{y} \text{ misclassified} > \epsilon(m, K, \delta)\right\} < \delta,$$

where $\epsilon(m, K, \delta) = \frac{1}{m}\left(D \log(4m) + \log \frac{2^K}{\delta}\right)$.
where $D = \sum_{i=1}^{K} k_i \log(4em/k_i)$ and $k_i = \mathrm{fat}(\gamma_i/8)$.

Proof: Using the standard permutation argument, we may fix a sequence **xy** and bound the probability under the uniform distribution on swapping permutations that the sequence satisfies the condition stated. We consider generating minimal $\gamma_k/2$-covers B_{xy}^k for each value of k, where $\gamma_k = \min\{\gamma' : \text{fat}(\gamma'/8) \le k\}$. Suppose that for node i of the tree the margin γ^i of the hyperplane w_i satisfies $\text{fat}(\gamma^i/8) = k_i$. We can therefore find $f_i \in B_{xy}^{k_i}$ whose output values are within $\gamma^i/2$ of w_i. We now consider the tree T' obtained by replacing the node perceptrons w_i of T with the corresponding f_i. This tree performs the same classification function on the first half of the sample, and the margin remains larger than $\gamma^i - \gamma_{k_i}/2 > \gamma_{k_i}/2$. If a point in the second half of the sample is incorrectly classified by T it will either still be incorrectly classified by the adapted tree T' or will at one of the decision nodes i in T' be closer to the decision boundary than $\gamma_{k_i}/2$. The point is thus distinguishable from left hand side points which are both correctly classified and have margin greater than $\gamma_{k_i}/2$ at node i. Hence, that point must be kept on the right hand side in order for the condition to be satisfied. Hence, the fraction of permutations that can be allowed for one choice of the functions from the covers is $2^{-\epsilon m}$. We must take the union bound over all choices of the functions from the covers. Using the techniques of [11] the numbers of these choices is bounded by Corollory 4.3 as follows

$$\Pi_{i=1}^K 2(8m)^{k_i \log(4em/k_i)} = 2^K (8m)^D,$$

where $D = \sum_{i=1}^K k_i \log(4em/k_i)$. The value of ϵ in the lemma statement therefore ensures that this the union bound is less than δ.

□

Using the standard lemma due to Vapnik [14, page 168] to bound the error probabilities in terms of the discrepancy on a double sample, combined with Lemma 4.4 gives the following result.

Theorem 4.5 *Suppose we are able to classify an m sample of labelled examples using a perceptron decision tree with K nodes and obtaining margins γ_i at node i, then we can bound the generalisation error with probability greater than $1 - \delta$ to be less than*

$$\frac{1}{m}\left(D\log(4m) + \log\frac{(8m)^K \binom{2K}{K}}{(K+1)\delta}\right)$$

where $D = \sum_{i=1}^K k_i \log(4em/k_i)$ and $k_i = \text{fat}(\gamma_i/8)$.

Proof: We must bound the probabilities over different architectures of trees and different margins. We simply have to choose the values of ϵ to ensure that the individual δ's are sufficiently small that the total over all possible choices is less than δ. The details are omitted in this abstract.

□

5   Experiments

The theoretical results obtained in the previous section imply that an algorithm which produces large margin splits should have a better generalization, since increasing the margins in the internal nodes, has the effect of decreasing the bound on the test error.

In order to test this strategy, we have performed the following experiment, divided in two parts: first run a standard perceptron decision tree algorithm and then for each decision node generate a maximal margin hyperplane implementing the same dichotomy in place of the decision boundary generated by the algorithm.

Input: Random m sample $\mathbf{x}$ with corresponding classification b.

Algorithm: Find a perceptron decision tree T which correctly classifies the sample
using a standard algorithm;
Let k = number of decision nodes of T;
From tree T create T' by executing the following loop:

> **For each decision node** i replace the weight vector w_i by the vector w_i'
> which realises the maximal margin hyperplane agreeing with w_i on the
> set of inputs reaching node i;

Let the margin of w_i' on the inputs reaching node i be γ_i;

Output: Classifier T', with bound on the generalisation error in terms of the number of decision nodes K and $D = \sum_{i=1}^{K} k_i \log(4em/k_i)$ where $k_i = \text{fat}(\gamma_i/8)$.

Note that the classification of T and T' agree on the sample and hence, that T' is consistent with the sample.

As a PDT learning algorithm we have used OC1 [8], created by Murthy, Kasif and Salzberg and freely available over the internet. It is a randomized algorithm, which performs simulated annealing for learning the perceptrons. The details about the randomization, the pruning, and the splitting criteria can be found in [8].

The data we have used for the test are 4 of the 5 sets used in the original OC1 paper, which are publicly available in the UCI data repository [16].

The results we have obtained on these data are compatible with the ones reported in the original OC1 paper, the differences being due to different divisions between training and testing sets and their sizes; the absence in our experiments of cross-validation and other techniques to estimate the predictive accuracy of the PDT; and the inherently randomized nature of the algorithm.

The second stage of the experiment involved finding - for each node - the hyperplane which performes *the same* split as performed by the OC1 tree but with the maximal margin. This can be done by considering the subsample reaching each node as perfectly divided in two parts, and feeding the data accordingly relabelled to an algorithm which finds the optimal split in the linearly separable case. The maximal margin hyperplanes are then placed in the decision nodes and the new tree is tested on the same testing set.

The data sets we have used are: *Wiscounsin Breast Cancer, Pima Indians Diabetes, Boston Housing* transformed into a classification problem by thresholding the price at $ 21.000 and the classical *Iris* studied by Fisher (More informations about the databases and their authors are in [8]). All the details about sample sizes, number of attributes and results (training and testing accuracy, tree size) are summarized in table 1.

We were not particularly interested in achieving a high testing accuracy, but rather in observing if improved performances can be obtained by increasing the margin. For this reason we did not try to optimize the performance of the original classifier by using cross-validation, or a convenient training/testing set ratio. The relevant quantity, in this experiment, is the different in the testing error between a PDT with arbitrary margins and the same tree with optimized margins. This quantity has turned out to be always positive, and to range from 1.7 to 2.8 percent of gain, on test errors which were already very low.

	train	OC1 test	FAT test	#trs	#ts	attrib.	classes	nodes
CANC	96.53	93.52	95.37	249	108	9	2	1
IRIS	96.67	96.67	98.33	90	60	4	3	2
DIAB	89.00	70.48	72.45	209	559	8	2	4
HOUS	95.90	81.43	84.29	306	140	13	2	7

References

[1] Ncga Alon, Shai Ben-David, Nicolò Cesa-Bianchi and David Haussler, "Scale-sensitive Dimensions, Uniform Convergence, and Learnability," in *Proceedings of the Conference on Foundations of Computer Science (FOCS)*, (1993). Also to appear in *Journal of the ACM*.

[2] Martin Anthony and Peter Bartlett, "Function learning from interpolation", Technical Report, (1994). (An extended abstract appeared in *Computational Learning Theory, Proceedings 2nd European Conference, EuroCOLT'95*, pages 211–221, ed. Paul Vitanyi, (Lecture Notes in Artificial Intelligence, 904) Springer-Verlag, Berlin, 1995).

[3] Peter L. Bartlett and Philip M. Long, "Prediction, Learning, Uniform Convergence, and Scale-Sensitive Dimensions," Preprint, Department of Systems Engineering, Australian National University, November 1995.

[4] Peter L. Bartlett, Philip M. Long, and Robert C. Williamson, "Fat-shattering and the learnability of Real-valued Functions," *Journal of Computer and System Sciences*, **52**(3), 434-452, (1996).

[5] Breiman L., Friedman J.H., Olshen R.A., Stone C.J., "Classification and Regression Trees", Wadsworth International Group, Belmont, CA, 1984.

[6] Brodley C.E., Utgoff P.E., Multivariate Decision Trees, Machine Learning 19, pp. 45-77, 1995.

[7] Michael J. Kearns and Robert E. Schapire, "Efficient Distribution-free Learning of Probabilistic Concepts," pages 382–391 in *Proceedings of the 31st Symposium on the Foundations of Computer Science*, IEEE Computer Society Press, Los Alamitos, CA, 1990.

[8] Murthy S.K., Kasif S., Salzberg S., A System for Induction of Oblique Decision Trees, Journal of Artificial Intelligence Research, 2 (1994), pp. 1-32.

[9] Quinlan J.R., "C4.5: Programs for Machine Learning", Morgan Kaufmann, 1993.

[10] Sankar A., Mammone R.J., Growing and Pruning Neural Tree Networks, IEEE Transactions on Computers, 42:291-299, 1993.

[11] John Shawe-Taylor, Peter L. Bartlett, Robert C. Williamson, Martin Anthony, Structural Risk Minimization over Data-Dependent Hierarchies, NeuroCOLT Technical Report NC-TR-96-053, 1996.
(ftp://ftp.dcs.rhbnc.ac.uk/pub/neurocolt/tech_reports).

[12] J.A. Sirat, and J.-P. Nadal, "Neural trees: a new tool for classification", Network, 1, pp. 423-438, 1990

[13] Utgoff P.E., Perceptron Trees: a Case Study in Hybrid Concept Representations, Connection Science 1 (1989), pp. 377-391.

[14] Vladimir N. Vapnik, *Estimation of Dependences Based on Empirical Data*, Springer-Verlag, New York, 1982.

[15] Vladimir N. Vapnik, *The Nature of Statistical Learning Theory*, Springer-Verlag, New York, 1995

[16] University of California, Irvine - Machine Learning Repository, http://www.ics.uci.edu/ mlearn/MLRepository.html

From Regularization Operators to Support Vector Kernels

Alexander J. Smola
GMD FIRST
Rudower Chaussee 5
12489 Berlin, Germany
smola@first.gmd.de

Bernhard Schölkopf
Max–Planck–Institut für biologische Kybernetik
Spemannstraße 38
72076 Tübingen, Germany
bs@mpik-tueb.mpg.de

Abstract

We derive the correspondence between regularization operators used in Regularization Networks and Hilbert Schmidt Kernels appearing in Support Vector Machines. More specifically, we prove that the Green's Functions associated with regularization operators are suitable Support Vector Kernels with equivalent regularization properties. As a by–product we show that a large number of Radial Basis Functions namely conditionally positive definite functions may be used as Support Vector kernels.

1 INTRODUCTION

Support Vector (SV) Machines for pattern recognition, regression estimation and operator inversion exploit the idea of transforming into a high dimensional feature space where they perform a linear algorithm. Instead of evaluating this map explicitly, one uses Hilbert Schmidt Kernels $k(\mathbf{x}, \mathbf{y})$ which correspond to dot products of the mapped data in high dimensional space, i.e.

$$k(\mathbf{x}, \mathbf{y}) = (\Phi(\mathbf{x}) \cdot \Phi(\mathbf{y})) \tag{1}$$

with $\Phi : \mathbb{R}^n \to \mathcal{F}$ denoting the map into feature space. Mostly, this map and many of its properties are unknown. Even worse, so far no general rule was available which kernel should be used, or why mapping into a very high dimensional space often provides good results, seemingly defying the curse of dimensionality. We will show that each kernel $k(\mathbf{x}, \mathbf{y})$ corresponds to a regularization operator $\hat{P}$, the link being that k is the Green's function of $\hat{P}^* \hat{P}$ (with $\hat{P}^*$ denoting the adjoint operator of $\hat{P}$). For the sake of simplicity we shall only discuss the case of regression — our considerations, however, also hold true for the other cases mentioned above.

We start by briefly reviewing the concept of SV Machines (section 2) and of Regularization Networks (section 3). Section 4 contains the main result stating the equivalence of both methods. In section 5, we show some applications of this finding to known SV machines. Section 6 introduces a new class of possible SV kernels, and, finally, section 7 concludes the paper with a discussion.

2   SUPPORT VECTOR MACHINES

The SV algorithm for regression estimation, as described in [Vapnik, 1995] and [Vapnik et al., 1997], exploits the idea of computing a linear function in high dimensional feature space $\mathcal{F}$ (furnished with a dot product) and thereby computing a nonlinear function in the space of the input data $\mathbb{R}^n$. The functions take the form $f(\mathbf{x}) = (\omega \cdot \Phi(\mathbf{x})) + b$ with $\Phi : \mathbb{R}^n \to \mathcal{F}$ and $\omega \in \mathcal{F}$.

In order to infer f from a training set $\{(\mathbf{x}_i, y_i) \mid i = 1, \ldots, \ell, \ \mathbf{x}_i \in \mathbb{R}^n, y_i \in \mathbb{R}\}$, one tries to minimize the empirical risk functional $R_{emp}[f]$ together with a complexity term $\|\omega\|^2$, thereby enforcing *flatness* in feature space, i.e. to minimize

$$R_{reg}[f] = R_{emp}[f] + \lambda\|\omega\|^2 = \frac{1}{\ell}\sum_{i=1}^{\ell} c(f(\mathbf{x}_i), y_i) + \lambda\|\omega\|^2 \tag{2}$$

with $c(f(\mathbf{x}_i), y_i)$ being the cost function determining how deviations of $f(\mathbf{x}_i)$ from the target values y_i should be penalized, and λ being a regularization constant. As shown in [Vapnik, 1995] for the case of ϵ–insensitive cost functions,

$$c(f(\mathbf{x}), y) = \begin{cases} |f(\mathbf{x}) - y| - \epsilon & \text{for } |f(\mathbf{x}) - y| \geq \epsilon \\ 0 & \text{otherwise} \end{cases}, \tag{3}$$

(2) can be minimized by solving a quadratic programming problem formulated in terms of dot products in $\mathcal{F}$. It turns out that the solution can be expressed in terms of *Support Vectors*, $\omega = \sum_{i=1}^{\ell} \alpha_i \Phi(\mathbf{x}_i)$, and therefore

$$f(\mathbf{x}) = \sum_{i=1}^{\ell} \alpha_i (\Phi(\mathbf{x}_i) \cdot \Phi(\mathbf{x})) + b = \sum_{i=1}^{\ell} \alpha_i k(\mathbf{x}_i, \mathbf{x}) + b, \tag{4}$$

where $k(\mathbf{x}_i, \mathbf{x})$ is a kernel function computing a dot product in feature space (a concept introduced by Aizerman et al. [1964]). The coefficients α_i can be found by solving a quadratic programming problem (with $K_{ij} := k(\mathbf{x}_i, \mathbf{x}_j)$ and $\alpha_i = \beta_i - \beta_i^*$):

$$\begin{aligned} \text{minimize} \quad & \frac{1}{2}\sum_{i,j=1}^{\ell}(\beta_i^* - \beta_i)(\beta_j^* - \beta_j)K_{ij} - \sum_{i=1}^{\ell}(\beta_i^* - \beta_i)y_i - (\beta_i^* + \beta_i)\epsilon \\ \text{subject to} \quad & \sum_{i=1}^{\ell}\beta_i - \beta_i^* = 0, \ \ \beta_i, \beta_i^* \in [0, \tfrac{1}{\lambda\ell}] \end{aligned} \tag{5}$$

Note that (3) is not the only possible choice of cost functions resulting in a quadratic programming problem (in fact quadratic parts and infinities are admissible, too). For a detailed discussion see [Smola and Schölkopf, 1998]. Also note that any continuous symmetric function $k(\mathbf{x}, \mathbf{y}) \in L_2 \otimes L_2$ may be used as an admissible Hilbert–Schmidt kernel if it satisfies Mercer's condition

$$\int\int k(\mathbf{x}, \mathbf{y})g(\mathbf{x})g(\mathbf{y})d\mathbf{x}d\mathbf{y} \geq 0 \ \text{ for all } \ g \in L_2(\mathbb{R}^n). \tag{6}$$

3   REGULARIZATION NETWORKS

Here again we start with minimizing the empirical risk functional $R_{emp}[f]$ plus a regularization term $\|\hat{P}f\|^2$ defined by a regularization operator $\hat{P}$ in the sense of Arsenin and

Tikhonov [1977]. Similar to (2), we minimize

$$R_{reg}[f] = R_{emp} + \lambda \|\hat{P}f\|^2 = \frac{1}{\ell} \sum_{i=1}^{\ell} c(f(\mathbf{x}_i), y_i) + \lambda \|\hat{P}f\|^2. \tag{7}$$

Using an expansion of f in terms of some symmetric function $k(\mathbf{x}_i, \mathbf{x}_j)$ (note here, that k need not fulfil Mercer's condition),

$$f(\mathbf{x}) = \sum_i \alpha_i k(\mathbf{x}_i, \mathbf{x}) + b, \tag{8}$$

and the cost function defined in (3), this leads to a quadratic programming problem similar to the one for SVs: by computing Wolfe's dual (for details of the calculations see [Smola and Schölkopf, 1998]), and using

$$D_{ij} := ((\hat{P}k)(\mathbf{x}_i, .) \cdot (\hat{P}k)(\mathbf{x}_j, .)) \tag{9}$$

$((f \cdot g)$ denotes the dot product of the functions f and g in Hilbert Space, i.e. $\int \bar{f}(\mathbf{x})g(\mathbf{x})d\mathbf{x})$, we get $\vec{\alpha} = D^{-1}K(\vec{\beta} - \vec{\beta}^*)$, with β_i, β_i^* being the solution of

minimize $\quad \frac{1}{2} \sum_{i,j=1}^{\ell} (\beta_i^* - \beta_i)(\beta_j^* - \beta_j)(KD^{-1}K)_{ij} - \sum_{i=1}^{\ell} (\beta_i^* - \beta_i)y_i - (\beta_i^* + \beta_i)\epsilon$

subject to $\quad \sum_{i=1}^{\ell} \beta_i - \beta_i^* = 0, \quad \beta_i, \beta_i^* \in [0, \frac{1}{\ell\lambda}]$

$$\tag{10}$$

Unfortunately this setting of the problem does not preserve sparsity in terms of the coefficients, as a potentially sparse decomposition in terms of β_i and β_i^* is spoiled by $D^{-1}K$, which in general is not diagonal (the expansion (4) on the other hand does typically have many vanishing coefficients).

4 THE EQUIVALENCE OF BOTH METHODS

Comparing (5) with (10) leads to the question if and under which condition the two methods might be equivalent and therefore also under which conditions regularization networks might lead to sparse decompositions (i.e. only a few of the expansion coefficients in f would differ from zero). A sufficient condition is $D = K$ (thus $KD^{-1}K = K$), i.e.

$$k(\mathbf{x}_i, \mathbf{x}_j) = ((\hat{P}k)(\mathbf{x}_i, .) \cdot (\hat{P}k)(\mathbf{x}_j, .)) \tag{11}$$

Our goal now is twofold:

- Given a regularization operator $\hat{P}$, find a kernel k such that a SV machine using k will not only enforce flatness in feature space, but also correspond to minimizing a regularized risk functional with $\hat{P}$ as regularization operator.

- Given a Hilbert Schmidt kernel k, find a regularization operator $\hat{P}$ such that a SV machine using this kernel can be viewed as a Regularization Network using $\hat{P}$.

These two problems can be solved by employing the concept of Green's functions as described in [Girosi et al., 1993]. These functions had been introduced in the context of solving differential equations. For our purpose, it is sufficient to know that the Green's functions $G_{\mathbf{x}_i}(\mathbf{x})$ of $\hat{P}^*\hat{P}$ satisfy

$$(\hat{P}^*\hat{P}G_{\mathbf{x}_i})(\mathbf{x}) = \delta_{\mathbf{x}_i}(\mathbf{x}). \tag{12}$$

Here, $\delta_{\mathbf{x}_i}(\mathbf{x})$ is the δ–distribution (not to be confused with the Kronecker symbol δ_{ij}) which has the property that $(f \cdot \delta_{\mathbf{x}_i}) = f(\mathbf{x}_i)$. Moreover we require for all $\mathbf{x}_i$ the projection of $G_{\mathbf{x}_i}(\mathbf{x})$ onto the null space of $\hat{P}^*\hat{P}$ to be zero. The relationship between kernels and regularization operators is formalized in the following proposition.

Proposition 1
Let $\hat{P}$ be a regularization operator, and G be the Green's function of $\hat{P}^*\hat{P}$. Then G is a Hilbert Schmidt–Kernel such that $D = K$. SV machines using G minimize risk functional (7) with $\hat{P}$ as regularization operator.

Proof: *Substituting (12) into $G_{\mathbf{x}_j}(\mathbf{x}_i) = \left(G_{\mathbf{x}_j}(.) \cdot \delta_{\mathbf{x}_i}(.)\right)$ yields*

$$G_{\mathbf{x}_j}(\mathbf{x}_i) = \left((\hat{P}G_{\mathbf{x}_i})(.) \cdot (\hat{P}G_{\mathbf{x}_j})(.)\right) = G_{\mathbf{x}_i}(\mathbf{x}_j), \tag{13}$$

hence $G(\mathbf{x}_i, \mathbf{x}_j) := G_{\mathbf{x}_i}(\mathbf{x}_j)$ is symmetric and satisfies (11). Thus the SV optimization problem (5) is equivalent to the regularization network counterpart (10). Furthermore G is an admissible positive kernel, as it can be written as a dot product in Hilbert Space, namely

$$G(\mathbf{x}_i, \mathbf{x}_j) = (\Phi(\mathbf{x}_i) \cdot \Phi(\mathbf{x}_j)) \quad with \quad \Phi : \mathbf{x}_i \longmapsto (\hat{P}G_{\mathbf{x}_i})(.). \tag{14}$$

In the following we will exploit this relationship in both ways: to compute Green's functions for a given regularization operator $\hat{P}$ and to infer the regularization operator from a given kernel k.

5   TRANSLATION INVARIANT KERNELS

Let us now more specifically consider regularization operators $\hat{P}$ that may be written as multiplications in Fourier space [Girosi et al., 1993]

$$\left(\hat{P}f \cdot \hat{P}g\right) = \frac{1}{(2\pi)^{n/2}} \int_\Omega \frac{\overline{\tilde{f}(\omega)}\tilde{g}(\omega)}{P(\omega)} d\omega \tag{15}$$

with $\tilde{f}(\omega)$ denoting the Fourier transform of $f(\mathbf{x})$, and $P(\omega) = P(-\omega)$ real valued, non-negative and converging uniformly to 0 for $|\omega| \to \infty$ and $\Omega = \text{supp}[P(\omega)]$. Small values of $P(\omega)$ correspond to a strong attenuation of the corresponding frequencies.

For regularization operators defined in Fourier Space by (15) it can be shown by exploiting $P(\omega) = P(-\omega) = \overline{P(\omega)}$ that

$$G(\mathbf{x}_i, \mathbf{x}) = \frac{1}{(2\pi)^{n/2}} \int_{\mathbb{R}^n} e^{i\omega(\mathbf{x}_i - \mathbf{x})} P(\omega) d\omega \tag{16}$$

is a corresponding Green's function satisfying translational invariance, i.e. $G(\mathbf{x}_i, \mathbf{x}_j) = G(\mathbf{x}_i - \mathbf{x}_j)$, and $\tilde{G}(\omega) = P(\omega)$. For the proof, one only has to show that G satisfies (11).

This provides us with an efficient tool for analyzing SV kernels and the types of capacity control they exhibit.

Example 1 (B_q-splines)
Vapnik et al. [1997] propose to use B_q-splines as building blocks for kernels, i.e.

$$k(\mathbf{x}) = \prod_{i=1}^n B_q(\mathbf{x}_i) \tag{17}$$

with $\mathbf{x} \in \mathbb{R}^n$. For the sake of simplicity, we consider the case $n = 1$. Recalling the definition

$$B_q = \otimes^{q+1} 1_{[-0.5, 0.5]} \tag{18}$$

($\otimes$ denotes the convolution and 1_X the indicator function on X), we can utilize the above result and the Fourier–Plancherel identity to construct the Fourier representation of the corresponding regularization operator. Up to a multiplicative constant, it equals

$$P(\omega) = \tilde{k}(\omega) = \text{sinc}^{(q+1)}\left(\frac{\omega_i}{2}\right). \tag{19}$$

This shows that only B-splines of odd order are admissible, as the even ones have negative parts in the Fourier spectrum (which would result in an amplification of the corresponding frequency components). The zeros in $\tilde{k}$ stem from the fact that B_l has only compact support $[-(k+1)/2, (k+1)/2]$. By using this kernel we trade reduced computational complexity in calculating f (we only have to take points with $\|\mathbf{x}_i - \mathbf{x}_j\| \leq c$ from some limited neighborhood determined by c into account) for a possibly worse performance of the regularization operator as it completely removes frequencies ω_p with $\tilde{k}(\omega_p) = 0$.

Example 2 (Dirichlet kernels)
In [Vapnik et al., 1997], a class of kernels generating Fourier expansions was introduced,

$$k(x) = \frac{\sin(2N+1)x/2}{\sin x/2}. \tag{20}$$

(As in example 1 we consider $\mathbf{x} \in \mathbb{R}^1$ to avoid tedious notation.) By construction, this kernel corresponds to $P(\omega) = \frac{1}{2}\sum_{i=-N}^{N} \delta(\omega - i)$. A regularization operator with these properties, however, may not be desirable as it only damps a finite number of frequencies and leaves all other frequencies unchanged which can lead to overfitting (Fig. 1).

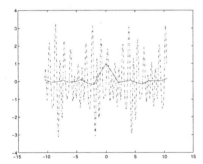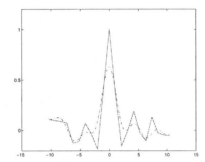

Figure 1: Left: Interpolation with a Dirichlet Kernel of order $N = 10$. One can clearly observe the overfitting (dashed line: interpolation, solid line: original data points, connected by lines). Right: Interpolation of the same data with a Gaussian Kernel of width $\sigma^2 = 1$.

Example 3 (Gaussian kernels)
Following the exposition of Yuille and Grzywacz [1988] as described in [Girosi et al., 1993], one can see that for

$$\|\hat{P}f\|^2 = \int d\mathbf{x} \sum_m \frac{\sigma^{2m}}{m!2^m} (\hat{O}^m f(\mathbf{x}))^2 \tag{21}$$

with $\hat{O}^{2m} = \Delta^m$ and $\hat{O}^{2m+1} = \nabla\Delta^m$, Δ being the Laplacian and ∇ the Gradient operator, we get Gaussians kernels

$$k(\mathbf{x}) = \exp\left(-\frac{\|\mathbf{x}\|^2}{2\sigma^2}\right). \tag{22}$$

Moreover, we can provide an equivalent representation of $\hat{P}$ in terms of its Fourier properties, i.e. $P(\omega) = \exp(-\frac{\sigma^2\|\mathbf{x}\|^2}{2})$ up to a multiplicative constant. Training a SV machine with Gaussian RBF kernels [Schölkopf et al., 1997] corresponds to minimizing the specific cost function with a regularization operator of type (21). This also explains the good performance of SV machines in this case, as it is by no means obvious that choosing a flat function in high dimensional space will correspond to a simple function in low dimensional space, as showed in example 2. Gaussian kernels tend to yield good performance under general smoothness assumptions and should be considered especially if no additional knowledge of the data is available.

6   A NEW CLASS OF SUPPORT VECTOR KERNELS

We will follow the lines of Madych and Nelson [1990] as pointed out by Girosi et al. [1993]. Our main statement is that conditionally positive definite functions (c.p.d.) generate admissible SV kernels. This is very useful as the property of being c.p.d. often is easier to verify than Mercer's condition, especially when combined with the results of Schoenberg and Micchelli on the connection between c.p.d. and completely monotonic functions [Schoenberg, 1938, Micchelli, 1986]. Moreover c.p.d. functions lead to a class of SV kernels that do not necessarily satisfy Mercer's condition.

Definition 1 (Conditionally positive definite functions)
A continuous function h, defined on $[0, \infty)$, is said to be conditionally positive definite (c.p.d.) of order m on $\mathbb{R}^n$ if for any distinct points $\mathbf{x}_1, \ldots, \mathbf{x}_\ell \in \mathbb{R}^n$ and scalars $c_1, \ldots, c_\ell$ the quadratic form $\sum_{i,j=1}^{\ell} c_i c_j h(\|\mathbf{x}_i - \mathbf{x}_j\|)$ is nonnegative provided that $\sum_{i=1}^{n} c_i p(\mathbf{x}_i) = 0$ for all polynomials p on $\mathbb{R}^n$ of degree lower than m.

Proposition 2 (c.p.d. functions and admissible kernels)
Define Π_m^n the space of polynomials of degree lower than m on $\mathbb{R}^n$. Every c.p.d. function h of order m generates an admissible Kernel for SV expansions on the space of functions f orthogonal to Π_m^n by setting $k(\mathbf{x}_i, \mathbf{x}_j) := h(\|\mathbf{x}_i - \mathbf{x}_j\|^2)$.

Proof: *In [Dyn, 1991] and [Madych and Nelson, 1990] it was shown that c.p.d. functions h generate semi–norms $\|.\|_h$ by*

$$\|f\|_h^2 := \int d\mathbf{x}_i d\mathbf{x}_j h(\|\mathbf{x}_i - \mathbf{x}_j\|) f(\mathbf{x}_i) f(\mathbf{x}_j). \tag{23}$$

Provided that the projection of f onto the space of polynomials of degree lower than m is zero. For these functions, this, however, also defines a dot product in some feature space. Hence they can be used as SV kernels.

Only c.p.d. functions of order m up to 2 are of practical interest for SV methods (for details see [Smola and Schölkopf, 1998]). Consequently, we may use kernels like the ones proposed in [Girosi et al., 1993] as SV kernels:

$$k(\mathbf{x}, \mathbf{y}) = e^{-\beta \|\mathbf{x}-\mathbf{y}\|^2} \qquad \text{Gaussian, } (m = 0); \tag{24}$$

$$k(\mathbf{x}, \mathbf{y}) = -\sqrt{\|\mathbf{x} - \mathbf{y}\|^2 + c^2} \qquad \text{multiquadric, } (m = 1) \tag{25}$$

$$k(\mathbf{x}, \mathbf{y}) = \frac{1}{\sqrt{\|\mathbf{x}-\mathbf{y}\|^2+c^2}} \qquad \text{inverse multiquadric, } (m = 0) \tag{26}$$

$$k(\mathbf{x}, \mathbf{y}) = \|\mathbf{x} - \mathbf{y}\|^2 \ln \|\mathbf{x} - \mathbf{y}\| \qquad \text{thin plate splines, } (m = 2) \tag{27}$$

7   DISCUSSION

We have pointed out a connection between SV kernels and regularization operators. As one of the possible implications of this result, we hope that it will deepen our understanding of SV machines and of why they have been found to exhibit high generalization ability. In Sec. 5, we have given examples where only the translation into the regularization framework provided insight in why certain kernels are preferable to others. Capacity control is one of the strengths of SV machines; however, this does not mean that the structure of the learning machine, i.e. the choice of a suitable kernel for a given task, should be disregarded. On the contrary, the rather general class of admissible SV kernels should be seen as another strength, provided that we have a means of choosing the right kernel. The newly established link to regularization theory can thus be seen as a tool for constructing the structure consisting of sets of functions in which the SV machine (approximately) performs structural risk minimization (e.g. [Vapnik, 1995]). For a treatment of SV kernels in a Reproducing Kernel Hilbert Space context see [Girosi, 1997].

Finally one should leverage the theoretical results achieved for regularization operators for a better understanding of SVs (and vice versa). By doing so this theory might serve as a bridge for connecting two (so far) separate threads of machine learning. A trivial example for such a connection would be a Bayesian interpretation of SV machines. In this case the choice of a special kernel can be regarded as a prior on the hypothesis space with $P[f] \propto \exp(-\lambda\|\hat{P}f\|^2)$. A more subtle reasoning probably will be necessary for understanding the capacity bounds [Vapnik, 1995] from a Regularization Network point of view. Future work will include an analysis of the family of polynomial kernels, which perform very well in Pattern Classification [Schölkopf et al., 1995].

Acknowledgements

AS is supported by a grant of the DFG (# Ja 379/51). BS is supported by the Studienstiftung des deutschen Volkes. The authors thank Chris Burges, Federico Girosi, Leo van Hemmen, Klaus–Robert Müller and Vladimir Vapnik for helpful discussions and comments.

References

M. A. Aizerman, E. M. Braverman, and L. I. Rozonoér. Theoretical foundations of the potential function method in pattern recognition learning. *Automation and Remote Control*, 25:821–837, 1964.

N. Dyn. Interpolation and approximation by radial and related functions. In C.K. Chui, L.L. Schumaker, and D.J. Ward, editors, *Approximation Theory, VI*, pages 211–234. Academic Press, New York, 1991.

F. Girosi. An equivalence between sparse approximation and support vector machines. A.I. Memo No. 1606, MIT, 1997.

F. Girosi, M. Jones, and T. Poggio. Priors, stabilizers and basis functions: From regularization to radial, tensor and additive splines. A.I. Memo No. 1430, MIT, 1993.

W.R. Madych and S.A. Nelson. Multivariate interpolation and conditionally positive definite functions. II. *Mathematics of Computation*, 54(189):211–230, 1990.

C. A. Micchelli. Interpolation of scattered data: distance matrices and conditionally positive definite functions. *Constructive Approximation*, 2:11–22, 1986.

I.J. Schoenberg. Metric spaces and completely monotone functions. *Ann. of Math.*, 39: 811–841, 1938.

B. Schölkopf, C. Burges, and V. Vapnik. Extracting support data for a given task. In U. M. Fayyad and R. Uthurusamy, editors, *Proc. KDD 1*, Menlo Park, 1995. AAAI Press.

B. Schölkopf, K. Sung, C. Burges, F. Girosi, P. Niyogi, T. Poggio, and V. Vapnik. Comparing support vector machines with gaussian kernels to radial basis function classifiers. *IEEE Trans. Sign. Processing*, 45:2758 – 2765, 1997.

A. J. Smola and B. Schölkopf. On a kernel–based method for pattern recognition, regression, approximation and operator inversion. *Algorithmica*, 1998. see also GMD Technical Report 1997-1064, URL: http://svm.first.gmd.de/papers.html.

V. Vapnik. *The Nature of Statistical Learning Theory*. Springer Verlag, New York, 1995.

V. Vapnik, S. Golowich, and A. Smola. Support vector method for function approximation, regression estimation, and signal processing. In *NIPS 9*, San Mateo, CA, 1997.

A. Yuille and N. Grzywacz. The motion coherence theory. In *Proceedings of the International Conference on Computer Vision*, pages 344–354, Washington, D.C., 1988. IEEE Computer Society Press.

The Rectified Gaussian Distribution

N. D. Socci, D. D. Lee and H. S. Seung
Bell Laboratories, Lucent Technologies
Murray Hill, NJ 07974
{nds|ddlee|seung}@bell-labs.com

Abstract

A simple but powerful modification of the standard Gaussian distribution is studied. The variables of the rectified Gaussian are constrained to be nonnegative, enabling the use of nonconvex energy functions. Two multimodal examples, the competitive and cooperative distributions, illustrate the representational power of the rectified Gaussian. Since the cooperative distribution can represent the translations of a pattern, it demonstrates the potential of the rectified Gaussian for modeling pattern manifolds.

1 INTRODUCTION

The *rectified* Gaussian distribution is a modification of the standard Gaussian in which the variables are constrained to be nonnegative. This simple modification brings increased representational power, as illustrated by two multimodal examples of the rectified Gaussian, the competitive and the cooperative distributions. The modes of the competitive distribution are well-separated by regions of low probability. The modes of the cooperative distribution are closely spaced along a nonlinear continuous manifold. Neither distribution can be accurately approximated by a single standard Gaussian. In short, the rectified Gaussian is able to represent both discrete and continuous variability in a way that a standard Gaussian cannot.

This increased representational power comes at the price of increased complexity. While finding the mode of a standard Gaussian involves solution of linear equations, finding the modes of a rectified Gaussian is a quadratic programming problem. Sampling from a standard Gaussian can be done by generating one dimensional normal deviates, followed by a linear transformation. Sampling from a rectified Gaussian requires Monte Carlo methods. Mode-finding and sampling algorithms are basic tools that are important in probabilistic modeling.

Like the Boltzmann machine[1], the rectified Gaussian is an undirected graphical model. The rectified Gaussian is a better representation for probabilistic modeling

(a)   (b)   (c)

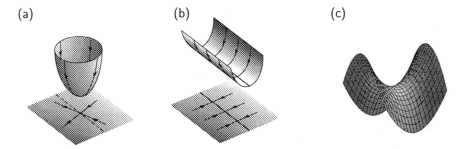

Figure 1: Three types of quadratic energy functions. (a) Bowl (b) Trough (c) Saddle

of continuous-valued data. It is unclear whether learning will be more tractable for the rectified Gaussian than it is for the Boltzmann machine.

A different version of the rectified Gaussian was recently introduced by Hinton and Ghahramani[2, 3]. Their version is for a single variable, and has a singularity at the origin designed to produce sparse activity in directed graphical models. Our version lacks this singularity, and is only interesting in the case of more than one variable, for it relies on undirected interactions between variables to produce the multimodal behavior that is of interest here.

The present work is inspired by biological neural network models that use continuous dynamical attractors[4]. In particular, the energy function of the cooperative distribution was previously studied in models of the visual cortex[5], motor cortex[6], and head direction system[7].

2   ENERGY FUNCTIONS: BOWL, TROUGH, AND SADDLE

The standard Gaussian distribution $P(x)$ is defined as

$$P(x) = Z^{-1}e^{-\beta E(x)} , \tag{1}$$

$$E(x) = \frac{1}{2}x^T A x - b^T x . \tag{2}$$

The symmetric matrix A and vector b define the quadratic energy function $E(x)$. The parameter $\beta = 1/T$ is an inverse temperature. Lowering the temperature concentrates the distribution at the minimum of the energy function. The prefactor Z normalizes the integral of $P(x)$ to unity.

Depending on the matrix A, the quadratic energy function $E(x)$ can have different types of curvature. The energy function shown in Figure 1(a) is convex. The minimum of the energy corresponds to the peak of the distribution. Such a distribution is often used in pattern recognition applications, when patterns are well-modeled as a single prototype corrupted by random noise.

The energy function shown in Figure 1(b) is flattened in one direction. Patterns generated by such a distribution come with roughly equal likelihood from anywhere along the trough. So the direction of the trough corresponds to the invariances of the pattern. Principal component analysis can be thought of as a procedure for learning distributions of this form.

The energy function shown in Figure 1(c) is saddle-shaped. It cannot be used in a Gaussian distribution, because the energy decreases without limit down the sides of the saddle, leading to a non-normalizable distribution. However, certain saddle-shaped energy functions can be used in the rectified Gaussian distribution, which is defined over vectors x whose components are all nonnegative. The class of energy functions that can be used are those where the matrix A has the property $x^T A x > 0$ for all $x > 0$, a condition known as *copositivity*. Note that this set of matrices is larger than the set of positive definite matrices that can be used with a standard Gaussian. The nonnegativity constraints block the directions in which the energy diverges to negative infinity. Some concrete examples will be discussed shortly. The energy functions for these examples will have multiple minima, and the corresponding distribution will be multimodal, which is not possible with a standard Gaussian.

3   MODE-FINDING

Before defining some example distributions, we must introduce some tools for analyzing them. The modes of a rectified Gaussian are the minima of the energy function (2), subject to nonnegativity constraints. At low temperatures, the modes of the distribution characterize much of its behavior.

Finding the modes of a rectified Gaussian is a problem in quadratic programming. Algorithms for quadratic programming are particularly simple for the case of non-negativity constraints. Perhaps the simplest algorithm is the projected gradient method, a discrete time dynamics consisting of a gradient step followed by a rectification

$$x_{t+1} = [x_t + \eta(b - Ax_t)]^+ \tag{3}$$

The rectification $[x]^+ = \max(x, 0)$ keeps x within the nonnegative orthant ($x \geq 0$). If the step size η is chosen correctly, this algorithm can provably be shown to converge to a stationary point of the energy function[8]. In practice, this stationary point is generally a local minimum.

Neural networks can also solve quadratic programming problems. We define the synaptic weight matrix $W = I - A$, and a continuous time dynamics

$$\dot{x} + x = [b + Wx]^+ \tag{4}$$

For any initial condition in the nonnegative orthant, the dynamics remains in the nonnegative orthant, and the quadratic function (2) is a Lyapunov function of the dynamics.

Both of these methods converge to a stationary point of the energy. The gradient of the energy is given by $g = Ax - b$. According to the Kühn-Tucker conditions, a stationary point must satisfy the conditions that for all i, either $g_i = 0$ and $x_i > 0$, or $g_i > 0$ and $x_i = 0$. The intuitive explanation is that in the interior of the constraint region, the gradient must vanish, while at the boundary, the gradient must point toward the interior. For a stationary point to be a local minimum, the Kühn-Tucker conditions must be augmented by the condition that the Hessian of the nonzero variables be positive definite.

Both methods are guaranteed to find a global minimum only in the case where A is positive definite, so that the energy function (2) is convex. This is because a convex energy function has a unique minimum. Convex quadratic programming is solvable in polynomial time. In contrast, for a nonconvex energy function (indefinite A), it is not generally possible to find the global minimum in polynomial time, because of the possible presence of local minima. In many practical situations, however, it is not too difficult to find a reasonable solution.

(a)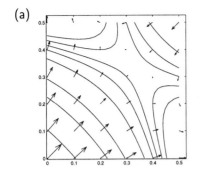

(b)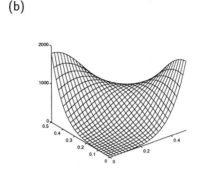

Figure 2: The competitive distribution for two variables. (a) A non-convex energy function with two constrained minima on the x and y axes. Shown are contours of constant energy, and arrows that represent the negative gradient of the energy. (b) The rectified Gaussian distribution has two peaks.

The rectified Gaussian happens to be most interesting in the nonconvex case, precisely because of the possibility of multiple minima. The consequence of multiple minima is a multimodal distribution, which cannot be well-approximated by a standard Gaussian. We now consider two examples of a multimodal rectified Gaussian.

4 COMPETITIVE DISTRIBUTION

The competitive distribution is defined by

$$A_{ij} = -\delta_{ij} + 2 \tag{5}$$
$$b_i = 1; \tag{6}$$

We first consider the simple case $N = 2$. Then the energy function given by

$$E(x, y) = -\frac{x^2 + y^2}{2} + (x + y)^2 - (x + y) \tag{7}$$

has two constrained minima at $(1, 0)$ and $(0, 1)$ and is shown in figure 2(a). It does not lead to a normalizable distribution unless the nonnegativity constraints are imposed. The two constrained minima of this nonconvex energy function correspond to two peaks in the distribution (fig 2(b)). While such a bimodal distribution could be approximated by a mixture of two standard Gaussians, a single Gaussian distribution cannot approximate such a distribution. In particular, the reduced probability density between the two peaks would not be representable at all with a single Gaussian.

The competitive distribution gets its name because its energy function is similar to the ones that govern winner-take-all networks[9]. When N becomes large, the N global minima of the energy function are singleton vectors (fig 3), with one component equal to unity, and the rest zero. This is due to a competitive interaction between the components. The mean of the zero temperature distribution is given by

$$\langle x_i \rangle = \frac{1}{N} \tag{8}$$

The eigenvalues of the covariance

$$\langle x_i x_j \rangle - \langle x_i \rangle \langle x_j \rangle = \frac{1}{N}\delta_{ij} - \frac{1}{N^2} \tag{9}$$

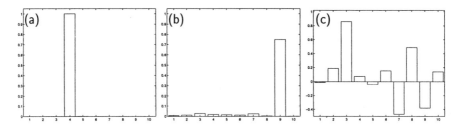

Figure 3: The competitive distribution for $N = 10$ variables. (a) One mode (zero temperature state) of the distribution. The strong competition between the variables results in only one variable on. There are N modes of this form, each with a different winner variable. (b) A sample at finite temperature ($\beta \approx 110$) using Monte Carlo sampling. There is still a clear winner variable. (c) Sample from a standard Gaussian with matched mean and covariance. Even if we cut off the negative values this sample still bears little resemblance to the states shown in (a) and (b), since there is no clear winner variable.

all equal to $1/N$, except for a single zero mode. The zero mode is $\mathbf{1}$, the vector of all ones, and the other eigenvectors span the $N-1$ dimensional space perpendicular to $\mathbf{1}$. Figure 3 shows two samples: one (b) drawn at finite temperature from the competitive distribution, and the other (c) drawn from a standard Gaussian distribution with the same mean and covariance. Even if the sample from the standard Gaussian is cut so negative values are set to zero the sample does not look at all like the original distribution. Most importantly a standard Gaussian will never be able to capture the strongly competitive character of this distribution.

5   COOPERATIVE DISTRIBUTION

To define the cooperative distribution on N variables, an angle $\theta_i = 2\pi i/N$ is associated with each variable x_i, so that the variables can be regarded as sitting on a ring. The energy function is defined by

$$A_{ij} = \delta_{ij} + \frac{1}{N} - \frac{4}{N}\cos(\theta_i - \theta_j) \tag{10}$$

$$b_i = 1; \tag{11}$$

The coupling A_{ij} between x_i and x_j depends only on the separation $\theta_i - \theta_j$ between them on the ring.

The minima, or ground states, of the energy function can be found numerically by the methods described earlier. An analytic calculation of the ground states in the large N limit is also possible[5]. As shown in Figure 4(a), each ground state is a lump of activity centered at some angle on the ring. This delocalized pattern of activity is different from the singleton modes of the competitive distribution, and arises from the cooperative interactions between neurons on the ring. Because the distribution is invariant to rotations of the ring (cyclic permutations of the variables x_i), there are N ground states, each with the lump at a different angle.

The mean and the covariance of the cooperative distribution are given by

$$\langle x_i \rangle = \text{const} \tag{12}$$

$$\langle x_i x_j \rangle - \langle x_i \rangle \langle x_j \rangle = C(\theta_i - \theta_j) \tag{13}$$

A given sample of x, shown in Figure 4(a), does not look anything like the mean, which is completely uniform. Samples generated from a Gaussian distribution with

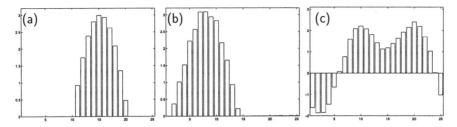

Figure 4: The cooperative distribution for $N = 25$ variables. (a) Zero temperature state. A cooperative interaction between the variables leads to a delocalized pattern of activity that can sit at different locations on the ring. (b) A finite temperature ($\beta = 50$) sample. (c) A sample from a standard Gaussian with matched mean and covariance.

the same mean and covariance look completely different from the ground states of the cooperative distribution (fig 4(c)).

These deviations from standard Gaussian behavior reflect fundamental differences in the underlying energy function. Here the energy function has N discrete minima arranged along a ring. In the limit of large N the barriers between these minima become quite small. A reasonable approximation is to regard the energy function as having a continuous line of minima with a ring geometry[5]. In other words, the energy surface looks like a curved trough, similar to the bottom of a wine bottle. The mean is the centroid of the ring and is not close to any minimum.

The cooperative distribution is able to model the set of all translations of the lump pattern of activity. This suggests that the rectified Gaussian may be useful in invariant object recognition, in cases where a continuous manifold of instantiations of an object must be modeled. One such case is visual object recognition, where the images of an object from different viewpoints form a continuous manifold.

6 SAMPLING

Figures 3 and 4 depict samples drawn from the competitive and cooperative distribution. These samples were generated using the Metropolis Monte Carlo algorithm. Since full descriptions of this algorithm can be found elsewhere, we give only a brief description of the particular features used here. The basic procedure is to generate a new configuration of the system and calculate the change in energy (given by eq. 2). If the energy decreases, one accepts the new configuration unconditionally. If it increases then the new configuration is accepted with probability $e^{-\beta \Delta E}$.

In our sampling algorithm one variable is updated at a time (analogous to single spin flips). The acceptance ratio is much higher this way than if we update all the spins simultaneously. However, for some distributions the energy function may have approximately marginal directions; directions in which there is little or no barrier. The cooperative distribution has this property. We can expect critical slowing down due to this and consequently some sort of collective update (analogous to multi-spin updates or cluster updates) might make sampling more efficient. However, the type of update will depend on the specifics of the energy function and is not easy to determine.

7 DISCUSSION

The competitive and cooperative distributions are examples of rectified Gaussians for which no good approximation by a standard Gaussian is possible. However, both distributions can be approximated by mixtures of standard Gaussians. The competitive distribution can be approximated by a mixture of N Gaussians, one for each singleton state. The cooperative distribution can also be approximated by a mixture of N Gaussians, one for each location of the lump on the ring. A more economical approximation would reduce the number of Gaussians in the mixture, but make each one anisotropic[10].

Whether the rectified Gaussian is superior to these mixture models is an empirical question that should be investigated empirically with specific real-world probabilistic modeling tasks. Our intuition is that the rectified Gaussian will turn out to be a good representation for nonlinear pattern manifolds, and the aim of this paper has been to make this intuition concrete.

To make the rectified Gaussian useful in practical applications, it is critical to find tractable learning algorithms. It is not yet clear whether learning will be more tractable for the rectified Gaussian than it was for the Boltzmann machine. Perhaps the continuous variables of the rectified Gaussian may be easier to work with than the binary variables of the Boltzmann machine.

Acknowledgments We would like to thank P. Mitra, L. Saul, B. Shraiman and H. Sompolinsky for helpful discussions. Work on this project was supported by Bell Laboratories, Lucent Technologies.

References

[1] D. H. Ackley, G. E. Hinton, and T. J. Sejnowski. A learning algorithm for Boltzmann machines. *Cognitive Science*, 9:147–169, 1985.

[2] G. E. Hinton and Z. Ghahramani. Generative models for discovering sparse distributed representations. *Phil. Trans. Roy. Soc.*, B352:1177–90, 1997.

[3] Z. Ghahramani and G. E. Hinton. Hierarchical non-linear factor analysis and topographic maps. *Adv. Neural Info. Proc. Syst.*, 11, 1998.

[4] H. S. Seung. How the brain keeps the eyes still. *Proc. Natl. Acad. Sci. USA*, 93:13339–13344, 1996.

[5] R. Ben-Yishai, R. L. Bar-Or, and H. Sompolinsky. Theory of orientation tuning in visual cortex. *Proc. Nat. Acad. Sci. USA*, 92:3844–3848, 1995.

[6] A. P. Georgopoulos, M. Taira, and A. Lukashin. Cognitive neurophysiology of the motor cortex. *Science*, 260:47–52, 1993.

[7] K. Zhang. Representation of spatial orientation by the intrinsic dynamics of the head-direction cell ensemble: a theory. *J. Neurosci.*, 16:2112–2126, 1996.

[8] D. P. Bertsekas. *Nonlinear programming*. Athena Scientific, Belmont, MA, 1995.

[9] S. Amari and M. A. Arbib. Competition and cooperation in neural nets. In J. Metzler, editor, *Systems Neuroscience*, pages 119–165. Academic Press, New York, 1977.

[10] G. E. Hinton, P. Dayan, and M. Revow. Modeling the manifolds of images of handwritten digits. *IEEE Trans. Neural Networks*, 8:65–74, 1997.

Online learning from finite training sets in nonlinear networks

Peter Sollich[*]

Department of Physics
University of Edinburgh
Edinburgh EH9 3JZ, U.K.
P.Sollich@ed.ac.uk

David Barber[†]

Department of Applied Mathematics
Aston University
Birmingham B4 7ET, U.K.
D.Barber@aston.ac.uk

Abstract

Online learning is one of the most common forms of neural network training. We present an analysis of online learning from *finite* training sets for *non-linear* networks (namely, soft-committee machines), advancing the theory to more realistic learning scenarios. Dynamical equations are derived for an appropriate set of order parameters; these are exact in the limiting case of either linear networks or infinite training sets. Preliminary comparisons with simulations suggest that the theory captures some effects of finite training sets, but may not yet account correctly for the presence of local minima.

1 INTRODUCTION

The analysis of online gradient descent learning, as one of the most common forms of supervised learning, has recently stimulated a great deal of interest [1, 5, 7, 3]. In online learning, the weights of a network ('student') are updated immediately after presentation of each training example (input-output pair) in order to reduce the error that the network makes on that example. One of the primary goals of online learning analysis is to track the resulting evolution of the generalization error - the error that the student network makes on a novel test example, after a given number of example presentations. In order to specify the learning problem, the training outputs are assumed to be generated by a teacher network of known architecture. Previous studies of online learning have often imposed somewhat restrictive and

---

[*]Royal Society Dorothy Hodgkin Research Fellow
[†]Supported by EPSRC grant GR/J75425: Novel Developments in Learning Theory for Neural Networks

unrealistic assumptions about the learning framework. These restrictions are, either that the size of the training set is infinite, or that the learning rate is small[1, 5, 4]. Finite training sets present a significant analytical difficulty as successive weight updates are correlated, giving rise to highly non-trivial generalization dynamics.

For linear networks, the difficulties encountered with finite training sets and non-infinitesimal learning rates can be overcome by extending the standard set of descriptive ('order') parameters to include the effects of weight update correlations[7]. In the present work, we extend our analysis to *nonlinear* networks. The particular model we choose to study is the soft-committee machine which is capable of representing a rich variety of input-output mappings. Its online learning dynamics has been studied comprehensively for infinite training sets[1, 5]. In order to carry out our analysis, we adapt tools originally developed in the statistical mechanics literature which have found application, for example, in the study of Hopfield network dynamics[2].

2 MODEL AND OUTLINE OF CALCULATION

For an N-dimensional input vector $\mathbf{x}$, the output of the soft committee machine is given by

$$y = \sum_{l=1}^{L} g\left(\sqrt{\frac{1}{N}}\mathbf{w}_l^{\mathrm{T}}\mathbf{x}\right) \tag{1}$$

where the nonlinear activation function $g(h_l) = \mathrm{erf}(h_l/\sqrt{2})$ acts on the activations $h_l = \mathbf{w}_l^{\mathrm{T}}\mathbf{x}/\sqrt{N}$ (the factor $1/\sqrt{N}$ is for convenience only). This is a neural network with L hidden units, input to hidden weight vectors $\mathbf{w}_l$, $l = 1..L$, and all hidden to output weights set to 1.

In online learning the student weights are adapted on a sequence of presented examples to better approximate the teacher mapping. The training examples are drawn, with replacement, from a finite set, $\{(\mathbf{x}^\mu, y^\mu), \mu = 1..p\}$. This set remains fixed during training. Its size relative to the input dimension is denoted by $\alpha = p/N$. We take the input vectors $\mathbf{x}^\mu$ as samples from an N dimensional Gaussian distribution with zero mean and unit variance. The training outputs y^μ are assumed to be generated by a teacher soft committee machine with hidden weight vectors $\mathbf{w}_m^*$, $m = 1..M$, with additive Gaussian noise corrupting its activations and output.

The discrepancy between the teacher and student on a particular training example $(\mathbf{x}, y)$, drawn from the training set, is given by the squared difference of their corresponding outputs,

$$E = \frac{1}{2}\left[\sum_l g(h_l) - y\right]^2 = \frac{1}{2}\left[\sum_l g(h_l) - \sum_m g(k_m + \xi_m) - \xi_0\right]^2$$

where the student and teacher activations are, respectively

$$h_l = \sqrt{\frac{1}{N}}\mathbf{w}_l^{\mathrm{T}}\mathbf{x} \qquad k_m = \sqrt{\frac{1}{N}}(\mathbf{w}_m^*)^{\mathrm{T}}\mathbf{x}, \tag{2}$$

and ξ_m, $m = 1..M$ and ξ_0 are noise variables corrupting the teacher activations and output respectively.

Given a training example $(\mathbf{x}, y)$, the student weights are updated by a gradient descent step with learning rate η,

$$\mathbf{w}_l' - \mathbf{w}_l = -\eta\nabla_{\mathbf{w}_l}E = -\frac{\eta}{\sqrt{N}}\mathbf{x}\partial_{h_l}E \tag{3}$$

The generalization error is defined to be the average error that the student makes on a test example selected at random (and uncorrelated with the training set), which we write as $\epsilon_g = \langle E \rangle$.

Although one could, in principle, model the student weight dynamics directly, this will typically involve too many parameters, and we seek a more compact representation for the evolution of the generalization error. It is straightforward to show that the generalization error depends, not on a detailed description of all the network weights, but only on the overlap parameters $Q_{ll'} = \frac{1}{N} \mathbf{w}_l^\mathrm{T} \mathbf{w}_{l'}$ and $R_{lm} = \frac{1}{N} \mathbf{w}_l^\mathrm{T} \mathbf{w}_m^*$ [1, 5, 7]. In the case of infinite α, it is possible to obtain a closed set of equations governing the overlap parameters Q, R [5]. For finite training sets, however, this is no longer possible, due to the correlations between successive weight updates[7].

In order to overcome this difficulty, we use a technique developed originally to study statistical physics systems[2]. Initially, consider the dynamics of a general vector of order parameters, denoted by Ω, which are functions of the network weights $\mathbf{w}$. If the weight updates are described by a transition probability $T(\mathbf{w} \to \mathbf{w}')$, then an approximate update equation for Ω is

$$\Omega' - \Omega = \left\langle \int d\mathbf{w}' \left(\Omega(\mathbf{w}') - \Omega(\mathbf{w}) \right) T(\mathbf{w} \to \mathbf{w}') \right\rangle_{P(\mathbf{w}) \propto \delta(\Omega(\mathbf{w}) - \Omega)} \tag{4}$$

Intuitively, the integral in the above equation expresses the average change[1] of Ω caused by a weight update $\mathbf{w} \to \mathbf{w}'$, starting from (given) initial weights $\mathbf{w}$. Since our aim is to develop a closed set of equations for the order parameter dynamics, we need to remove the dependency on the initial weights $\mathbf{w}$. The only information we have regarding $\mathbf{w}$ is contained in the chosen order parameters Ω, and we therefore average the result over the 'subshell' of all $\mathbf{w}$ which correspond to these values of the order parameters. This is expressed as the δ-function constraint in equation(4).

It is clear that if the integral in (4) depends on $\mathbf{w}$ only through $\Omega(\mathbf{w})$, then the average is unnecessary and the resulting dynamical equations are exact. This is in fact the case for $\alpha \to \infty$ and $\Omega = \{Q, R\}$, the standard order parameters mentioned above[5]. If this cannot be achieved, one should choose a set of order parameters to obtain approximate equations which are as close as possible to the exact solution. The motivation for our choice of order parameters is based on the linear perceptron case where, in addition to the standard parameters Q and R, the overlaps projected onto eigenspaces of the training input correlation matrix $\mathbf{A} = \frac{1}{N} \sum_{\mu=1}^p \mathbf{x}^\mu (\mathbf{x}^\mu)^\mathrm{T}$ are required[2]. We therefore split the eigenvalues of $\mathbf{A}$ into Γ equal blocks ($\gamma = 1 \ldots \Gamma$) containing $N' = N/\Gamma$ eigenvalues each, ordering the eigenvalues such that they increase with γ. We then define projectors $\mathbf{P}^\gamma$ onto the corresponding eigenspaces and take as order parameters:

$$Q_{ll'}^\gamma = \frac{1}{N'} \mathbf{w}_l^\mathrm{T} \mathbf{P}^\gamma \mathbf{w}_{l'} \qquad R_{lm}^\gamma = \frac{1}{N'} \mathbf{w}_l^\mathrm{T} \mathbf{P}^\gamma \mathbf{w}_m^* \qquad U_{ls}^\gamma = \frac{1}{N'} \mathbf{w}_l^\mathrm{T} \mathbf{P}^\gamma \mathbf{b}_s \tag{5}$$

where the $\mathbf{b}_s$ are linear combinations of the noise variables and training inputs,

$$\mathbf{b}_s = \frac{1}{\sqrt{N}} \sum_{\mu=1}^p \xi_s^\mu \mathbf{x}^\mu. \tag{6}$$

---

[1]Here we assume that the system size N is large enough that the mean values of the parameters alone describe the dynamics sufficiently well (*i.e.*, self-averaging holds).

[2]The order parameters actually used in our calculation for the linear perceptron[7] are Laplace transforms of these projected order parameters.

As $\Gamma \to \infty$, these order parameters become functionals of a continuous variable[3].

The updates for the order parameters (5) due to the weight updates (3) can be found by taking the scalar products of (3) with either projected student or teacher weights, as appropriate. This then introduces the following activation 'components',

$$h_l^\gamma = \sqrt{\frac{\Gamma}{N'}}\mathbf{w}_l^{\mathrm{T}}\mathbf{P}^\gamma\mathbf{x} \qquad k_m^\gamma = \sqrt{\frac{\Gamma}{N'}}(\mathbf{w}_m^*)^{\mathrm{T}}\mathbf{P}^\gamma\mathbf{x} \qquad c_s^\gamma = \sqrt{\frac{\Gamma}{N'}}\mathbf{x}^{\mathrm{T}}\mathbf{P}^\gamma\mathbf{b}_s \quad (7)$$

so that the student and teacher activations are $h_l = \frac{1}{\Gamma}\sum_\gamma h_l^\gamma$ and $k_m = \frac{1}{\Gamma}\sum_\gamma k_m^\gamma$, respectively. For the linear perceptron, the chosen order parameters form a complete set - the dynamical equations close, without need for the average in (4).

For the nonlinear case, we now sketch the calculation of the order parameter update equations (4). Taken together, the integral over $\mathbf{w}'$ (a sum of p discrete terms in our case, one for each training example) and the subshell average in (4), define an average over the activations (2), their components (7), and the noise variables ξ_m, ξ_0. These variables turn out to be Gaussian distributed with zero mean, and therefore only their covariances need to be worked out. One finds that these are in fact given by the naive training set averages. For example,

$$\begin{aligned}
\langle h_l^\gamma k_m \rangle &= \frac{1}{p}\sum_\mu \frac{\Gamma}{N}(\mathbf{w}_l)^{\mathrm{T}}\mathbf{P}^\gamma\mathbf{x}^\mu(\mathbf{x}^\mu)^{\mathrm{T}}\mathbf{w}_m^* \\
&= \frac{\Gamma}{\alpha N}(\mathbf{w}_l)^{\mathrm{T}}\mathbf{P}^\gamma\mathbf{A}\mathbf{w}_m^* = \frac{a_\gamma}{\alpha}R_{lm}^\gamma, \qquad (8)
\end{aligned}$$

where we have used $\mathbf{P}^\gamma\mathbf{A} = a_\gamma\mathbf{P}^\gamma$ with a_γ 'the' eigenvalue of $\mathbf{A}$ in the γ-th eigenspace; this is well defined for $\Gamma \to \infty$ (see [6] for details of the eigenvalue spectrum). The correlations of the activations and noise variables explicitly appearing in the error in (3) are calculated similarly to give,

$$\begin{aligned}
\langle h_l h_{l'} \rangle &= \frac{1}{\Gamma}\sum_\gamma \frac{a_\gamma}{\alpha}Q_{ll'}^\gamma \\
\langle h_l k_m \rangle &= \frac{1}{\Gamma}\sum_\gamma \frac{a_\gamma}{\alpha}R_{lm}^\gamma \qquad \langle k_m k_{m'} \rangle = \frac{1}{\Gamma}\sum_\gamma \frac{a_\gamma}{\alpha}T_{mm'}^\gamma \qquad (9) \\
\langle h_l \xi_s \rangle &= \frac{1}{\Gamma}\sum_\gamma \frac{1}{\alpha}U_{ls}^\gamma \qquad \langle k_m \xi_s \rangle = 0 \qquad \langle \xi_s \xi_{s'} \rangle = \delta_{ss'}\sigma_s^2
\end{aligned}$$

where the final equation defines the noise variances. The $T_{mm'}^\gamma$ are projected overlaps between teacher weight vectors, $T_{mm'}^\gamma = \frac{1}{N}(\mathbf{w}_m^*)^{\mathrm{T}}\mathbf{P}^\gamma\mathbf{w}_{m'}^*$. We will assume that the teacher weights and training inputs are uncorrelated, so that $T_{mm'}^\gamma$ is independent of γ. The required covariances of the 'component' activations are

$$\begin{aligned}
\langle k_m^\gamma h_l \rangle &= \frac{a_\gamma}{\alpha}R_{lm}^\gamma & \langle k_m^\gamma k_{m'} \rangle &= \frac{a_\gamma}{\alpha}T_{mm'}^\gamma & \langle k_m^\gamma \xi_s \rangle &= 0 \\
\langle c_s^\gamma h_l \rangle &= \frac{a_\gamma}{\alpha}U_{ls}^\gamma & \langle c_s^\gamma k_{m'} \rangle &= 0 & \langle c_s^\gamma \xi_{s'} \rangle &= \frac{a_\gamma}{\alpha}\sigma_s^2\delta_{ss'} \\
\langle h_l^\gamma h_{l'} \rangle &= \frac{a_\gamma}{\alpha}Q_{ll'}^\gamma & \langle h_l^\gamma k_{m'} \rangle &= \frac{a_\gamma}{\alpha}R_{lm}^\gamma & \langle h_l^\gamma \xi_s \rangle &= \frac{1}{\alpha}U_{ls}^\gamma
\end{aligned}$$
$$(10)$$

---

[3] Note that the limit $\Gamma \to \infty$ is taken *after* the thermodynamic limit, i.e., $\Gamma \ll N$. This ensures that the number of order parameters is always negligible compared to N (otherwise self-averaging would break down).

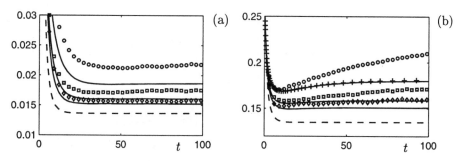

Figure 1: ϵ_g vs t for student and teacher with one hidden unit ($L = M = 1$); $\alpha = 2, 3, 4$ from above, learning rate $\eta = 1$. Noise of equal variance was added to both activations and output (a) $\sigma_1^2 = \sigma_0^2 = 0.01$, (b) $\sigma_1^2 = \sigma_0^2 = 0.1$. Simulations for $N = 100$ are shown by circles; standard errors are of the order of the symbol size. The bottom dashed lines show the infinite training set result for comparison. $\Gamma = 10$ was used for calculating the theoretical predictions; the curved marked "+" in (b), with $\Gamma = 20$ (and $\alpha = 2$), shows that this is large enough to be effectively in the $\Gamma \to \infty$ limit.

Using equation (3) and the definitions (7), we can now write down the dynamical equations, replacing the number of updates n by the continuous variable $t = n/N$ in the limit $N \to \infty$:

$$\partial_t R_{lm}^\gamma = -\eta \langle k_m^\gamma \partial_{h_l} E \rangle$$
$$\partial_t U_{ls}^\gamma = -\eta \langle c_s^\gamma \partial_{h_l} E \rangle$$
$$\partial_t Q_{ll'}^\gamma = -\eta \langle h_l^\gamma \partial_{h_{l'}} E \rangle - \eta \langle h_{l'}^\gamma \partial_{h_l} E \rangle + \eta^2 \frac{a_\gamma}{\alpha} \langle \partial_{h_l} E \partial_{h_{l'}} E \rangle \qquad (11)$$

where the averages are over zero mean Gaussian variables, with covariances (9,10). Using the explicit form of the error E, we have

$$\partial_{h_l} E = g'(h_l) \left[\sum_{l'} g(h_{l'}) - \sum_m g(k_m + \xi_m) - \xi_0 \right] \qquad (12)$$

which, together with the equations (11) completes the description of the dynamics. The Gaussian averages in (11) can be straightforwardly evaluated in a manner similar to the infinite training set case[5], and we omit the rather cumbersome explicit form of the resulting equations.

We note that, in contrast to the infinite training set case, the student activations h_l and the noise variables c_s and ξ_s are now correlated through equation (10). Intuitively, this is reasonable as the weights become correlated, during training, with the examples in the training set. In calculating the generalization error, on the other hand, such correlations are absent, and one has the same result as for infinite training sets. The dynamical equations (11), together with (9,10) constitute our main result. They are exact for the limits of either a linear network ($R, Q, T \to 0$, so that $g(x) \propto x$) or $\alpha \to \infty$, and can be integrated numerically in a straightforward way. In principle, the limit $\Gamma \to \infty$ should be taken but, as shown below, relatively small values of Γ can be taken in practice.

3   RESULTS AND DISCUSSION

We now discuss the main consequences of our result (11), comparing the resulting predictions for the generalization dynamics, $\epsilon_g(t)$, to the infinite training set theory

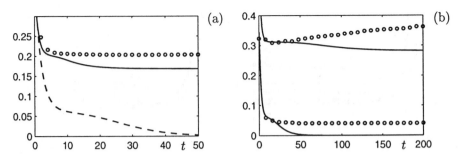

Figure 2: ϵ_g vs t for two hidden units ($L = M = 2$). Left: $\alpha = 0.5$, with $\alpha = \infty$ shown by dashed line for comparison; no noise. Right: $\alpha = 4$, no noise (bottom) and noise on teacher activations and outputs of variance 0.1 (top). Simulations for $N = 100$ are shown by small circles; standard errors are less than the symbol size. Learning rate $\eta = 2$ throughout.

and to simulations. Throughout, the teacher overlap matrix is set to $T_{ij} = \delta_{ij}$ (orthogonal teacher weight vectors of length $\sqrt{N}$).

In figure(1), we study the accuracy of our method as a function of the training set size for a nonlinear network with one hidden unit at two different noise levels. The learning rate was set to $\eta = 1$ for both (a) and (b). For small activation and output noise ($\sigma^2 = 0.01$), figure(1a), there is good agreement with the simulations for α down to $\alpha = 3$, below which the theory begins to underestimate the generalization error, compared to simulations. Our finite α theory, however, is still considerably more accurate than the infinite α predictions. For larger noise ($\sigma^2 = 0.1$, figure(1b)), our theory provides a reasonable quantitative estimate of the generalization dynamics for $\alpha > 3$. Below this value there is significant disagreement, although the qualitative behaviour of the dynamics is predicted quite well, including the overfitting phenomenon beyond $t \approx 10$. The infinite α theory in this case is qualitatively incorrect.

In the two hidden unit case, figure(2), our theory captures the initial evolution of $\epsilon_g(t)$ very well, but diverges significantly from the simulations at larger t; nevertheless, it provides a considerable improvement on the infinite α theory. One reason for the discrepancy at large t is that the theory predicts that different student hidden units will always specialize to individual teacher hidden units for $t \rightarrow \infty$, whatever the value of α. This leads to a decay of ϵ_g from a plateau value at intermediate times t. In the simulations, on the other hand, this specialization (or symmetry breaking) appears to be inhibited or at least delayed until very large t. This can happen even for zero noise and $\alpha \geq L$, where the training data should should contain enough information to force student and teacher weights to be equal asymptotically. The reason for this is not clear to us, and deserves further study. Our initial investigations, however, suggest that symmetry breaking may be strongly delayed due to the presence of saddle points in the training error surface with very 'shallow' unstable directions.

When our theory fails, which of its assumptions are violated? It is conceivable that multiple local minima in the training error surface could cause self-averaging to break down; however, we have found no evidence for this, see figure(3a). On the other hand, the simulation results in figure(3b) clearly show that the implicit assumption of Gaussian student activations – as discussed before eq. (8) – can be violated.

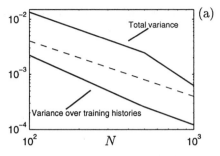 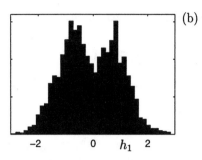

Figure 3: (a) Variance of $\epsilon_g(t = 20)$ vs input dimension N for student and teacher with two hidden units ($L = M = 2$), $\alpha = 0.5$, $\eta = 2$, and zero noise. The bottom curve shows the variance due to different random choices of training examples from a fixed training set ('training history'); the top curve also includes the variance due to different training sets. Both are compatible with the $1/N$ decay expected if self-averaging holds (dotted line). (b) Distribution (over training set) of the activation h_1 of the first hidden unit of the student. Histogram from simulations for $N = 1000$, all other parameter values as in (a).

In summary, the main theoretical contribution of this paper is the extension of online learning analysis for finite training sets to *nonlinear* networks. Our approximate theory does not require the use of replicas and yields ordinary first order differential equations for the time evolution of a set of order parameters. Its central implicit assumption (and its Achilles' heel) is that the student activations are Gaussian distributed. In comparison with simulations, we have found that it is more accurate than the infinite training set analysis at predicting the generalization dynamics for finite training sets, both qualitatively and also quantitatively for small learning times t. Future work will have to show whether the theory can be extended to cope with non-Gaussian student activations without incurring the technical difficulties of dynamical replica theory [2], and whether this will help to capture the effects of local minima and, more generally, 'rough' training error surfaces.

Acknowledgments : We would like to thank Ansgar West for helpful discussions.

References

[1] M. Biehl and H. Schwarze. *Journal of Physics A*, 28:643–656, 1995.

[2] A. C. C. Coolen, S. N. Laughton, and D. Sherrington. In NIPS 8, pp. 253-259, MIT Press, 1996; S.N. Laughton, A.C.C. Coolen, and D. Sherrington. *Journal of Physics A*, 29:763–786, 1996.

[3] See for example: The dynamics of online learning. Workshop at NIPS'95.

[4] T. Heskes and B. Kappen. *Physical Review A*, 44:2718–2762, 1994.

[5] D. Saad and S. A. Solla *Physical Review E*, 52:4225, 1995.

[6] P. Sollich. *Journal of Physics A*, 27:7771–7784, 1994.

[7] P. Sollich and D. Barber. In NIPS 9, pp.274-280, MIT Press, 1997; *Europhysics Letters*, 38:477-482, 1997.

Competitive On-Line Linear Regression

V. Vovk
Department of Computer Science
Royal Holloway, University of London
Egham, Surrey TW20 0EX, UK
vovk@dcs.rhbnc.ac.uk

Abstract

We apply a general algorithm for merging prediction strategies (the Aggregating Algorithm) to the problem of linear regression with the square loss; our main assumption is that the response variable is bounded. It turns out that for this particular problem the Aggregating Algorithm resembles, but is slightly different from, the well-known ridge estimation procedure. From general results about the Aggregating Algorithm we deduce a guaranteed bound on the difference between our algorithm's performance and the best, in some sense, linear regression function's performance. We show that the AA attains the optimal constant in our bound, whereas the constant attained by the ridge regression procedure in general can be 4 times worse.

1 INTRODUCTION

The usual approach to regression problems is to assume that the data are generated by some stochastic mechanism and make some, typically very restrictive, assumptions about that stochastic mechanism. In recent years, however, a different approach to this kind of problems was developed (see, e.g., DeSantis et al. [2], Littlestone and Warmuth [7]): in our context, that approach sets the goal of finding an on-line algorithm that performs not much worse than the best regression function found off-line; in other words, it replaces the usual statistical analyses by the competitive analysis of on-line algorithms.

DeSantis et al. [2] performed a competitive analysis of the Bayesian merging scheme for the log-loss prediction game; later Littlestone and Warmuth [7] and Vovk [10] introduced an on-line algorithm (called the Weighted Majority Algorithm by the former authors) for the simple binary prediction game. These two algorithms (the Bayesian merging scheme and the Weighted Majority Algorithm) are special cases of the Aggregating Algorithm (AA) proposed in [9, 11]. The AA is a member of a wide family of algorithms called "multiplicative weight" or "exponential weight" algorithms.

Closer to the topic of this paper, Cesa-Bianchi et al. [1] performed a competitive analysis, under the square loss, of the standard Gradient Descent Algorithm and Kivinen and Warmuth [6] complemented it by a competitive analysis of a modification of the Gradient Descent, which they call the Exponentiated Gradient Algorithm. The bounds obtained in [1, 6] are of the following type: at every trial T,

$$L_T \leq cL_T^* + O(1), \tag{1}$$

where L_T is the loss (over the first T trials) of the on-line algorithm, L_T^* is the loss of the best (by trial T) linear regression function, and c is a constant, $c > 1$; specifically, $c = 2$ for the Gradient Descent and $c = 3$ for the Exponentiated Gradient. These bounds hold under the following assumptions: for the Gradient Descent, it is assumed that the L_2 norm of the weights and of all data items are bounded by constant 1; for the Exponentiated Gradient, that the L_1 norm of the weights and the L_∞ norm of all data items are bounded by 1.

In many interesting cases bound (1) is weak. For example, suppose that our comparison class contains a "true" regression function, but its values are corrupted by an i.i.d. noise. Then, under reasonable assumptions about the noise, L_T^* will grow linearly in T, and inequality (1) will only bound the difference $L_T - L_T^*$ by a linear function of T. (Though in other situations bound (1) can be better than our bound (2), see below. For example, in the case of the Exponentiated Gradient, the $O(1)$ in (1) depends on the number of parameters n logarithmically whereas our bound depends on n linearly.)

In this paper we will apply the AA to the problem of linear regression. The AA has been proven to be optimal in some simple cases [5, 11], so we can also expect good performance in the problem of linear regression. The following is a typical result that can be obtained using the AA: Learner has a strategy which ensures that always

$$L_T \leq L_T^* + n\ln(T+1) + 1 \tag{2}$$

(n is the number of predictor variables). It is interesting that the assumptions for the last inequality are weaker than those for both the Gradient Descent and Exponentiated Gradient: we only assume that the L_2 norm of the weights and the L_∞ norm of all data items are bounded by constant 1 (these assumptions will be further relaxed later on). The norms L_2 and L_∞ are not dual, which casts doubt on the accepted intuition that the weights and data items should be measured by dual norms (such as L_1–L_∞ or L_2–L_2).

Notice that the logarithmic term $n\ln(T+1)$ of (2) is similar to the term $\frac{n}{2}\ln T$ occurring in the analysis of the log-loss game and its generalizations, in particular in Wallace's theory of minimum message length, Rissanen's theory of stochastic complexity, minimax regret analysis. In the case $n = 1$ and $x_t = 1$, $\forall t$, inequality (2) differs from Freund's [4] Theorem 4 only in the additive constant. In this paper we will see another manifestation of a phenomenon noticed by Freund [4]: for some important problems, the adversarial bounds of on-line competitive learning theory are only a tiny amount worse than the average-case bounds for some stochastic strategies for Nature.

A weaker variant of inequality (2) can be deduced from Foster's [3] Theorem 1 (if we additionally assume that the response variable take only two values, -1 or 1): Foster's result implies

$$L_T \leq L_T^* + 8n \ln(2n(T+1)) + 8$$

(a multiple of 4 arises from replacing Foster's set $\{0, 1\}$ of possible values of the response variable by our $\{-1, 1\}$; we also replaced Foster's d by $2n$: to span our set of possible weights we need $2n$ Foster's predictors).

Inequality (2) is also similar to Yamanishi's [12] result; in that paper, he considers a more general framework than ours but does not attempt to find optimal constants.

2   ALGORITHM

We consider the following protocol of interaction between Learner and Nature:

> FOR $t = 1, 2, \ldots$
>   Nature chooses $x_t \in \mathbb{R}^n$
>   Learner chooses prediction $p_t \in \mathbb{R}$
>   Nature chooses $y_t \in [-Y, Y]$
> END FOR.

This is a "perfect-information" protocol: either player can see the other player's moves. The parameters of our protocol are: a fixed positive number n (the dimensionality of our regression problem) and an upper bound $Y > 0$ on the value y_t returned by Nature. It is important, however, that our algorithm for playing this game (on the part of Learner) *does not need to know Y*.

We will only give a description of our regression algorithm; its derivation from the general AA will be given in the future full version of this paper. (It is usually a nontrivial task to represent the AA in a computationally efficient form, and the case of on-line linear regression is not an exception.) Fix n and $a > 0$. The algorithm is as follows:

> $A := aI;\ b := 0$
> FOR TRIAL $t = 1, 2, \ldots$:
>   read new $x_t \in \mathbb{R}^n$
> $A := A + x_t x_t'$
>   output prediction $p_t := b' A^{-1} x_t$
>   read new $y_t \in \mathbb{R}$
> $b := b + y_t x_t$
> END FOR.

In this description, A is an $n \times n$ matrix (which is always symmetrical and positive definite), $b \in \mathbb{R}^n$, I is the unit $n \times n$ matrix, and 0 is the all-0 vector.

The naive implementation of this algorithm would require $O(n^3)$ arithmetic operations at every trial, but the standard recursive technique allows us to spend only $O(n^2)$ arithmetic operations per trial. This is still not as good as for the Gradient Descent Algorithm and Exponentiated Gradient Algorithm (they require only $O(n)$

operations per trial); we seem to have a trade-off between the quality of bounds on predictive performance and computational efficiency. In the rest of the paper "AA" will mean the algorithm described in the previous paragraph (which is the Aggregating Algorithm applied to a particular uncountable pool of experts with a particular Gaussian prior).

3 BOUNDS

In this section we state, without proof, results describing the predictive performance of our algorithm. Our comparison class consists of the linear functions $y_t = w \cdot x_t$, where $w \in \mathbb{R}^n$. We will call the possible weights w "experts" (imagine that we have continuously many experts indexed by $w \in \mathbb{R}^n$; Expert w always recommends prediction $w \cdot x_t$ to Learner). At every trial t Expert w and Learner suffer loss $(y_t - w \cdot x_t)^2$ and $(y_t - p_t)^2$, respectively. Our notation for the total loss suffered by Expert w and Learner over the first T trials will be

$$L_T(w) := \sum_{t=1}^{T}(y_t - w \cdot x_t)^2$$

and

$$L_T(\text{Learner}) := \sum_{t=1}^{T}(y_t - p_t)^2,$$

respectively.

For compact pools of experts (which, in our setting, corresponds to the set of possible weights w being bounded and closed) it is usually possible to derive bounds (such as (2)) where the learner's loss is compared to the best expert's loss. In our case of non-compact pool, however, we need to give the learner a start on remote experts. Specifically, instead of comparing Learner's performance to $\inf_w L_T(w)$, we compare it to $\inf_w \left(L_T(w) + a\|w\|^2\right)$ (thus giving Learner a start of $a\|w\|^2$ on Expert w), where $a > 0$ is a constant reflecting our prior expectations about the "complexity" $\|w\| := \sqrt{\sum_{i=1}^{n} w_i^2}$ of successful experts.

This idea of giving a start to experts allows us to prove stronger results; e.g., the following elaboration of (2) holds:

$$L_T(\text{Learner}) \leq \inf_w \left(L_T(w) + \|w\|^2\right) + n\ln(T+1) \tag{3}$$

(this inequality still assumes that $\|x_t\|_\infty \leq 1$ for all t but w is unbounded).

Our notation for the transpose of matrix A will be A'; as usual, vectors are identified with one-column matrices.

Theorem 1 *For any fixed n, Learner has a strategy which ensures that always*

$$
\begin{aligned}
L_T(\text{Learner}) \;\leq\; & \inf_w \left(L_T(w) + a\|w\|^2\right) + Y^2 \ln \det\left(I + \frac{1}{a}\sum_{t=1}^{T} x_t x_t'\right) \\
\leq\; & \inf_w \left(L_T(w) + a\|w\|^2\right) + Y^2 \sum_{i=1}^{n} \ln\left(1 + \frac{1}{a}\sum_{t=1}^{T} x_{t,i}^2\right).
\end{aligned}
$$

If, in addition, $\|x_t\|_\infty \le X$, $\forall t$,

$$L_T(\text{Learner}) \le \inf_w \left(L_T(w) + a\|w\|^2\right) + nY^2 \ln\left(\frac{TX^2}{a} + 1\right). \tag{4}$$

The last inequality of this theorem implies inequality (3): it suffices to put $X = Y = a = 1$.

The term

$$\ln \det\left(I + \frac{1}{a}\sum_{t=1}^T x_t x_t'\right)$$

in Theorem 1 might be difficult to interpret. Notice that it can be rewritten as

$$n \ln T + \ln \det\left(\frac{1}{T}I + \frac{1}{a}\text{cov}(X_1, \ldots, X_n)\right),$$

where $\text{cov}(X_1, \ldots, X_n)$ is the empirical covariance matrix of the predictor variables (in other words, $\text{cov}(X_1, \ldots, X_n)$ is the covariance matrix of the random vector which takes the values $x_1, \ldots, x_T$ with equal probability $\frac{1}{T}$). We can see that this term is typically close to $n \ln T$.

Using standard transformations, it is easy to deduce from Theorem 1, e.g., the following results (for simplicity we assume $n = 1$ and $x_t, y_t \in [-1, 1]$, $\forall t$):

- if the pool of experts consists of all polynomials of degree d, Learner has a strategy guaranteeing

$$L_T(\text{Learner}) \le \inf_w \left(L_T(w) + \|w\|^2\right) + (d+1)\ln(T+1).$$

- if the pool of experts consists of all splines of degree d with k nodes (chosen *a priori*), Learner has a strategy guaranteeing

$$L_T(\text{Learner}) \le \inf_w \left(L_T(w) + \|w\|^2\right) + (d+k+1)\ln(T+1).$$

The following theorem shows that the constant n in inequality (4) cannot be improved.

Theorem 2 *Fix n (the number of attributes) and Y (the upper bound on $|y_t|$). For any $\epsilon > 0$ there exist a constant C and a stochastic strategy for Nature such that $\|x_t\|_\infty = 1$ and $|y_t| = Y$, for all t, and, for any stochastic strategy for Learner,*

$$\mathbf{E}\left(L_T(\text{Learner}) - \inf_{w:\|w\|\le Y} L_T(w)\right) \ge (n-\epsilon)Y^2 \ln T - C, \quad \forall T.$$

4   COMPARISONS

It is easy to see that the ridge regression procedure sometimes gives results that are not sensible in our framework where $y_t \in [-Y, Y]$ and the goal is to compete against the best linear regression function. For example, suppose $n = 1$, $Y = 1$, and Nature generates outcomes (x_t, y_t), $t = 1, 2, \ldots$, where

$$a \ll x_1 \ll x_2 \ll \cdots, \quad y_t = \begin{cases} 1, & \text{if } t \text{ odd}, \\ -1, & \text{if } t \text{ even}. \end{cases}$$

At trial $t = 2, 3, \ldots$ the ridge regression procedure (more accurately, its natural modification which truncates its predictions to $[-1, 1]$) will give prediction $p_t = y_{t-1}$ equal to the previous response, and so will suffer a loss of about $4T$ over T trials. On the other hand, the AA's prediction will be close to 0, and so the cumulative loss of the AA over the first T trials will be about T, which is close to the best expert's loss. We can see that the ridge regression procedure in this situation is forced to suffer a loss 4 times as big as the AA's loss.

The lower bound stated in Theorem 2 does not imply that our regression algorithm is better than the ridge regression procedure in our adversarial framework. (Moreover, the idea of our proof of Theorem 2 is to lower bound the performance of the ridge regression procedure in the situation where the expected loss of the ridge regression procedure is optimal.) Theorem 1 asserts that

$$L_T(\text{Learner}) \leq \inf_w \left(L_T(w) + a\|w\|^2 \right) + Y^2 \sum_{i=1}^{n} \ln \left(1 + \frac{1}{a} \sum_{t=1}^{T} x_{t,i}^2 \right) \tag{5}$$

when Learner follows the AA. The next theorem shows that the ridge regression procedure sometimes violates this inequality.

Theorem 3 *Let* $n = 1$ *(the number of attributes) and* $Y = 1$ *(the upper bound on* $|y_t|$*); fix* $a > 0$*. Nature has a strategy such that, when Learner plays the ridge regression strategy,*

$$L_T(\text{Learner}) = 4T + O(1), \tag{6}$$

$$\inf_w \left(L_T(w) + a\|w\|^2 \right) = T + O(1), \tag{7}$$

$$\ln \left(1 + \frac{1}{a} \sum_{t=1}^{T} x_t^2 \right) = T \ln 2 + O(1) \tag{8}$$

as $T \to \infty$ *(and, therefore, (5) is violated).*

5 CONCLUSION

A distinctive feature of our approach to linear regression is that our only assumption about the data is that $|y_t| \leq Y$, $\forall t$; we do not make any assumptions about stochastic properties of the data-generating mechanism. In some situations (if the data were generated by a partially known stochastic mechanism) this feature is a disadvantage, but often it will be an advantage.

This paper was greatly influenced by Vapnik's [8] idea of transductive inference. The algorithm analyzed in this paper is "transductive", in the sense that it outputs some prediction p_t for y_t after being given x_t, rather than to output a general rule for mapping x_t into p_t; in particular, p_t may depend non-linearly on x_t. (It is easy, however, to extract such a rule from the description of the algorithm once it is found.)

Acknowledgments

Kostas Skouras and Philip Dawid noticed that our regression algorithm is different from the ridge regression and that in some situations it behaves very differently. Manfred Warmuth's advice about relevant literature is also gratefully appreciated.

References

[1] N. Cesa-Bianchi, P. M. Long, and M. K. Warmuth (1996), Worst-case quadratic loss bounds for on-line prediction of linear functions by gradient descent, *IEEE Trans. Neural Networks* **7**:604–619.

[2] A. DeSantis, G. Markowsky, and M. N. Wegman (1988), Learning probabilistic prediction functions, *in* "Proceedings, 29th Annual IEEE Symposium on Foundations of Computer Science," pp. 110–119, Los Alamitos, CA: IEEE Comput. Soc.

[3] D. P. Foster (1991), Prediction in the worst case, *Ann. Statist.* **19**:1084–1090.

[4] Y. Freund (1996), Predicting a binary sequence almost as well as the optimal biased coin, *in* "Proceedings, 9th Annual ACM Conference on Computational Learning Theory", pp. 89–98, New York: Assoc. Comput. Mach.

[5] D. Haussler, J. Kivinen, and M. K. Warmuth (1994), Tight worst-case loss bounds for predicting with expert advice, University of California at Santa Cruz, Technical Report UCSC-CRL-94-36, revised December. Short version *in* "Computational Learning Theory" (P. Vitányi, Ed.), Lecture Notes in Computer Science, Vol. 904, pp. 69–83, Berlin: Springer, 1995.

[6] J. Kivinen and M. K. Warmuth (1997), Exponential Gradient versus Gradient Descent for linear predictors, *Inform. Computation* **132**:1–63.

[7] N. Littlestone and M. K. Warmuth (1994), The Weighted Majority Algorithm, *Inform. Computation* **108**:212–261.

[8] V. N. Vapnik (1995), *The Nature of Statistical Learning Theory*, New York: Springer.

[9] V. Vovk (1990), Aggregating strategies, *in* "Proceedings, 3rd Annual Workshop on Computational Learning Theory" (M. Fulk and J. Case, Eds.), pp. 371–383, San Mateo, CA: Morgan Kaufmann.

[10] V. Vovk (1992), Universal forecasting algorithms, *Inform. Computation* **96**:245–277.

[11] V. Vovk (1997), A game of prediction with expert advice, to appear in *J. Comput. Inform. Syst.* Short version *in* "Proceedings, 8th Annual ACM Conference on Computational Learning Theory," pp. 51–60, New York: Assoc. Comput. Mach., 1995.

[12] K. Yamanishi (1997), A decision-theoretic extension of stochastic complexity and its applications to learning, submitted to *IEEE Trans. Inform. Theory*.

On the infeasibility of training neural networks with small squared errors

Van H. Vu

Department of Mathematics, Yale University

vuha@math.yale.edu

Abstract

We demonstrate that the problem of training neural networks with small (average) squared error is computationally intractable. Consider a data set of M points (X_i, Y_i), $i = 1, 2, \ldots, M$, where X_i are input vectors from R^d, Y_i are real outputs ($Y_i \in R$). For a network f_0 in some class $\mathcal{F}$ of neural networks, $(1/M) \sum_{i=1}^{M} (f_0(X_i) - Y_i)^2)^{1/2} - \inf_{f \in \mathcal{F}} (1/M) \sum_{i=1}^{M} (f(X_i) - Y_i)^2)^{1/2}$ is the (avarage) relative error occurs when one tries to fit the data set by f_0. We will prove for several classes $\mathcal{F}$ of neural networks that achieving a relative error smaller than some fixed positive threshold (independent from the size of the data set) is NP-hard.

1 Introduction

Given a data set (X_i, Y_i), $i = 1, 2, \ldots, M$, X_i are input vectors from R^d, Y_i are real outputs ($Y_i \in R$). We call the points (X_i, Y_i) *data points*. The training problem for neural networks is to find a network from some class (usually with fixed number of nodes and layers), which fits the data set with small error. In the following we describe the problem with more details.

Let $\mathcal{F}$ be a class (set) of neural networks, and α be a metric norm in R^M. To each $f \in \mathcal{F}$, associate an *error vector* $E_f = (|f(X_i) - Y_i|)_{i=1}^{M}$ ($E_{\mathcal{F}}$ depends on the data set, of course, though we prefer this notation to avoid difficulty of having too many subindices). The norm of E_f in α shows how well the network f fits the data regarding to this particular norm. Furthermore, let $e_{\alpha, \mathcal{F}}$ denote the smallest error achieved by a network in $\mathcal{F}$, namely:

$$e_{\alpha, \mathcal{F}} = \min_{f \in \mathcal{F}} \|E_f\|_\alpha$$

In this context, the training problem we consider here is to find $f \in \mathcal{F}$ such that

$||E_f||_\alpha - e_{\alpha, \mathcal{F}} \leq \epsilon_{\mathcal{F}}$, where $\epsilon_{\mathcal{F}}$ is a positive number given in advance, and does not depend on the size M of the data set. We will call $\epsilon_{\mathcal{F}}$ *relative error*. The norm α is chosen by the nature of the training process, the most common norms are:

l_∞ norm: $||v||_\infty = max|v_i|$ (interpolation problem)

l_2 norm: $||v||_2 = (1/M \sum_{i=1}^{M} v_i^2)^{1/2}$, where $v = (v_i)_{i=1}^{M}$ (least square error problem).

The quantity $||E_f||_{l_2}$ is usually referred to as the *emperical error* of the training process. The first goal of this paper is to show that achieving small emperical error is NP-hard. From now on, we work with l_2 norm, if not otherwise specified.

A question of great importance is: given the data set, $\mathcal{F}$ and $\epsilon_{\mathcal{F}}$ in advance, could one find an efficient algorithm to solve the training problem formulated above. By efficiency we mean an algorithm terminating in polynomial time (polynomial in the size of the input). This question is closely related to the problem of learning neural networks in polynomial time (see [3]). The input in the algorithm is the data set, by its size we means the number of bits required to write down all (X_i, Y_i).

Question 1. *Given $\mathcal{F}$ and $\epsilon_{\mathcal{F}}$ and a data set. Could one find an efficient algorithm which produces a function $f \in \mathcal{F}$ such that $||E_f|| < e_{\mathcal{F}} + \epsilon_{\mathcal{F}}$*

Question 1 is very difficult to answer in general. In this paper we will investigate the following important sub-question:

Question 2. *Can one achieve arbitrary small relative error using polynomial algorithms ?*

Our purpose is to give a negative answer for Question 2. This question was posed by L. Jones in his seminar at Yale (1996). The crucial point here is that we are dealing with l_2 norm, which is very important from statistical point of view. Our investigation is also inspired by former works done in [2], [6], [7], etc, which show negative results in the l_∞ norm case.

Definition. *A positive number ϵ is a threshold of a class $\mathcal{F}$ of neural networks if the training problem by networks from $\mathcal{F}$ with relative error less than ϵ is NP-hard (i.e., computationally infeasible).*

In order to provide a negative answer to Question 2, we are going to show the existence of thresholds (which is independent from the size of the data set) for the following classes of networks.

- $\mathcal{F}_n = \{f | f(x) = (1/n)(\sum_{i=1}^{n} step\,(a_i x - b_i))\}$
- $\mathcal{F}'_n = \{f | f(x) = (\sum_{i=1}^{n} c_i step\,(a_i x - b_i))\}$
- $\mathcal{G}_n = \{g | g(x) = \sum_{i_1}^{n} c_i \phi_i(a_i x - b_i)\}$

where n is a positive integer, $step(x) = 1$ if x is positive and zero otherwise, a_i and x are vectors from R^d, b_i are real numbers, and c_i are positive numbers. It is clear that the class $\mathcal{F}'_n$ contains $\mathcal{F}_n$; the reason why we distinguish these two cases is that the proof for $\mathcal{F}_n$ is relatively easy to present, while contains the most important ideas. In the third class, the functions ϕ_i are sigmoid functions which satisfy certain Lipchitzian conditions (for more details see [9])

Main Theorem

(i) The classes $\mathcal{F}_1$, $\mathcal{F}_2$, $\mathcal{F}'_2$ and $\mathcal{G}_2$ have absolute constant (positive) thresholds

(ii) For every class $\mathcal{F}_{n+2}, n > 0$, there is a threshold of form $\zeta n^{-3/2} d^{-1/2}$.

(iii) For every $\mathcal{F}'_{n+2}, n > 0$, there is a threshold of form $\zeta n^{-3/2} d^{-3/2}$.

(iv) For every class $\mathcal{G}_{n+2}, n > 0$, there is a threshold of form $\zeta n^{-5/2} d^{-1/2}$.

In the last three statements, ζ is an absolute positive constant.

Here is the key argument of the proof. Assume that there is an algorithm A which solves the training problem in some class (say $\mathcal{F}_n$) with relative error ϵ. From some (properly chosen) NP-hard problem, we will construct a data set so that if ϵ is sufficiently small, then the solution found by A (given the constructed data set as input) in $\mathcal{F}_n$ implies a solution for the original NP-hard problem. This will give a lower bound on ϵ, if we assume that the algorithm A is polynomial. In all proofs the leading parameter is d (the dimension of data inputs). So by polynomial we mean a polynomial with d as variable. All the input (data) sets constructed will have polynomial size in d.

The paper is organized as follow. In the next Section, we discuss earlier results concerning the l_∞ norm. In Section 3, we display the NP-hard results we will use in the reduction. In Section 4, we prove the main Theorem for class $\mathcal{F}_2$ and mention the method to handle more general cases. We conclude with some remarks and open questions in Section 5.

To end this Section, let us mention one important corollary. The Main Theorem implies that learning $\mathcal{F}_n$, $\mathcal{F}'_n$ and $\mathcal{G}_n$ (with respect to l_2 norm) is hard. For more about the connection between the complexity of training and learning problems, we refer to [3], [5].

Notation: Through the paper U_d denotes the unit hypercube in R^d. For any number x, x_d denotes the vector $(x, x, .., x)$ of length d. In particular, 0_d denotes the origin of R^d. For any half space H, $\bar{H}$ is the complement of H. For any set A, $|A|$ is the number of elements in A. A function $y(d)$ is said to have order of magnitude $\Theta(F(d))$, if there are $c < C$ positive constants such that $c < y(d)/F(d) < C$ for all d.

2   Previous works in the l_∞ case

The case $\alpha = l_\infty$ (interpolation problem) was considered by several authors for many different classes of (usually) 2-layer networks (see [6],[2], [7], [8]). Most of the authors investigate the case when there is a perfect fit, i.e., $e_{l_\infty, \mathcal{F}} = 0$. In [2], the authors proved that training 2-layer networks containing 3 step function nodes with zero relative error is NP-hard. Their proof can be extended for networks with more inner nodes and various logistic output nodes. This generalized a former result of Maggido [8] on data set with rational inputs. Combining the techniques used in [2] with analysis arguments, Lee Jones [6] showed that the training problem with relative error $1/10$ by networks with two monotone Lipschitzian Sigmoid inner nodes and linear output node, is also NP-hard (NP-complete under certain circumstances). This implies a threshold (in the sense of our definition) $(1/10)M^{-1/2}$ for the class examined. However, this threshold is rather weak, since it is decreasing in M. This result was also extended for the n inner nodes case [6].

It is also interesting to compare our results with Judd's. In [7] he considered the following problem "Given a network and a set of training examples (a data set), does there exist a set of weights so that the network gives correct output for all training examples ?" He proved that this problem is NP-hard even if the network is required to produce the correct output for two-third of the traing examples. In fact, it was shown that there is a class of networks and a data sets so that any algorithm will produce poorly on some networks and data sets in the class. However, from this result one could not tell if there is a network which is "hard to train" for all algorithms. Moreover, the number of nodes in the networks grows with the size of the data set. Therefore, in some sense, the result is not independent from the size of the data set.

In our proofs we will exploit many techniques provided in these former works. The crucial one is the reduction used by A. Blum and R. Rivest, which involves the NP-hardness of the Hypergraph 2-Coloring problem.

3   Some NP hard problems

Definition *Let B be a CNF formula, where each clause has at most k literals. Let $max(B)$ be the maximum number of clauses which can be satisfied by a truth assignment. The APP MAX k-SAT problem is to find a truth assignment which satisfies $(1 - \epsilon)max(B)$ clauses.*

The following Theorem says that this approximation problem is NP -hard, for some small ϵ.

Theorem 3.1.1 *Fix $k \geq 2$. There is $\epsilon_1 > 0$, such that finding a truth assignment, which satisfies at least $(1 - \epsilon_1)max(B)$ clauses is NP-hard.*

The problem is still hard, when every literal in B appears in only few clauses, and every clause contains only few literals. Let $\mathcal{B}_3(5)$ denote the class of CNFs with at most 3 literals in a clause and every literal appears in at most 5 clauses (see [1]).

Theorem 3.1.2 *There is $\epsilon_2 > 0$ such that finding a truth assignment, which satisfies at least $(1 - \epsilon)max(B)$ clauses in a formula $B \in \mathcal{B}_3(5)$ is NP-hard.*

The optimal thresholds in these theorems can be computed, due to recent results in Thereotical Computer Science. Because of space limitation, we do not go into this matter.

Let $H = (V, E)$ be a hypergraph on the set V, and E is the set of edges (collection of subsets of V). Elements of V are called vertices. The degree of a vertex is the number of edges containing the vertex. We could assume that each edge contains at least two vertices. Color the vertices with color Blue or Red. An edge is *colorful* if it contains vertices of both colors, otherwise we call it *monochromatic*. Let $c(H)$ be the maximum number of colorful edges one can achieve by a coloring. By a probabilistic argument, it is easy to show that $c(H)$ is at least $|E|/2$ (in a random coloring, an edge will be colorful with probability at least $1/2$). Using 3.1.2, we could prove the following theorem (for the proof see [9])

Theorem 3.1.3 *There is a constant $\epsilon_3 > 0$ such that finding a coloring with at least $(1 - \epsilon_3)c(H)$ colorful edges is NP-hard. This statement holds even in the case when every but one degree in H is at most 10*

4   Proof for $\mathcal{F}_2$

We follow the reduction used in [2]. Consider a hypergraph $H(V, E)$ described Theorem 3.2.1. Let $V = \{1, 2, \ldots, d + 1\}$, where with the possible exception of the vertex $d + 1$, all other vertices have degree at most 10. Every edge will have at least 2 and at most 4 vertices. So the number of edges is at least $(d + 1)/4$.

Let p_i be the ith unit vector in R^{d+1}, $p_i = (0, 0, \ldots, 0, 1, 0, \ldots, 0)$. Furthermore, $\chi_C = \sum_{i \in C} p_i$ for every edge $C \in E$. Let S be a coloring with maximum number of colorful edges. In this coloring denote by A_1 the set of colorful edges and by A_2 the set of monochromatic edges. Clearly $|A_1| = c(H)$.

Our data set will be the following (inputs are from R^{d+1} instead of from R^d, but it makes no difference)

$$D = \{(p_i, 1/2)\}_{i=1}^{d} \cup \{(p_{d+1}, 1/2)^t\} \cup \{(0_{d+1}, 1)^t\} \cup \{(\chi_C, 1)|C \in A_1\} \cup \{(\chi_C, 1/2)|C \in A_2\}$$

where $(p_{d+1}, 1/2)^t$ and $(0_{d+1}, 1)^t$ means $(p_{d+1}, 1/2)$ and $(0_{d+1}, 1)$ are repeated t times in the data set, resp. Similarly to [2], consider two vectors a and b in R^{d+1} where

$$a = (a_1, \ldots, a_{d+1}), a_i = -1 \text{ if } i \text{ is Red and } a_i = d + 1 \text{ otherwise}$$
$$b = (b_1, \ldots, b_{d+1}), b_i = -1 \text{ if } i \text{ is Blue and } b_i = d + 1 \text{ otherwise}$$

It is not difficult to verify that the function $f_0 = (1/2)(\text{step}\,(ax + 1/2) + \text{step}\,(bx + 1/2))$ fits the data perfectly, thus $e_{\mathcal{F}_2} = ||E_{f_0}|| = 0$.

Suppose $f = (1/2)(\text{step}\,(cx - \gamma) + \text{step}\,(dx - \delta))$ satisfies

$$M||E_f||^2 = \sum_{i=1}^{M}(f(X_i) - Y_i)^2 < M\epsilon^2$$

Since if $f(X_i) \neq Y_i$ then $(f(X_i) - Y_i)^2 \geq 1/4$, the previous inequality implies: $\mu_0 = |\{i, f(X_i) \neq Y_i\}| < 4M\epsilon^2 = \mu$

The ratio μ_0/M is called misclassification ratio, and we will show that this ratio cannot be arbitrary small. In order to avoid unnecessary ceiling and floor symbols, we assume the upper-bound μ is an integer. We choose $t = \mu$ so that we can also assume that $(0_{d+1}, 1)$ and $(p_{d+1}, 1/2)$ are well classified. Let H_1 (H_2) be the half space consisting of x: $cx - \gamma > 0$ ($dx - \delta > 0$). Note that $0_d \in H_1 \cap H_2$ and $p_{d+1} \in \bar{H}_1 \cup \bar{H}_2$. Now let P_1 denote the set of i where $p_i \notin H_1$, and P_2 the set of i such that $p_i \in H_1 \cap H_2$. Clearly, if $j \in P_2$, then $f(p_j) \neq Y_j$, hence: $|P_2| \leq \mu$. Let $Q = \{C \in E|C \cap P_2 \neq \emptyset\}$. Note that for each $j \in P_2$ the degree of j is at most 10, thus: $|Q| \leq 10|P_2| \leq 10\mu$

Let $A_1' = \{C|f(\chi_C) = 1\}$. Since less than μ points are misclassified, $|A_1' \triangle A_1| < \mu$. Color V by the following rule: (1) if $p_i \in P_1$, then i is Red; (2) if $p_i \in P_2$, color i arbitrarily, either Red or Blue; (3) if $p_i \notin P_1 \cup P_2$, then i is Blue.

Now we can finish the proof by the following two claims:

Claim 1: *Every edge in $A_1' \backslash Q$ is colorful.* It is left to readers to verify this simple statement.

Claim 2: $|A_1' \backslash Q|$ *is close to* $|A_1|$.

Notice that:

$$|A_1 \backslash (A_1' \backslash Q)| \leq |A_1 \triangle A_1'| + |Q| \leq \mu + 10\mu = 11\mu$$

Observe that the size of the data set is $M = d + 2t + |E|$, so $|E| + d \geq M - 2t = M - 2\mu$. Moreover, $|E| \geq (d+1)/4$, so $|E| \geq (1/5)(M - 2\mu)$. On the other hand, $|A_1| \geq (1/2)|E|$, all together we obtain; $|A_1| \geq (1/10)(M - \mu)$, which yields:

$$|A_1' \backslash Q| \geq |A_1|(1 - 11\frac{\mu}{|A_1|}) \geq |A_1|(1 - 110(\frac{\mu}{(M - \mu)}))$$

$$\geq |A_1|(1 - 110(\frac{4\epsilon^2}{1 - 4\epsilon^2})) = |A_1|(1 - k(\epsilon))$$

Choose $\epsilon = \epsilon_4$ such that $k(\epsilon_4) \leq \epsilon_3$ (see Theorem 3.1.3). Then ϵ_4 will be a threshold for the class $\mathcal{F}_2$. This completes the proof. Q.E.D.

Due to space limitation, we omit the proofs for other classes and refer to [9]. However, let us at least describe (roughly) the general method to handle these cases. The method consists of following steps:

• Extend the data set in the previous proof by a set of (special) points.

• Set the multiplicities of the special points sufficiently high so that those points should be well-classified.

• If we choose the special points properly, the fact that these points are well-classified will determine (roughly) the behavior of all but 2 nodes. In general we will show that all but 2 nodes have little influence on the outputs of non-special data points.

• The problem basically reduces to the case of two nodes. By modifying the previous proof, we could achieve the desired thresholds.

5   Remarks and open problems

• Readers may argue about the existence of (somewhat less natural) data points of high multiplicities. We can avoid using these data points by a combinatorial trick described in [9].

• The proof in Section 4 could be carried out using Theorem 3.1.2. However, we prefer using the hypergraph coloring terminology (Theorem 3.1.3), which is more convenient and standard. Moreover, Theorem 3.1.3 itself is interesting, and has not been listed among well known "approximation is hard" theorems.

• It remains an open question to determine the right order of magnitude of thresholds for all the classes we considered. (see Section 1). By technical reasons, in the Main theorem, the thresholds for more than two nodes involve the dimension (d). We conjecture that there are dimension-free thresholds.

Acknowledgement We wish to thank A. Blum, A. Barron and L. Lovász for many useful ideas and discussions.

References

[1] S. Arora and C. Lund *Hardness of approximation*, book chapter, preprint

[2] A. Blum, R. Rivest *Training a 3-node neural network is NP-hard* Neutral Networks, Vol 5., p 117-127, 1992

[3] A. Blumer, A. Ehrenfeucht, D. Haussler, M. Warmuth, *Learnability and the Vepnik-Chervonenkis Dimension*, Journal of the Association for computing Machinery, Vol 36, No. 4, 929-965, 1989.

[4] M. Garey and D. Johnson, Computers and intractability: A guide to the theory of NP-completeness, San Francisco, W.H.Freeman, 1979

[5] D. Haussler, *Generalizing the PAC model for neural net and other learning applications* (Tech. Rep. UCSC-CRL-89-30). Santa Cruz. CA: University of California 1989.

[6] L. Jones, *The computational intractability of training sigmoidal neural networks* (preprint)

[7] J. Judd *Neutral Networks and Complexity of learning*, MIT Press 1990.

[8] N. Meggido, *On the complexity of polyhedral separability* (Tech. Rep. RJ 5252) IBM Almaden Research Center, San Jose, CA

[9] V. H. Vu, *On the infeasibility of training neural networks with small squared error*, manuscript.

The Storage Capacity
of a Fully-Connected Committee Machine

Yuansheng Xiong
Department of Physics, Pohang Institute of Science and Technology,
Hyoja San 31, Pohang, Kyongbuk, Korea
xiong@galaxy.postech.ac.kr

Chulan Kwon
Department of Physics, Myong Ji University,
Yongin, Kyonggi, Korea
ckwon@wh.myongji.ac.kr

Jong-Hoon Oh
Lucent Technologies, Bell Laboratories,
600 Mountain Ave., Murray Hill, NJ07974, U. S. A.
jhoh@physics.bell-labs.com

Abstract

We study the storage capacity of a fully-connected committee machine with a large number K of hidden nodes. The storage capacity is obtained by analyzing the geometrical structure of the weight space related to the internal representation. By examining the asymptotic behavior of order parameters in the limit of large K, the storage capacity α_c is found to be proportional to $K\sqrt{\ln K}$ up to the leading order. This result satisfies the mathematical bound given by Mitchison and Durbin, whereas the replica-symmetric solution in a conventional Gardner's approach violates this bound.

1 INTRODUCTION

Since Gardner's pioneering work on the storage capacity of a single layer perceptron[1], there have been numerous efforts to use the statistical mechanics formulation to study feed-forward neural networks. The storage capacity of multi-layer neural networks has been of particular interest, together with the generalization problem. Barkai, Hansel and Kanter[2] studied a parity machine with a non-overlapping receptive field of continuous weights within a one-step replica symmetry breaking (RSB) scheme, and their result agrees with a mathematical bound previously found by Mitchison and Durbin (MD)[3]. Subsequently Barkai, Hansel and Sompolinsky[4] and Engel et al.[5] have studied the committee machine, which is closer to the multi-layer perceptron architecture and is most frequently used in real-world applications. Though they have derived many interesting results, particularly for the case of a finite number of hidden units, it was found that their the replica-symmetric (RS) result violates the MD bound in the limit where the number of hidden units K is large.

Recently, Monasson and O'Kane[6] proposed a new statistical mechanics formalism which can analyze the weight-space structure related to the internal representations of hidden units. It was applied to single layer perceptrons[7, 8, 9] as well as multi-layer networks[10, 11, 12]. Monasson and Zecchina[10] have successfully applied this formalism to the case of both committee and parity machines with non-overlapping receptive fields (NRF)[10]. They suggested that analysis of the RS solution under this new statistical mechanics formalism can yield results just as good as the one-step RSB solution in the conventional Gardner's method.

In this letter, we apply this formalism for a derivation of the storage capacity of a fully-connected committee machine, which is also called a committee machine with overlapping receptive field (ORF) and is believed to be a more relevant architecture. In particular, we obtain the value of the critical storage capacity in the limit of large K, which satisfies the MD bound. It also agrees with a recent one-step RSB calculation, using the conventional Gardner method, to within a small difference of a numerical prefactor[13]. Finally we will briefly discuss the fully-connected parity machine.

2 WEIGHT SPACE STRUCTURE OF THE COMMITTEE MACHINE

We consider a fully-connected committee machine with N input units, K hidden units and one output unit, where weights between the hidden units and the output unit are set to 1. The network maps input vectors $\{x_i^\mu\}$, where $\mu = 1, ..., P$, to output y^μ as:

$$
\begin{aligned}
y^\mu &= \mathrm{sgn}\left(\sum_{j=1}^{K} h_j^\mu\right) \\
&= \mathrm{sgn}\left[\sum_{j=1}^{K} \mathrm{sgn}\left(\sum_{i=1}^{N} W_{ji} x_i^\mu\right)\right],
\end{aligned}
\tag{1}
$$

where W_{ji} is the weight between the ith input node and the jth hidden unit. $h_j^\mu \equiv \mathrm{sgn}(\sum_{i=1}^{N} W_{ji} x_i^\mu)$ is the jth component of the internal representation for input pattern $\{x_i^\mu\}$. We consider continuous weights with spherical constraint, $\sum_i^N W_{ji} = N$.

Given $P = \alpha N$ patterns, the learning process in a layered neural network can be interpreted as the selection of cells in the weight space corresponding to a set of suitable internal representations $\mathbf{h} = \{h_j^\mu\}$, each of which has a non-zero elementary volume defined by:

$$V_{\mathbf{h}} = \text{Tr}_{\{W_{ji}\}} \prod_{\mu} \Theta \left(y^{\mu} \sum_{j} h_j^{\mu} \right) \prod_{\mu,j} \Theta \left(h_j^{\mu} \sum_{i} W_{ji} x_i^{\mu} \right), \tag{2}$$

where $\Theta(x)$ is the Heaviside step function. The Gardner's volume V_G, that is, the volume of the weight space which satisfies the given input-output relations, can be written as the sum of the cells over all internal representations:

$$V_G = \sum_{\mathbf{h}} V_{\mathbf{h}}. \tag{3}$$

The method developed by Monasson and his collaborators [6, 10] is based on analysis of the detailed internal structure, that is, how the Gardner's volume V_G is decomposed into elementary volumes $V_{\mathbf{h}}$ associated with a possible internal representation. The distribution of the elementary volumes can be derived from the free energy,

$$g(r) = -\frac{1}{Nr} \left\langle\!\left\langle \ln \left(\sum_{\mathbf{h}} V_{\mathbf{h}}^r \right) \right\rangle\!\right\rangle, \tag{4}$$

where $\langle\!\langle \cdots \rangle\!\rangle$ denotes the average over patterns. The entropy $\mathcal{N}[w(r)]$ of the volumes whose average sizes are equal to $w(r) = -1/N \ln \langle\!\langle V_{\mathbf{h}} \rangle\!\rangle$, can be given by the Legendre relations

$$\mathcal{N}[w(r)] = -\frac{\partial g(r)}{\partial(1/r)}, \quad w(r) = \frac{\partial[rg(r)]}{\partial r} \tag{5}$$

respectively.

The entropies $\mathcal{N}_D = \mathcal{N}[w(r = 1)]$ and $\mathcal{N}_R = \mathcal{N}[w(r = 0)]$ are of most importance, and will be discussed below. In the thermodynamic limit, $1/N \langle\!\langle \ln(V_G) \rangle\!\rangle = -g(r = 1)$ is dominated by elementary volumes of size $w(r = 1)$, of which there are $\exp(N\mathcal{N}_D)$. Furthermore, the most numerous elementary volumes have the size $w(r = 0)$ and number $\exp(N\mathcal{N}_R)$. The vanishing condition for the entropies is related to the zero volume condition for V_G and thus gives the storage capacity. We focus on the entropy $\mathcal{N}_D$ of elementary volumes dominating the weight space V_G.

3   ORDER PARAMETERS AND PHASE TRANSITION

For a fully-connected machine, the overlaps between different hidden units should be taken into account, which makes this problem much more difficult than the tree-like (NRF) architecture studied in Ref. [10]. The replicated partition function for the fully-connected committee machine reads:

$$\left\langle\!\left\langle \left(\sum_{\mathbf{h}} V_{\mathbf{h}}^r \right)^n \right\rangle\!\right\rangle = \left\langle\!\left\langle \text{Tr}_{h_j^{\mu\alpha}} \text{Tr}_{W_j^{\mu\alpha}} \prod_{\mu\alpha} \Theta \left(\sum_{j} h_j^{\mu\alpha} \right) \prod_{\mu j \alpha a} \Theta \left(h_j^{\mu\alpha} \sum_{i} W_{ji}^{\alpha a} x_i^{\mu} \right) \right\rangle\!\right\rangle, \tag{6}$$

with $a = 1, \cdots, r$ and $\alpha = 1, \cdots, n$. Unlike Gardner's conventional approach, we need two sets of replica indices for the weights. We introduce the order parameters,

$$Q_{jk}^{\alpha\beta ab} = \frac{1}{N} \sum_{i} W_{ji}^{\alpha a} W_{ki}^{\beta b}, \tag{7}$$

where the indices a, b originate from the integer power r of elementary volumes, and α, β are the standard replica indices. The replica symmetry ansatz leads to five order parameters as:

$$
Q_{jk}^{\alpha\beta ab} = \begin{cases}
q^* & (j = k, \alpha = \beta, a \neq b), \\
q & (j = k, \alpha \neq \beta), \\
c & (j \neq k, \alpha = \beta, a = b), \\
d^* & (j \neq k, \alpha = \beta, a \neq b), \\
d & (j \neq k, \alpha \neq \beta),
\end{cases}
\tag{8}
$$

where q^* and q are, respectively, the overlaps between the weight vectors connected to the same hidden unit of the same ($\alpha = \beta$) and different ($\alpha \neq \beta$) replicas corresponding to the two different internal representations. The order parameters c, d^* and d describe the overlaps between weights that are connected to different hidden units, of which c and d^* are the overlaps within the same replica whereas d correlates different replicas.

Using a standard replica trick, we obtain the explicit form of $g(r)$. One may notice that the free energy evaluated at $r = 1$ is reduced to the RS results obtained by the conventional method on the committee machine[4, 5], which is independent of q^* and d^*. This means that the internal structure of the weight space is overlooked by conventional calculation of the Gardner's volume. When we take the limit $r \to 1$, the free energy can be expanded as:

$$
g(r, q^*, q, c, d^*, d) = g(1, q, c, d) + (r - 1) \left. \frac{\partial g(r, q^*, q, c, d^*, d)}{\partial r} \right|_{r=1}.
\tag{9}
$$

As noticed, $g(r, q^*, q, c, d^*, d)$ is the same as the RS free energy in the Gardner's method. From the relation:

$$
\mathcal{N}_D = - \left. \frac{\partial g(r)}{\partial(1/r)} \right|_{r=1} = \left. \frac{\partial g(r)}{\partial r} \right|_{r=1},
\tag{10}
$$

we obtain the explicit form of $\mathcal{N}_D$.

In the case of the NRF committee machine, where each of the hidden units is connected to different input units, we do not have a phase transition. Instead, a single solution is applicable for the whole range of α. In contrast, the phase-space structure of the fully-connected committee machine is more complicated than that of the NRF committee machine. When a small number of input patterns are given, the system is in the permutation-symmetry (PS) phase[4, 5, 14], where the role of each hidden unit is not specialized. In the PS phase, the Gardner's volume is a single connected region. The order parameters associated with different hidden units are equal to the corresponding ones associated with the same hidden unit. When a critical number of patterns is given, the Gardner's volume is divided into many islands, each one of which can be transformed into other ones by permutation of hidden units. This phenomenon is called permutation symmetry breaking (PSB), and is usually accompanied by a first-order phase transition. In the PSB phase, the role of each hidden unit is specialized to store a larger number of patterns effectively. A similar breaking of symmetry has been observed in the study of generalization[14, 15], where the first-order phase transition induces discontinuity of the learning curve. It was pointed out that the critical storage capacity is attained in the PSB phase[4, 5], and our recent one-step replica symmetry breaking calculation confirmed this picture[13]. Therefore, we will focus on the analysis of the PSB solution near the storage capacity, in which q^*, $q \to 1$, and c, d^*, d are of order $1/K$.

4   STORAGE CAPACITY

When we analyze the results for free energy, the case with $q(r = 1)$, $c(r = 1)$ and $d(r = 1)$ is reduced to the usual saddle-point solutions of the replica symmetric expression of the Gardner's volume $g(r = 1)$[4, 5]. When K is large, the trace over all allowed internal representations can be evaluated similarly to Ref.[4]. The saddle-point equations for q^* and d^* are derived from the derivative of the free energy in the limit $r \to 1$, as in Eq. (9). The details of the self-consistent equations are not shown for space consideration. In the following, we only summarize the asymptotic behavior of the order parameters for large α:

$$1 - q + d - c \sim \frac{128}{(\pi - 2)^2} \frac{K^2}{\alpha^2}, \tag{11}$$

$$1 - q + (K - 1)(c - d) \sim \frac{32}{\pi - 2} \frac{K}{\alpha^2}, \tag{12}$$

$$q + (K - 1)d \sim \frac{\pi - 2}{\alpha}, \tag{13}$$

$$1 - q^* + d^* - c \sim \frac{\pi^2 \Gamma^2}{2\alpha^2}, \tag{14}$$

$$1 - q^* + (K - 1)(c - d^*) \sim \frac{\pi^2 \Gamma^2}{2\alpha^2}, \tag{15}$$

where $\Gamma = -[\sqrt{\pi} \int du\, H(u) \ln H(u)]^{-1} \simeq 0.62$.

It is found that all the overlaps between weights connecting different hidden units have scaling of $-1/K$, whereas the typical overlaps between weights connecting the same hidden unit approach one. The order parameters c, d and d^* are negative, showing antiferromagnetic correlations between different hidden units, which implies that each hidden unit attempts to store patterns different from those of the others[4, 5].

Finally, the asymptotic behavior of the entropy $\mathcal{N}_D$ in the large K limit can be derived using the scaling given above. Near the storage capacity, $\mathcal{N}_D$ can be written, up to the leading order, as:

$$\mathcal{N}_D \simeq K \ln K - \frac{(\pi - 2)^2 \alpha^2}{256 K}. \tag{16}$$

Being the entropy of a discrete system, $\mathcal{N}_D$ cannot be negative. Therefore, $\mathcal{N}_D = 0$ gives an indication of the upper bound of storage capacity, that is, $\alpha_c \sim \frac{16}{\pi - 2} K \sqrt{\ln K}$. The storage capacity per synapse, $\frac{16}{\pi - 2} \sqrt{\ln K}$, satisfies the rigorous bound $\sim \ln K$ derived by Mitchison and Durbin (MD)[3], whereas the conventional RS result[4, 5], which scales as $\sqrt{K}$, violates the MD bound.

5   DISCUSSIONS

Recently, we have studied this problem using a conventional Gardner approach in the one-step RSB scheme[13]. The result yields the same scaling with respect to K, but a coefficient smaller by a factor $\sqrt{2}$. In the present paper, we are dealing with the fine structure of version space related to internal representations. On the other hand, the RSB calculation seems to handle this fine structure in association with symmetry breaking between replicas. Although the physics of the two approaches seems to be somehow related, it is not clear which of the two can yield a better estimate of the storage capacity. It is possible that the present RS calculation does not properly handle the RSB picture of the system. Monasson and his co-workers reported that the Almeida-Thouless instability of the RS solutions decreases with increasing K, in the NRF case[10, 11]. A similar analysis for the fully-connected case certainly deserves further research. On the other hand, the one-step RSB scheme also introduces approximation, and possibly it cannot fully explain the weight-space structure associated with internal representations.

It is interesting to compare our result with that of the NRF committee machine along the same lines[10]. Based on the conventional RS calculation, Angel et al. suggested that the same storage capacity per synapse for both fully-connected and NRF committee machines will be similar, as the overlap between the hidden nodes approaches zero.[5]. While the asymptotic scaling with respect to K is the same, the storage capacity in the fully-connected committee machine is larger than in the NRF one. It is also consistent with our result from one-step RSB calculation[13]. This implies that the small, but nonzero negative correlation between the weights associated with different hidden units, enhances the storage capacity. This may be good news for those people using a fully connected multi-layer perceptron in applications.

From the fact that the storage capacity of the NRF parity machine is $\ln K / \ln 2$[2, 10], which saturates the MD bound, one may guess that the storage capacity of a fully-connected parity machine is also proportional to $K \ln K$. It will be interesting to check whether the storage capacity per synapse of the fully-connected parity machine is also enhanced compared to the NRF machine[16].

Acknowledgements

This work was partially supported by the Basic Science Special Program of POSTECH and the Korea Ministry of Education through the POSTECH Basic Science Research Institute(Grant No. BSRI-96-2438). It was also supported by non-directed fund from Korea Research Foundation, 1995, and by KOSEF grant 971-0202-010-2.

References

[1] E. Gardner, Europhys, Lett. 4(4), 481 (1987); E. Gardner, J. Phys. A21, 257 (1988); E. Gardner and B. Derrida, J. Phys. A21, 271 (1988).

[2] E. Barkai, D. Hansel and I. Kanter, Phys. Rev. Lett. V 65, N18, 2312 (1990).

[3] G. J. Mitchison and R. M. Durbin, Boil. Cybern. 60, 345 (1989).

[4] E. Barkai, D. Hansel and H. Sompolinsky, Phys. Rev. E45, 4146 (1992).

[5] A. Engel, H. M. Köhler, F. Tschepke, H. Vollmayr, and A. Zippeelius, Phys. Rev. E45, 7590 (1992).

[6] R. Monasson and D. O'Kane, Europhys. Lett. 27, 85(1994).

[7] B. Derrida, R. B. Griffiths and A Prugel-Bennett, J. Phys. A 24, 4907 (1991).

[8] M. Biehl and M. Opper, *Neural Networks: The Statistical Mechanics Perspective*, Jong-Hoon Oh, Chulan Kwon, and Sungzoon Cho (eds.) (World Scientific, Singapore, 1995).

[9] A. Engel and M. Weigt, Phys. Rev. E53, R2064 (1996).

[10] R. Monasson and R. Zecchina, Phys. Rev. Lett. 75, 2432 (1995); 76, 2205 (1996).

[11] R. Monasson and R. Zecchina, Mod. Phys. B, Vol.9, 1887-1897 (1996).

[12] S. Cocco, R. Monasson and R. Zecchina, Phys. Rev. E54, 717 (1996).

[13] C. Kwon and J. H. Oh, J. Phys. A, in press.

[14] K. Kang, J. H. Oh, C. Kwon and Y. Park, Phys. Rev. E48, 4805 (1993).

[15] H. Schwarze and J. Hertz, Europhys. Lett. 21, 785 (1993).

[16] Y. Xiong, C. Kwon and J.-H. Oh, to be published (1997).

The Efficiency and The Robustness of Natural Gradient Descent Learning Rule

Howard Hua Yang
Department of Computer Science
Oregon Graduate Institute
PO Box 91000, Portland, OR 97291, USA
hyang@cse.ogi.edu

Shun-ichi Amari
Lab. for Information Synthesis
RIKEN Brain Science Institute
Wako-shi, Saitama 351-01, JAPAN
amari@zoo.brain.riken.go.jp

Abstract

The inverse of the Fisher information matrix is used in the natural gradient descent algorithm to train single-layer and multi-layer perceptrons. We have discovered a new scheme to represent the Fisher information matrix of a stochastic multi-layer perceptron. Based on this scheme, we have designed an algorithm to compute the natural gradient. When the input dimension n is much larger than the number of hidden neurons, the complexity of this algorithm is of order $O(n)$. It is confirmed by simulations that the natural gradient descent learning rule is not only efficient but also robust.

1 INTRODUCTION

The inverse of the Fisher information matrix is required to find the Cramer-Rao lower bound to analyze the performance of an unbiased estimator. It is also needed in the natural gradient learning framework (Amari, 1997) to design statistically efficient algorithms for estimating parameters in general and for training neural networks in particular. In this paper, we assume a stochastic model for multi-layer perceptrons. Considering a Riemannian parameter space in which the Fisher information matrix is a metric tensor, we apply the natural gradient learning rule to train single-layer and multi-layer perceptrons. The main difficulty encountered is to compute the inverse of the Fisher information matrix of large dimensions when the input dimension is high. By exploring the structure of the Fisher information matrix and its inverse, we design a fast algorithm with lower complexity to implement the natural gradient learning algorithm.

2   A STOCHASTIC MULTI-LAYER PERCEPTRON

Assume the following model of a stochastic multi-layer perceptron:

$$z = \sum_{i=1}^{m} a_i \varphi(w_i^T x + b_i) + \xi \tag{1}$$

where $(\cdot)^T$ denotes the transpose, $\xi \sim N(0, \sigma^2)$ is a Gaussian random variable, and $\varphi(x)$ is a differentiable output function for hidden neurons. Assume the multi-layer network has a n-dimensional input, m hidden neurons, a one dimensional output, and $m \leq n$. Denote $a = (a_1, \cdots, a_m)^T$ the weight vector of the output neuron, $w_i = (w_{1i}, \cdots, w_{ni})^T$ the weight vector of the i-th hidden neuron, and $b = (b_1, \cdots, b_m)^T$ the vector of thresholds for the hidden neurons. Let $W = [w_1, \cdots, w_m]$ be a matrix formed by column weight vectors w_i, then (1) can be rewritten as $z = a^T \varphi(W^T x + b) + \xi$. Here, the scalar function φ operates on each component of the vector $W^T x + b$.

The joint probability density function (pdf) of the input and the output is

$$p(x, z; W, a, b) = p(z|x; W, a, b)p(x).$$

Define a loss function:

$$L(x, z; \theta) = -\log p(x, z; \theta) = l(z|x; \theta) - \log p(x)$$

where $\theta = (w_1^T, \cdots, w_m^T, a^T, b^T)^T$ includes all the parameters to be estimated and

$$l(z|x; \theta) = -\log p(z|x; \theta) = \frac{1}{2\sigma^2}(z - a^T \varphi(W^T x + b))^2.$$

Since $\frac{\partial L}{\partial \theta} = \frac{\partial l}{\partial \theta}$, the Fisher information matrix is defined by

$$G(\theta) = E[\frac{\partial L}{\partial \theta}(\frac{\partial L}{\partial \theta})^T] = E[\frac{\partial l}{\partial \theta}(\frac{\partial l}{\partial \theta})^T] \tag{2}$$

The inverse of $G(\theta)$ is often used in the Cramer-Rao inequality:

$$E[\|\widehat{\theta} - \theta^*\|^2 \mid \theta^*] \geq \mathrm{Tr}(G^{-1}(\theta^*))$$

where $\widehat{\theta}$ is an unbiased estimator of a true parameter θ^*.

For the on-line estimator $\widehat{\theta}_t$ based on the independent examples $\{(x_s, z_s), s = 1, \cdots, t\}$ drawn from the probability law $p(x, z; \theta^*)$, the Cramer-Rao inequality for the on-line estimator is

$$E[\|\widehat{\theta}_t - \theta^*\|^2 \mid \theta^*] \geq \frac{1}{t}\mathrm{Tr}(G^{-1}(\theta^*)) \tag{3}$$

3   NATURAL GRADIENT LEARNING

Consider a parameter space $\Theta = \{\theta\}$ in which the divergence between two points θ_1 and θ_2 is given by the Kullback-Leibler divergence

$$D(\theta_1, \theta_2) = \mathrm{KL}[p(x, z; \theta_1)\|p(x, z; \theta_2)].$$

When the two points are infinitesimally close, we have the quadratic form

$$D(\theta, \theta + d\theta) = \frac{1}{2}d\theta^T G(\theta)d\theta. \tag{4}$$

This is regarded as the square of the length of $d\theta$. Since $G(\theta)$ depends on θ, the parameter space is regarded as a Riemannian space in which the local distance is defined by (4). Here, the Fisher information matrix $G(\theta)$ plays the role of the Riemannian metric tensor.

It is shown by Amari(1997) that the steepest descent direction of a loss function $C(\theta)$ in the Riemannian space Θ is

$$-\tilde{\nabla}C(\theta) = -G^{-1}(\theta)\nabla C(\theta).$$

The natural gradient descent method is to decrease the loss function by updating the parameter vector along this direction. By multiplying $G^{-1}(\theta)$, the covariant gradient $\nabla C(\theta)$ is converted into its contravariant form $G^{-1}(\theta)\nabla C(\theta)$ which is consistent with the contravariant differential form $dC(\theta)$.

Instead of using $l(z|x;\theta)$ we use the following loss function:

$$l_1(z|x;\theta) = \frac{1}{2}(z - a^T\varphi(W^Tx + b))^2.$$

We have proved in [5] that $G(\theta) = \frac{1}{\sigma^2}A(\theta)$ where $A(\theta)$ does not depend on the unknown σ. So $G^{-1}(\theta)\frac{\partial l}{\partial \theta} = A^{-1}(\theta)\frac{\partial l_1}{\partial \theta}$. The on-line learning algorithms based on the gradient $\frac{\partial l_1}{\partial \theta}$ and the natural gradient $A^{-1}(\theta)\frac{\partial l_1}{\partial \theta}$ are, respectively,

$$\theta_{t+1} = \theta_t - \frac{\mu}{t}\frac{\partial l_1}{\partial \theta}(z_t|x_t;\theta_t), \tag{5}$$

$$\theta_{t+1} = \theta_t - \frac{\mu'}{t}A^{-1}(\theta_t)\frac{\partial l_1}{\partial \theta}(z_t|x_t;\theta_t) \tag{6}$$

where μ and μ' are learning rates.

When the negative log-likelihood function is chosen as the loss function, the natural gradient descent algorithm (6) gives a Fisher efficient on-line estimator (Amari, 1997), i.e., the asymptotic variance of θ_t driven by (6) satisfies

$$E[(\theta_t - \theta^*)(\theta_t - \theta^*)^T \mid \theta^*] \approx \frac{1}{t}G^{-1}(\theta^*) \tag{7}$$

which gives the mean square error

$$E[\|\theta_t - \theta^*\|^2 \mid \theta^*] \approx \frac{1}{t}\mathrm{Tr}(G^{-1}(\theta^*)). \tag{8}$$

The main difficulty in implementing the natural gradient descent algorithm (6) is to compute the natural gradient on-line. To overcome this difficulty, we studied the structure of the matrix $A(\theta)$ in [5] and proposed an efficient scheme to represent this matrix. Here, we briefly describe this scheme.

Let $A(\theta) = [A_{ij}]_{(m+2)\times(m+2)}$ be a partition of $A(\theta)$ corresponding to the partition of $\theta = (w_1^T,\cdots,w_m^T,a^T,b^T)^T$. Denote $u_i = w_i/\|w_i\|, i = 1,\cdots,m$, $U_1 = [u_1,\cdots,u_m]$ and $[v_1,\cdots,v_m] = U_1(U_1^TU_1)^{-1}$. It has been proved in [5] that those blocks in $A(\theta)$ are divided into three classes: $C_1 = \{A_{ij}, i,j = 1,\cdots,m\}$, $C_2 = \{A_{i,m+1}, A_{m+1,i}^T, A_{i,m+2}, A_{m+2,i}^T, i = 1,\cdots,m\}$ and $C_3 = \{A_{m+i,m+j}, i,j = 1,2\}$. Each block in C_1 is a linear combination of matrices $u_kv_l^T, k,l = 1,\cdots,m$, and $\Omega_0 = I - \sum_{k=1}^m u_kv_k^T$. Each block in C_2 is a matrix whose column is a linear combination of $\{v_k, k = 1,\cdots,m.\}$. The coefficients in these combinations are integrals with respect to the multivariate Gaussian distribution $N(0, R_1)$ where

$R_1 = U_1^T U_1$ is $m \times m$. Each block in C_3 is an $m \times m$ matrix whose entries are also integrals with respect to $N(\mathbf{0}, R_1)$. Detail expressions for these integrals are given in [5]. When $\varphi(x) = \text{erf}(\frac{x}{\sqrt{2}})$, using the techniques in (Saad and Solla, 1995), we can find the analytic expressions for most of these integrals.

The dimension of $A(\theta)$ is $(nm + 2m) \times (nm + 2m)$. When the input dimension n is much larger than the number of hidden neurons, by using the above scheme, the space for storing this large matrix is reduced from $O(n^2)$ to $O(n)$. We also gave a fast algorithm in [5] to compute $A^{-1}(\theta)$ and the natural gradient with the time complexity $O(n^2)$ and $O(n)$ respectively. The trick is to make use of the structure of the matrix $A^{-1}(\theta)$.

4   SIMULATION

In this section, we give some simulation results to demonstrate that the natural gradient descent algorithm is efficient and robust .

4.1   Single-layer perceptron

Assume 7-dimensional inputs $x_t \sim N(\mathbf{0}, I)$ and $\varphi(u) = \frac{1-e^{-u}}{1+e^{-u}}$. For the single-layer perceptron, $z = \varphi(w^T x)$, the on-line gradient descent (GD) and the natural GD algorithms are respectively

$$w_{t+1} = w_t + \mu_0(t)(z_t - \varphi(w_t^T x_t))\varphi'(w_t^T x_t)x_t \quad \text{and} \tag{9}$$

$$w_{t+1} = w_t + \mu_1(t)A^{-1}(w_t)(z_t - \varphi(w_t^T x_t))\varphi'(w_t^T x_t)x_t \tag{10}$$

where

$$A^{-1}(w) = \frac{1}{d_1(w)}I + \left(\frac{1}{d_2(w)} - \frac{1}{d_1(w)}\right)\frac{ww^T}{w^2}, \quad w = \|w\|, \tag{11}$$

$$d_1(w) = \frac{1}{\sqrt{2\pi}}\int_{-\infty}^{\infty}(\varphi'(wx))^2 e^{-\frac{x^2}{2}}\,dx > 0, \tag{12}$$

$$d_2(w) = \frac{1}{\sqrt{2\pi}}\int_{-\infty}^{\infty}(\varphi'(wx))^2 x^2 e^{-\frac{x^2}{2}}\,dx > 0, \tag{13}$$

and $\mu_0(t)$ and $\mu_1(t)$ are two learning rate schedules defined by $\mu_i(t) = \mu(\eta_i, c_i, \tau_i; t), i = 0, 1$. Here,

$$\mu(\eta, c, \tau; t) = \eta(1 + \frac{c}{\eta}\frac{t}{\tau})/(1 + \frac{c}{\eta}\frac{t}{\tau} + \frac{t^2}{\tau}). \tag{14}$$

is the search-then-converge schedule proposed by (Darken and Moody, 1992) . Note that $t < \tau$ is a "search phase" and $t > \tau$ is a "converge phase". When $\tau_i = 1$, the learning rate function $\mu_i(t)$ has no search phase but a weaker converge phase when η_i is small. When t is large, $\mu_i(t)$ decreases as $\frac{c_i}{t}$.

Randomly choose a 7-dimensional vector as w^* for the teacher network:

$$w^* = [-1.1043, 0.4302, 1.1978, 1.5317, -2.2946, -0.7866, 0.4428]^T.$$

Choose $\eta_0 = 1.25$, $\eta_1 = 0.05$, $c_0 = 8.75$, $c_1 = 1$, and $\tau_0 = \tau_1 = 1$. These parameters are selected by trial and error to optimize the performance of the GD and the natural GD methods at the noise level $\sigma = 0.2$. The training examples $\{(x_t, z_t)\}$ are generated by $z_t = \varphi(w^{*T} x_t) + \xi_t$ where $\xi_t \sim N(0, \sigma^2)$ and σ^2 is unknown to the algorithms.

Let w_t and $\widetilde{w}_t$ be the weight vectors driven by the equations (9) and (10) respectively. $\|w_t - w^*\|$ and $\|\widetilde{w}_t - w^*\|$ are error functions for the GD and the natural GD.

Denote $w^* = \|w^*\|$. From the equation (11), we obtain the Cramer-Rao Lower Bound (CRLB) for the deviation at the true weight vector w^*:

$$\mathrm{CRLB}(t) = \frac{\sigma}{\sqrt{t}}\sqrt{\frac{n-1}{d_1(w^*)} + \frac{1}{d_2(w^*)}}. \tag{15}$$

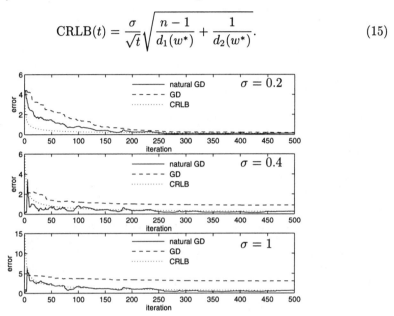

Figure 1: Performance of the GD and the natural GD at different noise levels $\sigma = 0.2, 0.4, 1$.

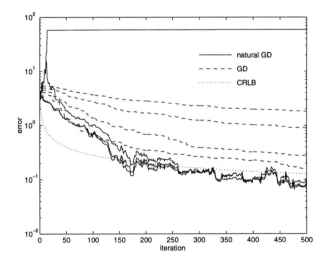

It is shown in Figure 1 that the natural GD algorithm reaches CRLB at different noise levels while the GD algorithm reaches the CRLB only at the noise level $\sigma = 0.2$. The robustness of the natural gradient descent against the additive noise in

Figure 2:   Performance of the GD and the natural GD when η_0 = 1.25, 1.75, 2.25, 2.75, η_1 = 0.05, 0.2, 0.4425, 0.443, and c_0 = 8.75 and c_1 = 1 are fixed.

the training examples is clearly shown by Figure 1. When the teacher signal is non-stationary, our simulations show that the natural GD algorithm also reaches the CRLB.

Figure 2 shows that the natural GD algorithm is more robust than the GD algorithm against the change of the learning rate schedule. The performance of the GD algorithm deteriorates when the constant η_0 in the learning rate schedule $\mu_0(t)$ is different from that optimal one. On the contrary, the natural GD algorithm performs almost the same for all η_1 within a interval $[0.05, 0.4425]$. Figure 2 also shows that the natural GD algorithm breaks down when η_1 is larger than the critical number 0.443. This means that the weak converge phase in the learning rate schedule is necessary.

4.2   Multi-layer perceptron

Let us consider the simple multi-layer perceptron with 2-dimensional input and 2-hidden neurons. The problem is to train the committee machine $y = \varphi(w_1^T x) + \varphi(w_2^T x)$ based on the examples $\{(x_t, z_t), t = 1, \cdots, T\}$ generated by the stochastic committee machine $z_t = \varphi(w_1^{*T} x_t) + \varphi(w_2^{*T} x_t) + \xi_t$. Assume $\|w_i^*\| = 1$. We can reparameterize the weight vector to decrease the dimension of the parameter space from 4 to 2:

$$w_i = \begin{bmatrix} \cos(\alpha_i) \\ \sin(\alpha_i) \end{bmatrix}, \quad w_i^* = \begin{bmatrix} \cos(\alpha_i^*) \\ \sin(\alpha_i^*) \end{bmatrix}, \quad i = 1, 2.$$

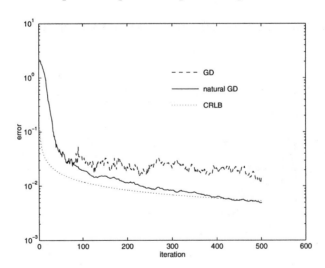

Figure 3: The GD vs. the natural GD

The parameter space is $\{\boldsymbol{\theta} = (\alpha_1, \alpha_2)\}$. Assume that the true parameters are $\alpha_1^* = 0$ and $\alpha_2^* = \frac{3\pi}{4}$. Due to the symmetry, both $\boldsymbol{\theta}_1^* = (0, \frac{3\pi}{4})$ and $\boldsymbol{\theta}_2^* = (\frac{3\pi}{4}, 0)$ are true parameters. Let $\boldsymbol{\theta}_t$ and $\boldsymbol{\theta}_t'$ be computed by the GD algorithm and the natural GD algorithm respectively. The errors are measured by

$$\varepsilon_t = \min\{\|\boldsymbol{\theta}_t - \boldsymbol{\theta}_1^*\|, \|\boldsymbol{\theta}_t - \boldsymbol{\theta}_2^*\|\}, \quad \text{and} \quad \varepsilon_t' = \min\{\|\boldsymbol{\theta}_t' - \boldsymbol{\theta}_1^*\|, \|\boldsymbol{\theta}_t' - \boldsymbol{\theta}_2^*\|\}.$$

In this simulation, using $\boldsymbol{\theta}_0 = (0.1, 0.2)$ as an initial estimate, we first start the GD algorithm and run it for 80 iterations. Then, we use the estimate obtained from the GD algorithm at the 80-th iteration as an initial estimate for the natural GD algorithm and run the latter algorithm for 420 iterations. The noise level is $\sigma = 0.05$. N independent runs are conducted to obtain the errors $\varepsilon_t(j)$ and $\varepsilon_t'(j)$, $j = 1, \cdots, N$. Define root mean square errors

$$\bar{\varepsilon}_t = \sqrt{\frac{1}{N} \sum_{j=1}^{N} (\varepsilon_t(j))^2}, \quad \text{and} \quad \bar{\varepsilon}'_t = \sqrt{\frac{1}{N} \sum_{j=1}^{N} (\varepsilon_t'(j))^2}.$$

Based on $N = 10$ independent runs, the errors $\bar{\varepsilon}_t$ and $\bar{\varepsilon}'_t$ are computed and compared with the CRLB in Figure 3. The search-then-converge learning schedule (14) is used in the GD algorithm while the learning rate for the natural GD algorithm is simply the annealing rate $\frac{1}{k}$.

5 CONCLUSIONS

The natural gradient descent learning rule is statistically efficient. It can be used to train any adaptive system. But the complexity of this learning rule depends on the architecture of the learning machine. The main difficulty in implementing this learning rule is to compute the inverse of the Fisher information matrix of large dimensions. For a multi-layer perceptron, we have shown an efficient scheme to represent the Fisher information matrix based on which the space for storing this large matrix is reduced from $O(n^2)$ to $O(n)$. We have also shown an algorithm to compute the natural gradient. Taking advantage of the structure of the inverse of the Fisher information matrix, we found that the complexity of computing the natural gradient is $O(n)$ when the input dimension n is much larger than the number of hidden neurons.

The simulation results have confirmed the fast convergence and statistical efficiency of the natural gradient descent learning rule. They have also verified that this learning rule is robust against the changes of the noise levels in the training examples and the parameters in the learning rate schedules.

References

[1] S. Amari. Natural gradient works efficiently in learning. *Accepted by Neural Computation*, 1997.

[2] S. Amari. Neural learning in structured parameter spaces – natural Riemannian gradient. In *Advances in Neural Information Processing Systems, 9, ed. M. C. Mozer, M. I. Jordan and T. Petsche, The MIT Press: Cambridge, MA.*, pages 127–133, 1997.

[3] C. Darken and J. Moody. Towards faster stochastic gradient search. In *Advances in Neural Information Processing Systems, 4, eds. Moody, Hanson, and Lippmann, Morgan Kaufmann, San Mateo*, pages 1009–1016, 1992.

[4] D. Saad and S. A. Solla. On-line learning in soft committee machines. *Physical Review E*, 52:4225–4243, 1995.

[5] H. H. Yang and S. Amari. Natural gradient descent for training multi-layer perceptrons. *Submitted to IEEE Tr. on Neural Networks*, 1997.

PART IV
ALGORITHMS AND ARCHITECTURE

Ensemble Learning
for Multi-Layer Networks

David Barber[*]   Christopher M. Bishop[†]

Neural Computing Research Group
Department of Applied Mathematics and Computer Science
Aston University, Birmingham B4 7ET, U.K.
http://www.ncrg.aston.ac.uk/

Abstract

Bayesian treatments of learning in neural networks are typically
based either on local Gaussian approximations to a mode of the
posterior weight distribution, or on Markov chain Monte Carlo
simulations. A third approach, called *ensemble learning*, was introduced by Hinton and van Camp (1993). It aims to approximate
the posterior distribution by minimizing the Kullback-Leibler divergence between the true posterior and a parametric approximating distribution. However, the derivation of a deterministic algorithm relied on the use of a Gaussian approximating distribution
with a *diagonal* covariance matrix and so was unable to capture
the posterior correlations between parameters. In this paper, we
show how the ensemble learning approach can be extended to full-
covariance Gaussian distributions while remaining computationally
tractable. We also extend the framework to deal with hyperparameters, leading to a simple re-estimation procedure. Initial results
from a standard benchmark problem are encouraging.

1 Introduction

Bayesian techniques have been successfully applied to neural networks in the context of both regression and classification problems (MacKay 1992; Neal 1996). In
contrast to the maximum likelihood approach which finds only a single estimate
for the regression parameters, the Bayesian approach yields a distribution of weight
parameters, $p(\mathbf{w}|D)$, conditional on the training data D, and predictions are ex-

---

[*]Present address: SNN, University of Nijmegen, Geert Grooteplein 21, Nijmegen, The
Netherlands. http://www.mbfys.kun.nl/snn/ email: davidb@mbfys.kun.nl

[†]Present address: Microsoft Research Limited, St George House, Cambridge CB2 3NH,
UK. http://www.research.microsoft.com email: cmbishop@microsoft.com

pressed in terms of expectations with respect to the posterior distribution (Bishop 1995). However, the corresponding integrals over weight space are analytically intractable. One well-established procedure for approximating these integrals, known as Laplace's method, is to approximate the posterior distribution by a Gaussian, centred at a mode of $p(\mathbf{w}|D)$, in which the covariance of the Gaussian is determined by the local curvature of the posterior distribution (MacKay 1995). The required integrations can then be performed analytically. More recent approaches involve Markov chain Monte Carlo simulations to generate samples from the posterior (Neal 1996). However, such techniques can be computationally expensive, and they also suffer from the lack of a suitable convergence criterion.

A third approach, called ensemble learning, was introduced by Hinton and van Camp (1993) and again involves finding a simple, analytically tractable, approximation to the true posterior distribution. Unlike Laplace's method, however, the approximating distribution is fitted globally, rather than locally, by minimizing a Kullback-Leibler divergence. Hinton and van Camp (1993) showed that, in the case of a Gaussian approximating distribution with a *diagonal* covariance, a deterministic learning algorithm could be derived. Although the approximating distribution is no longer constrained to coincide with a mode of the posterior, the assumption of a diagonal covariance prevents the model from capturing the (often very strong) posterior correlations between the parameters. MacKay (1995) suggested a modification to the algorithm by including linear preprocessing of the inputs to achieve a somewhat richer class of approximating distributions, although this was not implemented. In this paper we show that the ensemble learning approach can be extended to allow a Gaussian approximating distribution with an *general* covariance matrix, while still leading to a tractable algorithm.

1.1   The Network Model

We consider a two-layer feed-forward network having a single output whose value is given by

$$f(\mathbf{x}, \mathbf{w}) = \sum_{i=1}^{H} v_i \sigma(\mathbf{u}_i \cdot \mathbf{x}) \tag{1}$$

where $\mathbf{w}$ is a k-dimensional vector representing all of the adaptive parameters in the model, $\mathbf{x}$ is the input vector, $\{\mathbf{u}_i\}, i = 1, \ldots, H$ are the input-to-hidden weights, and $\{v_i\}, i = 1, \ldots, H$ are the hidden-to-output weights. The extension to multiple outputs is straightforward. For reasons of analytic tractability, we choose the sigmoidal hidden-unit activation function $\sigma(a)$ to be given by the error function

$$\sigma(a) = \sqrt{\frac{2}{\pi}} \int_0^a \exp\left(-s^2/2\right) ds \tag{2}$$

which (when appropriately scaled) is quantitatively very similar to the standard logistic sigmoid. Hidden unit biases are accounted for by appending the input vector with a node that is always unity. In the current implementation there are no output biases (and the output data is shifted to give zero mean), although the formalism is easily extended to include adaptive output biases (Barber and Bishop 1997). The data set consists of N pairs of input vectors and corresponding target output values $D = \{\mathbf{x}^\mu, t^\mu\}, \mu = 1, \ldots, N$. We make the standard assumption of Gaussian noise on the target values, with variance β^{-1}. The likelihood of the training data is then proportional to $\exp(-\beta E_D)$, where the training error E_D is

$$E_D(\mathbf{w}) = \frac{1}{2} \sum_\mu \left(f(\mathbf{x}^\mu, \mathbf{w}) - t^\mu\right)^2 . \tag{3}$$

The prior distribution over weights is chosen to be a Gaussian of the form

$$p(\mathbf{w}) \propto \exp\left(-E_w(\mathbf{w})\right) \tag{4}$$

where $E_w(\mathbf{w}) = \frac{1}{2}\mathbf{w}^T \mathbf{A} \mathbf{w}$, and $\mathbf{A}$ is a matrix of hyperparameters. The treatment of β and $\mathbf{A}$ is dealt with in Section 2.1. From Bayes' theorem, the posterior distribution over weights can then be written

$$p(\mathbf{w}|D) = \frac{1}{Z} \exp\left(-\beta E_D(\mathbf{w}) - E_w(\mathbf{w})\right) \tag{5}$$

where Z is a normalizing constant. Network predictions on a novel example are given by the posterior average of the network output

$$\langle f(\mathbf{x}) \rangle = \int f(\mathbf{x}, \mathbf{w}) p(\mathbf{w}|D) \, d\mathbf{w}. \tag{6}$$

This represents an integration over a high-dimensional space, weighted by a posterior distribution $p(\mathbf{w}|D)$ which is exponentially small except in narrow regions whose locations are unknown a-priori. The accurate evaluation of such integrals is thus very difficult.

2 Ensemble Learning

Integrals of the form (6) may be tackled by approximating $p(\mathbf{w}|D)$ by a simpler distribution $Q(\mathbf{w})$. In this paper we choose this approximating distribution to be a Gaussian with mean $\overline{\mathbf{w}}$ and covariance $\mathbf{C}$. We determine the values of $\overline{\mathbf{w}}$ and $\mathbf{C}$ by minimizing the Kullback-Leibler divergence between the network posterior and approximating Gaussian, given by

$$\mathcal{F}[Q] = \int Q(\mathbf{w}) \ln\left\{ \frac{Q(\mathbf{w})}{p(\mathbf{w}|D)} \right\} d\mathbf{w} \tag{7}$$

$$= \int Q(\mathbf{w}) \ln Q(\mathbf{w}) d\mathbf{w} - \int Q(\mathbf{w}) \ln p(\mathbf{w}|D) \, d\mathbf{w}. \tag{8}$$

The first term in (8) is the negative entropy of a Gaussian distribution, and is easily evaluated to give $\frac{1}{2} \ln \det(\mathbf{C}) + \text{const.}$

From (5) we see that the posterior dependent term in (8) contains two parts that depend on the prior and likelihood

$$\int Q(\mathbf{w}) E_w(\mathbf{w}) d\mathbf{w} + \int Q(\mathbf{w}) E_D(\mathbf{w}) d\mathbf{w}. \tag{9}$$

Note that the normalization coefficient Z^{-1} in (5) gives rise to a constant additive term in the KL divergence and so can be neglected. The prior term $E_w(\mathbf{w})$ is quadratic in $\mathbf{w}$, and integrates to give $\text{Tr}(\mathbf{CA}) + \frac{1}{2}\overline{\mathbf{w}}^T \mathbf{A} \overline{\mathbf{w}}$. This leaves the data dependent term in (9) which we write as

$$L = \int Q(\mathbf{w}) E_D(\mathbf{w}) d\mathbf{w} = \frac{\beta}{2} \sum_{\mu=1}^{N} l(\mathbf{x}^\mu, t^\mu) \tag{10}$$

where

$$l(\mathbf{x}, t) = \int Q(\mathbf{w}) \left(f(\mathbf{x}, \mathbf{w})\right)^2 d\mathbf{w} - 2t \int Q(\mathbf{w}) f(\mathbf{x}, \mathbf{w}) \, d\mathbf{w} + t^2. \tag{11}$$

For clarity, we concentrate only on the first term in (11), as the calculation of the term linear in $f(\mathbf{x}, \mathbf{w})$ is similar, though simpler. Writing the Gaussian integral over Q as an average, $\langle\ \rangle$, the first term of (11) becomes

$$\left\langle (f(\mathbf{x}, \mathbf{w}))^2 \right\rangle = \sum_{i,j=1}^{H} \left\langle v_i v_j \sigma(\mathbf{u}_i^\mathrm{T}\mathbf{x})\sigma(\mathbf{u}_j^\mathrm{T}\mathbf{x}) \right\rangle. \tag{12}$$

To simplify the notation, we denote the set of input-to-hidden weights $(\mathbf{u}_1, \ldots, \mathbf{u}_H)$ by $\mathbf{u}$ and the set of hidden-to-output weights, $(v_1, \ldots, v_H)$ by $\mathbf{v}$. Similarly, we partition the covariance matrix $\mathbf{C}$ into blocks, $\mathbf{C}_{uu}$, $\mathbf{C}_{vu}$, $\mathbf{C}_{vv}$, and $\mathbf{C}_{vu} = \mathbf{C}_{uv}^\mathrm{T}$. As the components of $\mathbf{v}$ do not enter the non-linear sigmoid functions, we can directly integrate over $\mathbf{v}$, so that each term in the summation (12) gives

$$\left\langle \left(\theta_{ij} + (\mathbf{u} - \overline{\mathbf{u}})^\mathrm{T} \boldsymbol{\Psi}_{ij} (\mathbf{u} - \overline{\mathbf{u}}) + \boldsymbol{\Omega}_{ij}^\mathrm{T} (\mathbf{u} - \overline{\mathbf{u}}) \right) \sigma \left(\mathbf{u}^\mathrm{T} \mathbf{x}^i \right) \sigma \left(\mathbf{u}^\mathrm{T} \mathbf{x}^j \right) \right\rangle \tag{13}$$

where

$$\theta_{ij} = \left(\mathbf{C}_{vv} - \mathbf{C}_{vu}\mathbf{C}_{uu}^{-1}\mathbf{C}_{uv} \right)_{ij} + \overline{v}_i\overline{v}_j \tag{14}$$

$$\boldsymbol{\Psi}_{ij} = \mathbf{C}_{uu}^{-1}\mathbf{C}_{u,v=i}\mathbf{C}_{v=j,u}\mathbf{C}_{uu}^{-1}, \tag{15}$$

$$\boldsymbol{\Omega}_{ij} = 2\mathbf{C}_{uu}^{-1}\mathbf{C}_{u,v=j}\overline{v}_i. \tag{16}$$

Although the remaining integration in (13) over $\mathbf{u}$ is not analytically tractable, we can make use of the following result to reduce it to a one-dimensional integration

$$\langle \sigma (\mathbf{z}\cdot\mathbf{a} + a_0)\, \sigma(\mathbf{z}\cdot\mathbf{b} + b_0) \rangle_\mathbf{z} = \left\langle \sigma(z|\mathbf{a}| + a_0)\, \sigma \left(\frac{z\mathbf{a}^\mathrm{T}\mathbf{b} + b_0|\mathbf{a}|}{\sqrt{|\mathbf{a}|^2 (1 + |\mathbf{b}|^2) - (\mathbf{a}^\mathrm{T}\mathbf{b})^2}} \right) \right\rangle_z \tag{17}$$

where $\mathbf{a}$ and $\mathbf{b}$ are vectors and a_0, b_0 are scalar offsets. The average on the left of (17) is over an isotropic multi-dimensional Gaussian, $p(\mathbf{z}) \propto \exp(-\mathbf{z}^\mathrm{T}\mathbf{z}/2)$, while the average on the right is over the one-dimensional Gaussian $p(z) \propto \exp(-z^2/2)$. This result follows from the fact that the vector $\mathbf{z}$ only occurs through the scalar product with $\mathbf{a}$ and $\mathbf{b}$, and so we can choose a coordinate system in which the first two components of $\mathbf{z}$ lie in the plane spanned by $\mathbf{a}$ and $\mathbf{b}$. All orthogonal components do not appear elsewhere in the integrand, and therefore integrate to unity.

The integral we desire, (13) is only a little more complicated than (17) and can be evaluated by first transforming the coordinate system to an isotopic basis $\mathbf{z}$, and then differentiating with respect to elements of the covariance matrix to 'pull down' the required linear and quadratic terms in the σ-independent pre-factor of (13). These derivatives can then be reduced to a form which requires only the numerical evaluation of (17). We have therefore succeeded in reducing the calculation of the KL divergence to analytic terms together with a single one-dimensional numerical integration of the form (17), which we compute using Gaussian quadrature[1].

Similar techniques can be used to evaluate the derivatives of the KL divergence with respect to the mean and covariance matrix (Barber and Bishop 1997). Together with the KL divergence, these derivatives are then used in a scaled conjugate gradient optimizer to find the parameters $\overline{\mathbf{w}}$ and $\mathbf{C}$ that represent the best Gaussian fit.

The number of parameters in the covariance matrix scales quadratically with the number of weight parameters. We therefore have also implemented a version with

---

[1]Although (17) appears to depend on 4 parameters, it can be expressed in terms of 3 independent parameters. An alternative to performing quadrature during training would therefore be to compute a 3-dimensional look-up table in advance.

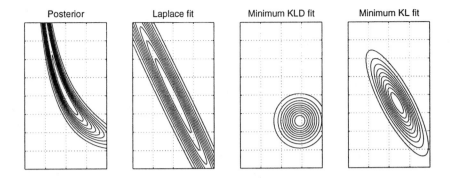

| Posterior | Laplace fit | Minimum KLD fit | Minimum KL fit |

Figure 1: Laplace and minimum Kullback-Leibler Gaussian fits to the posterior. The Laplace method underestimates the local posterior mass by basing the covariance matrix on the mode alone, and has KL value 41. The minimum Kullback-Leibler Gaussian fit with a diagonal covariance matrix (KLD) gives a KL value of 4.6, while the minimum Kullback-Leibler Gaussian with full covariance matrix achieves a value of 3.9.

a constrained covariance matrix

$$\mathbf{C} = \operatorname{diag}(d_1^2, \ldots, d_n^2) + \sum_{i=1}^{s} \mathbf{s}_i \mathbf{s}_i^{\mathrm{T}} \tag{18}$$

which is the form of covariance used in factor analysis (Bishop 1997). This reduces the number of free parameters in the covariance matrix from $k(k+1)/2$ to $k(s+1)$ (representing $k(s+1) - s(s-1)/2$ independent degrees of freedom) which is now linear in k. Thus, the number of parameters can be controlled by changing s and, unlike a diagonal covariance matrix, this model can still capture the strongest of the posterior correlations. The value of s should be as large as possible, subject only to computational cost limitations. There is no 'over-fitting' as s is increased since more flexible distributions $Q(\mathbf{w})$ simply better approximate the true posterior.

We illustrate the optimization of the KL divergence using a toy problem involving the posterior distribution for a two-parameter regression problem. Figure 1 shows the true posterior together with approximations obtained from Laplace's method, ensemble learning with a diagonal covariance Gaussian, and ensemble learning using an unconstrained Gaussian.

2.1 Hyperparameter Adaptation

So far, we have treated the hyperparameters as fixed. We now extend the ensemble learning formalism to include hyperparameters within the Bayesian framework. For simplicity, we consider a standard isotropic prior covariance matrix of the form $\mathbf{A} = \alpha \mathbf{I}$, and introduce hyperpriors given by Gamma distributions

$$\ln p(\alpha) = \ln \left\{ \alpha^{a-1} \exp\left(-\frac{\alpha}{b}\right) \right\} + \operatorname{const} \tag{19}$$

$$\ln p(\beta) = \ln \left\{ \beta^{c-1} \exp\left(-\frac{\beta}{d}\right) \right\} + \operatorname{const} \tag{20}$$

where a, b, c, d are constants. The joint posterior distribution of the weights and hyperparameters is given by

$$p(\mathbf{w}, \alpha, \beta | D) \propto p(D | \mathbf{w}, \beta) p(\mathbf{w} | \alpha) p(\alpha) p(\beta) \tag{21}$$

in which

$$\ln p(D | \mathbf{w}, \beta) = -\beta E_D + \frac{N}{2} \ln \beta + \text{const} \tag{22}$$

$$\ln p(\mathbf{w} | \alpha) = -\alpha |\mathbf{w}|^2 + \frac{k}{2} \ln \alpha + \text{const} \tag{23}$$

We follow MacKay (1995) by modelling the joint posterior $p(\mathbf{w}, \alpha, \beta | D)$ by a factorized approximating distribution of the form

$$Q(\mathbf{w}) R(\alpha) S(\beta) \tag{24}$$

where $Q(\mathbf{w})$ is a Gaussian distribution as before, and the functional forms of R and S are left unspecified. We then minimize the KL divergence

$$\mathcal{F}[Q, R, S] = \int Q(\mathbf{w}) R(\alpha) S(\beta) \ln \left\{ \frac{Q(\mathbf{w}) R(\alpha) S(\beta)}{p(\mathbf{w}, \alpha, \beta | D)} \right\} d\mathbf{w} \, d\alpha \, d\beta. \tag{25}$$

Consider first the dependence of (25) on $Q(\mathbf{w})$

$$\mathcal{F}[Q] = -\int Q(\mathbf{w}) R(\alpha) S(\beta) \left\{ -\beta E_D(\mathbf{w}) - \frac{\alpha}{2} |\mathbf{w}|^2 - \ln Q(\mathbf{w}) \right\} + \text{const} \tag{26}$$

$$= -\int Q(\mathbf{w}) \left\{ -\bar{\beta} E_D(\mathbf{w}) - \frac{\bar{\alpha}}{2} |\mathbf{w}|^2 - \ln Q(\mathbf{w}) \right\} + \text{const} \tag{27}$$

where $\bar{\alpha} = \int R(\alpha) \alpha \, d\alpha$ and $\bar{\beta} = \int S(\beta) \beta \, d\beta$. We see that (27) has the form of (8), except that the fixed hyperparameters are now replaced with their average values. To calculate these averages, consider the dependence of the functional $\mathcal{F}$ on $R(\alpha)$

$$\mathcal{F}[R] = -\int Q(\mathbf{w}) R(\alpha) S(\beta) \left\{ -\frac{\alpha}{2} |\mathbf{w}|^2 + \frac{k}{2} \ln \alpha + (a-1) \ln \alpha - \frac{\alpha}{b} \right\} d\mathbf{w} \, d\alpha \, d\beta$$

$$= -\int R(\alpha) \left\{ \frac{\alpha}{s} + (r-1) \ln \alpha - \ln R(\alpha) \right\} d\alpha + \text{const} \tag{28}$$

where $r = \frac{k}{2} + a$ and $1/s = \frac{1}{2} |\bar{\mathbf{w}}|^2 + \frac{1}{2} \text{Tr} \mathbf{C} + 1/b$. We recognise (28) as the Kullback-Leibler divergence between $R(\alpha)$ and a Gamma distribution. Thus the optimum $R(\alpha)$ is also Gamma distributed

$$R(\alpha) \propto \alpha^{r-1} \exp\left(-\frac{\alpha}{s}\right). \tag{29}$$

We therefore obtain $\bar{\alpha} = rs$.

A similar procedure for $S(\beta)$ gives $\bar{\beta} = uv$, where $u = \frac{N}{2} + c$ and $1/v = \langle E_D \rangle + 1/d$, in which $\langle E_D \rangle$ has already been calculated during the optimization of $Q(\mathbf{w})$.

This defines an iterative procedure in which we start by initializing the hyperparameters (using the mean of the hyperprior distributions) and then alternately optimize the KL divergence over $Q(\mathbf{w})$ and re-estimate $\bar{\alpha}$ and $\bar{\beta}$.

3 Results and Discussion

As a preliminary test of our method on a standard benchmark problem, we applied the minimum KL procedure to the Boston Housing dataset. This is a one

Method	Test Error
Ensemble ($s = 1$)	0.22
Ensemble (diagonal)	0.28
Laplace	0.33

Table 1: Comparison of ensemble learning with Laplace's method. The test error is defined to be the mean squared error over the test set of 378 examples.

dimensional regression problem, with 13 inputs, in which the data for 128 training examples was obtained from the DELVE archive[2]. We trained a network of four hidden units, with covariance matrix given by (18) with $s = 1$, and specified broad hyperpriors on α and β ($a = 0.25$, $b = 400$, $c = 0.05$, and $d = 2000$). Predictions are made by evaluating the integral in (6). This integration can be done analytically as a consequence of the form of the sigmoid function given in (2).

We compared the performance of the KL method against the Laplace framework of MacKay (1995) which also treats hyperparameters through a re-estimation procedure. In addition we also evaluated the performance of the ensemble method using a diagonal covariance matrix. Our results are summarized in Table 1.

Acknowledgements

We would like to thank Chris Williams for helpful discussions. Supported by EPSRC grant GR/J75425: *Novel Developments in Learning Theory for Neural Networks*.

References

Barber, D. and C. M. Bishop (1997). On computing the KL divergence for Bayesian neural networks. Technical report, Neural Computing Research Group, Aston University, Birmingham, U.K.

Bishop, C. M. (1995). *Neural Networks for Pattern Recognition*. Oxford University Press.

Bishop, C. M. (1997). Latent variables, mixture distributions and topographic mappings. Technical report, Aston University. To appear in *Proceedings of the NATO Advanced Study Institute on Learning in Graphical Models*, Erice.

Hinton, G. E. and D. van Camp (1993). Keeping neural networks simple by minimizing the description length of the weights. In *Proceedings of the Sixth Annual Conference on Computational Learning Theory*, pp. 5–13.

MacKay, D. J. C. (1992). A practical Bayesian framework for back-propagation networks. *Neural Computation 4*(3), 448–472.

MacKay, D. J. C. (1995). Developments in probabilistic modelling with neural networks—ensemble learning. In *Neural Networks: Artificial Intelligence and Industrial Applications. Proceedings of the 3rd Annual Symposium on Neural Networks, Nijmegen, Netherlands, 14-15 September 1995*, Berlin, pp. 191–198. Springer.

MacKay, D. J. C. (1995). Probable networks and plausible predictions – a review of practical Bayesian methods for supervised neural networks. *Network: Computation in Neural Systems 6*(3), 469–505.

Neal, R. M. (1996). *Bayesian Learning for Neural Networks*. Springer. Lecture Notes in Statistics 118.

---

[2]See http://www.cs.utoronto.ca/~delve/

Radial Basis Functions: a Bayesian treatment

David Barber[*]   Bernhard Schottky

Neural Computing Research Group
Department of Applied Mathematics and Computer Science
Aston University, Birmingham B4 7ET, U.K.
http://www.ncrg.aston.ac.uk/
{D.Barber,B.Schottky}@aston.ac.uk

Abstract

Bayesian methods have been successfully applied to regression and
classification problems in multi-layer perceptrons. We present a
novel application of Bayesian techniques to Radial Basis Function
networks by developing a Gaussian approximation to the posterior
distribution which, for fixed basis function widths, is analytic in
the parameters. The setting of regularization constants by cross-
validation is wasteful as only a single optimal parameter estimate
is retained. We treat this issue by assigning prior distributions to
these constants, which are then adapted in light of the data under
a simple re-estimation formula.

1   Introduction

Radial Basis Function networks are popular regression and classification tools[10].
For fixed basis function centers, RBFs are linear in their parameters and can therefore be trained with simple one shot linear algebra techniques[10]. The use of
unsupervised techniques to fix the basis function centers is, however, not generally
optimal since setting the basis function centers using density estimation on the input
data alone takes no account of the target values associated with that data. Ideally,
therefore, we should include the target values in the training procedure[7, 3, 9]. Unfortunately, allowing centers to adapt to the training targets leads to the RBF being
a nonlinear function of its parameters, and training becomes more problematic.

Most methods that perform supervised training of RBF parameters minimize the

---

[*]Present address: SNN, University of Nijmegen, Geert Grooteplein 21, Nijmegen, The
Netherlands. http://www.mbfys.kun.nl/snn/ email: davidb@mbfys.kun.nl

training error, or penalized training error in the case of regularized networks[7, 3, 9]. The setting of the associated regularization constants is often achieved by computationally expensive approaches such as cross-validation which search through a set of regularization constants chosen a priori. Furthermore, much of the information contained in such computation is discarded in favour of keeping only a single regularization constant. A single set of RBF parameters is subsequently found by minimizing the penalized training error with the determined regularization constant. In this work, we assign prior distributions over these regularization constants, both for the hidden to output weights and the basis function centers. Together with a noise model, this defines an ideal Bayesian procedure in which the beliefs expressed in the distribution of regularization constants are combined with the information in the data to yield a posterior *distribution* of network parameters[6]. The beauty of this approach is that none of the information is discarded, in contrast to cross-validation type procedures. Bayesian techniques applied to such non-linear, non-parametric models, however, can also be computationally extremely expensive, as predictions require averaging over the high-dimensional posterior parameter distribution. One approach is to use Markov chain Monte Carlo techniques to draw samples from the posterior[8]. A simpler approach is the Laplace approximation which fits a Gaussian distribution with mean set to a mode of the posterior, and covariance set to the inverse Hessian evaluated at that mode. This can be viewed as a local posterior approximation, as the form of the posterior away from the mode does not affect the Gaussian fit. A third approach, called ensemble learning, also fits a Gaussian, but is based on a less local fit criterion, the Kullback-Leibler divergence[4, 5]. As shown in [1], this method can be applied successfully to multi-layer perceptrons, whereby the KL divergence is an *almost* analytic quantity in the adaptable parameters. For fixed basis function widths, the KL divergence for RBF networks is *completely* analytic in the adaptable parameters, leading to a relatively fast optimization procedure.

2 Bayesian Radial Basis Function Networks

For an N dimensional input vector $\mathbf{x}$, we consider RBFs that compute the linear combination of K Gaussian basis functions,

$$f(\mathbf{x}, \mathbf{m}) = \sum_{l=1}^{K} w_l \exp\left\{-\lambda_l \|\mathbf{x} - \mathbf{c}_l\|^2\right\} \tag{1}$$

where we denote collectively the centers $\mathbf{c}_1 \dots \mathbf{c}_K$, and weights $\mathbf{w} = w_1 \dots w_k$ by the parameter vector $\mathbf{m} = [\mathbf{c}_1', \dots, \mathbf{c}_K', w_1, \dots, w_K]'$. We consider the basis function widths $\lambda_1, \dots \lambda_k$ to be fixed although, in principle, they can also be adapted by a similar technique to the one presented below. The data set that we wish to regress is a set of P input-output pairs $D = \{\mathbf{x}^\mu, y^\mu, \mu = 1 \dots P\}$. Assuming that the target outputs y have been corrupted with additive Gaussian noise of variance β^{-1}, the likelihood of the data is[1]

$$p(D|\mathbf{m}, \beta) = \exp\left(-\beta E_D\right)/Z_D, \tag{2}$$

where the training error is defined,

$$E_D = \frac{1}{2} \sum_{\mu=1}^{P} (f(\mathbf{x}^\mu, \mathbf{m}) - y^\mu)^2 \tag{3}$$

To discourage overfitting, we choose a prior regularizing distribution for $\mathbf{m}$

$$p(\mathbf{m}|\alpha) = \exp\left(-E_m(\mathbf{m})\right)/Z_P \tag{4}$$

---

[1]In the following, Z_D, Z_P and Z_F are normalising constants

where we take $E_m(\mathbf{m}) = \frac{1}{2}\mathbf{m}^{\mathrm{T}}\mathrm{A}\mathbf{m}$ for a matrix A of hyperparameters. More complicated regularization terms, such as those that penalize centers that move away from specified points are easily incorporated in our formalism. For expositional clarity, we deal here with only the simple case of a diagonal regularizer matrix $\mathrm{A} = \alpha\mathrm{I}$.

The conditional distribution $p(\mathbf{m}|D, \alpha, \beta)$ is then given by

$$p(\mathbf{m}|D, \alpha, \beta) = \exp(-\beta E_D(\mathbf{m}) - E_m(\mathbf{m}))/Z_F \tag{5}$$

We choose to model the hyperparameters α and β by Gamma distributions,

$$p(\alpha) \propto \alpha^{a-1}e^{-\alpha/b} \qquad p(\beta) \propto \alpha^{c-1}e^{-\beta/d}, \tag{6}$$

where a, b, c, d are chosen constants. This completely specifies the joint posterior,

$$p(\mathbf{m}, \alpha, \beta|D) = p(\mathbf{m}|D, \alpha, \beta)p(\alpha)p(\beta). \tag{7}$$

A Bayesian prediction for a new test point $\mathbf{x}$ is then given by the posterior average $\langle f(\mathbf{x}, \mathbf{m})\rangle_{p(\mathbf{m},\alpha,\beta|D)}$. If the centers are fixed, $p(\mathbf{w}|D, \alpha, \beta)$ is Gaussian and computing the posterior average is trivial. However, with adaptive centers,the posterior distribution is typically highly complex and computing this average is difficult[2]. We describe below approaches that approximate the posterior by a simpler distribution which can then be used to find the Bayesian predictions and error bars analytically.

3   Approximating the posterior

3.1   Laplace's method

Laplace's method is an approximation to the Bayesian procedure that fits a Gaussian to the mode $\mathbf{m}_0$ of $p(\mathbf{m}, |D, \alpha, \beta)$ by extremizing the exponent in (5)

$$T = \frac{\alpha}{2}\|\mathbf{m}\|^2 + \beta E_D(\mathbf{m}) \tag{8}$$

with respect to $\mathbf{m}$. The mean of the approximating distribution is then set to the mode $\mathbf{m}_0$, and the covariance is taken to be the inverse Hessian around $\mathbf{m}_0$; this is then used to approximately compute the posterior average. This is a local method as no account is taken for the fit of the Gaussian away from the mode.

3.2   Kullback-Leibler method

The Kullback-Leibler divergence between the posterior $p(\mathbf{m}, \alpha, \beta|D)$ and an approximating distribution $q(\mathbf{m}, \alpha, \beta)$ is defined by

$$KL[q] = -\int q(\mathbf{m}, \alpha, \beta)\ln\left(\frac{p(\mathbf{m}, \alpha, \beta|D)}{q(\mathbf{m}, \alpha, \beta)}\right). \tag{9}$$

$KL[q]$ is zero only if p and q are identical, and is greater than zero otherwise. Since in (5) Z_F is unknown, we can compute the KL divergence only up to an additive constant, $L[q] = KL[q] - \ln Z_F$. We seek then a posterior approximation of the form $q(\mathbf{m}, \alpha, \beta) = Q(\mathbf{m})R(\alpha)S(\beta)$ where $Q(\mathbf{m})$ is Gaussian and the distributions R and S are determined by minimization of the functional $L[q]$[5].

We first consider optimizing L with respect to the mean $\overline{\mathbf{m}}$ and covariance C of the Gaussian distribution $Q(\mathbf{m}) \propto \exp\left\{-\frac{1}{2}(\mathbf{m} - \overline{\mathbf{m}})^{\mathrm{T}}\mathrm{C}^{-1}(\mathbf{m} - \overline{\mathbf{m}})\right\}$. Omitting all constant terms and integrating out α and β, the $Q(\mathbf{m})$ dependency in L is,

$$L[Q(\mathbf{m})] = -\int Q(\mathbf{m})\left[-\bar{\beta}E_D(\mathbf{m}) - \frac{1}{2}\bar{\alpha}\|\mathbf{m}\|^2 - \ln Q(\mathbf{m})\right]d\mathbf{m} + \text{const}. \tag{10}$$

---

[2]The fixed and adaptive center Bayesian approaches are contrasted more fully in [2].

where

$$\bar{\alpha} = \int \alpha R(\alpha) d\alpha, \qquad \bar{\beta} = \int \beta S(\beta) d\beta \qquad (11)$$

are the mean values of the hyperparameters. For Gaussian basis functions, the remaining integration in (10) over $Q(\mathbf{m})$ can be evaluated analytically, giving[3]

$$L[Q(\mathbf{m})] = \frac{1}{2}\bar{\alpha}\left\{\mathrm{tr}(\mathbf{C}) + ||\overline{\mathbf{m}}||^2\right\} + \bar{\beta}\langle E_D(\mathbf{m})\rangle_Q - \frac{1}{2}\ln(\det \mathbf{C}) + \mathrm{const.} \qquad (12)$$

where

$$\langle E_D(\mathbf{m})\rangle_Q = \frac{1}{2}\sum_{\mu=1}^{P}\left((y^\mu)^2 - 2y^\mu\sum_{l=1}^{K} s_l^\mu + \sum_{kl=1}^{K} s_{kl}^\mu\right) \qquad (13)$$

The analytical formulae for

$$s_l^\mu = \langle w_l \exp\{-\lambda_l||\mathbf{x}^\mu - \mathbf{c}_l||^2\}\rangle_Q \qquad (14)$$
$$s_{kl}^\mu = \langle w_k w_l \exp\{-\lambda_k||\mathbf{x}^\mu - \mathbf{c}_k||^2\}\exp\{-\lambda_l||\mathbf{x}^\mu - \mathbf{c}_l||^2\}\rangle_Q \qquad (15)$$

are straightforward to compute, requiring only Gaussian integration[2]. The values for $\mathbf{C}$ and $\overline{\mathbf{m}}$ can then be found by optimizing (12).

We now turn to the functional optimisation of (9) with respect to R. Integrating out $\mathbf{m}$ and β leaves, up to a constant,

$$L[R] = \int R(\alpha)\left\{\alpha\left[\frac{||\overline{\mathbf{m}}||^2}{2} + \frac{\mathrm{tr}(\mathbf{C})}{2} + \frac{1}{b}\right] + \left[\frac{K(N+1)}{4} + a - 1\right]\ln\alpha + \ln R(\alpha)\right\}d\alpha \qquad (16)$$

As the first two terms in (16) constitute the log of a Gamma distribution (6), the functional (16) is optimized by choosing a Gamma distribution for α,

$$R(\alpha) \propto \alpha^{r-1}e^{-\alpha/s} \qquad (17)$$

with

$$r = \frac{K(N+1)}{2} + a, \qquad \frac{1}{s} = \frac{||\overline{\mathbf{m}}||^2}{2} + \frac{1}{2}\mathrm{tr}(\mathbf{C}) + \frac{1}{b}, \qquad \bar{\alpha} = rs. \qquad (18)$$

The same procedure for $S(\beta)$ yields

$$S(\beta) \propto \beta^{u-1}e^{-\beta/v} \qquad (19)$$

with

$$u = \frac{P}{2} + c, \qquad \frac{1}{v} = \langle E_D(\mathbf{m})\rangle_Q + \frac{1}{d}, \qquad \bar{\beta} = uv, \qquad (20)$$

where the averaged training error is given by (13). The optimization of the approximating distribution $Q(\mathbf{m})R(\alpha)S(\beta)$ can then be performed using an iterative procedure in which we first optimize (12) with respect to $\overline{\mathbf{m}}$ and $\mathbf{C}$ for fixed $\bar{\alpha}, \bar{\beta}$, and then update $\bar{\alpha}$ and $\bar{\beta}$ according to the re-estimation formulae (18,20).

After this iterative procedure has converged, we have an approximating distribution of parameters, both for the hidden to output weights and center positions (figure 1(a)). The actual predictions are then given by the posterior average over this distribution of networks. The model averaging effect inherent in the Bayesian procedure produces a final function potentially much more complex than that achievable by a single network.

A significant advantage of our procedure over the Laplace procedure is that we can lower bound model the likelihood $\ln p(D|\mathrm{model}) \geq -(L + \ln Z_D + \ln Z_P)$. Hence, decreasing L increases $p(D|\mathrm{model})$. We can use this bound to rank different models, leading to principled Bayesian model selection.

---

[3]$\langle \ldots \rangle_Q$ denotes $\int Q(\mathbf{m})\ldots d\mathbf{m}$

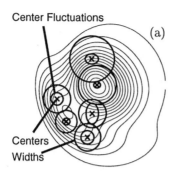
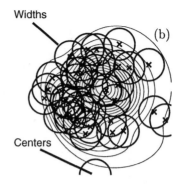

Figure 1: Regressing a surface from 40 noisy training examples. (a) The KL approximate Bayesian treatment fits 6 basis functions to the data. The posterior distribution for the parameters gives rise to a posterior weighted average of a distribution of the 6 Gaussians. We plot here the posterior standard deviation of the centers (center fluctuations) and the mean centers. The widths were fixed a priori using Maximum Likelihood. (b) Fixing a basis function on each training point with fixed widths. The hidden-output weights were determined by cross-validation of the penalised training error.

4   Relation to non-Bayesian treatments

One non-Bayesian approach to training RBFs is to minimze the training error (3) plus a regularizing term of the form (8) for fixed centers[7, 3, 9]. In figure 1(b) we fix a center on each training input. For fixed hyperparameters α and β, the optimal hidden-to-output weights can then be found by minimizing (8). To set the hyperparameters, we iterate this procedure using cross-validation. This results in a single estimate for the parameters $\mathbf{m}_0$ which is then used for predictions $f(\mathbf{x}, \mathbf{m}_0)$. In figure(1), both the Bayesian adaptive center and the fixed center methods have similar performance in terms of test error on this problem. However, the parsimonious representation of the data by the Bayesian adaptive center method may be advantageous if interpreting the data is important.

In principle, in the Bayesian approach, there is no need to carry out a cross-validation type procedure for the regularization parameters α, β. After deciding on a particular Bayesian model with suitable hyperprior constants (here a, b, c, d), our procedure will combine these beliefs about the regularity of the RBF with the dataset in a principled manner, returning a-posteriori probabilities for the values of the regularization constants. Error bars on the predictions are easily calculated as the posterior distribution quantifies our uncertainty in the parameter estimates.

One way of viewing the connection between the CV and Bayesian approaches, is to identify the a-priori choice of CV regularization coefficients α_i that one wishes to examine as a uniform prior over the set $\{\alpha_i\}$. The posterior regularizer distribution is then a delta peak centred at that α_* with minimal CV error. This delta peak represents a loss of information regarding the performance of all the other networks trained with $\alpha_i \neq \alpha_*$. In contrast, in our Bayesian approach we assign a continuous prior distribution on α, which is updated according to the evidence in the data. Any loss of information then occurs in approximating the resulting posterior distribution.

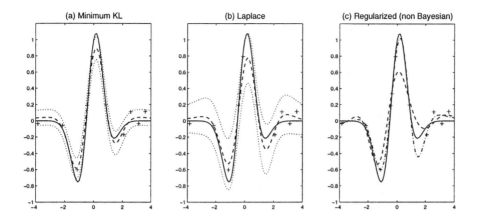

Figure 2: Minimal KL Gaussian fit, Laplace Gaussian, and a non-Bayesian procedure on regressing with 6 Gaussian basis functions. The training points are labelled
by crosses and the target function g is given by the solid lines. For both (a) and (b),
the mean prediction is given by the dashed lines, and standard errors are given by
the dots. (a) Approximate Bayesian solution based on Kullback-Leibler divergence.
The regularization constant α and inverse noise level β are adapted as described
in the text. (b) Laplace method based on equation (8). Both α and β are set to
the mean of the hyperparameter distributions (6). The mean prediction is given
by averaging over the locally approximated posterior. Note that the error bars are
somewhat large, suggesting that the local posterior mass has been underestimated.
(c) The broken line is the Laplace solution without averaging over the posterior,
showing much greater variation than the averaged prediction in (b). The dashed line
corresponds to fixing the basis function centers at each data point, and estimating
the regularization constants α by cross-validation.

5 Demonstration

We apply the above outlined Bayesian framework to a simple one-dimensional regression problem. The function to be learned is given by

$$g(x) = (1 + x - 2x^2)\exp\{-x^2\}, \tag{21}$$

and is plotted in figure(2). The training patterns are sampled uniformly between $[-4, 4]$ and the output is corrupted with additive Gaussian noise of variance
$\sigma^2 = 0.005$. The number of basis function is $K = 6$, giving a reasonably flexible model for this problem. In figure(2), we compare the Bayesian approaches
(a),(b) to non-Bayesian approaches(c). In this demonstration, the basis function
widths were chosen by penalised training error minimization and fixed throughout all experiments. For the Bayesian procedures, we chose hyperprior constants,
$a = 2, b = 1/4, c = 4, d = 50$, corresponding to mean values $\bar{\alpha} = 0.5$ and $\bar{\beta} = 200$.
In (c), we plot a more conventional approach using cross-validation to set the regularization constant.

A useful feature of the Bayesian approaches lies in the principled theory for the error
bars. In (c), although we know the test error for each regularization constant in the
set of constants we choose to examine, we do not know any principled procedure
for using these values for error bar assessment.

6   Conclusions

We have incorporated Radial Basis Functions within a Bayesian framework, arguing that the selection of regularization constants by non-Bayesian methods such as cross-validation is wasteful of the information contained in our prior beliefs and the data set. Our framework encompasses flexible priors such as hard assigning a basis function center to each data point or penalizing centers that wander far from pre-assigned points. We have developed an approximation to the ideal Bayesian procedure by fitting a Gaussian distribution to the posterior based on minimizing the Kullback-Leibler divergence. This is an objectively better and more controlled approximation to the Bayesian procedure than the Laplace method. Furthermore, the KL divergence is an analytic quantity for fixed basis function widths. This framework also includes the automatic adaptation of regularization constants under the influence of data and provides a rigorous lower bound on the likelihood of the model.

Acknowledgements

We would like to thank Chris Bishop and Chris Williams for useful discussions. BS thanks the Leverhulme Trust for support (F/250/K).

References

[1] D. Barber and C. M. Bishop. On computing the KL divergence for Bayesian Neural Networks. Technical report, Neural Computing Research Group, Aston University, Birmingham, 1998. See also D. Barber and C. M. Bishop *These proceedings.*

[2] D. Barber and B. Schottky. Bayesian Radial Basis Functions. Technical report, Neural Computing Research Group, Aston University, Birmingham, 1998.

[3] C. M. Bishop. Improving the Generalization Properties of Radial Basis Function Networks. *Neural Computation*, 4(3):579–588, 1991.

[4] G. E. Hinton and D. van Camp. Keeping neural networks simple by minimizing the description length of the weights. In *Proceedings of the Seventh Annual ACM Workshop on Computational Learning Theory (COLT '93)*, 1993.

[5] D. J. C. MacKay. Developments in probabilistic modelling with neural networks – ensemble learning. In *Neural Networks: Artificial Intelligence and Industrial Applications. Proceedings of the 3rd Annual Symposium on Neural Networks, Nijmegan, Netherlands, 14-15 September 1995*, pages 191–198. Springer.

[6] D. J. C. MacKay. Bayesian Interpolation. *Neural Computation*, 4(3):415–447, 1992.

[7] J. Moody and C. J. Darken. Fast Learning in Networks of Locally-Tuned Processing Units. *Neural Computation*, 1:281–294, 1989.

[8] Neal, R. M. *Bayesian Learning for Neural Networks*. Springer, New York, 1996. Lecture Notes in Statistics 118.

[9] M. J. L. Orr. Regularization in the Selection of Radial Basis Function Centers. *Neural Computation*, 7(3):606–623, 1995.

[10] M. J. L. Orr. Introduction to Radial Basis Function Networks. Technical report, Centre for Cognitive Science, Univeristy of Edinburgh, Edinburgh, EH8 9LW, U.K., 1996.

Shared Context Probabilistic Transducers

Yoshua Bengio[*]
Dept. IRO,
Université de Montréal,
Montréal (QC), Canada, H3C 3J7
bengioy@iro.umontreal.ca

Samy Bengio[†]
Microcell Labs,
1250, René Lévesque Ouest,
Montréal (QC), Canada, H3B 4W8
samy.bengio@microcell.ca

Jean-François Isabelle[‡]
Microcell Labs,
1250, René Lévesque Ouest,
Montréal (QC), Canada, H3B 4W8
jean-francois.isabelle@microcell.ca

Yoram Singer
AT&T Laboratories,
Murray Hill, NJ 07733, USA,
singer@research.att.com

Abstract

Recently, a model for supervised learning of probabilistic transducers represented by suffix trees was introduced. However, this algorithm tends to build very large trees, requiring very large amounts of computer memory. In this paper, we propose a new, more compact, transducer model in which one shares the parameters of distributions associated to contexts yielding similar conditional output distributions. We illustrate the advantages of the proposed algorithm with comparative experiments on inducing a noun phrase recognizer.

1   Introduction

Learning algorithms for sequential data modeling are important in many applications such as natural language processing and time-series analysis, in which one has to learn a model from one or more sequences of training data. Many of these algorithms can be cast as *weighted transducers* (Pereira, Riley and Sproat, 1994), which associate input sequences to output sequences, with weights for each input/output

---

[*] Yoshua Bengio is also with AT&T Laboratories, Holmdel, NJ 07733, USA.

[†] This work was performed while Samy Bengio was at INRS-Télécommunication, Iledes-Soeurs, Québec, Canada, H3E 1H6

[‡] This work was performed while Jean-François Isabelle was at INRS-Télécommunication, Ile-des-Soeurs, Québec, Canada, H3E 1H6

sequence pair. When these weights are interpreted as probabilities, such models are called *probabilistic transducers*. In particular, a probabilistic transducer can represent the conditional probability distribution of output sequences given an input sequence. For example, algorithms for combining several transducers were found useful in natural language and speech processing (Riley and Pereira, 1994). Very often, weighted transducers use an intermediate variable that represents "context", such as the state variable of Hidden Markov Models (Baker, 1975; Jelinek, 1976). A particular type of weighted transducer, called *Input/Output Hidden Markov Model*, is one in which the input-to-context distribution and context-to-output distribution are represented by flexible parameterized models (such as neural networks) (Bengio and Frasconi, 1996). In this paper, we will study probabilistic transducers with a deterministic input-to-state mapping (i.e., a function from the past input subsequence to the current value of the context variable). One such transducer is the one which assigns a value of the context variable to every value of the past input subsequence already seen in the data. This input-to-state mapping can be efficiently represented by a tree. Such transducers are called *suffix tree transducers* (Singer, 1996).

A problem with suffix tree transducers is that they tend to yield very large trees (whose size may grow as $O(n^2)$ for a sequence of data of length n). For example, in the application studied in this paper, one obtains trees requiring over a gigabyte of memory. Heuristics may be used to limit the growth of the tree (e.g., by limiting the maximum depth of the context, i.e., of the tree, and by limiting the maximum number of contexts, i.e., nodes of the tree). In this paper, instead, we propose a new model for a probabilistic transducer with deterministic input-to-state function in which this function is compactly represented, by sharing parameters of contexts which are associated to similar output distributions. Another way to look at the proposed algorithm is that it searches for a clustering of the nodes of a suffix tree transducer. The data structure that represents the contexts is not anymore a tree but a single-root acyclic directed graph.

2   Background: Suffix Tree Probabilistic Transducers

The learning algorithm for suffix tree probabilistic transducers (Singer, 1996) constructs the model $P(y_1^n|x_1^n)$ from **discrete input** sequences $x_1^n = \{x_1, x_2, \ldots, x_n\}$ to output sequences $y_1^n = \{y_1, y_2, \ldots, y_n\}$, where x_t are elements of a finite alphabet Σ_{in}. This distribution is represented by a tree in which each internal node may have a child for every element of Σ_{in}, therefore associating a label $\in \Sigma_{in}$ to each arc. A node at depth d is labeled with the sequence σ_1^d of labels on arcs from root to node, corresponding to a particular *input context*, e.g., at some position n in the sequence a context of length d is the value σ_1^d of the preceding subsequence x_{n-d+1}^n. Each node at depth d is therefore associated with a model of the output distribution in this context, $P(y_n|x_{n-d+1}^n = \sigma_1^d)$ (independent of n).

To obtain a local output probability for y_n (i.e., given x_1^n), one follows the longest possible path from the root to a node a depth d according to the labels x_n, x_{n-1}, ... x_{n-d+1}. The local output probability at this node is used to model y_n. Since $P(y_1^T|x_1^T)$ can always be written $\prod_{n=1}^T P(y_n|x_1^n)$, the overall input/output conditional distribution can be decomposed, according to this model, as follows:

$$P(y_1^T|x_1^T) = \prod_{n=1}^T P(y_n|x_{n-d(x_1^n)+1}^n), \tag{1}$$

where $d(x_1^n)$ is the depth of the node of the tree associated with the longest suffix $\sigma_1^d = x_{n-d+1}^n$ of x_1^n. Figure 1 gives a simple example of a suffix tree transducer.

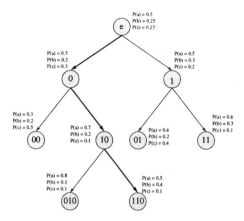

Figure 1: *Example of suffix tree transducer (Singer, 1996). The input alphabet,* $\Sigma_{in} = \{0, 1\}$ *and the output alphabet,* $\Sigma_{out} = \{a, b, c\}$. *For instance,* $P(a|00110) = P(a|110) = 0.5$.

3 Proposed Model and Learning Algorithm

In the model proposed here, the input/output conditional distribution $P(y_1^T|x_1^T)$ is represented by *a single-root acyclic directed graph*. Each *node* of this graph is associated with a *set of contexts* $C_{node} = \{\sigma_1^{d_i}\}$, corresponding to all the paths i (of various lengths d_i) from the root of the tree to this *node*. All these contexts are associated with the same local output distribution $P(y_n|x_1^n$ has a suffix in C_{node}).

Like in suffix tree transducers, each internal node may have a child for every element of Σ_{in}. The arc is labeled with the corresponding element of Σ_{in}. Also like in suffix tree transducers, to obtain $P(y_n|x_1^n)$, one follows the path from the root to the deepest node called $deepest(x_1^n)$ according to the labels x_n, x_{n-1}, etc... The local output distribution at this node is used to predict y_n or its probability. The overall conditional distribution is therefore given by

$$P(y_1^T|x_1^T) = \prod_{n=1}^{T} P(y_n|deepest(x_1^n)) \tag{2}$$

where the set of contexts $C_{deepest(x_1^n)}$ associated to the deepest node $deepest(x_1^n)$ contains a suffix of x_1^n. The model can be used both to compute the conditional probability of a given input/output sequence pair, or to guess an output sequence given an input sequence. Note that the input variable can contain delayed values of the output variable (as in Variable Length Markov Models).

3.1 Proposed Learning Algorithm

We present here a constructive learning algorithm for building the graph of the model and specify which data points are used to update each local output model (associated to nodes of the graph). The algorithm is on-line and operates according to two regimes: (1) adding new nodes and simply updating the local output distributions at existing nodes, and (2) merging parts of the graph which represent similar distributions. If there are multiple sequences in the training data they are concatenated in order to obtain a single input/output sequence pair.

(1) After every observation (x_n, y_n), the algorithm updates the output distributions

of the nodes for which $C_{node(x_1^n)}$ contains a suffix of x_1^n, possibly adding new nodes (with labels $x_{n-d_i}^n$) until $x_1^n \in C_{node}$ for some $node$.

(2) Every τ_{merge} observations, the algorithm attempts to merge sub-graphs which are found similar enough, by comparing the $N(N-1)/2$ pairs of sub-graphs rooted at the N nodes that have seen at least $\min_n$ observations. Merging two subgraphs is equivalent to forcing them to share parameters (as well as reducing the size of the representation of the distribution). A merge is performed between the graphs rooted at nodes a and b if $\Delta(a,b) < \min_\Delta$ and the merge succeeds. The details of the similarity measure and merging algorithm are given in the next subsections.

3.2 Similarity Measure Between Rooted Subgraphs

In order to compare (asymmetrically) output distributions $P(y|a)$ and $P(y|b)$ at two nodes a and b, one can use the Kullback-Liebler divergence:

$$KL(a,b) = \sum_{y \in \Sigma_{out}} P(y|b) \log \frac{P(y|b)}{P(y|a)} \tag{3}$$

However, we want to compare the whole acyclic graphs rooted at these 2 nodes. In order to do so, let us define the following. Let s be a string of input labels, and b a node. Define $desc(b,s)$ as the most remote descendant of b obtained by following from b the arcs whose labels correspond to the sequence s. Let $descendents(a)$ be the set of strings obtained by following the arcs starting from node a until reaching the leaves which have a as an ancestor. Let $P(s|a)$ be the probability of following the arcs according to string s, starting from node a. This distribution can be estimated by counting the relative number of descendents through each of the children of each node.

To compare the graphs rooted at two nodes a and b, we extend the KL divergence by weighing each of the descendents of a, as follows:

$$WKL(a,b) = \sum_{s \in descendents(a)} P(s|a) KL(desc(a,s), desc(b,s)) \tag{4}$$

Finally, to obtain a symmetric measure, we define

$$\Delta(a,b) = WKL(a,b) + WKL(b,a) \tag{5}$$

that is used in the merge phase of the constructive learning algorithm to decide whether the subgraphs rooted at a and b should be merged.

3.3 Merging Two Rooted Subgraphs

If $\Delta(a,b) < \min_\Delta$ (a predefined threshold) we want to merge the two subgraphs rooted at a and b and create a new subgraph rooted at c. The local output distribution at c is obtained from the local output distributions at a and b as follows:

$$P(y_n|c) = P(y_n|a)P(a|a \text{ or } b) + P(y_n|b)P(b|a \text{ or } b) \tag{6}$$

where we define

$$P(a|a \text{ or } b) = \frac{\alpha^{d(a)}}{\alpha^{d(a)} + \alpha^{d(b)}}, \tag{7}$$

where $d(a)$ is the length of the longest path from the root to node a, and α represents a prior parameter (between 0 and 1) on the depth of the acyclic graphs. This prior parameter can be used to induce a prior distribution over possible rooted acyclic graphs structures which favors smaller graphs and shorter contexts (see the mixture of probabilistic transducers of (Singer, 1996)).

The merging algorithm can then be summarized as follows:

- The parents of a and b become parents for c.

- Some verifications are made to prevent merges which would yield to cycles in the graph. The nodes a and b are not merged if they are parents of one another.

- We make each child of a a child of c. For each child u of b (following an arc labeled l), look for the corresponding child v of c (also following the arc labeled l). If there is no such child, and u is not a parent of c, make u a new child of c. Else, if u and v are not parents of each other, recursively merge them.

- Delete nodes a and b, as well as all the links from and to these nodes.

This algorithm is symmetric with respect to a and b except when a merge cannot be done because a and b are parents of one another. In this case, an asymmetric decision must be taken: we chose to keep only a and reject b. Figure 2 gives a simple example of merge.

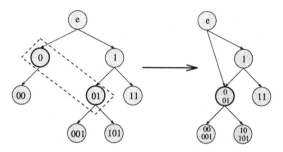

Figure 2: *This figure shows how two nodes are merged. The result is no longer a tree, but a directed graph. Some verifications are done to avoid cycles in the graph. Each node can have multiple labels, corresponding to the multiple possible paths from the root to the node.*

4   Comparative Experiments

We compared experimentally our model to the one proposed in (Singer, 1996) on mixtures of suffix tree transducers, using the same task. Given a text where each word is assigned an appropriate part-of-speech value (verb, noun, adjective, etc), the task is to identify the noun phrases in the text. The UPENN tree-bank corpus database was used in these experiments. The input vocabulary size, $|\Sigma_{in}| = 41$, is the number of possible part-of-speech tags, and the output vocabulary size is $|\Sigma_{out}| = 2$. The model was trained over 250000 marked tags, constraining the tree to be of maximal depth 15. The model was then tested (freezing the model structure and its parameters) over 37000 other tags. Using the mixture of suffix tree transducers (Singer, 1996) and thresholding the output probability at 0.5 to take output decisions, yielded an accuracy rate of 97.6% on the test set, but required over 1 gigabyte of computer memory.

To make interesting comparisons with the shared context transducers, we chose the following experimental scheme. Not only did we fix the maximal depth of the directed graph to 15, but we also fixed the maximal number of allocated nodes, i.e., simulating fixed memory resources. When this number was reached, we froze the structure but continued to update the parameters of the model until the end of the training database was reached. For the shared context version, whenever a merge freed some nodes, we let the graph grow again to its maximal node size. At the end of this process, we evaluated the model on the test set.

We tested this method for various values of the maximum number of nodes in the graph. For each experiment, we tried different values of the other parameters (the similarity threshold $\min_\Delta$ for merging, the minimum number of observations $\min_n$ at a node before it can be considered for a merge, and the delay τ_{merge} between two merging phases), and we picked the one which performed the best *on the training set*. Results are reported in figure 3.

maximal number of nodes	with merge (%)	without merge (%)
20	0.762	0.584
50	0.827	0.624
100	0.861	0.727
500	0.924	0.867
1000	0.949	0.917
2000	0.949	0.935
5000	0.952	0.948

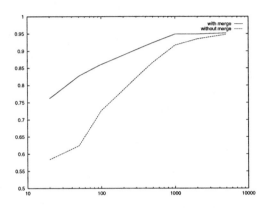

Figure 3: *This figure shows the generalization accuracy rate of a transducer with merges (shared contexts graph) against one without merges (suffix tree), with different maximum number of nodes. The maximum number of nodes are in a logarithmic scale, and the accuracy rates are expressed in relative frequency of correct classification.*

As can be seen from the results, the accuracy rate over the test set is better for transducers with shared contexts than without. More precisely, the gain is greater when the maximum number of nodes is smaller. When we fix the maximum number of nodes to a very small value (20), a shared context transducer performs 1.3 times better (in classification error) than a non-shared one. This gain becomes smaller and smaller as the maximum size increases. Beyond a certain maximum size, there is almost no gain, and one could probably observe a loss for some large sizes. We also need to keep in mind that the larger the transducer is, the slower the program to create the shared context transducer is, compared to the non-shared one. Finally, it is interesting to note that using only 5000 nodes, we were able to obtain 95.2% accuracy, which is only 2.4% less than those obtained with no constraint on the number of nodes.

5   Conclusion

In this paper, we have presented the following:

- A new probabilistic model for probabilistic transducers with deterministic input-to-state function, represented by a rooted acyclic directed graph with nodes associated to a set of contexts and children associated to the different input symbols. This is a generalization of the suffix tree transducer.

- A constructive learning algorithm for this model, based on construction and merging phases. The merging is obtained by clustering parts of the graph which represent a similar conditional distribution.

- Experimental results on a natural-language task showing that when the size of the graph is constrained, this algorithm performs better than the purely constructive (no merge) suffix tree algorithm.

References

Baker, J. (1975). Stochastic modeling for automatic speech understanding. In Reddy, D., editor, *Speech Recognition*, pages 521–542. Academic Press, New York.

Bengio, S. and Bengio, Y. (1996). An EM algorithm for asynchronous input/output hidden markov models. In *Proceedings of the International Conference on Neural Information Processing*, Honk Kong.

Bengio, Y. and Frasconi, P. (1996). Input/Output HMMs for sequence processing. *IEEE Transactions on Neural Networks*, 7(5):1231–1249.

Jelinek, F. (1976). Continuous speech recognition by statistical methods. *Proceedings of the IEEE*, 64:532–556.

Pereira, F., Riley, M., and Sproat, R. (1994). Weighted rational transductions and their application to human language processing. In *ARPA Natural Language Processing Workshop*.

Riley, M. and Pereira, F. (1994). Weighted-finite-automata tools with applications to speech and language processing. Technical Report Technical Memorandum 11222-931130-28TM, AT&T Bell Laboratories.

Singer, Y. (1996). Adaptive mixtures of probabilistic transducers. In Mozer, M., Touretzky, D., and Perrone, M., editors, *Advances in Neural Information Processing Systems 8*. MIT Press, Cambridge, MA.

Approximating Posterior Distributions in Belief Networks using Mixtures

Christopher M. Bishop   **Neil Lawrence**

Neural Computing Research Group
Dept. Computer Science & Applied Mathematics
Aston University
Birmingham, B4 7ET, U.K.

Tommi Jaakkola   **Michael I. Jordan**

Center for Biological and Computational Learning
Massachusetts Institute of Technology
79 Amherst Street, E10-243
Cambridge, MA 02139, U.S.A.

Abstract

Exact inference in densely connected Bayesian networks is computationally intractable, and so there is considerable interest in developing effective approximation schemes. One approach which has been adopted is to
bound the log likelihood using a mean-field approximating distribution.
While this leads to a tractable algorithm, the mean field distribution is assumed to be factorial and hence unimodal. In this paper we demonstrate
the feasibility of using a richer class of approximating distributions based
on *mixtures* of mean field distributions. We derive an efficient algorithm
for updating the mixture parameters and apply it to the problem of learning in sigmoid belief networks. Our results demonstrate a systematic
improvement over simple mean field theory as the number of mixture
components is increased.

1   Introduction

Bayesian belief networks can be regarded as a fully probabilistic interpretation of feed-
forward neural networks. Maximum likelihood learning for Bayesian networks requires
the evaluation of the likelihood function $P(V|\boldsymbol{\theta})$ where V denotes the set of instantiated
(visible) variables, and $\boldsymbol{\theta}$ represents the set of parameters (weights and biases) in the net-
work. Evaluation of $P(V|\boldsymbol{\theta})$ requires summing over exponentially many configurations of

the hidden variables H, and is computationally intractable except for networks with very sparse connectivity, such as trees. One approach is to consider a rigorous lower bound on the log likelihood, which is chosen to be computationally tractable, and to optimize the model parameters so as to maximize this bound instead.

If we introduce a distribution $Q(H)$, which we regard as an approximation to the true posterior distribution, then it is easily seen that the log likelihood is bounded below by

$$\mathcal{F}[Q] = \sum_{\{H\}} Q(H) \ln \frac{P(V, H)}{Q(H)}. \tag{1}$$

The difference between the true log likelihood and the bound given by (1) is equal to the Kullback-Leibler divergence between the true posterior distribution $P(H|V)$ and the approximation $Q(H)$. Thus the correct log likelihood is reached when $Q(H)$ exactly equals the true posterior. The aim of this approach is therefore to choose an approximating distribution which leads to computationally tractable algorithms and yet which is also flexible so as to permit a good representation of the true posterior. In practice it is convenient to consider parametrized distributions, and then to adapt the parameters to maximize the bound. This gives the best approximating distribution within the particular parametric family.

1.1 Mean Field Theory

Considerable simplification results if the model distribution is chosen to be factorial over the individual variables, so that $Q(H) = \prod_i Q(h_i)$, which gives *mean field theory*. Saul *et al.* (1996) have applied mean field theory to the problem of learning in sigmoid belief networks (Neal, 1992). These are Bayesian belief networks with binary variables in which the probability of a particular variable S_i being on is given by

$$P(S_i = 1|\text{pa}(S_i)) = \sigma\left(\sum_j J_{ij} S_j + b_i\right) \tag{2}$$

where $\sigma(z) \equiv (1 + e^{-z})^{-1}$ is the logistic sigmoid function, $\text{pa}(S_i)$ denote the parents of S_i in the network, and J_{ij} and b_i represent the adaptive parameters (weights and biases) in the model. Here we briefly review the framework of Saul *et al.* (1996) since this forms the basis for the illustration of mixture modelling discussed in Section 3. The mean field distribution is chosen to be a product of Bernoulli distributions of the form

$$Q(H) = \prod_i \mu_i^{h_i} (1 - \mu_i)^{1 - h_i} \tag{3}$$

in which we have introduced mean-field parameters μ_i. Although this leads to considerable simplification of the lower bound, the expectation over the log of the sigmoid function, arising from the use of the conditional distribution (2) in the lower bound (1), remains intractable. This can be resolved by using variational methods (Jaakkola, 1997) to find a lower bound on $\mathcal{F}(Q)$, which is therefore itself a lower bound on the true log likelihood. In particular, Saul *et al.* (1996) make use of the following inequality

$$\langle \ln[1 + e^{z_i}] \rangle \leq \xi_i \langle z_i \rangle + \ln \langle e^{-\xi_i z_i} + e^{(1 - \xi_i) z_i} \rangle \tag{4}$$

where z_i is the argument of the sigmoid function in (2), and $\langle \rangle$ denotes the expectation with respect to the mean field distribution. Again, the quality of the bound can be improved by adjusting the variational parameter ξ_i. Finally, the derivatives of the lower bound with respect to the J_{ij} and b_i can be evaluated for use in learning. In summary, the algorithm involves presenting training patterns to the network, and for each pattern adapting the μ_i and ξ_i to give the best approximation to the true posterior within the class of separable distributions of the form (3). The gradients of the log likelihood bound with respect to the model parameters J_{ij} and b_i can then be evaluated for this pattern and used to adapt the parameters by taking a step in the gradient direction.

2   Mixtures

Although mean field theory leads to a tractable algorithm, the assumption of a completely factorized distribution is a very strong one. In particular, such representations can only effectively model posterior distributions which are uni-modal. Since we expect multi-modal distributions to be common, we therefore seek a richer class of approximating distributions which nevertheless remain computationally tractable. One approach (Saul and Jordan, 1996) is to identify a tractable substructure within the model (for example a chain) and then to use mean field techniques to approximate the remaining interactions. This can be effective where the additional interactions are weak or are few in number, but will again prove to be restrictive for more general, densely connected networks. We therefore consider an alternative approach[1] based on mixture representations of the form

$$Q_{\text{mix}}(H) = \sum_{m=1}^{M} \alpha_m Q(H|m) \tag{5}$$

in which each of the components $Q(H|m)$ is itself given by a mean-field distribution, for example of the form (3) in the case of sigmoid belief networks. Substituting (5) into the lower bound (1) we obtain

$$\mathcal{F}[Q_{\text{mix}}] = \sum_m \alpha_m \mathcal{F}[Q(H|m)] + I(m, H) \tag{6}$$

where $I(m, H)$ is the mutual information between the component label m and the set of hidden variables H, and is given by

$$I(m, H) = \sum_m \sum_{\{H\}} \alpha_m Q(H|m) \ln \frac{Q(H|m)}{Q_{\text{mix}}(H)}. \tag{7}$$

The first term in (6) is simply a convex combination of standard mean-field bounds and hence is no greater than the largest of these and so gives no useful improvement over a single mean-field distribution. It is the second term, i.e. the mutual information, which characterises the gain in using mixtures. Since $I(m, H) \geq 0$, the mutual information increases the value of the bound and hence improves the approximation to the true posterior.

2.1   Smoothing Distributions

As it stands, the mutual information itself involves a summation over the configurations of hidden variables, and so is computationally intractable. In order to be able to treat it efficiently we first introduce a set of 'smoothing' distributions $R(H|m)$, and rewrite the mutual information (7) in the form

$$\begin{aligned} I(m, H) \quad = \quad & \sum_m \sum_{\{H\}} \alpha_m Q(H|m) \ln R(H|m) - \sum_m \alpha_m \ln \alpha_m \\ & - \sum_m \sum_{\{H\}} \alpha_m Q(H|m) \ln \left\{ \frac{R(H|m)}{\alpha_m} \frac{Q_{\text{mix}}(H)}{Q(H|m)} \right\}. \end{aligned} \tag{8}$$

It is easily verified that (8) is equivalent to (7) for arbitrary $R(H|m)$. We next make use of the following inequality

$$- \ln x \geq -\lambda x + \ln \lambda + 1 \tag{9}$$

---

[1]Here we outline the key steps. A more detailed discussion can be found in Jaakkola and Jordan (1997).

to replace the logarithm in the third term in (8) with a linear function (conditionally on the component label m). This yields a lower bound on the mutual information given by $I(m, H) \geq I_\lambda(m, H)$ where

$$I_\lambda(m, H) = \sum_m \sum_{\{H\}} \alpha_m Q(H|m) \ln R(H|m) - \sum_m \alpha_m \ln \alpha_m$$

$$- \sum_m \lambda_m \sum_{\{H\}} R(H|m) Q_{\text{mix}}(H) + \sum_m \alpha_m \ln \lambda_m + 1. \quad (10)$$

With $I_\lambda(m, H)$ substituted for $I(m, H)$ in (6) we again obtain a rigorous lower bound on the true log likelihood given by

$$\mathcal{F}_\lambda[Q_{\text{mix}}(H)] = \sum_m \alpha_m \mathcal{F}[Q(H|m)] + I_\lambda(m, H). \quad (11)$$

The summations over hidden configurations $\{H\}$ in (10) can be performed analytically if we assume that the smoothing distributions $R(H|m)$ factorize. In particular, we have to consider the following two summations over hidden variable configurations

$$\sum_{\{H\}} R(H|m) Q(H|k) = \prod_i \sum_{h_i} R(h_i|m) Q(h_i|k) \overset{\text{def}}{=} \pi_{R,Q}(m, k) \quad (12)$$

$$\sum_{\{H\}} Q(H|m) \ln R(H|m) = \sum_i \sum_{h_i} Q(h_i|m) \ln R(h_i|m) \overset{\text{def}}{=} H(Q\|R|m). \quad (13)$$

We note that the left hand sides of (12) and (13) represent sums over exponentially many hidden configurations, while on the right hand sides these have been re-expressed in terms of expressions requiring only polynomial time to evaluate by making use of the factorization of $R(H|m)$.

It should be stressed that the introduction of a factorized form for the smoothing distributions still yields an improvement over standard mean field theory. To see this, we note that if $R(H|m) = \text{const.}$ for all $\{H, m\}$ then $I(m, H) = 0$, and so optimization over $R(H|m)$ can only improve the bound.

2.2 Optimizing the Mixture Distribution

In order to obtain the tightest bound within the class of approximating distributions, we can maximize the bound with respect to the component mean-field distributions $Q(H|m)$, the mixing coefficients α_m, the smoothing distributions $R(H|m)$ and the variational parameters λ_m, and we consider each of these in turn.

We will assume that the choice of a single mean field distribution leads to a tractable lower bound, so that the equations

$$\frac{\partial \mathcal{F}[Q]}{\partial Q(h_j)} = \text{const} \quad (14)$$

can be solved efficiently[2]. Since $I_\lambda(m, H)$ in (10) is linear in the marginals $Q(h_j|m)$, it follows that its derivative with respect to $Q(h_j|m)$ is independent of $Q(h_j|m)$, although it will be a function of the other marginals, and so the optimization of (11) with respect to individual marginals again takes the form (14) and by assumption is therefore soluble.

Next we consider the optimization with respect to the mixing coefficients α_m. Since all of the terms in (11) are linear in α_m, except for the entropy term, we can write

$$\mathcal{F}_\lambda[Q_{\text{mix}}(H)] = \sum_m \alpha_m(-E_m) - \sum_m \alpha_m \ln \alpha_m + 1 \quad (15)$$

---

[2]In standard mean field theory the constant would be zero, but for many models of interest the slightly more general equations given by (14) will again be soluble.

where we have used (10) and defined

$$
\begin{aligned}
-E_m \;=\; & \mathcal{F}[Q(H|m)] + \sum_{\{H\}} Q(H|m) \ln R(H|m) \\
& + \sum_k \lambda_k \sum_{\{H\}} R(H|k) Q(H|m) + \ln \lambda_m.
\end{aligned}
\tag{16}
$$

Maximizing (15) with respect to α_m, subject to the constraints $0 \le \alpha_m \le 1$ and $\sum_m \alpha_m = 1$, we see that the mixing coefficients which maximize the lower bound are given by the Boltzmann distribution

$$
\alpha_m = \frac{\exp(-E_m)}{\sum_k \exp(-E_k)}.
\tag{17}
$$

We next maximize the bound (11) with respect to the smoothing marginals $R(h_j|m)$. Some manipulation leads to the solution

$$
R(h_j|m) = \frac{\alpha_m Q(h_j|m)}{\lambda_m} \left[\sum_k \alpha_k \pi_{R,Q}^j(m,k) Q(h_j|k) \right]^{-1}
\tag{18}
$$

in which $\pi_{R,Q}^j(m,k)$ denotes the expression defined in (12) but with the j term omitted from the product.

The optimization of the μ_{mj} takes the form of a re-estimation formula given by an extension of the result obtained for mean-field theory by Saul *et al.* (1996). For simplicity we omit the details here.

Finally, we optimize the bound with respect to the λ_m, to give

$$
\frac{1}{\lambda_m} = \frac{1}{\alpha_m} \sum_k \pi_{R,Q}(m,k).
\tag{19}
$$

Since the various parameters are coupled, and we have optimized them individually keeping the remainder constant, it will be necessary to maximize the lower bound iteratively until some convergence criterion is satisfied. Having done this for a particular instantiation of the visible nodes, we can then determine the gradients of the bound with respect to the parameters governing the original belief network, and use these gradients for learning.

3   Application to Sigmoid Belief Networks

We illustrate the mixtures formalism by considering its application to sigmoid belief networks of the form (2). The components of the mixture distribution are given by factorized Bernoulli distributions of the form (3) with parameters μ_{mi}. Again we have to introduce variational parameters ξ_{mi} for each component using (4). The parameters $\{\mu_{mi}, \xi_{mi}\}$ are optimized along with $\{\alpha_m, R(h_j|m), \lambda_m\}$ for each pattern in the training set.

We first investigate the extent to which the use of a mixture distribution yields an improvement in the lower bound on the log likelihood compared with standard mean field theory. To do this, we follow Saul *et al.* (1996) and consider layered networks having 2 units in the first layer, 4 units in the second layer and 6 units in the third layer, with full connectivity between layers. In all cases the six final-layer units are considered to be visible and have their states clamped at zero. We generate 5000 networks with parameters $\{J_{ij}, b_i\}$ chosen randomly with uniform distribution over $(-1, 1)$. The number of hidden variable configurations is $2^6 = 64$ and is sufficiently small that the true log likelihood can be computed directly by summation over the hidden states. We can therefore compare the value of the lower bound $\mathcal{F}$ with the true log likelihood L, using the normalized error $(L - \mathcal{F})/L$. Figure 1 shows histograms of the relative log likelihood error for various numbers of mixture components, together with the mean values taken from the histograms. These show a systematic improvement in the quality of the approximation as the number of mixture components is increased.

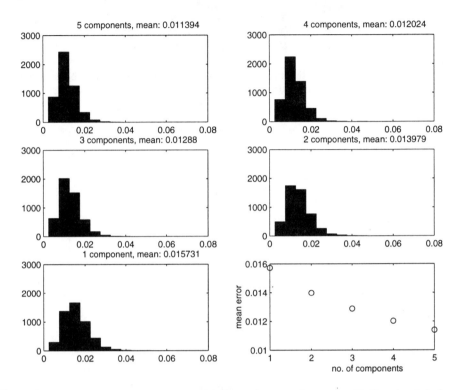

Figure 1: Plots of histograms of the normalized error between the true log likelihood and the lower bound, for various numbers of mixture components. Also shown is the mean values taken from the histograms, plotted against the number of components.

Next we consider the impact of using mixture distributions on learning. To explore this we use a small-scale problem introduced by Hinton *et al.* (1995) involving binary images of size 4×4 in which each image contains either horizontal or vertical bars with equal probability, with each of the four possible locations for a bar occupied with probability 0.5. We trained networks having architecture 1–8–16 using distributions having between 1 and 5 components. Randomly generated patterns were presented to the network for a total of 500 presentations, and the μ_{mi} and ξ_{mi} were initialised from a uniform distribution over $(0, 1)$. Again the networks are sufficiently small that the exact log likelihood for the trained models can be evaluated directly. A Hinton diagram of the hidden-to-output weights for the eight units in a network trained with 5 mixture components is shown in Figure 2. Figure 3 shows a plot of the true log likelihood versus the number M of components in the mixture for a set of experiments in which, for each value of M, the model was trained 10 times starting from different random parameter initializations. These results indicate that, as the number of mixture components is increased, the learning algorithm is able to find a set of network parameters having a larger likelihood, and hence that the improved flexibility of the approximating distribution is indeed translated into an improved training algorithm. We are currently applying the mixture formalism to the large-scale problem of hand-written digit classification.

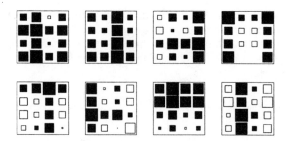

Figure 2: Hinton diagrams of the hidden-to-output weights for each of the 8 hidden units in a network trained on the 'bars' problem using a mixture distribution having 5 components.

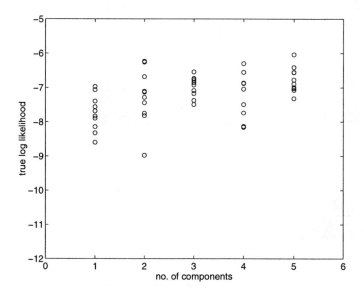

Figure 3: True log likelihood (divided by the number of patterns) versus the number M of mixture components for the 'bars' problem indicating a systematic improvement in performance as M is increased.

References

Hinton, G. E., P. Dayan, B. J. Frey, and R. M. Neal (1995). The wake-sleep algorithm for unsupervised neural networks. *Science* **268**, 1158–1161.

Jaakkola, T. (1997). *Variational Methods for Inference and Estimation in Graphical Models*. Ph.D. thesis, MIT.

Jaakkola, T. and M. I. Jordan (1997). Approximating posteriors via mixture models. To appear in Proceedings NATO ASI *Learning in Graphical Models*, Ed. M. I. Jordan. Kluwer.

Neal, R. (1992). Connectionist learning of belief networks. *Artificial Intelligence* **56**, 71–113.

Saul, L. K., T. Jaakkola, and M. I. Jordan (1996). Mean field theory for sigmoid belief networks. *Journal of Artificial Intelligence Research* **4**, 61–76.

Saul, L. K. and M. I. Jordan (1996). Exploiting tractable substructures in intractable networks. In D. S. Touretzky, M. C. Mozer, and M. E. Hasselmo (Eds.), *Advances in Neural Information Processing Systems*, Volume 8, pp. 486–492. MIT Press.

Receptive field formation in natural scene environments: comparison of single cell learning rules

Brian S. Blais
Brown University Physics Department
Providence, RI 02912

N. Intrator
School of Mathematical Sciences
Tel-Aviv University
Ramat-Aviv, 69978 ISRAEL

H. Shouval
Institute for Brain and Neural Systems
Brown University
Providence, RI 02912

Leon N Cooper
Brown University Physics Department and
Institute for Brain and Neural Systems
Brown University
Providence, RI 02912

Abstract

We study several statistically and biologically motivated learning rules using the same visual environment, one made up of natural scenes, and the same single cell neuronal architecture. This allows us to concentrate on the feature extraction and neuronal coding properties of these rules. Included in these rules are kurtosis and skewness maximization, the quadratic form of the BCM learning rule, and single cell ICA. Using a structure removal method, we demonstrate that receptive fields developed using these rules depend on a small portion of the distribution. We find that the quadratic form of the BCM rule behaves in a manner similar to a kurtosis maximization rule when the distribution contains kurtotic directions, although the BCM modification equations are computationally simpler.

1   INTRODUCTION

Recently several learning rules that develop simple cell-like receptive fields in a natural image environment have been proposed (Law and Cooper, 1994; Olshausen and Field, 1996; Bell and Sejnowski, 1997). The details of these rules are different as well as their computational reasoning, however they all depend on statistics of order higher than two and they all produce sparse distributions.

In what follows we investigate several specific modification functions that have the general properties of BCM synaptic modification functions (Bienenstock et al., 1982), and study their feature extraction properties in a natural scene environment. Several of the rules we consider are derived from standard statistical measures (Kendall and Stuart, 1977), such as skewness and kurtosis, based on polynomial moments. We compare these with the quadratic form of BCM (Intrator and Cooper, 1992), though one should note that this is not the only form that could be used. By subjecting all of the learning rules to the same input statistics and retina/LGN preprocessing and by studying in detail the single neuron case, we eliminate possible network/lateral interaction effects and can examine the properties of the learning rules themselves.

We compare the learning rules and the receptive fields they form, and introduce a procedure for directly measuring the sparsity of the representation a neuron learns. This gives us another way to compare the learning rules, and a more quantitative measure of the concept of sparse representations.

2   MOTIVATION

We use two methods for motivating the use of the particular rules. One comes from Projection Pursuit (Friedman, 1987) and the other is Independent Component Analysis (Comon, 1994). These methods are related, as we shall see, but they provide two different approaches for the current work.

2.1   EXPLORATORY PROJECTION PURSUIT

Diaconis and Freedman (1984) show that for most high-dimensional clouds (of points), most low-dimensional projections are approximately Gaussian. This finding suggests that important information in the data is conveyed in those directions whose single dimensional projected distribution is far from Gaussian.

Intrator (1990) has shown that a BCM neuron can find structure in the input distribution that exhibits deviation from Gaussian distribution in the form of multimodality in the projected distributions. This type of deviation is particularly useful for finding clusters in high dimensional data. In the natural scene environment, however, the structure does not seem to be contained in clusters. In this work we show that the BCM neuron can still find interesting structure in non-clustered data.

The most common measures for deviation from Gaussian distribution are skewness and kurtosis which are functions of the first three and four moments of the distribution respectively. Rules based on these statistical measures satisfy the BCM conditions proposed in Bienenstock et al. (1982), including a threshold-based stabilization. The details of these rules and some of the qualitative features of the stabilization are different, however. In addition, there are some learning rules, such as the ICA rule of Bell and Sejnowski (1997) and the sparse coding algorithm of Olshausen and Field (1995), which have been used with natural scene inputs to produce oriented receptive fields. We do not include these in our comparison because they are not single cell learning rules, and thus detract from our immediate goal of comparing rules with the same input structure and neuronal architecture.

2.2   INDEPENDENT COMPONENT ANALYSIS

Recently it has been claimed that the independent components of natural scenes are the edges found in simple cells (Bell and Sejnowski, 1997). This was achieved through the maximization of the mutual entropy of a set of mixed signals. Others (Hyvarinen and Oja, 1996) have claimed that maximizing kurtosis can also lead to the separation of mixed signals into independent components. This alternate connection between kurtosis and receptive fields leads us into a discussion of ICA.

Independent Component Analysis (ICA) is a statistical signal processing technique whose goal is to express a set of random variables as a linear mixture of statistically independent variables. The problem of ICA is then to find the transformation from the observed mixed signals to the "unmixed" independent sources. The search for independent components relies on the fact that a linear mixture of two non-Gaussian distributions will become more Gaussian than either of them. Thus, by seeking projections which maximize deviations from Gaussian distribution, we recover the original (independent) signals. This explains the connection of ICA to the framework of exploratory projection pursuit.

3   SYNAPTIC MODIFICATION RULES

In this section we outline the derivation for the learning rules in this study. Neural activity is assumed to be a positive quantity, so for biological plausibility we denote by c the rectified activity $\sigma(\mathbf{d} \cdot \mathbf{m})$, where $\sigma(\cdot)$ is a smooth monotonic function with a positive output (a slight negative output is also allowed). σ' denotes the derivative of the sigmoidal. The rectification is required for all rules that depend on odd moments because these vanish in symmetric distributions such as natural scenes. We study the following measures(Kendall and Stuart, 1977, for review):

Skewness 1   This measures the deviation from symmetry, and is of the form:

$$S_1 = E[c^3]/E^{1.5}[c^2]. \tag{1}$$

A maximization of this measure via gradient ascent gives

$$\nabla S_1 = \frac{1}{\Theta_M^{1.5}} E\left[c\left(c - E[c^3]/E[c^2]\right)\sigma'\mathbf{d}\right] = \frac{1}{\Theta_M^{1.5}} E\left[c\left(c - E[c^3]/\Theta_M\right)\sigma'\mathbf{d}\right] \tag{2}$$

where Θ_m is defined as $E[c^2]$.

Skewness 2   Another skewness measure is given by

$$S_2 = E[c^3] - E^{1.5}[c^2]. \tag{3}$$

This measure requires a stabilization mechanism which we achieve by requiring that the vector of weights, denoted by m, has norm of 1. The gradient of S_2 is

$$\nabla S_2 = 3E\left[c^2 - c\sqrt{E[c^2]}\right] = 3E\left[c\left(c - \sqrt{\Theta_M}\right)\sigma'\mathbf{d}\right], \parallel \mathbf{m} \parallel = 1 \tag{4}$$

Kurtosis 1   Kurtosis measures deviation from Gaussian distribution mainly in the tails of the distribution. It has the form

$$K_1 = E[c^4]/E^2[c^2] - 3. \tag{5}$$

This measure has a gradient of the form

$$\nabla K_1 = \frac{1}{\Theta_M^2} E\left[c\left(c^2 - E[c^4]/E[c^2]\right)\sigma'\mathbf{d}\right] = \frac{1}{\Theta_M^2} E\left[c\left(c^2 - E[c^4]/\Theta_M\right)\sigma'\mathbf{d}\right]. \tag{6}$$

Kurtosis 2 As before, there is a similar form which requires some stabilization:

$$K_2 = E[c^4] - 3E^2[c^2]. \tag{7}$$

This measure has a gradient of the form

$$\nabla K_2 = 4E\left[c^3 - cE[c^2]\right] = 3E\left[c(c^2 - \Theta_M)]\sigma'\mathbf{d}\right], \quad \| \mathbf{m} \| = 1. \tag{8}$$

Kurtosis 2 and ICA It has been shown that kurtosis, defined as

$$K_2 = E\left[\mathbf{c}^4\right] - 3E^2\left[\mathbf{c}^2\right]$$

can be used for ICA(Hyvarinen and Oja, 1996). Thus, finding the extrema of kurtosis of the projections enables the estimation of the independent components. They obtain the following expression

$$\mathbf{m} = \frac{2}{\lambda}\left(E^{-1}\left[\mathbf{dd}^T\right]E\left[\mathbf{d}(\mathbf{m}\cdot\mathbf{d})^3\right] - 3\mathbf{m}\right). \tag{9}$$

which leads to an iterative "fixed-point algorithm".

Quadratic BCM The Quadratic BCM (QBCM) measure as given in (Intrator and Cooper, 1992) is of the form

$$\text{QBCM} = \frac{1}{3}E[c^3] - \frac{1}{4}E^2[c^2]. \tag{10}$$

Maximizing this form using gradient ascent gives the learning rule:

$$\nabla\text{QBCM} = E\left[c^2 - cE[c^2]\right] = E[c(c - \Theta_M)\sigma'\mathbf{d}]. \tag{11}$$

4 METHODS

We use 13x13 circular patches from 12 images of natural scenes, presented to the neuron each iteration of the learning. The natural scenes are preprocessed either with a Difference of Gaussians (DOG) filter(Law and Cooper, 1994) or a whitening filter(Oja, 1995; Bell and Sejnowski, 1995), which eliminates the second order correlations. The moments of the output, c, are calculated iteratively, and when it is needed (i.e. K_2 and S_2) we also normalize the weights at each iteration.

For Oja's fixed-point algorithm, the learning was done in batches of 1000 patterns over which the expectation values were performed. However, the covariance matrix was calculated over the entire set of input patterns.

5 RESULTS

5.1 RECEPTIVE FIELDS

The resulting receptive fields (RFs) formed are shown in Figure 1 for both the DOGed and whitened images. Every learning rule developed oriented receptive fields, though some were more sensitive to the preprocessing than others. The additive versions of kurtosis and skewness, K_2 and S_2 respectively, developed RFs with a higher spatial frequency, and more orientations, in the whitened environment than in the DOGed environment.

The multiplicative versions of kurtosis and skewness, K_1 and S_1 respectively, as well as QBCM, sampled from many orientations regardless of the preprocessing. S_1 gives receptive fields with lower spatial frequencies than either QBCM or K_1.

This disappears with the whitened inputs, which implies that the spatial frequency of the RF is related to the dependence of the learning rule on the second moment. Example receptive fields using Oja's fixed-point ICA algorithm not surprisingly look qualitatively similar to those found using the stochastic maximization of K_2.

The output distributions for all of the rules appear to be double exponential. This distribution is one which we would consider sparse, but it would be difficult to compare the sparseness of the distributions merely on the appearance of the output distribution alone. In order to determine the sparseness of the code, we introduce a method for measuring it directly.

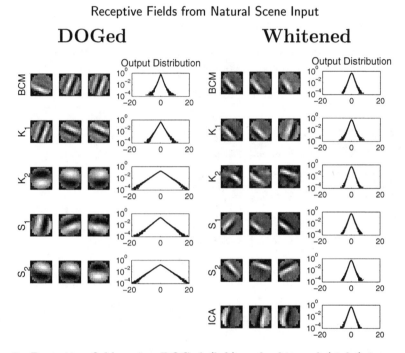

Figure 1: Receptive fields using DOGed (left) and whitened (right) image input obtained from learning rules maximizing (from top to bottom) the Quadratic BCM objective function, Kurtosis (multiplicative), Kurtosis (additive), Skewness (multiplicative), and Skewness (additive). Shown are three examples (left to right) from each learning rule as well as the log of the normalized output distribution, before the application of the rectifying sigmoid.

5.2 STRUCTURE REMOVAL: SENSITIVITY TO OUTLIERS

Learning rules which are dependent on large polynomial moments, such as Quadratic BCM and kurtosis, tend to be sensitive to the tails of the distribution. In the case of a sparse code the outliers, or the rare and interesting events, are what is important. Measuring the degree to which the neurons form a sparse code can be done in a straightforward and systematic fashion.

The procedure involves simply eliminating from the environment those patterns for which the neuron responds strongly. These patterns tend to be the high contrast edges, and are thus the structure found in the image. The percentage of patterns that needs to be removed in order to cause a change in the receptive field gives a direct measure of the sparsity of the coding. The results of this structure removal are shown in Figure 2.

For Quadratic BCM and kurtosis, one need only eliminate *less than one half of a percent* of the input patterns to change the receptive field significantly. To make this more precise, we define a normalized difference between two *mean zero* vectors as $\mathcal{D} \equiv \frac{1}{2}(1 - \cos\alpha)$, where α is the angle between the two vectors. This measure has a value of zero for identical vectors, and a maximum value of one for orthogonal vectors.

Also shown in Figure 2 is the normalized difference as a function of the percentage eliminated, for the different learning rules. RF differences can be seen with as little as a tenth of a percent, which suggests that the neuron is coding the information in a very sparse manner. Changes of around a half a percent and above are visible as significant orientation, phase, or spatial frequency changes. Although both skewness and Quadratic BCM depend primarily on the third moment, QBCM behaves more like kurtosis with regards to sparse coding.

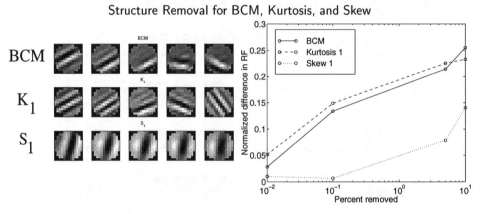

Figure 2: Example receptive fields (left), and normalized difference measure (right), resulting from structure removal using QBCM, K_1, and S_1. The RFs show the successive deletion of top 1% of the distribution. On the right is the normalized difference between RFs as a function of the percentage deleted in structure removal. The maximum possible value of the difference is 1.

6   DISCUSSION

This study attempts to compare several learning rules which have some statistical or biological motivation, or both. For a related study discussing projection pursuit and BCM see (Press and Lee, 1996). We have used natural scenes to gain some more insight about the statistics underlying natural images. There are several outcomes from this study:

- All rules used, found kurtotic distributions.

- The single cell ICA rule we considered, which used the subtractive form of kurtosis, achieved receptive fields qualitatively similar to other rules discussed.

- The Quadratic BCM and the multiplicative version of kurtosis are less sensitive to the second moments of the distribution and produce oriented RFs even when the data is not whitened. The subtractive versions of kurtosis and skewness are sensitive and produces oriented RFs only after sphering the data (Friedman, 1987; Field, 1994).

- Both Quadratic BCM and kurtosis are sensitive to the elimination of the upper 1/2% portion of the distribution. The sensitivity to small portions of the distribution represents the other side of the coin of sparse coding.

- The skew rules' sensitivity to the upper parts of the distribution is not so strong.

- Quadratic BCM learning rule, which has been advocated as a projection index for finding multi-modality in high dimensional distribution, can find projections emphasizing high kurtosis when no cluster structure is present in the data.

ACKNOWLEDGMENTS

This work, was supported by the Office of Naval Research, the DANA Foundation and the National Science Foundation.

References

Bell, A. J. and Sejnowski, T. J. (1995). An information-maximisation approach to blind separation and blind deconvolution. *Neural Computation*, 7(6):1129–1159.

Bell, A. J. and Sejnowski, T. J. (1997). The independent components of natural scenes are edge filters. *Vision Research*. in press.

Bienenstock, E. L., Cooper, L. N., and Munro, P. W. (1982). Theory for the development of neuron selectivity: orientation specificity and binocular interaction in visual cortex. *Journal of Neuroscience*, 2:32–48.

Comon, P. (1994). Independent component analysis, a new concept? *Signal Processing*, 36:287–314.

Field, D. J. (1994). What is the goal of sensory coding. *Neural Computation*, 6:559–601.

Friedman, J. H. (1987). Exploratory projection pursuit. *Journal of the American Statistical Association*, 82:249–266.

Hyvarinen, A. and Oja, E. (1996). A fast fixed-point algorithm for independent component analysis. *Int. Journal of Neural Systems*, 7(6):671–687.

Intrator, N. (1990). A neural network for feature extraction. In Touretzky, D. S. and Lippmann, R. P., editors, *Advances in Neural Information Processing Systems*, volume 2, pages 719–726. Morgan Kaufmann, San Mateo, CA.

Intrator, N. and Cooper, L. N. (1992). Objective function formulation of the BCM theory of visual cortical plasticity: Statistical connections, stability conditions. *Neural Networks*, 5:3–17.

Kendall, M. and Stuart, A. (1977). *The Advanced Theory of Statistics*, volume 1. MacMillan Publishing, New York.

Law, C. and Cooper, L. (1994). Formation of receptive fields according to the BCM theory in realistic visual environments. *Proceedings National Academy of Sciences*, 91:7797–7801.

Oja, E. (1995). The nonlinear pca learning rule and signal separation - mathematical analysis. Technical Report A26, Helsinki University, CS and Inf. Sci. Lab.

Olshausen, B. A. and Field, D. J. (1996). Emergence of simple cell receptive field properties by learning a sparse code for natural images. *Nature*, 381:607–609.

Press, W. and Lee, C. W. (1996). Searching for optimal visual codes: Projection pursuit analysis of the statistical structure in natural scenes. In *The Neurobiology of Computation: Proceedings of the fifth annual Computation and Neural Systems conference*. Plenum Publishing Corporation.

An Annealed Self-Organizing Map for Source Channel Coding

Matthias Burger, Thore Graepel, and Klaus Obermayer
Department of Computer Science
Technical University of Berlin
FR 2-1, Franklinstr. 28/29, 10587 Berlin, Germany
{burger, graepel2, oby}@cs.tu-berlin.de

Abstract

We derive and analyse robust optimization schemes for noisy vector quantization on the basis of deterministic annealing. Starting from a cost function for central clustering that incorporates distortions from channel noise we develop a soft topographic vector quantization algorithm (STVQ) which is based on the maximum entropy principle and which performs a maximum-likelihood estimate in an expectation-maximization (EM) fashion. Annealing in the temperature parameter β leads to phase transitions in the existing code vector representation during the cooling process for which we calculate critical temperatures and modes as a function of eigenvectors and eigenvalues of the covariance matrix of the data and the transition matrix of the channel noise. A whole family of vector quantization algorithms is derived from STVQ, among them a deterministic annealing scheme for Kohonen's self-organizing map (SOM). This algorithm, which we call SSOM, is then applied to vector quantization of image data to be sent via a noisy binary symmetric channel. The algorithm's performance is compared to those of LBG and STVQ. While it is naturally superior to LBG, which does not take into account channel noise, its results compare very well to those of STVQ, which is computationally much more demanding.

1 INTRODUCTION

Noisy vector quantization is an important lossy coding scheme for data to be transmitted over noisy communication lines. It is especially suited for speech and image data which in many applications have to be transmitted under low bandwidth / high noise level conditions. Following the idea of (Farvardin, 1990) and (Luttrell, 1989) of jointly optimizing the codebook and the data representation w.r.t. to a given channel noise we apply a deterministic annealing scheme (Rose, 1990; Buhmann, 1997) to the problem and develop a soft topographic vector quantization algorithm (STVQ) (cf. Heskes, 1995; Miller, 1994). From STVQ we can derive a class of vector quantization algorithms, among which we find SSOM, a deterministic annealing variant of Kohonen's self-organizing map (Kohonen, 1995), as an approximation. While the SSOM like the SOM does not minimize any known energy function (Luttrell, 1989) it is computationally less demanding than STVQ. The deterministic annealing scheme enables us to use the neighborhood function of the SOM solely to encode the desired transition probabilities of the channel noise and thus opens up new possibilities for the usage of SOMs with arbitrary neighborhood functions. We analyse phase transitions during the annealing and demonstrate the performance of SSOM by applying it to lossy image data compression for transmission via noisy channels.

2 DERIVATION OF A CLASS OF VECTOR QUANTIZERS

Vector quantization is a method of encoding data by grouping the data vectors and providing a representative in data space for each group. Given a set $\mathcal{X}$ of data vectors $\mathbf{x}_i \in \Re^d$, $i = 1, \ldots, D$, the objective of vector quantization is to find a set $\mathcal{W}$ of code vectors $\mathbf{w}_r$, $r = 0, \ldots, N - 1$, and a set $\mathcal{M}$ of binary assignment variables m_{ir}, $\sum_r m_{ir} = 1$, $\forall i$, such that a given cost function

$$E\left(\mathcal{M}, \mathcal{W} \mid \mathcal{X}\right) = \sum_i \sum_r m_{ir} E_r(\mathbf{x}_i, \mathcal{W}) \tag{1}$$

is minimized. $E_r(\mathbf{x}_i, \mathcal{W})$ denotes the cost of assigning data point $\mathbf{x}_i$ to code vector $\mathbf{w}_r$.

Following an idea by (Luttrell, 1994) we consider the case that the code labels r form a compressed encoding of the data for the purpose of transmission via a noisy channel (see Figure 1). The distortion caused by the channel noise is modeled by a matrix $\mathbf{H}$ of transition probabilities h_{rs}, $\sum_s h_{rs} = 1$, $\forall r$, for the noise induced change of assignment of a data vector $\mathbf{x}_i$ from code vector $\mathbf{w}_r$ to code vector $\mathbf{w}_s$. After transmission the received index s is decoded using its code vector $\mathbf{w}_s$. Averaging the squared Euclidean distance $\|\mathbf{x}_i - \mathbf{w}_s\|^2$ over all possible transitions yields the assignment costs

$$E_r(\mathbf{x}_i, \mathcal{W}) = \frac{1}{2} \sum_s h_{rs} \|\mathbf{x}_i - \mathbf{w}_s\|^2 , \tag{2}$$

where the factor $1/2$ is introduced for computational convenience.

Starting from the cost function E given in Eqs. (1), (2) the Gibbs-distribution $P\left(\mathcal{M}, \mathcal{W} \mid \mathcal{X}\right) = \frac{1}{Z} \exp\left(-\beta E\left(\mathcal{M}, \mathcal{W} \mid \mathcal{X}\right)\right)$ can be obtained via the principle of maximum entropy under the constraint of a given average cost $\langle E \rangle$. The Lagrangian multiplier β is associated with $\langle E \rangle$ and is interpreted as an inverse temperature that determines the fuzziness of assignments. In order to generalize from the given training set $\mathcal{X}$ we calculate the most likely set of code vectors from the probability distribution $P\left(\mathcal{M}, \mathcal{W} \mid \mathcal{X}\right)$ marginalized over all legal sets of assignments $\mathcal{M}$. For a given value of β we obtain

$$\mathbf{w}_r = \frac{\sum_i \mathbf{x}_i \sum_s h_{rs} P(\mathbf{x}_i \in s)}{\sum_i \sum_s h_{rs} P(\mathbf{x}_i \in s)} , \qquad \forall r , \tag{3}$$

where $P(\mathbf{x}_i \in s) = \langle m_{is} \rangle$,

$$P(\mathbf{x}_i \in s) = \frac{\exp\left(-\frac{\beta}{2} \sum_t h_{st} \|\mathbf{x}_i - \mathbf{w}_t\|^2\right)}{\sum_u \exp\left(-\frac{\beta}{2} \sum_t h_{ut} \|\mathbf{x}_i - \mathbf{w}_t\|^2\right)} , \tag{4}$$

is the assignment probability of data vector $\mathbf{x}_i$ to code vector $\mathbf{w}_s$. Solving Eqs. (3), (4) by fixed-point iteration comprises an expectation-maximization algorithm, where the E-step,

Figure 1: Cartoon of a generic data communication problem. The encoder assigns input vectors $\mathbf{x}_i$ to labeled code vectors $\mathbf{w}_r$. Their indices $\mathbf{r}$ are then transmitted via a noisy channel which is characterized by a set of transition probabilities $h_{\mathbf{rs}}$. The decoder expands the received index $\mathbf{s}$ to its code vector $\mathbf{w}_s$ which represents the data vectors assigned to it during encoding. The total error is measured via the squared Euclidean distance between the original data vector $\mathbf{x}_i$ and its representative $\mathbf{w}_s$ averaged over all transitions $\mathbf{r} \to \mathbf{s}$.

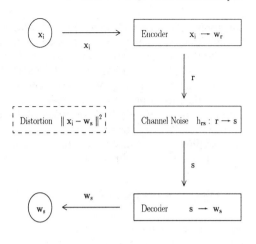

Eq. (4), determines the assignment probabilities $P(\mathbf{x}_i \in \mathbf{s})$ for all data points $\mathbf{x}_i$ and the old code vectors $\mathbf{w}_s$ and the M-step, Eq. (3), determines the new code vectors $\mathbf{w}_r$ from the new assignment probabilities $P(\mathbf{x}_i \in \mathbf{s})$. In order to find the global minimum of E, $\beta = 0$ is increased according to an annealing schedule which tracks the solution from the easily solvable convex problem at low β to the exact solution of Eqs. (1), (2) at infinite β. In the following we call the solution of Eqs. (3), (4) soft topographic vector quantizer (STVQ).

Eqs. (3), (4) are the starting point for a whole class of vector quantization algorithms (Figure 2). The approximation $h_{\mathbf{rs}} \to \delta_{\mathbf{rs}}$ applied to Eq. (4) leads to a soft version of Kohonen's self-organzing map (SSOM), if additionally applied to Eq. (3) soft-clustering (SC) (Rose, 1990) is recovered. $\beta \to \infty$ leads to the corresponding "hard" versions topographic vector quantisation (TVQ) (Luttrell, 1989), self-organizing map (SOM) (Kohonen, 1995), and LBG. In the following, we will focus on the soft self-organizing map (SSOM). SSOM is computationally less demanding than STVQ, but offers – in contrast to the traditional SOM – a robust deterministic annealing optimization scheme. Hence it is possible to extend the SOM approach to arbitrary non-trivial neighborhood functions $h_{\mathbf{rs}}$ as required, e.g. for source channel coding problems for noisy channels.

3   PHASE TRANSITIONS IN THE ANNEALING

From (Rose, 1990) it is known that annealing in β changes the representation of the data. Code vectors split with increasing β and the size of the codebook for a fixed β is given by the number of code vectors that have split up to that point. With non-diagonal $\mathbf{H}$, however, permutation symmetry is broken and the "splitting" behavior of the code vectors changes.

At infinite temperature every data vector $\mathbf{x}_i$ is assigned to every code vector $\mathbf{w}_r$ with equal probability $P^0(\mathbf{x}_i \in \mathbf{r}) = 1/N$, where N is the size of the codebook. Hence all code vectors are located in the center of mass, $\mathbf{w}_r^0 = \frac{1}{D} \sum_i \mathbf{x}_i$, $\forall \mathbf{r}$, of the data. Expanding the r.h.s. of Eq. (3) to first order around the fixed point $\{\mathbf{w}_r^0\}$ and assuming $h_{\mathbf{rs}} = h_{\mathbf{sr}}$, $\forall \mathbf{r}, \mathbf{s}$, we obtain the critical value

$$\beta^* = \frac{1}{\lambda_{\max}^{\mathbf{C}} \lambda_{\max}^{\mathbf{G}}} \tag{5}$$

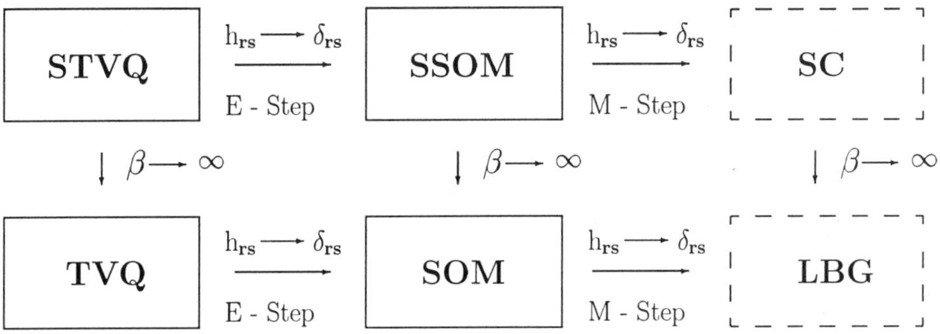

Figure 2: Class of vector quantizers derived from STVQ, together with approximations and limits (see text). The "S" in front stands for "soft" to indicate the probabilistic approach.

for the inverse temperature, at which the center of mass solution becomes unstable. $\lambda_{\max}^{C}$ is the largest eigenvalue of the covariance matrix $C = \frac{1}{D} \sum_i x_i x_i^T$ of the data and corresponds to their variance $\lambda_{\max}^{C} = \sigma_{\max}^2$ along the principal axis which is given by the associated eigenvector $v_{\max}^{C}$ and along which code vectors split. $\lambda_{\max}^{G}$ is the largest eigenvalue of a matrix G whose elements are given by $g_{rt} = \sum_s h_{rs} \left(h_{st} - \frac{1}{N} \right)$. The rth component of the corresponding eigenvector $v_{\max}^{G}$ determines for each code vector w_r in which direction along the principal axis it departs from w_r^0 and how it moves relative to the other code vectors. For SSOM a similar result is obtained with G in Eq. (5) simply being replaced by $G^{SSOM}, g_{rt}^{SSOM} = h_{rt} - \frac{1}{N}$. See (Graepel, 1997) for details.

4 NUMERICAL RESULTS

In the following we consider a binary symmetric channel (BSC) with a bit error rate (BER) ϵ. Assuming that the length of the code indices is n bits, the matrix elements of the transition matrix H are

$$h_{rs} = (1 - \epsilon)^{n - d_H(r,s)} \epsilon^{d_H(r,s)},\qquad(6)$$

where $d_H(r, s)$ is the Hamming-distance between the binary representations of r and s.

4.1 TOY PROBLEM

The numerical analysis of the phase transitions described in the previous section was performed on a toy data set consisting of 2000 data vectors drawn from a two-dimensional elongated Gaussian distribution $P(x) = (2\pi)^{-1} |C|^{-\frac{1}{2}} \exp(-\frac{1}{2} x^T C^{-1} x)$ with diagonal covariance matrix $C = \text{diag}(1, 0.04)$. The size of the codebook was $N = 4$ corresponding to $n = 2$ bits. Figure 3 (left) shows the x-coordinates of the positions of the code vectors in data space as functions of the inverse temperature β. At a critical inverse temperature β^* the code vectors split along the x-axis which is the principal axis of the distribution of data points. In accordance with the eigenvector $v_{\max}^{G} = (1, 0, 0, -1)^T$ for the largest eigenvalue $\lambda_{\max}^{G}$ of the matrix G two code vectors with Hamming distance $d_H = 2$ move to opposite positions along the principal axis, and two remain at the center. Note the degeneracy of eigenvalues for matrix (6). Figure 3 (right) shows the critical inverse temperature β^* as a function of the BER for both STVQ (crosses) and SSOM (dots). Results are in very good agreement with the theoretical predictions of Eq. (5) (solid line). The inset displays the average cost $\langle E \rangle = \frac{1}{2} \sum_i \sum_r P(x_i \in r) \sum_s h_{rs} \|x_i - w_s\|^2$ as a function of β for

$\epsilon = 0.08$ for STVQ and SSOM. The drop of the average cost occurs at the critical inverse temperature β^*.

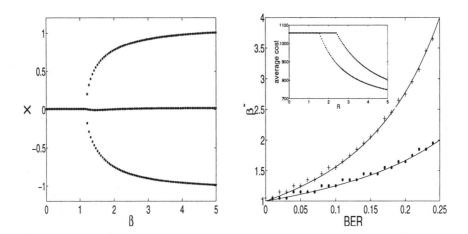

Figure 3: Phase transitions in the 2 bit "toy" problem. (**left**) X-coordinate of code vectors for the SSOM case plotted vs. inverse temperature β, $\epsilon = 0.08$. The splitting of the four code vectors occurs at $\beta = 1.25$ which is in very good accordance with the theory. (**right**) Critical values of β for SSOM (dots) and STVQ (crosses), determined via the kink in the average cost (inset: $\epsilon = 0.08$, top line STVQ), which indicates the phase transition. Solid lines denote theoretical predictions. Convergence parameter for the fixed-point iteration, giving the upper limit for the difference in successive code vector positions per dimension, was $\delta = 5.0\text{E} - 10$.

4.2   SOURCE CHANNEL CODING FOR IMAGE DATA

In order to demonstrate the applicability of STVQ and in particular of SSOM to source channel coding we employed both algorithms to the compression of image data, which were then sent via a noisy channel and decoded after transmission. As a training set we used three 512×512 pixel 256 gray-value images from different scenes with blocksize $d = 2 \times 2$. The size of the codebook was chosen to be $N = 16$ in order to achieve a compression to 1 bpp. We applied an exponential annealing schedule given by $\beta_{t+1} = 2\,\beta_t$ and determined the start value β_0 to be just below the critical β^* for the first split as given in Eq. (5). Note that with the transition matrix as given in Eq. (6) this optimization corresponds to the embedding of an $n = 4$ dimensional hypercube in the $d = 4$ dimensional data space. We tested the resulting codebooks by encoding our test image Lena[1] (Figure 5), which had not been used for determining the codebook, simulating the transmission of the indices via a noisy binary symmetric channel with given bit error rate and reconstructing the image using the codebook.

The results are summarized in Figure 4 which shows a plot of the signal-to-noise-ratio (SNR) as a function of the bit-error rate for STVQ (dots), SSOM (vertical crosses), and LBG (oblique crosses). STVQ shows the best performance especially for high BERs, where it is naturally far superior to the LBG-algorithm which does not take into account channel noise. SSOM, however, performs only slightly worse (approx. 1 dB) than STVQ. Considering the fact that SSOM is computationally much less demanding than STVQ

---

[1]The Lenna Story can be found at http://www.isr.com/ chuck/lennapg/lenna.shtml

($\mathcal{O}(N)$ for encoding) - due to the omission of the convolution with h_{rs} in Eq. (4) - the result demonstrates the efficiency of SSOM for source channel coding. Figure 4 also shows the generalization behavior of a SSOM codebook optimized for a BER of 0.05 (rectangles). Since this codebook was optimized for $\epsilon = 0.05$ it performs worse than appropriately trained SSOM codebooks for other values of BER, but still performs better than LBG except for low values of BERs. At low values, SSOMs trained for the noisy case are outperformed by LBG because robustness w.r.t. channel noise is achieved at the expense of an optimal data representation in the noise free case. Figure 5, finally, provides a visual impression of the performance of the different vector quantizers at a BER of 0.033. While the reconstruction for STVQ is only slightly better than the one for SSOM, both are clearly superior to the reconstruction for LBG.

Figure 4: Comparison between different vector quantizers for image compression, noisy channel (BSC) transmission and reconstruction. The plot shows the signal-to-noise-ratio (SNR), defined as $10 \log_{10}(\sigma_{signal}/\sigma_{noise})$, as a function of bit-error rate (BER) for STVQ and SSOM, each optimized for the given channel noise, for SSOM, optimized for a BER of 0.05, and for LBG. The training set consisted of three 512×512 pixel 256 gray-value images with blocksize $d = 2 \times 2$. The codebook size was N = 16 corresponding to 1 bpp. The annealing schedule was given by $\beta_{t+1} = 2\beta_t$ and Lena was used as a test image. Convergence parameter δ was $1.0E - 5$.

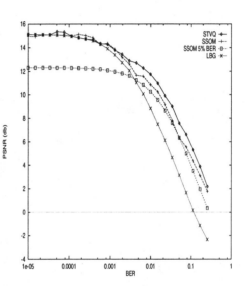

5 CONCLUSION

We presented an algorithm for noisy vector quantization which is based on deterministic annealing (STVQ). Phase transitions in the annealing process were analysed and a whole class of vector quantizers could be derived, includings standard algorithms such as LBG and "soft" versions as special cases of STVQ. In particular, a fuzzy version of Kohonen's SOM was introduced, which is computationally more efficient than STVQ and still yields very good results as demonstrated for noisy vector quantization of image data. The deterministic annealing scheme opens up many new possibilities for the usage of SOMs, in particular, when its neighborhood function represents non-trivial neighborhood relations.

Acknowledgements This work was supported by TU Berlin (FIP 13/41). We thank H. Bartsch for help and advice with regard to the image processing example.

References

J. M. Buhmann and T. Hofmann. *Robust Vector Quantization by Competitive Learning.* Proceedings of ICASSP'97, Munich, (1997).

N. Farvardin. *A Study of Vector Quantization for Noisy Channels.* IEEE Transactions on Information Theory, vol. 36, p. 799-809 (1990).

Figure 5: Lena transmitted over a binary symmetric channel with BER of 0.033 encoded and reconstructed using different vector quantization algorithms.

T. Graepel, M. Burger, and K. Obermayer. *Phase Transitions in Stochastic Self-Organizing Maps.* Physical Review E, vol. 56, no. 4, p. 3876-3890 (1997).

T. Heskes and B. Kappen. *Self-Organizing and Nonparametric Regression.* Artificial Neural Networks - ICANN'95, vol.1,p. 81-86 (1995).

T. Kohonen. *Self-Organizing Maps.* Springer-Verlag, 1995.

S. P. Luttrell. *Self-Organisation: A Derivation from first Principles of a Class of Learning Algorithms.* Proceedings of IJCNN'89, Washington DC, vol. 2, p. 495-498 (1989).

S. P. Luttrell. *A Baysian Analysis of Self-Organizing Maps.* Neural Computation, vol. 6, p. 767-794 (1994).

D. Miller and K. Rose. *Combined Source-Channel Vector Quantization Using Deterministic Annealing.* IEEE Transactions on Communications, vol. 42, p. 347-356 (1994).

K. Rose, E. Gurewitz, and G. C. Fox. *Statistical Mechanics and Phase Transitions in Clustering.* Physical Review Letters, vol. 65, No. 8, p. 945-948 (1990).

Incorporating Test Inputs into Learning

Zehra Cataltepe
Learning Systems Group
Department of Computer Science
California Institute of Technology
Pasadena, CA 91125
zehra@cs.caltech.edu

Malik Magdon-Ismail
Learning Systems Group
Department of Electrical Engineering
California Institute of Technology
Pasadena, CA 91125
magdon@cco.caltech.edu

Abstract

In many applications, such as credit default prediction and medical image recognition, test inputs are available in addition to the labeled training examples. We propose a method to incorporate the test inputs into learning. Our method results in solutions having smaller test errors than that of simple training solution, especially for noisy problems or small training sets.

1 Introduction

We introduce an estimator of test error that takes into consideration the test inputs. The new estimator, augmented error, is composed of the training error and an additional term computed using the test inputs. In some applications, such as credit default prediction and medical image recognition, we do have access to the test inputs. In our experiments, we found that the augmented error (which is computed without looking at the test outputs but only test inputs and training examples) can result in a smaller test error. In particular, it tends to increase when the test error increases (overtraining) even if the simple training error does not. (see figure (1)).

In this paper, we provide an analytic solution for incorporating test inputs into learning in the case of linear, noisy targets and linear hypothesis functions. We also show experimental results for the nonlinear case.

Previous results on the use of unlabeled inputs include Castelli and Cover [2] who show that the labeled examples are exponentially more valuable than unlabeled examples in reducing the classification error. For mixture models, Shahshahani and Landgrebe [7] and Miller and Uyar [6] investigate incorporating unlabeled examples into learning for classification problems and using EM algorithm, and show that unlabeled examples are useful especially when input dimensionality is high and the number of examples is small. In our work we only concentrate on estimating the test error better using the test inputs and our method

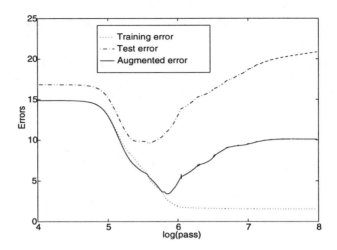

Figure 1: The augmented error, computed not looking at the test outputs at all, follows the test error as overtraining occurs.

extends to the case of unlabeled inputs or input distribution information. Our method is also applicable for regression or classification problems.

In figure 1, we show the training, test and augmented errors, while learning a nonlinear noisy target function with a nonlinear hypothesis. As overtraining occurs, the augmented error follows the test error. In section 2, we explain our method of incorporating test inputs into learning and give the analytical solutions for linear target and hypothesis functions. Section 3 includes theory about the existence and general form of the new solution. Section 4 discusses experimental results. Section 5 extends our solution to the case of knowing the input distribution, or knowing extra inputs that are not necessarily test inputs.

2   Incorporating Test Inputs into Learning

In learning-from-examples, we assume we have a **training set**: $\{(\mathbf{x}_1, f_1), \ldots, (\mathbf{x}_N, f_N)\}$ with inputs $\mathbf{x}_n$ and possibly noisy targets f_n. Our goal is to choose a hypothesis $g_\mathbf{v}$, among a class of hypotheses G, minimizing the test error on an unknown **test set** $\{(\mathbf{y}_1, h_1), \ldots, (\mathbf{y}_M, h_M)\}$.

Using the sample mean square error as our error criterion, the **training error** of hypothesis $g_\mathbf{v}$ is:

$$E_0(g_\mathbf{v}) \;=\; \frac{1}{N} \sum_{n=1}^{N} (g_\mathbf{v}(\mathbf{x}_n) - f_n)^2$$

Similarly the **test error** of $g_\mathbf{v}$ is:

$$E(g_\mathbf{v}) \;=\; \frac{1}{M} \sum_{m=1}^{M} (g_\mathbf{v}(\mathbf{y}_m) - h_m)^2$$

Expanding the test error:

$$E(g_\mathbf{v}) \;=\; \frac{1}{M} \sum_{m=1}^{M} g_\mathbf{v}^2(\mathbf{y}_m) - \frac{2}{M} \sum_{m=1}^{M} g_\mathbf{v}(\mathbf{y}_m) h_m + \frac{1}{M} \sum_{m=1}^{M} h_m^2$$

The main observation is that, when we know the test inputs, we know the first term exactly. Therefore we need only approximate the remaining terms using the training set:

$$E(g_{\mathbf{v}}) \approx \frac{1}{M}\sum_{m=1}^{M} g_{\mathbf{v}}^2(\mathbf{y}_m) - \frac{2}{N}\sum_{n=1}^{N} g_{\mathbf{v}}(\mathbf{x}_n) f_n + \frac{1}{N}\sum_{n=1}^{N} f_n^2 \qquad (1)$$

$$= E_0(g_{\mathbf{v}}) + \frac{1}{M}\sum_{m=1}^{M} g_{\mathbf{v}}^2(\mathbf{y}_m) - \frac{1}{N}\sum_{n=1}^{N} g_{\mathbf{v}}^2(\mathbf{x}_n)$$

We scale the addition to the training error by an **augmentation parameter** α to obtain a more general error function that we call the **augmented error**:

$$E_\alpha(g_{\mathbf{v}}) = E_0(g_{\mathbf{v}}) + \alpha\left(\frac{1}{M}\sum_{m=1}^{M} g_{\mathbf{v}}^2(\mathbf{y}_m) - \frac{1}{N}\sum_{n=1}^{N} g_{\mathbf{v}}^2(\mathbf{x}_n)\right)$$

where $\alpha = 0$ corresponds to the training error E_0 and $\alpha = 1$ corresponds to equation (1).

The best value of the augmentation parameter depends on a number of factors including the target function, the noise distribution and the hypothesis class. In the following sections we investigate properties of the best augmentation parameter and give a method of finding the best augmentation parameter when the hypothesis is linear.

3 Augmented Solution for the Linear Hypothesis

In this section we assume hypothesis functions of the form $g_{\mathbf{v}}(\mathbf{x}) = \mathbf{v}^T\mathbf{x}$. From here onwards we will denote the functions by the vector that multiplies the inputs. When the hypothesis is linear we can find the minimum of the augmented error analytically.

Let $X_{d\times N}$ be the matrix of training inputs, $Y_{d\times M}$ be the matrix of test inputs and $\mathbf{f}_{N\times 1}$ contain the training targets. The solution $\mathbf{w}_0$ minimizing the training error E_0 is the least squares solution [5]: $\mathbf{w}_0 = \left(\frac{XX^T}{N}\right)^{-1}\frac{X\mathbf{f}}{N}$.

The augmented error $E_\alpha(\mathbf{v}) = E_0(\mathbf{v}) + \alpha\mathbf{v}^T\left(\frac{YY^T}{M} - \frac{XX^T}{N}\right)\mathbf{v}$ is minimized at the augmented error $\mathbf{w}_\alpha$:

$$\mathbf{w}_\alpha = (I - \alpha R)^{-1}\mathbf{w}_0 \qquad (2)$$

where $R = I - \left(\frac{XX^T}{N}\right)^{-1}\frac{YY^T}{M}$. When $\alpha = 0$, the augmented solution $\mathbf{w}_\alpha$ is equal to the least mean squares solution $\mathbf{w}_0$.

4 Properties of the Augmentation Parameter

Assume a linear target and possibly noisy training outputs: $\mathbf{f} = \mathbf{w}^{*T}X + \mathbf{e}$ where $\langle\mathbf{e}\mathbf{e}^T\rangle = \sigma_e^2 I_{N\times N}$.

Since the specific realization of noise $\mathbf{e}$ is unknown, instead of minimizing the test error directly, we focus on minimizing $\langle E(\mathbf{w}_\alpha)\rangle_{\mathbf{e}}$, the expected value of the test error of the augmented solution with respect to the noise distribution:

$$\langle E(\mathbf{w}_\alpha)\rangle_{\mathbf{e}} = \mathbf{w}^{*T}\left((I - \alpha R^T)^{-1} - I\right)\frac{YY^T}{M}\left((I - \alpha R)^{-1} - I\right)\mathbf{w}^*$$

$$+ \frac{\sigma_e^2}{N}tr\left((I - \alpha R^T)^{-1}\frac{YY^T}{M}(I - \alpha R)^{-1}\left(\frac{XX^T}{N}\right)^{-1}\right) \qquad (3)$$

where we have used $\langle e^T A e \rangle_e = \sigma_e^2 tr(A)$ and $tr(A)$ denotes the trace of matrix A. When $\alpha = 0$, we have:

$$\langle E(\mathbf{w}_0) \rangle_{\mathbf{e}} \;=\; \frac{\sigma_e^2}{N} tr\left(\frac{YY^T}{M} \left(\frac{XX^T}{N} \right)^{-1} \right) \tag{4}$$

Now, we prove the existence of a nonzero augmentation parameter α when the outputs are noisy.

Theorem 1: If $\sigma_e^2 > 0$ and $tr(R(I-R)) \neq 0$, then there is an $\alpha \neq 0$ that minimizes the expected test error $\langle E(\mathbf{w}_\alpha) \rangle_{\mathbf{e}}$.

Proof: Since $\frac{\partial B^{-1}(\alpha)}{\partial \alpha} = -B^{-1}(\alpha) \frac{\partial B(\alpha)}{\partial \alpha} B^{-1}(\alpha)$ for any matrix B whose elements are scalar functions of α [3], the derivative of $\langle E(\mathbf{w}_\alpha) \rangle_{\mathbf{e}}$ with respect to α at $\alpha = 0$ is:

$$\left. \frac{d \langle E(\mathbf{w}_\alpha) \rangle_{\mathbf{e}}}{d\alpha} \right|_{\alpha=0} \;=\; 2 \frac{\sigma_e^2}{N} tr\left(R\left(\frac{XX^T}{N} \right)^{-1} \frac{YY^T}{M} \right) = 2 \frac{\sigma_e^2}{N} tr(R(I-R))$$

If the derivative is < 0 (> 0 respectively), then $\langle E(\mathbf{w}_\alpha) \rangle_{\mathbf{e}}$ is minimized at some $\alpha > 0$ ($\alpha < 0$ respectively). $\square$

The following proposition gives an approximate formula for the best α.

Theorem 2: If N and M are large, and the training and test inputs are drawn i.i.d from an input distribution with covariance matrix $\langle \mathbf{xx}^T \rangle = \sigma_x^2 I$, then the α^* minimizing $\langle E(\mathbf{w}_\alpha) \rangle_{\mathbf{e},\mathbf{x},\mathbf{y}}$, the expected test error of the augmented solution with respect to noise and inputs, is approximately:

$$\alpha^* \approx \frac{d}{N} \frac{\sigma_e^2}{\sigma_x^2 \mathbf{w}^{*T} \mathbf{w}^*} \tag{5}$$

Proof: is given in the appendix. $\square$

This formula determines the behavior of the best α. The best α:

- decreases as the signal-to-noise ratio increases.
- increases as $\frac{d}{N}$ increases, i.e. as we have less examples per input dimension.

4.1 $\mathbf{w}_\alpha$ as an Estimator of $\mathbf{w}^*$

The mean squared error (m.s.e.) of any estimator $\hat{\mathbf{w}}$ of $\mathbf{w}^*$, can be written as [1]:

$$\left\langle ||\mathbf{w}^* - \hat{\mathbf{w}}||^2 \right\rangle_{\mathbf{e}} \;=\; ||\mathbf{w}^* - \langle \hat{\mathbf{w}} \rangle_{\mathbf{e}}||^2 + \left\langle ||\hat{\mathbf{w}} - \langle \hat{\mathbf{w}} \rangle_{\mathbf{e}}||^2 \right\rangle_{\mathbf{e}}$$

$$m.s.e(\hat{\mathbf{w}}) \;=\; bias^2(\hat{\mathbf{w}}) + variance(\hat{\mathbf{w}})$$

When α is independent of the specific realization $\mathbf{e}$ of the noise:

$$m.s.e.(\mathbf{w}_\alpha) \;=\; \mathbf{w}^{*T} \left(I - (I - \alpha R^T)^{-1} \right) \left(I - (I - \alpha R)^{-1} \right) \mathbf{w}^*$$
$$+ \frac{\sigma_e^2}{N} tr\left(\left(\frac{XX^T}{N} \right)^{-1} (I - \alpha R^T)^{-1} (I - \alpha R)^{-1} \right)$$

Hence the *m.s.e.* of the least square estimator $\mathbf{w}_0$ is:

$$m.s.e.(\mathbf{w}_0) \quad = \quad \frac{\sigma_e^2}{N} tr\left(\left(\frac{XX^T}{N}\right)^{-1}\right)$$

$\mathbf{w}_0$ is the minimum variance unbiased linear estimator of $\mathbf{w}^*$. Although $\mathbf{w}_\alpha$ is a biased estimator if $\alpha R \neq 0$, the following proposition shows that, when there is noise, there is an $\alpha \neq 0$ minimizing the *m.s.e.* of $\mathbf{w}_\alpha$:

Theorem 3: If $\sigma_e^2 > 0$ and $tr\left(\left(\frac{XX^T}{N}\right)^{-1}(R + R^T)\right) \neq 0$, then there is an $\alpha \neq 0$ that minimizes the m.s.e. of $\mathbf{w}_\alpha$.

Proof: is similar to the proof of proposition 1 and will be skipped □.

As N and M get large, $R = I - \left(\frac{XX^T}{N}\right)^{-1}\frac{YY^T}{M} \to 0$ and $\mathbf{w}_\alpha = (I - \alpha R)^{-1}\mathbf{w}_0 \to \mathbf{w}_0$. Hence, for large N and M, the bias and variance of $\mathbf{w}_\alpha$ approach 0, making $\mathbf{w}_\alpha$ an unbiased and consistent estimator of $\mathbf{w}^*$.

5 A Method to Find the Best Augmentation Parameter

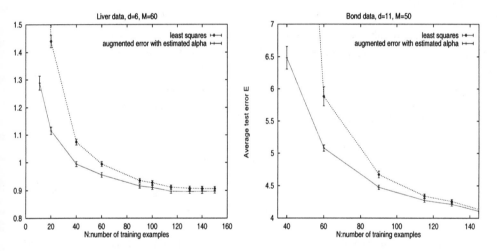

Figure 2: Using the augmented error results in smaller test error especially when the number of training examples is small.

Given only the training and test inputs X and Y, and the training outputs $\mathbf{f}$, in this section we propose a method to find the best α minimizing the test error of $\mathbf{w}_\alpha$.

Equation (3) gives a formula for the expected test error which we want to minimize. However, we do not know the target $\mathbf{w}^*$ and the noise variance σ_e^2. In equation (3), we replace $\mathbf{w}^*$ by $\mathbf{w}_\alpha$ and σ_e^2 by $\frac{(X^T\mathbf{w}_\alpha-\mathbf{f})^T(X^T\mathbf{w}_\alpha-\mathbf{f})}{N-d-1}$, where $\mathbf{w}_\alpha$ is given by equation (2). Then we find the α minimizing the resulting approximation to the expected test error.

We experimented with this method of finding the best α on artificial and real data. The results of experiments for liver data[1] and bond data[2] are shown in figure 2. In the liver

---

[1] ftp://ftp.ics.uci.edu/pub/machine-learning-databases/liver-disorders/bupa.data
[2] We thank Dr. John Moody for providing the bond data.

database the inputs are different blood test results and the output is the number of drinks per day. The bond data consists of financial ratios as inputs and rating of the bond from AAA to B- or lower as the output.

We also compared our method to the least squares ($\mathbf{w}_0$) and early stopping using different validation set sizes for linear and noisy problems. The table below shows the results.

SNR	mean $\frac{E(\mathbf{w}_\alpha)}{E(\mathbf{w}_0)}$	mean $\frac{E(\mathbf{w}_{early\ stop})}{E(\mathbf{w}_0)}, N_v = \frac{N}{3}$	mean $\frac{E(\mathbf{w}_{early\ stop})}{E(\mathbf{w}_0)}, N_v = \frac{N}{6}$
0.01	0.650 ± 0.006	0.126 ± 0.003	0.192 ± 0.004
1	0.830 ± 0.007	1.113 ± 0.021	1.075 ± 0.020
100	1.001 ± 0.002	2.373 ± 0.040	2.073 ± 0.042

Table 1: Augmented solution is consistently better than the least squares whereas early stopping gives worse results as the signal-to-noise ratio (SNR) increases. Even averaging early stopping solutions did not help when SNR = 100 ($\frac{E(\mathbf{w}_{early\ stop})}{E(\mathbf{w}_0)} = 1.245 \pm 0.018$ when $N_v = \frac{N}{3}$ and 1.307 ± 0.021 for $N_v = \frac{N}{6}$). For the results shown, $d = 11$, $N = 30$ training examples were used, N_v is the number of validation examples.

6   Extensions

When the input probability distribution or the covariance matrix of inputs, instead of test inputs are known, $\frac{YY^T}{M}$ can be replaced by $\langle \mathbf{x}\mathbf{x}^T \rangle = \Sigma$ and our methods are still applicable.

If the inputs available are not test inputs but just some extra inputs, they can still be incorporated into learning. Let us denote the extra K inputs $\{\mathbf{z}_1, \ldots, \mathbf{z}_K\}$ by the matrix $Z_{d \times K}$. Then the augmented error becomes:

$$E_\alpha (\mathbf{v}) = E_0 (\mathbf{v}) + \alpha \frac{K}{K + N} \mathbf{v}^T \left(\frac{ZZ^T}{K} - \frac{XX^T}{N} \right) \mathbf{v}$$

The augmented new solution and its expected test error are same as in equations (2) and (3), except we have $R_Z = I - \left(\frac{XX^T}{N} \right)^{-1} \frac{ZZ^T}{K}$ instead of R.

Note that for the linear hypothesis case, the augmented error is not necessarily a regularized version of the training error, because the matrix $\frac{YY^T}{M} - \frac{XX^T}{N}$ is not necessarily a positive definite matrix.

7   Conclusions and Future Work

We have demonstrated a method of incorporating inputs into learning when the target and hypothesis functions are linear, and the target is noisy. We are currently working on extending our method to nonlinear target and hypothesis functions.

Appendix

Proof of Theorem 2: When the spectral radius of αR is less than 1 (α is small and/or N and M are large), we can approximate $(I - \alpha R)^{-1} \approx I + \alpha R$ [4], and similarly, $\left(I - \alpha R^T \right)^{-1} \approx I + \alpha R^T$. Discarding any terms with powers of α greater than 1, and solving for α in $\frac{d\langle E(\mathbf{w}_\alpha)\rangle_{\mathbf{e},\mathbf{x},\mathbf{y}}}{d\alpha} = \left\langle \frac{d\langle E(\mathbf{w}_\alpha)\rangle_{\mathbf{e}}}{d\alpha} \right\rangle_{\mathbf{x},\mathbf{y}} = 0$:

$$\alpha^* \approx \frac{\sigma_e^2}{N} \frac{\langle tr\left(R\left(R - I\right)\right)\rangle_{\mathbf{x},\mathbf{y}}}{\left\langle \mathbf{w}^T \frac{YY^T}{M} R^2 \mathbf{w}\right\rangle_{\mathbf{x},\mathbf{y}}} \approx \frac{\sigma_e^2}{N} \frac{tr\left(\langle R^2 - R\rangle_{\mathbf{x},\mathbf{y}}\right)}{\sigma_x^2 \mathbf{w}^T \langle R^2\rangle_{\mathbf{x},\mathbf{y}} \mathbf{w}}$$

The last step follows since we can write $\frac{YY^T}{M} = \sigma_x^2\left(I + \frac{V_y}{\sqrt{M}}\right)$, $\frac{XX^T}{N} = \sigma_x^2\left(I - \frac{V_x}{\sqrt{N}}\right)$ and $\left(\frac{XX^T}{N}\right)^{-1} = \frac{1}{\sigma_x^2}\left(I + \frac{V_x}{\sqrt{N}} + \frac{V_x^2}{N}\right) + O\left(\frac{1}{N^{1.5}}\right)$ for matrices V_x and V_y such that $\langle V_x\rangle_\mathbf{x} = \langle V_y\rangle_\mathbf{y} = 0$ and $\langle V_x^2\rangle_x$ and $\langle V_y^2\rangle_y$ are constant with respect to N and M. For large M we can approximate $\left\langle \frac{YY^T}{M}R^2\right\rangle_{\mathbf{x},\mathbf{y}} = \sigma_x^2\langle R^2\rangle_{\mathbf{x},\mathbf{y}}$.

Ignoring terms of $O\left(\frac{1}{N^{1.5}}\right)$, $\langle R^2 - R\rangle_{\mathbf{x},\mathbf{y}} = \left\langle 2\frac{V_x^2}{N} + \frac{V_y^2}{M}\right\rangle_{\mathbf{x},\mathbf{y}}$ and $\langle R^2\rangle_{\mathbf{x},\mathbf{y}} = \left\langle \frac{V_x^2}{N} + \frac{V_y^2}{M}\right\rangle_{\mathbf{x},\mathbf{y}}$. It can be shown that $\left\langle \frac{V_x^2}{N}\right\rangle_x = \frac{\lambda}{N}I$ for a constant λ depending on the input distribution. Similarly $\left\langle \frac{V_y^2}{M}\right\rangle_y = \frac{\lambda}{M}I$. Therefore:

$$\alpha^* \approx \frac{d}{N}\frac{\sigma_e^2}{\sigma_x^2\mathbf{w}^T\mathbf{w}}\frac{\frac{2}{N} + \frac{1}{M}}{\frac{1}{N} + \frac{1}{M}} \approx \frac{d}{N}\frac{\sigma_e^2}{\sigma_x^2\mathbf{w}^T\mathbf{w}}$$

□

Acknowledgments

We would like to thank the Caltech Learning Systems Group: Prof. Yaser Abu-Mostafa, Dr. Amir Atiya, Alexander Nicholson, Joseph Sill and Xubo Song for many useful discussions.

References

[1] Bishop, C. (1995) *Neural Networks for Pattern Recognition*, Clarendon Press, Oxford, 1995.

[2] Castelli, V. & Cover T. (1995) On the Exponential Value of Labeled Samples. *Pattern Recognition Letters*, Vol. 16, Jan. 1995, pp. 105-111.

[3] Devijver, P. A. & Kittler, J. (1982) *Pattern Recognition: A Statistical Approach*, pp. 434. Prentice-Hall International, London.

[4] Golub, G. H. & Van Loan C. F. (1993) *Matrix Computations*, The Johns-Hopkins University Press, Baltimore, MD.

[5] Hocking, R. R. (1996) *Methods and Applications of Linear Models*. John Wiley & Sons, NY.

[6] Miller, D. J. & Uyar, S. (1996), A Mixture of Experts Classifier with Learning Based on Both Labeled and Unlabeled Data. In G. Tesauro, D. S. Touretzky and T.K. Leen (eds.), *Advances in Neural Information Processing Systems 9*. Cambridge, MA: MIT Press.

[7] Shahshahani, B. M. & Landgrebe, D. A. (1994) The Effect of Unlabeled Samples in Reducing Small Sample Size Problem and Mitigating the Hughes Phenemenon. *IEEE Transactions on Geoscience and Remote Sensing*, Vol. 32 No. 5, Sept 1994, pp. 1087–1095.

On Efficient Heuristic Ranking of Hypotheses

Steve Chien, Andre Stechert, and Darren Mutz
Jet Propulsion Laboratory, California Institute of Technology
4800 Oak Grove Drive, M/S 525-3660, Pasadena, CA 91109-8099
steve.chien@jpl.nasa.gov, Voice: (818) 306-6144 FAX: (818) 306-6912
Content Areas: Applications (Stochastic Optimization),Model Selection Algorithms

Abstract

This paper considers the problem of learning the ranking of a set
of alternatives based upon incomplete information (e.g., a limited
number of observations). We describe two algorithms for hypothesis ranking and their application for probably approximately correct (PAC) and expected loss (EL) learning criteria. Empirical
results are provided to demonstrate the effectiveness of these ranking procedures on both synthetic datasets and real-world data from
a spacecraft design optimization problem.

1 INTRODUCTION

In many learning applications, the cost of information can be quite high, imposing
a requirement that the learning algorithms glean as much usable information as
possible with a minimum of data. For example:

- In speedup learning, the expense of processing each training example can
  be significant [Tadepalli92].
- In decision tree learning, the cost of using all available training examples
  when evaluating potential attributes for partitioning can be computationally expensive [Musick93].
- In evaluating medical treatment policies, additional training examples imply suboptimal treatment of human subjects.
- In data-poor applications, training data may be very scarce and learning
  as well as possible from limited data may be key.

This paper provides a statistical decision-theoretic framework for the ranking of
parametric distributions. This framework will provide the answers to a wide range
of questions about algorithms such as: how much information is enough? At what
point do we have adequate information to rank the alternatives with some requested
confidence?

The remainder of this paper is structured as follows. First, we describe the hypothesis ranking problem more formally, including definitions for the probably approximately correct (PAC) and expected loss (EL) decision criteria. We then define two algorithms for establishing these criteria for the hypothesis ranking problem – a recursive hypothesis selection algorithm and an adjacency based algorithm. Next, we describe empirical tests demonstrating the effectiveness of these algorithms as well as documenting their improved performance over a standard algorithm from the statistical ranking literature. Finally, we describe related work and future extensions to the algorithms.

2 HYPOTHESIS RANKING PROBLEMS

Hypothesis ranking problems, an extension of hypothesis selection problems, are an abstract class of learning problems where an algorithm is given a set of hypotheses to rank according to *expected utility* over some unknown distribution, where the expected utility must be estimated from training data.

In many of these applications, a system chooses a single alternative and never revisits the decision. However, some systems require the ability to investigate several options (either serially or in parallel), such as in beam search or iterative broadening, where the ranking formulation is most appropriate. Also, as is the case with evolutionary approaches, a system may need to populate future alternative hypotheses on the basis of the ranking of the current population[Goldberg89].

In any hypothesis evaluation problem, always achieving a correct ranking is impossible in practice, because the actual underlying probability distributions are unavailable and there is always a (perhaps vanishingly) small chance that the algorithms will be unlucky because only a finite number of samples can be taken. Consequently, rather than always requiring an algorithm to output a correct ranking, we impose probabilistic criteria on the rankings to be produced. While several families of such requirements exist, in this paper we examine two, the *probably approximately correct* (PAC) requirement from the computational learning theory community [Valiant84] and the *expected loss* (EL) requirement frequently used in decision theory and gaming problems [Russell92].

The expected utility of a hypothesis can be estimated by observing its values over a finite set of training examples. However, to satisfy the PAC and EL requirements, an algorithm must also be able to reason about the potential difference between the estimated and true utilities of each hypotheses. Let U_i be the true expected utility of hypothesis i and let $\hat{U}_i$ be the estimated expected utility of hypothesis i. Without loss of generality, let us presume that the proposed ranking of hypotheses is $U_1 > U_2 >, ..., > U_{k-1} > U_k$. The PAC requirement states that for some user-specified ϵ with probability $1 - \delta$:

$$\bigwedge_{i=1}^{k-1} [(U_i + \epsilon) > MAX(U_{i+1}, ..., U_k)] \tag{1}$$

Correspondingly, let the loss L of selecting a hypothesis H_1 to be the best from a set of k hypotheses $H_1, ..., H_k$ be as follows.

$$L(H_1, \{H_1, ..., H_k\}) = MAX(0, MAX(U_2, ..., U_k) - U_1) \tag{2}$$

and let the loss RL of a ranking $H_1, ..., H_k$ be as follows.

$$RL(H_1, ..., H_k) = \sum_{i=1}^{k-1} L(H_i, \{H_{i+1}, ..., H_k\}) \tag{3}$$

A hypothesis ranking algorithm which obeys the expected loss requirement must produce rankings that on average have less than the requested expected loss bound.

Consider ranking the hypotheses with expected utilities: $U_1 = 1.0, U_2 = 0.95, U_3 = 0.86$. The ranking $U_2 > U_1 > U_3$ is a valid PAC ranking for $\epsilon = 0.06$ but not for $\epsilon = 0.01$ and has an observed loss of $0.05 + 0 = 0.05$.

However, while the confidence in a pairwise comparison between two hypotheses is well understood, it is less clear how to ensure that desired confidence is met in the set of comparisons required for a selection or the more complex set of comparisons required for a ranking. Equation 4 defines the confidence that $U_i + \epsilon > U_j$, when the distribution underlying the utilities is normally distributed with unknown and unequal variances.

$$\gamma = \phi \left((\hat{U}_{i-j} + \epsilon) \frac{\sqrt{n}}{\hat{S}_{i-j}} \right) \tag{4}$$

where ϕ represents the cumulative standard normal distribution function, and n, $\hat{U}_{i-j}$, and $\hat{S}_{i-j}$ are the size, sample mean, and sample standard deviation of the blocked differential distribution, respectively[1].

Likewise, computation of the expected loss for asserting an ordering between a pair of hypotheses is well understood, but the estimation of expected loss for an entire ranking is less clear. Equation 5 defines the expected loss for drawing the conclusion $U_i > U_j$, again under the assumption of normality (see [Chien95] for further details).

$$EL[U_i > U_j] = \frac{\hat{S}_{i-j} e^{-0.5n(\frac{\hat{U}_{i-j}}{\hat{S}_{i-j}})^2}}{\sqrt{2\pi n}} + \frac{\hat{U}_{i-j}}{\sqrt{2\pi}} \int_{-\frac{\hat{U}_{i-j}\sqrt{n}}{\hat{S}_{i-j}}}^{\infty} e^{-0.5z^2} dz \tag{5}$$

In the next two subsections, we describe two interpretations for estimating the likelihood that an overall ranking satisfies the PAC or EL requirements by estimating and combining pairwise PAC errors or EL estimates. Each of these interpretations lends itself directly to an algorithmic implementation as described below.

2.1 RANKING AS RECURSIVE SELECTION

One way to determine a ranking $H_1, ..., H_k$ is to view ranking as recursive selection from the set of remaining candidate hypotheses. In this view, the overall ranking error, as specified by the desired confidence in PAC algorithms and the loss threshhold in EL algorithms, is first distributed among $k - 1$ *selection errors* which are then further subdivided into *pairwise comparison errors*. Data is then sampled until the estimates of the pairwise comparison error (as dictated by equation 4 or 5) satisfy the bounds set by the algorithm.

Thus, another degree of freedom in the design of recursive ranking algorithms is the method by which the overall ranking error is ultimately distributed among individual pairwise comparisons between hypotheses. Two factors influence the way in which we compute error distribution. First, our model of error combination determines how the error allocated for individual comparisons or selections combines into overall ranking error and thus how many candidates are available as targets for the distribution. Using Bonferroni's inequality, one combine errors additively, but a more conservative approach might be to assert that because the predicted "best" hypothesis may change during sampling in the worst case the conclusion might depend on all possible pairwise comparisons and thus the error should be distributed among all $\binom{n}{2}$ pairs of hypotheses[2]).

---

[1]Note that in our approach we *block* examples to further reduce sampling complexity. Blocking forms estimates by using the difference in utility between competing hypotheses on each observed example. Blocking can significantly reduce the variance in the data when the hypotheses are not independent. It is trivial to modify the formulas to address the cases in which it is not possible to block data (see [Moore94, Chien95] for further details).

[2]For a discussion of this issue, see pp. 18-20 of [Gratch93].

Second, our policy with respect to allocation of error among the candidate comparisons or selections determines how samples will be distributed. For example, in some contexts, the consequences of early selections far outweigh those of later selections. For these scenarios, we have implemented ranking algorithms that divide overall ranking error unequally in favor of earlier selections[3]. Also, it is possible to divide selection error into pairwise error unequally based on estimates of hypothesis parameters in order to reduce sampling cost (for example, [Gratch94] allocates error rationally).

Within the scope of this paper, we only consider algorithms that: (1) combine pairwise error into selection error additively, (2) combine selection error into overall ranking error additively and (3) allocate error equally at each level.

One disadvantage of recursive selection is that once a hypothesis has been selected, it is removed from the pool of candidate hypotheses. This causes problems in rare instances when, while sampling to increase the confidence of some later selection, the estimate for a hypothesis' mean changes enough that some previously selected hypothesis no longer dominates it. In this case, the algorithm is restarted taking into account the data sampled so far.

These assumptions result in the following formulations (where $\delta(U_1 \rhd_\epsilon \{U_2, ..., U_k\})$ is used to denote the error due to the action of selecting hypothesis 1 under Equation 1 from the set $\{H_1, ..., H_k\}$ and $\delta(U_1 \rhd \{U_2, ..., U_k\})$ denotes the error due to selection loss in situations where Equation 2 applies):

$$\begin{aligned} \delta_{rec}(U_1 > U_2 > ... > U_k) = \ & \delta_{rec}(U_2 > U_3 > ... > U_k) \\ & +\delta(U_1 \rhd_\epsilon \{U_2, ..., U_k\}) \end{aligned} \tag{6}$$

where $\delta_{rec}(U_k) = 0$ (the base case for the recursion) and the selection error is as defined in [Chien95]:

$$\delta(U_1 \rhd_\epsilon \{U_2, ..., U_k\}) = \sum_{i=2}^{k} \delta_{1,i} \tag{7}$$

using Equation 4 to compute pairwise confidence.

Algorithmically, we implement this by:

1. sampling a default number of times to seed the estimates for each hypothesis mean and variance,
2. allocating the error to selection and pairwise comparisons as indicated above,
3. sampling until the desired confidences for successive selections is met, and
4. restarting the algorithm if any of the hypotheses means changed significantly enough to change the overall ranking.

An analogous recursive selection algorithm based on expected loss is defined as follows.

$$\begin{aligned} EL_{rec}(U_1 > U_2 > ... > U_k) = \ & EL_{rec}(U_2 > U_3 > ... > U_k) \\ & +EL(U_1 \rhd \{U_2, ..., U_k\}) \end{aligned} \tag{8}$$

where $EL_{rec}(U_k) = 0$ and the selection EL is as defined in [Chien95]:

$$EL(U_1 \rhd \{U_2, ..., U_k\}) = \sum_{i=2}^{k} EL(U_1, U_i) \tag{9}$$

---

[3]Space constraints preclude their description here.

2.2   RANKING BY COMPARISON OF ADJACENT ELEMENTS

Another interpretation of ranking confidence (or loss) is that only adjacent elements in the ranking need be compared. In this case, the overall ranking error is divided directly into $k-1$ pairwise comparison errors. This leads to the following confidence equation for the PAC criteria:

$$\delta_{adj}(U_1 > U_2 > ... > U_k) = \sum_{i=1}^{k-1} \delta_{i,i+1} \tag{10}$$

And the following equation for the EL criteria.

$$EL_{adj}(U_1 > U_2 > ... > U_k) = \sum_{i=1}^{k-1} EL(U_i, U_{i+1}) \tag{11}$$

Because ranking by comparison of adjacent hypotheses does not establish the dominance between non-adjacent hypotheses (where the hypotheses are ordered by observed mean utility), it has the advantage of requiring fewer comparisons than recursive selection (and thus may require fewer samples than recursive selection). However, for the same reason, adjacency algorithms may be less likely to correctly bound probability of correct selection (or average loss) than the recursive selection algorithms. In the case of the PAC algorithms, this is because ϵ-dominance is not necessarily transitive. In the case of the EL algorithms, it is because expected loss is not additive when considering two hypothesis relations sharing a common hypothesis. For instance, the size of the blocked differential distribution may be different for each of the pairs of hypotheses being compared.

2.3   OTHER RELEVANT APPROACHES

Most standard statistical ranking/selection approaches make strong assumptions about the form of the problem (e.g., the variances associated with underlying utility distribution of the hypotheses might be assumed known and equal). Among these, Turnbull and Weiss [Turnbull84] is most comparable to our PAC-based approach[4]. Turnbull and Weiss treat hypotheses as normal random variables with unknown mean and unknown and unequal variance. However, they make the additional stipulation that hypotheses are independent. So, while it is still reasonable to use this approach when the candidate hypotheses are not independent, excessive statistical error or unnecessarily large training set sizes may result.

3   EMPIRICAL PERFORMANCE EVALUATION

We now turn to empirical evaluation of the hypothesis ranking techniques on real-world datasets. This evaluation serves three purposes. First, it demonstrates that the techniques perform as predicted (in terms of bounding the probability of incorrect selection or expected loss). Second, it validates the performance of the techniques as compared to standard algorithms from the statistical literature. Third, the evaluation demonstrates the robustness of the new approaches to real-world hypothesis ranking problems.

An experimental trial consists of solving a hypothesis ranking problem with a given technique and a given set of problem and control parameters. We measure performance by (1) how well the algorithms satisfy their respective criteria; and (2) the number of samples taken. Since the performance of these statistical algorithms on any single trial provides little information about their overall behavior, each trial is repeated multiple times and the results are averaged across 100 trials. Because

---

[4]PAC-based approaches have been investigated extensively in the statistical ranking and selection literature under the topic of *confidence interval based* algorithms (see [Haseeb85] for a review of the recent literature).

Table 1: Estimated expected total number of observations to rank DS-2 spacecraft designs. Achieved probability of correct ranking is shown in parenthesis.

k	$\gamma^{\bullet}$	$\frac{\sigma}{\epsilon}$	TURNBULL	PAC_{rec}	PAC_{adj}
10	0.75	2	534 (0.96)	144 (1.00)	92 (0.98)
10	0.90	2	667 (0.98)	160 (1.00)	98 (1.00)
10	0.95	2	793 (0.99)	177 (1.00)	103 (0.99)

Table 2: Estimated expected total number of observations and expected loss of an incorrect ranking of DS-2 penetrator designs.

Parameters		EL_{rec}		EL_{adj}	
k	$H^{\bullet}$	Samples	Loss	Samples	Loss
10	0.10	152	0.005	77	0.014
10	0.05	200	0.003	90	0.006
10	0.02	378	0.003	139	0.003

the PAC and expected loss criteria are not directly comparable, the approaches are analyzed separately.

Experimental results from synthetic datasets are reported in [Chien97]. The evaluation of our approach on artificially generated data is used to show that: (1) the techniques correctly bound probability of incorrect ranking and expected loss as predicted when the underlying assumptions are valid even when the underlying utility distributions are inherently hard to rank, and (2) that the PAC techniques compare favorably to the algorithm of Turnbull and Weiss in a wide variety of problem configurations.

The test of real-world applicability is based on data drawn from an actual NASA spacecraft design optimization application. This data provides a strong test of the applicability of the techniques in that all of the statistical techniques make some form of normality assumption - yet the data in this application is highly non-normal.

Tables 1 and 2 show the results of ranking 10 penetrator designs using the PAC-based, Turnbull, and expected loss algorithms In this problem the utility function is the depth of penetration of the penetrator, with those cases in which the penetrator does not penetrate being assigned zero utility. As shown in Table 1, both PAC algorithms significantly outperformed the Turnbull algorithm, which is to be expected because the hypotheses are somewhat correlated (via impact orientations and soil densities). Table 2 shows that the EL_{rec} expected loss algorithm effectively bounded actual loss but the EL_{adj} algorithm was inconsistent.

4   DISCUSSION AND CONCLUSIONS

There are a number of areas of related work. First, there has been considerable analysis of hypothesis selection problems. Selection problems have been formalized using a Bayesian framework [Moore94, Rivest88] that does not require an initial sample, but uses a rigorous encoding of prior knowledge. Howard [Howard70] also details a Bayesian framework for analyzing learning cost for selection problems. If one uses a hypothesis selection framework for ranking, allocation of pairwise errors can be performed rationally [Gratch94]. Reinforcement learning work [Kaelbling93] with immediate feedback can also be viewed as a hypothesis selection problem.

In summary, this paper has described the hypothesis ranking problem, an extension to the hypothesis selection problem. We defined the application of two decision criteria, *probably approximately correct* and *expected loss*, to this problem. We then defined two families of algorithms, recursive selection and adjacency, for solution of hypothesis ranking problems. Finally, we demonstrated the effectiveness of these algorithms on both synthetic and real-world datasets, documenting improved performance over existing statistical approaches.

References

[Bechhofer54] R.E. Bechhofer, "A Single-sample Multiple Decision Procedure for Ranking Means of Normal Populations with Known Variances," *Annals of Math. Statistics* (25) 1, 1954 pp. 16-39.

[Chien95] S. A. Chien, J. M. Gratch and M. C. Burl, "On the Efficient Allocation of Resources for Hypothesis Evaluation: A Statistical Approach," *IEEE Trans. Pattern Analysis and Machine Intelligence 17 (7)*, July 1995, pp. 652-665.

[Chien97] S. Chien, A. Stechert, and D. Mutz, "Efficiently Ranking Hypotheses in Machine Learning," JPL-D-14661, June 1997. *Available online at http://www-aig.jpl.nasa.gov/public/www/pas-bibliography.html*

[Goldberg89] D. Goldberg, Genetic Algorithms in Search, Optimization and Machine Learning, Add. Wes., 1989.

[Govind81] Z. Govindarajulu, "The Sequential Statistical Analysis," American Sciences Press, Columbus, OH, 1981.

[Gratch92] J. Gratch and G. DeJong, "COMPOSER: A Probabilistic Solution to the Utility Problem in Speed-up Learning," Proc. AAAI92, San Jose, CA, July 1992, pp. 235-240.

[Gratch93] J. Gratch, "COMPOSER: A Decision-theoretic Approach to Adaptive Problem Solving," Tech. Rep. UIUCDCS-R-93-1806, Dept. Comp. Sci., Univ. Illinois, May 1993.

[Gratch94] J. Gratch, S. Chien, and G. DeJong, "Improving Learning Performance Through Rational Resource Allocation," Proc. AAAI94, Seattle, WA, August 1994, pp. 576-582.

[Greiner92] R. Greiner and I. Jurisica, "A Statistical Approach to Solving the EBL Utility Problem," Proc. AAAI92, San Jose, CA, July 1992, pp. 241-248.

[Haseeb85] R. M. Haseeb, *Modern Statistical Selection*, Columbus, OH: Am. Sciences Press, 1985.

[Hogg78] R. V. Hogg and A. T. Craig, Introduction to Mathematical Statistics, Macmillan Inc., London, 1978.

[Howard70] R. A. Howard, Decision Analysis: Perspectives on Inference, Decision, and Experimentation," Proceedings of the IEEE 58, 5 (1970), pp. 823-834.

[Kaelbling93] L. P. Kaelbling, Learning in Embedded Systems, MIT Press, Cambridge, MA, 1993.

[Minton88] S. Minton, Learning Search Control Knowledge: An Explanation-Based Approach, Kluwer Academic Publishers, Norwell, MA, 1988.

[Moore94] A. W. Moore and M. S. Lee, "Efficient Algorithms for Minimizing Cross Validation Error," Proc. ML94, New Brunswick, MA, July 1994.

[Musick93] R. Musick, J. Catlett and S. Russell, "Decision Theoretic Subsampling for Induction on Large Databases," Proc. ML93, Amhert, MA, June 1993, pp. 212-219.

[Rivest88] R. L. Rivest and R. Sloan, A New Model for Inductive Inference," Proc. 2nd Conference on Theoretical Aspects of Reasoning about Knowledge, 1988.

[Russell92] S. Russell and E. Wefald, Do the Right Thing: Studies in Limited Rationality, MIT Press, MA.

[Tadepalli92] P. Tadepalli, "A theory of unsupervised speedup learning," Proc. AAAI92,, pp. 229-234.

[Turnbull84] Turnbull and Weiss, "A class of sequential procedures for k-sample problems concerning normal means with unknown unequal variances," in *Design of Experiments: ranking and selection*, T. J. Santner and A. C. Tamhane (eds.), Marcel Dekker, 1984.

[Valiant84] L. G. Valiant, "A Theory of the Learnable," Communications of the ACM 27, (1984), pp. 1134-1142.

Learning to Order Things

William W. Cohen   Robert E. Schapire   Yoram Singer
AT&T Labs, 180 Park Ave., Florham Park, NJ 07932
{wcohen,schapire,singer}@research.att.com

Abstract

There are many applications in which it is desirable to order rather than classify instances. Here we consider the problem of learning how to order, given feedback in the form of preference judgments, i.e., statements to the effect that one instance should be ranked ahead of another. We outline a two-stage approach in which one first learns by conventional means a *preference function*, of the form PREF(u, v), which indicates whether it is advisable to rank u before v. New instances are then ordered so as to maximize agreements with the learned preference function. We show that the problem of finding the ordering that agrees best with a preference function is NP-complete, even under very restrictive assumptions. Nevertheless, we describe a simple greedy algorithm that is guaranteed to find a good approximation. We then discuss an on-line learning algorithm, based on the "Hedge" algorithm, for finding a good linear combination of ranking "experts." We use the ordering algorithm combined with the on-line learning algorithm to find a combination of "search experts," each of which is a domain-specific query expansion strategy for a WWW search engine, and present experimental results that demonstrate the merits of our approach.

1 Introduction

Most previous work in inductive learning has concentrated on learning to classify. However, there are many applications in which it is desirable to order rather than classify instances. An example might be a personalized email filter that gives a priority ordering to unread mail. Here we will consider the problem of learning how to construct such orderings, given feedback in the form of *preference judgments*, i.e., statements that one instance should be ranked ahead of another.

Such orderings could be constructed based on a learned classifier or regression model, and in fact often are. For instance, it is common practice in information retrieval to rank documents according to their estimated probability of relevance to a query based on a learned classifier for the concept "relevant document." An advantage of learning orderings directly is that preference judgments can be much easier to obtain than the labels required for classification learning.

For instance, in the email application mentioned above, one approach might be to rank messages according to their estimated probability of membership in the class of "urgent" messages, or by some numerical estimate of urgency obtained by regression. Suppose, however, that a user is presented with an ordered list of email messages, and elects to read the third message first. Given this election, it is not necessarily the case that message three is urgent, nor is there sufficient information to estimate any numerical urgency measures; however, it seems quite reasonable to infer that message three should have been ranked ahead of the others. Thus, in this setting, obtaining preference information may be easier and more natural than obtaining the information needed for classification or regression.

In the remainder of this paper, we will investigate the following two-stage approach to learning how to order. In stage one, we learn a *preference function*, a two-argument function $\text{PREF}(u, v)$ which returns a numerical measure of how certain it is that u should be ranked before v. In stage two, we use the learned preference function to order a set of new instances U; to accomplish this, we evaluate the learned function $\text{PREF}(u, v)$ on all pairs of instances $u, v \in U$, and choose an ordering of U that agrees, as much as possible, with these pairwise preference judgments. This general approach is novel; for related work in various fields see, for instance, references [2, 3, 1, 7, 10].

As we will see, given an appropriate feature set, learning a preference function can be reduced to a fairly conventional classification learning problem. On the other hand, finding a total order that agrees best with a preference function is NP-complete. Nevertheless, we show that there is an efficient greedy algorithm that always finds a good approximation to the best ordering. After presenting these results on the complexity of ordering instances using a preference function, we then describe a specific algorithm for learning a preference function. The algorithm is an on-line weight allocation algorithm, much like the weighted majority algorithm [9] and Winnow [8], and, more directly, Freund and Schapire's [4] "Hedge" algorithm. We then present some experimental results in which this algorithm is used to combine the results of several "search experts," each of which is a domain-specific query expansion strategy for a WWW search engine.

2 Preliminaries

Let X be a set of instances (possibly infinite). A *preference function* PREF is a binary function $\text{PREF} : X \times X \to [0, 1]$. A value of $\text{PREF}(u, v)$ which is close to 1 or 0 is interpreted as a strong recommendation that u should be ranked before v. A value close to $1/2$ is interpreted as an abstention from making a recommendation. As noted above, the hypothesis of our learning system will be a preference function, and new instances will be ranked so as to agree as much as possible with the preferences predicted by this hypothesis.

In standard classification learning, a hypothesis is constructed by combining primitive features. Similarly, in this paper, a preference function will be a combination of other preference functions. In particular, we will typically assume the availability of a set of N primitive preference functions $R_1, \ldots, R_N$. These can then be combined in the usual ways, e.g., with a boolean or linear combination of their values; we will be especially interested in the latter combination method.

It is convenient to assume that the R_i's are well-formed in certain ways. To this end, we introduce a special kind of preference function called a *rank ordering*. Let S be a totally ordered set[1] with '$>$' as the comparison operator. An *ordering function into* S is a function $f : X \to S$. The function f induces the preference function R_f, defined as

$$R_f(u, v) \stackrel{\text{def}}{=} \begin{cases} 1 & \text{if } f(u) > f(v) \\ 0 & \text{if } f(u) < f(v) \\ \frac{1}{2} & \text{otherwise.} \end{cases}$$

We call R_f a *rank ordering for* X *into* S. If $R_f(u, v) = 1$, then we say that u is preferred to v, or u is ranked higher than v.

It is sometimes convenient to allow an ordering function to "abstain" and not give a preference for a pair u, v. Let ϕ be a special symbol not in S, and let f be a function into $S \cup \{\phi\}$. We will interpret the mapping $f(u) = \phi$ to mean that u is "unranked," and let $R_f(u, v) = \frac{1}{2}$ if either u or v is unranked.

To give concrete examples of rank ordering, imagine learning to order documents based on the words that they contain. To model this, let X be the set of all documents in a repository,

---

[1]That is, for all pairs of distinct elements $s_1, s_2 \in S$, either $s_1 < s_2$ or $s_1 > s_2$.

and for N words $w_1, \ldots, w_N$, let $f_i(u)$ be the number of occurrences of w_i in u. Then R_{f_i} will prefer u to v whenever w_i occurs more often in u than v. As a second example, consider a meta-search application in which the goal is to combine the rankings of several WWW search engines. For N search engines $e_1, \ldots, e_N$, one might define f_i so that R_{f_i} prefers u to v whenever u is ranked ahead of v in the list L_i produced by the corresponding search engine. To do this, one could let $f_i(u) = -k$ for the document u appearing in the k-th position in the list L_i, and let $f_i(u) = \phi$ for any document not appearing in L_i.

3   Ordering instances with a preference function

We now consider the complexity of finding the total order that agrees best with a learned preference function. To analyze this, we must first quantify the notion of agreement between a preference function PREF and an ordering. One natural notion is the following: Let X be a set, PREF be a preference function, and let ρ be a total ordering of X, expressed again as an ordering function (i.e., $\rho(u) > \rho(v)$ iff u precedes v in the order). We define AGREE(ρ, PREF) to be the sum of PREF(u, v) over all pairs u, v such that u is ranked ahead of v by ρ:

$$\text{AGREE}(\rho, \text{PREF}) = \sum_{u,v:\rho(u)>\rho(v)} \text{PREF}(u, v). \qquad (1)$$

Ideally, one would like to find a ρ that maximizes AGREE(ρ, PREF). This general optimization problem is of little interest since in practice, there are many constraints imposed by learning: for instance PREF must be in some restricted class of functions, and will generally be a combination of relatively well-behaved preference functions R_i. A more interesting question is whether the problem remains hard under such constraints.

The theorem below gives such a result, showing that the problem is NP-complete even if PREF is restricted to be a linear combination of rank orderings. This holds even if all the rank orderings map into a set S with only three elements, one of which may or may not be ϕ. (Clearly, if S consists of more than three elements then the problem is still hard.)

Theorem 1 *The following decision problem is NP-complete:*

Input: *A rational number κ; a set X; a set S with $|S| \geq 3$; a collection of N ordering functions $f_i : X \to S$; and a preference function* PREF *defined as* PREF$(u, v) = \sum_{i=1}^{N} w_i R_{f_i}(u, v)$ *where* $\mathbf{w} = (w_1, \ldots, w_N)$ *is a weight vector in $[0, 1]^N$ with $\sum_{i=1}^{N} w_i = 1$.*

Question: *Does there exist a total order ρ such that* AGREE$(\rho, \text{PREF}) \geq \kappa$?

The proof (omitted) is by reduction from CYCLIC-ORDERING [5, 6].

Although this problem is hard when $|S| \geq 3$, it becomes tractable for linear combinations of rank orderings into a set S of size two. In brief, suppose one is given X, S and PREF as in Theorem 1, save that S is a two-element set, which we assume without loss of generality to be $S = \{0, 1\}$. Now define $\rho(u) = \sum_i w_i f_i(u)$. It can be shown that the total order defined by ρ maximizes AGREE(ρ, PREF). (In case of a tie, $\rho(u) = \rho(v)$ for distinct u and v, ρ defines only a partial order. The claim still holds in this case for any total order which is consistent with this partial order.)   Of course, when $|S| = 2$, the rank orderings are really only binary classifiers. The fact that this special case is tractable underscores the fact that manipulating orderings can be computationally more difficult than performing the corresponding operations on binary classifiers.

Theorem 1 implies that we are unlikely to find an efficient algorithm that finds the optimal total order for a weighted combination of rank orderings. Fortunately, there do exist efficient algorithms for finding an *approximately* optimal total order. Figure 1 summarizes a greedy

Algorithm Order-By-Preferences
Inputs: an instance set X; a preference function PREF
Output: an approximately optimal ordering function $\hat{\rho}$
let $V = X$
for each $v \in V$ **do** $\pi(v) = \sum_{u \in V} \text{PREF}(v, u) - \sum_{u \in V} \text{PREF}(u, v)$
while V is non-empty **do**
    let $t = \arg \max_{u \in V} \pi(u)$
    let $\hat{\rho}(t) = |V|$
    $V = V - \{t\}$
    for each $v \in V$ **do** $\pi(v) = \pi(v) + \text{PREF}(t, v) - \text{PREF}(v, t)$
endwhile

Figure 1: A greedy ordering algorithm

algorithm that produces a good approximation to the best total order, as we will shortly demonstrate. The algorithm is easiest to describe by thinking of PREF as a directed weighted graph where, initially, the set of vertices V is equal to the set of instances X, and each edge $u \to v$ has weight $\text{PREF}(u, v)$. We assign to each vertex $v \in V$ a *potential* value $\pi(v)$, which is the weighted sum of the outgoing edges *minus* the weighted sum of the ingoing edges. That is, $\pi(v) = \sum_{u \in V} \text{PREF}(v, u) - \sum_{u \in V} \text{PREF}(u, v)$. The greedy algorithm then picks some node t that has maximum potential, and assigns it a rank by setting $\hat{\rho}(t) = |V|$, effectively ordering it ahead of all the remaining nodes. This node, together with all incident edges, is then deleted from the graph, and the potential values π of the remaining vertices are updated appropriately. This process is repeated until the graph is empty; notice that nodes removed in subsequent iterations will have progressively smaller and smaller ranks.

The next theorem shows that this greedy algorithm comes within a factor of two of optimal. Furthermore, it is relatively simple to show that the approximation factor of 2 is tight.

Theorem 2 *Let* OPT(PREF) *be the weighted agreement achieved by an optimal total order for the preference function* PREF *and let* APPROX(PREF) *be the weighted agreement achieved by the greedy algorithm. Then* APPROX(PREF) $\geq \frac{1}{2}$OPT(PREF).

4   Learning a good weight vector

In this section, we look at the problem of learning a good linear combination of a set of preference functions. Specifically, we assume access to a set of *ranking experts* which provide us with preference functions R_i of a set of instances. The problem, then, is to learn a preference function of the form $\text{PREF}(u, v) = \sum_{i=1}^{N} w_i R_i(u, v)$. We adopt the on-line learning framework first studied by Littlestone [8] in which the weight w_i assigned to each ranking expert R_i is updated incrementally.

Learning is assumed to take place in a sequence of rounds. On the t-th round, the learning algorithm is provided with a set X^t of instances to be ranked and to a set of N preference functions R_i^t of these instances. The learner may compute $R_i^t(u, v)$ for any and all preference functions R_i^t and pairs $u, v \in X^t$ before producing a final ordering ρ_t of X^t. Finally, the learner receives feedback from the environment. We assume that the feedback is an arbitrary set of assertions of the form "u should be preferred to v." That is, formally we regard the feedback on the t-th round as a set F^t of pairs (u, v) indicating such preferences.

The algorithm we propose for this problem is based on the "weighted majority algorithm" [9] and, more directly, on the "Hedge" algorithm [4]. We define the *loss* of a preference function

Allocate Weights for Ranking Experts
Parameters:
$\beta \in [0, 1]$, initial weight vector $\mathbf{w}^1 \in [0, 1]^N$ with $\sum_{i=1}^N w_i^1 = 1$
N ranking experts, number of rounds T
Do for $t = 1, 2, \ldots, T$

1. Receive a set of elements X^t and preference functions $R_1^t, \ldots, R_N^t$.

2. Use algorithm Order-By-Preferences to compute ordering function $\hat{\rho}_t$ which approximates $\text{PREF}_t(u, v) = \sum_{i=1}^N w_i R_i^t(u, v)$.

3. Order X^t using $\hat{\rho}_t$.

4. Receive feedback F^t from the user.

5. Evaluate losses $\text{Loss}(R_i^t, F^t)$ as defined in Eq. (2).

6. Set the new weight vector $w_i^{t+1} = w_i^t \cdot \beta^{\text{Loss}(R_i^t, F^t)} / Z_t$ where Z_t is a normalization constant, chosen so that $\sum_{i=1}^N w_i^{t+1} = 1$.

Figure 2: The on-line weight allocation algorithm.

R with respect to the user's feedback F as

$$\text{Loss}(R, F) \overset{\text{def}}{=} \frac{\sum_{(u,v) \in F} (1 - R(u, v))}{|F|}. \tag{2}$$

This loss has a natural probabilistic interpretation. If R is viewed as a randomized prediction algorithm that predicts that u will precede v with probability $R(u, v)$, then $\text{Loss}(R, F)$ is the probability of R disagreeing with the feedback on a pair (u, v) chosen uniformly at random from F.

We now can use the Hedge algorithm almost verbatim, as shown in Figure 2. The algorithm maintains a positive weight vector whose value at time t is denoted by $\mathbf{w}^t = (w_1^t, \ldots, w_N^t)$. If there is no prior knowledge about the ranking experts, we set all initial weights to be equal so that $w_i^1 = 1/N$. The weight vector $\mathbf{w}^t$ is used to combine the preference functions of the different experts to obtain the preference function $\text{PREF}_t = \sum_{i=1}^N w_i^t R_i^t$. This, in turn, is converted into an ordering $\hat{\rho}_t$ on the current set of elements X^t using the method described in Section 3. After receiving feedback F^t, the loss for each preference function $\text{Loss}(R_i^t, F^t)$ is evaluated as in Eq. (2) and the weight vector $\mathbf{w}^t$ is updated using the multiplicative rule $w_i^{t+1} = w_i^t \cdot \beta^{Loss(R_i^t, F^t)} / Z_t$ where $\beta \in [0, 1]$ is a parameter, and Z_t is a normalization constant, chosen so that the weights sum to one after the update. Thus, based on the feedback, the weights of the ranking experts are adjusted so that experts producing preference functions with relatively large agreement with the feedback are promoted.

We will briefly sketch the theoretical rationale behind this algorithm. Freund and Schapire [4] prove general results about Hedge which can be applied directly to this loss function. Their results imply almost immediately a bound on the cumulative loss of the preference function PREF_t in terms of the loss of the best ranking expert, specifically

$$\sum_{t=1}^T \text{Loss}(\text{PREF}_t, F^t) \leq a_\beta \min_i \sum_{t=1}^T \text{Loss}(R_i^t, F^t) + c_\beta \ln N$$

where $a_\beta = \ln(1/\beta)/(1 - \beta)$ and $c_\beta = 1/(1 - \beta)$. Thus, if one of the ranking experts has low loss, then so will the combined preference function PREF_t.

However, we are not interested in the loss of PREF_t (since it is not an ordering), but rather in the performance of the actual ordering $\hat{\rho}_t$ computed by the learning algorithm. Fortunately, the losses of these can be related using a kind of triangle inequality. It can be shown that, for any PREF, F and ρ:

$$\mathrm{Loss}(R_\rho, F) \leq \frac{\mathrm{DISAGREE}(\rho, \mathrm{PREF})}{|F|} + \mathrm{Loss}(\mathrm{PREF}, F) \tag{3}$$

where, similar to Eq. (1), $\mathrm{DISAGREE}(\rho, \mathrm{PREF}) = \sum_{u,v:\rho(u)>\rho(v)}(1 - \mathrm{PREF}(u,v))$. Not surprisingly, maximizing AGREE is equivalent to minimizing DISAGREE.

So, in sum, we use the greedy algorithm of Section 3 to minimize (approximately) the first term on the right hand side of Eq. (3), and we use the learning algorithm Hedge to minimize the second term.

5   Experimental results for metasearch

We now present some experiments in learning to combine the results of several WWW searches. We note that this problem exhibits many facets that require a general approach such as ours. For instance, approaches that learn to combine similarity scores are not applicable since the similarity scores of WWW search engines are often unavailable.

We chose to simulate the problem of learning a domain-specific search engine. As test cases we picked two fairly narrow classes of queries—retrieving the home pages of machine learning researchers (ML), and retrieving the home pages of universities (UNIV). We obtained a listing of machine learning researchers, identified by name and affiliated institution, together with their home pages, and a similar list for universities, identified by name and (sometimes) geographical location. Each entry on a list was viewed as a query, with the associated URL the sole relevant document.

We then constructed a series of special-purpose "search experts" for each domain. These were implemented as query expansion methods which converted a name, affiliation pair (or a name, location pair) to a likely-seeming Altavista query. For example, one expert for the ML domain was to search for all the words in the person's name plus the words "machine" and "learning," and to further enforce a strict requirement that the person's last name appear. Overall we defined 16 search experts for the ML domain and 22 for the UNIV domain. Each search expert returned the top 30 ranked documents. In the ML domain there were 210 searches for which at least one search expert returned the named home page; for the UNIV domain, there were 290 such searches.

For each query t, we first constructed the set X^t consisting of all documents returned by all of the expanded queries defined by the search experts. Next, each search expert i computed a preference function R_i^t. We chose these to be rank orderings defined with respect to an ordering function f_i^t in the natural way: We assigned a rank of $f_i^t = 30$ to the first listed document, $f_i = 29$ to the second-listed document, and so on, finally assigning a rank of $f_i = 0$ to every document not retrieved by the expanded query associated with expert i.

To encode feedback, we considered two schemes. In the first we simulated complete relevance feedback—that is, for each query, we constructed feedback in which the sole relevant document was preferred to all other documents. In the second, we simulated the sort of feedback that could be collected from "click data," i.e., from observing a user's interactions with a metasearch system. For each query, after presenting a ranked list of documents, we noted the rank of the one relevant document. We then constructed a feedback ranking in which the relevant document is preferred to all preceding documents. This would correspond to observing which link the user actually followed, and making the assumption that this link was preferred to previous links.

To evaluate the expected performance of a fully-trained system on novel queries in this domain, we employed leave-one-out testing. For each query q, we removed q from the

	ML Domain				University Domain			
	Top 1	Top 10	Top 30	Av. rank	Top 1	Top 10	Top 30	Av. rank
Learned System (Full Feedback)	114	185	198	4.9	111	225	253	7.8
Learned System ("Click Data")	93	185	198	4.9	87	229	259	7.8
Naive	89	165	176	7.7	79	157	191	14.4
Best (Top 1)	**119**	170	184	6.7	**112**	221	247	8.2
Best (Top 10)	114	**182**	190	5.3	111	**223**	249	8.0
Best (Top 30)	97	181	**194**	5.6	111	223	**249**	8.0
Best (Av. Rank)	114	182	190	**5.3**	111	223	249	**8.0**

Table 1: Comparison of learned systems and individual search queries

query set, and recorded the rank of q after training (with $\beta = 0.5$) on the remaining queries. For click data feedback, we recorded the median rank over 100 randomly chosen permutations of the training queries.

We the computed an approximation to average rank by artificially assigning a rank of 31 to every document that was either unranked, or ranked above rank 30. (The latter case is to be fair to the learned system, which is the only one for which a rank greater than 30 is possible.) A summary of these results is given in Table 1, together with some additional data on "top-k performance"—the number of times the correct homepage appears at rank no higher than k. In the table we give the top-k performance (for three values of k) and average rank for several ranking systems: the two learned systems, the naive query (the person or university's name), and the single search expert that performed best with respect to each performance measure. The table illustrates the robustness of the learned systems, which are nearly always competitive with the best expert for every performance measure listed; the only exception is that the system trained on click data trails the best expert in top-k performance for small values of k. It is also worth noting that in both domains, the naive query (simply the person or university's name) is not very effective. Even with the weaker click data feedback, the learned system achieves a 36% decrease in average rank over the naive query in the ML domain, and a 46% decrease in the UNIV domain.

To summarize the experiments, on these domains, the learned system not only performs much better than naive search strategies; it also consistently performs at least as well as, and perhaps slightly better than, any single domain-specific search expert. Furthermore, the performance of the learned system is almost as good with the weaker "click data" training as with complete relevance feedback.

References

[1] D.S. Hochbaum (Ed.). *Approximation Algorithms for NP-hard problems*. PWS Publishing Company, 1997.

[2] O. Etzioni, S. Hanks, T. Jiang, R. M. Karp, O. Madani, and O. Waarts. Efficient information gathering on the internet. In *37th Ann. Symp. on Foundations of Computer Science*, 1996.

[3] P.C Fishburn. *The Theory of Social Choice*. Princeton University Press, Princeton, NJ, 1973.

[4] Y. Freund and R.E. Schapire. A decision-theoretic generalization of on-line learning and an application to boosting. *Journal of Computer and System Sciences*, 1997.

[5] Z. Galil and N. Megido. Cyclic ordering is NP-complete. *Theor. Comp. Sci.*, 5:179–182, 1977.

[6] M.R. Gary and D.S. Johnson. *Computers and Intractibility: A Guide to the Theory of NP-completeness*. W. H. Freeman and Company, New York, 1979.

[7] P.B. Kantor. Decision level data fusion for routing of documents in the TREC3 context: a best case analysis of worste case results. In *TREC-3*, 1994.

[8] N. Littlestone. Learning quickly when irrelevant attributes abound: A new linear-threshold algorithm. *Machine Learning*, 2(4), 1988.

[9] N. Littlestone and M.K. Warmuth. The weighted majority algorithm. *Information and Computation*, 108(2):212–261, 1994.

[10] K.E. Lochbaum and L.A. Streeter. Comparing and combining the effectiveness of latent semantic indexing and the ordinary vector space model for information retrieval. *Information processing and management*, 25(6):665–676, 1989.

Regularisation in Sequential Learning Algorithms

João FG de Freitas
Cambridge University
Engineering Department
Cambridge CB2 1PZ England
jfgf@eng.cam.ac.uk
[**Corresponding author**]

Mahesan Niranjan
Cambridge University
Engineering Department
Cambridge CB2 1PZ England
niranjan@eng.cam.ac.uk

Andrew H Gee
Cambridge University
Engineering Department
Cambridge CB2 1PZ England
ahg@eng.cam.ac.uk

Abstract

In this paper, we discuss regularisation in online/sequential learning algorithms. In environments where data arrives sequentially, techniques such as cross-validation to achieve regularisation or model selection are not possible. Further, bootstrapping to determine a confidence level is not practical. To surmount these problems, a minimum variance estimation approach that makes use of the extended Kalman algorithm for training multi-layer perceptrons is employed. The novel contribution of this paper is to show the theoretical links between extended Kalman filtering, Sutton's variable learning rate algorithms and Mackay's Bayesian estimation framework. In doing so, we propose algorithms to overcome the need for heuristic choices of the initial conditions and noise covariance matrices in the Kalman approach.

1 INTRODUCTION

Model estimation involves building mathematical representations of physical processes using measured data. This problem is often referred to as system identification, time-series modelling or machine learning. In many occasions, the system being modelled varies with time. Under this circumstance, the estimator needs to be updated sequentially. Online or sequential learning has many applications in tracking and surveillance, control systems, fault detection, communications, econometric systems, operations research, navigation and other areas where data sequences are often non-stationary and difficult to obtain before the actual estimation process.

To achieve acceptable generalisation, the complexity of the estimator needs to be judiciously controlled. Although there are various reliable schemes for controlling model complexity when training *en bloc* (batch processing), the same cannot be said about sequential learning. Conventional regularisation techniques cannot be applied simply because there is no data to cross-validate. Consequently, there is ample scope for the design of sequential methods of controlling model complexity.

2 NONLINEAR ESTIMATION

A dynamical system may be described by the following discrete, stochastic state space representation:

$$\mathbf{w}_{k+1} = \mathbf{w}_k + \mathbf{d}_k \tag{1}$$

$$y_k = \mathbf{g}(\mathbf{w}_k, t_k) + v_k \tag{2}$$

where it has been assumed that the model parameters ($\mathbf{w}_k \in \Re^q$) constitute the states of the system, which in our case represent the weights of a multi-layer perceptron (MLP). $\mathbf{g}$ is a nonlinear vector function that may change at each estimation step k, t_k denotes the time at the k-th estimation step and d_k and v_k represent zero mean white noise with covariances given by Q_k and R_k respectively. The noise terms are often called the process noise (d_k) and the measurement noise (v_k). The system measurements are encoded in the output vector $y_k \in \Re^m$.

The estimation problem may be reformulated as having to compute an estimate $\hat{\mathbf{w}}_k$ of the states $\mathbf{w}_k$ using the set of measurements $Y_k = \{y_1, y_2, \cdots, y_k\}$. The estimate $\hat{\mathbf{w}}_k$ can be used to predict future values of the output y. We want $\hat{\mathbf{w}}_k$ to be an unbiased, minimum variance and consistent estimate (Gelb 1984). A minimum variance (unbiased) estimate is one that has its variance less than or equal to that of any other unbiased estimator. Since the variance of the output y depends directly on the variance of the parameter estimates (Åström 1970), the minimum variance framework constitutes a regularisation scheme for sequential learning.

The conditional probability density function of $\mathbf{w}_k$ given Y_k ($p(\mathbf{w}_k|Y_k)$) constitutes the complete solution of the estimation problem (Bar-Shalom and Li 1993, Ho and Lee 1964, Jazwinski 1970). This is simply because $p(\mathbf{w}_k|Y_k)$ embodies all the statistical information about $\mathbf{w}_k$ given the measurements Y_k and the initial condition $\mathbf{w}_0$. This is essentially the Bayesian approach to estimation, where instead of describing a model by a single set of parameters, it is expressed in terms of the conditional probability $p(\mathbf{w}_k|Y_k)$ (Jaynes 1986, Jazwinski 1970). The estimate $\hat{\mathbf{w}}_k$ can be computed from $p(\mathbf{w}_k|Y_k)$ according to several criteria, namely MAP estimation (peak of the posterior), minimum variance estimation (centroid of the posterior) and minimax estimation (median of the posterior).

The Bayesian solution to the optimal estimation problem is (Ho and Lee 1964):

$$p(\mathbf{w}_{k+1}|Y_{k+1}) = \frac{p(\mathbf{w}_{k+1}, y_{k+1}|Y_k)}{p(y_{k+1}|Y_k)}$$

$$= \frac{\int p(y_{k+1}|Y_k, \mathbf{w}_{k+1})p(\mathbf{w}_{k+1}|\mathbf{w}_k)p(\mathbf{w}_k|Y_k)d\mathbf{w}_k}{\int \int p(y_{k+1}|Y_k, \mathbf{w}_{k+1})p(\mathbf{w}_{k+1}|\mathbf{w}_k)p(\mathbf{w}_k|Y_k)d\mathbf{w}_{k+1}d\mathbf{w}_k} \tag{3}$$

where the integrals run over the parameter space. This functional integral difference equation governing the evolution of the posterior density function is not suitable for practical implementation (Bar-Shalom and Li 1993, Jazwinski 1970). It involves propagating a quantity (the posterior density function) that cannot be described by a finite number of parameters. The situation in the linear case is vastly simpler. There the mean and covariance are sufficient statistics for describing the Gaussian posterior density function.

In view of the above statements, it would be desirable to have a framework for non-linear estimation similar to the one for linear-Gaussian estimation. The extended Kalman filter (EKF) constitutes an attempt in this direction (Bar-Shalom and Li 1993, Gelb 1984). The EKF is a minimum variance estimator based on a Taylor series expansion of the nonlinear function $\mathbf{g}(\mathbf{w})$ around the previous estimate. The EKF equations for a linear expansion are given by:

$$K_{k+1} = (P_k + Q_k)G_{k+1}[R_k + G_{k+1}^T(P_k + Q_k)G_{k+1}]^{-1} \qquad (4)$$

$$\hat{\mathbf{w}}_{k+1} = \hat{\mathbf{w}}_k + K_{k+1}(y_{k+1} - G_{k+1}^T\hat{\mathbf{w}}_k) \qquad (5)$$

$$P_{k+1} = P_k + Q_k - K_{k+1}G_{k+1}^T(P_k + Q_k) \qquad (6)$$

where P_k denotes the covariance of the weights. In the general multiple input, multiple output (MIMO) case, $\mathbf{g} \in \Re^m$ is a vector function and G represents the Jacobian of the network outputs with respect to the weights.

The EKF provides a minimum variance Gaussian approximation to the posterior probability density function. In many cases, $p(\mathbf{w}_k|Y_k)$ is a multi-modal (several peaks) function. In this scenario, it is possible to use a committee of Kalman filters, where each individual filter approximates a particular mode, to produce a more accurate approximation (Bar-Shalom and Li 1993, Kadirkamanathan and Kadirkamanathan 1995). The parameter covariances of the individual estimators may be used to determine the contribution of each estimator to the committee. In addition, the parameter covariances serve the purpose of placing confidence intervals on the output prediction.

3   TRAINING MLPs WITH THE EKF

One of the earliest implementations of EKF trained MLPs is due to Singhal and Wu (Singhal and Wu 1988). In their method, the network weights are grouped into a single vector $\mathbf{w}$ that is updated in accordance with the EKF equations. The entries of the Jacobian matrix are calculated by back-propagating the m output values through the network.

The algorithm proposed by Singhal and Wu requires a considerable computational effort. The complexity is of the order mq^2 multiplications per estimation step. Shah, Palmieri and Datum (1992) and Puskorius and Feldkamp (1991) have proposed strategies for decoupling the global EKF estimation algorithm into local EKF estimation sub-problems, thereby reducing the computational time. The EKF is an improvement over conventional MLP estimation techniques, such as back-propagation, in that it makes use of second order statistics (covariances). These statistics are essential for placing error bars on the predictions and for combining separate networks into committees of networks. Further, it has been proven elsewhere that the back-propagation algorithm is simply a degenerate of the EKF algorithm (Ruck, Rogers, Kabrisky, Maybeck and Oxley 1992).

However, the EKF algorithm for training MLPs suffers from serious difficulties, namely choosing the initial conditions $(\mathbf{w}_0, P_0)$ and the noise covariance matrices R and Q. In this work, we propose the use of maximum likelihood techniques, such as back-propagation computed over a small set of initial data, to initialise the

EKF-MLP estimator. The following two subsections· describe ways of overcoming the difficulty of choosing R and Q.

3.1 ELIMINATING Q BY UPDATING P WITH BACK-PROPAGATION

To circumvent the problem of choosing the process noise covariance Q, while at the same time increasing computational efficiency, it is possible to extend an algorithm proposed by Sutton (Sutton 1992) to the nonlinear case. In doing so, the weights co-variance is approximated by a diagonal matrix with entries given by $p_{qq} = \exp(\beta_q)$, where β is updated by error back-propagation (de Freitas, Niranjan and Gee 1997).

The Kalman gain K_k and the weights estimate $\hat{\mathbf{w}}_k$ are updated using a variation of the Kalman equations, where the Kalman gain and weights update equations are independent of Q (Gelb 1984), while the weights covariance P is updated by back-propagation. This algorithm lessens the burden of choosing the matrix Q by only having to choose the learning rate scalar η. The performance of the EKF algorithm with P updated by back-propagation will be analysed in Section 4.

3.2 KALMAN FILTERING AND BAYESIAN TECHNIQUES

A further improvement on the EKF algorithm for training MLPs would be to update R and Q automatically each estimation step. This can be done by borrowing some ideas from the Bayesian estimation field. In particular, we shall attempt to link Mackay's work (Mackay 1992, Mackay 1994) on Bayesian estimation for neural networks with the EKF estimation framework. This theoretical link should serve to enhance both methods.

Mackay expresses the prior, likelihood and posterior density functions in terms of the following Gaussian approximations:

$$p(\mathbf{w}) = \frac{1}{(2\pi)^{q/2}\alpha^{-q/2}} \exp\left(-\frac{\alpha}{2}\|\mathbf{w}\|^2 \right) \tag{7}$$

$$p(Y_k|\mathbf{w}) = \frac{1}{(2\pi)^{n/2}\beta^{-n/2}} \exp\left(-\frac{\beta}{2}\sum_{k=1}^{n}(y_k - \hat{f}_{n,q}(\mathbf{w}, \Phi_k))^2 \right) \tag{8}$$

$$p(\mathbf{w}|Y_k) = \frac{1}{(2\pi)^{q/2}|A|^{-1/2}} \exp\left(-\frac{1}{2}(\mathbf{w} - \mathbf{w}_{MP})^T A(\mathbf{w} - \mathbf{w}_{MP}) \right) \tag{9}$$

where $\hat{f}_{n,q}(\mathbf{w}, \Phi_k)$ represents the estimator and the hyper-parameters α and β control the variance of the prior distribution of weights and the variance of the measurement noise. α also plays the role of the regularisation coefficient. The posterior is obtained by approximating it with a Gaussian function, whose mean $\mathbf{w}_{MP}$ is given by a minimum of the following regularised error function:

$$S(\mathbf{w}) = \frac{\alpha}{2}\|\mathbf{w}\|^2 + \frac{\beta}{2}\sum_{k=1}^{n}(y_k - \hat{f}_{n,q}(\mathbf{w}, \Phi_k))^2 \tag{10}$$

The posterior covariance A is the Hessian of the above error function.

In Mackay's estimation framework, also known as the evidence framework, the parameters $\mathbf{w}$ are obtained by minimising equation (10), while the hyper-parameters α and β are obtained by maximising the evidence $p(Y_k|\alpha,\beta)$ after approximating the posterior density function by a Gaussian function. In doing so, the following recursive formulas for α and β are obtained:

$$\alpha_{k+1} = \frac{\gamma}{\sum_{i=1}^{q} w_i^2} \qquad \text{and} \qquad \beta_{k+1} = \frac{n - \gamma}{\sum_{k=1}^{n}(y_k - \hat{f}_{n,q}(\mathbf{w}_k, \Phi_k))^2}$$

The quantity γ represents the effective number of parameters $\gamma = \sum_{i=1}^{q} \frac{\lambda_i}{\lambda_i + \alpha}$, where the λ_i correspond to the eigenvalues of the Hessian of the error function without the regularisation term.

Instead of adopting Mackay's evidence framework, it is possible to maximise the posterior density function by performing integrations over the hyper-parameters analytically (Buntine and Weigend 1991, Mackay 1994). The latter approach is known as the MAP framework for α and β. The hyper-parameters computed by the MAP framework differ from the ones computed by the evidence framework in that the former makes use of the total number of parameters and not only the effective number of parameters. That is, α and β are updated according to:

$$\alpha_{k+1} = \frac{q}{\sum_{i=1}^{q} w_i^2} \qquad \text{and} \qquad \beta_{k+1} = \frac{n}{\sum_{k=1}^{n} (y_k - \hat{f}_{n,q}(\mathbf{w}_k, \Phi_k))^2}$$

By comparing the equations for the prior, likelihood and posterior density functions in the Kalman filtering framework (Ho and Lee 1964) with equations (7), (8) and (9) we can establish the following relations:

$$P = A^{-1} \; , \qquad\qquad Q = \alpha^{-1} I_q - A^{-1} \qquad \text{and} \qquad R = \beta^{-1} I_m$$

where I_q and I_m represent identity matrices of sizes q and m respectively. Therefore, it is possible to update Q and R sequentially by expressing them in terms of the sequential updates of α and β.

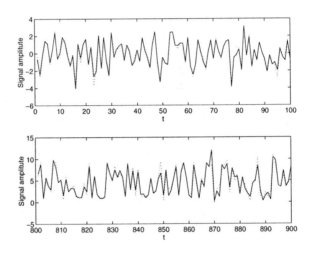

Figure 1: Prediction using the conventional EKF algorithm for a network with 20 hidden neurons. Actual output $[\cdots]$ and estimated output $[—]$.

4   RESULTS

To compare the performance of the conventional EKF algorithm, the EKF algorithm with P updated by back-propagation, and the EKF algorithm with R and Q updated sequentially according to the Bayesian MAP framework, noisy data was generated from the following nonlinear, non-stationary, multivariate process:

$$y(t) = \begin{cases} x_1(t) + x_2(t) + v(t) & 1 \leq t \leq 200 \\ 4\sin(x_1(t)) + x_2(t)\sin(0.03(t-200)) + v(t) & 200 < t \leq 1000 \end{cases}$$

where the inputs x_i are uniformly distributed random sequences with variance equal to 1 and $v(t)$ corresponds to uniformly distributed noise with variance equal to 0.1. Figure 1 shows the prediction obtained using the conventional EKF algorithm. To

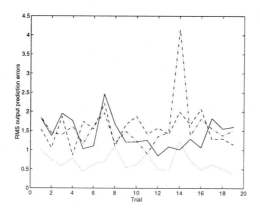

Figure 2: Output error for the conventional EKF algorithm [···], the EKF algorithm with P updated by back-propagation [- . -], the EKF algorithm with R and Q updated sequentially according to the Bayesian MAP framework [—], and the EKF algorithm with the Bayesian evidence framework [- - -].

compare the four estimation frameworks, an MLP with 20 neurons in the hidden layer was selected. The initial conditions were obtained by using back-propagation on the first 100 samples and assigning to P a diagonal matrix with diagonal elements equal to 10. The matrices R and Q in the conventional EKF algorithm were chosen, by trial and error, to be identity matrices. In the EKF algorithm with P updated by back-propagation, R was chosen to be equal to the identity matrix, while the learning rate was set to 0.01. Finally, in the EKF algorithm with R and Q updated sequentially, the initial R and Q matrices were chosen to be identity matrices. The prediction errors obtained for each method with random input data are shown in Figure 2.

It is difficult to make a fair comparison between the four nonlinear estimation methods because their parameters were optimised independently. However, the results suggest that the prediction obtained with the conventional EKF training outperforms the predictions of the other methods. This may be attributed to the facts that, firstly, in this simple problem it is possible to guess the optimal values for R and Q and, secondly, the algorithms to update the noise covariances may affect the regularisation performance of the EKF algorithm. This issue, and possible solutions, is explored in depth by the authors in (de Freitas et al. 1997).

5 Conclusions

In this paper, we point out the links between Kalman filtering, gradient descent algorithms with variable learning rates and Bayesian estimation. This results in two algorithms for eliminating the problem of choosing the initial conditions and the noise covariance matrices in the training of MLPs with the EKF. These algorithms are illustrated on a toy problem here, but more extensive experiments have been reported in (de Freitas et al. 1997).

Improved estimates may be readily obtained by combining the estimators into committees or extending the training methods to recurrent networks. Finally, the computational time may be reduced by decoupling the network weights.

Acknowledgements

João FG de Freitas is financially supported by two University of the Witwatersrand Merit Scholarships, a Foundation for Research Development Scholarship (South Africa) and a Trinity College External Studentship (Cambridge).

References

Åström, K. J. (1970). *Introduction to Stochastic Control Theory*, Academic Press.

Bar-Shalom, Y. and Li, X. R. (1993). *Estimation and Tracking: Principles, Techniques and Software*, Artech House, Boston.

Buntine, W. L. and Weigend, A. S. (1991). Bayesian back-propagation, *Complex Systems* **5**: 603–643.

de Freitas, J., Niranjan, M. and Gee, A. (1997). Hierarchichal Bayesian-Kalman models for regularisation and ARD in sequential learning, *Technical Report CUED/F-INFENG/TR 307*, Cambridge University, http://svr-www.eng.cam.ac.uk/~jfgf.

Gelb, A. (ed.) (1984). *Applied Optimal Estimation*, MIT Press.

Ho, Y. C. and Lee, R. C. K. (1964). A Bayesian approach to problems in stochastic estimation and control, *IEEE Transactions on Automatic Control* **AC-9**: 333–339.

Jaynes, E. T. (1986). Bayesian methods: General background, *in* J. H. Justice (ed.), *Maximum Entropy and Bayesian Methods in Applied Statistics*, Cambridge University Press, pp. 1–25.

Jazwinski, A. H. (1970). *Stochastic Processes and Filtering Theory*, Academic Press.

Kadirkamanathan, V. and Kadirkamanathan, M. (1995). Recursive estimation of dynamic modular RBF networks, *in* D. S. Touretzky, M. C. Mozer and M. E. Hasselmo (eds), *Advances in Neural Information Processing Systems 8*, pp. 239–245.

Mackay, D. J. C. (1992). Bayesian interpolation, *Neural Computation* **4**(3): 415–447.

Mackay, D. J. C. (1994). Hyperparameters: Optimise or integrate out?, *in* G. Heidbreder (ed.), *Maximum Entropy and Bayesian Methods*.

Puskorius, G. V. and Feldkamp, L. A. (1991). Decoupled extended Kalman filter training of feedforward layered networks, *International Joint Conference on Neural Networks*, Seattle, pp. 307–312.

Ruck, D. W., Rogers, S. K., Kabrisky, M., Maybeck, P. S. and Oxley, M. E. (1992). Comparative analysis of backpropagation and the extended Kalman filter for training multilayer perceptrons, *IEEE Transactions on Pattern Analysis and Machine Intelligence* **14**(6): 686–690.

Shah, S., Palmieri, F. and Datum, M. (1992). Optimal filtering algorithms for fast learning in feedforward neural networks, *Neural Networks* **5**: 779–787.

Singhal, S. and Wu, L. (1988). Training multilayer perceptrons with the extended Kalman algorithm, *in* D. S. Touretzky (ed.), *Advances in Neural Information Processing Systems*, Vol. 1, San Mateo, CA, pp. 133–140.

Sutton, R. S. (1992). Gain adaptation beats least squares?, *Proceedings of the Seventh Yale Workshop on Adaptive Learning Systems*, pp. 161–166.

Agnostic Classification of Markovian Sequences

Ran El-Yaniv   **Shai Fine**   **Naftali Tishby**[*]
Institute of Computer Science and Center for Neural Computation
The Hebrew University
Jerusalem 91904, Israel
E-mail: {ranni,fshai,tishby}@cs.huji.ac.il
Category: Algorithms.

Abstract

Classification of finite sequences without explicit knowledge of their statistical nature is a fundamental problem with many important applications. We propose a new information theoretic approach to this problem which is based on the following ingredients: (i) sequences are similar when they are likely to be generated by the same source; (ii) cross entropies can be estimated via "universal compression"; (iii) Markovian sequences can be asymptotically-optimally merged.

With these ingredients we design a method for the classification of discrete sequences whenever they can be compressed. We introduce the method and illustrate its application for hierarchical clustering of languages and for estimating similarities of protein sequences.

1 Introduction

While the relationship between compression (minimal description) and supervised learning is by now well established, no such connection is generally accepted for the unsupervised case. Unsupervised classification is still largely based on ad-hock distance measures with often no explicit statistical justification. This is particularly true for unsupervised classification of sequences of discrete symbols which is encountered in numerous important applications in machine learning and data mining, such as text categorization, biological sequence modeling, and analysis of spike trains.

The emergence of "universal" (i.e. asymptotically distribution independent) se-

---

[*]Corresponding author.

quence compression techniques suggests the existence of "universal" classification methods that make minimal assumptions about the statistical nature of the data. Such techniques are potentially more robust and appropriate for real world applications.

In this paper we introduce a specific method that utilizes the connection between universal compression and unsupervised classification of sequences. Our only underlying assumption is that the sequences can be approximated (in the information theoretic sense) by *some* finite order Markov sources. There are three ingredients to our approach. The first is the assertion that two sequences are statistically similar if they are likely to be independently generated by the same source. This likelihood can then be estimated, given a typical sequence of the most likely joint source, using any good compression method for the sequence samples. The third ingredient is a novel and simple randomized sequence merging algorithm which provably generates a *typical sequence* of the most likely joint source of the sequences, under the above Markovian approximation assumption.

Our similarity measure is also motivated by the known "two sample problem" [Leh59] of estimating the probability that two given samples are taken from the same distribution. In the i.i.d. (Bernoulli) case this problem was thoroughly investigated and the optimal statistical test is given by the sum of the empirical *cross entropies* between the two samples and their *most likely joint source*. We argue that this measure can be extended for arbitrary order Markov sources and use it to construct and sample the most likely joint source.

The similarity measure and the statistical merging algorithm can be naturally combined into classification algorithms for sequences. Here we apply the method to hierarchical clustering of short text segments in 18 European languages and to evaluation of similarities of protein sequences. A complete analysis of the method, with further applications, will be presented elsewhere [EFT97].

2 Measuring the statistical similarity of sequences

Estimating the statistical similarity of two individual sequences is traditionally done by training a statistical model for each sequence and then measuring the likelihood of the other sequence by the model. Training a model entails an assumption about the nature of the noise in the data and this is the rational behind most "edit distance" measures, even when the noise model is not explicitly stated.

Estimating the log-likelihood of a sequence-sample over a discrete alphabet Σ by a statistical model can be done through the *Cross Entropy* or *Kullback-Leibler Divergence*[CT91] between the sample empirical distribution p and model distribution q, defined as:

$$D_{KL}(p\|q) = \sum_{\sigma \in \Sigma} p(\sigma) \log \frac{p(\sigma)}{q(\sigma)} . \tag{1}$$

The KL-divergence, however, has some serious practical drawbacks. It is non-symmetric and unbounded unless the model distribution q is absolutely continuous with respect to p (i.e. $q = 0 \Rightarrow p = 0$). The KL-divergence is therefore highly sensitive to low probability events under q. Using the "empirical" (sample) distributions for both p and q can result in very unreliable estimates of the true divergences. Essentially, $D_{KL}[p\|q]$ measures the asymptotic coding inefficiency when coding the sample p with an optimal code for the model distribution q.

The symmetric divergence, i.e. $D(p, q) = D_{KL}[p\|q] + D_{KL}[q\|p]$, suffers from similar sensitivity problems and lacks the clear statistical meaning.

2.1 The "two sample problem"

Direct Bayesian arguments, or alternately the method of types [CK81], suggest that the probability that there exists one source distribution $\hat{M}$ for two independently drawn samples, x and y [Leh59], is proportional to

$$\int d\mu\,(M)\,\Pr\,(x|M)\cdot\Pr\,(y|M) = \int d\mu\,(M)\cdot 2^{-(|x|D_{KL}[p_x||M]+|y|D_{KL}[p_y||M])}, \quad (2)$$

where $d\mu(M)$ is a prior density of all candidate distributions, p_x and p_y are the empirical (sample) distributions, and $|x|$ and $|y|$ are the corresponding sample sizes.

For large enough samples this integral is dominated (for any non-vanishing prior) by the maximal exponent in the integrand, or by *the most likely joint source* of x and y, M_λ, defined as

$$M_\lambda = \arg\min_{M'}\left\{|x|D_{KL}\,(p_x||M') + |y|D_{KL}\,(p_y||M')\right\}. \quad (3)$$

where $0 \le \lambda = |x|/(|x| + |y|) \le 1$ is the sample *mixture ratio*. The convexity of the KL-divergence guarantees that this minimum is unique and is given by

$$M_\lambda = \lambda p_x + (1 - \lambda)\,p_y,$$

the $\lambda - mixture$ of p_x and p_y.

The similarity measure between two samples, $d(x,y)$, naturally follows as the minimal value of the above exponent. That is,

Definition 1 *The similarity measure, $d(x,y) = \mathcal{D}_\lambda(p_x, p_y)$, of two samples x and y, with empirical distributions p_x and p_y respectively, is defined as*

$$d(x,y) = \mathcal{D}_\lambda(p_x, p_y) = \lambda D_{KL}\,(p_x||M_\lambda) + (1 - \lambda)\,D_{KL}\,(p_y||M_\lambda) \quad (4)$$

where M_λ is the λ-mixture of p_x and p_y.

The function $\mathcal{D}_\lambda\,(p, q)$ is an extension of the Jensen-Shannon divergence (see e.g. [Lin91]) and satisfies many useful analytic properties, such as symmetry and boundedness on both sides by the L_1-norm, in addition to its clear statistical meaning. See [Lin91, EFT97] for a more complete discussion of this measure.

2.2 Estimating the $\mathcal{D}_\lambda$ similarity measure

The key component of our classification method is the estimation of $\mathcal{D}_\lambda$ for individual finite sequences, without an explicit model distribution.

Since cross entropies, D_{KL}, express code-length differences, they can be estimated using any efficient compression algorithm for the two sequences. The existence of "universal" compression methods, such as the Lempel-Ziv algorithm (see e.g. [CT91]) which are provably asymptotically optimal for any sequence, give us the means for asymptotically optimal estimation of $\mathcal{D}_\lambda$, provided that we can obtain a typical sequence of the most-likely joint source, M_λ.

We apply an improvement of the method of Ziv and Merhav [ZM93] for the estimation of the two cross-entropies using the Lempel-Ziv algorithm given two sample sequences [BE97]. Notice that our estimation of $\mathcal{D}_\lambda$ is as good as the compression method used, namely, closer to optimal compression yields better estimation of the similarity measure.

It remains to show how a typical sequence of the most-likely joint source can be generated.

3   Joint Sources of Markovian Sequences

In this section we first explicitly generalize the notion of the joint statistical source to finite order Markov probability measures. We identify the joint source of Markovian sequences and show how to construct a typical random sample of this source.

More precisely, let x and y be two sequences generated by Markov processes with distributions P and Q, respectively. We present a novel algorithm for the merging the two sequences, by generating a typical sequence of an approximation to the most likely joint source of x and y. The algorithm does not require the parameters of the true sources P and Q and the computation of the sequence is done directly from the sequence samples x and y.

As before, Σ denotes a finite alphabet and P and Q denote two ergodic Markov sources over Σ of orders K_P and K_Q, respectively. By equation 3, the λ-*mixture joint source* M_λ of P and Q is $M_\lambda = \arg\min_{M'} \lambda D_{KL}(P||M') + (1-\lambda)D_{KL}(Q||M')$, where for sequences $D_{KL}(P||M) = \limsup_{n\to\infty} \frac{1}{n} \sum_{x\in\Sigma^n} P(x) \log \frac{P(x)}{M(x)}$. The following theorem identifies the joint source of P and Q.

Theorem 1 *The unique λ-mixture joint source M_λ of P and Q, of order $K = \max\{K_P, K_Q\}$, is given by the following conditional distribution. For each $s \in \Sigma^K, a \in \Sigma$,*

$$M_\lambda(a|s) = \frac{\lambda P(s)}{\lambda P(s) + (1 - \lambda)Q(s)} P(a|s) + \frac{(1 - \lambda)Q(s)}{\lambda P(s) + (1 - \lambda)Q(s)} Q(a|s) .$$

This distribution can be naturally extended to n sources with priors $\lambda_1, \ldots, \lambda_n$.

3.1   The "sequence merging" algorithm

The above theorem can be easily translated into an algorithm. Figure 1 describes a randomized algorithm that generates from the given sequences x and y, an asymptotically typical sequence z of the most likely joint source, as defined by Theorem 1, of P and Q.

Initialization:
- $z[0]$ = choose a symbol from x with probability λ or y with probability $1 - \lambda$
- $i = 0$

Loop:
Repeat until the approximation error is lower then a prescribe threshold
- $s_x :=$ max length suffix of z appearing somewhere in x
- $s_y :=$ max length suffix of z appearing somewhere in y
- $\Lambda(\lambda, s_x, s_y) = \frac{\lambda Pr_x(s_x)}{\lambda Pr_x(s_x) + (1-\lambda)Pr_y(s_y)}$
- $r =$ choose x with probability $\Lambda(\lambda, s_x, s_y)$ or y with probability $1 - \Lambda(\lambda, s_x, s_y)$
- $r(s_r) =$ randomly choose one of the occurrences of s_r in r
- $z[i + 1] =$ the symbol appearing immediately after $r(s_r)$ at r
- $i = i + 1$

End Repeat

Figure 1: The most-likely joint source algorithm

Notice that the algorithm is completely unparameterized, even the sequence alphabets, which may differ from one sequence to another, are not explicitly needed. The algorithm can be efficiently implemented by pre-preparing suffix trees for the given sequences, and the merging algorithm is naturally generalizable to any number of sequences.

4 Applications

There are several possible applications of our sequence merging algorithm and similarity measure. Here we focus on three possible applications: the source merging problem, estimation of sequence similarity, and bottom-up sequence-classification. These algorithms are different from most existing approaches because they rely only on the sequenced data, similar to universal compression, without explicit modeling assumptions. Further details, analysis, and applications of the method will be presented elsewhere [EFT97].

4.1 Merging and synthesis of sequences

An immediate application of the source merging algorithm is for synthesis of typical sequences of the joint source from some given data sequences, *without any access to an explicit model of the source.*

To illustrate this point consider the sequence in Figure 2. This sequence was randomly generated, *character by character*, from two natural excerpts: a 47,655-character string from Dickens' Tale of Two Cities, and a 59,097-character string from Twain's The King and the Pauper.

```
      Do your way to her breast, and sent a treason's sword- and not empty.
  "I am particularly and when the stepped of his own commits place.  No; yes,
  of course, and he passed behind that by turns ascended upon him, and my bone
  to touch it, less to say:  'Remove thought, every one!  Guards!  In miness?"
  The books third time.  There was but pastened her unave misg his ruined head
  than they had known to keep his saw whether think" The feet our grace he
  called offer information?
```

[Twickens, 1997]

Figure 2: A typical excerpt of random text generated by the "joint source" of Dickens and Twain.

4.2 Pairwise similarity of proteins

The joint source algorithm, combined with the new similarity measure, provide natural means for computing the similarity of sequences over any alphabet. In this section we illustrate this application[1] for the important case of protein sequences (sequences over the set of the 20 amino-acids).

From a database of all known proteins we selected 6 different families and within each family we randomly chose 10 proteins. The families chosen are: *Chaperonin, MHC1, Cytochrome, Kinase, Globin Alpha and Globin Beta.* Our pairwise distances between all 60 proteins were computed using our agnostic algorithm and are depicted in the 60x60 matrix of Figure 3. As can be seen, the algorithm succeeds to

---

[1]The protein results presented here are part of an ongoing work with G. Yona and E. Ben-Sasson.

identify the families (the success with the Kinase and Cytochrome families is more limited).

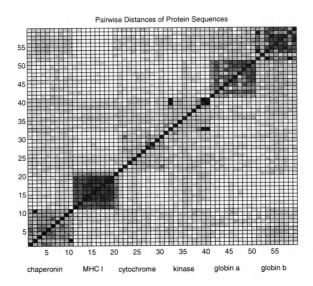

Figure 3: A 60x60 symmetric matrix representing the pairwise distances, as computed by our agnostic algorithm, between 60 proteins, each consecutive 10 belong to a different family. Darker gray represent higher similarity.

In another experiment we considered all the 200 proteins of the Kinase family and computed the pairwise distances of these proteins using the agnostic algorithm. For comparison we computed the pairwise similarities of these sequences using the widely used Smith-Waterman algorithm (see e.g. [HH92]).[2] The resulting agnostic similarities, computed with no biological information whatsoever, are very similar to the Smith-Waterman similarities.[3] Furthermore, our agnostic measure discovered some biological similarities not detected by the Smith-Waterman method.

4.3 Agnostic classification of languages

The sample of the joint source of two sequences can be considered as their "average" or "centroid", capturing a mixture of their statistics. Averaging and measuring distance between objects are sufficient for most standard clustering algorithms such as bottom-up greedy clustering, vector quantization (VQ), and clustering by deterministic annealing. Thus, our merging method and similarity measure can be directly applied for the classification of finite sequences via standard clustering algorithms.

To illustrate the power of this new sequence clustering method we give the result of a rudimentary linguistic experiment using a greedy bottom-up (conglomerative) clustering of short excerpts (1500 characters) from eighteen languages. Specifically, we took sixteen random excerpts from the following Porto-Indo-European languages: *Afrikaans, Catalan, Danish, Dutch, English, Flemish, French, German, Italian, Latin, Norwegian, Polish, Portuguese, Spanish, Swedish* and *Welsh*, together with

---

[2]we applied the Smith-Waterman for computing local-alignment costs using the state-of-the-art *blosum62* biological cost matrix.

[3]These results are not given here due to space limitations and will be discussed elsewhere.

two artificial languages: *Esperanto* and *Klingon*[4].

The resulting hierarchical classification tree is depicted in Figure 4. This entirely unsupervised method, when applied to these short random excerpts, clearly agrees with the "standard" philologic tree of these languages, both in terms of the grouping and the levels of similarity (depth of the split) of the languages (the Polish-Welsh "similarity" is probably due to the specific transcription used).

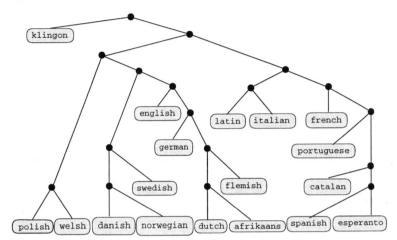

Figure 4: Agnostic bottom-up greedy clustering of eighteen languages

Acknowledgments

We sincerely thank Ran Bachrach and Golan Yona for helpful discussions. We also thank Sageev Oore for many useful comments.

References

[BE97]   R. Bachrach and R. El-Yaniv, An Improved Measure of Relative Entropy Between Individual Sequences, unpublished manuscript.

[CK81]   I. Csiszár and J. Krörner. Information Theory: Coding Theorems for Discrete Memoryless Systems, Academic Press, New-York 1981.

[CT91]   T. M. Cover and J. A. Thomas. Elements of Information Theory, John Wiley & Sons, New-York 1991.

[EFT97] R. El-Yaniv, S. Fine and N. Tishby. Classifying Markovian Sources, in preparations, 1997.

[HH92]   S. Henikoff and J. G. Henikoff (1992). Amino acid substitution matrices from protein blocks. *Proc. Natl. Acad. Sci. USA* **89**, 10915-10919.

[Leh59] E. L. Lehmann. Testing Statistical Hypotheses, John Wiley & Sons, New-York 1959.

[Lin91] J. Lin, 1991. Divergence measures based on the Shannon entropy. *IEEE Transactions on Information Theory*, 37(1):145–151.

[ZM93]   J. Ziv and N. Merhav, 1993. A Measure of Relative Entropy Between Individual Sequences with Application to Universal Classification, *IEEE Transactions on Information Theory*, 39(4).

---

[4]Klingon is a synthetic language that was invented for the Star-Trek TV series.

Ensemble and Modular Approaches for Face Detection: a Comparison

Raphaël Feraud *and **Olivier Bernier** [†]
France-Télécom CNET DTL/DLI
Technopole Anticipa, 2 avenue Pierre Marzin, 22307 Lannion cedex, FRANCE

Abstract

A new learning model based on autoassociative neural networks is developped and applied to face detection. To extend the detection ability in orientation and to decrease the number of false alarms, different combinations of networks are tested: ensemble, conditional ensemble and conditional mixture of networks. The use of a conditional mixture of networks allows to obtain *state of the art* results on different benchmark face databases.

1 A constrained generative model

Our purpose is to classify an extracted window x from an image as a face ($x \in \mathcal{V}$) or non-face ($x \in \mathcal{N}$). The set of all possible windows is $\mathcal{E} = \mathcal{V} \cup \mathcal{N}$, with $\mathcal{V} \cap \mathcal{N} = \emptyset$. Since collecting a representative set of non-face examples is impossible, face detection by a statistical model is a difficult task. An autoassociative network, using five layers of neurons, is able to perform a non-linear dimensionnality reduction [Kramer, 1991]. However, its use as an estimator, to classify an extracted window as face or non-face, raises two problems:

1. $\mathcal{V}'$, the obtained sub-manifold can contain non-face examples ($\mathcal{V} \subset \mathcal{V}'$),

2. owing to local minima, the obtained solution can be close to the linear solution: the principal components analysis.

Our approach is to use counter-examples in order to find a sub-manifold as close as possible to $\mathcal{V}$ and to constrain the algorithm to converge to a non-linear solution [Feraud, R. et al., 1997]. Each non-face example is constrained to be reconstructed as its projection on $\mathcal{V}$. The projection $\mathcal{P}$ of a point x of the input space $\mathcal{E}$ on $\mathcal{V}$, is defined by:

---

*email: feraud@lannion.cnet.fr
[†]email: bernier@lannion.cnet.fr

- if $x \in \mathcal{V}$, then $\mathcal{P}(x) = x$,
- if $x \notin \mathcal{V}$: $\mathcal{P}(x) = \arg\min_{y \in \mathcal{V}}(d(x, y))$, where d is the Euclidian distance.
  During the learning process, the projection $\mathcal{P}$ of x on $\mathcal{V}$ is approximated by: $\mathcal{P}(x) \sim \frac{1}{n}\sum_{i=1}^{n} v_i$, where $v_1, v_2, \ldots, v_n$, are the n nearest neighbours, in the training set of faces, of v, the nearest face example of x.

The goal of the learning process is to approximate the distance $\mathcal{D}$ of an input space element x to the set of faces $\mathcal{V}$:

- $\mathcal{D}(x, \mathcal{V}) = \|x - \mathcal{P}(x)\| \sim \frac{1}{M}(x - \hat{x})^2$, where M is the size of input image x and $\hat{x}$ the image reconstructed by the neural network,
- let $x \in \mathcal{E}$, then $x \in \mathcal{V}$ if and only if $\mathcal{D}(x, \mathcal{V}) \leq \tau$, with $\tau \in \mathbb{R}$, where τ is a threshold used to adjust the sensitivity of the model.

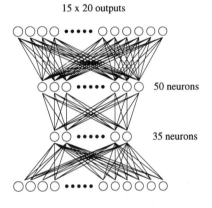

15 x 20 outputs

50 neurons

35 neurons

15 x 20 inputs

Figure 1: The use of two hidden layers and counter-examples in a compression neural network allows to realize a non-linear dimensionality reduction.

In the case of non-linear dimensionnality reduction, the reconstruction error is related to the position of a point to the non-linear principal components in the input space. Nevertheless, a point can be near to a principal component and far from the set of faces. With the algorithm proposed, the reconstruction error is related to the distance between a point to the set of faces. As a consequence, if we assume that the learning process is consistent [Vapnik, 1995], our algorithm is able to evaluate the probability that a point belongs to the set of faces. Let y be a binary random variable: $y = 1$ corresponds to a face example and $y = 0$ to a non-face example, we use:

$$P(y = 1|x) = e^{-\frac{(x - \hat{x})^2}{\sigma^2}}$$, where σ depends on the threshold τ

The size of the training windows is 15x20 pixels. The faces are normalized in position and scale. The windows are enhanced by histogram equalization to obtain a relative independence to lighting conditions, smoothed to remove the noise and normalized by the average face, evaluated on the training set. Three face databases are used: after vertical mirroring, B_{f1} is composed of 3600 different faces with orientation between 0 degree and 20 degree, B_{f2} is composed of 1600 different faces with orientation between 20 degree and 60 degree and B_{f3} is the concatenation of B_{f1} and B_{f2}, giving a total of 5200 faces. All of the training faces are extracted from the *usenix face database*(**), from the test set B of CMU(**), and from 100 images containing faces and complex backgrounds.

Figure 2: Left to right: the counter-examples successively chosen by the algorithm are increasingly similar to real faces (iteration 1 to 8).

The non-face databases $(B_{nf1}, B_{nf2}, B_{nf3})$, corresponding to each face database, are collected by an iterative algorithm similar to the one used in [Sung, K. and Poggio, T., 1994] or in [Rowley, H. et al., 1995]:

- **1)** $B_{nf} = \emptyset$, $\tau = \tau_{min}$,
- **2)** the neural network is trained with $B_f + B_{nf}$,
- **3)** the face detection system is tested on a set of background images,
- **4)** a maximum of 100 subimages x_i are collected with $\mathcal{D}(x_i, \mathcal{V}) \leq \tau$,
- **5)** $B_{nf} = B_{nf} + \{x_0, \ldots, x_n\}$, $\tau = \tau + \mu$, with $\mu > 0$,
- **6)** while $\tau < \tau_{max}$ go back to step 2.

After vertical mirroring, the size of the obtained set of non-face examples is respectively 1500 for B_{nf1}, 600 for B_{nf2} and 2600 for B_{nf3}. Since the non-face set $(\mathcal{N})$ is too large, it is not possible to prove that this algorithm converge in a finite time. Nevertheless, in only 8 iterations, collected counter-examples are close to the set of faces (Figure 2). Using this algorithm, three elementary face detectors are constructed: the front view face detector trained on B_{f1} and B_{nf1} (CGM1), the turned face detector trained on B_{f2} and B_{nf2} (CGM2) and the general face detector trained on B_{f3} and B_{nf3} (CGM3).

To obtain a non-linear dimensionnality reduction, five layers are necessary. However, our experiments show that four layers are sufficient. Consequently, each CGM has four layers (Figure 1). The first and last layers consist each of 300 neurons, corresponding to the image size 15x20. The first hidden layer has 35 neurons and the second hidden layer 50 neurons. In order to reduce the false alarm rate and to extend the face detection ability in orientation, different combinations of networks are tested. The use of ensemble of networks to reduce false alarm rate was shown by [Rowley, H. et al., 1995]. However, considering that to detect a face in an image, there are two subproblems to solve, detection of front view faces and turned faces, a modular architecture can also be used.

2   Ensemble of CGMs

Generalization error of an estimator can be decomposed in two terms: the bias and the variance [Geman, S. et al., 1992]. The bias is reduced with prior knowledge. The use of an ensemble of estimators can reduce the variance when these estimators are independently and identically distributed [Raviv, Y. and Intrator, N., 1996]. Each face detector i produces:

$$E_i[y|x] = P_i(y = 1|x)$$

Assuming that the three face detectors (CGM1,CGM2,CGM3) are independently and identically distributed (iid), the ouput of the ensemble is:

$$E[y|x] = \frac{1}{3} \sum_{i=1}^{3} E_i[y|x]$$

3   Conditional mixture of CGMs

To extend the detection ability in orientation, a conditional mixture of CGMs is tested. The training set is separated in two subsets: front view faces and the corresponding counter-examples ($\theta = 1$) and turned faces and the corresponding counter-examples ($\theta = 0$). The first subnetwork (CGM1) evaluates the probability of the tested image to be a front view face, knowing the label equals 1 ($P(y = 1|x, \theta = 1)$). The second (CGM2) evaluates the probability of the tested image to be a turned face, knowing the label equals 0 ($P(y = 1|x, \theta = 0)$). A gating network is trained to evaluate $P(\theta = 1|x)$, supposing that the partition $\theta = 1, \theta = 0$ can be generalized to every input:

$$E[y|x] = E[y|\theta = 1, x]f(x) + E[y|\theta = 0, x](1 - f(x))$$

Where $f(x)$ is the estimated value of $P(\theta = 1|x)$.

This system is different from a mixture of experts introduced by [Jacobs, R. A. et al., 1991]: each module is trained separately on a subset of the training set and then the gating network learns to combine the outputs.

4   Conditional ensemble of CGMs

To reduce the false alarm rate and to detect front view and turned faces, an original combination, using (CGM1,CGM2) and a gate network, is proposed. Four sets are defined:

- $\mathcal{F}$ is the front view face set,
- $\mathcal{P}$ is the turned face set, with $\mathcal{F} \cap \mathcal{P} = \emptyset$,
- $\mathcal{V} = \mathcal{F} \cup \mathcal{P}$ is the face set,
- $\mathcal{N}$ is the non-face set, with $\mathcal{V} \cap \mathcal{N} = \emptyset$,

Our goal is to evaluate $P(x \in V|x)$. Each estimator computes respectively:

- $P(x \in F|x \in \mathcal{F} \cup \mathcal{N}, x)$ $(CGM1(x))$,
- $P(x \in P|x \in \mathcal{P} \cup \mathcal{N}, x)$ $(CGM2(x))$,

Using the Bayes theorem, we obtain:

$$P(x \in \mathcal{F}|x \in \mathcal{F} \cup \mathcal{N}, x) = \frac{P(x \in \mathcal{F}|x)}{P(x \in \mathcal{F} \cup \mathcal{N}|x)} P(x \in \mathcal{F} \cup \mathcal{N}|x \in \mathcal{F}, x)$$

Since $x \in \mathcal{F} \Rightarrow x \in \mathcal{F} \cup \mathcal{N}$, then:

$$P(x \in \mathcal{F}|x, x \in \mathcal{F} \cup \mathcal{N}) = \frac{P(x \in \mathcal{F}|x)}{P(x \in \mathcal{F} \cup \mathcal{N}|x)}$$

$$\Leftrightarrow P(x \in \mathcal{F}|x) = P(x \in \mathcal{F}|x \in \mathcal{F} \cup \mathcal{N}, x)P(x \in \mathcal{F} \cup \mathcal{N}|x)$$

$$\Leftrightarrow P(x \in \mathcal{F}|x) = P(x \in \mathcal{F}|x \in \mathcal{F} \cup \mathcal{N}, x)[P(x \in \mathcal{F}|x) + P(x \in \mathcal{N}|x)]$$

In the same way, we have:

$$P(x \in \mathcal{P}|x) = P(x \in \mathcal{P}|x \in \mathcal{P} \cup \mathcal{N}, x)[P(x \in \mathcal{P}|x) + P(x \in \mathcal{N}|x)]$$

Then:

$$P(x \in \mathcal{V}|x) = P(x \in \mathcal{N}|x)[P(x \in \mathcal{P}|x \in \mathcal{P} \cup \mathcal{N}, x) + P(x \in \mathcal{F}|x \in \mathcal{F} \cup \mathcal{N}, x)]$$
$$+P(x \in \mathcal{P}|x)P(x \in \mathcal{P}|x \in \mathcal{P} \cup \mathcal{N}, x) + P(x \in \mathcal{F}|x)P(x \in \mathcal{F}|x \in \mathcal{F} \cup \mathcal{N}, x)$$

Rewriting the previous equation using the following notation, $CGM1(x)$ for $P(x \in \mathcal{F}|x \in \mathcal{F} \cup \mathcal{N}, x)$ and $CGM1(x)$ for $P(x \in \mathcal{P}|x \in \mathcal{P} \cup \mathcal{N}, x)$, we have:

$$P(x \in \mathcal{V}|x) = P(x \in \mathcal{N}|x)[CGM1(x) + CGM2(x)] \quad (1)$$
$$+P(x \in \mathcal{P}|x)CGM2(x) + P(x \in \mathcal{F}|x)CGM1(x) \quad (2)$$

Then, we can deduce the behaviour of the conditional ensemble:

- in $\mathcal{N}$, if the output of the gate network is 0.5, as in the case of ensembles, the conditional ensemble reduces the variance of the error (first term of the right side of the equation (1)),
- in $\mathcal{V}$, as in the case of the conditional mixture, the conditional ensemble permits to combine two different tasks (second term of the right side of the equation (2)): detection of turned faces and detection of front view faces.

The gate network $f(x)$ is trained to calculate the probability that the tested image is a face ($P(x \in \mathcal{V}|x)$), using the following cost function:

$$C = \sum_{x_i \in \mathcal{V}} ([f(x_i)MGC1(x) + (1 - f(x_i))]MGC2(x) - y_i)^2 + \sum_{x_i \in \mathcal{N}} (f(x_i) - 0.5)^2$$

5   Discussion

Each 15x20 subimage is extracted and normalized by enhancing, smoothing and substracting the average face, before being processed by the network. The detection threshold τ is fixed for all the tested images. To detect a face at different scales, the image is subsampled.

The first test allows to evaluate the limits in orientation of the face detectors. The *sussex face database*(**), containing different faces with ten orientations betwen 0 degree and 90 degrees, is used (Table 1). The general face detector (CGM3) uses the same learning face database than the different mixtures of CGMs. Nevertheless, CGM3 has a smaller orientation range than the conditional mixtures of CGMs, and the conditional ensemble of CGMs. Since the performances of the ensemble of CGMS are low, the corresponding hypothesis (the CGMs are iid) is invalid. Moreover, this test shows that the combination by a gating neural network of CGMs,

Table 1:Results on *Sussex face database*

orientation (degree)	CGM1	CGM2	CGM3	Ensemble (1,2,3)	Conditional ensemble (1,2,gate)	Conditional mixture (1,2,gate)
0	100.0 %	100.0 %	100.0 %	100.0 %	100.0 %	100.0 %
10	62.5 %	100.0 %	87.5 %	100.0 %	100.0 %	100.0 %
20	50.0 %	100.0 %	87.5 %	87.5 %	100.0 %	100.0 %
30	12.5 %	100.0 %	62.5 %	62.5 %	100.0 %	100.0 %
40	0.0 %	100.0 %	50.0 %	12.5 %	62.5.0 %	87.5 %
50	0.0 %	75.0 %	0.0 %	0.0 %	37.5 %	62.5 %
60	0.0 %	37.5 %	0.0 %	0.0 %	0.0 %	37.5 %
70	0.0 %	37.5 %	0.0 %	0.0 %	0.0 %	25.0 %

trained on different training set, allows to extend the detection ability to both front view and turned faces. The conditional mixture of CGMs obtains results in term of orientation and false alarm rate close to the best CGMs used to contruct it (see Table 1 and Table 2).

The second test allows to evaluate the false alarms rate and to compare our results with the best results published so far on the test set *A* [Rowley, H. et al., 1995] of the CMU (**), containing 42 images of various quality. First, these results show that the model, trained without counter-examples (GM), overestimates the distribution of faces and its false alarm rate is too important to use it as a face detector. Second, the estimation of the probability distribution of the face performed by one CGM (CGM3) is more precise than the one obtained by [Rowley, H. et al., 1995] with one SWN (see Table 2). The conditional ensemble of CGMs and the conditional mixture of CGMs obtained a similar detection rate than an ensemble of SWNs [Rowley, H. et al., 1995], but with a false alarm rate two or three times lower. Since the results of the conditional ensemble of CGMs and the conditional mixture of CGMs are close on this test, the detection rate versus the number of false alarms is plotted (Figure 3), for different thresholds. The conditional mixture of CGMs curve is above the one for the conditional ensemble of CGMs.

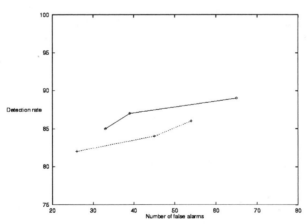

Figure 3: Detection rate versus number of false alarms on the CMU test set A. In dashed line conditional ensemble and in solid line conditional mixture.

The conditionnal mixture of CGMs is used in an application called LISTEN [Collobert, M. et al., 1996]: a camera detects, tracks a face and controls a micro-phone array towards a speaker, in real time. The small size of the subimages (15x20) processed allows to detect a face far from the camera (with an aperture of 60 degrees, the maximum distance to the camera is 6 meters). To detect a face in real time, the number of tested hypothesis is reduced by motion and color analysis.

Table 2:Results on the CMU test set A
GM: the model trained without counter-examples, CGM1: face detector, CGM2:
turned face detector, CGM3: general face detector. SWN: shared weight network.
(*) Considering that our goal is to detect human faces, non-human faces and rough
face drawings have not been taken into account.

Model	Detection rate		False alarms rate	
GM	84 %	+/- 5 %	1/1,000	+/- 0.1/1,00
CGM1	77 %	+/- 5 %	5.43/1,000,000	+/- 0.38/1,0
	127/164		47/33,700,000	
CGM2	85 %	+/- 5 %	6.3/1,000,000	+/- 0.37/1,0
	139/164		212/33,700,000	
CGM3	85 %	+/- 5 %	1.36/1,000,000	+/- 0.41/1,0
	139/164		46/33,700,000	
[Rowley,1995]	84 %	+/- 5 %	8.13/1,000,000	+/- 0.4/1,00
(one SWN)	142/169*		179/22,000,000	
Ensemble	74 %	+/- 5 %	0.71/1,000,000	+/- 0.43/1,0
(CGM1,CGM2,CGM3)	121/164		24/33,700,000	
Conditional ensemble	82 %	+/- 5 %	0.77/1,000,000	+/- 0.38/1,0
(CGM1,CGM2,gate)	134/164		26/33,700,000	
[Rowley,1995]	85 %	+/- 5 %	2.13/1,000,000	+/- 0.42/1,0
(three SWNs)	144/169*		47/22,000,000	
Conditional mixture	87 %	+/- 5 %	1.15/1,000,000	+/- 0.35/1,0
(CGM1,CGM2,gate)	142/164		39/33,700,000	

(**) *usenix face database, sussex face database* and CMU test sets can be retrieved at
www.cs.rug.nl/ peterkr/FACE/face.html.

References

[Collobert, M. et al., 1996] Collobert, M., Feraud, R., Le Tourneur, G., Bernier, O., Vial-
    let, J.E, Mahieux, Y., and Collobert, D. (1996). Listen: a system for locating and
    tracking individual speaker. In *Second International Conference On Automatic Face
    and Gesture Recognition*.

[Feraud, R. et al., 1997] Feraud, R., Bernier, O., and Collobert, D. (1997). A constrained
    generative model applied to face detection. *Neural Processing Letters*.

[Geman, S. et al., 1992] Geman, S., Bienenstock, E., and Doursat, R. (1992). Neural
    networks and the bias-variance dilemma. *Neural Computation*, 4:1–58.

[Jacobs, R. A. et al., 1991] Jacobs, R. A., Jordan, M. I., Nowlan, S. J., and Hinton, G. E.
    (1991). Adaptative mixtures of local experts. *Neural Computation*, 3:79–87.

[Kramer, 1991] Kramer, M. (1991). Nonlinear principal component analysis using autoas-
    sociative neural networks. *AIChE Journal*, 37:233–243.

[Raviv, Y. and Intrator, N., 1996] Raviv, Y. and Intrator, N. (1996). Bootstrapping with
    noise: An effective regularization technique. *Connection Science*, 8:355–372.

[Rowley, H. et al., 1995] Rowley, H., Baluja, S., and Kanade, T. (1995). Human face
    detection in visual scenes. In *Neural Information Processing Systems 8*.

[Sung, K. and Poggio, T., 1994] Sung, K. and Poggio, T. (1994). Example-based learning
    for view-based human face detection. Technical report, M.I.T.

[Vapnik, 1995] Vapnik, V. (1995). *The Nature of Statistical Learning Theory*. Springer-
    Verlag New York Heidelberg Berlin.

A Revolution: Belief Propagation in Graphs With Cycles

Brendan J. Frey*
http://www.cs.utoronto.ca/~frey
Department of Computer Science
University of Toronto

David J. C. MacKay
http://wol.ra.phy.cam.ac.uk/mackay
Department of Physics, Cavendish Laboratory
Cambridge University

Abstract

Until recently, artificial intelligence researchers have frowned upon
the application of probability propagation in Bayesian belief networks that have cycles. The probability propagation algorithm is
only exact in networks that are cycle-free. However, it has recently
been discovered that the two *best* error-correcting decoding algorithms are actually performing probability propagation in belief
networks with cycles.

1 Communicating over a noisy channel

Our increasingly wired world demands efficient methods for communicating bits of
information over physical channels that introduce errors. Examples of real-world
channels include twisted-pair telephone wires, shielded cable-TV wire, fiber-optic
cable, deep-space radio, terrestrial radio, and indoor radio. Engineers attempt
to correct the errors introduced by the noise in these channels through the use
of *channel coding* which adds protection to the information source, so that some
channel errors can be corrected. A popular model of a physical channel is shown
in Fig. 1. A vector of K information bits $\mathbf{u} = (u_1, \ldots, u_K)$, $u_k \in \{0, 1\}$ is encoded,
and a vector of N codeword bits $\mathbf{x} = (x_1, \ldots, x_N)$ is transmitted into the channel.
Independent Gaussian noise with variance σ^2 is then added to each codeword bit,

---

*Brendan Frey is currently a Beckman Fellow at the Beckman Institute for Advanced
Science and Technology, University of Illinois at Urbana-Champaign.

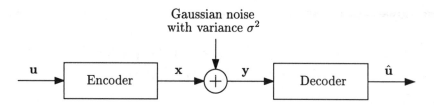

Figure 1: A communication system with a channel that adds Gaussian noise to the transmitted discrete-time sequence.

producing the real-valued channel output vector $\mathbf{y} = (y_1, \ldots, y_N)$. The decoder must then use this received vector to make a guess $\hat{\mathbf{u}}$ at the original information vector. The probability $P_b(e)$ of bit error is minimized by choosing the u_k that maximizes $P(u_k|\mathbf{y})$ for $k = 1, \ldots, K$. The *rate* K/N of a code is the number of information bits communicated per codeword bit. We will consider rate $\sim 1/2$ systems in this paper, where $N = 2K$.

The simplest rate $1/2$ encoder duplicates each information bit: $x_{2k-1} = x_{2k} = u_k$, $k = 1, \ldots, K$. The optimal decoder for this *repetition code* simply averages together pairs of noisy channel outputs and then applies a threshold:

$$\hat{u}_k = 1 \quad \text{if} \quad (y_{2k-1} + y_{2k})/2 > 0.5, \quad 0 \text{ otherwise.} \tag{1}$$

Clearly, this procedure has the effect of reducing the noise variance by a factor of $1/2$. The resulting probability $P_b(e)$ that an information bit will be erroneously decoded is given by the area under the tail of the noise Gaussian:

$$P_b(e) = \Phi\left(\frac{-0.5}{\sigma^2/2}\right), \tag{2}$$

where $\Phi()$ is the cumulative standard normal distribution. A plot of $P_b(e)$ versus σ for this repetition code is shown in Fig. 2, along with a thumbnail picture that shows the distribution of noisy received signals at the noise level where the repetition code gives $P_b(e) = 10^{-5}$.

More sophisticated channel encoders and decoders can be used to increase the tolerable noise level without increasing the probability of a bit error. This approach can in principle improve performance up to a bound determined by Shannon (1948). For a given probability of bit error $P_b(e)$, this limit gives the maximum noise level that can be tolerated, no matter what channel code is used. Shannon's proof was non-constructive, meaning that he showed that there exist channel codes that achieve his limit, but did not present practical encoders and decoders. The curve for Shannon's limit is also shown in Fig. 2.

The two curves described above define the region of interest for practical channel coding systems. For a given $P_b(e)$, if a system requires a lower noise level than the repetition code, then it is not very interesting. At the other extreme, it is impossible for a system to tolerate a higher noise level than Shannon's limit.

2   Decoding Hamming codes by probability propagation

One way to *detect* errors in a string of bits is to add a parity-check bit that is chosen so that the sum modulo 2 of all the bits is 0. If the channel flips one bit, the receiver will find that the sum modulo 2 is 1, and can detect than an error occurred. In a simple Hamming code, the codeword $\mathbf{x}$ consists of the original vector

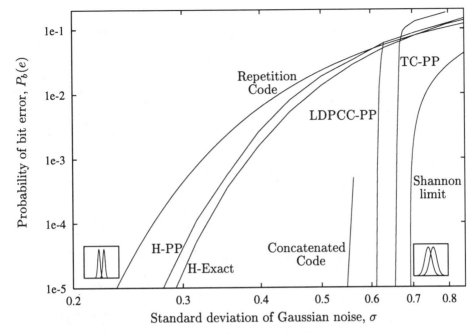

Figure 2: Probability of bit error $P_b(e)$ versus noise level σ for several codes with rates near $1/2$, using $0/1$ signalling. It is impossible to obtain a $P_b(e)$ below Shannon's limit (shown on the far right for rate $1/2$). "H-PP" = Hamming code (rate $4/7$) decoded by probability propagation (5 iterations); "H-Exact" = Hamming code decoded exactly; "LDPCC-PP" = low-density parity-check coded decoded by probability propagation; "TC-PP" = turbocode decoded by probability propagation. The thumbnail pictures show the distribution of noisy received signals at the noise levels where the repetition code and the Shannon limit give $P_b(e) = 10^{-5}$.

u in addition to several parity-check bits, each of which depends on a different *subset* of the information bits. In this way, the Hamming code can not only detect errors but also *correct* them.

The code can be cast in the form of the conditional probabilities that specify a Bayesian network. The Bayesian network for a $K = 4$, $N = 7$ rate $4/7$ Hamming code is shown in Fig. 3a. Assuming the information bits are uniformly random, we have $P(u_k) = 0.5$, $u_k \in \{0,1\}$, $k = 1,2,3,4$. Codeword bits 1 to 4 are direct copies of the information bits: $P(x_k|u_k) = \delta(x_k, u_k)$, $k = 1,2,3,4$, where $\delta(a,b) = 1$ if $a = b$ and 0 otherwise. Codeword bits 5 to 7 are parity-check bits: $P(x_5|u_1,u_2,u_3) = \delta(x_5, u_1 \oplus u_2 \oplus u_3)$, $P(x_6|u_1,u_2,u_4) = \delta(x_6, u_1 \oplus u_2 \oplus u_4)$, $P(x_7|u_2,u_3,u_4) = \delta(x_7, u_2 \oplus u_3 \oplus u_4)$, where $\oplus$ indicates addition modulo 2 (XOR). Finally, the conditional channel probability densities are

$$p(y_n|x_n) = \frac{1}{\sqrt{2\pi\sigma^2}} e^{-(y_n - x_n)^2/2\sigma^2}, \tag{3}$$

for $n = 1, \ldots, 7$.

The probabilities $P(u_k|\mathbf{y})$ can be computed exactly in this belief network, using Lauritzen and Spiegelhalter's algorithm (1988) or just brute force computation. However, for the more powerful codes discussed below, exact computations are intractable. Instead, one way the decoder can approximate the probabilities $P(u_k|\mathbf{y})$ is by applying the probability propagation algorithm (Pearl 1988) to the Bayesian network. Probability propagation is only approximate in this case because the

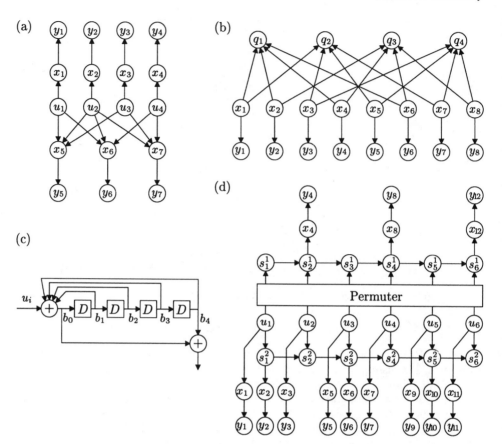

Figure 3: (a) The Bayesian network for a $K = 4$, $N = 7$ Hamming code. (b) The Bayesian network for a $K = 4$, $N = 8$ low-density parity-check code. (c) A block diagram for the turbocode linear feedback shift register. (d) The Bayesian network for a $K = 6$, $N = 12$ turbocode.

network contains cycles (*ignoring* edge directions), *e.g.*, u_1-x_5-u_2-x_6-u_1. Once a channel output vector **y** is observed, propagation begins by sending a message from y_n to x_n for $n = 1, \ldots, 7$. Then, a message is sent from x_k to u_k for $k = 1, 2, 3, 4$. An *iteration* now begins by sending messages from the information variables u_1, u_2, u_3, u_4 to the parity-check variables x_5, x_6, x_7 in parallel. The iteration finishes by sending messages from the parity-check variables back to the information variables in parallel. Each time an iteration is completed, new estimates of $P(u_k|\mathbf{y})$ for $k = 1, 2, 3, 4$ are obtained.

The $P_b(e)$ — σ curve for optimal decoding and the curve for the probability propagation decoder (5 iterations) are shown in Fig. 2. Quite surprisingly, the performance of the iterative decoder is quite close to that of the optimal decoder. Our expectation was that short cycles would confound the probability propagation decoder. However, it seems that good performance can be obtained even when there are short cycles in the code network.

For this simple Hamming code, the complexities of the probability propagation decoder and the exact decoder are comparable. However, the similarity in performance between these two decoders prompts the question: "Can probability propagation decoders give performances comparable to exact decoding in cases where exact decoding is computationally intractable?"

3   A leap towards the limit: Low-density parity-check codes

Recently, there has been an explosion of interest in the channel coding community in two new coding systems that have brought us a leap closer to Shannon's limit. Both of these codes can be described by Bayesian networks with cycles, and it turns out that the corresponding iterative decoders are performing probability propagation in these networks.

Fig. 3b shows the Bayesian network for a simple *low-density parity-check code* (Gallager 1963). In this network, the information bits are not represented explicitly. Instead, the network defines a set of allowed configurations for the codewords. Each parity-check vertex q_i requires that the codeword bits $\{x_n\}_{n \in Q_i}$ to which q_i is connected have even parity:

$$P(q_i | \{x_n\}_{n \in Q_i}) = \delta(q_i, \bigoplus_{n \in Q_i} x_n), \qquad (4)$$

where **q** is clamped to **0** to ensure even parity. Here, Q_i is the set of indices of the codeword bits to which parity-check vertex q_i is connected. The conditional probability densities for the channel outputs are the same as in Eq. 3.

One way to view the above code is as N binary codeword variables along with a set of linear (modulo 2) equations. If in the end we want there to be K degrees of freedom, then the number of linearly independent parity-check equations should be $N - K$. In the above example, there are $N = 8$ codeword bits and 4 parity-checks, leaving $K = 8 - 4 = 4$ degrees of freedom. It is these degrees of freedom that we use to represent the information vector **u**. Because the code is linear, a K-dimensional vector **u** can be mapped to a valid **x** simply by multiplying by an $N \times K$ matrix (using modulo 2 addition). This is how an encoder can produce a low-density parity-check codeword for an input vector.

Once a channel output vector **y** is observed, the iterative probability propagation decoder begins by sending messages from **y** to **x**. An iteration now begins by sending messages from the codeword variables **x** to the parity-check constraint variables **q**. The iteration finishes by sending messages from the parity-check constraint variables back to the codeword variables. Each time an iteration is completed, new estimates of $P(x_n | \mathbf{y})$ for $n = 1, \ldots, N$ are obtained. After a valid (but not necessarily correct) codeword has been found, or a prespecified limit on the number of iterations has been reached, decoding stops. The estimate of the codeword is then mapped back to an estimate **û** of the information vector.

Fig. 2 shows the performance of a $K = 32,621$, $N = 65,389$ low-density parity-check code when decoded as described above. (See MacKay and Neal (1996) for details.) It is impressively close to Shannon's limit — significantly closer than the "Concatenated Code" (described in Lin and Costello (1983)) which was considered the best practical code until recently.

4   Another leap: Turbocodes

The codeword for a turbocode (Berrou *et al.* 1996) consists of the original information vector, plus two sets of bits used to protect the information. Each of these two sets is produced by feeding the information bits into a linear feedback shift register (LFSR), which is a type of finite state machine. The two sets differ in that one set is produced by a *permuted* set of information bits; *i.e.*, the order of the bits is scrambled in a fixed way before the bits are fed into the LFSR. Fig. 3c shows a block diagram (*not* a Bayesian network) for the LFSR that was used in our experiments.

Each box represents a delay (memory) element, and each circle performs addition modulo 2. When the kth information bit arrives, the machine has a state s_k which can be written as a binary string of state bits $b_4 b_3 b_2 b_1 b_0$ as shown in the figure. b_0 of the state s_k is determined by the current input u_k and the previous state s_{k-1}. Bits b_1 to b_4 are just shifted versions of the bits in the previous state.

Fig. 3d shows the Bayesian network for a simple turbocode. Notice that each state variable in the two constituent chains depends on the previous state and an information bit. In each chain, every second LFSR output is not transmitted. In this way, the overall rate of the code is $1/2$, since there are $K = 6$ information bits and $N = 6 + 3 + 3 = 12$ codeword bits. The conditional probabilities for the states of the nonpermuted chain are

$$P(s_k^1 | s_{k-1}^1, u_k) = 1 \quad \text{if state } s_k^1 \text{ follows } s_{k-1}^1 \text{ for input } u_k, \quad 0 \quad \text{otherwise.} \quad (5)$$

The conditional probabilities for the states in the other chain are similar, except that the inputs are permuted. The probabilities for the information bits are uniform, and the conditional probability densities for the channel outputs are the same as in Eq. 3.

Decoding proceeds with messages being passed from the channel output variables to the constituent chains and the information bits. Next, messages are passed from the information variables to the first constituent chain, $\mathbf{s}^1$. Messages are passed forward and then backward along this chain, in the manner of the forward-backward algorithm (Smyth *et al.* 1997). After messages are passed from the first chain to the second chain $\mathbf{s}^2$, the second chain is processed using the forward-backward algorithm. To complete the iteration, messages are passed from $\mathbf{s}^2$ to the information bits.

Fig. 2 shows the performance of a $K = 65,536$, $N = 131,072$ turbocode when decoded as described above, using a fixed number (18) of iterations. (See Frey (1998) for details.) Its performance is significantly closer to Shannon's limit than the performances of both the low-density parity-check code and the textbook standard "Concatenated Code".

5   Open questions

We are certainly not claiming that the NP-hard problem (Cooper 1990) of probabilistic inference in general Bayesian networks can be solved in polynomial time by probability propagation. However, the results presented in this paper do show that there are practical problems which can be solved using *approximate* inference in graphs with cycles. Iterative decoding algorithms are using probability propagation in graphs with cycles, and it is still not well understood why these decoders work so well. Compared to other approximate inference techniques such as variational methods, probability propagation in graphs with cycles is unprincipled. How well do more principled decoders work? In (MacKay and Neal 1995), a variational decoder that maximized a lower bound on $\prod_{k=1}^{K} P(u_k | \mathbf{y})$ was presented for low-density parity-check codes. However, it was found that the performance of the variational decoder was *not* as good as the performance of the probability propagation decoder.

It is not difficult to design small Bayesian networks with cycles for which probability propagation is unstable. Is there a way to easily distinguish between those graphs for which propagation will work and those graphs for which propagation is unstable? A belief that is not uncommon in the graphical models community is that short cycles are particularly apt to lead probability propagation astray. Although it is possible to design networks where this is so, there seems to be a variety of interesting networks (such as the Hamming code network described above) for which propagation works well, despite short cycles.

The probability distributions that we deal with in decoding are very special distributions: the true posterior probability mass is actually concentrated in one microstate in a space of size 2^M where M is large (*e.g.*, 10,000). The decoding problem is to find this most probable microstate, and it may be that iterative probability propagation decoders work because the true probability distribution is concentrated in this microstate.

We believe that there are many interesting and contentious issues in this area that remain to be resolved.

Acknowledgements

We thank Frank Kschischang, Bob McEliece, and Radford Neal for discussions related to this work, and Zoubin Ghahramani for comments on a draft of this paper. This research was supported in part by grants from the Gatsby foundation, the Information Technology Research Council, and the Natural Sciences and Engineering Research Council.

References

C. Berrou and A. Glavieux 1996. Near optimum error correcting coding and decoding: Turbo-codes. *IEEE Transactions on Communications* **44**, 1261–1271.

G. F. Cooper 1990. The computational complexity of probabilistic inference using Bayesian belief networks. *Artificial Intelligence* **42**, 393–405.

B. J. Frey 1998. *Graphical Models for Machine Learning and Digital Communication*, MIT Press, Cambridge, MA. See http://www.cs.utoronto.ca/~frey.

R. G. Gallager 1963. *Low-Density Parity-Check Codes*, MIT Press, Cambridge, MA.

S. Lin and D. J. Costello, Jr. 1983. *Error Control Coding: Fundamentals and Applications*, Prentice-Hall Inc., Englewood Cliffs, NJ.

S. L. Lauritzen and D. J. Spiegelhalter 1988. Local computations with probabilities on graphical structures and their application to expert systems. *Journal of the Royal Statistical Society B* **50**, 157–224.

D. J. C. MacKay and R. M. Neal 1995. Good codes based on very sparse matrices. In *Cryptography and Coding. 5th IMA Conference*, number 1025 in Lecture Notes in Computer Science, 100-111, Springer, Berlin Germany.

D. J. C. MacKay and R. M. Neal 1996. Near Shannon limit performance of low density parity check codes. *Electronics Letters* **32**, 1645–1646. Due to editing errors, reprinted in *Electronics Letters* **33**, 457–458.

J. Pearl 1988. *Probabilistic Reasoning in Intelligent Systems*, Morgan Kaufmann, San Mateo, CA.

C. E. Shannon 1948. A mathematical theory of communication. *Bell System Technical Journal* **27**, 379–423, 623–656.

P. Smyth, D. Heckerman, and M. I. Jordan 1997. Probabilistic independence networks for hidden Markov probability models. *Neural Computation* **9**, 227–270.

Hierarchical Non-linear Factor Analysis and Topographic Maps

Zoubin Ghahramani and Geoffrey E. Hinton
Dept. of Computer Science, University of Toronto
Toronto, Ontario, M5S 3H5, Canada
http://www.cs.toronto.edu/neuron/
{zoubin,hinton}@cs.toronto.edu

Abstract

We first describe a hierarchical, generative model that can be viewed as a non-linear generalisation of factor analysis and can be implemented in a neural network. The model performs perceptual inference in a probabilistically consistent manner by using top-down, bottom-up and lateral connections. These connections can be learned using simple rules that require only locally available information. We then show how to incorporate lateral connections into the generative model. The model extracts a sparse, distributed, hierarchical representation of depth from simplified random-dot stereograms and the localised disparity detectors in the first hidden layer form a topographic map. When presented with image patches from natural scenes, the model develops topographically organised local feature detectors.

1 Introduction

Factor analysis is a probabilistic model for real-valued data which assumes that the data is a linear combination of real-valued uncorrelated Gaussian sources (the factors). After the linear combination, each component of the data vector is also assumed to be corrupted by additional Gaussian noise. A major advantage of this generative model is that, given a data vector, the probability distribution in the space of factors is a multivariate Gaussian whose mean is a linear function of the data. It is therefore tractable to compute the posterior distribution exactly and to use it when learning the parameters of the model (the linear combination matrix and noise variances). A major disadvantage is that factor analysis is a linear model that is insensitive to higher order statistical structure of the observed data vectors.

One way to make factor analysis non-linear is to use a mixture of factor analyser modules, each of which captures a different linear regime in the data [3]. We can view the factors of *all* of the modules as a large set of basis functions for describing the data and the process of selecting one module then corresponds to selecting an appropriate subset of the basis functions. Since the number of subsets under consideration is only linear in the number of modules, it is still tractable to compute the full posterior distribution when given a data point. Unfortunately, this mixture model is often inadequate. Consider, for example, a typical image that contains multiple objects. To represent the pose and deformation of each object we want a componential representation of the object's parameters which could be obtained from an appropriate factor analyser. But to represent the multiple objects we need several of these componential representations at once, so the pure mixture idea is not tenable. A more powerful non-linear generalisation of factor analysis is to have a large set of factors and to allow *any* subset of the factors to be selected. This can be achieved by using a generative model in which there is a high probability of generating factor activations of exactly zero.

2   Rectified Gaussian Belief Nets

The Rectified Gaussian Belief Net (RGBN) uses multiple layers of units with states that are either positive real values or zero [5]. Its main disadvantage is that computing the posterior distribution over the factors given a data vector involves Gibbs sampling. In general, Gibbs sampling can be very time consuming, but in practice 10 to 20 samples per unit have proved adequate and there are theoretical reasons for believing that learning can work well even when the Gibbs sampling fails to reach equilibrium [10].

We first describe the RGBN without considering neural plausibility. Then we show how lateral interactions within a layer can be used to perform probabilistic inference correctly using locally available information. This makes the RGBN far more plausible as a neural model than a sigmoid belief net [9, 8] because it means that Gibbs sampling can be performed without requiring units in one layer to see the total top-down input to units in the layer below.

The generative model for RGBN's consists of multiple layers of units each of which has a real-valued unrectified state, y_j, and a rectified state, $[y_j]^+$, which is zero if y_j is negative and equal to y_j otherwise. This rectification is the only non-linearity in the network.[1] The value of y_j is Gaussian distributed with a standard deviation σ_j and a mean, $\hat{y}_j$ that is determined by the generative bias, g_{0j}, and the combined effects of the rectified states of units, k, in the layer above:

$$\hat{y}_j = g_{0j} + \sum_k g_{kj}[y_k]^+ \qquad (1)$$

The rectified state $[y_j]^+$ therefore has a Gaussian distribution above zero, but all of the mass of the Gaussian that falls below zero is concentrated in an infinitely dense spike at zero as shown in Fig. 1a. This infinite density creates problems if we attempt to use Gibbs sampling over the rectified states, so, following a suggestion by Radford Neal, we perform Gibbs sampling on the unrectified states.

Consider a unit, j, in some intermediate layer of a multilayer RGBN. Suppose that we fix the unrectified states of all the other units in the net. To perform Gibbs sampling, we need to stochastically select a value for y_j according to its distribution given the unrectified states of all the other units. If we think in terms of energy functions, which are equal to negative log probabilities (up to a constant), the rectified states of the units in the layer above contribute a quadratic energy term by determining $\hat{y}_j$. The unrectified states of units, i, in the layer below contribute a constant if $[y_j]^+$ is 0, and if $[y_j]^+$ is positive they each contribute a quadratic term

---

[1]The key arguments presented in this paper hold for general nonlinear belief networks as long as the noise is Gaussian; they are not specific to the rectification nonlinearity.

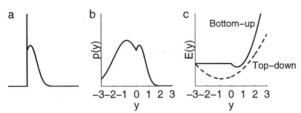

Figure 1: **a)** Probability density in which all the mass of a Gaussian below zero has been replaced by an infinitely dense spike at zero. **b)** Schematic of the density of a unit's unrectified state. **c)** Bottom-up and top-down energy functions corresponding to **b**.

because of the effect of $[y_j]^+$ on $\hat{y}_i$.

$$E(y_j) = \frac{(y_j - \hat{y}_j)^2}{2\sigma_j^2} + \sum_i \frac{(y_i - \sum_h g_{hi}[y_h]^+)^2}{2\sigma_i^2} \qquad (2)$$

where h is an index over all the units in the same layer as j including j itself. Terms that do not depend on y_j have been omitted from Eq. 2. For values of y_j below zero there is a quadratic energy function which leads to a Gaussian distribution. The same is true for values of y_j above zero, but it is a different quadratic (Fig. 1c). The Gaussian distributions corresponding to the two quadratics must agree at $y_j = 0$ (Fig. 1b). Because this distribution is piecewise Gaussian it is possible to perform Gibbs sampling exactly.

Given samples from the posterior, the generative weights of a RGBN can be learned by using the online delta rule to maximise the log probability of the data.[2]

$$\Delta g_{ji} = \epsilon \, [y_j]^+ \, (y_i - \hat{y}_i) \qquad (3)$$

The variance of the local Gaussian noise of each unit, σ_j^2, can also be learned by an online rule, $\Delta \sigma_j^2 = \epsilon \, [(y_j - \hat{y}_j)^2 - \sigma_j^2]$. Alternatively, σ_j^2 can be fixed at 1 for all hidden units and the effective local noise level can be controlled by scaling the generative weights.

3   The Role of Lateral Connections in Perceptual Inference

In RGBNs and other layered belief networks, fixing the value of a unit in one layer causes correlations between the parents of that unit in the layer above. One of the main reasons why purely bottom-up approaches to perceptual inference have proven inadequate for learning in layered belief networks is that they fail to take into account this phenomenon, which is known as "explaining away."

Lee and Seung (1997) introduced a clever way of using lateral connections to handle explaining away effects during perceptual inference. Consider the network shown in Fig. 2. One contribution, E_{below}, to the energy of the state of the network is the squared difference between the unrectified states of the units in one layer, y_j, and the top-down expectations generated by the states of units in the layer above. Assuming the local noise models for the lower layer units all have unit variance, and

---

[2]If Gibbs sampling has not been run long enough to reach equilibrium, the delta rule follows the gradient of the *penalized* log probability of the data [10]. The penalty term is the Kullback-Liebler divergence between the equilibrium distribution and the distribution produced by Gibbs sampling. Other things being equal, the delta rule therefore adjusts the parameters that determine the equilibrium distribution to reduce this penalty, thus favouring models for which Gibbs sampling works quickly.

ignoring biases and constant terms that are unaffected by the states of the units

$$E_{\text{below}} = \frac{1}{2} \sum_j (y_j - \hat{y}_j)^2 = \frac{1}{2} \sum_j (y_j - \sum_k [y_k]^+ g_{kj})^2. \tag{4}$$

Rearranging this expression and setting $r_{jk} = g_{kj}$ and $m_{kl} = -\sum_j g_{kj} g_{lj}$ we get

$$E_{\text{below}} = \frac{1}{2} \sum_j y_j^2 - \sum_k [y_k]^+ \sum_j y_j r_{jk} - \frac{1}{2} \sum_k [y_k]^+ \sum_l [y_l]^+ m_{kl}. \tag{5}$$

This energy function can be exactly implemented in a network with recognition weights, r_{jk}, and symmetric lateral interactions, m_{kl}. The lateral and recognition connections allow a unit, k, to compute how E_{below} for the layer below depends on its own state and therefore they allow it to follow the gradient of E or to perform Gibbs sampling in E.

Figure 2: A small segment of a network, showing the generative weights (dashed) and the recognition and lateral weights (solid) which implement perceptual inference and correctly handle explaining away effects.

Seung's trick can be used in an RGBN and it eliminates the most neurally implausible aspect of this model which is that a unit in one layer appears to need to send both its state y and the top-down prediction of its state $\hat{y}$ to units in the layer above. Using the lateral connections, the units in the layer above can, in effect, compute all they need to know about the top-down predictions. In computer simulations, we can simply set each lateral connection m_{kl} to be the dot product $-\sum_j g_{kj} g_{lj}$. It is also possible to learn these lateral connections in a more biologically plausible way by driving units in the layer below with unit-variance independent Gaussian noise and using a simple anti-Hebbian learning rule. Similarly, a purely local learning rule can learn recognition weights equal to the generative weights. If units at one layer are driven by unit-variance, independent Gaussian noise, and these in turn drive units in the layer below using the generative weights, then Hebbian learning between the two layers will learn the correct recognition weights [5].

4 Lateral Connections in the Generative Model

When the generative model contains only top-down connections, lateral connections make it possible to do perceptual inference using locally available information. But it is also possible, and often desirable, to have lateral connections in the generative model. Such connections can cause nearby units in a layer to have *a priori* correlated activities, which in turn can lead to the formation of redundant codes and, as we will see, topographic maps.

Symmetric lateral interactions between the unrectified states of units within a layer have the effect of adding a quadratic term to the energy function

$$E_{\text{MRF}} = \frac{1}{2} \sum_k \sum_l M_{kl} \, y_k y_l, \tag{6}$$

which corresponds to a Gaussian Markov Random Field (MRF). During sampling, this term is simply added to the top-down energy contribution. Learning is more difficult. The difficulty stems from the need to know the derivatives of the partition function of the MRF for each data vector. This partition function depends on the top-down inputs to a layer so it varies from one data vector to the next, even if the lateral connections themselves are non-adaptive. Fortunately, since both the MRF and the top-down prediction define Gaussians over the states of the units in a layer, these derivatives can be easily calculated. Assuming unit variances,

$$\Delta g_{ji} = \epsilon \left([y_j]^+ (y_i - \hat{y}_i) + [y_j]^+ \sum_k \left[M(I+M)^{-1} \right]_{ik} \hat{y}_k \right) \tag{7}$$

where M is the MRF matrix for the layer including units i and k, and I is the identity matrix. The first term is the delta rule (Eq. 3); the second term is the derivative of the partition function which unfortunately involves a matrix inversion. Since the partition function for a multivariate Gaussian is analytical it is also possible to learn the lateral connections in the MRF.

Lateral interactions between the *rectified* states of units add the quadratic term $\frac{1}{2} \sum_k \sum_l M_{kl} [y_k]^+ [y_l]^+$. The partition function is no longer analytical, so computing the gradient of the likelihood involves a two-phase Boltzmann-like procedure:

$$\Delta g_{ji} = \epsilon \left(\left\langle [y_j]^+ y_i \right\rangle^* - \left\langle [y_j]^+ y_i \right\rangle^- \right), \tag{8}$$

where $\langle \cdot \rangle^*$ averages with respect to the posterior distribution of y_i and y_j, and $\langle \cdot \rangle^-$ averages with respect to the posterior distribution of y_j and the prior of y_i given units in the same layer as j. This learning rule suffers from all the problems of the Boltzmann machine, namely it is slow and requires two-phases. However, there is an approximation which results in the familiar one-phase delta rule that can be described in three equivalent ways: (1) it treats the lateral connections in the generative model as if they were additional lateral connections in the recognition model; (2) instead of lateral connections in the generative model it assumes some fictitious children with clamped values which affect inference but whose likelihood is not maximised during learning; (3) it maximises a penalized likelihood of the model without the lateral connections in the generative model.

5   Discovering depth in simplified stereograms

Consider the following generative process for stereo pairs. Random dots of uniformly distributed intensities are scattered sparsely on a one-dimensional surface, and the image is blurred with a Gaussian filter. This surface is then randomly placed at one of two different depths, giving rise to two possible left-to-right disparities between the images seen by each eye. Separate Gaussian noise is then added to the image seen by each eye. Some images generated in this manner are shown in Fig. 3a.

a 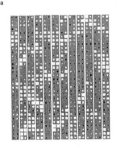 b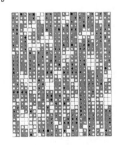

Figure 3: a) Sample data from the stereo disparity problem. The left and right column of each 2×32 image are the inputs to the left and right eye, respectively. Periodic boundary conditions were used. The value of a pixel is represented by the size of the square, with white being positive and black being negative. Notice that pixel noise makes it difficult to infer the disparity, *i.e.* the vertical shift between the left and right columns, in some images. b) Sample images generated by the model after learning.

We trained a three-layer RGBN consisting of 64 visible units, 64 units in the first hidden layer and 1 unit in the second hidden layer on the 32-pixel wide stereo disparity problem. Each of the hidden units in the first hidden layer was connected to the entire array of visible units, *i.e.* it had inputs from both eyes. The hidden units in this layer were also laterally connected in an MRF over the unrectified units. Nearby units excited each other and more distant units inhibited each other, with the net pattern of excitation/inhibition being a difference of two Gaussians. This MRF was initialised with large weights which decayed exponentially to zero over the course of training. The network was trained for 30 passes through a data set of 2000 images. For each image we used 16 iterations of Gibbs sampling to approximate the posterior distribution over hidden states. Each iteration consisted of sampling every hidden unit once in a random order. The states after the fourth iteration of Gibbs sampling were used for learning, with a learning rate of 0.05 and a weight decay parameter of 0.001. Since the top level of the generative process makes a discrete decision between left and right global disparity we used a trivial extension of the RGBN in which the top level unit saturates both at 0 and 1.

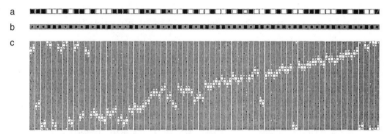

Figure 4: Generative weights of a three-layered RGBN after being trained on the stereo disparity problem. **a)** Weights from the top layer hidden unit to the 64 middle-layer hidden units. **b)** Biases of the middle-layer hidden units, and **c)** weights from the hidden units to the 2×32 visible array.

Thirty-two of the hidden units learned to become local left-disparity detectors, while the other 32 became local right-disparity detectors (Fig. 4c). The unit in the second hidden layer learned positive weights to the left-disparity detectors in the layer below, and negative weights to the right detectors (Fig. 4a). In fact, the activity of this top unit discriminated the true global disparity of the input images with 99% accuracy. A random sample of images generated by the model after learning is shown in Fig. 3b. In addition to forming a hierarchical distributed representation of disparity, units in the hidden layer self-organised into a topographic map. The MRF caused high correlations between nearby units early in learning, which in turn resulted in nearby units learning similar weight vectors. The emergence of topography depended on the strength of the MRF and on the speed with which it decayed. Results were relatively insensitive to other parametric changes.

We also presented image patches taken from natural images [1] to a network with units in the first hidden layer arranged in laterally-connected 2D grid. The network developed local feature detectors, with nearby units responding to similar features (Fig. 5). Not all units were used, but the unused units all clustered into one area.

6   Discussion

Classical models of topography formation such as Kohonen's self-organising map [6] and the elastic net [2, 4] can be thought of as variations on mixture models where additional constraints have been placed to encourage neighboring hidden units to have similar generative weights. The problem with a mixture model is that it cannot handle images in which there are several things going on at once. In contrast, we

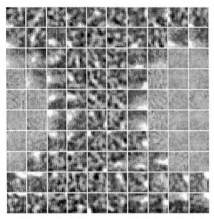

Figure 5: Generative weights of an RGBN trained on 12 × 12 natural image patches: weights from each of the 100 hidden units which were arranged in a 10 × 10 sheet with toroidal boundary conditions.

have shown that topography can arise in much richer hierarchical and componential generative models by inducing correlations between neighboring units.

There is a sense in which topography is a necessary consequence of the lateral connection trick used for perceptual inference. It is infeasible to interconnect all pairs of units in a cortical area. If we assume that direct lateral interactions (or interactions mediated by interneurons) are primarily local, then widely separated units will not have the apparatus required for explaining away. Consequently the computation of the posterior distribution will be incorrect unless the generative weight vectors of widely separated units are orthogonal. If the generative weights are constrained to be positive, the only way two vectors can be orthogonal is for each to have zeros wherever the other has non-zeros. Since the redundancies that the hidden units are trying to model are typically spatially localised, it follows that widely separated units must attend to different parts of the image and units can only attend to overlapping patches if they are laterally interconnected. The lateral connections in the generative model assist in the formation of the topography required for correct perceptual inference.

Acknowledgements. We thank P. Dayan, B. Frey, G. Goodhill, D. MacKay, R. Neal and M. Revow. The research was funded by NSERC and ITRC. GEH is the Nesbitt-Burns fellow of CIAR.

References

[1] A. Bell & T. J. Sejnowski. The 'Independent components' of natural scenes are edge filters. *Vision Research*, In Press.

[2] R. Durbin & D. Willshaw. An analogue approach to the travelling salesman problem using an elastic net method. *Nature*, 326(16):689–691, 1987.

[3] Z. Ghahramani & G. E. Hinton. The EM algorithm for mixtures of factor analyzers. Univ. Toronto Technical Report CRG-TR-96-1, 1996.

[4] G. J. Goodhill & D. J. Willshaw. Application of the elatic net algorithm to the formation of ocular dominance stripes. *Network: Comp. in Neur. Sys.*, 1:41–59, 1990.

[5] G. E. Hinton & Z. Ghahramani. Generative models for discovering sparse distributed representations. *Philos. Trans. Roy. Soc. B*, 352:1177–1190, 1997.

[6] T. Kohonen. Self-organized formation of topologically correct feature maps. *Biological Cybernetics*, 43:59–69, 1982.

[7] D. D. Lee & H. S. Seung. Unsupervised learning by convex and conic coding. In M. Mozer, M. Jordan, & T. Petsche, eds., *NIPS 9*. MIT Press, Cambridge, MA, 1997.

[8] M. S. Lewicki & T. J. Sejnowski. Bayesian unsupervised learning of higher order structure. In *NIPS 9*. MIT Press, Cambridge, MA, 1997.

[9] R. M. Neal. Connectionist learning of belief networks. *Artif. Intell.*, 56:71–113, 1992.

[10] R. M. Neal & G. E. Hinton. A new view of the EM algorithm that justifies incremental and other variants. *Unpublished Manuscript*, 1993.

Regression with Input-dependent Noise: A Gaussian Process Treatment

Paul W. Goldberg
Department of Computer Science
University of Warwick
Coventry, CV4 7AL, UK
pwg@dcs.warwick.ac.uk

Christopher K.I. Williams
Neural Computing Research Group
Aston University
Birmingham B4 7ET, UK
c.k.i.williams@aston.ac.uk

Christopher M. Bishop
Microsoft Research
St. George House
1 Guildhall Street
Cambridge, CB2 3NH, UK
cmbishop@microsoft.com

Abstract

Gaussian processes provide natural non-parametric prior distributions over regression functions. In this paper we consider regression problems where there is noise on the output, and the variance of the noise depends on the inputs. If we assume that the noise is a smooth function of the inputs, then it is natural to model the noise variance using a second Gaussian process, in addition to the Gaussian process governing the noise-free output value. We show that prior uncertainty about the parameters controlling both processes can be handled and that the posterior distribution of the noise rate can be sampled from using Markov chain Monte Carlo methods. Our results on a synthetic data set give a posterior noise variance that well-approximates the true variance.

1 Background and Motivation

A very natural approach to regression problems is to place a prior on the kinds of function that we expect, and then after observing the data to obtain a posterior. The prior can be obtained by placing prior distributions on the weights in a neural network, although we would argue that it is perhaps more natural to place priors directly over functions. One tractable way of doing this is to create a *Gaussian process prior*. This has the advantage that predictions can be made from the posterior using only matrix multiplication for fixed hyperparameters and a global noise level. In contrast, for neural networks (with fixed hyperparameters and a global noise level) it is necessary to use approximations or Markov chain Monte Carlo (MCMC) methods. Rasmussen (1996) has demonstrated that predictions obtained with Gaussian processes are as good as or better than other state-of-the art predictors.

In much of the work on regression problems in the statistical and neural networks literatures, it is assumed that there is a global noise level, independent of the input vector x. The book by Bishop (1995) and the papers by Bishop (1994), MacKay (1995) and Bishop and Qazaz (1997) have examined the case of input-dependent noise for parametric models such as neural networks. (Such models are said to *heteroscedastic* in the statistics literature.) In this paper we develop the treatment of an input-dependent noise model for Gaussian process regression, where the noise is assumed to be Gaussian but its variance depends on x. As the noise level is non-negative we place a Gaussian process prior on the log noise level. Thus there are two Gaussian processes involved in making predictions: the usual Gaussian process for predicting the function values (the y-process), and another one (the z-process) for predicting the log noise level. Below we present a Markov chain Monte Carlo method for carrying out inference with this model and demonstrate its performance on a test problem.

1.1   Gaussian processes

A stochastic process is a collection of random variables $\{Y(x)|x \in X\}$ indexed by a set X. Often X will be a space such as $\mathcal{R}^d$ for some dimension d, although it could be more general. The stochastic process is specified by giving the probability distribution for every finite subset of variables $Y(x_1), \ldots, Y(x_k)$ in a consistent manner. A Gaussian process is a stochastic process which can be fully specified by its mean function $\mu(x) = E[Y(x)]$ and its covariance function $C_P(x, x') = E[(Y(x) - \mu(x))(Y(x') - \mu(x'))]$; any finite set of points will have a joint multivariate Gaussian distribution. Below we consider Gaussian processes which have $\mu(x) \equiv 0$. This assumes that any known offset or trend in the data has been removed. A non-zero $\mu(x)$ is easily incorporated into the framework at the expense of extra notational complexity.

A *covariance function* is used to define a Gaussian process; it is a parametrised function from pairs of x-values to their covariance. The form of the covariance function that we shall use for the prior over functions is given by

$$C_Y(x^{(i)}, x^{(j)}) = v_Y \exp\left(-\frac{1}{2}\sum_{l=1}^{d} w_{Yl}(x_l^{(i)} - x_l^{(j)})^2\right) + J_Y\delta(i,j) \qquad (1)$$

where v_Y specifies the overall y-scale and $w_{Yl}^{-1/2}$ is the length-scale associated with the lth coordinate. J_Y is a "jitter" term (as discussed by Neal, 1997), which is added to prevent ill-conditioning of the covariance matrix of the outputs. J_Y is a typically given a small value, e.g. 10^{-6}.

For the prediction problem we are given n data points $\mathcal{D} = ((x_1, t_1), (x_2, t_2),$

$\ldots, (x_n, t_n))$, where t_i is the observed output value at x_i. The t's are assumed to have been generated from the true y-values by adding independent Gaussian noise whose variance is x-dependent. Let the noise variance at the n data points be $r = (r(x_1), r(x_2), \ldots, r(x_n))$. Given the assumption of a Gaussian process prior over functions, it is a standard result (e.g. Whittle, 1963) that the predictive distribution $P(t^*|x^*)$ corresponding to a new input x^* is $t^* \sim N(\hat{t}(x^*), \sigma^2(x^*))$, where

$$\hat{t}(x^*) = k_Y^T(x^*)(K_Y + K_N)^{-1}t \tag{2}$$
$$\sigma^2(x^*) = C_Y(x^*, x^*) + r(x^*) - k_Y^T(x^*)(K_Y + K_N)^{-1}k_Y(x^*) \tag{3}$$

where the noise-free covariance matrix K_Y satisfies $[K_Y]_{ij} = C_Y(x_i, x_j)$, and $k_Y(x^*) = (C_Y(x^*, x_1), \ldots, C_Y(x^*, x_n))^T$, $K_N = \text{diag}(r)$ and $t = (t_1, \ldots, t_n)^T$, and $\sqrt{\sigma^2(x^*)}$ gives the "error bars" or confidence interval of the prediction.

In this paper we do not specify a functional form for the noise level $r(x)$ but we do place a prior over it. An independent Gaussian process (the z-process) is defined to be the log of the noise level. Its values at the training data points are denoted by $z = (z_1, \ldots, z_n)$, so that $r = (\exp(z_1), \ldots, \exp(z_n))$. The prior for z has a covariance function $C_Z(x^{(i)}, x^{(j)})$ similar to that given in equation 1, although the parameters v_Z and the w_{Zl}'s can be chosen to be different to those for the y-process. We also add the jitter term $J_Z\delta(i, j)$ to the covariance function for Z, where J_Z is given the value 10^{-2}. This value is larger than usual, for technical reasons discussed later.

We use a zero-mean process for z which carries a prior assumption that the average noise rate is approximately 1 (being e to the power of components of z). This is suitable for the experiment described in section 3. In general it is easy to add an offset to the z-process to shift the prior noise rate.

2   An input-dependent noise process

We discuss, in turn, sampling the noise rates and making predictions with fixed values of the parameters that control both processes, and sampling from the posterior on these parameters.

2.1   Sampling the Noise Rates

The predictive distribution for t^*, the output at a point x^*, is $P(t^*|t) = \int P(t^*|t, r(z))P(z|t)dz$. Given a z vector, the prediction $P(t^*|t, r(z))$ is Gaussian with mean and variance given by equations 2 and 3, but $P(z|t)$ is difficult to handle analytically, so we use a Monte Carlo approximation to the integral. Given a representative sample $\{z_1, \ldots, z_k\}$ of log noise rate vectors we can approximate the integral by the sum $\frac{1}{k}\sum_j P(t^*|t, r(z_j))$.

We wish to sample from the distribution $P(z|t)$. As this is quite difficult, we sample instead from $P(y, z|t)$; a sample for $P(z|t)$ can then be obtained by ignoring the y values. This is a similar approach to that taken by Neal (1997) in the case of Gaussian processes used for classification or robust regression with t-distributed noise. We find that

$$P(y, z|t) \propto P(t|y, r(z))P(y)P(z). \tag{4}$$

We use Gibbs sampling to sample from $P(y, z|t)$ by alternately sampling from $P(z|y, t)$ and $P(y|z, t)$. Intuitively were are alternating the "fitting" of the curve (or

y-process) with "fitting" the noise level (z-process). These two steps are discussed in turn.

• *Sampling from $P(y|t, z)$*

For y we have that

$$P(y|t, z) \propto P(t|y, r(z))P(y) \tag{5}$$

where

$$P(t|y, r(z)) = \prod_{i=1}^{n} \frac{1}{(2\pi r_i)^{1/2}} \exp\left(-\frac{(t_i - y_i)^2}{2r_i}\right). \tag{6}$$

Equation (6) can also be written as $P(t|y, r(z)) \sim N(t, K_N)$. Thus $P(y|t, z)$ is a multivariate Gaussian with mean $(K_Y^{-1} + K_N^{-1})^{-1} K_N^{-1} t$ and covariance matrix $(K_Y^{-1} + K_N^{-1})^{-1}$ which can be sampled by standard methods.

• *Sampling from $P(z|t, y)$*

For fixed y and t we obtain

$$P(z|y, t) \propto P(t|y, z)P(z). \tag{7}$$

The form of equation 6 means that it is not easy to sample z as a vector. Instead we can sample its components separately, which is a standard Gibbs sampling algorithm. Let z_i denote the ith component of z and let z_{-i} denote the remaining components. Then

$$P(z_i|z_{-i}, y, t) \propto \frac{1}{(2\pi \exp(z_i))^{1/2}} \exp\left(-\frac{(t_i - y_i)^2}{2\exp(z_i)}\right) P(z_i|z_{-i}). \tag{8}$$

$P(z_i|z_{-i})$ is the distribution of z_i conditioned on the values of z_{-i}. The computation of $P(z_i|z_{-i})$ is very similar to that described by equations (2) and (3), except that $C_Y(\cdot, \cdot)$ is replaced by $C_Z(\cdot, \cdot)$ and there is no noise so that $r(\cdot)$ will be identically zero.

We sample from $P(z_i|z_{-i}, y, t)$ using rejection sampling. We first sample from $P(z_i|z_{-i})$, and then reject according to the term $\exp\{-z_i/2 - \frac{1}{2}(t_i - y_i)^2 \exp(-z_i)\}$ (the likelihood of local noise rate z_i), which can be rescaled to have a maximum value of 1 over z_i. Note that it is not necessary to perform a separate matrix inversion for each i when computing the $P(z_i|z_{-i})$ terms; the required matrices can be computed efficiently from the inverse of K_Z. We find that the average rejection rate is approximately two-thirds, which makes the method we currently use reasonably efficient. Note that it is also possible to incorporate the term $\exp(-z_i/2)$ from the likelihood into the mean of the Gaussian $P(z_i|z_{-i})$ to reduce the rejection rate.

As an alternative approach, it is possible to carry out Gibbs sampling for $P(z_i|z_{-i}, t)$ without explicitly representing y, using the fact that $\log P(t|z) = -\frac{1}{2}\log|K| - \frac{1}{2}t^T K^{-1} t + const$, where $K = K_Y + K_N$. We have implemented this and found similar results to those obtained using sampling of the y's. However, explicitly representing the y-process is useful when adapting the parameters, as described in section 2.3.

2.2 Making predictions

So far we have explained how to obtain a sample from $P(z|t)$. To make predictions we use

$$P(t^*|t) \simeq \frac{1}{k} \sum_j P(t^*|t, r(z_j)). \tag{9}$$

However, $P(t^*|t, r(z_j))$ is not immediately available, as z^*, the noise level at x^* is unknown. In fact

$$P(t^*|t, r(z_j)) = \int P(t^*|z^*, t, r(z_j)) P(z^*|z_j, t) \, dz^*. \tag{10}$$

$P(z^*|z_j, t)$ is simply a Gaussian distribution for z^* conditioned on z_j, and is obtained in a similar way to $P(z_i|z_{-i})$. As $P(t^*|z^*, t, r(z_j))$ is a Gaussian distribution as given by equations (2) and (3), $P(t^*|t, r(z_j))$ is an infinite mixture of Gaussians with weights $P(z^*|z_j)$. Note, however, that each of these components has the same mean $\hat{t}(x^*)$ as given by equation (2), but a different variance.

We approximate $P(t^*|t, r(z_j))$ by taking $s = 10$ samples of $P(z^*|z_j)$ and thus obtain a mixture of s Gaussians as the approximating distribution. The approximation for $P(t^*|t)$ is then obtained by averaging these s-component mixtures over the k samples $z_1, \ldots, z_k$ to obtain an sk-component mixture of Gaussians.

2.3 Adapting the parameters

Above we have described how to obtain a sample from the posterior distribution $P(z|t)$ and to use this to make predictions, based on the assumption that the parameters θ_Y (i.e. $v_Y, J_Y, w_{Y1}, \ldots, w_{Yd}$) and θ_Z (i.e. $v_Z, J_Z, w_{Z1}, \ldots, w_{Zd}$) have been set to the correct values. In practice we are unlikely to know what these settings should be, and so introduce a hierarchical model, as shown in Figure 1. This graphical model shows that the joint probability distribution decomposes as $P(\theta_Y, \theta_Z, y, z, t) = P(\theta_Y) P(\theta_Z) P(y|\theta_Y) P(z|\theta_Z) P(t|y, z)$.

Our goal now becomes to obtain a sample from the posterior $P(\theta_Y, \theta_Z, y, z|t)$, which can be used for making predictions as before. (Again, the y samples are not needed for making predictions, but they will turn out to be useful for sampling θ_Y.) Sampling from the joint posterior can be achieved by interleaving updates of θ_Y and θ_Z with y and z updates. Gibbs sampling for θ_Y and θ_Z is not feasible as these parameters are buried deeply in the K_Y and K_N matrices, so we use the Metropolis algorithm for their updates. As usual, we consider moving from our current state $\theta = (\theta_Y, \theta_Z)$ to a new state $\tilde{\theta}$ using a proposal distribution $J(\theta, \tilde{\theta})$. In practice we take J to be an isotropic Gaussian centered on θ. Denote the ratio of $P(\theta_Y) P(\theta_Z) P(y|\theta_Y) P(z|\theta_Z)$ in states $\tilde{\theta}$ and θ by r. Then the proposed state $\tilde{\theta}$ is accepted with probability $\min\{r, 1\}$.

It would also be possible to use more sophisticated MCMC algorithms such as the Hybrid Monte Carlo algorithm which uses derivative information, as discussed in Neal (1997).

3 Results

We have tested the method on a one-dimensional synthetic problem. 60 data points

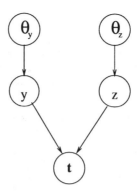

Figure 1: The hierarchical model including parameters.

were generated from the function $y = 2\sin(2\pi x)$ on $[0, 1]$ by adding independent Gaussian noise. This noise has a standard deviation that increases linearly from 0.5 at $x = 0$ to 1.5 at $x = 1$. The function and the training data set are illustrated in Figure 2(a).

As the parameters are non-negative quantities, we actually compute with their log values. $\log v_Y, \log v_Z, \log w_Y$ and $\log w_Z$ were given $N(0, 1)$ prior distributions. The jitter values were fixed at $J_Y = 10^{-6}$ and $J_Z = 10^{-2}$. The relatively large value for J_Z assists the convergence of the Gibbs sampling, since it is responsible for most of the variance of the conditional distribution $P(z_i | z_{-i})$. The broadening of this distribution leads to samples whose likelihoods are more variable, allowing the likelihood term (used for rejection) to be more influential.

In our simulations, on each iteration we made three Metropolis updates for the parameters, along with sampling from all of the y and z variables. The Metropolis proposal distribution was an isotropic Gaussian with variance 0.01. We ran for 3000 iterations, and discarded the first one-third of iterations as "burn-in", after which plots of each of the parameters seemed to have settled down. The parameters and z values were stored every 100 iterations. In Figure 2(b) the average standard deviation of the inferred noise has been plotted, along with with two standard deviation error-bars. Notice how the standard deviation increases from left to right, in close agreement with the data generator.

Studying the posterior distributions of the parameters, we find that the y-lengthscale $\lambda_Y \stackrel{def}{=} (w_Y)^{-1/2}$ is well localized around 0.22 ± 0.1, in good agreement with the wavelength of the sinusoidal generator. (For the covariance function in equation 1, the expected number of zero crossings per unit length is $1/\pi\lambda_Y$.) $(w_Z)^{-1/2}$ is less tightly constrained, which makes sense as it corresponds to a longer wavelength process, and with only a short segment of data available there is still considerable posterior uncertainty.

4   Conclusions

We have introduced a natural non-parametric prior on variable noise rates, and given an effective method of sampling the posterior distribution, using a MCMC

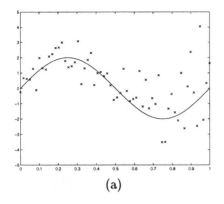
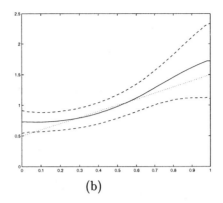

(a)   (b)

Figure 2: (a) shows the training set (crosses); the solid line depicts the x-dependent mean of the output. (b) The solid curve shows the average standard deviation of the noise process, with two standard deviation error bars plotted as dashed lines. The dotted line indicates the true standard deviation of the data generator.

method. When applied to a data set with varying noise, the posterior noise rates obtained are well-matched to the known structure. We are currently experimenting with the method on some more challenging real-world problems.

Acknowledgements

This work was carried out at Aston University under EPSRC Grant Ref. GR/K 51792 *Validation and Verification of Neural Network Systems.*

References

[1] C.M. Bishop (1994). Mixture Density Networks. Technical report NCRG/94/001, Neural Computing Research Group, Aston University, Birmingham, UK.

[2] C.M. Bishop (1995). *Neural Networks for Pattern Recognition.* Oxford University Press.

[3] C.M. Bishop and C. Qazaz (1997). Regression with Input-dependent Noise: A Bayesian Treatment. In M. C. Mozer, M. I. Jordan and T. Petsche (Eds) *Advances in Neural Information Processing Systems 9* Cambridge MA MIT Press.

[4] D. J. C. MacKay (1995). Probabilistic networks: new models and new methods. In F. Fogelman-Soulie and P. Gallinari (Eds), *Proceedings ICANN'95 International Conference on Neural Networks*, pp. 331-337. Paris, EC2 & Cie.

[5] R. Neal (1997). Monte Carlo Implementation of Gaussian Process Models for Bayesian Regression and Classification. Technical Report 9702, Department of Statistics, University of Toronto. Available from `http://www.cs.toronto.edu/~radford/`.

[6] C.E. Rasmussen (1996). *Evaluation of Gaussian Processes and Other Methods for Nonlinear Regression.* PhD thesis, Department of Computer Science, University of Toronto. Available from `http://www.cs.utoronto.ca/~carl/`.

[7] C.K.I. Williams and C.E. Rasmussen (1996). Gaussian Processes for Regression. In D. S. Touretzky, M. C. Mozer and M. E. Hasselmo *Advances in Neural Information Processing Systems 8* pp. 514-520, Cambridge MA MIT Press.

[8] P. Whittle (1963). *Prediction and regulation by linear least-square methods.* English Universities Press.

Linear concepts and hidden variables:
An empirical study

Adam J. Grove
NEC Research Institute
4 Independence Way
Princeton NJ 08540
grove@research.nj.nec.com

Dan Roth*
Department of Computer Science
University of Illinois at Urbana-Champaign
1304 W. Springfield Ave. Urbana 61801
danr@cs.uiuc.edu

Abstract

Some learning techniques for classification tasks work indirectly, by first trying to fit a full probabilistic model to the observed data. Whether this is a good idea or not depends on the robustness with respect to deviations from the postulated model. We study this question experimentally in a restricted, yet non-trivial and interesting case: we consider a *conditionally independent attribute* (CIA) model which postulates a single binary-valued *hidden variable* z on which all other attributes (i.e., the target and the observables) depend. In this model, finding the most likely value of any one variable (given known values for the others) reduces to testing a linear function of the observed values.

We learn CIA with two techniques: the standard EM algorithm, and a new algorithm we develop based on covariances. We compare these, in a controlled fashion, against an algorithm (a version of *Winnow*) that attempts to find a good linear classifier directly. Our conclusions help delimit the fragility of using the CIA model for classification: once the data departs from this model, performance quickly degrades and drops below that of the directly-learned linear classifier.

1 Introduction

We consider the classic task of predicting a *binary* (0/1) target variable x_0, based on the values of some n other binary variables $x_1 \ldots x_n$. We can distinguish between two styles of learning approach for such tasks. *Parametric* algorithms postulate some form of probabilistic model underlying the data, and try to fit the model's parameters. To classify an example we can compute the conditional probability distribution for x_0 given the values of the known variables, and then predict the most probable value. *Non-parametric* algorithms do not assume that the training data has a particular form. They instead search directly in the space of possible classification functions, attempting to find one with small error on the training set of examples.

An important advantage of parametric approaches is that the induced model can be used to support a wide range of inferences, aside from the specified classification task. On the other hand, to postulate a particular form of probabilistic model can be a very strong assumption.

*Partly supported by ONR grant N00014-96-1-0550 while visiting Harvard University.

So it is important to understand how robust such methods are when the real world deviates from the assumed model.

In this paper, we report on some experiments that test this issue. We consider the specific case of $n + 1$ *conditionally independent attributes* x_i together with a single *unobserved* variable z, also assumed to be binary valued, on which the x_i depend (henceforth, the binary CIA model); see Section 2. In fact, such models are plausible in many domains (for instance, in some language interpretation tasks; see [GR96]). We fit the parameters of the CIA model using the well-known *expectation-maximization* (EM) technique [DLR77], and also with a new algorithm we have developed based on estimating covariances; see Section 4. In the nonparametric case, we simply search for a good *linear separator*. This is because the optimal predictors for the binary CIA model (i.e., for predicting one variable given known values for the rest) are also linear. This means that our comparison is "fair" in the sense that neither strategy can choose from classifiers with more expressive power than the other. As a representative of the non-parametric class of algorithms, we use the Winnow algorithm of [Lit88], with some modifications (see Section 6). Winnow works directly to find a "good" linear separator. It is guaranteed to find a perfect separator if one exists, and empirically seems to be fairly successful even when there is no perfect separator [GR96, Blu97]. It is also very fast.

Our experimental methodology is to first generate synthetic data from a true CIA model and test performance; we then study various deviations from the model. There are various interesting issues involved in constructing good experiments, including the desirability of controlling the inherent "difficulty" of learning a model. Since we cannot characterize the entire space, we consider here only deviations in which the data is drawn from a CIA model in which the hidden variable can take more than two values. (Note that the optimal classifier given x_0 is generally not linear in this case.)

Our observations are not *qualitatively* surprising. CIA does well when the assumed model is correct, but performance degrades when the world departs from the model. But as we discuss, we found it surprising how fragile this model can sometimes be, when compared against algorithms such as Winnow. This is even though the data is not linearly separable either, and so one might expect the direct learning techniques to degrade in performance as well. But it seems that Winnow and related approaches are far less fragile. Thus the main contribution of this work is that our results shed light on the specific tradeoff between fitting parameters to a probabilistic model, versus direct search for a good classifier. Specifically, they illustrate the dangers of predicting using a model that is even "slightly" simpler than the distribution actually generating the data, vs. the relative robustness of directly searching for a good predictor. This would seem to be an important practical issue, and highlights the need for some better theoretical understanding of the notion of "robustness".

2 Conditionally Independent Attributes

Throughout we assume that each example is a binary vector $\tilde{x} \in \{0, 1\}^{n+1}$, and that each example is generated independently at random according to some unknown distribution on $\{0, 1\}^{n+1}$. We use X_i to denote the i'th attribute, considered as a random variable, and x_i to denote a value for X_i. In the conditionally independent attribute (CIA) model, examples are generated as follows. We postulate a "hidden" variable Z with k values, which takes values z for $0 \leq z < k$ with probability $\alpha_z \geq 0$. Since we must have $\sum_{z=0}^{k-1} \alpha_z = 1$ there are $k - 1$ independent parameters. Having randomly chosen a value z for the hidden variable, we choose the value x_i for each observable X_i: the value is 1 with probability $p_i^{(z)}$, and 0 otherwise. Here $p_i^{(z)} \in [0, 1]$. The attributes' values are chosen independently of each other, although z remains fixed. Note that there are thus $(n + 1)k$ probability parameters $p_i^{(z)}$. In the following, let $\mathcal{P}$ denote the set of all $(n + 1)k + k - 1$ parameters in the model. From this point, and until Section 7, we always assume that $k = 2$ and in this case, to simplify notation, we write α_1 as α, α_0 ($= 1 - \alpha$) as α', p_i^1 as p_i and p_i^0 as q_i.

3 The Expectation-Maximization algorithm (EM)

One traditional unsupervised approach to learning the parameters of this model is to find the maximum-likelihood parameters of the distribution given the data. That is, we attempt to find the set of parameters that maximizes the probability of the data observed.

Finding the maximum likelihood parameterization analytically appears to be a difficult problem, even in this rather simple setting. However, a practical approach is to use the well-known *Expectation-Maximization* algorithm (EM) [DLR77], which is an iterative approach that always converges to a local maximum of the likelihood function. In our setting, the procedure is as follows. We simply begin with a randomly chosen parameterization $\mathcal{P}$, and then we iterate until (apparent) convergence:[1]

Expectation: For all $\tilde{x}^i$, compute $u_i = P_{\mathcal{P}}(\tilde{x}^i \wedge z = 1)$ and $v_i = P_{\mathcal{P}}(\tilde{x}^i \wedge z = 0)$.

Maximization: Reestimate $\mathcal{P}$ as follows (writing $U = \sum_i u_i$ and $V = \sum_i v_i$):

$$\alpha \leftarrow \sum_{i=1}^{s} u_i/(U+V) \qquad p_j \leftarrow \sum_{\{i : \tilde{x}_j^i = 1\}} u_i/U \qquad q_j \leftarrow \sum_{\{i : \tilde{x}_j^i = 1\}} v_i/V.$$

After convergence has been detected all we know is that we are near a *local* minima of the likelihood function. Thus it is prudent to repeat the process with many different restarts. (All our experiments were extremely conservative concerning the stopping criteria at each iteration, and in the number of iterations we tried.) But in practice, we are never sure that the true optimum has been located.

4 Covariances-Based approach

Partly in response to concern just expressed, we also developed another heuristic technique for learning $\mathcal{P}$. The algorithm, which we call COV, is based on measuring the covariance between pairs of attributes. Since we do not see Z, attributes will appear to be correlated. In fact, if the CIA model is correct, it is easy to show that covariance between X_i and X_j (defined as $y_{i,j} = \mu_{i,j} - \mu_i\mu_j$ where $\mu_i, \mu_j, \mu_{i,j}$ are the expectations of $X_i, X_j, (X_i$ and $X_j)$, respectively), will be $y_{i,j} = \alpha\alpha'\delta_i\delta_j$ where δ_i denotes $p_i - q_i$. We also know that the expected value of X_i is $\mu_i = \alpha p_i + \alpha' q_i$. Furthermore, we will be able to get very accurate estimates of μ_i just by observing the proportion of samples in which x_i is 1. Thus, if we could estimate both α and δ_i it would be trivial to solve for estimates of p_i and q_i.

To estimate δ_i, suppose we have computed all the pairwise covariances using the data; we use $\hat{y}_{i,j}$ to denote our estimate of $y_{i,j}$. For any distinct $j, k \neq i$ we clearly have $\alpha\alpha'\delta_i^2 = |\frac{y_{i,j}y_{i,k}}{y_{j,k}}|$ so we could estimate δ_i^2 using this equation. A better estimate would be to consider *all* pairs j, k and average the individual estimates. However, not all individual estimates are equally good. It can be shown that the smaller $y_{j,k}$ is, the less reliable we should expect the estimate to be (and in the limit, where X_j and X_k are perfectly uncorrelated, we get no valid estimate at all). This suggests that we use a weighted average, with the weights proportional to $y_{j,k}$. Using these weights leads us to the next equation for determining δ_i, which, after simplification, is:

$$\alpha\alpha'\delta_i^2 = \frac{\sum_{j,k:j\neq k\neq i} |y_{i,j}y_{i,k}|}{\sum_{j,k:j\neq k\neq i} |y_{j,k}|} = \frac{(\sum_{j:j\neq i} |y_{i,j}|)^2 - \sum_{j:j\neq i} y_{i,j}^2}{\sum_{j,k:j\neq k} |y_{j,k}| - 2\sum_{j:j\neq i} |y_{j,i}|}$$

By substituting the estimates $\hat{y}_{i,j}$ we get an estimate for $\alpha\alpha'\delta_i^2$. This estimate can be computed in linear time except for the determination of $\sum_{j,k:j\neq k} |y_{j,k}|$ which, although quadratic, does not depend on i and so can be computed once and for all. Thus it takes $O(n^2)$ time in total to estimate $\alpha\alpha'\delta_i^2$ for all i.

It remains only to estimate α and the signs of the δ_i's. Briefly, to determine the signs we first stipulate that δ_0 is positive. (Because we never see z, one sign can be chosen at random.)

---

[1]The maximization phase works as though we were estimating parameters by taking averages based on weighted *labeled* data (i.e., in which we see z). If $\tilde{x}_i$ is a sample point, these fictional data points are $(\tilde{x}_i, z = 1)$ with weight u_i/U and $(\tilde{x}_i, z = 0)$ with weight v_i/V.

In principle, then, the sign of δ_j will then be equal to the sign of $y_{0,j}$, which we have an estimate for. In practice, this can statistically unreliable for small sample sizes and so we use a more involved "voting" procedure (details omitted here). Finally we estimate α. We have found no better method of doing this than to simply search for the optimal value, using likelihood as the search criterion. However, this is only a 1-dimensional search and it turns out to be quite efficient in practice.

5 Linear Separators and CIA

Given a fully parameterized CIA model, we may be interested in predicting the value of one variable, say X_0, given known values for the remaining variables. One can show that in fact the optimal prediction region is given by a linear separator in the other variables, although we omit details of this derivation here.[2] This suggest an obvious learning strategy: simply try to find the line which minimizes this loss on the training set. Unfortunately, in general the task of finding a linear separator that minimizes disagreements on a collection of examples is known to be NP-hard [HS92]. So instead we use an algorithm called *Winnow* that is known to produce good results when a linear separator exists, as well as under certain more relaxed assumptions [Lit91], and appears to be quite effective in practice.

6 Learning using a Winnow-based algorithm

The basic version of the Winnow algorithm [Lit88] keeps an n-dimensional vector $w = (w_1, \ldots w_n)$ of positive weights (i.e., w_i is the weight associated with the ith feature), which it updates whenever a mistake is made. Initially, the weight vector is typically set to assign equal positive weight to all features. The algorithm has 3 parameters, a promotion parameter $\alpha > 1$, a demotion parameter $0 < \beta < 1$ and a threshold θ. For a given instance $(x_1, \ldots, x_n)$ the algorithm predicts that $x_0 = 1$ iff $\sum_{i=1}^{m} w_i x_i > \theta$. If the algorithm predicts 0 and the label (i.e., x_0) is 1 (positive example) then the weights which correspond to active attributes ($x_i = 1$) are promoted—the weight w_i is replaced by a larger weight $\alpha \cdot w_i$. Conversely, if algorithm predicts 1 and the received label is 0, then the weights which correspond to active features are demoted by factor β. We allow for negative weights as follows. Given an example $(x_1, \ldots, x_n)$, we rewrite it as an example over $2n$ variables $(y_1, y_2, \ldots, y_{2n})$ where $y_i = x_i$ and $y_{n+i} = 1 - x_i$. We then apply Winnow just as above to learn $2n$ (positive) weights. If w_i^+ is the weight associated with x_i and w_i^- is the weight associated with x_{n+i} (i.e., $1 - x_i$), then the prediction rule is simply to compare $\sum_{i=1}^{n} (w_i^+ x_i + w_i^- (1 - x_i))$ with the threshold.

In the experiments described here we have made two significant modifications to the basic algorithm. To reduce variance, our final classifier is a weighted average of several classifiers; each is trained using a subsample from the training set, and its weight is based based on how well it was doing on that sample. Second, we biased the algorithm so as to look for "thick" classifiers. To understand this, consider the case in which the data is perfectly linearly separable. Then there will generally be many linear concepts that separate the training data we actually see. Among these, it seems plausible that we have a better chance of doing well on the unseen test data if we choose a linear concept that separates the positive and negative training examples as "widely" as possible. The idea of having a wide separation is less clear when there is no perfect separator, but we can still appeal to the basic intuition. To bias the search towards "thick" separators, we change Winnow's training rule somewhat. We now have a new margin parameter τ. As before, we always update when our current hypothesis makes a mistake, but now we *also* update if $|\sum_{i=1}^{n} w_i x_i - \theta|$ is less than τ, even if the prediction is correct. In our experiments, we found that performance when using this version of Winnow is better than that of the basic algorithm, so in this paper we present results for the former.

---

[2] A derivation for the slightly different case, for predicting z, can be found in [MP69].

7 Experimental Methodology

Aside from the choice of algorithm used, the number of attributes n, and the sample size s, our experiments also differed in two other dimensions. These are the type of process generating the data (we will be interested in various deviations from CIA), and the "difficulty" of the problem. These features are determined by the *data model* we use (i.e., the distribution over $\{0, 1\}^n$ used to generate data sets).

Our first experiments consider the case where the data really is drawn from a binary CIA distribution. We associated with any such distribution a "difficulty" parameter B, which is the accuracy with which one could predict the value of Z if one actually knew the correct model. (Of course, even with knowledge of the correct model we should not expect 100% accuracy.) The ability to control B allows us to select and study models with different qualitative characteristics. In particular, this has allowed us concentrated most of our experiments on fairly "hard" instances[3], and to more meaningfully compare trials with differing numbers of attributes. We denote by $\text{CIA}(n, 2, b)$ the class of all data models which are binary CIA distributions over n variables with difficulty b.[4] The next family of data models we used are also CIA models, but now using more than two values for the hidden variable. We denote the family using k values as $\text{CIA}(n, k, b)$ where n and b are as before. When $k > 2$ there are more complex correlation patterns between the X_i than when $k = 2$. Furthermore, the optimal predictor is not necessarily linear. The specific results we discuss in the next section have concentrated on this case.

Given any set of parameters, including a particular class of data models, our experiments are designed with the goal of good statistical accuracy. We repeatedly (typically 100 to 300 times) choose a data model at random from the chosen class, choose a sample of the appropriate size from this model, and then run all our algorithms. Each algorithm produces a (linear) hypothesis. We measure the success rate S_{alg} (i.e., the proportion of times a hypothesis makes the correct prediction of x_0) by drawing yet more random samples from the data model being used. In the test phase we always draw enough new samples so that the confidence interval for S_{alg}, *for the results on a single model*, has width at most $\pm 1\%$. We use the S_{alg} values to construct a *normalized* measure of performance (denoted T) as follows. Let S_{best} be the best possible accuracy attainable for predicting x_0 (i.e., the accuracy achieved by the actual model generating the data). Let S_{const} denote the performance of the best possible constant prediction rule (i.e., the rule that predicts the most likely *a priori* value for x_0). Note that S_{const} and S_{best} can vary from model to model. For each model we compute $\frac{S_{alg} - S_{const}}{S_{best} - S_{const}}$, and our normalized statistic T is the average of these values. It can be thought of as measuring the percentage of the *possible* predictive power, over a plausible baseline, that an algorithm achieves.

8 Results

We only report on a small, but representative, selection of our experiments in any detail. For instance, although we have considered many values of n ranging from 10 to 500, here we show six graphs giving the learning curves for $\text{CIA}(n, k, 0.90)$ for $n = 10, 75$, and for $k = 2, 3, 5$; as noted, we display the T statistic. The error bars show the standard error,[5] providing a rough indication of accuracy. Not surprisingly, when the data model is binary

---

[3]Note that if one simply chooses parameters of a CIA model independently at random, without examining the difficulty of the model or adjusting for n, one will get many trivial problems, in which it is easy to predict Z with nearly 100% accuracy, and thus predict optimally for X_0.

[4]It is nontrivial to efficiently select random models from this class. Briefly, our scheme is to choose each parameter in a CIA model independently from a symmetric beta distribution. Thus, the model parameters will have expected value 0.5. We choose the parameter of the beta distribution (which determines concentration about 0.5) so that the average B value, of the models thus generated, equals b. Finally, we use rejection sampling to find CIA models with B values that are exactly $b \pm 1\%$.

[5]Computed as the observed standard deviation, divided by the square root of the number of trials.

CIA, the EM algorithm does extremely well, learning significantly (if not overwhelmingly) faster than Winnow. But as we depart from the binary CIA assumption, the performance of EM quickly degrades.

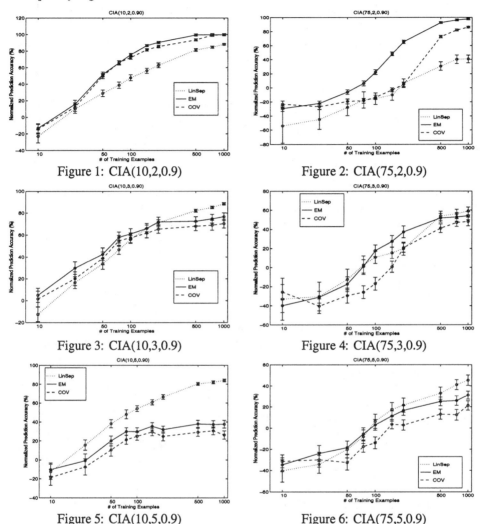

Figure 1: CIA(10,2,0.9)

Figure 2: CIA(75,2,0.9)

Figure 3: CIA(10,3,0.9)

Figure 4: CIA(75,3,0.9)

Figure 5: CIA(10,5,0.9)

Figure 6: CIA(75,5,0.9)

When $k = 3$ performances is, on the whole, very similar for Winnow and EM. But when $k = 5$ Winnow is already superior to EM; significantly and uniformly so for $n = 10$. For fixed k the difference seems to become somewhat less dramatic as n increases; in Figure 6 (for $n = 75$) Winnow is less obviously dominant, and in fact is not better than EM until the sample size has reached 100. (But when $s \leq n$, meaning that we have fewer samples than attributes, the performance is uniformly dismal anyway.)

Should we attribute this degradation to the binary CIA assumption, or to the EM itself? This question is our reason for also considering the covariance algorithm. We see that the results for COV are generally similar to EM's, supporting our belief that the phenomena we see are properties inherent to the model rather than to the specific algorithm being used. Similarly (the results are omitted) we have tried several other algorithms that try to find good linear separators directly, including the classic *Perceptron* algorithm [MP69]; our version of Winnow was the best on the experiments we tried and thus we conjecture that its performance is (somewhat) indicative of what is possible for any such approach.

As the comparison between $n = 10$ and $n = 75$ illustrates, there is little qualitative difference between the phenomena observed as the number of attributes increases. Nevertheless, as n grows it does seem that Winnow needs more examples before its performance surpasses that of the other algorithms (for any fixed k). As already noted, this may be due simply to the very "noisy" nature of the region $s \leq n$. We also have reasons to believe that this is partially an artifact of way we select models.

As previously noted, we also experimented with varying "difficulty" (B) levels. Although we omit the corresponding figures we mentioned that the main difference is that Winnow is a little faster in surpassing EM when the data deviates from the assumed model, but when the data model really is binary CIA, and EM converge even faster to an optimal performance.

These patterns were confirmed when we tried to compare the approaches on real data. We have used data that originates from a problem in which assuming a hidden "context" variable seems somewhat plausible. The data is taken from the context-sensitive spelling correction domain. We used one data set from those that were used in [GR96]. For example, given sentences in which the word *passed* or *past* appear, the task is to determine, for each such occurrence, which of the two it should be. This task may be modeled by thinking of the "context" as a hidden variable in our sense. Yet when we tried to learn in this case under the CIA model, with a binary valued hidden variable, the results were no better than just predicting the most likely classification (around 70%). Winnow, in contrast, performed extremely well and exceeds 95% on this task. We hesitate to read much into our limited real-data experiments, other than to note that so far they are consistent with the more careful experiments on synthetic data.

9   Conclusion

By restricting to a binary hidden variable, we have been able to consider a "fair" comparison between probabilistic model construction, and more traditional algorithms that directly learn a classification—at least in the sense that both have the same expressive power. Our conclusions concerning the fragility of the former should not be surprising but we believe that given the importance of the problem it is valuable to have some idea of the true significance of the effect. As we have indicated, in many real-world cases, where a model of the sort we have considered here seems plausible, it is impossible to nail down more specific characterizations of the probabilistic model. Our results exhibit how important it is to use the correct model and how sensitive are the results to deviations from it, when attempting to learn using model construction. The purpose of this paper is not to advocate that in practice one should use either Winnow or binary CIA in exactly the form considered here. A richer probabilistic model should be used along with a model selection phase. However, studying the problem in a restricted and controlled environment in crucial so as to understand the nature and significance of this fundamental problem.

References

[Blu97] A. Blum. Empirical support for winnow and weighted majority based algorithms: results on a calendar scheduling domain. *Machine Learning*, 26:1–19, 1997.

[DLR77] A. P. Dempster, N. M. Laird, and D. B. Rubin. Maximum likelihood from incomplete data via the EM algorithm. *Royal Statistical Society B*, 39:1–38, 1977.

[GR96] A. R. Golding and D. Roth. Applying winnow to context-sensitive spelling correcton. In *Proc. 13th International Conference on Machine Learning (ML'96)*, pages 182–190, 1996.

[HS92] K. Höffgen and H. Simon. Robust trainability of single neurons. In *Proc. 5th Annu. Workshop on Comput. Learning Theory*, pages 428–439, New York, New York, 1992. ACM Press.

[Lit88] N. Littlestone. Learning quickly when irrelevant attributes abound: A new linear-threshold algorithm. *Machine Learning*, 2:285–318, 1988.

[Lit91] N. Littlestone. Redundant noisy attributes, attribute errors, and linear threshold learning using Winnow. In *Proc. 4th Annu. Workshop on Comput. Learning Theory*, pages 147–156, San Mateo, CA, 1991. Morgan Kaufmann.

[MP69] M. L. Minsky and S. A. Papert. *Perceptrons*. MIT Press, Cambridge, MA, 1969.

Classification by Pairwise Coupling

TREVOR HASTIE *
Stanford University
and
ROBERT TIBSHIRANI †
University of Toronto

Abstract

We discuss a strategy for polychotomous classification that involves
estimating class probabilities for each pair of classes, and then coupling the estimates together. The coupling model is similar to the
Bradley-Terry method for paired comparisons. We study the nature of the class probability estimates that arise, and examine the
performance of the procedure in simulated datasets. The classifiers
used include linear discriminants and nearest neighbors: application to support vector machines is also briefly described.

1 Introduction

We consider the discrimination problem with K classes and N training observations.
The training observations consist of predictor measurements $\mathbf{x} = (x_1, x_2, \ldots x_p)$ on
p predictors and the known class memberships. Our goal is to predict the class
membership of an observation with predictor vector $\mathbf{x}_0$

Typically K-class classification rules tend to be easier to learn for $K = 2$ than for
$K > 2$ — only one decision boundary requires attention. Friedman (1996) suggested
the following approach for the the K-class problem: solve each of the two-class
problems, and then for a test observation, combine all the pairwise decisions to
form a K-class decision. Friedman's combination rule is quite intuitive: assign to
the class that wins the most pairwise comparisons.

Department of Statistics, Stanford University, Stanford California 94305;
trevor@playfair.stanford.edu

Department of Preventive Medicine and Biostatistics, and Department of Statistics;
tibs@utstat.toronto.edu

Friedman points out that this rule is equivalent to the Bayes rule when the class posterior probabilities p_i (at the test point) are known:

$$\text{argmax}_i [p_i] = \text{argmax}_i [\sum_{j \neq i} I\left(p_i/(p_i + p_j) > p_j/(p_i + p_j)\right)]$$

Note that Friedman's rule requires only an estimate of each pairwise decision. Many (pairwise) classifiers provide not only a rule, but estimated class probabilities as well. In this paper we argue that one can improve on Friedman's procedure by combining the pairwise class probability estimates into a joint probability estimate for all K classes.

This leads us to consider the following problem. Given a set of events $A_1, A_2, \ldots A_K$, some experts give us pairwise probabilities $r_{ij} = \text{Prob}(A_i | A_i \text{ or } A_j)$. Is there a set of probabilities $p_i = \text{Prob}(A_i)$ that are compatible with the r_{ij}?

In an exact sense, the answer is no. Since $\text{Prob}(A_i | A_i \text{ or } A_j) = p_j/(p_i + p_j)$ and $\sum p_i = 1$, we are requiring that $K-1$ free parameters satisfy $K(K-1)/2$ constraints and, this will not have a solution in general. For example, if the r_{ij} are the ijth entries in the matrix

$$\begin{pmatrix} \cdot & 0.9 & 0.4 \\ 0.1 & \cdot & 0.7 \\ 0.6 & 0.3 & \cdot \end{pmatrix} \tag{1}$$

then they are not compatible with any p_i's. This is clear since $r_{12} > .5$ and $r_{23} > .5$, but also $r_{31} > .5$.

The model $\text{Prob}(A_i | A_i \text{ or } A_j) = p_j/(p_i + p_j)$ forms the basis for the Bradley-Terry model for paired comparisons (Bradley & Terry 1952). In this paper we fit this model by minimizing a Kullback-Leibler distance criterion to find the best approximation $\hat{r}_{ij} = \hat{p}_i/(\hat{p}_i + \hat{p}_j)$ to a given set of r_{ij}'s. We carry this out at each predictor value $\mathbf{x}$, and use the estimated probabilities to predict class membership at $\mathbf{x}$.

In the example above, the solution is $\hat{\mathbf{p}} = (0.47, 0.25, 0.28)$. This solution makes qualitative sense since event A_1 "beats" A_2 by a larger margin than the winner of any of the other pairwise matches.

Figure 1 shows an example of these procedures in action. There are 600 data points in three classes, each class generated from a mixture of Gaussians. A linear discriminant model was fit to each pair of classes, giving pairwise probability estimates r_{ij} at each $\mathbf{x}$. The first panel shows Friedman's procedure applied to the pairwise rules. The shaded regions are areas of indecision, where each class wins one vote. The coupling procedure described in the next section was then applied, giving class probability estimates $\hat{\mathbf{p}}(\mathbf{x})$ at each $\mathbf{x}$. The decision boundaries resulting from these probabilities are shown in the second panel. The procedure has done a reasonable job of resolving the confusion, in this case producing decision boundaries similar to the three-class LDA boundaries shown in panel 3. The numbers in parentheses above the plots are test-error rates based on a large test sample from the same population. Notice that despite the indeterminacy, the max-wins procedure performs no worse than the coupling procedure, and both perform better than LDA. Later we show an example where the coupling procedure does substantially better than max-wins.

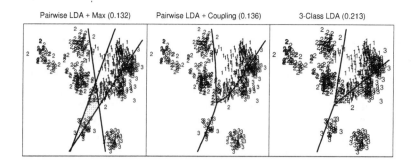

Figure 1: *A three class problem, with the data in each class generated from a mixture of Gaussians. The first panel shows the maximum-win procedure. The second panel shows the decision boundary from coupling of the pairwise linear discriminant rules based on $\hat{d}$ in (6). The third panel shows the three-class LDA boundaries. Test-error rates are shown in parentheses.*

This paper is organized as follows. The coupling model and algorithm are given in section 2. Pairwise threshold optimization, a key advantage of the pairwise approach, is discussed in section 3. In that section we also examine the performance of the various methods on some simulated problems, using both linear discriminant and nearest neighbour rules. The final section contains some discussion.

2 Coupling the probabilities

Let the probabilities at feature vector $\mathbf{x}$ be $\mathbf{p}(\mathbf{x}) = (p_1(\mathbf{x}), \ldots p_K(\mathbf{x}))$. In this section we drop the argument $\mathbf{x}$, since the calculations are done at each $\mathbf{x}$ separately.

We assume that for each $i \neq j$, there are n_{ij} observations in the training set and from these we have estimated conditional probabilities $r_{ij} = \text{Prob}(i|i \text{ or } j)$.

Our model is

$$
\begin{aligned}
n_{ij}r_{ij} &\sim \text{Binomial}(n_{ij}, \mu_{ij}) \\
\mu_{ij} &= \frac{p_i}{p_i + p_j}
\end{aligned}
\tag{2}
$$

or equivalently

$$
\log \mu_{ij} = \log(p_i) - \log(p_i + p_j),
\tag{3}
$$

a *log-nonlinear model*.

We wish to find $\hat{p}_i$'s so that the $\hat{u}_{ij}$'s are close to the r_{ij}'s. There are $K - 1$ independent parameters but $K(K - 1)/2$ equations, so it is not possible in general to find $\hat{p}_i$'s so that $\hat{\mu}_{ij} = r_{ij}$ for all i, j.

Therefore we must settle for $\hat{\mu}_{ij}$'s that are close to the observed r_{ij}'s. Our closeness criterion is the average (weighted) Kullback-Leibler distance between r_{ij} and μ_{ij}:

$$
\ell(\mathbf{p}) = \sum_{i<j} n_{ij} \left[r_{ij} \log \frac{r_{ij}}{\mu_{ij}} + (1 - r_{ij}) \log \frac{1 - r_{ij}}{1 - \mu_{ij}} \right]
\tag{4}
$$

and we find **p** to minimize this function.

This model and criterion is formally equivalent to the Bradley-Terry model for preference data. One observes a proportion r_{ij} of n_{ij} preferences for item i, and the sampling model is binomial, as in (2). If each of the r_{ij} were independent, then $\ell(\mathbf{p})$ would be equivalent to the log-likelihood under this model. However our r_{ij} are not independent as they share a common training set and were obtained from a common set of classifiers. Furthermore the binomial models do not apply in this case; the r_{ij} are evaluations of functions at a point, and the randomness arises in the way these functions are constructed from the training data. We include the n_{ij} as weights in (4); this is a crude way of accounting for the different precisions in the pairwise probability estimates.

The score (gradient) equations are:

$$\sum_{j \neq i} n_{ij} \mu_{ij} = \sum_{j \neq i} n_{ij} r_{ij}; \ i = 1, 2, \ldots K \tag{5}$$

subject to $\sum p_i = 1$. We use the following iterative procedure to compute the $\hat{p}_i$'s:

Algorithm

1. Start with some guess for the $\hat{p}_i$, and corresponding $\hat{\mu}_{ij}$.

2. Repeat ($i = 1, 2, \ldots, K, 1, \ldots$) until convergence:

$$\hat{p}_i \leftarrow \hat{p}_i \cdot \frac{\sum_{j \neq i} n_{ij} r_{ij}}{\sum_{j \neq i} n_{ij} \hat{\mu}_{ij}}$$

renormalize the $\hat{p}_i$, and recompute the $\hat{\mu}_{ij}$.

3. $\hat{\mathbf{p}} \leftarrow \hat{\mathbf{p}} / \sum \hat{p}_i$

The algorithm also appears in Bradley & Terry (1952). The updates in step 2 attempt to modify **p** so that the sufficient statistics match their expectation, but go only part of the way. We prove in Hastie & Tibshirani (1996) that $\ell(\mathbf{p})$ increases at each step. Since $\ell(\mathbf{p})$ is bounded above by zero, the procedure converges. At convergence, the score equations are satisfied, and the $\hat{\mu}_{ij}$s and $\hat{\mathbf{p}}$ are consistent. This algorithm is similar in flavour to the Iterative Proportional Scaling (IPS) procedure used in log-linear models. IPS has a long history, dating back to Deming & Stephan (1940). Bishop, Fienberg & Holland (1975) give a modern treatment and many references.

The resulting classification rule is

$$\hat{d}(\mathbf{x}) = \mathrm{argmax}_i [\hat{p}_i(\mathbf{x})] \tag{6}$$

Figure 2 shows another example similar to Figure 1, where we can compare the performance of the rules $\hat{d}$ and $\tilde{d}$. The hatched area in the top left panel is an indeterminate region where there is more than one class achieving $\max(\tilde{p}_i)$. In the top right panel the coupling procedure has resolved this indeterminacy in favor of class 1 by weighting the various probabilities. See the figure caption for a description of the bottom panels.

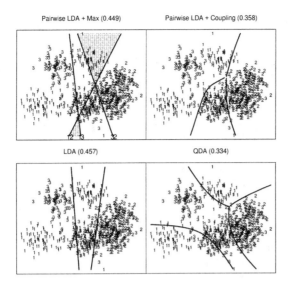

Figure 2: *A three class problem similar to that in figure 1, with the data in each class generated from a mixture of Gaussians. The first panel shows the maximum-wins procedure d̃). The second panel shows the decision boundary from coupling of the pairwise linear discriminant rules based on d̂ in (6). The third panel shows the three-class LDA boundaries, and the fourth the QDA boundaries. The numbers in the captions are the error rates based on a large test set from the same population.*

3   Pairwise threshold optimization

As pointed out by Friedman (1996), approaching the classification problem in a pairwise fashion allows one to optimize the classifier in a way that would be computationally burdensome for a K-class classifier. Here we discuss optimization of the classification threshold.

For each two class problem, let logit $p_{ij}(x) = d_{ij}(x)$. Normally we would classify to class i if $d_{ij}(x) > 0$. Suppose we find that $d_{ij}(x) > t_{ij}$ is better. Then we define $d'_{ij}(x) = d_{ij}(x) - t_{ij}$, and hence $p'_{ij}(x) = \text{logit}^{-1} d'_{ij}(x)$. We do this for all pairs, and then apply the coupling algorithm to the $p'_{ij}(x)$ to obtain probabilities $p'_i(x)$. In this way we can optimize over $K(K-1)/2$ parameters separately, rather than optimize jointly over K parameters. With nearest neigbours, there are other approaches to threshold optimization, that bias the class probability estimates in different ways. See Hastie & Tibshirani (1996) for details. An example of the benefit of threshold optimization is given next.

Example: ten Gaussian classes with unequal covariance

In this simulated example taken from Friedman (1996), there are 10 Gaussian classes in 20 dimensions. The mean vectors of each class were chosen as 20 independent uniform $[0,1]$ random variables. The covariance matrices are constructed from eigenvectors whose square roots are uniformly distributed on the 20-dimensional unit sphere (subject to being mutually orthogonal), and eigenvalues uniform on $[0.01, 1.01]$. There are 100 observations per class in the training set, and 200 per class in the test set. The optimal decision boundaries in this problem are quadratic, and neither linear nor nearest-neighbor methods are well-suited. Friedman states that the Bayes error rate is less than 1%.

Figure 3 shows the test error rates for linear discriminant analysis, J-nearest neighbor and their paired versions using threshold optimization. We see that the coupled classifiers nearly halve the error rates in each case. In addition, the coupled rule works a little better than Friedman's max rule in each task. Friedman (1996) reports a median test error rate of about 16% for his thresholded version of pairwise nearest neighbor.

Why does the pairwise thresholding work in this example? We looked more closely at the pairwise nearest neighbour rules rules that were constructed for this problem. The thresholding biased the pairwise distances by about 7% on average. The average number of nearest neighbours used per class was 4.47 (.122), while the standard J-nearest neighbour approach used 6.70 (.590) neighbours for all ten classes. For all ten classes, the 4.47 translates into 44.7 neighbours. Hence relative to the standard J-NN rule, the pairwise rule, in using the threshold optimization to reduce bias, is able to use about six times as many near neighbours.

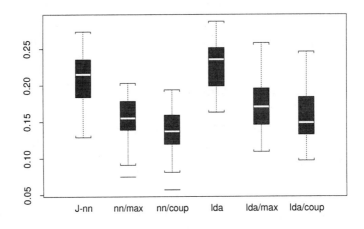

Figure 3: *Test errors for 20 simulations of ten-class Gaussian example.*

4   Discussion

Due to lack of space, there are a number of issues that we did not discuss here. In Hastie & Tibshirani (1996), we show the relationship between the pairwise coupling and the max-wins rule: specifically, if the classifiers return 0 or 1s rather than probabilities, the two rules give the same classification. We also apply the pairwise coupling procedure to nearest neighbour and support vector machines. In the latter case, this provides a natural way of extending support vector machines, which are defined for two-class problems, to multi-class problems.

The pairwise procedures, both Friedman's max-win and our coupling, are most likely to offer improvements when additional optimization or efficiency gains are possible in the simpler 2-class scenarios. In some situations they perform exactly like the multiple class classifiers. Two examples are: a) each of the pairwise rules are based on QDA: i.e. each class modelled by a Gaussian distribution with separate covariances, and then the r_{ij}s derived from Bayes rule; b) a generalization of the above, where the density in each class is modelled in some fashion, perhaps nonparametrically via density estimates or near-neighbor methods, and then the density estimates are used in Bayes rule.

Pairwise LDA followed by coupling seems to offer a nice compromise between LDA and QDA, although the decision boundaries are no longer linear. For this special case one might derive a different coupling procedure globally on the *logit* scale, which would guarantee linear decision boundaries. Work of this nature is currently in progress with Jerry Friedman.

Acknowledgments

We thank Jerry Friedman for sharing a preprint of his pairwise classification paper with us, and acknowledge helpful discussions with Jerry, Geoff Hinton, Radford Neal and David Tritchler. Trevor Hastie was partially supported by grant DMS-9504495 from the National Science Foundation, and grant ROI-CA-72028-01 from the National Institutes of Health. Rob Tibshirani was supported by the Natural Sciences and Engineering Research Council of Canada and the IRIS Centr of Excellence.

References

Bishop, Y., Fienberg, S. & Holland, P. (1975), *Discrete multivariate analysis*, MIT Press, Cambridge.

Bradley, R. & Terry, M. (1952), 'The rank analysis of incomplete block designs. i. the method of paired comparisons', *Biometrics* pp. 324–345.

Deming, W. & Stephan, F. (1940), 'On a least squares adjustment of a sampled frequency table when the expected marginal totals are known', *Ann. Math. Statist.* pp. 427–444.

Friedman, J. (1996), Another approach to polychotomous classification, Technical report, Stanford University.

Hastie, T. & Tibshirani, R. (1996), Classification by pairwise coupling, Technical report, University of Toronto.

Unsupervised On-Line Learning of Decision Trees for Hierarchical Data Analysis

Marcus Held and Joachim M. Buhmann
Rheinische Friedrich–Wilhelms–Universität
Institut für Informatik III, Römerstraße 164
D-53117 Bonn, Germany
email: {held, jb}.cs.uni-bonn.de
WWW: http://www-dbv.cs.uni-bonn.de

Abstract

An adaptive on–line algorithm is proposed to estimate hierarchical data structures for non–stationary data sources. The approach is based on the principle of *minimum cross entropy* to derive a decision tree for data clustering and it employs a *metalearning* idea (learning to learn) to adapt to changes in data characteristics. Its efficiency is demonstrated by grouping non–stationary artifical data and by hierarchical segmentation of LANDSAT images.

1   Introduction

Unsupervised learning addresses the problem to detect structure inherent in un-labeled and unclassified data. The simplest, but not necessarily the best approach for extracting a grouping structure is to represent a set of data samples $\mathcal{X} = \left\{ x_i \in \mathbb{R}^d | i = 1, \ldots, N \right\}$ by a set of prototypes $\mathcal{Y} = \left\{ y_\alpha \in \mathbb{R}^d | \alpha = 1, \ldots, K \right\}$, $K \ll N$. The encoding usually is represented by an assignment matrix $\mathbf{M} = (M_{i\alpha})$, where $M_{i\alpha} = 1$ if and only if x_i belongs to cluster α, and $M_{i\alpha} = 0$ otherwise. According to this encoding scheme, the cost function $\mathcal{H}(\mathbf{M}, \mathcal{Y}) = \frac{1}{N} \sum_{i=1}^{N} M_{i\alpha} \mathcal{D}(x_i, y_\alpha)$ measures the quality of a data partition, i.e., optimal assignments and prototypes $(\mathbf{M}, \mathcal{Y})^{\text{opt}} = \arg \min_{\mathbf{M}, \mathcal{Y}} \mathcal{H}(\mathbf{M}, \mathcal{Y})$ minimize the inhomogeneity of clusters w.r.t. a given distance measure $\mathcal{D}$. For reasons of simplicity we restrict the presentation to the *sum–of–squared–error criterion* $\mathcal{D}(x, y) = \|x - y\|^2$ in this paper. To facilitate this minimization a deterministic annealing approach was proposed in [5] which maps the discrete optimization problem, i.e. how to determine the data assignments, via the *Maximum Entropy Principle* [2] to a continuous parameter estimation problem. Deterministic annealing introduces a Lagrange multiplier β to control the approximation of $\mathcal{H}(\mathbf{M}, \mathcal{Y})$ in a probabilistic sense. Equivalently to maximize the entropy at fixed expected K-means costs we minimize the free energy $\mathcal{F} = \frac{1}{\beta} \sum_{i=1}^{N} \ln \left(\sum_{\mu=1}^{K} \exp\left(-\beta \mathcal{D}\left(x_i, y_\alpha\right)\right) \right)$ w.r.t. the prototypes y_α. The assignments $M_{i\alpha}$ are treated as random variables yielding a fuzzy centroid rule

$$y_\alpha = \sum_{i=1}^{N} \langle M_{i\alpha} \rangle x_i / \sum_{i=1}^{N} \langle M_{i\alpha} \rangle, \tag{1}$$

where the expected assignments $\langle M_{i\alpha} \rangle$ are given by Gibbs distributions

$$\langle M_{i\alpha} \rangle = \frac{\exp\left(-\beta \mathcal{D}\left(x_i, y_\alpha\right)\right)}{\sum_{\mu=1}^{K} \exp\left(-\beta \mathcal{D}\left(x_i, y_\alpha\right)\right)}. \tag{2}$$

For a more detailed discussion of the DA approach to data clustering cf. [1, 3, 5].

In addition to assigning data to clusters (1,2), hierarchical clustering provides the partitioning of data space with a tree structure. Each data sample x is sequentially assigned to a nested structure of partitions which hierarchically cover the data space $\mathbb{R}^d$. This sequence of special decisions is encoded by decision rules which are attached to nodes along a path in the tree (see also fig. 1).

Therefore, learning a decision tree requires to determine a tree topology, the accompanying assignments, the inner node labels S and the prototypes $\mathcal{Y}$ at the leaves. The search of such a hierarchical partition of the data space should be guided by an optimization criterion, i.e., minimal distortion costs.

This problem is solvable by a two–stage approach, which on the one hand minimizes the distortion costs at the leaves given the tree structure and on the other hand optimizes the tree structure given the leaf induced partition of $\mathbb{R}^d$. This approach, due to Miller & Rose [3], is summarized in section 2. The extensions for adaptive on–line learning and experimental results are described in sections 3 and 4, respectively.

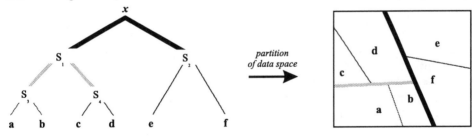

Figure 1: Right: Topology of a decision tree. Left: Induced partitioning of the data space (positions of the letters also indicate the positions of the prototypes). Decisions are made according to the nearest neighbor rule.

2 Unsupervised Learning of Decision Trees

Deterministic annealing of hierarchical clustering treats the assignments of data to inner nodes of the tree in a probabilistic way analogous to the expected assignments of data to leaf prototypes. Based on the maximum entropy principle, the probability $\Phi_{i,j}^{\mathrm{H}}$ that data point x_i reaches inner node s_j is recursively defined by (see [3]):

$$\Phi_{i,\mathrm{root}}^{\mathrm{H}} := 1, \quad \Phi_{i,j}^{\mathrm{H}} = \Phi_{i,\mathrm{parent}(j)}^{\mathrm{H}} \pi_{i,j}, \quad \pi_{i,j} = \frac{\exp\left(-\gamma \mathcal{D}\left(x_i, s_j\right)\right)}{\sum\limits_{k \in \mathrm{siblings}(j)} \exp\left(-\gamma \mathcal{D}\left(x_i, s_k\right)\right)}, \tag{3}$$

where the Lagrange multiplier γ controls the fuzziness of all the transitions $\pi_{i,j}$. On the other hand, given the tree topology and the prototypes at the leaves, the maximum entropy principle naturally recommends an *ideal probability* $\Phi^{\mathrm{I}}_{i,\alpha}$ at leaf y_α, resp. at an inner node s_j,

$$\Phi^{\mathrm{I}}_{i,\alpha} = \frac{\exp\left(-\beta \mathcal{D}\left(x_i, y_\alpha\right)\right)}{\sum\limits_{\mu \in \mathcal{Y}} \exp\left(-\beta \mathcal{D}\left(x_i, y_\mu\right)\right)} \quad \text{and} \quad \Phi^{\mathrm{I}}_{i,j} = \sum_{k \in \text{descendants}(j)} \Phi^{\mathrm{I}}_{i,k}. \tag{4}$$

We apply the principle of minimum cross entropy for the calculation of the prototypes at the leaves given a priori the probabilities for the parents of the leaves. Minimization of the cross entropy with fixed expected costs $\langle H_{x_i} \rangle = \sum_\alpha \langle M_{i\alpha} \rangle \mathcal{D}\left(x_i, y_\alpha\right)$ for the data point x_i yields the expression

$$\min_{\{\langle M_{i\alpha} \rangle\}} \mathcal{I}\left(\{\langle M_{i\alpha} \rangle\} \| \{\Phi^{\mathrm{H}}_{i,\text{parent}(\alpha)}/K\}\right) = \min_{\{\langle M_{i\alpha} \rangle\}} \sum_\alpha \langle M_{i\alpha} \rangle \ln \frac{\langle M_{i\alpha} \rangle}{\Phi^{\mathrm{H}}_{i,\text{parent}(\alpha)}}, \tag{5}$$

where $\mathcal{I}$ denotes the Kullback–Leibler divergence and K defines the degree of the inner nodes. The *tilted distribution*

$$\langle M_{i\alpha} \rangle = \frac{\Phi^{\mathrm{H}}_{i,\text{parent}(\alpha)} \exp\left(-\beta \mathcal{D}\left(x_i, y_\alpha\right)\right)}{\sum_\mu \Phi^{\mathrm{H}}_{i,\text{parent}(\mu)} \exp\left(-\beta \mathcal{D}\left(x_i, y_\mu\right)\right)}. \tag{6}$$

generalizes the probabilistic assignments (2). In the case of Euclidian distances we again obtain the centroid formula (1) as the minimum of the free energy $\mathcal{F} = -\frac{1}{\beta} \sum_{i=1}^{N} \ln\left[\sum_{\alpha \in \mathcal{Y}} \Phi^{\mathrm{H}}_{i,\text{parent}(\alpha)} \exp\left(-\beta \mathcal{D}\left(x_i, y_\alpha\right)\right)\right]$. Constraints induced by the tree structure are incorporated in the assignments (6). For the optimization of the hierarchy, Miller and Rose in a second step propose the minimization of the distance between the hierarchical probabilities $\Phi^{\mathrm{H}}_{\cdot,\cdot}$ and the ideal probabilities $\Phi^{\mathrm{I}}_{\cdot,\cdot}$, the distance being measured by the Kullback–Leibler divergence

$$\min_{\gamma, \mathcal{S}} \sum_{s_j \in \text{parent}(\mathcal{Y})} \mathcal{I}\left(\{\Phi^{\mathrm{I}}_{\cdot,j}\} \| \{\Phi^{\mathrm{H}}_{\cdot,j}\}\right) \equiv \min_{\gamma, \mathcal{S}} \sum_{s_j \in \text{parent}(\mathcal{Y})} \sum_{i=1}^{N} \Phi^{\mathrm{I}}_{i,j} \ln \frac{\Phi^{\mathrm{I}}_{i,j}}{\Phi^{\mathrm{H}}_{i,j}}. \tag{7}$$

Equation (7) describes the minimization of the sum of cross entropies between the probability densities $\Phi^{\mathrm{I}}_{\cdot,\cdot}$ and $\Phi^{\mathrm{H}}_{\cdot,\cdot}$ over the parents of the leaves. Calculating the gradients for the inner nodes s_j and the Lagrange multiplier γ we receive

$$\frac{\partial}{\partial s_j} \mathcal{I} = -2\gamma \sum_{i=1}^{N} \left(x_i - s_j\right) \left\{\Phi^{\mathrm{I}}_{i,j} - \Phi^{\mathrm{I}}_{i,\text{parent}(j)} \pi_{i,j}\right\} := -2\gamma \sum_{i=1}^{N} \Delta_1\left(x_i, s_j\right), \tag{8}$$

$$\frac{\partial}{\partial \gamma} \mathcal{I} = \sum_{i=1}^{N} \sum_{j \in \mathcal{S}} \mathcal{D}\left(x_i, s_j\right) \left\{\Phi^{\mathrm{I}}_{i,j} - \Phi^{\mathrm{I}}_{i,\text{parent}(j)} \pi_{i,j}\right\} := \sum_{i=1}^{N} \sum_{j \in \mathcal{S}} \Delta_2\left(x_i, s_j\right). \tag{9}$$

The first gradient is a weighted average of the difference vectors $\left(x_i - s_j\right)$, where the weights measure the mismatch between the probability $\Phi^{\mathrm{I}}_{i,j}$ and the probability induced by the transition $\pi_{i,j}$. The second gradient (9) measures the scale $- \mathcal{D}\left(x_i, s_j\right)$ – on which the transition probabilities are defined, and weights them with the mismatch between the ideal probabilities. This procedure yields an algorithm which starts at a small value β with a complete tree and identical test vectors attached to all nodes. The prototypes at the leaves are optimized according to (6) and the centroid rule (1), and the hierarchy is optimized by (8) and (9). After convergence one increases β and optimizes the hierarchy and the prototypes at the leaves again. The increment of β leads to phase transitions where test vectors separate from each other and the formerly completely degenerated tree evolves its structure. For a detailed description of this algorithm see [3].

3 On-Line Learning of Decision Trees

Learning of decision trees is refined in this paper to deal with unbalanced trees and on-line learning of trees. Updating identical nodes according to the gradients (9) with assignments (6) weighs parameters of unbalanced tree structures in an unsatisfactory way. A detailed analysis reveals that degenerated test vectors, i.e., test vectors with identical components, still contribute to the assignments and to the evolution of γ. This artefact is overcome by using dynamic tree topologies instead of a predefined topology with indistinguishable test vectors. On the other hand, the development of an on–line algorithm makes it possible to process huge data sets and non–stationary data. For this setting there exists the need of on–line learning rules for the prototypes at the leaves, the test vectors at the inner nodes and the parameters γ and β. Unbalanced trees also require rules for splitting and merging nodes.

Following Buhmann and Kühnel [1] we use an expansion of order $O(1/n)$ of (1) to estimate the prototypes for the Nth datapoint

$$y_\alpha^N \approx y_\alpha^{N-1} + \eta_\alpha \frac{\langle M_{N\alpha}^{N-1}\rangle}{p_\alpha^{N-1} M}\left(x_N - y_\alpha^{N-1}\right), \tag{10}$$

where $p_\alpha^N \approx p_\alpha^{N-1} + 1/M\left(\langle M_{N\alpha}^{N-1}\rangle - p_\alpha^{N-1}\right)$ denotes the probability of the occurence of class α. The parameters M and η_α are introduced in order to take the possible non–stationarity of the data source into account. M denotes the size of the data window, and η_α is a node specific learning rate.

Adaptation of the inner nodes and of the parameter γ is performed by stochastic approximation using the gradients (8) and (9)

$$s_j^N := s_j^{N-1} + \eta_j \gamma^{N-1} \Delta_1\left(x_N, s_j^{N-1}\right), \tag{11}$$

$$\gamma^N := \gamma^{N-1} - \eta_\gamma \sum_{s_j \in S} \Delta_2\left(x_N, s_j^{N-1}\right). \tag{12}$$

For an appropriate choice of the learning rates η, the *learning to learn* approach of Murata et al. [4] suggests the learning algorithm

$$w^N = w^{N-1} - \eta^{N-1} f\left(x_N, w^{N-1}\right). \tag{13}$$

The flow f in parameter space determines the change of w^{N-1} given a new datapoint x_N. Murata et al. derive the following update scheme for the learning rate:

$$r^N = (1-\delta)r^{N-1} + \delta f\left(x_N, w^{N-1}\right), \tag{14}$$

$$\eta^N = \eta^{N-1} + \nu_1 \eta^{N-1}\left(\nu_2\|r^N\| - \eta^{N-1}\right), \tag{15}$$

where ν_1, ν_2 and δ are control parameters to balance the tradeoff between accuracy and convergence rate. r^N denotes the leaky average of the flow at time N.

The adaptation of β has to observe the necessary condition for a phase transition $\beta > \beta_{\text{crit}} \equiv 1/2\delta_{\max}$, $\delta_{\max}$ being the largest eigenvalue of the covariance matrix [3]

$$\Sigma_\alpha = \sum_{i=1}^M (x_i - y_\alpha)(x_i - y_\alpha)^t \langle M_{i\alpha}\rangle / \sum_{i=1}^M \langle M_{i\alpha}\rangle. \tag{16}$$

Rules for splitting and merging nodes of the tree are introduced to deal with un-balanced trees and non–stationary data. Simple rules measure the distortion costs at the prototypes of the leaves. According to these costs the leaf with highest distortion costs is split. The merging criterion combines neighboring leaves with minimal distance in a greedy fashion. The parameter M (10), the typical time scale for changes in the data distribution is used to fix the time between splitting resp. merging nodes and the update of β. Therefore, M controls the time scale for changes of the tree topology. The learning parameters for the learning to learn rules (13)-(15) are chosen empirically and are kept constant for all experiments.

4   Experiments

The first experiment demonstrates how a drifting two dimensional data source can be tracked. This data source is generated by a fixed tree augmented with transition probabilities at the edges and with Gaussians at the leaves. By descending the tree structure this generates an i.i.d. random variable $X \in \mathbb{R}^2$, which is rotated around the origin of $\mathbb{R}^2$ to obtain a random variable $T(N) = R(\omega, N)X$. R is an orthogonal matrix, N denotes the number of the actual data point and ω denotes the angular velocity, $M = 500$. Figure 2 shows 45 degree snapshots of the learning of this non–stationary data source. We start to take these snapshots after the algorithm has developed its final tree topology (after $\approx$ 8000 datapoints). Apart from fluctuations of the test vectors at the leaves, the whole tree structure is stable while tracking the rotating data source.

Additional experiments with higher dimensional data sources confirm the robustness of the algorithm w.r.t. the dimension of the data space, i. e. similiar tracking performances for different dimensions are observed, where differences are explained as differences in the data sources (figure 3). This performance is measured by the variance of the mean of the distances between the data source trajectory and the trajectories of the test vectors at the nodes of the tree.

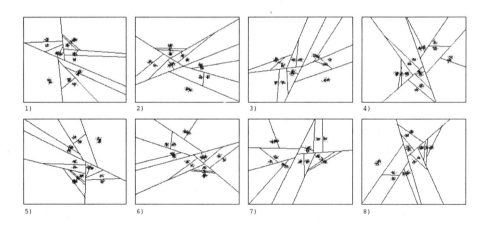

Figure 2: 45 degree snapshots of the learning of a data source which rotates with a velocity $\omega = 2\pi/30000$ (360 degree per 30000 data samples).

A second experiment demonstrates the learning of a switching data source. The results confirm a good performance concerning the restructuring of the tree (see figure 4). In this experiment the algorithm learns a given data source and after 10000 data points we switch to a different source.

As a real–world example of on–line learning of huge data sources the algorithm is applied to the hierarchical clustering of 6–dimensional LANDSAT data. The heat

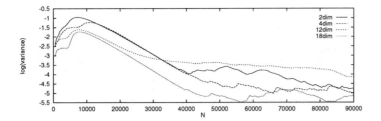

Figure 3: Tracking performance for different dimensions. As data sources we use *d*–dimensional Gaussians which are attached to a unit sphere. To the components of every random sample X we add $\sin(\omega N)$ in order to introduce non stationarity. The first 8000 samples are used for the development of the tree topology.

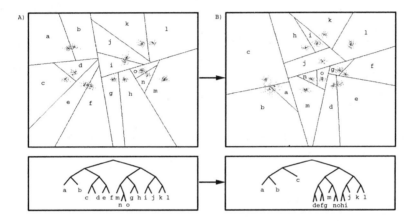

Figure 4: Learning a switching data source: top: a) the partition of the data space after 10000 data samples given the first source, b) the restructured partition after additional 2500 samples. Below: accompanying tree topologies.

channel has been discarded because of its reduced resolution. In a preprocessing step all channels are rescaled to unit variance, which alternatively could be established by using a Mahalanobis distance. Note that the decision tree which clusters this data supplies us with a hierarchical segmentation of the corresponding LANDSAT image. A tree of 16 leaves has been learned on a training set of 128 × 128 data samples, and it has been applied to a test set of 128 × 128 LANDSAT pixels. The training is established by 15 sequential runs through the test set, where after each $M = 16384$ run a split of one node is carried out. The resulting empirical errors (0.49 training distortion and 0.55 test distortion) differ only slightly from the errors obtained by the LBG algorithm applied to the whole training set (0.42 training distortion and 0.52 test distortion). This difference is due to the fact that not every data point is assigned to the nearest leaf prototype by a decision tree induced partition. The segmentation of the test image is depicted in figure 5.

5 Conclusion

This paper presents a method for unsupervised on–line learning of decision trees. We overcome the shortcomings of the original decision tree approach and extend

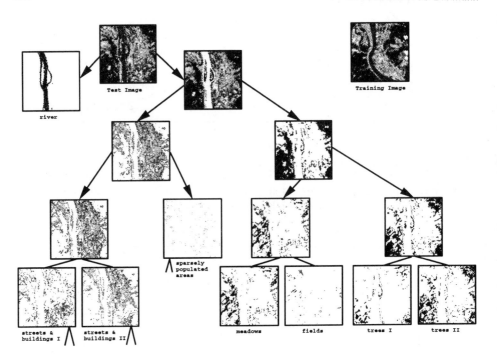

Figure 5: Hierarchical segmentation of the test image. The root represents the original image, i.e., the gray scale version of the three color channels.

it to the realm of on–line learning of huge data sets and of adaptive learning of non–stationary data. Our experiments demonstrate that the approach is capable of tracking gradually changing or switching environments. Furthermore, the method has been successfully applied to the hierarchical segmentation of LANDSAT images. Future work will address active data selection issues to significantly reduce the uncertainty of the most likely tree parameters and the learning questions related to different tree topologies.

Acknowledgement: This work has been supported by the German Israel Foundation for Science and Research Development (GIF) under grant #I–0403–001.06/95 and by the Federal Ministry for Education, Science and Technology (BMBF #01 M 3021 A/4).

References

[1] J. M. Buhmann and H. Kühnel. Vector quantization with complexity costs. *IEEE Transactions on Information Theory*, 39(4):1133–1145, July 1993.

[2] T.M. Cover and J. Thomas. *Elements of Information Theory*. Wiley & Sons, 1991.

[3] D. Miller and K. Rose. Hierarchical unsupervised learning with growing via phase transitions. *Neural Computation*, 8:425–450, February 1996.

[4] N. Murata, K.-R. Müller, A. Ziehe, and S. Amari. Adaptive on-line learning in changing environments. In M.C. Mozer, M.I. Jordan, and T. Petsche, editors, *Advances in Neural Information Processing Systems*, number 9, pages 599–605. MIT Press, 1997.

[5] K. Rose, E. Gurewitz, and G.C. Fox. A deterministic annealing approach to clustering. *Pattern Recognition Letters*, 11(9):589–594, September 1990.

Nonlinear Markov Networks for Continuous Variables

Reimar Hofmann and Volker Tresp*
Siemens AG, Corporate Technology
Information and Communications
81730 München, Germany

Abstract

We address the problem of learning structure in nonlinear Markov networks with continuous variables. This can be viewed as non-Gaussian multidimensional density estimation exploiting certain conditional independencies in the variables. Markov networks are a graphical way of describing conditional independencies well suited to model relationships which do not exhibit a natural causal ordering. We use neural network structures to model the quantitative relationships between variables. The main focus in this paper will be on learning the structure for the purpose of gaining insight into the underlying process. Using two data sets we show that interesting structures can be found using our approach. Inference will be briefly addressed.

1 Introduction

Knowledge about independence or conditional independence between variables is most helpful in "understanding" a domain. An intuitive representation of independencies is achieved by graphical models in which independency statements can be extracted from the structure of the graph. The two most popular types of graphical stochastical models are Bayesian networks which use a directed graph, and Markov networks which use an undirected graph. Whereas Bayesian networks are well suited to represent causal relationships, Markov networks are mostly used in cases where the user wants to express statistical correlation between variables. This is the case in image processing where the variables typically represent the grey levels of pixels and the graph encourages smoothness in the values of neighboring pixels (Markov random fields, Geman and Geman, 1984). We believe that Markov networks might be a useful representation in many domains where the concept of cause and effect is somewhat artificial. The learned structure of a Markov network also seems to be more easily communicated to non-experts; in a Bayesian network not all arc directions can be uniquely identified based on training data alone which makes a meaningful interpretation for the non-expert rather difficult.

As in Bayesian networks, direct dependencies between variables in Markov networks are represented by an arc between those variables and missing edges represent independencies (in Section 2 we will be more precise about the independencies represented in Markov networks). Whereas the graphical structure in Markov networks might be known a priori in some cases,

---

Reimar.Hofmann@mchp.siemens.de Volker.Tresp@mchp.siemens.de

the focus of this work is the case that structure is unknown and must be inferred from data. For both discrete variables and linear relationships between continuous variables algorithms for structure learning exist (Whittaker, 1990). Here we address the problem of learning structure for Markov networks of continuous variables where the relationships between variables are nonlinear. In particular we use neural networks for approximating the dependency between a variable and its Markov boundary. We demonstrate that structural learning can be achieved without a direct reference to a likelihood function and show how inference in such networks can be performed using Gibbs sampling. From a technical point of view, these *Markov boundary networks* perform multi-dimensional density estimation for a very general class of non-Gaussian densities.

In the next section we give a mathematical description of Markov networks and a formulation of the joint probability density as a product of compatibility functions. In Section 3.1 we discuss strucural learning in Markov networks based on a maximum likelihood approach and show that this approach is in general unfeasible. We then introduce our approach which is based on learning the Markov boundary of each variable. We also show how belief update can be performed using Gibbs sampling. In Section 4 we demonstrate that useful structures can be extraced from two data sets (Boston housing data, financial market) using our approach.

2 Markov Networks

The following brief introduction to Markov networks is adapted from Pearl (1988). Consider a strictly positive[1] joint probability density $p(x)$ over a set of variables $\mathcal{X} := \{x_1, \ldots, x_N\}$. For each variable x_i, let the *Markov boundary* of x_i, $\mathcal{B}_i \subseteq \mathcal{X} - \{x_i\}$, be the smallest set of variables that renders x_i and $\mathcal{X} - (\{x_i\} \cup \mathcal{B}_i)$ independent under $p(x)$ (the Markov boundary is unique for strictly positive distributions). Let the *Markov network* $\mathcal{G}$ be the undirected graph with nodes $x_1, \ldots, x_N$ and edges between x_i and x_j if and only if $x_i \in \mathcal{B}_j$ (which also implies $x_j \in \mathcal{B}_i$). In other words, a Markov network is generated by connecting each node to the nodes in its Markov boundary. Then for any set $Z \subseteq (\mathcal{X} - \{x_i, x_j\})$, x_i is independent of x_j given Z if and only if every path from x_i to x_j goes through at least one node in Z. In other words, two variables are independent if any path between those variables is "blocked" by a known variable. In particular a variable is independent of the remaining variables if the variables in its Markov boundary are known.

A *clique* in G is a maximal fully connected subgraph. Given a Markov Network G for $p(x)$ it can be shown that p can be factorized as a product of *positive* functions on the cliques of G, i.e.

$$p(x) = \frac{1}{K} \prod_i g_i(x_{clique_i}) \tag{1}$$

where the product is over all cliques in the graph. x_{clique_i} is the projection of x to the variables of the i-th clique and the g_i are the *compatibility functions* w.r.t. $clique_i$. $K = \int \prod_i g_i(x_{clique_i}) dx$ is the normalization constant. Note, that a state whose clique functions have large values has high probability. The theorem of Hammersley and Clifford states that the normalized product in equation 1 embodies all the conditional independencies portrayed by the graph (Pearl, 1988)[2] for any choice of the g_i.

If the graph is sparse, i.e. if many conditional independencies exist then the cliques might

---

[1] To simplify the discussion we will assume strict positivity for the rest of this paper. For some of the statements weaker conditions may also be sufficient. Note that strict positivity implies that functional constraints (for example, $a = b$) are excluded.

[2] In terms of graphical models: The graph G is an I-map of p.

be small and the product will be over low dimensional functions. Similar to Bayesian networks where the complexity of describing a joint probability density is greatly reduced by decomposing the joint density in a product of ideally low-dimensional conditional densities, equation 1 describes the decomposition of a joint probability density function into a product of ideally low-dimensional compatibility functions. It should be noted that Bayesian networks and Markov networks differ in which specific independencies they can represent (Pearl, 1988).

3 Learning the Markov Network

3.1 Likelihood Function Based Learning

Learning graphical stochastical models is usually decomposed into the problems of learning structure (that is the edges in the graph) and of learning the parameters of the joint density function under the constraint that it obeys the independence statements made by the graph. The idea is to generate candidate structures according to some search strategy, learn the parameters for this structure and then judge the structure on the basis of the (penalized) likelihood of the model or, in a fully Bayesian approach, using a Bayesian scoring metric.

Assume that the compatibility functions in equation 1 are approximated using a function approximator such as a neural network $g_i() \approx g_i^w(x)$. Let $\{x^p\}_{p=1}^N$ be a training set. With likelihood $L = \prod_{p=1}^N p^M(x^p)$ (where the M in p^M indicates a probability density *model* in contrast to the true distribution), the gradient of the log-likelihood with respect to weight w_i in $g_i(.)$ becomes

$$\frac{\partial}{\partial w_i} \sum_{p=1}^N \log p^M(x^p) = \sum_{p=1}^N \frac{\partial}{\partial w_i} \log g_i^w(x_{clique_i}^p) - N \frac{\int (\frac{\partial}{\partial w_i} \log g_i^w(x_{clique_i})) \prod_j g_j^w(x_{clique_j}) dx}{\int \prod_j g_j^w(x_{clique_j}) dx}$$

(2)

where the sums are over N training patterns. The gradient decomposes into two terms. Note, that only in the first term the training patterns appear explicitly and that, conveniently, the first term is only dependent on the clique i which contains parameter w_i. The second term emerges from the normalization constant K in equation 1. The difficulty is that the integrals in the second term can not be solved in closed form for universal types of compatibility functions g_i and have to be approximated numerically, typically using a form of Monte Carlo integration. This is exactly what is done in the Boltzmann machine, which is a special case of a Markov network with discrete variables.[3]

Currently, we consider maximum likelihood learning based on the compatibility functions unsuitable, considering the complexity and slowness of Monte Carlo integration (i.e. stochastic sampling). Note, that for structural learning the maximum likelihood learning is in the inner loop and would have to be executed repeatedly for a large number of structures.

3.2 Markov Boundary Learning

The difficulties in using maximum likelihood learning for finding optimal structures motivated the approach pursued in this paper. If the underlying true probability density is known the structure in a Markov network can be found using either the *edge deletion method* or the

---

[3] A fully connected Boltzmann machine does not display any independencies and we only have one clique consisting of all variables. The compatibility function is $g() = \exp(-\sum w_{ij} s_i s_j)$. The Boltzmann machine typically contains hidden variables, such that not only the second term (corresponding to the unclamped phase) in equation 2 has to be approximated using stochastic sampling but also the first term. (In this paper we only consider the case that data are complete).

Markov boundary method (Pearl, 1988). The edge deletion method uses the fact that variables a and b are *not* connected by an edge if and only if a and b are independent given all other variables. Evaluating this test for each pair of variables reveals the structure of the network. The Markov boundary method consists of determining - for each variable a - its Markov boundary and connecting a to each variable in its Markov boundary. Both approaches are simple if we have a reliable test for true conditional independence.

Both methods cannot be applied directly for learning structure from data since here tests for conditional independence cannot be based on the true underlying probability distribution (which is unknown) but has to be inferred from a finite data set. The hope is that dependencies which are strong enough to be supported by the data can still be reliably identified. It is, however not difficult to construct cases where simply using an (unreliable) statistical test for conditional independence with the edge deletion method does not work well.[4]

We now describe our approach, which is motivated by the Markov boundary method. First, we start with a fully connected graph. We train a model p_i^M to approximate the conditional density of each variable i, given the current candidate variables for its Markov boundary $\mathcal{B}'_i$ which initially are all other variables. For this we can use a wide variety of neural networks. We use conditional Parzen windows

$$p_i^M\left(x_i|x_{\mathcal{B}'_i}\right) = \frac{\sum_{p=1}^{N} G(x_{\{i\}\cup\mathcal{B}'_i}; x_{\{i\}\cup\mathcal{B}'_i}^p, \Sigma_i)}{\sum_{p=1}^{N} G(x_{\mathcal{B}'_i}; x_{\mathcal{B}'_i}^p, \Sigma_{i,\mathcal{B}'_i})}, \tag{3}$$

where $\{x^p\}_{p=1}^{N}$ is the training set and $G(x; \mu, \Sigma)$ is our notation for a multidimensional Gaussian centered at μ with covariance matrix Σ evaluated at x. The Gaussians in the nominator are centered at $x_{\{i\}\cup\mathcal{B}'_i}^p$ which is the location of the p-th sample in the joint input/output ($\{x_i\}\cup\mathcal{B}'_i$) space and the Gaussians in the denominator are centered at $x_{\mathcal{B}'_i}^p$ which is the location of the p-th sample in the input space ($\mathcal{B}'_i$). There is one covariance matrix Σ_i for each conditional density model which is shared between all the Gaussians in that model. Σ_i is restricted to a diagonal matrix where the diagonal elements in all dimensions except the output dimension i, are the same. So there are only two free parameters in the matrix: The variance in the output dimension and the variance in all input dimensions. $\Sigma_{i,\mathcal{B}'_i}$ is equal to Σ_i except that the row and column corresponding to the output dimension have been deleted. For each conditional model p_i^M, Σ_i was optimized on the basis of the leave-one-out cross validation log-likelihood.

Our approach is based on tentatively removing edges from the model. Removing an edge decreases the size of the Markov boundary candidates of both affected variables and thus decreases the number of inputs in the corresponding two conditional density models. With the inputs removed, we retrain the two models (in our case, we simply find the optimal Σ_i for the two conditional Parzen windows). If the removal of the edge was correct, the leave-one-out cross validation log-likelihood (*model-score*) of the two models should improve since an unnecessary input is removed. (Removing an unnecessary input typically decreases model variance.) We therefore remove an edge if the model-scores of both models improve. Let's define as *edge-removal-score* the smaller of the two improvements in model-score.

Here is the algorithm in pseudo code:

- Start with a fully connected network

---

[4]The problem is that in the edge deletion method the decision is made independently for each edge whether or not it should be present. There are however cases where it is obvious that at least one of two edges must be present although the edge deletion method which tests each edge individually removes both.

- Until no edge-removal-score is positive:
  - for all edges $edge_{ij}$ in the network
    * calculate the model-scores of the reduced models $p_i^M(x_i|\mathcal{B}_i' - \{j\})$ and $p_i^M(x_j|\mathcal{B}_j' - \{i\})$
    * compare with the model-scores of the current models $p_i^M(x_i|\mathcal{B}_i')$ and $p_i^M(x_j|\mathcal{B}_j')$
    * set the edge-removal-score to the smaller of both model-score improvements
  - remove the edge for which the edge-removal-score is in maximum.

- end

3.3 Inference

Note that we have learned the structure of the Markov network without an explicit representation of the probability density. Although the conditional densities $p(x_i|\mathcal{B}_i)$ provide sufficient information to calculate the joint probability density the latter can not be easily computed. More precisely, the conditional densities overdetermine the joint density which might lead to problems if the conditional densities are estimated from data. For inference, we are typically interested in the expected value of an unknown variable, given an arbitrary set of known variables, which can be calculated using Gibbs sampling. Note, that the conditional densities $p^M(x_i|\mathcal{B}_i)$ which are required for Gibbs sampling are explicitly modeled in our approach by the conditional Parzen windows. Also note, that sampling from the conditional Parzen model (as well as many other neural networks, such as mixture of experts models) is easy.[5] In Hofmann (1997) we show that Gibbs sampling from the conditional Parzen models gives significantly better results than running inference using either a kernel estimator or a Gaussian mixture model of the joint density.

4 Experiments

In our first experiment we used the Boston housing data set, which contains 506 samples. Each sample consists of the housing price and 13 other variables which supposedly influence the housing price in a Boston neighborhood. Maximizing the cross validation log-likelihood as score as described in the previous chapters results in a Markov network with 68 edges.

While cross validation gives an unbiased estimate of whether a direct dependency exists between two variables the estimate can have a large variance depending on the size of the given data set. If the goal of the experiment is to interpret the resulting structure one would prefer to see only those edges corresponding to direct dependencies which can be clearly identified from the given data set. In other words, if the relationship between two variables observed on the given data set is so weak that we can not be sure that it is not just an effect of the finite data set size, then we do not want to display the corresponding edge. This can be achieved by adding a penalty per edge to the score of the conditional density models. (figure 1).

Figure 2 shows the resulting Markov network for a penalty per edge of 0.2. The goal of the original experiment for which the Boston housing data were collected was to examine whether the air quality (5) has direct influence on the housing price (14). Our algorithm did not find such an influence - in accordance with the original study. It found that the percentage of low status population (13) and the average number of rooms (6) are in direct relationship with the housing price. The pairwise relationships between these three variables are displayed in figure 3.

---

[5] Readers not familiar with Gibbs sampling, please consult Geman and Geman (1984).

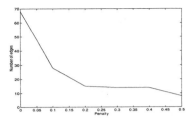

Figure 1: Number of edges in the Markov network for the Boston housing data as a function of the penalty per edge.

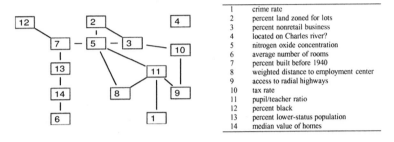

1	crime rate
2	percent land zoned for lots
3	percent nonretail business
4	located on Charles river?
5	nitrogen oxide concentration
6	average number of rooms
7	percent built before 1940
8	weighted distance to employment center
9	access to radial highways
10	tax rate
11	pupil/teacher ratio
12	percent black
13	percent lower-status population
14	median value of homes

Figure 2: Final structure of a run on the full Boston housing data set (penalty = 0.2).

The scatter plots visualize the relationship between variables 13 and 14, 6 and 14 and between 6 and 13 (from left to right). The left and the middle correspond to edges in the Markov network whereas for the right diagram the corresponding edge (6-13) is missing even though both variables are clearly dependent. The reason is, that the dependency between 6 and 13 can be explained as indirect relationship via variable 14. The Markov network tells us that 13 and 6 are independent given 14, but dependent if 14 is unknown.

In a second experiment we used a financial dataset. Each pattern corresponds to one business day. The variables in our model are relative changes in certain economic variables from the last business day to the present day which were expected to possibly influence the development of the German stock index DAX and the composite DAX, which contains a larger selection of stocks than the DAX. We used 500 training patterns consisting of 12 variables (figure 4). In comparison to the Boston housing data set most relationships are very weak. Using a penalty per edge of 0.2 leads to a very sparse model with only three edges (2-12, 12-1,5-11) (not shown). A penalty of 0.025 results in the model shown in figure 4. Note, that the composite

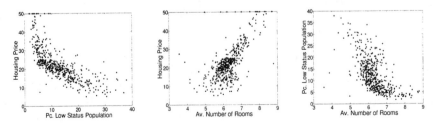

Figure 3: Pairwise relationship between the variables 6, 13 and 14. Displayed are all data points in the Boston housing data set.

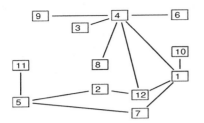

1	DAX
2	composite DAX
3	3 month interest rates Germany
4	return Germany
5	Morgan Stanley index Germany
6	Dow Jones industrial index
7	DM-USD exchange rate
8	US treasury bonds
9	gold price in DM
10	Nikkei index Japan
11	Morgan Stanley index Europe
12	price earning ratio (DAX stocks)

Figure 4: Final structure of a run on the financial data set with a penalty of 0.025. The small numbers next to the edges indicate the strength of the connection, i.e. the decrease in score (excluding the penalty) when the edge is removed. All variables are relative changes - not absolute values.

DAX is connected to the DAX mainly through the price earning ratio. While the DAX has direct connections to the Nikkei index and to the DM-USD exchange rate the composite DAX has a direct connection to the Morgan Stanley index for Germany. Recall, that composite DAX contains the stocks of many smaller companies in addition to the DAX stocks. The graph structure might be interpreted (with all caution) in the way that the composite DAX (including small companies) has a stronger dependency on national business whereas the DAX (only including the stock of major companies) reacts more to international indicators.

5   Conclusions

We have demonstrated, to our knowledge for the first time, how nonlinear Markov networks can be learned for continuous variables and we have shown that the resulting structures can give interesting insights into the underlying process. We used a representation based on models of the conditional probability density of each variable given its Markov boundary. These models can be trained locally. We showed how searching in the space of all possible structures can be done using this representation.

We suggest to use the conditional densities of each variable given its Markov boundary also for inference by Gibbs sampling. Since the required conditional densities are modeled explicitly by our approach and sampling from these is easy, Gibbs sampling is easier and faster to realize than with a direct representation of the joint density.

A topic of further research is the variance in resulting structures, i.e. the fact that different structures can lead to almost equally good models. It would for example be desirable to indicate to the user in a principled way the certainty of the existence or nonexistence of edges.

References

Geman, S., and Geman, D. (1984). Stochastic relaxations, Gibbs distributions and the Bayesian restoration of images. *IEEE Trans. on Pattern Analysis and Machine Intelligence* PAMI-6 (no. 6):721-42

Hofmann, R. (1997). *Inference in Markov Blanket Models.* Technical report, in preparation.

Monti, S., and Cooper, G. (1997). Learning Bayesian belief networks with neural network estimators. In *Neural Information Processing Systems 9.*, MIT Press.

Pearl, J. (1988). *Probabilistic reasoning in intelligent systems.* San Mateo: Morgan Kaufmann.

Whittaker, J. (1990). *Graphical models in applied multivariate statistics.* Chichester, UK: John Wiley and Sons.

Active Data Clustering

Thomas Hofmann
Center for Biological and Computational Learning, MIT
Cambridge, MA 02139, USA, hofmann@ai.mit.edu

Joachim M. Buhmann
Institut für Informatik III, Universität Bonn
Römerstraße 164, D-53117 Bonn, Germany, jb@cs.uni-bonn.de

Abstract

Active data clustering is a novel technique for clustering of proximity data which utilizes principles from sequential experiment design in order to interleave data generation and data analysis. The proposed active data sampling strategy is based on the *expected value of information*, a concept rooting in statistical decision theory. This is considered to be an important step towards the analysis of large-scale data sets, because it offers a way to overcome the inherent data sparseness of proximity data. We present applications to unsupervised texture segmentation in computer vision and information retrieval in document databases.

1 Introduction

Data clustering is one of the core methods for numerous tasks in pattern recognition, exploratory data analysis, computer vision, machine learning, data mining, and in many other related fields. Concerning the data representation it is important to distinguish between *vectorial data* and *proximity data*, cf. [Jain, Dubes, 1988]. In vectorial data each measurement corresponds to a certain 'feature' evaluated at an external scale. The elementary measurements of proximity data are, in contrast, (dis-)similarity values obtained by comparing pairs of entities from a given data set. Generating proximity data can be advantageous in cases where 'natural' similarity functions exist, while extracting features and supplying a meaningful vector-space metric may be difficult. We will illustrate the data generation process for two exemplary applications: unsupervised segmentation of textured images and data mining in a document database.

Textured image segmentation deals with the problem of partitioning an image into regions of homogeneous texture. In the unsupervised case, this has to be achieved on the basis of texture similarities without prior knowledge about the occuring textures. Our approach follows the ideas of [Geman *et al.*, 1990] to apply a *statistical test* to empirical distributions of image features at different sites. Suppose we decided to work with the gray-scale representation directly. At every image location $p = (x, y)$ we consider a local sample of gray-values, e.g., in a squared neighborhood around p. Then, the dissimilarity between two sites p_i and p_j is measured by the significance of rejecting the hypothesis that both samples were generated from the same probability distribution. Given a suitable binning $(t_k)_{1 \leq k \leq R}$ and histograms f_i, f_j, respectively, we propose to apply a χ^2-test, i.e.,

$$D_{ij} = \sum_k \frac{(f_i(t_k) - f_{ij}(t_k))^2}{f_{ij}(t_k)}, \quad \text{with } f_{ij}(t_k) = \frac{f_i(t_k) + f_j(t_k)}{2} . \tag{1}$$

In fact, our experiments are based on a multi-scale Gabor filter representation instead of the raw data, cf. [Hofmann *et al.*, 1997] for more details. The main advantage of the similarity-based approach is that it does not reduce the distributional information, e.g., to some simple first and second order statistics, *before* comparing textures. This preserves more information and also avoids the ad hoc specification of a suitable metric like a weighted Euclidean distance on vectors of extracted moment statistics.

As a second application we consider structuring a database of documents for improved information retrieval. Typical *measures of association* are based on the number of shared index terms [Van Rijsbergen, 1979]. For example, a document is represented by a (sparse) binary vector B, where each entry corresponds to the occurrence of a certain index term. The dissimilarity can then be defined by the cosine measure

$$D_{ij} = 1 - (B_i^t B_j / \sqrt{|B_i||B_j|}) . \tag{2}$$

Notice, that this measure (like many other) may violate the triangle inequality.

2 Clustering Sparse Proximity Data

In spite of potential advantages of similarity-based methods, their major drawback seems to be the scaling behavior with the number of data: given a dataset with N entities, the number of potential pairwise comparisons scales with $\mathcal{O}(N^2)$. Clearly, it is prohibitive to exhaustively perform or store all dissimilarities for large datasets, and the crucial problem is how to deal with this unavoidable data sparseness. More fundamentally, it is already the data generation process which has to solve the problem of *experimental design*, by selecting a subset of pairs (i, j) for evaluation. Obviously, a meaningful selection strategy could greatly profit from any knowledge about the grouping structure of the data. This observation leads to the concept of performing a *sequential* experimental design which interleaves the data clustering with the data acquisition process. We call this technique *active data clustering*, because it actively selects new data, and uses tentative knowledge to estimate the relevance of missing data. It amounts to inferring from the available data not only a grouping structure, but also to learn which future data is most relevant for the clustering problem. This fundamental concept may also be applied to other unsupervised learning problems suffering from data sparseness.

The first step in deriving a clustering algorithm is the specification of a suitable objective function. In the case of similarity-based clustering this is not at all a trivial problem and we have systematically developed an axiomatic approach based on invariance and robustness principles [Hofmann *et al.*, 1997]. Here, we can only give some informal justifications for our choice. Let us introduce indicator functions to represent data partitionings, $M_{i\nu}$ being the indicator function for entity $\mathbf{o}_i$ belonging to cluster $\mathcal{C}_\nu$. For a given number K of clusters, all Boolean functions are summarized in terms of an assignment matrix $\mathbf{M} \in \{0,1\}^{N \times K}$. Each row of $\mathbf{M}$ is required to sum to one in order to guarantee a unique cluster membership. To distinguish between known and unknown dissimilarities, index sets or *neighborhoods* $\mathcal{N} = (\mathcal{N}_1, \ldots, \mathcal{N}_N)$ are introduced. If $j \in \mathcal{N}_i$ this means the value of D_{ij} is available, otherwise it is not known. For simplicity we assume the dissimilarity measure (and in turn the neighborhood relation) to be symmetric, although this is not a necessary requirement. With the help of these definition the proposed criterion to assess the quality of a clustering configuration is given by

$$\mathcal{H}(\mathbf{M}; \mathbf{D}, \mathcal{N}) \;=\; \sum_{i=1}^{N}\sum_{\nu=1}^{K} M_{i\nu} d_{i\nu}, \quad d_{i\nu} = \frac{\sum_{j \in \mathcal{N}_i} M_{j\nu} D_{ij}}{\sum_{j \in \mathcal{N}_i} M_{j\nu}}. \tag{3}$$

$\mathcal{H}$ additively combines contributions $d_{i\nu}$ for each entity, where $d_{i\nu}$ corresponds to the average dissimilarity to entities belonging to cluster $\mathcal{C}_\nu$. In the sparse data case, averages are restricted to the fraction of entities with known dissimilarities, i.e., the subset of entities belonging to $\mathcal{C}_\nu \cap \mathcal{N}_i$.

3   Expected Value of Information

To motivate our active data selection criterion, consider the simplified sequential problem of inserting a new entity (or object) $\mathbf{o}_N$ to a database of $N-1$ entities with a given fixed clustering structure. Thus we consider the decision problem of optimally assigning the new object to one of the K clusters. If all dissimilarities between objects $\mathbf{o}_i$ and object $\mathbf{o}_N$ are known, the optimal assignment only depends on the average dissimilarities to objects in the different clusters, and hence is given by

$$M_{N\alpha^*} = 1 \;\Longleftrightarrow\; \alpha^* = \arg\min_{\nu} d^*_{N\nu}, \quad \text{where } d^*_{N\nu} = \frac{\sum_{j=1}^{N-1} M_{j\nu} D_{Nj}}{\sum_{j=1}^{N-1} M_{j\nu}}. \tag{4}$$

For incomplete data, the total population averages $d^*_{N\nu}$ are replaced by point estimators $d_{N\nu}$ obtained by restricting the sums in (4) to $\mathcal{N}_N$, the neighborhood of $\mathbf{o}_N$. Let us furthermore assume we want to compute a fixed number L of dissimilarities before making the terminal decision. If the entities in each cluster are not further distinguished, we can pick a member at random, once we have decided to sample from a cluster $\mathcal{C}_\nu$. The selection problem hence becomes equivalent to the problem of optimally distributing L measurements among K populations, such that the risk of making the wrong decision based on the resulting estimates $d_{N\nu}$ is minimal. More formally, this risk is given by $\mathcal{R} = d^*_{N\alpha} - d^*_{N\alpha^*}$, where α is the decision based on the subpopulation estimates $\{d_{N\nu}\}$ and α^* is the true optimum.

To model the problem of selecting an optimal experiment we follow the Bayesian approach developed by Raiffa & Schlaifer [Raiffa, Schlaifer, 1961] and compute the so-called *Expected Value of Sampling Information* (EVSI). As a fundamental step this involves the calculation of distributions for the quantities $d_{N\nu}$. For reasons of computational efficiency we are assuming that dissimilarities resulting from a comparison with an object in cluster $\mathcal{C}_\nu$ are normally distributed[1] with mean $d^*_{N\nu}$ and variance $\sigma^*_{N\nu}{}^2$. Since the variances are nuisance parameters the risk function $\mathcal{R}$ does not depend on, it suffices to calculate the marginal distribution of

---

[1]Other computationally more expensive choices to model within cluster dissimilarities are skewed distributions like the Gamma–distribution.

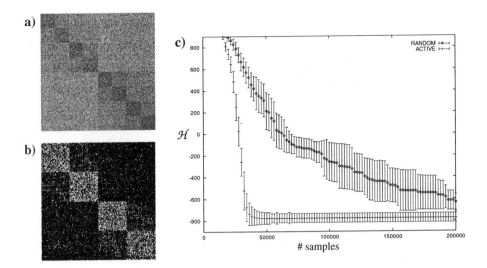

Figure 1: (a) Gray-scale visualization of the generated proximity matrix ($N = 800$). Dark/light gray values correspond to low/high dissimilarities respectively, D_{ij} being encoded by pixel (i, j). (b) Sampling snapshot for active data clustering after 60000 samples, queried values are depicted in white. (c) Costs evaluated on the **complete** data for sequential active and random sampling.

$d^*_{N\nu}$. For the class of statistical models we will consider in the sequel the empirical mean $d_{N\nu}$, the unbiased variance estimator $\sigma^2_{N\nu}$ and the sample size $m_{N\nu}$ are a sufficient statistic. Depending on these empirical quantities the marginal posterior distribution of $d^*_{N\nu}$ for uninformative priors is a Student t distribution with $t = \sqrt{m_{N\nu}}(d^*_{N\nu} - d_{N\nu})/\sigma_{N\nu}$ and $m_{N\nu} - 1$ degrees of freedom. The corresponding density will be denoted by $f_\nu(d^*_{N\nu}|d_{N\nu}, \sigma^2_{N\nu}, m_{N\nu})$. With the help of the posterior densities f_ν we define the *Expected Value of Perfect Information* (EVPI) after having observed $(d_{N\nu}, \sigma^2_{N\nu}, m_{N\nu})$ by

$$\text{EVPI} = \int_{-\infty}^{+\infty} \cdots \int_{-\infty}^{+\infty} \max_\nu \{d^*_{N\alpha} - d^*_{N\nu}\} \prod_{\nu=1}^{K} f_\nu(d^*_{N\nu}|d_{N\nu}, \sigma^2_{N\nu}, m_{N\nu}) \, d\, d^*_{N\nu}, \qquad (5)$$

where $\alpha = \arg\min_\nu d_{N\nu}$. The EVPI is the loss one expects to incur by making the decision α based on the incomplete information $\{d_{N\nu}\}$ instead of the optimal decision α^*, or, put the other way round, the expected gain we would obtain if α^* was revealed to us.

In the case of experimental design, the main quantity of interest is not the EVPI but the *Expected Value of Sampling Information* (EVSI). The EVSI quantifies how much gain we are expecting from additional data. The outcome of additional experiments can only be anticipated by making use of the information which is already available. This is known as *preposterior analysis*. The linearity of the utility measure implies that it suffices to calculate averages with respect to the *preposterous* distribution [Raiffa, Schlaifer, 1961, Chapter 5.3]. Drawing $m^+_{N\nu}$ additional samples from the ν-th population, and averaging possible outcomes with the (prior) distribution $f_\nu(d^*_{N\nu}|d_{N\nu}, \sigma^2_{N\nu}, m_{N\nu})$ will not affect the unbiased estimates $d_{N\nu}, \sigma^2_{N\nu}$, but only increase the number of samples $m_{N\nu} \to m_{N\nu} + m^+_{N\nu}$. Thus, we can compute the EVSI from (5) by replacing the prior densities with its preposterous counterparts.

To evaluate the K-dimensional integral in (5) or its EVSI variant we apply Monte-Carlo techniques, sampling from the Student t densities using Kinderman's re-

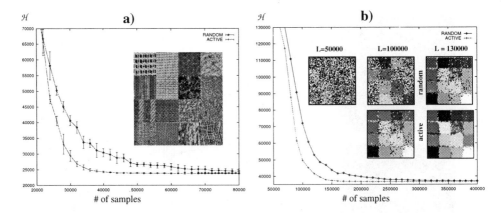

Figure 2: (a) Solution quality for active and random sampling on data generated from a mixture image of 16 Brodatz textures ($N = 1024$). (b) Cost trajectories and segmentation results for an active and random sampling example run ($N = 4096$).

jection sampling scheme, to get an empirical estimate of the random variable $\psi_\alpha(d^*_{N1}, \ldots, d^*_{NK}) = \max_\nu \{d^*_{N\alpha} - d^*_{N\nu}\}$. Though this enables us in principle to approximate the EVSI of any possible experiment, we cannot efficiently compute it for all possible ways of distributing the L samples among K populations. In the large sample limit, however, the EVSI becomes a concave function of the sampling sizes. This motivates a greedy design procedure of drawing new samples incrementally one by one.

4   Active Data Clustering

So far we have assumed the assignments of all but one entity $\mathbf{o}_N$ to be given in advance. This might be realistic in certain on-line applications, but more often we want to simultaneously find assignments for all entities in a dataset. The active data selection procedure hence has to be combined with a recalculation of clustering solutions, because additional data may help us not only to improve our terminal decision, but also with respect to our sampling strategy. A local optimization of $\mathcal{H}$ for assignments of a single object $\mathbf{o}_i$ can rely on the quantities

$$ g_{i\nu} = \sum_{j \in \mathcal{N}_i} \left[\frac{1}{n_{i\nu}} + \frac{1}{n^{+i}_{j\nu}} \right] M_{j\nu} D_{ij} - \sum_{j \in \mathcal{N}_i} \frac{1}{n^{+i}_{j\nu} n^{-i}_{j\nu}} \sum_{k \in \mathcal{N}_j - \{i\}} M_{j\nu} M_{k\nu} D_{jk} \, , \quad (6) $$

where $n_{j\nu} = \sum_{j \in \mathcal{N}_i} M_{j\nu}$, $n^{-i}_{j\nu} = n_{j\nu} - M_{i\nu}$, and $n^{+i}_{j\nu} = n^{-i}_{j\nu} + 1$, by setting $M_{i\alpha} = 1 \iff \alpha = \arg\min_\nu g_{i\nu} = \arg\min_\nu \mathcal{H}(\mathbf{M}|M_{i\nu} = 1)$, a claim which can be proved by straightforward algebraic manipulations (cf. [Hofmann et al., 1997]). This effectively amounts to a cluster readjustment by reclassification of objects. For additional evidence arising from new dissimilarities, one thus performs local reassignments, e.g., by cycling through all objects in random order, until no assignment is changing.

To avoid unfavorable local minima one may also introduce a computational temperature T and utilize $\{g_{i\nu}\}$ for simulated annealing based on the Gibbs sampler [Geman, Geman, 1984], $P\{M_{i\alpha} = 1\} = \exp\left[-\frac{1}{T} g_{i\alpha}\right] / \sum_{\nu=1}^{K} \exp\left[-\frac{1}{T} g_{i\nu}\right]$. Alternatively, Eq. (6) may also serve as the starting point to derive mean-field equations in a deterministic annealing framework, cf. [Hofmann, Buhmann, 1997]. These local

1	2	3	4	5	6	7	8	9	10
cluster	cluster	cluster	cluster	task	cluster	cluster	model	fuzzi	network
model	state	atom	algorithm	schedul	structur	object	cluster	cluster	cluster
distribu	sup	result	propos	cluster	method	approach	method	algorithm	neural
process	particl	temperatur	method	algorithm	base	algorithm	object	data	learn
studi	studi	degre	new	graph	gener	base	data	method	algorithm
cloud	sup	alloi	speech	schedul	loop	user	model	fuzzi	neural
fractal	alpha	atom	continu	task	video	queri	context	membership	network
event	state	ion	error	placem	famili	access	decision	rule	competit
random	particl	electron	construct	connect	softwar	softwar	manufactur	control	selforgan
particl	interac	temperatur	speaker	qualiti	variabl	placem	physical	identif	learn

11	12	13	14	15	16	17	18	19	20
algorithm	algorithm	cluster	method	cluster	robust	imag	cluster	model	galaxi
problem	cluster	data	docum	data	cluster	cluster	data	cluster	function
cluster	fuzzi	propos	signatur	techniqu	system	segment	algorithm	scale	correl
method	propos	result	cluster	result	complex	algorithm	set	nonlinear	redshift
optim	data	method	file	paper	eigenvalu	method	method	simul	hsup
heurist	converg	link	docum	visual	uncertainti	pixel	dissimilar	nbodi	hsup
solv	cmean	singl	retriev	video	robust	segment	point	gravit	redshift
tool	algorithm	method	previou	target	perturb	imag	data	dark	mpc
program	fcm	retriev	analyt	processor	bound	motion	center	mass	galaxi
machin	criteria	hierarchi	literatur	queri	matrix	color	kmean	matter	survei

Figure 3: Clustering solution with 20 clusters for 1584 documents on 'clustering'. Clusters are characterized by their 5 most topical and 5 most typical index terms.

optimization algorithms are well-suited for an incremental update after new data has been sampled, as they do not require a complete recalculation from scratch. The probabilistic reformulation in an annealing framework has the further advantage to provide assignment probabilities which can be utilized to improve the randomized 'partner' selection procedure. For any of these algorithms we sequentially update data assignments until a convergence criterion is fulfilled.

5 Results

To illustrate the behavior of the active data selection criterion we have run a series of repeated experiments on artificial data. For $N = 800$ the data has been divided into 8 groups of 100 entities. Intra-group dissimilarities have been set to zero, while inter-group dissimilarities were defined hierarchically. All values have been corrupted by Gaussian noise. The proximity matrix, the sampling performance, and a sampling snapshot are depicted in Fig. 1. The sampling exactly performs as expected: after a short initial phase the active clustering algorithm spends more samples to disambiguate clusters which possess a higher mean similarity, while less dissimilarities are queried for pairs of entities belonging to well separated clusters. For this type of structured data the gain of active sampling increases with the depth of the hierarchy. The final solution variance is due to local minima. Remarkably the active sampling strategy not only shows a faster improvement, it also finds on average significantly better solution. Notice that the sampling has been decomposed into stages, refining clustering solutions after sampling of 1000 additional dissimilarities.

The results of an experiment for unsupervised texture segmentation is shown Fig. 2. To obtain a close to optimal solution the active sampling strategy roughly needs less than 50% of the sample size required by random sampling for both, a resolution of $N = 1024$ and $N = 4096$. At a 64×64 resolution, for $L = 100K, 150K, 200K$ actively selected samples the random strategy needs on average $\bar{L} = 120K, 300K, 440K$ samples, respectively, to obtain a comparable solution quality. Obviously, active sampling can only be successful in an intermediate regime: if too little is known, we cannot infer additional information to improve our sampling, if the sample is large enough to reliably detect clusters, there is no need to sample any more. Yet, this intermediate regime significantly increases with K (and N).

Finally, we have clustered 1584 documents containing abstracts of papers with *clustering* as a title word. For $K = 20$ clusters[2] active clustering needed 120000 samples ($< 10\%$ of the data) to achieve a solution quality within 1% of the asymptotic solution. A random strategy on average required 230000 samples. Fig. 3 shows the achieved clustering solution, summarizing clusters by topical (most frequent) and typical (most characteristic) index terms. The found solution gives a good overview over areas dealing with clusters and clustering[3].

6 Conclusion

As we have demonstrated, the concept of *expected value of information* fits nicely into an optimization approach to clustering of proximity data, and establishes a sound foundation of active data clustering in statistical decision theory. On the medium size data sets used for validation, active clustering achieved a consistently better performance as compared to random selection. This makes it a promising technique for automated structure detection and data mining applications in large data bases. Further work has to address stopping rules and speed-up techniques to accelerate the evaluation of the selection criterion, as well as a unification with annealing methods and hierarchical clustering.

Acknowledgments

This work was supported by the Federal Ministry of Education and Science BMBF under grant # 01 M 3021 A/4 and by a M.I.T. Faculty Sponser's Discretionary Fund.

References

[Geman *et al.*, 1990] Geman, D., Geman, S., Graffigne, C., Dong, P. (1990). Boundary Detection by Constrained Optimization. *IEEE Transactions on Pattern Analysis and Machine Intelligence*, **12**(7), 609–628.

[Geman, Geman, 1984] Geman, S., Geman, D. (1984). Stochastic Relaxation, Gibbs Distributions, and the Bayesian Restoration of Images. *IEEE Transactions on Pattern Analysis and Machine Intelligence*, **6**(6), 721–741.

[Hofmann, Buhmann, 1997] Hofmann, Th., Buhmann, J. M. (1997). Pairwise Data Clustering by Deterministic Annealing. *IEEE Transactions on Pattern Analysis and Machine Intelligence*, **19**(1), 1–14.

[Hofmann *et al.*, 1997] Hofmann, Th., Puzicha, J., Buhmann, J.M. 1997. Deterministic Annealing for Unsupervised Texture Segmentation. *Pages 213–228 of: Proceedings of the International Workshop on Energy Minimization Methods in Computer Vision and Pattern Recognition*. Lecture Notes in Computer Science, vol. 1223.

[Jain, Dubes, 1988] Jain, A. K., Dubes, R. C. (1988). *Algorithms for Clustering Data*. Englewood Cliffs, NJ 07632: Prentice Hall.

[Raiffa, Schlaifer, 1961] Raiffa, H., Schlaifer, R. (1961). *Applied Statistical Decision Theory*. Cambridge MA: MIT Press.

[Van Rijsbergen, 1979] Van Rijsbergen, C. J. (1979). *Information Retrieval*. Butterworths, London Boston.

---

[2]The number of clusters was determined by a criterion based on complexity costs.

[3]Is it by chance, that 'fuzzy' techniques are 'softly' distributed over two clusters?

Function Approximation with the Sweeping Hinge Algorithm

Don R. Hush, Fernando Lozano
Dept. of Elec. and Comp. Engg.
University of New Mexico
Albuquerque, NM 87131

Bill Horne
MakeWaves, Inc.
832 Valley Road
Watchung, NJ 07060

Abstract

We present a computationally efficient algorithm for function approximation with piecewise linear sigmoidal nodes. A one hidden layer network is constructed one node at a time using the method of fitting the residual. The task of fitting individual nodes is accomplished using a new algorithm that searchs for the best fit by solving a sequence of Quadratic Programming problems. This approach offers significant advantages over derivative–based search algorithms (e.g. backpropagation and its extensions). Unique characteristics of this algorithm include: finite step convergence, a simple stopping criterion, a deterministic methodology for seeking "good" local minima, good scaling properties and a robust numerical implementation.

1 Introduction

The learning algorithm developed in this paper is quite different from the traditional family of derivative–based descent methods used to train Multilayer Perceptrons (MLPs) for function approximation. First, a *constructive* approach is used, which builds the network one node at a time. Second, and more importantly, we use *piecewise linear* sigmoidal nodes instead of the more popular (continuously differentiable) logistic nodes. These two differences change the nature of the learning problem entirely. It becomes a *combinatorial* problem in the sense that the number of feasible solutions that must be considered in the search is *finite*. We show that this number is exponential in the input dimension, and that the problem of finding the global optimum admits no polynomial–time solution. We then proceed to develop a heuristic algorithm that produces good approximations with reasonable efficiency. This algorithm has a simple stopping criterion, and very few user specified parameters. In addition, it produces solutions that are comparable to (and sometimes better than) those produced by local descent methods, and it does so using a deterministic methodology, so that the results are independent of initial conditions.

2   Background and Motivation

We wish to approximate an unknown continuous function $f(\mathbf{x})$ over a compact set with a one–hidden layer network described by

$$\hat{f}_n(\mathbf{x}) = a_0 + \sum_{i=1}^{n} a_i \sigma(\mathbf{x}, \mathbf{w}_i) \tag{1}$$

where n is the number of hidden layer nodes (basis functions), $\mathbf{x} \in \Re^d$ is the input vector, and $\{\sigma(\mathbf{x}, \mathbf{w})\}$ are sigmoidal functions parameterized by a weight vector $\mathbf{w}$. A set of example data, $S = \{\mathbf{x}_i, y_i\}$, with a total of N samples is available for training and test.

The models in (1) have been shown to be universal approximators. More importantly, (Barron, 1993) has shown that for a special class of continuous functions, Γ_C, the generalization error satisfies

$$E[\|f - f_{n,N}\|^2] \leq \|f - f_n\|^2 + E[\|f_n - f_{n,N}\|^2]$$

$$= O\left(\tfrac{1}{n}\right) + O\left(\tfrac{nd \log N}{N}\right)$$

where $\|\cdot\|$ is the appropriate two–norm, f_n is the the best n–node approximation to f, and $f_{n,N}$ is the approximation that best fits the samples in S. In this equation $\|f - f_n\|^2$ and $E[\|f_n - f_{n,N}\|^2]$ correspond to the *approximation* and *estimation* error respectively. Of particular interest is the $O(1/n)$ bound on approximation error, which for fixed basis functions is of the form $O(1/n^{2/d})$ (Barron, 1993). Barron's result tells us that the (tunable) sigmoidal bases are able to avoid the curse of dimensionality (for functions in Γ_C). Further, it has been shown that the $O(1/n)$ bound can be achieved *constructively* (Jones, 1992), that is by designing the basis functions (nodes) one at a time. The proof of this result is itself constructive, and thus provides a framework for the development of an algorithm which can (in principle) achieve this bound. One manifestation of this algorithm is shown in Figure 1. We call this the *iterative approximation algorithm* (IIA) because it builds the approximation by iterating on the residual (i.e. the unexplained portion of the function) at each step. This is the same algorithmic strategy used to form bases in numerous other settings, e.g. Grahm-Schmidt, Conjugate Gradient, and Projection Pursuit. The difficult part of the IIA algorithm is in the determination of the best fitting basis function σ_n in step 2. This is the focus of the remainder of this paper.

3   Algorithmic Development

We begin by defining the *hinging sigmoid* (HS) node on which our algorithms are based. An HS node performs the function

$$\sigma_h(\mathbf{x}, \mathbf{w}) = \begin{cases} w_+, & \tilde{\mathbf{w}}_l^T \tilde{\mathbf{x}} \geq w_+ \\ \tilde{\mathbf{w}}_l^T \tilde{\mathbf{x}}, & w_- \leq \tilde{\mathbf{w}}_l^T \tilde{\mathbf{x}} \leq w_+ \\ w_-, & \tilde{\mathbf{w}}_l^T \tilde{\mathbf{x}} \leq w_- \end{cases} \tag{2}$$

where $\mathbf{w}^T = [\tilde{\mathbf{w}}_l \; w_+ \; w_-]$ and $\tilde{\mathbf{x}}$ is an augmented input vector with a 1 in the first component. An example of the surface formed by an HS node on a two–dimensional input is shown in Figure 2. It is comprised of three hyperplanes joined pairwise

Initialization: $f_0(\mathbf{x}) = 0$
for $n = 1$ **to** n_{max} **do**
    1. Compute Residual: $e_n(\mathbf{x}) = f(\mathbf{x}) - f_{n-1}(\mathbf{x})$
    2. Fit Residual: $\sigma_n(\mathbf{x}) = \arg\min_{\sigma \in \Sigma} \|e_n(\mathbf{x}) - \sigma(\mathbf{x})\|$
    3. Update Estimate: $f_n(\mathbf{x}) = \alpha f_{n-1}(\mathbf{x}) + \beta \sigma_n(\mathbf{x})$
       where α and β are chosen to minimize $\|f(\mathbf{x}) - f_n(\mathbf{x})\|$
endloop

Figure 1: Iterative Approximation Algorithm (IIA).

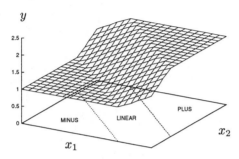

Figure 2: A Sigmoid Hinge function in two dimensions.

continuously at two hinge locations. The upper and middle hyperplanes are joined at "Hinge 1" and the lower and middle hyperplanes are joined at "Hinge 2". These hinges induce linear partitions on the input space that divide the space into three regions, and the samples in S into three subsets,

$$
\begin{aligned}
S_+ &= \left\{ (\mathbf{x}_i, y_i) : \tilde{\mathbf{w}}_l^T \tilde{\mathbf{x}}_i \geq w_+ \right\} \\
S_l &= \left\{ (\mathbf{x}_i, y_i) : w_- \leq \tilde{\mathbf{w}}_l^T \tilde{\mathbf{x}}_i \leq w_+ \right\} \\
S_- &= \left\{ (\mathbf{x}_i, y_i) : \tilde{\mathbf{w}}_l^T \tilde{\mathbf{x}}_i \leq w_- \right\}
\end{aligned}
\tag{3}
$$

These subsets, and the corresponding regions of the input space, are referred to as the PLUS, LINEAR and MINUS subsets/regions respectively. We refer to this type of partition as a *sigmoidal partition*. A sigmoidal partition of S will be denoted $P = \{S_+, S_l, S_-\}$, and the set of all such partitions will be denoted $\Pi = \{P_i\}$. Input samples that fall on the boundary between two regions can be assigned to the set on either side. These points are referred to as *hinge samples* and play a crucial role in subsequent development. Note that once a weight vector $\mathbf{w}$ is specified, the partition P is completely determined, but the reverse is not necessarily true. That is, there are generally an infinite number of weight vectors that induce the same partition.

We begin our quest for a learning algorithm with the development of an expression for the empirical risk. The empirical risk (squared error over the sample set) is defined

$$
E_P(\mathbf{w}) = \frac{1}{2} \sum_S \left(y_i - \sigma_h(\mathbf{x}_i, \mathbf{w}) \right)^2
\tag{4}
$$

This expression can be expanded into three terms, one for each set in the partition,

$$E_P(\mathbf{w}) = \frac{1}{2}\sum_{S_-}(y_i - w_-)^2 + \frac{1}{2}\sum_{S_+}(y_i - w_+)^2 + \frac{1}{2}\sum_{S_l}(y_i - \tilde{\mathbf{w}}_l^T \tilde{\mathbf{x}}_i)^2$$

After further expansion and rearrangement of terms we obtain

$$E_P(\mathbf{w}) = \frac{1}{2}\mathbf{w}^T\mathbf{R}\mathbf{w} - \mathbf{w}^T\mathbf{r} + s_y^2 \tag{5}$$

where

$$\mathbf{R}_l = \sum_{S_l}\tilde{\mathbf{x}}_i\tilde{\mathbf{x}}_i^T \quad \mathbf{r}_l = \sum_{S_l}\tilde{\mathbf{x}}_i y_i \tag{6}$$

$$s_y^2 = \tfrac{1}{2}\sum_S y_i^2 \quad s_y^+ = \sum_{S_+} y_i \quad s_y^- = \sum_{S_-} y_i \tag{7}$$

$$\mathbf{R} = \begin{pmatrix} \mathbf{R}_l & 0 & 0 \\ 0 & N_+ & 0 \\ 0 & 0 & N_- \end{pmatrix} \quad \mathbf{r} = \begin{pmatrix} \mathbf{r}_l \\ s_y^+ \\ s_y^- \end{pmatrix} \quad \mathbf{w} = \begin{pmatrix} \tilde{\mathbf{w}}_l \\ w_+ \\ w_- \end{pmatrix} \tag{8}$$

and N_+, N_l and N_- are the number of samples in S_+, S_l and S_- respectively. The subscript P is used to emphasize that this criterion is dependent on the partition (i.e. P is required to form $\mathbf{R}$ and $\mathbf{r}$). In fact, the nature of the partition plays a critical role in determining the properties of the solution. When $\mathbf{R}$ is positive *definite* (i.e. full rank), P is referred to as a *stable* partition, and when $\mathbf{R}$ has reduced rank P is referred to as an *unstable* partition. A stable partition requires that $\mathbf{R}_l > 0$. For purposes of algorithm development we will assume that $\mathbf{R}_l > 0$ when $|S_l| > N_{min}$, where N_{min} is a suitably chosen value greater than or equal to $d + 1$. With this, a necessary condition for a stable partition is that there be at least one sample in S_+ and S_- and $N_l \geq N_{min}$. When seeking a minimizing solution for $E_P(\mathbf{w})$ we restrict ourselves to stable partitions because of the potential nonuniqueness associated with solutions to unstable partitions.

Determining a weight vector that simultaneously minimizes $E_P(\mathbf{w})$ and preserves the current partition can be posed as a constrained optimization problem. This problem takes on the form

$$\begin{aligned} \min \tfrac{1}{2}\mathbf{w}^T\mathbf{R}\mathbf{w} - \mathbf{w}^T\mathbf{r} \\ \text{subject to } \mathbf{A}\mathbf{w} \leq \mathbf{0} \end{aligned} \tag{9}$$

where the inequality constraints are designed to maintain the current partition defined by (3). This is a *Quadratic Programming* problem with *inequality constraints*, and because $\mathbf{R} > 0$ it has a unique global minimum. The general Quadratic Programming problem is NP–hard and also hard to approximate (Bellare and Rogaway, 1993). However, the convex case which we restrict ourselves to here (i.e. $\mathbf{R} > 0$) admits a polynomial time solution. In this paper we use the *active set* algorithm (Luenberger, 1984) to solve (9). With the proper implementation, this algorithm runs in $O(k(d^2 + Nd))$ time, where k is typically on the order of d or less.

The solution to the quadratic programming problem in (9) is only as good as the current partition allows. The more challenging aspect of minimizing $E_P(\mathbf{w})$ is in the search for a good partition. Unfortunately there is no ordering or arrangement of partitions that is convex in $E_P(\mathbf{w})$, so the search for the optimal partition will be a computationally challenging problem. An exhaustive search is usually out of the question because of the prohibitively large number of partitions, as given by the following lemma.

Lemma 1: *Let S contain a total of N samples in $\Re^d$ that lie in general position. Then the number of sigmoidal partitions defined in (3) is $\Theta(N^{d+1})$.*

Proof: A detailed proof is beyond the scope of this paper, but an intuitive proof follows. It is well–known that the number of linear dichotomies of N points in d dimensions is $\Theta(N^d)$ (Edelsbrunner, 1987). Each sigmoidal partition is comprised of two linear dichotomies, one formed by Hinge 1 and the other by Hinge 2, and these dichotomies are constrained to be simple translations of one another. Thus, to enumerate all sigmoidal partitions we allow one of the hinges, say Hinge 1, can take on $\Theta(N^d)$ different positions. For each of these the other hinge can occupy only $\sim N$ unique positions. The total is therefore $\Theta(N^{d+1})$.

The search algorithm developed here employs a Quadratic Programming (QP) algorithm at each new partition to determine the optimal weight vector for that partition (i.e. the optimal orientation for the separating hyperplanes). Transitions are made from one partition to the next by allowing hinge samples to flip from one side of the hinge boundary to the next. The search is terminated when a minimum value of $E_P(\mathbf{w})$ is found (i.e. it can no longer be reduced by flipping hinge samples). Such an algorithm is shown in Figure 3. We call this the `HingeDescent` algorithm because it allows the hinges to "walk across" the data in a manner that descends the $E_P(\mathbf{w})$ criterion. Note that provisions are made within the algorithm to avoid unstable partitions. Note also that it is easy to modify this algorithm to descend only one hinge at a time, simply by omitting one of the blocks of code that flips samples across the corresponding hinge boundary.

```
{This routine is invoked with a stable feasible solution W = {w, R, r, A, S₊, Sₗ, S₋}.}
procedure HingeDescent (W)
        { Allow hinges to walk across the data until a minimizing partition is found. }
        E = ½wᵀRw − wᵀr
        do
                Emin = E
                {Flip Hinge 1 Samples.}
                for each ((xᵢ, yᵢ) on Hinge 1) do
                        if ((xᵢ, yᵢ) ∈ S₊ and N₊ > 1) then
                                Move (xᵢ, yᵢ) from S₊ to Sₗ, and update R, r, and A
                        elseif ((xᵢ, yᵢ) ∈ Sₗ and Nₗ > Nmin) then
                                Move (xᵢ, yᵢ) from Sₗ to S₊, and update R, r, and A
                        endif
                endloop
                {Flip Hinge 2 Samples.}
                for each ((xᵢ, yᵢ) on Hinge 2) do
                        if ((xᵢ, yᵢ) ∈ S₋ and N₋ > 1) then
                                Move (xᵢ, yᵢ) from S₋ to Sₗ, and update R, r, and A
                        elseif ((xᵢ, yᵢ) ∈ Sₗ and Nₗ > Nmin) then
                                Move (xᵢ, yᵢ) from Sₗ to S₋, and update R, r, and A
                        endif
                endloop
                {Compute optimal solution for new partition.}
                W = QPSolve(W);
                E = ½wᵀRw − wᵀr
        while (E < Emin) ;
        return(W);
    end ;     {HingeDescent}
```

Figure 3: The `HingeDescent` Algorithm.

Lemma 2: *When started at a stable partition, the* `HingeDescent` *algorithm will* *converge to a stable partition of $E_P(\mathbf{w})$ in a finite number of steps.*

Proof: First note that when $\mathbf{R} > 0$, a QP solution can always be found in a finite number of steps. The proof of this result is beyond the scope of this paper, but can easily be found in the literature (Luenberger, 1984). Now, by design, HingeDescent always moves from one stable partition to the next, maintaining the $\mathbf{R} > 0$ property at each step so that all QP solutions can be produced in a finite number of steps. In addition, $E_P(\mathbf{w})$ is reduced at each step (except the last one) so no partitions are revisited, and since there are a finite number of partitions (see Lemma 1) this algorithm must terminate in a finite number of steps. QED.

Assume that QPSolve runs in $O(k(d^2+Nd))$ time as previously stated. Then the run time of HingeDescent is given by $O(N_p((k+N_h)d^2+kNd))$, where N_h is the number of samples flipped at each step and N_p is the total number of partitions explored. Typical values for k and N_h are on the order of d, simplifying this expression to $O(N_p(d^3 + Nd^2))$. N_p can vary widely, but is often substantially less than N.

HingeDescent seeks a local minimum over Π, and may produce a poor solution, depending on the starting partition. One way to remedy this is to start from several different initial partitions, and then retain the best solution overall. We take a different approach here, that always starts with the same initial condition, visits several local minima along the way, and always ends up with the same final solution each time.

The SweepingHinge algorithm works as follows. It starts by placing one of the hinges, say Hinge 1, at the outer boundary of the data. It then sweeps this hinge across the data, M samples at a time (e.g. $M = 1$), allowing the other hinge (Hinge 2) to descend to an optimal position at each step. The initial hinge locations are determined as follows. A linear fit is formed to the entire data set and the hinges are positioned at opposite ends of the data so that the PLUS and MINUS regions meet the LINEAR region at the two data samples on either end. After the initial linear fit, the hinges are allowed to descend to a local minimum using HingeDescent. Then Hinge 1 is swept across the data M samples at a time. Mechanically this is achieved by moving M additional samples from S_l to S_+ at each step. Hinge 2 is allowed to descend to an optimal position at each of these steps using the Hinge2Descent algorithm. This algorithm is identical to HingeDescent except that the code that flips samples across Hinge 1 is omitted. The best overall solution from the sweep is retained and "fine–tuned" with one final pass through the HingeDescent algorithm to produce the final solution.

The run time of SweepingHinge is no worse than N/M times that of HingeDescent. Given this, an upper bound on the (typical) run time for this algorithm (with $M = 1$) is $O(NN_p(d^3 + Nd^2))$. Consequently, SweepingHinge scales reasonably well in both N and d, considering the nature of the problem it is designed to solve.

4   Empirical Results

The following experiment was adapted from (Breiman, 1993). The function $f(\mathbf{x}) = e^{-\|\mathbf{x}\|^2}$ is sampled at $100d$ points $\{\mathbf{x}_i\}$ such that $\|\mathbf{x}\| \leq 3$ and $\|\mathbf{x}\|$ is uniform on $[0, 3]$. The dimension d is varied from 4 to 10 (in steps of 2) and models of size 1 to 20 nodes are trained using the IIA/SweepingHinge algorithm. The number of samples traversed at each step of the sweep in SweepingHinge was set to $M = 10$. N_{min} was set equal to $3d$ throughout. A refitting pass was employed after each new node was added in the IIA. The refitting algorithm used HingeDescent to "fine–tune" each node each node before adding the next node. The average sum of squared

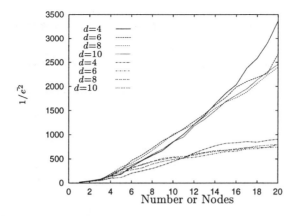

Figure 4: Upper (lower) curves are for training (test) data.

error, $\bar{e}^2$, was computed for both the training data and an independent set of test data of size $200d$. Plots of $1/\bar{e}^2$ versus the number of nodes are shown in Figure 4. The curves for the training data are clearly bounded below by a linear function of n (as suggested by inverting the $O(1/n)$ result of Barron's). More importantly however, they show no significant dependence on the dimension d. The curves for the test data show the effect of the estimation error as they start to "bend over" around $n = 10$ nodes. Again however, they show no dependence on dimension.

Acknowledgements

This work was inspired by the theoretical results of (Barron, 1993) for sigmoidal networks as well as the "Hinging Hyperplanes" work of (Breiman, 1993) , and the "Ramps" work of (Friedman and Breiman, 1994). This work was supported in part by ONR grant number N00014–95–1–1315.

References

Barron, A.R. (1993) Universal approximation bounds for superpositions of a sigmoidal function. *IEEE Transactions on Information Theory* **39**(3):930–945.

Bellare, M. & Rogaway, P. (1993) The complexity of approximating a nonlinear program. In P.M. Pardalos (ed.), *Complexity in numerical optimization*, pp. 16–32, World Scientific Pub. Co.

Breiman, L. (1993) Hinging hyperplanes for regression, classification and function approximation. *IEEE Transactions on Information Theory* **39**(3):999–1013.

Breiman, L. & Friedman, J.H. (1994) Function approximation using RAMPS. *Snowbird Workshop on Machines that Learn.*

Edelsbrunner, H. (1987) In EATCS Monographs on Theoretical Computer Science V. 10, *Algorithms in Combinatorial Geometry*. Springer–Verlag.

Jones, L.K. (1992) A simple lemma on greedy approximation in Hilbert space and convergence rates for projection pursuit regression and neural network training. *The Annals of Statistics*, **20**:608–613.

Luenberger, D.G. (1984) *Introduction to Linear and Nonlinear Programming.* Addison–Wesley.

The Error Coding and Substitution PaCTs

GARETH JAMES
and
TREVOR HASTIE
Department of Statistics, Stanford University

Abstract

A new class of *plug in* classification techniques have recently been developed in the statistics and machine learning literature. A plug in classification technique (PaCT) is a method that takes a standard classifier (such as LDA or TREES) and plugs it into an algorithm to produce a new classifier. The standard classifier is known as the *Plug in Classifier* (PiC). These methods often produce large improvements over using a single classifier. In this paper we investigate one of these methods and give some motivation for its success.

1 Introduction

Dietterich and Bakiri (1995) suggested the following method, motivated by Error Correcting Coding Theory, for solving k class classification problems using binary classifiers.

- Produce a k by B (B large) binary coding matrix, ie a matrix of zeros and ones. We will denote this matrix by Z, its i,jth component by Z_{ij}, its ith row by $\mathbf{Z}_i$ and its jth column by $\mathbf{Z}^j$.

- Use the first column of the coding matrix ($\mathbf{Z}^1$) to create two *super* groups by assigning all groups with a one in the corresponding element of $\mathbf{Z}^1$ to super group one and all other groups to super group zero.

- Train your plug in classifier (PiC) on the new two class problem.

- Repeat the process for each of the B columns ($\mathbf{Z}^1, \mathbf{Z}^2, \ldots, \mathbf{Z}^B$) to produce B trained classifiers.

- For a new test point apply each of the B classifiers to it. Each classifier will produce a $\hat{p}_j$ which is the estimated probability the test point comes from the jth super group one. This will produce a vector of probability estimates, $\hat{\mathbf{p}} = (\hat{p}_1, \hat{p}_2, \ldots, \hat{p}_B)^T$.

- To classify the point calculate $L_i = \sum_{j=1}^{B} |\hat{p}_j - Z_{ij}|$ for each of the k groups (ie for i from 1 to k). This is the L1 distance between $\hat{p}$ and $\mathbf{Z}_i$ (the ith row of Z). Classify to the group with lowest L1 distance or equivalently $\arg_i \min L_i$

We call this the ECOC PaCT. Each row in the coding matrix corresponds to a unique (non-minimal) coding for the appropriate class. Dietterich's motivation was that this allowed *errors* in individual classifiers to be *corrected* so if a small number of classifiers gave a bad fit they did not unduly influence the final classification. Several PiC's have been tested. The best results were obtained by using *tree's*, so all the experiments in this paper are stated using a standard CART PiC. Note however, that the theorems are general to any PiC.

In the past it has been assumed that the improvements shown by this method were attributable to the error coding structure and much effort has been devoted to choosing an *optimal* coding matrix. In this paper we develop results which suggest that a randomized coding matrix should match (or exceed) the performance of a *designed* matrix.

2 The Coding Matrix

Empirical results (see Dietterich and Bakiri (1995)) suggest that the ECOC PaCT can produce large improvements over a standard k class tree classifier. However, they do not shed any light on why this should be the case. To answer this question we need to explore its probability structure. The coding matrix, Z, is central to the PaCT. In the past the usual approach has been to choose one with as large a separation between rows ($\mathbf{Z}_i$) as possible (in terms of hamming distance) on the basis that this allows the largest number of *errors* to be corrected. In the next two sections we will examine the tradeoffs between a *designed* (*deterministic*) and a *completely randomized* matrix.

Some of the results that follow will make use of the following assumption.

$$E[\hat{p}_j \mid Z, X] = \sum_{i=1}^{k} Z_{ij} q_i = \mathbf{Z}^{j^T} q \quad j = 1, \ldots, B \tag{1}$$

where $q_i = P(G_i \mid X)$ is the posterior probability that the test observation is from group i given that our predictor variable is X. This is an unbiasedness assumption. It states that on average our classifier will estimate the probability of being in super group one correctly. The assumption is probably not too bad given that trees are considered to have low bias.

2.1 Deterministic Coding Matrix

Let $\bar{D}_i = 1 - 2L_i/B$ for $i = 1 \ldots k$. Notice that $\arg_i \min L_i = \arg_i \max \bar{D}_i$ so using $\bar{D}_i$ to classify is identical to the ECOC PaCT. Theorem 3 in section 2.2 explains why this is an intuitive transformation to use.

Obviously no PaCT can outperform the Bayes Classifier. However we would hope that it would achieve the Bayes Error Rate when we use the Bayes Classifier as our PiC for each 2 class problem. We have defined this property as Bayes Optimality. Bayes Optimality is essentially a consistency result. It states, if our PiC converges to the Bayes Classifier, as the training sample size increases, then so will the PaCT.

Definition 1 *A PaCT is said to be Bayes Optimal if, for any test set, it always classifies to the bayes group when the Bayes Classifier is our PiC.*

For the ECOC PaCT this means that $\arg_i \max q_i = \arg_i \max \bar{D}_i$, for all points in the predictor space, when we use the Bayes Classifier as our PiC. However it can be shown that in this case

$$\bar{D}_i = 1 - \frac{2}{B} \sum_{l \neq i} q_l \sum_{j=1}^{B} (Z_{lj} - Z_{ij})^2 \quad i = 1, \ldots, k$$

It is not clear from this expression why there should be any guarantee that $\arg_i \max \bar{D}_i = \arg_i \max q_i$. In fact the following theorem tells us that only in very restricted circumstances will the ECOC PaCT be Bayes Optimal.

Theorem 1 *The Error Coding method is Bayes Optimal iff the Hamming distance between every pair of rows of the coding matrix is equal.*

The hamming distance between two binary vectors is the number of points where they differ. For general B and k there is no known way to generate a matrix with this property so the ECOC PaCT will not be Bayes Optimal.

2.2   Random Coding Matrix

We have seen in the previous section that there are potential problems with using a deterministic matrix. Now suppose we randomly generate a coding matrix by choosing a zero or one with equal probability for every coordinate. Let $\mu_i = E(1 - 2|\hat{p}_1 - Z_{i1}| \mid \mathcal{T})$ where $\mathcal{T}$ is the training set. Then μ_i is the conditional expectation of $\bar{D}_i$ and we can prove the following theorem.

Theorem 2 *For a random coding matrix, conditional on $\mathcal{T}$, $\arg_i \max \bar{D}_i \to \arg_i \max \mu_i$ a.s. as $B \to \infty$. Or in other words the classification from the ECOC PaCT approaches the classification from just using $\arg_i \max \mu_i$ a.s.*

This leads to corollary 1 which indicates we have eliminated the main concern of a deterministic matrix.

Corollary 1 *When the coding matrix is randomly chosen the ECOC PaCT is asymptotically Bayes Optimal ie $\arg_i \max \bar{D}_i \to \arg_i \max q_i$ a.s. as $B \to \infty$*

This theorem is a consequence of the strong law. Theorems 2 and 3 provide motivation for the ECOC procedure.

Theorem 3 *Under assumption 1 for a randomly generated coding matrix*

$$E\bar{D}_i = E\mu_i = q_i \quad i = 1 \ldots k$$

This tells us that $\bar{D}_i$ is an unbiased estimate of the conditional probability so classifying to the maximum is in a sense an unbiased estimate of the Bayes classification.
Now theorem 2 tells us that for *large B* the ECOC PaCT will be similar to classifying using $\arg_i \max \mu_i$ only. However what we mean by large depends on the rate of convergence. Theorem 4 tells us that this rate is in fact exponential.

Theorem 4 *If we randomly choose Z then, conditional on $\mathcal{T}$, for any fixed X*

$$Pr(\arg_i \max \bar{D}_i \neq \arg_i \max \mu_i) \leq (k - 1) \cdot e^{-mB}$$

for some constant m.

Note that theorem 4 does not depend on assumption 1. This tells us that the error rate for the ECOC PaCT is equal to the error rate using $\arg_i \max \mu_i$ plus a term which decreases exponentially in the limit. This result can be proved using Hoeffding's inequality (Hoeffding (1963)).
Of course this only gives an upper bound on the error rate and does not necessarily indicate the behavior for smaller values of B. Under certain conditions a Taylor expansion indicates that $Pr(\arg_i \max \bar{D}_i \neq \arg_i \max \mu_i) \approx 0.5 - m\sqrt{B}$ for small values of $m\sqrt{B}$. So we

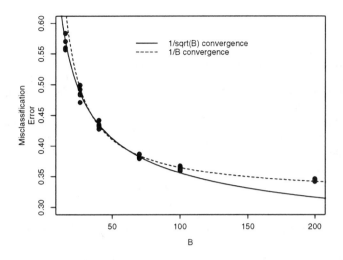

Figure 1: Best fit curves for rates $1/\sqrt{B}$ and $1/B$

might expect that for smaller values of B the error rate decreases as some power of B but that as B increases the change looks more and more exponential.

To test this hypothesis we calculated the error rates for 6 different values of B $(15, 26, 40, 70, 100, 200)$ on the LETTER data set (available from the Irvine Repository of machine learning). Each value of B contains 5 points corresponding to 5 random matrices. Each point is the average over 20 random training sets. Figure 1 illustrates the results. Here we have two curves. The lower curve is the best fit of $1/\sqrt{B}$ to the first four groups. It fits those groups well but under predicts errors for the last two groups. The upper curve is the best fit of $1/B$ to the last four groups. It fits those groups well but over predicts errors for the first two groups. This supports our hypothesis that the error rate is moving through the powers of B towards an exponential fit.

We can see from the figure that even for relatively low values of B the reduction in error rate has slowed substantially. This indicates that almost all the remaining errors are a result of the error rate of $\arg_i \max \mu_i$ which we can not reduce by changing the coding matrix.

The coding matrix can be viewed as a method for sampling from the distribution of $1 - 2|\hat{p}_j - Z_{ij}|$. If we sample randomly we will estimate μ_i (its mean). It is well known that the optimal way to estimate such a parameter is by random sampling so it is not possible to improve on this by *designing* the coding matrix. Of course it may be possible to improve on $\arg_i \max \mu_i$ by using the training data to influence the sampling procedure and hence estimating a different quantity. However a designed coding matrix does not use the training data. It should not be possible to improve on random sampling by using such a procedure (as has been attempted in the past).

3   Why does the ECOC PaCT work?

The easiest way to motivate why the ECOC PaCT works, in the case of tree classifiers, is to consider a very similar method which we call the Substitution PaCT. We will show that under certain conditions the ECOC PaCT is very similar to the Substitution PaCT and then motivate the success of the later.

3.1 Substitution PaCT

The Substitution PaCT uses a coding matrix to form many different trees just as the ECOC PaCT does. However, instead of using the transformed training data to form a probability estimate for each two class problem, we now plug the original (ie k-class) training data back into the new tree. We use this training data to form probability estimates and classifications just as we would with a regular tree. The only difference is in how the tree is formed. Therefore, unlike the ECOC PaCT, each tree will produce a probability estimate for each of the k classes. For each class we simply average the probability estimate for that class over our B trees. So if p_i^S is the probability estimate for the Substitution PaCT, then

$$p_i^S = \frac{1}{B} \sum_{j=1}^{B} p_{ij} \tag{2}$$

where p_{ij} is the probability estimate for the ith group for the tree formed from the jth column of the coding matrix.

Theorem 5 shows that under certain conditions the ECOC PaCT can be thought of as an approximation to the Substitution PaCT.

Theorem 5 *Suppose that p_{ij} is independent from the jth column of the coding matrix, for all i and j. Then as B approaches infinity the ECOC PaCT and Substitution PaCT will converge ie they will give identical classification rules.*

The theorem depends on an unrealistic assumption. However, empirically it is well known that trees are unstable and a small change in the data set can cause a large change in the structure of the tree so it may be reasonable to suppose that there is a low correlation.

To test this empirically we ran the ECOC and Substitution PaCT's on a simulated data set. The data set was composed of 26 classes. Each class was distributed as a bivariate normal with identity covariance matrix and uniformly distributed means. The training data consisted of 10 observations from each group. Figure 2 shows a plot of the estimated probabilities for each of the 26 classes and 1040 test data points averaged over 10 training data sets. Only points where the true posterior probability is greater than 0.01 have been plotted since groups with insignificant probabilities are unlikely to affect the classification. If the two groups were producing identical estimates we would expect the data points to lie on the dotted 45 degree line. Clearly this is not the case. The Substitution PaCT is systematically shrinking the probability estimates. However there is a very clear linear relationship ($R^2 \approx 95\%$) and since we are only interested in the $\arg\max$ for each test point we might expect similar classifications. In fact this is the case with fewer than 4% of points correctly classified by one group but not the other.

3.2 Why does the Substitution PaCT work?

The fact that p_i^S is an average of probability estimates suggests that a reduction in variability may be an explanation for the success of the Substitution PaCT. Unfortunately it has been well shown (see for example Friedman (1996)) that a reduction in variance of the probability estimates does not necessarily correspond to a reduction in the error rate. However theorem 6 provides simplifying assumptions under which a relationship between the two quantities exists.

Theorem 6 *Suppose that*

$$
\begin{aligned}
p_i^T &= \alpha_0^T + \alpha_1^T q_i + \sigma_T \epsilon_i^T \quad (\alpha_1^T > 0) \tag{3}\\
\text{and} \quad p_i^S &= \alpha_0^S + \alpha_1^S q_i + \sigma_S \epsilon_i^S \quad (\alpha_1^S > 0) \tag{4}
\end{aligned}
$$

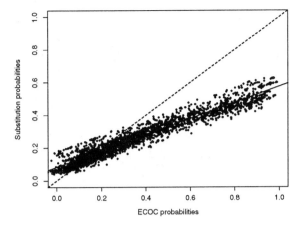

Figure 2: Probability estimates from both the ECOC and Substitution PaCT's

where ϵ^S and ϵ^T have identical joint distributions with variance 1. p_i^T is the probability estimate of the ith group for a k class tree method, α_0 and α_1 are constants and q_i is the true posterior probability. Let

$$\gamma = \frac{Var(p_i^T/\alpha_1^T)}{Var(p_{i1}/\alpha_1^S)}$$

and $\rho = corr(p_{i1}, p_{i2})$ (assumed constant for all i). Then

$$Pr(\arg\max p_i^S = \arg\max q_i) \geq Pr(\arg\max p_i^T = \arg\max q_i) \tag{5}$$

if

$$\rho < \gamma \tag{6}$$

and

$$B \geq \frac{1-\rho}{\gamma - \rho} \tag{7}$$

The theorem states that under fairly general conditions, the probability that the Substitution PaCT gives the same classification as the Bayes classifier is at least as great as that for the tree method provided that the standardized variability is low enough. It should be noted that only in the case of two groups is there a direct correspondence between the error rate and 5. The inequality in 5 is strict for most common distributions (e.g. normal, uniform, exponential and gamma) of ϵ.

Now there is reason to believe that in general ρ will be small. This is a result of the empirical variability of tree classifiers. A small change in the training set can cause a large change in the structure of the tree and also the final probability estimates. So by changing the super group coding we might expect a probability estimate that is fairly unrelated to previous estimates and hence a low correlation.

To test the accuracy of this theory we examined the results from the simulation performed in section 3.1. We wished to estimate γ and ρ. The following table summarizes our estimates for the variance and standardizing (α_1) terms from the simulated data set.

Classifier	$Var(p_i)$	α_1	$Var(p_i/\alpha_1)$
Substitution PaCT	0.0515	0.3558	0.4068
Tree Method	0.0626	0.8225	0.0925

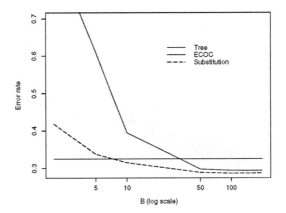

Figure 3: Error rates on the simulated data set for tree method, Substitution PaCT and ECOC PaCT plotted against B (on log scale)

These quantities give us an estimate for γ of $\hat{\gamma} = 0.227$ We also derived an estimate for ρ of $\hat{\rho} = 0.125$

We see that ρ is less than γ so provided $B \geq \frac{1-\hat{\rho}}{\hat{\gamma}-\hat{\rho}} \approx 8.6$ we should see an improvement in the Substitution PaCT over a k class tree classifier. Figure 3 shows that the Substitution error rate drops below that of the tree classifier at almost exactly this point.

4 Conclusion

The ECOC PaCT was originally envisioned as an adaption of error coding ideas to classification problems. Our results indicate that the error coding matrix is simply a method for randomly sampling from a fixed distribution. This idea is very similar to the Bootstrap where we randomly sample from the empirical distribution for a fixed data set. There you are trying to estimate the variability of some parameter. Your estimate will have two sources of error, randomness caused by sampling from the empirical distribution and the randomness from the data set itself. In our case we have the same two sources of error, error caused by sampling from $1 - 2|\hat{p}_j - Z_{ij}|$ to estimate μ_i and error's caused by μ itself. In both cases the first sort of error will reduce rapidly and it is the second type we are really interested in. It is possible to motivate the reduction in error rate of using $\arg_i \max \mu_i$ in terms of a decrease in variability, provided B is large enough and our correlation (ρ) is small enough.

References

Dieterich, T.G. and Bakiri G. (1995) Solving Multiclass Learning Problems via Error-Correcting Output Codes, Journal of Artificial Intelligence Research 2 (1995) 263-286

Dietterich, T. G. and Kong, E. B. (1995) Error-Correcting Output Coding Corrects Bias and Variance, Proceedings of the 12th International Conference on Machine Learning pp. 313-321 Morgan Kaufmann

Friedman, J.H. (1996) On Bias, Variance, 0/1-loss, and the Curse of Dimensionality, Dept. of Statistics, Stanford University, Technical Report

Hoeffding, W. (1963) Probability Inequalities for Sums of Bounded Random Variables. "Journal of the American Statistical Association", March, 1963

S-Map: A network with a simple self-organization algorithm for generative topographic mappings

Kimmo Kiviluoto
Laboratory of Computer and
Information Science
Helsinki University of Technology
P.O. Box 2200
FIN-02015 HUT, Espoo, Finland
Kimmo.Kiviluoto@hut.fi

Erkki Oja
Laboratory of Computer and
Information Science
Helsinki University of Technology
P.O. Box 2200
FIN-02015 HUT, Espoo, Finland
Erkki.Oja@hut.fi

Abstract

The S-Map is a network with a simple learning algorithm that combines the self-organization capability of the Self-Organizing Map (SOM) and the probabilistic interpretability of the Generative Topographic Mapping (GTM). The simulations suggest that the S-Map algorithm has a stronger tendency to self-organize from random initial configuration than the GTM. The S-Map algorithm can be further simplified to employ pure Hebbian learning, without changing the qualitative behaviour of the network.

1 Introduction

The self-organizing map (SOM; for a review, see [1]) forms a topographic mapping from the data space onto a (usually two-dimensional) output space. The SOM has been succesfully used in a large number of applications [2]; nevertheless, there are some open theoretical questions, as discussed in [1, 3]. Most of these questions arise because of the following two facts: the SOM is not a generative model, i.e. it does not generate a density in the data space, and it does not have a well-defined objective function that the training process would strictly minimize.

Bishop et al. [3] introduced the generative topographic mapping (GTM) as a solution to these problems. However, it seems that the GTM requires a careful initialization to self-organize. Although this can be done in many practical applications, from a theoretical point of view the GTM does not yet offer a fully satisfactory model for natural or artificial self-organizing systems.

In this paper, we first briefly review the SOM and GTM algorithms (section 2); then we introduce the S-Map, which may be regarded as a crossbreed of SOM and GTM (section 3); finally, we present some simulation results with the three algorithms (section 4), showing that the S-Map manages to combine the computational simplicity and the ability to self-organize of the SOM with the probabilistic framework of the GTM.

2 SOM and GTM

2.1 The SOM algorithm

The self-organizing map associates each data vector $\boldsymbol{\xi}^t$ with that map unit that has its weight vector closest to the data vector. The *activations* η_i^t of the map units are given by

$$\eta_i^t = \begin{cases} 1, & \text{when } ||\boldsymbol{\mu}_i - \boldsymbol{\xi}^t|| < ||\boldsymbol{\mu}_j - \boldsymbol{\xi}^t||, \ \forall j \neq i \\ 0, & \text{otherwise} \end{cases} \tag{1}$$

where $\boldsymbol{\mu}_i$ is the weight vector of the ith map unit $\boldsymbol{\zeta}_i$, $i = 1, \ldots, K$. Using these activations, the SOM weight vector update rule can be written as

$$\boldsymbol{\mu}_j := \boldsymbol{\mu}_j + \delta^t \sum_{i=1}^{K} \eta_i^t h(\boldsymbol{\zeta}_i, \boldsymbol{\zeta}_j; \beta^t)(\boldsymbol{\xi}^t - \boldsymbol{\mu}_j) \tag{2}$$

Here parameter δ^t is a learning rate parameter that decreases with time. The *neighborhood function* $h(\boldsymbol{\zeta}_i, \boldsymbol{\zeta}_j; \beta^t)$ is a decreasing function of the distance between map units $\boldsymbol{\zeta}_i$ and $\boldsymbol{\zeta}_j$; β^t is a width parameter that makes the neighborhood function get narrower as learning proceeds. One popular choice for the neighborhood function is a Gaussian with inverse variance β^t.

2.2 The GTM algorithm

In the GTM algorithm, the map is considered as a *latent space*, from which a nonlinear mapping to the data space is first defined. Specifically, a point $\boldsymbol{\zeta}$ in the latent space is mapped to the point $\boldsymbol{v}$ in the data space according to the formula

$$\boldsymbol{v}(\boldsymbol{\zeta}; \mathbf{M}) = \mathbf{M}\boldsymbol{\phi}(\boldsymbol{\zeta}) = \sum_{j=1}^{L} \phi_j(\boldsymbol{\zeta})\boldsymbol{\mu}_j \tag{3}$$

where $\boldsymbol{\phi}$ is a vector consisting of L Gaussian basis functions, and $\mathbf{M}$ is a $D \times L$ matrix that has vectors $\boldsymbol{\mu}_j$ as its columns, D being the dimension of the data space.

The probability density $p(\boldsymbol{\zeta})$ in the latent space generates a density to the manifold that lies in the data space and is defined by (3). If the latent space is of lower dimension than the data space, the manifold would be singular, so a Gaussian noise model is added. A single point in the latent space generates thus the following density in the data space:

$$p(\boldsymbol{\xi}|\boldsymbol{\zeta}; \mathbf{M}, \beta) = \left(\frac{\beta}{2\pi}\right)^{D/2} \exp\left[-\frac{\beta}{2}||\boldsymbol{v}(\boldsymbol{\zeta}; \mathbf{M}) - \boldsymbol{\xi}||^2\right] \tag{4}$$

where β is the inverse of the variance of the noise.

The key point of the GTM is to approximate the density in the data space by assuming the latent space prior $p(\boldsymbol{\zeta})$ to consist of equiprobable delta functions that form a regular lattice in the latent space. The centers $\boldsymbol{\zeta}_i$ of the delta functions are called the *latent vectors* of the GTM, and they are the GTM equivalent to the SOM map units. The approximation of the density generated in the data space is thus given by

$$p(\boldsymbol{\xi}|\mathbf{M},\beta) = \frac{1}{K}\sum_{i=1}^{K} p(\boldsymbol{\xi}|\boldsymbol{\zeta}_i;\mathbf{M},\beta) \tag{5}$$

The parameters of the GTM are determined by minimizing the negative log likelihood error

$$\mathcal{E}(\mathbf{M},\beta) = -\sum_{t=1}^{T} \ln\left[\frac{1}{K}\sum_{i=1}^{K} p(\boldsymbol{\xi}^t|\boldsymbol{\zeta}_i;\mathbf{M},\beta)\right] \tag{6}$$

over the set of sample vectors $\{\boldsymbol{\xi}^t\}$. The batch version of the GTM uses the EM algorithm [4]; for details, see [3]. One may also resort to an on-line gradient descent procedure that yields the GTM update steps

$$\boldsymbol{\mu}_j^{t+1} := \boldsymbol{\mu}_j^t + \delta^t \beta^t \sum_{i=1}^{K} \eta_i^t(\mathbf{M}^t,\beta^t)\phi_j(\boldsymbol{\zeta}_i)[\boldsymbol{\xi}^t - \boldsymbol{v}(\boldsymbol{\zeta}_i;\mathbf{M}^t)] \tag{7}$$

$$\beta^{t+1} := \beta^t + \delta^t\left[\frac{1}{2}\sum_{i=1}^{K} \eta_i^t(\mathbf{M}^t,\beta^t)\|\boldsymbol{\xi}^t - \boldsymbol{v}(\boldsymbol{\zeta}_i;\mathbf{M}^t)\|^2 - \frac{D}{2\beta^t}\right] \tag{8}$$

where $\eta_i^t(\mathbf{M},\beta)$ is the GTM counterpart to the SOM unit activation, the posterior probability $p(\boldsymbol{\zeta}_i|\boldsymbol{\xi}^t;\mathbf{M},\beta)$ of the latent vector $\boldsymbol{\zeta}_i$ given data vector $\boldsymbol{\xi}^t$:

$$\begin{aligned}
\eta_i^t(\mathbf{M},\beta) &= p(\boldsymbol{\zeta}_i|\boldsymbol{\xi}^t;\mathbf{M},\beta) \\
&= \frac{p(\boldsymbol{\xi}^t|\boldsymbol{\zeta}_i;\mathbf{M},\beta)}{\sum_{i'=1}^{K} p(\boldsymbol{\xi}^t|\boldsymbol{\zeta}_{i'};\mathbf{M},\beta)} \\
&= \frac{\exp[-\frac{\beta}{2}\|\boldsymbol{v}(\boldsymbol{\zeta}_i;\mathbf{M}) - \boldsymbol{\xi}^t\|^2]}{\sum_{i'=1}^{K} \exp[-\frac{\beta}{2}\|\boldsymbol{v}(\boldsymbol{\zeta}_{i'};\mathbf{M}) - \boldsymbol{\xi}^t\|^2]}
\end{aligned} \tag{9}$$

2.3 Connections between SOM and GTM

Let us consider a GTM that has an equal number of latent vectors and basis functions[1], each latent vector $\boldsymbol{\zeta}_i$ being the center for one Gaussian basis function $\phi_i(\boldsymbol{\zeta})$. Latent vector locations may be viewed as units of the SOM, and consequently the basis functions may be interpreted as connection strengths between the units. Let us use the shorthand notation $\phi_j^i \equiv \phi_j(\boldsymbol{\zeta}_i)$. Note that $\phi_j^i = \phi_i^j$, and assume that the basis functions be normalized so that $\sum_{j=1}^{K} \phi_j^i = \sum_{i=1}^{K} \phi_j^i = 1$.

At the zero-noise limit, or when $\beta \to \infty$, the softmax activations of the GTM given in (9) approach the winner-take-all function (1) of the SOM. The winner unit $\boldsymbol{\zeta}_{c(t)}$ for the data vector $\boldsymbol{\xi}^t$ is the map unit that has its *image* closest to the data vector, so that the index $c(t)$ is given by

$$c(t) = \operatorname*{argmin}_i \|\boldsymbol{v}(\boldsymbol{\zeta}_i) - \boldsymbol{\xi}^t\| = \operatorname*{argmin}_i \left\|\left(\sum_{j=1}^{K} \phi_j^i \boldsymbol{\mu}_j\right) - \boldsymbol{\xi}^t\right\| \tag{10}$$

---

[1]Note that this choice serves the purpose of illustration only; to use GTM properly, one should choose much more latent vectors than basis functions.

The GTM weight update step (7) then becomes

$$\boldsymbol{\mu}_j^{t+1} := \boldsymbol{\mu}_j^t + \delta^t \phi_j^{c(t)} [\boldsymbol{\xi}^t - \boldsymbol{v}(\boldsymbol{\zeta}_{c(t)}; \mathbf{M}^t)] \tag{11}$$

This resembles the variant of SOM, in which the winner is searched with the rule (10) and weights are updated as

$$\boldsymbol{\mu}_j^{t+1} := \boldsymbol{\mu}_j^t + \delta^t \phi_j^{c(t)} (\boldsymbol{\xi}^t - \boldsymbol{\mu}_j^t) \tag{12}$$

Unlike the original SOM rules (1) and (2), the modified SOM with rules (10) and (12) does minimize a well-defined objective function: the *SOM distortion measure* [5, 6, 7, 1]. However, there is a difference between GTM and SOM learning rules (11) and (12). With SOM, each individual weight vector moves towards the data vector, but with GTM, the *image* of the winner latent vector $\boldsymbol{v}(\boldsymbol{\zeta}_{c(t)}; \mathbf{M})$ moves towards the data vector, and all weight vectors $\boldsymbol{\mu}_j$ move to the same direction.

For nonzero noise, when $0 < \beta < \infty$, there is more difference between GTM and SOM: with GTM, not only the winner unit but activations from other units as well contribute to the weight update.

3 S-Map

Combining the softmax activations of the GTM and the learning rule of the SOM, we arrive at a new algorithm: the S-Map.

3.1 The S-Map algorithm

The S-Map resembles a GTM with an equal number of latent vectors and basis functions. The position of the ith unit on the map is is given by the latent vector $\boldsymbol{\zeta}_i$; the connection strength of the unit to another unit j is ϕ_j^i, and a weight vector $\boldsymbol{\mu}_i$ is associated with the unit. The activation of the unit is obtained using rule (9).

The S-Map weights learn proportionally to the activation of the unit that the weight is associated with, and the activations of the neighboring units:

$$\boldsymbol{\mu}_j^{t+1} := \boldsymbol{\mu}_j^t + \delta^t \left(\sum_{i=1}^{K} \phi_j^i \eta_i^t \right) (\boldsymbol{\xi}^t - \boldsymbol{\mu}_j^t) \tag{13}$$

which can be further simplified to a fully Hebbian rule, updating each weight proportionally to the activation of the corresponding unit only, so that

$$\boldsymbol{\mu}_j^{t+1} := \boldsymbol{\mu}_j^t + \delta^t \eta_j^t (\boldsymbol{\xi}^t - \boldsymbol{\mu}_j^t) \tag{14}$$

The parameter β value may be adjusted in the following way: start with a small value, slowly increase it so that the map unfolds and spreads out, and then keep increasing the value as long as the error (6) decreases. The parameter adjustment scheme could also be connected with the topographic error of the mapping, as proposed in [9] for the SOM.

Assuming normalized input and weight vectors, the "dot-product metric" form of the learning rules (13) and (14) may be written as

$$\boldsymbol{\mu}_j^{t+1} := \boldsymbol{\mu}_j^t + \delta^t \left(\sum_{i=1}^{K} \phi_j^i \eta_i^t \right) (\mathbf{I} - \boldsymbol{\mu}_j^t \boldsymbol{\mu}_j^{tT}) \boldsymbol{\xi}^t \tag{15}$$

and

$$\boldsymbol{\mu}_j^{t+1} := \boldsymbol{\mu}_j^t + \delta^t \eta_j^t (\mathbf{I} - \boldsymbol{\mu}_j^t \boldsymbol{\mu}_j^{tT}) \boldsymbol{\xi}^t \qquad (16)$$

respectively; the matrix in the second parenthesis keeps the weight vectors normalized to unit length, assuming a small value for the learning rate parameter δ^t [8]. The dot-product metric form of a unit activity is

$$\eta_i^t = \frac{\exp\left[\beta \left(\sum_{j=1}^K \phi_j^i \boldsymbol{\mu}_j\right)^T \boldsymbol{\xi}^t\right]}{\sum_{i'=1}^K \exp\left[\beta \left(\sum_{j=1}^K \phi_j^{i'} \boldsymbol{\mu}_j\right)^T \boldsymbol{\xi}^t\right]} \qquad (17)$$

which approximates the posterior probability $p(\boldsymbol{\zeta}_i | \boldsymbol{\xi}^t; \mathbf{M}, \beta)$ that the data vector were generated by that specific unit. This is based on the observation that if the data vectors $\{\boldsymbol{\xi}^t\}$ are normalized to unit length, the density generated in the data space (unit sphere in $\mathbb{R}^D$) becomes

$$p(\boldsymbol{\xi} | \boldsymbol{\zeta}_i; \mathbf{M}, \beta) = \left(\begin{array}{c} \text{normalizing} \\ \text{constant} \end{array}\right)^{-1} \times \exp\left[\beta \left(\sum_{j=1}^K \phi_j^i \boldsymbol{\mu}_j\right)^T \boldsymbol{\xi}\right] \qquad (18)$$

3.2 S-Map algorithm minimizes the GTM error function in dot-product metric

The GTM error function is the negative log likelihood, which is given by (6) and is reproduced here:

$$\mathcal{E}(\mathbf{M}, \beta) = -\sum_{t=1}^T \ln\left[\frac{1}{K} \sum_{i=1}^K p(\boldsymbol{\xi}^t | \boldsymbol{\zeta}_i; \mathbf{M}, \beta)\right] \qquad (19)$$

When the weights are updated using a batch version of (15), accumulating the updates for one epoch, the expected value of the error [4] for the unit $\boldsymbol{\zeta}_i$ is

$$\mathrm{E}(\mathcal{E}_i^{\mathrm{new}}) = -\sum_{t=1}^T \underbrace{p^{\mathrm{old}}(\boldsymbol{\zeta}_i | \boldsymbol{\xi}^t; \mathbf{M}, \beta)}_{\eta_i^{\mathrm{old},t}} \ln[\underbrace{p^{\mathrm{new}}(\boldsymbol{\zeta}_i)}_{=1/K} p^{\mathrm{new}}(\boldsymbol{\xi}^t | \boldsymbol{\zeta}_i; \mathbf{M}, \beta)]$$

$$= -\sum_{t=1}^T \eta_i^{\mathrm{old},t} \beta \left(\sum_{j=1}^K \phi_j^i \boldsymbol{\mu}_j^{\mathrm{new}}\right)^T \boldsymbol{\xi}^t + \text{terms not involving the weight vectors} \qquad (20)$$

The change of the error for the whole map after one epoch is thus

$$\mathrm{E}(\mathcal{E}^{\mathrm{new}} - \mathcal{E}^{\mathrm{old}}) = -\sum_{i=1}^K \sum_{t=1}^T \sum_{j=1}^K \eta_i^{\mathrm{old},t} \beta \phi_j^i (\boldsymbol{\mu}_j^{\mathrm{new}} - \boldsymbol{\mu}_j^{\mathrm{old}})^T \boldsymbol{\xi}^t$$

$$= -\beta\delta \sum_{j=1}^K \underbrace{\left(\sum_{t=1}^T \sum_{i=1}^K \eta_i^{\mathrm{old},t} \phi_j^i \boldsymbol{\xi}^t\right)}_{\boldsymbol{\sigma}_j^T} (\mathbf{I} - \boldsymbol{\mu}_j^{\mathrm{old}} \boldsymbol{\mu}_j^{\mathrm{old}\,T}) \underbrace{\left(\sum_{t'=1}^T \sum_{i'=1}^K \eta_{i'}^{\mathrm{old},t'} \phi_j^{i'} \boldsymbol{\xi}^{t'}\right)}_{\boldsymbol{\sigma}_j} \qquad (21)$$

$$= -\beta\delta \sum_{j=1}^K [\boldsymbol{\sigma}_j^T \boldsymbol{\sigma}_j - (\boldsymbol{\sigma}_j^T \boldsymbol{\mu}_j^{\mathrm{old}})^2] \leq 0$$

with equality only when the weights are already in the error minimum.

4   Experimental results

The self-organization ability of the SOM, the GTM, and the S-Map was tested on an artificial data set: 500 points from a uniform random distribution in the unit square.

The initial weight vectors for all models were set to random values, and the final configuration of the map was plotted on top of the data (figure 1). For all the algorithms, the batch version was used. The SOM was trained as recommended in [1] – in two phases, the first starting with a wide neighborhood function, the second with a narrow neighborhood. The GTM was trained using the Matlab implementation by Svensén, following the recommendations given in [10]. The S-Map was trained in two ways: using the "full" rule (13), and the simplified rule (14). In both cases, the parameter β value was slowly increased every epoch; by monitoring the error (6) of the S-Map (see the error plot in the figure) the suitable value for β can be found.

In the GTM simulations, we experimented with many different choices for basis function width and their number, both with normalized and unnormalized basis functions. It turned out that GTM is somewhat sensitive to these choices: it had difficulties to unfold after a random initialization, unless the basis functions were set so wide (with respect to the weight matrix prior) that the map was well-organized already in its initial configuration. On the other hand, using very wide basis functions with the GTM resulted in a map that was too rigid to adapt well to the data. We also tried to update the parameter β according to an annealing schedule, as with the S-Map, but this did not seem to solve the problem.

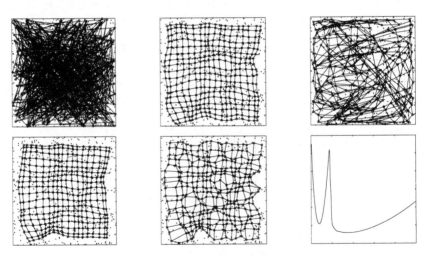

Figure 1: Random initialization (top left), SOM (top middle), GTM (top right), "full" S-Map (bottom left), simplified S-Map (bottom middle). On bottom right, the S-Map error as a function of epochs is displayed; the parameter β was slightly increased every epoch, which causes the error to increase in the early (unfolding) phase of the learning, as the weight update only minimizes the error for a given β.

5   Conclusions

The S-Map and SOM seem to have a stronger tendency to self-organize from random initialization than the GTM. In data analysis applications, when the GTM can be properly initialized, SOM, S-Map, and GTM yield comparable results; those obtained using the latter two algorithms are also straightforward to interpret in probabilistic terms. In Euclidean metric, the GTM has the additional advantage of guaranteed convergence to some error minimum; the convergence of the S-Map in Euclidean metric is still an open question. On the other hand, the batch GTM is computationally clearly heavier per epoch than the S-Map, while the S-Map is somewhat heavier than the SOM.

The SOM has an impressive record of proven applications in a variety of different tasks, and much more experimenting is needed for any alternative method to reach the same level of practicality. SOM is also the basic bottom-up procedure of self-organization in the sense that it starts from a minimum of functional principles realizable in parallel neural networks. This makes it hard to analyze, however. A probabilistic approach like the GTM stems from the opposite point of view by emphasizing the statistical model, but as a trade-off, the resulting algorithm may not share all the desirable properties of the SOM. Our new approach, the S-map, seems to have succeeded in inheriting the strong self-organization capability of the SOM, while offering a sound probabilistic interpretation like the GTM.

References

[1] T. Kohonen, *Self-Organizing Maps.* Springer Series in Information Sciences 30, Berlin Heidelberg New York: Springer, 1995.

[2] T. Kohonen, E. Oja, O. Simula, A. Visa, and J. Kangas, "Engineering applications of the self-organizing map," *Proceedings of the IEEE*, vol. 84, pp. 1358–1384, Oct. 1996.

[3] C. M. Bishop, M. Svensen, and C. K. I. Williams, "GTM: A principled alternative to the self-organizing map," in *Advances in Neural Information Processing Systems* (to appear) (M. C. Mozer, M. I. Jordan, and T. Petche, eds.), vol. 9, MIT Press, 1997.

[4] A. P. Dempster, N. M. Laird, and D. B. Rubin, "Maximum likelihood from incomplete data via the EM algorithm," *Journal of the Royal Statistical Society*, vol. B 39, no. 1, pp. 1–38, 1977.

[5] S. P. Luttrell, "Code vector density in topographic mappings," Memorandum 4669, Defense Research Agency, Malvern, UK, 1992.

[6] T. M. Heskes and B. Kappen, "Error potentials for self-organization," in *Proceedings of the International Conference on Neural Networks (ICNN'93)*, vol. 3, (Piscataway, New Jersey, USA), pp. 1219–1223, IEEE Neural Networks Council, Apr. 1993.

[7] S. P. Luttrell, "A Bayesian analysis of self-organising maps," *Neural Computation*, vol. 6, pp. 767–794, 1994.

[8] E. Oja, "A simplified neuron model as a principal component analyzer," *Journal of Mathematical Biology*, vol. 15, pp. 267–273, 1982.

[9] K. Kiviluoto, "Topology preservation in self-organizing maps," in *Proceedings of the International Conference on Neural Networks (ICNN'96)*, vol. 1, (Piscataway, New Jersey, USA), pp. 294–299, IEEE Neural Networks Council, June 1996.

[10] M. Svensén, *The GTM toolbox – user's guide.* Neural Computing Research Group / Aston University, Birmingham, UK, 1.0 ed., Oct. 1996. Available at URL `http://neural-server.aston.ac.uk/GTM/MATLAB_Impl.html`.

Learning nonlinear overcomplete representations for efficient coding

Michael S. Lewicki
lewicki@salk.edu

Terrence J. Sejnowski
terry@salk.edu

Howard Hughes Medical Institute
Computational Neurobiology Lab
The Salk Institute
10010 N. Torrey Pines Rd.
La Jolla, CA 92037

Abstract

We derive a learning algorithm for inferring an overcomplete basis by viewing it as probabilistic model of the observed data. Overcomplete bases allow for better approximation of the underlying statistical density. Using a Laplacian prior on the basis coefficients removes redundancy and leads to representations that are sparse and are a *nonlinear* function of the data. This can be viewed as a generalization of the technique of independent component analysis and provides a method for blind source separation of fewer mixtures than sources. We demonstrate the utility of overcomplete representations on natural speech and show that compared to the traditional Fourier basis the inferred representations potentially have much greater coding efficiency.

A traditional way to represent real-values signals is with Fourier or wavelet bases. A disadvantage of these bases, however, is that they are not specialized for any particular dataset. Principal component analysis (PCA) provides one means for finding an basis that is adapted for a dataset, but the basis vectors are restricted to be orthogonal. An extension of PCA called independent component analysis (Jutten and Herault, 1991; Comon et al., 1991; Bell and Sejnowski, 1995) allows the learning of non-orthogonal bases. All of these bases are complete in the sense that they span the input space, but they are limited in terms of how well they can approximate the dataset's statistical density.

Representations that are overcomplete, *i.e.* more basis vectors than input variables, can provide a better representation, because the basis vectors can be specialized for a larger variety of features present in the entire ensemble of data. A criticism of overcomplete representations is that they are redundant, *i.e.* a given data point may have many possible representations, but this redundancy is removed by the prior probability of the basis coefficients which specifies the *probability* of the alternative representations.

Most of the overcomplete bases used in the literature are fixed in the sense that they are not adapted to the structure in the data. Recently Olshausen and Field (1996) presented an algorithm that allows an overcomplete basis to be learned. This algorithm relied on an approximation to the desired probabilistic objective that had several drawbacks, including tendency to breakdown in the case of low noise levels and when learning bases with higher degrees of overcompleteness. In this paper, we present an improved approximation to the desired probabilistic objective and show that this leads to a simple and robust algorithm for learning optimal overcomplete bases.

1 Inferring the representation

The data, $x_{1:L}$, are modeled with an overcomplete linear basis plus additive noise:

$$\mathbf{x} = \mathbf{As} + \epsilon \tag{1}$$

where $\mathbf{A}$ is an $L \times M$ matrix, whose columns are the basis vectors, where $M \geq L$. We assume Gaussian additive noise so that $\log P(\mathbf{x}|\mathbf{A}, \mathbf{s}) \propto -\lambda(\mathbf{x} - \mathbf{As})^2/2$, where $\lambda = 1/\sigma^2$ defines the precision of the noise.

The redundancy in the overcomplete representation is removed by defining a density for the basis coefficients, $P(\mathbf{s})$, which specifies the *probability* of the alternative representations. The most probable representation, $\hat{\mathbf{s}}$, is found by maximizing the posterior distribution

$$\hat{\mathbf{s}} = \max_{\mathbf{s}} P(\mathbf{s}|\mathbf{A}, \mathbf{x}) = \max_{\mathbf{s}} P(\mathbf{s})P(\mathbf{x}|\mathbf{A}, \mathbf{s}) \tag{2}$$

$P(\mathbf{s})$ influences how the data are fit in the presence of noise and determines the uniqueness of the representation. In this model, the data is a linear function of $\mathbf{s}$, but $\mathbf{s}$ is *not*, in general, a linear function of the data. If the basis function is complete ($\mathbf{A}$ is invertible) then, assuming broad priors and low noise, the most probable internal state can be computed simply by inverting $\mathbf{A}$. In the case of an overcomplete basis, however, $\mathbf{A}$ can not be inverted. Figure 1 shows how different priors induce different representations.

Unlike the Gaussian prior, the optimal representation under the Laplacian prior cannot be obtained by a simple linear operation. One approach for optimizing $\mathbf{s}$ is to use the gradient of the log posterior in an optimization algorithm. An alternative method for finding the most probable internal state is to view the problem as the linear program: $\min \mathbf{1}^T \mathbf{s}$ such that $\mathbf{As} = \mathbf{x}$. This can be generalized to handle both positive and negative $\mathbf{s}$ and solved efficiently and exactly with interior point linear programming methods (Chen et al., 1996).

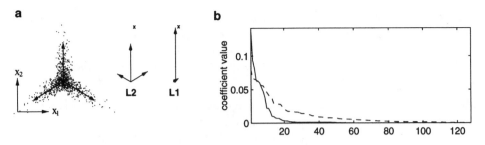

Figure 1: Different priors induce different representations. (a) The 2D data distribution has three main axes which form an overcomplete representation. The graphs marked "L2" and "L1" show the optimal scaled basis vectors for the data point x under the Gaussian and Laplacian prior, respectively. Assuming zero noise, a Gaussian for $P(\mathbf{s})$ is equivalent to finding the exact fitting $\mathbf{s}$ with minimum L_2 norm, which is given by the pseudoinverse $\mathbf{s} = \mathbf{A}^+\mathbf{x}$. A Laplacian prior ($P(s_m) \propto \exp[-\theta|s_m|]$) yields the exact fit with minimum L_1 norm, which is a *nonlinear* operation which essentially selects a subset of the basis vectors to represent the data (Chen et al., 1996). The resulting representation is sparse. (b) A 64-sample segment of speech was fit to a 2× overcomplete Fourier representation (128 basis vectors). The plot shows rank order distribution of the coefficients of $\mathbf{s}$ under a Gaussian prior (dashed); and a Laplacian prior (solid). Far more significantly positive coefficients are required under the Gaussian prior than under the Laplacian prior.

2   Learning

The learning objective is to adapt $\mathbf{A}$ to maximize the probability of the data which is computed by marginalizing over the internal states

$$P(\mathbf{x}|\mathbf{A}) = \int d\mathbf{s}\, P(\mathbf{s})P(\mathbf{x}|\mathbf{A}, \mathbf{s}) \tag{3}$$

general, this integral cannot be evaluated analytically but can be approximated with a Gaussian integral around $\hat{\mathbf{s}}$, yielding

$$\log P(\mathbf{x}|\mathbf{A}) \approx \text{const.} + \log P(\hat{\mathbf{s}}) - \frac{\lambda}{2}(\mathbf{x} - \mathbf{A}\hat{\mathbf{s}})^2 - \frac{1}{2}\log\det\mathbf{H} \tag{4}$$

where $\mathbf{H}$ is the Hessian of the log posterior at $\hat{\mathbf{s}}$, given by $\lambda\mathbf{A}^{\mathrm{T}}\mathbf{A} - \nabla\nabla\log P(\hat{\mathbf{s}})$. To avoid a singularity under the Laplacian prior, we use the approximation $(\log P(s_m))' \approx -\theta\tanh(\beta s_m)$ which gives the Hessian full rank and positive determinant. For large β this approximates the true Laplacian prior. A learning rule can be obtained by differentiating $\log P(\mathbf{x}|\mathbf{A})$ with respect to $\mathbf{A}$.

In the following discussion, we will present the derivations of the three terms in (4) and simplifying assumptions that lead to the following simple form of the learning rule

$$\Delta\mathbf{A} = \mathbf{A}\mathbf{A}^{\mathrm{T}}\nabla\log P(\mathbf{x}|\mathbf{A}) \approx -\mathbf{A}(\mathbf{z}\hat{\mathbf{s}}^{\mathrm{T}} + \mathbf{I}) \tag{5}$$

where $z_k = \partial\log P(s_k)/\partial s_k$.

2.1 Deriving $\nabla \log P(\hat{s})$

This term specifies how to change $\mathbf{A}$ so as to make the probability of the representation $\hat{s}$ more probable. If we assume a Laplacian prior, this component changes $\mathbf{A}$ to make the representation more sparse.

We assume $P(\hat{s}) = \prod_m P(\hat{s}_m)$. In order to obtain $\partial \hat{s}_m / \partial a_{ij}$, we need to describe $\hat{s}$ as a function of $\mathbf{A}$. If the basis is complete (and we assume low noise), then we may simply invert $\mathbf{A}$ to obtain $\hat{s} = \mathbf{A}^{-1}\mathbf{x}$. When $\mathbf{A}$ is overcomplete, however, there is no simple expression, but we may still make an approximation.

Under priors, the most probable solution, $\hat{s}$, will yield at most L non-zero elements. In effect, this selects a complete basis from $\mathbf{A}$. Let $\check{\mathbf{A}}$ represent this reduced basis under $\hat{s}$. We then have $\check{s} = \check{\mathbf{A}}^{-1}(\mathbf{x} - \epsilon)$ where $\check{s}$ is equal to $\hat{s}$ with $M - L$ zero-valued elements removed. $\check{\mathbf{A}}^{-1}$ obtained by removing the columns of $\mathbf{A}$ corresponding to the $M - L$ zero-valued elements of $\hat{s}$. This allows us to use results obtained for the case when $\mathbf{A}$ is invertible. Following MacKay (1996) we obtain

$$\frac{\partial \check{s}_k}{\partial \check{a}_{ij}} = -\sum_l \check{A}_{ki}^{-1} \check{A}_{jl}^{-1}(x_l - \epsilon_l) = -\check{A}_{ki}^{-1}\check{s}_j \tag{6}$$

Rewriting in matrix notation we have

$$\frac{\partial \log P(\check{s})}{\partial \mathbf{A}} = -\check{\mathbf{A}}^{-\mathrm{T}}\check{z}\check{s}^{\mathrm{T}} \tag{7}$$

We can use this to obtain an expression in terms of the original variables. We simply invert the mapping $\hat{s} \to \check{s}$ to obtain $z \leftarrow \check{z}$ and $\mathbf{W}^{\mathrm{T}} \leftarrow \check{\mathbf{A}}^{-\mathrm{T}}$ (row-wise) with $z_m = 0$ and row m of $\mathbf{W}^{\mathrm{T}} = 0$ if $\check{s}_m = 0$. We then have

$$\frac{\partial \log P(s)}{\partial \mathbf{A}} = -\mathbf{W}^{\mathrm{T}}zs^{\mathrm{T}} \tag{8}$$

2.2 Deriving $\nabla(\mathbf{x} - \mathbf{A}\hat{s})^2$

The second term specifies how to change $\mathbf{A}$ so as to minimize the data misfit. Letting $e_k = [\mathbf{x} - \mathbf{A}s]_k$ and using the results and notation from above we have:

$$\frac{\partial}{\partial a_{ij}} \frac{\lambda}{2} \sum_k e_k^2 = \lambda e_i s_j + \lambda \sum_k e_k \sum_l a_{kl} \frac{\partial s_l}{\partial a_{ij}} \tag{9}$$

$$= \lambda e_i s_j + \lambda \sum_k e_k \sum_l -a_{kl}w_{li}s_j \tag{10}$$

$$= \lambda e_i s_j - \lambda e_i s_j = 0 \tag{11}$$

Thus no gradient component arises from the error term.

2.3 Deriving $\nabla \log \det \mathbf{H}$

The third term in the learning rule specifies how to change the weights so as to minimize the width of the posterior distribution $P(\mathbf{x}|\mathbf{A})$ and thus increase the overall probability of the data. An element of $\mathbf{H}$ is defined by $\mathbf{H}_{mn} = c_{mn} + b_{mn}$

where $c_{mn} = \sum_k \lambda a_{km} a_{kn}$ and $b_{mn} = [-\nabla\nabla \log P(\hat{s})]_{mn}$. This gives

$$\frac{\partial \log \det \mathbf{H}}{\partial a_{ij}} = \sum_{mn} \mathbf{H}_{nm}^{-1} \left[\frac{\partial c_{mn}}{\partial a_{ij}} + \frac{\partial b_{mn}}{\partial a_{ij}} \right] \tag{12}$$

First considering $\partial c_{mn}/\partial a_{ij}$, we can obtain

$$\sum_{mn} \mathbf{H}_{mn}^{-1} \frac{\partial c_{mn}}{\partial a_{ij}} = \sum_{m \neq j} \mathbf{H}_{mj}^{-1} \lambda a_{im} + \sum_{m \neq j} \mathbf{H}_{jm}^{-1} \lambda a_{im} + \mathbf{H}_{jj}^{-1} 2\lambda a_{ij} \tag{13}$$

Using the fact that $\mathbf{H}_{mj}^{-1} = \mathbf{H}_{jm}^{-1}$ due to the symmetry of the Hessian, we have

$$\sum_{mn} \mathbf{H}_{mn}^{-1} \frac{\partial c_{mn}}{\partial \mathbf{A}} = 2\lambda \mathbf{A} \mathbf{H}^{-1} \tag{14}$$

Next we derive $\partial b_{mn}/\partial a_{ij}$. We have that $\nabla\nabla \log P(\hat{s})$ is diagonal, because we assume $P(\hat{s}) = \prod_m P(\hat{s}_m)$. Letting $2y_m = \mathbf{H}_{mm}^{-1} \partial b_{mm}/\partial \hat{s}_m$ and using the result under the reduced representation (6) we can obtain

$$\sum_{mm} \mathbf{H}_{mm}^{-1} \frac{\partial b_{mm}}{\partial \mathbf{A}} = -2\mathbf{W}^{\mathrm{T}} \mathbf{y} \hat{s}^{\mathrm{T}} \tag{15}$$

2.4 Stabilizing and simplifying the learning rule

Putting the terms together yields a problematic expression due to the matrix inverses. This can be alleviated by multiplying the gradient by an appropriate positive definite matrix, which rescales the gradient components but preserves a direction valid for optimization. Noting that $\mathbf{A}^{\mathrm{T}} \mathbf{W}^{\mathrm{T}} = \mathbf{I}$ we have

$$\mathbf{A}\mathbf{A}^{\mathrm{T}} \nabla \log P(\mathbf{x}|\mathbf{A}) = -\mathbf{A}z\hat{s}^{\mathrm{T}} - \lambda \mathbf{A}\mathbf{A}^{\mathrm{T}}\mathbf{A}\mathbf{H}^{-1} + \mathbf{A}\mathbf{y}\hat{s}^{\mathrm{T}} \tag{16}$$

If λ is large (low noise) then the Hessian is dominated by $\lambda \mathbf{A}^{\mathrm{T}}\mathbf{A}$ and we have

$$-\lambda \mathbf{A}\mathbf{A}^{\mathrm{T}}\mathbf{A}\mathbf{H}^{-1} = -\mathbf{A}\lambda \mathbf{A}^{\mathrm{T}}\mathbf{A}(\lambda \mathbf{A}^{\mathrm{T}}\mathbf{A} + \mathbf{B})^{-1} \approx -\mathbf{A} \tag{17}$$

The vector $\mathbf{y}$ hides a computation involving the inverse Hessian. If the basis vectors in $\mathbf{A}$ are randomly distributed, then as the dimensionality of $\mathbf{A}$ increases the basis vectors become approximately orthogonal and consequently the Hessian becomes approximately diagonal. It can be shown that if $\log P(\mathbf{s})$ and its derivatives are smooth, y_m vanishes for large λ. Combining the remaining terms yields equation (5). Note that this rule contains no matrix inverses and the vector $\mathbf{z}$ involves only the derivative of the log prior.

In the case where $\mathbf{A}$ is square, this form of the rule is similar to the natural gradient independent component analysis (ICA) learning rule (Amari et al., 1996). The difference in the more general case where $\mathbf{A}$ is rectangular is that $\hat{s}$ must maximize the posterior distribution $P(\mathbf{s}|\mathbf{x}, \mathbf{A})$ which cannot be done simply with the filter matrix as in standard ICA algorithms.

3 Examples

More sources than inputs. In these 2D examples, the bases were initialized to random, normalized vectors. The coefficients were solved using BPMPD and publicly available interior point linear programming package (Meszaros, 1997) which gives the most probable solution under the Laplacian prior assuming zero noise. The algorithm was run for 30 iterations using equation (5) with a stepsize of 0.001 and a batchsize of 200. Convergence was rapid, typically requiring less than 20 iterations. In all cases, the direction of the learned vectors matched those of the true generating distribution; the magnitude was estimated less precisely, possibly due to the approximation of $\log P(\mathbf{x}|\mathbf{A})$. This can be viewed as a source separation problem, but true separation will be limited due to the projection of the sources down to a smaller subspace which necessarily loses information.

Figure 2: Examples illustrating the fitting of 2D distributions with overcomplete bases. The first example is equivalent to 3 sources mixed into 2 channels; the second to 4 sources mixed into 2 channels. The data in both examples were generated from the true basis $\mathbf{A}$ using $\mathbf{x} = \mathbf{As}$ with the elements of $\mathbf{s}$ distributed according to an exponential distribution with unit mean. Identical results were obtained by drawing $\mathbf{s}$ from a Laplacian prior (positive and negative coefficients). The overcomplete bases allow the model to capture the true underlying statistical structure in the 2D data space.

Overcomplete representations of speech. Speech data were obtained from the TIMIT database, using a single speaker was speaking ten different example sentences with no preprocessing. The basis was initialized to an overcomplete Fourier basis. A conjugate gradient routine was used to obtain the most probable basis coefficients. The stepsize was gradually reduced over 10000 iterations. Figure 3 shows that the learned basis is quite different from the Fourier representation. The power spectrum for the learned basis vectors can be multimodal and/or broadband. The learned basis achieves greater coding efficiency: 2.19 ± 0.59 bits per sample compared to 3.86 ± 0.28 bits per sample for a $2\times$ overcomplete Fourier basis.

4 Summary

Learning overcomplete representations allows a basis to better approximate the underlying statistical density of the data and consequently the learned representations have better encoding and denoising properties than generic bases. Unlike the case for complete representations and the standard ICA algorithm, the transformation

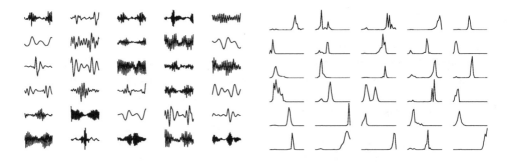

Figure 3: An example of fitting a 2x overcomplete representation to segments of from natural speech. Each segment consisted of 64 samples, sampled at a frequency of 8000 Hz (8 msecs). The plot shows a random sample of 30 of the 128 basis vectors (each scaled to full range). The right graph shows the corresponding power spectral densities (0 to 4000 Hz).

from the data to the internal representation is non-linear. The probabilistic formulation of the basis inference problem offers the advantages that assumptions about the prior distribution on the basis coefficients are made explicit and that different models can be compared objectively using $\log P(\mathbf{x}|\mathbf{A})$.

References

Amari, S., Cichocki, A., and Yang, H. H. (1996). A new learning algorithm for blind signal separation. In *Advances in Neural and Information Processing Systems*, volume 8, pages 757–763, San Mateo. Morgan Kaufmann.

Bell, A. J. and Sejnowski, T. J. (1995). An information maximization approach to blind separation and blind deconvolution. *Neural Computation*, 7(6):1129–1159.

Chen, S., Donoho, D. L., and Saunders, M. A. (1996). Atomic decomposition by basis pursuit. Technical report, Dept. Stat., Stanford Univ., Stanford, CA.

Comon, P., Jutten, C., and Herault, J. (1991). Blind separation of sources .2. problems statement. *Signal Processing*, 24(1):11–20.

Jutten, C. and Herault, J. (1991). Blind separation of sources .1. an adaptive algorithm based on neuromimetic architecture. *Signal Processing*, 24(1):1–10.

MacKay, D. J. C. (1996). Maximum likelihood and covariant algorithms for independent component analysis. University of Cambridge, Cavendish Laboratory. Available at ftp://wol.ra.phy.cam.ac.uk/pub/mackay/ica.ps.gz.

Meszaros, C. (1997). BPMPD: An interior point linear programming solver. Code available at ftp://ftp.netlib.org/opt/bpmpd.tar.gz.

Olshausen, B. A. and Field, D. J. (1996). Emergence of simple-cell receptive-field properties by learning a sparse code for natural images. *Nature*, 381:607–609.

Factorizing Multivariate Function Classes

Juan K. Lin*
Department of Physics
University of Chicago
Chicago, IL 60637

Abstract

The mathematical framework for factorizing equivalence classes of multivariate functions is formulated in this paper. Independent component analysis is shown to be a special case of this decomposition. Using only the local geometric structure of a class representative, we derive an analytic solution for the factorization. We demonstrate the factorization solution with numerical experiments and present a preliminary tie to decorrelation.

1 FORMALISM

In independent component analysis (ICA), the goal is to find an unknown linear coordinate system where the joint distribution function admits a factorization into the product of one dimensional functions. However, this decomposition is only rarely possible. To formalize the notion of multivariate function factorization, we begin by defining an equivalence relation.

Definition. We say that two functions $f, g : \mathbb{R}^n \to \mathbb{R}$ are *equivalent* if there exists $A, \vec{b}$ and c such that: $f(\vec{x}) = cg(A\vec{x} + \vec{b})$, where A is a non-singular matrix and $c \neq 0$.

Thus, the equivalence class of a function consists of all invertible linear transformations of it. To avoid confusion, equivalence classes will be denoted in upper case, and class representatives in lower case. We now define the *product* of two equivalence classes. Consider representatives $b : \mathbb{R}^n \to \mathbb{R}$, and $c : \mathbb{R}^m \to \mathbb{R}$ of corresponding equivalence classes B and C. Let $\vec{x_1} \in \mathbb{R}^n$, $\vec{x_2} \in \mathbb{R}^m$, and $\vec{x} = (\vec{x_1}, \vec{x_2})$. From the scalar product of the two functions, define the function $a : \mathbb{R}^{n+m} \to \mathbb{R}$ by $a(\vec{x}) = b(\vec{x_1})c(\vec{x_2})$. Let the product of B and C be the equivalence class A with

---

*Current address: E25-201, MIT, Cambridge, MA 02139. Email: jklin@ai.mit.edu

representative $a(\vec{x})$. This product is independent of the choice of representatives of B and C, and hence is a well defined operation on equivalence classes. We proceed to define the notion of an *irreducible* class.

Definition. Denote the equivalence class of constants by I. We say that A is *irreducible* if $A = BC$ implies either $B = A, C = I$, or $B = I, C = A$.

From the way products of equivalence classes are defined, we know that all equivalence classes of one dimensional functions are irreducible. Our formulation of the factorization of multivariate function classes is now complete. Given a multivariate function, we seek a factorization of the equivalence class of the given representative into a product of irreducibles. Intuitively, in the context of joint distribution functions, the irreducible classes constitute the underlying sources. This factorization generalizes independent component analysis to allow for higher dimensional "vector" sources. Consequently, this decomposition is well–defined for *all* multivariate function classes. We now present a local geometric approach to accomplishing this factorization.

2   LOCAL GEOMETRIC INFORMATION

Given that the joint distribution factorizes into a product in the "source" coordinate system, what information can be extracted locally from the joint distribution in a "mixed" coordinate frame? We assume that the relevant multivariate function is twice differentiable in the region of interest, and denote H^f, the Hessian of f, to be the matrix with elements $H_{ij}^f = \partial_i \partial_j f$, where $\partial_k = \frac{\partial}{\partial s_k}$.

Proposition: H^f is block diagonal everywhere, $\partial_i \partial_j f|_{\vec{s_0}} = 0$ for all points $\vec{s_0}$ and all $i \leq k$, $j > k$, *if and only if* f is separable into a sum $f(s_1, \ldots, s_n) = g(s_1, \ldots, s_k) + h(s_{k+1}, \ldots, s_n)$ for some functions g and h.

Proof – Sufficiency:
Given $f(s_1, \ldots, s_n) = g(s_1, \ldots, s_k) + h(s_{k+1}, \ldots, s_n)$,

$$\frac{\partial^2 f}{\partial s_i \partial s_j} = \frac{\partial}{\partial s_i} \frac{\partial h(s_{k+1}, \ldots, s_n)}{\partial s_j} = 0$$

everywhere for all $i \leq k$, $j > k$.

Necessity:
From $H_{1n}^f = 0$, we can decompose f into

$$f(s_1, s_2, \ldots, s_n) = \hat{g}(s_1, \ldots, s_{n-1}) + \hat{h}(s_2, \ldots, s_n),$$

for some functions $\hat{g}$ and $\hat{h}$. Continuing by imposing the constraints $H_{1j}^f = 0$ for all $j > k$, we find

$$f(s_1, s_2, \ldots, s_n) = \breve{g}(s_1, \ldots, s_k) + \breve{h}(s_2, \ldots, s_n).$$

Combining with $H_{2j}^f = 0$ for all $j > k$ yields

$$f(s_1, s_2, \ldots, s_n) = \tilde{g}(s_1, \ldots, s_k) + \tilde{h}(s_3, \ldots, s_n).$$

Finally, inducting on i, from the constraints $H_{ij}^f = 0$ for all $i \leq k$ and $j > k$, we arrive at the desired functional form

$$f(s_1, s_2, \ldots, s_n) = g(s_1, \ldots, s_k) + h(s_{k+1}, \ldots, s_n).$$

More explicitly, a twice–differentiable function satisfies the set of coupled partial differential equations represented by the block diagonal structure of H if and only if it admits the corresponding separation of variables decomposition. By letting $\log p = f$, the additive decomposition of f translates to a product decomposition of p. The more general decomposition into an arbitrary number of factors is obtained by iterative application of the above proposition. The special case of independent component analysis corresponds to a strict diagonalization of H. Thus, in the context of smooth joint distribution functions, pairwise conditional independence is necessary and sufficient for statistical independence.

To use this information in a transformed "mixture" frame, we must understand how the matrix $H^{\log p}$ transforms. From the relation between the mixture and source coordinate systems given by $\vec{x} = A\vec{s}$, we have $\frac{\partial}{\partial s_i} = A_{ji}\frac{\partial}{\partial x_j}$, where we use Einstein's convention of summation over repeated indices. From the relation between the joint distributions in the mixture and source frames, $p_s(\vec{s}) = |A| p_x(\vec{x})$, direct differentiation gives

$$\frac{\partial^2 \log p_s(\vec{s})}{\partial s_i \partial s_l} = A_{ji} A_{kl} \frac{\partial^2 \log p_x(\vec{x})}{\partial x_j \partial x_k}.$$

Letting $H_{ij} = \frac{\partial^2 \log p_s(\vec{s})}{\partial s_i \partial s_j}$ and $\tilde{H}_{ij} = \frac{\partial^2 \log p_x(\vec{x})}{\partial x_i \partial x_j}$, in matrix notation we have $H = A^T \tilde{H} A$. In other words, H is a second rank (symmetric) covariant tensor. The joint distribution admits a product decomposition in the source frame if and only if H and hence $A^T \tilde{H} A$ has the corresponding block diagonal structure. Thus multivariate function class factorization is solved by joint block diagonalization of symmetric matrices, with constraints on A of the form $A_{ji} \tilde{H}_{jk} A_{kl} = 0$.

Because the Hessian is symmetric, its diagonalization involves only (n choose 2) constraints. Consequently, in the independent component analysis case where the joint distribution function admits a factorization into one dimensional functions, if the mixing transformation is orthogonal, the independent component coordinate system will lie along the eigenvector directions of $\tilde{H}$. Generally however, $n(n-1)$ independent constraints corresponding to information from the Hessian at two points are needed to determine the n arbitrary coordinate directions.

3   NUMERICAL EXPERIMENTS

In the simplest attack on the factorization problem, we solve the constraint equations from two points simultaneously. The analytic solution is demonstrated in two dimensions. Without loss of generality, the mixing matrix A is taken to be of the form

$$A = \begin{pmatrix} 1 & x \\ y & 1 \end{pmatrix}.$$

The constraints from the two points are: $ax + b(xy + 1) + cy = 0$, and $a'x + b'(xy + 1) + c'y = 0$, where $H_{11} = a$, $H_{21} = H_{12} = b$ and $H_{22} = c$ at the first point, and the primed coefficients denote the values at the second point.

Solving the simultaneous quadratic equations, we find

$$x = \frac{a'c - ac' \pm \sqrt{(a'c - ac')^2 - 4(a'b - ab')(b'c - bc')}}{2(ab' - a'b)},$$

$$y = \frac{a'c - ac' \pm \sqrt{(a'c - ac')^2 - 4(a'b - ab')(b'c - bc')}}{2(bc' - b'c)}.$$

The $\pm$ double roots is indicative of the $(x, y) \to (1/y, 1/x)$ symmetry in the equations, and together only give two distinct orientation solutions. These independent component orientation solutions are given by $\theta_1 = \tan^{-1}(1/x)$ and $\theta_2 = \tan^{-1}(y)$.

3.1 Natural Audio Sources

To demonstrate the analytic factorization solution, we present some proof of concept numerics. Generality is pursued over optimization concerns. First, we perform the standard separation of two linearly mixed natural audio sources. The input dataset consists of 32000 un–ordered datapoints, since no use will be made of the temporal information. The process for obtaining estimates of the Hessian matrix $\tilde{H}$ is as follows. A histogram of the input distribution was first acquired and smoothed by a low–pass Gaussian mask in spatial–frequency space. The elements of $\tilde{H}$ were then obtained via convolution with a discrete approximation of the derivative operator. The width of the Gaussian mask and the support of the derivative operator were chosen to reduce sensitivity to low spatial–frequency uncertainty. It should be noted that the analytic factorization solution makes no assumptions about the mixing transformation, consequently, a blind determination of the smoothing length scale is not possible because of the multiplicative degree of freedom in each source.

Because of the need to take the logarithm of p before differentiation, or equivalently to divide by p afterwards, we set a threshold and only extracted information from points where the number of counts was greater than threshold. This is justified from a counting uncertainty perspective, and also from the understanding that regions with vanishing probability measure contain no information.

With our sample of 32000 datapoints, we considered only the bin–points with a corresponding bin count greater than 30. From the 394 bin locations that satisfied this constraint, the solutions (θ_1, θ_2) for all (394 choose 2) $= (394 \cdot 393/2)$ pairs of the corresponding factorization equations are plotted in Fig. 1. A histogram of these solutions are shown in Fig. 2. The two peaks in the solution histogram correspond to orientations that differ from the two actual independent component orientations by 0.008 and 0.013 radians. The signal to mixture ratio of the two outputs generated from the solution are 158 and 49.

3.2 Effect of Noise

Because the solution is analytic, uncertainty in the sampling just propagates through to the solution, giving rise to a finite width in the solution's distribution. We investigated the effect of noise and counting uncertainty by performing numerics starting from analytic forms for the source distributions. The joint distribution in the source frame was taken to be:

$$p_s(s_1, s_2) = (2 + \sin(s_1)) * (2 + \sin(s_2)).$$

Normalization is irrelevant since a function's decomposition into product form is preserved in scalar multiplication. This is also reflected in the equivalence between $H^{\log p}$ and $H^{\log cp}$ for c an arbitrary positive constant. The joint distribution in the mixture frame was obtained from the relation $p_x(\vec{x}) = |A|^{-1} p_s(\vec{s})$. To simulate

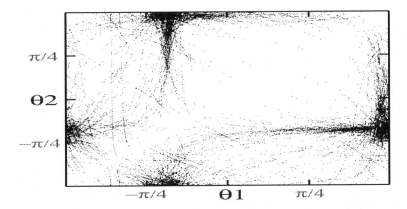

Figure 1: Scatterplot of the independent component orientation solutions. All unordered solution pairs (θ_1, θ_2) are plotted. The solutions are taken in the range from $-\pi/2$ to $\pi/2$.

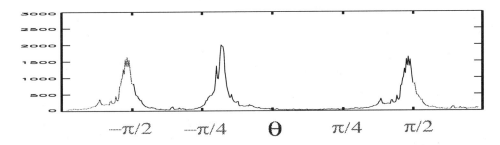

Figure 2: Histogram of the orientation solutions plotted in the previous figure. The range is still taken from $-\pi/2$ to $\pi/2$, with the histogram wrapped around to ease the circular identification. The mixing matrix used was: $a_{11} = 0.0514$, $a_{21} = 0.779$, $a_{12} = 0.930$, $a_{22} = -0.579$, giving independent component orientations at -0.557 and 1.505 radians. Gaussian fit to the centers of the two solution peaks give -0.570 ± 0.066 and 1.513 ± 0.077 radians for the two orientations.

sampling, $p_x(\vec{x})$ was multiplied with the number of samples M, onto which was added Gaussian distributed noise with amplitude given by the $(M\, p_x(\vec{x}))^{1/2}$. This reflects the fact that counting uncertainty scales as the square root of the number of counts. The result was rounded to the nearest integer, with all negative count values set to zero. The subsequent processing coincided with that for natural audio sources. From the source distribution equation above, the minimum number of expected counts is M, and the maximum is $9M$. The results in Figures 3 and 4 show that, as expected, increasing the number of samplings decreases the widths of the solution peaks. By fitting Gaussians to the two peaks, we find that the uncertainty (peak widths) in the independent component orientations changes from 0.06 to 0.1 radians as the sampling is decreased from for $M = 20$ to $M = 2$. So even with few samplings, a relatively accurate determination of the independent component coordinate system can be made.

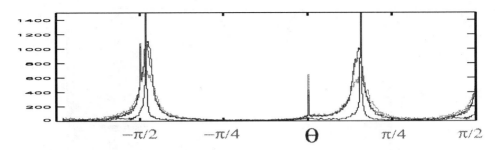

Figure 3: Histogram of the independent component orientation solutions for four different samplings. Solutions were generated from 20000 randomly chosen pairs of positions. The curves, from darkest to lightest, correspond to solutions for the noiseless, $M = 20, 11$ and 2 simulations. The noiseless solution histogram curve extends to a height of approximately 15000 counts, and is accurate to the width of the bin. The slight scatter is due to discretization noise. Spikes at $\theta = 0$ and $-\pi/2$ correspond to pairs of positions which contain no information.

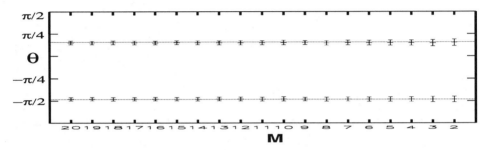

Figure 4: The centers and widths of the solution peaks as a function of the minimum expected number of counts M. From the source distribution, the maximum expected number of counts is $9M$. Information was only extracted from regions with more than $2M$ counts. The actual independent component orientation as determined from the mixing matrix A are shown by the two dashed lines. The solutions are very accurate even for small samplings.

4   RELATION TO DECORRELATION

Ideally, if a mixed tensor (transforms as $J = A^{-1}\tilde{J}A$) with the full degrees of freedom can be found which is diagonal if and only if the joint distribution appears in product form, then the independent component coordinate directions will coincide with that of the tensor's eigenvectors. However, the preceding analysis shows that a maximum of $n(n-1)/2$ constraints contain all the information that exists locally. This, however, provides a nice connection with decorrelation.

Starting with the characteristic function of $\log p(\vec{x})$, $\phi(\vec{k}) = \int e^{i\vec{k}\cdot\vec{x}} \log p(\vec{x})\, d\vec{x}$, the off diagonal terms of $H^{\log p}$ are given by

$$\frac{\partial^2 \log p}{\partial x_i \partial x_j} \propto \int k_i k_j e^{-i\vec{k}\cdot\vec{x}}\, \phi(\vec{k})\, d\vec{k},$$

which can loosely be seen as the second order cross–moments in $\phi(\vec{k})$. Thus diagonalization of $H^{\log p}$ roughly translates into decorrelation in $\phi(\vec{k})$. It should be noted that $\phi(\vec{k})$ is not a proper distribution function. In fact, it is a complex valued function with $\phi(\vec{k}) = \phi^*(-\vec{k})$. Consequently, the summation in the above equation is not an expectation value, and needs to be interpreted as a superposition of plane waves with specified wavelengths, amplitudes and phases.

5   DISCUSSION

The introduced functional decomposition defines a generalization of independent component analysis which is valid for all multivariate functions. A rigorous notion of the decomposition of a multivariate function into a set of lower dimensional factors is presented. With only the assumption of local twice differentiability, we derive an analytic solution for this factorization [1]. A new algorithm is presented, which in contrast to iterative non–local parametric density estimation ICA algorithms [2, 3, 4], performs the decomposition analytically using local geometric information. The analytic nature of this approach allows for a proper treatment of source separation in the presence of uncertainty, while the local nature allows for a local determination of the source coordinate system. This leaves open the possibility of describing a position dependent independent component coordinate system with local linear coordinates patches.

The presented class factorization formalism removes the decomposition assumptions needed for independent component analysis, and reinforces the well known fact that sources are recoverable only up to linear transformation. By modifying the equivalence class relation, a rich underlying algebraic structure with both multiplication and addition can be constructed. Also, it is clear that the matrix of second derivatives reveals an even more general combinatorial undirected graphical structure of the multivariate function. These topics, as well as uniqueness issues of the factorization will be addressed elsewhere [5].

The author is grateful to Jack Cowan, David Grier and Robert Wald for many invaluable discussions.

References

[1] J. K. Lin, *Local Independent Component Analysis*, Ph. D. thesis, University of Chicago, 1997.

[2] A. J. Bell and T. J. Sejnowski, Neural Computation **7**, 1129 (1995).

[3] S. Amari, A. Cichocki, and H. Yang, in *Advances in Neural and Information Processing Systems, 8*, edited by D. S. Touretzky, M. C. Mozer, and M. E. Hasselmo (MIT Press, Cambridge, MA, 1996), pp. 757–763.

[4] B. A. Pearlmutter and L. Parra, in *Advances in Neural and Information Processing Systems, 9*, edited by M. C. Mozer, M. I. Jordan, and T. Petsche (MIT Press, Cambridge, MA, 1997), pp. 613–619.

[5] J. K. Lin, *Graphical Structure of Multivariate Functions*, in preparation.

A Framework for Multiple-Instance Learning

Oded Maron
NE43-755
AI Lab, M.I.T.
Cambridge, MA 02139
oded@ai.mit.edu

Tomás Lozano-Pérez
NE43-836a
AI Lab, M.I.T.
Cambridge, MA 02139
tlp@ai.mit.edu

Abstract

Multiple-instance learning is a variation on supervised learning, where the task is to learn a concept given positive and negative *bags* of instances. Each bag may contain many instances, but a bag is labeled positive even if only one of the instances in it falls within the concept. A bag is labeled negative only if all the instances in it are negative. We describe a new general framework, called *Diverse Density*, for solving multiple-instance learning problems. We apply this framework to learn a simple description of a person from a series of images (bags) containing that person, to a stock selection problem, and to the drug activity prediction problem.

1 Introduction

One of the drawbacks of applying the supervised learning model is that it is not always possible for a teacher to provide labeled examples for training. Multiple-instance learning provides a new way of modeling the teacher's weakness. Instead of receiving a set of instances which are labeled positive or negative, the learner receives a set of *bags* that are labeled positive or negative. Each bag contains many instances. A bag is labeled negative if all the instances in it are negative. On the other hand, a bag is labeled positive if there is at least one instance in it which is positive. From a collection of labeled bags, the learner tries to induce a concept that will label individual instances correctly. This problem is harder than even noisy supervised learning since the ratio of negative to positive instances in a positively-labeled bag (the noise ratio) can be arbitrarily high.

The first application of multiple-instance learning was to drug activity prediction. In the activity prediction application, one objective is to predict whether a candidate drug molecule will bind strongly to a target protein known to be involved in some disease state. Typically, one has examples of molecules that bind well to the target protein and also of molecules that do not bind well. Much as in a lock and key, shape is the most important factor in determining whether a drug molecule and the target protein will bind. However, drug molecules are flexible, so they can adopt a wide range of shapes. A positive example does not convey what shape the molecule took in order to bind – only that *one* of the shapes that the molecule can take was the right one. However, a negative example means that none of the shapes that the molecule can achieve was the right key.

The multiple-instance learning model was only recently formalized by [Dietterich *et al.*, 1997]. They assume a hypothesis class of axis-parallel rectangles, and develop algorithms for dealing with the drug activity prediction problem described above. This work was followed by [Long and Tan, 1996], where a high-degree polynomial PAC bound was given for the number of examples needed to learn in the multiple-instance learning model. [Auer, 1997] gives a more efficient algorithm, and [Blum and Kalai, 1998] shows that learning from multiple-instance examples is reducible to PAC-learning with two sided noise and to the Statistical Query model. Unfortunately, the last three papers make the restrictive assumption that all instances from all bags are generated independently.

In this paper, we describe a framework called *Diverse Density* for solving multiple-instance problems. Diverse Density is a measure of the intersection of the positive bags minus the union of the negative bags. By maximizing Diverse Density we can find the point of intersection (the desired concept), and also the set of feature weights that lead to the best intersection. We show results of applying this algorithm to a difficult synthetic training set as well as the "musk" data set from [Dietterich *et al.*, 1997]. We then use Diverse Density in two novel applications: one is to learn a simple description of a person from a series of images that are labeled positive if the person is somewhere in the image and negative otherwise. The other is to deal with a high amount of noise in a stock selection problem.

2   Diverse Density

We motivate the idea of Diverse Density through a molecular example. Suppose that the shape of a candidate molecule can be adequately described by a feature vector . One instance of the molecule is therefore represented as a point in n-dimensional feature space. As the molecule changes its shape (through both rigid and non-rigid transformations), it will trace out a manifold through this n-dimensional space[1]. Figure 1(a) shows the paths of four molecules through a 2-dimensional feature space.

If a candidate molecule is labeled positive, we know that in at least one place along the manifold, it took on the right shape for it to fit into the target protein. If the molecule is labeled negative, we know that none of the conformations along its manifold will allow binding with the target protein. If we assume that there is only one shape that will bind to the target protein, what do the positive and negative manifolds tell us about the location of the correct shape in feature space? The answer: it is where all positive feature-manifolds intersect without intersecting any negative feature-manifolds. For example, in Figure 1(a) it is point A.

Unfortunately, a multiple-instance bag does not give us complete distribution information, but only some arbitrary sample from that distribution. In fact, in applications other than drug discovery, there is not even a notion of an underlying continuous manifold. Therefore, Figure 1(a) becomes Figure 1(b). The problem of trying to find an intersection changes

---

[1]In practice, one needs to restrict consideration to shapes of the molecule that have sufficiently low potential energy. But, we ignore this restriction in this simple illustration.

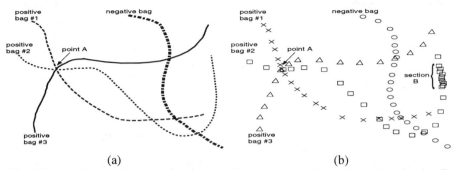

<table>
<tr><td>(a)</td><td>(b)</td></tr>
</table>

The different shapes that a molecule can Samples taken along the paths. Section B
take on are represented as a path. The inter- is a high density area, but point A is a high
section point of positive paths is where they Diverse Density area.
took on the same shape.

Figure 1: A motivating example for Diverse Density

to a problem of trying to find an area where there is both high density of positive points
and low density of negative points. The difficulty with using regular density is illustrated in
Figure 1(b), Section B. We are not just looking for high density, but high "Diverse Density".
We define Diverse Density at a point to be a measure of how many *different* positive bags have
instances near that point, and how far the negative instances are from that point.

2.1 Algorithms for multiple-instance learning

In this section, we derive a probabilistic measure of Diverse Density, and test it on a difficult
artificial data set. We denote positive bags as B_i^+, the jth point in that bag as B_{ij}^+, and the
value of the kth feature of that point as B_{ijk}^+. Likewise, B_{ij}^- represents a negative point.
Assuming for now that the true concept is a single point t, we can find it by maximizing
$\Pr(x = t \mid B_1^+, \cdots, B_n^+, B_1^-, \cdots, B_m^-)$ over all points x in feature space. If we use Bayes'
rule and an uninformative prior over the concept location, this is equivalent to maximizing
the likelihood $\Pr(B_1^+, \cdots, B_n^+, B_1^-, \cdots, B_m^- \mid x = t)$. By making the additional assumption
that the bags are conditionally independent given the target concept t, the best hypothesis is
$\arg\max_x \prod_i \Pr(B_i^+ \mid x = t) \prod_i \Pr(B_i^- \mid x = t)$. Using Bayes' rule once more (and again
assuming a uniform prior over concept location), this is equivalent to

$$\arg\max_x \prod_i \Pr(x = t \mid B_i^+) \prod_i \Pr(x = t \mid B_i^-). \tag{1}$$

This is a general definition of maximum Diverse Density, but we need to define the terms in the
products to instantiate it. One possibility is a noisy-or model: the probability that not all points
missed the target is $\Pr(x = t \mid B_i^+) = \Pr(x = t \mid B_{i1}^+, B_{i2}^+, \ldots) = 1 - \prod_j (1 - \Pr(x = t \mid B_{ij}^+))$,
and likewise $\Pr(x = t \mid B_i^-) = \prod_j (1 - \Pr(x = t \mid B_{ij}^-))$. We model the causal probability of
an individual instance on a potential target as related to the distance between them. Namely,
$\Pr(x = t \mid B_{ij}) = \exp(- \parallel B_{ij} - x \parallel^2)$. Intuitively, if one of the instances in a positive bag
is close to x, then $\Pr(x = t \mid B_i^+)$ is high. Likewise, if every positive bag has an instance
close to x and no negative bags are close to x, then x will have high Diverse Density. Diverse
Density at an intersection of n bags is exponentially higher than it is at an intersection of $n - 1$
bags, yet all it takes is one well placed negative instance to drive the Diverse Density down.

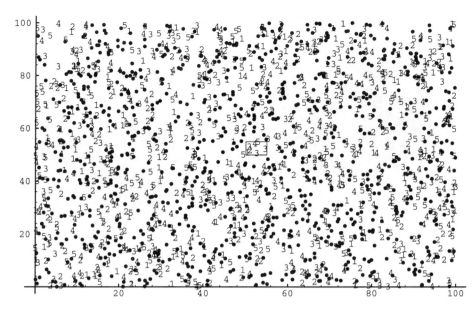

Figure 2: Negative and positive bags drawn from the same distribution, but labeled according to their intersection with the middle square. Negative instances are dots, positive are numbers. The square contains at least one instance from every positive bag and no negatives,

The Euclidean distance metric used to measure "closeness" depends on the features that describe the instances. It is likely that some of the features are irrelevant, or that some should be weighted to be more important than others. Luckily, we can use the same framework to find not only the best location in feature space, but also the best weighting of the features. Once again, we find the best scaling of the individual features by finding the scalings that maximize Diverse Density. The algorithm returns both a location x and a scaling vector s, where $\| B_{ij} - x \|^2 = \sum_k s_k^2 (B_{ijk} - x_k)^2$.

Note that the assumption that all bags intersect at a single point is not necessary. We can assume more complicated concepts, such as for example a disjunctive concept $t_a \vee t_b$. In this case, we maximize over a pair of locations x_a and x_b and define $\Pr(x_a = t_a \vee x_b = t_b \mid B_{ij}) = \max_{x_a, x_b}(\Pr(x_a = t_a \mid B_{ij}), \Pr(x_b = t_b \mid B_{ij}))$.

To test the algorithm, we created an artificial data set: 5 positive and 5 negative bags, each with 50 instances. Each instance was chosen uniformly at randomly from a $[0, 100] \times [0, 100] \in \mathcal{R}^2$ domain, and the concept was a 5×5 square in the middle of the domain. A bag was labeled positive if at least one of its instances fell within the square, and negative if none did, as shown in Figure 2. The square in the middle contains at least one instance from every positive bag and no negative instances. This is a difficult data set because both positive and negative bags are drawn from the same distribution. They only differ in a small area of the domain.

Using regular density (adding up the contribution of every positive bag and subtracting negative bags; this is roughly what a supervised learning algorithm such as nearest neighbor performs), we can plot the density surface across the domain. Figure 3(a) shows this surface for the data set in Figure 2, and it is clear that finding the peak (a candidate hypothesis) is difficult. However, when we plot the Diverse Density surface (using the noisy-or model) in Figure 3(b), it is easy to pick out the global maximum which is within the desired concept. The other

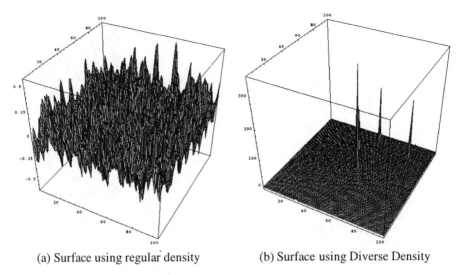

(a) Surface using regular density   (b) Surface using Diverse Density

Figure 3: Density surfaces over the example data of Figure 3

major peaks in Figure 3(b) are the result of a chance concentration of instances from different bags. With a bit more bad luck, one of those peaks could have eclipsed the one in the middle. However, the chance of this decreases as the number of bags (training examples) increases.

One remaining issue is how to find the maximum Diverse Density. In general, we are searching an arbitrary density landscape and the number of local maxima and size of the search space could prohibit any efficient exploration. In this paper, we use gradient ascent with multiple starting points. This has worked succesfully in every test case because we know what starting points to use. The maximum Diverse Density peak is made of contributions from some set of positive points. If we start an ascent from every positive point, one of them is likely to be closest to the maximum, contribute the most to it and have a climb directly to it. While this heuristic is sensible for maximizing with respect to location, maximizing with respect to scaling of feature weights may still lead to local maxima.

3   Applications of Diverse Density

By way of benchmarking, we tested the Diverse Density approach on the "musk" data sets from [Dietterich et al., 1997], which were also used in [Auer, 1997]. We also have begun investigating two new applications of multiple-instance learning. We describe preliminary results on all of these below. The musk data sets contain feature vectors describing the surfaces of a variety of low-energy shapes from approximately 100 molecules. Each feature vector has 166 dimensions. Approximately half of these molecules are known to smell "musky," the remainder are very similar molecules that do not smell musky. There are two musk data sets; the Musk-1 data set is smaller, both in having fewer molecules and many fewer instances per molecule. Many (72) of the molecules are shared between the two data sets, but the second set includes more instances for the shared molecules.

We approached the problem as follows: for each run, we held out a randomly selected 1/10 of the data set as a test set. We computed the maximum Diverse Density on the training set by multiple gradient ascents, starting at each positive instance. This produces a maximum feature point as well as the best feature weights corresponding to that point. We note that typically less than half of the 166 features receive non-zero weighting. We then computed a distance threshold that optimized classification performance under leave-one-out cross validation within the training set. We used the feature weights and distance threshold to classify the examples of the test set; an example was deemed positive if the weighted distance from the maximum density point to any of its instances was below the threshold.

The table below lists the average accuracy of twenty runs, compared with the performance of the two principal algorithms reported in [Dietterich *et al.*, 1997] (`iterated-discrim APR` and `GFS elim-kde` APR), as well as the `MULTINST` algorithm from [Auer, 1997]. We note that the performances reported for `iterated-discrim` APR involves choosing parameters to maximize *test set* performance and so probably represents an upper bound for accuracy on this data set. The `MULTINST` algorithm assumes that all instances from all bags are generated independently. The Diverse Density results, which required no tuning, are comparable or better than those of `GFS elim-kde` APR and `MULTINST`.

Musk Data Set 1		Musk Data Set 2	
algorithm	accuracy	algorithm	accuracy
iterated-discrim APR	92.4	iterated-discrim APR	89.2
GFS elim-kde APR	91.3	MULTINST	84.0
Diverse Density	88.9	Diverse Density	82.5
MULTINST	76.7	GFS elim-kde APR	80.4

We also investigated two new applications of multiple-instance learning. The first of these is to learn a simple description of a person from a series of images that are labeled positive if they contain the person and negative otherwise. For a positively labeled image we only know that the person is somewhere in it, but we do not know where. We sample 54 subimages of varying centers and sizes and declare them to be instances in one positive bag since one of them contains the person. This is repeated for every positive and negative image.

We use a very simple representation for the instances. Each subimage is divided into three parts which roughly correspond to where the head, torso and legs of the person would be. The three dominant colors (one for each subsection) are used to represent the image. Figure 4 shows a training set where every bag included two people, yet the algorithm learned a description of the person who appears in all the images. This technique is expanded in [Maron and LakshmiRatan, 1998] to learn descriptions of natural images and use the learned concept to retrieve similar images from a large image database.

Another new application uses Diverse Density in the stock selection problem. Every month, there are stocks that perform well for fundamental reasons and stocks that perform well because of flukes; there are many more of the latter, but we are interested in the former. For every month, we take the 100 stocks with the highest return and put them in a positive bag, hoping that at least one of them did well for fundamental reasons. Negative bags are created from the bottom 5 stocks in every month. A stock instance is described by 17 features such as momentum, price to fair-value, etc. Grantham, Mayo, Van Otterloo & Co. kindly provided us with data on the 600 largest US stocks since 1978. We tested the algorithm through five runs of training for ten years, then testing on the next year. In each run, the algorithm returned the stock description (location in feature space and a scaling of the features) that maximized Diverse Density. The test stocks were then ranked and decilized by distance (in weighted feature space) to the max-DD point. Figure 5 shows the average return of every decile. The return in the top decile (stocks that are most like the "fundamental stock") is positive and

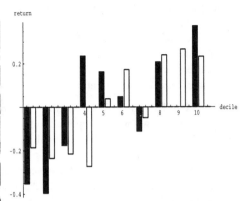

Figure 5: A training set of images with one person in common.

Figure 6: Black bars show Diverse Density's average return on a decile, and the white bars show GMO's predictor's return.

higher than the average return of a GMO predictor. Likewise, the return in the bottom decile is negative and below that of a GMO predictor.

4   Conclusion

In this paper, we have shown that Diverse Density is a general tool with which to learn from Multiple-Instance examples. In addition, we have shown that Multiple-Instance problems occur in a wide variety of domains. We attempted to show the various ways in which ambiguity can lead to the Multiple-Instance framework: through lack of knowledge in the drug discovery example, through ambiguity of representation in the vision example, and through a high degree of noise in the stock example.

Acknowledgements
We thank Peter Dayan and Paul Viola at MIT and Tom Hancock and Chris Darnell at GMO for helpful discussions and the AFOSR ASSERT program, Parent Grant#:F49620-93-1-0263 for their support of this research.

References

[Auer, 1997] P. Auer. On Learning from Multi-Instance Examples: Empirical Evaluation of a theoretical Approach. NeuroCOLT Technical Report Series, NC-TR-97-025, March 1997.

[Blum and Kalai, 1998] A. Blum and A. Kalai. A Note on Learning from Multiple-Instance Examples. *To appear in Machine Learning*, 1998.

[Dietterich *et al.*, 1997] T. G. Dietterich, R. H. Lathrop, and T. Lozano-Pérez. Solving the Multiple-Instance Problem with Axis-Parallel Rectangles. *Artificial Intelligence Journal*, 89, 1997.

[Long and Tan, 1996] P. M. Long and L. Tan. PAC-learning axis alligned rectangles with respect to product distributions from multiple-instance examples. In *Proceedings of the 1996 Conference on Computational Learning Theory*, 1996.

[Maron and LakshmiRatan, 1998] O. Maron and A. LakshmiRatan. Multiple-Instance Learning for Natural Scene Classification. In *Submitted to CVPR-98*, 1998.

An application of Reversible-Jump MCMC to multivariate spherical Gaussian mixtures

Alan D. Marrs
Signal & Information Processing Dept.
Defence Evaluation & Research Agency
Gt. Malvern, UK WR14 3PS
marrs@signal.dra.hmg.gb

Abstract

Applications of Gaussian mixture models occur frequently in the fields of statistics and artificial neural networks. One of the key issues arising from any mixture model application is how to estimate the optimum number of mixture components. This paper extends the Reversible-Jump Markov Chain Monte Carlo (MCMC) algorithm to the case of multivariate spherical Gaussian mixtures using a hierarchical prior model. Using this method the number of mixture components is no longer fixed but becomes a parameter of the model which we shall estimate. The Reversible-Jump MCMC algorithm is capable of moving between parameter subspaces which correspond to models with different numbers of mixture components. As a result a sample from the full joint distribution of all unknown model parameters is generated. The technique is then demonstrated on a simulated example and a well known vowel dataset.

1 Introduction

Applications of Gaussian mixture models regularly appear in the neural networks literature. One of their most common roles in the field of neural networks, is in the placement of centres in a radial basis function network. In this case the basis functions are used to model the distribution of input data ($\mathbf{X}_i = [x_1, x_2, ..., x_d]^T$, ($i = 1, n$)), and the problem is one of mixture density estimation.

$$p(\mathbf{X}_i) = \sum_{j=1}^{k} \pi_j p(\mathbf{X}_i | \mathbf{\Theta_j}), \tag{1}$$

where k is the number of mixture components, π_j the weight or mixing proportion for component j and Θ_j the component parameters (mean & variance in this case). The mixture components represent the basis functions of the neural network and their parameters (centres & widths) may be estimated using the expectation-maximisation (EM) algorithm.

One of the key issues arising in the use of mixture models is how to estimate the number of components. This is a model selection problem: the problem of choosing the 'correct' number of components for a mixture model. This may be thought of as one of comparing two (or more) mixture models with different components, and choosing the model that is 'best' based upon some criterion. For example, we might compare a two component model to one with a single component.

$$\mathbf{H_o} : p(\mathbf{X}_i | \Theta) \;\; ; \;\; \mathbf{H_a} : \pi p(\mathbf{X}_i | \Theta_1) + (1 - \pi) p(\mathbf{X}_i | \Theta_2). \tag{2}$$

This may appear to be a case of testing of nested hypotheses. However, it has been noted [5] that the standard frequentist hypothesis testing theory (generalised likelihood ratio test) does not apply to this problem because the desired regularity conditions do not hold. In addition, if the models being tested have 2 and 3 components respectively, they are not strictly nested. For example, we could equate any pair of components in the three component model to the components in the two component model, yet how do we choose which component to 'leave out'?

2   Bayesian approach to Gaussian mixture models

A full Bayesian analysis treats the number of mixture components as one of the parameters of the model for which we wish to find the conditional distribution. In this case we would represent the joint distribution as a hierarchical model where we may introduce prior distributions for the model parameters, ie.

$$p(k, \pi, z, \mathbf{\Theta}, \mathbf{X}) = p(k)p(\pi|k)p(z|\pi, k)p(\mathbf{\Theta}|z, \pi, k)p(\mathbf{X}|\mathbf{\Theta}, z, \pi, k), \tag{3}$$

where $\pi = (\pi_j)_{j=1}^{k}$, $\mathbf{\Theta} = (\Theta_j)_{j=1}^{k}$ and $z = (z_i)_{i=1}^{n}$ are allocation variables introduced by treating mixture estimation as a hidden data problem with z_i allocating the ith observation to a particular component. A simplified version of this model can be derived by imposing further conditional independencies, leading to the following expression for the joint distribution

$$p(k, \pi, z, \mathbf{\Theta}, \mathbf{X}) = p(k)p(\pi|k)p(z|\pi, k)p(\mathbf{\Theta}|k)p(\mathbf{X}|\mathbf{\Theta}, z). \tag{4}$$

In addition, we add an extra layer to the hierarchy representing priors on the model parameters giving the final form for the joint distribution

$$\begin{aligned} p(\lambda, \delta, \eta, k, \pi, z, \mathbf{\Theta}, \mathbf{X}) = p(\lambda)p(\delta)p(\eta)p(k|\lambda)p(\pi|k, \delta)p(z|\pi, k) \times \\ p(\mathbf{\Theta}|k, \eta)p(\mathbf{X}|\mathbf{\Theta}, z). \end{aligned} \tag{5}$$

Until recently a full Bayesian analysis has been mathematically intractable. Model comparison was carried out by conducting an extensive search over all possible model orders comparing Bayes factors for all possible pairs of models. What we really desire is a method which will estimate the model order along with the other model parameters. Two such methods based upon Markov Chain Monte Carlo (MCMC) techniques are reversible-jump MCMC [2] and jump-diffusion [3].

In the following sections, we extend the reversible-jump MCMC technique to multivariate spherical Gaussian mixture models. Results are then shown for a simulated example and an example using the Peterson-Barney vowel data.

3   Reversible-jump MCMC algorithm

Following [4] we define the priors for our hierarchical model and derive a set of 5 move types for the reversible jump MCMC sampling scheme. To simplify some of the MCMC steps we choose a prior model where the prior on the weights is Dirichlet and the prior model for $\boldsymbol{\mu}_j = [\mu_{j_1}, ..., \mu_{j_d}]^T$ and σ_j^{-2} is that they are drawn independently with normal and gamma priors,

$$\pi \sim D(\delta, ..., \delta) \ , \ \boldsymbol{\mu}_j \sim N(\boldsymbol{\eta}, \mathbf{A}^{-1}) \ , \ \sigma_j \sim \Gamma(\alpha, \beta), \tag{6}$$

where for the purposes of this study we follow[4] and define the hyper-parameters thus: $\delta = 1.0$; $\boldsymbol{\eta}$ is set to be the mean of the data; $\mathbf{A}$ is the diagonal precision matrix for the prior on $\boldsymbol{\mu}_j$ with components a_j which are taken to be $1/r_j^2$ where r_j is the data range in dimension j; $\alpha = 2.0$ and β is some small multiple of $1/r_j^2$.

The moves then consist of: **I**: updating the weights; **II**: updating the parameters $(\boldsymbol{\mu}, \sigma)$; **III**: updating the allocation; **IV**: updating the hyper-parameters; **V**: splitting one component into two, or combining two into one.

The first 4 moves are relatively simple to define, since the conjugate nature of the priors leads to relatively simple forms for the full conditional distribution of the desired parameter. Thus the first 4 moves are Gibbs sampling moves and the full conditional distributions for the weights π_j, means $\boldsymbol{\mu}_j$, variances σ_j and allocation variables z_i are given by:

$$p(\pi_j|...) \sim D(\delta + n_1, ..., \delta + n_k), \tag{7}$$

where n_k is the number of observations allocated to component k;

$$p(\boldsymbol{\mu}_j|...) = \prod_{m=1}^{d} p(\mu_{j_m}|...) : p(\mu_{j_m}|...) \sim N(\frac{n_j \bar{x}_{i_m} \sigma_j^{-2} + a_m \eta_m}{(n_j \sigma_j^{-2} + a_m)}, (n_j \sigma_j^{-2} + a_m)^{-1}), \tag{8}$$

where we recognise that $\boldsymbol{\mu}_j$ is an d dimensional vector with components μ_{j_m} ($m = 1, d$), η_m are the components of the $\boldsymbol{\mu}_j$ prior mean and a_m represent the diagonal components of $\mathbf{A}$.

$$p(\sigma_j^{-2}|...) = \Gamma(\nu + n_j - 1, \frac{1}{2} \sum_{i=1:z_{ij}=1}^{n} (\mathbf{X}_i - \boldsymbol{\mu}_j)^T (\mathbf{X}_i - \boldsymbol{\mu}_j) + \beta); \tag{9}$$

and

$$p(z_i = j|...) \propto \frac{\pi_j}{\sigma_j} \exp\left(-\sum_{m=1}^{d} \frac{(x_i - \mu_{j_m})^2}{\sigma_j^2}\right). \tag{10}$$

The final move involves splitting/combining model components. The main criteria which need to be met when designing these moves are that they are irreducible, aperiodic, form a reversible pair and satisfy detailed balance[1]. The MCMC step for this move takes the form of a Metropolis-Hastings step where a move from state y to state y' is proposed, with $\pi(y)$ the target probability distribution and $q_m(y, y')$ the proposal distribution for the move m. The resulting move is then accepted with probability α_m

$$\alpha_m = min\left\{1, \frac{\pi(y')q_m(y', y)}{\pi(y)q_m(y, y')}\right\}. \tag{11}$$

In the case of a move from state y to a state y' which lies in a higher dimensional space, the move may be implemented by drawing a vector of continuous random variables u, independent of y. The new state y' is then set using an invertible deterministic function of x and u. It can be shown [2] that the acceptance probability is then given by

$$\alpha_m = min\left\{1, \frac{\pi(y')r_m(y')}{\pi(y)r_m(y)q(u)}\left|\frac{\partial y'}{\partial(y, u)}\right|\right\}, \tag{12}$$

where $r_m(y)$ is the probability of choosing move type m when in state y, and $q(u)$ is the density function of u.

The initial application of the reversible jump MCMC technique to normal mixtures [4] was limited to the univariate case. This yielded relatively simple expressions for the split/combine moves, and, most importantly, the determinant of the Jacobian of the transformation from a model with k components to one with $k+1$ components was simple to derive. In the more general case of multivariate normal models care must be taken in prescribing move transformations. A complicated transformation will lead to problems when the |Jacobian| for a d-dimensional model is required.

For multivariate spherical Gaussian models, we randomly choose a model component from the current k component model. The decision is then made to split or combine with one of its neighbours with probability p_{s_k} and p_{c_k} respectively (where $p_{c_k} = 1 - p_{s_k}$). If the choice is to combine the component, we label the chosen component z_1, and choose z_2 to be a neighbouring component j with probability $\propto 1/r_j$ where r_j is the distance from the component z_1. The new component resulting from the combination of z_1 and z_2 is labelled z_c and its parameters are calculated from:

$$\pi_{z_c} = \pi_{z_1} + \pi_{z_2} \quad ; \quad \mu_{z_{c_j}:(j=1,d)} = \frac{(\pi_{z_1}\mu_{z_{c1_j}} + \pi_{z_2}\mu_{z_{c_j}})}{(\pi_{z_1} + \pi_{z_1})} ;$$
$$\sigma_{z_c}^2 = \frac{(\pi_{z_1}\sigma_{z_1}^2 + \pi_{z_2}\sigma_{z_2})}{(\pi_{z_1} + \pi_{z_2})}. \tag{13}$$

If the decision is to split, the chosen component is labelled z_c and it is used to define two new model components z_1 and z_2 with weights and parameters conforming to (13). In making this transformation there are $2 + d$ degrees of freedom, so we need to generate $2 + d$ random numbers to enable the specification of the new component parameters. The random numbers are denoted u_1, $\mathbf{u_2} = [u_{2_1}, ..., u_{2_d}]^T$ and u_3. All are drawn from $Beta(2, 2)$ distributions while the components of $\mathbf{u_2}$ each have probability 0.5 of being negative. The split transformation is then defined by:

$$\pi_{z_1} = u_1\pi_{z_c} \quad , \quad \pi_{z_2} = (1 - u_1)\pi_{z_c}$$
$$\mu_{z_{1_j}} = \mu_{z_{c_j}} - u_{2_j}\sigma_{z_c}\sqrt{\frac{\pi_{z_2}}{\pi_{z_1}}} \quad , \quad \mu_{z_{2_j}} = \mu_{z_{c_j}} + u_{2_j}\sigma_{z_c}\sqrt{\frac{\pi_{z_1}}{\pi_{z_2}}}$$

$$\sigma_{z_1}^2 = u_3 \sigma_{z_c}^2 \frac{\pi_{z_2}}{\pi_{z_1}} \quad , \quad \sigma_{z_2}^2 = (1 - u_3) \sigma_{z_c}^2 \frac{\pi_{z_1}}{\pi_{z_2}}. \tag{14}$$

Once the new components have been defined it is necessary to evaluate the probability of choosing to combine component z_1 with component z_2 in this new model.

Having proposed the split/combine move all that remains is to calculate the Metropolis-Hastings acceptance probability α, where $\alpha = min(1, R)$ for the split move and $\alpha = min(1, 1/R)$ for the combine move. Where in the case of a split move from a model with k components to one with $k + 1$ components, or a combine move from $k + 1$ to k, R is given by:

$$
\begin{aligned}
R = \quad & \frac{\prod_{i=1:z_{ij}=z_1}^{n} p(\mathbf{X}_i|\Theta,c) \prod_{i=1:z_{ij}=z_2}^{n} p(\mathbf{X}_i|\Theta,c)}{\prod_{i=1:z_{ij}=z_c}^{n} p(\mathbf{X}_i|\Theta,c)} \times \\
& \frac{\pi_{z_1}^{\delta-1+n_1} \pi_{z_2}^{\delta-1+n_2}}{\pi_{z_c}^{\delta-1+n_1+n_2} B(\delta, k\delta)} \times \\
& \prod_{m=1}^{d} \sqrt{\frac{a_m}{(2\pi)}} \exp\left(-\frac{1}{2} a_m \left((\mu_{z_{1m}} - \eta_m)^2 + (\mu_{z_{2m}} - \eta_m)^2 - (\mu_{z_{cm}} - \eta_m)\right)\right) \times \\
& \frac{\beta^\alpha}{\Gamma(\alpha)} \left(\frac{\sigma_{z_c}^2}{\sigma_{z_1}^2 \sigma_{z_2}^2}\right)^{(\alpha-1)} \exp\left(-\beta(\sigma_{z_1}^{-2} + \sigma_{z_2}^{-2} - \sigma_{z_c}^{-2})\right) \times \\
& \frac{p_{c_{k+1}}}{p_{s_k} P_{alloc}} \left(g_{2,2}(u_1) g_{1,1}(u_3) \prod_{j=1}^{d} g_{2,2}(u_{2_j})\right) \times \\
& \frac{\pi_{z_c} \sigma_{z_c}^{d+1}}{(2((1-u_1)u_1)^{(d+1)/2} \sqrt{(1-u_3)u_3}}, \tag{15}
\end{aligned}
$$

where $g_{2,2}()$ denotes a $Beta(2, 2)$ density function. The first line on the R.H.S is due to the ratio of likelihoods for those observations assigned to the components in question, the subsequent three lines are due to the prior ratios, the fifth line is due to the the proposal ratio and the last line due to the |Jacobian| of the transformation. The term p_{alloc} represents a combination of the probability of obtaining the current allocation of data to the components in question and the probability of choosing to combine components z_1 and z_2.

4 Results

To assess this approach to the estimation of multivariate spherical Gaussian mixture models, we firstly consider a toy problem where 1000 bivariate samples were generated from a known 20 component mixture model. This is followed by an analysis of the Peterson-Barney vowel data set comprising 780 samples of the measured amplitude of four formant frequencies for 10 utterances. For this mixture estimation example, we ignore the class labels and consider the straight forward density estimation problem.

4.1 Simulated data

The resulting reversible-jump MCMC chain of model order can be seen in figure 1, along with the resulting histogram (after rejecting the first 2000 MCMC samples). The histogram shows that the *maximum a posteriori* value for model order is 17. The MAP estimate of model parameters was obtained by averaging all the 17 component model samples, the estimated model is shown in figure 2 alongside the original generating model. The results are rather encouraging given the large number of model components and the relatively small number of samples.

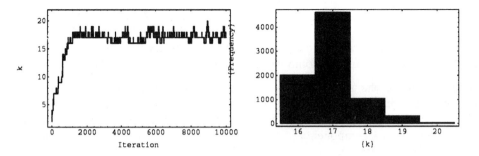

Figure 1: Reversible-jump MCMC chain and histogram of model order for simulated data.

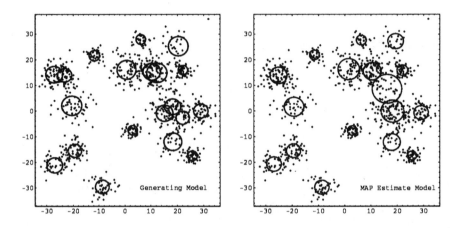

Figure 2: Example of model estimation for simulated data.

4.2 Vowel data

The reversible-jump MCMC chain of model order for the Peterson-Barney vowel data example is shown in figure 3, alongside the resulting MAP model estimate. For ease of visualisation, the estimated model and data samples have been projected onto the first two principal components of the data. Again, the results are encouraging.

5 Conclusion

One of the key problems when using Gaussian mixture models is estimation of the optimum number of components to include in the model. In this paper we extend the reversible-jump MCMC technique for estimating the parameters of Gaussian mixtures with an unknown number of components to the multivariate spherical Gaussian case. The technique is then demonstrated on a simulated data example and an example using a well known dataset.

The attraction of this approach is that the number of mixture components is not fixed at the outset but becomes a parameter of the model. The reversible-jump MCMC approach is then capable of moving between parameter subspaces which

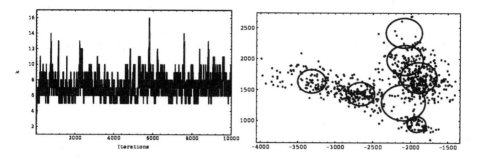

Figure 3: Reversible-jump MCMC chain of model order and MAP estimate of model (projected onto first two principal components) for vowel data.

correspond to models with different numbers of mixture components. As a result a sample of the full joint distribution is generated from which the posterior distribution for the number of model components can be derived. This information may then either be used to construct a Bayesian classifier or to define the centres in a radial basis function network.

References

[1] W.R. Gilks, S. Richardson, and D.J. Spiegelhalter Eds. *Markov Chain Monte Carlo in Practice*. Chapman and Hall, 1995.

[2] P.J. Green. Reversible jump MCMC computation and Bayesian model determination. *Boimetrika*, 82:711–732, 1995.

[3] D.B. Phillips and A.F.M. Smith. Bayesian model comparison via jump diffusions. In W.R. Gilks, S. Richardson, and D.J. Spiegelhalter, editors, *Markov Chain Monte Carlo in Practice*. Chapman and Hall, 1995.

[4] S. Richardson and P. J. Green. On Bayesian analysis of mixtures with an unknown number of components. *J. Royal Stat. Soc. Series B*, 59(4), 1997.

[5] D.M. Titterington, A.F.M. Smith, and U.E. Makov. *Statistical Analysis of Finite Mixture Distributions*. Wiley, 1985.

Estimating Dependency Structure as a Hidden Variable

Marina Meilă and Michael I. Jordan
{mmp, jordan}@ai.mit.edu
Center for Biological & Computational Learning
Massachusetts Institute of Technology
45 Carleton St. E25-201
Cambridge, MA 02142

Abstract

This paper introduces a probability model, the *mixture of trees* that can account for sparse, dynamically changing dependence relationships. We present a family of efficient algorithms that use EM and the Minimum Spanning Tree algorithm to find the ML and MAP mixture of trees for a variety of priors, including the Dirichlet and the MDL priors.

1 INTRODUCTION

A fundamental feature of a good model is the ability to uncover and exploit independencies in the data it is presented with. For many commonly used models, such as neural nets and belief networks, the dependency structure encoded in the model is fixed, in the sense that it is not allowed to vary depending on actual values of the variables or with the current case. However, dependency structures that are conditional on values of variables abound in the world around us. Consider for example bitmaps of handwritten digits. They obviously contain many dependencies between pixels; however, the pattern of these dependencies will vary across digits. Imagine a medical database recording the body weight and other data for each patient. The body weight could be a function of age and height for a healthy person, but it would depend on other conditions if the patient suffered from a disease or was an athlete.

Models that are able to represent data conditioned dependencies are decision trees and mixture models, including the soft counterpart of the decision tree, the mixture of experts. Decision trees however can only represent certain patterns of dependecy, and in particular are designed to represent a set of conditional probability tables and not a joint probability distribution. Mixtures are more flexible and the rest of this paper will be focusing on one special case called the *mixtures of trees*.

We will consider domains where the observed variables are related by pairwise dependencies only and these dependencies are sparse enough to contain no cycles. Therefore they can be represented graphically as a *tree*. The structure of the dependencies may vary from one instance to the next. We index the set of possible dependecy structures by a discrete *structure variable z* (that can be observed or hidden) thereby obtaining a *mixture*.

In the framework of graphical probability models, tree distributions enjoy many properties that make them attractive as modelling tools: they have a flexible topology, are intuitively appealing, sampling and computing likelihoods are linear time, simple efficient algorithms for marginalizing and conditioning ($\mathcal{O}(|V|^2)$ or less) exist. Fitting the best tree to a given distribution can be done exactly and efficiently (Chow and Liu, 1968). Trees can capture simple pairwise interactions between variables but they can prove insufficient for more complex distributions. Mixtures of trees enjoy most of the computational advantages of trees and, in addition, they are universal approximators over the space of all distributions. Therefore, they are fit for domains where the dependency patterns become tree like when a possibly hidden variable is instantiated.

Mixture models have been extensively used in the statistics and neural network literature. Of relevance to the present work are the mixtures of Gaussians, whose distribution space, in the case of continuous variables overlaps with the space of mixtures of trees. Work on fitting a tree to a distribution in a Maximum-Likelihood (ML) framework has been pioneered by (Chow and Liu, 1968) and was extended to polytrees by (Pearl, 1988) and to mixtures of trees with observed structure variable by (Geiger, 1992; Friedman and Goldszmidt, 1996). Mixtures of factorial distributions were studied by (Kontkanen et al., 1996) whereas (Thiesson et al., 1997) discusses mixtures of general belief nets. Multinets (Geiger, 1996) which are essentially mixtures of Bayes nets include mixtures of trees as a special case. It is however worth studying mixtures of trees separately for their special computational advantages.

This work presents efficient algorithms for learning mixture of trees models with unknown or hidden structure variable. The following section introduces the model; section 3 develops the basic algorithm for its estimation from data in the ML framework. Section 4 discusses the introduction of priors over mixtures of trees models and presents several realistic factorized priors for which the MAP estimate can be computed by a modified versions of the basic algorithm. The properties of the model are verified by simulation in section 5 and section 6 concludes the paper.

2 THE MIXTURE OF TREES MODEL

In this section we will introduce the mixture of trees model and the notation that will be used throughout the paper. Let V denote the set of variables of interest. According to the graphical model paradigm, each variable is viewed as a vertex of a graph. Let r_v denote the number of values of variable $v \in V$, x_v a particular value of V, x_A an assignment to the variables in the subset A of V. To simplify notation x_V will be denoted by x.

We use trees as graphical representations for families of probability distributions over V that satisfy a common set of independence relationships encoded in the tree topology. In this representation, an edge of the tree shows a direct dependence, or, more precisely, the absence of an edge between two variables signifies that they are independent, conditioned on all the other variables in V. We shall call a graph that has no cycles a *tree*[1] and shall denote by E the set of its (undirected) edges. A probability distribution T that is conformal with the tree (V, E) is a distribution that can be factorized as:

$$T(x) = \frac{\prod_{(u,v) \in E} T_{uv}(x_u, x_v)}{\prod_{v \in V} T_v(x_v)^{\deg v - 1}} \tag{1}$$

Here deg v denotes the *degree* of v, e.g. the number of edges incident to node $v \in V$. The

---

[1]In the graph theory literature, our definition corresponds to a *forest*. The connected components of a forest are called trees.

factors T_{uv} and T_v are the marginal distributions under T:

$$T_{uv}(x_u, x_v) = \sum_{x_{V-\{u,v\}}} T(x_u, x_v, x_{V-\{u,v\}}), \quad T_v(x_v) = \sum_{x_{V-\{v\}}} T(x_v, x_{V-\{v\}}). \quad (2)$$

The distribution itself will be called a tree when no confusion is possible. Note that a tree distribution has for each edge $(u, v) \in E$ a factor depending on x_u, x_v onlyl If the tree is connected, e.g. it *spans* all the nodes in V, it is often called a *spanning tree*.

An equivalent representation for T in terms of conditional probabilities is

$$T(x) = \prod_{v \in V} T_{v|pa(v)}(x_v | x_{pa(v)}) \quad (3)$$

The form (3) can be obtained from (1) by choosing an arbitrary root in each connected component and recursively substituting $\frac{T_{v pa(v)}}{T_v}$ by $T_{v|pa(v)}$ starting from the root. $pa(v)$ represents the parent of v in the thus directed tree or the empty set if v is the root of a connected component. The directed tree representation has the advantage of having independent parameters. The total number of free parameters in either representation is $\sum_{(u,v) \in E_T} r_u r_v - \sum_{v \in V} (\deg v - 1) r_v$.

Now we define a mixture of trees to be a distribution of the form

$$Q(x) = \sum_{k=1}^{m} \lambda_k T^k(x); \quad \lambda_k \geq 0, \ k = 1, \ldots, m; \quad \sum_{k=1}^{m} \lambda_k = 1. \quad (4)$$

From the graphical models perspective, a mixture of trees can be viewed as a containing an unobserved choice variable z, taking value $k \in \{1, \ldots m\}$ with probability λ_k. Conditioned on the value of z the distribution of the visible variables x is a tree. The m trees may have different structures and different parameters. Note that because of the structure variable, a mixture of trees is not properly a belief network, but most of the results here owe to the belief network perspective.

3   THE BASIC ALGORITHM: ML FITTING OF MIXTURES OF TREES

This section will show how a mixture of trees can be fit to an observed dataset in the Maximum Likelihood paradigm via the EM algorithm (Dempster et al., 1977). The observations are denoted by $\{x^1, x^2, \ldots, x^N\}$; the corresponding values of the structure variable are $\{z^i, i = 1, \ldots N\}$.

Following a usual EM procedure for mixtures, the Expectation (E) step consists in estimating the posterior probability of each tree to generate datapoint x^i

$$Pr[z^i = k | x^{1,\ldots,N}, model] = \gamma_k(i) = \frac{\lambda_k T^k(x^i)}{\sum_{k'} \lambda_{k'} T^{k'}(x^i)} \quad (5)$$

Then the expected complete log-likelihood to be maximized by the M step of the algorithm is

$$E[l_c | x^{1,\ldots N}, model] = \sum_{k=1}^{m} \Gamma_k [\log \lambda_k + \sum_{i=1}^{N} P^k(x^i) \log T^k(x^i)] \quad (6)$$

$$\Gamma_k = \sum_{i=1}^{N} \gamma_k(x^i), \quad k = 1, \ldots m \text{ and } P^k(x^i) = \gamma_k(i)/\Gamma_k. \quad (7)$$

The maximizing values for the parameters λ are $\lambda_k^{new} = \Gamma_k/N$. To obtain the new distributions T^k, we have to maximize for each k the expression that is the negative of the

Figure 1: **The Basic Algorithm: ML Fitting of a Mixture of Trees**

Input: Dataset $\{x^1, \ldots x^N\}$

　　Initial model m, T^k, λ^k, $k = 1, \ldots m$

　　Procedure MST(weights) that fits a maximum weight spanning tree over V

Iterate until convergence

E step: 　compute γ_k^i, $P^k(x^i)$ for $k = 1, \ldots m$, $i = 1, \ldots N$ by (5), (7)

M step:

　M1. 　$\lambda_k \leftarrow \Gamma_k / N$, $k = 1, \ldots m$

　M2. 　compute marginals P_v^k, P_{uv}^k, $u, v \in V$, $k = 1, \ldots m$

　M3. 　compute mutual information $I_{uv}^k u, v \in V$, $k = 1, \ldots m$

　M4. 　call MST($\{ I_{uv}^k \}$) to generate E_{T^k} for $k = 1, \ldots m$

　M5. 　$T_{uv}^k \leftarrow P_{uv}^k$, ; $T_v^k \leftarrow P_v^k$ for $(u, v) \in E_{T^k}$, $k = 1, \ldots m$

crossentropy between P^k and T^k.

$$\sum_{i=1}^{N} P^k(x^i) \log T^k(x^i) \tag{8}$$

This problem can be solved exactly as shown in (Chow and Liu, 1968). Here we will give a brief description of the procedure. First, one has to compute the mutual information between each pair of variables in V under the target distribution P

$$I_{uv} = I_{vu} = \sum_{x_u x_v} P_{uv}(x_u, x_v) \log \frac{P_{uv}(x_u, x_v)}{P_u(x_u) P_v(x_v)}, \quad u, v \in V, u \neq v. \tag{9}$$

Second, the optimal tree structure is found by a *Maximum Spanning Tree* (MST) algorithm using I_{uv} as the weight for edge (u, v), $\forall u, v \in V$. Once the tree is found, its marginals T_{uv} (or $T_{u|v}$), $(u, v) \in E_T$ are exactly equal to the corresponding marginals P_{uv} of the target distribution P. They are already computed as an intermediate step in the computation of the mutual informations I_{uv} (9).

In our case, the target distribution for T^k is represented by the posterior sample distribution P^k. Note that although each tree fit to P^k is optimal, for the encompassing problem of fitting a mixture of trees to a sample distribution only a local optimum is guaranteed to be reached. The algorithm is summarized in figure 1.

This procedure is based on one important assumption that should be made explicit now. It is the **Parameter independence assumption**: *The distribution* $T_{v|pa(v)}^k$ *for any* k, v *and value of* $pa(v)$ *is a multinomial with* $r_v - 1$ *free parameters that are independent of any other parameters of the mixture.*

It is possible to constrain the m trees to share the same structure, thus constructing a truly Bayesian network. To achieve this, it is sufficient to replace the weights in step **M4** by $\sum_k I_{uv}^k$ and run the MST algorithm only once to obtain the common structure E_T. The tree stuctures obtained by the basic algorithm are connected. The following section will give reasons and ways to obtain disconnected tree structures.

4　MAP MIXTURES OF TREES

In this section we extend the basic algorithm to the problem of finding the Maximum a Posteriori (MAP) probability mixture of trees for a given dataset. In other words, we will consider a nonuniform prior $P[model]$ and will be searching for the mixture of trees that maximizes

$$\log P[model|x^{1, \ldots N}] = \log P[x^{1, \ldots N}|model] + \log P[model] + \text{constant}. \tag{10}$$

Factorized priors The present maximization problem differs from the ML problem solved in the previous section only by the addition of the term $\log P[model]$. We can as well approach it from the EM point of view, by iteratively maximizing

$$E\left[\log P[model|x^{1,\dots N}, z^{1,\dots N}]\right] = E[l_c(x^{1,\dots N}, z^{1,\dots N}|model)] + \log P[model] \quad (11)$$

It is easy to see that the added term does not have any influence on the E step, which will proceed exactly as before. However, in the M step, we must be able to successfully maximize the r.h.s. of (11). Therefore, we look for priors of the form

$$P[model] = P[\lambda_{1,\dots m}] \prod_{k=1}^{m} P[T_k] \quad (12)$$

This class of priors is in agreement with the parameter independence assumption and includes the conjugate prior for the multinomial distribution which is the Dirichlet prior. A Dirichlet prior over a tree can be represented as a table of fictitious marginal probabilities P'^k_{uv} for each pair u, v of variables plus an *equivalent sample size* N' that gives the strength of the prior (Heckerman et al., 1995). However, for Dirichlet priors, the maximization over tree structures (corresponding to step **M4**) can only be performed iteratively (Meilă et al., 1997).

MDL (Minimum Description Length) priors are less informative priors. They attempt to balance the number of parameters that are estimated with the amount of data available, usually by introducing a penalty on model complexity. For the experiments in section 5 we used *edge pruning*. More smoothing methods are presented in (Meilă et al., 1997). To penalize the number of parameters in each component we introduce a prior that penalizes each edge that is added to a tree, thus encouraging the algorithm to produce disconnected trees. The edge pruning prior is $P[T] \propto \exp\left[-\beta \sum_{uv \in E_T} \Delta_{uv}\right]$. We choose a uniform penalty $\Delta_{uv} = 1$. Another possible choice is $\Delta_{uv} = (r_u - 1)(r_v - 1)$ which is the number of parameters introduced by the presence of edge (u, v) w.r.t. a factorized distribution. Using this prior is equivalent to maximizing the following expression in step **M4** of the Basic Algorithm (the index k being dropped for simplicity)

$$\underset{E_T}{\operatorname{argmax}} \sum_{uv \in E_T} \max[0, \Gamma I_{uv} - \beta \Delta_{uv}] = \underset{E_T}{\operatorname{argmax}} \sum_{uv \in E_T} W_{uv} \quad (13)$$

5 EMPIRICAL RESULTS

We have tested our model and algorithms for their ability to retrieve the dependency structure in the data, as classifiers and as density estimators.

For the first objective, we sampled 30,000 datapoints from a mixture of 5 trees over 30 variables with $r_v = 4$ for all vertices. All the other parameters of the generating model and the initial points for the algorithm were picked at random. The results on retrieving the original trees were excellent: out of 10 trials, the algorithm failed to retrieve correctly only 1 tree in 1 trial. This bad result can be accounted for by sampling noise. The tree that wasn't recovered had a λ of only 0.02. The difference between the log likelihood of the samples of the generating tree and the approximating tree was 0.41 bits per example.

For classification, we investigated the performance of mixtures of trees on a the Australian Credit dataset from the UCI repository[2]. The data set has 690 instances of 14-dimensional attribute vectors. Nine attributes are discrete ($2 - 14$ values) and 5 are continuous. The class variable has 6 values. The continuous variables were discretized in $3 - 5$ uniform bins each. We tested mixtures with different values for m and for the edge pruning parameter β. For comparison we tried also mixtures of factorial distributions of different sizes. One tenth of the data, picked randomly at each trial, was used for testing and the rest for training. In the training phase, we learned a MT model of the joint distribution of all the 15 variables.

---

[2] http://www.ics.uci.edu/~mlearn/MLRepository.html

Figure 2: Performance of different algorithms on the Australian Credit dataset. – is mixture of trees with $\beta = 10$, - - is mixture of trees with $beta = 1/m$, --- is mixture of factorial distributions.

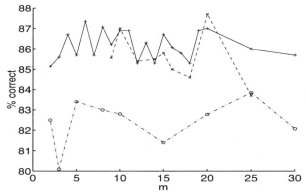

Table 1: a) Mixture of trees compression rates $[\log l_{test}/N_{test}]$. b) Compression rates (bits/digit) for the single digit (Digit) and double digit (Pairs) datasets. MST is mixtures of trees, MF is a mixture of factorial distributions, BR is base rate model, H-WS is Helmholtz Machine trained with the wake-sleep algorithm (Frey et al., 1996), H-MF is Helmholtz Machine trained with the Mean Field approximation, FV is a fully visible bayes net. (*=best)

(a)

m	Digits	Pairs
16	*34.72	79.25
32	34.48	*78.99
64	34.84	79.70
128	34.88	81.26

(b)

Algorithm	Digits	Pairs
gzip	44.3	89.2
BR	59.2	118.4
MF	37.5	92.7
H-MF	39.5	80.7
H-WS	39.1	80.4
FV	35.9	*72.9
MT	*34.7	79.0

In the testing phase, the output of our classifier was chosen to be the class value with the largest posterior probability given the inputs. Figure 2 shows that the results obtained for mixtures of trees are superior to those obtained for mixtures of factorial distributions.For comparison, correct classification rates obtained and cited in (Kontkanen et al., 1996) on training/test sets of the same size are: 87.2next best model (a decision tree called Cal50).

We also tested the basic algorithm as a density estimator by running it on a subset of binary vector representations of handwritten digits and measuring the compression rate. One dataset contained images of single digits in 64 dimensions, the second contained 128 dimensional vectors representing randomly paired digit images. The training, validation and test set contained 6000, 2000, and 5000 exemplars respectively. The data sets, the training conditions and the algorithms we compared with are described in (Frey et al., 1996). We tried mixtures of 16, 32, 64 and 128 trees, fitted by the basic algorithm. The results (shown in table1 averaged over 3 runs) are very encouraging: the mixture of trees is the absolute winner for compressing the simple digits and comes in second as a model for pairs of digits. This suggests that our model (just like the mixture of factorized distributions) is able to perform good compression of the digit data but is unable to discover the independency in the double digit set.

6 CONCLUSIONS

This paper has shown a method of modeling and exploiting sparse dependency structure that is conditioned on values of the data. By using trees, our method avoids the exponential computation demands that plague both inference and structure finding in wider classes of belief nets. The algorithms presented here are linear in m and N and quadratic in $|V|$. Each M step is performing exact maximization over the space of all the tree structures and parameters. The possibility of pruning the edges of the components of a mixture of trees can play a role in classification, as a means of automatically selecting the variables that are relevant for the task.

The importance of using the right priors in constructing models for real-world problems can hardly be understated. In this context, the present paper has presented a broad class of priors that are efficiently handled in the framework of our algorithm and it has shown that this class includes important priors like the MDL prior and the Dirichlet prior.

Acknowledgements

Thanks to Quaid Morris for running the digits and structure finding experiments and to Brendan Frey for providing the digits datasets.

References

Chow, C. K. and Liu, C. N. (1968). Approximating discrete probability distributions with dependence trees. *"IEEE Transactions on Information Theory"*, IT-14(3):462–467.

Dempster, A. P., Laird, N. M., and Rubin, D. B. (1977). Maximum likelihood from incomplete data via the EM algorithm. *Journal of the Royal Statistical Society, B*, 39:1–38.

Frey, B. J., Hinton, G. E., and Dayan, P. (1996). Does the wake-sleep algorithm produce good density estimators? In Touretsky, D., Mozer, M., and Hasselmo, M., editors, *Neural Information Processing Systems*, number 8, pages 661–667. MIT Press.

Friedman, N. and Goldszmidt, M. (1996). Building classifiers using Bayesian networks. In *Proceedings of the National Conference on Artificial Intelligence (AAAI 96)*, pages 1277–1284, Menlo Park, CA. AAAI Press.

Geiger, D. (1992). An entropy-based learning algorithm of bayesian conditional trees. In *Proceedings of the 8th Conference on Uncertainty in AI*, pages 92–97. Morgan Kaufmann Publishers.

Geiger, D. (1996). Knowledge representation and inference in similarity networks and bayesian multinets. *"Artificial Intelligence"*, 82:45–74.

Heckerman, D., Geiger, D., and Chickering, D. M. (1995). Learning Bayesian networks: the combination of knowledge and statistical data. *Machine Learining*, 20(3):197–243.

Kontkanen, P., Myllymaki, P., and Tirri, H. (1996). Constructing bayesian finite mixture models by the EM algorithm. Technical Report C-1996-9, Univeristy of Helsinky, Department of Computer Science.

Meilă, M., Jordan, M. I., and Morris, Q. D. (1997). Estimating dependency structure as a hidden variable. Technical Report AIM–1611,CBCL–151, Massachusetts Institute of Technology, Artificial Intelligence Laboratory.

Pearl, J. (1988). *Probabilistic Reasoning in Intelligent Systems: Networks of Plausible Inference.* Morgan Kaufman Publishers, San Mateo, CA.

Thiesson, B., Meek, C., Chickering, D. M., and Heckerman, D. (1997). Learning mixtures of Bayes networks. Technical Report MSR–POR–97–30, Microsoft Research.

Combining Classifiers Using Correspondence Analysis

Christopher J. Merz
Dept. of Information and Computer Science
University of California, Irvine, CA 92697-3425 U.S.A.
cmerz@ics.uci.edu

Category: Algorithms and Architectures.

Abstract

Several effective methods for improving the performance of a single learning algorithm have been developed recently. The general approach is to create a set of learned models by repeatedly applying the algorithm to different versions of the training data, and then combine the learned models' predictions according to a prescribed voting scheme. Little work has been done in combining the predictions of a collection of models generated by many learning algorithms having different representation and/or search strategies. This paper describes a method which uses the strategies of stacking and correspondence analysis to model the relationship between the learning examples and the way in which they are classified by a collection of learned models. A nearest neighbor method is then applied within the resulting representation to classify previously unseen examples. The new algorithm consistently performs as well or better than other combining techniques on a suite of data sets.

1 Introduction

Combining the predictions of a set of learned models[1] to improve classification and regression estimates has been an area of much research in machine learning and neural networks [Wolpert, 1992, Merz and Pazzani, 1997, Perrone, 1994, Breiman, 1996, Meir, 1995]. The challenge of this problem is to decide which models to rely on for prediction and how much weight to give each. The goal of combining learned models is to obtain a more accurate prediction than can be obtained from any single source alone.

---

[1] A learned model may be anything from a decision/regression tree to a neural network.

Recently, several effective methods have been developed for improving the performance of a single learning algorithm by combining multiple learned models generated using the algorithm. Some examples include bagging [Breiman, 1996], boosting [Freund, 1995], and error correcting output codes [Kong and Dietterich, 1995]. The general approach is to use a particular learning algorithm and a model generation technique to create a set of learned models and then combine their predictions according to a prescribed voting scheme. The models are typically generated by varying the training data using resampling techniques such as bootstrapping [Efron and Tibshirani, 1993] or data partitioning [Meir, 1995]. Though these methods are effective, they are limited to a single learning algorithm by either their model generation technique or their method of combining.

Little work has been done in combining the predictions of a collection of models generated by many learning algorithms each having different representation and/or search strategies. Existing approaches typically place more emphasis on the model generation phase rather than the combining phase [Opitz and Shavlik, 1996]. As a result, the combining method is rather limited. The focus of this work is to present a more elaborate combining scheme, called SCANN, capable of handling any set of learned models, and evaluate it on some real-world data sets. A more detailed analytical and empirical study of the SCANN algorithm is presented in [Merz, 1997].

This paper describes a combining method applicable to model sets that are homogeneous or heterogeneous in their representation and/or search techniques. Section 2 describes the problem and explains some of the caveats of solving it. The SCANN algorithm (Section 3), uses the strategies of stacking [Wolpert, 1992] and correspondence analysis [Greenacre, 1984] to model the relationship between the learning examples and the way in which they are classified by a collection of learned models. A nearest neighbor method is then applied to the resulting representation to classify previously unseen examples.

In an empirical evaluation on a suite of data sets (Section 4), the naive approach of taking the plurality vote (PV) frequently exceeds the performance of the constituent learners. SCANN, in turn, matches or exceeds the performance of PV and several other stacking-based approaches. The analysis reveals that SCANN is not sensitive to having many poor constituent learned models, and it is not prone to overfit by reacting to insignificant fluctuations in the predictions of the learned models.

2   Problem Definition and Motivation

The problem of generating a set of learned models is defined as follows. Suppose two sets of data are given: a learning set $\mathcal{L} = \{(\mathbf{x}_i, y_i), i = 1, \ldots, I\}$ and a test set $\mathcal{T} = \{(\mathbf{x}_t, y_t), t = 1, \ldots, T\}$. $\mathbf{x}_i$ is a vector of input values which are either nominal or numeric values, and $y_i \in \{\mathcal{C}_1, \ldots, \mathcal{C}_C\}$ where C is the number of classes. Now suppose $\mathcal{L}$ is used to build a set of N functions, $\mathcal{F} = \{f_n(x)\}$, each element of which approximates $f(x)$, the underlying function.

The goal here is to combine the predictions of the members of $\mathcal{F}$ so as to find the best approximation of $f(x)$. Previous work [Perrone, 1994] has indicated that the ideal conditions for combining occur when the errors of the learned models are uncorrelated. The approaches taken thus far attempt to generate learned models which make uncorrelated errors by using the same algorithm and presenting different samples of the training data [Breiman, 1996, Meir, 1995], or by adjusting the search heuristic slightly [Opitz and Shavlik, 1996, Ali and Pazzani, 1996].

No single learning algorithm has the right bias for a broad selection of problems.

Therefore, another way to achieve diversity in the errors of the learned models generated is to use completely different learning algorithms which vary in their method of search and/or representation. The intuition is that the learned models generated would be more likely to make errors in different ways. Though it is not a requirement of the combining method described in the next section, the group of learning algorithms used to generate $\mathcal{F}$ will be heterogeneous in their search and/or representation methods (i.e., neural networks, decision lists, Bayesian classifiers, decision trees with and without pruning, etc.). In spite of efforts to diversify the errors committed, it is still likely that some of the errors will be correlated because the learning algorithms have the same goal of approximating f, and they may use similar search strategies and representations. A robust combining method must take this into consideration.

3 Approach

The approach taken consists of three major components: Stacking, Correspondence Analysis, and Nearest Neighbor (SCANN). Sections 3.1-3.3 give a detailed description of each component, and section 3.4 explains how they are integrated to form the SCANN algorithm.

3.1 Stacking

Once a diverse set of models has been generated, the issue of how to combine them arises. Wolpert [Wolpert, 1992] provided a general framework for doing so called *stacked generalization* or *stacking*. The goal of stacking is to combine the members of $\mathcal{F}$ based on information learned about their particular biases with respect to $\mathcal{L}^2$.

The basic premise of stacking is that this problem can be cast as another induction problem where the input space is the (approximated) outputs of the learned models, and the output space is the same as before, i.e.,

$$\mathcal{L}_1 = \{((\hat{f}_1(\mathbf{x}_i), \hat{f}_2(\mathbf{x}_i), \ldots, \hat{f}_N(\mathbf{x}_i)), y_i), i = 1, \ldots, I\}$$

The approximated outputs of each learned model, represented as $\hat{f}_n(\mathbf{x}_i)$, are generated using the following in-sample/out-of-sample approach:

1. Divide the $\mathcal{L}_0$ data up into V partitions.
2. For each partition, v,
   - Train each algorithm on all but partition v to get $\{\hat{f}_n^{-v}\}$.
   - Test each learned model in $\{\hat{f}_n^{-v}\}$ on partition v.
   - Pair the predictions on each example in partition v (i.e., the new *input space*) with the corresponding output, and append the new examples to $\mathcal{L}_1$
3. Return $\mathcal{L}_1$

3.2 Correspondence Analysis

Correspondence Analysis (CA) [Greenacre, 1984] is a method for geometrically exploring the relationship between the rows and columns of a matrix whose entries are categorical. The goal here is to explore the relationship between the training

---

[2] Henceforth $\mathcal{L}$ will be referred to as $\mathcal{L}_0$ for clarity.

Table 1: Correspondence Analysis calculations.

Stage	Symbol	Definition	Description
1	$\mathbf{N}$	$(I \times J)$ indicator matrix	Records votes of learned models.
	n	$\sum_{i=1}^{I} \sum_{j=1}^{J} n_{ij}$	Grand total of table $\mathbf{N}$.
	$\mathbf{r}$	$r_i = n_{i+}/n$	Row masses.
	$\mathbf{c}$	$c_j = n_{+j}/n$	Column masses.
	$\mathbf{P}$	$(1/n)\mathbf{N}$	Correspondence matrix.
	$\mathbf{D_c}$	$(J \times J)$ diagonal matrix	Masses $\mathbf{c}$ on diagonal.
	$\mathbf{D_r}$	$(I \times I)$ diagonal matrix	Masses $\mathbf{r}$ on diagonal.
	$\mathbf{A}$	$\mathbf{D_r}^{-1/2}(\mathbf{P} - \mathbf{rc}^T)\mathbf{D_c}^{-1/2}$	Standardized residuals.
2	$\mathbf{A}$	$\mathbf{U\Gamma V^T}$	SVD of $\mathbf{A}$.
3	$\mathbf{F}$	$\mathbf{D_r}^{-1/2}\mathbf{U\Gamma}$	Principal coordinates of rows.
	$\mathbf{G}$	$\mathbf{D_c}^{-1/2}\mathbf{V\Gamma}$	Principal coordinates of columns.

examples and how they are classified by the learned models. To do this, the prediction matrix, $\mathbf{M}$, is explored where $m_{in} = \hat{f}_n(\mathbf{x}_i)$ ($1 \leq i \leq I$, and $1 \leq n \leq N$). It is also important to see how the predictions for the training examples relate to their true class labels, so the class labels are appended to form $\mathbf{M'}$, an $(I \times J)$ matrix (where $J = N + 1$). For proper application of correspondence analysis, $\mathbf{M'}$ must be converted to an $(I \times (J \cdot C))$ *indicator matrix*, $\mathbf{N}$, where $n_{i,(j \cdot J+c)}$ is a one exactly when $m_{ij} = \mathcal{C}_c$, and zero otherwise.

The calculations of CA may be broken down into three stages (see Table 1). Stage one consists of some preprocessing calculations performed on $\mathbf{N}$ which lead to the *standardized residual matrix*, $\mathbf{A}$. In the second stage, a singular value decomposition (SVD) is performed on $\mathbf{A}$ to redefine it in terms of three matrices: $\mathbf{U}_{(I \times K)}$, $\mathbf{\Gamma}_{(K \times K)}$, and $\mathbf{V}_{(K \times J)}$, where $K = min(I - 1, J - 1)$. These matrices are used in the third stage to determine $\mathbf{F}_{(I \times K)}$ and $\mathbf{G}_{(J \times K)}$, the coordinates of the rows and columns of $\mathbf{N}$, respectively, in the new space. It should be noted that not all K dimensions are necessary. Section 3.4, describes how the final number of dimensions, $K*$, is determined.

Intuitively, in the new geometric representation, two rows, $\mathbf{f}_{p*}$ and $\mathbf{f}_{q*}$, will lie close to one another when examples p and q receive similar predictions from the collection of learned models. Likewise, rows $\mathbf{g}_{r*}$ and $\mathbf{g}_{s*}$ will lie close to to one another when the learned models corresponding to r and s make similar predictions for the set of examples. Finally, each column, r, has a learned model, j', and a class label, c', with which it is associated; $\mathbf{f}_{p*}$ will lie closer to $\mathbf{g}_{r*}$ when model j' predicts class c'.

3.3 Nearest Neighbor

The nearest neighbor algorithm is used to classify points in a weighted Euclidean space. In this scenario, each possible class will be assigned coordinates in the space derived by correspondence analysis. Unclassified examples will be mapped into the new space (as described below), and the class label corresponding to the closest class point is assigned to the example.

Since the actual class assignments for each example reside in the last C columns of $\mathbf{N}$, their coordinates in the new space can be found by looking in the last C *rows* of $\mathbf{G}$. For convenience, these class points will be called $Class_1, \ldots, Class_C$.

To classify an unseen example, $\mathbf{x}_{Test}$, the predictions of the learned models on $\mathbf{x}_{Test}$ must be converted to a *row profile*, $\tilde{\mathbf{r}}^T$, of length $J \cdot C$, where $\tilde{r}^T_{(j \cdot J+c)}$ is $1/J$ exactly

Table 2: Experimental results.

Data set	PV error	SCANN vs PV ratio	S-BP vs PV ratio	S-BAYES vs PV ratio	Best Ind. vs PV ratio
abalone	80.35	**.490**	**.499**	.487	$.535^{BP}$
bal	13.81	**.900**	.859	.992	$.911^{BP}$
breast	4.31	**.886**	.920	.881	$.938^{BP}$
credit	13.99	.999	1.012	1.001	1.054^{BP}
dementia	32.78	.989	1.037	.932	$1.048^{C4.5}$
glass	31.44	1.008	**1.158**	**1.215**	$\mathbf{1.155}^{OC1}$
heart	18.17	.964	.998	.972	$.962^{BP}$
ionosphere	3.05	**.691**	**1.289**	**1.299**	$\mathbf{2.175}^{C4.5}$
iris	4.44	1.017	1.033	**1.467**	1.150^{OC1}
krk	6.67	1.030	1.080	**1.149**	1.159^{NN}
liver	29.33	1.035	1.077	1.024	$\mathbf{1.138}^{CN2}$
lymphography	17.78	1.017	**1.162**	1.100	$.983^{Pebls}$
musk	13.51	**.812**	.889	.835	1.113^{Pebls}
retardation	32.64	**.970**	.960	.990	$.936^{Bayes}$
sonar	23.02	.990	1.079	1.007	1.048^{BP}
vote	5.24	**.903**	.908	.893	$.927^{C4.5}$
wave	21.94	1.008	**1.109**	1.008	$\mathbf{1.200}^{Pebls}$
wdbc	4.27	1.000	1.103	1.007	1.164^{NN}

when $m_{ij} = \mathcal{C}_c$, and zero otherwise. However, since the example is unclassified, $\mathbf{x}_{Test}$ is of length $(J - 1)$ and can only be used to fill the first $((J - 1) \cdot C)$ entries in $\tilde{\mathbf{r}}^T$. For this reason, C different versions are generated, i.e., $\tilde{\mathbf{r}}_1^T, \ldots, \tilde{\mathbf{r}}_C^T$, where each one "hypothesizes" that $\mathbf{x}_{Test}$ belongs to one of the C classes (by putting $1/J$ in the appropriate column). Locating these profiles in the scaled space is a matter of simple matrix multiplication, i.e., $\mathbf{f}_c^T = \tilde{\mathbf{r}}_c^T \mathbf{G}\mathbf{\Gamma}^{-1}$. The $\mathbf{f}_c^T$ which lies closest to a class point, say $Class_{c'}$, is considered the "correct" hypothesized class, and $\mathbf{x}_{Test}$ is assigned the class label c'.

3.4 The SCANN Algorithm

Now that the three main parts of the approach have been described, a summary of the SCANN algorithm can be given as a function of $\mathcal{L}_0$ and the constituent learning algorithms, $\mathcal{A}$. The first step is to use $\mathcal{L}_0$ and $\mathcal{A}$ to generate the stacking data, $\mathcal{L}_1$, capturing the approximated predictions of each learned model. Next, $\mathcal{L}_1$ is used to form the indicator matrix, $\mathbf{N}$. A correspondence analysis is performed on $\mathbf{N}$ to derive the scaled space, $\mathbf{A} = \mathbf{U}\mathbf{\Gamma}\mathbf{V}^T$. The number of dimensions retained from this new representation, $K*$, is the value which optimizes classification on $\mathcal{L}_1$. The resulting scaled space is used to derive the row/column coordinates $\mathbf{F}$ and $\mathbf{G}$, thus geometrically capturing the relationships between the examples, the way in which they are classified, and their position relative to the true class labels. Finally, the nearest neighbor strategy exploits the new representation by predicting which class is most likely according to the predictions made on a novel example.

4 Experimental Results

The constituent learning algorithms, $\mathcal{A}$, spanned a variety of search and/or representation techniques: Backpropagation (BP) [Rumelhart et al., 1986], CN2 [Clark and Niblett, 1989], C4.5 [Quinlan, 1993], OC1 [Salzberg; and Beigel, 1993], PEBLS [Cost, 1993], nearest neighbor (NN), and naive Bayes. Depending on the data set, anywhere from five to eight instantiations of algorithms were applied. The combining strategies evaluated were PV, SCANN, and two other learners trained on $\mathcal{L}_1$: S-BP, and S-Bayes.

The data sets used were taken from the UCI Machine Learning Database Repository [Merz and Murphy, 1996], except for the unreleased medical data sets: *retardation* and *dementia*. Thirty runs per data set were conducted using a training/test partition of 70/30 percent. The results are reported in Table 2. The first column gives the mean error rate over the 30 runs of the baseline combiner, PV. The next three columns ("SCANN vs PV", "S-BP vs PV", and "S-Bayes vs PV") report the ratio of the other combining strategies to the error rate of PV. The column labeled "Best Ind. vs PV" reports the ratio with respect to the model with the best average error rate. The superscript of each entry in this column denotes the winning algorithm. A value less than 1 in the "a vs b" columns represents an improvement by method a over method b. Ratios reported in **boldface** indicate the difference between method a and method b is significant at a level better than 1 percent using a two-tailed sign test.

It is clear that, over the 18 data sets, SCANN holds a statistically significant advantage on 7 sets improving upon PV's classification error by 3-50 percent. Unlike the other combiners, SCANN posts no statistically significant losses to PV (i.e., there were 4 losses each for S-BP and S-Bayes). With the exception of the *retardation* data set, SCANN consistently performs as well or better than the best individual learned model. In the direct comparison of SCANN with the S-BP and S-Bayes, SCANN posts 5 and 4 significant wins, respectively, and no losses.

The most dramatic improvement of the combiners over PV came in the *abalone* data set. A closer look at the results revealed that 7 of the 8 learned models were very poor classifiers with error rates around 80 percent, and the errors of the poor models were highly correlated. This empirically demonstrates PV's known sensitivity to learned models with highly correlated errors. On the other hand, PV performs well on the *glass* and *wave* data sets where the errors of the learned models are measured to be fairly uncorrelated. Here, SCANN performs similarly to PV, but S-BP and S-Bayes appear to be overfitting by making erroneous predictions based on insignificant variations on the predictions of the learned models.

5 Conclusion

A novel method has been introduced for combining the predictions of heterogeneous or homogeneous classifiers. It draws upon the methods of stacking, correspondence analysis and nearest neighbor. In an empirical analysis, the method proves to be insensitive to poor learned models and matches the performance of plurality voting as the errors of the learned models become less correlated.

References

[Ali and Pazzani, 1996] Ali, K. and Pazzani, M. (1996). Error reduction through learning multiple descriptions. *Machine Learning*, 24:173.

[Breiman, 1996] Breiman, L. (1996). Bagging predictors. *Machine Learning*, 24(2):123–40.

[Clark and Niblett, 1989] Clark, P. and Niblett, T. (1989). The CN2 induction algorithm. *Machine Learning*, 3(4):261–283.

[Cost, 1993] Cost, S.; Salzberg, S. (1993). A weighted nearest neighbor algorithm for learning with symbolic features. *Machine Learning*, 10(1):57–78.

[Efron and Tibshirani, 1993] Efron, B. and Tibshirani, R. (1993). *An Introduction to the Bootstrap*. Chapman and Hall, London and New York.

[Freund, 1995] Freund, Y. (1995). Boosting a weak learning algorithm by majority. *Information and Computation*, 121(2):256–285. Also appeared in COLT90.

[Greenacre, 1984] Greenacre, M. J. (1984). *Theory and Application of Correspondence Analysis*. Academic Press, London.

[Kong and Dietterich, 1995] Kong, E. B. and Dietterich, T. G. (1995). Error-correcting output coding corrects bias and variance. In *Proceedings of the 12th International Conference on Machine Learning*, pages 313–321. Morgan Kaufmann.

[Meir, 1995] Meir, R. (1995). Bias, variance and the combination of least squares estimators. In Tesauro, G., Touretzky, D., and Leen, T., editors, *Advances in Neural Information Processing Systems*, volume 7, pages 295–302. The MIT Press.

[Merz, 1997] Merz, C. (1997). Using correspondence analysis to combine classifiers. *Submitted to Machine Learning*.

[Merz and Murphy, 1996] Merz, C. and Murphy, P. (1996). UCI repository of machine learning databases.

[Merz and Pazzani, 1997] Merz, C. J. and Pazzani, M. J. (1997). Combining neural network regression estimates with regularized linear weights. In Mozer, M., Jordan, M., and Petsche, T., editors, *Advances in Neural Information Processing Systems*, volume 9. The MIT Press.

[Opitz and Shavlik, 1996] Opitz, D. W. and Shavlik, J. W. (1996). Generating accurate and diverse members of a neural-network ensemble. In Touretzky, D. S., Mozer, M. C., and Hasselmo, M. E., editors, *Advances in Neural Information Processing Systems*, volume 8, pages 535–541. The MIT Press.

[Perrone, 1994] Perrone, M. P. (1994). Putting it all together: Methods for combining neural networks. In Cowan, J. D., Tesauro, G., and Alspector, J., editors, *Advances in Neural Information Processing Systems*, volume 6, pages 1188–1189. Morgan Kaufmann Publishers, Inc.

[Quinlan, 1993] Quinlan, R. (1993). *C4.5 Programs for Machine Learning*. Morgan Kaufmann, San Mateo, CA.

[Rumelhart et al., 1986] Rumelhart, D. E., Hinton, G. E., and Williams, R. J. (1986). Learning internal representations by error propagation. In Rumelhart, D. E., McClelland, J. L., and the PDP research group., editors, *Parallel distributed processing: Explorations in the microstructure of cognition, Volume 1: Foundations*. MIT Press.

[Salzberg; and Beigel, 1993] Salzberg;, S. M. S. K. S. and Beigel, R. (1993). OC1: Randomized induction of oblique decision trees. In *Proceedings of AAAI-93*. AAAI Pres.

[Wolpert, 1992] Wolpert, D. H. (1992). Stacked generalization. *Neural Networks*, 5:241–259.

Learning Path Distributions using Nonequilibrium Diffusion Networks

Paul Mineiro *
pmineiro@cogsci.ucsd.edu
Department of Cognitive Science
University of California, San Diego
La Jolla, CA 92093-0515

Javier Movellan
movellan@cogsci.ucsd.edu
Department of Cognitive Science
University of California, San Diego
La Jolla, CA 92093-0515

Ruth J. Williams
williams@math.ucsd.edu
Department of Mathematics
University of California, San Diego
La Jolla, CA 92093-0112

Abstract

We propose diffusion networks, a type of recurrent neural network
with probabilistic dynamics, as models for learning natural signals
that are continuous in time and space. We give a formula for the
gradient of the log-likelihood of a path with respect to the drift
parameters for a diffusion network. This gradient can be used to
optimize diffusion networks in the nonequilibrium regime for a wide
variety of problems paralleling techniques which have succeeded in
engineering fields such as system identification, state estimation
and signal filtering. An aspect of this work which is of particular interest to computational neuroscience and hardware design is
that with a suitable choice of activation function, e.g., quasi-linear
sigmoidal, the gradient formula is local in space and time.

1 Introduction

Many natural signals, like pixel gray-levels, line orientations, object position, velocity and shape parameters, are well described as continuous–time continuous–valued
stochastic processes; however, the neural network literature has seldom explored the
continuous stochastic case. Since the solutions to many decision theoretic problems
of interest are naturally formulated using probability distributions, it is desirable
to have a flexible framework for approximating probability distributions on continuous path spaces. Such a framework could prove as useful for problems involving
continuous–time continuous–valued processes as conventional hidden Markov models have proven for problems involving discrete–time sequences.

Diffusion networks are similar to recurrent neural networks, but have probabilistic
dynamics. Instead of a set of ordinary differential equations (ODEs), diffusion
networks are described by a set of stochastic differential equations (SDEs). SDEs
provide a rich language for expressing stochastic temporal dynamics and have proven

---

*To whom correspondence should be addressed.

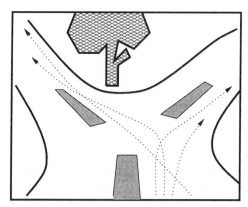

Figure 1: An example where the average of desirable paths yields an undesirable path, namely one that collides with the tree.

useful in formulating continuous–time statistical inference problems, resulting in such solutions as the continuous Kalman filter and generalizations of it like the condensation algorithm (Isard & Blake, 1996).

A formula is given here for the gradient of the log-likelihood of a path with respect to the drift parameters for a diffusion network. Using this gradient we can potentially optimize the model to approximate an entire probability distribution of continuous paths, not just average paths or equilibrium points. Figure 1 illustrates the importance of this kind of learning by showing a case in which learning average paths would have undesirable results, namely collision with a tree. Experience has shown that learning distributions of paths, not just averages, is crucial for dynamic perceptual tasks in realistic environments, e.g., visual contour tracking (Isard & Blake, 1996). Interestingly, with a suitable choice of activation function, e.g., quasi-linear sigmoidal, the gradient formula depends only upon local computations, i.e., no time unfolding or explicit backpropagation of error is needed. The fact that noise localizes the gradient is of potential interest for domains such as theoretical neuroscience, cognitive modeling and hardware design.

2 Diffusion Networks

Hereafter C_n refers to the space of continuous $\mathbf{R}^n$-valued functions over the time interval $[0, T]$, with $T \in \mathbf{R}$, $T > 0$ fixed throughout this discussion.

A diffusion network with parameter $\lambda \in \mathbf{R}^p$ is a random process defined via an Itô SDE of the form

$$dX(t) = \mu(t, X(t), \lambda)dt + \sigma dB(t), \tag{1}$$
$$X(0) \sim \nu,$$

where X is a C_n-valued process that represents the temporal dynamics of the n nodes in the network; $\mu : [0, T] \times \mathbf{R}^n \times \mathbf{R}^p \to \mathbf{R}^n$ is a deterministic function called the drift; $\lambda \in \mathbf{R}^p$ is the vector of drift parameters, e.g., synaptic weights, which are to be optimized; B is a Brownian motion process which provides the random driving term for the dynamics; ν is the initial distribution of the solution; and $\sigma \in \mathbf{R}$, $\sigma > 0$, is a *fixed* constant called the dispersion coefficient, which determines the strength of the noise term. In this paper we do not address the problem of optimizing the dispersion or the initial distribution of X. For the existence and uniqueness in law of the solution to (1) $\mu(\cdot, \cdot, \lambda)$ must satisfy some conditions. For example, it is sufficient that it is Borel measurable and satisfies a linear growth condition: $|\mu(t, x, \lambda)| \leq K_\lambda(1 + |x|)$ for some $K_\lambda > 0$ and all $t \in [0, T]$, $x \in \mathbf{R}^n$; see

(Karatzas & Shreve, 1991, page 303) for details.

It is typically the case that the n-dimensional diffusion network will be used to model d-dimensional observations with $n > d$. In this case we divide X into hidden and observable[1] components, denoted H and O respectively, so that $X = (H, O)$.

Note that with $\sigma = 0$ in equation (1), the model becomes equivalent to a continuous–time deterministic recurrent neural network. Diffusion networks can therefore be thought of as neural networks with "synaptic noise" represented by a Brownian motion process. In addition, diffusion networks have Markovian dynamics, and hidden states if $n > d$; therefore, they are also continuous–time continuous–state hidden Markov models. As with conventional hidden Markov models, the probability density of an observable state sequence plays an important role in the optimization of diffusion networks. However, because X is a continuous–time process, care must taken in defining a probability density.

2.1 Density of a continuous observable path

Let (X^λ, B^λ) defined on some filtered probability space $(\tilde{\Omega}, \tilde{F}, \{\tilde{F}_t\}, \tilde{P})$ be a (weak) solution of (1) with fixed parameter λ. Here $X^\lambda = (H^\lambda, O^\lambda)$ represents the states of the network and is adapted to the filtration $\{\tilde{F}_t\}$, B^λ is an n-dimensional $\{\tilde{F}_t\}$-martingale Brownian motion and the filtration $\{\tilde{F}_t\}$ satisfies the usual conditions (Karatzas and Shreve, 1991, page 300). Let Q^λ be the unique probability law generated by any weak solution of (1) with fixed parameter λ

$$Q^\lambda(A) = \tilde{P}(X^\lambda \in A) \quad \text{for all } A \in \mathcal{F}, \tag{2}$$

where $\mathcal{F}$ is the Borel sigma algebra generated by the open sets of C_n. Setting $\Omega = C_n$, $\Omega_h = C_{n-d}$, and $\Omega_o = C_d$ with associated Borel σ-algebras $\mathcal{F}$, $\mathcal{F}_h$ and $\mathcal{F}_o$, respectively, we have $\Omega = \Omega_h \times \Omega_o$, $\mathcal{F} = \mathcal{F}_h \otimes \mathcal{F}_o$, and we can define the marginal laws for the hidden and observable components of the network by

$$Q_h^\lambda(A_h) = Q^\lambda(A_h \times C_d) \triangleq \tilde{P}(H^\lambda \in A_h) \quad \text{for all } A_h \in \mathcal{F}_h, \tag{3}$$

$$Q_o^\lambda(A_o) = Q^\lambda(C_{n-d} \times A_o) \triangleq \tilde{P}(O^\lambda \in A_o) \quad \text{for all } A_o \in \mathcal{F}_o. \tag{4}$$

For our purposes the appropriate generalization of the notion of a probability density on $\mathbf{R}^m$ to the general probability spaces considered here is the Radon-Nikodym derivative with respect to a reference measure that dominates all members of the family $\{Q^\lambda\}_{\lambda \in \mathbf{R}^p}$ (Poor, 1994, p.264ff). A suitable reference measure P is the law of the solution to (1) with zero drift ($\mu = 0$). The measures induced by this reference measure over $\mathcal{F}_h$ and $\mathcal{F}_o$ are denoted by P_h and P_o, respectively. Since in the reference model there are no couplings between any of the nodes in the network, the hidden and observable processes are independent and it follows that

$$P(A_h \times A_o) = P_h(A_h)P_o(A_o) \quad \text{for all } A_h \in \mathcal{F}_h, A_o \in \mathcal{F}_o. \tag{5}$$

The conditions on μ mentioned above are sufficient to ensure a Radon-Nikodym derivative for each Q^λ with respect to the reference measure. Using Girsanov's Theorem (Karatzas & Shreve, 1991, p.190ff) its form can be shown to be

$$Z^\lambda(\omega) = \frac{dQ^\lambda}{dP}(\omega) = \exp\left\{ \frac{1}{\sigma^2} \int_0^T \mu(t, \omega(t), \lambda) \cdot d\omega(t) \right.$$

$$\left. - \frac{1}{2\sigma^2} \int_0^T |\mu(t, \omega(t), \lambda)|^2 dt \right\}, \quad \omega \in \Omega, \tag{6}$$

---

[1]In our treatment we make no distinction between observables which are inputs and those which are outputs. Inputs can be conceptualized as observables under "environmental control," i.e., whose drifts are independent of both λ and the hidden and output processes.

where the first integral is an Itô stochastic integral. The random variable Z^λ can be interpreted as a likelihood or probability density with respect to the reference model[2]. However equation (6) defines the density of $\mathbf{R}^n$-valued paths of the entire network, whereas our real concern is the density of $\mathbf{R}^d$-valued observable paths. Denoting $\omega \in \Omega$ as $\omega = (\omega_h, \omega_o)$ where $\omega_h \in \Omega_h$ and $\omega_o \in \Omega_o$, note that

$$Q_o^\lambda(A) = \int_{\Omega_h \times \Omega_o} 1_A(\omega_o)\, Q^\lambda(d(\omega_h, \omega_o)) \tag{7}$$

$$= \int_{\Omega_o} 1_A(\omega_o) \left(\int_{\Omega_h} P_h(d\omega_h) Z^\lambda(\omega_h, \omega_o) \right) P_o(d\omega_o), \tag{8}$$

and therefore the Radon-Nikodym derivative of Q_o^λ with respect to P_o, the density of interest, is given by

$$Z_o^\lambda(\omega_o) = \frac{dQ_o^\lambda}{dP_o}(\omega_o) = E^{P_h}[Z^\lambda(\cdot, \omega_o)], \ \omega_o \in \Omega_o. \tag{9}$$

2.2   Gradient of the density of an observable path

The gradient of Z_o^λ with respect to λ is an important quantity for iterative optimization of cost functionals corresponding to a variety of problems of interest, e.g., maximum likelihood estimation of diffusion parameters for continuous path density estimation. Formal differentiation[3] of (9) yields

$$\nabla_\lambda \log Z_o^\lambda(\omega_o) = E^{P_h}[Z_{h|o}^\lambda(\cdot, \omega_o) \nabla_\lambda \log Z^\lambda(\cdot, \omega_o)], \tag{10}$$

where

$$Z_{h|o}^\lambda(\omega) \triangleq \frac{Z^\lambda(\omega)}{Z_o^\lambda(\omega_o)}, \tag{11}$$

$$\nabla_\lambda \log Z^\lambda(\omega) = \frac{1}{\sigma^2} \int_0^T J(t, \omega(t), \lambda) \cdot dI(\omega, t), \tag{12}$$

$$J_{jk}(t, x, \lambda) \triangleq \frac{\partial \mu_k(t, x, \lambda)}{\partial \lambda_j}, \tag{13}$$

$$I(\omega, t) \triangleq \omega(t) - \omega(0) - \int_0^t \mu(s, \omega(s), \lambda) ds. \tag{14}$$

Equation (10) states that the gradient of the density of an observable path can be found by clamping the observable nodes to that path and performing an average of $Z_{h|o}^\lambda \nabla_\lambda \log Z^\lambda$ with respect to P_h, i.e., average with respect to the hidden paths distributed as a scaled Brownian motion. This makes intuitive sense: the output gradient of the log density is a weighted average of the total gradient of the log density, where each hidden path contributes according to its likelihood $Z_{h|o}^\lambda$ given the output.

In practice to evaluate the gradient, equation (10) must be approximated. Here we use Monte Carlo techniques, the efficiency of which can be improved by sampling according to a density which reduces the variance of the integrand. Such a density

---

[2]To ease interpretation of (6) consider the simpler case of a one-dimensional Gaussian random variable with mean μ and variance σ^2. The ratio of the density of such a model with respect to an equivalent model with zero mean is $\exp(\frac{1}{\sigma^2}\mu x - \frac{1}{2\sigma^2}\mu^2)$. Equation (6) can be viewed as a generalization of this same idea to Brownian motion.

[3]See (Levanony et al., 1990) for sufficient conditions for the differentiation in equation (10) to be valid.

is available for models with hidden dynamics which do not explicitly depend upon the observables, i.e., the observable nodes do not send feedback connections to the hidden states. Models which obey this constraint are henceforth denoted *factorial*. Denoting μ_h and μ_o as the hidden and observable components, respectively, of the drift vector, and B_h and B_o as the hidden and observable components, respectively, of the Brownian motion, for a factorial network we have

$$dH(t) = \mu_h(t, H(t), \lambda)dt + \sigma dB_h(t), \tag{15}$$

$$dO(t) = \mu_o(t, H(t), O(t), \lambda)dt + \sigma dB_o(t). \tag{16}$$

The drift for the hidden variables does not depend on the observables, and Girsanov's theorem gives us an explicit formula for the density of the hidden process.

$$Z_h^\lambda(\omega_h) = \frac{dQ_h^\lambda}{dP_h}(\omega_h) = \exp\left\{ \frac{1}{\sigma^2} \int_0^T \mu_h(t, \omega_h(t), \lambda) \cdot d\omega_h(t) \right.$$
$$\left. - \frac{1}{2\sigma^2} \int_0^T |\mu_h(t, \omega_h(t), \lambda)|^2 dt \right\}. \tag{17}$$

Equations (9) and (10) can then be written in the form

$$Z_o^\lambda(\omega_o) = E^{Q_h^\lambda}[Z_{o|h}(\cdot, \omega_o)], \tag{18}$$

$$\nabla_\lambda \log Z_o^\lambda(\omega_o) = E^{Q_h^\lambda}\left[\frac{Z_{o|h}^\lambda(\cdot, \omega_o)}{Z_o^\lambda(\omega_o)} \nabla_\lambda \log Z^\lambda(\cdot, \omega_o) \right], \tag{19}$$

where

$$Z_{o|h}^\lambda(\omega) \triangleq \frac{Z^\lambda(\omega)}{Z_h^\lambda(\omega_h)} = \exp\left\{ \frac{1}{\sigma^2} \int_0^T \mu_o(t, \omega(t), \lambda) \cdot d\omega_o(t) \right.$$
$$\left. - \frac{1}{2\sigma^2} \int_0^T |\mu_o(t, \omega(t), \lambda)|^2 dt \right\}. \tag{20}$$

Note the expectations are now performed using the measure Q_h^λ. We can easily generate samples according to Q_h^λ by numerically integrating equation (15), and in practice this leads to more efficient Monte Carlo approximations of the likelihood and gradient.

3   Example: Noisy Sinusoidal Detection

This problem is a simple example of using diffusion networks for signal detection. The task was to detect a sinusoid in the presence of additive Gaussian noise. Stimuli were generated according to the following process

$$Y(t, \omega) = 1_A(\omega)\frac{1}{\pi}\sin(4\pi t) + B(t, \omega), \tag{21}$$

where $t \in [0, 1/2]$. Here Y is assumed anchored in a probability space $(\Omega, \mathcal{F}, P)$ large enough to accommodate the event A which indicates a signal or noise trial. Note that under P, B is a Brownian motion on C_d independent of A.

A model was optimized using 100 samples of equation (21) given $\omega \in A$, i.e., 100 stimuli containing a signal. The model had four hidden units and one observable unit ($n = 5$, $d = 1$). The drift of the model was given by

$$\mu(t, x, \lambda) = \theta + W \cdot g(x), \tag{22}$$

$$g_j(x) = \frac{1}{1 + e^{-x_j}} \, , \, j \in \{1, 2, 3, 4, 5\},$$

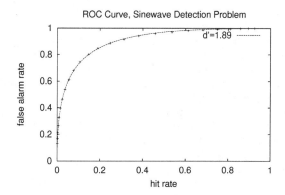

Figure 2: Receiver operating characteristic (ROC) curve for a diffusion network performing a signal detection task involving noisy sinusoids. Dotted line: Detection performance estimated numerically using 10000 novel stimuli. Solid line: Best fit curve corresponding to $d' = 1.89$. This value of d' corresponds to performance within 1.5% of the Bayesian limit.

where $\theta \in \mathbf{R}^5$ and W is a 5x5 real-valued connection matrix. In this case $\lambda = \{\{\theta_i\}, \{W_{ij}\}, i, j = 1, \ldots, 5\}$. The connections from output to hidden units were set to zero, allowing use of the more efficient techniques for factorial networks described above. The initial distribution for the model was a δ-function at $(1, -1, 1, -1, 0)$. The model was numerically simulated with $\Delta t = 0.01$, and 100 hidden samples were used to approximate the likelihood and gradient of the log–likelihood, according to equations (18) and (19). The conjugate gradient algorithm was used for training, with the log-likelihood of the data as the cost function.

Once training was complete, the parameter estimation was tested using 10000 novel stimuli and the following procedure. Given a new stimuli y we used the model to estimate the likelihood $\hat{Z}_o(Y \mid A) \triangleq Z_o^{\hat{\lambda}}(Y)$, where $\hat{\lambda}$ is the parameter vector at the end of training. The decision rule employed was

$$D(Y) = \begin{cases} \text{signal} & \text{if } \hat{Z}_o(Y \mid A) > b, \\ \text{noise} & \text{otherwise,} \end{cases} \tag{23}$$

where $b \in \mathbf{R}$ is a bias term representing assumptions about the apriori probability of a signal trial. By sweeping across different values of b the receiver-operator characteristic (ROC) curve is generated. This curve shows how the probability of a hit, $P(D = \text{signal} \mid A)$, and the probability of a false alarm, $P(D = \text{signal} \mid A^c)$, are related. From this curve the parameter d', a measure of sensitivity independent of apriori assumptions, can be estimated. Figure 2 shows the ROC curve as found by numerical simulation, and the curve obtained by the best fit value $d' = 1.89$. This value of d' corresponds to a 82.7% correct detection rate for equal prior signal probabilities.

The theoretically ideal observer can be derived for this problem, since the profile of the unperturbed signal is known exactly (Poor, 1994, p. 278ff). For this problem the optimal observer achieves $d'_{max} = 2$, which implies at equal probabilities for signal and noise trials, the Bayesian limit corresponds to a 84.1% correct detection rate. The detection system based upon the diffusion network is therefore operating close to the Bayesian limit, but was designed using only implicit information, i.e., 100 training examples, about the structure of the signal to be detected, in contrast to the explicit information required to design the optimal Bayesian classifier.

4 Discussion

As a hybrid of neural networks and hidden Markov models, diffusion networks combine the power of continuous–time continuous–state representation and the robustness of a probabilistic approach. In this paper we present a framework for identifying the drift parameters of a diffusion network, which builds upon previous work on diffusion, stochastic filtering, and artificial neural networks (Feigin, 1976; Campillo & Le Gland, 1989; Levanony et al., 1990; Apolloni & de Falco, 1991; Movellan, 1994). We have not treated the problems of identifying the initial distribution or the dispersion of the network, both of which are probably important for achieving good performance on realistic tasks. Identification of the dispersion is especially intriguing since it is (with appropriate scaling of the drift) equivalent to identifying the timescale of the model. An obvious application would be in speech recognition, where normalization of timescale is needed to correct for variable utterance speed, even for single-speaker systems (Rabiner & Juang, 1993, p.200).

Future work will focus on developing techniques for identifying the dispersion and initial distribution, improving numerical procedures used for computing the likelihood, and applying diffusions to continuous–time continuous–state perceptual problems such as visual contour tracking (Isard & Blake, 1996).

Acknowledgements

The authors thank Anthony Gamst for helpful discussion. Paul Mineiro is supported by an NSF Minority Graduate Fellowship. Research of R. J. Williams is supported in part by NSF Grants GER 9023335 and DMS 9703891.

References

Apolloni, B. & de Falco, D. (1991). Learning by asymmetric parallel Boltzmann machines. *Neural Computation*, *3*(3), 402–408.

Campillo, F. & Le Gland, F. (1989). MLE For Partially Observed Diffusions – Direct Maximization vs. the EM Algorithm. *Stochastic Processes and Their Applications*, *33*(2), 245–274.

Feigin, P. (1976). Maximum Likelihood Estimation for Continuous–Time Stochastic Processes. *Advances in Applied Probability*, *8*, 712–736.

Isard, M. & Blake, A. (1996). Contour Tracking by Stochastic Propagation of Conditional Density. *Proc. European Conf. Computer Vision*, 343–356.

Karatzas, I. & Shreve, S. (1991). *Brownian Motion and Stochastic Calculus*. Springer.

Levanony, D., Shwartz, A., & Zeitouni, O. (1990). Continuous-Time Recursive Estimation. In E. Arikan (Ed.), *Communication, Control, and Signal Processing*. Elsevier Science Publishers.

Movellan, J. (1994). A Local Algorithm to Learn Trajectories with Stochastic Neural Networks. In J. Cowan, G. Tesauro, & J. Alspector (Eds.), *Advances in Neural Information Processing Systems*, volume 6, pages 83–87. Morgan Kaufmann.

Poor, H. V. (1994). *An Introduction to Signal Detection and Estimation*. Springer-Verlag.

Rabiner, L. R. & Juang, H. (1993). *Fundamentals of Speech Recognition*. Prentice Hall.

Learning Generative Models with the Up-Propagation Algorithm

Jong-Hoon Oh and H. Sebastian Seung
Bell Labs, Lucent Technologies
Murray Hill, NJ 07974
{jhoh|seung}@bell-labs.com

Abstract

Up-propagation is an algorithm for inverting and learning neural network generative models. Sensory input is processed by inverting a model that generates patterns from hidden variables using top-down connections. The inversion process is iterative, utilizing a negative feedback loop that depends on an error signal propagated by bottom-up connections. The error signal is also used to learn the generative model from examples. The algorithm is benchmarked against principal component analysis in experiments on images of handwritten digits.

In his doctrine of unconscious inference, Helmholtz argued that perceptions are formed by the interaction of bottom-up sensory data with top-down expectations. According to one interpretation of this doctrine, perception is a procedure of sequential hypothesis testing. We propose a new algorithm, called up-propagation, that realizes this interpretation in layered neural networks. It uses top-down connections to generate hypotheses, and bottom-up connections to revise them.

It is important to understand the difference between up-propagation and its ancestor, the backpropagation algorithm[1]. Backpropagation is a learning algorithm for *recognition* models. As shown in Figure 1a, bottom-up connections recognize patterns, while top-down connections propagate an error signal that is used to learn the recognition model.

In contrast, up-propagation is an algorithm for inverting and learning *generative* models, as shown in Figure 1b. Top-down connections generate patterns from a set of hidden variables. Sensory input is processed by inverting the generative model, recovering hidden variables that could have generated the sensory data. This operation is called either pattern recognition or pattern analysis, depending on the meaning of the hidden variables. Inversion of the generative model is done iteratively, through a negative feedback loop driven by an error signal from the bottom-up connections. The error signal is also used for learning the connections

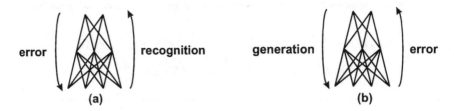

Figure 1: Bottom-up and top-down processing in neural networks. (a) Backprop network (b) Up-prop network

in the generative model.

Up-propagation can be regarded as a generalization of principal component analysis (PCA) and its variants like Conic[2] to nonlinear, multilayer generative models. Our experiments with images of handwritten digits demonstrate that up-propagation learns a global, nonlinear model of a pattern manifold. With its global parametrization, this model is distinct from locally linear models of pattern manifolds[3].

1   INVERTING THE GENERATIVE MODEL

The generative model is a network of $L + 1$ layers of neurons, with layer 0 at the bottom and layer L at the top. The vectors x_t, $t = 0 \ldots L$, are the activations of the layers. The pattern x_0 is generated from the hidden variables x_L by a top-down pass through the network,

$$x_{t-1} = f(W_t x_t), \qquad t = L, \ldots, 1 . \tag{1}$$

The nonlinear function f acts on vectors component by component. The matrix W_t contains the synaptic connections from the neurons in layer t to the neurons in layer $t - 1$. A bias term b_{t-1} can be added to the argument of f, but is omitted here. It is convenient to define auxiliary variables $\hat{x}_t$ by $x_t = f(\hat{x}_t)$. In terms of these auxiliary variables, the top-down pass is written as

$$\hat{x}_{t-1} = W_t f(\hat{x}_t) \tag{2}$$

Given a sensory input d, the top-down generative model can be inverted by finding hidden variables x_L that generate a pattern x_0 matching d. If some of the hidden variables represent the identity of the pattern, the inversion operation is called *recognition*. Alternatively, the hidden variables may just be a more compact representation of the pattern, in which case the operation is called *analysis* or *encoding*. The inversion is done iteratively, as described below.

In the following, the operator $*$ denotes elementwise multiplication of two vectors, so that $z = x * y$ means $z_i = x_i y_i$ for all i. The bottom-up pass starts with the mismatch between the sensory data d and the generated pattern x_0,

$$\delta_0 = f'(\hat{x}_0) * (d - x_0) , \tag{3}$$

which is propagated upwards by

$$\delta_t = f'(\hat{x}_t) * (W_t^T \delta_{t-1}) . \tag{4}$$

When the error signal reaches the top of the network, it is used to update the hidden variables x_L,

$$\Delta x_L \propto W_L^T \delta_{L-1} . \tag{5}$$

This update closes the negative feedback loop. Then a new pattern x_0 is generated by a top-down pass (1), and the process starts over again.

This iterative inversion process performs gradient descent on the cost function $\frac{1}{2}|d - x_0|^2$, subject to the constraints (1). This can be proved using the chain rule, as in the traditional derivation of the backprop algorithm. Another method of proof is to add the equations (1) as constraints, using Lagrange multipliers,

$$\frac{1}{2}|d - f(\hat{x}_0)|^2 + \sum_{t=1}^{L} \delta_{t-1}^T [\hat{x}_{t-1} - W_t f(\hat{x}_t)] . \tag{6}$$

This derivation has the advantage that the bottom-up activations δ_t have an interpretation as Lagrange multipliers.

Inverting the generative model by negative feedback can be interpreted as a process of sequential hypothesis testing. The top-down connections generate a hypothesis about the sensory data. The bottom-up connections propagate an error signal that is the disagreement between the hypothesis and data. When the error signal reaches the top, it is used to generate a revised hypothesis, and the generate-test-revise cycle starts all over again. Perception is the convergence of this feedback loop to the hypothesis that is most consistent with the data.

2 LEARNING THE GENERATIVE MODEL

The synaptic weights W_t determine the types of patterns that the network is able to generate. To learn from examples, the weights are adjusted to improve the network's generation ability. A suitable cost function for learning is the reconstruction error $\frac{1}{2}|d - x_0|^2$ averaged over an ensemble of examples. Online gradient descent with respect to the synaptic weights is performed by a learning rule of the form

$$\Delta W_t \propto \delta_{t-1} x_t^T . \tag{7}$$

The same error signal δ that was used to invert the generative model is also used to learn it.

The batch form of the optimization is compactly written using matrix notation. To do this, we define the matrices $D, X_0, \ldots, X_L$ whose columns are the vectors d, $x_0, \ldots, x_L$ corresponding to examples in the training set. Then computation and learning are the minimization of

$$\min_{X_L, W_t} \frac{1}{2}|D - X_0|^2 , \tag{8}$$

subject to the constraint that

$$X_{t-1} = f(W_t X_t) , \qquad t = 1, \ldots, L . \tag{9}$$

In other words, up-prop is a dual minimization with respect to hidden variables and synaptic connections. Computation minimizes with respect to the hidden variables X_L, and learning minimizes with respect to the synaptic weight matrices W_t.

From the geometric viewpoint, up-propagation is an algorithm for learning pattern manifolds. The top-down pass (1) maps an n_L-dimensional vector x_L to an n_0-dimensional vector x_0. Thus the generative model parametrizes a continuous n_L-dimensional manifold embedded in n_0-dimensional space. Inverting the generative model is equivalent to finding the point on the manifold that is closest to the sensory data. Learning the generative model is equivalent to deforming the manifold to fit a database of examples.

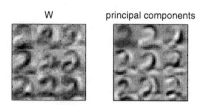

Figure 2: One-step generation of handwritten digits. Weights of the 256-9 up-prop network (left) versus the top 9 principal components (right)

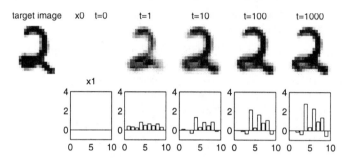

Figure 3: Iterative inversion of a generative model as sequential hypothesis testing. A fully trained 256–9 network is inverted to generate an approximation to a target image that was not previously seen during training. The stepsize of the dynamics was fixed to 0.02 to show time evolution of the system.

Pattern manifolds are relevant when patterns vary continuously. For example, the variations in the image of a three-dimensional object produced by changes of viewpoint are clearly continuous, and can be described by the action of a transformation group on a prototype pattern. Other types of variation, such as deformations in the shape of the object, are also continuous, even though they may not be readily describable in terms of transformation groups. Continuous variability is clearly not confined to visual images, but is present in many other domains. Many existing techniques for modeling pattern manifolds, such as PCA or PCA mixtures[3], depend on linear or locally linear approximations to the manifold. Up-prop constructs a globally parametrized, nonlinear manifold.

3   ONE-STEP GENERATION

The simplest generative model of the form (1) has just one step ($L = 1$). Up-propagation minimizes the cost function

$$\min_{X_1, W_1} \frac{1}{2} |D - f(W_1 X_1)|^2 \ . \tag{10}$$

For a linear f this reduces to PCA, as the cost function is minimized when the vectors in the weight matrix W_1 span the same space as the top principal components of the data D.

Up-propagation with a one-step generative model was applied to the USPS database[4], which consists of example images of handwritten digits. Each of the 7291 training and 2007 testing images was normalized to a 16×16 grid with pixel intensities in the range $[0, 1]$. A separate model was trained for each digit class. The nonlinearity f was the logistic function. Batch optimization of (10) was done by

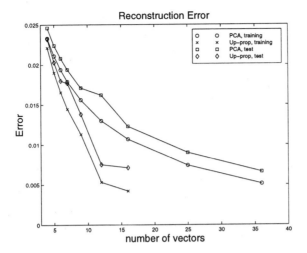

Figure 4: Reconstruction error for 256–n networks as a function of n. The error of PCA with n principal components is shown for comparison. The up-prop network performs better on both the training set and test set.

gradient descent with adaptive stepsize control by the Armijo rule[5]. In most cases, the stepsize varied between 10^{-1} and 10^{-3}, and the optimization usually converged within 10^3 epochs. Figure 2 shows the weights of a 256–9 network that was trained on 731 different images of the digit "two." Each of the 9 subimages is the weight vector of a top-level neuron. The top 9 principal components are also shown for comparison.

Figure 3 shows the time evolution of a fully trained 256–9 network during iterative inversion. The error signal from the bottom layer x_0 quickly activates the top layer x_1. At early times, all the top layer neurons have similar activation levels. However, the neurons with weight vectors more relevant to the target image become dominant soon, and the other neurons are deactivated.

The reconstruction error (10) of the up-prop network was much better than that of PCA. We trained 10 different up-prop networks, one for each digit, and these were compared with 10 corresponding PCA models. Figure 4 shows the average squared error per pixel that resulted. A 256–12 up-prop network performed as well as PCA with 36 principal components.

4   TWO-STEP GENERATION

Two-step generation is a richer model, and is learned using the cost function

$$\min_{X_2, W_1, W_2} \frac{1}{2} |D - f(W_1 f(W_2 X_2))|^2 . \tag{11}$$

Note that a nonlinear f is necessary for two-step generation to have more representational power than one-step generation. When this two-step generative model was trained on the USPS database, the weight vectors in W_1 learned features resembling principal components. The activities of the X_1 neurons tended to be close to their saturated values of one or zero.

The reconstruction error of the two-step generative network was compared to that of the one-step generative network with the same number of neurons in the top layer.

Our 256–25–9 network outperformed our 256–9 network on the test set, though both networks used nine hidden variables to encode the sensory data. However, the learning time was much longer, and iterative inversion was also slow. While up-prop for one-step generation converged within several hundred epochs, up-prop for two-step generation often needed several thousand epochs or more to converge. We often found long plateaus in the learning curves, which may be due to the permutation symmetry of the network architecture[6].

5 DISCUSSION

To summarize the experiments discussed above, we constructed separate generative models, one for each digit class. Relative to PCA, each generative model was superior at encoding digits from its corresponding class. This enhanced generative ability was due to the use of nonlinearity.

We also tried to use these generative models for recognition. A test digit was classified by inverting all the generative models, and then choosing the one best able to generate the digit. Our tests of this recognition method were not encouraging. The nonlinearity of up-propagation tended to improve the generation ability of models corresponding to all classes, not just the model corresponding to the correct classification of the digit. Therefore the improved encoding performance did not immediately transfer to improved recognition.

We have not tried the experiment of training one generative model on all the digits, with some of the hidden variables representing the digit class. In this case, pattern recognition could be done by inverting a single generative model. It remains to be seen whether this method will work.

Iterative inversion was surprisingly fast, as shown in Figure 3, and gave solutions of surprisingly good quality in spite of potential problems with local minima, as shown in Figure 4. In spite of these virtues, iterative inversion is still a problematic method. We do not know whether it will perform well if a single generative model is trained on multiple pattern classes. Furthermore, it seems a rather indirect way of doing pattern recognition.

The up-prop generative model is deterministic, which handicaps its modeling of pattern variability. The model can be dressed up in probabilistic language by defining a prior distribution $P(x_L)$ for the hidden variables, and adding Gaussian noise to x_0 to generate the sensory data. However, this probabilistic appearance is only skin deep, as the sequence of transformations from x_L to x_0 is still completely deterministic. In a truly probabilistic model, like a belief network, every layer of the generation process adds variability.

In conclusion, we briefly compare up-propagation to other algorithms and architectures.

1. In backpropagation[1], only the recognition model is explicit. Iterative gradient descent methods can be used to invert the recognition model, though this implicit generative model generally appears to be inaccurate[7, 8].

2. Up-propagation has an explicit generative model, and recognition is done by inverting the generative model. The accuracy of this implicit recognition model has not yet been tested empirically. Iterative inversion of generative models has also been proposed for linear networks[2, 9] and probabilistic belief networks[10].

3. In the autoencoder[11] and the Helmholtz machine[12], there are separate

models of recognition and generation, both explicit. Recognition uses only bottom-up connections, and generation uses only top-down connections. Neither process is iterative. Both processes can operate completely independently; they only interact during learning.

4. In attractor neural networks[13, 14] and the Boltzmann machine[15], recognition and generation are performed by the same recurrent network. Each process is iterative, and each utilizes both bottom-up and top-down connections. Computation in these networks is chiefly based on positive, rather than negative feedback.

Backprop and up-prop suffer from a lack of balance in their treatment of bottom-up and top-down processing. The autoencoder and the Helmholtz machine suffer from inability to use iterative dynamics for computation. Attractor neural networks lack these deficiencies, so there is incentive to solve the problem of learning attractors[14].

This work was supported by Bell Laboratories. JHO was partly supported by the Research Professorship of the LG-Yonam Foundation. We are grateful to Dan Lee for helpful discussions.

References

[1] D. E. Rumelhart, G. E. Hinton, and R. J. Williams. Learning internal representations by back-propagating errors. *Nature*, 323:533–536, 1986.

[2] D. D. Lee and H. S. Seung. Unsupervised learning by convex and conic coding. *Adv. Neural Info. Proc. Syst.*, 9:515–521, 1997.

[3] G. E. Hinton, P. Dayan, and M. Revow. Modeling the manifolds of images of handwritten digits. *IEEE Trans. Neural Networks*, 8:65–74, 1997.

[4] Y. LeCun et al. Learning algorithms for classification: a comparison on handwritten digit recognition. In J.-H. Oh, C. Kwon, and S. Cho, editors, *Neural networks: the statistical mechanics perspective*, pages 261–276, Singapore, 1995. World Scientific.

[5] D. P. Bertsekas. *Nonlinear programming*. Athena Scientific, Belmont, MA, 1995.

[6] K. Kang, J.-H. Oh, C. Kwon, and Y. Park. Generalization in a two-layer neural network. *Phys. Rev.*, E48:4805–4809, 1993.

[7] J. Kindermann and A. Linden. Inversion of neural networks by gradient descent. *Parallel Computing*, 14:277–286, 1990.

[8] Y. Lee. Handwritten digit recognition using K nearest-neighbor, radial-basis function, and backpropagation neural networks. *Neural Comput.*, 3:441–449, 1991.

[9] R. P. N. Rao and D. H. Ballard. Dynamic model of visual recognition predicts neural response properties in the visual cortex. *Neural Comput.*, 9:721–63, 1997.

[10] L. K. Saul, T. Jaakkola, and M. I. Jordan. Mean field theory for sigmoid belief networks. *J. Artif. Intell. Res.*, 4:61–76, 1996.

[11] G. W. Cottrell, P. Munro, and D. Zipser. Image compression by back propagation: an example of extensional programming. In N. E. Sharkey, editor, *Models of cognition: a review of cognitive science*. Ablex, Norwood, NJ, 1989.

[12] G. E. Hinton, P. Dayan, B. J. Frey, and R. M. Neal. The "wake-sleep" algorithm for unsupervised neural networks. *Science*, 268:1158–1161, 1995.

[13] H. S. Seung. Pattern analysis and synthesis in attractor neural networks. In K.-Y. M. Wong, I. King, and D.-Y. Yeung, editors, *Theoretical Aspects of Neural Computation: A Multidisciplinary Perspective*, Singapore, 1997. Springer-Verlag.

[14] H. S. Seung. Learning continuous attractors in recurrent networks. *Adv. Neural Info. Proc. Syst.*, 11, 1998.

[15] D. H. Ackley, G. E. Hinton, and T. J. Sejnowski. A learning algorithm for Boltzmann machines. *Cognitive Science*, 9:147–169, 1985.

An Incremental Nearest Neighbor Algorithm with Queries

Joel Ratsaby*
N.A.P. Inc.
Hollis, New York

Abstract

We consider the general problem of learning multi-category classification from labeled examples. We present experimental results for a nearest neighbor algorithm which actively selects samples from different pattern classes according to a querying rule instead of the *a priori* class probabilities. The amount of improvement of this query-based approach over the passive batch approach depends on the complexity of the Bayes rule. The principle on which this algorithm is based is general enough to be used in any learning algorithm which permits a model-selection criterion and for which the error rate of the classifier is calculable in terms of the complexity of the model.

1 INTRODUCTION

We consider the general problem of learning multi-category classification from labeled examples. In many practical learning settings the time or sample size available for training are limited. This may have adverse effects on the accuracy of the resulting classifier. For instance, in learning to recognize handwritten characters typical time limitation confines the training sample size to be of the order of a few hundred examples. It is important to make learning more efficient by obtaining only training data which contains significant information about the separability of the pattern classes thereby letting the learning algorithm participate actively in the sampling process. Querying for the class labels of specificly selected examples in the input space may lead to significant improvements in the generalization error (cf. Cohn, Atlas & Ladner, 1994, Cohn, 1996). However in learning pattern recognition this is not always useful or possible. In the handwritten recognition problem, the computer could ask the user for labels of selected patterns generated by the computer

---

*The author's coordinates are: Address: Hamered St. #2, Ra'anana, ISRAEL. Email: jer@ee.technion.ac.il

however labeling such patterns are not necessarily representative of his handwriting style but rather of his reading recognition ability. On the other hand it is possible to let the computer (learner) select particular pattern classes, not necessarily according to their *a priori* probabilities, and then obtain randomly drawn patterns according to the underlying unknown class-conditional probability distribution. We refer to such selective sampling as *sample querying*. Recent theory (cf. Ratsaby, 1997) indicates that such freedom to select different classes at any time during the training stage is beneficial to the accuracy of the classifier learnt. In the current paper we report on experimental results for an incremental algorithm which utilizes this sample-querying procedure.

2 THEORETICAL BACKGROUND

We use the following setting: Given M distinct pattern classes each with a class conditional probability density $f_i(x)$, $1 \le i \le M$, $x \in \mathbb{R}^d$, and a priori probabilities p_i, $1 \le i \le M$. The functions $f_i(x)$, $1 \le i \le M$, are assumed to be unknown while the p_i are assumed to be known or easily estimable as is the case of learning character recognition. For a sample-size vector $m = [m_1, \ldots, m_M]$ where $\sum_{i=1}^{M} m_i = \overline{m}$ denote by $\zeta^m = \{(x_j, y_j)\}_{j=1}^{\overline{m}}$ a sample of labeled examples consisting of m_i example from pattern class i where y_j, $1 \le j \le \overline{m}$, are chosen *not* necessarily at random from $\{1, 2, \ldots, M\}$, and the corresponding x_j are drawn at random i.i.d. according to the class conditional probability density $f_{y_j}(x)$. The expected misclassification error of a classifier c is referred to as the *loss* of c and is denoted by $L(c)$. It is defined as the probability of misclassification of a randomly drawn x with respect to the underlying mixture probability density function $f(x) = \sum_{i=1}^{M} p_i f_i(x)$. The loss is commonly represented as $L(c) = \mathrm{E} 1_{\{x: c(x) \ne y(x)\}}$, where $1_{\{x \in A\}}$ is the indicator function of a set A, expectation is taken with respect to the joint probability distribution $f_y(x) p(y)$ where $p(y)$ is a discrete probability distribution taking values p_i over $1 \le i \le M$, while y denotes the label of the class whose distribution $f_y(x)$ was used to draw x. The loss $L(c)$ may also be written as $L(c) = \sum_{i=1}^{M} p_i \mathrm{E}_i 1_{\{c(x) \ne i\}}$ where E_i denotes expectation with respect to $f_i(x)$. The pattern recognition problem is to learn based on ζ^m the optimal classifier, also known as the *Bayes classifier*, which by definition has minimum loss which we denote by L^*.

A multi-category classifier c is represented as a vector $c(x) = [c_1(x), \ldots, c_M(x)]$ of *boolean classifiers*, where $c_i(x) = 1$ if $c(x) = i$, and $c_i(x) = 0$ otherwise, $1 \le i \le M$. The loss $L(c)$ of a multi-category classifier c may then be expressed as the average of the losses of its component classifiers, i.e., $L(c) = \sum_{i=1}^{M} p_i L(c_i)$ where for a boolean classifier c_i the loss is defined as $L(c_i) = \mathrm{E}_i 1_{\{c_i(x) \ne 1\}}$. As an estimate of $L(c)$ we define the *empirical loss* $L_m(c) = \sum_{i=1}^{M} p_i L_{m_i}(c)$ where $L_{m_i}(c) = \frac{1}{m_i} \sum_{j: y_j = i} 1_{\{c(x_j) \ne i\}}$ which may also can be expressed as $L_{m_i}(c_i) = \frac{1}{m_i} \sum_{j: y_j = i} 1_{\{c_i(x_j) \ne 1\}}$.

The family of all classifiers is assumed to be decomposed into a multi-structure $S = S_1 \times S_2 \times \cdots \times S_M$, where S_i is a nested structure (cf. Vapnik, 1982) of boolean families $\mathcal{B}_{k_{j_i}}$, $j_i = 1, 2, \ldots$, for $1 \le i \le M$, i.e., $S_1 = \mathcal{B}_{k_1}, \mathcal{B}_{k_2}, \ldots, \mathcal{B}_{k_{j_1}}, \ldots$, $S_2 = \mathcal{B}_{k_1}, \mathcal{B}_{k_2}, \ldots, \mathcal{B}_{k_{j_2}}, \ldots$, up to $S_M = \mathcal{B}_{k_1}, \mathcal{B}_{k_2}, \ldots, \mathcal{B}_{k_{j_M}}, \ldots$, where $k_{j_i} \in \mathbb{Z}_+$ denotes the VC-dimension of $\mathcal{B}_{k_{j_i}}$ and $\mathcal{B}_{k_{j_i}} \subseteq \mathcal{B}_{k_{j_i+1}}$, $1 \le i \le M$. For any fixed positive integer vector $j \in \mathbb{Z}_+^M$ consider the class of vector classifiers $\mathcal{H}_{k(j)} = \mathcal{B}_{k_{j_1}} \times \mathcal{B}_{k_{j_2}} \times \cdots \times \mathcal{B}_{k_{j_M}} \equiv \mathcal{H}_k$ where we take the liberty in dropping the multi-index j and write k instead of $k(j)$. Define by $\mathcal{G}_k$ the subfamily of $\mathcal{H}_k$ consisting of classifiers c that are well-defined, i.e., ones whose components c_i, $1 \leq i \leq M$ satisfy $\bigcup_{i=1}^{M}\{x : c_i(x) = 1\} = \mathbb{R}^d$ and $\{x : c_i(x) = 1\} \bigcap \{x : c_j(x) = 1\} = \emptyset$, for $1 \leq i \neq j \leq M$.

From the Vapnik-Chervonenkis theory (cf. Vapnik, 1982, Devroye, Gyorfi & Lugosi, 1996) it follows that the loss of any boolean classifier $c_i \in \mathcal{B}_{k_{j_i}}$ is, with high confidence, related to its empirical loss as $L(c_i) \leq L_{m_i}(c_i) + \epsilon(m_i, k_{j_i})$ where $\epsilon(m_i, k_{j_i}) = const \sqrt{k_{j_i} \ln m_i / m_i}$, $1 \leq i \leq M$, where henceforth we denote by $const$ any constant which does not depend on the relevant variables in the expression. Let the vectors $m = [m_1, \ldots, m_M]$ and $k \equiv k(j) = [k_{j_1}, \ldots, k_{j_M}]$ in $\mathbb{Z}_{+}^{M}$. Define $\epsilon(m, k) = \sum_{i=1}^{M} p_i \epsilon(m_i, k_{j_i})$. It follows that the deviation between the empirical loss and the loss is bounded uniformly over all multi-category classifiers in a class $\mathcal{G}_k$ by $\epsilon(m, k)$. We henceforth denote by c_k^* the optimal classifier in $\mathcal{G}_k$, i.e., $c_k^* = \mathrm{argmin}_{c \in \mathcal{G}_k} L(c)$ and $\hat{c}_k = \mathrm{argmin}_{c \in \mathcal{G}_k} L_m(c)$ is the empirical loss minimizer over the class $\mathcal{G}_k$.

The above implies that the classifier $\hat{c}_k$ has a loss which is no more than $L(c_k^*) + \epsilon(m, k)$. Denote by k^* the minimal complexity of a class $\mathcal{G}_k$ which contains the Bayes classifier. We refer to it as the *Bayes complexity* and henceforth assume $k_i^* < \infty$, $1 \leq i \leq M$. If k^* was known then based on a sample of size $\overline{m}$ with a sample size vector $m = [m_1, \ldots, m_M]$ a classifier $\hat{c}_{k^*}$ whose loss is bounded from above by $L^* + \epsilon(m, k^*)$ may be determined where $L^* = L(c_{k^*}^*)$ is the Bayes loss. This bound is minimal with respect to k by definition of k^* and we refer to it as the *minimal criterion*. It can be further minimized by selecting a sample of size vector $m^* = \mathrm{argmin}_{\{m \in \mathbb{Z}_{+}^{M} : \sum_{i=1}^{M} m_i = \overline{m}\}} \epsilon(m, k^*)$. This basically says that more examples should be queried from pattern classes which require more complex discriminating rules within the Bayes classifier. Thus sample-querying via minimization of the minimal criterion makes learning more efficient through tuning the subsample sizes to the complexity of the Bayes classifier. However the Bayes classifier depends on the underlying probability distributions which in most interesting scenarios are unknown thus k^* should be assumed unknown. In (Ratsaby, 1997) an incremental learning algorithm, based on Vapnik's structural risk minimization, generates a random complexity sequence $\hat{k}(n)$, corresponding to a sequence of empirical loss minimizers $\hat{c}_{\hat{k}(n)}$ over $\mathcal{G}_{\hat{k}(n)}$, which converges to k^* with increasing time n for learning problems with a zero Bayes loss. Based on this, a sample-query rule which achieves the same minimization is defined without the need to know k^*. We briefly describe the main ideas next.

At any time n, the criterion function is $\epsilon(\cdot, \hat{k}(n))$ and is defined over the m-domain $\mathbb{Z}_{+}^{M}$. A gradient descent step of a fixed size is taken to minimize the current criterion. After a step is taken, a new sample-size vector $m(n + 1)$ is obtained and the difference $m(n + 1) - m(n)$ dictates the sample-query at time n, namely, the increment in subsample size for each of the M pattern classes. With increasing n the vector sequence $m(n)$ gets closer to an *optimal path* defined as the set which is comprised of the solutions to the minimization of $\epsilon(m, k^*)$ under all different constraints of $\sum_{i=1}^{M} m_i = \overline{m}$, where $\overline{m}$ runs over the positive integers. Thus for all large n the sample-size vector $m(n)$ is optimal in that it minimizes the minimal criterion $\epsilon(\cdot, k^*)$ for the current total sample size $\overline{m}(n)$. This constitutes the sample-querying procedure of the learning algorithm. The remaining part does empirical loss minimization over the current class $\mathcal{G}_{\hat{k}(n)}$ and outputs $\hat{c}_{\hat{k}(n)}$. By assumption, since the Bayes classifier is contained in $\mathcal{G}_{k^*}$, it follows that for all large n, the loss $L(\hat{c}_{\hat{k}(n)}) \leq L^* + \min_{\{m \in \mathbb{Z}_{+}^{M} : \sum_{i=1}^{M} m_i = \overline{m}(n)\}} \epsilon(m, k^*)$, which is basically the minimal criterion mentioned above. Thus the algorithm produces a classifier $\hat{c}_{\hat{k}(n)}$ with a minimal loss even when the Bayes complexity k^* is unknown.

In the next section we consider specific model classes consisting of nearest-neighbor classifiers on which we implement this incremental learning approach.

3 INCREMENTAL NEAREST-NEIGHBOR ALGORITHM

Fix and Hodges , cf. Silverman & Jones (1989), introduced the simple but powerful nearest-neighbor classifier which based on a labeled training sample $\{(x_i, y_i)\}_{i=1}^{\overline{m}}$, $x_i \in \mathbb{R}^d$, $y_i \in \{1, 2, \ldots, M\}$, when given a pattern x, it outputs the label y_j corresponding to the example whose x_j is closest to x. Every example in the training sample is used for this decision (we denote such an example as a *prototype*) thus the empirical loss is zero. The condensed nearest-neighbor algorithm (Hart, 1968) and the reduced nearest neighbor algorithm (Gates, 1972) are procedures which aim at reducing the number of prototypes while maintaining a zero empirical loss. Thus given a training sample of size $\overline{m}$, after running either of these procedures, a nearest neighbor classifier having a zero empirical loss is generated based on $\overline{s} \leq \overline{m}$ prototypes. Learning in this manner may be viewed as a form of empirical loss minimization with a complexity regularization component which puts a penalty proportional to the number of prototypes.

A cell boundary $e_{i,j}$ of the voronoi diagram (cf. Preparata & Shamos, 1985) corresponding to a multi-category nearest-neighbor classifier c is defined as the $(d-1)$-dimensional perpendicular-bisector hyperplane of the line connecting the x-component of two prototypes x_i and x_j. For a fixed $l \in \{1, \ldots, M\}$, the collection of voronoi cell-boundaries based on pairs of prototypes of the form (x_i, l), (x_j, q) where $q \neq l$, forms the boundary which separates the decision region labeled l from its complement and represents the boolean nearest-neighbor classifier c_l. Denote by k_l the number of such cell-boundaries and denote by s_l the number of prototypes from a total of m_l examples from pattern class l. The value of k_l may be calculated directly from the knowledge of the s_l prototypes, $1 \leq l \leq M$, using various algorithms. The boolean classifier c_l is an element of an infinite class of boolean classifiers based on partitions of $\mathbb{R}^d$ by arrangements of k_l hyperplanes of dimensionality $d-1$ where each of the cells of a partition is labeled either 0 or 1. It follows, cf. Devroye et. al. (1996), that the loss of a multi-category nearest-neighbor classifier c which consists of s_l prototypes out of m_l examples, $1 \leq l \leq M$, is bounded as $L(c) \leq L_m(c) + \epsilon(m, k)$, where the *a priori* probabilities are taken as known, $m = [m_1, \ldots, m_M]$, $k = [k_1, \ldots, k_M]$ and $\epsilon(m, k) = \sum_{l=1}^{M} p_l \epsilon(m_l, k_l)$, where $\epsilon(m_l, k_l) = const \sqrt{((d+1)k_l \ln m_l + (ek_l/d)^d)/m_l}$. Letting k^* denote the Bayes complexity then $\epsilon(\cdot, k^*)$ represents the minimal criterion.

The next algorithm uses the Condense and Reduce procedures in order to generate a sequence of classifiers $\hat{c}_{\hat{k}(n)}$ with a complexity vector $\hat{k}(n)$ which tends to k^* as $n \to \infty$. A sample-querying procedure referred to as Greedy Query (GQ) chooses at any time n to increment the single subsample of pattern class $j^*(n)$ where $m_{j^*(n)}$ is the direction of maximum descent of the criterion $\epsilon(\cdot, \hat{k}(n))$ at the current sample-size vector $m(n)$. For the part of the algorithm which utilizes a Delaunay-Triangulation procedure we use the fast Fortune's algorithm (cf. O'Rourke) which can be used only for dimensionality $d = 2$. Since all we are interested is in counting Voronoi borders between all adjacent Voronoi cells then an efficient computation is possible also for dimensions $d > 2$ by resorting to linear programming for computing the adjacencies of facets of a polyhedron, cf. Fukuda (1997).

Incremental Nearest Neighbor (INN) Algorithm

Initialization: (Time $n = 0$)

Let increment-size Δ be a fixed small positive integer. Start with $m(0) = [c, \ldots, c]$, where c is a small positive integer. Draw $\zeta^{m(0)} = \{\zeta^{m_j(0)}\}_{j=1}^{M}$ where $\zeta^{m_j(0)}$ consists of $m_j(0)$ randomly drawn i.i.d. examples from pattern class j.

While (number of available examples $\geq \Delta$) **Do:**

   1. **Call Procedure CR**: $\hat{c}_{\hat{k}(n)} = CR(\zeta^{m(n)})$.

   2. **Call Procedure GQ**: $m(n+1) = GQ(n)$.

   3. $n := n + 1$.

End While

//Used up all examples.

Output: NN-classifier $\hat{c}_{\hat{k}(n)}$.

Procedure Condense-Reduce (CR)

Input: Sample $\zeta^{m(n)}$ stored in an array $A[]$ of size $\overline{m}(n)$.

Initialize: Make only the first example $A[1]$ be a prototype.

//Condense

Do:

$ChangeOccured := $ FALSE.

For $i = 1, \ldots, \overline{m}(n)$:

   • **Classify** $A[i]$ based on available prototypes using the NN-Rule.

   • **If** not correct **then**

      – Let $A[i]$ be a prototype.

      – $ChangeOccured := $ TRUE.

   • **End If**

End For

While ($ChangeOccured$).

//Reduce

Do:

$ChangeOccured := $ FALSE.

For $i = 1, \ldots, \overline{m}(n)$:

   • **If** $A[i]$ is a prototype **then** classify it using the remaining prototypes by the NN-Rule.

   • **If** correct **then**

      – Make $A[i]$ be not a prototype.

      – $ChangeOccured := $ TRUE.

   • **End If**

End For

While ($ChangeOccured$).

Run Delaunay-Triangulation Let $\hat{k}(n) = [\hat{k}_1, \ldots, \hat{k}_M]$, $\hat{k}_i$ denotes the number of Voronoi-cell boundaries associated with the $\hat{s}_i$ prototypes.

Return (NN-classifier with complexity vector $\hat{k}(n)$).

Procedure Greedy-Query (GQ)

Input: Time n.

$$j^*(n) := \mathrm{argmax}_{1 \leq j \leq M} \left| \frac{\partial}{\partial m_j} \epsilon(m, \hat{k}(n)) \right|_{|_{m(n)}}$$

Draw: Δ new i.i.d. examples from class $j^*(n)$. Denote them by ζ.

Update Sample: $\zeta^{m_{j^*}(n)(n+1)} := \zeta^{m_{j^*}(n)(n)} \bigcup \zeta$, while $\zeta^{m_i(n+1)} := \zeta^{m_i(n)}$, for $1 \leq i \neq j^*(n) \leq M$.

Return: $(m(n) + \Delta\, e_{j^*(n)})$, where e_j is an all zero vector except 1 at j^{th} element.

3.1 EXPERIMENTAL RESULTS

We ran algorithm INN on several two-dimensional ($d = 2$) multi-category classification problems and compared its generalization error versus total sample size $\overline{m}$ with that of batch learning, the latter uses Procedure CR (but not Procedure GQ) with uniform subsample proportions, i.e., $m_i = \frac{\overline{m}}{M}$, $1 \leq i \leq M$.

We ran three classification problems consisting of 4 equiprobable pattern classes with a zero Bayes loss. The generalization curves represent the average of 15 independent learning runs of the empirical error on a fixed size test set. Each run (both for INN and Batch learning) consists of 80 independent experiments where each differs by 10 in the sample size used for training where the maximum sample size is 800. We call an experiment a success if INN results in a lower generalization error than Batch. Let p be the probability of INN beating Batch. We wish to reject the hypothesis H that $p = \frac{1}{2}$ which says that INN and Batch are approximately equal in performance. The results are displayed in Figure 1 as a series of pairs, the first picture showing the pattern classes of the specific problem while the second shows the learning curves for the two learning algorithms. Algorithm INN outperformed the simple Batch approach with a reject level of less than 1%, the latter ignoring the inherent Bayes complexity and using an equal subsample size for each of the pattern classes. In contrast, the INN algorithm learns, incrementally over time, which of the classes are harder to separate and queries more from these pattern classes.

References

Cohn D., Atlas L., Ladner R. (1994), Improving Generalization with Active Learning. *Machine Learning*, Vol 15, p.201-221.

Devroye L., Gyorfi L. Lugosi G. (1996). "A Probabilistic Theory of Pattern Recognition", Springer Verlag.

Fukuda K. (1997). Frequently Asked Questions in Geometric Computation. Technical report, Swiss Federal Institute of technology, Lausanne. Available at `ftp://ftp.ifor.ethz.ch/pub/fukuda/reports`.

Gates, G. W. (1972) The Reduced Nearest Neighbor Rule. *IEEE Trans. Info. Theo.*, p.431-433.

Hart P. E. (1968) The Condensed Nearest Neighbor Rule. *IEEE Trans. on Info. Theo.*, Vol. IT-14, No. 3.

O'rourke J. (1994). "Computational Geometry in C". Cambridge University Press.

Ratsaby, J. (1997) Learning Classification with Sample Queries. Electrical Engineering Dept., Technion, CC PUB #196. Available at URL http://www.ee.technion.ac.il/ jer/iandc.ps.

Rivest R. L., Eisenberg B. (1990), On the sample complexity of pac-learning using random and chosen examples. *Proceedings of the 1990 Workshop on Computational Learning Theory*, p. 154-162, Morgan Kaufmann, San Maeto, CA.

B. W. Silverman and M. C. Jones. E. Fix and J. l. Hodges (1951): An important contribution to nonparametric discriminant analysis and density estimation— commentary on Fix and Hodges (1951). *International statistical review*, 57(3), p.233-247, 1989.

Vapnik V.N., (1982), "Estimation of Dependences Based on Empirical Data", Springer-Verlag, Berlin.

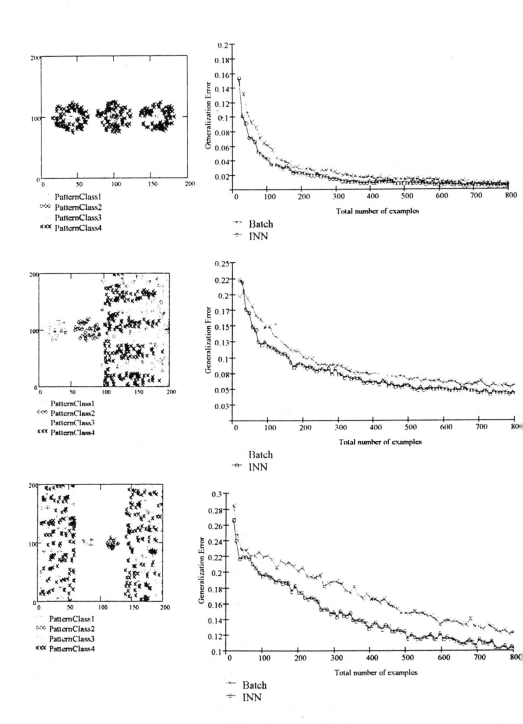

Figure 1. Three different Pattern Classification Problems and Learning
Curves of the INN-Algorithm compared to Batch Learning.

RCC Cannot Compute Certain FSA, Even with Arbitrary Transfer Functions

Mark Ring
RWCP Theoretical Foundation GMD Laboratory
GMD — German National Research Center for Information Technology
Schloss Birlinghoven
D-53 754 Sankt Augustin, Germany
email: Mark.Ring@GMD.de

Abstract

Existing proofs demonstrating the computational limitations of Recurrent Cascade Correlation and similar networks (Fahlman, 1991; Bachrach, 1988; Mozer, 1988) explicitly limit their results to units having sigmoidal or hard-threshold transfer functions (Giles et al., 1995; and Kremer, 1996). The proof given here shows that *for any* finite, discrete transfer function used by the units of an RCC network, there are finite-state automata (FSA) that the network cannot model, no matter how many units are used. The proof also applies to *continuous* transfer functions with a finite number of fixed-points, such as sigmoid and radial-basis functions.

1 Introduction

The Recurrent Cascade Correlation (RCC) network was proposed by Fahlman (1991) to offer a fast and efficient alternative to fully connected recurrent networks. The network is arranged such that each unit has only a single recurrent connection: the connection that goes from itself to itself. Networks with the same structure have been proposed by Mozer (Mozer, 1988) and Bachrach (Bachrach, 1988). This structure is intended to allow simplified training of recurrent networks in the hopes of making them computationally feasible. However, this increase in efficiency comes at the cost of computational power: the networks' computational capabilities are limited *regardless of the power of their activation functions*. The remaining input to each unit consists of the input to the network as a whole together with the outputs from all units lower in the RCC network. Since it is the structure of the network and not the learning algorithm that is of interest here, only the structure will be described in detail.

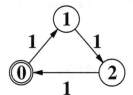

Figure 1: This finite-state automaton was shown by Giles et al. (1995) to be un-representable by an RCC network whose units have hard-threshold or sigmoidal transfer functions. The arcs are labeled with transition labels of the FSA which are given as input to the RCC network. The nodes are labeled with the output values that the network is required to generate. The node with an inner circle is an accepting or *halting* state.

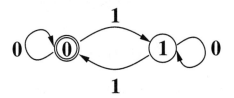

Figure 2: This finite-state automaton is one of those shown by Kremer (1996) not to be representable by an RCC network whose units have a hard-threshold or sigmoidal transfer function. This FSA computes the parity of the inputs seen so far.

The functionality of a network of N RCC units, $U_0, ..., U_{N-1}$ can be described in the following way:

$$V_0(t) = f_0(\vec{i}(t), V_0(t-1)) \tag{1}$$

$$V_x(t) = f_x(\vec{i}(t), V_x(t-1), V_{x-1}(t), V_{x-2}(t), ..., V_0(t)), \tag{2}$$

where $V_x(t)$ is the output value of U_x at time step t, and $\vec{i}(t)$ is the input to the network at time step t. The value of each unit is determined from: (1) the network input at the current time step, (2) its own value at the previous time step, and (3) the output values of the units lower in the network at the current time step. Since learning is not being considered here, the weights are assumed to be constant.

2   Existing Proofs

The proof of Giles, et al (1995) showed that an RCC network whose units had a hard-threshold or sigmoidal transfer function cannot produce outputs that oscillate with a period greater than two when the network input is constant. (An oscillation has a period of x if it repeats itself every x steps.) Thus, the FSA shown in Figure 1 cannot be modeled by such an RCC network, since its output (shown as node labels) oscillates at a period greater than two given constant input. Kremer (1996) refined the class of FSA representable by an RCC network showing that, if the input to the net oscillates with period p, then the output can only oscillate with a period of ω, where ω is one of p's factors (or of $2p$'s factors if p is odd). An unrepresentable example, therefore, is the parity FSA shown in Figure 2, whose output has a period of four given the following input (of period two): $0, 1, 0, 1, ...$

Both proofs, that by Giles et al. and that by Kremer, are explicitly designed with

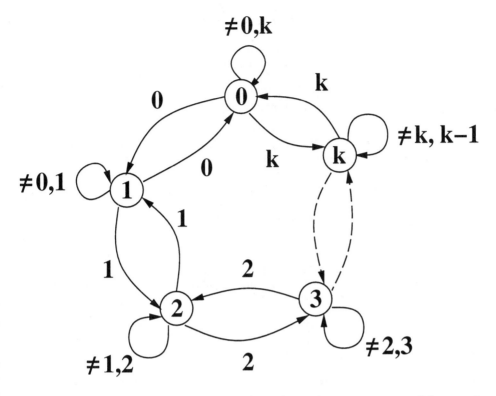

Figure 3: This finite-state automaton cannot be modeled with any RCC network whose units are capable of representing only k discrete outputs. The values within the circles are the state names and the output expected from the network. The arcs describe transitions from state to state, and their values represent the input given to the network when the transition is made. The dashed lines indicate an arbitrary number of further states between state 3 and state k which are connected in the same manner as states 1, 2, and 3. (All states are halting states.)

hard-threshold and sigmoidal transfer functions in mind, and can say nothing about other transfer functions. In other words, these proofs do not demonstrate the limitations of the RCC-type network *structure*, but about the use of threshold units within this structure. The following proof is the first that actually demonstrates the limitations of the single-recurrent-link network structure.

3   Details of the Proof

This section proves that RCC networks are incapable even in principle of modeling certain kinds of FSA, regardless of the sophistication of each unit's transfer function, provided only that the transfer function be discrete and finite, meaning only that the units of the RCC network are capable of generating a fixed number, k, of distinct output values. (Since all functions implemented on a discrete computer fall into this category, this assumption is minor. Furthermore, as will be discussed in Section 4, the outputs of most interesting continuous transfer functions reduce to only a small number of distinct values.) This generalized RCC network is proven here to be incapable of modeling the finite-state automaton shown in Figure 3.

For ease of exposition, let us call any FSA of the form shown in Figure 3 an RF^{k+1} for *Ring FSA with $k+1$ states*.[1] Further, call a unit whose output can be any of k distinct values and whose input includes its own previous output, a DRU^k for *Discrete Recurrent Unit*. These units are a generalization of the units used by RCC networks in that the specific transfer function is left unspecified. By proving the network is limited when its units are DRU^k's proves the limitations of the network's *structure* regardless of the transfer function used.

Clearly, a DRU^{k+1} with a sufficiently sophisticated transfer function could by itself model an RF^{k+1} by simply allocating one of its $k+1$ output values for each of the $k+1$ states. At each step it would receive as input the last state of the FSA and the next transition and could therefore compute the next state. By restricting the units in the least conceivable manner, i.e., by reducing the number of distinct output values to k, the RCC network becomes incapable of modeling any RF^{k+1} regardless of how many DRU^k's the network contains. This will now be proven.

The proof is inductive and begins with the first unit in the network, which, after being given certain sequences of inputs, becomes incapable of distinguishing among any states of the FSA. The second step, the inductive step, proves that no finite number of such units can assist a unit higher in the RCC network in making a distinction between any states of the RF^{k+1}.

Lemma 1 *No DRU^k whose input is the current transition of an RF^{k+1} can reliably distinguish among any states of the RF^{k+1}. More specifically, at least one of the DRU^k's k output values can be generated in all of the RF^{k+1}'s $k+1$ states.*

Proof: Let us name the DRU^k's k distinct output values $V^0, V^1, ..., V^{k-1}$. The mapping function implemented by the DRU^k can be expressed as follows:

$$(V^x, i) \Rightarrow V^y,$$

which indicates that when the unit's last output was V^x and its current input is i, then its next output is V^y.

Since an RF^k is cyclical, the arithmetic in the following will also be cyclical (i.e., modular):

$$x \oplus y \equiv \begin{cases} x + y & \text{if } x + y < k \\ x + y - k & \text{if } x + y \geq k \end{cases}$$

$$x \ominus y \equiv \begin{cases} x - y & \text{if } x \geq y \\ x + k - y & \text{if } x < y \end{cases}$$

where $0 \leq x < k$ and $0 \leq y < k$.

Since it is impossible for the DRU^k to represent each of the RF^{k+1}'s $k+1$ states with a distinct output value, at least two of these states must be represented ambiguously by the same value. That is, there are two RF^{k+1} states a and b and one DRU^k value $V^{a/b}$ such that $V^{a/b}$ can be generated by the unit both when the FSA is in state a and when it is in state b. Furthermore, this value *will* be generated by the unit given an appropriate sequence of inputs. (Otherwise the value is *unreachable*, serves no purpose, and can be discarded, reducing the unit to a DRU^{k-1}.)

Once the DRU^k has generated $V^{a/b}$, it cannot in the next step distinguish whether the FSA's current state is a or b. Since the FSA could be in either state a or b, the next state after a b transition could be either a or $b \oplus 1$. That is:

$$(V^{a/b}, b) \Rightarrow V^{a/b \oplus 1}, \tag{3}$$

---

[1] Thanks to Mike Mozer for suggesting this catchy name.

where $a \ominus b \geq b \ominus a$ and $k > 1$. This new output value $V^{a/b\oplus1}$ can therefore be generated when the FSA is in either state a or state $b \oplus 1$. By repeatedly replacing b with $b \oplus 1$ in Equation 3, all states from b to $a \ominus 1$ can be shown to share output values with state a, i.e., $V^{a/b}, V^{a/b\oplus1}, V^{a/b\oplus2}, ..., V^{a/a\ominus2}, V^{a/a\ominus1}$ all exist.

Repeatedly substituting $a \ominus 1$ and a for a and b respectively in the last paragraph produces values $V^{x/y}$ $\forall x, y \in 0, 1, ..., k+1$. There is, therefore, at least one value that can be generated by the unit in both states of every possible pair of states.

Since there are $\binom{k+1}{2}$ distinct pairs but only k distinct output values, and since

$$\left\lceil \frac{\binom{k+1}{2}}{k} \right\rceil > 1,$$

when $k > 1$, then not all of these pairs can be represented by unique V values. At least two of these pairs must share the same output value, and this implies that some $V^{a/b/c}$ exists that can be output by the unit in any of the three FSA states $a, b,$ and c.

Starting with

$$(V^{a/b/c}, c) \Rightarrow V^{a/b/c\oplus1},$$

and following the same argument given above for $V^{a/b}$, there must be a $V^{x/y/z}$ for all triples of states $x, y,$ and z. Since there are $\binom{k+1}{3}$ distinct triples but only k distinct output values, and since

$$\left\lceil \frac{\binom{k+1}{3}}{k} \right\rceil > 1,$$

where $k > 3$, some $V^{a/b/c/d}$ must also exist.

This argument can be followed repeatedly since:

$$\left\lceil \frac{\binom{k+1}{m}}{k} \right\rceil > 1,$$

for all $m < k + 1$, including when $m = k$. Therefore, there is at least one $V^{0/1/2/../k/k+1}$ that can be output by the unit in all $k + 1$ states of the RF^{k+1}. Call this value and any other that can be generated in all FSA states V^k. All V^k's are reachable (else they could be discarded and the above proof applied for $\text{DRU}^l, l < k$). When a V^k is output by a DRU^k, it does not distinguish any states of the RF^{k+1}.

Lemma 2 *Once a DRU^k outputs a V^k, all future outputs will also be V^k 's.*

Proof: The proof is simply by inspection, and is shown in the following table:

Actual State	Transition	Next State
x	x	$x \oplus 1$
$x \oplus 1$	x	x
$x \oplus 2$	x	$x \oplus 2$
$x \oplus 3$	x	$x \oplus 3$
...	...	...
$x \ominus 2$	x	$x \ominus 2$
$x \ominus 1$	x	$x \ominus 1$

If the unit's last output value was a V^k, then the FSA might be in any of its $k+1$ possible states. As can be seen, if at this point any of the possible transitions is given as input, the next state can also be any of the $k+1$ possible states. Therefore, no future input can ever serve to lessen the unit's ambiguity.

Theorem 1 *An RCC network composed of any finite number of DRU^k's cannot model an RF^{k+1}.*

Proof: Let us describe the transitions of an RCC network of N units by using the following notation:

$$(\langle V_{N-1}, V_{N-2}, ..., V_1, V_0 \rangle, i) \Rightarrow \langle V'_{N-1}, V'_{N-2}, ..., V'_1, V'_0 \rangle,$$

where V_m is the output value of the m'th unit (i.e., U_m) before the given input, i, is seen by the network, and V'_m is U_m's value after i has been processed by the network. The first unit, U_0, receives only i and V_0 as input. Every other unit U_x receives as input i and V_x as well as $V'_y, y < x$.

Lemma 1 shows that the first unit, U_0, will eventually generate a value V_0^k, which can be generated in any of the RF^{k+1} states. From Lemma 2, the unit will continue to produce V_0^k values after this point.

Given any finite number N of DRU^k's, $U_{m-1}, ..., U_0$ that are producing their V_k values, $V_{N-1}^k, ..., V_0^k$, the next higher unit, U_N, will be incapable of disambiguating all states by itself, i.e., at least two FSA states, a and b, will have overlapping output values, $V_N^{a/b}$. Since none of the units $U_{N-1}, ..., U_0$ can distinguish between any states (including a and b),

$$(\langle V_N^{a/b}, V_{N-1}^k, ..., V_1^k, V_0^k \rangle, b) \Rightarrow \langle V_N^{a/b \oplus 1}, V_{N-1}^k, ..., V_1^k, V_0^k \rangle,$$

assuming that $b \ominus a \geq a \ominus b$ and $k > 1$. The remainder of the proof follows identically along the lines developed for Lemmas 1 and 2. The result of this development is that U_N also has a set of reachable output values V_N^k that can be produced in any state of the FSA. Once one such value is produced, no less-ambiguous value is ever generated. Since no RCC network containing any number of DRU^k's can over time distinguish among any states of an RF^{k+1}, no such RCC network can model such an FSA.

4 Continuous Transfer Functions

Sigmoid functions can generate a theoretically infinite number of output values; if represented with 32 bits, they can generate 2^{32} outputs. This hardly means, however, that all such values are of use. In fact, as was shown by Giles et al. (1995), if the input remains constant for a long enough period of time (as it can in all RF^{k+1}'s), the output of sigmoid units will converge to a constant value (a fixed point) or oscillate between two values. This means that a unit with a sigmoid transfer function is in principle a DRU^2. Most useful continuous transfer functions (radial-basis functions, for example), exhibit the same property, reducing to only a small number of distinct output values when given the same input repeatedly. The results shown here are therefore not merely theoretical, but are of real practical significance and apply to any network whose recurrent links are restricted to self connections.

5 Conclusion

No RCC network can model any FSA containing an RF^{k+1} (such as that shown in Figure 3), given units limited to generating k possible output values, regardless of the sophistication of the transfer function that generates these values. This places an upper bound on the computational capabilities of an RCC network. Less sophisticated transfer functions, such as the sigmoid units investigated by Giles et al. and Kremer may have even greater limitations. Figure 2, for example, could be modeled by a single sufficiently sophisticated DRU^2, but cannot be modeled by an RCC network composed of hard-threshold or sigmoidal units (Giles et al., 1995; Kremer, 1996) because these units cannot exploit all mappings from inputs to outputs. By not assuming arbitrary transfer functions, previous proofs could not isolate the network's structure as the source of RCC's limitations.

References

Bachrach, J. R. (1988). Learning to represent state. Master's thesis, Department of Computer and Information Sciences, University of Massachusetts, Amherst, MA 01003.

Fahlman, S. E. (1991). The recurrent cascade-correlation architecture. In Lippmann, R. P., Moody, J. E., and Touretzky, D. S., editors, *Advances in Neural Information Processing Systems 3*, pages 190–196, San Mateo, California. Morgan Kaufmann Publishers.

Giles, C., Chen, D., Sun, G., Chen, H., Lee, Y., and Goudreau, M. (1995). Constructive learning of recurrent neural networks: Problems with recurrent cascade correlation and a simple solution. *IEEE Transactions on Neural Networks*, 6(4):829.

Kremer, S. C. (1996). Finite state automata that recurrent cascade-correlation cannot represent. In Touretzky, D. S., Mozer, M. C., and Hasselno, M. E., editors, *Advances in Neural Information Processing Systems 8*, pages 679–686. MIT Press. In Press.

Mozer, M. C. (1988). A focused back-propagation algorithm for temporal pattern recognition. Technical Report CRG–TR–88–3, Department of Psychology, University of Toronto.

EM Algorithms for PCA and SPCA

Sam Roweis[*]

Abstract

I present an expectation-maximization (EM) algorithm for principal component analysis (PCA). The algorithm allows a few eigenvectors and eigenvalues to be extracted from large collections of high dimensional data. It is computationally very efficient in space and time. It also naturally accommodates missing information. I also introduce a new variant of PCA called *sensible* principal component analysis (SPCA) which defines a proper density model in the data space. Learning for SPCA is also done with an EM algorithm. I report results on synthetic and real data showing that these EM algorithms correctly and efficiently find the leading eigenvectors of the covariance of datasets in a few iterations using up to hundreds of thousands of datapoints in thousands of dimensions.

1 Why EM for PCA?

Principal component analysis (PCA) is a widely used dimensionality reduction technique in data analysis. Its popularity comes from three important properties. First, it is the *optimal* (in terms of mean squared error) *linear* scheme for compressing a set of high dimensional vectors into a set of lower dimensional vectors and then reconstructing. Second, the model parameters can be computed *directly* from the data – for example by diagonalizing the sample covariance. Third, compression and decompression are easy operations to perform given the model parameters – they require only matrix multiplications.

Despite these attractive features however, PCA models have several shortcomings. One is that naive methods for finding the principal component directions have trouble with high dimensional data or large numbers of datapoints. Consider attempting to diagonalize the sample covariance matrix of n vectors in a space of p dimensions when n and p are several hundred or several thousand. Difficulties can arise both in the form of computational complexity and also data scarcity.[1] Even computing the sample covariance itself is very costly, requiring $O(np^2)$ operations. In general it is best to avoid altogether computing the sample

---

[*]roweis@cns.caltech.edu; Computation & Neural Systems, California Institute of Tech.

[1]On the data scarcity front, we often do not have enough data in high dimensions for the sample covariance to be of full rank and so we must be careful to employ techniques which do not require full rank matrices. On the complexity front, direct diagonalization of a symmetric matrix thousands of rows in size can be extremely costly since this operation is $O(p^3)$ for $p \times p$ inputs. Fortunately, several techniques exist for efficient matrix diagonalization when only the first few leading eigenvectors and eigenvalues are required (for example the power method [10] which is only $O(p^2)$).

covariance explicitly. Methods such as the *snap-shot* algorithm [7] do this by assuming that the eigenvectors being searched for are linear combinations of the datapoints; their complexity is $O(n^3)$. In this note, I present a version of the expectation-maximization (EM) algorithm [1] for learning the principal components of a dataset. The algorithm does not require computing the sample covariance and has a complexity limited by $O(knp)$ operations where k is the number of leading eigenvectors to be learned.

Another shortcoming of standard approaches to PCA is that it is not obvious how to deal properly with missing data. Most of the methods discussed above cannot accommodate missing values and so incomplete points must either be discarded or completed using a variety of ad-hoc interpolation methods. On the other hand, the EM algorithm for PCA enjoys all the benefits [4] of other EM algorithms in terms of estimating the maximum likelihood values for missing information directly at each iteration.

Finally, the PCA model itself suffers from a critical flaw which is independent of the technique used to compute its parameters: it does not define a proper probability model in the space of inputs. This is because the density is not normalized within the principal subspace. In other words, if we perform PCA on some data and then ask how well *new* data are fit by the model, the only criterion used is the squared distance of the new data from their projections into the principal subspace. A datapoint far away from the training data but nonetheless near the principal subspace will be assigned a high "pseudo-likelihood" or low error. Similarly, it is not possible to generate "fantasy" data from a PCA model. In this note I introduce a new model called *sensible* principal component analysis (SPCA), an obvious modification of PCA, which *does* define a proper covariance structure in the data space. Its parameters can also be learned with an EM algorithm, given below.

In summary, the methods developed in this paper provide three advantages. They allow *simple and efficient* computation of a few eigenvectors and eigenvalues when working with many datapoints in high dimensions. They permit this computation even in the presence of missing data. On a real vision problem with missing information, I have computed the 10 leading eigenvectors and eigenvalues of 2^{17} points in 2^{12} dimensions in a few hours using MATLAB on a modest workstation. Finally, through a small variation, these methods allow the computation not only of the principal subspace but of a complete Gaussian probabilistic model which allows one to generate data and compute true likelihoods.

2 Whence EM for PCA?

Principal component analysis can be viewed as a limiting case of a particular class of linear-Gaussian models. The goal of such models is to capture the covariance structure of an observed p-dimensional variable $\mathbf{y}$ using fewer than the $p(p+1)/2$ free parameters required in a full covariance matrix. Linear-Gaussian models do this by assuming that $\mathbf{y}$ was produced as a linear transformation of some k-dimensional latent variable $\mathbf{x}$ plus additive Gaussian noise. Denoting the transformation by the $p \times k$ matrix $\mathbf{C}$, and the (p-dimensional) noise by $\mathbf{v}$ (with covariance matrix $\mathbf{R}$) the generative model can be written[2] as

$$\mathbf{y} = \mathbf{Cx} + \mathbf{v} \qquad \mathbf{x} \sim \mathcal{N}(\mathbf{0}, \mathbf{I}) \qquad \mathbf{v} \sim \mathcal{N}(\mathbf{0}, \mathbf{R}) \tag{1a}$$

The latent or cause variables $\mathbf{x}$ are assumed to be independent and identically distributed according to a unit variance spherical Gaussian. Since $\mathbf{v}$ are also independent and normal distributed (and assumed independent of $\mathbf{x}$), the model reduces to a single Gaussian model

---

[2] All vectors are column vectors. To denote the transpose of a vector or matrix I use the notation $\mathbf{x}^T$. The determinant of a matrix is denoted by $|\mathbf{A}|$ and matrix inversion by $\mathbf{A}^{-1}$. The zero matrix is $\mathbf{0}$ and the identity matrix is $\mathbf{I}$. The symbol $\sim$ means "distributed according to". A multivariate normal (Gaussian) distribution with mean μ and covariance matrix $\mathbf{\Sigma}$ is written as $\mathcal{N}(\mu, \mathbf{\Sigma})$. The same Gaussian evaluated at the point $\mathbf{x}$ is denoted $\mathcal{N}(\mu, \mathbf{\Sigma})|_{\mathbf{x}}$.

for $\mathbf{y}$ which we can write explicitly:

$$\mathbf{y} \sim \mathcal{N}\left(\mathbf{0}, \mathbf{CC}^T + \mathbf{R}\right) \qquad (1b)$$

In order to save parameters over the direct covariance representation in p-space, it is necessary to choose $k < p$ and also to restrict the covariance structure of the Gaussian noise $\mathbf{v}$ by constraining the matrix $\mathbf{R}$.[3] For example, if the shape of the noise distribution is restricted to be axis aligned (its covariance matrix is diagonal) the model is known as *factor analysis*.

2.1 Inference and learning

There are two central problems of interest when working with the linear-Gaussian models described above. The first problem is that of *state inference* or *compression* which asks: *given* fixed model parameters $\mathbf{C}$ and $\mathbf{R}$, what can be said about the unknown hidden states $\mathbf{x}$ given some observations $\mathbf{y}$? Since the datapoints are independent, we are interested in the posterior probability $P\left(\mathbf{x}|\mathbf{y}\right)$ over a single hidden state given the corresponding single observation. This can be easily computed by linear matrix projection and the resulting density is itself Gaussian:

$$P\left(\mathbf{x}|\mathbf{y}\right) = \frac{P\left(\mathbf{y}|\mathbf{x}\right)P\left(\mathbf{x}\right)}{P\left(\mathbf{y}\right)} = \frac{\mathcal{N}\left(\mathbf{Cx}, \mathbf{R}\right)|_{\mathbf{y}}\,\mathcal{N}\left(\mathbf{0}, \mathbf{I}\right)|_{\mathbf{x}}}{\mathcal{N}\left(\mathbf{0}, \mathbf{CC}^T + \mathbf{R}\right)|_{\mathbf{y}}} \qquad (2a)$$

$$P\left(\mathbf{x}|\mathbf{y}\right) = \mathcal{N}\left(\beta\mathbf{y}, I - \beta\mathbf{C}\right)|_{\mathbf{x}}, \qquad \beta = \mathbf{C}^T(\mathbf{CC}^T + \mathbf{R})^{-1} \qquad (2b)$$

from which we obtain not only the expected value $\beta\mathbf{y}$ of the unknown state but also an estimate of the uncertainty in this value in the form of the covariance $I - \beta\mathbf{C}$. Computing $\mathbf{y}$ from $\mathbf{x}$ (*reconstruction*) is also straightforward: $P\left(\mathbf{y}|\mathbf{x}\right) = \mathcal{N}\left(\mathbf{Cx}, \mathbf{R}\right)|_{\mathbf{y}}$. Finally, computing the likelihood of any datapoint $\mathbf{y}$ is merely an evaluation under (1b).

The second problem is that of *learning*, or *parameter fitting* which consists of identifying the matrices $\mathbf{C}$ and $\mathbf{R}$ that make the model assign the highest likelihood to the observed data. There are a family of EM algorithms to do this for the various cases of restrictions to $\mathbf{R}$ but all follow a similar structure: they use the inference formula (2b) above in the **e-step** to estimate the unknown state and then choose $\mathbf{C}$ and the restricted $\mathbf{R}$ in the **m-step** so as to maximize the expected joint likelihood of the estimated $\mathbf{x}$ and the observed $\mathbf{y}$.

2.2 Zero noise limit

Principal component analysis is a limiting case of the linear-Gaussian model as the covariance of the noise $\mathbf{v}$ becomes infinitesimally small and equal in all directions. Mathematically, PCA is obtained by taking the limit $\mathbf{R} = \lim_{\epsilon \to 0} \epsilon\mathbf{I}$. This has the effect of making the likelihood of a point $\mathbf{y}$ dominated solely by the squared distance between it and its reconstruction $\mathbf{Cx}$. The directions of the columns of $\mathbf{C}$ which minimize this error are known as the *principal components*. Inference now reduces to[4] simple least squares projection:

$$P\left(\mathbf{x}|\mathbf{y}\right) = \mathcal{N}\left(\beta\mathbf{y}, I - \beta\mathbf{C}\right)|_{\mathbf{x}}, \qquad \beta = \lim_{\epsilon \to 0} \mathbf{C}^T(\mathbf{CC}^T + \epsilon\mathbf{I})^{-1} \qquad (3a)$$

$$P\left(\mathbf{x}|\mathbf{y}\right) = \mathcal{N}\left((\mathbf{C}^T\mathbf{C})^{-1}\mathbf{C}^T\mathbf{y}, \mathbf{0}\right)|_{\mathbf{x}} = \delta(\mathbf{x} - (\mathbf{C}^T\mathbf{C})^{-1}\mathbf{C}^T\mathbf{y}) \qquad (3b)$$

Since the noise has become infinitesimal, the posterior over states collapses to a single point and the covariance becomes zero.

---

[3]This restriction on $\mathbf{R}$ is not merely to save on parameters: the covariance of the observation noise *must* be restricted in some way for the model to capture any interesting or informative projections in the state $\mathbf{x}$. If $\mathbf{R}$ were not restricted, the learning algorithm could simply choose $\mathbf{C} = \mathbf{0}$ and then set $\mathbf{R}$ to be the covariance of the data thus trivially achieving the maximum likelihood model by explaining all of the structure in the data as noise. (Remember that since the model has reduced to a single Gaussian distribution for $\mathbf{y}$ we can do no better than having the covariance of our model equal the sample covariance of our data.)

[4]Recall that if $\mathbf{C}$ is $p \times k$ with $p > k$ and is rank k then left multiplication by $\mathbf{C}^T(\mathbf{CC}^T)^{-1}$ (which appears not to be well defined because $(\mathbf{CC}^T)$ is not invertible) is *exactly equivalent to* left multiplication by $(\mathbf{C}^T\mathbf{C})^{-1}\mathbf{C}^T$. The intuition is that even though $\mathbf{CC}^T$ truly is not invertible, the directions along which it is not invertible are exactly those which $\mathbf{C}^T$ is about to project out.

3 An EM algorithm for PCA

The key observation of this note is that even though the principal components can be computed explicitly, there is still an EM algorithm for learning them. It can be easily derived as the zero noise limit of the standard algorithms (see for example [3, 2] and section 4 below) by replacing the usual **e-step** with the projection above. The algorithm is:

- **e-step**: $\mathbf{X} = (\mathbf{C}^T\mathbf{C})^{-1}\mathbf{C}^T\mathbf{Y}$
- **m-step**: $\mathbf{C}^{new} = \mathbf{Y}\mathbf{X}^T(\mathbf{X}\mathbf{X}^T)^{-1}$

where $\mathbf{Y}$ is a $p \times n$ matrix of all the observed data and $\mathbf{X}$ is a $k \times n$ matrix of the unknown states. The columns of $\mathbf{C}$ will span the space of the first k principal components. (To compute the corresponding eigenvectors and eigenvalues explicitly, the data can be projected into this k-dimensional subspace and an ordered orthogonal basis for the covariance in the subspace can be constructed.) Notice that the algorithm can be performed *online* using only a single datapoint at a time and so its storage requirements are only $O(kp) + O(k^2)$. The workings of the algorithm are illustrated graphically in figure 1 below.

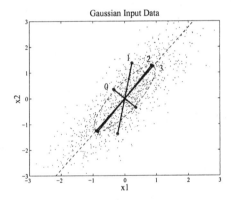 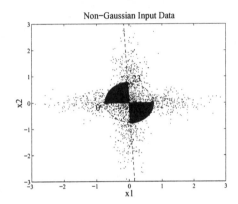

Figure 1: Examples of iterations of the algorithm. The left panel shows the learning of the first principal component of data drawn from a Gaussian distribution, while the right panel shows learning on data from a non-Gaussian distribution. The dashed lines indicate the direction of the leading eigenvector of the sample covariance. The dashed ellipse is the one standard deviation contour of the sample covariance. The progress of the algorithm is indicated by the solid lines whose directions indicate the guess of the eigenvector and whose lengths indicate the guess of the eigenvalue at each iteration. The iterations are numbered; number 0 is the initial condition. Notice that the difficult learning on the right does not get stuck in a local minimum, although it does take more than 20 iterations to converge which is unusual for Gaussian data (see figure 2).

The intuition behind the algorithm is as follows: guess an orientation for the principal subspace. *Fix* the guessed subspace and project the data **y** into it to give the values of the hidden states **x**. Now *fix* the values of the hidden states and choose the subspace orientation which minimizes the squared reconstruction errors of the datapoints. For the simple two-dimensional example above, I can give a physical analogy. Imagine that we have a rod pinned at the origin which is free to rotate. Pick an orientation for the rod. Holding the rod still, project every datapoint onto the rod, and attach each projected point to its original point with a spring. Now release the rod. Repeat. The direction of the rod represents our guess of the principal component of the dataset. The energy stored in the springs is the reconstruction error we are trying to minimize.

3.1 Convergence and Complexity

The EM learning algorithm for PCA amounts to an iterative procedure for finding the subspace spanned by the k leading eigenvectors without explicit computation of the sample covariance. It is attractive for small k because its complexity is limited by $O(knp)$ per iteration and so depends only linearly on *both* the dimensionality of the data and the number of points. Methods that explicitly compute the sample covariance matrix have complexities limited by $O(np^2)$, while methods like the snap-shot method that form linear combinations of the data must compute and diagonalize a matrix of all possible inner products between points and thus are limited by $O(n^2p)$ complexity. The complexity scaling of the algorithm compared to these methods is shown in figure 2 below. For each dimensionality, a random covariance matrix Σ was generated[5] and then $10p$ points were drawn from $\mathcal{N}(\mathbf{0}, \Sigma)$. The number of floating point operations required to find the first principal component was recorded using MATLAB's flops function. As expected, the EM algorithm scales more favourably in cases where k is small and both p and n are large. If $k \approx p \approx n$ (we want all the eigenvectors) then all methods are $O(p^3)$.

The standard convergence proofs for EM [1] apply to this algorithm as well, so we can be sure that it will always reach a local maximum of likelihood. Furthermore, Tipping and Bishop have shown [8, 9] that the only stable local extremum is the *global maximum* at which the true principal subspace is found; so it converges to the correct result. Another possible concern is that the number of iterations required for convergence may scale with p or n. To investigate this question, I have explicitly computed the leading eigenvector for synthetic datasets (as above, with $n = 10p$) of varying dimension and recorded the number of iterations of the EM algorithm required for the inner product of the eigendirection with the current guess of the algorithm to be 0.999 or greater. Up to 450 dimensions (4500 datapoints), the number of iterations remains roughly constant with a mean of 3.6. The ratios of the first k eigenvalues seem to be the critical parameters controlling the number of iterations until convergence (For example, in figure 1b this ratio was 1.0001.)

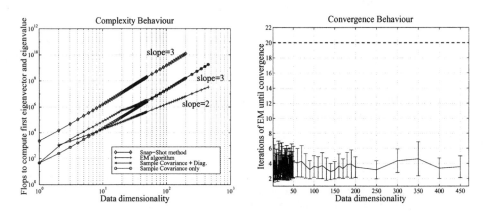

Figure 2: Time complexity and convergence behaviour of the algorithm. In all cases, the number of datapoints n is 10 times the dimensionality p. For the left panel, the number of floating point operations to find the leading eigenvector and eigenvalue were recorded. The EM algorithm was always run for exactly 20 iterations. The cost shown for diagonalization of the sample covariance uses the MATLAB functions cov and eigs. The snap-shot method is show to indicate scaling only; one would not normally use it when $n > p$. In the right hand panel, convergence was investigated by explicitly computing the leading eigenvector and then running the EM algorithm until the dot product of its guess and the true eigendirection was 0.999 or more. The error bars show $\pm$ one standard deviation across many runs. The dashed line shows the number of iterations used to produce the EM algorithm curve ('+') in the left panel.

---

[5]First, an axis-aligned covariance is created with the p eigenvalues drawn at random from a uniform distribution in some positive range. Then $(p - 1)$ points are drawn from a p-dimensional zero mean spherical Gaussian and the axes are aligned in space using these points.

3.2 Missing data

In the complete data setting, the values of the projections or hidden states $\mathbf{x}$ are viewed as the "missing information" for EM. During the **e-step** we compute these values by projecting the observed data into the current subspace. This minimizes the model error given the observed data and the model parameters. However, if some of the input points are missing certain coordinate values, we can easily estimate those values in the same fashion. Instead of estimating only $\mathbf{x}$ as the value which minimizes the squared distance between the point and its reconstruction we can generalize the **e-step** to:

- **generalized e-step**: For each (possibly incomplete) point $\mathbf{y}$ find the unique pair of points $\mathbf{x}^*$ and $\mathbf{y}^*$ (such that $\mathbf{x}^*$ lies in the current principal subspace and $\mathbf{y}^*$ lies in the subspace defined by the known information about $\mathbf{y}$) which minimize the norm $\|\mathbf{Cx}^* - \mathbf{y}^*\|$. Set the corresponding column of $\mathbf{X}$ to $\mathbf{x}^*$ and the corresponding column of $\mathbf{Y}$ to $\mathbf{y}^*$.

If $\mathbf{y}$ is complete, then $\mathbf{y}^* = \mathbf{y}$ and $\mathbf{x}^*$ is found exactly as before. If not, then $\mathbf{x}^*$ and $\mathbf{y}^*$ are the solution to a least squares problem and can be found by, for example, QR factorization of a particular constraint matrix. Using this generalized **e-step** I have found the leading principal components for datasets in which *every* point is missing some coordinates.

4 Sensible Principal Component Analysis

If we require $\mathbf{R}$ to be a multiple $\epsilon\mathbf{I}$ of the identity matrix (in other words the covariance ellipsoid of $\mathbf{v}$ is spherical) but *do not* take the limit as $\epsilon \to 0$ then we have a model which I shall call *sensible principal component analysis* or SPCA. The columns of $\mathbf{C}$ are still known as the *principal components* (it can be shown that they are the same as in regular PCA) and we will call the scalar value ϵ on the diagonal of $\mathbf{R}$ the *global noise level*. Note that SPCA uses $1 + pk - k(k-1)/2$ free parameters to model the covariance. Once again, inference is done with equation (2b). Notice however, that even though the principal components found by SPCA are the same as those for PCA, the mean of the posterior is not in general the same as the point given by the PCA projection (3b). Learning for SPCA also uses an EM algorithm (given below).

Because it has a *finite* noise level ϵ, SPCA defines a proper generative model and probability distribution in the data space:

$$\mathbf{y} \sim \mathcal{N}\left(0, \mathbf{CC}^T + \epsilon\mathbf{I}\right) \tag{4}$$

which makes it possible to generate data from or to evaluate the actual *likelihood* of *new* test data under an SPCA model. Furthermore, this likelihood will be much lower for data far from the training set even if they are near the principal subspace, unlike the reconstruction error reported by a PCA model.

The EM algorithm for learning an SPCA model is:

- **e-step**: $\beta = \mathbf{C}^T(\mathbf{CC}^T + \epsilon\mathbf{I})^{-1}$ $\quad \mu_\mathbf{x} = \beta\mathbf{Y} \quad \Sigma_\mathbf{x} = n\mathbf{I} - n\beta\mathbf{C} + \mu_\mathbf{x}\mu_\mathbf{x}^T$
- **m-step**: $\mathbf{C}^{new} = \mathbf{Y}\mu_\mathbf{x}^T\Sigma^{-1}$ $\quad \epsilon^{new} = \text{trace}[\mathbf{XX}^T - \mathbf{C}\mu_\mathbf{x}\mathbf{Y}^T]/n^2$

Two subtle points about complexity[6] are important to notice; they show that learning for SPCA also enjoys a complexity limited by $O(knp)$ and not worse.

---

[6]First, since $\epsilon\mathbf{I}$ is diagonal, the inversion in the **e-step** can be performed efficiently using the matrix inversion lemma: $(\mathbf{CC}^T + \epsilon\mathbf{I})^{-1} = (\mathbf{I}/\epsilon - \mathbf{C}(\mathbf{I} + \mathbf{C}^T\mathbf{C}/\epsilon)^{-1}\mathbf{C}^T/\epsilon^2)$. Second, since we are only taking the trace of the matrix in the **m-step**, we do not need to compute the full sample covariance $\mathbf{XX}^T$ but instead can compute only the variance along each coordinate.

5 Relationships to previous methods

The EM algorithm for PCA, derived above using probabilistic arguments, is closely related to two well know sets of algorithms. The first are *power iteration* methods for solving matrix eigenvalue problems. Roughly speaking, these methods iteratively update their eigenvector estimates through repeated multiplication by the matrix to be diagonalized. In the case of PCA, explicitly forming the sample covariance and multiplying by it to perform such power iterations would be disastrous. However since the sample covariance is in fact a sum of outer products of individual vectors, we can multiply by it efficiently without ever computing it. In fact, the EM algorithm is exactly equivalent to performing power iterations for finding C using this trick. Iterative methods for partial least squares (e.g. the NIPALS algorithm) are doing the same trick for regression. Taking the singular value decomposition (SVD) of the data matrix directly is a related way to find the principal subspace. If Lanczos or Arnoldi methods are used to compute this SVD, the resulting iterations are similar to those of the EM algorithm. Space prohibits detailed discussion of these sophisticated methods, but two excellent general references are [5, 6]. The second class of methods are the competitive learning methods for finding the principal subspace such as Sanger's and Oja's rules. These methods enjoy the same storage and time complexities as the EM algorithm; however their update steps reduce but do not minimize the cost and so they typically need more iterations and require a learning rate parameter to be set by hand.

Acknowledgements

I would like to thank John Hopfield and my fellow graduate students for constant and excellent feedback on these ideas. In particular I am grateful to Erik Winfree for significant contributions to the missing data portion of this work, to Dawei Dong who provided image data to try as a real problem, as well as to Carlos Brody, Sanjoy Mahajan, and Maneesh Sahani. The work of Zoubin Ghahramani and Geoff Hinton was an important motivation for this study. Chris Bishop and Mike Tipping are pursuing independent but yet unpublished work on a virtually identical model. The comments of three anonymous reviewers and many visitors to my poster improved this manuscript greatly.

References

[1] A. P. Dempster, N. M. Laird, and D. B. Rubin. Maximum likelihood from incomplete data via the EM algorithm. *Journal of the Royal Statistical Society series B*, 39:1–38, 1977.

[2] B. S. Everitt. *An Introducction to Latent Variable Models*. Chapman and Hill, London, 1984.

[3] Zoubin Ghahramani and Geoffrey Hinton. The EM algorithm for mixtures of factor analyzers. Technical Report CRG-TR-96-1, Dept. of Computer Science, University of Toronto, Feb. 1997.

[4] Zoubin Ghahramani and Michael I. Jordan. Supervised learning from incomplete data via an EM approach. In Jack D. Cowan, Gerald Tesauro, and Joshua Alspector, editors, *Advances in Neural Information Processing Systems*, volume 6, pages 120–127. Morgan Kaufmann, 1994.

[5] Gene H. Golub and Charles F. Van Loan. *Matrix Computations*. The Johns Hopkins University Press, Baltimore, MD, USA, second edition, 1989.

[6] R. B. Lehoucq, D. C. Sorensen, and C. Yang. Arpack users' guide: Solution of large scale eigenvalue problems with implicitly restarted Arnoldi methods. Technical Report from http://www.caam.rice.edu/software/ARPACK/, Computational and Applied Mathematics, Rice University, October 1997.

[7] L. Sirovich. Turbulence and the dynamics of coherent structures. *Quarterly Applied Mathematics*, 45(3):561–590, 1987.

[8] Michael Tipping and Christopher Bishop. Mixtures of probabilistic principal component analyzers. Technical Report NCRG/97/003, Neural Computing Research Group, Aston University, June 1997.

[9] Michael Tipping and Christopher Bishop. Probabilistic principal component analysis. Technical Report NCRG/97/010, Neural Computing Research Group, Aston University, September 1997.

[10] J. H. Wilkinson. *The Algebraic Eigenvalue Problem*. Claredon Press, Oxford, England, 1965.

Local Dimensionality Reduction

Stefan Schaal [1,2,4]
sschaal@usc.edu
http://www-slab.usc.edu/sschaal

Sethu Vijayakumar [3,1]
sethu@cs.titech.ac.jp
http://ogawa-
www.cs.titech.ac.jp/~sethu

Christopher G. Atkeson [4]
cga@cc.gatech.edu
http://www.cc.gatech.edu/
fac/Chris.Atkeson

[1] ERATO Kawato Dynamic Brain Project (JST), 2-2 Hikaridai, Seika-cho, Soraku-gun, 619-02 Kyoto
[2] Dept. of Comp. Science & Neuroscience, Univ. of South. California HNB-103, Los Angeles CA 90089-2520
[3] Department of Computer Science, Tokyo Institute of Technology, Meguro-ku, Tokyo-152
[4] College of Computing, Georgia Institute of Technology, 801 Atlantic Drive, Atlanta, GA 30332-0280

Abstract

If globally high dimensional data has locally only low dimensional distributions, it is advantageous to perform a local dimensionality reduction before further processing the data. In this paper we examine several techniques for local dimensionality reduction in the context of locally weighted linear regression. As possible candidates, we derive local versions of factor analysis regression, principle component regression, principle component regression on joint distributions, and partial least squares regression. After outlining the statistical bases of these methods, we perform Monte Carlo simulations to evaluate their robustness with respect to violations of their statistical assumptions. One surprising outcome is that locally weighted partial least squares regression offers the best average results, thus outperforming even factor analysis, the theoretically most appealing of our candidate techniques.

1 INTRODUCTION

Regression tasks involve mapping a n-dimensional continuous input vector $\mathbf{x} \in \mathfrak{R}^n$ onto a m-dimensional output vector $\mathbf{y} \in \mathfrak{R}^m$. They form a ubiquitous class of problems found in fields including process control, sensorimotor control, coordinate transformations, and various stages of information processing in biological nervous systems. This paper will focus on spatially localized learning techniques, for example, kernel regression with Gaussian weighting functions. Local learning offer advantages for real-time incremental learning problems due to fast convergence, considerable robustness towards problems of negative interference, and large tolerance in model selection (Atkeson, Moore, & Schaal, 1997; Schaal & Atkeson, in press). Local learning is usually based on interpolating data from a local neighborhood around the query point. For high dimensional learning problems, however, it suffers from a bias/variance dilemma, caused by the nonintuitive fact that "... [in high dimensions] if neighborhoods are *local*, then they are almost surely *empty*, whereas if a neighborhood is not *empty*, then it is not *local*." (Scott, 1992, p.198). Global learning methods, such as sigmoidal feedforward networks, do not face this problem as they do not employ neighborhood relations, although they require strong prior knowledge about the problem at hand in order to be successful.

Assuming that local learning in high dimensions is a hopeless, however, is not necessarily warranted: being *globally* high dimensional does not imply that data remains high dimensional if viewed *locally*. For example, in the control of robot arms and biological arms we have shown that for estimating the inverse dynamics of an arm, a globally 21-dimensional space reduces on average to 4-6 dimensions locally (Vijayakumar & Schaal, 1997). A local learning system that can robustly exploit such locally low dimensional distributions should be able to avoid the curse of dimensionality.

In pursuit of the question of what, in the context of local regression, is the "right" method to perform local dimensionality reduction, this paper will derive and compare several candidate techniques under i) perfectly fulfilled statistical prerequisites (e.g., Gaussian noise, Gaussian input distributions, perfectly linear data), and ii) less perfect conditions (e.g., non-Gaussian distributions, slightly quadratic data, incorrect guess of the dimensionality of the true data distribution). We will focus on nonlinear function approximation with locally weighted linear regression (LWR), as it allows us to adapt a variety of global linear dimensionality reduction techniques, and as LWR has found widespread application in several local learning systems (Atkeson, Moore, & Schaal, 1997; Jordan & Jacobs, 1994; Xu, Jordan, & Hinton, 1996). In particular, we will derive and investigate locally weighted principal component regression (LWPCR), locally weighted joint data principal component analysis (LWPCA), locally weighted factor analysis (LWFA), and locally weighted partial least squares (LWPLS). Section 2 will briefly outline these methods and their theoretical foundations, while Section 3 will empirically evaluate the robustness of these methods using synthetic data sets that increasingly violate some of the statistical assumptions of the techniques.

2 METHODS OF DIMENSIONALITY REDUCTION

We assume that our regression data originate from a generating process with two sets of observables, the "inputs" $\tilde{\mathbf{x}}$ and the "outputs" $\tilde{\mathbf{y}}$. The characteristics of the process ensure a functional relation $\tilde{\mathbf{y}} = f(\tilde{\mathbf{x}})$. Both $\tilde{\mathbf{x}}$ and $\tilde{\mathbf{y}}$ are obtained through some measurement device that adds independent mean zero noise of different magnitude in each observable, such that $\mathbf{x} = \tilde{\mathbf{x}} + \varepsilon_x$ and $\mathbf{y} = \tilde{\mathbf{y}} + \varepsilon_y$. For the sake of simplicity, we will only focus on one-dimensional output data ($m=1$) and functions f that are either linear or slightly quadratic, as these cases are the most common in nonlinear function approximation with locally linear models. Locality of the regression is ensured by weighting the error of each data point with a weight from a Gaussian kernel:

$$w_i = \exp\left(-0.5\left(\mathbf{x}_i - \mathbf{x}_q\right)^T \mathbf{D}\left(\mathbf{x}_i - \mathbf{x}_q\right)\right) \tag{1}$$

$\mathbf{x}_q$ denotes the query point, and $\mathbf{D}$ a positive semi-definite distance metric which determines the size and shape of the neighborhood contributing to the regression (Atkeson et al., 1997). The parameters $\mathbf{x}_q$ and $\mathbf{D}$ can be determined in the framework of nonparametric statistics (Schaal & Atkeson, in press) or parametric maximum likelihood estimations (Xu et al, 1995)— for the present study they are determined manually since their origin is secondary to the results of this paper. Without loss of generality, all our data sets will set $\mathbf{x}_q$ to the zero vector, compute the weights, and then translate the input data such that the locally weighted mean, $\bar{\mathbf{x}} = \sum w_i \mathbf{x}_i / \sum w_i$, is zero. The output data is equally translated to be mean zero. Mean zero data is necessary for most of techniques considered below. The (translated) input data is summarized in the rows of the matrix $\mathbf{X}$, the corresponding (translated) outputs are the elements of the vector $\mathbf{y}$, and the corresponding weights are in the diagonal matrix $\mathbf{W}$. In some cases, we need the joint input and output data, denoted as $\mathbf{Z}=[\mathbf{X}\ \mathbf{y}]$.

2.1 FACTOR ANALYSIS (LWFA)

Factor analysis (Everitt, 1984) is a technique of dimensionality reduction which is the most appropriate given the generating process of our regression data. It assumes the observed data z was produced by a mean zero independently distributed k -dimensional vector of factors v, transformed by the matrix U, and contaminated by mean zero independent noise ε with diagonal covariance matrix Ω:

$$z = Uv + \varepsilon, \quad \text{where} \quad z = \left[x^T, y\right]^T \quad \text{and} \quad \varepsilon = \left[\varepsilon_x^T, \varepsilon_y\right]^T \tag{2}$$

If both v and ε are normally distributed, the parameters Ω and U can be obtained iteratively by the Expectation-Maximization algorithm (EM) (Rubin & Thayer, 1982). For a linear regression problem, one assumes that z was generated with $U=[I, \beta]^T$ and $v = \tilde{x}$, where β denotes the vector of regression coefficients of the linear model $y = \beta^T x$, and I the identity matrix. After calculating Ω and U by EM in joint data space as formulated in (2), an estimate of β can be derived from the conditional probability $P(y \mid x)$. As all distributions are assumed to be normal, the expected value of y is the mean of this conditional distribution. The locally weighted version (LWFA) of β can be obtained together with an estimate of the factors v from the joint weighted covariance matrix Ψ of z and v:

$$E\left\{\begin{bmatrix} y \\ v \end{bmatrix} \middle| x \right\} = \begin{bmatrix} \hat{\beta}^T \\ B \end{bmatrix} x = \Psi_{21}\Psi_{11}^{-1}x, \quad \text{where} \quad \Psi = \left[Z^T, V^T\right]W\begin{bmatrix} Z \\ V \end{bmatrix}\bigg/ \sum w_i = \tag{3}$$

$$= \begin{bmatrix} \Omega + UU^T & U \\ U^T & I \end{bmatrix} = \begin{bmatrix} \Psi_{11}(= n \times n) & \Psi_{12}(= n \times (m + k)) \\ \Psi_{21}(= (m + k) \times n) & \Psi_{22}(= (m + k) \times (m + k)) \end{bmatrix}$$

where $E\{\cdot\}$ denotes the expectation operator and B a matrix of coefficients involved in estimating the factors v. Note that unless the noise ε is zero, the estimated β is different from the true β as it tries to average out the noise in the data.

2.2 JOINT-SPACE PRINCIPAL COMPONENT ANALYSIS (LWPCA)

An alternative way of determining the parameters β in a reduced space employs locally weighted principal component analysis (LWPCA) in the joint data space. By defining the largest $k+1$ principal components of the weighted covariance matrix of Z as U:

$$U = \left[eigenvectors\left(\sum w_i(z_i - \bar{z})(z_i - \bar{z})^T \bigg/ \sum w_i\right)\right]_{\max(1:k+1)} \tag{4}$$

and noting that the eigenvectors in U are unit length, the matrix inversion theorem (Horn & Johnson, 1994) provides a means to derive an efficient estimate of β

$$\beta = U_x\left(U_y^T - U_y^T\left(U_y U_y^T - I\right)^{-1}U_y U_y^T\right), \quad \text{where} \quad U = \begin{bmatrix} U_x(= n \times k) \\ U_y(= m \times k) \end{bmatrix} \tag{5}$$

In our one dimensional output case, U_y is just a $(1 \times k)$-dimensional row vector and the evaluation of (5) does not require a matrix inversion anymore but rather a division.

If one assumes normal distributions in all variables as in LWFA, LWPCA is the special case of LWFA where the noise covariance Ω is spherical, i.e., the same magnitude of noise in all observables. Under these circumstances, the subspaces spanned by U in both methods will be the same. However, the regression coefficients of LWPCA will be different from those of LWFA unless the noise level is zero, as LWFA optimizes the coefficients according to the noise in the data (Equation (3)). Thus, for normal distributions and a correct guess of k, LWPCA is always expected to perform worse than LWFA.

2.3 PARTIAL LEAST SQUARES (LWPLS, LWPLS_1)

Partial least squares (Wold, 1975; Frank & Friedman, 1993) recursively computes orthogonal projections of the input data and performs single variable regressions along these projections on the residuals of the previous iteration step. A locally weighted version of partial least squares (LWPLS) proceeds as shown in Equation (6) below.

As all single variable regressions are ordinary univariate least-squares minimizations, LWPLS makes the same statistical assumption as ordinary linear regressions, i.e., that only output variables have additive noise, but input variables are noiseless. The choice of the projections **u**, however, introduces an element in LWPLS that remains statistically still debated (Frank & Friedman, 1993), although, interestingly, there exists a strong similarity with the way projections are chosen in Cascade Correlation (Fahlman & Lebiere, 1990). A peculiarity of LWPLS is that it also regresses the inputs of the previous step against the projected inputs **s** in order to ensure the orthogonality of all the projections **u**. Since LWPLS chooses projections in a very powerful way, it can accomplish optimal function fits with only one single projections (i.e.,

For Training :	**For Lookup :**
Initialize :	Initialize :
$\mathbf{D}_0 = \mathbf{X}, \quad \mathbf{e}_0 = \mathbf{y}$	$\mathbf{d}_0 = \mathbf{x}, \ y = 0$
For i = 1 to k :	For i = 1 to k :
$\mathbf{u}_i = \mathbf{D}_{i-1}^T \mathbf{W} \mathbf{e}_{i-1}$	$s_i = \mathbf{d}_{i-1}^T \mathbf{u}_i$
$\mathbf{s}_i = \mathbf{D}_{i-1} \mathbf{u}_i$	$y = y + \beta_i s_i$
$\beta_i = \dfrac{\mathbf{s}_i^T \mathbf{W} \mathbf{e}_{i-1}}{\mathbf{s}_i^T \mathbf{W} \mathbf{s}_i}$	$\mathbf{d}_i = \mathbf{d}_{i-1} - s_i \mathbf{p}_i$
$\mathbf{p}_i = \dfrac{\mathbf{D}_{i-1}^T \mathbf{W} \mathbf{s}_i}{\mathbf{s}_i^T \mathbf{W} \mathbf{s}_i}$	
$\mathbf{D}_i = \mathbf{D}_{i-1} - \mathbf{s}_i \mathbf{p}_i^T$	(6)

$k=1$) for certain input distributions. We will address this issue in our empirical evaluations by comparing k-step LWPLS with 1-step LWPLS, abbreviated LWPLS_1.

2.4 PRINCIPAL COMPONENT REGRESSION (LWPCR)

Although not optimal, a computationally efficient techniques of dimensionality reduction for linear regression is principal component regression (LWPCR) (Massy, 1965). The inputs are projected onto the largest k principal components of the weighted covariance matrix of the input data by the matrix $\mathbf{U}$:

$$\mathbf{U} = \left[eigenvectors\left(\sum w_i (\mathbf{x}_i - \bar{\mathbf{x}})(\mathbf{x}_i - \bar{\mathbf{x}})^T / \sum w_i \right) \right]_{max(1:k)} \tag{7}$$

The regression coefficients β are thus calculated as:

$$\beta = \left(\mathbf{U}^T \mathbf{X}^T \mathbf{W} \mathbf{X} \mathbf{U} \right)^{-1} \mathbf{U}^T \mathbf{X}^T \mathbf{W} \mathbf{y} \tag{8}$$

Equation (8) is inexpensive to evaluate since after projecting $\mathbf{X}$ with $\mathbf{U}$, $\mathbf{U}^T \mathbf{X}^T \mathbf{W} \mathbf{X} \mathbf{U}$ becomes a diagonal matrix that is easy to invert. LWPCR assumes that the inputs have additive spherical noise, which includes the zero noise case. As during dimensionality reduction LWPCR does not take into account the output data, it is endangered by clipping input dimensions with low variance which nevertheless have important contribution to the regression output. However, from a statistical point of view, it is less likely that low variance inputs have significant contribution in a linear regression, as the confidence bands of the regression coefficients increase inversely proportionally with the variance of the associated input. If the input data has non-spherical noise, LWPCR is prone to focus the regression on irrelevant projections.

3 MONTE CARLO EVALUATIONS

In order to evaluate the candidate methods, data sets with 5 inputs and 1 output were randomly generated. Each data set consisted of 2,000 training points and 10,000 test points, distributed either uniformly or nonuniformly in the unit hypercube. The outputs were generated by either a linear or quadratic function. Afterwards, the 5-dimensional input space was projected into a 10-dimensional space by a randomly chosen distance preserving linear transformation. Finally, Gaussian noise of various magnitudes was added to both the 10-dimensional inputs and one dimensional output. For the test sets, the additive noise in the outputs was omitted. Each regression technique was localized by a Gaussian kernel (Equation (1)) with a 10-dimensional distance metric **D**=10***I** (**D** was manually chosen to ensure that the Gaussian kernel had sufficiently many data points and no "data holes" in the fringe areas of the kernel) . The precise experimental conditions followed closely those suggested by Frank and Friedman (1993):

- 2 kinds of linear functions $y = \beta_{lin}^T \mathbf{x}$ for: i) $\beta_{lin} = [1,1,1,1,1]^T$,   ii) $\beta_{lin} = [1,2,3,4,5]^T$

- 2 kinds of quadratic functions $y = \beta_{lin}^T \mathbf{x} + \beta_{quad}^T [x_1^2, x_2^2, x_3^2, x_4^2, x_5^2]^T$ for:

  i) $\beta_{lin} = [1,1,1,1,1]^T$ and $\beta_{quad} = 0.1[1,1,1,1,1]^T$, and ii) $\beta_{lin} = [1,2,3,4,5]^T$ and $\beta_{quad} = 0.1[1,4,9,16,25]^T$

- 3 kinds of noise conditions, each with 2 sub-conditions:
  i) only output noise: a) low noise: *local* signal/noise ratio lsnr=20,
                 and   b) high noise: lsnr=2,
  ii) equal noise in inputs and outputs:
         a) low noise $\varepsilon_{x,n} = \varepsilon_y = N(0, 0.01^2)$, $n \in [1,2,...,10]$,

     and   b) high noise $\varepsilon_{x,n} = \varepsilon_y = N(0, 0.1^2)$, $n \in [1,2,...,10]$,

  iii) unequal noise in inputs and outputs:
         a) low noise: $\varepsilon_{x,n} = N(0, (0.01n)^2)$, $n \in [1,2,...,10]$ and lsnr=20,
     and   b) high noise: $\varepsilon_{x,n} = N(0, (0.01n)^2)$, $n \in [1,2,...,10]$ and lsnr=2,

- 2 kinds of input distributions: i) uniform in unit hyper cube, ii) uniform in unit hyper cube excluding data points which activate a Gaussian weighting function (1) at $c = [0.5, 0, 0, 0, 0]^T$ with **D**=10***I** more than w=0.2 (this forms a "hyper kidney" shaped distribution)

Every algorithm was run[*] 30 times on each of the 48 combinations of the conditions. Additionally, the complete test was repeated for three further conditions varying the dimensionality—called factors in accordance with LWFA—that the algorithms assumed to be the true dimensionality of the 10-dimensional data from k=4 to 6, i.e., too few, correct, and too many factors. The average results are summarized in Figure 1.

Figure 1a,b,c show the summary results of the three factor conditions. Besides averaging over the 30 trials per condition, each mean of these charts also averages over the two input distribution conditions and the linear and quadratic function condition, as these four cases are frequently observed violations of the statistical assumptions in nonlinear function approximation with locally linear models. In Figure 1b the number of factors equals the underlying dimensionality of the problem, and all algorithms are essentially performing equally well. For perfectly Gaussian distributions in all random variables (not shown separately), LWFA's assumptions are perfectly fulfilled and it achieves the best results, however, almost indistinguishable closely followed by LWPLS. For the "unequal noise condition", the two PCA based techniques, LWPCA and LWPCR, perform the worst since—as expected—they choose suboptimal projections. However, when violating the statistical assumptions, LWFA loses parts of its advantages, such that the summary results become fairly balanced in Figure 1b.

The quality of function fitting changes significantly when violating the correct number of factors, as illustrated in Figure 1a,c. For too few factors (Figure 1a), LWPCR performs worst because it randomly omits one of the principle components in the input data, without respect to how important it is for the regression. The second worse is LWFA: according to its assumptions it believes that the signal it cannot model must be noise, leading to a degraded estimate of the data's subspace and, consequently, degraded regression results. LWPLS has a clear lead in this test, closely followed by LWPCA and LWPLS_1.

---

[*] Except for LWFA, all methods can evaluate a data set in non-iterative calculations. LWFA was trained with EM for maximally 1000 iterations or until the log-likelihood increased less than 1.e-10 in one iteration.

For too many factors than necessary (Figure 1c), it is now LWPCA which degrades. This effect is due to its extracting one very noise contaminated projection which strongly influences the recovery of the regression parameters in Equation (4). All other algorithms perform almost equally well, with LWFA and LWPLS taking a small lead.

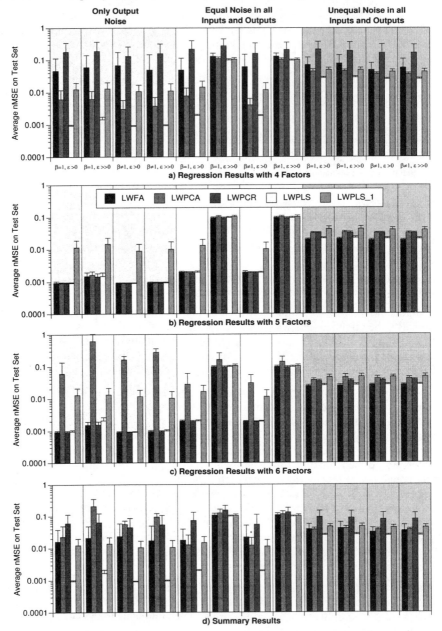

Figure 1: Average summary results of Monte Carlo experiments. Each chart is primarily divided into the three major noise conditions, cf. headers in chart (a). In each noise condition, there are four further subdivision: i) coefficients of linear or quadratic model are equal with low added noise; ii) like i) with high added noise; iii) coefficients of linear or quadratic model are different with low noise added; iv) like iii) with high added noise. Refer to text and descriptions of Monte Carlo studies for further explanations.

4 SUMMARY AND CONCLUSIONS

Figure 1d summarizes all the Monte Carlo experiments in a final average plot. Except for LWPLS, every other technique showed at least one clear weakness in one of our "robustness" tests. It was particularly an incorrect number of factors which made these weaknesses apparent. For high-dimensional regression problems, the local dimensionality, i.e., the number of factors, is not a clearly defined number but rather a varying quantity, depending on the way the generating process operates. Usually, this process *does not need* to generate locally low dimensional distributions, however, it often "*chooses*" to do so, for instance, as human arm movements follow stereotypic patterns despite they could generate arbitrary ones. Thus, local dimensionality reduction needs to find *autonomously* the appropriate number of local factor. Locally weighted partial least squares turned out to be a surprisingly robust technique for this purpose, even outperforming the statistically appealing probabilistic factor analysis. As in principal component analysis, LWPLS's number of factors can easily be controlled just based on a variance-cutoff threshold in input space (Frank & Friedman, 1993), while factor analysis usually requires expensive cross-validation techniques. Simple, variance-based control over the number of factors can actually improve the results of LWPCA and LWPCR in practice, since, as shown in Figure 1a, LWPCR is more robust towards overestimating the number of factors, while LWPCA is more robust towards an underestimation. If one is interested in dynamically growing the number of factors while obtaining already good regression results with too few factors, LWPCA and, especially, LWPLS seem to be appropriate—it should be noted how well one factor LWPLS (LWPLS_1) already performed in Figure 1!

In conclusion, since locally weighted partial least squares was equally robust as local weighted factor analysis towards additive noise in both input and output data, and, moreover, superior when mis-guessing the number of factors, it seems to be a most favorable technique for local dimensionality reduction for high dimensional regressions.

Acknowledgments

The authors are grateful to Geoffrey Hinton for reminding them of partial least squares. This work was supported by the ATR Human Information Processing Research Laboratories. S. Schaal's support includes the German Research Association, the Alexander von Humboldt Foundation, and the German Scholarship Foundation. S. Vijayakumar was supported by the Japanese Ministry of Education, Science, and Culture (Monbusho). C. G. Atkeson acknowledges the Air Force Office of Scientific Research grant F49-6209410362 and a National Science Foundation Presidential Young Investigators Award.

References

Atkeson, C. G., Moore, A. W., & Schaal, S, (1997a). "Locally weighted learning." *Artificial Intelligence Review*, 11, 1-5, pp.11-73.

Atkeson, C. G., Moore, A. W., & Schaal, S, (1997c). "Locally weighted learning for control." *Artificial Intelligence Review*, 11, 1-5, pp.75-113.

Belsley, D. A., Kuh, E., & Welsch, R. E, (1980). *Regression diagnostics: Identifying influential data and sources of collinearity*. New York: Wiley.

Everitt, B. S, (1984). *An introduction to latent variable models*. London: Chapman and Hall.

Fahlman, S. E. , Lebiere, C, (1990). "The cascade-correlation learning architecture." In: Touretzky, D. S. (Ed.), *Advances in Neural Information Processing Systems II*, pp.524-532. Morgan Kaufmann.

Frank, I. E., & Friedman, J. H, (1993). "A statistical view of some chemometric regression tools." *Technometrics*, 35, 2, pp.109-135.

Geman, S., Bienenstock, E., & Doursat, R, (1992). "Neural networks and the bias/variance dilemma." *Neural Computation*, 4, pp.1-58.

Horn, R. A., & Johnson, C. R, (1994). *Matrix analysis*. Press Syndicate of the University of Cambridge.

Jordan, M. I., & Jacobs, R, (1994). "Hierarchical mixtures of experts and the EM algorithm." *Neural Computation*, 6, 2, pp.181-214.

Massy, W. F, (1965). "Principle component regression in exploratory statistical research." *Journal of the American Statistical Association*, 60, pp.234-246.

Rubin, D. B., & Thayer, D. T, (1982). "EM algorithms for ML factor analysis." *Psychometrika*, 47, 1, 69-76.

Schaal, S., & Atkeson, C. G, (in press). "Constructive incremental learning from only local information." *Neural Computation*.

Scott, D. W, (1992). *Multivariate Density Estimation*. New York: Wiley.

Vijayakumar, S., & Schaal, S, (1997). "Local dimensionality reduction for locally weighted learning." In: *International Conference on Computational Intelligence in Robotics and Automation*, pp.220-225, Monteray, CA, July 10-11, 1997.

Wold, H. (1975). "Soft modeling by latent variables: the nonlinear iterative partial least squares approach." In: Gani, J. (Ed.), *Perspectives in Probability and Statistics, Papers in Honour of M. S. Bartlett*. Acad. Press.

Xu, L., Jordan, M. I., & Hinton, G. E, (1995). "An alternative model for mixture of experts." In: Tesauro, G., Touretzky, D. S., & Leen, T. K. (Eds.), *Advances in Neural Information Processing Systems 7*, pp.633-640. Cambridge, MA: MIT Press.

Prior Knowledge in Support Vector Kernels

Bernhard Schölkopf[*†], **Patrice Simard**[‡], **Alex Smola**[†], **& Vladimir Vapnik**[‡]
[*]Max-Planck-Institut für biologische Kybernetik, Tübingen, Germany
[†]GMD FIRST, Rudower Chaussee 5, 12489 Berlin, Germany
[‡]AT&T Research, 100 Schulz Drive, Red Bank, NJ, USA
bs@first.gmd.de

Abstract

We explore methods for incorporating prior knowledge about a problem at hand in Support Vector learning machines. We show that both invariances under group transformations and prior knowledge about locality in images can be incorporated by constructing appropriate kernel functions.

1 INTRODUCTION

When we are trying to extract regularities from data, we often have additional knowledge about functions that we estimate. For instance, in image classification tasks, there exist transformations which leave class membership *invariant* (e.g. local translations); moreover, it is usually the case that images have a *local* structure in that not all correlations between image regions carry equal amounts of information.

The present study investigates the question how to make use of these two sources of knowledge by designing appropriate Support Vector (SV) kernel functions. We start by giving a brief introduction to SV machines (Vapnik & Chervonenkis, 1979; Vapnik, 1995) (Sec. 2). Regarding prior knowledge about invariances, we present a method to design kernel functions for invariant classification hyperplanes (Sec. 3). The method is applicable to invariances under the action of differentiable local 1-parameter groups of local transformations, e.g. translational invariance in pattern recognition. In Sec. 4, we describe kernels which take into account image locality by using localized receptive fields. Sec. 5 presents experimental results on both types of kernels, followed by a discussion (Sec. 6).

2 OPTIMAL MARGIN HYPERPLANES

For linear hyperplane decision functions $f(\mathbf{x}) = \mathrm{sgn}\left((\mathbf{w} \cdot \mathbf{x}) + b\right)$, the VC-dimension can be controlled by controlling the norm of the weight vector $\mathbf{w}$. Given training data $(\mathbf{x}_1, y_1), \ldots, (\mathbf{x}_\ell, y_\ell)$, $\mathbf{x}_i \in \mathbf{R}^N, y_i \in \{\pm 1\}$, a separating hyperplane which generalizes well can be found by minimizing

$$\frac{1}{2}\|\mathbf{w}\|^2 \quad \text{subject to} \quad y_i \cdot ((\mathbf{x}_i \cdot \mathbf{w}) + b) \geq 1 \quad \text{for } i = 1, \ldots, \ell, \tag{1}$$

the latter being the conditions for separating the training data with a margin. Nonseparable cases are dealt with by introducing slack variables (Cortes & Vapnik 1995), but we shall omit this modification to simplify the exposition. All of the following also applies for the nonseparable case.

To solve the above convex optimization problem, one introduces a Lagrangian with multipliers α_i and derives the dual form of the optimization problem: maximize

$$\sum_{i=1}^{\ell} \alpha_i - \frac{1}{2} \sum_{i,k=1}^{\ell} \alpha_i y_i \alpha_k y_k (\mathbf{x}_i \cdot \mathbf{x}_k) \quad \text{subject to} \quad \alpha_i \geq 0, \quad \sum_{i=1}^{\ell} \alpha_i y_i = 0. \tag{2}$$

It turns out that the solution vector has an expansion in terms of training examples, $\mathbf{w} = \sum_{i=1}^{\ell} \alpha_i y_i \mathbf{x}_i$, where only those α_i corresponding to constraints (1) which are met can become nonzero; the respective examples $\mathbf{x}_i$ are called *Support Vectors*. Substituting this expansion for $\mathbf{w}$ yields the decision function

$$f(\mathbf{x}) = \text{sgn} \left(\sum_{i=1}^{\ell} \alpha_i y_i (\mathbf{x} \cdot \mathbf{x}_i) + b \right). \tag{3}$$

It can be shown that minimizing (2) corresponds to minimizing an upper bound on the VC dimension of separating hyperplanes, or, equivalently, to maximizing the separation margin between the two classes. In the next section, we shall depart from this and modify the dot product used such that the minimization of (2) corresponds to enforcing transformation invariance, while at the same time the constraints (1) still hold.

3 INVARIANT HYPERPLANES

Invariance by a self-consistency argument. We face the following problem: to express the condition of invariance of the decision function, we already need to know its coefficients which are found only during the optimization, which in turn should already take into account the desired invariances. As a way out of this circle, we use the following ansatz: consider decision functions $f = (\text{sgn} \circ g)$, where g is defined as

$$g(\mathbf{x}_j) := \sum_{i=1}^{\ell} \alpha_i y_i (B\mathbf{x}_j \cdot B\mathbf{x}_i) + b, \tag{4}$$

with a matrix B to be determined below. This follows Vapnik (1995), who suggested to incorporate invariances by modifying the dot product used. Any nonsingular B defines a dot product, which can equivalently be written as $(\mathbf{x}_j \cdot A\mathbf{x}_i)$, with a positive definite matrix $A = B^\top B$.

Clearly, invariance of g under local transformations of all $\mathbf{x}_j$ is a sufficient condition for the local invariance of f, which is what we are aiming for. Strictly speaking, however, invariance of g is not necessary at points which are not Support Vectors, since these lie in a region where $(\text{sgn} \circ g)$ is constant — however, before training, it is hard to predict which examples will turn out to become SVs. In the Virtual SV method (Schölkopf, Burges, & Vapnik, 1996), a first run of the standard SV algorithm is carried out to obtain an initial SV set; similar heuristics could be applied in the present case.

Local invariance of g for each pattern $\mathbf{x}_j$ under transformations of a differentiable local 1-parameter group of local transformations $\mathcal{L}_t$,

$$\left. \frac{\partial}{\partial t} \right|_{t=0} g(\mathcal{L}_t \mathbf{x}_j) = 0, \tag{5}$$

can be approximately enforced by minimizing the regularizer

$$\frac{1}{\ell} \sum_{j=1}^{\ell} \left(\frac{\partial}{\partial t} \Big|_{t=0} g(\mathcal{L}_t \mathbf{x}_j) \right)^2 . \tag{6}$$

Note that the sum may run over labelled as well as unlabelled data, so in principle one could also require the decision function to be invariant with respect to transformations of elements of a *test* set. Moreover, we could use different transformations for different patterns.

For (4), the local invariance term (5) becomes

$$\cdot \frac{\partial}{\partial t} \Big|_{t=0} \left(\sum_{i=1}^{\ell} \alpha_i y_i (B\mathcal{L}_t \mathbf{x}_j \cdot B\mathbf{x}_i) + b \right) = \sum_{i=1}^{\ell} \alpha_i y_i \partial_1 (B\mathcal{L}_0 \mathbf{x}_j \cdot B\mathbf{x}_i) \cdot B \frac{\partial}{\partial t} \Big|_{t=0} \mathcal{L}_t \mathbf{x}_j, \tag{7}$$

using the chain rule. Here, $\partial_1 (B\mathcal{L}_0 \mathbf{x}_j \cdot B\mathbf{x}_i)$ denotes the gradient of $(\mathbf{x} \cdot \mathbf{y})$ with respect to $\mathbf{x}$, evaluated at the point $(\mathbf{x} \cdot \mathbf{y}) = (B\mathcal{L}_0 \mathbf{x}_j \cdot B\mathbf{x}_i)$. Substituting (7) into (6), using the facts that $\mathcal{L}_0 = I$ and $\partial_1 (\mathbf{x}, \mathbf{y}) = \mathbf{y}^\top$, yields the regularizer

$$\frac{1}{\ell} \sum_{j=1}^{\ell} \left(\sum_{i=1}^{\ell} \alpha_i y_i (B\mathbf{x}_i)^\top B \frac{\partial}{\partial t} \Big|_{t=0} \mathcal{L}_t \mathbf{x}_j \right)^2 = \sum_{i,k=1}^{\ell} \alpha_i y_i \alpha_k y_k (B\mathbf{x}_i \cdot BCB^\top B\mathbf{x}_k) \tag{8}$$

where

$$C := \frac{1}{\ell} \sum_{j=1}^{\ell} \left(\frac{\partial}{\partial t} \Big|_{t=0} \mathcal{L}_t \mathbf{x}_j \right) \left(\frac{\partial}{\partial t} \Big|_{t=0} \mathcal{L}_t \mathbf{x}_j \right)^\top . \tag{9}$$

We now choose B such that (8) reduces to the standard SV target function $\|\mathbf{w}\|^2$ in the form obtained by substituting the expansion $\mathbf{w} = \sum_{i=1}^{\ell} \alpha_i y_i \mathbf{x}_i$ into it (cf. the quadratic term of (2)), utilizing the dot product chosen in (4), i.e. such that $(B\mathbf{x}_i \cdot BCB^\top B\mathbf{x}_k) = (B\mathbf{x}_i \cdot B\mathbf{x}_k)$. Assuming that the $\mathbf{x}_i$ span the whole space, this condition becomes $B^\top BCB^\top B = B^\top B$, or, by requiring B to be nonsingular, i.e. that no information get lost during the preprocessing, $BCB^\top = I$. This can be satisfied by a preprocessing (whitening) matrix

$$B = C^{-\frac{1}{2}} \tag{10}$$

(modulo a unitary matrix, which we disregard), the nonnegative square root of the inverse of the nonnegative matrix C defined in (9). In practice, we use a matrix

$$C_\lambda := (1 - \lambda)C + \lambda I, \tag{11}$$

$0 < \lambda \le 1$, instead of C. As C is nonnegative, C_λ is invertible. For $\lambda = 1$, we recover the standard SV optimal hyperplane algorithm, other values of λ determine the trade-off between invariance and model complexity control. It can be shown that using C_λ corresponds to using an objective function $\Phi(\mathbf{w}) = (1 - \lambda) \sum_i (\mathbf{w} \cdot \frac{\partial}{\partial t} |_{t=0} \mathcal{L}_t \mathbf{x}_i)^2 + \lambda \|\mathbf{w}\|^2$.

By choosing the preprocessing matrix B according to (10), we have obtained a formulation of the problem where the standard SV quadratic optimization technique does in effect minimize the tangent regularizer (6): the maximum of (2), using the modified dot product as in (4), coincides with the minimum of (6) subject to the separation conditions $y_i \cdot g(\mathbf{x}_i) \ge 1$, where g is defined as in (4).

Note that preprocessing with B does not affect classification speed: since $(B\mathbf{x}_j \cdot B\mathbf{x}_i) = (\mathbf{x}_j \cdot B^\top B\mathbf{x}_i)$, we can precompute $B^\top B\mathbf{x}_i$ for all SVs $\mathbf{x}_i$ and thus obtain a machine (with modified SVs) which is as fast as a standard SV machine (cf. (4)).

Relationship to Principal Component Analysis (PCA). Let us now provide some interpretation of (10) and (9). The tangent vectors $\pm \frac{\partial}{\partial t} |_{t=0} \mathcal{L}_t \mathbf{x}_j$ have zero mean, thus C is a sample estimate of the covariance matrix of the random vector $s \cdot \frac{\partial}{\partial t}|_{t=0}\mathcal{L}_t\mathbf{x}$, $s \in \{\pm 1\}$ being a random sign. Based on this observation, we call C (9) the *Tangent Covariance Matrix* of the data set $\{\mathbf{x}_i : i = 1, \ldots, \ell\}$ with respect to the transformations $\mathcal{L}_t$.

Being positive definite,[1] C can be diagonalized, $C = SDS^\top$, with an orthogonal matrix S consisting of C's Eigenvectors and a diagonal matrix D containing the corresponding positive Eigenvalues. Then we can compute $B = C^{-\frac{1}{2}} = SD^{-\frac{1}{2}}S^\top$, where $D^{-\frac{1}{2}}$ is the diagonal matrix obtained from D by taking the inverse square roots of the diagonal elements. Since the dot product is invariant under orthogonal transformations, we may drop the leading S and (4) becomes

$$g(\mathbf{x}_j) = \sum_{i=1}^{\ell} \alpha_i y_i (D^{-\frac{1}{2}}S^\top\mathbf{x}_j \cdot D^{-\frac{1}{2}}S^\top\mathbf{x}_i) + b. \tag{12}$$

A given pattern $\mathbf{x}$ is thus first transformed by projecting it onto the Eigenvectors of the tangent covariance matrix C, which are the rows of $S^\top$. The resulting feature vector is then rescaled by dividing by the square roots of C's Eigenvalues.[2] In other words, the directions of main variance of the random vector $\frac{\partial}{\partial t}|_{t=0}\mathcal{L}_t\mathbf{x}$ are scaled back, thus more emphasis is put on features which are less variant under $\mathcal{L}_t$. For example, in image analysis, if the $\mathcal{L}_t$ represent translations, more emphasis is put on the relative proportions of ink in the image rather than the positions of lines. The PCA interpretation of our preprocessing matrix suggests the possibility to regularize and reduce dimensionality by discarding part of the features, as it is common usage when doing PCA.

In the present work, the ideas described in this section have only been tested in the linear case. More generally, SV machines use a nonlinear *kernel function* which can be shown to compute a dot product in a high-dimensional space F nonlinearly related to input space via some map Φ, i.e. $k(\mathbf{x}, \mathbf{y}) = (\Phi(\mathbf{x}) \cdot \Phi(\mathbf{y}))$. In that case, the above analysis leads to a tangent covariance matrix C in F, and it can be shown that (12) can be evaluated in terms of the kernel function (Schölkopf, 1997). To this end, one diagonalizes C using techniques of kernel PCA (Schölkopf, Smola, & Müller, 1996).

4   KERNELS USING LOCAL CORRELATIONS

By using a kernel $k(\mathbf{x}, \mathbf{y}) = (\mathbf{x} \cdot \mathbf{y})^d$, one implicitly constructs a decision boundary in the space of all possible products of d pixels. This may not be desirable, since in natural images, correlations over short distances are much more reliable as features than long-range correlations are. To take this into account, we define a kernel $k_p^{d_1, d_2}$ as follows (cf. Fig. 1):

1. compute a third image $\mathbf{z}$, defined as the pixel-wise product of $\mathbf{x}$ and $\mathbf{y}$

2. sample $\mathbf{z}$ with pyramidal receptive fields of diameter p, centered at all locations (i, j), to obtain the values $\mathbf{z}_{ij}$

3. raise each $\mathbf{z}_{ij}$ to the power d_1, to take into account local correlations within the range of the pyramid

4. sum $\mathbf{z}_{ij}^{d_1}$ over the whole image, and raise the result to the power d_2 to allow for longe-range correlations of order d_2

---

[1] It is understood that we use C_λ if C is not definite (cf. (11)). Alternatively, we can below use the pseudoinverse.

[2] As an aside, note that our goal to build invariant SV machines has thus serendipitously provided us with an approach for an open problem in SV learning, namely the one of scaling: in SV machines, there has so far been no way of automatically assigning different weight to different directions in input space — in a trained SV machine, the weights of the first layer (the SVs) form a subset of the training set. Choosing these Support Vectors from the training set only gives rather limited possibilities for appropriately dealing with different scales in different directions of input space.

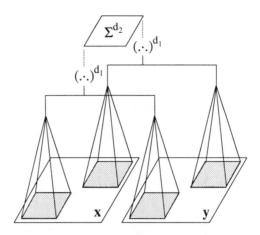

Figure 1: Kernel utilizing local correlations in images, corresponding to a dot product in a polynomial space which is spanned mainly by local correlations between pixels (see text).

The resulting kernel will be of order $d_1 \cdot d_2$, however, it will *not* contain *all* possible correlations of $d_1 \cdot d_2$ pixels.

5   EXPERIMENTAL RESULTS

In the experiments, we used a subset of the MNIST data base of handwritten characters (Bottou et al., 1994), consisting of 5000 training examples and 10000 test examples at a resolution of 20x20 pixels, with entries in $[-1, 1]$. Using a linear SV machine (i.e. a separating hyperplane), we obtain a test error rate of 9.8% (training 10 binary classifiers, and using the maximum value of g (cf. (4)) for 10-class classification); by using a polynomial kernel of degree 4, this drops to 4.0%. In all of the following experiments, we used degree 4 kernels of various types. The number 4 was chosen as it can be written as a product of two integers, thus we could compare results to a kernel $k_p^{d_1, d_2}$ with $d_1 = d_2 = 2$. For the considered classification task, results for higher polynomial degrees are very similar.

In a series of experiments with a homogeneous polynomial kernel $k(\mathbf{x}, \mathbf{y}) = (\mathbf{x} \cdot \mathbf{y})^4$, using preprocessing with Gaussian smoothing kernels of standard deviation $0.1, 0.2, \ldots, 1.0$, we obtained error rates which gradually increased from 4.0% to 4.3%; thus no improvement of this performance was possible by a simple smoothing operation. Applying the Virtual SV method (retraining the SV machine on translated SVs; Schölkopf, Burges, & Vapnik, 1996) to this problem results in an improved error rate of 2.8%. For training on the full 60000 pattern set, the Virtual SV performance is 0.8% (Schölkopf, 1997).

Invariant hyperplanes. Table 1 reports results obtained by preprocessing all patterns with B (cf. (10)), choosing different values of λ (cf. (11)). In the experiments, the patterns were first rescaled to have entries in $[0, 1]$, then B was computed, using horizontal and vertical translations, and preprocessing was carried out; finally, the resulting patterns were scaled back again. This was done to ensure that patterns and derivatives lie in comparable regions of $\mathbf{R}^N$ (note that if the pattern background level is a constant -1, then its derivative is 0). The results show that even though (9) was derived for the linear case, it can lead to improvements in the nonlinear case (here, for a degree 4 polynomial), too.

Dimensionality reduction. The above $[0, 1]$ scaling operation is affine rather than linear, hence the argument leading to (12) does not hold for this case. We thus only report results on dimensionality reduction for the case where the data is kept in $[0, 1]$ scaling from the very

Table 1: Classification error rates for modifying the kernel $k(\mathbf{x}, \mathbf{y}) = (\mathbf{x} \cdot \mathbf{y})^4$ with the invariant hyperplane preprocessing matrix $B_\lambda = C_\lambda^{-\frac{1}{2}}$; cf. (10) and (11). Enforcing invariance with $0.1 < \lambda < 1$ leads to improvements over the original performance ($\lambda = 1$).

λ	0.1	0.2	0.3	0.4	0.5	0.6	0.7	0.8	0.9	1.0
error rate in %	4.2	3.8	3.6	3.6	3.7	3.8	3.8	3.9	3.9	4.0

Table 2: Dropping directions corresponding to small Eigenvalues of C (cf. (12)) leads to substantial improvements. All results given are for the case $\lambda = 0.4$ (cf. Table 1); degree 4 homogeneous polynomial kernel.

principal components discarded	0	50	100	150	200	250	300	350
error rate in %	8.7	5.4	4.9	4.4	4.2	3.9	3.7	3.9

beginning on. Dropping principal components which are less important leads to substantial improvements (Table 2); cf. the explanation following (12). The results in Table 2 are somewhat distorted by the fact that the polynomial kernel is not translation invariant, and performs poorly on the $[0, 1]$ data, which becomes evident in the case where none of the principal components are discarded. Better results have been obtained using translation invariant kernels, e.g. Gaussian RBFs (Schölkopf, 1997).

Kernels using local correlations. To exploit locality in images, we used a pyramidal receptive field kernel $k_p^{d_1, d_2}$ with diameter $p = 9$ (cf. Sec. 4). For $d_1 = d_2 = 2$, we obtained an improved error rate of 3.1%, another degree 4 kernel with *only* local correlations ($d_1 = 4, d_2 = 1$) led to 3.4%. Albeit significantly better than the 4.0% for the degree 4 homogeneous polynomial (the error rates on the 10000 element test set have an accuracy of about 0.1%, cf. Bottou et al., 1994), this is still worse than the Virtual SV result of 2.8%. As the two methods, however, exploit different types of prior knowledge, it could be expected that combining them leads to still better performance; and indeed, this yielded the best performance of all (2.0%).

For the purpose of benchmarking, we also ran our system on the US postal service database of 7291+2007 handwritten digits at a resolution of 16 × 16. In that case, we obtained the following test error rates: SV with degree 4 polynomial kernel 4.2%, Virtual SV (same kernel) 3.5%, SV with $k_7^{2,2}$ 3.6%, Virtual SV with $k_7^{2,2}$ 3.0%. The latter compares favourably to almost all known results on that data base, and is second only to a memory-based tangent-distance nearest neighbour classifier at 2.6% (Simard, LeCun, & Denker, 1993).

6 DISCUSSION

With its rather general class of admissible kernel functions, the SV algorithm provides ample possibilities for constructing task-specific kernels. We have considered an image classification task and used two forms of domain knowledge: first, pattern classes were required to be locally translationally invariant, and second, local correlations in the images were assumed to be more reliable than long-range correlations. The second requirement can be seen as a more general form of prior knowledge — it can be thought of as arising partially from the fact that patterns possess a whole variety of transformations; in object recognition, for instance, we have object rotations and deformations. Typically, these transformations are continuous, which implies that local relationships in an image are fairly stable, whereas global relationships are less reliable.

We have incorporated both types of domain knowledge into the SV algorithm by constructing appropriate kernel functions, leading to substantial improvements on the considered pattern recognition tasks. Our method for constructing kernels for *transformation invariant* SV machines, put forward to deal with the first type of domain knowledge, so far has only been applied in the linear case, which partially explains why it only led to moderate improvements (also, we so far only used translational invariance). It is applicable for differentiable transformations — other types, e.g. for mirror symmetry, have to be dealt with using other techniques, e.g. Virtual SVs (Schölkopf, Burges, & Vapnik, 1996). Its main advantages compared to the latter technique is that it does not slow down testing speed, and that using more invariances leaves training time almost unchanged. The proposed kernels respecting *locality* in images led to large improvements; they are applicable not only in image classification but in all cases where the relative importance of subsets of products features can be specified appropriately. They do, however, slow down both training and testing by a constant factor which depends on the specific kernel used.

Both described techniques should be directly applicable to other kernel-based methods as SV regression (Vapnik, 1995) and kernel PCA (Schölkopf, Smola, & Müller, 1996). Future work will include the nonlinear case (cf. our remarks in Sec. 3), the incorporation of invariances other than translation, and the construction of kernels incorporating local feature extractors (e.g. edge detectors) different from the pyramids described in Sec. 4.

Acknowledgements. We thank Chris Burges and Léon Bottou for parts of the code and for helpful discussions, and Tony Bell for his remarks.

References

B. E. Boser, I .M. Guyon, and V. N. Vapnik. A training algorithm for optimal margin classifiers. In D. Haussler, editor, *Proceedings of the 5th Annual ACM Workshop on Computational Learning Theory*, pages 144–152, Pittsburgh, PA, 1992. ACM Press.

L. Bottou, C. Cortes, J. S. Denker, H. Drucker, I. Guyon, L. D. Jackel, Y. LeCun, U. A. Müller, E. Säckinger, P. Simard, and V. Vapnik. Comparison of classifier methods: a case study in handwritten digit recognition. In *Proceedings of the 12th International Conference on Pattern Recognition and Neural Networks, Jerusalem*, pages 77 – 87. IEEE Computer Society Press, 1994.

C. Cortes and V. Vapnik. Support vector networks. *Machine Learning*, 20:273 – 297, 1995.

B. Schölkopf. *Support Vector Learning*. R. Oldenbourg Verlag, Munich, 1997. ISBN 3-486-24632-1.

B. Schölkopf, C. Burges, and V. Vapnik. Incorporating invariances in support vector learning machines. In C. von der Malsburg, W. von Seelen, J. C. Vorbrüggen, and B. Sendhoff, editors, *Artificial Neural Networks — ICANN'96*, pages 47 – 52, Berlin, 1996a. Springer Lecture Notes in Computer Science, Vol. 1112.

B. Schölkopf, A. Smola, and K.-R. Müller. Nonlinear component analysis as a kernel eigenvalue problem. Technical Report 44, Max-Planck-Institut für biologische Kybernetik, 1996b. in press *(Neural Computation)*.

P. Simard, Y. LeCun, and J. Denker. Efficient pattern recognition using a new transformation distance. In S. J. Hanson, J. D. Cowan, and C. L. Giles, editors, *Advances in Neural Information Processing Systems 5*, pages 50–58, San Mateo, CA, 1993. Morgan Kaufmann.

P. Simard, B. Victorri, Y. LeCun, and J. Denker. Tangent prop — a formalism for specifying selected invariances in an adaptive network. In J. E. Moody, S. J. Hanson, and R. P. Lippmann, editors, *Advances in Neural Information Processing Systems 4*, pages 895–903, San Mateo, CA, 1992. Morgan Kaufmann.

V. Vapnik. *The Nature of Statistical Learning Theory*. Springer Verlag, New York, 1995.

V. Vapnik and A. Chervonenkis. *Theory of Pattern Recognition [in Russian]*. Nauka, Moscow, 1974. (German Translation: W. Wapnik & A. Tscherwonenkis, *Theorie der Zeichenerkennung*, Akademie-Verlag, Berlin, 1979).

Training Methods for Adaptive Boosting
of Neural Networks

Holger Schwenk
Dept. IRO
Université de Montréal
2920 Chemin de la Tour,
Montreal, Qc, Canada, H3C 3J7
schwenk@iro.umontreal.ca

Yoshua Bengio
Dept. IRO
Université de Montréal
and *AT&T Laboratories, NJ*
bengioy@iro.umontreal.ca

Abstract

"Boosting" is a general method for improving the performance of any learning algorithm that consistently generates classifiers which need to perform only slightly better than random guessing. A recently proposed and very promising boosting algorithm is *AdaBoost* [5]. It has been applied with great success to several benchmark machine learning problems using rather simple learning algorithms [4], and decision trees [1, 2, 6]. In this paper we use AdaBoost to improve the performances of neural networks. We compare training methods based on sampling the training set and weighting the cost function. Our system achieves about 1.4% error on a data base of online handwritten digits from more than 200 writers. Adaptive boosting of a multi-layer network achieved 1.5% error on the UCI Letters and 8.1% error on the UCI satellite data set.

1 Introduction

AdaBoost [4, 5] (for *Ada*ptive *Boost*ing) constructs a composite classifier by sequentially training classifiers, while putting more and more emphasis on certain patterns. AdaBoost has been applied to rather weak learning algorithms (with low capacity) [4] and to decision trees [1, 2, 6], and not yet, until now, to the best of our knowledge, to artificial neural networks. These experiments displayed rather intriguing generalization properties, such as continued decrease in generalization error after training error reaches zero. Previous workers also disagree on the reasons for the impressive generalization performance displayed by AdaBoost on a large array of tasks. One issue raised by Breiman [1] and the authors of AdaBoost [4] is whether some of this effect is due to a reduction in variance similar to the one obtained from the Bagging algorithm.

In this paper we explore the application of AdaBoost to Diabolo (auto-associative) networks and multi-layer neural networks (MLPs). In doing so, we also compare three different versions of AdaBoost: (R) training each classifier with a fixed training set obtained by resampling with replacement from the original training set (as in [1]), (E) training by resampling after each epoch a new training set from the original training set, and (W) training by directly weighting the cost function (here the squared error) of the neural network. Note that the second version (E) is a better approximation of the weighted cost function than the first one (R), in particular when many epochs are performed. If the variance reduction induced by averaging the hypotheses from very different models explains a good part of the generalization performance of AdaBoost, then the weighted training version (W) should perform worse then the resampling versions, and the fixed sample version (R) should perform better then the continuously resampled version (E).

2 AdaBoost

AdaBoost combines the hypotheses generated by a set of classifiers trained one after the other. The tth classifier is trained with more emphasis on certain patterns, using a cost function weighted by a probability distribution D_t over the training data ($D_t(i)$ is positive and $\sum_i D_t(i) = 1$). Some learning algorithms don't permit training with respect to a weighted cost function. In this case sampling with replacement (using the probability distribution D_t) can be used to approximate a weighted cost function. Examples with high probability would then occur more often than those with low probability, while some examples may not occur in the sample at all although their probability is not zero. This is particularly true in the simple resampling version (labeled "R" earlier), and unlikely when a new training set is resampled after each epoch ("E" version). Neural networks can be trained directly with respect to a distribution over the learning data by weighting the cost function (this is the "W" version): the squared error on the i-th pattern is weighted by the probability $D_t(i)$. The result of training the tth classifier is a *hypothesis* $h_t : X \to Y$ where $Y = \{1, ..., k\}$ is the space of labels, and X is the space of input features. After the tth round the weighted error ϵ_t of the resulting classifier is calculated and the distribution D_{t+1} is computed from D_t, by increasing the probability of incorrectly labeled examples. The global decision f is obtained by weighted voting. Figure 1 (left) summarizes the basic AdaBoost algorithm. It converges (learns the training set) if each classifier yields a weighted error that is less than 50%, i.e., better than chance in the 2-class case. There is also a multi-class version, called *pseudoloss*-AdaBoost, that can be used when the classifier computes confidence scores for each class. Due to lack of space, we give only the algorithm (see figure 1, right) and we refer the reader to the references for more details [4, 5].

AdaBoost has very interesting theoretical properties, in particular it can be shown that the error of the composite classifier on the training data decreases exponentially fast to zero [5] as the number of combined classifiers is increased. More importantly, however, bounds on the *generalization error* of such a system have been formulated [7]. These are based on a notion of *margin* of classification, defined as the difference between the score of the correct class and the strongest score of a wrong class. In the case in which there are just two possible labels $\{-1, +1\}$, this is $yf(x)$, where f is the composite classifier and y the correct label. Obviously, the classification is correct if the margin is positive. We now state the theorem bounding the generalization error of Adaboost [7] (and any classifier obtained by a convex combination of a set of classifiers). Let H be a set of hypotheses (from which the h_t hare chosen), with VC-dimenstion d. Let f be any convex combination of hypotheses from H. Let S be a sample of N examples chosen independently at random according to a distribution D. Then with probability at least $1 - \delta$ over the random choice of the training set S from D, the following bound is satisfied for all $\theta > 0$:

$$P_D[yf(x) \leq 0] \ \leq \ P_S[yf(x) \leq \theta] + O\left(\frac{1}{\sqrt{N}}\sqrt{\frac{d\log^2(N/d)}{\theta^2} + \log(1/\delta)}\right) \quad (1)$$

Note that this bound is independent of the number of combined hypotheses and how they

Input: sequence of N examples $(x_1, y_1), \ldots, (x_N, y_N)$ with labels $y_i \in Y = \{1, \ldots, k\}$	
Init: $D_1(i) = 1/N$ for all i	**Init:** let $B = \{(i, y): i \in \{1, \ldots, N\}, y \neq y_i\}$ $D_1(i, y) = 1/|B|$ for all $(i, y) \in B$
Repeat:	**Repeat:**
1. Train neural network with respect to distribution D_t and obtain hypothesis $h_t : X \to Y$	1. Train neural network with respect to distribution D_t and obtain hypothesis $h_t : X \times Y \to [0, 1]$
2. calculate the weighted error of h_t: $$\epsilon_t = \sum_{i:h_t(x_i) \neq y_i} D_t(i) \quad \begin{array}{c}\text{abort loop}\\ \text{if } \epsilon_t > \frac{1}{2}\end{array}$$	2. calculate the pseudo-loss of h_t: $$\epsilon_t = \frac{1}{2} \sum_{(i,y) \in B} D_t(i, y)(1 - h_t(x_i, y_i) + h_t(x_i, y))$$
3. set $\beta_t = \epsilon_t/(1 - \epsilon_t)$	3. set $\beta_t = \epsilon_t/(1 - \epsilon_t)$
4. update distribution D_t $$D_{t+1}(i) = \frac{D_t(i)}{Z_t} \beta_t^{\delta_i}$$ with $\delta_i = (h_t(x_i) = y_i)$ and Z_t a normalization constant	4. update distribution D_t $$D_{t+1}(i, y) = \frac{D_t(i,y)}{Z_t} \beta_t^{\frac{1}{2}((1+h_t(x_i,y_i)-h_t(x_i,y))}$$ where Z_t is a normalization constant
Output: final hypothesis: $$f(x) = \arg\max_{y \in Y} \sum_{t:h_t(x)=y} \log \frac{1}{\beta_t}$$	**Output:** final hypothesis: $$f(x) = \arg\max_{y \in Y} \sum_t \left(\log \frac{1}{\beta_t}\right) h_t(x, y)$$

Figure 1: AdaBoost algorithm (left), multi-class extension using confidence scores (right)

are chosen from H. The distribution of the margins however plays an important role. It can be shown that the AdaBoost algorithm is especially well suited to the task of maximizing the number of training examples with large margin [7].

3 The Diabolo Classifier

Normally, neural networks used for classification are trained to map an input vector to an output vector that encodes directly the classes, usually by the so called "1-out-of-N encoding". An alternative approach with interesting properties is to use auto-associative neural networks, also called autoencoders or *Diabolo networks*, to learn a model of each class. In the simplest case, each autoencoder network is trained only with examples of the corresponding class, i.e., it learns to reconstruct all examples of one class at its output. The distance between the input vector and the reconstructed output vector expresses the likelihood that a particular example is part of the corresponding class. Therefore classification is done by choosing the best fitting model. Figure 2 summarizes the basic architecture. It shows also typical classification behavior for an online character recognition task. The input and output vectors are (x, y)-coordinate sequences of a character. The visual representation in the figure is obtained by connecting these points. In this example the "1" is correctly classified since the network for this class has the smallest reconstruction error.

The Diabolo classifier uses a *distributed representation* of the models which is much more compact than the enumeration of references often used by distance-based classifiers like nearest-neighbor or RBF networks. Furthermore, one has to calculate only one distance measure for each class to recognize. This allows to incorporate knowledge by a domain specific distance measure at a very low computational cost. In previous work [8], we have shown that the well-known tangent-distance [11] can be used in the objective function of the autoencoders. This Diabolo classifier has achieved state-of-the-art results in handwritten OCR [8, 9]. Recently, we have also extended the idea of a transformation invariant distance

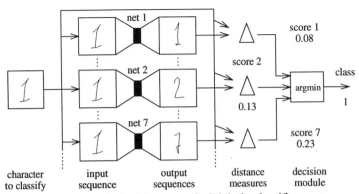

Figure 2: Architecture of a Diabolo classifier

measure to online character recognition [10]. One autoencoder alone, however, can not learn efficiently the model of a character if it is written in many different stroke orders and directions. The architecture can be extended by using several autoencoders per class, each one specializing on a particular writing style (subclass). For the class "0", for instance, we would have one Diabolo network that learns a model for zeros written clockwise and another one for zeros written counterclockwise. The assignment of the training examples to the different subclass models should ideally be done in an unsupervised way. However, this can be quite difficult since the number of writing styles is not known in advance and usually the number of examples in each subclass varies a lot. Our training data base contains for instance 100 zeros written counterclockwise, but only 3 written clockwise (there are also some more examples written in other strange styles). Classical clustering algorithms would probably tend to ignore subclasses with very few examples since they aren't responsible for much of the error, but this may result in poor generalization behavior. Therefore, in previous work we have manually assigned the subclass labels [10]. Of course, this is not a generally satisfactory approach, and certainly infeasible when the training set is large. In the following, we will show that the emphasizing algorithm of AdaBoost can be used to train multiple Diabolo classifiers per class, performing a soft assignment of examples of the training set to each network.

4   Results with Diabolo and MLP Classifiers

Experiments have been performed on three data sets: a data base of online handwritten digits, the UCI *Letters* database of offline machine-printed alphabetical characters and the UCI *satellite* database that is generated from Landsat Multi-spectral Scanner image data. All data sets have a pre-defined training and test set. The Diabolo classifier was only applied to the online data set (since it takes advantage of the structure of the input features).

The online data set was collected at Paris 6 University [10]. It is writer-independent (different writers in training and test sets) and there are 203 writers, 1200 training examples and 830 test examples. Each writer gave only one example per class. Therefore, there are many different writing styles, with very different frequencies. We only applied a simple preprocessing: the characters were resampled to 11 points, centered and size normalized to a (x,y)-coordinate sequence in $[-1, 1]^{22}$. Since the Diabolo classifier with tangent distance [10] is invariant to small transformations we don't need to extract further features.

Table 1 summarizes the results on the test set of different approaches before using Ada-Boost. The Diabolo classifier with hand-selected sub-classes in the training set performs best since it is invariant to transformations and since it can deal with the different writing styles. The experiments suggest that fully connected neural networks are not well suited for this task: small nets do poorly on both training and test sets, while large nets overfit.

Table 1: Online digits data set error rates for different unboosted classifiers

	Diabolo classifier		fully connected MLP		
	no subclasses	hand-selected	22-10-10	22-30-10	22-50-10
train:	2.2%	0.6%	5.7%	0.8%	0.4%
test:	3.3%	1.2%	8.8%	3.3%	2.8%

10-fold cross-validation was used to find the optimal number of training epochs (typically about 200). If training is continued until 1000 epochs, the test error increases by more than 1 %.

Table 2 shows the results of bagged and boosted multi-layer perceptrons with 10, 30 or 50 hidden units, trained for either 100, 200, 500 or 1000 epochs, and using either the ordinary resampling scheme (R), resampling with different random selections at each epoch (E), or training with weights D_t on the squared error criterion for each pattern (W). 100 neural networks were combined. The multi-class version of the AdaBoost algorithm was used in all the experiments with MLPs: it yielded considerably better results than the basic version. Pseudoloss-AdaBoost was however not useful for the Diabolo classifier since it uses a powerful discriminant learning algorithm [9].

Table 2: Online digits test error rates for boosted MLPs

architecture version:	22-10-10			22-30-10			22-50-10		
	R	E	W	R	E	W	R	E	W
Bagging: 500 it	5.4%			2.8%			1.8%		
AdaBoost:									
100 it	2.9%	3.2%	6.0%	1.7%	1.8%	5.1%	2.1%	1.8%	4.9%
200 it	3.0%	2.8%	5.6%	1.8%	1.8%	4.2%	1.8%	1.7%	3.5%
500 it	2.5%	2.7%	3.3%	1.7%	1.5%	3.0%	1.7%	1.7%	2.8%
1000 it	2.8%	2.7%	3.2%	1.8%	1.6%	2.6%	1.6%	1.5%	2.2%
5000 it	-	-	2.9%	-	-	1.6%	-	-	1.6%

AdaBoost improved in all cases the generalization error of the MLPs, for instance from 8.8 % to about 2.7 % for the 22-10-10 architecture. Boosting was also always superior to Bagging. Furthermore, it seems that the number of iterations of each *individual* classifier has no significant importance on the results of the combined classifier, at least on this database. Note that the test set has only 830 examples and small differences in the error rate are not statistically significant. AdaBoost with weighted training of MLPs, however, doesn't work if the learning of each individual MLP is stopped too early (1000 epochs): the networks didn't learn well enough the weighted examples and ϵ_t rapidly approached 0.5. When training each MLP for 5000 epochs, however, the weighted training (W) version achieved the same low test error. AdaBoost is less useful for very big networks (50 or more hidden units for this data) since each individual classifier achieves zero training error. In this case the probability distribution D_t doesn't change any more and AdaBoost reduces to Bagging (with eventually unequal probabilities).

Figure 3 shows the error rate of some of the boosted classifiers as the number of machines is increased, as well as examples of the margin distributions obtained after training. AdaBoost brings training error to zero after only a few steps, even with a MLP with only 10 hidden units. The generalization error is also considerably improved and it continues to decrease asymptotically after zero training error has been reached. The Diabolo classifier performs

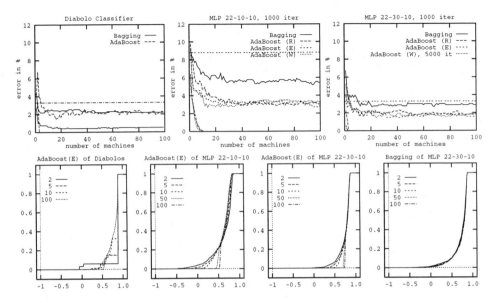

Figure 3:   top: error rates of the boosted classifiers for increasing number of networks
bottom: margin distributions using 2, 5, 10 and 100 machines respectively

best when combining 16 classifiers (**1.4%** error = 12 errors) which is almost as good as
the Diabolo classifier using hand-selected subclasses (1.2% = 10 errors). Since we know
that one autoencoder can't learn a model of the different writing style within one class, this
seems to be evidence that the example emphasizing of AdaBoost was able to assign them
automatically to different machines. Bagging yields 2.2 % error in this case. The surprising
effect of continuously decreasing generalization error even after training error reaches zero
has already been observed by others [1, 2, 4, 6]. This seems to contradict Occam's razor, but
it may be explained by the recently proven theorem of Schapire et al. [7]: the bound on the
generalization error (equation 1) depends only on the margin distribution and on the VC-
dimension of the basic learning machine (one Diabolo classifier or MLP respectively), not
on the number of machines combined by AdaBoost. Figure 3 bottom shows the margins
distributions, i.e. the fraction of examples whose margin is at most x as a function of
$x \in [-1, 1]$. It is clearly visible that AdaBoost increases the number of examples with
high margin: with 100 machines all examples have a margin higher than 0.5. Note that the
margin distribution using hundred 22-30-10 MLPs is better as the one from 100 Diabolo
classifiers, but not the error rate. We hypothesize that the difference in performance may
be due in part to a lower effective VC-dimension of the Diabolo classifier. It may also
be that the generalization error bounds of Freund et al. are too far away from the actual
generalization error. Similar experiments were performed with MLPs on the "Letters" data

Table 3: Test error rates on the UCI data sets

	CART [1]			C4.5 [4]			MLP		
	alone	bagged	boosted	alone	bagged	boosted	alone	bagged	boosted
letter	12.4 %	6.4 %	3.4 %	13.8 %	6.8 %	3.3 %	6.1 %	4.3 %	**1.5 %**
satellite	14.8 %	10.3 %	8.8 %	14.8 %	10.6 %	8.9 %	12.8 %	8.7 %	**8.1 %**

set from the UCI Machine Learning database. It has 16000 training and 4000 test patterns,
16 input features, and 26 classes (A-Z) of distorted machine-printed characters from 20
different fonts. The experiments were performed with a 16-70-50-26 MLP using 500 online
back-propagation epochs and resampling after each epoch (E), which performed best on

the experiments with the online data set. Each input feature was normalized according to its mean and variance on the training set. The plain, bagged and boosted networks are compared to decision trees (results from [1, 4]), Table 3. In all experiments 100 classifiers were combined. The results obtained with the boosted network are extremely good (**1.5%** error) and are the best that the authors know to be published for this data set. The best performance reported in STATLOG [3] is 6.4%. Note also that we need to combine only few neural networks to get already important improvements: with 20 neural networks the error falls already under 2 % whereas boosted decision trees typically "converge" later. The W-version of AdaBoost yields also the same results on this data, but again, the networks have to be trained longer. Similar conclusions hold for the UCI "satellite" data set (Table 3).

5 Conclusion

As demonstrated in three real-world applications, AdaBoost can significantly improve neural classifiers such as multi-layer networks and Diabolo networks. The behavior of Ada-Boost for neural networks confirms previous observations on other learning algorithms [1, 2, 4, 6, 7], such as the continued generalization improvement after zero training error has been reached, and the associated improvement in the margin distribution. It seems also that AdaBoost is little sensitive to overtraining of the individual classifiers, so that the neural networks can be trained for a fixed (preferably high) number of training epochs. This makes the choice of neural networks design parameters easier.

Another interesting finding of this paper is that the "weighted training" version of AdaBoost works well for MLPs, but requires many more training epochs (because of the weights on the cost function terms, the conditioning of the Hessian matrix is probably worse). These results add credence to the view of Freund and Schapire that the improvement in generalization error brought by AdaBoost is mainly due to the emphasizing (that increases the margin), rather than to a variance reduction due to the randomization of the resampling process.

References

[1] L. Breiman. Bias, variance, and Arcing classifiers. Technical Report 460, Statistics Department, University of California at Berkeley, 1996.

[2] H. Drucker and C. Cortes, Boosting decision trees. In *NIPS*8*, pages 479–485, 1996.

[3] Feng. C., Sutherland, A., King, R., Muggleton, S., & Henery, R. (1993). Comparison of machine learning classifiers to statistics and neural networks. In *Proceedings of the Fourth International Workshop on Artificial Intelligence and Statistics* (pages 41–52).

[4] Y. Freund and R.E. Schapire. Experiments with a new boosting algorithm. In *Machine Learning: Proceedings of Thirteenth International Conference*, pages 148–156, 1996.

[5] Y. Freund and R.E. Schapire. A decision theoretic generalization of on-line learning and an application to boosting. *Journal of Computer and System Science*, to appear.

[6] J.R. Quinlan. Bagging, Boosting and C4.5. In *14th Ntnl Conf. on Artificial Intelligence*, 1996.

[7] R.E. Schapire, Y. Freund, P. Bartlett, and W.S. Lee. Boosting the margin: A new explanation for the effectiveness of voting methods. In *Machine Learning: Proceedings of Fourteenth International Conference*, in press, 1997.

[8] H. Schwenk and M. Milgram. Transformation invariant autoassociation with application to handwritten character recognition. *NIPS*7*, pages 991–998. MIT Press, 1995.

[9] H. Schwenk and M. Milgram. Learning discriminant tangent models for handwritten character recognition. In *ICANN*96*, pages 585–590. Springer Verlag, 1995.

[10] H. Schwenk and M. Milgram. Constraint tangent distance for online character recognition. In *International Conference on Pattern Recognition*, pages D 520–524, 1996.

[11] P. Simard, Y. Le Cun, and J. Denker. Efficient pattern recognition using a new transformation distance. *NIPS*5*, pages 50–58. Morgan Kaufmann, 1993.

Learning Continuous Attractors in Recurrent Networks

H. Sebastian Seung
Bell Labs, Lucent Technologies
Murray Hill, NJ 07974
seung@bell-labs.com

Abstract

One approach to invariant object recognition employs a recurrent neural network as an associative memory. In the standard depiction of the network's state space, memories of objects are stored as attractive fixed points of the dynamics. I argue for a modification of this picture: if an object has a continuous family of instantiations, it should be represented by a continuous attractor. This idea is illustrated with a network that learns to complete patterns. To perform the task of filling in missing information, the network develops a continuous attractor that models the manifold from which the patterns are drawn. From a statistical viewpoint, the pattern completion task allows a formulation of unsupervised learning in terms of regression rather than density estimation.

A classic approach to invariant object recognition is to use a recurrent neural network as an associative memory[1]. In spite of the intuitive appeal and biological plausibility of this approach, it has largely been abandoned in practical applications. This paper introduces two new concepts that could help resurrect it: object representation by continuous attractors, and learning attractors by pattern completion.

In most models of associative memory, memories are stored as attractive fixed points at discrete locations in state space[1]. Discrete attractors may not be appropriate for patterns with continuous variability, like the images of a three-dimensional object from different viewpoints. When the instantiations of an object lie on a continuous *pattern manifold*, it is more appropriate to represent objects by attractive manifolds of fixed points, or continuous attractors.

To make this idea practical, it is important to find methods for learning attractors from examples. A naive method is to train the network to retain examples in short-term memory. This method is deficient because it does not prevent the network from storing spurious fixed points that are unrelated to the examples. A superior method is to train the network to restore examples that have been corrupted, so that it learns to complete patterns by filling in missing information.

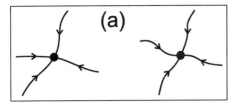
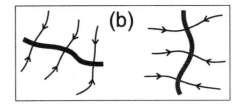

Figure 1: Representing objects by dynamical attractors. (a) Discrete attractors. (b) Continuous attractors.

Learning by pattern completion can be understood from both dynamical and statistical perspectives. Since the completion task requires a large basin of attraction around each memory, spurious fixed points are suppressed. The completion task also leads to a formulation of unsupervised learning as the regression problem of estimating functional dependences between variables in the sensory input.

Density estimation, rather than regression, is the dominant formulation of unsupervised learning in stochastic neural networks like the Boltzmann machine[2]. Density estimation has the virtue of suppressing spurious fixed points automatically, but it also has the serious drawback of being intractable for many network architectures. Regression is a more tractable, but nonetheless powerful, alternative to density estimation.

In a number of recent neurobiological models, continuous attractors have been used to represent continuous quantities like eye position [3], direction of reaching[4], head direction[5], and orientation of a visual stimulus[6]. Along with these models, the present work is part of a new paradigm for neural computation based on continuous attractors.

1 DISCRETE VERSUS CONTINUOUS ATTRACTORS

Figure 1 depicts two ways of representing objects as attractors of a recurrent neural network dynamics. The standard way is to represent each object by an attractive fixed point[1], as in Figure 1a. Recall of a memory is triggered by a sensory input, which sets the initial conditions. The network dynamics converges to a fixed point, thus retrieving a memory. If different instantiations of one object lie in the same basin of attraction, they all trigger retrieval of the same memory, resulting in the many-to-one map required for invariant recognition.

In Figure 1b, each object is represented by a continuous manifold of fixed points. A one-dimensional manifold is shown, but generally the attractor should be multidimensional, and is parametrized by the instantiation or pose parameters of the object. For example, in visual object recognition, the coordinates would include the viewpoint from which the object is seen.

The reader should be cautioned that the term "continuous attractor" is an idealization and should not be taken too literally. In real networks, a continuous attractor is only approximated by a manifold in state space along which drift is very slow. This is illustrated by a simple example, a descent dynamics on a trough-shaped energy landscape[3]. If the bottom of the trough is perfectly level, it is a line of fixed points and an ideal continuous attractor of the dynamics. However, any slight imperfections cause slow drift along the line. This sort of approximate continuous attractor is what is found in real networks, including those trained by the learning

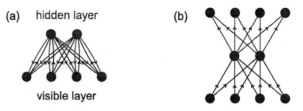

Figure 2: (a) Recurrent network. (b) Feedforward autoencoder.

algorithms to be discussed below.

2   DYNAMICS OF MEMORY RETRIEVAL

The preceding discussion has motivated the idea of representing pattern manifolds by continuous attractors. This idea will be further developed with the simple network shown in Figure 2a, which consists of a visible layer $x_1 \in R^{n_1}$ and a hidden layer $x_2 \in R^{n_2}$. The architecture is recurrent, containing both bottom-up connections (the $n_2 \times n_1$ matrix W_{21}) and top-down connections (the $n_1 \times n_2$ matrix W_{12}). The vectors b_1 and b_2 represent the biases of the neurons. The neurons have a rectification nonlinearity $[x]^+ = \max\{x, 0\}$, which acts on vectors component by component.

There are many variants of recurrent network dynamics: a convenient choice is the following discrete-time version, in which updates of the hidden and visible layers alternate in time. After the visible layer is initialized with the input vector $x_1(0)$, the dynamics evolves as

$$
\begin{aligned}
x_2(t) &= [b_2 + W_{21}x_1(t-1)]^+ , \\
x_1(t) &= [b_1 + W_{12}x_2(t)]^+ .
\end{aligned}
\tag{1}
$$

If memories are stored as attractors, iteration of this dynamics can be regarded as memory retrieval.

Activity circulates around the feedback loop between the two layers. One iteration of this loop is the map $x_1(t-1) \to x_2(t) \to x_1(t)$. This single iteration is equivalent to the feedforward architecture of Figure 2b. In the case where the hidden layer is smaller than the visible layers, this architecture is known as an autoencoder network[7]. Therefore the recurrent network dynamics (1) is equivalent to repeated iterations of the feedforward autoencoder. This is just the standard trick of unfolding the dynamics of a recurrent network in time, to yield an equivalent feedforward network with many layers[7]. Because of the close relationship between the recurrent network of Figure 2a and the autoencoder of Figure 2b, it should not be surprising that learning algorithms for these two networks are also related, as will be explained below.

3   LEARNING TO RETAIN PATTERNS

Little trace of an arbitrary input vector $x_1(0)$ remains after a few time steps of the dynamics (1). However, the network can retain some input vectors in short-term memory as "reverberating" patterns of activity. These correspond to fixed points of the dynamics (1); they are patterns that do not change as activity circulates around the feedback loop.

This suggests a formulation of learning as the optimization of the network's ability to retain examples in short-term memory. Then a suitable cost function is the squared difference $|x_1(T) - x_1(0)|^2$ between the example pattern $x_1(0)$ and the network's short-term memory $x_1(T)$ of it after T time steps. Gradient descent on this cost function can be done via backpropagation through time[7].

If the network is trained with patterns drawn from a continuous family, then it can learn to perform the short-term memory task by developing a continuous attractor that lies near the examples it is trained on. When the hidden layer is smaller than the visible layer, the dimensionality of the attractor is limited by the size of the hidden layer.

For the case of a single time step ($T = 1$), training the recurrent network of Figure 2a to retain patterns is equivalent to training the autoencoder of Figure 2b by minimizing the squared difference between its input and output layers, averaged over the examples[8]. From the information theoretic perspective, the small hidden layer in Figure 2b acts as a bottleneck between the input and output layers, forcing the autoencoder to learn an efficient encoding of the input.

For the special case of a linear network, the nature of the learned encoding is understood completely. Then the input and output vectors are related by a simple matrix multiplication. The rank of the matrix is equal to the number of hidden units. The average distortion is minimized when this matrix becomes a projection operator onto the subspace spanned by the principal components of the examples[9].

From the dynamical perspective, the principal subspace is a continuous attractor of the dynamics (1). The linear network dynamics converges to this attractor in a single iteration, starting from any initial condition. Therefore we can interpret principal component analysis and its variants as methods of learning continuous attractors[10].

4 LEARNING TO COMPLETE PATTERNS

Learning to retain patterns in short-term memory only works properly for architectures with a small hidden layer. The problem with a large hidden layer is evident when the hidden and visible layers are the same size, and the neurons are linear. Then the cost function for learning can be minimized by setting the weight matrices equal to the identity, $W_{21} = W_{12} = I$. For this trivial minimum, every input vector is a fixed point of the recurrent network (Figure 2a), and the equivalent feedforward network (Figure 2b) exactly realizes the identity map. Clearly these networks have not learned anything.

Therefore in the case of a large hidden layer, learning to retain patterns is inadequate. Without the bottleneck in the architecture, there is no pressure on the feedforward network to learn an efficient encoding. Without constraints on the dimension of the attractor, the recurrent network develops spurious fixed points that have nothing to do with the examples.

These problems can be solved by a different formulation of learning based on the task of pattern completion. In the completion task of Figure 3a, the network is initialized with a corrupted version of an example. Learning is done by minimizing the completion error, which is the squared difference $|x_1(T) - d|^2$ between the uncorrupted pattern d and the final visible vector $x_1(T)$. Gradient descent on completion error can be done with backpropagation through time[11].

This new formulation of learning eliminates the trivial identity map solution men-

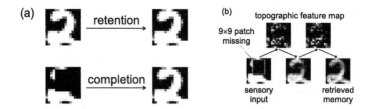

Figure 3: (a) Pattern retention versus completion. (b) Dynamics of pattern completion.

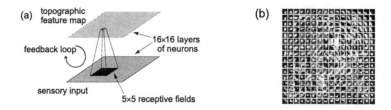

Figure 4: (a) Locally connected architecture. (b) Receptive fields of hidden neurons.

tioned above: while the identity network can retain any example, it cannot restore corrupted examples to their pristine form. The completion task forces the network to enlarge the basins of attraction of the stored memories, which suppresses spurious fixed points. It also forces the network to learn associations between variables in the sensory input.

5   LOCALLY CONNECTED ARCHITECTURE

Experiments were conducted with images of handwritten digits from the USPS database described in [12]. The example images were 16×16, with a gray scale ranging from 0 to 1. The network was trained on a specific digit class, with the goal of learning a single pattern manifold. Both the network architecture and the nature of the completion task were chosen to suit the topographic structure present in visual images.

The network architecture was given a topographic organization by constraining the synaptic connectivity to be local, as shown in Figure 4a. Both the visible and hidden layers of the network were 16×16. The visible layer represented an image, while the hidden layer was a topographic feature map. Each neuron had 5×5 receptive and projective fields, except for neurons near the edges, which had more restricted connectivity.

In the pattern completion task, example images were corrupted by zeroing the pixels inside a 9×9 patch chosen at a random location, as shown in Figure 3a. The location of the patch was randomized for each presentation of an example. The size of the patch was a substantial fraction of the 16×16 image, and much larger than the 5×5 receptive field size. This method of corrupting the examples gave the completion task a topographic nature, because it involved a set of spatially contiguous pixels. This topographic nature would have been lacking if the examples had been corrupted by, for example, the addition of spatially uncorrelated noise.

Figure 3b illustrates the dynamics of pattern completion performed by a network trained on examples of the digit class "two." The network is initialized with a corrupted example of a "two." After the first iteration of the dynamics, the image is partially restored. The second iteration leads to superior restoration, with further sharpening of the image. The "filling in" phenomenon is also evident in the hidden layer.

The network was first trained on a retrieval dynamics of one iteration. The resulting biases and synaptic weights were then used as initial conditions for training on a retrieval dynamics of two iterations. The hidden layer developed into a topographic feature map suitable for representing images of the digit "two." Figure 4b depicts the bottom-up receptive fields of the 256 hidden neurons. The top-down projective fields of these neurons were similar, but are not shown.

This feature map is distinct from others[13] because of its use of top-down and bottom-up connections in a feedback loop. The bottom-up connections analyze images into their constituent features, while the top-down connections synthesize images by composing features. The features in the top-down connections can be regarded as a "vocabulary" for synthesis of images. Since not all combinations of features are proper patterns, there must be some "grammatical" constraints on their combination. The network's ability to complete patterns suggests that some of these constraints are embedded in the dynamical equations of the network. Therefore the relaxation dynamics (1) can be regarded as a process of massively parallel constraint satisfaction.

6   CONCLUSION

I have argued that continuous attractors are a natural representation for pattern manifolds. One method of learning attractors is to train the network to retain examples in short-term memory. This method is equivalent to autoencoder learning, and does not work if the number of hidden units is large. A better method is to train the network to complete patterns. For a locally connected network, this method was demonstrated to learn a topographic feature map. The trained network is able to complete patterns, indicating that syntactic constraints on the combination of features are embedded in the network dynamics.

Empirical evidence that the network has indeed learned a continuous attractor is obtained by local linearization of the network (1). The linearized dynamics has many eigenvalues close to unity, indicating the existence of an approximate continuous attractor. Learning with an increased number of iterations in the retrieval dynamics should improve the quality of the approximation.

There is only one aspect of the learning algorithm that is specifically tailored for *continuous* attractors. This aspect is the limitation of the retrieval dynamics (1) to a few iterations, rather than iterating it all the way to a true fixed point. As mentioned earlier, a continuous attractor is only an idealization; in a real network it does not consist of true fixed points, but is just a manifold to which relaxation is fast and along which drift is slow. Adjusting the shape of this manifold is the goal of learning; the exact locations of the true fixed points are not relevant.

The use of a fast retrieval dynamics removes one long-standing objection to attractor neural networks, which is that true convergence to a fixed point takes too long. If all that is desired is fast relaxation to an approximate continuous attractor, attractor neural networks are not much slower than feedforward networks.

In the experiments discussed here, learning was done with backpropagation through time. Contrastive Hebbian learning[14] is a simpler alternative. Part of the image is held clamped, the missing values are filled in by convergence to a fixed point, and an anti-Hebbian update is made. Then the missing values are clamped at their correct values, the network converges to a new fixed point, and a Hebbian update is made. This procedure has the disadvantage of requiring true convergence to a fixed point, which can take many iterations. It also requires symmetric connections, which may be a representational handicap.

This paper addressed only the learning of a single attractor to represent a single pattern manifold. The problem of learning multiple attractors to represent multiple pattern classes will be discussed elsewhere, along with the extension to network architectures with many layers.

Acknowledgments   This work was supported by Bell Laboratories. I thank J. J. Hopfield, D. D. Lee, L. K. Saul, N. D. Socci, H. Sompolinsky, and D. W. Tank for helpful discussions.

References

[1] J. J. Hopfield. Neural networks and physical systems with emergent collective computational abilities. *Proc. Nat. Acad. Sci. USA*, 79:2554–2558, 1982.

[2] D. H. Ackley, G. E. Hinton, and T. J. Sejnowski. A learning algorithm for Boltzmann machines. *Cognitive Science*, 9:147–169, 1985.

[3] H. S. Seung. How the brain keeps the eyes still. *Proc. Natl. Acad. Sci. USA*, 93:13339–13344, 1996.

[4] A. P. Georgopoulos, M. Taira, and A. Lukashin. Cognitive neurophysiology of the motor cortex. *Science*, 260:47–52, 1993.

[5] K. Zhang. Representation of spatial orientation by the intrinsic dynamics of the head-direction cell ensemble: a theory. *J. Neurosci.*, 16:2112–2126, 1996.

[6] R. Ben-Yishai, R. L. Bar-Or, and H. Sompolinsky. Theory of orientation tuning in visual cortex. *Proc. Nat. Acad. Sci. USA*, 92:3844–3848, 1995.

[7] D.E. Rumelhart, G.E. Hinton, and R.J. Williams. Learning internal representations by error propagation. In D.E. Rumelhart and J.L. McClelland, editors, *Parallel Distributed Processing*, volume 1, chapter 8, pages 318–362. MIT Press, Cambridge, 1986.

[8] G. W. Cottrell, P. Munro, and D. Zipser. Image compression by back propagation: an example of extensional programming. In N. E. Sharkey, editor, *Models of cognition: a review of cognitive science*. Ablex, Norwood, NJ, 1989.

[9] P. Baldi and K. Hornik. Neural networks and principal component analysis: Learning from examples without local minima. *Neural Networks*, 2:53–58, 1989.

[10] H. S. Seung. Pattern analysis and synthesis in attractor neural networks. In K.-Y. M. Wong, I. King, and D.-Y. Yeung, editors, *Theoretical Aspects of Neural Computation: A Multidisciplinary Perspective*, Singapore, 1997. Springer-Verlag.

[11] F.-S. Tsung and G. W. Cottrell. Phase-space learning. *Adv. Neural Info. Proc. Syst.*, 7:481–488, 1995.

[12] Y. LeCun et al. Learning algorithms for classification: a comparison on handwritten digit recognition. In J.-H. Oh, C. Kwon, and S. Cho, editors, *Neural networks: the statistical mechanics perspective*, pages 261–276, Singapore, 1995. World Scientific.

[13] T. Kohonen. The self-organizing map. *Proc. IEEE*, 78:1464–1480, 1990.

[14] J. J. Hopfield, D. I. Feinstein, and R. G. Palmer. "Unlearning" has a stabilizing effect in collective memories. *Nature*, 304:158–159, 1983.

Monotonic Networks

Joseph Sill
Computation and Neural Systems program
California Institute of Technology
MC 136-93, Pasadena, CA 91125
email: joe@cs.caltech.edu

Abstract

Monotonicity is a constraint which arises in many application domains. We present a machine learning model, the monotonic network, for which monotonicity can be enforced exactly, i.e., by virtue of functional form. A straightforward method for implementing and training a monotonic network is described. Monotonic networks are proven to be universal approximators of continuous, differentiable monotonic functions. We apply monotonic networks to a real-world task in corporate bond rating prediction and compare them to other approaches.

1 Introduction

Several recent papers in machine learning have emphasized the importance of priors and domain-specific knowledge. In their well-known presentation of the bias-variance tradeoff (Geman and Bienenstock, 1992), Geman and Bienenstock conclude by arguing that the crucial issue in learning is the determination of the "right biases" which constrain the model in the appropriate way given the task at hand. The No-Free-Lunch theorem of Wolpert (Wolpert, 1996) shows, under the 0-1 error measure, that if all target functions are equally likely a priori, then all possible learning methods do equally well in terms of average performance over all targets. One is led to the conclusion that consistently good performance is possible only with some agreement between the modeler's biases and the true (non-flat) prior. Finally, the work of Abu-Mostafa on learning from hints (Abu-Mostafa, 1990) has shown both theoretically (Abu-Mostafa, 1993) and experimentally (Abu-Mostafa, 1995) that the use of prior knowledge can be highly beneficial to learning systems.

One piece of prior information that arises in many applications is the monotonicity constraint, which asserts that an increase in a particular input cannot result in a decrease in the output. A method was presented in (Sill and Abu-Mostafa, 1996) which enforces monotonicity approximately by adding a second term measuring "monotonicity error" to the usual error measure. This technique was shown to yield improved error rates on real-world applications. Unfortunately, the method can be quite expensive computationally. It would be useful to have a model which obeys monotonicity exactly, i.e., by virtue of functional form.

We present here such a model, which we will refer to as a monotonic network. A monotonic network implements a piecewise-linear surface by taking maximum and minimum operations on groups of hyperplanes. Monotonicity constraints are enforced by constraining the signs of the hyperplane weights. Monotonic networks can be trained using the usual gradient-based optimization methods typically used with other models such as feedforward neural networks. Armstrong (Armstrong et. al. 1996) has developed a model called the adaptive logic network which is capable of enforcing monotonicity and appears to have some similarities to the approach presented here. The adaptive logic network, however, is available only through a commercial software package. The training algorithms are proprietary and have not been fully disclosed in academic journals. The monotonic network therefore represents (to the best of our knowledge) the first model to be presented in an academic setting which has the ability to enforce monotonicity.

Section II describes the architecture and training procedure for monotonic networks. Section III presents a proof that monotonic networks can uniformly approximate any continuous monotonic function with bounded partial derivatives to an arbitrary level of accuracy. Monotonic networks are applied to a real-world problem in bond rating prediction in Section IV. In Section V, we discuss the results and consider future directions.

2   Architecture and Training Procedure

A monotonic network has a feedforward, three-layer (two hidden-layer) architecture (Fig. 1). The first layer of units compute different linear combinations of the input vector. If increasing monotonicity is desired for a particular input, then all the weights connected to that input are constrained to be positive. Similarly, weights connected to an input where decreasing monotonicity is required are constrained to be negative. The first layer units are partitioned into several groups (the number of units in each group is not necessarily the same). Corresponding to each group is a second layer unit, which computes the maximum over all first-layer units within the group. The final output unit computes the minimum over all groups.

More formally, if we have K groups with outputs $g_1, g_2, \ldots g_K$, and if group k consists of h_k hyperplanes $\mathbf{w}^{(\mathbf{k},\mathbf{1})}, \mathbf{w}^{(\mathbf{k},\mathbf{2})}, \ldots \mathbf{w}^{(\mathbf{k},\mathbf{h_k})}$, then

$$g_k(\mathbf{x}) = \max_j \mathbf{w}^{(\mathbf{k},\mathbf{j})} \cdot \mathbf{x} - t^{(k,j)}, 1 \leq j \leq h_k$$

Let y be the final output of the network. Then

$$y = \min_k g_k(\mathbf{x})$$

or, for classification problems,

$$y = \sigma(\min_k g_k(\mathbf{x}))$$

where $\sigma(u) = $ e.g. $\frac{1}{1+e^{-u}}$.

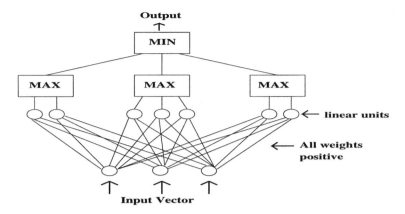

Figure 1: This monotonic network obeys increasing monotonicity in all 3 inputs because all weights in the first layer are constrained to be positive.

In the discussions which follow, it will be useful to define the term *active*. We will call a group l active at $\mathbf{x}$ if

$$g_l(\mathbf{x}) = \min_k g_k(\mathbf{x})$$

, i.e., if the group determines the output of the network at that point. Similarly, we will say that a hyperplane is active at $\mathbf{x}$ if its group is active at $\mathbf{x}$ and the hyperplane is the maximum over all hyperplanes in the group.

As will be shown in the following section, the three-layer architecture allows a monotonic network to approximate any continuous, differentiable monotonic function arbitrarily well, given sufficiently many groups and sufficiently many hyperplanes within each group. The maximum operation within each group allows the network to approximate convex (positive second derivative) surfaces, while the minimum operation over groups enables the network to implement the concave (negative second derivative) areas of the target function (Figure 2).

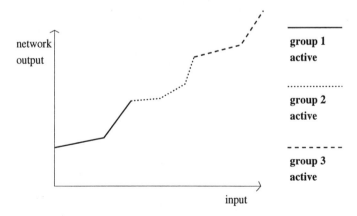

Figure 2: This surface is implemented by a monotonic network consisting of three groups. The first and third groups consist of three hyperplanes, while the second group has only two.

Monotonic networks can be trained using many of the standard gradient-based optimization techniques commonly used in machine learning. The gradient for each hyperplane is found by computing the error over all examples for which the hyperplane is active. After the parameter update is made according to the rule of the optimization technique, each training example is reassigned to the hyperplane that is now active at that point. The set of examples for which a hyperplane is active can therefore change during the course of training.

The constraints on the signs of the weights are enforced using an exponential transformation. If increasing monotonicity is desired in input variable i, then $\forall j, k$ the weights corresponding to the input are represented as $w_i^{(j,k)} = e^{z_i^{(j,k)}}$. The optimization algorithm can modify $z_i^{(j,k)}$ freely during training while maintaining the constraint. If decreasing monotonicity is required, then $\forall j, k$ we take $w_i^{(j,k)} = -e^{z_i^{(j,k)}}$.

3   Universal Approximation Capability

In this section, we demonstrate that monotonic networks have the capacity to approximate uniformly to an arbitrary degree of accuracy any continuous, bounded, differentiable function on the unit hypercube $[0, 1]^D$ which is monotonic in all variables and has bounded partial derivatives. We will say that $\mathbf{x}'$ *dominates* $\mathbf{x}$ if $\forall 1 \leq d \leq D, x_d' \geq x_d$. A function m is monotonic in all variables if it satisfies the constraint that $\forall \mathbf{x}, \mathbf{x}'$, if $\mathbf{x}'$ dominates $\mathbf{x}$ then $m(\mathbf{x}') \geq m(\mathbf{x})$.

Theorem 3.1 Let $m(\mathbf{x})$ be any continuous, bounded monotonic function with bounded partial derivatives, mapping $[0, 1]^D$ to $\mathbf{R}$. Then there exists a function $m_{net}(\mathbf{x})$ which can be implemented by a monotonic network and is such that, for any ϵ and any $\mathbf{x} \in [0, 1]^D$, $|m(\mathbf{x}) - m_{net}(\mathbf{x})| < \epsilon$.

Proof:

Let b be the maximum value and a be the minimum value which m takes on $[0, 1]^D$. Let α bound the magnitude of all partial first derivatives of m on $[0, 1]^D$. Define an equispaced grid of points on $[0, 1]^D$, where $\delta = \frac{1}{n}$ is the spacing between grid points along each dimension. I.e., the grid is the set S of points $(i_1\delta, i_2\delta, \ldots i_D\delta)$ where $1 \leq i_1 \leq n, 1 \leq i_2 \leq n, \ldots 1 \leq i_D \leq n$. Corresponding to each grid point $\mathbf{x}' = (x_1', x_2', \ldots x_D')$, assign a group consisting of $D+1$ hyperplanes. One hyperplane in the group is the constant output plane $y = m(\mathbf{x}')$. In addition, for each dimension d, place a hyperplane $y = \gamma(x_d - x_d') + m(\mathbf{x}')$, where $\gamma > \frac{b-a}{\delta}$. This construction ensures that the group associated with $\mathbf{x}'$ cannot be active at any point $\mathbf{x}^*$ where there exists a d such that $x_d^* - x_d' > \delta$, since the group's output at such a point must be greater than b and hence greater than the output of a group associated with another grid point.

Now consider any point $\mathbf{x} \in [0, 1]^D$. Let $\mathbf{s}^{(1)}$ be the unique grid point in S such that $\forall d, 0 \leq x_d - s_d^{(1)} < \delta$, i.e., $\mathbf{s}^{(1)}$ is the closest grid point to $\mathbf{x}$ which $\mathbf{x}$ dominates. Then we can show that $m_{net}(\mathbf{x}) \geq m(\mathbf{s}^{(1)})$. Consider an arbitrary grid point $\mathbf{s}' \neq \mathbf{s}^{(1)}$. By the monotonicity of m, if $\mathbf{s}'$ dominates $\mathbf{s}^{(1)}$, then $m(\mathbf{s}') \geq m(\mathbf{s}^{(1)})$, and hence, the group associated with $\mathbf{s}'$ has a constant output hyperplane $y = m(\mathbf{s}') \geq m(\mathbf{s}^{(1)})$ and therefore outputs a value $\geq m(\mathbf{s}^{(1)})$ at $\mathbf{x}$. If $\mathbf{s}'$ does not dominate $\mathbf{s}^{(1)}$, then there exists a d such that $s_d^{(1)} > s_d'$. Therefore, $x_d - s_d' \geq \delta$, meaning that the output of the group associated with $\mathbf{s}'$ is at least $b \geq m(\mathbf{s}^{(1)})$. All groups have output at least as large as $m(\mathbf{s}^{(1)})$, so we have indeed shown that $m_{net}(\mathbf{x}) \geq m(\mathbf{s}^{(1)})$. Now consider the grid point $\mathbf{s}^{(2)}$ that is obtained by adding δ to each coordinate of $\mathbf{s}^{(1)}$. The group associated with $\mathbf{s}^{(2)}$ outputs $m(\mathbf{s}^{(2)})$ at $\mathbf{x}$, so $m_{net}(\mathbf{x}) \leq m(\mathbf{s}^{(2)})$. Therefore, we have $m(\mathbf{s}^{(1)}) \leq m_{net}(\mathbf{x}) \leq m(\mathbf{s}^{(2)})$. Since $\mathbf{x}$ dominates $\mathbf{s}^{(1)}$ and is dominated by $\mathbf{s}^{(2)}$, by monotonicity we also have $m(\mathbf{s}^{(1)}) \leq m(\mathbf{x}) \leq m(\mathbf{s}^{(2)})$. $|m(\mathbf{x}) - m_{net}(\mathbf{x})|$ is therefore bounded by $|m(\mathbf{s}^{(2)}) - m(\mathbf{s}^{(1)})|$. By Taylor's theorem for multivariate functions, we know that

$$m(\mathbf{s}^{(2)}) - m(\mathbf{s}^{(1)}) = \delta \sum_{d=1}^{D} \frac{\partial m(\mathbf{c})}{\partial x_d}$$

for some point $\mathbf{c}$ on the line segment between $\mathbf{s}^{(1)}$ and $\mathbf{s}^{(2)}$. Given the assumptions made at the outset, $|m(\mathbf{s}^{(2)}) - m(\mathbf{s}^{(1)})|$, and hence, $|m(\mathbf{x}) - m_{net}(\mathbf{x})|$ can be bounded by $d\delta\alpha$. We take $\delta < \frac{\epsilon}{d\alpha}$ to complete the proof ∎.

4 Experimental Results

We tested monotonic networks on a real-world problem concerning the prediction of corporate bond ratings. Rating agencies such as Standard & Poors (S & P) issue bond ratings intended to assess the level of risk of default associated with the bond. S & P ratings can range from AAA down to B- or lower.

A model which accurately predicts the S & P rating of a bond given publicly available financial information about the issuer has considerable value. Rating agencies do not rate all bonds, so an investor could use the model to assess the risk associated with a bond which S & P has not rated. The model can also be used to anticipate rating changes before they are announced by the agency.

The dataset, which was donated by a Wall Street firm, is made up of 196 examples. Each training example consists of 10 financial ratios reflecting the fundamental characteristics of the issuing firm, along with an associated rating. The meaning of the financial ratios was not disclosed by the firm for proprietary reasons. The rating labels were converted into integers ranging from 1 to 16. The task was treated as a single-output regression problem rather than a 16-class classification problem.

Monotonicity constraints suggest themselves naturally in this context. Although the meanings of the features are not revealed, it is reasonable to assume that they consist of quantities such as profitability, debt, etc. It seems intuitive that, for instance, the higher the profitability of the firm is , the stronger the firm is, and hence, the higher the bond rating should be. Monotonicity was therefore enforced in all input variables.

Three different types of models (all trained on squared error) were compared: a linear model, standard two-layer feedforward sigmoidal neural networks, and monotonic networks. The 196 examples were split into 150 training examples and 46 test examples. In order to get a statistically significant evaluation of performance, a leave-k-out procedure was implemented in which the 196 examples were split 200 different ways and each model was trained on the training set and tested on the test set for each split. The results shown are averages over the 200 splits.

Two different approaches were used with the standard neural networks. In both cases, the networks were trained for 2000 batch-mode iterations of gradient descent with momentum and an adaptive learning rate, which sufficed to allow the networks to approach minima of the training error. The first method used all 150 examples for direct training and minimized the training error as much as possible. The second technique split the 150 examples into 110 for direct training and 40 used for validation, i.e., to determine when to stop training. Specifically, the mean-squared-error on the 40 examples was monitored over the course of the 2000 iterations, and the state of the network at the iteration where lowest validation error was obtained was taken as the final network to be tested on the test set. In both cases, the networks were initialized with small random weights. The networks had direct input-output connections in addition to hidden units in order to facilitate the implementation of the linear aspects of the target function.

The monotonic networks were trained for 1000 batch-mode iterations of gradient descent with momentum and an adaptive learning rate. The parameters of each hyperplane in the network were initialized to be the parameters of the linear model obtained from the training set, plus a small random perturbation. This procedure ensured that the network was able to find a reasonably good fit to the data. Since the meanings of the features were not known, it was not known *a priori* whether increasing or decreasing monotonicity should hold for each feature. The directions of monotonicity were determined by observing the signs of the weights of the linear model obtained from the training data.

Model	training error	test error
Linear	$3.45 \pm .02$	$4.09 \pm .06$
10-2-1 net	$1.83 \pm .01$	$4.22 \pm .14$
10-4-1 net	$1.22 \pm .01$	$4.86 \pm .16$
10-6-1 net	$0.87 \pm .01$	$5.57 \pm .20$
10-8-1 net	$0.65 \pm .01$	$5.56 \pm .16$

Table 1: Performance of linear model and standard networks on bond rating problem

The results support the hypothesis of a monotonic (or at least roughly monotonic) target function. As Table 1 shows, standard neural networks have sufficient flexibility to fit the training data quite accurately (n-k-1 network means a 2-layer network with n inputs, k hidden units, and 1 output). However, their excessive, non-monotonic degrees of freedom lead to overfitting, and their out-of-sample performance is even worse than that of a linear model. The use of early stopping alleviates the overfitting and enables the networks to outperform the linear model. Without the monotonicity constraint, however, standard neural networks still do not perform as well as the monotonic networks. The results seem to be quite robust with respect to the choice of number of hidden units for the standard networks and number and size of groups for the monotonic networks.

Model	training error	test error
10-2-1 net	$2.46 \pm .04$	$3.83 \pm .09$
10-4-1 net	$2.19 \pm .05$	$3.82 \pm .08$
10-6-1 net	$2.14 \pm .05$	$3.77 \pm .07$
10-8-1 net	$2.13 \pm .06$	$3.86 \pm .09$

Table 2: Performance of standard networks using early stopping on bond rating problem

5 Conclusion

We presented a model, the monotonic network, in which monotonicity constraints can be enforced exactly, without adding a second term to the usual objective function. A straightforward method for implementing and training such models was

Model	training error	test error
2 groups, 2 planes per group	$2.78 \pm .05$	$3.71 \pm .07$
3 groups, 3 planes per group	$2.64 \pm .04$	$3.56 \pm .06$
4 groups, 4 planes per group	$2.50 \pm .04$	$3.48 \pm .06$
5 groups, 5 planes per group	$2.44 \pm .03$	$3.43 \pm .06$

Table 3: Performance of monotonic networks on bond rating problem

demonstrated, and the method was shown to outperform other methods on a real-world problem.

Several areas of research regarding monotonic networks need to be addressed in the future. One issue concerns the choice of the number of groups and number of planes in each group. In general, the usual bias-variance tradeoff that holds for other models will apply here, and the optimal number of groups and planes will be quite difficult to determine *a priori*. There may be instances where additional prior information regarding the convexity or concavity of the target function can guide the decision, however. Another interesting observation is that a monotonic network could also be implemented by reversing the maximum and minimum operations, i.e., by taking the maximum over groups where each group outputs the minimum over all of its hyperplanes. It will be worthwhile to try to understand when one approach or the other is most appropriate.

Acknowledgments

The author is very grateful to Yaser Abu-Mostafa for considerable guidance. I also thank John Moody for supplying the data. Amir Atiya, Eric Bax, Zehra Cataltepe, Malik Magdon-Ismail, Alexander Nicholson, and Xubo Song supplied many useful comments.

References

[1] S. Geman and E. Bienenstock (1992). Neural Networks and the Bias-Variance Dilemma. *Neural Computation 4*, pp 1-58.

[2] D. Wolpert (1996). The Lack of A Priori Distinctions Between Learning Algorithms. *Neural Computation 8*, pp 1341-1390.

[3] Y. Abu-Mostafa (1990). Learning from Hints in Neural Networks *Journal of Complexity 6*, 192-198.

[4] Y. Abu-Mostafa (1993) Hints and the VC Dimension *Neural Computation* **4**, 278-288

[5] Y. Abu-Mostafa (1995) Financial Market Applications of Learning from Hints *Neural Networks in the Capital Markets*, A. Refenes, ed., 221-232. Wiley, London, UK.

[6] J. Sill and Y. Abu-Mostafa (1996) Monotonicity Hints. To appear in it Advances in Neural Information Processing Systems 9.

[7] W.W. Armstrong, C. Chu, M. M. Thomas (1996) Feasibility of using Adaptive Logic Networks to Predict Compressor Unit Failure *Applications of Neural Networks in Environment, Energy, and Health*, Chapter 12. P. Keller, S. Hashem, L. Kangas, R. Kouzes, eds, World Scientific Publishing Company, Ltd., London.

Stacked Density Estimation

Padhraic Smyth *
Information and Computer Science
University of California, Irvine
CA 92697-3425
smyth@ics.uci.edu

David Wolpert
NASA Ames Research Center
Caelum Research
MS 269-2, Mountain View, CA 94035
dhw@ptolemy.arc.nasa.gov

Abstract

In this paper, the technique of stacking, previously only used for supervised learning, is applied to unsupervised learning. Specifically, it is used for non-parametric multivariate density estimation, to combine finite mixture model and kernel density estimators. Experimental results on both simulated data and real world data sets clearly demonstrate that stacked density estimation outperforms other strategies such as choosing the single best model based on cross-validation, combining with uniform weights, and even the single best model chosen by "cheating" by looking at the data used for independent testing.

1 Introduction

Multivariate probability density estimation is a fundamental problem in exploratory data analysis, statistical pattern recognition and machine learning. One frequently estimates density functions for which there is little prior knowledge on the shape of the density and for which one wants a flexible and robust estimator (allowing multimodality if it exists). In this context, the methods of choice tend to be finite mixture models and kernel density estimation methods. For mixture modeling, mixtures of Gaussian components are frequently assumed and model choice reduces to the problem of choosing the number k of Gaussian components in the model (Titterington, Smith and Makov, 1986) . For kernel density estimation, kernel shapes are typically chosen from a selection of simple unimodal densities such as Gaussian, triangular, or Cauchy densities, and kernel bandwidths are selected in a data-driven manner (Silverman 1986; Scott 1994).

As argued by Draper (1996), model uncertainty can contribute significantly to pre-

---

*Also with the Jet Propulsion Laboratory 525-3660, California Institute of Technology, Pasadena, CA 91109

dictive error in estimation. While usually considered in the context of supervised learning, model uncertainty is also important in unsupervised learning applications such as density estimation. Even when the model class under consideration contains the true density, if we are only given a finite data set, then there is always a chance of selecting the wrong model. Moreover, even if the correct model is selected, there will typically be estimation error in the parameters of that model. These difficulties are summarized by writing

$$P(f \mid D) = \sum_M \int d\theta_M P(\theta_M \mid D, M) \times P(M \mid D) \times f_{M,\theta_M}, \tag{1}$$

where f is a density, D is the data set, M is a model, and θ_M is a set of values for the parameters for model M. The posterior probability $P(M \mid D)$ reflects model uncertainty, and the posterior $P(\theta_M \mid D, M)$ reflects uncertainty in setting the parameters even once one knows the model. Note that if one is privy to $P(M, \theta_M)$, then Bayes' theorem allows us to write out both of our posteriors explicitly, so that we explicitly have $P(f \mid D)$ (and therefore the Bayes-optimal density) given by a weighted average of the f_{M,θ_M}. (See also Escobar and West (1995)). However even when we know $P(M, \theta_M)$, calculating the combining weights can be difficult. Thus, various approximations and sampling techniques are often used, a process that necessarily introduces extra error (Chickering and Heckerman 1997). More generally, consider the case of mis-specified models where the model class does not include the true model, so our presumption for $P(M, \theta_M)$ is erroneous. In this case often one should again average.

Thus, a natural approach to improving density estimators is to consider empirically-driven combinations of multiple density models. There are several ways to do this, especially if one exploits previous combining work in supervised learning. For example, Ormontreit and Tresp (1996) have shown that "bagging" (uniformly weighting different parametrizations of the same model trained on different bootstrap samples), originally introduced for supervised learning (Breiman 1996a), can improve accuracy for mixtures of Gaussians with a fixed number of components. Another supervised learning technique for combining different types of models is "stacking" (Wolpert 1992), which has been found to be very effective for both regression and classification (e.g., Breiman (1996b)). This paper applies stacking to density estimation, in particular to combinations involving kernel density estimators together with finite mixture model estimators.

2 Stacked Density Estimation

2.1 Background on Density Estimation with Mixtures and Kernels

Consider a set of d real-valued random variables $\underline{X} = \{X^1, \dots, X^d\}$ Upper case symbols denote variable names (such as X^j) and lower-case symbols a particular value of a variable (such as x^j). $\underline{x}$ is a realization of the vector variable $\underline{X}$. $f(\underline{x})$ is shorthand for $f(\underline{X} = \underline{x})$ and represents the joint probability distribution of $\underline{X}$. $D = \{\underline{x}_1, \dots, \underline{x}_N\}$ is a training data set where each sample $\underline{x}_i, 1 \le i \le N$ is an independently drawn sample from the underlying density function $\bar{f}(\underline{x})$.

A commonly used model for density estimation is the *finite mixture model* with k components, defined as:

$$f^k(\underline{x}) = \sum_{j=1}^k \alpha_j g_j(\underline{x}), \tag{2}$$

where $\sum_{j=1}^{k} \alpha_j = 1$. The component g_j's are usually relatively simple unimodal densities such as Gaussians. Density estimation with mixtures involves finding the locations, shapes, and weights of the component densities from the data (using for example the Expectation-Maximization (EM) procedure). *Kernel density estimation* can be viewed as a special case of mixture modeling where a component is centered at each data point, given a weight of $1/N$, and a common covariance structure (kernel shape) is estimated from the data.

The quality of a particular probabilistic model can be evaluated by an appropriate scoring rule on independent out-of-sample data, such as the test set log-likelihood (also referred to as the log-scoring rule in the Bayesian literature). Given a test data set D^{test}, the test log likelihood is defined as

$$\log f(D^{test}|f^k(\underline{x})) = \sum_{D^{test}} \log f^k(\underline{x}_i) \tag{3}$$

This quantity can play the role played by classification error in classification or squared error in regression. For example, cross-validated estimates of it can be used to find the best number of clusters to fit to a given data set (Smyth, 1996).

2.2 Background on Stacking

Stacking can be used either to combine models or to improve a single model. In the former guise it proceeds as follows. First, subsamples of the training set are formed. Next the models are all trained on one subsample and resultant joint predictive behavior on another subsample is observed, together with information concerning the optimal predictions on the elements in that other subsample. This is repeated for other pairs of subsamples of the training set. Then an additional ("stacked") model is trained to learn, from the subsample-based observations, the relationship between the observed joint predictive behavior of the models and the optimal predictions. Finally, this learned relationship is used in conjunction with the predictions of the individual models being combined (now trained on the entire data set) to determine the full system's predictions.

2.3 Applying Stacking to Density Estimation

Consider a set of M different density models, $f_m(\underline{x}), 1 \leq m \leq M$. In this paper each of these models will be either a finite mixture with a fixed number of component densities or a kernel density estimate with a fixed kernel and a single fixed global bandwidth in each dimension. (In general though no such restrictions are needed.) The procedure for stacking the M density models is as follows:

1. Partition the training data set D v times, exactly as in v-fold cross validation (we use $v = 10$ throughout this paper), and for each fold:

   (a) Fit each of the M models to the training portion of the partition of D.

   (b) Evaluate the likelihood of each data point in the test partition of D, for each of the M fitted models.

2. After doing this one has M density estimates for each of N data points, and therefore a matrix of size $N \times M$, where each entry is $f_m(\underline{x}_i)$, the out-of-sample likelihood of the mth model on the ith data point.

3. Use that matrix to estimate the combination coefficients $\{\beta_1, \ldots, \beta_M\}$ that maximize the log-likelihood at the points $\underline{x}_i$ of a stacked density model of

the form:

$$f_{\text{stacked}}(\underline{x}) = \sum_{m=1}^{M} \beta_m f_m(\underline{x}).$$

Since this is itself a mixture model, but where the $f_m(\underline{x}_i)$ are fixed, the EM algorithm can be used to (easily) estimate the β_m.

4. Finally, re-estimate the parameters of each of the m component density models using *all* of the training data D. The stacked density model is then the linear combination of those density models, with combining coefficients given by the β_m.

3 Experimental Results

In our stacking experiments $M = 6$: three triangular kernels with bandwidths of $0.1, 0.4$, and 1.5 of the standard deviation (of the full data set) in each dimension, and three Gaussian mixture models with $k = 2, 4$, and 8 components. This set of models was chosen to provide a reasonably diverse representational basis for stacking. We follow roughly the same experimental procedure as described in Breiman (1996b) for stacked regression:

- Each data set is randomly split into training and test partitions 50 times, where the test partition is chosen to be large enough to provide reasonable estimates of out-of-sample log-likelihood.

- The following techniques are run on each training partition:

  1. **Stacking:** The stacked combination of the six constituent models.
  2. **Cross-Validation:** The single best model as indicated by the maximum likelihood score of the $M = 6$ single models in the $N \times M$ cross-validated table of likelihood scores.
  3. **Uniform Weighting:** A uniform average of the six models.
  4. **"Cheating:"** The best single model, i.e., the model having the largest likelihood on the *test* data partition,
  5. **Truth:** The true model structure, if the true model is one of the six generating the data (only valid for simulated data).

- The log-likelihoods of the models resulting from these techniques are calculated on the test data partition. The log-likelihood of a single Gaussian model (parameters determined on the training data) is subtracted from each model's log-likelihood to provide some normalization of scale.

3.1 Results on Real Data Sets

Four real data sets were chosen for experimental evaluation. The diabetes data set consists of 145 data points used in Gaussian clustering studies by Banfield and Raftery (1991) and others. Fisher's iris data set is a classic data set in 4 dimensions with 150 data points. Both of these data sets are thought to consist roughly of 3 clusters which can be reasonably approximated by 3 Gaussians. The Barney and Peterson vowel data (2 dimensions, 639 data points) contains 10 distinct vowel sounds and so is highly multi-modal. The star-galaxy data (7 dimensions, 499 data points) contains non-Gaussian looking structure in various 2d projections.

Table 1 summarizes the results. In all cases stacking had the highest average log-likelihood, even out-performing "cheating" (the single best model chosen from the test data). (Breiman (1996b) also found for regression that stacking outperformed

Table 1: Relative performance of stacking multiple mixture models, for various data sets, measured (relative to the performance of a single Gaussian model) by mean log-likelihood on test data partitions. The maximum for each data set is underlined.

Data Set	Gaussian	Cross-Validation	"Cheating"	Uniform	Stacking
Diabetes	-352.9	27.8	30.4	29.2	<u>31.8</u>
Fisher's Iris	-52.6	18.3	21.2	18.3	<u>22.5</u>
Vowel	128.9	53.5	54.6	40.2	<u>55.8</u>
Star-Galaxy	-257.0	678.9	721.6	789.1	<u>888.9</u>

Table 2: Average across 20 runs of the stacked weights found for each constituent model. The columns with $h = \ldots$ are for the triangular kernels and the columns with $k = \ldots$ are for the Gaussian mixtures.

Data Set	$h=0.1$	$h=0.4$	$h=1.5$	$k = 2$	$k = 4$	$k = 8$
Diabetes	0.01	0.09	0.03	0.13	0.41	0.32
Fisher's Iris	0.02	0.16	0.00	0.26	0.40	0.16
Vowel	0.00	0.25	0.00	0.02	0.20	0.53
Star-Galaxy	0.00	0.04	0.03	0.03	0.27	0.62

the "cheating" method.) We considered two null hypotheses: stacking has the same predictive accuracy as cross-validation, and it has the same accuracy as uniform weighting. Each hypothesis can be rejected with a chance of less than 0.01% of being incorrect, according to the Wilcoxon signed-rank test i.e., the observed differences in performance are extremely strong even given the fact that this particular test is not strictly applicable in this situation.

On the vowel data set uniform weighting performs much worse than the other methods: it is closer in performance to stacking on the other 3 data sets. On three of the data sets, using cross-validation to select a single model is the worst method. "Cheating" is second-best to stacking except on the star-galaxy data, where it is worse than uniform weighting also: this may be because the star-galaxy data probably induces the greatest degree of mis-specification relative to this 6-model class (based on visual inspection).

Table 2 shows the averages of the stacked weight vectors for each data set. The mixture components generally got higher weight than the triangular kernels. The vowel and star-galaxy data sets have more structure than can be represented by any of the component models and this is reflected in the fact that for each most weight is placed on the most complex mixture model with $k = 8$.

3.2   Results on Simulated Data with no Model Mis-Specification

We simulated data from a 2-dimensional 4-Gaussian mixture model with a reasonable degree of overlap (this is the data set used in Ripley (1994) with the class labels removed) and compared the same models and combining/selection schemes as before, except that "truth" is also included, i.e., the scheme which always selects the true model structure with $k = 4$ Gaussians. For each training sample size, 20 different training data sets were simulated, and the mean likelihood on an independent test data set of size 1000 was reported.

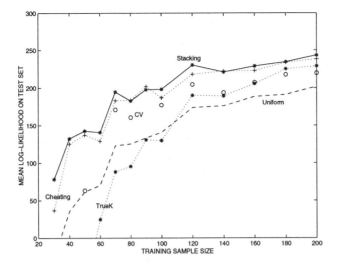

Figure 1: Plot of mean log-likelihood (relative to a single Gaussian model) for various density estimation schemes on data simulated from a 4-component Gaussian mixture.

Note that here we are assured of having the true model in the set of models being considered, something that is presumably never exactly the case in the real world (and presumably was not the case for the experiments recounted in Table 1.) Nonetheless, as indicated in (Figure 1), stacking performed about the same as the "cheating" method and significantly outperformed the other methods, including "truth." (Results where some of the methods had log-likelihoods *lower* than the single Gaussian are not shown for clarity).

The fact that "truth" performed poorly on the smaller sample sizes is due to the fact that with smaller sample sizes it was often better to fit a simpler model with reliable parameter estimates (which is what "cheating" typically would do) than a more complex model which may overfit (even when it is the true model structure). As the sample size increases, both "truth" and cross-validation approach the performance of "cheating" and stacking: uniform weighting is universally poorer as one would expect when the true model is within the model class. The stacked weights at the different sample sizes (not shown) start out with significant weight on the triangular kernel model and gradually shift to the $k = 2$ Gaussian mixture model and finally to the (true) $k = 4$ Gaussian model as sample size grows. Thus, stacking is seen to incur no penalty when the true model is within the model class being fit. In fact the opposite is true; for small sample sizes stacking outperforms other density estimation techniques which place full weight on a single (but poorly parametrized) model.

4 Discussion and Conclusions

Selecting a global bandwidth for kernel density estimation is still a topic of debate among statisticians. Stacking allows the possibility of side-stepping the issue of a single bandwidth by combining kernels with different bandwidths and different kernel shapes. A stacked combination of such kernel estimators is equivalent to using a single composite kernel that is a convex combination of the underlying kernels. For example, kernel estimators based on finite support kernels can be regularized in a data-driven manner by combining them with infinite support kernels. The key point is that the shape and width of the resulting "effective" kernel is driven by the data.

It is also worth noting that by combining Gaussian mixture models with different k values one gets a hierarchical "mixture of mixtures" model. This hierarchical model can provide a natural multi-scale representation of the data, which is clearly similar in spirit to wavelet density estimators, although the functional forms and estimation methodologies for each technique can be quite different. There is also a representational similarity to Jordan and Jacob's (1994) "mixture of experts" model where the weights are allowed to depend directly on the inputs. Exploiting that similarity, one direction for further work is to investigate adaptive weight parametrizations in the stacked density estimation context.

Acknowledgements

The work of P.S. was supported in part by NSF Grant IRI-9703120 and in part by the Jet Propulsion Laboratory, California Institute of Technology, under a contract with the National Aeronautics and Space Administration.

References

Banfield, J. D., and Raftery, A. E., 'Model-based Gaussian and non-Gaussian clustering,' *Biometrics*, 49, 803–821, 1993.

Breiman, L., 'Bagging predictors,' *Machine Learning*, 26(2), 123–140, 1996a.

Breiman, L., 'Stacked regressions,' *Machine Learning*, 24, 49–64, 1996b.

Chickering, D. M., and Heckerman, D., 'Efficient approximations for the marginal likelihood of Bayesian networks with hidden variables,' *Machine Learning*, in press.

Draper, D, 'Assessment and propagation of model uncertainty (with discussion),' *Journal of the Royal Statistical Society B*, 57, 45–97, 1995.

Escobar, M. D., and West, M., 'Bayesian density estimation and inference with mixtures,' *J. Am. Stat. Assoc.*, 90, 577-588, 1995.

Jordan, M. I. and Jacobs, R. A., 'Hierarchical mixtures of experts and the EM algorithm,' *Neural Computation*, 6, 181–214, 1994.

Madigan, D., and Raftery, A. E., 'Model selection and accounting for model uncertainty in graphical models using Occam's window,' *J. Am. Stat. Assoc.*, 89, 1535–1546, 1994.

Ormeneit, D., and Tresp, V., 'Improved Gaussian mixture density estimates using Bayesian penalty terms and network averaging,' in *Advances in Neural Information Processing 8*, 542–548, MIT Press, 1996.

Ripley, B. D. 1994. 'Neural networks and related methods for classification (with discussion),' *J. Roy. Stat. Soc. B*, 56, 409–456.

Smyth, P.,'Clustering using Monte-Carlo cross-validation,' in *Proceedings of the Second International Conference on Knowledge Discovery and Data Mining*, Menlo Park, CA: AAAI Press, pp.126–133, 1996.

Titterington, D. M., A. F. M. Smith, U. E. Makov, *Statistical Analysis of Finite Mixture Distributions*, Chichester, UK: John Wiley and Sons, 1985

Wolpert, D. 1992. 'Stacked generalization,' *Neural Networks*, 5, 241–259.

Bidirectional Retrieval from Associative Memory

Friedrich T. Sommer and Günther Palm
Department of Neural Information Processing
University of Ulm, 89069 Ulm, Germany
{sommer,palm}@informatik.uni-ulm.de

Abstract

Similarity based fault tolerant retrieval in neural associative memories (NAM) has not lead to wiedespread applications. A drawback of the efficient Willshaw model for sparse patterns [Ste61, WBLH69], is that the high asymptotic information capacity is of little practical use because of high cross talk noise arising in the retrieval for finite sizes. Here a new bidirectional iterative retrieval method for the Willshaw model is presented, called crosswise bidirectional (CB) retrieval, providing enhanced performance. We discuss its asymptotic capacity limit, analyze the first step, and compare it in experiments with the Willshaw model. Applying the very efficient CB memory model either in information retrieval systems or as a functional model for reciprocal cortico-cortical pathways requires more than robustness against random noise in the input: Our experiments show also the segmentation ability of CB-retrieval with addresses containing the superposition of pattens, provided even at high memory load.

1 INTRODUCTION

From a technical point of view neural associative memories (NAM) provide data storage and retrieval. Neural models naturally imply parallel implementation of storage and retrieval algorithms by the correspondence to synaptic modification and neural activation. With distributed coding of the data the recall in NAM models is fault tolerant: It is robust against noise or superposition in the addresses and against local damage in the synaptic weight matrix. As biological models NAM have been proposed as general working schemes of networks of pyramidal cells in many places of the cortex.

An important property of a NAM model is its information capacity, measuring how efficient the synaptic weights are used. In the early sixties Steinbuch realized under the name "Lernmatrix" a memory model with binary synapses which is now known as Willshaw model [Ste61, WBLH69]. The great variety of NAM models proposed since then, many triggered by Hopfield's work [Hop82], do not reach the high asymptotic information capacity of the Willshaw model.

For finite network size, the Willshaw model does not optimally retrieve the stored information, since the inner product between matrix colum and input pattern determines the activity for each output neuron independently. For autoassociative pattern completion iterative retrieval can reduce cross talk noise [GM76, GR92, PS92, SSP96]. A simple bidirectional iteration – as in bidirectional associative memory (BAM) [Kos87] – can, however, not improve heteroassociative pattern mapping. For this task we propose CB-retrieval where each retrieval step forms the resulting activity pattern in an autoassociative process that uses the connectivity matrix twice before thresholding, thereby exploiting the stored information more efficiently.

2   WILLSHAW MODEL AND CB EXTENSION

Here pattern mapping tasks $x^\nu \to y^\nu$ are considered for a set of *memory patterns*: $\{(x^\nu, y^\nu) : x^\nu \in \{0,1\}^n, y^\nu \in \{0,1\}^m, \nu = 1, ..., M\}$. The number of 1-components in a pattern is called *pattern activity*. The Willshaw model works efficiently, if the memories are *sparse*, i.e., if the memory patterns have the same activities: $|x^\nu| = \sum_{i=1}^n x_i^\nu = a, |y^\nu| = \sum_{i=1}^m y_i^\nu = b \ \forall \ \nu$ with $a << n$ and $b << m$. During learning the set of memory patterns is transformed to the weight matrix by

$$C_{ij} = \min(1, \sum_\nu x_i^\nu y_j^\nu) = \sup_\nu x_i^\nu y_j^\nu.$$

For a given initial pattern $\tilde{x}^\mu$ the retrieval yields the output pattern $\hat{y}^\mu$ by forming in each neuron the dendritic sum $[C\tilde{x}^\mu]_j = \sum_i C_{ij}\tilde{x}_i^\mu$ and by calculating the activity value by threshold comparison

$$\hat{y}_j^\mu = H([C\tilde{x}^\mu]_j - \theta) \ \forall j, \tag{1}$$

with the global threshold value θ and $H(x)$ denoting the Heaviside function.

For finite sizes and with high memory load, i.e., $0 << P_1 := \text{Prob}\,[Cij = 1]\,(< 0.5)$, the Willshaw model provides no tolerance with respect to errors in the address, see Fig. 1 and 2. A bidirectional iteration of standard *simple retrieval* (1), as proposed in BAM models [Kos87], can therefore be ruled out for further retrieval error reduction [SP97]. In the energy function of the Willshaw BAM

$$E(x,y) = -\sum_{ij} C_{ij} x_i y_j + \Theta' \sum_i x_i + \Theta \sum_j y_j$$

we now indroduce a factor accounting for the magnitudes of dendritic potentials at activated neurons

$$E(x,y) = -\sum_{ij} C_{ij} x_i y_j \frac{a[C^T y]_i + b[Cx]_j}{a+b} + \Theta' \sum_i x_i + \Theta \sum_j y_j. \tag{2}$$

Differentiating the energy function (2) yields the gradient descent equations

$$y_j^{new} = H([Cx]_j^2 + \underbrace{\sum_k \sum_i C_{ij}C_{ik}x_i\, y_k}_{=:w_{jk}^x} - \Theta) \qquad (3)$$

$$x_i^{new} = H([C^T y]_i^2 + \underbrace{\sum_l \sum_j C_{ij}C_{lj}y_j\, x_l}_{=:w_{il}^y} - \Theta') \qquad (4)$$

As new terms in (3) and (4) sums over pattern components weighted with the quantities w_{jk}^x and w_{il}^y occur. w_{jk}^x is the overlap between the matrix columns j and k conditioned by the pattern x, which we call a *conditioned link* between y-units. Restriction on the conditioned link terms yields a new iterative retrieval scheme which we denote as *crosswise bidirectional (CB) retrieval*

$$y(r+1)_j = H(\sum_{i \in x(r)} C_{ij}[C^T y(r-1)]_i - \Theta) \qquad (5)$$

$$x(r+1)_i = H(\sum_{j \in y(r)} C_{ij}[C x(r-1)]_j - \Theta') \qquad (6)$$

For $r = 0$ pattern $y(r-1)$ has to be replaced by $H([Cx(0)] - \theta)$, for $r > 2$ Boolean ANDing with results from timestep $r - 1$ can be applied which has been shown to improve iterative retrieval in the Willshaw model for autoassociation [SSP96].

3   MODEL EVALUATION

Two possible retrieval error types can be distinguished: a *"miss"* error converts a 1-entry in y^μ to '0' and a *"add"* error does the opposite.

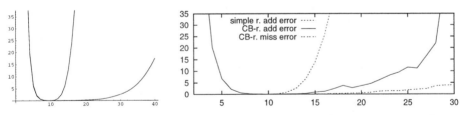

Figure 1: Mean retrieval error rates for $n = 2000$, $M = 15000$, $a = b = 10$ corresponding to a memory load of $P_1 = 0.3$. The x-axes display the address activity: $|\tilde{x}^\mu| = 10$ corresponds to a errorfree learning pattern, lower activities are due to miss errors, higher activities due to add errors. Left: Theory – Add errors for simple retrieval, eq. (7) (upper curve) and lower bound for the first step of CB-retrieval, eq. (9). Right: Simulations – Errors for simple and CB retrieval.

The analysis of simple retrieval from the address $\tilde{x}^\mu$ yields with optimal threshold setting $\theta = \tilde{k}$ the add error rate, i.e, the expectation of spurious ones:

$$\hat{\alpha} = (m - b)\text{Prob}\left[r \geq \tilde{k}\right], \qquad (7)$$

with the binomial random variable $\text{Prob}[r=l] = B(|\tilde{x}^\mu|, P_1)_l$, where $B(n,p)_l := \binom{n}{l} p^l (1-p)^{n-l}$. $\tilde{\alpha}$ denotes the add error rate and $k = |\tilde{x}^\mu| - \tilde{\alpha}$ the number of correct 1-s in the address.

For the first step of CB-retrieval a lower bound of the add error rate $\alpha(1)$ can be derived by the analysis of CB-retrieval with fixed address $x(0) = \tilde{x}^\mu$ and the perfect learning pattern y^μ as starting patterns in the y-layer. In this case the add error rate is:

$$\alpha = (m-b)\text{Prob}\left[r_1 + r_2 \geq \tilde{k}b\right], \tag{8}$$

where the random variables r_1 and r_2 have the distributions:
$\text{Prob}[r_1 = l/b] = B(\tilde{k}, P_1)_l$ and $\text{Prob}[r_2 = l] = B(\tilde{\alpha}b, (P_1)^2)_l$. Thus,

$$\alpha(1) \geq (m-b)\sum_{s=0}^{\tilde{k}} B(\tilde{k}, P_1)_s BS\left[\tilde{\alpha}b, (P_1)^2, (\tilde{k}-s)b\right], \tag{9}$$

where $BS[n,p,t] := \sum_{l=t}^{n} B(n,p)_l$ is the binomial sum.

In Fig. 1 the analytic results for the first step (7) and (9) can be compared with simulations (left versus right diagram). In the experiments simple retrieval is performed with threshold $\theta = \tilde{k}$. CB-retrieval is iterated in the y-layer (with fixed address $\tilde{x}$) starting with three randomly chosen 1-s from the simple retrieval result $\hat{y}^\mu$. The iteration is stopped, if a stable pattern at threshold $\Theta = b\tilde{k}$ is reached.

The memory capacity can be calculated per pattern component under the assumption that in the memory patterns each component is independent, i.e., the probabilities for a 1 are $p = a/n$ or $q = b/m$ respectively, and the probabilities of an add and a miss error are simply the renormalized rates denoted by α', β' and $\tilde{\alpha}'$, $\tilde{\beta}'$ for x-patterns and by γ', δ' for y-patterns. The information about the stored pattern contained in noisy initial or retrieved patterns is then given by the transinformation $t(p, \alpha', \beta') := i(p) - i(p, \alpha', \beta')$, where $i(p)$ is the Shannon information, and $i(p, \alpha', \beta')$ the conditional information. The heteroassociative mapping is evaluated by the *output capacity*: $A(\tilde{\alpha}', \tilde{\beta}') := Mm\, t(q, \gamma', \delta')/mn$ (in units bit/synapse). It depends on the initial noise since the performance drops with growing initial errors and assumes the maximum, if no fault tolerance is provided, that is, with noiseless initial patterns, see Fig. 2. Autoassociative completion of a distorted x-pattern is evaluated by the *completion capacity*: $C(\tilde{\alpha}', \tilde{\beta}') := Mn(t(p, \alpha', \beta') - t(p, \tilde{\alpha}', \tilde{\beta}'))/mn$. A BAM maps and completes at the same time and should be therefore evaluated by the *search capacity* $S := C + A$.

The asymptotic capacity of the Willshaw model is strikingly high: The completion capacity (for autoassociation) is $C^+ = \ln[2]/4$, the mapping capacity (for heteroassociation with input noise) is $A^+ = \ln[2]/2$ bit/syn [Pal91], leading to a value for the search capacity of $(3\ln[2])/4 = 0.52$ bit/syn. To estimate S for general retrieval procedures one can consider a recognition process of stored patterns in the whole space of sparse initial patterns; an initial pattern is "recognized", if it is invariant under a bidirectional retrieval cycle. The so-called *recognition capacity* of this process is an upper bound of the completion capacity and it had been determined as $\ln[2]/2$, see [PS92]. This is achieved again with parameters M, p, q providing $A = \ln[2]/2$ yielding $\ln[2]$ bit/syn as upper bound of the asymptotic search capacity. In summary, we know about the asymptotic search capacity of the CB-model: $0.52 \leq S^+ \leq 0.69$ bit/syn. For experimental results, see Fig. 4.

4   EXPERIMENTAL RESULTS

The CB model has been tested in simulations and compared with the Willshaw model (simple retrieval) for addresses with random noise (Fig. 2) and for addresses composed by two learning patterns (Fig. 3). In Fig. 2 the widely enlarged range of high qualtity retrieval in the CB-model is demonstrated for different system sizes.

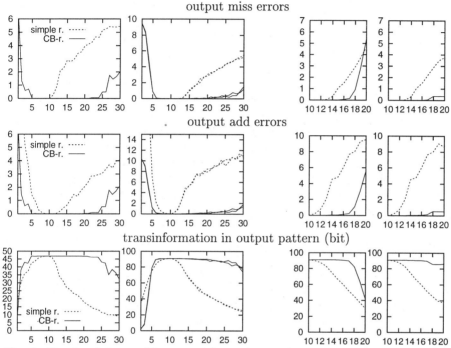

Fig. 2: Retrieval from addresses with random noise. The x-axis labeling is as in Fig. 1. Small system with $n = 100$, $M = 35$ (left), system size as in Fig. 1, two trials (right). Output activities adjusted near $|y| = \tilde{k}$ by threshold setting.

Fig. 3: Retrieval from addresses composed by two learning patterns. Parameters as in right column of Fig. 2, explanation of left and right column, see text.

In Fig. 3 the address contains one learning pattern and 1-components of a second learning pattern successively added with increasing abscissae. On the right end of each diagram both patterns are completely superimposed. Diagrams in the left column show errors and transinformation, if retrieval results are compared with the learning pattern which is for $|\tilde{x}^{\mu}| < 20$ dominantly addressed. Simple retrieval errors behave similiar as for random noise in the address (Fig. 2) while the error level of CB-retrieval raises faster if more than 7 adds from the second pattern are present. Diagrams in the right column show the same quantities, if the retrieval result is compared with the closest of the two learning patterns. It can be observed i) that a learning pattern is retrieved even if the address is a complete superposition and ii) if the second pattern is almost complete in the address the retrieved pattern corresponds in some cases to the second pattern. However, in all cases CB-retrieval yields one of the learning pattern pairs and it could be used to generate a good address for further retrieval of the other by deletion of the corresponding 1-components in the original address.

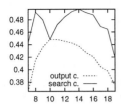

Fig. 4: Output and search capacity of CB retrieval in bit/syn with x-axis labeling as in Fig. 2 for $n = m = 2000$, $a = b = 10$ $M = 20000$. The difference between both curves is the contribution due to x-pattern completion, the completion capacity C. It is zero for $|x(0)| = 10$, if the initial pattern is errorfree.

The search capacity of the CB model in Fig. 4 is close to the theoretical expectations from Sect. 3, increasing with input noise due to the address completion.

5 SPARSE CODING

To apply the proposed NAM model, for instance, in information retrieval, a coding of the data to be accessed into sparse binary patterns is required. A useful extraction of sparse features should take account of statistical data properties and the way the user is acting on them. There is evidence from cognitive psychology that such a coding is typically quite easy to find. The feature encoding, where a person is extracting feature sets to characterize complex situations by a few present features, is one of the three basic classes of cognitive processes defined by Sternberg [Ste77]. Similarities in the data are represented by feature patterns having a large number of present features in common, that is a high overlap: $o(x, x') := \sum_i x_i x'_i$. For text retrieval word fragments used in existing indexing techniques can be directly taken as sparse binary features [Geb87]. For image processing sparse coding strategies [Zet90], and neural models for sparse feature extraction by anti-Hebbian learning [Föl90] have been proposed. Sparse patterns extracted from different data channels in heterogeneous data can simply be concatenated and processed simultaneously in NAM. If parts of the original data should be held in a conventional memory, also these addresses have to be represented by distributed and sparse patterns in order to exploit the high performance of the proposed NAM.

6 CONCLUSION

A new bidirectional retrieval method (CB-retrieval) has been presented for the Willshaw neural associative memory model. Our analysis of the first CB-retrieval step indicates a high potential for error reduction and increased input fault tolerance. The asymptotic capacity for bidirectional retrieval in the binary Willshaw matrix has been determined between 0.52 and 0.69 bit/syn. In experiments CB-retrieval showed significantly increased input fault tolerance with respect to the standard model leading to a practical information capacity in the order of the theoretical expectations (0.5 bit/syn). Also the segmentation ability of CB-retrieval with ambiguous addresses has been shown. Even at high memory load such input patterns can be decomposed and corresponding memory entries returned individually. The model improvement does not require sophisticated individual threshold setting [GW95], strategies proposed for BAM like more complex learning procedures, or "dummy augmentation" in the pattern coding [WCM90, LCL95].

The demonstrated performance of the CB-model encourages applications as massively parallel search strategies in Information Retrieval. The sparse coding requirement has been briefly discussed regarding technical strategies and psychological plausibility. Biologically plausible variants of CB-retrieval contribute to more refined cell assembly theories, see [SWP98].

Acknowledgement: One of the authors (F.T.S.) was supported by grant SO352/3-1 of the Deutsche Forschungsgemeinschaft.

References

[Föl90]   P. Földiak. Forming sparse representations by local anti-hebbian learning. *Biol. Cybern.*, 64:165–170, 1990.

[Geb87]   F. Gebhardt. Text signatures by superimposed coding of letter triplets and quadruplets. *Information Systems*, 12(2):151–156, 1987.

[GM76]   A.R. Gardner-Medwin. The recall of events through the learning of associations between their parts. *Proceedings of the Royal Society of London B*, 194:375–402, 1976.

[GR92]   W.G. Gibson and J. Robinson. Statistical analysis of the dynamics of a sparse associative memory. *Neural Networks*, 5:645–662, 1992.

[GW95]   B. Graham and D. Willshaw. Improving recall from an associative memory. *Biological Cybernetics*, 72:337–346, 1995.

[Hop82]   J.J. Hopfield. Neural networks and physical systems with emergent collective computational abilities. *Proceedings of the National Academy of Sciences, USA*, 79, 1982.

[Kos87]   B. Kosko. Adaptive bidirectional associative memories. *Applied Optics*, 26(23):4947–4971, 1987.

[LCL95]   C.-S. Leung, L.-W. Chan, and E. Lai. Stability, capacity and statistical dynamics of second-order bidirectional associative memory. *IEEE Trans. Syst, Man Cybern.*, 25(10):1414–1424, 1995.

[Pal91]   G. Palm. Memory Capacities of Local Rules for Synaptic Modification. *Concepts in Neuroscience*, 2:97–128, 1991.

[PS92]   G. Palm and F. T. Sommer. Information capacity in recurrent McCulloch-Pitts networks with sparsely coded memory states. *Network*, 3:1–10, 1992.

[SP97]   F. T. Sommer and G. Palm. Improved bidirectional retrieval of sparse patterns stored by Hebbian learning. *Submitted to Neural Networks*, 1997.

[SSP96]   F. Schwenker, F. T. Sommer, and G. Palm. Iterative retrieval of sparsely coded associative memory patterns. *Neural Networks*, 9(3):445 – 455, 1996.

[Ste61]   K. Steinbuch. Die Lernmatrix. *Kybernetik*, 1:36–45, 1961.

[Ste77]   R. J. Sternberg. *Intelligence, information processing and analogical reasoning.* Hillsdale, NJ, 1977.

[SWP98]   F. T. Sommer, T. Wennekers, and G. Palm. Bidirectional completion of Cell Assemblies in the cortex. In *Computational Neuroscience: Trends in Research.* Plenum Press, 1998.

[WBLH69]   D. J. Willshaw, O. P. Buneman, and H. C. Longuet-Higgins. Nonholographic associative memory. *Nature*, 222:960–962, 1969.

[WCM90]   Y. F. Wang, J. B. Cruz, and J. H. Mulligan. Two coding stragegies for bidirectional associative memory. *IEEE Trans. Neural Networks*, 1(1):81–92, 1990.

[Zet90]   C. Zetsche. Sparse coding: the link between low level vision and associative memory. In R. Eckmiller, G. Hartmann, and G. Hauske, editors, *Parallel Processing in Neural Systems and Computers*. Elsevier Science Publishers B. V. (North Holland), 1990.

Mapping a manifold of perceptual observations

Joshua B. Tenenbaum
Department of Brain and Cognitive Sciences
Massachusetts Institute of Technology, Cambridge, MA 02139
jbt@psyche.mit.edu

Abstract

Nonlinear dimensionality reduction is formulated here as the problem of trying to find a Euclidean feature-space embedding of a set of observations that preserves as closely as possible their intrinsic metric structure – the distances between points on the observation manifold as measured along geodesic paths. Our *isometric feature mapping* procedure, or isomap, is able to reliably recover low-dimensional nonlinear structure in realistic perceptual data sets, such as a manifold of face images, where conventional global mapping methods find only local minima. The recovered map provides a canonical set of globally meaningful features, which allows perceptual transformations such as interpolation, extrapolation, and analogy – highly nonlinear transformations in the original observation space – to be computed with simple linear operations in feature space.

1 Introduction

In psychological or computational research on perceptual categorization, it is generally taken for granted that the perceiver has *a priori* access to a representation of stimuli in terms of some perceptually meaningful features that can support the relevant classification. However, these features will be related to the raw sensory input (e.g. values of retinal activity or image pixels) only through a very complex transformation, which must somehow be acquired through a combination of evolution, development, and learning. Fig. 1 illustrates the feature-discovery problem with an example from visual perception. The set of views of a face from all possible viewpoints is an extremely high-dimensional data set when represented as image arrays in a computer or on a retina; for example, 32 x 32 pixel grey-scale images can be thought of as points in a 1,024-dimensional observation space. The perceptually meaningful structure of these images, however, is of much lower dimensionality; all of the images in Fig. 1 lie on a two-dimensional manifold parameterized by viewing angle. A perceptual system that discovers this manifold structure has learned a model of the appearance of this face that will support a wide range of recognition, classification, and imagery tasks (some demonstrated in Fig. 1), despite the absence of any prior physical knowledge about three-dimensional object geometry, surface texture, or illumination conditions.

Learning a manifold of perceptual observations is difficult because these observations

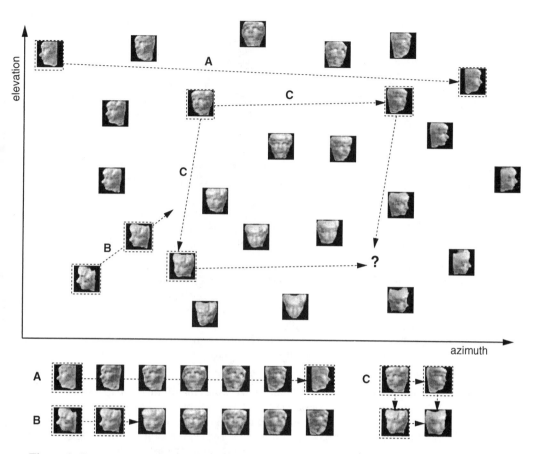

Figure 1: Isomap recovers a global topographic map of face images varying in two viewing angle parameters, azimuth and elevation. Image interpolation (A), extrapolation (B), and analogy (C) can then be carried out by linear operations in this feature space.

usually exhibit significant nonlinear structure. Fig. 2A provides a simplified version of this problem. A flat two-dimensional manifold has been nonlinearly embedded in a three-dimensional observation space, [1] and must be "unfolded" by the learner. For linearly embedded manifolds, principal component analysis (PCA) is guaranteed to discover the dimensionality of the manifold and produce a compact representation in the form of an orthonormal basis. However, PCA is completely insensitive to the higher-order, nonlinear structure that characterizes the points in Fig. 2A or the images in Fig. 1.

Nonlinear dimensionality reduction – the search for intrinsically low-dimensional structures embedded nonlinearly in high-dimensional observations – has long been a goal of computational learning research. The most familiar nonlinear techniques, such as the self-organizing map (SOM; Kohonen, 1988), the generative topographic mapping (GTM; Bishon, Svensen, & Williams, 1998), or autoencoder neural networks (DeMers & Cottrell, 1993), try to generalize PCA by discovering a single *global* low-dimensional nonlinear model of the observations. In contrast, *local* methods (Bregler & Omohundro, 1995; Hinton, Revow, & Dayan, 1995) seek a set of low-dimensional models, usually linear and hence valid only for a limited range of data. When appropriate, a single global model is

---

[1]Given by $x_1 = z_1 \cos(z_1)$, $x_2 = z_1 \sin(z_1)$, $x_3 = z_2$, for $z_1 \in [3\pi/2, 9\pi/2]$, $z_2 \in [0, 15]$.

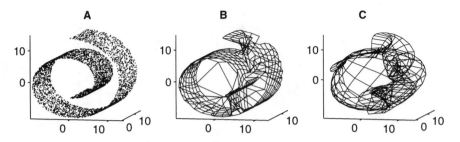

Figure 2: A nonlinearly embedded manifold may create severe local minima for "top-down" mapping algorithms. (A) Raw data. (B) Best SOM fit. (C) Best GTM fit.

more revealing and useful than a set of local models. However, local linear methods are in general far more computationally efficient and reliable than global methods.

For example, despite the visually obvious structure in Fig. 2A, this manifold was not successfuly modeled by either of two popular global mapping algorithms, SOM (Fig. 2B) and GTM (Fig. 2C), under a wide range of parameter settings. Both of these algorithms try to fit a grid of predefined (usually two-dimensional) topology to the data, using greedy optimization techniques that first fit the large-scale (linear) structure of the data, before making small-scale (nonlinear) refinements. The coarse structure of such "folded" data sets as Fig. 2A hides their nonlinear structure from greedy optimizers, virtually ensuring that top-down mapping algorithms will become trapped in highly suboptimal solutions.

Rather than trying to force a predefined map onto the data manifold, this paper shows how a perceptual system may map a set of observations in a "bottom-up" fashion, by first learning the topological structure of the manifold (as in Fig. 3A) and only then learning a metric map of the data (as in Fig. 3C) that respects this topology. The next section describes the goals and steps of the mapping procedure, and subsequent sections demonstrate applications to two challenging learning tasks: recovering a five-dimensional manifold embedded nonlinearly in 50 dimensions, and recovering the manifold of face images depicted in Fig. 1.

2   Isometric feature mapping

We assume our data lie on an unknown manifold M embedded in a high-dimensional observation space X. Let $x^{(i)}$ denote the coordinates of the ith observation. We seek a mapping $f : X \rightarrow Y$ from the observation space X to a low-dimensional Euclidean feature space Y that preserves as well as possible the intrinsic metric structure of the observations, i.e. the distances between observations as measured along geodesic (locally shortest) paths of M. The *isometric feature mapping*, or isomap, procedure presented below generates an implicit description of the mapping f, in terms of the corresponding feature points $y^{(i)} = f(x^{(i)})$ for sufficiently many observations $x^{(i)}$. Explicit parametric descriptions of f or f^{-1} can be found with standard techniques of function approximation (Poggio & Girosi, 1990) that interpolate smoothly between the known corresponding pairs $\{x^{(i)}, y^{(i)}\}$.

A Euclidean map of the data's intrinsic geometry has several important properties. First, intrinsically similar observations should map to nearby points in feature space, supporting efficient similarity-based classification and informative visualization. Moreover, the geodesic paths of the manifold, which are highly nonlinear in the original observation space, should map onto straight lines in feature space. Then perceptually natural transformations along these paths, such as the interpolation, extrapolation and analogy demonstrated in Figs. 1A-C, may be computed by trivial linear operations in feature space.

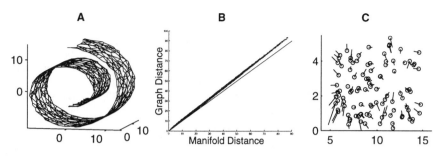

Figure 3: The results of the three-step isomap procedure. (A) Discrete representation of manifold in Fig. 2A. (B) Correlation between measured graph distances and true manifold distances. (C) Correspondence of recovered two-dimensional feature points $\{y_1, y_2\}$ (circles) with original generating vectors $\{z_1, z_2\}$ (line ends).

The isomap procedure consists of three main steps, each of which might be carried out by more or less sophisticated techniques. The crux of isomap is finding an efficient way to compute the true geodesic distance between observations, given only their Euclidean distances in the high-dimensional observation space. Isomap assumes that distance between points in observation space is an accurate measure of manifold distance only locally and must be integrated over paths on the manifold to obtain global distances. As preparation for computing manifold distances, we first construct a discrete representation of the manifold in the form of a topology-preserving network (Fig. 3A). Given this network representation, we then compute the shortest-path distance between any two points in the network using dynamic programming. This polynomial-time computation provides a good approximation to the actual manifold distances (Fig. 3B) without having to search over all possible paths in the network (let alone the infinitely many paths on the unknown manifold!). Finally, from these manifold distances, we construct a global geometry-preserving map of the observations in a low-dimensional Euclidean space, using multidimensional scaling (Fig. 3C). The implementation of this procedure is detailed below.

Step 1: Discrete representation of manifold (Fig. 3A). From the input data of n observations $\{x^{(1)}, \ldots, x^{(n)}\}$, we randomly select a subset of r points to serve as the nodes $\{g^{(1)}, \ldots, g^{(r)}\}$ of the topology-preserving network. We then construct a graph G over these nodes by connecting $g^{(i)}$ and $g^{(j)}$ if and only if there exists at least one $\mathbf{x}^{(k)}$ whose two closest nodes (in observation space) are $g^{(i)}$ and $g^{(j)}$ (Martinetz & Schulten, 1994). The resulting graph for the data in Fig. 2A is shown in Fig. 3A (with $n = 10^4, r = 10^3$). This graph clearly respects the topology of the manifold far better than the best fits with SOM (Fig. 2B) or GTM (Fig. 2C). In the limit of infinite data, the graph thus produced converges to the Delaunay triangulation of the nodes, restricted to the data manifold (Martinetz & Schulten, 1994). In practice, $n = 10^4$ data points have proven sufficient for all examples we have tried. This number may be reduced significantly if we know the dimensionality d of the manifold, but here we assume no *a priori* information about dimensionality. The choice of r, the number of nodes in G, is the only free parameter in isomap. If r is too small, the shortest-path distances between nodes in G will give a poor approximation to their true manifold distance. If r is too big (relative to n), G will be missing many appropriate links (because each data point $\mathbf{x}^{(i)}$ contributes at most one link). In practice, choosing a satisfactory r is not difficult – all three examples presented in this paper use $r = n/10$, the first value tried. I am currently exploring criteria for selecting the optimal value r based on statistical arguments and dimensionality considerations.

Step 2: Manifold distance measure (Fig. 3B). We first assign a weight to each link w_{ij} in the graph G, equal to $d_X^{ij} = \|x^{(i)} - x^{(j)}\|$, the Euclidean distance between nodes i and j in the observation space X. The length of a path in G is defined to be the sum of link weights along that path. We then compute the geodesic distance d_G^{ij} (i.e. shortest path length) between all pairs of nodes i and j in G, using Floyd's $O(r^3)$ algorithm (Foster, 1995). Initialize $d_G^{ij} = d_X^{ij}$ if nodes i and j are connected

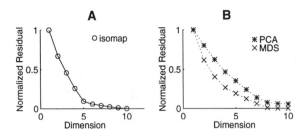

Figure 4: Given a 5–dimensional manifold embedded nonlinearly in a 50–dimensional space, isomap identifies the intrinsic dimensionality (A), while PCA and MDS alone do not (B).

and ∞ otherwise. Then for each node k, set each $d_G^{ij} = \min(d_G^{ij}, d_G^{ik} + d_G^{kj})$. Fig. 3B plots the distances d_G^{ij} computed between nodes i and j in the graph of Fig. 3A versus their actual manifold distances d_M^{ij}. Note that the correlation is almost perfect ($R > .99$), but d_G^{ij} tends to overestimate d_M^{ij} by a constant factor due to the discretization introduced by the graph. As the density of observations increases, so does the possible graph resolution. Thus, in the limit of infinite data, the graph-based approximation to manifold distance may be made arbitrarily accurate.

Step 3: Isometric Euclidean embedding (Fig. 3C). We use ordinal multidimensional scaling (MDS; Cox & Cox, 1994; code provided by Brian Ripley), also called "nonmetric" MDS, to find a k-dimensional Euclidean embedding that preserves as closely as possible the graph distances d_G^{ij}. In contrast to classical "metric" MDS, which explicitly tries to preserve distances, ordinal MDS tries to preserve only the rank ordering of distances. MDS finds a configuration of k-dimensional feature vectors $\{y^{(1)}, \ldots, y^{(r)}\}$, corresponding to the high-dimensional observations $\{x^{(1)}, \ldots, x^{(r)}\}$, that minimizes the stress function,

$$S = \min_{\hat{d}_G^{ij}} \sqrt{\frac{\sum_{i<j}(d_Y^{ij} - \hat{d}_G^{ij})^2}{\sum_{i<j}(d_Y^{ij})^2}}. \tag{1}$$

Here $d_Y^{ij} = \|y^{(i)} - y^{(j)}\|$, the Euclidean distance between feature vectors i and j, and the $\hat{d}_G^{ij}$ are some monotonic transformation of the graph distances d_G^{ij}. We use ordinal MDS because it is less senstitive to noisy estimates of manifold distance. Moreover, when the number of points scaled is large enough (as it is in all our examples), ordinal constraints alone are sufficient to reconstruct a precise metric map. Fig. 3C shows the projections of 100 random points on the manifold in Fig. 2A onto a two-dimensional feature space computed by MDS from the graph distances output by step 2 above. These points are in close correspondence (after rescaling) with the original two-dimensional vectors used to generate the manifold (see note 1), indicating that isomap has successfully unfolded the manifold onto a 2-dimensional Euclidean plane.

3   Example 1: Five-dimensional manifold

This section demonstrates isomap's ability to discover and model a noisy five-dimensional manifold embedded within a 50-dimensional space. As the dimension of the manifold increases beyond two, SOM, GTM, and other constrained clustering approaches become impractical due to the exponential proliferation of cluster centers. Isomap, however, is quite practical for manifolds of moderate dimensionality, because the estimates of manifold distance for a fixed graph size degrade gracefully as dimensionality increases. Moreover, isomap is able to automatically discover the intrinsic dimensionality of the data, while conventional methods must be initialized with a fixed dimensionality.

We consider a 5-dimensional manifold parameterized by $\{z_1, \ldots, z_5\} \in [0, 4]^5$. The first 10 of 50 observation dimensions were determined by nonlinear functions of these parameters. [2]

---

[2] $x_1 = \cos(\pi z_1)$, $x_2 = \sin(\pi z_1)$, $x_3 = \cos(\frac{2\pi}{3} z_1)$, $x_4 = \sin(\frac{2\pi}{3} z_1)$, $x_5 = \cos(\frac{\pi}{3} z_1)$, $x_6 = \sin(\frac{\pi}{3} z_1)$, $x_7 = z_2 \cos^2(\frac{\pi}{32} z_1) + z_3 \sin^2(\frac{\pi}{32} z_1)$, $x_8 = z_2 \sin^2(\frac{\pi}{32} z_1) + z_3 \cos^2(\frac{\pi}{32} z_1)$, $x_9 = z_4 \cos^2(\frac{\pi}{32} z_1) + z_5 \sin^2(\frac{\pi}{32} z_1)$, $x_{10} = z_4 \sin^2(\frac{\pi}{32} z_1) + z_5 \cos^2(\frac{\pi}{32} z_1)$.

Low-amplitude gaussian noise (4-5% of variance) was added to each of these dimensions, and the remaining 40 dimensions were set to pure noise of similar variance. The isomap procedure applied to this data ($n = 10^4, r = 10^3$) correctly recognized its intrinsic five-dimensionality, as indicated by the sharp decrease of stress (see Eq. 1) for embedding dimensions up to 5 and only gradual decrease thereafter (Fig. 4A). In contrast, both PCA and raw MDS (using distances in observation space rather than manifold distances) identify the 10-dimensional linear subspace containing the data, but show no sensitivity to the underlying five-dimensional manifold (Fig. 4B).

4   Example 2: Two-dimensional manifold of face images

This section illustrates the performance of isomap on the two-dimensional manifold of face images shown in Fig. 1. To generate this map, 32 x 32-pixel images of a face were first rendered in MATLAB in many different poses (azimuth $\in [-90°, 90°]$, elevation $\in [-10°, 10°]$), using a 3-D range image of an actual head and a combination of lambertian and specular reflectance models. To save computation, the data ($n = 10^4$ images) were first reduced to 60 principal components and then submitted to isomap ($r = 10^3$). The plot of stress S vs. dimension indicated a dimensionality of two (even more clearly than Fig. 4A). Fig. 1 shows the two-dimensional feature space that results from applying MDS to the computed graph distances, with 25 face images placed at their corresponding points in feature space. Note the clear topographic representation of similar views at nearby feature points. The principal axes of the feature space can be identified as the underlying viewing angle parameters used to generate the data. The correlations of the two isomap dimensions with the two pose angles are $R = .99$ and $R = .95$ respectively. No other global mapping procedure tried (PCA, MDS, SOM, GTM) produced interpretable results for these data.

The human visual system's implicit knowledge of an object's appearance is not limited to a representation of view similarity, and neither is isomap's. As mentioned in Section 2, an isometric feature map also supports analysis and manipulation of data, as a consequence of mapping geodesics of the observation manifold to straight lines in feature space. Having found a number of corresponding pairs $\{x^{(i)}, y^{(i)}\}$ of images $x^{(i)}$ and feature vectors $y^{(i)}$, it is easy to learn an explicit inverse mapping $f^{-1} : Y \to X$ from low-dimensional feature space to high-dimensional observation space, using generic smooth interpolation techniques such as generalized radial basis function (GRBF) networks (Poggio & Girosi, 1990). All images in Fig. 1 have been synthesized from such a mapping. [3]

Figs. 1A-C show how learning this inverse mapping allows interpolation, extrapolation, and analogy to be carried out using only linear operations. We can interpolate between two images $x^{(1)}$ and $x^{(2)}$ by synthesizing a sequence of images along their connecting line $(y^{(2)} - y^{(1)})$ in feature space (Fig. 1A). We can extrapolate the transformation from one image to another and far beyond, by following the line to the edge of the manifold (Fig. 1B). We can map the transformation between two images $x^{(1)}$ and $x^{(2)}$ onto an analogous transformation of another image $x^{(3)}$, by adding the transformation vector $(y^{(2)} - y^{(1)})$ to $y^{(3)}$ and synthesizing a new image at the resulting feature coordinates (Fig. 1C).

A number of authors (Bregler & Omohundro, 1995; Saul & Jordan, 1997; Beymer & Poggio, 1995) have previously shown how learning from examples allows sophisticated

---

[3]The map from feature vectors to images was learned by fitting a GRBF net to 1000 corresponding points in both spaces. Each point corresponds to a node in the graph G used to measure manifold distance, so the feature-space distances required to fit the GRBF net are given (approximately) by the graph distances d_G^{ij} computed in step 2 of isomap. A subset C of $m = 300$ points were randomly chosen as RBF centers, and the standard deviation of the RBFs was set equal to $\max_{i,j \in C} d_G^{ij} / \sqrt{2m}$ (as prescribed by Haykin, 1994).

image manipulations to be carried out efficiently. However, these approaches do not support as broad a range of transformations as isomap does, because of their use of only locally valid models and/or the need to compute special-purpose image features such as optical flow. See Tenenbaum (1997) for further discussion, as well as examples of isomap applied to more complex manifolds of visual observations.

5 Conclusions

The essence of the isomap approach to nonlinear dimensionality reduction lies in the novel problem formulation: to seek a low-dimensional Euclidean embedding of a set of observations that captures their intrinsic similarities, as measured along geodesic paths of the observation manifold. Here I have presented an efficient algorithm for solving this problem and shown that it can discover meaningful feature-space models of manifolds for which conventional "top-down" approaches fail. As a direct consequence of mapping geodesics to straight lines in feature space, isomap learns a representation of perceptual observations in which it is easy to perform interpolation and other complex transformations. A negative consequence of this strong problem formulation is that isomap will not be applicable to every data manifold. However, as with the classic technique of PCA, we can state clearly the general class of data for which isomap is appropriate – manifolds with no "holes" and no intrinsic curvature – with a guarantee that isomap will succeed on data sets from this class, given enough samples from the manifold. Future work will focus on generalizing this domain of applicability to allow for manifolds with more complex topologies and significant curvature, as would be necessary to model certain perceptual manifolds such as the complete view space of an object.

Acknowledgements

Thanks to M. Bernstein, W. Freeman, S. Gilbert, W. Richards, and Y. Weiss for helpful discussions. The author is a Howard Hughes Medical Institute Predoctoral Fellow.

References

Beymer, D. & Poggio, T. (1995). Representations for visual learning, *Science* **272**, 1905.

Bishop, C., Svensen, M., & Williams, C. (1998). GTM: The generative topographic mapping. *Neural Computation* **10(1)**.

Bregler, C. & Omohundro, S. (1995). Nonlinear image interpolation using manifold learning. *NIPS 7*. MIT Press.

Cox, T. & Cox, M. (1994). *Multidimensional scaling*. Chapman & Hall.

DeMers, D. & Cottrell, G. (1993). Nonlinear dimensionality reduction. *NIPS 5*. Morgan Kauffman.

Foster, I. (1995). *Designing and building parallel programs*. Addison-Wesley.

Haykin, S. (1994). *Neural Networks: A Comprehensive Foundation*. Macmillan.

Hinton, G., Revow, M., & Dayan, P. (1995). Recognizing handwritten digits using mixtures of linear models. *NIPS 7*. MIT Press.

Kohonen, T. (1988). *Self-Organization and Associative Memory*. Berlin: Springer.

Martinetz, T. & Schulten, K. (1994). Topology representing networks. *Neural Networks* **7**, 507.

Poggio, T. & Girosi, F. (1990). Networks for approximation and learning. *Proc. IEEE* **78**, 1481.

Saul, L. & Jordan, M. (1997). A variational principle for model-based morphing. *NIPS 9*. MIT Press.

Tenenbaum, J. (1997). Unsupervised learning of appearance manifolds. Manuscript submitted.

Graph Matching with Hierarchical Discrete Relaxation

Richard C. Wilson and Edwin R. Hancock
Department of Computer Science, University of York
York, Y01 5DD, UK.

Abstract

Our aim in this paper is to develop a Bayesian framework for matching hierarchical relational models. The goal is to make discrete label assignments so as to optimise a global cost function that draws information concerning the consistency of match from different levels of the hierarchy. Our Bayesian development naturally distinguishes between intra-level and inter-level constraints. This allows the impact of reassigning a match to be assessed not only at its own (or peer) level of representation, but also upon its parents and children in the hierarchy.

1   Introduction

Hierarchical graphical structures are of critical importance in the interpretation of sensory or perceptual data. For instance, following the influential work of Marr [6] there has been sustained efforts at effectively organising and processing hierarchical information in vision systems. There are a plethora of concrete examples which include pyramidal hierarchies [3] that are concerned with multi-resolution information processing and conceptual hierarchies [4] which are concerned with processing at different levels of abstraction. Key to the development of techniques for hierarchical information processing is the desire to exploit not only the intra-level constraints applying at the individual levels of representation but also inter-level constraints operating between different levels of the hierarchy. If used effectively these inter-level constraints can be brought to bear on the interpretation of uncertain image entities in such a way as to improve the fidelity of interpretation achieved by single level means. Viewed as an additional information source, inter-level constraints can be used to resolve ambiguities that would persist if single-level constraints alone were used.

In the connectionist literature graphical structures have been widely used to represent probabilistic causation in hierarchical systems [5, 9]. Although this literature has provided a powerful battery of techniques, they have proved to be of limited use in practical sensory processing systems. The main reason for this is that the underpinning independence assumptions and the resulting restrictions on graph topology are rarely realised in practice. In particular there are severe technical problems in dealing with structures that contain loops or are not tree-like. One way to overcome this difficulty is to edit intractable structures to produce tractable ones [8].

Our aim in this paper is to extend this discrete relaxation framework to hierarchical graphical structures. We develop a label-error process to model the violation of both inter-level and intra-level constraints. These two sets of constraints have distinct probability distributions. Because we are concerned with directly comparing the topology graphical structures rather than propagating causation, the resulting framework is not restricted by the topology of the hierarchy. In particular, we illustrate the effectiveness of the method on amoral graphs used to represent scene-structure in an image interpretation problem. This is a heterogeneous structure [2, 4] in which different label types and different classes of constraint operate at different levels of abstraction. This is to be contrasted with the more familiar pyramidal hierarchy which is effectively homogeneous [1, 3]. Since we are dealing with discrete entities inter-level information communication is via a symbolic interpretation of the objects under consideration.

2 Hierarchical Consistency

The hierarchy consists of a number of levels, each containing objects which are fully described by their children at the level below. Formally each level is described by an attributed relational graph $G^l = (V^l, E^l, \mathbf{X}^l)$, $\forall l \in L$, with L being the index-set of levels in the hierarchy; the indices t and b are used to denote the top and bottom levels of the hierarchy respectively. According to our notation for level l of the hierarchy, V^l is the set of nodes, E^l is the set of intra-level edges and $\mathbf{X}^l = \{\underline{x}_u^l, \forall u \in V^l\}$ is a set of unary attributes residing on the nodes. The children or descendents which form the representation of an element j at a lower level are denoted by $\mathcal{D}_j$. In other words, if u^{l-1} is in $\mathcal{D}_j$ then there is a link in the hierarchy between element j at level l and element u at level $l - 1$. According to our assumptions, the elements of $\mathcal{D}_j$ are drawn exclusively from V^{l-1}. The goal of performing relaxation operations is to find the match between scene graph G_1 and model graph G_2. At each individual level of the hierarchy this match is represented by a mapping function f^l, $\forall l \in L$, where $f^l : V_1^l \to V_2^l$.

The development of a hierarchical consistency measure proceeds along a similar line to the single-level work of Wilson and Hancock [10]. The quantity of interest is the MAP estimate for the mapping function f given the available unary attributes, i.e. $f = \arg\max_{\hat{f}} P(\hat{f}^l, \forall l \in L | \mathbf{X}^l, \forall l \in L)$. We factorize the measurement information over the set of nodes by application of Bayes rule under the assumption of measurement independence on the nodes. As a result

$$P(f^l, \forall l \in L | \mathbf{X}^l, \forall l \in L) = \frac{1}{p(\mathbf{X}^l, \forall l \in L)} \left\{ \prod_{l \in L} \prod_{u \in V^l} p(\mathbf{x}_u^l | f^l(u)) \right\} P(f^l, \forall l \in L) \quad (1)$$

The critical modelling ingredient in developing a discrete relaxation scheme from the above MAP criterion is the joint prior for the mapping function, i.e. $P(f^l, \forall l \in L)$

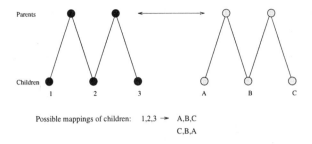

Possible mappings of children: 1,2,3 → A,B,C
                                           C,B,A

Figure 1: Example constrained children mappings

which represents the influence of structural information on the matching process. The joint measurement density, $p(\mathbf{X}^l, \forall l \in L)$, on the other hand is a fixed property of the hierarchy and can be eliminated from further consideration.

Raw perceptual information resides on the lowest level of the hierarchy. Our task is to propagate this information upwards through the hierarchy. To commence our development, we assume that individual levels are conditionally dependent only on the immediately adjacent descendant and ancestor levels. This assumption allows the factorisation of the joint probability in a manner analogous to a Markov chain [3]. Since we wish to draw information from the bottom upwards, the factorisation commences from the highest level of labelling. The expression for the joint probability of the hierarchical labelling is

$$P(f^l, \forall l \in L) = P(f^b) \prod_{l \in L, l \neq t} P(f^{l+1}|f^l) \tag{2}$$

We can now focus our attention on the conditional probabilities $P(f^{l+1}|f^l)$. These quantities express the probability of a labelling at the level $l+1$ given the previously defined labelling at the descendant level l. We develop tractable expressions for these probabilities by decomposing the hierarchical graph into convenient structural units. Here we build on the idea of decomposing single-level graphs into super-cliques that was successfully exploited in our previous work [10]. Super-cliques are the sets of nodes connected to a centre-object by intra-level edges. However, in the hierarchical case the relational units are more complex since we must also consider the graph-structure conveyed by inter-level edges.

We follow the philosophy adopted in the single-level case [10] by averaging the super-clique probabilities to estimate the conditional matching probabilities $P(f^{l+1}|f^l)$. If $\Gamma_j^l \subset f^l$ denotes the current match of the super-clique centred on the object $j \in V_1^l$ then we write

$$P(f^l|f^{l-1}) = \frac{1}{|V^l|} \sum_{j \in V^l} P(\Gamma_j^l|f^{l-1}) \tag{3}$$

In order to model this probability, we require a dictionary of constraint relations for the corresponding graph sub-units (super-cliques) from the model graph G_2. The allowed mappings between the model graph and the data graph which preserve the topology of the graph structure at a particular level of representation are referred to as "structure preserving mappings" or SPM's. It is important to note that we need only explore those mappings which are topologically identical to the super-clique centred on object j and therefore the possible mappings of the child nodes are heavily constrained by the mappings of their parents (Figure 1). We denote the set of SPM's by $\mathcal{P}$. Since the set $\mathcal{P}$ is effectively the state-space of legal matching, we can apply the Bayes theorem to compute the conditional super-clique probability in the following manner

$$P(\Gamma_j^l | f^{l-1}) = \sum_{S \in \mathcal{P}} P(\Gamma_j^l | S, f^{l-1}) P(S | f^{l-1}) \qquad (4)$$

According to this expression, there are two distinct components to our model. The first involves the comparison between our mapped realisation of the super-clique from graph G_1, i.e. Γ_j^l, with the selected unit from graph G_2 and the mapping from level $l-1$. Here we take the view that once we have hypothesised a particular mapping S from $\mathcal{P}$, the mapping f^{l-1} provides us with no further information, i.e. $P(\Gamma_j^l | S, f^{l-1}) = P(\Gamma_j^l | S)$. The matched super-clique Γ_j^l is conditionally independent given a mapping from the set of SPM's and we may write the first term as $P(\Gamma_j^l | S)$. In other words, this first conditional probability models only intra-level constraints. The second term is the significant one in evaluating the impact inter-level constraints on the labelling at the previous level. In this term the probability of the hypothesised mapping S is conditioned according to the match of the child level l.

All that remains now is to evaluate the conditional probabilities. Under the assumption of memoryless matching errors, the first term may be factorised over the marginal probabilities for the assigned matches γ_i^l on the individual nodes of the matched super-clique Γ_j^l given their counterparts s_i belonging to the structure preserving mapping S. In other words,

$$P(\Gamma_j^l | S) = \prod_{\gamma_i^l \in \Gamma_j^l} P(\gamma_i^l | s_i) \qquad (5)$$

In order to proceed we need to specify a probability distribution for the different matching possibilities. There are three cases. Firstly, the match γ_i^l may be to a dummy-node d inserted into Γ_j^l to raise it to the same size as S so as to facilitate comparison. This process effectively models structural errors in the data-graph. The second and third cases, relate to whether the match is correct or in error. Assuming that dummy node insertions may be made with probability P_s and that matching errors occur with probability P_e, then we can write down the following distribution rule

$$P(\gamma_i^l | s_i) = \begin{cases} P_s & \text{if } \gamma_i^l = d \text{ or } s_i = d \\ (1 - P_e)(1 - P_s) & \text{if } \gamma_i^l = s_i \\ P_e(1 - P_s) & \text{otherwise} \end{cases} \qquad (6)$$

The second term in Equation (5) is more subtle; it represents the conditional probability of the SPM S given a previously determined labelling at the level below. However, the mapping contains labels only from the current level l, not labels from level $l-1$. We can reconcile this difference by noting that selection of a particular mapping at level l limits the number of consistent mappings allowed topologically at the level below. In other words if one node is mapped to another at level l, the consistent interpretation is that the children of the nodes must match to each other. Provided that a set of mappings is available for the child-nodes, then this constraint can be used to model $P(S|f^{l-1})$. The required child-node mappings are referred to as "Hierarchy Preserving Mappings" or HPM's. It is these hierarchical mappings that lift the requirements for moralization in our matching scheme, since they effectively encode potentially incestuous vertical relations. We will denote the set of HPM's for the descendants of the SPM S as $\mathcal{Q}_S$ and a member of this set as $Q = \{q_i, \forall i \in \mathcal{D}_j\}$. Using this model the conditional probability $P(S|f^{l-1})$ is given by

$$P(S|f^{l-1}) = \sum_{Q \in \mathcal{Q}_S} P(S|Q, f^{l-1})P(Q|f^{l-1}) \tag{7}$$

Following our modelling of the intra-level probabilities, in this inter-level case assume that S is conditionally independent of f^{l-1} given Q, i.e. $P(S|Q, f^{l-1}) = P(S|Q)$.

Traditionally, dictionary based hierarchical schemes have operated by using a labelling determined at a preceding level to prune the dictionary set by elimination of vertically inconsistent items [4]. This approach can easily be incorporated into our scheme by setting $P(Q|f^{l-1})$ equal to unity for consistent items and to zero for those which are inconsistent. However we propose a different approach; by adopting the same kind of label distribution used in Equation 6 we can grade the SPM's according to their consistency with the match at level $l - 1$, i.e. f^{l-1}. The model is developed by factorising over the child nodes $q_i \in Q$ in the following manner

$$P(Q|f^{l-1}) = \prod_{q_i \in Q} P(q_i|\gamma_i^{l-1}) \tag{8}$$

The conditional probabilities are assigned by a re-application of the distribution rule given in Equation (6), i.e.

$$P(q_i|f^{l-1}) = \begin{cases} P_s & \text{if dummy node match} \\ (1 - P_e)(1 - P_s) & \text{if } q_i = \gamma_i^{l-1} \\ P_e(1 - P_s) & \text{otherwise} \end{cases} \tag{9}$$

For the conditional probability of the SPM given the HPM Q, we adopt a simple uniform model under the assumption that all legitimate mappings are equivalent, i.e. $P(S|Q) = P(S) = \frac{1}{|\mathcal{P}|}$.

The various simplifications can be assembled along the lines outlined in [10] to develop a discrete update rule for matching the two hierarchical structures. The MAP update decision depends only on the label configurations residing on levels $l - 1$, l and $l + 1$ together with the measurements residing on level l. Specifically, the level l matching configuration satisfies the condition

$$f^l = \arg\max_{\hat{f}^l} \left\{ \prod_{j \in V_1^l} p(\underline{x}_j^l | \hat{f}^l(j)) \right\} P(f^{l-1}|\hat{f}^l) P(\hat{f}^l|f^{l+1}) \tag{10}$$

Here consistency of match between levels l and $l - l$ of the hierarchy is gauged by the quantity

$$P(f^{l-1}|f^l) = \frac{1}{V_1^l} \sum_{i \in V_1^l} \sum_{S \in \mathcal{P}} \frac{K(\Gamma_i^l)}{\mathcal{Q}_S} \quad \exp \quad \left[-(k_e H(\Gamma_i^l, S) + k_s \Phi(\Gamma_i^l, S)) \right]$$

$$\sum_{Q \in \mathcal{Q}_S} K(\Gamma_i^{l-1}) \quad \exp \quad \left[-(k_e H(\Gamma_i^{l-1}, Q) + k_s \Phi(\Gamma_i^{l-1}, Q)) \right] \tag{11}$$

In the above expression $H(\Gamma_j, S)$ is the "Hamming distance" which counts the number of label conflicts between the assigned match Γ_j and the structure preserving mapping S. This quantity measures the consistency of the matched labels. The number of dummy nodes inserted into Γ_j by the mapping S is denoted by $\Phi(\Gamma_j, S)$. This second quantity measures the structural compatibility of the two hierarchical graphs. The exponential constants $k_e = \ln \frac{(1-P_e)(1-P_s)}{P_e}$ and $k_s = \ln \frac{1-P_s}{P_s}$ are related to the probabilities of structural errors and mis-assignment errors. Finally, $K(\Gamma_j) = (1 - P_e)(1 - P_e)^{|\Gamma_j|}$ is a normalisation constant. Finally, it is worth pointing out that the discrete relaxation scheme of Equation (10) can be applied at any level in the hierarchy. In other words the process can be operated in top-down or bottom-up modes if required.

3   Matching SAR Data

In our experimental evaluation of the discrete relaxation scheme we will focus on the matching of perceptual groupings of line-segments in radar images. Here the model graph is elicited from a digital map for the same area as the radar image. The line tokens extracted from the radar data correspond to hedges in the landscape. These are mapped as quadrilateral field boundaries in the cartographic model. To support this application, we develop a hierarchical matching scheme based on line-segments and corner groupings. The method used to extract these features from the radar images is explained in detail in [10]. Straight line segments extracted from intensity ridges are organised into corner groupings. The intra-level graph is a constrained Delaunay triangulation of the line-segments. Inter-level relations represent the subsumption of the bottom-level line segments into corners.

The raw image data used in this study is shown in Figure 2a. The extracted line-segments are shown in Figure 2c. The map used for matching is shown in Figure 2b. The experimental matching study is based on 95 linear segments in the SAR data and 30 segments contained in the map. However only 23 of the SAR segments have feasible matches within the map representation. Figure 2c shows the matches obtained by non-hierarchical means. The lines are coded as follows; the black lines are correct matches while the grey lines are matching errors. With the same coding scheme Figure 2d. shows the result obtained using the hierarchical method outlined in this paper. Comparing Figures 2c and 2d it is clear that the hierarchical method has been effective at grouping significant line structure and excluding clutter. To give some idea of relative performance merit, in the case of the non-hierarchical method, 20 of the 23 matchable segments are correctly identified with 75 incorrect matches. Application of the hierarchical method gives 19 correct matches, only 17 residual clutter segments with 59 nodes correctly labelled as clutter.

4   Conclusions

We have developed graph matching technique which is tailored to hierarchical relational descriptions. The key element is this development is to quantify the match-

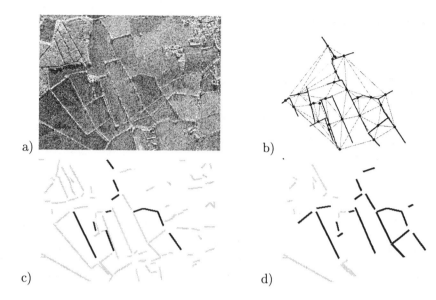

Figure 2: Graph editing: a) Original image, b) Digital map, c) Non hierarchical match , d) Hierarchical match.

ing consistency using the concept of hierarchy preserving mappings between two graphs. Central to the development of this novel technique is the idea of computing the probability of a particular node match by drawing on the topologically allowed mappings of the child nodes in the hierarchy. Results on image data with lines and corners as graph nodes reveal that the technique is capable of matching perceptual groupings under moderate levels of corruption.

References

[1] F. Cohen and D. Cooper. *Simple Parallel Hierarchical and Relaxation Algorithms for Segmenting Non-Causal Markovian Random Fields.* IEEE PAMI, **9**, 1987, pp.195–219.

[2] L. Davis and T. Henderson. *Hierarchical Constraint Processes for Shape Analysis.* IEEE PAMI, **3**, 1981, pp.265–277.

[3] B. Gidas. *A Renormalization Group Approach to Image Processing Problems.* IEEE PAMI, **11**, 1989, pp.164–180.

[4] T. Henderson. *Discrete Relaxation Techniques.* Oxford University Press, 1990.

[5] D.J. Spiegelhalter and S.L. Lauritzen, *Sequential updating of conditional probabilities on directed Graphical structures*, Networks, 1990, **20**, pp.579-605.

[6] D. Marr, *Vision.* W.H. Freeman and Co., San Francisco.

[7] J. Pearl, *Probabilistic Reasoning in Intelligent Systems*, Morgan Kaufmann, 1988.

[8] M. Meila and M. Jordan, *Optimal triangulation with continuous cost functions*, Advances in Neural Information Processing Systems 9, to appear 1997.

[9] P.Smyth, D. Heckerman, M.I. Jordan, *Probabilistic independence networks for hidden Markov probability models*, Neural Computation, **9**, 1997, pp. 227-269.

[10] R.C. Wilson and E. R. Hancock, *Structural Matching by Discrete Relaxation.* IEEE PAMI, **19**, 1997, pp.634–648.

IEEE PAMI, June 1997.

Multiplicative Updating Rule for Blind Separation Derived from the Method of Scoring

Howard Hua Yang
Department of Computer Science
Oregon Graduate Institute
PO Box 91000, Portland, OR 97291, USA
hyang@cse.ogi.edu

Abstract

For blind source separation, when the Fisher information matrix is used as the Riemannian metric tensor for the parameter space, the steepest descent algorithm to maximize the likelihood function in this Riemannian parameter space becomes the serial updating rule with equivariant property. This algorithm can be further simplified by using the asymptotic form of the Fisher information matrix around the equilibrium.

1 Introduction

The relative gradient was introduced by (Cardoso and Laheld, 1996) to design multiplicative updating algorithms with equivariant property for blind separation problems. The idea is to calculate differentials by using a relative increment instead of an absolute increment in the parameter space. This idea has been extended to compute the relative Hessian by (Pham, 1996).

For a matrix function $f = f(\boldsymbol{W})$, the relative gradient is defined by

$$\widehat{\nabla} f = \frac{\partial f}{\partial \boldsymbol{W}} \boldsymbol{W}^T. \tag{1}$$

From the differential of $f(\boldsymbol{W})$ based on the relative gradient, the following learning rule is given by (Cardoso and Laheld, 1996) to maximize the function f:

$$\frac{d\boldsymbol{W}}{dt} = \eta \widehat{\nabla} f \boldsymbol{W} = \eta \frac{\partial f}{\partial \boldsymbol{W}} \boldsymbol{W}^T \boldsymbol{W} \tag{2}$$

Also motivated by designing blind separation algorithms with equivariant property, the natural gradient defined by

$$\widetilde{\nabla} f = \frac{\partial f}{\partial W} W^T W \tag{3}$$

was introduced in (Amari et al, 1996) which yields the same learning rule (2). The geometrical meaning of the natural gradient is given by (Amari, 1996). More details about the natural gradient can be found in (Yang and Amari, 1997) and (Amari, 1997).

The framework of the natural gradient learning was proposed by (Amari, 1997). In this framework, the ordinary gradient descent learning algorithm in the Euclidean space is not optimal in minimizing a function defined in a Riemannian space. The ordinary gradient should be replaced by the natural gradient which is defined by operating the inverse of the metric tensor in the Riemannian space on the ordinary gradient. Let w denote a parameter vector. It is proved by (Amari, 1997) that if $C(w)$ is a loss function defined on a Riemannian space $\{w\}$ with a metric tensor G, the negative natural gradient of $C(w)$, namely, $-G^{-1}\frac{\partial C}{\partial w}$ is the steepest descent direction to decrease this function in the Riemannian space. Therefore, the steepest descent algorithm in this Riemannian space has the following form:

$$\frac{dw}{dt} = -\eta G^{-1} \frac{\partial C}{\partial w}.$$

If the Fisher information matrix is used as the metric tensor for the Riemannian space and $C(w)$ is replaced by the negative log-likelihood function, the above learning rule becomes the method of scoring (Kay, 1993) which is the focus of this paper.

Both the relative gradient $\widehat{\nabla}$ and the natural gradient $\widetilde{\nabla}$ were proposed in order to design the multiplicative updating algorithms with the equivariant property. The former is due to a multiplicative increment in calculating differential while the latter is due to an increment based on a nonholonomic basis (Amari, 1997). Neither $\widehat{\nabla}$ nor $\widetilde{\nabla}$ depends on the data model. The Fisher information matrix is a special and important choice for the Riemannian metric tensor for statistical estimation problems. It depends on the data model. Operating the inverse of the Fisher information matrix on the ordinary gradient, we have another gradient operator. It is called a natural gradient induced by the Fisher information matrix.

In this paper, we show how to derive a multiplicative updating algorithm from the method of scoring. This approach is different from those based on the relative gradient and the natural gradient defined by (3).

2 Fisher Information Matrix For Blind Separation

Consider a linear mixing system:

$$x = As$$

where $A \in \Re^{n \times n}$, $x = (x_1, \cdots, x_n)^T$ and $s = (s_1, \cdots, s_n)^T$. Assume that sources are independent with a factorized joint pdf:

$$r(s) = \prod_{i=1}^{n} r(s_i).$$

The likelihood function is

$$p(x; A) = \frac{r(A^{-1}x)}{|A|}$$

where $|A| = |det(A)|$. Let $W = A^{-1}$ and $y = Wx$ (a demixing system), then we have the log-likelihood function

$$L(W) = \sum_{i=1}^{n} \log r_i(y_i) + \log |W|.$$

It is easy to obtain

$$\frac{\partial L}{\partial w_{ij}} = \frac{r_i'(y_i)}{r_i(y_i)} x_j + W_{ij}^{-T} \tag{4}$$

where W_{ij}^{-T} is the (i,j) entry in $W^{-T} = (W^{-1})^T$. Writing (4) in a matrix form, we have

$$\frac{\partial L}{\partial W} = W^{-T} - \Phi(y)x^T = (I - \Phi(y)y^T)W^{-T} = F(y)W^{-T} \tag{5}$$

where $\Phi(y) = (\phi_1(y_1), \cdots, \phi_n(y_n))^T$, $\phi_i(y_i) = -\frac{r_i'(y_i)}{r_i(y_i)}$ and $F(y) = I - \Phi(y)y^T$.

The maximum likelihood algorithm based on the ordinary gradient $\frac{\partial L}{\partial W}$ is

$$\frac{dW}{dt} = \eta(I - \Phi(y)y^T)W^{-T} = \eta F(y)W^{-T}$$

which has the high computational complexity due to the matrix inverse W^{-1}. The maximum likelihood algorithm based on the natural gradient of matrix functions is

$$\frac{dW}{dt} = \eta\widetilde{\nabla}L = \eta(I - \Phi(y)y^T)W. \tag{6}$$

The same algorithm is obtained from $\frac{dW}{dt} = \eta\widehat{\nabla}LW$ by using the relative gradient. An apparent reason for using this algorithm is to avoid the matrix inverse W^{-1}. Another good reason for using it is due to the fact that the matrix W driven by (6) never becomes singular if the initial matrix W is not singular. This is proved by (Yang and Amari, 1997). In fact, this property holds for any learning rule of the following type:

$$\frac{dW}{dt} = H(y)W. \tag{7}$$

Let $< U, V >= \text{Tr}(U^T V)$ denote the inner product of U and $V \in \Re^{n \times n}$. When $W(t)$ is driven by the equation (7), we have
$$\frac{d|W|}{dt} = < \frac{\partial|W|}{\partial W}, \frac{dW}{dt} > = < |W|(W^{-1})^T, \frac{dW}{dt} >$$
$$= \text{Tr}(|W|W^{-1}H(y)W) = \text{Tr}(H(y))|W|.$$

Therefore,

$$|W(t)| = |W(0)| \exp\{\int_0^t \text{Tr}(H(y(\tau)))d\tau\} \tag{8}$$

which is non-singular when the initial matrix $W(0)$ is non-singular.

The matrix function $F(y)$ is also called an estimating function. At the equilibrium of the system (6), it satisfies the zero condition $E[F(y)] = 0$, i.e.,

$$E[\phi_i(y_i)y_j] = \delta_{ij} \tag{9}$$

where $\delta_{ij} = 1$ if $i = j$ and 0 otherwise.

To calculate the Fisher information matrix, we need a vector form of the equation (5). Let $\text{Vec}(\cdot)$ denote an operator on a matrix which cascades the columns of the matrix from the left to the right and forms a column vector. This operator has the following property:

$$\text{Vec}(\boldsymbol{ABC}) = (\boldsymbol{C}^T \otimes \boldsymbol{A})\text{Vec}(\boldsymbol{B}) \tag{10}$$

where $\otimes$ denotes the Kronecker product. Applying this property, we first rewrite (5) as

$$\frac{\partial L}{\partial \text{Vec}(\boldsymbol{W})} = \text{Vec}(\frac{\partial L}{\partial \boldsymbol{W}}) = (\boldsymbol{W}^{-1} \otimes \boldsymbol{I})\text{Vec}(\boldsymbol{F}(\boldsymbol{y})), \tag{11}$$

and then obtain the Fisher information matrix

$$\begin{aligned} \boldsymbol{G} &= E[\frac{\partial L}{\partial \text{Vec}(\boldsymbol{W})}(\frac{\partial L}{\partial \text{Vec}(\boldsymbol{W})})^T] \\ &= (\boldsymbol{W}^{-1} \otimes \boldsymbol{I})E[\text{Vec}(\boldsymbol{F}(\boldsymbol{y}))\text{Vec}^T(\boldsymbol{F}(\boldsymbol{y}))](\boldsymbol{W}^{-T} \otimes \boldsymbol{I}). \end{aligned} \tag{12}$$

The inverse of $\boldsymbol{G}$ is

$$\boldsymbol{G}^{-1} = (\boldsymbol{W}^T \otimes \boldsymbol{I})\boldsymbol{D}^{-1}(\boldsymbol{W} \otimes \boldsymbol{I}) \tag{13}$$

where $\boldsymbol{D} = E[\text{Vec}(\boldsymbol{F}(\boldsymbol{y}))\text{Vec}^T(\boldsymbol{F}(\boldsymbol{y}))]$.

3 Natural Gradient Induced By Fisher Information Matrix

Define a Riemannian space

$$\mathcal{V} = \{\text{Vec}(\boldsymbol{W}); \quad \boldsymbol{W} \in Gl(n)\}$$

in which the Fisher information matrix $\boldsymbol{G}$ is used as its metric. Here, $Gl(n)$ is the space of all the $n \times n$ invertible matrices.

Let $C(\boldsymbol{W})$ be a matrix function to be minimized. It is shown by (Amari, 1997) that the steepest descent direction in the Riemannian space $\mathcal{V}$ is $-\boldsymbol{G}^{-1}\frac{\partial C}{\partial \text{Vec}(\boldsymbol{W})}$.

Let us define the natural gradient in $\mathcal{V}$ by

$$\overline{\nabla}C(\boldsymbol{W}) = (\boldsymbol{W}^T \otimes \boldsymbol{I})\boldsymbol{D}^{-1}(\boldsymbol{W} \otimes \boldsymbol{I})\frac{\partial C}{\partial \text{Vec}(\boldsymbol{W})} \tag{14}$$

which is called the natural gradient induced by the Fisher information matrix. The time complexity of computing the natural gradient in the space $\mathcal{V}$ is high since inverting the matrix $\boldsymbol{D}$ of $n^2 \times n^2$ is needed.

Using the natural gradient in $\mathcal{V}$ to maximize the likelihood function $L(\boldsymbol{W})$ or the method of scoring, from (11) and (14) we have the following learning rule

$$\text{Vec}(\frac{d\boldsymbol{W}}{dt}) = \eta(\boldsymbol{W}^T \otimes \boldsymbol{I})\boldsymbol{D}^{-1}\text{Vec}(\boldsymbol{F}(\boldsymbol{y})) \tag{15}$$

We shall prove that the above learning rule has the equivariant property.

Denote Vec^{-1} the inverse of the operator Vec. Let matrices $\boldsymbol{B}$ and $\boldsymbol{A}$ be of $n^2 \times n^2$ and $n \times n$, respectively. Denote $\boldsymbol{B}(i, \cdot)$ the i-th row of $\boldsymbol{B}$ and $\boldsymbol{B}_i = \text{Vec}^{-1}(\boldsymbol{B}(i, \cdot))$, $i = 1, \cdots, n^2$. Define an operator $\boldsymbol{B}\star$ as a mapping from $\Re^{n \times n}$ to $\Re^{n \times n}$:

$$\boldsymbol{B} \star \boldsymbol{A} = \begin{bmatrix} <\boldsymbol{B}_1, \boldsymbol{A}> & \cdots & <\boldsymbol{B}_{n^2-n+1}, \boldsymbol{A}> \\ \cdots & \cdots & \cdots \\ <\boldsymbol{B}_n, \boldsymbol{A}> & \cdots & <\boldsymbol{B}_{n^2}, \boldsymbol{A}> \end{bmatrix}$$

where $< \cdot, \cdot >$ is the inner product in $\Re^{n \times n}$. With the operation $\star$, we have

$$\boldsymbol{B}\text{Vec}(\boldsymbol{A}) = \begin{bmatrix} <\boldsymbol{B}_1, \boldsymbol{A}> \\ \vdots \\ <\boldsymbol{B}_{n^2}, \boldsymbol{A}> \end{bmatrix} = \text{Vec}(\text{Vec}^{-1}(\begin{bmatrix} <\boldsymbol{B}_1, \boldsymbol{A}> \\ \vdots \\ <\boldsymbol{B}_{n^2}, \boldsymbol{A}> \end{bmatrix})) = \text{Vec}(\boldsymbol{B} \star \boldsymbol{A}),$$

i.e.,
$$B\text{Vec}(A) = \text{Vec}(B \star A).$$

Applying the above relation, we first rewrite the equation (15) as

$$\text{Vec}(\frac{dW}{dt}) = \eta(W^T \otimes I)\text{Vec}(D^{-1} \star F(y)),$$

then applying (10) to the above equation we obtain

$$\frac{dW}{dt} = \eta(D^{-1} \star F(y))W. \tag{16}$$

Theorem 1 *For the blind separation problem, the maximum likelihood algorithm based on the natural gradient induced by the Fisher information matrix or the method of scoring has the form (16) which is a multiplicative updating rule with the equivariant property.*

To implement the algorithm (16), we estimate D by sample average. Let $f_{ij}(y)$ be the (i,j) entry in $F(y)$. A general form for the entries in D is

$$d_{ij,kl} = E[f_{ij}(y)f_{kl}(y)]$$

which depends on the source pdfs $r_i(s_i)$. When the source pdfs are unknown, in practice we choose $r_i(s_i)$ as our prior assumptions about the source pdfs. To simplify the algorithm (16), we replace D by its asymptotic form at the solution points $a = (c_1 s_{\sigma(1)}, \cdots, c_n s_{\sigma(n)})^T$ where $(\sigma(1), \cdots, \sigma(n))$ is a permutation of $(1, \cdots, n)$.

Regarding the structure of the asymptotic D, we have the following theorem:

Theorem 2 *Assume that the pdfs of the sources s_i are even functions.*

Then at the solution point $a = (c_1 s_{\sigma(1)}, \cdots, c_n s_{\sigma(n)})^T$, D is a diagonal matrix and its n^2 diagonal entries have two forms, namely,

$$E[f_{ij}(a)f_{ij}(a)] = \mu_i \lambda_j, \quad \text{for } i \neq j \text{ and}$$
$$E[(f_{ii}(a))^2] = \nu_i$$

where $\mu_i = E[\phi_i^2(a_i)]$, $\lambda_i = E[a_i^2]$ and $\nu_i = E[\phi_i^2(a_i)a_i^2] - 1$. More concisely, we have

$$D = diag(Vec(H)) \tag{17}$$

where

$$H = (\mu_i \lambda_j)_{n \times n} - diag(\mu_1 \lambda_1, \cdots, \mu_n \lambda_n) + diag(\nu_1, \cdots, \nu_n)$$

The proof of Theorem 2 is given in Appendix 1.

Let $H = (h_{ij})_{n \times n}$. Since all μ_i, λ_i, and ν_i are positive, and so are all h_{ij}. We define

$$\frac{1}{H} = (\frac{1}{h_{ij}})_{n \times n}.$$

Then from (17), we have

$$D^{-1} = diag(\text{Vec}(\frac{1}{H})).$$

The results in Theorem 2 enable us to simplify the algorithm (16) to obtain a low complexity learning rule. Since D^{-1} is a diagonal matrix, for any $n \times n$ matrix A we have

$$D^{-1}\text{Vec}(A) = \text{Vec}(\frac{1}{H} \odot A) \tag{18}$$

where $\odot$ denotes the componentwise multiplication of two matrices of the same dimension. Applying (18) to the learning rule (15), we obtain the following learning rule

$$\mathrm{Vec}(\frac{d\boldsymbol{W}}{dt}) = \eta(\boldsymbol{W}^T \otimes \boldsymbol{I})\mathrm{Vec}(\frac{1}{\boldsymbol{H}} \odot \boldsymbol{F}(\boldsymbol{y})).$$

Again, applying (10) to the above equation we have the following learning rule

$$\frac{d\boldsymbol{W}}{dt} = \eta(\frac{1}{\boldsymbol{H}} \odot \boldsymbol{F}(\boldsymbol{y}))\boldsymbol{W}. \tag{19}$$

Like the learning rule (16), the algorithm (19) is also multiplicative; but unlike (16), there is no need to inverse the $n^2 \times n^2$ matrix in (19). The computation of $\frac{1}{\boldsymbol{H}}$ is straightforward by computing the reciprocals of the entries in $\boldsymbol{H}$.

$(\mu_i, \lambda_i, \nu_i)$ are $3n$ unknowns in $\boldsymbol{G}$. Let us impose the following constraint

$$\nu_i = \mu_i\lambda_i. \tag{20}$$

Under this constraint, the number of unknowns in $\boldsymbol{G}$ is $2n$, and $\boldsymbol{D}$ can be written as

$$\boldsymbol{D} = \boldsymbol{D}_\lambda \otimes \boldsymbol{D}_\mu \tag{21}$$

where $\boldsymbol{D}_\lambda = \mathrm{diag}(\lambda_1, \cdots, \lambda_n)$ and $\boldsymbol{D}_\mu = \mathrm{diag}(\mu_1, \cdots, \mu_n)$.

From (14), using (21) we have the natural gradient descent rule in the Riemannian space $\mathcal{V}$

$$\frac{d\mathrm{Vec}(\boldsymbol{W})}{dt} = -\eta(\boldsymbol{W}^T\boldsymbol{D}_\lambda^{-1}\boldsymbol{W} \otimes \boldsymbol{D}_\mu^{-1})\frac{\partial C}{\partial \mathrm{Vec}(\boldsymbol{W})}. \tag{22}$$

Applying the property (10), we rewrite the above equation in a matrix form

$$\frac{d\boldsymbol{W}}{dt} = -\eta\boldsymbol{D}_\mu^{-1}\frac{\partial C}{\partial \boldsymbol{W}}\boldsymbol{W}^T\boldsymbol{D}_\lambda^{-1}\boldsymbol{W}. \tag{23}$$

Since μ_i and λ_i are unknown, $\boldsymbol{D}_\mu$ and $\boldsymbol{D}_\lambda$ are replaced by the identity matrix in practice. Therefore, the algorithm (2) is an approximation of the algorithm (23).

Taking $C = -L(\boldsymbol{W})$ as the negative likelihood function and applying the expression (5), we have the following maximum likelihood algorithm based on the natural gradient in $\mathcal{V}$:

$$\frac{d\boldsymbol{W}}{dt} = \eta\boldsymbol{D}_\mu^{-1}(\boldsymbol{I} - \Phi(\boldsymbol{y})\boldsymbol{y}^T)\boldsymbol{D}_\lambda^{-1}\boldsymbol{W}. \tag{24}$$

Again, replacing $\boldsymbol{D}_\mu$ and $\boldsymbol{D}_\lambda$ by the identity matrix we obtain the maximum likelihood algorithm (6) based on the relative gradient or natural gradient of matrix functions.

In the context of the blind separation, the source pdfs are unknown. The prior assumption $r_i(s_i)$ used to define the functions $\phi_i(y_i)$ may not match the true pdfs of the sources. However, the algorithm (24) is generally robust to the mismatch between the true pdfs and the pdfs employed by the algorithm if the mismatch is not too large. See (Cardoso, 1997) and (Pham, 1996) for example.

4 Conclusion

In the context of blind separation, when the Fisher information matrix is used as the Riemannian metric tensor for the parameter space, maximizing the likelihood function in this Riemannian space based on the steepest descent method is the method of scoring. This method yields a multiplicative updating rule with the equivariant property. It is further simplified by using the asymptotic form of the Fisher information matrix around the equilibrium.

5   Appendix

Appendix 1 *Proof of Theorem 2:*

By definition $f_{ij}(\boldsymbol{y}) = \delta_{ij} - \phi_i(y_i)y_j$. At the equilibrium $\boldsymbol{a} = (c_1 s_{\sigma(1)}, \cdots, c_n s_{\sigma(n)})^T$, we have $E[\phi_i(a_i)a_j] = 0$ for $i \neq j$ and $E[\phi_i(a_i)a_i] = 1$. So $E[f_{ij}(\boldsymbol{a})] = 0$. Since the source pdfs are even functions, we have $E[a_i] = 0$ and $E[\phi_i(a_i)] = 0$. Applying these equalities , it is not difficult to verify that

$$E[f_{ij}(\boldsymbol{a})f_{kl}(\boldsymbol{a})] = 0, \quad \text{for } (i,j) \neq (k,l). \tag{25}$$

So, $\boldsymbol{D}$ is a diagonal matrix and

$$E[f_{ii}(\boldsymbol{a})f_{ii}(\boldsymbol{a})] = E[(1 - \phi_i(a_i)a_i)^2] = E[\phi_i^2(a_i)a_i^2] - 1,$$

$$E[f_{ij}(\boldsymbol{a})f_{ij}(\boldsymbol{a})] = E[\phi_i^2(a_i)a_j^2] = \mu_i \lambda_j$$

for $i \neq j$.
Q.E.D.

References

[1] S. Amari. Natural gradient works efficiently in learning. *Accepted by Neural Computation*, 1997.

[2] S. Amari. Neural learning in structured parameter spaces – natural Riemannian gradient. In *Advances in Neural Information Processing Systems, 9, ed. M. C. Mozer, M. I. Jordan and T. Petsche, The MIT Press: Cambridge, MA.*, pages 127–133, 1997.

[3] S. Amari, A. Cichocki, and H. H. Yang. A new learning algorithm for blind signal separation. In *Advances in Neural Information Processing Systems, 8, eds. David S. Touretzky, Michael C. Mozer and Michael E. Hasselmo, MIT Press: Cambridge, MA.*, pages 757–763, 1996.

[4] J.-F. Cardoso. Infomax and maximum likelihood for blind source separation. *IEEE Signal Processing Letters*, April 1997.

[5] J.-F. Cardoso and B. Laheld. Equivariant adaptive source separation. *IEEE Trans. on Signal Processing*, 44(12):3017–3030, December 1996.

[6] S. M. Kay. *Fundamentals of Statistical Signal Processing: Estimation Theory.* PTR Prentice Hall, Englewood Cliffs, 1993.

[7] D. T. Pham. Blind separation of instantaneous mixture of sources via an ica. *IEEE Trans. on Signal Processing*, 44(11):2768–2779, November 1996.

[8] H. H. Yang and S. Amari. Adaptive on-line learning algorithms for blind separation: Maximum entropy and minimum mutual information. *Neural Computation*, 9(7):1457–1482, 1997.

PART V
IMPLEMENTATION

A 1,000-Neuron System with One Million 7-bit Physical Interconnections

Yuzo Hirai

Institute of Information Sciences and Electronics
University of Tsukuba
1-1-1 Ten-nodai, Tsukuba, Ibaraki 305, Japan
e-mail: hirai@is.tsukuba.ac.jp

Abstract

An asynchronous PDM (Pulse-Density-Modulating) digital neural network system has been developed in our laboratory. It consists of one thousand neurons that are physically interconnected via one million 7-bit synapses. It can solve one thousand simultaneous nonlinear first-order differential equations in a fully parallel and continuous fashion. The performance of this system was measured by a winner-take-all network with one thousand neurons. Although the magnitude of the input and network parameters were identical for each competing neuron, one of them won in 6 milliseconds. This processing speed amounts to 360 billion connections per second. A broad range of neural networks including spatiotemporal filtering, feedforward, and feedback networks can be run by loading appropriate network parameters from a host system.

1 INTRODUCTION

The hardware implementation of neural networks is crucial in order to realize the real-time operation of neural functions such as spatiotemporal filtering, learning and constraint processings. Since the mid eighties, many VLSI chips and systems have been reported in the literature, e.g. [1] [2]. Most of the chips and the systems including analog and digital implementations, however, have focused on *feedforward* neural networks. Little attention has been paid to the dynamical aspect of *feedback* neural networks, which is especially important in order to realize constraint processings, e.g. [3]. Although there were a small number of exceptions that used analog circuits [4] [5], their network sizes were limited as compared to those of their feedforward counterparts because of wiring problems that are inevitable in regard to full and physical interconnections. To relax this problem, a pulse-stream system has been used in analog [6] and digital implementations [7].

The author developed a fully interconnected 54-neuron system that uses an asynchronous PDM (Pulse-Density-Modulating) digital circuit system [8]. The present paper describes a thousand-neuron system in which all of the neurons are physically interconnected via one million 7-bit synapses in order to create a fully parallel feedback system. The outline of this project was described in [10]. In addition to the enlargement of system size, synapse circuits were improved and time constant of each neuron was made variable. The PDM system was used because it can accomplish faithful analog data transmission between neurons and can relax wiring problems. An asynchronous digital circuit was used because it can solve scaling problems, and we could also use it to connect more than one thousand VLSI chips, as described below.

2   NEURON MODEL AND THE CIRCUITS

2.1   SINGLE NEURON MODEL

The behavior of each neuron in the system can be described by the following non-linear first-order differential equation:

$$\mu_i \frac{dy_i^*(t)}{dt} = -y_i^*(t) + \sum_{j=1}^{N} w_{ij} y_j(t) + I_i(t), \tag{1}$$

$$y_i(t) = \varphi[y_i^*(t)], \text{ and} \tag{2}$$

$$\varphi[a] = \begin{cases} a & \text{if } a > 0 \\ 0 & \text{otherwise,} \end{cases} \tag{3}$$

where μ_i is a time constant of the i-th neuron, $y_i^*(t)$ is an internal potential of the i-th neuron at time t, w_{ij} is a synaptic weight from the j-th to the i-th neurons, and $I_i(t)$ is an external input to the i-th neuron. $\varphi[a]$ is an analog threshold output function which becomes saturated at a given maximum value.

The system solves Eq.(1) in the following integral form:

$$y_i^*(t) = \int_0^t \left\{ -y_i^*(\tau) + \sum_{j=1}^{N} w_{ij} y_j(\tau) + I_i(\tau) \right\} \frac{d\tau}{\mu_i} + y_i^*(0), \tag{4}$$

where $y_i^*(0)$ is an initial value. An analog output of a neuron is expressed by a pulse stream whose frequency is proportional to the positive, instantaneous internal potential.

2.2   SINGLE NEURON CIRCUIT

2.2.1   Synapse circuits

The circuit diagrams for a single neuron are shown in Fig. 1. As shown in Fig.1(a), it consists of synapse circuits, excitatory and inhibitory dendrite OR circuits, and a cell body circuit. Each synapse circuit transforms the instantaneous frequency of the input pulses to a frequency that is proportional to the synaptic weight. This transformation is carried out by a 6-bit rate multiplier, as shown in Fig.1(b). The behavior of a rate multiplier is illustrated in Fig.1(c) using a 3-bit case for brevity. A rate multiplier is a counter and its state transits to the next state when an input pulse occurs. Each binary bit of a given weight specifies at which states the output pulses are generated. When the LSB is on, an output pulse is generated at the fourth state. When the second bit is on, output pulses are generated at the second

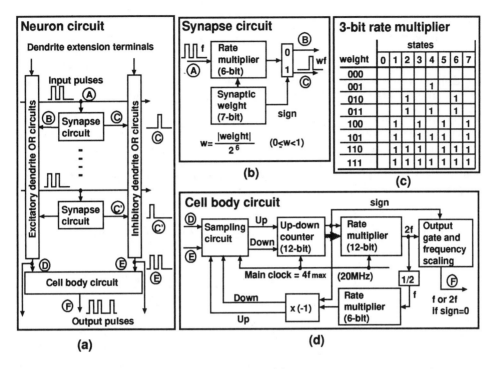

Figure 1: Circuit diagram of a single neuron. (a) Circuit diagram of a single neuron and (b) that of a synapse circuit. (c) To illustrate the function of a rate multiplier, the multiplication table for a 3-bit case is shown. (d) Circuit diagram of a cell body circuit. See details in text.

and at the sixth states. When the MSB is on, they are generated at all of the odd states. Therefore, the magnitude of synaptic weight that can be represented by a rate multiplier is less than one. In our circuit, this limitation was overcome by increasing the frequency of a neuron output by a factor of two, as described below.

2.2.2   Dendrite circuits

Output pulses from a synapse circuit are fed either to an excitatory dendrite OR circuit or to an inhibitory one, according to the synaptic weight sign. In each dendrite OR circuit, the synaptic output pulses are summed by OR gates, as is shown along the right side of Fig.1(a). Therefore, if these output pulses are synchronized, they are counted as one pulse and linear summation cannot take place. In our circuit, each neuron is driven by an individual clock oscillator. Therefore, they will tend to become desynchronized. The summation characteristic was analysed in [9], and it was shown to have a saturation characteristic that is similar to the positive part of a hyperbolic tangent function.

2.2.3   Cell body circuit

A cell body circuit performs the integration given by Eq.(4) as follows. As shown in Fig.1(d), integration was performed by a 12-bit up-down counter. Input pulses from an excitatory dendrite OR circuit are fed into the up-input of the counter and those from an inhibitory one are fed into the down-input after conflicts between excitatory and inhibitory pulses have been resolved by a sampling circuit. A 12-bit rate multiplier produces internal pulses whose frequency is $2f$, where f is proportional to the absolute value of the counter. The rate multiplier is driven by a main clock whose frequency is $4f_{max}$, f_{max} being the maximum output frequency. When the counter value is positive, an output pulse train whose frequency is either f or $2f$, according to the scale factor is transmitted from a cell body circuit.

The negative feedback term that appeared in the integrand of Eq.(4) can be realized by feeding the internal pulses into the down-input of the counter when the counter value is positive and feeding them into the up-input when it is negative. The 6-bit rate multiplier inserted in this feedback path changes the time constant of a neuron. Let β_i be the rate value of the rate multiplier, where $0 \le \beta_i < 2^6$. The Eq.(4) becomes:

$$
\begin{aligned}
y_i^*(t) &= \int_0^t \left\{ -\frac{\beta}{2^6} y_i^*(\tau) + \sum_{j=1}^{N} w_{ij} y_j(\tau) + I_i(\tau) \right\} \frac{d\tau}{\mu_i} + y_i^*(0) \\
&= \int_0^t \left\{ -y_i^*(\tau) + \frac{2^6}{\beta} \left(\sum_{j=1}^{N} w_{ij} y_j(\tau) + I_i(\tau) \right) \right\} \frac{d\tau}{\frac{\mu_i 2^6}{\beta}} + y_i^*(0).
\end{aligned}
\tag{5}
$$

Therefore, the time constant changes to $\frac{\mu_i 2^6}{\beta}$, where μ_i was given by $\frac{2^{11}}{f_{max}}$ seconds. It should be noted that, since the magnitude of the total input was increased by a factor of $\frac{2^6}{\beta}$, the strength of the input should be decreased by the inverse of that factor in order to maintain an appropriate output level. If it is not adjusted, we can increase the input strength. Therefore, the system has both input and output scaling functions. The time constant varies from about $416\mu sec$ for $\beta = 63$ to $26.2msec$ for $\beta = 1$. When $\beta = 0$, the negative feedback path is interrupted and the circuit operates as a simple integrator, and every feedforward network can be run in this mode of operation.

3   THE 1,000-NEURON SYSTEM

3.1   VLSI CHIP

A single type of VLSI chip was fabricated using a $0.7\mu m$ CMOS gate array with 250,000 gates. A single chip contains 18 neurons and 51 synapses for each neuron. Therefore, each chip has a total of 918 synapses. About 85% of the gates in a gate array could be used, which was an extremely efficient value. A chip was mounted on a flat package with 256 pins. Among them, 216 pins were used for signals and the others were used for twenty pairs of $V_{CC}(=3.3V)$ and GND.

3.2   THE SYSTEM

As illustrated in Fig.2(a), this system consists of $56 \times 20 = 1,120$ chips. 56 chips are used for both cell bodies and synapses, and the others are used to extend dendrite circuits and increase the number of synapses. In order to extend the dendrites, the dendrite signals in a chip can be directly transmitted to the dendrite extention terminals of another chip by bypassing the cell body circuits. There are $51 \times 20 = 1,020$ synapses per neuron. Among them, 1,008 synapses are used for fully hard-wired interconnections and the other 12 synapses are used to receive external signals. There are a total of 1,028,160 synapses in this system. It is controlled by a personal computer. The synaptic weights, the contents of the up-down counters

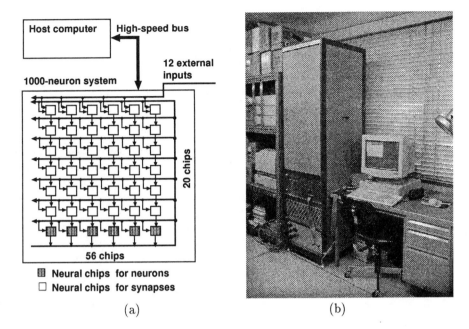

Figure 2: Structure of the system. (a) System configuration. The down arrows emitted from the open squares designate signal lines that are extending dendrites. The others designate neuron outputs. (b) Exterior of the system. It is controlled by a personal computer.

and the control registers can be read and written by the host system. It takes about 6 seconds to set all the network parameters from the host system.

The exterior of this system is shown in Fig.2(b). Inside the cabinet, there are four shelves. In each shelf, fourteen circuit boards were mounted and on each board 20 chips were mounted. One chip was used for 18 neurons and the other chips were used to extend the dendrites. Each neuron is driven by an individual 20MHz clock oscillator.

4 SYSTEM PERFORMANCE

In order to measure the performance of this system, one neuron was used as a signal generator. By setting all the synaptic weights and the internal feedback gain of a signal neuron to zero, and by setting the content of the up-down counter to a given value, it can produce an output with a constant frequency that is proportional to the counter value. The input strength of the other neurons can be adjusted by changing the counter value of a signal neuron or the synaptic weights from it.

The step reponses of a neuron to different inputs are shown in Fig.3(a). As seen in the figure, the responses exactly followed Eq.(1) and the time constant was about 400μsec. Figure 3(b) shows responses with different time constants. The inputs were identical for all cases.

Figure 3(c) shows the response of a temporal filter that was obtained by the difference between a fast and a slow neuron. By combining two low-pass filters that had different cutoff frequencies, a band-pass filter was created. A variety of spatiotem-

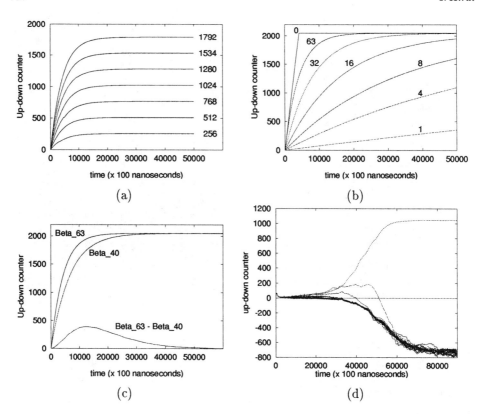

Figure 3: Responses obtained by the system. (a) Step responses to different input levels. Parameters are the values that are set in the up-down counter of a signal neuron. (b) Step responses for different time constants. Parameters are the values of β_i in Eq.5. Inputs were identical in all cases. (c) Response of a temporal filter that was obtain by the difference between a fast and a slow neuron. (d) Response of a winner-take-all network among 1,007 neurons. The responses of a winner neuron and 24 of the 1,006 defeated neurons are shown.

poral filters can be implemented in this way.

Figure 3(d) shows the responses of a winner-take-all network among 1,007 neurons. The time courses of the responses of a winner neuron and 24 of the 1,006 defeated neurons are shown in the figure. The strength of all of the inhibitory synaptic weights between neurons was set to $2 \times \left(-\frac{48}{64}\right)$, where 2 is an output scale factor. The synaptic weights from a signal neuron to the 1,007 competing ones were identical and were $\frac{32}{64}$. Although the network parameters and the inputs to all competing neurons were identical, one of them won in 6 msec. Since the system operates asynchronously and the spatial summation of the synaptic output pulses is probabilistic, one of the competing neurons can win in a stochastic manner.

In order to derive the processing speed in terms of *connections per second*, the same winner-take-all network was solved by the Euler method on a latest workstation. Since it took about 76.2 seconds and 2,736 iterations to converge, the processing speed of the workstation was about 36 million connections per second $\left(\approx \frac{1,007 \times 1,007 \times 2,736}{76.2}\right)$. Since this system is 10,000 times faster than the workstation, the processing speed amounts to 360 billion connections per second.

Various kinds of neural networks including spatiotemporal filtering, feedforward and feedback neural networks can be run in this single system by loading appropriate network parameters from the host system. The second version of this system, which can be used via the Internet, will be completed by the end of March, 1998.

Acknowledgements

The author is grateful to Mr. Y. Kuwabara and Mr. T. Ochiai of Hitachi Micro-computer System Ltd. for their collaboration in developing this system and to Dr. M. Yasunaga and Mr. M. Takahashi for their help in testing it. The author is also grateful to Mr. H. Toda for his collaboration in measuring response data. This work was supported by "Proposal-Based Advanced Industrial Technology R&D Program" from NEDO in Japan.

References

[1] C. Mead: *Analog VLSI and Neural Systems*. Addison-Wesley Publishing Company, Massachusetts, 1989

[2] K.W.Przytula and V.K.Prasanna, Eds.: *Parallel Digital Implementations of Neural Networks*. Prentice Hall, New Jersey, 1993

[3] J.J. Hopfield: Neurons with graded response have collective computational properties like those of two-state neurons. *Proc. Natl. Acad. Sci. U.S.A.*, **81**, pp.3088-3092, 1984

[4] P. Mueller, J. van der Spiegel, V. Agami, D. Blackman, P. Chance, C. Donham, R. Etienne, J. Kim. M. Massa and S. Samarasekera: Design and performance of a prototype analog neural computer. *Proc. the 2nd International Conf. on Microelectronics for Neural Networks*, pp.347-357, 1991

[5] G. Cauwenberghs: A learning analog neural network chip with continuous-time recurrent dynamics. In J. D. Cowan, G. Tesauro and J. Alspector, Eds., *Advances in Neural Information Processing Systems 6*, Morgan Kaufmann Publishers, San Mateo, CA, pp.858-865, 1994

[6] S. Churcher, D. J. Baxter, A. Hamilton, A. F. Murry, and H. M. Reekie: Generic analog neural computation – The EPSILON chip. In S. J. Hanson, J. D. Cowan and C. L. Giles, Eds., *Advances in Neural Information Processing Systems 6*, Morgan Kaufmann Publishers, San Mateo, CA, pp.773-780, 1993

[7] H. Eguchi, T. Furuta, H. Horiguchi, S. Oteki and T. Kitaguchi: Neural network LSI chip with on-chip learning. *Proceedings of IJCNN'91 Seattle*, Vol.I/453-456, 1991

[8] Y. Hirai, et al.: A digital neuro-chip with unlimited connectability for large scale neural networks. *Proc. International Joint Conf. on Neural Networks'89 Washington D.C.*, Vol.II/163-169, 1989

[9] Y.Hirai, *VLSI Neural Network Systems* (Gordon and Breach Science Publishers, Birkshire, 1992)

[10] Y. Hirai and M. Yasunaga: A PDM digital neural network system with 1,000 neurons fully interconnected via 1,000,000 6-bit synapses. *Proc. International Conference on Neural Information Processings'96*, Vol.II/1251, 1996

Silicon Retina with Adaptive Filtering Properties

Shih-Chii Liu
Computation and Neural Systems
136-93 California Institute of Technology
Pasadena, CA 91125
shih@pcmp.caltech.edu

Abstract

This paper describes a small, compact circuit that captures the temporal and adaptation properties both of the photoreceptor and of the laminar layers of the fly. This circuit uses only six transistors and two capacitors. It is operated in the subthreshold domain. The circuit maintains a high transient gain by using adaptation to the background intensity as a form of gain control. The adaptation time constant of the circuit can be controlled via an external bias. Its temporal filtering properties change with the background intensity or signal-to-noise conditions. The frequency response of the circuit shows that in the frequency range of 1 to 100 Hz, the circuit response goes from highpass filtering under high light levels to lowpass filtering under low light levels (i.e., when the signal-to-noise ratio is low). A chip with 20×20 pixels has been fabricated in 1.2μm ORBIT CMOS nwell technology.

1 BACKGROUND

The first two layers in the fly visual system are the retina layer and the laminar layer. The photoreceptors in the retina synapse onto the monopolar cells in the laminar layer. The photoreceptors adapt to the background intensity, and use this adaptation as a form of gain control in maintaining a high response to transient signals. The laminar layer performs bandpass filtering under high background intensities, and reverts to lowpass filtering in the case of low background intensities where the signal-to-noise (S/N) ratio is low. This adaptive filtering response in the temporal domain is analogous to the spatial center-surround response of the bipolar cells in the vertebrate retina.

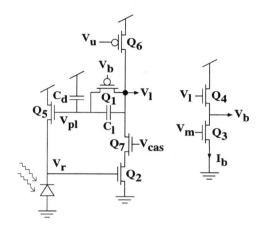

Figure 1: Circuit diagram of retino-laminar circuit. The feedback consists of a resistor implemented by a pFET transistor, Q_1. The conductance of the resistor is controlled by the external bias, V_m.

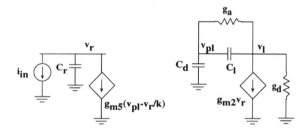

Figure 2: Small signal model of the circuit shown in Figure 1. C_r is the parasitic capacitance at the node, V_r.

The Delbrück silicon receptor circuit (Delbrück, 1994) modeled closely the step responses and the adaptation responses of the biological receptors. By including two additional transistors, the **retino-laminar (RL) circuit** described here captures the properties of both the photoreceptor layer (i.e., the adaptation properties and phototransduction) and the cells in the laminar layer (i.e., the adaptive filtering). The time constant of the circuit is controllable via an external bias, and the adaptation behavior of the circuit over different background intensities is more symmetrical than that of Delbrück's photoreceptor circuit.

2   CIRCUIT DESCRIPTION

The RL circuit which has the basic form of Delbrück's receptor circuit is shown in Figure 1. I have replaced the adaptive element in his receptor circuit by a nonlinear resistor consisting of a pFET transistor, Q_1. The implementation of a floating, voltage-controlled resistor has been described earlier by (Banu and Tsividis, 1982). The bias for Q_1, V_b, is generated by Q_3 and Q_4. The conductance of Q_1 is determined by the output voltage, V_l, and an external bias, V_m. We give a brief description of the circuit operation here; details are described in (Delbrück, 1994). The receptor node, V_r, is clamped to the voltage needed to sink the current sourced

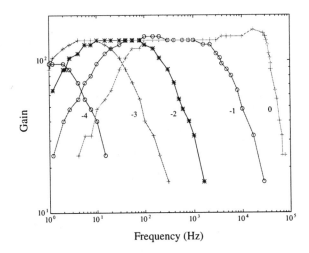

Figure 3: Frequency plot of the RL circuit over five decades of background intensity. The number next to each curve corresponds to the log intensity of the mean value; 0 log corresponds to the intensity of a red LED. The plot shows that, in the range of 1 to 100 Hz, the circuit is a bandpass filter at high light levels, and reduces to a lowpass filter at low light levels.

by Q_6, which is biased by an external voltage, V_u. Changes in the photocurrent are amplified by the transistors, Q_2 and Q_6, resulting in a change in V_l. This change in V_l is capacitively coupled through the capacitive divider, consisting of C_l and C_d, into V_{pl}, so that Q_5 supplies the extra increase in photocurrent.

The feedback transistor, Q_5, is operated in subthreshold so that V_r and V_l is logarithmic in the photocurrent. A large change in the photocurrent resulting from a change in the background intensity, leads to a large change in the circuit output, V_l. Significant current then flows through Q_1, thus charging or discharging V_{pl}.

3 PROPERTIES OF RL CIRCUIT

The temporal responses and adaptation properties of this circuit are expounded in the following sections. In Section 3.1, we solve for the transfer function of the circuit and in Section 3.2, we describe the dependence of the conductance of Q_1 on the background intensity. In Sections 3.3 and 3.4, we describe the temporal responses of this circuit, and compare the adaptation response of RL circuit with that of Delbrück's circuit.

3.1 TRANSFER FUNCTION

We can solve for the transfer function of the RL circuit in Figure 1 by writing the KCL equations of the small-signal model shown in Figure 2. The transfer function, $\frac{v_l}{i_{in}}$, is given by:

$$\frac{v_l}{i_{in}} = \frac{1}{g_{m5}} \left[\frac{\frac{s(\tau_{ld}+\tau_l)+g_a/g_{m2}}{s\tau_l+g_a/g_{m2}}}{(s\tau_r + 1/\kappa)(1/A_{amp} + s\tau_{ld} + \frac{s\tau_{ld}}{A_{amp}(s\tau_l+g_a/g_{m2})}) + 1} \right], \tag{1}$$

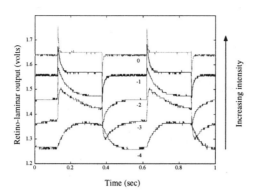

Time (sec)

Figure 4: Temporal responses of the circuit over five decades of background intensity. The input stimulus is a square-wave-modulated red LED of contrast 0.15. The circuit acts as a highpass filter (that is, a differentiator) at high intensities, and as a lowpass filter as the intensity drops.

where $A_{amp} = \frac{g_{m2}}{g_d}$, g_m is the transconductance, and g_d is the output conductance of a transistor. We define the time constants, τ_l, τ_r, and τ_{ld}, as follows:

$$\tau_l = \frac{C_l}{g_{m2}}; \tau_r = \frac{C_r}{g_{m5}}; \tau_{ld} = \frac{C_d}{g_{m2}},$$

where g_a is the output conductance of Q_1 and C_r is the parasitic capacitance at the node, V_r.

The frequency response curves in Figure 3 are measured from the fabricated circuit over five decades of background intensity. We obtain the curves by using a sine-wave–modulated red LED source. The number next to each curve is the log intensity of the mean value; 0 log is the intensity of a red LED. We obtain the remaining curves by interposing neutral density filters between the LED source and the chip. Figure 3 shows that, in the range of 1 to 100 Hz, the circuit is a bandpass filter at high light levels, and reduces to a lowpass filter at low light levels. For each frequency curve, the gain is flat in the middle, and is given by $A_{cl} = \frac{C_1 + C_d}{C_1}$. The cutoff frequencies change with the background intensity; this change is analyzed in Section 3.2.

3.2 DEPENDENCE OF CIRCUIT'S TIME CONSTANT ON BACKGROUND INTENSITY

The cutoff frequencies of the circuit depend on the conductance, g_a, of Q_1. Here, we analyze the dependence of g_a on the background intensity. Since Q_1 is operated in subthreshold, the conductance depends on the current flowing through Q_1. The I–V relationship for Q_1 can be written as

$$I = 2I_{op}\left(\frac{I_b}{I_{on}}\right)^{\kappa_p} e^{(1-\kappa_n\kappa_p)\overline{V}} e^{-\kappa_n\kappa_p\Delta V/2} \sinh(\Delta V/2) \qquad (2)$$

$$= I_\alpha I_{ph}^{(1-\kappa_n\kappa_p)/\kappa_n} e^{(1-2\kappa_n\kappa_p)\Delta V/2} \sinh(\Delta V/2) \qquad (3)$$

where $\overline{V} = \frac{V_1+V_{pl}}{2}$, $\Delta V = V_1 - V_{pl}$, I_{ph} is the photocurrent, and $I_\alpha = 2I_{op}\left(\frac{I_b}{I_{on}}\right)^{\kappa_p}\left(\frac{e^{V_r}}{I_{on}}\right)^{(1-\kappa_n\kappa_p)/\kappa_n}$. The exponential relationship for Equations 2 and 3 is for a FET transistor operating in subthreshold, where I_{op} is the quiescent leakage current of the transistor, and κ is the effectiveness of the gate in controlling

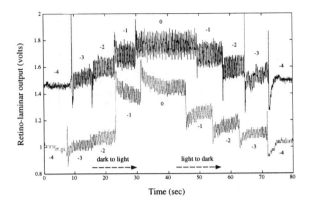

Figure 5: Plots of adaptation responses of the RL circuit and of Delbrück's circuit. The input stimulus is a red LED driven by a square wave of contrast 0.18. The bottom curve corresponding to Delbrück's receptor has been shifted down so that we can compare the two curves. The adaptation response of the RL circuit is more symmetrical than that of Delbrück's circuit when the circuit goes from dark to light conditions and back.

the surface potential of the channel of the transistor. Equation 3 shows that g_a is proportional to the photocurrent, I_{ph}, hence, the background intensity. A more intuitive way of understanding how g_a changes with I_{ph} is that the change in V_b with a fixed change in the output, V_1, depends on the output level of V_1. The change in V_b is larger for a higher DC output, V_1, because of the increased body effect at Q_4 due to its higher source voltage. The larger change in V_b leads to an increase in the conductance, g_a.

As I_{ph} increases, g_a increases, so the cutoff frequencies shift to the right, as seen in Figure 3. If we compare both the "0" curve and the "-1" curve, we can see that the cutoff frequencies are approximately different by a factor of 10. Thus, the exponent of I_{ph}, $(1 - \kappa_n \kappa_p)/\kappa_n \approx 1$. Since the κ values change with the current through the transistor, the exponent also changes. The different values of the exponent with I_{ph} can be seen from the different amounts of shifts in the cutoff frequencies of the curves.

3.3 TEMPORAL RESPONSES

The adaptive temporal filtering of the circuit over five decades of background intensity can also be observed from the step response of the RL circuit to a square-wave-modulated LED of contrast 0.15, as shown in Figure 4. The data in Figure 4 show that the time constant of the circuit increases as the light level decreases. The temporal responses observed in these circuits are comparable to the contrast responses recorded from the LMCs by Juusola and colleagues (Juusola et al., 1995).

3.4 ADAPTATION PROPERTIES

The RL circuit also differs from Delbrück's circuit in that the adaptation time constant can be set by an external bias. In the Delbrück circuit, the adaptation time constant is predetermined at the design phase and by process parameters. In Figure 5, we compare the adaptation properties of the RL circuit with those of Delbrück's

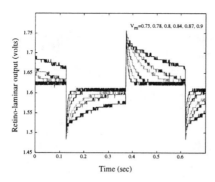

Figure 6: Step response of the RL circuit for different values of V_m. The input stimulus is a square-wave-modulated red LED source. The value of V_m was varied from 0.73 to 0.9 V. The curve with the longest time constant of decay corresponds to the lowest value of V_m.

circuit. The input stimulus consists of a square-wave-modulated LED source with a contrast of about 0.18. We take the circuit from dark to light conditions, and back again, by using neutral density filters. The top curve corresponds to the response from the RL circuit, and the bottom curve corresponds to the response from the Delbrück circuit. The RL circuit adapts symmetrically, when it goes from light to dark conditions and back. In contrast, Delbrück's circuit shows an asymmetrical adaptative behavior; it adapts more slowly when it goes from dark to light conditions.

The adaptation time constant of the RL circuit depends on the conductance, g_a, and the capacitors, C_l and C_d. From Equation 3, we see that g_a is dependent on I_b which is set by the bias, V_m. Hence, we can change the adaptation time constant by varying V_m. The dependence of the time constant on V_m is further demonstrated by recording the step response of the circuit to a LED source of contrast 0.15 for various values of V_m. The output data is shown in Figure 6 for five different values of V_m. The time constant of the circuit decreases as V_m increases.

A chip consisting of 20×20 pixels was fabricated in $1.2 \mu m$ ORBIT CMOS nwell technology. An input stimulus consisting of a rotating flywheel, with black strips on a white background, was initially presented to the imager. The flywheel was then stopped, and the response of the chip was recorded one sec after the motion was ceased. I repeated the experiment for two adaptation time constants by changing the value of V_m. Figure 7a shows the output of the chip with the longer adaptation time constant. We see that the image is still present, whereas the image in Figure 7b has almost faded away; that is, the chip has adapted away the stationary image.

4   CONCLUSIONS

I have described a small circuit captures the temporal and adaptation properties of both the photoreceptor and the laminar layers in the fly retina. By adapting to the background intensity, the circuit maintains a high transient gain. The temporal behavior of the circuit also changes with the background intensity, such that, at high S/N ratios, the circuit acts as a highpass filter and, at low S/N ratios, the circuit acts as a lowpass filter to average out the noise. The circuit uses only six transistors and two capacitors and is compact. The adaptation time constant of the

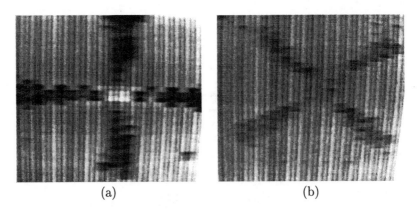

(a)   (b)

Figure 7: Adaptation results from a two-dimensional array of 20 × 20 pixels. The output of the array was recorded one sec after cessation of the pattern motion. The experiment was repeated for two different adaptation time constants. Figure (a) corresponds to the longer adaptation time constant. The image is still present, whereas the image in Figure (b) has almost faded away.

circuit can be controlled via an external bias.

Acknowledgments

I thank Bradley A. Minch for discussions of this work, Carver Mead for supporting this work, and the MOSIS foundation for fabricating this circuit. I also thank Lyn Dupre for editing this document. This work was supported in part by the Office of Naval Research, by DARPA, and by the Beckman Foundation.

References

T. Delbrück, "Analog VLSI phototransduction by continous-time, adaptive, logarithmic photoreceptor circuits," *CNS Memo No.30*, California Institute of Technology, Pasadena, CA, 1994.

M. Banu and Y. Tsividis, "Floating voltage-controlled resistors in CMOS technology," *Electronics Letters*, **18:15**, pp. 678–679, 1982.

M. Juusola, R.O. Uusitola, and M. Weckstrom, " Transfer of graded potentials at the photoreceptor-interneuron synapse," *J. of General Physiology*, **105**, pp. 115–148, 1995.

Analog VLSI Model of Intersegmental Coordination With Nearest-Neighbor Coupling

Girish N. Patel
girish@ece.gatech.edu

Jeremy H. Holleman
jeremy@ece.gatech.edu

Stephen P. DeWeerth
steved@ece.gatech.edu

School of Electrical and Computer Engineering
Georgia Institute of Technology
Atlanta, Ga. 30332-0250

Abstract

We have a developed an analog VLSI system that models the coordination of neurobiological segmental oscillators. We have implemented and tested a system that consists of a chain of eleven pattern generating circuits that are synaptically coupled to their nearest neighbors. Each pattern generating circuit is implemented with two silicon Morris-Lecar neurons that are connected in a reciprocally inhibitory network. We discuss the mechanisms of oscillations in the two-cell network and explore system behavior based on isotropic and anisotropic coupling, and frequency gradients along the chain of oscillators.

1 INTRODUCTION

In recent years, neuroscientists and modelers have made great strides towards illuminating structure and computational properties in biological motor systems. For example, much progress has been made toward understanding the neural networks that elicit rhythmic motor behaviors, including leech heartbeat (Calabrese and De Schutter, 1992), crustacean stomatogastric mill (Selverston, 1989) and tritonia swimming (Getting, 1989). In particular, segmented locomotory systems, such as those that underlie swimming in the lamprey (Cohen and Kiemel, 1993, Sigvardt, 1993, Grillner et al, 1991) and in the leech (Friesen and Pearce, 1993), are interesting from an quantitative perspective. In these systems, it is clear that coordinated motor behaviors are a result of complex interactions among membrane, synaptic, circuit, and system properties. However, because of the lack of sufficient neural underpinnings, a complete understanding of the computational principles in these systems is still lacking. Abstracting the biophysical complexity by modeling segmented systems as coupled nonlinear oscillators is one approach that has provided much insight into the operation of these systems (Cohen et al, 1982). More specifically, this type of modeling work has illuminated computational properties that give rise to *phase constancy*, a motor behavior that is characterized by intersegmental phase lags that are maintained at constant values independent of swimming frequency. For example, it has been shown that frequency gradients and asymmetrical coupling play an important role in establishing phase lags of correct sign and amplitude (Kopell and Ermentrout, 1988) as well as appropriate boundary conditions (Williams and Sigvardt, 1994).

Although theoretical modeling has provided much insight into the operation of intersegmental systems, these models have limited capacity for incorporating biophysical properties and complex interconnectivity. Software and/or hardware emulation provides the potential to add such complexity to system models. Additionally, the modularity and regularity in the anatomical and computational structures of intersegmental systems facilitate scalable representations. These factors make segmented systems particularly viable for modeling using neuromorphic analog very large-scale integrated (aVLSI) technology. In general, biological motor systems have a number of properties that make their real-time modeling using aVLSI circuits interesting and approachable. Like their sensory counterparts, they exhibit rich emergent properties that are generated by collective architectures that are regular and modular. Additionally, the fact that motor processing is at the periphery of the nervous system makes the analysis of the system behavior accessible due to the fact that output of the system (embodied in the motor actions) is observable and facilitates functional analysis.

The goals in this research are i) to study how the properties of individual neurons in a network affect the overall system behavior; (ii) to facilitate the validation of the principles underlying intersegmental coordination; and (iii) to develop a real-time, low power, motion control system. We want to exploit these principles and architectures both to improve our understanding of the biology and to design artificial systems that perform autonomously in various environments. In this paper we present an analog VLSI model of intersegmental coordination that addresses the role of frequency gradients and asymmetrical coupling. Each segment in our system is implemented with two silicon model neurons that are connected in a reciprocally inhibitory network. A model of intersegmental coordination is implemented by connecting eleven such oscillators, with nearest neighbor coupling. We present the neuron model, and we investigate the role of frequency gradients and asymmetrical coupling in the establishment of phase lags along a chain these neural oscillators.

2 NEURON MODEL

In order to produce bursting activity, a neuron must possess "slow" intrinsic time constants in addition to the "fast" time constants that are necessary for the generation of spikes. Hardware models of neurons with both slow and fast time constants have been designed based upon previously described Hodgkin–Huxley neuron models (Mahowald and Douglas, 1991). Although these circuits are good models of their biological counterparts, they are relatively complex, with a large parameter space and transistor count, limiting their usefulness in the development of large-scale systems. It has been shown (Skinner, 1994), however, that pattern generation can be represented with only the slow time constants, creating a system that represents the envelope of the bursting oscillations without the individual spikes. Model neurons with only slow time constants have been proposed by Morris and Lecar (1981).

We have implemented an analog VLSI model of the Morris-Lecar Neuron (Patel and DeWeerth, 1997). Figure 1 shows the circuit diagram of this neuron. The model consists of two state variables: one corresponding to the membrane potential (V) and one corresponding to a slow variable (N). The slow variable is obtained by delaying the mem-

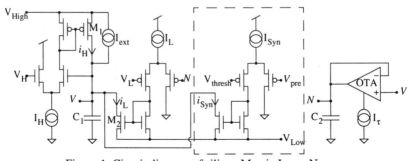

Figure 1: Circuit diagram of silicon Morris-Lecar Neuron

brane potential by way of an operational transconductance amplifier (OTA) connected in unity gain configuration with load capacitor C_2. The membrane potential is obtained by injecting two positive currents (I_{ext} and i_H) and two negative currents (i_L and i_{syn}) into capacitor C_1. Current i_H raises the membrane potential towards V_{High} when the membrane potential increases above V_H, whereas current i_L lowers the membrane potential towards V_{Low} when the delayed membrane potential increases above V_L. The synaptic current, i_{syn}, activates when the presynaptic input, V_{Pre}, increases above V_{thresh}. Assuming operation of transistors in weak inversion and synaptic coupling turned off ($i_{syn} = 0$) the equations of motion for the system are.

$$C_1 \dot{V} = I_1(V, N) = I_{ext}\alpha_P + I_H \frac{\exp(\kappa(V - V_H)/U_T)}{1 + \exp(\kappa(V - V_H)/U_T)}\alpha_P - I_L \frac{\exp(\kappa(N - V_L)/U_T)}{1 + \exp(\kappa(N - V_L)/U_T)}\alpha_N$$

$$C_2 \dot{N} = I_2(V, N) = I_\tau \tanh(\kappa(V - N)/(2U_T))(1 - \exp((N - V_{dd})/U_T)))$$

The terms α_P and α_N, where $\alpha_P = 1 - \exp(V - V_{High})/U_T$ and $\alpha_N = 1 - \exp(V_{Low} - V)/U_T$, correspond to the ohmic effect of transistor M1 and M2 respectively. κ corresponds to the back-gate effect of a MOS transistor operated in weak inversion, and U_T corresponds to the thermal voltage. We can understand the behavior of this circuit by analyzing the geometry of the curves that yield zero motion (i.e., when $I_1(V, N) = I_2(V, N) = 0$). These curves, referred to as nullclines, are shown in Figure 2 for various values of external current.

The externally applied constant current (I_{ext}), which has the effect of shifting the V nullcline in the positive vertical direction (see Figure 2), controls the mode of operation of the neuron. When the V- and N nullclines intersect between the local minimum and local maximum of the V nullcline (P2 in Figure 2), the resulting fixed point is unstable and the trajectories of the system approach a stable limit-cycle (an *endogenous bursting* mode). Fixed points to the left of the local minimum (P1 in Figure 2) or to the right of the local maximum (P3 in Figure 2) are stable and correspond to a *silent* mode and a *tonic* mode of the neuron respectively. An inhibitory synaptic current (i_{syn}) has the effect of shifting the V nullcline in the negative vertical direction; depending on the state of a presynaptic cell, i_{Syn} can dynamically change the mode of operation of the neuron.

3 TWO-CELL NETWORK

When two cells are connected in a reciprocally inhibitory network, the two cells will oscillate in antiphase depending on the conditions of the free and inhibited cells and the value of the synaptic threshold (Skinner et. al, 1994). We assume that the turn-on characteristics of the synaptic current is sharp (valid for large $V_{High} - V_{Low}$) such that when the membrane potential of a presynaptic cell reaches above V_{thresh}, the postsynaptic cell is immediately inhibited by application of negative current I_{Syn} to its membrane potential.

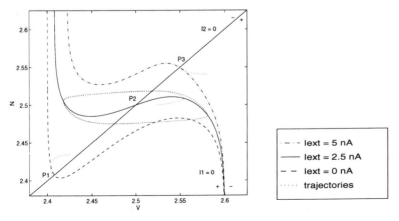

Figure 2: Nullcline and corresponding trajectories of silicon Morris-Lecar neuron.

If the free cell is an endogenous burster, the inhibited cell is silent, and the synaptic threshold is between the local maximum of the free cell and the local minimum in the inhibited cell, the mechanism for oscillation is due to *intrinsic release*. This mechanism can be understood by observing that the free cell undergoes rapid depolarization when its state approaches the local maximum thus facilitating the release of the inhibited cell. If the free cell is tonic and the inhibited cell is an endogenous burster (and conditions on synaptic threshold are the same as in the intrinsic release case), then the oscillations are due to an *intrinsic escape* mechanism. This mechanism is understood by observing that the inhibited cell undergoes rapid hyperpolarization, thus escaping inhibition, when its state approaches the local minimum. Note, in both intrinsic release and intrinsic escape mechanisms, the synaptic threshold has no effect on oscillator period because rapid changes in membrane potential occur before the effect of synaptic threshold.

When the free cell is an endogenous burster, the inhibited cell is silent, and the synaptic threshold is to the right of the local maximum of the free cell, then the oscillations are due to a *synaptic release* mechanism. This mechanism can be understood by observing that when the membrane potential of the free cell reaches below the synaptic threshold, the free cell ceases to inhibit the other cell which causes the release of the inhibited cell. When the free cell is tonic, and the inhibited cell is an endogenous burster, and the synaptic threshold is to the left of the local minimum of the inhibited cell, then the oscillations are due to a *synaptic escape* mechanism. This mechanism can be understood by observing that when the membrane potential of the inhibited cell crosses above the synaptic threshold, then the membrane potential of the inhibited cell is large enough to inhibit the free cell. Note, increasing the synaptic threshold has the effect of increasing oscillator frequency for the synaptic release mechanism, however, oscillator frequency under the synaptic escape mechanism will decrease with an increase in the synaptic threshold.

By setting $V_{High} - V_{Low}$ to a large value, the synaptic currents appear to have a sharp cutoff. However, because transistor currents saturate within a few thermal voltages, the nullclines due to the membrane potential appear less cubic-like and more square-like. This does not effect the qualitative behavior of the circuit, as we are able to produce antiphasic oscillations due to all four mechanisms. Figure 3 illustrates the four modes of oscillations under various parameter regimes. Figure 3A show typical waveforms from two silicon neurons when they are configured in a reciprocally inhibitory network. The oscillations in this case are due to intrinsic release mechanism and the frequency of oscillations are insensitive to the synaptic threshold. When the synaptic threshold is increased above 2.5 volts, the oscillations are due to the synaptic release mechanism and the oscillator frequency will increase as the synaptic threshold is increased, as shown in Figure 3C. By adjusting I_{ext} such that the free cell is tonic and the inhibited cell bursts endogenously, we are able to produce oscillations due to the intrinsic escape mechanism, as

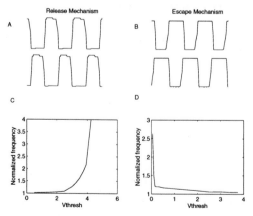

Figure 3: Experimental results from two neurons connected in a reciprocally inhibitory network. Antiphasic oscillations due to intrinsic release mechanism (A), and intrinsic escape mechanism (B). Dependence of oscillator frequency on synaptic threshold for the synaptic release mechanism (C) and synaptic escape mechanism (D)

shown in Figure 3B. As the synaptic threshold is decreased below 0.3 volts, the oscillations are caused by the synaptic escape mechanism and oscillator frequency increases as the synaptic threshold is decreased. The sharp transition between intrinsic and synaptic mechanisms is due to nullclines that appear square-like.

4   CHAIN OF COUPLED NEURAL OSCILLATORS

In order to build a chain of pattern generating circuits with nearest neighbor coupling, we designed our silicon neurons with five synaptic connections. The connections are made using the synaptic spread rule proposed by Williams (1990). The rule states that a neuron in any given segment can only connect to neurons in other segments that are homologues to the neurons it connects to in the local segment. Therefore, each neuron makes two inhibitory, contralateral connections and two excitatory, ipsilateral connections (as well a single inhibitory connection in the local segment). The synaptic circuit, shown in the dashed box in Figure 1, is repeated for each inhibitory synapse and its complementary version is repeated for the excitatory synapses. In order to investigate the role of frequency gradients, each neural oscillator has an independent parameter, I_{ext}, for setting the intrinsic oscillator period. A set of global parameters, I_L, I_H, I_τ, V_H, V_L, V_{High}, and V_{Low} control the mechanism of oscillation. These parameters are set such that the mechanism of oscillation is intrinsic release.

Because of inherent mismatch of devices in CMOS technology, a consequence in our model is that neurons with equal parameters do not necessarily behave with similar performance. Figure 4A illustrates the intrinsic oscillator period along the length of system when all neurons receive the same parameters. When the oscillators are symmetrically coupled, the resulting phase differences along the chain are nonzero, as shown in Figure 4B. The phase lags are negative with respect to the head position, thus the default swim direction is backward. As the coupling strength is increased, indicated by the lowermost curves in Figure 4B, the phase lags become smaller, as expected, but do not diminish to produce synchronous oscillations. When the oscillators are locked to one common frequency, Ω, theory predicts (Kopell and Ermentrout, 1988) that the common frequency is dependent on intrinsic oscillator frequencies, and coupling from neighboring oscillators. In addition, under the condition of weak coupling, the effect of coupling can be quantified with coupling functions that depends on the phase difference between neighboring oscillators:

$$\Omega = \omega_i + H_A^i(\phi_i) + H_D^i(-\phi_{i-1})$$

where, ω_i is the intrinsic frequency of a given oscillator, H_A and H_D are coupling functions in the ascending and descending directions respectively, and ϕ_i is the phase difference between the (i+1)th and ith oscillator. This equation suggests that the phase lags must be large in order to compensate for large variations in the intrinsic oscillator fre-

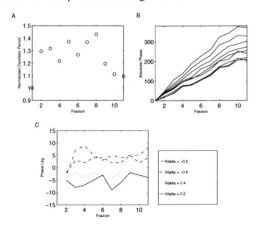

Figure 4: Experimental data obtained from system of coupled oscillators.

quencies.

Another factor that can effect the intersegmental phase lag is the degree of anisotropic coupling. To investigate the effect of asymmetrical coupling, we adjusted I_{ext} in each segment so to produce uniform intrinsic oscillator periods (to within ten percent of 115 ms) along the length of the system. Asymmetrical coupling is established by maintaining $V_{avg} \equiv (V_{ASC} - V_{DES})/2$ at 0.7 volts and varying $V_{delta} \equiv V_{ASC} - V_{DES}$ from 0.4 to - 0.4 volts. V_{ASC} and V_{DES} correspond to the bias voltage that sets the synaptic conductance of presynaptic inputs arriving from the ascending and descending directions respectively. Throughout the experiment, the average of inhibitory (contralateral) and excitatory (ipsilateral) connections from one direction are maintained at equal levels. Figure 4C shows the intersegmental phase lags at different levels of anisotropic coupling. Stronger ascending weights (V_{delta} = 0.4, 0.2 volts) produced negative phase lags, corresponding to backward swimming, while stronger descending connections (V_{delta} = -0.4, -0.2 volts) produce positive phase lags, corresponding to backward swimming. Although mathematical models suggest that stronger ascending coupling should produce forward swimming, we feel that the type of coupling (inhibitory contralateral and excitatory ipsilateral connections) and the oscillatory mode (intrinsic release) of the segmental oscillators may account for this discrepancy.

To study the effects of frequency gradients, we adjusted I_{ext} at each segment such that the that the oscillator period from the head to the tail (from segment 1 to segment 11) varied from 300 ms to 100 ms in 20 ms increments. In addition, to minimize the effect of asymmetrical coupling, we set V_{avg} = 0.8 volts and V_{delta} = 0 volts. The absolute phase under these conditions are shown in Figure 5A. The phase lags are negative with respect to the head position, which corresponds to backward swimming. With a positive frequency gradient, head oscillator at 100 ms and tail oscillator at 300 ms, the resulting phases are in the opposite direction, as shown in Figure 5B. These results are consistent with mathematical models and the *trailing oscillator hypothesis* as expounded by Grillner et. al. (1991).

5 CONCLUSIONS AND FUTURE WORK

We have implemented and tested an analog VLSI model of intersegmental coordination with nearest neighbor coupling. We have explored the effects of anisotropic coupling and frequency gradients on system behavior. One of our results—stronger ascending connections produced backward swimming instead of forward swimming—is contrary to theory. There are two factors that may account for this discrepancy: i) our system exhibits inherent spatial disorder in the parameter space due to device mismatch, and ii) the operating point at which we performed the experiments retains high sensitivity to neuron parameter variations and oscillatory modes. We are continuing to explore the parameter space to determine if there are more robust operating points.

We expect that the limitation of our system to only including nearest-neighbor connections is a major factor in the large phase-lag variations that we observed. The importance of both short and long distance connections in the regulation of constant phase under conditions of large variability in the parameter space has been shown by Cohen and Kiemel (1993). To address these issues, we are currently designing a system that facilitates both short and long distance connections (DeWeerth et al, 1997). Additionally, to study the

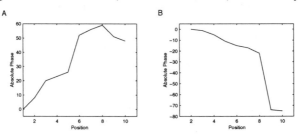

Figure 5: Absolute phase with negative (A) and positive (B) frequency gradients.

role of sensory feedback and to close the loop between neural control and motor behavior, we are also building a mechanical segmented system into which we will incorporate our aVLSI models.

Acknowledgments

This research is supported by NSF grant IBN-9511721. We would like to thank Avis Cohen for discussion on computational properties that underlie coordinated motor behavior in the lamprey swim system. We would also like to thank Mario Simoni for discussions on pattern generating circuits. We thank the Georgia Tech Analog Consortium for supporting students with travel funds.

References

Calabrese, R. and De Schutter, E. (1992). Motor-pattern-generating networks in Invertebrates: Modeling Our Way Toward Understanding. *TINS*, 15.11:439–445.

Cohen, A, Holms, P. and Rand R. (1982). The nature of coupling between segmental oscillators of the lamprey spinal generator for locomotion: A mathematical model. J. Math Biol. 13:345–369.

Cohen, A. and Kiemel, T. (1993). Intersegmental coordination: lessons from modeling systems of coupled non-linear oscillators. *Amer. Zool.*, 33:54–65.

DeWeerth, S., Patel, G., Schimmel, D., Simoni, M. and Calabrese, R. (1997). In *Proceedings of the Seventeenth Conference on Advanced Research in VLSI*, R.B. Brown and A.T. Ishii (eds), Los Alamitos, CA: IEEE Computer Society, 182–200.

Friesen, O and Pearce, R. (1993). Mechanisms of intersegmental coordination in leech locomotion. *SINS* 5:41-47.

Getting, P. (1989). A network oscillator underlying swimming in Tritonia. In *Cellular and Neuronal Oscillators*, J.W. Jacklet (ed), New York: Marcel Dekker, 101–128.

Grillner, S. Wallén, P., Brodin, L. and Lansner, A. (1991). Neuronal network generating locomotor behavior in lamprey: circuitry, transmitter, membrane properties, and simulation. *Ann. Rev. Neurosci.*, 14:169–169.

Kopell, N. and Ermentrout, B. (1988). Coupled oscillators and the design of central pattern generators. *Math Biosci.* 90:87–109.

Mahowald, M. and Douglas, R. (1991) A silicon neuron. *Nature,* 354:515–518.

Morris, C. and Lecar, H. (1981) Voltage oscillations in the barnacle giant muscle fiber. *Biophys. J,* 35: 193–213.

Patel, G., DeWeerth, S. (1997). Analogue VLSI Morris-Lecar neuron. *Electronic Letters,* IEE. 33.12: 997-998.

Sigvardt, K.(1993). Intersegmental coordination in the lamprey central pattern generator for locomotion. *SINS* 5:3-15.

Selverston, A. (1989) The Lobster Gastric Mill Oscillator, In *Cellular and Neuronal Oscillators*, J.W. Jacklet (ed), New York: Marcel Dekker, 338–370.

Skinner, F., Kopell, N., and Marder E. (1994) Mechanisms for Oscillation and Frequency Control in Reciprocally Inhibitory Model Neural Networks., *J. of Comp. Neuroscience,* 1:69–87.

Willams, T. (1992). Phase Coupling and Synaptic Spread in Chains of Coupled Neuronal Oscillators. *Science,* vol. 258.

Williams, T., Sigvardt, K. (1994) intersegmental phase lags in the lamprey spinal cord: experimental confirmation of the existence of a boundary region. *J. of Comp. Neuroscience,* 1:61–67.

An Analog VLSI Neural Network for Phase-based Machine Vision

Bertram E. Shi
Department of Electrical and Electronic
Engineering
Hong Kong University of Science and
Technology
Clear Water Bay, Kowloon, Hong Kong

Kwok Fai Hui
Fujitsu Microelectronics Pacific Asia Ltd.
Suite 1015-20, Tower 1
Grand Century Place
193 Prince Edward Road West
Mongkok, Kowloon, Hong Kong.

Abstract

We describe the design, fabrication and test results of an analog CMOS VLSI neural network prototype chip intended for phase-based machine vision algorithms. The chip implements an image filtering operation similar to Gabor-filtering. Because a Gabor filter's output is complex valued, it can be used to define a phase at every pixel in an image. This phase can be used in robust algorithms for disparity estimation and binocular stereo vergence control in stereo vision and for image motion analysis. The chip reported here takes an input image and generates two outputs at every pixel corresponding to the real and imaginary parts of the output.

1 INTRODUCTION

Gabor filters are used as preprocessing stages for different tasks in machine vision and image processing. Their use has been partially motivated by findings that two dimensional Gabor filters can be used to model receptive fields of orientation selective neurons in the visual cortex (Daugman, 1980) and three dimensional spatio-temporal Gabor filters can be used to model biological image motion analysis (Adelson, 1985).

A Gabor filter has a complex valued impulse response which is a complex exponential modulated by a Gaussian function. In one dimension,

$$g(x) = \frac{1}{\sqrt{2\pi}\sigma} e^{-\frac{x^2}{2\sigma^2}} e^{j\omega_{xo}x} = \frac{1}{\sqrt{2\pi}\sigma} e^{-\frac{x^2}{2\sigma^2}} (\cos(\omega_{xo}x) + j\sin(\omega_{xo}x))$$

where ω_{xo} and σ are real constants corresponding to the angular frequency of the complex exponential and the standard deviation of the Gaussian.

The phase of the complex valued filter output at a given pixel is related to the location of edges and other features in the input image near that pixel. Because translating the image input results in a phase shift in the Gabor output, several authors have developed "phase-based" approaches to disparity estimation (Westelius, 1995) and binocular vergence control (Theimer, 1994) in stereo vision and image motion analysis (Fleet, 1992). Barron et. al.'s comparison (Barron, 1992) of algorithms for optical flow estimation indicates that Fleet's algorithm is the most accurate among those tested.

The remainder of this paper describes the design, fabrication and test results of a prototype analog VLSI continuous time neural network which implements a complex valued filter similar to the Gabor.

2   NETWORK AND CIRCUIT ARCHITECTURE

The prototype implements a Cellular Neural Network (CNN) architecture for Gabor-type image filtering (Shi, 1996). It consists of an array of neurons, called "cells," each corresponding to one pixel in the image to be processed. Each cell has two outputs $v_r(n)$ and $v_i(n)$ which evolve over time according to the equation

$$\begin{bmatrix} \dot{v}_r(n) \\ \dot{v}_i(n) \end{bmatrix} = \begin{bmatrix} \cos\omega_{xo} & -\sin\omega_{xo} \\ \sin\omega_{xo} & \cos\omega_{xo} \end{bmatrix} \begin{bmatrix} v_r(n-1) \\ v_i(n-1) \end{bmatrix} - \begin{bmatrix} 2+\lambda^2 & 0 \\ 0 & 2+\lambda^2 \end{bmatrix} \begin{bmatrix} v_r(n) \\ v_i(n) \end{bmatrix} + \begin{bmatrix} \cos\omega_{xo} & \sin\omega_{xo} \\ -\sin\omega_{xo} & \cos\omega_{xo} \end{bmatrix} \begin{bmatrix} v_r(n+1) \\ v_i(n+1) \end{bmatrix} + \begin{bmatrix} \lambda^2 u(n) \\ 0 \end{bmatrix}$$

where $\lambda > 0$ and $\omega_o \in [0, 2\pi]$ are real constants and $u(n)$ is the input image. The feedback from neighbouring cells' outputs enables information to be spread globally throughout the array. This network has a unique equilibrium point where the outputs correspond to the real and imaginary parts of the result of filtering the image with a complex valued discrete space convolution kernel which can be approximated by

$$g(n) = \frac{\lambda}{2} e^{-\lambda|n|} e^{j\omega_{xo}(n)} .$$

The Gaussian function of the Gabor filter has been replaced by $(\lambda/2) \, e^{-\lambda|x|}$. The larger λ is, the narrower the impulse response and the larger the bandwidth. Figure 1 shows the real (a) and imaginary (b) parts of $g(n)$ for $\lambda = 0.3$ and $\omega_{xo} = 0.93$. The dotted lines show the function which modulates the complex exponential.

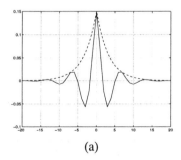
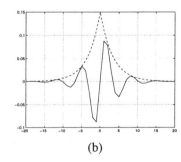

(a)   (b)

Figure 1: The Real and Imaginary Parts of the Impulse Response.

In the circuit implementation of this CNN, each output corresponds to the voltage across a capacitor. We selected the circuit architecture in Figure 2 because it was the least sensitive to the effects of random parameter variations among those we considered (Hui, 1996). In the figure, resistor labels denote conductances and trapezoidal blocks represent transconductance amplifiers labelled by their gains.

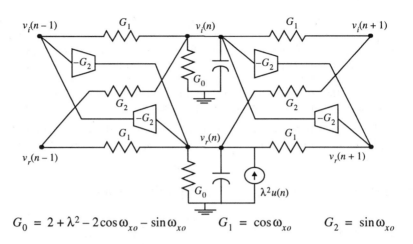

$$G_0 = 2 + \lambda^2 - 2\cos\omega_{xo} - \sin\omega_{xo} \qquad G_1 = \cos\omega_{xo} \qquad G_2 = \sin\omega_{xo}$$

Figure 2: Circuit Implementation of One Neuron.

The circuit implementation also gives good intuitive understanding of the CNN's operation. Assume that the input image is an impulse at pixel n. In the circuit, this corresponds to setting the current source $\lambda^2 u(n)$ to λ^2 amps and setting the remaining current sources to zero. If the gains and conductances were chosen so that $\lambda = 0.3$ and $\omega_{xo} = 0.93$, then the steady state voltages across the lower capacitors would follow the spatial distribution shown in Figure 1(a) where the center peak occurs at cell n and the voltages across the upper capacitors would follow the distribution shown in Figure 1(b). To see how this would arise in the circuit, consider the current supplied by the source $\lambda^2 u(n)$. Part of the current flows through the conductance G_0 pushing the voltage $v_r(n)$ positive. As this voltage increases, the two resistors with conductance G_1 cause a smoothing effect which pulls the voltages $v_r(n-1)$ and $v_r(n+1)$ up towards $v_r(n)$. Current also flows through the diagonal resistor with conductance G_2 pulling $v_i(n+1)$ positive as well. At the same time, the transconductance amplifier with input $v_r(n)$ draws current from node $v_i(n-1)$ pushing $v_i(n-1)$ negative. The larger G_2, the more the voltages at nodes $v_i(n-1)$ and $v_i(n+1)$ are pushed negative and positive. On the other hand, the larger G_1, the greater the smoothing between nodes. Thus, the larger the ratio

$$\frac{G_2}{G_1} = \frac{\sin\omega_{xo}}{\cos\omega_{xo}} = \tan\omega_{xo},$$

the higher the spatial frequency ω_{xo} at which the impulse response oscillates.

3   DESIGN OF CMOS BUILDING BLOCKS

This section describes CMOS transistor circuits which implement the transconductance amplifiers and resistors in Figure 2. It is not necessary to implement the capacitors explicitly. Since the equilibrium point of the CNN is unique, the parasitic capacitances of the circuit are sufficient to ensure the circuit operates correctly.

3.1   TRANSCONDUCTANCE AMPLIFIER

The transconductance amplifiers can be implemented using the circuit shown in Figure 3(a). For $V_{in} \approx V_{GND}$, the output current is approximately $I_{out} = \sqrt{\beta_n I_{SS}} V_{in}$ where $\beta_n = \mu_n C_{ox}(W/L)$ and (W/L) is the width/length ratio of the differential pair. The transistors in the current mirrors are assumed to be matched. Using cascoded current mirrors decreases static errors such as offsets caused by the finite output impedance of the MOS transistors in saturation.

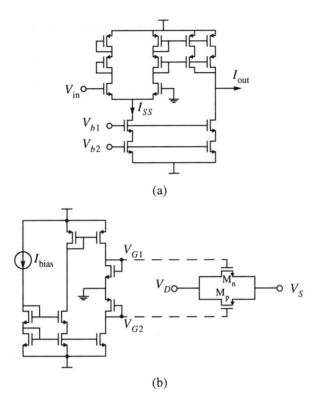

(a)

(b)

Figure 3: The CMOS Circuits Implementing OTAs and Resistors

3.2 RESISTORS

Since the convolution kernels implemented are modulated sine and cosine functions, the nodal voltages $v_e(n)$ and $v_o(n)$ can be both positive and negative with respect to the ground potential. The resistors in the circuit must be floating and exhibit good linearity and invariance to common mode offsets for voltages around the ground potential. Many MOS resistor circuits require bias circuitry implemented at every resistor. Since for image processing tasks, we are interested in maximizing the number of pixels processed, eliminating the need for bias circuitry at each cell will decrease its area and in turn increase the number of cells implementable within a given area.

Figure 3(b) shows a resistor circuit which satisfies the requirements above. This circuit is essentially a CMOS transmission gate with adjustable gate voltages. The global bias circuit which generates the gate voltages in the CMOS resistor is shown on the left. The gate bias voltages V_{G1} and V_{G2} are distributed to each resistor designed with the same value. Both transistors M_n and M_p operate in the conduction region where (Enz, 1995)

$$I_{Dn} = n_n \beta_n \left(V_{Pn} - \frac{V_D + V_S}{2} \right)(V_D - V_S) \text{ and } I_{Dp} = -n_p \beta_p \left(V_{Pp} - \frac{V_D + V_S}{2} \right)(V_D - V_S)$$

and V_{Pn} and V_{Pp} are nonlinear functions of the gate and threshold voltages. The sizing of the NMOS and PMOS transistors can be chosen to decrease the effect of the nonlinearity due to the $(V_D + V_S)/2$ terms. The conductance of the resistors can be adjusted using I_{bias}.

3.3 LIMITATIONS

Due to the physical constraints of the circuit realizations, not all values of λ and ω_{xo} can be realized. Because the conductance values are non-negative and the OTA gains are non-positive both G_1 and G_2 must be non-negative. This implies that ω_{xo} must lie between 0 and $\pi/2$. Because the conductance G_0 is non-negative, $\lambda^2 \geq -2 + 2\cos\omega_{xo} + \sin\omega_{xo}$. Figure 4 shows the range of center frequencies ω_{xo} (normalized by π) and relative band-widths $(2\lambda/\omega_{xo})$ achievable by this realization. Not all bandwidths are achievable for $\omega_{xo} \leq 2\text{atan}\,0.5 \approx 0.3\pi$.

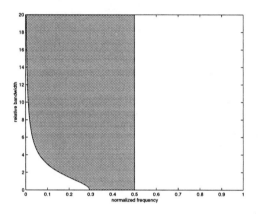

Figure 4: The filter parameters implementable by the circuit realization.

4 TEST RESULTS

The circuit architecture and CMOS building blocks described above were fabricated using the Orbit 2µm n-well process available through MOSIS. In this prototype, a 13 cell one dimensional array was fabricated on a 2.2mm square die. The value of ω_{xo} is fixed at $2\text{atan}\,0.5 \approx 0.927$ by transistor sizing. This is the smallest spatial frequency for which all bandwidths can be obtained. In addition, $G_0 = \lambda^2$ for this value of ω_{xo}. The width of the impulse response is adjustable by changing the externally supplied bias current shown in Figure 3(b) controlling G_0.

The transconductance amplifiers and resistors are designed to operate between $\pm300\text{mV}$. The currents representing the input image are provided by transconductance amplifiers internal to the chip which are controlled by externally applied voltages. Outputs are read off the chip in analog form through two common read-out amplifiers: one for the real part of the impulse response and one for the imaginary part. The outputs of the cells are con-nected in turn to the inputs of the read-out amplifier through transmission gates controlled by a shift register. The chip requires $\pm4\text{V}$ supplies and dissipates 35mW.

To measure the impulse response of the filters, we applied 150mV to the input correspond-ing to the middle cell of the array and 0V to the remaining inputs. The output voltages from one chip as a function of cell number are shown as solid lines in Figure 5(a, b). To correct for DC offsets, we also measured the output voltages when all of the inputs were grounded, as shown by the dashed lines in the figure. The DC offsets can be separated into two components: a constant offset common to all cells in the array and a small offset which varies from cell to cell. For the chip shown, the constant offset is approximately

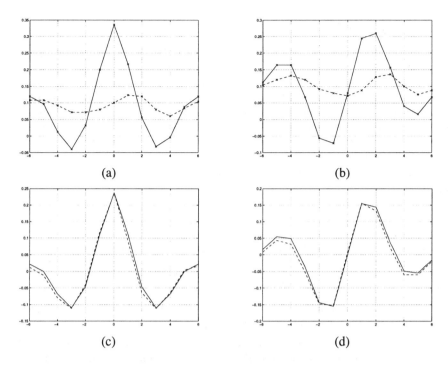

Figure 5: DC Measurements from the Prototype

100mV and the small variations have a standard deviation of 20mV. These results are consistent with the other chips. The constant offset is primarily due to the offset voltage in the read-out amplifier. The small variations from cell to cell are the result of both parameter variations from cell to cell and offsets in the transconductance amplifiers of each cell.

By subtracting the DC zero-input offsets at each cell from the outputs, we can observe that the impulse response closely matches that predicted by the theory. The dotted lines in Figure 5(c, d) show the offset corrected outputs for the same chip as shown in Figure 5(a, b). The solid lines shows the theoretical output of the chip using parameters λ and ω_{xo} chosen to minimize the mean squared error between the theory and the data. The chip was designed for $\lambda = 0.210$ and $\omega_{xo} = 0.927$. The parameters for the best fit are $\lambda = 0.175$ and $\omega_{xo} = 0.941$. The signal to noise ratio, as defined by the energy in the theoretical output divided by the energy in the error between theory and data, is 19.3dB. Similar measurements from two other chips gave signal to noise ratios of 29.0dB ($\lambda = 0.265$, $\omega_{xo} = 0.928$) and 30.6dB ($\lambda = 0.200$, $\omega_{xo} = 0.938$).

To measure the speed of the chips, we grounded all of the inputs except that of the middle cell to which we attached a function generator generating a square wave switching between $\pm 200\text{mV}$. The rise times (10% to 90%) at the output of the chip for each cell were measured and ranged between 340 and 528 nanoseconds. The settling times will not increase if the number of cells increases since the outputs are computed in parallel. The settling time is primarily determined by the width of the impulse response. The wider the impulse response, the farther information must propagate through the array and the slower the settling time.

5 CONCLUSION

We have described the architecture, design and test results from an analog VLSI prototype of a neural network which filters images with convolution kernels similar to those of the Gabor filter. Our future work on chip design includes fabricating chips with larger numbers of cells, two dimensional arrays and chips with integrated photosensors which acquire and process images simultaneously. We are also investigating the use of these neural network chips in binocular vergence control of an active stereo vision system.

Acknowledgements

This work was supported by the Hong Kong Research Grants Council (RGC) under grant number HKUST675/95E.

References

E. H. Adelson, and J. R. Bergen, "Spatiotemporal energy models for the perception of motion", J. *Optical Society of America A*, vol. 2, pp. 284-299, Feb. 1985.

J. Barron, D. S. Fleet, S. S. Beauchemin, and T. A. Burkitt, "Performance of optical flow techniques," in *Proc. of CVPR*, (Champaign, IL), pp. 236-242, IEEE, 1992.

J. G. Daugman, "Two-dimensional spectral analysis of cortical receptive field profiles," *Vision Research*, vol. 20, pp. 847-856, 1980.

C. C. Enz, F. Krummenacher, and E. A. Vittoz, "An analytical MOS transistor model valid in all regions of operation and dedicated to low-voltage and low-current applications," *Analog Integrated Circuits and Signal Processing,* vol.8, no.1, p83-114, Jul. 1995.

D. J. Fleet, *Measurement of Image Velocity*, Boston. MA: Kluwer Academic Publishers, 1992.

K. F. Hui and B. E. Shi, "Robustness of CNN Implementations for Gabor-type Filtering," *Proc. of Asia Pacific Conference on Circuits and Systems*, pp. 105-108, Nov. 1996.

B. E. Shi, "Gabor-type image filtering with cellular neural networks," *Proceedings of the 1996 IEEE International Symposium on Circuits and Systems*, vol. 3, pp. 558-561, May 1996.

W. M. Theimer and H. A Mallot, "Phase-based binocular vergence control and depth reconstruction using active vision," *CVGIP: Image Understanding*, vol. 60, no. 3, pp. 343-358, Nov. 1994.

C.-J. Westelius, H. Knutsson, J. Wiklund and C.-F. Westin, "Phase-based disparity estimation," in J. L. Crowley and H. I. Christensen, eds., *Vision as Process*, chap. 11, pp. 157-178, Springer-Verlag, Berlin, 1995.

PART VI
SPEECH, HANDWRITING AND SIGNAL PROCESSING

Analysis of Drifting Dynamics with Neural Network Hidden Markov Models

J. Kohlmorgen
GMD FIRST
Rudower Chaussee 5
12489 Berlin, Germany

K.-R. Müller
GMD FIRST
Rudower Chaussee 5
12489 Berlin, Germany

K. Pawelzik
MPI f. Strömungsforschung
Bunsenstr. 10
37073 Göttingen, Germany

Abstract

We present a method for the analysis of nonstationary time series with multiple operating modes. In particular, it is possible to detect and to model both a switching of the dynamics and a less abrupt, time consuming drift from one mode to another. This is achieved in two steps. First, an unsupervised training method provides prediction experts for the inherent dynamical modes. Then, the trained experts are used in a hidden Markov model that allows to model drifts. An application to physiological wake/sleep data demonstrates that analysis and modeling of real-world time series can be improved when the drift paradigm is taken into account.

1 Introduction

Modeling dynamical systems through a measured time series is commonly done by reconstructing the state space with time-delay coordinates [10]. The prediction of the time series can then be accomplished by training neural networks [11]. If, however, a system operates in multiple modes and the dynamics is *drifting* or *switching*, standard approaches like multi-layer perceptrons are likely to fail to represent the underlying input-output relations. Moreover, they do not reveal the dynamical structure of the system. Time series from alternating dynamics of this type can originate from many kinds of systems in physics, biology and engineering.

In [2, 6, 8], we have described a framework for time series from *switching* dynamics, in which an ensemble of neural network predictors specializes on the respective operating modes. We now extend the ability to describe a mode change not only as a switching but – if appropriate – also as a drift from one predictor to another. Our results indicate that physiological signals contain drifting dynamics, which underlines the potential relevance of our method in time series analysis.

2   Detection of Drifts

The detection and analysis of drifts is performed in two steps. First, an unsupervised (hard-)segmentation method is applied. In this approach, an ensemble of competing prediction experts f_i, $i = 1, ..., N$, is trained on a given time series. The optimal choice of function approximators f_i depends on the specific application. In general, however, neural networks are a good choice for the prediction of time series [11]. In this paper, we use radial basis function (RBF) networks of the Moody-Darken type [5] as predictors, because they offer a fast and robust learning method.

Under a gaussian assumption, the probability that a particular predictor i would have produced the observed data y is given by

$$p(y \mid i) = K e^{-\beta(y-f_i)^2},\tag{1}$$

where K is the normalization term for the gaussian distribution. If we assume that the experts are mutually exclusive and exhaustive, we have $p(y) = \sum_i p(y \mid i)p(i)$. We further assume that the experts are – a priori – equally probable,

$$p(i) = 1/N.\tag{2}$$

In order to train the experts, we want to maximize the likelihood that the ensemble would have generated the time series. This can be done by a gradient method. For the derivative of the log-likelihood $\log L = \log(p(y))$ with respect to the output of an expert, we get

$$\frac{\partial \log L}{\partial f_i} \propto \left[\frac{e^{-\beta(y-f_i)^2}}{\sum_j e^{-\beta(y-f_j)^2}} \right] (y - f_i).\tag{3}$$

This learning rule can be interpreted as a weighting of the learning rate of each expert by the expert's relative prediction performance. It is a special case of the Mixtures of Experts [1] learning rule, with the gating network being omitted. Note that according to Bayes' rule the term in brackets is the posterior probability that expert i is the correct choice for the given data y, i.e. $p(i \mid y)$. Therefore, we can simply write

$$\frac{\partial \log L}{\partial f_i} \propto p(i \mid y)(y - f_i).\tag{4}$$

Furthermore, we imposed a low-pass filter on the prediction errors $\varepsilon_i = (y - f_i)^2$ and used deterministic annealing of β in the training process (see [2, 8] for details). We found that these modifications can be essential for a successful segmentation and prediction of time series from switching dynamics.

As a prerequisite of this method, mode changes should occur infrequent, i.e. between two mode changes the dynamics should operate stationary in one mode for a certain number of time steps. Applying this method to a time series yields a (hard) segmentation of the series into different operating modes together with prediction experts for each mode. In case of a drift between two modes, the respective segment tends to be subdivided into several parts, because a single predictor is not able to handle the nonstationarity.

The second step takes the drift into account. A segmentation algorithm is applied that allows to model drifts between two stationary modes by combining the two respective predictors, f_i and f_j. The drift is modeled by a weighted superposition

$$f(\vec{x}_t) = a(t) f_i(\vec{x}_t) + (1 - a(t)) f_j(\vec{x}_t), \quad 0 \le a(t) \le 1, \tag{5}$$

where $a(t)$ is a mixing coefficient and $\vec{x}_t = (x_t, x_{t-\tau}, \ldots, x_{t-(m-1)\tau})^T$ is the vector of time-delay coordinates of a (scalar) time series $\{x_t\}$. Furthermore, m is the embedding dimension and τ is the delay parameter of the embedding. Note that the use of multivariate time series is straightforward.

3 A Hidden Markov Model for Drift Segmentation

In the following, we will set up a hidden Markov model (HMM) that allows us to use the Viterbi algorithm for the analysis of drifting dynamics. For a detailed description of HMMs, see [9] and the references therein. An HMM consists of (1) a set S of states, (2) a matrix $A = \{p_{\hat{s},s}\}$ of state transition probabilities, (3) an observation probability distribution $p(y|s)$ for each state s, which is a continuous density in our case, and (4) the initial state distribution $\pi = \{\pi_s\}$.

Let us first consider the construction of S, the set of states, which is the crucial point of this approach. Consider a set P of 'pure' states (dynamical modes). Each state $s \in P$ represents one of the neural network predictors $f_{k(s)}$ trained in the first step. The predictor of each state performs the predictions autonomously. Next, consider a set M of mixture states, where each state $s \in M$ represents a linear mixture of two nets $f_{i(s)}$ and $f_{j(s)}$. Then, given a state $s \in S, S = P \cup M$, the prediction of the overall system is performed by

$$g_s(\vec{x}_t) = \begin{cases} f_{k(s)}(\vec{x}_t) & ; \text{if } s \in P \\ a(s) f_{i(s)}(\vec{x}_t) + b(s) f_{j(s)}(\vec{x}_t) & ; \text{if } s \in M \end{cases} \tag{6}$$

For each mixture state $s \in M$, the coefficients $a(s)$ and $b(s)$ have to be set together with the respective network indices $i(s)$ and $j(s)$. For computational feasibility, the number of mixture states has to be restricted. Our intention is to allow for drifts between any two network outputs of the previously trained ensemble. We choose $a(s)$ and $b(s)$ such that $0 < a(s) < 1$ and $b(s) = 1 - a(s)$. Moreover, a discrete set of $a(s)$ values has to be defined. For simplicity, we use equally distant steps,

$$a_r = \frac{r}{R+1}, \quad r = 1, \ldots, R. \tag{7}$$

R is the number of intermediate mixture levels. A given resolution R between any two out of N nets yields a total number of mixed states $|M| = R \cdot N \cdot (N-1)/2$. If, for example, the resolution $R = 32$ is used and we assume $N = 8$, then there are $|M| = 896$ mixture states, plus $|P| = N = 8$ pure states.

Next, the transition matrix $A = \{p_{\hat{s},s}\}$ has to be chosen. It determines the transition probability for each pair of states. In principle, this matrix can be found using a training procedure, as e.g. the Baum-Welch method [9]. However, this is hardly feasible in this case, because of the immense size of the matrix. In the above example, the matrix A has $(896 + 8)^2 = 817216$ elements that would have to be estimated. Such an exceeding number of free parameters is prohibitive for any adaptive method. Therefore, we use a *fixed* matrix. In this way, prior knowledge about the dynamical system can be incorporated. In our applications either switches or smooth drifts between two nets are allowed, in such a way that a (monotonous) drift from one net to another is *a priori* as likely as a switch. All the other transitions are disabled by setting $p_{\hat{s},s} = 0$. Defining $p(y \mid s)$ and π is straightforward. Following eq.(1) and eq.(2), we assume gaussian noise

$$p(y \mid s) = Ke^{-\beta(y-g_s)^2}, \tag{8}$$

and equally probable initial states, $\pi_s = |S|^{-1}$.

The Viterbi algorithm [9] can then be applied to the above stated HMM, without any further training of the HMM parameters. It yields the drift segmentation of a given time series, i.e. the most likely state sequence (the sequence of predictors or linear mixtures of two predictors) that could have generated the time series, in our case with the assumption that mode changes occur either as (smooth) drifts or as infrequent switches.

4   Drifting Mackey-Glass Dynamics

As an example, consider a high-dimensional chaotic system generated by the Mackey-Glass delay differential equation

$$\frac{dx(t)}{dt} = -0.1x(t) + \frac{0.2x(t - t_d)}{1 + x(t - t_d)^{10}}. \tag{9}$$

It was originally introduced as a model of blood cell regulation [4]. Two stationary operating modes, A and B, are established by using different delays, $t_d = 17$ and 23, respectively. After operating 100 time steps in mode A (with respect to a subsampling step size $\tau = 6$), the dynamics is drifting to mode B. The drift takes another 100 time steps. It is performed by mixing the equations for $t_d = 17$ and 23 during the integration of eq.(9). The mixture is generated according to eq.(5), using an exponential drift

$$a(t) = \exp\left(\frac{-4\,t}{100}\right), \quad t = 1, \dots, 100. \tag{10}$$

Then, the system runs stationary in mode B for the following 100 time steps, whereupon it is *switching* back to mode A at $t = 300$, and the loop starts again (Fig.1(a)). The competing experts algorithm is applied to the first 1500 data points of the generated time series, using an ensemble of 6 predictors $f_i(\vec{x}_t)$, $i = 1, ..., 6$. The input to each predictor is a vector $\vec{x}_t$ of time-delay coordinates of the scalar time series $\{x_t\}$. The embedding dimension is $m = 6$ and the delay parameter is $\tau = 1$ on the subsampled data. The RBF predictors consist of 40 basis functions each.

After training, nets 2 and 3 have specialized on mode A, nets 5 and 6 on mode B. This is depicted in the drift segmentation in Fig.1(b). Moreover, the removal of four nets does not increase the root mean squared error (RMSE) of the prediction significantly (Fig.1(c)), which correctly indicates that two predictors completely describe the dynamical system. The sequence of nets to be removed is obtained by repeatedly computing the RMSE of all n subsets with $n - 1$ nets each, and then selecting the subset with the lowest RMSE of the respective drift segmentation. The segmentation of the remaining nets, 2 and 5, nicely reproduces the evolution of the dynamics, as seen in Fig.1(d).

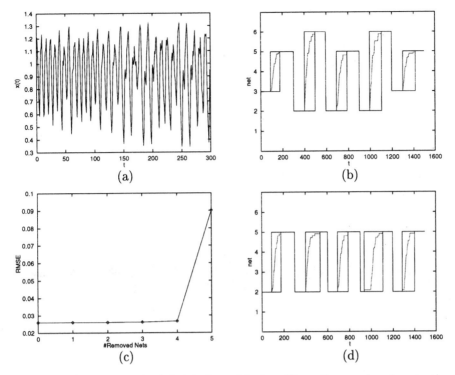

Figure 1: *(a) One 'loop' of the drifting Mackey-Glass time series (see text). (b) The resulting drift segmentation invokes four nets. The dotted line indicates the evolution of the mixing coefficient a(t) of the respective nets. For example, between t = 100 and 200 it denotes a drift from net 3 to net 5, which appears to be exponential. (c) Increase of the prediction error when predictors are successively removed. (d) The two remaining predictors model the dynamics of the time series properly.*

5 Wake/Sleep EEG

In [7], we analyzed physiological data recorded from the wake/sleep transition of a human. The objective was to provide an unsupervised method to detect the sleep onset and to give a detailed approximation of the signal dynamics with a high time resolution, ultimately to be used in diagnosis and treatment of sleep disorders. The application of the drift segmentation algorithm now yields a more detailed modeling of the dynamical system.

As an example, Fig. 2 shows a comparison of the drift segmentation ($R = 32$) with a manual segmentation by a medical expert. The experimental data was measured during an afternoon nap of a healthy human. The computer-based analysis is performed on a single-channel EEG recording (occipital-1), whereas the manual segmentation was worked out using several physiological recordings (EEG, EOG, ECG, heart rate, blood pressure, respiration).

The two-step drift segmentation method was applied using 8 RBF networks. However, as shown in Fig. 2, three nets (4, 6, and 8) are finally found by the Viterbi algorithm to be sufficient to represent the most likely state sequence. Before the sleep onset, at $t \approx 3500$ (350s) in the manual analysis, a mixture of two wake-state

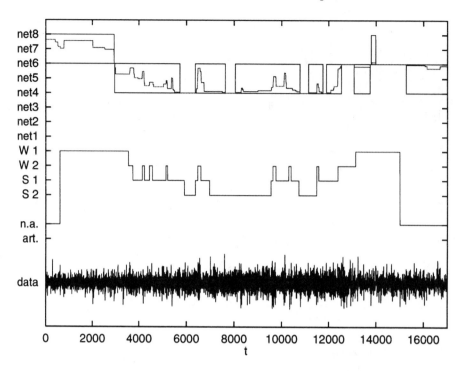

Figure 2: *Comparison of the drift segmentation obtained by the algorithm (upper plot), and a manual segmentation by a medical expert (middle). Only a single-channel EEG recording (occipital-1, time resolution 0.1s) of an afternoon nap is given for the algorithmic approach, while the manual segmentation is based on all available measurements. In the manual analysis, $W1$ and $W2$ indicate two wake-states (eyes open/closed), and $S1$ and $S2$ indicate sleep stage I and II, respectively. (n.a.: no assessment, art.: artifacts)*

nets, 6 and 8, performs the best reconstruction of the EEG dynamics. Then, at $t = 3000$ (300s), there starts a drift to net 4, which apparently represents the dynamics of sleep stage II (S2). Interestingly, sleep stage I (S1) is not represented by a separate net but by a linear mixture of net 4 and net 6, with much more weight on net 4. Thus, the process of falling asleep is represented as a drift from the state of being awake directly to sleep stage II.

During sleep there are several wake-up spikes indicated in the manual segmentation. At least the last four are also clearly indicated in the drift segmentation, as drifts back to net 6. Furthermore, the detection of the final arousal after $t = 12000$ (1200s) is in good accordance with the manual segmentation: there is a fast drift back to net 6 at that point.

Considering the fact that our method is based only on the recording of a single EEG channel and does not use any medical expert knowledge, the drift algorithm is in remarkable accordance with the assessment of the medical expert. Moreover, it resolves the dynamical structure of the signal to more detail. For a more comprehensive analysis of wake/sleep data, we refer to our forthcoming publication [3].

6 Summary and Discussion

We presented a method for the unsupervised segmentation and identification of nonstationary drifting dynamics. It applies to time series where the dynamics is drifting or switching between different operating modes. An application to physiological wake/sleep data (EEG) demonstrates that drift can be found in natural systems. It is therefore important to consider this aspect of data description.

In the case of wake/sleep data, where the physiological state transitions are far from being understood, we can extract the shape of the dynamical drift from wake to sleep in an unsupervised manner. By applying this new data analysis method, we hope to gain more insights into the underlying physiological processes. Our future work is therefore dedicated to a comprehensive analysis of large sets of physiological wake/sleep recordings. We expect, however, that our method will be also applicable in many other fields.

Acknowledgements: We acknowledge support of the DFG (grant Ja379/51) and we would like to thank J. Rittweger for the EEG data and for fruitful discussions.

References

[1] Jacobs, R.A., Jordan, M.A., Nowlan, S.J., Hinton, G.E. (1991). Adaptive Mixtures of Local Experts, *Neural Computation* **3**, 79–87.

[2] Kohlmorgen, J., Müller, K.-R., Pawelzik, K. (1995). Improving short-term prediction with competing experts. ICANN'95, EC2 & Cie, Paris, 2:215–220.

[3] Kohlmorgen, J., Müller, K.-R., Rittweger, J., Pawelzik, K., in preparation.

[4] Mackey, M., Glass, L. (1977). Oscillation and Chaos in a Physiological Control System, Science **197**, 287.

[5] Moody, J., Darken, C. (1989). Fast Learning in Networks of Locally-Tuned Processing Units. *Neural Computation* **1**, 281–294.

[6] Müller, K.-R., Kohlmorgen, J., Pawelzik, K. (1995). Analysis of Switching Dynamics with Competing Neural Networks, *IEICE Trans. on Fundamentals of Electronics, Communications and Computer Sc.*, E78-A, No.10, 1306–1315.

[7] Müller, K.-R., Kohlmorgen, J., Rittweger, J., Pawelzik, K. (1995). Analysing Physiological Data from the Wake-Sleep State Transition with Competing Predictors, NOLTA'95: Symposium on Nonlinear Theory and its Appl., 223–226.

[8] Pawelzik, K., Kohlmorgen, J., Müller, K.-R. (1996). Annealed Competition of Experts for a Segmentation and Classification of Switching Dynamics, *Neural Computation*, **8:2**, 342–358.

[9] Rabiner, L.R. (1988). A Tutorial on Hidden Markov Models and Selected Applications in Speech Recognition. In *Readings in Speech Recognition*, ed. A. Waibel, K. Lee, 267–296. San Mateo: Morgan Kaufmann, 1990.

[10] Takens, F. (1981). Detecting Strange Attractors in Turbulence. In: Rand, D., Young, L.-S., (Eds.), *Dynamical Systems and Turbulence*, Springer Lecture Notes in Mathematics, **898**, 366.

[11] Weigend, A.S., Gershenfeld, N.A. (Eds.) (1994). *Time Series Prediction: Forecasting the Future and Understanding the Past*, Addison-Wesley.

Bayesian Robustification for Audio Visual Fusion

Javier Movellan *
movellan@cogsci.ucsd.edu
Department of Cognitive Science
University of California, San Diego
La Jolla, CA 92092-0515

Paul Mineiro
pmineiro@cogsci.ucsd.edu
Department of Cognitive Science
University of California, San Diego
La Jolla, CA 92092-0515

Abstract

We discuss the problem of catastrophic fusion in multimodal recognition systems. This problem arises in systems that need to fuse different channels in non-stationary environments. Practice shows that when recognition modules within each modality are tested in contexts inconsistent with their assumptions, their influence on the fused product tends to increase, with catastrophic results. We explore a principled solution to this problem based upon Bayesian ideas of competitive models and inference robustification: each sensory channel is provided with simple white-noise context models, and the perceptual hypothesis and context are jointly estimated. Consequently, context deviations are interpreted as changes in white noise contamination strength, automatically adjusting the influence of the module. The approach is tested on a fixed lexicon automatic audiovisual speech recognition problem with very good results.

1 Introduction

In this paper we address the problem of catastrophic fusion in automatic multimodal recognition systems. We explore a principled solution based on the Bayesian ideas of competitive models and inference robustification (Clark & Yuille, 1990; Box, 1980; O'Hagan, 1994). For concreteness, consider an audiovisual car telephony task which we will simulate in later sections. The task is to recognize spoken phone numbers based on input from a camera and a microphone. We want the recognition system to work on environments with non-stationary statistical properties: at times the video signal (V) may be relatively clean and the audio signal (A) may be contaminated by sources like the radio, the engine, and friction with the road. At other times the A signal may be more reliable than the V signal, e.g., the radio is off, but the talker's mouth is partially occluded. Ideally we want the audio-visual system to combine the A and V sources optimally given the conditions at hand, e.g., give more weight to whichever channel is more reliable at that time. At a minimum we expect that for a wide variety of contexts, the performance after fusion should not be worse than the independent unimodal systems (Bernstein & Benoit, 1996). When component modules can significantly outperform the overall system after fusion, *catastrophic fusion* is said to have occurred.

---

* To whom correspondence should be addressed.

Fixed vocabulary audiovisual speech recognition (AVSR) systems typically consist of two independent modules, one dedicated to A signals and one to V signals (Bregler, Hild, Manke & Waibel, 1993; Wolff, Prasad, Stork & Hennecke, 1994; Adjondani & Benoit, 1996; Movellan & Chadderdon, 1996). From a Bayesian perspective this modularity reflects an assumption of conditional independence of A and V signals (i.e., the likelihood function factorizes)

$$p(x_a x_v | \omega_i \lambda_a \lambda_v) \propto p(x_a | \omega_i \lambda_a) p(x_v | \omega_i \lambda_v), \tag{1}$$

where x_a and x_v are the audio and video data, ω_i is a perceptual interpretation of the data (e.g., the word "one") and $\{\lambda_a, \lambda_v\}$ are the audio and video models according to which these probabilities are calculated, e.g., a hidden Markov model, a neural network, or an exemplar model. Training is also typically modularized: the A module is trained to maximize the likelihood of a sample of A signals while the V module is trained on the corresponding sample of V signals. At test time new data are presented to the system and each module typically outputs the log probability of its input given each perceptual alternative. Assuming conditional independence, Bayes' rule calls for an affine combination of modules

$$\begin{aligned}\hat{w} &= \underset{\omega_i}{\operatorname{argmax}} \{\log p(\omega_i | x_a x_v \lambda_a \lambda_v)\} \\ &= \underset{\omega_i}{\operatorname{argmax}} \{\log p(x_a | \omega_i \lambda_a) + \log p(x_v | \omega_i \lambda_v) + \log p(\omega_i)\} \end{aligned} \tag{2}$$

where $\hat{w}$ is the interpretation chosen by the system, and $p(w_i)$ is the prior probability of each alternative. This fusion rule is optimal in the sense that it minimizes the expected error: no other fusion rule produces smaller error rates, provided the models $\{\lambda_a, \lambda_v\}$ and the assumption of conditional independence are correct.

Unfortunately a naive application of Bayes' rule to AVSR produces catastrophic fusion. The A and V modules make assumptions about the signals they receive, either explicitly, e.g., a well defined statistical model, or implicitly, e.g., a black-box trained with a particular data sample. In our notation these assumptions are reflected by the fact that the log-likelihoods are conditional on models: $\{\lambda_a, \lambda_v\}$. The fact that modules make assumptions implies that they will operate correctly only within a restricted *context*, i.e, the collection of situations that meet the assumptions. In practice one typically finds that Bayes' rule assigns more weight to modules operating outside their valid context, the opposite of what is desired.

2   Competitive Models and Bayesian Robustification

Clark and Yuille (1990) and Yuille and Bulthoff (1996) analyzed information integration in sensory systems from a Bayesian perspective. Modularity is justified in their view by the need to make assumptions that disambiguate the data available to the perceptual system (Clark & Yuille, 1990, p. 5). However, this produces modules which are valid only within certain contexts. The solution proposed by Clark and Yuille (1990) is the creation of an ensemble of models each of which specializes on a restricted context and automatically checks whether the context is correct. The hope is that by working with such an ensemble of models, robustness under a variety of contexts can be achieved (Clark & Yuille, 1990, p. 13).

Box (1980) investigated the problem of robust statistical inference from a Bayesian perspective. He proposed extending inference models with additional "nuisance" parameters σ, a process he called Bayesian robustification. The idea is to replace an implicit assumption about the specific value of σ with a prior distribution over σ, representing uncertainty about that parameter.

The approach here combines the ideas of competitive models and robustification. Each of the channels in the multimodal recognition system is provided with extra parameters that represent non-stationary properties of the environment, what we call a context model. By doing so we effectively work with an infinite ensemble of models each of which compete on-line to explain the data. As we will see later even unsophisticated context models provide superior performance when the environment is non-stationary.

We redefine the estimation problem as simultaneously choosing the most probable A and V context parameters and the most probable perceptual interpretation

$$\hat{w} = \operatorname*{argmax}_{\omega_i} \left\{ \max_{\sigma_a, \sigma_v} p(\omega_i \sigma_a \sigma_v | x_a x_v \lambda_a \lambda_v) \right\} \tag{3}$$

where σ_a and σ_v are the context parameters for the audio and visual channels and ω_i are the different perceptual interpretations. One way to think of this joint decision approach is that we let all context models compete and we let only the most probable context models have an influence on the fused percept. Hereafter we refer to this approach as *competitive fusion*.

Assuming conditional independence of the audio and video data and uninformative priors for (σ_a, σ_v), we have

$$\hat{w} = \operatorname*{argmax}_{\omega_i} \left\{ \log p(\omega_i) + \left[\max_{\sigma_a} \log p(x_a | \omega_i \sigma_a \lambda_a) \right] + \left[\max_{\sigma_v} \log p(x_v | \omega_i \sigma_v \lambda_v) \right] \right\}. \tag{4}$$

Thus conditional independence allows a modular implementation of competitive fusion, i.e., the A and V channels do not need to talk to each other until the time to make a joint decision, as follows.

1. For each ω_i obtain conditional estimates of the context parameters for the audio and video signals:

$$\hat{\sigma}^2_{a|\omega_i} \triangleq \operatorname*{argmax}_{\sigma_a} \left\{ \log p(x_a | \omega_i \sigma_a \lambda_a) \right\}, \tag{5}$$

and

$$\hat{\sigma}^2_{v|\omega_i} \triangleq \operatorname*{argmax}_{\sigma_v} \left\{ \log p(x_v | \omega_i \sigma_v \lambda_v) \right\}. \tag{6}$$

2. Find the best ω_i using the conditional context estimates.

$$\hat{w} = \operatorname*{argmax}_{\omega_i} \left\{ \log p(\omega_i) + \log p(x_a | \omega_i \hat{\sigma}_{a|\omega_i} \lambda_a) + \log p(x_v | \omega_i \hat{\sigma}_{v|\omega_i} \lambda_v) \right\} \tag{7}$$

3 Application to AVSR

Competitive fusion can be easily applied to Hidden Markov Models (HMM), an architecture closely related to stochastic neural networks and arguably the most successful for AVSR. Typical hidden Markov models used in AVSR are defined by

- Markovian state dynamics: $p(q_{t+1}|\underline{q}_t) = p(q_{t+1}|q_t)$, where q_t is the state at time t and $\underline{q}_t = (q_1, \cdots q_t)$,

- Conditionally independent sensor models linking observations to states $f(x_t|q_t)$, typically a mixture of multivariate Gaussian densities

$$f(x_t|q_t) = \sum_i p(m_i|q_t)(2\pi)^{-N/2} |\Sigma|^{-1/2} \exp(d(x_t, q_t, \mu_i, \Sigma)), \tag{8}$$

where N is the dimensionality of the data, m_i is the mixture label, $p(m_i|q_t)$ is the mixture distribution for state q_t, μ_i is the centroid for mixture m_i, Σ is a covariance matrix, and d is the Mahalanobis norm

$$d(x_t, q_t, \mu_i, \Sigma) = (x_t - \mu_i)'\Sigma^{-1}(x_a - \mu_i). \tag{9}$$

The approach explored here consists on modeling contextual changes as variations on the variance parameters. This corresponds to modeling non-stationary properties of the environments as variations in white noise power within each channel. Competitive fusion calls for on-line maximization of the variance parameters at the same time we optimize with respect to the response alternative.

$$\hat{w} = \underset{\omega_i}{\operatorname{argmax}} \left\{ \log p(\omega_i) + \left[\max_{\Sigma_a} \log p(x_a|\omega_i\Sigma_a\lambda_a) \right] + \left[\max_{\Sigma_v} \log p(x_v|\omega_i\Sigma_v\lambda_v) \right] \right\}. \tag{10}$$

The maximization with respect to the variances can be easily integrated into standard HMM packages by simply applying the EM learning algorithm (Dampster, Laird & Rubin, 1977) on the variance parameters at test time. Thus the only difference between the standard approach and competitive fusion is that we retrain the variance parameters of each HMM at test time. In practice this training takes only one or two iterations of the EM algorithm and can be done on-line. We tested this approach on the following AVSR problem.

Training database We used Tulips1 (Movellan, 1995) a database consisting of 934 images of 9 male and 3 female undergraduate students from the Cognitive Science Department at the University of California, San Diego. For each of these, two samples were taken for each of the digits "one" through "four". Thus, the total database consists of 96 digit utterances. The specifics of this database are explained in (Movellan, 1995). The database is available at http://cogsci.ucsd.edu.

Visual processing We have tried a wide variety of visual processing approaches on this database, including decomposition with local Gaussian templates (Movellan, 1995), PCA-based templates (Gray, Movellan & Sejnowski, 1997), and Gabor energy templates (Movellan & Prayaga, 1996). To date, best performance was achieved with the local Gaussian approach. Each frame of the video track is soft-thresholded and symmetrized along the vertical axis, and a temporal difference frame is obtained by subtracting the previous symmetrized frame from the current symmetrized frame. We calculate the inner-products between the symmetrized images and a set of basis images. Our basis images were 10x15 shifted Gaussian kernels with a standard deviation of 3 pixels. The loadings of the symmetrized image and the differential image are combined to form the final observation frame. Each of these composite frames has 300 dimensions (2x10x15). The process is explained in more detail in Movellan (1995).

Auditory processing LPC/cepstral analysis is used for the auditory front-end. First, the auditory signal is passed through a first-order emphasizer to spectrally flatten it. Then the signal is separated into non-overlapping frames at 30 frames per second. This is done so that there are an equal number of visual and auditory feature vectors for each utterance, which are then synchronized with each other. On each frame we perform the standard LPC/cepstral analysis. Each 30 msec auditory frame is characterized by 26 features: 12 cepstral coefficients, 12 delta-cepstrals, 1 log-power, and 1 delta-log-power. Each of the 26 features is encoded with 8-bit accuracy.

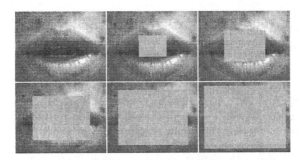

Figure 1: Examples of the different occlusion levels, from left to right: 0%, 10%, 20%, 40%, 60%, 80%. Percentages are in terms of area.

Recognition Engine   In previous work (Chadderdon & Movellan, 1995) a wide variety of HMM architectures were tested on this database including architectures that did not assume conditional independence. Optimal performance was found with independent A and V modules using variance matrices of the form σI, where σ is a scalar and I the identity matrix. The best A models had 5 states and 7 mixtures per state and the best V models had 3 states and 3 mixtures per state. We also determined the optimal weight of A and V modules. Optimal performance is obtained by weighting the output of V times 0.18.

Factorial Contamination Experiment   In this experiment we used the previously optimized architecture and compared its performance under 64 different conditions using the standard and the competitive fusion approaches. We used a $2 \times 8 \times 8$ factorial design, the first factor being the fusion rule, and the second and third factors the context in the audio and video channels. To our knowledge this is the first time an AVSR system is tested with a factorial experimental design with both A and V contaminated at various levels. The independent variables were:

1. Fusion rule: Classical, and competitive fusion.
2. Audio Context: Inexistent, clean, or contaminated at one of the following signal to noise ratios: 12 Db, 6 Db, 0 Db, -6 Db, -12 Db and -100 Db. The contamination was done with audio digitally sampled from the interior of a car while running on a busy highway with the doors open and the radio on a talk-show station.
3. Video Context: Inexistent, clean or occluded by a grey level patch. The percentages of visual area occupied by the patch were 10%, 20%, 40%, 60%, 80% and 100% (see Figure 1).

The dependent variable was performance on the digit recognition task evaluated in terms of generalization to new speakers. In all cases training was done with clean signals and testing was done with one of the 64 contexts under study. Since the training sample is small, generalization performance was estimated using a jackknife procedure (Efron, 1982). Models were trained with 11 subjects, leaving a different subject out for generalization testing. The entire procedure was repeated 12 times, each time leaving a different subject out for testing. Statistics of generalization performance are thus based on 96 generalization trials (4 digits × 12 subjects × 2 observations per subject). Standard statistical tests were used to compare the classical and competitive context rules.

The results of this experiment are displayed in Table 1. Note how the experiment replicates the phenomenon of catastrophic fusion. With the classic approach, when one of the channels is contaminated, performance after fusion can be significantly

Performance with Competitive Fusion

Video	None	Clean	12 Db	6 Db	0 Db	-6 Db	-12 Db	-100 Db
None	—	95.83	95.83	90.62	80.20	67.70	42.70	19.80
Clean	84.37	97.92	97.92	94.80	90.62	89.58	81.25	82.20
10%	73.95	93.75	93.75	94.79	87.50	80.20	71.87	64.58
20%	62.50	96.87	96.87	94.79	89.58	80.20	62.50	41.66
40%	37.50	93.75	89.58	87.50	83.30	70.83	43.75	30.20
60%	34.37	93.75	91.66	88.54	82.29	65.62	42.70	26.04
80%	27.00	95.83	90.62	86.45	79.16	64.58	46.87	25.00
100%	25.00	93.75	92.71	84.37	78.12	63.54	44.79	26.04

Performance with Classic Fusion

Video	None	Clean	12 Db	6 Db	0 Db	-6 Db	-12 Db	-100 Db
None	—	95.83	94.79	89.58	79.16	65.62	40.62	20.83
Clean	86.45	98.95	96.87	95.83	93.75	87.50	79.16	70.83
10%	73.95	93.75	93.75	93.75	89.58	79.16	70.83	52.58
20%	54.16	89.58	84.41	84.37	84.37	75.00	51.00	43.00
40%	29.16	81.25	78.12	78.12	67.20	52.08	38.54	34.37
60%	32.29	77.08	77.08	72.91	62.50	47.91	37.50	29.16
80%	29.16	70.83	72.91	68.75	54.16	44.79	33.83	28.12
100%	25.00	61.46	61.45	58.33	51.04	42.70	38.54	29.16

Table 1: Average generalization performance with standard and competitive fusion. Boxed cells indicate a statistically significant difference $\alpha = 0.05$ between the two fusion approaches.

worse than performance with the clean channel alone. For example, when the audio is clean, the performance of the audio-only system is 95.83%. When combined with bad video (100% occlusion), this performance drops down to 61.46%, a statistically significant difference, $F(1,11) = 132.0$, $p < 10^{-6}$. Using competitive fusion, the performance of the joint system is 93.75%, which is not significantly different from the performance of the A system only, $F(1,11) = 2.4$, $p = 0.15$. The table shows in boxes the regions for which the classic and competitive fusion approaches were significantly different ($\alpha = 0.05$). Contrary to the classic approach, the competitive approach behaves robustly in all tested conditions.

4 Discussion

Catastrophic fusion may occur when the environment is non-stationary forcing modules to operate outside their assumed context. The reason for this problem is that in the absence of a context model, deviations from the expected context are interpreted as information about the different perceptual interpretations instead of information about contextual changes. We explored a principled solution to this problem inspired by the Bayesian ideas of robustification (Box, 1980) and competitive models (Clark & Yuille, 1990). Each module was provided with simple white-noise context models and the most probable context and perceptual hypothesis were jointly estimated. Consequently, context deviations are interpreted as changes in the white noise contamination strength, automatically adjusting the influence of the module. The approach worked very well on a fixed lexicon AVSR problem.

References

Adjondani, A. & Benoit, C. (1996). On the Integration of Auditory and Visual Parameters in an HMM-based ASR. In D. G. Stork & M. E. Hennecke (Eds.), *Speechreading by Humans and Machines: Models, Systems, and Applications*, pages 461–471. New York: NATO/Springer-Verlag.

Bernstein, L. & Benoit, C. (1996). For Speech Perception Three Senses are Better than One. In *Proc. of the 4th Int. Conf. on Spoken Language Processing*, Philadelphia, PA., USA.

Box, G. E. P. (1980). Sampling and Bayes inference in scientific modeling. *J. Roy. Stat. Soc., A., 143*, 383–430.

Bregler, C., Hild, H., Manke, S., & Waibel, A. (1993). Improving Connected Letter Recognition by Lipreading. In *Proc. Int. Conf. on Acoust., Speech, and Signal Processing*, volume 1, pages 557–560, Minneapolis. IEEE.

Bülthoff, H. H. & Yuille, A. L. (1996). A Bayesian framework for the integration of visual modules. In T. Inui & J. L. McClelland (Eds.), *Attention and performance XVI: Information integration in perception and communication*, pages 49–70. Cambridge, MA: MIT Press.

Chadderdon, G. & Movellan, J. (1995). Testing for Channel Independence in Bimodal Speech Recognition. In *Proceedings of 2nd Joint Symposium on Neural Computation*, pages 84–90.

Clark, J. J. & Yuille, A. L. (1990). *Data Fusion for Sensory Information Processing Systems*. Boston: Kluwer Academic Publishers.

Dampster, A. P., Laird, N. M., & Rubin, D. B. (1977). Maximum likelihood from incomplete data via the EM algorithm. *J. Roy. Stat. Soc., 39*, 1–38.

Efron, A. (1982). *The jacknife, the bootstrap and other resampling plans*. Philadelphia, Pennsylvania: SIAM.

Gray, M. S., Movellan, J. R., & Sejnowski, T. (1997). Dynamic features for visual speechreading: A systematic comparison. In Mozer, Jordan, & Petsche (Eds.), *Advances in Neural Information Processing Systems*, volume 9. MIT Press.

Movellan, J. R. (1995). Visual speech recognition with stochastic neural networks. In G. Tesauro, D. Touretzky, & T. Leen (Eds.), *Advances in neural information processing systems*. Cambridge,Massacusetts: MIT Press.

Movellan, J. R. & Chadderdon, G. (1996). Channel Separability in the Audio Visual Integration of Speech: A Bayesian Approach. In D. G. Stork & M. E. Hennecke (Eds.), *Speechreading by Humans and Machines: Models, Systems, and Applications*, pages 473–487. New York: NATO/Springer-Verlag.

Movellan, J. R. & Prayaga, R. S. (1996). Gabor Mosaics: A description of Local Orientation Statistics with Applications to Machine Perception. In G. W. Cottrell (Ed.), *proceedings of the Eight Annual Conference of the Cognitive Science Society*, page 817. Mahwah, New Jersey: LEA.

O'Hagan, A. (1994). *Kendall's Advanced Theory of Statistics: Volume 2B, Bayesian Inference*. volume 2B. Cambridge University Press.

Wolff, G. J., Prasad, K. V., Stork, D. G., & Hennecke, M. E. (1994). Lipreading by Neural Networks: Visual Preprocessing, Learning and Sensory Integration. In J. D. Cowan, G. Tesauro, & J. Alspector (Eds.), *Advances in Neural Information Processing Systems*, volume 6, pages 1027–1034. Morgan Kaufmann.

Modeling acoustic correlations by factor analysis

Lawrence Saul and Mazin Rahim
{lsaul,mazin}@research.att.com
AT&T Labs — Research
180 Park Ave, D-130
Florham Park, NJ 07932

Abstract

Hidden Markov models (HMMs) for automatic speech recognition rely on high dimensional feature vectors to summarize the short-time properties of speech. Correlations between features can arise when the speech signal is non-stationary or corrupted by noise. We investigate how to model these correlations using factor analysis, a statistical method for dimensionality reduction. Factor analysis uses a small number of parameters to model the covariance structure of high dimensional data. These parameters are estimated by an Expectation-Maximization (EM) algorithm that can be embedded in the training procedures for HMMs. We evaluate the *combined* use of mixture densities and factor analysis in HMMs that recognize alphanumeric strings. Holding the total number of parameters fixed, we find that these methods, properly combined, yield better models than either method on its own.

1 Introduction

Hidden Markov models (HMMs) for automatic speech recognition[1] rely on high dimensional feature vectors to summarize the short-time, acoustic properties of speech. Though front-ends vary from recognizer to recognizer, the spectral information in each frame of speech is typically codified in a feature vector with thirty or more dimensions. In most systems, these vectors are conditionally modeled by mixtures of Gaussian probability density functions (PDFs). In this case, the correlations between different features are represented in two ways[2]: implicitly by the use of two or more mixture components, and explicitly by the non-diagonal elements in each covariance matrix. Naturally, these strategies for modeling correlations—implicit versus explicit—involve tradeoffs in accuracy, speed, and memory. This paper examines these tradeoffs using the statistical method of factor analysis.

The present work is motivated by the following observation. Currently, most HMM-based recognizers do not include any explicit modeling of correlations; that is to say—conditioned on the hidden states, acoustic features are modeled by mixtures of Gaussian PDFs with *diagonal* covariance matrices. The reasons for this practice are well known. The use of full covariance matrices imposes a heavy computational burden, making it difficult to achieve real-time recognition. Moreover, one rarely has enough data to (reliably) estimate full covariance matrices. Some of these disadvantages can be overcome by parameter-tying[3]—e.g., sharing the covariance matrices across different states or models. But parameter-tying has its own drawbacks: it considerably complicates the training procedure, and it requires some artistry to know which states should and should not be tied.

Unconstrained and diagonal covariance matrices clearly represent two extreme choices for the hidden Markov modeling of speech. The statistical method of factor analysis[4, 5] represents a compromise between these two extremes. The idea behind factor analysis is to map systematic variations of the data into a lower dimensional subspace. This enables one to represent, in a very compact way, the covariance matrices for high dimensional data. These matrices are expressed in terms of a small number of parameters that model the most significant correlations without incurring much overhead in time or memory. Maximum likelihood estimates of these parameters are obtained by an Expectation-Maximization (EM) algorithm that can be embedded in the training procedures for HMMs.

In this paper we investigate the use of factor analysis in continuous density HMMs. Applying factor analysis at the state and mixture component level[6, 7] results in a powerful form of dimensionality reduction, one tailored to the local properties of speech. Briefly, the organization of this paper is as follows. In section 2, we review the method of factor analysis and describe what makes it attractive for large problems in speech recognition. In section 3, we report experiments on the speaker-independent recognition of connected alpha-digits. Finally, in section 4, we present our conclusions as well as ideas for future research.

2   Factor analysis

Factor analysis is a linear method for dimensionality reduction of Gaussian random variables[4, 5]. Many forms of dimensionality reduction (including those implemented as neural networks) can be understood as variants of factor analysis. There are particularly close ties to methods based on principal components analysis (PCA) and the notion of tangent distance[8]. The combined use of mixture densities and factor analysis—resulting in a *non-linear* form of dimensionality reduction—was first applied by Hinton et al[6] to the modeling of handwritten digits. The EM procedure for mixtures of factor analyzers was subsequently derived by Ghahramani et al[7]. Below we describe the method of factor analysis for Gaussian random variables, then show how it can be applied to the hidden Markov modeling of speech.

2.1   Gaussian model

Let $\mathbf{x} \in \mathcal{R}^D$ denote a high dimensional Gaussian random variable. For simplicity, we will assume that $\mathbf{x}$ has zero mean. If the number of dimensions, D, is very large, it may be prohibitively expensive to estimate, store, multiply, or invert a full covariance matrix. The idea behind factor analysis is to find a subspace of much lower dimension, $f \ll D$, that captures most of the variations in $\mathbf{x}$. To this end, let $\mathbf{z} \in \mathcal{R}^f$ denote a low dimensional Gaussian random variable with zero mean and identity covariance matrix:

$$P(\mathbf{z}) = \frac{1}{(2\pi)^{f/2}} e^{-z^2/2}. \tag{1}$$

We now imagine that the variable $\mathbf{x}$ is generated by a random process in which $\mathbf{z}$ is a latent (or hidden) variable; the elements of $\mathbf{z}$ are known as the *factors*. Let Λ denote an arbitrary $D \times f$ matrix, and let Ψ denote a diagonal, positive-definite $D \times D$ matrix. We imagine that $\mathbf{x}$ is generated by sampling $\mathbf{z}$ from eq. (1), computing the D-dimensional vector $\Lambda \mathbf{z}$, then adding independent Gaussian noise (with variances Ψ_{ii}) to each component of this vector. The matrix Λ is known as the *factor loading* matrix. The relation between $\mathbf{x}$ and $\mathbf{z}$ is captured by the conditional distribution:

$$P(\mathbf{x}|\mathbf{z}) = \frac{|\Psi|^{-1/2}}{(2\pi)^{D/2}} e^{-\frac{1}{2}(\mathbf{x}-\Lambda\mathbf{z})^T \Psi^{-1}(\mathbf{x}-\Lambda\mathbf{z})}. \tag{2}$$

The marginal distribution for $\mathbf{x}$ is found by integrating out the hidden variable $\mathbf{z}$. The calculation is straightforward because both $P(\mathbf{z})$ and $P(\mathbf{x}|\mathbf{z})$ are Gaussian:

$$P(\mathbf{x}) = \int d\mathbf{z} \, P(\mathbf{x}|\mathbf{z})P(\mathbf{z}) \tag{3}$$

$$= \frac{|\Psi + \Lambda\Lambda^T|^{-1/2}}{(2\pi)^{D/2}} e^{-\frac{1}{2}\mathbf{x}^T(\Psi+\Lambda\Lambda^T)^{-1}\mathbf{x}}. \tag{4}$$

From eq. (4), we see that $\mathbf{x}$ is normally distributed with mean zero and covariance matrix $\Psi + \Lambda\Lambda^T$. It follows that when the diagonal elements of Ψ are small, most of the variation in $\mathbf{x}$ occurs in the subspace spanned by the columns of Λ. The variances Ψ_{ii} measure the typical size of componentwise fluctuations outside this subspace.

Covariance matrices of the form $\Psi + \Lambda\Lambda^T$ have a number of useful properties. Most importantly, they are expressed in terms of a small number of parameters, namely the $D(f+1)$ non-zero elements of Λ and Ψ. If $f \ll D$, then storing Λ and Ψ requires much less memory than storing a full covariance matrix. Likewise, estimating Λ and Ψ also requires much less data than estimating a full covariance matrix. Covariance matrices of this form can be efficiently inverted using the matrix inversion lemma[9],

$$(\Psi + \Lambda\Lambda^T)^{-1} = \Psi^{-1} - \Psi^{-1}\Lambda(I + \Lambda^T\Psi^{-1}\Lambda)^{-1}\Lambda^T\Psi^{-1} \tag{5}$$

where I is the $f \times f$ identity matrix. This decomposition also allows one to compute the probability $P(\mathbf{x})$ with only $O(fD)$ multiplies, as opposed to the $O(D^2)$ multiplies that are normally required when the covariance matrix is non-diagonal.

Maximum likelihood estimates of the parameters Λ and Ψ are obtained by an EM procedure[4]. Let $\{\mathbf{x}_t\}$ denote a sample of data points (with mean zero). The EM procedure is an iterative procedure for maximizing the log-likelihood, $\sum_t \ln P(\mathbf{x}_t)$, with $P(\mathbf{x}_t)$ given by eq. (4). The E-step of this procedure is to compute:

$$Q(\Lambda', \Psi'; \Lambda, \Psi) = \sum_t \int d\mathbf{z} \, P(\mathbf{z}|\mathbf{x}_t, \Lambda, \Psi) \ln P(\mathbf{z}, \mathbf{x}_t|\Lambda', \Psi'). \tag{6}$$

The right hand side of eq. (6) depends on Λ and Ψ through the statistics[7]:

$$E[\mathbf{z}|\mathbf{x}_t] = [I + \Lambda^T\Psi^{-1}\Lambda]^{-1}\Lambda^T\Psi^{-1}\mathbf{x}_t, \tag{7}$$

$$E[\mathbf{z}\mathbf{z}^T|\mathbf{x}_t] = [I + \Lambda^T\Psi^{-1}\Lambda]^{-1} + E[\mathbf{z}|\mathbf{x}_t]E[\mathbf{z}^T|\mathbf{x}_t]. \tag{8}$$

Here, $E[\cdot|\mathbf{x}_t]$ denotes an average with respect to the posterior distribution, $P(\mathbf{z}|\mathbf{x}_t, \Lambda, \Psi)$. The M-step of the EM algorithm is to maximize the right hand side of eq. (6) with respect to Ψ' and Λ'. This leads to the iterative updates[7]:

$$\Lambda' = \left(\sum_t \mathbf{x}_t \mathrm{E}[\mathbf{z}^T|\mathbf{x}_t]\right)\left(\sum_t \mathrm{E}[\mathbf{z}\mathbf{z}^T|\mathbf{x}_t]\right)^{-1}, \tag{9}$$

$$\Psi' = \mathrm{diag}\left\{\frac{1}{N}\sum_t [\mathbf{x}_t\mathbf{x}_t^T - \Lambda'\mathrm{E}[\mathbf{z}|\mathbf{x}_t]\mathbf{x}_t^T]\right\}, \tag{10}$$

where N is the number of data points, and Ψ' is constrained to be purely diagonal. These updates are guaranteed to converge monotonically to a (possibly local) maximum of the log-likelihood.

2.2   Hidden Markov modeling of speech

Consider a continuous density HMM whose feature vectors, conditioned on the hidden states, are modeled by mixtures of Gaussian PDFs. If the dimensionality of the feature space is very large, we can make use of the parameterization in eq. (4). Each mixture component thus obtains its own means, variances, and factor loading matrix. Taken together, these amount to a total of $C(f+2)D$ parameters per mixture model, where C is the number of mixture components, f the number of factors, and D the dimensionality of the feature space. Note that these models capture feature correlations in two ways: implicitly, by using two or more mixture components, and explicitly, by using one or more factors. Intuitively, one expects the mixture components to model *discrete* types of variability (e.g., whether the speaker is male or female), and the factors to model *continuous* types of variability (e.g., due to coarticulation or noise). Both types of variability are important for building accurate models of speech.

It is straightforward to integrate the EM algorithm for factor analysis into the training of HMMs. Suppose that $\mathcal{S} = \{\mathbf{x}_t\}$ represents a sequence of acoustic vectors. The forward-backward procedure enables one to compute the posterior probability, $\gamma_t^{sc} = P(s_t = s, c_t = c|\mathcal{S})$, that the HMM used state s and mixture component c at time t. The updates for the matrices Λ^{sc} and Ψ^{sc} (within each state and mixture component) have essentially the same form as eqs. (9-10), except that now each observation $\mathbf{x}_t$ is weighted by the posterior probability, γ_t^{sc}. Additionally, one must take into account that the mixture components have non-zero means[7]. A complete derivation of these updates (along with many additional details) will be given in a longer version of this paper.

Clearly, an important consideration when applying factor analysis to speech is the choice of acoustic features. A standard choice—and the one we use in our experiments—is a thirty-nine dimensional feature vector that consists of twelve cepstral coefficients (with first and second derivatives) and the normalized log-energy (with first and second derivatives). There are known to be correlations[2] between these features, especially between the different types of coefficients (e.g., cepstrum and delta-cepstrum). While these correlations have motivated our use of factor analysis, it is worth emphasizing that the method applies to arbitrary feature vectors. Indeed, whatever features are used to summarize the short-time properties of speech, one expects correlations to arise from coarticulation, background noise, speaker idiosyncrasies, etc.

3   Experiments

Continuous density HMMs with diagonal and factored covariance matrices were trained to recognize alphanumeric strings (e.g., N Z 3 V J 4 E 3 U 2). Highly

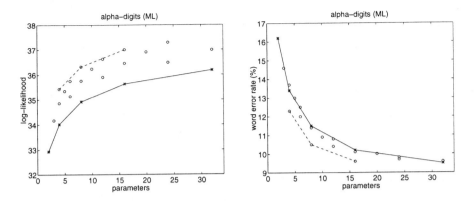

Figure 1: Plots of log-likelihood scores and word error rates on the test set versus the number of parameters per mixture model (divided by the number of features). The stars indicate models with diagonal covariance matrices; the circles indicate models with factor analysis. The dashed lines connect the recognizers in table 2.

confusable letters such as B/V, C/Z, and M/N make this a challenging problem in speech recognition. The training and test data were recorded over a telephone network and consisted of 14622 and 7255 utterances, respectively. Recognizers were built from 285 left-to-right HMMs trained by maximum likelihood estimation; each HMM modeled a context-dependent sub-word unit. Testing was done with a free grammar network (i.e., no grammar constraints). We ran several experiments, varying both the number of mixture components and the number of factors. The goal was to determine the best model of acoustic feature correlations.

Table 1 summarizes the results of these experiments. The columns from left to right show the number of mixture components, the number of factors, the number of parameters per mixture model (divided by the feature dimension), the word error rates (including insertion, deletion, and substitution errors) on the test set, the average log-likelihood per frame of speech on the test set, and the CPU time to recognize twenty test utterances (on an SGI R4000). Not surprisingly, the word accuracies and likelihood scores increase with the number of modeling parameters; likewise, so do the CPU times. The most interesting comparisons are between models with the same number of parameters—e.g., four mixture components with no factors versus two mixture components with two factors. The left graph in figure 1 shows a plot of the average log-likelihood versus the number of parameters per mixture model; the stars and circles in this plot indicate models with and without diagonal covariance matrices. One sees quite clearly from this plot that given a *fixed* number of parameters, models with non-diagonal (factored) covariance matrices tend to have higher likelihoods. The right graph in figure 1 shows a similar plot of the word error rates versus the number of parameters. Here one does not see much difference; presumably, because HMMs are such poor models of speech to begin with, higher likelihoods do not necessarily translate into lower error rates. We will return to this point later.

It is worth noting that the above experiments used a *fixed* number of factors per mixture component. In fact, because the variability of speech is highly context-dependent, it makes sense to vary the number of factors, even across states within the same HMM. A simple heuristic is to adjust the number of factors depending on the amount of training data for each state (as determined by an initial segmentation of the training utterances). We found that this heuristic led to more pronounced

C	f	$C(f+2)$	word error (%)	log-likelihood	CPU time (sec)
1	0	2	16.2	32.9	25
1	1	3	14.6	34.2	30
1	2	4	13.7	34.9	30
1	3	5	13.0	35.3	38
1	4	6	12.5	35.8	39
2	0	4	13.4	34.0	30
2	1	6	12.0	35.1	44
2	2	8	11.4	35.8	48
2	3	10	10.9	36.2	61
2	4	12	10.8	36.6	67
4	0	8	11.5	34.9	46
4	1	12	10.4	35.9	80
4	2	16	10.1	36.5	93
4	3	20	10.0	36.9	132
4	4	24	9.8	37.3	153
8	0	16	10.2	35.6	93
8	1	24	9.7	36.5	179
8	2	32	9.6	37.0	226
16	0	32	9.5	36.2	222

Table 1: Results for different recognizers. The columns indicate the number of mixture components, the number of factors, the number of parameters per mixture model (divided by the number of features), the word error rates and average log-likelihood scores on the test set, and the CPU time to recognize twenty utterances.

C	f	$C(f+2)$	word error (%)	log-likelihood	CPU time (sec)
1	2	4	12.3	35.4	32
2	2	8	10.5	36.3	53
4	2	16	9.6	37.0	108

Table 2: Results for recognizers with variable numbers of factors; f denotes the *average* number of factors per mixture component.

differences in likelihood scores and error rates. In particular, substantial improvements were observed for three recognizers whose HMMs employed an *average* of two factors per mixture component; see the dashed lines in figure 1. Table 2 summarizes these results. The reader will notice that these recognizers are extremely competitive in all aspects of performance—accuracy, memory, and speed—with the baseline (zero factor) models in table 1.

4   Discussion

In this paper we have studied the combined use of mixture densities and factor analysis for speech recognition. This was done in the framework of hidden Markov modeling, where acoustic features are conditionally modeled by mixtures of Gaussian PDFs. We have shown that mixture densities and factor analysis are complementary means of modeling acoustic correlations. Moreover, when used together, they can lead to smaller, faster, and more accurate recognizers than either method on its own. (Compare the last lines of tables 1 and 2.)

Several issues deserve further investigation. First, we have seen that increases in likelihood scores do not always correspond to reductions in error rates. (This is a common occurrence in automatic speech recognition.) We are currently investigating *discriminative* methods[10] for training HMMs with factor analysis; the idea here is to optimize an objective function that more directly relates to the goal of minimizing classification errors. Second, it is important to extend our results to large vocabulary tasks in speech recognition. The extreme sparseness of data in these tasks makes factor analysis an appealing strategy for dimensionality reduction. Finally, there are other questions that need to be answered. Given a limited number of parameters, what is the best way to allocate them among factors *and* mixture components? Do the cepstral features used by HMMs throw away informative correlations in the speech signal? Could such correlations be better modeled by factor analysis? Answers to these questions can only lead to further improvements in overall performance.

Acknowledgements

We are grateful to A. Ljolje (AT&T Labs), Z. Ghahramani (University of Toronto) and H. Seung (Bell Labs) for useful discussions. We also thank P. Modi (AT&T Labs) for providing an initial segmentation of the training utterances.

References

[1] Rabiner, L., and Juang, B. (1993) *Fundamentals of Speech Recognition.* Englewood Cliffs: Prentice Hall.

[2] Ljolje, A. (1994) The importance of cepstral parameter correlations in speech recognition. *Computer Speech and Language* **8**:223-232.

[3] Bellegarda, J., and Nahamoo, D. (1990) Tied mixture continuous parameter modeling for speech recognition. *IEEE Transactions on Acoustics, Speech, and Signal Processing* **38**:2033-2045.

[4] Rubin, D., and Thayer, D. (1982) EM algorithms for factor analysis. *Psychometrika* **47**:69–76.

[5] Everitt, B. (1984) *An introduction to latent variable models.* London: Chapman and Hall.

[6] Hinton, G., Dayan, P., and Revow, M. (1996) Modeling the manifolds of images of handwritten digits. To appear in *IEEE Transactions on Neural Networks.*

[7] Ghahramani, Z. and Hinton, G. (1996) The EM algorithm for mixtures of factor analyzers. *University of Toronto Technical Report* CRG-TR-96-1.

[8] Simard, P., LeCun, Y., and Denker, J. (1993) Efficient pattern recognition using a new transformation distance. In J. Cowan, S. Hanson, and C. Giles, eds. *Advances in Neural Information Processing Systems* **5**:50–58. Cambridge: MIT Press.

[9] Press, W., Teukolsky, S., Vetterling, W., and Flannery, B. (1992) *Numerical Recipes in C: The Art of Scientific Computing.* Cambridge: Cambridge University Press.

[10] Bahl, L., Brown, P., deSouza, P., and Mercer, L. (1986) Maximum mutual information estimation of hidden Markov model parameters for speech recognition. In *Proceedings of ICASSP 86*: 49-52.

Blind Separation of Radio Signals in Fading Channels

Kari Torkkola

Motorola, Phoenix Corporate Research Labs,

2100 E. Elliot Rd, MD EL508, Tempe, AZ 85284, USA

email: A540AA@email.mot.com

Abstract

We apply information maximization / maximum likelihood blind source separation [2, 6] to complex valued signals mixed with complex valued nonstationary matrices. This case arises in radio communications with baseband signals. We incorporate known source signal distributions in the adaptation, thus making the algorithms less "blind". This results in drastic reduction of the amount of data needed for successful convergence. Adaptation to rapidly changing signal mixing conditions, such as to fading in mobile communications, becomes now feasible as demonstrated by simulations.

1 Introduction

In SDMA (spatial division multiple access) the purpose is to separate radio signals of interfering users (either intentional or accidental) from each others on the basis of the spatial characteristics of the signals using smart antennas, array processing, and beamforming [5, 8]. Supervised methods typically use a variant of LMS (least mean squares), either gradient based, or algebraic, to adapt the coefficients that describe the channels or their inverses. This is usually a robust way of estimating the channel but a part of the signal is wasted as predetermined training data, and the methods might not be fast enough for rapidly varying fading channels.

Unsupervised methods either rely on information about the antenna array manifold, or properties of the signals. Former approaches might require calibrated antenna arrays or special array geometries. Less restrictive methods use signal properties only, such as constant modulus, finite alphabet, spectral self-coherence, or cyclostationarity. Blind source separation (BSS) techniques typically rely only on source signal independence and non-Gaussianity assumptions.

Our aim is to separate simultaneous radio signals occupying the same frequency band, more specifically, radio signals that carry digital information. Since linear mixtures of antenna signals end up being linear mixtures of (complex) baseband signals due to the linearity of the downconversion process, we will apply BSS at the baseband stage of the receiver. The main contribution of this paper is to show that by making better use of the known signal properties, it is possible to devise algorithms that adapt much faster than algorithms that rely only on weak assumptions, such as source signal independence.

We will first discuss how the probability density functions (pdf) of baseband DPSK signals could be modelled in a way that can efficiently be used in blind separation algorithms. We will incorporate those models into information maximization and into maximum likelihood approaches [2, 6]. We will then continue with the maximum likelihood approach and other modulation techniques, such as QAM. Finally, we will show in simulations, how this approach results in an adaptation process that is fast enough for fading channels.

2 Models of baseband signal distributions

In digital communications the binary (or n-ary) information is transmitted as discrete combinations of the amplitude and/or the phase of the carrier signal. After downconversion to baseband the instantaneous amplitude of the carrier can be observed as the length of a complex valued sample of the baseband signal, and the phase of the carrier is discernible as the phase angle of the same sample. Possible combinations that depend on the modulation method employed, are called symbol constellations. N-QAM (quadrature amplitude modulation) utilizes both the amplitude and the phase, whereby the baseband signals can only take one of N possible locations on a grid on the complex plane. In N-PSK (phase shift keying) the amplitude of the baseband signal stays constant, but the phase can take any of N discrete values. In DPSK (differential phase shift keying) the information is encoded as the difference between phases of two consecutive transmitted symbols. The phase can thus take any value, and since the amplitude remains constant, the baseband signal distribution is a circle on the complex plane.

Information maximization BSS requires a nonlinear function that models the cumulative density function (cdf) of the data. This function and its derivative need to be differentiable. In the case of a circular complex distribution with uniformly distributed phase, there is only one important direction of deviation, the radial direction. A smooth cdf G for a circular distribution at the unit circle can be constructed using the hyperbolic tangent function as

$$G(z) = tanh(w(|z| - 1)) \qquad (1)$$

and the pdf, differentiated in the radial direction, that is, with respect to $|z|$ is

$$g(z) = \frac{\partial}{\partial |z|} tanh(w(|z| - 1)) = w(1 - tanh^2(w(|z| - 1))) \qquad (2)$$

where $z = x + iy$ is a complex valued variable, and the parameter w controls the steepness of the slope of the *tanh* function. Note that this is in contrast to more commonly used coordinate axis directions to differentiate and to integrate to get the pdf from the cdf and vice versa. These functions are plotted in Fig. 1.

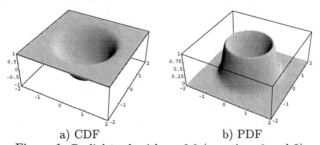

a) CDF   b) PDF

Figure 1: Radial *tanh* with w=2.0 (equations 1 and 2).

Note that we have not been worrying about the pdf integrating to unity. Thus we could leave the first multiplicative constant w out of the definition of g. Scaling will not be important for our purposes of using these functions as the nonlinearities in the information maximization BSS. Note also that when the steepness w approaches infinity, the densities approach the ideal density of a DPSK source, the unit circle. Many other equally good choices are possible where the ideal density is reached as a limit of a parameter value. For example, the radial section of the circular "ridge" of the pdf could be a Gaussian.

3   The information maximization adaptation equation

The information maximization adaptation equation to learn the unmixing matrix W using the natural gradient is [2]

$$\Delta W \propto (\hat{y}u^T + I)W \quad \text{where} \quad \hat{y}_j = \frac{\partial}{\partial y_j}\frac{\partial y_j}{\partial u_j} \tag{3}$$

Vector $u = Wx$ denotes a time sample of the separated sources, x denotes the corresponding time sample of the observed mixtures, and y_j is the nonlinear function approximating the cdf of the data, which is applied to each component of the u.

Now we can insert (1) into y_j. Making use of $\partial|z|/\partial z = z/|z|$ this yields for $\hat{y}_j$:

$$\hat{y}_j = \frac{\partial}{\partial y_j}\frac{\partial}{\partial u_j} tanh(w(|u_j| - 1)) = -2wy_j\frac{u_j}{|u_j|} \tag{4}$$

When (4) is inserted into (3) we get

$$\Delta W \propto \left(I - 2\left(\frac{w_j tanh(w_j(|u_j| - 1))u_j}{|u_j|}\right)_j u^H\right)W. \tag{5}$$

where $(.)_j$ denotes a vector with elements of varying j. Here, we have replaced the transpose operator by the hermitian operator H, since we will be processing complex data. We have also added a subscript to w as these parameters can be learned, too. We will not show the adaptation equations due to lack of space.

4   Connection to the maximum likelihood approach

Pearlmutter and Parra have shown that (3) can be derived from the maximum likelihood approach to density estimation [6]. The same fact has also been pointed out by others, for example, by Cardoso [3]. We will not repeat their straightforward derivation, but the final adaptation equation is of the following form:

$$\Delta W \propto -\frac{d\hat{G}}{dW}W^T W = \left(\left(\frac{f_j'(u_j; w_j)}{f_j(u_j; w_j)}\right)_j u^T + I\right)W. \tag{6}$$

where $u = Wx$ are the sources separated from mixtures x, and $f_j(u_j; w_j)$ is the pdf of source j parametrized by w_j. This is exactly the form of Bell and Sejnowski when f_j is taken to be the derivative of the necessary nonlinearity g_j, which was assumed to be "close" to the true cdf of the source. Thus the information maximization approach makes implicit assumptions about the cdf's of the sources in the form of the nonlinear squashing function, and does implicit density estimation, whereas in the ML approach the density assumptions are made explicit. This fact makes it more intuitive and lucid to derive the adaptation for other forms of densities, and also to extend it to complex valued variables.

Now, we can use the circular pdf's (2) depicted in Fig. 1 as the densities f_j (omitting scaling) $f_j(u_j; w_j) = 1 - tanh^2(w_j(|u_j| - 1))$. where the steepness w_j acts as the single parameter of the density. Now we need to compute its derivative

$$f_j'(u_j; w_j) = \frac{\partial}{\partial u_j}f_j(u_j; w_j) = -2\,tanh(w_j(|u_j| - 1))f_j(u_j; w_j)w_j\frac{u_j}{|u_j|} \tag{7}$$

Inserting this into (6) and changing transpose operators into hermitians yields

$$\Delta W \propto \left(I - 2\left(\frac{w_j tanh(w_j(|u_j| - 1))u_j}{|u_j|}\right)_j u^H\right)W, \tag{8}$$

which is exactly the information maximization rule (5). Notice that at this time we did not have to ponder what would be an appropriate way to construct the cdf from the pdf for complex valued distributions.

5 Modifications for QAM and other signal constellations

So far we have only looked at signals that lie on the unit circle, or that have a constant modulus. Now we will take a look at other modulation techniques, in which the alphabet is constructed as discrete points on the complex plane. An example is the QAM (quadrature amplitude modulation), in which the signal alphabet is a regular grid. For example, in 4-QAM, the alphabet could be $A_4 = \{1+i, -1+i, -1-i, 1-i\}$, or any scaled version of A_4.

In the ideal pdf of 4-QAM, each symbol is represented just as a point. Again, we can construct a smoothed version of the ideal pdf as the sum of "bumps" over all of the alphabet where the ideal pdf will be approached by increasing w.

$$g(u) = \sum_k (1 - tanh^2(w_k|u - u_k|)) \qquad (9)$$

Now the density for each source j will be

$$f_j(u_j; \mathbf{w}_j) = \sum_k (1 - tanh^2(w_k|u_j - u_k|)) \qquad (10)$$

where $\mathbf{w}_j$ is now a vector of parameters w_k. In practice each w_k would be equal in which case a single parameter w will suffice.

This density function could now be inserted into (6) resulting in the weight update equation. However, since $f_j(u_j; \mathbf{w}_j)$ is a sum of multiple components, f'/f will not have a particularly simple form. In essence, for each sample to be processed, we would need to evaluate all the components of the pdf model of the constellation. This can be avoided by evaluating only the component of the pdf corresponding to that symbol of the alphabet u_c which is nearest to the current separated sample u. This is a very good approximation when w is large. But the approximation does not even have to be a good one when w is small, since the whole purpose of using "wide" pdf components is to be able to evaluate the gradients on the whole complex plane. Figure 2 depicts examples of this approximation with two different values of w. The discontinuities are visible at the real and imaginary axes for the smaller w.

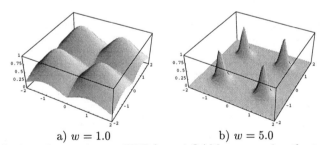

a) $w = 1.0$ \qquad b) $w = 5.0$

Figure 2: A piecewise continuous PDF for a 4-QAM source using the *tanh* function.

Thus for the 4-QAM, the complex plane will be divided into 4 quadrants, each having its own adaptation rule corresponding to the single pdf component in that quadrant. Evaluating (6) for each component of the sum gives

$$\Delta_k W \propto \left(I - 2\left(\frac{w_k tanh(w_k|u_j - u_k|)u_j}{|u_j|}\right)_j u^H\right) W, \qquad (11)$$

for each symbol k of the alphabet or for the corresponding location u_k on the complex plane. This equation can be applied as such when the baseband signal is sampled at the symbol rate. With oversampling, it may be necessary to include in the pdf model the transition paths between the symbols, too.

6   Practical simplifications

To be able to better vectorize the algorithm, it is practical to accumulate ΔW from a number of samples before updating the W. This amounts to computing an expectation of ΔW over a number, say, 10-500 samples of the mixtures. Looking at the DPSK case, (5) or (8) the expectation of $|u_i|$ in the denominator equals one "near" convergence since we assume baseband signals that are distributed on the unit circle.

Also, near the solution we can assume that the separated outputs u_j are close to true distributions, the exact unit circle, which can be derived from f_j by increasing its steepness. At the limit the *tanh* will equal the *sign* function, when the whole adaptation, ignoring scaling, is

$$\Delta W \propto \left(I - 2(sign(|u_j| - 1)u_j)_j u^H \right) W, \tag{12}$$

However, this simplification can only be used when the W is not too far off from the correct solution. This is especially true when the number of available samples of the mixtures is small. The smooth *tanh* is needed in the beginning of the adaptation to give the correct direction to the gradient in the algorithm since the pdfs of the outputs u_j are far from the ideal ones in the beginning.

7   Performance with static and fading signals

We have tested the performance of the proposed algorithm both with static and dynamic (changing) mixing conditions. In the static case with four DPSK signals (8 x oversampled) mixed with random matrices the algorithm needs only about 80 sample points (corresponding to 10 symbols) of the mixtures to converge to a separating solution, whereas a more general algorithm, such as [4], needs about 800-1200 samples for convergence. We attribute this improvement to making much better use of the baseband signal distributions.

In mobile communications the signals are subject to *fading*. If there is no direct line of sight from the transmitter to the receiver, only multiple reflected and diffracted signal components reach the receiver. When either the receiver or the transmitter is moving, for example, in an urban environment, these components are changing very rapidly. If the phases of the carrier signals in these components are aligned the components add constructively at the receiver. If the phases of carriers are 180 degrees off the components add destructively.

Note that a half of a wavelength difference in the lengths of the paths of the received components corresponds to a 180 degree phase shift. This is only about 0.17 m at 900 MHz. Since this small a spatial difference can cause the signal to change from constructive interference to a null received signal, the result is that both the amplitude and the phase of the received signal vary seemingly randomly at a rate that is proportional to relative speeds of the transmitter and the receiver. The amplitude of the received signal follows a Rayleigh distribution, hence the name *Rayleigh fading*. As an example, Figure 3 depicts a 0.1 second fragment of the amplitude of a fading channel.

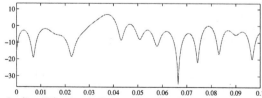

Figure 3: Amplitude (in dB) of a fading radio channel corresponding to a vehicle speed of 60 mph, when the carrier is 900 Mhz. Horizontal axis is time in seconds.

With fading sources, the problem is to be able to adapt to changing conditions, keeping up with the fading rate. In the signal of Fig. 3 it takes less than 5 milliseconds to move from a peak of the amplitude into a deep fade. Assuming a symbol rate of 20000 symbols/second, this corresponds to a mere 100 symbols during this change.

We simulated again DPSK sources oversampling by 8 relative to the symbol rate. The received sampled mixtures are

$$x_i[n] = \sum_j f_{ij}[n]s_j[n] + n_i[n] \tag{13}$$

where $s_j[n]$ are the source signals, $f_{ij}[n]$ represents the fading channel from transmitter j to receiver i, and $n_i[n]$ represents the noise observed by receiver i.

In our experiments, we used a sliding window of 80 samples centered at the current sample. The weight matrix update (the gradient) was calculated using all the samples of the window, the weight matrix was updated, the window was slid one sample forward, and the same was repeated. Using this technique we were able to keep up with the fading rate corresponding to 60 mph relative speed of the transmitter and the receiver. Figure 4 depicts how the algorithm tracks the fading channels in the case of three simultaneous source signals.

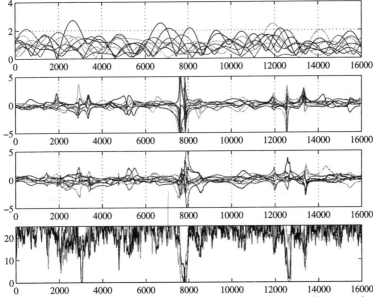

Figure 4: Separation of three signals subject to fading channels. Top graph: The real parts 16 independent fading channels. 2nd graph: The inverse of the instantaneous fading conditions (only the real part is depicted). This is one example of an ideal separation solution. 3rd graph: The separation solution tracked by the algorithm. (only the real part is depicted). Bottom graph: The resulting signal/interference (S/I) ratio in dB for each of the four separated source signals. Horizontal axis is samples. 16000 samples (8 x oversampled) corresponds to 0.1 seconds.

On the average, the S/I to start with is zero. The average output S/I is 20 dB for the worst of the three separated signals. Since the mixing is now dynamic the instantaneous mixing matrix, as determined by the instantaneous fades, can occasionally be singular and cannot be inverted. Thus the signals at this instance cannot be separated. In our 0.1 second test signal this occurred four times in the three source signal case (9 independent fading paths), at which instances the output

S/I bounced to or near zero momentarily for one or more of the separated signals. Durations of these instances are short, lasting about 15 symbols, and covering about 3 per cent of the total signal time.

8   Related work and discussion

Although the whole field of blind source separation has started around 1985, rather surprisingly, no application to radio communications has yet emerged. Most of the source separation algorithms are based on higher-order statistics, and these should be relatively straightforward to generalize for complex valued baseband data. Perhaps the main reason is that all theoretical work has concentrated in the case of static mixing, not in the dynamic case. Many communications channels are dynamic in nature, and thus rapidly adapting methods are necessary.

Making use of all available knowledge of the sources, in this case the pdf's of the source signals, allows successful adaptation based on a very small number of samples, much smaller than by just incorporating the coarse shapes of the pdf's into the algorithm. It is not unreasonable to presume this knowledge, on the contrary, the modulation method of a communications system must certainly be known. To our knowledge, no successful blind separation of signals subject to rapidly varying mixing conditions, such as fading, has been reported in the literature.

Different techniques applied to separation of various simulated radio signals under static mixing conditions have been described, for example, in [9, 4]. The maximum likelihood method reported recently by Yellin and Friedlander [9] seems to be the closest to our approach, but they only apply it to simulated baseband radio signals with static mixing conditions.

It must also be noted that channel time dispersion is not taken into account in our current simulations. This is valid only in cases where the delay spread is short compared to the inverse of the signal bandwidths. If this is not a valid assumption, separation techniques for convolutive mixtures, such as in [7] or [1], need to be combined with the methods developed in this paper.

References

[1] S. Amari, S. Douglas, A. Cichocki, and H. H. Yang. Multichannel blind deconvolution and equalization using the natural gradient. In *Proc. 1st IEEE Signal Processing Workshop on Signal Processing Advances in Wireless Communications*, pages 101–104, Paris, France, April 16-18 1997.

[2] A. Bell and T. Sejnowski. An information-maximisation approach to blind separation and blind deconvolution. *Neural Computation*, 7(6):1129–1159, 1995.

[3] J.-F. Cardoso. Infomax and maximum likelihood for source separation. *IEEE Letters on Signal Processing*, 4(4):112–114, April 1997.

[4] J.-F. Cardoso and B. Laheld. Equivariant adaptive source separation. *IEEE Transactions on Signal Processing*, 44(12):3017–3030, December 1996.

[5] A. Paulraj and C. B. Papadias. Array processing in mobile communications. In *Handbook of Signal Processing*. CRC Press, 1997.

[6] B. A. Pearlmutter and L. C. Parra. A context-sensitive generalization of ICA. In *International Conference on Neural Information Processing*, Hong Kong, Sept. 24–27 1996. Springer.

[7] K. Torkkola. Blind separation of convolved sources based on information maximization. In *IEEE Workshop on Neural Networks for Signal Processing*, pages 423–432, Kyoto, Japan, September 4-6 1996.

[8] A.-J. van der Veen and A. Paulraj. An analytical constant modulus algorithm. *IEEE Transactions on Signal Processing*, 44(5), May 1996.

[9] D. Yellin and B. Friedlander. A maximum likelihood approach to blind separation of narrowband digital communication signals. In *Proc. 30th Asilomar Conf. on Signals, Systems, and Computers*, 1996.

Hybrid NN/HMM-Based Speech Recognition with a Discriminant Neural Feature Extraction

Daniel Willett, Gerhard Rigoll

Department of Computer Science
Faculty of Electrical Engineering
Gerhard-Mercator-University Duisburg, Germany
{willett,rigoll}@fb9-ti.uni-duisburg.de

Abstract

In this paper, we present a novel hybrid architecture for continuous speech recognition systems. It consists of a continuous HMM system extended by an arbitrary neural network that is used as a preprocessor that takes several frames of the feature vector as input to produce more discriminative feature vectors with respect to the underlying HMM system. This hybrid system is an extension of a state-of-the-art continuous HMM system, and in fact, it is the first hybrid system that really is capable of outperforming these standard systems with respect to the recognition accuracy. Experimental results show an relative error reduction of about 10% that we achieved on a remarkably good recognition system based on continuous HMMs for the Resource Management 1000-word continuous speech recognition task.

1 INTRODUCTION

Standard state-of-the-art speech recognition systems utilize Hidden Markov Models (HMMs) to model the acoustic behavior of basic speech units like phones or words. Most commonly the probabilistic distribution functions are modeled as mixtures of Gaussian distributions. These mixture distributions can be regarded as output nodes of a Radial-Basis-Function (RBF) network that is embedded in the HMM system [1]. Contrary to neural training procedures the parameters of the HMM system, including the RBF network, are usually estimated to maximize the training observations' likelihood. In order to combine the time-warping abilities of HMMs and the more discriminative power of neural networks, several hybrid approaches arose during the past five years, that combine HMM systems and neural networks. The best known approach is the one proposed by Bourlard [2]. It replaces the HMMs' RBF-net with a Multi-Layer-Perceptron (MLP) which is trained to output each HMM state's posterior probability. At last year's NIPS our group presented a novel hybrid speech recognition approach that combines a discrete HMM speech recognition system and a neural quantizer [3]. By maximizing the mutual information between the VQ-labels and the assigned phoneme-classes, this approach outperforms standard discrete recognition systems. We showed that this approach is capable of building up very accurate systems with an extremely fast likelihood computation, that only consists of a quantization and a table lookup. This resulted in a hybrid system with recognition performance equivalent to the best

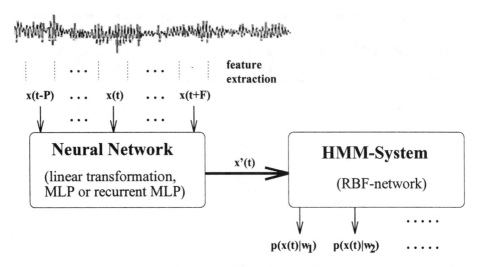

Figure 1: Architecture of the hybrid NN/HMM system

continuous systems, but with a much faster decoding. Nevertheless, it has turned out that this hybrid approach is not really capable of substantially outperforming very good continuous systems with respect to the recognition accuracy. This observation is similar to experiences with Bourlard's MLP approach. For the decoding procedure, this architecture offers a very efficient pruning technique (phone deactivation pruning [4]) that is much more efficient than pruning on likelihoods, but until today this approach did not outperform standard continuous HMM systems in recognition performance.

2 HYBRID CONTINUOUS HMM/MLP APPROACH

Therefore, we followed a different approach, namely the extension of a state-of-the-art continuous system that achieves extremely good recognition rates with a neural net that is trained with MMI-methods related to those in [5]. The major difference in this approach is the fact that the acoustic processor is not replaced by a neural network, but that the Gaussian probability density component is retained and combined with a neural component in an appropriate manner. A similar approach was presented in [6] to improve a speech recognition system for the TIMIT database. We propose to regard the additional neural component as being part of the feature extraction, and to reuse it in recognition systems of higher complexity where discriminative training is extremely expensive.

2.1 ARCHITECTURE

The basic architecture of this hybrid system is illustrated in Figure 1. The neural net functions as a feature transformation that takes several additional past and future feature vectors into account to produce an improved more discriminant feature vector that is fed into the HMM system. This architecture allows (at least) three ways of interpretation; 1. as a hybrid system that combines neural nets and continuous HMMs, 2. as an LDA-like transformation that incorporates the HMM parameters into the calculation of the transformation matrix and 3. as feature extraction method, that allows the extraction of features according to the underlying HMM system. The considered types of neural networks are linear transformations, MLPs and recurrent MLPs. A detailed description of the possible topologies is given in Section 3.

With this architecture, additional past and future feature vectors can be taken into account in the probability estimation process without increasing the dimensionality of the Gaussian mixture components. Instead of increasing the HMM system's number of parameters the neural net is trained to produce more discriminant feature vectors with respect to the trained HMM system. Of course, adding some kind of neural net increases the number of parameters too, but the increase is much more moderate than it would be when increasing each Gaussian's dimensionality.

2.2 TRAINING OBJECTIVE

The original purpose of this approach was the intention to transfer the hybrid approach presented in [3], based on MMI neural network, to (semi-) continuous systems. This way, we hoped to be able to achieve the same remarkable improvements that we obtained on discrete systems now on continuous systems, which are the much better and more flexible baseline systems. The most natural way to do this would be the re-estimation of the code-book of Gaussian mean vectors of a semi-continuous system using the neural MMI training algorithm presented in [3]. Unfortunately though, this won't work, as this codebook of a semi-continuous system does not determine a separation of the feature space, but is used as means of Gaussian densities. The MMI-principle can be retained, however, by leaving the original HMM system unmodified and instead extending it with a neural component, trained according to a frame-based MMI approach, related to the one in [3]. The MMI criterion is usually formulated in the following way:

$$\hat{\lambda}_{MMI} = \operatorname*{argmax}_{\lambda} I_\lambda(X, W) = \operatorname*{argmax}_{\lambda}(H_\lambda(X) - H_\lambda(X|W)) = \operatorname*{argmax}_{\lambda} \frac{p_\lambda(X|W)}{p_\lambda(X)}$$
(1)

This means that following the MMI criterion the system's free parameters λ have to be estimated to maximize the quotient of the observation's likelihood $p_\lambda(X|W)$ for the known transcription W and its overall likelihood $p_\lambda(X)$. With $X = (x(1), x(2), ...x(T))$ denoting the training observations and $W = (w(1), w(2), ...w(T))$ denoting the HMM states - assigned to the observation vectors in a Viterbi-alignment - the frame-based MMI criterion becomes

$$\hat{\lambda}_{MMI} \approx \operatorname*{argmax}_{\lambda} \sum_{i=1}^{T} I_\lambda(x(i), w(i))$$

$$= \operatorname*{argmax}_{\lambda} \prod_{i=1}^{T} \frac{p_\lambda(x(i)|w(i))}{p_\lambda(x(i))} \approx \operatorname*{argmax}_{\lambda} \prod_{i=1}^{T} \frac{p_\lambda(x(i)|w(i))}{\sum_{k=1}^{S} p_\lambda(x(i)|w_k)p(w_k)}$$
(2)

where S is the total number of HMM states, $(w_1, ...w_S)$ denotes the HMM states and $p(w_k)$ denotes each states' prior-probability that is estimated on the alignment of the training data or by an analysis of the language model.

Eq. 2 can be used to re-estimate the Gaussians of a continuous HMM system directly. In [7] we reported the slight improvements in recognition accuracy that we achieved with this parameter estimation. However, it turned out, that only the incorporation of additional features in the probability calculation pipeline can provide more discriminative emission probabilities and a major advance in recognition accuracy. Thus, we experienced it to be more convenient to train an additional neural net in order to maximize Eq. 2. Besides, this approach offers the possibility of improving a recognition system by applying a trained feature extraction network taken from a different system. Section 5 will report our positive experiences with this procedure.

At first, for matter of simplicity, we will consider a linear network that takes P past feature vectors and F future feature vectors as additional input. With the linear net denoted as a $(P + F + 1) \times N$ matrix NET, each component $x'(t)[c]$ of the network output $x'(t)$ computes to

$$x'(t)[c] = \sum_{i=0}^{P+F} \sum_{j=1}^{N} x(t - P + i)[j] \cdot NET[i * N + j][c] \qquad \forall c \in \{1...N\}$$
(3)

so that the derivative with respect to a component of NET easily computes to

$$\frac{\partial x'(t)[c]}{\partial NET[i * N + j][\hat{c}]} = \delta_{c,\hat{c}} x(t - P + i)[j]$$
(4)

In a continuous HMM system with diagonal covariance matrices the pdf of each HMM state w is modeled by a mixture of Gaussian components like

$$p_\lambda(x|w) = \sum_{j=1}^{C_w} d_{wj} \frac{1}{\sqrt{(2\pi)^n |\sigma_j|}} e^{-\frac{1}{2} \sum_{l=1}^{N} \frac{(m_j[l] - x[l])^2}{\sigma_j[l]}}$$
(5)

A pdf's derivative with respect to a component $x'[c]$ of the net's output becomes

$$\frac{\partial p_\lambda(x'|w)}{\partial x'[c]} = \sum_{j=1}^{C_w} d_{wj} \frac{(x[c] - m_j[c])}{\sigma_j[c]} \frac{1}{\sqrt{(2\pi)^n |\sigma_j|}} e^{-\frac{1}{2} \sum_{l=1}^{N} \frac{(m_j[l] - x'[l])^2}{\sigma_j[l]}} \quad (6)$$

With $x(t)$ in Eq. 2 now replaced by the net output $x'(t)$ the partial derivative of Eq. 2 with respect to a probabilistic distribution function $p(x'(i)|w_k)$ computes to

$$\frac{\partial I_\lambda(x'(i), w(i))}{\partial p_\lambda(x'(i)|w_k)} = \frac{\delta_{w(i), w_k}}{p_\lambda(x(i)|w_k)} - \frac{p(w_k)}{\sum_{l=1}^{S} p_\lambda(x(i)|w_l)p(w_l)} \quad (7)$$

Thus, using the chain rule the derivative of the net's parameters with respect to the frame-based MMI criterion can be computed as displayed in Eq. 8

$$\frac{\partial I_\lambda(X, W)}{\partial NET[l][c]} = \sum_{i=1}^{T} \left(\sum_{k=1}^{S} \left(\frac{\partial I_\lambda(x(i)|w(i)))}{\partial p_\lambda(x'(i)|w_k)} \frac{\partial p_\lambda(x'(i)|w_k)}{\partial x'(i)[c]} \frac{\partial x'(i)[c]}{\partial NET[l][c]} \right) \right) \quad (8)$$

and a gradient descent procedure can be used to determine the optimal parameter estimates.

2.3   ADVANTAGES OF THE PROPOSED APPROACH

When using a linear network, the proposed approach strongly resembles the well known Linear Discriminant Analysis (LDA) [8] in architecture and training objective. The main difference is the way the transformation is set up. In the proposed approach the transformation is computed by taking directly the HMM parameters into account whereas the LDA only tries to separate the features according to some class assignment. With the incorporation of a trained continuous HMM system the net's parameters are estimated to produce feature vectors that not only have a good separability in general, but also have a distribution that can be modeled with mixtures of Gaussians very well. Our experiments given at the end of this paper prove this advantage. Furthermore, contrary to LDA, that produces feature vectors that don't have much in common with the original vectors, the proposed approach only slightly modifies the input vectors. Thus, a well trained continuous system can be extended by the MMI-net approach, in order to improve its recognition performance without the need for completely rebuilding it. In addition to that, the approach offers a fairly easy extension to nonlinear networks (MLP) and recurrent networks (recurrent MLP). This will be outlined in the following Section. And, maybe as the major advantage, the approach allows keeping up the division of the input features into streams of features that are strongly uncorrelated and which are modeled with separate pdfs. The case of multiple streams is discussed in detail in Section 4. Besides, the MMI approach offers the possibility of a unified training of the HMM system and the feature extraction network or an iterative procedure of training each part alternately.

3   NETWORK TOPOLOGIES

Section 2 explained how to train a linear transformation with respect to the frame-based MMI criterion. However, to exploit all the advantages of the proposed hybrid approach the network should be able to perform a nonlinear mapping, in order to produce features whose distribution is (closer to) a mixture of Gaussians although the original distribution is not.

3.1   MLP

When using a fully connected MLP as displayed in Figure 2 with one hidden layer of H nodes, that perform the nonlinear function f, the activation of one of the output nodes $x'(t)[c]$ becomes

$$x'(t)[c] = \sum_{h=1}^{H} L2[h][c] \cdot f\left(BIAS_h + \sum_{i=0}^{P+F} \sum_{j=1}^{N} x(t - P + i)[j] \cdot L1[i * N + j][h] \right) \quad (9)$$

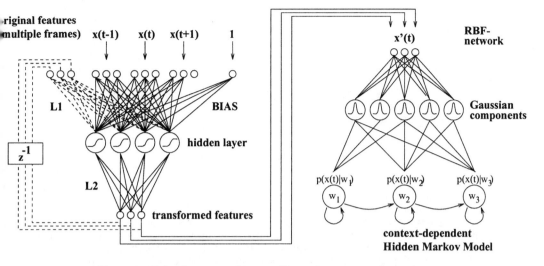

Figure 2: Hybrid system with a nonlinear feature transformation

which is easily differentiable with respect to the nonlinear network's parameters. In our experiments we chose f to be defined as the hyperbolic tangents $f(x) := tanh(x) = (2(1+ e^{-x})^{-1} - 1)$ so that the partial derivative with respect to i.e. a weight $L1[\hat{i} \cdot N + \hat{j}][h]$ of the first layer computes to

$$\frac{\partial x'(t)[c]}{\partial L1[\hat{i} \cdot N + \hat{j}][h]} = x(t - P + \hat{i})[\hat{j}] \cdot L2[h][c] \tag{10}$$

$$\cdot cosh\left(BIAS_h + \sum_{i=0}^{P+F} \sum_{j=1}^{N} x(t - P + i)[j] \cdot L1[i * N + j][h] \right)^{-2}$$

and the gradient can be set up according to Eq. 8.

3.2 RECURRENT MLP

With the incorporation of several additional past feature vectors as explained in Section 2, more discriminant feature vectors can be generated. However, this method is not capable of modeling longer term relations, as it can be achieved by extending the network with some recurrent connections. For the sake of simplicity, in our experiments we simply extended the MLP as indicated with the dashed lines in Figure 2 by propagating the output $x(t)$ back to the input of the network (with a delay of one discrete time step). This type of recurrent neural net is often referred to as a 'Jordan'-network. Certainly, the extension of the network with additional hidden nodes in order to model the recurrence more independently would be possible as well.

4 MULTI STREAM SYSTEMS

In HMM-based recognition systems the extracted features are often divided into streams that are modeled independently. This is useful the less correlated the divided features are. In this case the overall likelihood of an observation computes to

$$p_\lambda(x|w) = \prod_{s=1}^{M} p_{s\lambda}(x|w)^{w_s} \tag{11}$$

where each of the stream pdfs $p_{s\lambda}(x|w)$ only uses a subset of the features in x. The stream weights w_s are usually set to unity.

system	baseline system	LDA	linear MMI-net	MLP (H=36)	Jordan-Network
monophones one stream	24%	21%	21%	21%	-
monophones four streams	11.8%	11.0%	10.9%	10.8%	10,9%
triphones four streams	5.2%	5.3%	4.8%	4.7%	4.7%

Table 1: Word error rates achieved in the experiments

A multi stream system can be improved by a neural extraction for each stream and an independent training of these neural networks. However, it has to be considered that the subdivided features usually are not totally independent and by considering multiple input frames as illustrated in Figure 1 this dependence often increases. It is a common practice, for instance, to model the features' first and second order delta coefficients in independent streams. So, for sure the streams lose independence when considering multiple frames, as these coefficients are calculated using the additional frames. Nevertheless, we found it to give best results to maintain this subdivision into streams, but to consider the stronger correlation by training each stream's net dependent on the other nets' outputs. A training criterion follows straight from Eq. 11 inserted in Eq. 2.

$$\hat{\lambda}_{MMI} = \operatorname*{argmax}_{\lambda} \prod_{i=1}^{T} \frac{p_\lambda(x(i)|w(i))}{p_\lambda(x(i))} = \operatorname*{argmax}_{\lambda} \prod_{i=1}^{T} \prod_{s=1}^{M} \left(\frac{p_{s\lambda}(x(i)|w(i))}{p_{s\lambda}(x(i))} \right)^{w_s} \quad (12)$$

The derivative of this equation with respect to the pdf $p_{\hat{s}\lambda}(x|w)$ of a specific stream $\hat{s}$ depends on the other streams' pdfs. With the w_s set to unity it is

$$\frac{\partial I_\lambda(x'(i), w(i))}{\partial p_{\hat{s}\lambda}(x'(i)|w_k)} = \left(\prod_{s\neq\hat{s}} \frac{p_{s\lambda}(x(i)|w(i))}{p_{s\lambda}(x(i))} \right) \left(\frac{\delta_{w(i),w_k}}{p_{\hat{s}\lambda}(x(i)|w_k)} - \frac{p(w_k)}{\sum_{l=1}^{S} p_{\hat{s}\lambda}(x(i)|w_l)p(w_l)} \right)$$

$$(13)$$

Neglecting the correlation among the streams the training of each stream's net can be done independently. However, the more the incorporation of additional features increases the streams' correlation, the more important it gets to train the nets in a unified training procedure according to Eq. 13.

5 EXPERIMENTS AND RESULTS

We applied the proposed approach to improve a context-independent (monophones) and a context-dependent (triphones) continuous speech recognition system for the 1000-word Resource Management (RM) task. The systems used linear HMMs of three emitting states each. The tying of Gaussian mixture components was performed with an adaptive procedure according to [9]. The HMM states of the word-internal triphone system were clustered in a tree-based phonetic clustering procedure. Decoding was performed with a Viterbi-decoder and the standard wordpair-grammar of perplexity 60. Training of the MLP was performed with the RPROP algorithm. For training the weights of the recurrent connections we chose real-time recurrent learning. The average error rates were computed using the test-sets Feb89, Oct89, Feb91 and Sep92.

The table above shows the recognition results with single stream systems in its first section. These systems simply use a 12-value Cepstrum feature vector without the incorporation of delta coefficients. The systems with an input transformation use one additional past and one additional future feature vector as input. The proposed approach achieves the same performance as the LDA, but it is not capable of outperforming it.

The second section of the table lists the recognition results with four stream systems that use the first and second order delta coefficients in additional streams plus log energy and this values' delta coefficients in a forth stream. The MLP system trained according to Eq.

11 slightly outperforms the other approaches. The incorporation of recurrent network connections does not improve the system's performance.

The third section of the table lists the recognition results with four stream systems with a context-dependent acoustic modeling (triphones). The applied LDA and the MMI-networks were taken from the monophone four stream system. On the one hand, this was done to avoid the computational complexity that the MMI training objective causes on context-dependent systems. On the other hand, this demonstrates that the feature vectors produced by the trained networks have a good discrimination for continuous systems in general. Again, the MLP system outperforms the other approaches and achieves a very remarkable word error rate. It should be pointed out here, that the structure of the continuous system as reported in [9] is already highly optimized and it is almost impossible to further reduce the error rate by means of any acoustic modeling method. This is reflected in the fact that even a standard LDA cannot improve this system. Only the new neural approach leads to a 10% reduction in error rate which is a large improvement considering the fact that the error rate of the baseline system is among the best ever reported for the RM database,

6 CONCLUSION

The paper has presented a novel approach to discriminant feature extraction. A MLP network has successfully been used to compute a feature transformation that outputs extremely suitable features for continuous HMM systems. The experimental results have proven that the proposed approach is an appropriate method for including several feature frames in the probability estimation process without increasing the dimensionality of the Gaussian mixture components in the HMM system. Furthermore did the results on the triphone speech recognition system prove that the approach provides discriminant features, not only for the system that the mapping is computed on, but for HMM systems with a continuous modeling in general. The application of recurrent networks did not improve the recognition accuracy. The longer range relations seem to be very weak and they seem to be covered well by using the neighboring feature vectors and first and second order delta coefficients. The proposed unified training procedure for multiple nets in multi-stream systems allows keeping up the subdivision of features of weak correlations, and gave us best profits in recognition accuracy.

References

[1] H. Ney, "Speech Recognition in a Neural Network Framework: Discriminative Training of Gaussian Models and Mixture Densities as Radial Basis Functions", *Proc. IEEE-ICASSP,* 1991, pp. 573–576.

[2] H Bourlard, N. Morgan, "Connectionist Speech Recognition - A Hybrid Approach", *Kluwer Academic Press*, 1994.

[3] G. Rigoll, C. Neukirchen, "A new approach to hybrid HMM/ANN speech recognition using mutual information neural networks", *Advances in Neural Information Processing Systems (NIPS-96),* Denver, Dec. 1996, pp. 772–778.

[4] M. M. Hochberg, G. D. Cook, S. J. Renals, A. J. Robinson, A. S. Schechtman, "The 1994 ABBOT Hybrid Connectionist-HMM Large-Vocabulary Recognition System", *Proc. ARPA Spoken Language Systems Technology Workshop,* 1995.

[5] G. Rigoll, "Maximum Mutual Information Neural Networks for Hybrid Connectionist-HMM Speech Recognition", *IEEE-Trans. Speech Audio Processing,* Vol. 2, No. 1, Jan. 1994, pp. 175–184.

[6] Y. Bengio et al., "Global Optimization of a Neural Network - Hidden Markov Model Hybrid" *IEEE-Transcations on NN,* Vol. 3, No. 2, 1992, pp. 252–259.

[7] D. Willett, C. Neukirchen, R. Rottland, "Dictionary-Based Discriminative HMM Parameter Estimation for Continuous Speech Recognition Systems", *Proc. IEEE-ICASSP,* 1997, pp. 1515–1518.

[8] X. Aubert, R. Haeb-Umbach, H. Ney, "Continuous mixture densities and linear discriminant analysis for improved context-dependent acoustic models", *Proc. IEEE-ICASSP,* 1993, pp. II 648–651.

[9] D. Willett, G. Rigoll, "A New Approach to Generalized Mixture Tying for Continuous HMM-Based Speech Recognition", *Proc. EUROSPEECH,* Rhodes, 1997.

PART VII
VISUAL PROCESSING

A Non-parametric Multi-Scale Statistical Model for Natural Images

Jeremy S. De Bonet & Paul Viola
Artificial Intelligence Laboratory
Learning & Vision Group
545 Technology Square Massachusetts Institute of Technology
Cambridge, MA 02139

EMAIL: jsd@ai.mit.edu & viola@ai.mit.edu
HOMEPAGE: http://www.ai.mit.edu/projects/lv

Abstract

The observed distribution of natural images is far from uniform. On the contrary, real images have complex and important structure that can be exploited for image processing, recognition and analysis. There have been many proposed approaches to the principled statistical modeling of images, but each has been limited in either the complexity of the models or the complexity of the images. We present a non-parametric multi-scale statistical model for images that can be used for recognition, image de-noising, and in a "generative mode" to synthesize high quality textures.

1   Introduction

In this paper we describe a multi-scale statistical model which can capture the structure of natural images across many scales. Once trained on example images, it can be used to recognize novel images, or to generate new images. Each of these tasks is reasonably efficient, requiring no more than a few seconds or minutes on a workstation.

The statistical modeling of images is an endeavor which reaches back to the 60's and 70's (Duda and Hart, 1973). Statistical approaches are alluring because they provide a unified view of learning, classification and generation. To date however, a generic, efficient and unified statistical model for natural images has yet to appear. Nevertheless, many approaches have shown significant competence in specific areas.

Perhaps the most influential statistical model for generic images is the Markov random field (MRF) (Geman and Geman, 1984). MRF's define a distribution over images that is based on simple and local interactions between pixels. Though MRF's have been very successfully used for restoration of images, their generative properties are weak. This is due to the inability of the MRF's to capture long range (low frequency) interactions between pixels. Recently there has been a great deal of interest in hierarchical models such as the Helmholtz machine (Hinton et al., 1995; Dayan et al., 1995). Though the Helmholtz machine can be trained to discover long range structure, it is not easily applied to natural images.

Multi-scale wavelet models have emerged as an effective technique for modeling realistic natural images. These techniques hypothesize that the wavelet transform measures the underlying causes of natural images which are assumed to be statistically independent. The primary evidence for this conjecture is that the coefficients of wavelet transformed images are uncorrelated and low in entropy (hence the success of wavelet compression). These insights have been used for noise reduction (Donoho and Johnstone, 1993; Simoncelli and Adelson, 1996), and example driven texture synthesis (Heeger and Bergen, 1995). The main drawback of wavelet algorithms is the assumption of complete independence between coefficients. We conjecture that in fact there is strong cross-scale dependence between the wavelet coefficients of an image, which is consistent with observations in (De Bonet, 1997) and (Buccigrossi and Simoncelli, 1997).

2   Multi-scale Statistical Models

Multi-scale wavelet techniques assume that images are a linear transform of a collection of statistically independent random variables: $I = W^{-1}\vec{C}$, where I is an image, W^{-1} is the inverse wavelet transform, and $\vec{C} = \{c_k\}$ is a vector of random variable "causes" which are assumed to be independent. The distribution of each cause c_k is $p_k(\cdot)$, and since the c_k's are independent it follows that: $p(\vec{C}) = \prod_k p_k(c_k)$. Various wavelet transforms have been developed, but all share the same type of multi-scale structure — each row of the wavelet matrix W is a spatially localized filter that is a shifted and scaled version of a single basis function.

The wavelet transform is most efficiently computed as an iterative convolution using a bank of filters. First a "pyramid" of low frequency downsampled images is created: $G_0 = I$, $G_1 = 2\downarrow(g \otimes G_0)$, and $G_{i+1} = 2\downarrow(g \otimes G_i)$, where $2\downarrow$ downsamples an image by a factor of 2 in each dimension, $\otimes$ is the convolution operation, and g is a low pass filter. At each level a series of filter functions are applied: $F_j^i = f_i \otimes G_j$, where the f_i's are various types of filters. Computation of the F_j^i's is a linear transformation that can thought of as a single matrix W. With careful selection of g and f_i this matrix can be constructed so that $W^{-1} = W^\top$ (Simoncelli et al., 1992)[1]. Where convenient we will combine the pixels of the feature images $F_j^i(x, y)$ into a single cause vector $\vec{C}$.

The expected distribution of causes, c_k, is a function of the image classes that are being modeled. For example it is possible to attempt to model the space of all natural images. In that case it appears as though the most accurate $p_k(\cdot)$'s are highly kurtotic which indicates that the c_k's are most often zero but in rare cases take on very large values (Donoho and Johnstone, 1993; Simoncelli and Adelson, 1996). This is in direct contrast to the distribution of c_k's for white-noise images – which is gaussian. The difference in these distributions can be used as the basis of noise reduction algorithms, by reducing the wavelet coefficients which are more

---

[1]Computation of the inverse wavelet transform is algorithmically similar to the computation of the forward wavelet transform.

likely to be noise than signal.

Specific image classes can be modeled using similar methods (Heeger and Bergen, 1995)[2]. For a given set of input images the empirical distribution of the c_k's is observed. To generate a novel example of a texture a new set of causes, $\vec{C}'$ is sampled from the assumed independent empirical distributions $p_k(\cdot)$. The generated images are computed using the inverse wavelet transform: $I' = W^{-1}\vec{C}'$. Bergen and Heeger have used this approach to build a probabilistic model of a texture from a single example image. To do this they assume that textures are *spatially ergodic* – that the expected distribution is not a function of position in the image. As a result the pixels in any one feature image, $F_j^i(x, y)$, are samples from the same distribution and can be combined[3].

Heeger and Bergen's work is at or near the current state of the art in texture generation. Figure 1 contains some example textures. Notice however, that this technique is much better at generating smooth or noise-like textures than those with well defined structure. Image structures, such as the sharp edges at the border of the tiles in the rightmost texture can not be modeled with their approach. These image features directly contradict the assumption that the wavelet coefficients, or causes, of the image are independent.

For many types of natural images the coefficients of the wavelet transform are not independent, for example images which contain long edges. While wavelets are local both in frequency and space, a long edge is not local in frequency nor in space. As a result the wavelet representation of such a feature requires many coefficients. The high frequencies of the edge are captured by many small high frequency wavelets. The long scale is captured by a number of larger low frequency wavelets. A model which assumes these coefficients are independent can never accurately model images which contain these non-local features. Conversely a model which captures the conditional dependencies between coefficients will be much more effective. We chose to approximate the joint distribution of coefficients as a chain, in which coefficients that occur higher in the wavelet pyramid condition the distribution of coefficients at lower levels (i.e. low frequencies condition the generation of higher frequencies).

For every pixel in an image define the *parent vector* of that pixel:

$$\vec{V}(x,y) = \left[F_0^0(x,y), F_0^1(x,y), \ldots, F_0^N(x,y), \right.$$
$$F_1^0(\lfloor\tfrac{x}{2}\rfloor, \lfloor\tfrac{y}{2}\rfloor), F_1^1(\lfloor\tfrac{x}{2}\rfloor, \lfloor\tfrac{y}{2}\rfloor), \ldots, F_1^N(\lfloor\tfrac{x}{2}\rfloor, \lfloor\tfrac{y}{2}\rfloor), \ldots$$
$$\left. F_M^0(\lfloor\tfrac{x}{2^M}\rfloor, \lfloor\tfrac{y}{2^M}\rfloor), F_M^1(\lfloor\tfrac{x}{2^M}\rfloor, \lfloor\tfrac{y}{2^M}\rfloor), \ldots, F_M^N(\lfloor\tfrac{x}{2^M}\rfloor, \lfloor\tfrac{y}{2^M}\rfloor) \right] \quad (1)$$

where M is the top level of the pyramid and N is the number of features. Rather than generating each of these coefficients independently, we define a chain across scale. In this chain the generation of the lower levels depend on the higher levels:

$$p(\vec{V}(x,y)) = p(\vec{V}_M(x,y)) \times p(\vec{V}_{M-1}(x,y)|\vec{V}_M(x,y))$$
$$\times p(\vec{V}_{M-2}(x,y)|\vec{V}_{M-1}(x,y), \vec{V}_M(x,y)) \times \ldots$$
$$\times p(\vec{V}_0(x,y)|\vec{V}_1(x,y), \ldots, \vec{V}_{M-1}(x,y), \vec{V}_M(x,y)) \quad (2)$$

---

[2]See (Zhu, Wu and Mumford, 1996) for a related but more formal model.

[3]Their generation process is slightly more complex than this, involving a iteration designed to match the pixel histogram. The implementation used for generating the images in Figure 1 incorporates this, but we do not discuss it here.

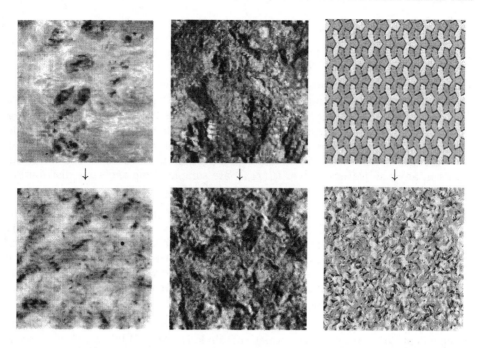

Figure 1: Synthesis results for the Heeger and Bergen (1995) model. TOP: Input textures. BOTTOM: Synthesis results. This technique is much better at generating fine or noisy textures then it is at generating textures which require co-occurrence of wavelets at multiple scales.

Figure 2: Synthesis results using our technique for the input textures shown in Figure 1 (TOP).

where $\vec{V}_l(x,y)$ is the a subset of the elements of $\vec{V}(x,y)$ computed from G_l. Usually we will assume ergodicity, i.e. that $p(\vec{V}(x,y))$ is independent of x and y. The generative process starts from the top of the pyramid, choosing values for the $\vec{V}_M(x,y)$ at all points. Once these are generated the values at the next level, $\vec{V}_{M-1}(x,y)$, are generated. The process continues until all of the wavelet coefficients are generated. Finally the image is computed using the inverse wavelet transform.

It is important to note that this probabilistic model is not made up of a collection of independent chains, one for each $\vec{V}(x,y)$. Parent vectors for neighboring pixels have substantial overlap as coefficients in the higher pyramid levels (which are lower resolution) are shared by neighboring pixels at lower pyramid levels. Thus, the generation of nearby pixels will be strongly dependent. In a related approach a similar arrangement of generative chains has been termed a Markov tree (Basseville et al., 1992).

2.1 Estimating the Conditional Distributions

The additional descriptive power of our generative model does not come without cost. The conditional distributions that appear in (2) must be estimated from observations. We choose to do this directly from the data in a non-parametric fashion. Given a sample of parent vectors $\left\{\vec{S}(x,y)\right\}$ from an example image we estimate the conditional distribution as a ratio of Parzen window density estimators:

$$p(\vec{V}_l(x,y)|\vec{V}_{l+1}^M(x,y)) = \frac{p(\vec{V}_l^M(x,y))}{p(\vec{V}_{l+1}^M(x,y))} \approx \frac{\sum_{x',y'} R(\vec{V}_l^M(x,y), \vec{S}_l^M(x',y'))}{\sum_{x',y'} R(\vec{V}_{l+1}^M(x,y), \vec{S}_{l+1}^M(x',y'))} \quad (3)$$

where $\vec{V}_l^k(x,y)$ is a subset of the parent vector $\vec{V}(x,y)$ that contains information from level l to level k, and $R(\cdot)$ is a function of two vectors that returns maximal values when the vectors are similar and smaller values when the vectors are dissimilar. We have explored various $R(\cdot)$ functions. In the results presented the $R(\cdot)$ function returns a fixed constant $1/z$ if all of the coefficients of the vectors are within some threshold θ and zero otherwise. Given this simple definition for $R(\cdot)$ sampling from $p(\vec{V}_l(x,y)|\vec{V}_{l+1}^M(x,y))$ is very straightforward: find all x',y' such that $R(\vec{S}_{l+1}^M(x',y'), \vec{S}_{l+1}^M(x,y)) = 1/z$ and pick from among them to set $\vec{V}_l(x,y) = \vec{S}_l(x',y')$.

3 Experiments

We have applied this approach to the problems of texture generation, texture recognition, target recognition, and signal de-noising. In each case our results are competitive with the best published approaches.

In Figure 2 we show the results of our technique on the textures from Figure 1. For these textures we are better able to model features which are caused by a conjunction of wavelets. This is especially striking in the rightmost texture where the geometrical tiling is almost, but not quite, preserved. In our model, knowledge of the joint distribution provides constraints which are critical in the overall perceived appearance of the synthesized texture.

Using this same model, we can measure the textural similarity between a known and novel image. We do this by measuring the likelihood of generating the parent vectors in the novel image under the chain model of the known image. On "easy" data sets, such as the the the MeasTex `Brodatz` texture test suite, performance is slightly higher than other techniques, our approach achieved 100% correct classification compared to 97% achieved by a gaussian MRF approach (Chellappa and Chatterjee, 1985). The MeasTex `lattice` test suite is slightly more difficult because each texture is actually a composition of textures containing different spatial frequencies. Our approach achieved 97% while the best alternate method, in this case Gabor Convolution Energy method (Fogel and Sagi, 1989) achieved 89%. Gaussian MRF's explicitly assume that the texture is a unimodal distribution and as a result achieve only 79% correct recognition. We also measured performance on a set of 20 types of natural texture and compared the classification power of this model to that of human observers (humans discriminate textures extremely accurately.) On this

Original   Denoise Shrinkage   Shrinkage Residual

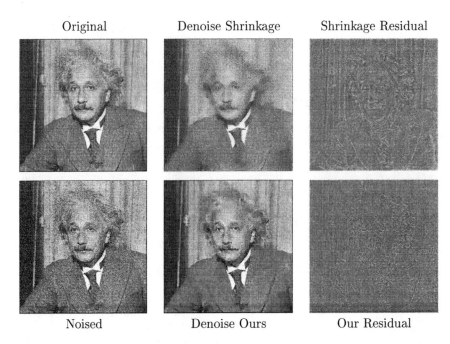

Noised   Denoise Ours   Our Residual

Figure 3: (Original) the original image; (Noised) the image corrupted with white gaussian noise (SNR 8.9 dB); (Denoise Shrinkage) the results of de-noising using wavelet shrinkage or coring (Donoho and Johnstone, 1993; Simoncelli and Adelson, 1996) (SNR 9.8 dB); (Shrinkage Residual) the residual error between the shrinkage de-noised result and the original — notice that the error contains a great deal of interpretable structure; (Denoise Ours) our de-noising approach (SNR 13.2 dB); and (Our Residual) the residual error — these errors are much less structured.

test, humans achieved 86% accuracy, our approach achieved an accuracy of 81%, and GMRF's achieved 68%.

A strong probabilistic model for images can be used to perform a variety of image processing tasks including de-noising and sharpening. De-noising of an observed image $\hat{I}$ can be performed by Monte Carlo averaging: draw a number of sample images according to the prior density $P(I)$, compute the likelihood of the noise for each image $P(\nu = \hat{I}) - I)$, and then find the weighted average over these images. The weighted average is the estimated mean over all possible ways that the image might have been generated given the observation.

Image de-noising frequently relies on generic image models which simply enforce image smoothness. These priors either leave a lot of residual noise or remove much of the original image. In contrast, we construct a probability density model from the noisy image itself. In effect we assume that the image is redundant, containing many examples of the same visual structures, as if it were a texture. The value of this approach is directly related to the redundancy in the image. If the redundancy in the image is very low, then the parent structures will be everywhere different, and the only resampled images with significant likelihood will be the original image. But if there is some redundancy in the image — that might arise from a regular texture or smoothly varying patch — the resampling will freely average across these similar regions. This will have the effect of reducing noise in these images. In Figure 3 we show results of this de-noising approach.

4 Conclusions

We have presented a statistical model of texture which can be trained using example images. The form of the model is a conditional chain across scale on a pyramid of wavelet coefficients. The cross scale condtional distributions are estimated non-parametrically. This is important because many of the observed conditional distributions are complex and contain multiple modes. We believe that there are two main weaknesses of the current approach: i) the tree on which the distributions are defined are fixed and non-overlapping; and ii) the conditional distributions are estimated from a small number of samples. We hope to address these limitations in future work.

Acknowledgments

In this research, Jeremy De Bonet is supported by the DOD Multidisciplinary Research Program of the University Research Initiative, and Paul Viola by Office of Naval Research Grant No. N00014-96-1-0311.

References

Basseville, M., Benveniste, A., Chou, K. C., Golden, S. A., Nikoukhah, R., and Willsky, A. S. (1992). Modeling and estimation of multiresolution stochastic processes. *IEEE Transactions on Information Theory*, 38(2):766–784.

Buccigrossi, R. W. and Simoncelli, E. P. (1997). Progressive wavelet image coding based on a conditional probability model. In *Proceedings ICASSP-97*, Munich, Germany.

Chellappa, R. and Chatterjee, S. (1985). Classification of textures using gaussian markov random fields. In *Proceedings of the International Joint Conference on Acoustics, Speech and Signal Processing*, volume 33, pages 959–963.

Dayan, P., Hinton, G., Neal, R., and Zemel, R. (1995). The helmholtz machine. *Neural Computation*, 7:1022–1037.

De Bonet, J. S. (1997). Multiresolution sampling procedure for analysis and synthesis of texture images. In *Computer Graphics*. ACM SIGGRAPH.

Donoho, D. L. and Johnstone, I. M. (1993). Adaptation to unknown smoothness via wavelet shrinkage. Technical report, Stanford University, Department of Statistics. Also Tech. Report 425.

Duda, R. and Hart, P. (1973). *Pattern Classification and Scene Analysis*. John Wiley and Sons.

Fogel, I. and Sagi, D. (1989). Gabor filters as texture discriminator. *Biological Cybernetics*, 61:103–113.

Geman, S. and Geman, D. (1984). Stochastic relaxation, gibbs distributions, and the bayesian restoration of images. *IEEE Transactions on Pattern Analysis and Machine Intelligence*, 6:721–741.

Heeger, D. J. and Bergen, J. R. (1995). Pyramid-based texture analysis/synthesis. In *Computer Graphics Proceedings*, pages 229–238.

Hinton, G., Dayan, P., Frey, B., and Neal, R. (1995). The "wake-sleep" algorithm for unsupervised neural networks. *Science*, 268:1158–1161.

Simoncelli, E. P. and Adelson, E. H. (1996). Noise removal via bayesian wavelet coring. In *IEEE Third Int'l Conf on Image Processing*, Laussanne Switzerland. IEEE.

Simoncelli, E. P., Freeman, W. T., Adelson, E. H., and Heeger, D. J. (1992). Shiftable multiscale transforms. *IEEE Transactions on Information Theory*, 38(2):587–607.

Zhu, S. C., Wu, Y., and Mumford, D. (1996). Filters random fields and maximum entropy(frame): To a unified theory for texture modeling. *To appear in Int'l Journal of Computer Vision*.

Recovering Perspective Pose with a Dual Step EM Algorithm

Andrew D.J. Cross and Edwin R. Hancock,
Department of Computer Science,
University of York,
York, Y01 5DD, UK.

Abstract

This paper describes a new approach to extracting 3D perspective structure from 2D point-sets. The novel feature is to unify the tasks of estimating transformation geometry and identifying point-correspondence matches. Unification is realised by constructing a mixture model over the bi-partite graph representing the correspondence match and by effecting optimisation using the EM algorithm. According to our EM framework the probabilities of structural correspondence gate contributions to the expected likelihood function used to estimate maximum likelihood perspective pose parameters. This provides a means of rejecting structural outliers.

1   Introduction

The estimation of transformational geometry is key to many problems of computer vision and robotics [10]. Broadly speaking the aim is to recover a matrix representation of the transformation between image and world co-ordinate systems. In order to estimate the matrix requires a set of correspondence matches between features in the two co-ordinate systems [11]. Posed in this way there is a basic chicken-and-egg problem. Before good correspondences can be estimated, there need to be reasonable bounds on the transformational geometry. Yet this geometry is, after all, the ultimate goal of computation. This problem is usually overcome by invoking constraints to bootstrap the estimation of feasible correspondence matches [5, 8]. One of the most popular ideas is to use the epipolar constraint to prune the space of potential correspondences [5]. One of the drawbacks of this pruning strategy is that residual outliers may lead to ill-conditioned or singular parameter matrices [11].

The aim in this paper is to pose the two problems of estimating transformation geometry and locating correspondence matches using an architecture that is reminiscent of the hierarchical mixture of experts algorithm [6]. Specifically, we use a bi-partite graph to represent the current configuration of correspondence match. This graphical structure provides an architecture that can be used to gate contributions to the likelihood function for the geometric parameters using structural constraints. Correspondence matches and transformation parameters are estimated by applying the EM algorithm to the gated likelihood function. In this way we arrive at dual maximisation steps. Maximum likelihood parameters are found by minimising the structurally gated squared residuals between features in the two images being matched. Correspondence matches are updated so as to maximise the *a posteriori* probability of the observed structural configuration on the bi-partite association graph.

We provide a practical illustration in the domain of computer vision which is aimed at matching images of floppy discs under severe perspective foreshortening. However, it is important to stress that the idea of using a graphical model to provide structural constraints on parameter estimation is a task of generic importance. Although the EM algorithm has been used to extract affine and Euclidean parameters from point-sets [4] or line-sets [9], there has been no attempt to impose structural constraints of the correspondence matches. Viewed from the perspective of graphical template matching [1, 7] our EM algorithm allows an explicit deformational model to be imposed on a set of feature points. Since the method delivers statistical estimates for both the transformation parameters and their associated covariance matrix it offers significant advantages in terms of its adaptive capabilities.

2 Perspective Geometry

Our basic aim is to recover the perspective transformation parameters which bring a set of model or fiducial points into correspondence with their counterparts in a set of image data. Each point in the image data is represented by an augmented vector of co-ordinates $\underline{w}_i = (x_i, y_i, 1)^T$ where i is the point index. The available set of image points is denoted by $\mathbf{w} = \{\underline{w}_i, \forall i \in \mathcal{D}\}$ where $\mathcal{D}$ is the point index-set. The fiducial points constituting the model are similarly represented by the set of augmented co-ordinate vectors $\mathbf{z} = \{\underline{z}_j, \forall j \in \mathcal{M}\}$. Here $\mathcal{M}$ is the index-set for the model feature-points and the $\underline{z}_j$ represent the corresponding image co-ordinates.

Perspective geometry is distinguished from the simpler Euclidean (translation, rotation and scaling) and affine (the addition of shear) cases by the presence of significant foreshortening. We represent the perspective transformation by the parameter matrix

$$\Phi^{(n)} = \begin{pmatrix} \phi_{1,1}^{(n)} & \phi_{1,2}^{(n)} & \phi_{1,3}^{(n)} \\ \phi_{2,1}^{(n)} & \phi_{2,2}^{(n)} & \phi_{2,3}^{(n)} \\ \phi_{3,1}^{(n)} & \phi_{3,2}^{(n)} & \phi_{3,3}^{(n)} \end{pmatrix} \tag{1}$$

Using homogeneous co-ordinates, the transformation between model and data is $\underline{z}_j^{(n)} = (\frac{1}{\underline{z}_j^T \cdot \Psi^{(n)}})^{-1} \Phi^{(n)} \underline{z}_j$, where $\Psi^{(n)} = (\phi_{3,1}^{(n)}, \phi_{3,2}^{(n)}, 1)^T$ is a column-vector formed from the elements in bottom row of the transformation matrix.

3 Relational Constraints

One of our goals in this paper is to exploit structural constraints to improve the recovery of perspective parameters from sets of feature points. We abstract the process as bi-partite graph matching. Because of its well documented robustness to noise and change of viewpoint, we adopt the Delaunay triangulation as our basic representation of image structure [3]. We establish Delaunay triangulations on the data and the model, by seeding Voronoi tessellations from the feature-points.

The process of Delaunay triangulation generates relational graphs from the two sets of point-features. More formally, the point-sets are the nodes of a data graph $G_D = \{\mathcal{D}, E_D\}$ and a model graph $G_M = \{\mathcal{M}, E_M\}$. Here $E_D \subseteq \mathcal{D} \times \mathcal{D}$ and $E_M \subseteq \mathcal{M} \times \mathcal{M}$ are the edge-sets of the data and model graphs. Key to our matching process is the idea of using the edge-structure of Delaunay graphs to constrain the correspondence matches between the two point-sets. This correspondence matching is denoted by the function $f : \mathcal{M} \to \mathcal{D}$ from the nodes of the data-graph to those of the model graph. According to this notation the statement $f^{(n)}(i) = j$ indicates that there is a match between the node $i \in \mathcal{D}$ of the model-graph to the node $j \in \mathcal{M}$ of the model graph at iteration n of the algorithm. We use the binary indicator

$$s_{i,j}^{(n)} = \begin{cases} 1 & \text{if } f^{(n)}(i) = j \\ 0 & \text{otherwise} \end{cases} \tag{2}$$

to represent the configuration of correspondence matches.

We exploit the structure of the Delaunay graphs to compute the consistency of match using the Bayesian framework for relational graph-matching recently reported by Wilson and Hancock [12]. Suffice to say that consistency of a configuration of matches residing on the neighbourhood $R_i = i \cup \{k \; ; \; (i,k) \in E_D\}$ of the node i in the data-graph and its counterpart $S_j = j \cup \{l \; ; \; (j,l) \in E_m\}$ for the node j in the model-graph is gauged by Hamming distance. The Hamming distance $H(i,j)$ counts the number of matches on the data-graph neighbourhood R_i that are inconsistently matched onto the model-graph neighbourhood S_j. According to Wilson and Hancock [12] the structural probability for the correspondence match $f(i) = j$ at iteration n of the algorithm is given by

$$\zeta_{i,j}^{(n)} = \frac{\exp\left[-\beta H(i,j)\right]}{\sum_{j \in \mathcal{M}} \exp\left[-\beta H(i,j)\right]} \tag{3}$$

In the above expression, the Hamming distance is given by $H(i,j) = \sum_{(k,l) \in R_i \bullet S_j} (1 - s_{k,l}^{(n)})$ where the symbol $\bullet$ denotes the composition of the data-graph relation R_i and the model-graph relation S_j. The exponential constant $\beta = \ln \frac{1 - P_e}{P_e}$ is related to the uniform probability of structural matching errors P_e. This probability is set to reflect the overlap of the two point-sets. In the work reported here we set $P_e = \frac{2||\mathcal{M}| - |\mathcal{D}||}{||\mathcal{M}| + |\mathcal{D}||}$.

4 The EM Algorithm

Our aim is to extract perspective pose parameters and correspondences matches from the two point-sets using the EM algorithm. According to the original work of Dempster, Laird and Rubin [2] the expected likelihood function is computed by weighting the current log-probability density by the *a posteriori* measurement probabilities computed from the preceding maximum likelihood parameters. Jordan and Jacobs [6] augment the process with a graphical model which effectively gates contributions to the expected log-likelihood function. Here we provide a variant of this idea in which the bi-partite graph representing the correspondences matches gate the log-likelihood function for the perspective pose parameters.

4.1   Mixture Model

Our basic aim is to jointly maximize the data-likelihood $p(\mathbf{w}|\mathbf{z}, f, \Phi)$ over the space of correspondence matches f and the matrix of perspective parameters Φ. To commence our development, we assume observational independence and factorise the conditional measurement density over the set of data-items

$$p(\mathbf{w}|\mathbf{z}, f, \Phi) = \prod_{i \in \mathcal{D}} p(\underline{w}_i|\mathbf{z}, f, \Phi) \qquad (4)$$

In order to apply the apparatus of the EM algorithm to maximising $p(\mathbf{w}|\mathbf{z}, f, \Phi)$ with respect to f and Φ, we must establish a mixture model over the space of correspondence matches. Accordingly, we apply Bayes theorem to expand over the space of match indicator variables. In other words,

$$p(\underline{w}_i|\mathbf{z}, f, \Phi) = \sum_{s_{i,j} \in f} p(\underline{w}_i, s_{i,j}|\mathbf{z}, f, \Phi) \qquad (5)$$

In order to develop a tractable likelihood function, we apply the chain rule of conditional probability. In addition, we use the indicator variables to control the switching of the conditional measurement densities via exponentiation. In other words we assume $p(\underline{w}_i|s_{i,j}, \underline{z}_j, \Phi) = p(\underline{w}_i|\underline{z}_j, \Phi)^{s_{i,j}}$.

With this simplification, the mixture model for the correspondence matching process leads to the following expression for the expected likelihood function

$$Q(f^{(n+1)}, \Phi^{(n+1)}|f^{(n)}, \Phi^{(n)}) = \sum_{i \in \mathcal{D}} \sum_{i \in \mathcal{M}} P(s_{i,j}|\mathbf{w}, \mathbf{z}, f^{(n)}, \Phi^{(n)}) s_{i,j}^{(n)} \ln p(\underline{w}_i|\underline{z}_j, \Phi^{(n+1)})$$

$$(6)$$

To further simplify matters we make a mean-field approximation and replace $s_{i,j}^{(n)}$ by its average value, i.e. we make use of the fact that $E(s_{i,j}^{(n)}) = \zeta_{i,j}^{(n)}$. In this way the structural matching probabilities gate contributions to the expected likelihood function. This mean-field approximation alleviates problems associated with local optima which are likely to occur if the likelihood function is discretised by gating with $s_{i,j}$.

4.2   Expectation

Using the Bayes rule, we can re-write the *a posteriori* measurement probabilities in terms of the components of the conditional measurement densities appearing in the mixture model in equation (5)

$$P(s_{i,j}|\mathbf{w}, \mathbf{z}, f^{(n)}, \Phi^{(n+1)}) = \frac{\zeta_{i,j}^{(n)} p(\underline{w}_i|\underline{z}_j, \Phi^{(n)})}{\sum_{j' \in \mathcal{M}} \zeta_{i,j'}^{(n)} p(\underline{w}_i|\underline{z}_{j'}, \Phi^{(n)})} \qquad (7)$$

In order to proceed with the development of a point registration process we require a model for the conditional measurement densities, i.e. $p(\underline{w}_i|\underline{z}_j, \Phi^{(n)})$. Here we assume that the required model can be specified in terms of a multivariate Gaussian distribution. The random variables appearing in these distributions are the error residuals for the position predictions of the jth model line delivered by the current estimated transformation parameters. Accordingly we write

$$p(\underline{w}_i|\underline{z}_j, \Phi^{(n)}) = \frac{1}{(2\pi)^{\frac{3}{2}}\sqrt{|\Sigma|}} \exp\left[-\frac{1}{2}(\underline{w}_i - \underline{z}_j^{(n)})^T \Sigma^{-1} (\underline{w}_i - \underline{z}_j^{(n)})\right] \tag{8}$$

In the above expression Σ is the variance-covariance matrix for the vector of error-residuals $\epsilon_{i,j}(\Phi^{(n)}) = \underline{w}_i - \underline{z}_j^{(n)}$ between the components of the predicted measurement vectors $\underline{z}_j'$ and their counterparts in the data, i.e. $\underline{w}_i$. Formally, the matrix is related to the expectation of the outer-product of the error-residuals i.e. $\Sigma = E[\epsilon_{i,j}(\Phi^{(n)})\epsilon_{i,j}(\Phi^{(n)})^T]$.

4.3   Maximisation

The maximisation step of our matching algorithm is based on two coupled update processes. The first of these aims to locate maximum *a posteriori* probability correspondence matches. The second class of update operation is concerned with locating maximum likelihood transformation parameters. We effect the coupling by allowing information flow between the two processes. Correspondences located by maximum *a posteriori* graph-matching are used to constrain the recovery of maximum likelihood transformation parameters. *A posteriori* measurement probabilities computed from the updated transformation parameters are used to refine the correspondence matches.

In terms of the indicator variables matches the configuration of maximum *a posteriori* probability correspondence matches is updated as follows

$$f^{(n+1)}(i) = \arg\max_{j \in \mathcal{M}} P(\underline{z}_j|\underline{w}_i, \Phi^{(n)}) \frac{\exp\left[-\beta \sum_{(k,l) \in R_i \bullet S_j}(1 - s_{k,l}^{(n)})\right]}{\sum_{j \in \mathcal{M}} \exp\left[-\beta \sum_{(k,l) \in R_i \bullet S_j}(1 - s_{k,l}^{(n)})\right]} \tag{9}$$

The maximum likelihood transformation parameters satisfy the condition

$$\Phi^{(n+1)} = \arg\min_{\Phi} \sum_{i \in \mathcal{D}} \sum_{i \in \mathcal{M}} P(\underline{z}_j|\underline{w}_i, \Phi^{(n)})\varsigma_{i,j}^{(n)}(\underline{w}_i - \underline{z}_j^{(n)})^T \Sigma^{-1}(\underline{w}_i - \underline{z}_j^{(n)}) \tag{10}$$

In the case of perspective geometry where we have used homogeneous co-ordinates the saddle-point equations are not readily amenable in a closed-form linear fashion. Instead, we solve the non-linear maximisation problem using the Levenberg-Marquardt technique. This non-linear optimisation technique offers a compromise between the steepest gradient and inverse Hessian methods. The former is used when close to the optimum while the latter is used far from it.

5   Experiments

The real-world evaluation of our matching method is concerned with recognising planer objects in different 3D poses. The object used in this study is a 3.5 inch floppy disk which is placed on a desktop. The scene is viewed with a low-quality SGI IndyCam. The feature points used to triangulate the object are corners. Since the imaging process is not accurately modelled by a perspective transformation under pin-hole optics, the example provides a challenging test of our matching process.

Our experiments are illustrated in Figure 1. The first two columns show the views under match. In the first example (the upper row of Figure 1) we are concerned with matching when there is a significant difference in perspective forshortening. In the example shown in the lower row of Figure 1, there is a rotation of the object in addition to the foreshortening. The images in the third column are the initial matching configurations. Here the perspective parameter matrix has been selected at random. The fourth column in Figure 1 shows the final matching configuration after the EM algorithm has converged. In both cases the final registration is accurate. The algorithm appears to be capable of recovering good matches even when the initial pose estimate is poor.

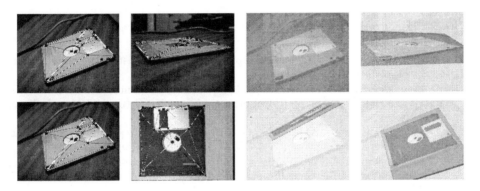

Figure 1: Images Under Match, Initial and Final Configurations.

We now turn to measuring the sensitivity of our method. In order to illustrate the benefits offered by the structural gating process, we compare its performance with a conventional least-squares parameter estimation process. Figure 2 shows a comparison of the two algorithms for a problem involving a point-set of 20 nodes. Here we show the RMS error as a function of the number of points which have correct correspondence matches. The break-even point occurs when 8 nodes are initially matched correctly and there are 12 errors. Once the number of initially correct correspondences exceeds 8 then the EM method consistently outperforms the least-squares estimation.

6 Conclusions

Our main contributions in this paper are twofold. The theoretical contribution has been to develop a mixture model that allows a graphical structure to to constrain the estimation of maximum likelihood model parameters. The second contribution is a practical one, and involves the application of the mixture model to the estimation of perspective pose parameters. There are a number of ways in which the ideas developed in this paper can be extended. For instance, the framework is readily extensible to the recognition of more complex non-planar objects.

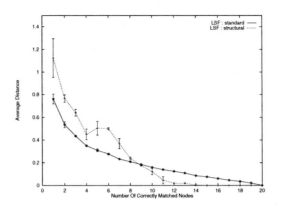

Figure 2: Structural Sensitivity.

References

[1] Y. Amit and A. Kong, "Graphical Templates for Model Registration", *IEEE PAMI*, **18**, pp. 225–236, 1996.

[2] A.P. Dempster, Laird N.M. and Rubin D.B., "Maximum-likelihood from incomplete data via the EM algorithm", J. Royal Statistical Soc. Ser. B (methodological),**39**, pp 1-38, 1977.

[3] O.D. Faugeras, E. Le Bras-Mehlman and J-D. Boissonnat, "Representing Stereo Data with the Delaunay Triangulation", *Artificial Intelligence*, **44**, pp. 41–87, 1990.

[4] S. Gold, Rangarajan A. and Mjolsness E., "Learning with pre-knowledge: Clustering with point and graph-matching distance measures", *Neural Computation*, **8**, pp. 787–804, 1996.

[5] R.I. Hartley, "Projective Reconstruction and Invariants from Multiple Images", *IEEE PAMI*, **16**, pp. 1036—1041, 1994.

[6] M.I. Jordan and R.A. Jacobs, "Hierarchical Mixtures of Experts and the EM Algorithm", *Neural Computation*, **6**, pp. 181-214, 1994.

[7] M. Lades, J.C. Vorbruggen, J. Buhmann, J. Lange, C. von der Maalsburg, R.P. Wurtz and W.Konen, "Distortion-invariant object-recognition in a dynamic link architecture", *IEEE Transactions on Computers*, **42**, pp. 300–311, 1993

[8] D.P. McReynolds and D.G. Lowe, "Rigidity Checking of 3D Point Correspondences under Perspective Projection", *IEEE PAMI*, **18** , pp. 1174–1185, 1996.

[9] S. Moss and E.R. Hancock, "Registering Incomplete Radar Images with the EM Algorithm", *Image and Vision Computing*, **15**, 637–648, 1997.

[10] D. Oberkampf, D.F. DeMenthon and L.S. Davis, "Iterative Pose Estimation using Coplanar Feature Points", *Computer Vision and Image Understanding*, **63**, pp. 495–511, 1996.

[11] P. Torr, A. Zisserman and S.J. Maybank, "Robust Detection of Degenerate Configurations for the Fundamental Matrix", *Proceedings of the Fifth International Conference on Computer Vision*, pp. 1037-1042, 1995.

[12] R.C. Wilson and E.R. Hancock, "Structural Matching by Discrete Relaxation", *IEEE PAMI*, **19**, pp.634–648, 1997.

Bayesian model of surface perception

William T. Freeman
MERL, Mitsubishi Electric Res. Lab.
201 Broadway
Cambridge, MA 02139
freeman@merl.com

Paul A. Viola
Artificial Intelligence Lab
Massachusetts Institute of Technology
Cambridge, MA 02139
viola@ai.mit.edu

Abstract

Image intensity variations can result from several different object surface effects, including shading from 3-dimensional relief of the object, or paint on the surface itself. An essential problem in vision, which people solve naturally, is to attribute the proper physical cause, e.g. surface relief or paint, to an observed image. We addressed this problem with an approach combining psychophysical and Bayesian computational methods.

We assessed human performance on a set of test images, and found that people made fairly consistent judgements of surface properties. Our computational model assigned simple prior probabilities to different relief or paint explanations for an image, and solved for the most probable interpretation in a Bayesian framework. The ratings of the test images by our algorithm compared surprisingly well with the mean ratings of our subjects.

1 Introduction

When people study a picture, they can judge whether it depicts a shaded, 3-dimensional surface, or simply a flat surface with markings or paint on it. The two images shown in Figure 1 illustrate this distinction [1]. To many observers Figure 1a appears to be a raised plateau lit from the left. Figure 1b is simply a re-arrangement of the local features of 1a, yet it does not give an impression of shape or depth. There is no simple correct answer for this problem; either of these images could be explained as marks on paper, or as illuminated shapes. Nevertheless people tend to make particular judgements of shape or reflectance. We seek an algorithm to arrive at those same judgements.

There are many reasons to study this problem. Disentangling shape and reflectance is a prototypical underdetermined vision problem, which biological vision systems routinely solve. Insights into this problem may apply to other vision problems as well. A machine that could interpret images as people do would have many applications, such as the interactive editing and manipulation of images. Finally, there is a large body of computer vision work on "shape from shading"–inferring the 3-dimensional shape of a shaded object [4]. Virtually every algorithm assumes that all image intensity changes are caused by shading; these algorithms fail for any image with reflectance changes. To bring this body of work into practical use, we need to be able to disambiguate shading from reflectance changes.

There has been very little work on this problem. Sinha and Adelson [9] examined a world of painted polyhedra, and used consistancy constraints to identify regions of shape and reflectance changes. Their consistancy constraints involved specific assumptions which need not always hold and may be better described in a probabilistic framework. In addition, we seek a solution for more general, greyscale images.

Our approach combines psychophysics and computational modeling. First we will review the physics of image formation and describe the under-constrained surface perception problem. We then describe an experiment to measure the interpretations of surface shading and reflectance among different individuals. We will see that the judgements are fairly consistent across individuals and can be averaged to define "ground truth" for a set of test images. Our approach to modeling the human judgements is Bayesian. We begin by formulating prior probabilities for shapes and reflectance images, in the spirit of recent work on the statistical modeling of images [5, 8, 11]. Using these priors, the algorithm then determines whether an image is more likely to have been generated by a 3D shape or as a pattern of reflectance. We compare our algorithm's performance to that of the human subjects.

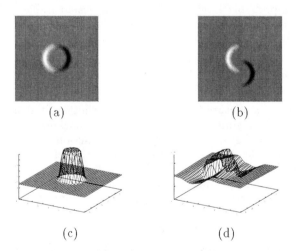

(a)   (b)

(c)   (d)

Figure 1: Images (a) and (b), designed by Adelson [1], are nearly the same everywhere, yet give different percepts of shading and reflectance. (a) looks like a plateau, lit from the left; (b) looks like marks on paper. Illustrating the under-constrained nature of perception, both images can be explained either by reflectance changes on paper (they are), or, under appropriate lighting conditions, by the shapes (c) and (d), respectively (vertical scale exaggerated).

2   Physics of Imaging

One simple model for the generation of an image from a three dimensional shape is the Lambertian model:

$$I(x, y) = R(x, y) \left(\hat{l} \cdot \hat{n}(x, y) \right), \tag{1}$$

where $I(x, y)$ is an image indexed by pixel location, $\hat{n}(x, y)$ is the surface normal at every point on the surface conveniently indexed by the pixel to which that surface patch projects, $\hat{l}$ is a unit vector that points in the direction of the light source, and $R(x, y)$ is the reflectance at every point on the surface[1]. A patch of surface is brighter if the light shines onto it directly and darker if the light shines on it obliquely. A patch can also be dark simply because it is painted with a darker pigment. The shape of the object is probably more easily described as a depth map $z(x, y)$ from which $\hat{n}(x, y)$ is computed.

The classical "shape from shading" task attempts to compute z from I given knowledge of $\hat{l}$ and assuming R is everywhere constant. Notice that the problem is "ill-posed"; while $I(x, y)$ does constrain $\hat{n}(x, y)$ it is not sufficient to uniquely determine the surface normal at each pixel. Some assumption about global properties of z is necessary to *condition* the problem. If R is allowed to vary, the problem becomes even more under-constrained. For example, $R = I$ and $\hat{n}(x, y) = \hat{l}$ is a valid solution for every image. This is the "all reflectance" hypothesis, where the inferred surface is flat and all of the image variation is due to reflectance. Interestingly there is also an "all shape" solution for every image where $R = 1$ and $I(x, y) = \hat{l} \cdot \hat{n}(x, y)$ (see Figure 1 for examples of such shapes).

Since the relationship between z and I is non-linear, "shape from shading" cannot be solved directly and requires a time consuming search procedure. For our computational experiments we seek a rendering model for shapes which simplifies the mathematics, yet maintains the essential ambiguities of the problem. We use the approximations of linear shading [6]. This involves two sets of approximations. First, that the rendered image $I(x, y)$ is some function, $G(\frac{\partial z}{\partial x}, \frac{\partial z}{\partial y})$, only of the surface slope at any point:

$$I(x, y) \approx G(\frac{\partial z}{\partial x}, \frac{\partial z}{\partial y}). \tag{2}$$

The second approximation is that the rendering function G itself is a linear function of the surface slopes,

$$G(\frac{\partial z}{\partial x}, \frac{\partial z}{\partial y}) \approx k_1 + k_2 \frac{\partial z}{\partial x} + k_3 \frac{\partial z}{\partial y}. \tag{3}$$

Under linear shading, finding a shape which explains a given image is a trivial integration along the direction of the assumed light source. Despite this simplicity, images rendered under linear shading appear fairly realistically shaded [6].

3   Psychophysics

We used a survey to assess subjects' image judgements. We made a set of 60 test images, using Canvas and Photoshop programs to generate and manipulate the images. Our goal was to create a set of images with varying degrees of shadedness. We sought to assess to what extent each subject saw each image as created by

---

[1] Note: we assume orthographic projection, a distant light source, and no shadowing.

shading changes or reflectance changes. Each of our 18 naive observers was given a 4 page survey showing the images in a different random order.

To explain the problem of image interpretation quickly to naive subjects, we used a concrete story (Adelson's Theater Set Shop analogy [2] is a related didactic example). The survey instructions were as follows:

> *Pretend that each of the following pictures is a photograph of work made by either a painter or a sculptor.*
>
> *The painter could use paint, markers, air brushes, computer, etc., to make any kind of mark on a flat canvas. The paint had no 3-dimensionality; everything was perfectly flat.*
>
> *The sculptor could make 3-dimensional objects, but could make no markings on them. She could mold, sculpt, and scrape her sculptures, but could not draw or paint. All the objects were made out of a uniform plaster material and were made visible by lighting and shading effects.*

The subjects used a 5-point rating scale to indicate whether each image was made by the painter (P) or sculptor (S): S, S?, ?, P?, P.

3.1   Survey Results

We examined a non-parametric comparison of the image ratings, the rank order correlation (the linear correlation of image rankings in order of shapeness by each observer) [7]. Over all possible pairings of subjects, the rank order correlations ranged from 0.3 to 0.9, averaging 0.65. All of these correlations were statistically significant, most at the 0.0001 level. We concluded that for our set of test images, people do give a very similar set of interpretations of shading and reflectance.

We assigned a numerical value to each of the 5 survey responses (S=2; S?=1; ?=0; P?=-1; P=-2) and found the average numerical "shadedness" score for each image. Figure 2 shows a histogram of the survey responses for each image, ordered in decreasing order of shadedness. The two images of Figure 1 had average scores of 1.7 and -1.6, respectively, confirming the impressions of shading and reflectance. There was good consensus for the rankings of the most paint-like and most sculpture-like images; the middle images showed a higher score variance. The rankings by each individual showed a strong correlation with the rankings by the average of the remaining subjects, ranging from 0.6 to 0.9. Figure 4 shows the histogram of those correlations. The ordering of the images by the average of the subjects' responses provides a "ground truth" with which to compare the rankings of our algorithm. Figure 3, left, shows a randomly chosen subset of the sorted images, in decreasing order of assessed sculptureness.

4   Algorithm

We will assume that people are choosing the most probable interpretation of the observed image. We will adopt a Bayesian approach and calculate the most probable interpretation for each image under a particular set of prior probabilities for images and shapes. To parallel the choices we gave our subjects, we will choose between interpretations that account for the image entirely by shape changes, or entirely by reflectance changes. Thus, our images are either a rendered shape, multiplied by a uniform reflectance image, or a flat shape, multiplied by some non-uniform reflectance image.

intensity: score frequency for each image

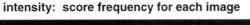
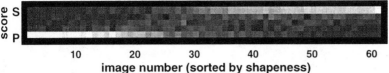

Figure 2: Histogram of survey responses. Intensity shows the number of responses of each score (vertical scale) for each image (horizontal, sorted in increasing order of shapeness).

To find the most probable interpretation, given an image, we need to assign prior probabilities to shape and reflectance configurations. There has been recent interest in characterizing the probabilities of images by the expected distributions of subband coefficient values [5, 8, 11]. The statistical distribution of bandpass linear filter outputs, for natural images, is highly kurtotic; the output is usually small, but in rare cases it takes on very large values. This non-gaussian behavior is not a property of the filter operation, because filtered "random" images appear gaussian. Rather it is a property of the structure of natural images. An exponential distribution, $P(c) \propto e^{-|c|}$, where c is the filter coefficient value, is a reasonable model. These priors have been used in texture synthesis, noise removal, and receptive field modeling. Here, we apply them to the task of scene interpretation.

We explored using a very simple image prior:

$$P(I) \propto \exp\left(-\sum_{x,y} \sqrt{\frac{\partial I(x,y)}{\partial x}^2 + \frac{\partial I(x,y)}{\partial y}^2}\right) \tag{4}$$

Here we treat the image derivative as an image subband corresponding to a very simple filter. We applied this image prior to both reflectance images, $I(x,y)$, as well as range images, $z(x,y)$.

For any given picture, we seek to decide whether a shape or a reflectance explanation is more probable. The proper Bayesian approach would be to integrate the prior probabilities of all shapes which could explain the image in order to arrive at the total probability of a shape explanation. (The reflectance explanation, $\hat{R}$ is unique; the image itself). We employed a computationally simpler procedure, a very rough approximation to the proper calculation: we evaluated the prior probability, $P(\hat{S})$ of the single, most probable shape explanation, $\hat{S}$, for the image. Using the ratio test of a binary hypothesis, we formed a shapeness index, J, by the ratio of the probabilities for the shape and reflectance explanations, $J = \frac{P(\hat{S})}{P(\hat{R})}$. The index J was used to rank the test images by shapeness.

We need to find the most probable shape explanation. The overall log likelihood of a shape, z, given an image is, using the linear shading approximations of Eq. (3):

$$
\begin{aligned}
\log P(z, k_1, k_2, k_3 | I) &= \log P(I | z, k_1, k_2, k_3) + \log P(z) + c \\
&= \sum_{x,y} (I - k_1 + k_2 \frac{\partial z}{\partial x} + k_3 \frac{\partial z}{\partial y})^2 + \sum_{x,y} \sqrt{\frac{\partial z}{\partial x}^2 + \frac{\partial z}{\partial y}^2} + c,
\end{aligned}
\tag{5}
$$

where c is a normalization constant. We use a multi-scale gradient descent algorithm that simultaneously determines the optimal shape and illumination parameters for an image (similar to that used by [10]). The optimization procedure has three stages starting with a quarter resolution version of I, and moving to the half and

Human Rankings   Algorithm Rankings

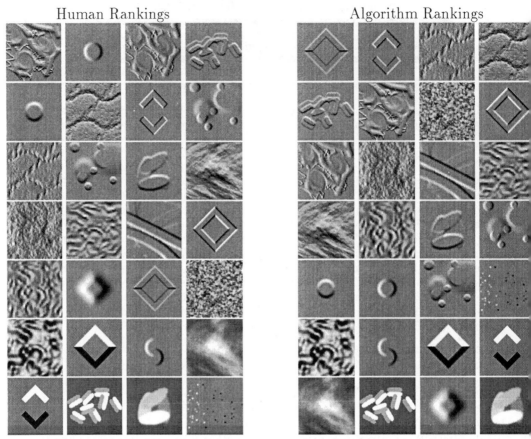

Figure 3: 28 of the 60 test images, arranged in decreasing order of subjects'
shapeness ratings. Left: Subjects' rankings. Right: Algorithm's rankings.

then full resolution. The solution found at the low resolution is interpolated up to
the next level and is used as a starting point for the next step in the optimization.
In our experiments images are 128x128 pixels. The optimization procedure takes
4000 descent steps at each resolution level.

5   Results

Surprisingly, the simple prior probability of Eq. (4) accounts for much of the ratings
of shading or paint by our human subjects. Figure 3 compares the rankings (shown
in raster scan order) of a subset of the test images for our algorithm and the average
of our subjects. The overall agreement is good. Figure 4 compares two measures: (1)
the correlations (dark bars) of the subjects' individual ratings to the mean subject
rating with (2) the correlation of our algorithm's ratings to the mean subject rating.
Subjects show correlations between 0.6 and 0.9; our Bayesian algorithm showed a
correlation of 0.64. Treating the mean subjects' ratings as the right answer, our
algorithm did worse than most subjects but not as badly as some subjects.

Figure 1 illustrates how our algorithm chooses an interpretation for an image. If a
simple shape explains an image, such as the shape explanation (c) for image (a),
the shape gradient penalties will be small, assigning a high prior probability to that
shape. If a complicated shape (d) is required to explain a simple image (b), the

low prior probability of the shape and the high prior probability of the reflectance image will favor a "paint" explanation.

We noted that many of the shapes inferred from paint-like images showed long ridges coincidently aligned with the assumed light direction. The assumption of generic light direction can be applied in a Bayesian framework [3] to penalize such coincidental alignments. We speculate that such a term would further penalize those unlikely shape interpretations and may improve algorithm performance.

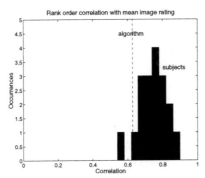

Figure 4: Correlation of individual subjects' image ratings compared with the mean rating (bars) compared with correlation of algorithm's rating with the mean rating (dashed line).

Acknowledgements

We thank E. Adelson, D. Brainard, and J. Tenenbaum for helpful discussions.

References

[1] E. H. Adelson, 1995. personal communication.

[2] E. H. Adelson and A. P. Pentland. The perception of shading and reflectance. In B. Blum, editor, *Channels in the Visual Nervous System: Neurophysiology, Psychophysics, and Models*, pages 195–207. Freund Publishing, London, 1991.

[3] W. T. Freeman. The generic viewpoint assumption in a framework for visual perception. *Nature*, 368(6471):542–545, April 7 1994.

[4] B. K. P. Horn and M. J. Brooks. *Shape from shading*. MIT Press, Cambridge, MA, 1989.

[5] B. A. Olshausen and D. J. Field. Emergence of simple-cell receptive field properties by learning a sparse code for natural images. *Nature*, 381:607–609, 1996.

[6] A. P. Pentland. Linear shape from shading. *Intl. J. Comp. Vis.*, 1(4):153–162, 1990.

[7] W. H. Press, S. A. Teukolsky, W. T. Vetterling, and B. P. Flannery. *Numerical Recipes in C*. Cambridge Univ. Press, 1992.

[8] E. P. Simoncelli and E. H. Adelson. Noise removal via Bayesian wavelet coring. In *3rd Annual Intl. Conf. on Image Processing*, Laussanne, Switzerland, 1996. IEEE.

[9] P. Sinha and E. H. Adelson. Recovering reflectance and illumination in a world of painted polyhedra. In *Proc. 4th Intl. Conf. Computer Vision*, pages 156–163. IEEE, 1993.

[10] D. Terzopoulos. Multilevel computational processes for visual surface reconstruction. *Comp. Vis., Graphics, Image Proc.*, 24:52–96, 1983.

[11] S. C. Zhu and D. Mumford. Learning generic prior models for visual computation. Submitted to IEEE Trans. PAMI, 1997.

Features as Sufficient Statistics

D. Geiger [*]
Department of Computer Science
Courant Institute
and Center for Neural Science
New York University
geiger@cs.nyu.edu

A. Rudra [†]
Department of Computer Science
Courant Institute
New York University
archi@cs.nyu.edu

L. Maloney [‡]
Departments of Psychology and Neural Science
New York University
ltm@cns.nyu.edu

Abstract

An image is often represented by a set of detected features. We get an enormous compression by representing images in this way. Furthermore, we get a representation which is little affected by small amounts of noise in the image. However, features are typically chosen in an ad hoc manner. We show how a good set of features can be obtained using sufficient statistics. The idea of sparse data representation naturally arises. We treat the 1-dimensional and 2-dimensional signal reconstruction problem to make our ideas concrete.

1 Introduction

Consider an image, I, that is the result of a stochastic image-formation process. The process depends on the precise state, f, of an environment. The image, accordingly, contains information about the environmental state f, possibly corrupted by noise. We wish to choose feature vectors $\phi(I)$ derived from the image that summarize this information concerning the environment. We are not otherwise interested in the contents of the image and wish to discard any information concerning the image that does not depend on the environmental state f.

---

[*]Supported by NSF grant 5274883 and AFOSR grants F 49620-96-1-0159 and F 49620-96-1-0028

[†]Partially supported by AFOSR grants F 49620-96-1-0159 and F 49620-96-1-0028

[‡]Supported by NIH grant EY08266

We develop criteria for choosing sets of features (based on information theory and statistical estimation theory) that extract from the image precisely the information concerning the environmental state.

2 Image Formation, Sufficient Statistics and Features

As above, the image I is the realization of a random process with distribution $P_{Environment}(f)$. We are interested in estimating the parameters f of the environmental model given the image (compare [4]). We assume in the sequel that f, the environmental parameters, are themselves a random vector with known prior distribution. Let $\phi(I)$ denote a feature vector derived from the the image I. Initially, we assume that $\phi(I)$ is a deterministic function of I.

For any choice of random variables, X, Y, define[2] the *mutual information* of X and Y to be $M(X;Y) = \sum_{X,Y} P(X,Y) log \frac{P(X,Y)}{P(X)P(Y)}$. The information about the environmental parameters contained in the image is then $M(f;I)$, while the information about the environmental parameters contained in the feature vector $\phi(I)$ is then $M(f;\phi(I))$. As a consequence of the *data processing inequality*[2], $M(f;\phi(I)) \leq M(f;I)$.

A vector $\phi(I)$, of features is defined to be *sufficient* if the inequality above is an equality. We will use the terms *feature* and *statistic* interchangeably. The definition of a sufficient feature vector above is then just the usual definition of a set of *jointly sufficient statistics*[2].

To summarize, a feature vector $\phi(I)$ captures all the information about the environmental state parameters f precisely when it is sufficent. [1]

Graded Sufficiency: A feature vector either is or is not sufficient. For every possible feature vector $\phi(I)$, we define a measure of its failure to be sufficent: $\text{Suff}(\phi(I)) = M(f;I) - M(f;\phi(I))$. This *sufficency measure* is always non-negative and it is zero precisely when ϕ is sufficient. We wish to find feature vectors $\phi(I)$ where $\text{Suff}(\phi(I))$ is close to 0. We define $\phi(I)$ to be ϵ-sufficient if $\text{Suff}(\phi(I)) \leq \epsilon$. In what follows, we will ordinarily say sufficient, when we mean ϵ-sufficient.

The above formulation of feature vectors as jointly sufficient statistics, maximizing the mutual information, $M(f,\phi(I))$, can be expressed as the *Kullback-Leibler distance* between the conditional distributions, $P(f|I)$ and $P(f|\phi(I))$:

$$E_I[D(P(f|I) \| P(f|\phi(I)))] = M(f;I) - M(f;\phi(I)), \tag{1}$$

where the symbol E_I denotes the expectation with respect to I, D denotes the *Kullback-Leibler (K-L) distance*, defined by $D(f\|g) = \sum_x f(x) \log(f(x)/g(x))$ [2].

Thus, we seek feature vectors $\phi(I)$ such that the conditional distributions, $P(f|I)$ and $P(f|\phi(I))$ in the K-L sense, averaged across the set of images. However, this optimization for each image could lead to over-fitting.

3 Sparse Data and Sufficient Statistics

The notion of sufficient statistics may be described by how much data can be removed without increasing the K-L distance between $P(f|\phi(I))$ and $P(f|I)$. Let us

---

[1]An information-theoretic framework has been adopted in neural networks by others; e.g., [5] [9][6] [1][8]. However, the connection between features and sufficiency is new.

[2]We won't prove the result here. The proof is simple and uses the Markov chain property to say that $P(f,I,\phi(I)) = P(I,\phi(I))P(f|I,\phi(I)) = P(I)P(f|I)$.

formulate the approach more precisely, and apply two methods to solve it.

3.1   Gaussian Noise Model and Sparse Data

We are required to construct $P(f|I)$ and $P(f|\phi(I))$. Note that according to Bayes'
rule $P(f|\phi(I)) = P(\phi(I)|f) P(f) / P(\phi(I))$. We will assume that the form of
the model $P(f)$ is known. In order to obtain $P(\phi(I)|f)$ we write $P(\phi(I)|f) =
\sum_I P(\phi(I)|I)P(I|f)$.

Computing $P(f|\phi(I))$: Let us first assume that the generative process of the image
I, given the model f, is Gaussian i.i.d. , i.e., $P(I|f) = (1/\sqrt{2\pi\sigma_i^2}) \prod_i e^{-(f_i-I_i)^2/2\sigma_i^2}$
where $i = 0, 1, ..., N - 1$ are the image pixel index for an image of size N. Fur-
ther, $P(I_i|f_i)$ is a function of $(I_i - f_i)$ and I_i varies from $-\infty$ to $+\infty$, so that the
normalization constant does not depend on f_i. Then, $P(f|I)$ can be obtained by
normalizing $P(f)P(I|f)$.

$$P(f|I) = (1/Z)(\prod_i e^{-(f_i-I_i)^2/2\sigma_i^2})P(f),$$

where Z is the normalization constant.

Let us introduce a binary decision variable $s_i = 0, 1$, which at every image pixel i
decides if that image pixel contains "important" information or not regarding the
model f. Our statistic ϕ is actually a (multivariate) random variable generated
from I according to

$$P_s(\phi|I) = \prod_i \sqrt{\frac{(1-s_i)}{2\pi\sigma_i^2 s_i}} e^{-\frac{1}{2\sigma_i^2}(I_i-\phi_i)^2 \frac{(1-s_i)}{s_i}}.$$

This distribution gives $\phi_i = I_i$ with probability 1 (Dirac delta function) when $s_i = 0$
(data is kept) and gives ϕ_i uniformly distributed otherwise ($s_i = 1$, data is removed).
We then have

$$
\begin{aligned}
P_s(\phi|f) &= \int P(\phi, I|f) \, dI = \int P(I|f) \, P_s(\phi|I) \, dI \\
&= \prod_i \frac{1}{\sqrt{2\pi\sigma_i^2}} \int e^{-\frac{1}{2\sigma_i^2}(f_i-I_i)^2} \sqrt{\frac{(1-s_i)}{2\pi\sigma_i^2 s_i}} e^{-\frac{1}{2\sigma_i^2}(I_i-\phi_i)^2 \frac{(1-s_i)}{s_i}} \, dI_i \\
&= \prod_i \sqrt{\frac{(1-s_i)}{2\pi\sigma_i^2}} e^{-\frac{1}{2\sigma_i^2}(f_i-\phi_i)^2(1-s_i)}.
\end{aligned}
$$

The conditional distribution of ϕ on f satisfies the properties that we mentioned in
connection with the posterior distribution of f on I. Thus,

$$P_s(f|\phi) = (1/Z_s) P(f) \left(\prod_i e^{-\frac{1}{2\sigma_i^2}(f_i-I_i)^2(1-s_i)}\right) \qquad (2)$$

where Z_s is a normalization constant.

It is also plausible to extend this model to non-Gaussian ones, by simply modifying
the quadratic term $(f_i - I_i)^2$ and keeping the sparse data coefficient $(1 - s_i)$.

3.2   Two Methods

We can now formulate the problem of finding a feature-set, or finding a sufficient
statistics, in terms of the variables s_i that can remove data. More precisely, we can
find s by minimizing

$$E(s, I) = D(P(f|I) \| P_s(f|\phi(I))) + \lambda \sum_i (1 - s_i). \tag{3}$$

It is clear that the *K-L* distance is minimized when $s_i = 0$ everywhere and all the data is kept. The second term is added on to drive the solution towards a minimal sufficient statistic, where the parameter λ has to be estimated. Note that, for λ very large, all the data is removed ($s_i = 1$), while for $\lambda = 0$ all the data is kept.

We can further write (3) as

$$
\begin{aligned}
E(s, I) &= \sum_f P(f|I) \log(P(f|I)/P_s(f|\phi(I))) + \lambda \sum_i (1 - s_i) \\
&= \sum_f P(f|I) log\left((Z_s/Z) \prod_i e^{-\frac{1}{2\sigma_i^2}(f_i - I_i)^2(1-(1-s_i))}\right) + \lambda \sum_i (1 - s_i) \\
&= log\frac{Z_s}{Z} - E_P[\sum_i \frac{s_i}{2\sigma_i^2}(f_i - I_i)^2)] + \lambda \sum_i (1 - s_i).
\end{aligned}
$$

where $E_P[.]$ denotes the expectation taken with respect to the distribution P.

If we let s_i be a continuous variable the minimum $E(s, I)$ will occur when

$$0 = \frac{\partial E}{\partial s_i} = (E_{P_s}[(f_i - I_i)^2] - E_P[(f_i - I_i)^2]) - \lambda. \tag{4}$$

We note that the Hessian matrix

$$H_s[i, j] = \frac{\partial^2 E}{\partial s_i \partial s_j} = E_{P_s}[(f_i - I_i)^2(f_j - I_j)^2] - E_{P_s}[(f_i - I_i)^2]E_{P_s}[(f_j - I_j)^2], \tag{5}$$

is a correlation matrix, i.e., it is positive semi-definite. Consequently, $E(s)$ is convex.

Continuation Method on λ:

In order to solve for the optimal vector s we consider the continuation method on the parameter λ. We know that $s = 0$, for $\lambda = 0$. Then, taking derivatives of (4) with respect to λ, we obtain

$$\sum_j \frac{\partial^2 E}{\partial s_i \partial s_j} \frac{\partial s_j}{\partial \lambda} - \frac{\partial^2 E}{\partial \lambda \partial s_i} = 0 \quad \rightarrow \quad \frac{\partial s_j}{\partial \lambda} = \sum_i H_s^{-1}[i, j].$$

It was necessary the Hessian to be invertible, i.e., the continuation method works because E is convex. The computations are expected to be mostly spent on estimating the Hessian matrix, i.e., on computing the averages $E_{P_s}[(f_i - I_i)^2(f_j - I_j)^2]$, $E_{P_s}[(f_i - I_i)^2]$, and $E_{P_s}[(f_j - I_j)^2]$. Sometimes these averages can be exactly computed, for example for one dimensional graph lattices. Otherwise these averages could be estimated via Gibbs sampling.

The above method can be very slow, since these computations for H_s have to be repeated at each increment in λ. We then investigate an alternative direct method.

A Direct Method:

Our approach seeks to find a "large set" of $s_i = 1$ and to maintain a distribution $P_s(f|\phi(I))$ close to $P(f|I)$, i.e., to remove as many data points as possible. For this

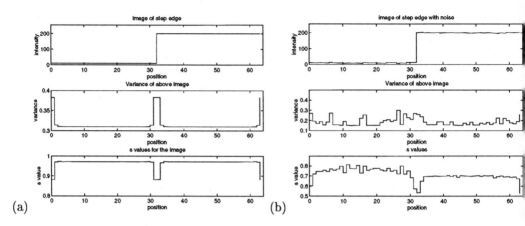

Figure 1: (a). Complete results for step edge showing the image, the effective variance and the computed s-value (using the continuation method). (b) Complete results for step edge with added noise.

goal, we can investigate the marginal distribution

$$
\begin{aligned}
P(f_i|I) &= \int df_0 \dots df_{i-1}\, df_{i+1} \dots df_{N-1}\, P(f|I) \\
&= \frac{1}{Z}\, e^{-\frac{1}{2\sigma_i^2}(f_i - I_i)^2} \int \prod_{j\neq i} df_j\, P(f) \left(\prod_{j\neq i} e^{-\frac{1}{2\sigma_j^2}(f_j - I_j)^2} \right) \\
&= P_{I_i}(f_i)\, P_{eff}(f_i), \quad \text{(after rearranging the normalization constants)}
\end{aligned}
$$

where $P_{eff}(f_i)$ is an effective marginal distribution that depends on all the other values of I besides the one at pixel i.

How to decide if $s_i = 0$ or $s_i = 1$ directly from this marginal distribution $P(f_i|I)$? The entropy of the first term $H_{I_i}(f_i) = \int df_i P_{I_i}(f_i)\, log P_{I_i}(f_i)$ indicates how much f_i is conditioned by the data. The larger the entropy the less the data constrain f_i, thus, there is less need to keep this data. The second term entropy $H_{eff}(f_i) = \int df_i P_{eff}(f_i)\, log P_{eff}(f_i)$ works the opposite direction. The more f_i is constrained by the neighbors, the lesser the entropy and the lesser the need to keep that data point. Thus, the decision to keep the data, $s_i = 0$, is driven by minimizing the "data" entropy $H_I(f_i)$ and maximizing the neighbor entropy $H_{eff}(f_i)$. The relevant quantity is $H_{eff}(f_i) - H_{I_i}(f_i)$. When this is large, the pixel is kept. Later, we will see a case where the second term is constant, and so the effective entropy is maximized.

For Gaussian models, the entropy is the logarithm of the variance and the appropriate ratio of variances may be considered.

4   Example: Surface Reconstruction

To make this approach concrete we apply to the problem of surface reconstruction. First we consider the 1 dimensional case to conclude that edges are the important features. Then, we apply to the two dimensional case to conclude that junctions followed by edges are the important features.

4.1 1D Case: Edge Features

Various simplifications and manipulations can be applied for the case that *the model f is described by a first order Markov model*, i.e., $P(f) = \prod_i P_i(f_i, f_{i-1})$. Then the posterior distribution is

$$P(f|I) = \frac{1}{Z} \prod_i e^{-[\frac{1}{2\sigma^2}(f_i - I_i)^2 + \mu_i(f_i - f_{i-1})^2]},$$

where μ_i are smoothing coefficients that may vary from pixel to pixel according to how much intensity change occurs ar pixel i, e.g., $\mu_i = \mu\frac{1}{1+\rho(I_i - I_{i-1})^2}$ with μ and ρ to be estimated. We have assumed that the standard deviation of the noise is homogeneous, to simplify the calculations and analysis of the direct method. Let us now consider both methods, the continuation one and the direct one to estimate the features.

Continuation Method: Here we apply $\frac{\partial s_i}{\partial \lambda} = \sum_i H_s^{-1}[i,j]$ by computing $H_s[i,j]$, given by (5), straight forwardly. We use the Baum-Welch method [2] for Markov chains to exactly compute $E_{P_s}[(f_i - I_i)^2(f_j - I_j)^2]$, $E_{P_s}[(f_i - I_i)^2]$, and $E_{P_s}[(f_j - I_j)^2]$. The final result of this algorithm, applied to a step-edge data (and with noise added) is shown in Figure 1. Not surprisingly, the edge data, both pixels, as well as the data boundaries, were the most important data, i.e., the features.

Direct Method: We derive the same result, that edges and boundaries are the most important data via an analysis of this model. We use the result that

$$P(f_i|I) = \int df_0 \dots df_{i-1}\, df_{i+1} \dots df_{N-1}\, P(f|I) = \frac{1}{Z^N} e^{-\frac{1}{2\sigma^2}(f_i - I_i)^2}\, e^{-\lambda_i^N(f_i - \Gamma_i^N)^2},$$

where λ_i^N is obtained recursively, in $\log_2 N$ steps (for simplicity, we are assuming N to be an exact power of 2), as follows

$$\lambda_i^{2K} = (\lambda_i^K + \frac{\lambda_{i+K}^K \mu_{i+K}^K}{\lambda_i^K + \mu_i^K + \mu_{i+K}^K} + \frac{\lambda_{i-K}^K \mu_i^K}{\lambda_i + \mu_i^K + \mu_{i-K}^K}) \quad (6)$$

where $K \in \{1,2,4,8,\dots,N\}$, $\mu_i^{2K} = \frac{\mu_i^K \mu_{i+K}^K}{\lambda_i^K + \mu_i^K + \mu_{i+K}^K}$, $\Gamma_i^{2K} = \frac{\lambda_i^K \Gamma_i^K + \mu_i^K \Gamma_{i-K}^K + \mu_{i+K}^K \Gamma_{i+K}^K}{\lambda_i^K + \mu_i^K + \mu_{i+K}^K}$, and $\lambda_i^1 = 1/(2\sigma^2)$, $\mu_i^1 = \mu_i$, $\Gamma_i^1 = I_i$ $\forall i$.

The effective variance is given by $var_{eff}(f_i) = 1/(2\lambda_i^N)$ while the data variance is given by $var_I(f_i) = \sigma^2$. Since $var_I(f_i)$ does not depend on any pixel i, maximizing the ratio var_{eff}/var_I (as the direct method suggested) as equivalent to maximizing either the effective variance, or the total variance (see figure(1)).

Thus, the lower is λ_i^N the lower is s_i. We note that λ_i^K increases with K, and μ_i^K decreases with K. Consequently λ^K increases less and less as K increases. In a perturbative sense λ_i^2 most contribute to λ_i^N and is defined by the two neighbors values μ_i and μ_{i+1}, i.e., by the edge information. The larger are the intensity edges the smaller are μ_i and therefore, the smaller will λ_i^2 be. Moreover, λ_i^N is mostly defined by λ_i^2 (in a perturbative sense, this is where most of the contribution comes). Thus, we can argue that the pixels i with intensity edges will have smaller values for λ_i^N and therefore are likely to have the data kept as a feature ($s_i = 0$).

4.2 2D Case: Junctions, Corners, and Edge Features

Let us investigate the two dimensional version of the 1D problem for surface reconstruction. Let us assume the posterior

$$P(f|I) = \frac{1}{Z} e^{-[\frac{1}{2\sigma^2}(f_{ij} - I_{ij})^2 + \mu_{ij}^v(f_{ij} - f_{i-1,j})^2 + \mu_{ij}^h(f_{ij} - f_{i,j-1})^2]},$$

where $\mu_{ij}^{v,h}$ are the smoothing coefficients along vertical and horizontal direction, that vary inversely according to the ∇I along these direction. We can then approximately compute (e.g., see [3])

$$P(f_{ij}|I) \approx \frac{1}{Z}\, e^{-\frac{1}{2\sigma^2}(f_{ij}-I_{ij})^2}\, e^{-\lambda_{ij}^N(f_{ij}-\Gamma_{ij}^N)^2}$$

where, analogously to the 1D case, we have

$$\lambda_{ij}^{2K} \;=\; \lambda_{ij}^K + \frac{\lambda_{i,j-K}^K \mu_{ij}^{h,K}}{\chi_{i,j-K}^K} + \frac{\lambda_{i,j+K}^K \mu_{i,j+K}^{h,K}}{\chi_{i,j+K}^K} + \frac{\lambda_{i-K,j}^K \mu_{ij}^{v,K}}{\chi_{i-K,j}^K} + \frac{\lambda_{i+K,j}^K \mu_{i+K,j}^{v,K}}{\chi_{i+K,j}^K} \quad (7)$$

where $\chi_{i,j}^K = \lambda_{ij}^K + \mu_{ij}^{h,K} + \mu_{ij}^{v,K} + \mu_{i,j+K}^{h,K} + \mu_{i+K,j}^{v,K}$, and $\mu_{ij}^{h,2K} = \frac{\mu_{ij}^{h,K}\mu_{i,j+K}^{h,K}}{\chi_{i,j}^K}$

The larger is the effective variance at one site (i,j), the smaller is λ^N, the more likely that image portion to be a feature. The larger the intensity gradient along h, v, at (i,j), the smaller $\mu_{ij}^{h,v}$. The smaller is $\mu_{ij}^{h,v}$ the smaller will be contribution to λ^2. In a perturbative sense ([3]) λ^2 makes the largest contribution to λ^N. Thus, at one site, the more intensity edges it has the larger will be the effective variance. Thus, T-junctions will produce very large effective variances, followed by corners, followed by edges. These will be, in order of importance, the features selected to reconstruct 2D surfaces.

5   Conclusion

We have proposed an approach to specify when a feature set has sufficient information in them, so that we can represent the image using it. Thus, one can, in principle, tell what kind of feature is likely to be important in a given model. Two methods of computation have been proposed and a concrete analysis for a simple surface reconstruction was carried out.

References

[1] A. Berger and S. Della Pietra and V. Della Pietra "A Maximum Entropy Approach to Natural Language Processing" *Computational Linguistics*, Vol.22 (1), pp 39–71, 1996.

[2] T. Cover and J. Thomas. *Elements of Information Theory.* Wiley Interscience, New York, 1991.

[3] D. Geiger and J. E. Kogler. Scaling Images and Image Feature via the Renormalization Group. In *Proc. IEEE Conf. on Computer Vision & Pattern Recognition* , New York, NY, 1993.

[4] G. Hinton and Z. Ghahramani. Generative Models for Discovering Sparse Distributed Representations To Appear *Phil. Trans. of the Royal Society* B, 1997.

[5] R. Linsker. Self-Organization in a Perceptual Network. *Computer*, March 1988, 105-117.

[6] J. Principe, U. of Florida at Gainesville Personal Communication

[7] T. Sejnowski. Computational Models and the Development of Topographic Projections *Trends Neurosci*, **10**, 304-305.

[8] S.C. Zhu, Y.N. Wu, D. Mumford. Minimax entropy principle and its application to texture modeling *Neural Computation* 1996 B.

[9] P. Viola and W.M. Wells III. "Alignment by Maximization of Mutual Information". In *Proceedings of the International Conference on Computer Vision.* Boston. 1995.

Detection of first and second order motion

Alexander Grunewald
Division of Biology
California Institute of Technology
Mail Code 216-76
Pasadena, CA 91125
alex@vis.caltech.edu

Heiko Neumann
Abteilung Neuroinformatik
Universität Ulm
89069 Ulm
Germany
hneumann@neuro.informatik.uni-ulm.de

Abstract

A model of motion detection is presented. The model contains three stages. The first stage is unoriented and is selective for contrast polarities. The next two stages work in parallel. A phase *insensitive* stage pools across different contrast polarities through a spatiotemporal filter and thus can detect first and second order motion. A phase *sensitive* stage keeps contrast polarities separate, each of which is filtered through a spatiotemporal filter, and thus only first order motion can be detected. Differential phase sensitivity can therefore account for the detection of first and second order motion. Phase insensitive detectors correspond to cortical complex cells, and phase sensitive detectors to simple cells.

1 INTRODUCTION

In our environment objects are constantly in motion, and the visual system faces the task of identifying the motion of objects. This task can be subdivided into two components: motion detection and motion integration. In this study we will look at motion detection. Recent psychophysics has made a useful distinction between first and second order motion. In first order motion an absolute image feature is moving. For example, a bright bar moving on a dark background is an absolute feature because luminance is moving. In second order motion a relative image feature is moving, for example a contrast reversing bar. No longer is it possible to identify the moving object through its luminance, but only that it has different luminance with respect to the background. Humans are very sensitive to first order motion, but can they detect second order motion? Chubb & Sperling (1988) showed that subjects are in fact able to detect second order motion. These findings have since been confirmed in many psychophysical experiments, and it has become clear that the parameters that yield detection of first and second order motion are different, suggesting that separate motion detection systems exist.

1.1   Detection of first and second order motion

First order motion, which is what we encounter in our daily lives, can be easily detected by finding the peak in the Fourier energy distribution. The motion energy detector developed by Adelson & Bergen (1985) does this explicitly, and it turns out that it is also equivalent to a Reichardt detector (van Santen & Sperling, 1985). However, these detectors cannot adequately detect second order motion, because second order motion stimuli often contain the maximum Fourier energy in the opposite direction (possibly at a different velocity) as the actual motion. In other words, purely linear filters, should have opposite directional tuning for first and second order motion. This is further illustrated in Figure 1.

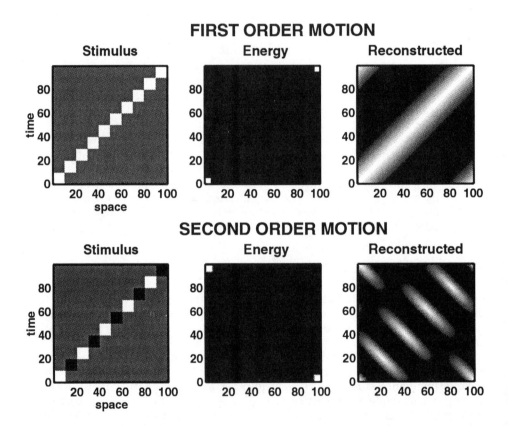

Figure 1: Schematic of first and second order motion, their peak Fourier energy, and the reconstruction. The peak Fourier energy is along the direction of motion for first order motion, and in the opposite direction for second order motion. For this reason a linear filter cannot detect second order motion.

One way to account for second order motion detection is to transform the second order motion signal into a first order signal. If second order motion is defined by contrast reversals, then detecting contrast edges and then rectifying the resulting signal of contrast will yield a first order motion signal. Thus this approach includes three steps: orientation detection, rectification and finally motion detection (Wilson et al., 1992).

1.2 Visual physiology

Cells in the retina and the lateral geniculate nucleus (LGN) have concentric (and hence unoriented) receptive fields which are organized in an opponent manner. While the center of such an ON cell is excited by a light increment, the surround is excited by a light decrement, and vice versa for OFF cells. It is only at the cortex that direction and orientation selectivity arise. Cortical simple cells are sensitive to the phase of the stimulus, while complex cells are not (Hubel & Wiesel, 1962).

Most motion models take at least partial inspiration from known physiology and anatomy, by relating the kernels of the motion detectors to the physiology of cortical cells. The motion energy model in particular detects orientation and first order motion at the same time. Curiously, all motion models essentially ignore the concentric opponency of receptive fields in the LGN. This is usually justified by pointing to the linearity of simple cells with respect to stimulus parameters. However, it has been shown that simple cells in fact exhibit strong nonlinearities (Hammond & MacKay, 1983). Moreover, motion detection does require at least one stage of nonlinearity (Poggio & Reichardt, 1973). The present study develops a model of first and second order motion detection which explicitly includes an unoriented processing stage, and phase sensitive and phase insensitive motion detectors are built from these unoriented signals. The former set of detectors only responds to first order motion, while the second set of detectors responds to both types of motion. We further show the analogies that can be drawn between these detector types and simple and complex cells in cat visual cortex.

2 MODEL DESCRIPTION

The model is two-dimensional, one dimension is space, which means that space has been collapsed onto a line, and the other dimension is time. The input image to the model is a space-time matrix of luminances, as shown in figure 1. At each processing stage essentially the same operations are performed. First the input signal is convolved with the appropriate kernel. At each stage there are multiple kernels, to generate the different signal types at that stage. For example, there are ON and OFF signals at the unoriented stage. Next the convolved responses are subtracted from each other. At the unoriented stage this means ON-OFF and OFF-ON. In the final step these results are half-wave rectified to only yield positive signals.

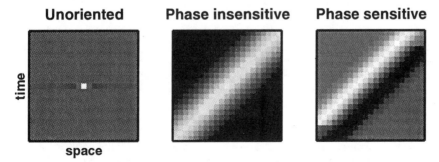

Figure 2: The kernels in the model. For the unoriented (left plot) and phase sensitive (right plot) kernel plots black indicates OFF regions, white ON regions, and grey zero input. For the phase insensitive plot (middle) grey denotes ON and OFF input, and black denotes zero input.

At the unoriented stage the input pattern is convolved with a difference of Gaussians kernel. This kernel has only a spatial dimension, no temporal dimension (see figure 2). As described earlier, competition is between ON and OFF signals, followed by half-wave rectification. This ensures that at each location only one set of unoriented signals is present. A simulation of the signals at the unoriented stage is shown in figure 3. For first order motion, ON signals are at locations corresponding to the inside of the moving bar. With each shift of the bar the signals also move. Similarly, the OFF signals correspond to the outside of the bar, and also move with the bar. For second order motion the contrast polarity reverses. Thus ON signals correspond to the inside when the bar is bright, and to the outside when the bar is dark, and vice versa for OFF signals. Thus any ON or OFF signals to the leading edge of the bar will remain active after the bar moves.

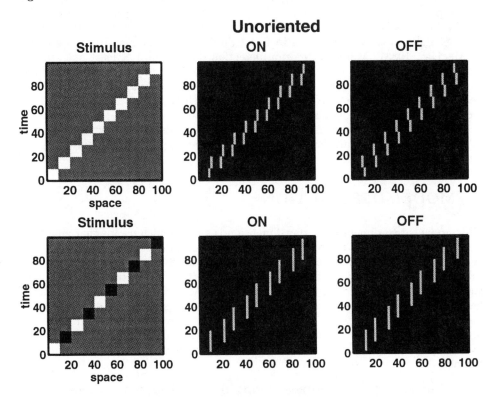

Figure 3: Unoriented signals to first and second order motion. ON signals are at the bright side of any contrast transition, while OFF signals are at the dark side. In first order motion ON and OFF move synchronously to the moving stimulus. In second order motion ON and OFF signals persist, since the leading edge becomes the trailing edge, and at the same time the contrast reverses, which means that at a particular spatial location the contrast remains constant.

At the phase insensitive stage the unoriented ON and OFF signals are added, and then the result is convolved with an energy detection filter. The pooling of ON and OFF signals means that the contrast transitions in the image are essentially full-wave rectified. This causes phase insensitivity. These pooled signals are then convolved with a space-time oriented filter (see figure 2). Competition between opposite directions of motion ensures that only one direction is active. A consequence of the pooling of unoriented ON and OFF signals at this stage is that the resulting signals are invariant to first or second order motion. Thus phase insensitivity makes this stage able to detect both first and second order motion. These signals are shown in figure 4. In a two-dimensional extension of this model these detectors would also be orientation selective. The simplest way to obtain this would be via elongation along the preferred orientation.

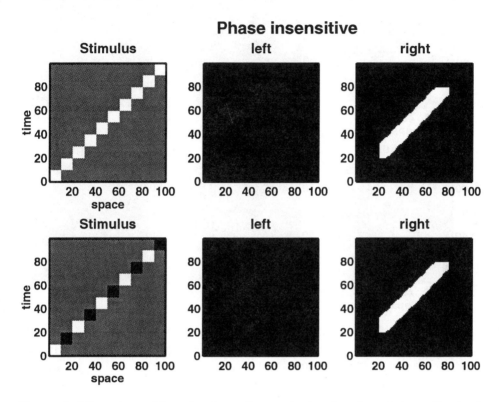

Figure 4: Phase insensitive signals to first and second order motion. For both stimuli there are no leftwards signals, and robust rightwards signals.

At the phase sensitive stage unoriented ON and OFF signals are separately convolved with space-time oriented kernels which are offset with respect to each other (see figure 2). The separate treatment of ON and OFF signals yields phase sensitivity. At each location there are four kernels: two for the two directions of motion, and two for the two phases. Competition occurs between signals of opposite direction tuning, and opposite phase preference. To avoid activation in the opposite direction of motion slightly removed from the location of the edge spatially broadly tuned inhibition is necessary. This is provided by the phase insensitive signals, thus avoiding feedback loops among phase sensitive detectors. First order signals from the unoriented stage match the spatiotemporal filters in the preferred direction, and thus phase sensitive signals arise. However, due to their phase reversal, second order motion input, provides poor motion signals, which are quenched through phase insensitive inhibition. These signals are shown in figure 5.

These simulations show that first and second order motion are detected differently. First order motion is detected by phase sensitive and phase insensitive motion detectors, while second order motion is only detected by the latter. From this we conclude that first order motion is a more potent stimulus, and that the detection of second order is more restricted, since it depends on a single type of detector. In particular, the size of the stimulus and its velocity have to be matched to the energy

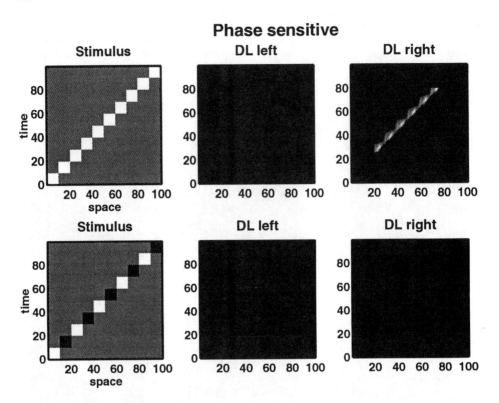

Figure 5: Phase sensitive signals to first and second order motion. Only the dark-light signals are shown. First order motion causes a consistent rightward motion signal, while second order motion does not.

filters for motion signals to arise.

3   RELATION TO PHYSIOLOGY

The relationship between the model and physiology is straightforward. Unoriented signals correspond to LGN responses, phase insensitive signals to complex cell responses, and phase sensitive signals to simple cell responses. Thus the model suggests that both simple and some complex cells receive direct LGN input. Moreover these complex cells inhibit simple cells. With an additional threshold in simple cells this inhibition could also be obtained via complex to simple cell excitation. We stress that we are not ruling out that many complex cells receive only simple cell input. Rather, the present research shows that if all complex cells receive only simple cell input, second order motion cannot be detected. Hence at least some complex cell responses need to be built up directly from LGN responses. Several lines of evidence from cat physiology support this suggestion. First, the mean latencies of simple and complex cells are about equal (Bullier & Henry, 1979), suggesting that at least some complex cells receive direct LGN input. Second, noise stimuli can selectively activate complex cells, without activation of simple cells (Hammond, 1991). Third, cross-correlation analyses show that complex cells do receive simple cell input (Ghose *et al.*, 1994).

The present model predicts that some cortical complex cells should respond to second order motion. Zhou & Baker (1993) investigated this, and found that some complex cells in area 17 respond to second order motion. Moreover, they found that simple cells of a particular first order motion preference did not reverse their motion preference when stimulated with second order motion, which would occur if simple cells were just linear filters. We interpret this as further evidence that complex cells provide inhibitory input to simple cells. If complex cells are built up from LGN input, then orientation selectivity in two-dimensional space cannot be obtained based on simple cell input, but rather requires complex cells with elongated receptive fields. Thus we predict that there ought to be a correlation in complex cells between elongated receptive fields and dependence on direct LGN input.

In conclusion we have shown how the phase sensitivity of motion detectors can be mapped onto the ability to detect only first order motion, or both first and second order motion. This suggests that it is not necessary to introduce a orientation detection stage before motion detection can take place, thus simplifying the model of motion detection. Furthermore we have shown that the proposed model is in accord with known physiology.

Acknowledgments

This work was supported by the McDonnell-Pew program in Cognitive Neuroscience.

References

Adelson, E. & Bergen (1985). Spatiotemporal energy models for the perception of motion. *J. Opt. Soc. Am. A*, **2**, 284-299.

Bullier, J. & Henry, G. H. (1979). Ordinal position of neurons in cat striate cortex. *J. Neurophys.*, **42**, 1251-1263.

Chubb, C. & Sperling, G. (1988). Drift-balanced random stimuli: a general basis for studying non-Fourier motion perception. *J. Opt. Soc. Am. A*, **5**, 1986-2007.

Ghose, G. M., Freeman, R. D. & Ohzawa, I. (1994). Local intracortical connections in the cat's visual cortex: postnatal development and plasticity. *J. Neurophys.*, **72**, 1290-1303.

Hammond, P. (1991). On the response of simple and complex cells to random dot patterns. *Vis. Res.*, **31**, 47-50.

Hammond, P. & MacKay, D. (1983). Influence of luminance gradient reversal on simple cells in feline striate cortex. *J. Physiol.*, **337**, 69-87.

Hubel, D. H. & Wiesel, T. N. (1962). Receptive fields, binocular interaction and functional architecture in the cat's visual cortex. *J. Physiol.*, **160**, 106-154.

Poggio, T. & Reichardt, W. (1973). Considerations on models of movement detection. *Kybernetik*, **12**, 223-227.

van Santen & Sperling, G. (1985). Elaborated Reichardt detectors. *J. Opt. Soc. Am. A*, **2**, 300-321.

Wilson, H. R., Ferrera, V. P. & Yo, C. (1992). A psychophysically motivated model for two-dimensional motion perception. *Vis. Neurosci.*, **9**, 79-97.

Zhou, Y.X. & Baker, C. L. (1993). A processing stream in mammalian visual cortex neurons for non-Fourier responses. *Science*, **261**, 98-101.

A Simple and Fast Neural Network Approach to Stereovision

Rolf D. Henkel
Institute of Theoretical Physics
University of Bremen
P.O. Box 330 440, D-28334 Bremen
`http://axon.physik.uni-bremen.de/~rdh`

Abstract

A neural network approach to stereovision is presented based on aliasing effects of simple disparity estimators and a fast coherence-detection scheme. Within a single network structure, a dense disparity map with an associated validation map and, additionally, the fused cyclopean view of the scene are available. The network operations are based on simple, biological plausible circuitry; the algorithm is fully parallel and non-iterative.

1 Introduction

Humans experience the three-dimensional world not as it is seen by either their left or right eye, but from a position of a virtual cyclopean eye, located in the middle between the two real eye positions. The different perspectives between the left and right eyes cause slight relative displacements of objects in the two retinal images (disparities), which make a simple superposition of both images without diplopia impossible. Proper fusion of the retinal images into the cyclopean view requires the registration of both images to a common coordinate system, which in turn requires calculation of disparities for all image areas which are to be fused.

1.1 The Problems with Classical Approaches

The estimation of disparities turns out to be a difficult task, since various random and systematic image variations complicate this task. Several different techniques have been proposed over time, which can be loosely grouped into feature-, area-

and phase-based approaches. All these algorithms have a number of computational problems directly linked to the very assumptions inherent in these approaches.

In feature-based stereo, intensity data is first converted to a set of features assumed to be a more stable image property than the raw image intensities. Matching primitives used include zerocrossings, edges and corner points (Frisby, 1991), or higher order primitives like topological fingerprints (see for example: Fleck, 1991). Generally, the set of feature-classes is *discrete*, causing the two primary problems of feature-based stereo algorithms: the famous "false-matches"-problem and the problem of missing disparity estimates.

False matches are caused by the fact that a single feature in the left image can potentially be matched with every feature of the same class in the right image. This problem is basic to all feature-based stereo algorithms and can only be solved by the introduction of additional constraints to the solution. In conjunction with the extracted features these constraints define a complicated error measure which can be minimized by cooperative processes (Marr, 1979) or by direct (Ohta, 1985) or stochastic search techniques (Yuille, 1991). While cooperative processes and stochastic search techniques can be realized easily on a neural basis, it is not immediately clear how to implement the more complicated algorithmic structures of direct search techniques neuronally. Cooperative processes and stochastic search techniques turn out to be slow, needing many iterations to converge to a local minimum of the error measure.

The requirement of features to be a stable image property causes the second problem of feature-based stereo: stable features can only be detected in a fraction of the whole image area, leading to missing disparity estimates for most of the image area. For those image parts, disparity estimates can only be guessed.

Dense disparity maps can be obtained with area-based approaches, where a suitable chosen correlation measure is maximized between small image patches of the left and right view. However, a neuronally plausible implementation of this seems to be not readily available. Furthermore, the maximization turns out to be a computationally expensive process, since extensive search is required in configuration space.

Hierarchical processing schemes can be utilized for speed-up, by using information obtained at coarse spatial scales to restrict searching at finer scales. But, for general image data, it is not guaranteed that the disparity information obtained at some coarse scale is valid. The disparity data might be wrong, might have a different value than at finer scales, or might not be present at all. Furthermore, by processing data from coarse to fine spatial scales, hierarchical processing schemes are intrinsically sequential. This creates additional algorithmic overhead which is again difficult to realize with neuronal structures.

The same comments apply to phase-based approaches, where a locally extracted Fourier-phase value is used for matching. Phase values are only defined modulo 2π, and this wrap-around makes the use of hierarchical processing essential for these types of algorithms. Moreover, since data is analyzed in different spatial frequency channels, it is nearly certain that some phase values will be undefined at intermediate scales, due to missing signal energy in this frequency band (Fleet, 1993). Thus, in addition to hierarchical processing, some kind of exception handling is needed with these approaches.

2   Stereovision by Coherence Detection

In summary, classical approaches to stereovision seem to have difficulties with the fast calculation of dense disparity-maps, at least with plausible neural circuitry. In the following, a neural network implementation will be described which solves this task by using simple disparity estimators based on motion-energy mechanisms (Adelson, 1985; Qian, 1997), closely resembling responses of complex cells in visual cortex (DeAngelis, 1991). Disparity units of these type belong to a class of disparity estimators which can be derived from optical flow methods (Barron, 1994). Clearly, disparity calculations and optical flow estimation share many similarities. The two stereo views of a (static) scene can be considered as two time-slices cut out of the space-time intensity pattern which would be recorded by an imaginary camera moving from the position of the left to the position of the right eye. However, compared to optical flow, disparity estimation is complicated by the fact that only two discrete "time"-samples are available, namely the images of the left and right view positions.

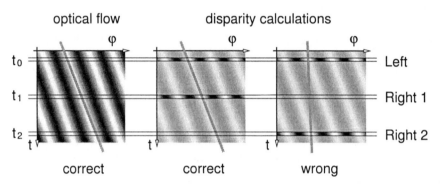

Figure 1: The velocity of an image patch manifests itself as principal texture direction in the space-time flow field traced out by the intensity pattern in time (left). Sampling such flow patterns at discrete times can create aliasing-effects which lead to wrong estimates. If one is using optical flow estimation techniques for disparity calculations, this problem is always present.

For an explanation consider Fig. 1. A surface patch shifting over time traces out a certain flow pattern. The principal texture direction of this flow indicates the relative velocity of the image patch (Fig. 1, left). Sampling the flow pattern only at discrete time points, the shift between two "time-samples" can be estimated without ambiguity provided the shift is not too large (Fig. 1, middle). However, if a certain limit is exceeded, it becomes impossible to estimate the shift correctly, given the data (Fig. 1, right). This is a simple aliasing-effect in the "time"-direction; an everyday example can be seen as motion reversal in movies.

In the case of stereovision, aliasing-effects of this type are always present, and they limit the range of disparities a simple disparity unit can estimate. Sampling theory gives a relation between the maximal spatial wavevector $k^{\varphi}_{\max}$ (or, equivalently, the minimum spatial wavelength $\lambda^{\varphi}_{\min}$) present in the data and the largest disparity which can be estimated reliably (Henkel, 1997):

$$|d| < \frac{\pi}{k^{\varphi}_{\max}} = \frac{1}{2}\lambda^{\varphi}_{\min}. \tag{1}$$

A well-known example of the size-disparity scaling expressed in equation (1) is found in the context of the spatial frequency channels assumed to exist in the visual cortex. Cortical cells respond to spatial wavelengths down to about half their peak wavelength λ_{opt}; therefore, they can estimate reliable only disparities less than $1/4\,\lambda_{opt}$. This is known as Marr's quarter-cycle limit (Blake, 1991).

Equation (1) immediately suggests a way to extend the limited working range of disparity estimators: a spatial smoothing of the image data before or during disparity calculation reduces k_{max}^φ, and in turn increases the disparity range. However, spatial smoothing reduces also the spatial resolution of the resulting disparity map. Another way of modifying the usable range of disparity estimators is the application of a fixed preshift to the input data before disparity calculation. This would require prior knowledge of the correct preshift to be applied, which is a nontrivial problem. One could resort to hierarchical coarse-to-fine schemes, but the difficulties with hierarchical schemes have already been elaborated.

The aliasing effects discussed are a general feature of sampling visual space with only two eyes; instead of counteracting, one can exploit them in a simple coherence-detection scheme, where the multi-unit activity in stacks of disparity detectors tuned to a common view direction is analyzed.

Assuming that all disparity units i in a stack have random preshifts or presmoothing applied to their input data, these units will have different, but slightly overlapping working ranges $D_i = [d_i^{min}, d_i^{max}]$ for valid disparity estimates. An object with true disparity d, seen in the common view direction of such a stack, will therefore split the stack into two disjunct classes: the class $\mathcal{C}$ of estimators with $d \in D_i$ for all $i \in \mathcal{C}$, and the rest of the stack, $\overline{\mathcal{C}}$, with $d \notin D_i$. All disparity estimators $\in \mathcal{C}$ will code more or less the true disparity $d_i \approx d$, but the estimates of units belonging to $\overline{\mathcal{C}}$ will be subject to the random aliasing effects discussed, depending in a complicated way on image content and disparity range D_i of the unit.

We will thus have $d_i \approx d \approx d_j$ whenever units i and j belong to $\mathcal{C}$, and random relationships otherwise. A simple coherence detection within each stack, i.e. searching for all units with $d_i \approx d_j$ and extracting the largest cluster found, will be sufficient to single out $\mathcal{C}$. The true disparity d in the view direction of the stack can be simply estimated as an average over all coherently coding units:

$$d \approx \langle d_i \rangle_{i \in \mathcal{C}} \, .$$

3   Neural Network Implementation

Repeating this coherence detection scheme in every view direction results in a fully parallel network structure for disparity calculation. Neighboring disparity stacks responding to different view directions estimate disparity values independently from each other, and within each stack, disparity units operate independently from each other. Since coherence detection is an opportunistic scheme, extensions of the basic algorithm to multiple spatial scales and combinations of different types of disparity estimators are trivial. Additional units are simply included in the appropriate coherence stacks. The coherence scheme will combine only the information from the coherently coding units and ignore the rest of the data. For this reason, the scheme also turns out to be extremely robust against single-unit failures.

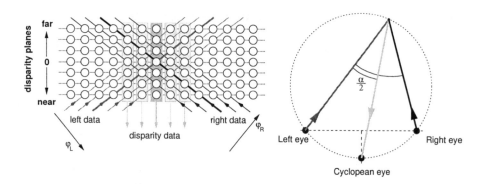

Figure 2: The network structure for a single horizontal scan-line (left). The view directions of the disparity stacks split the angle between the left and right lines of sight in the network and 3D-space in half, therefore analyzing space along the cyclopean view directions (right).

In the current implementation (Fig. 2), disparity units at a single spatial scale are arranged into horizontal disparity layers. Left and right image data is fed into this network along diagonally running data lines. This causes every disparity layer to receive the stereo data with a certain fixed preshift applied, leading to the required, slightly different working-ranges of neighboring layers. Disparity units stacked vertically above each other are collected into a single disparity stack which is then analyzed for coherent activity.

4   Results

The new stereo network performs comparable on several standard test image sets (Fig. 3). The calculated disparity maps are similar to maps obtained by classical area-based approaches, but they display subpixel-precision. Since no smoothing or regularization is performed by the coherence-based stereo algorithm, sharp disparity edges can be observed at object borders.

Within the network, a simple validation map is available locally. A measure of local

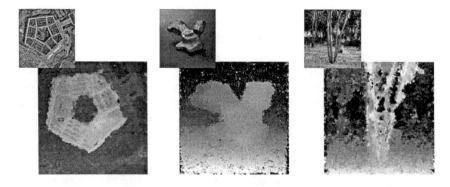

Figure 3: Disparity maps for some standard test images (small insets), calculated by the coherence-based stereo algorithm.

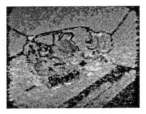

Figure 4: The performance of coherence-based stereo on a difficult scene with specular highlights, transparency and repetitive structures (left). The disparity map (middle) is dense and correct, except for a few structure-less image regions. These regions, as well as most object borders, are indicated in the validation map (right) with a low [dark] validation count.

coherence can be obtained by calculating the relative number of coherently acting disparity units in each stack, i.e. by calculating the ratio $N(\mathcal{C})/N(\mathcal{C}\cup\overline{\mathcal{C}})$, where $N(\mathcal{C})$ is the number of units in class $\mathcal{C}$. In most cases, this validation map clearly marks image areas where the disparity calculations failed (for various reasons, notably at occlusions caused by object borders, or in large structure-less image regions, where no reliable matching can be obtained — compare Fig 4).

Close inspection of disparity and validation maps reveals that these image maps are not aligned with the left or the right view of the scene. Instead, both maps are registered with the cyclopean view. This is caused by the structural arrangement of data lines and disparity stacks in the network. Reprojecting data lines and stacks back into 3D-space shows that the stacks analyze three-dimensional space along lines splitting the angle between the left and right view directions in half. This is the cyclopean view direction as defined by (Hering, 1879).

It is easy to obtain the cyclopean view of the scene itself. With I_i^L and I_i^R denoting the left and right input data at the position of disparity-unit i, a summation over all coherently coding disparity units in a stack, i.e.,

$$I^{\mathcal{C}} = \left\langle I_i^L + I_i^R \right\rangle_{i \in \mathcal{C}} ,$$

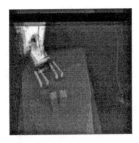

Figure 5: A simple superposition of the left and right stereo images results in diplopia (left). By using a vergence system, the two stereo images can be aligned better (middle), but diplopia is still prominent in most areas of the visual field. The fused cyclopean view of the scene (left) was calculated by the coherence-based stereo network.

gives the image intensity I^C in the cyclopean view-direction of this stack. Collecting I^C from all disparity stacks gives the complete cyclopean view as the third co-registered map of the network (Fig 5).

Acknowledgements

Thanks to Helmut Schwegler and Robert P. O'Shea for interesting discussions. Image data courtesy of G. Medoni, UCS Institute for Robotics & Intelligent Systems, B. Bolles, AIC, SRI International, and G. Sommer, Kiel Cognitive Systems Group, Christian-Albrechts-Universität Kiel. An internet-based implementation of the algorithm presented in this paper is available at http://axon.physik.uni-bremen.de/~rdh/online_calc/stereo/.

References

Adelson, E.H. & Bergen, J.R. (1985): Spatiotemporal Energy Models for the Perception of Motion. *J. Opt. Soc. Am.* **A2**: 284–299.

Barron, J.L., Fleet, D.J. & Beauchemin, S.S. (1994): Performance of Optical Flow Techniques. *Int. J. Comp. Vis.* **12**: 43–77.

Blake, R. & Wilson, H.R. (1991): Neural Models of Stereoscopic Vision. *TINS* **14**: 445–452.

DeAngelis, G.C., Ohzawa, I. & Freeman, R.D. (1991): Depth is Encoded in the Visual Cortex by a Specialized Field Structure. *Nature* **11**: 156–159.

Fleck, M.M. (1991): A Topological Stereo Matcher. *Int. J. of Comp. Vis.* **6**: 197–226.

Fleet, D.J. & Jepson, A.D. (1993): Stability of Phase Information. *IEEE PAMI* **2**: 333-340.

Frisby, J.P. & and S. B. Pollard, S.B. (1991): Computational Issues in Solving the Stereo Correspondence Problem. eds. M.S. Landy and J. A. Movshon, *Computational Models of Visual Processing*, pp. 331, MIT Press, Cambridge 1991.

Henkel, R.D. (1997): Fast Stereovision by Coherence Detection, in *Proc. of CAIP'97, Kiel*, LCNS 1296, eds. G. Sommer, K. Daniilidis and J. Pauli, pp. 297, LCNS 1296, Springer, Heidelberg 1997.

E. Hering (1879): Der Raumsinn und die Bewegung des Auges, in Handbuch der Psychologie, ed. L. Hermann, Band 3, Teil 1, Vogel, Leipzig 1879.

Marr, D. & Poggio, T. (1979): A Computational Theory of Human Stereo Vision. *Proc. R. Soc. Lond.* **B 204**: 301–328.

Ohta, Y, & Kanade, T. (1985): Stereo by Intra- and Inter-scanline Search using dynamic programming. *IEEE PAMI* **7**: 139–154.

Qian, N. & Zhu, Y. (1997): Physiological Computation of Binocular Disparity, to appear in *Vision Research*.

Yuille, A.L., Geiger, D. & Bülthoff, H.H. (1991): Stereo Integration, Mean Field Theory and Psychophysics. *Network* **2**: 423–442.

Inferring sparse, overcomplete image codes using an efficient coding framework

Michael S. Lewicki
lewicki@salk.edu

Howard Hughes Medical Institute
Computational Neurobiology Lab
The Salk Institute
10010 N. Torrey Pines Rd.
La Jolla, CA 92037

Bruno A. Olshausen
bruno@redwood.ucdavis.edu

Center for Neuroscience
University of California, Davis
1544 Newton Ct.,
Davis, CA

Abstract

We apply a general technique for learning overcomplete bases (Lewicki and Sejnowski, 1998) to the problem of finding efficient image codes. The bases learned by the algorithm are localized, oriented, and bandpass, consistent with earlier results obtained using different methods (Olshausen and Field, 1996; Bell and Sejnowski, 1997). We show that the learned bases are Gabor-like in structure and that higher degrees of overcompleteness produce greater sampling density in position, orientation, and scale. The efficient coding framework provides a method for comparing different bases objectively by calculating their probability given the observed data. Compared to complete and overcomplete Fourier and wavelet bases, the learned bases have much better coding efficiency. We demonstrate the improvement in the representation of the learned bases by showing superior noise reduction properties.

The problem of encoding sensory information efficiently is relevant both to the design of practical vision systems and also to advancing our understanding of how biological nervous systems process information. Within the image processing community, much work has been done on image codes that utilize a linear basis function expansion, and considerable effort has gone into choosing basis sets with desirable coding properties such as ease of computability and compression. An approach that has been largely overlooked, however, is to consider the *efficiency* of the image code as defined by Shannon's theorem—i.e, in terms of how well the basis set captures the data's probability density. Even bases that are chosen for their low-entropy coding properties, such as Gabor functions or wavelets, are still hand-designed rather than being adapted to the data so as to optimize efficiency. If the bases could be *adapted* to better model the statistical structure of images, it will allow for more efficient coding and better noise reduction properties.

Among existing techniques for adapting bases to the data are principal component analysis (PCA), which assumes the data have Gaussian structure and fits an appropriate orthogonal basis, and more recently independent component analysis (ICA), which allows for non-Gaussian distributions and non-orthogonal bases. These techniques are limited, however, in that they form a complete or critically sampled basis, *i.e.* the number of basis vectors is equal to the dimensionality of the input.

Codes based on so-called "overcomplete" bases, which allow a greater number of basis vectors than inputs, have been proposed because they allow certain advantages in terms of interpolation (Simoncelli et al., 1992) or in achieving sparsity in the representation (Chen et al., 1996). Like the bases discussed above, however, they are set by hand and not adapted to the data. Our point of departure from these previous approaches is that, by treating the basis as a probabilistic model, it is possible to adapt an overcomplete basis to the underlying statistics of the dataset.

An important aspect of the probabilistic framework is that it offers a new perspective on overcomplete representations: They are better because they allow greater flexibility in modeling the underlying probability density function of images. A common misconception is that overcomplete codes are redundant, but this is true only in the sense that there are multiple ways to describe a particular image. The prior probability on the basis coefficients yields a non-linear input-output relationship and gives different probabilities to different representations.

In this paper, we apply the algorithm described by Lewicki and Sejnowski (1998) which adapts arbitrary overcomplete bases. It also allows for comparing different bases objectively in terms of their relative probabilities. We demonstrate that learned bases form more efficient codes and have better denoising properties than traditional complete and overcomplete Fourier and wavelet bases.

1   A model for images

We assume data, $x_{1:L}$, can be described with an overcomplete linear basis plus additive noise:

$$\mathbf{x} = \mathbf{A}\mathbf{s} + \epsilon \tag{1}$$

where $\mathbf{A}$ is an $L \times M$ matrix, whose columns form the basis set, with $M > L$ and ϵ is assumed to be Gaussian white noise. Under this model the log probability of the data given the coefficients $\mathbf{s}$, is given by $\log P(\mathbf{x}|\mathbf{A},\mathbf{s}) \propto -\frac{\lambda}{2}(\mathbf{x} - \mathbf{A}\mathbf{s})^2$ where $\lambda = 1/\sigma^2$ defines the precision of the noise.

The probability of the data, independent of any particular $\mathbf{s}$, is given by marginalizing over the internal states $\mathbf{s}$

$$P(\mathbf{x}|\mathbf{A}) = \int d\mathbf{s}\, P(\mathbf{x}|\mathbf{A},\mathbf{s})P(\mathbf{s}) \tag{2}$$

where $P(\mathbf{s})$ is the prior distribution of the basis coefficients. We choose $P(s_m)$ to be Laplacian $(P(s_m) \propto \exp[-\theta_m |s_m|])$ which assumes sparse structure. The internal state is found by maximizing the posterior of $\mathbf{s}$

$$\hat{\mathbf{s}} = \max_{\mathbf{s}} P(\mathbf{s}|\mathbf{A}, \mathbf{x}) = \max_{\mathbf{s}} P(\mathbf{x}|\mathbf{A}, \mathbf{s})P(\mathbf{s}) \tag{3}$$

Under the Laplacian prior (or other priors with high-kurtosis), finding the most probable basis coefficients essentially selects out a complete basis and sets the coefficients for the remaining vectors to zero. Thus, in this model the data is a linear function of the basis vectors, but the basis coefficients are a *nonlinear* function of the data.

Adapting the basis set consists of maximizing the probability of the data (equation 2). In general this integral cannot be evaluated exactly, but can be approximated with a Gaussian integral around $\hat{\mathbf{s}}$

$$\log P(\mathbf{x}|\mathbf{A}) \approx \text{const.} - \frac{\lambda}{2}(\mathbf{x} - \mathbf{A}\hat{\mathbf{s}})^2 + \log P(\hat{\mathbf{s}}) - \frac{1}{2}\log \det \mathbf{H} \tag{4}$$

where $\mathbf{H}$ is the Hessian of the log posterior at $\hat{\mathbf{s}}$, given by $\lambda \mathbf{A}^T \mathbf{A} - \nabla\nabla \log P(\hat{\mathbf{s}})$. We assume the image patches $\mathbf{x}_{1:K}$ to be independent. Lewicki and Sejnowski (1998) have shown that $\mathbf{A}$ can be optimized using the learning rule

$$\Delta \mathbf{A} = \mathbf{A}\mathbf{A}^T \frac{\partial}{\partial \mathbf{A}} \log P(\mathbf{x}|\mathbf{A}) \approx -\mathbf{A}(\mathbf{z}\hat{\mathbf{s}}^T + \mathbf{A}^T \mathbf{A} \mathbf{H}^{-1}) \tag{5}$$

where $z_m = \partial \log P(s_m)/\partial s_m$. Using the approximation $\mathbf{A}^T \mathbf{A} \mathbf{H}^{-1} = \mathbf{I}$ usually produces acceptable results. We have found, however, the following approximation to be somewhat more robust: $-\lambda \mathbf{A}^T \mathbf{A} \mathbf{H}^{-1} \approx \mathbf{I} - \mathbf{B}\mathbf{Q} \, \text{diag}^{-1}[\mathbf{V} + \mathbf{Q}^T \mathbf{B}\mathbf{Q}]\mathbf{Q}^T$ where $\mathbf{B} = \nabla\nabla \log P(\hat{\mathbf{s}})$ and $\mathbf{Q}$ and $\mathbf{V}$ are obtained from the singular value decomposition $\lambda \mathbf{A}^T \mathbf{A} = \mathbf{Q}\mathbf{V}\mathbf{Q}^T$.

2 Learning overcomplete representations of natural scenes

We learn 1× and 2× overcomplete representations using the natural scenes data set from (Olshausen and Field, 1996). The bases were initialized to random vectors modulated by Gaussian blobs with a spatial standard deviation of 1 pixel whose position was evenly distributed. Similar results were obtained using random initial conditions, but convergence was slower. Choice of stepsize during learning was important for rapid and reliable convergence. In these examples, for each stepsize δ was chosen so that the absolute change in a_{ij} along the direction given by equation 5 was at most a fixed percentage of the data standard deviation. This stepsize was reduced from 2% to 0.1% over the first 1000 iterations and fixed at 0.1% for the remaining iterations. To ensure smoothness, the stepsize was also exponentially averaged using $\epsilon(t) = 0.9\epsilon(t-1) + 0.1\delta$. Both bases learned here were stable after 5000 gradient steps. Results are shown in Figures 1 and 2.

2.1 Comparison to alternative basis sets

An advantage of the probabilistic framework is that alternative bases can be compared objectively in terms of their coding efficiency. We used two methods to

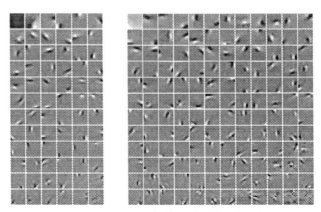

Figure 1: Results from training 1× (left) and 2× overcomplete (right) bases trained on 12x12 image patches extracted from natural scenes. Only every other basis function is shown in descending order of L2 norm left-right, top-bottom.

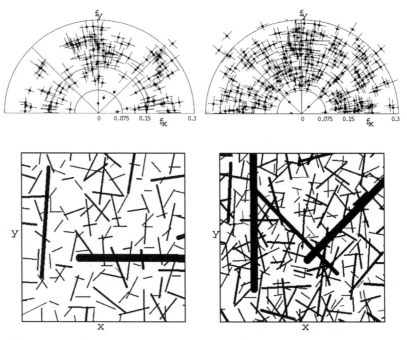

Figure 2: Basis function characteristics for the 1× (left panel) and 2× (right panel) overcomplete case. Each basis function was fitted with a Gabor function (i.e., a Gaussian-modulated sine grating) to characterize its position, spatial frequency selectivity, and orientation. At the top is a polar plot of the spatial-frequency and orientation selectivity. Each dot denotes the center spatial-frequency and orientation of a fitted basis function. The crosshairs indicate the spread in spatial-frequency and orientation. The plots at bottom show the spatial layout of the same set of basis functions. Each bar denotes the center position and orientation of a fitted basis function within the 12x12 grid. The thickness and length of the line denotes its spatial-frequency band (lower spatial frequencies are represented with thicker lines, and vice-versa). Increasing the degree of overcompleteness results in a denser tiling of the joint 4-D space of position, orientation, and spatial-frequency.

estimate how well a particular basis represented a given set of data. One approach is to calculate the entropy of the basis vector coefficients, s, assuming a discretization of the observed density required to maintain an encoding noise level of σ_x. Another approach is to use $-\log_2 P(\mathbf{x}|\mathbf{A}) - L\log_2(\sigma_x)$. Shannon's coding theorem states that this will give a lower bound on coding length if the model is correct. The entropy method has the drawback that it does not including the cost of misfitting the data, but, because it uses the observed distribution $P(\mathbf{s})$, it can yield a more accurate estimate if the data are well fit. For the examples below, the basis coefficients were optimized using a modified conjugate gradient procedure with a tolerance of 10^{-4}. The Laplacian prior parameter θ_m was adapted to fit the density of s_m obtained from the images. The noise level was assumed to be approximately 1 bit out of 8.

Comparison of complete bases ($\mathbf{A}_{64\times64}$). Table 1 shows the value of $\log P(\mathbf{x}|\mathbf{A})$ for various bases: the learned basis, a Gabor wavelet basis fit to the learned basis, a basis obtained using principal component analysis (PCA), the standard Fourier basis, the Haar wavelet basis, a pixel basis ($\mathbf{A}$ is the identity), and a Gabor wavelet basis designed to evenly tile the joint space of position, frequency, orientation, and phase). The table entries represent ten different estimates using 100 8×8 image patches randomly sampled from the dataset of natural images. The table shows that the learned basis is about 1.5 bits/pixel more efficient than any of the non-adapted bases. Note that although the fitted Gabor basis achieves the best coding efficiency in terms entropy, it is among the worst in terms of probability. This reflects the fact that this basis does not fully span the dataspace and cannot fit all of the data which is not accounted for in the entropy estimate. The large difference between the hand-generated and fitted Gabor clearly shows that there are a large number of free parameters in the Gabor basis and that hand-setting them to optimally tile the space is difficult.

To check the consistency of the coding efficiency estimates, an artificial dataset was generated by synthesizing data from the pixel basis using a Laplacian distribution for the coefficients. This produced images that consisted of independent pixels with a Laplacian intensity distribution. The right two columns show the estimated coding efficiencies for the same set of bases. For this dataset, the pixel basis achieves the best coding efficiency (as expected), and the learned basis performs much worse than any of the fixed basis.

Comparison of $2\times$ overcomplete bases ($\mathbf{A}_{64\times128}$) Again the learned basis achieves better coding efficiency than the fixed Fourier or Gabor basis on the same image dataset. The fitted Gabor basis performs better in terms of entropy but worse in terms of probability, reflecting the fact that even the $2\times$ overcomplete basis does not fully span the input space. One might expect that as more basis functions are added to the overcomplete representation, the coding efficiency should increase, because the basis functions can become more and more specific and obtain a better approximation to the underlying density. The tables show, however, that this is not the case. A likely reason for this is that the assumptions of the model are breaking down for higher degrees of overcompleteness. In particular, the present model assumes that the coefficients, s, are independent, an assumption that becomes increasingly inaccurate for higher degrees of overcompleteness. Models that can capture a greater variety of structure in the coefficients, such as with hierarchical priors, could achieve better representation and greater coding efficiency.

Table 1: Bits per pixel for complete bases

Basis	Image dataset		Pixel dataset	
	entropy	$-\log P(\mathbf{x}|\mathbf{A})$	entropy	$-\log P(\mathbf{x}|\mathbf{A})$
learned	3.43 ± 0.08	4.74 ± 0.05	5.21 ± 0.05	7.52 ± 0.27
GaborFit	2.82 ± 0.07	5.65 ± 0.02	4.27 ± 0.05	9.78 ± 0.36
PCA	4.77 ± 0.07	5.43 ± 0.07	4.76 ± 0.03	5.06 ± 0.03
Fourier	4.99 ± 0.08	5.48 ± 0.08	4.76 ± 0.03	5.06 ± 0.03
Haar	5.14 ± 0.08	5.55 ± 0.07	4.74 ± 0.03	5.03 ± 0.03
pixel	5.55 ± 0.09	5.79 ± 0.08	4.54 ± 0.02	4.89 ± 0.02
Gabor	7.18 ± 0.12	11.12 ± 3.33	6.51 ± 0.08	9.09 ± 0.26

Table 2: Bits per pixel for 2× overcomplete bases

Basis	Image dataset	
	entropy	$-\log P(\mathbf{x}|\mathbf{A})$
learned	4.57 ± 0.20	6.70 ± 0.04
GaborFit	4.00 ± 0.26	6.88 ± 0.05
Fourier	5.61 ± 0.15	7.69 ± 0.16
Gabor	6.36 ± 0.13	8.13 ± 0.13

3 Noise removal

In order to demonstrate the ability of the adapted bases to capture typical structure in the data, we applied the algorithm toward the problem of noise removal in images. This task is a natural fit for the algorithm, because Gaussian additive noise is incorporated into the specification of the image model. A set of bases that characterizes well the probability distribution of the data should have improved noise removal properties, since they will be better at inferring the most probable image in the face of uncertainty.

An image was tiled into non-overlapping 12x12 blocks and Gaussian noise was added to each of the sub-images. For each of these sub-images, the coefficients were fit so as to maximize the posterior probability of the coefficients (3), using an exponential prior on the coefficients (i.e., the same as in learning), and with λ set according to the level of noise added. The resulting image reconstructions are shown in Figure 3 using the learned bases with a Laplacian prior and standard Wiener filtering. Although the mean squared error (the mean difference between the original and reconstructed pixels) is roughly equal for both methods, they yield perceptually different reconstructions.

4 Conclusion

We have shown in this paper how the framework of probabilistic inference may be employed both for learning efficient image codes (5) and also for inferring the most probable representation for a given image (3). We have demonstrated moderate success in learning bases that capture the underlying statistical structure of images, and have demonstrated this using quantitative comparison with alternative, standard image codes. Importantly, the probabilistic framework provides a new

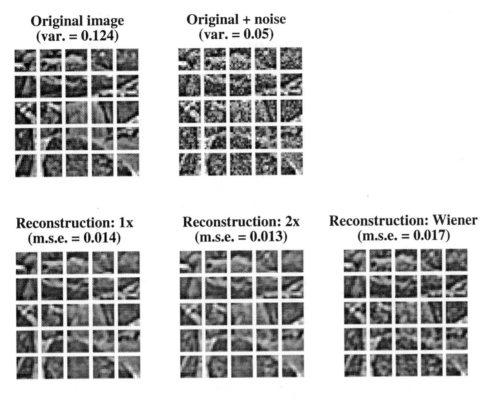

Figure 3: Application to image-denoising. An image is shown tiled into non-overlapping 12x12 blocks, and the image model was applied to each of these blocks separately.

perspective on the utility of working with overcomplete codes – better modeling of the underlying probability density. The combination of a sparse prior together with an overcomplete bases set results in representations that are a non-linear function of the image. This leads to practical advantages for de-noising and also to compression which we are currently pursuing.

References

Bell, A. J. and Sejnowski, T. J. (1997). The 'independent components' of natural scenes are edge filters. *Vision Research*, 37: 3327–3338.

Chen, S., Donoho, D. L., and Saunders, M. A. (1996). Atomic decomposition by basis pursuit. Technical report, Dept. Stat., Stanford Univ., Stanford, CA.

Lewicki, M. S. and Sejnowski, T. J. (1998). Learning nonlinear overcomplete representations for efficient coding. In *Advances in Neural and Information Processing Systems*, volume 10, San Mateo. Morgan Kaufmann.

Olshausen, B. A. and Field, D. J. (1996). Emergence of simple-cell receptive-field properties by learning a sparse code for natural images. *Nature*, 381:607–609.

Simoncelli, E. P., Freeman, W. T., Adelson, E. H., and J., H. D. (1992). Shiftable multiscale transforms. *IEEE Trans. Info. Theory*, 38:587–607.

Visual Navigation in a Robot using Zig-Zag Behavior

M. Anthony Lewis

Beckman Institute
405 N. Mathews Avenue
University of Illinois
Urbana, Illinois 61801

Abstract

We implement a model of obstacle avoidance in flying insects on a small, monocular robot. The result is a system that is capable of rapid navigation through a dense obstacle field. The key to the system is the use of zigzag behavior to articulate the body during movement. It is shown that this behavior compensates for a parallax blind spot surrounding the focus of expansion normally found in systems without parallax behavior. The system models the cooperation of several behaviors: halteres-ocular response (similar to VOR), optomotor response, and the parallax field computation and mapping to motor system. The resulting system is neurally plausible, very simple, and should be easily hosted on aVLSI hardware.

1 INTRODUCTION

Srinivasan and Zhang (1993) describe behavioral evidence for two distinct movement detecting systems in bee: (1) A direction selective pathway with low frequency response characteristics serving the optomotor response and (2) A non-direction selective movement system with higher frequency response serving functions of obstacle avoidance and the 'tunnel centering' response where the animal seeks a flight path along the centerline of a narrow corridor. Recently, this parallel movement detector view has received support from anatomical evidence in fly (Douglass and Strausfeld, 1996). We are concerned here with the implications of using non-direction selective movement detectors for tasks such as obstacle avoidance.

A reasonable model of a non-direction selective pathway would be that this pathway is computing the absolute value of the optic flow, i.e. $s = \|[\dot{x}, \dot{y}]\|$ where $\dot{x}, \dot{y}$ are the components of the optic flow field on the retina at the point $[x, y]$.

What is the effect of using the absolute value of the flow field and throwing away direction information? In section 2 we analyze the effect of a non-direction selective movement field. We understand from this analysis that rotational information, and the limited dynamic range of real sensors contaminates the non-direction selective field and probably prevents the use of this technique in an area around the direction heading of the observer.

One technique to compensate for this 'parallax blind spot' is by periodically changing the direction of the observer. Such periodic movements are seen in insects as well as lower vertebrates and it is suggestive that these movements may compensate for this basic problem.

In Section 3, we describe a robotic implementation using a crude non-direction selective movement detector based on a rectified temporal derivative of luminosity. Each 'neuron' in the model retina issues a vote to control the motors of the robot. This system, though seemingly naively simple, compares favorably with other robotic implementations that rely on the optic flow or a function of the optic flow (divergence). These techniques typically require a large degree of spatial temporal averaging and seem computationally complex. In addition, our model agrees better with with the biological evidence.

Finally, the technique presented here is amenable to implementation in custom aVLSI or mixed aVLSI/dVLSI chips. Thus it should be possible to build a subminiature visually guided navigation system with several (one?) low-power simple custom chips.

2 ANALYSIS OF NON-DIRECTION SELECTIVE MOVEMENT DETECTION SYSTEM

Let us assume a perspective projection

$$\begin{bmatrix} x \\ y \end{bmatrix} = \frac{\lambda}{Z}\begin{bmatrix} X \\ Y \end{bmatrix} \tag{1}$$

where λ is the focal length of the lens, X, Y, Z is the position of a point in the environment, and x, y is the projection of that point on the retinal plane. The velocity of the image of a moving point in the world can be found by differentiating (1) with respect to time:

$$\begin{bmatrix} \dot{x} \\ \dot{y} \end{bmatrix} = \frac{\lambda}{Z^2}\begin{bmatrix} Z\dot{X} - X\dot{Z} \\ Z\dot{Y} - Y\dot{Z} \end{bmatrix} \tag{2}$$

If we assume that objects in the environment are fixed in relation to one-and-other and that the observer is moving with relative translational velocity ${}^c V_e = \begin{bmatrix} V_x & V_y & V_z \end{bmatrix}^T$ and relative rotational velocity ${}^c \Omega_e = \begin{bmatrix} \omega_x & \omega_y & \omega_z \end{bmatrix}^T$ to the environment given in frame c, a point in the environment has relative velocity:

$$ {}^c\dot{P} = \begin{bmatrix} \dot{X} \\ \dot{Y} \\ \dot{Z} \end{bmatrix} = -\left({}^c\Omega_e \times {}^c P + {}^c V_e\right) \tag{3}$$

Now substituting in (2):

$$\begin{bmatrix} \dot{x} \\ \dot{y} \end{bmatrix} = \frac{\lambda}{Z}\begin{bmatrix} -1 & 0 & x \\ 0 & -1 & y \end{bmatrix}{}^c V_e + \lambda\begin{bmatrix} xy & -1-x^2 & y \\ 1+y^2 & -xy & -x \end{bmatrix}{}^c\Omega_e \tag{4}$$

and taking the absolute value of the optic flow:

$$\sqrt{\dot{s}^2} = \sqrt{\frac{\lambda^2 V_z^2}{Z^2}\left[\left(-\alpha + x - \frac{Z}{V_z}\left(xy\omega_x + \omega_y(x^2+1) + y\omega_z\right)\right)^2 + \left(-\beta + y + \frac{Z}{V_z}\left(-\omega_x(y^2+1) + xy\omega_y + x\omega_z\right)\right)^2\right]} \tag{5}$$

where we have made the substitution: $\begin{bmatrix} \dot{X}/Z & \dot{Y}/Z \end{bmatrix} \rightarrow \begin{bmatrix} \alpha & \beta \end{bmatrix}$ (that is, the heading direction).

We can see that the terms involving $\begin{bmatrix} \omega_x & \omega_y & \omega_z \end{bmatrix}$ cannot be separated from the x, y terms. If we assume that $\begin{bmatrix} \omega_x & \omega_y & \omega_z \end{bmatrix} = \mathbf{0}$ then we can rearrange the equation as:

$$\Delta^{-1}(s) = \frac{|T_z|}{|Z|} = \frac{|s|}{\lambda\sqrt{\left[(x-\alpha)^2 + (y-\beta)^2\right]}} \qquad (6)$$

in the case of Z translation. If $|T_z| = 0$ then we have:

$$\Delta^{-1}(s) = \frac{1}{|Z|} = \frac{|s|}{\lambda\sqrt{T_x^2 + T_y^2}} \qquad (7)$$

this corresponds to the case of pure lateral translations. Locusts (as well as some vertebrates) use *peering* or side to side movements to gauge distances before jumping.

We call the quantity in (6) inverse relative depth. Under the correct circumstances it is equivalent to the reciprocal of time to contact.

Equation (6) can be restated as: $\Delta^{-1}(s) = g_i s$ where g is a gain factor that depends on the current direction heading and the position in the retina. This gain factor can be implemented neurally as a shunting inhibition, for example.

This has the following implications. If the observer is using a non-direction sensitive movement detector then (A) it must rotationally stabilize its eyes (B) it must dynamically alter the gain of this information in a pathway between the retinal input and motor output or it must always have a constant direction heading and use constant gain factors.

In real systems there is likely to be imperfection in rotational stabilization of the observer as well as sensors with limited dynamic range. To understand the effect of these, let us assume that there is a base-line noise level δ and we assume that this defines a minimum threshold substituting $s = \delta$, we can find a level curve for the minimum detectability of an object, i.e.:

$$\frac{\delta|Z|}{\lambda|T_z|} = \sqrt{\left[(u-\alpha)^2 + (v-\beta)^2\right]} \qquad (8)$$

Thus, for constant depth and for δ independent of the spatial position on the retina, the level curve is a circle. The circle increases in radius with increasing distance, and noise, and decreases with increasing speed. The circle is centered around the direction heading.

The solution to the problem of a 'parallax blind spot' is to make periodic changes of direction. This can be accomplished in an open loop fashion or, perhaps, in an image driven fashion as suggested by Sobey (1994).

3 ROBOT MODEL

Figure 1a is a photograph of the robot model. The robot's base is a Khepera Robot. The Khepera is a small wheeled robot a little over 2" in diameter and uses differential drive motors. The robot has been fitted with a solid-state gyro attached to its body. This gyroscope senses angular velocities about the body axis and is aligned with the axis of the camera joint. A camera, capable of rotation about an axis perpendicular to the ground plane, is also attached. The camera has a field of view of about 90° and can swing of ±90°. The angle of the head rotation is sensed by a small potentiometer.

For convenience, each visual process is implemented on a separate Workstation (SGI Indy) as a heavyweight process. Interprocess communication is via PVM distributed computing library. Using a distributed processing model, behaviors can be dynamically added and deleted facilitating analysis and debugging.

3.1 ROBOT CONTROL SYSTEM

The control is divided into control modules as illustrated in Fig 2. At the top of the drawing we see a gaze stabilization pathway. This uses a gyro (imitating a halteres organ) for stabilization of rapid head movements. In addition, a visual pathway, using direction selective movement detector (DSMD) maps is used for slower optomotor response. Each of the six maps uses correlation type detectors (Borst and Egelhaaf,1989). Each map is

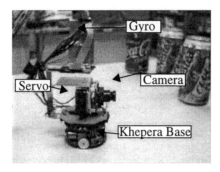 

Figure 1. Physical setup. (A) Modified Khepera Robot with camera and gyro mounted. (B) Typical obstacle field run experiment.

tuned to a different horizontal velocity (three for left image translations and three for right image translations).

The lower half of the drawing shows the obstacle avoidance pathway. A crude non-direction selective movement detector is created using a simple temporal derivative. The use of this as a movement detector was motivated by the desire to eventually replace the camera front end with a Neuromorphic chip. Temporal derivative chips are readily available (Delbrück and Mead, 1991).

Next we reason that the temporal derivative gives a crude estimate of the absolute value of the optic flow. For example if we expect only horizontal flows then: $E_x x = -E_t$ (Horn and Shunck, 1981). Here E_t is the temporal derivative of the luminosity and E_x is the spatial derivative. If we sample over a patch of the image, E_x will take on a range of values. If we take the average rectified temporal derivative over a patch then $|\dot{x}| = |-E_t| / |E_x|$. Thus the average rectified temporal derivative over a patch will give a velocity proportional the absolute value of the optic flow.

In order to make the change to motor commands, we use a voting scheme. Each pixel in the nondirection selective movement detector field (NDSMD) votes on a direction for the robot. The left pixels for a right turn and the right pixels vote for a left turn. The left and right votes are summed. In certain experiments described below the difference of the left and right votes was used to drive the rotation of the robot. In others a symmetry breaking scheme was used. It was observed that with an object dead ahead of the robot, often the left and right activation would have high but nearly equal activation. In the symmetry breaking scheme, the side with the lower activation was further decrease by a factor of 50%. This admittedly ad hoc solution remarkably improved the performance *in the non-zig-zag case* as noted below.

The zig-zag behavior is implemented as a feedforward command to the motor system and is modeled as:

$$\omega_{ZigZag}^{Khepera} = \sin(\omega t)K$$

Finally, a constant forward bias is added to each wheel so the robot makes constant progress. K is chosen empirically but in principle one should be able to derive it using the analysis in section 2.

As described above, the gaze stabilization module has control of head rotation and the zig-zag behavior and the depth from parallax behavior control the movement of the robot's body. During normal operation, the head may exceed the $\pm 90°$ envelope defined by the mechanical system. This problem can be addressed in several ways among them are by making a body saccade to bring the body under the head or making a head saccade to align the head with the body. We choose the later approach solely because it seemed to work better in practice.

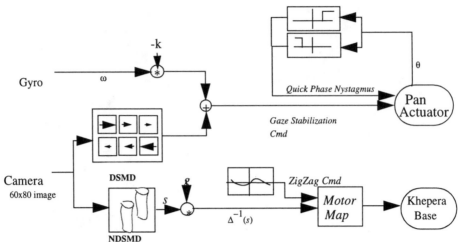

Figure 2. ZigZag Navigation model is composed of a gaze stabilization system (top) and an obstacle avoidance system (bottom). See text.

3.2 BIOLOGICAL INSPIRATION FOR MODEL

Course-grained visual pathways are modeled using inspiration from insect neurobiology. The model of depth from parallax is inspired by details given in Srinivasan & Zhang (1993) on work done in bees. Gaze stabilization using a fast channel, mediated by the halteres organs, and a slow optomotor response is inspired by a description of the blowfly *Calliphora* as reviewed by Hengstenberg (1991).

4 EXPERIMENTS

Four types of experimental setups were used. These are illustrated in Fig 3. In setup 1 the robot must avoid a dense field of obstacles (empty soda cans). This is designed to test the basic competence of this technique. In setup 2, thin dowels are place in the robot's path. This tests the spatial resolving capability of the robot. Likewise setup 3 uses a dense obstacle field with one opening replaced by a lightly textured surface.

Finally, experimental setup 4 uses a single small object (1cm black patch) and tests the distance at which the robot can 'lock-on' to a target. In this experiment, the avoidance field is sorted for a maximal element over a given threshold. A target cross is placed at this maximal element. The closest object should correspond with this maximal element. If a maximal element over a threshold is identified for a continuous 300ms and the target cross is on the correct target, the robot is stopped and its distance to the object is measured. The larger the distance, the better.

5 RESULTS

The results are described briefly here. In the setup 1 without the use of symmetry breaking, the scores were ZigZag: 10 Success, 0 Failures and the non-ZigZag: 4 Success and 6 Failures. With Symmetry Breaking installed the results were: ZigZag: 49 Success, 3 Failures and the non-ZigZag: 44 Success and 9 failures.

In the case palisades test: ZigZag: 22 Success, 4 Failures and the non-ZigZag: 14 Success and 11 failures.

In the false opening case: ZigZag: 8 Success, 2 Failures and the non-ZigZag: 6 Success and 4 Failures.

Finally, in the distance-to-lock setup, a lock was achieved at an average distance 21.3 CM (15 data points) for zigzag and 9.6 cm (15 data points) for the non-zigzag case.

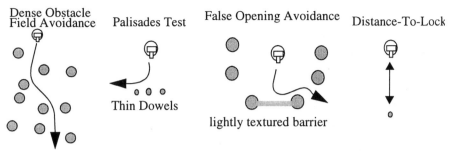

Figure 3. Illustrations of the four experimental setups.

We tentatively conclude that zig-zag behavior should improve performance in robot and in animal navigation.

6 DISCUSSION

In addition to the robotic implementation presented here, there have been many other techniques presented in the literature. Most relevant is Sobey (1994) who uses a zigzag behavior for obstacle avoidance. In this work, optic flow is computed through a process of discrete movements where 16 frames are collected, the robot stops, and the stored frames are analyzed for optic flow. The basic strategy is very clever: Always choose the next move in the direction of an identified object. The reasoning is that since we know the distance to the object in this direction, we can confidently move toward the object, stopping before collision. The basic idea of using zig-zag behavior is similar except that the zig-zagging is driven by perceptual input. In addition, the implementation requires estimation of the flow field requiring smoothing over numerous images. Finally, Sobey uses Optic Flow and we use the absolute value of the Optic Flow as suggested by biology.

Franceschini et al (1992) reports an analog implementation that uses elementary movement detectors. A unique feature is the non-uniform sampling and the use of three separate arrays. One array uses a sampling around the circumference. The other two sampling systems are mounted laterally on the robot and concentrate in the 'blind-spot' immediately in front of the robot. It is not clear that the strategy of using three sensor arrays, spatially separated, and direction selective movement detectors is in accord with the biological constraints.

Santos-Victor et al (1995) reports a system using optic flow and having lateral facing cameras. Here the authors were reproducing the centering reflex and did not focus on avoiding obstacles in front of the robot. Coombs and Roberts (1992,1993) use a similar technique. Weber et al (1996) describe wall following and stopping in front of an obstacle using an optic flow measure.

Finally, a number of papers report the use of flow field divergence, apparently first suggested by Nelson and Aloimonos (1989). This requires the computation of higher derivatives and requires significant smoothing. Even in this case, there is a problem of a 'parallax hole.' See Fig. 3 of that article, for example. In any case they did not implement their idea on a mobile robot. However, this approach has been followed up with an implementation in a robot by Camus et al (1996) reporting good results.

The system described here presents a physical model of insect like behavior integrated on a small robotic platform. Using results derived from an analysis of optic flow, we concluded that a zig-zag behavior in the robot would allow it to detect obstacles in front of the robot by periodically articulating the blind spot.

The complexity of the observed behavior and the simplicity of the control is striking. The robot is able to navigate through a field of obstacles, always searching out a freeway for movement.

The integrated behavior outlined here should be a good candidate for a neuromorphic implementation. A multichip (or single chip?) system could be envisioned using a relatively simple non-directional 2-d movement detector. Two arrays of perpendicular 1-d array of movement detectors should be sufficient for the optomotor response. This information could then be mapped to a circuit comprised of a few op-amp adder circuits and then sent to the head and body motors. Even the halteres organ could be simulated with a silicon fabricated gyroscope. The results would be an extremely compact robot capable of autonomous, visually guided navigation.

Finally, from our analysis of optic flow, we can make a reasonable prediction about the neural wiring in flying insects. The estimated depth of objects in the environment depends on where the object falls on the optic array as well as the ratio of translation to forward movement. Thus a bee or a fly should probably modulate its incoming visual signal to account for this time varying interpretation of the scene. We would predict that there should be motor information, related to the ratio of forward to lateral velocities would be projected to the non-directional selective motion detector array. This would allow a valid time varying interpretation of the scene in a zig-zagging animal.

Acknowledgments

The author acknowledges the useful critique of this work by Narendra Ahuja, Mark Nelson, John Hart and Lucia Simo. Special thanks to Garrick Kremesic and Barry Stout who assisted with the experimental setup and the modification of the Khepera. The author acknowledges the support of ONR grant N000149610657. The author also acknowledges the loan of the Khepera from UCLA (NSF grant CDA-9303148).

References

A. Borst and M. Egelhaaf (1989), Principles of Visual Motion Detection, Trends in Neurosciences, **12**(8):297-306

T. Camus, D. Coombs, M. Herman, and T.-H. Hong (1996), "Real-time Single-Workstation Obstacle Avoidance Using Only Wide-Field Flow Divergence", Proceedings of the 13th International Conference on Pattern Recognition. pp. 323-30 vol.3

D. Coombs and K. Roberts (1992), "'Bee-Bot': Using Peripheral Optical Flow to Avoid Obstacles", SPIE Vol 1825, Intelligent Robots and Computer Vision XI, pp 714-721.

D. Coombs and K. Roberts (1993), "Centering behavior using peripheral vision", Proc. 1993 IEEE Computer Society Conf. CVPR pp. 440-5, 16 refs. 1993

T. Delbrück and C. A. Mead (1991), Time-derivative adaptive silicon photoreceptor array. Proc. SPIE - Int. Soc. Opt. Eng. (USA). vol 1541, pp. 92-9.

J. K. Douglass and N. J. Strausfeld (1996), Visual Motion-Detection Circuits in Flies: Parallel Direction- and Non-Direction-Sensitive Pathways between the Medulla and Lobula Plate, J. of Neuroscience **16**(15):4551-4562.

N. Franceschini, J. M. Pichon and C. Blanes (1992), "From Insect Vision to Robot Vision", Phil. Trans. R. Soc Lond. B. **337**, pp 283-294.

R. Hengstenberg (1991), Gaze Control in the Blowfly *Calliphora*: a Multisensory, Two-Stage Integration Process, Seminars, in the Neurosciences, Vol3,pp 19-29.

B. K. P. Horn and B. G. Shunck (1981), "Determining Optic Flow", Artificial Intelligence, **17**(1-3):185-204.

R. C. Nelson and J. Y. Aloimonos (1989) Obstacle Avoidance Using Flow Field Divergence, IEEE Trans. on Pattern Anal. and Mach. Intel. **11**(10):1102-1106.

J. Santos-Victor, G. Sandini, F. Curotto and S. Garibaldi (1995), "Divergent Stereo in Autonomous Navigation: From Bees to Robots," Int. J. of Comp. Vis. **14**, pp 159-177.

P. J. Sobey (1994), "Active Navigation With a Monocular Robot" Biol. Cybern, **71**:433-440

M. V. Srinivasan and S. W. Zhang (1993), Evidence for Two Distinct Movement-Detecting Mechanisms in Insect Vision, Naturwissenschaften, **80**, pp 38-41.

K. Weber, S. Venkatash and M.V. Srinivasan (1996), "Insect Inspired Behaviours for the Autonomous Control of Mobile Robots" Proc. of ICPR'96, pp 156-160.

2D Observers for Human 3D Object Recognition?

Zili Liu
NEC Research Institute

Daniel Kersten
University of Minnesota

Abstract

Converging evidence has shown that human object recognition depends on familiarity with the images of an object. Further, the greater the similarity between objects, the stronger is the dependence on object appearance, and the more important two-dimensional (2D) image information becomes. These findings, however, do not rule out the use of 3D structural information in recognition, and the degree to which 3D information is used in visual memory is an important issue. Liu, Knill, & Kersten (1995) showed that any model that is restricted to rotations in the image plane of independent 2D templates could not account for human performance in discriminating novel object views. We now present results from models of generalized radial basis functions (GRBF), 2D nearest neighbor matching that allows 2D affine transformations, and a Bayesian statistical estimator that integrates over all possible 2D affine transformations. The performance of the human observers relative to each of the models is better for the novel views than for the familiar template views, suggesting that humans generalize better to novel views from template views. The Bayesian estimator yields the optimal performance with 2D affine transformations and independent 2D templates. Therefore, models of 2D affine matching operations with independent 2D templates are unlikely to account for human recognition performance.

1 Introduction

Object recognition is one of the most important functions in human vision. To understand human object recognition, it is essential to understand how objects are represented in human visual memory. A central component in object recognition is the matching of the stored object representation with that derived from the image input. But the nature of the object representation has to be inferred from recognition performance, by taking into account the contribution from the image information. When evaluating human performance, how can one separate the contributions to performance of the image information from the representation? Ideal observer analysis provides a precise computational tool to answer this question. An ideal observer's recognition performance is restricted only by the available image information and is otherwise optimal, in the sense of statistical decision theory, irrespective of how the model is implemented. A comparison of human to ideal performance (often in terms of efficiency) serves to normalize performance with respect to the image information for the task. We consider the problem of viewpoint dependence in human recognition.

A recent debate in human object recognition has focused on the dependence of recognition performance on viewpoint [1, 6]. Depending on the experimental conditions, an observer's ability to recognize a familiar object from novel viewpoints is impaired to varying degrees. A central assumption in the debate is the equivalence in viewpoint dependence and recognition performance. In other words, the assumption is that viewpoint dependent performance implies a viewpoint dependent representation, and that viewpoint independent performance implies a viewpoint independent representation. However, given that any recognition performance depends on the input image information, which is necessarily viewpoint dependent, the viewpoint dependence of the performance is neither necessary nor sufficient for the viewpoint dependence of the representation. Image information has to be factored out first, and the ideal observer provides the means to do this.

The second aspect of an ideal observer is that it is implementation free. Consider the GRBF model [5], as compared with human object recognition (see below). The model stores a number of 2D templates $\{T_i\}$ of a 3D object O, and recognizes or rejects a stimulus image S by the following similarity measure $\Sigma_i c_i \exp\left(\|T_i - S\|^2/2\sigma^2\right)$, where c_i and σ are constants. The model's performance as a function of viewpoint parallels that of human observers. This observation has led to the conclusion that the human visual system may indeed, as does the model, use 2D stored views with GRBF interpolation to recognize 3D objects [2]. Such a conclusion, however, overlooks implementational constraints in the model, because the model's performance also depends on its implementations. Conceivably, a model with some 3D information of the objects can also mimic human performance, so long as it is appropriately implemented. There are typically too many possible models that can produce the same pattern of results.

In contrast, an ideal observer computes the optimal performance that is only limited by the stimulus information and the task. We can define constrained ideals that are also limited by explicitly specified assumptions (e.g., a class of matching operations). Such a model observer therefore yields the best possible performance among the class of models with the same stimulus input and assumptions. In this paper, we are particularly interested in constrained ideal observers that are restricted in functionally significant aspects (e.g., a 2D ideal observer that stores independent 2D templates and has access only to 2D affine transformations). The key idea is that a constrained ideal observer is the best in its class. So if humans outperform this ideal observer, they must have used more than what is available to the ideal. The conclusion that follows is strong: not only does the constrained ideal fail to account for human performance, but the whole class of its implementations are also falsified.

A crucial question in object recognition is the extent to which human observers model the geometric variation in images due to the projection of a 3D object onto a 2D image. At one extreme, we have shown that any model that compares the image to independent views (even if we allow for 2D rigid transformations of the input image) is insufficient to account for human performance . At the other extreme, it is unlikely that variation is modeled in terms of rigid transformation of a 3D object template in memory. A possible intermediate solution is to match the input image to stored views, subject to 2D affine deformations. This is reasonable because 2D affine transformations approximate 3D variation over a limited range of viewpoint change.

In this study, we test whether any model limited to the independent comparison of 2D views, but with 2D affine flexibility, is sufficient to account for viewpoint dependence in human recognition. In the following section, we first define our experimental task, in which the computational models yield the provably best possible performance under their specified conditions. We then review the 2D ideal observer and GRBF model derived in [4], and the 2D affine nearest neighbor model in [8]. Our principal theoretical result is a closed-form solution of a Bayesian 2D affine ideal observer. We then compare human performance with the 2D affine ideal model, as well as the other three models. In particular, if humans can classify novel views of an object better than the 2D affine ideal, then our human observers must have used more information than that embodied by that ideal.

2 The observers

Let us first define the task. An observer looks at the 2D images of a 3D wire frame object from a number of viewpoints. These images will be called templates $\{\mathbf{T}_i\}$. Then two distorted copies of the original 3D object are displayed. They are obtained by adding 3D Gaussian positional noise (i.i.d.) to the vertices of the original object. One distorted object is called the target, whose Gaussian noise has a constant variance. The other is the distractor, whose noise has a larger variance that can be adjusted to achieve a criterion level of performance. The two objects are displayed from the same viewpoint in parallel projection, which is either from one of the template views, or a novel view due to 3D rotation. The task is to choose the one that is more similar to the original object. The observer's performance is measured by the variance (threshold) that gives rise to 75% correct performance. The optimal strategy is to choose the stimulus $\mathbf{S}$ with a larger probability $p(\mathbf{O}|\mathbf{S})$. From Bayes' rule, this is to choose the larger of $p(\mathbf{S}|\mathbf{O})$.

Assume that the models are restricted to 2D transformations of the image, and cannot reconstruct the 3D structure of the object from its independent templates $\{\mathbf{T}_i\}$. Assume also that the prior probability $p(\mathbf{T}_i)$ is constant. Let us represent $\mathbf{S}$ and $\mathbf{T}_i$ by their (x, y) vertex coordinates: $(\ \mathbf{X}\quad\mathbf{Y}\ )^T$, where $\mathbf{X} = (x^1, x^2, \ldots, x^n)$, $\mathbf{Y} = (y^1, y^2, \ldots, y^n)$. We assume that the correspondence between $\mathbf{S}$ and $\mathbf{T}_i$ is solved up to a reflection ambiguity, which is equivalent to an additional template: $\mathbf{T}_i^r = (\ \mathbf{X}^r\quad\mathbf{Y}^r\ )^T$, where $\mathbf{X}^r = (x^n, \ldots, x^2, x^1)$, $\mathbf{Y}^r = (y^n, \ldots, y^2, y^1)$. We still denote the template set as $\{\mathbf{T}_i\}$. Therefore,

$$p(\mathbf{S}|\mathbf{O}) = \Sigma p(\mathbf{S}|\mathbf{T}_i)p(\mathbf{T}_i). \tag{1}$$

In what follows, we will compute $p(\mathbf{S}|\mathbf{T}_i)p(\mathbf{T}_i)$, with the assumption that $\mathbf{S} = \mathcal{F}(\mathbf{T}_i) + \mathbf{N}(0, \sigma\mathbf{I}_{2n})$, where $\mathbf{N}$ is the Gaussian distribution, $\mathbf{I}_{2n}$ the $2n \times 2n$ identity matrix, and $\mathcal{F}$ a 2D transformation. For the 2D ideal observer, $\mathcal{F}$ is a rigid 2D rotation. For the GRBF model, $\mathcal{F}$ assigns a linear coefficient to each template $\mathbf{T}_i$, in addition to a 2D rotation. For the 2D affine nearest neighbor model, $\mathcal{F}$ represents the 2D affine transformation that minimizes $\|\mathbf{S} - \mathbf{T}_i\|^2$, after $\mathbf{S}$ and $\mathbf{T}_i$ are normalized in size. For the 2D affine ideal observer, $\mathcal{F}$ represents all possible 2D affine transformations applicable to $\mathbf{T}_i$.

2.1   The 2D ideal observer

The templates are the original 2D images, their mirror reflections, and 2D rotations (in angle ϕ) in the image plane. Assume that the stimulus S is generated by adding Gaussian noise to a template, the probability $p(\mathbf{S}|\mathbf{O})$ is an integration over all templates and their reflections and rotations. The detailed derivation for the 2D ideal and the GRBF model can be found in [4].

$$\Sigma p(\mathbf{S}|\mathbf{T}_i)p(\mathbf{T}_i) \propto \Sigma \int d\phi \exp\left(-\|\mathbf{S} - \mathbf{T}_i(\phi)\|^2/2\sigma^2\right). \tag{2}$$

2.2   The GRBF model

The model has the same template set as the 2D ideal observer does. Its training requires that $\Sigma_i \int_0^{2\pi} d\phi c_i(\phi) N(\|\mathbf{T}_j - \mathbf{T}_i(\phi)\|, \sigma) = 1$, $j = 1, 2, \ldots$, with which $\{c_i\}$ can be obtained optimally using singular value decomposition. When a pair of new stimuli $\{\mathbf{S}\}$ are presented, the optimal decision is to choose the one that is closer to the learned prototype, in other words, the one with a smaller value of

$$\|1 - \Sigma \int_0^{2\pi} d\phi c_i(\phi) \exp\left(-\frac{\|\mathbf{S} - \mathbf{T}_i(\phi)\|^2}{2\sigma^2}\right)\|. \tag{3}$$

2.3   The 2D affine nearest neighbor model

It has been proved in [8] that the smallest Euclidean distance $D(\mathbf{S}, \mathbf{T})$ between $\mathbf{S}$ and $\mathbf{T}$ is, when $\mathbf{T}$ is allowed a 2D affine transformation, $\mathbf{S} \to \mathbf{S}/\|\mathbf{S}\|$, $\mathbf{T} \to \mathbf{T}/\|\mathbf{T}\|$,

$$D^2(\mathbf{S}, \mathbf{T}) = 1 - tr(\mathbf{S}^+\mathbf{S} \cdot \mathbf{T}^T\mathbf{T})/\|\mathbf{T}\|^2, \tag{4}$$

where tr strands for $trace$, and $\mathbf{S}^+ = \mathbf{S}^T(\mathbf{S}\mathbf{S}^T)^{-1}$. The optimal strategy, therefore, is to choose the $\mathbf{S}$ that gives rise to the larger of $\Sigma \exp\left(-D^2(\mathbf{S}, \mathbf{T}_i)/2\sigma^2\right)$, or the smaller of $\Sigma D^2(\mathbf{S}, \mathbf{T}_i)$. (Since no probability is defined in this model, both measures will be used and the results from the better one will be reported.)

2.4   The 2D affine ideal observer

We now calculate the Bayesian probability by assuming that the prior probability distribution of the 2D affine transformation, which is applied to the template $\mathbf{T}_i$, $\mathbf{AT} + \mathbf{T_r} = \begin{pmatrix} a & b \\ c & d \end{pmatrix} \mathbf{T}_i + \begin{pmatrix} t_x & \cdots & t_x \\ t_y & \cdots & t_y \end{pmatrix}$, obeys a Gaussian distribution $N(\mathbf{X_0}, \gamma\mathbf{I}_6)$, where $\mathbf{X_0}$ is the identity transformation $\mathbf{X}_0^T = (a, b, c, d, t_x, t_y) = (1, 0, 0, 1, 0, 0)$. We have

$$\Sigma p(\mathbf{S}|\mathbf{T}_i) = \Sigma \int_{-\infty}^{\infty} d\mathbf{X} \exp\left(-\|\mathbf{AT}_i + \mathbf{T_r} - \mathbf{S}\|^2/2\sigma^2\right) \tag{5}$$

$$= \Sigma C(n, \sigma, \gamma) det^{-1}\left(\mathbf{Q}_i'\right) \exp\left(tr\left(\mathbf{K}_i^T\mathbf{Q}_i(\mathbf{Q}_i')^{-1}\mathbf{Q}_i\mathbf{K}_i\right)/2\sigma^2\right), \tag{6}$$

where $C(n, \sigma, \gamma)$ is a function of n, σ, γ; $\mathbf{Q}' = \mathbf{Q} + \gamma^{-2}\mathbf{I}_2$, and

$$\mathbf{Q} = \begin{pmatrix} \mathbf{X_T} \cdot \mathbf{X_T} & \mathbf{X_T} \cdot \mathbf{Y_T} \\ \mathbf{Y_T} \cdot \mathbf{X_T} & \mathbf{Y_T} \cdot \mathbf{Y_T} \end{pmatrix}, \mathbf{QK} = \begin{pmatrix} \mathbf{X_T} \cdot \mathbf{X_S} & \mathbf{Y_T} \cdot \mathbf{X_S} \\ \mathbf{X_T} \cdot \mathbf{Y_S} & \mathbf{Y_T} \cdot \mathbf{Y_S} \end{pmatrix} + \gamma^{-2}\mathbf{I}_2. \tag{7}$$

The free parameters are γ and the number of 2D rotated copies for each $\mathbf{T}_i$ (since a 2D affine transformation implicitly includes 2D rotations, and since a specific prior probability distribution $N(\mathbf{X_0}, \gamma\mathbf{I})$ is assumed, both free parameters should be explored together to search for the optimal results).

Figure 1: Stimulus classes with increasing structural regularity: Balls, Irregular, Symmetric, and V-Shaped. There were three objects in each class in the experiment.

2.5 The human observers

Three naive subjects were tested with four classes of objects: Balls, Irregular, Symmetric, and V-Shaped (Fig. 1). There were three objects in each class. For each object, 11 template views were learned by rotating the object 60°/step, around the X- and Y-axis, respectively. The 2D images were generated by orthographic projection, and viewed monocularly. The viewing distance was 1.5 m. During the test, the standard deviation of the Gaussian noise added to the target object was $\sigma_t = 0.254$ cm. No feedback was provided.

Because the image information available to the humans was more than what was available to the models (shading and occlusion in addition to the (x, y) positions of the vertices), both learned and novel views were tested in a randomly interleaved fashion. Therefore, the strategy that humans used in the task for the learned and novel views should be the same. The number of self-occlusions, which in principle provided relative depth information, was counted and was about equal in both learned and novel view conditions. The shading information was also likely to be equal for the learned and novel views. Therefore, this additional information was about equal for the learned and novel views, and should not affect the comparison of the performance (humans relative to a model) between learned and novel views. We predict that if the humans used a 2D affine strategy, then their performance relative to the 2D affine ideal observer should not be higher for the novel views than for the learned views. One reason to use the four classes of objects with increasing structural regularity is that structural regularity is a 3D property (e.g., 3D Symmetric vs. Irregular), which the 2D models cannot capture. The exception is the planar V-Shaped objects, for which the 2D affine models completely capture 3D rotations, and are therefore the "correct" models. The V-Shaped objects were used in the 2D affine case as a benchmark. If human performance increases with increasing structural regularity of the objects, this would lend support to the hypothesis that humans have used 3D information in the task.

2.6 Measuring performance

A stair-case procedure [7] was used to track the observers' performance at 75% correct level for the learned and novel views, respectively. There were 120 trials for the humans, and 2000 trials for each of the models. For the GRBF model, the standard deviation of the Gaussian function was also sampled to search for the best result for the novel views for each of the 12 objects, and the result for the learned views was obtained accordingly. This resulted in a conservative test of the hypothesis of a GRBF model for human vision for the following reasons: (1) Since no feedback was provided in the human experiment and the learned and novel views were randomly intermixed, it is not straightforward for the model to find the best standard deviation for the novel views, particularly because the best standard deviation for the novel views was not the same as that for the learned ones. The performance for the novel views is therefore the upper limit of the model's performance. (2) The subjects' performance relative to the model will be defined as statistical efficiency (see below). The above method will yield the lowest possible efficiency for the novel views, and a higher efficiency for the learned views, since the best standard deviation for the novel views is different from that for the learned views. Because our hypothesis depends on a higher statistical efficiency for the novel views than for the learned views, this method will make such a putative difference even smaller. Likewise, for the 2D affine ideal, the number of 2D rotated copies of each template $\mathbf{T}_i$ and the value γ were both extensively sampled, and the best performance for the novel views was selected accordingly. The result for the learned views corresponding to the same parameters was selected. This choice also makes it a conservative hypothesis test.

3   Results

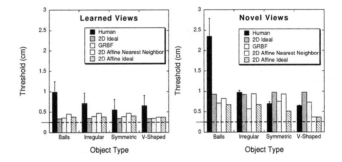

Figure 2: The threshold standard deviation of the Gaussian noise, added to the distractor in the test pair, that keeps an observer's performance at the 75% correct level, for the learned and novel views, respectively. The dotted line is the standard deviation of the Gaussian noise added to the target in the test pair.

Fig. 2 shows the threshold performance. We use statistical efficiency $\mathcal{E}$ to compare human to model performance. $\mathcal{E}$ is defined as the information used by humans relative to the ideal observer [3] : $\mathcal{E} = (d'_{human}/d'_{ideal})^2$, where d' is the discrimination index. We have shown in [4] that, in our task, $\mathcal{E} = \left((\sigma^{ideal}_{distractor})^2 - (\sigma_{target})^2 \right) / \left((\sigma^{human}_{distractor})^2 - (\sigma_{target})^2 \right)$, where σ is the threshold. Fig. 3 shows the statistical efficiency of the human observers relative to each of the four models.

We note in Fig. 3 that the efficiency for the novel views is higher than those for the learned views (several of them even exceeded 100%), except for the planar V-Shaped objects. We are particularly interested in the Irregular and Symmetric objects in the 2D affine ideal case, in which the pairwise comparison between the learned and novel views across the six objects and three observers yielded a significant difference (binomial, $p < 0.05$). This suggests that the 2D affine ideal observer cannot account for the human performance, because if the humans used a 2D affine template matching strategy, their relative performance for the novel views cannot be better than for the learned views. We suggest therefore that 3D information was used by the human observers (e.g., 3D symmetry). This is supported in addition by the increasing efficiencies as the structural regularity increased from the Balls, Irregular, to Symmetric objects (except for the V-Shaped objects with 2D affine models).

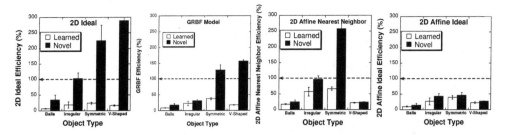

Figure 3: Statistical efficiencies of human observers relative to the 2D ideal observer, the GRBF model, the 2D affine nearest neighbor model, and the 2D affine ideal observer.

4 Conclusions

Computational models of visual cognition are subject to information theoretic as well as implementational constraints. When a model's performance mimics that of human observers, it is difficult to interpret which aspects of the model characterize the human visual system. For example, human object recognition could be simulated by both a GRBF model and a model with partial 3D information of the object. The approach we advocate here is that, instead of trying to mimic human performance by a computational model, one designs an implementation-free model for a specific recognition task that yields the best possible performance under explicitly specified computational constraints. This model provides a well-defined benchmark for performance, and if human observers outperform it, we can conclude firmly that the humans must have used better computational strategies than the model. We showed that models of independent 2D templates with 2D linear operations cannot account for human performance. This suggests that our human observers may have used the templates to reconstruct a representation of the object with some (possibly crude) 3D structural information.

References

[1] Biederman I and Gerhardstein P C. Viewpoint dependent mechanisms in visual object recognition: a critical analysis. J. Exp. Psych.: HPP, 21:1506–1514, 1995.

[2] Bülthoff H H and Edelman S. Psychophysical support for a 2D view interpolation theory of object recognition. Proc. Natl. Acad. Sci., 89:60–64, 1992.

[3] Fisher R A. Statistical Methods for Research Workers. Oliver and Boyd, Edinburgh, 1925.

[4] Liu Z, Knill D C, and Kersten D. Object classification for human and ideal observers. Vision Research, 35:549–568, 1995.

[5] Poggio T and Edelman S. A network that learns to recognize three-dimensional objects. Nature, 343:263–266, 1990.

[6] Tarr M J and Bülthoff H H. Is human object recognition better described by geon-structural-descriptions or by multiple-views? J. Exp. Psych.: HPP, 21:1494–1505, 1995.

[7] Watson A B and Pelli D G. QUEST: A Bayesian adaptive psychometric method. Perception and Psychophysics, 33:113–120, 1983.

[8] Werman M and Weinshall D. Similarity and affine invariant distances between 2D point sets. IEEE PAMI, 17:810–814, 1995.

Self-similarity properties of natural images

Antonio Turiel,[*] Germán Mato,[†] Néstor Parga [‡]
Departamento de Física Teórica . Universidad Autónoma de Madrid
Cantoblanco, 28049 Madrid, Spain
and Jean-Pierre Nadal[§]
Laboratoire de Physique Statistique de l'E.N.S. [¶] Ecole Normale Supérieure
24, rue Lhomond, F-75231 Paris Cedex 05, France

Abstract

Scale invariance is a fundamental property of ensembles of natural images [1]. Their non Gaussian properties [15, 16] are less well understood, but they indicate the existence of a rich statistical structure. In this work we present a detailed study of the marginal statistics of a variable related to the edges in the images. A numerical analysis shows that it exhibits extended self-similarity [3, 4, 5]. This is a scaling property stronger than self-similarity: all its moments can be expressed as a power of any given moment. More interesting, all the exponents can be predicted in terms of a multiplicative log-Poisson process. This is the very same model that was used very recently to predict the correct exponents of the structure functions of turbulent flows [6]. These results allow us to study the underlying multifractal singularities. In particular we find that the most singular structures are one-dimensional: the most singular manifold consists of sharp edges.

Category: *Visual Processing.*

1 Introduction

An important motivation for studying the statistics of natural images is its relevance for the modeling of the visual system. In particular, the epigenetic development

---

[*]e-mail: amturiel@delta.ft.uam.es

[†]e-mail: matog@cab.cnea.edu.ar

[‡]To whom correspondence should be addressed. e-mail: parga@delta.ft.uam.es

[§]e-mail: nadal@lps.ens.fr

[¶]Laboratoire associé au C.N.R.S. (U.R.A. 1306), à l'ENS, et aux Universités Paris VI et Paris VII.

could lead to the adaptation of visual processing to the statistical regularities in the visual scenes [8, 9, 10, 11, 12, 13]. Most of these predictions on the development of receptive fields have been obtained using a gaussian description of the environment contrast statistics. However non Gaussian properties like the ones found by [15, 16] could be important. To gain further insight into non Gaussian aspects of natural scenes we investigate the self similarity properties of an edge type variable [14].

Scale invariance in natural images is a well-established property. In particular it appears as a power law behaviour of the power spectrum of luminosity contrast: $S(f) \propto \frac{1}{|f|^{2-\eta}}$ (the parameter η depends on the particular images that has been included in the dataset). A more detailed analysis of the scaling properties of the luminosity contrast was done by [15; 16]. These authors noted the possible analogy between the statistics of natural images and turbulent flows. There is however no model to explain the scaling behaviour that they observed.

On the other hand, a large amount of effort has been put to understand the statistics of turbulent flows and to develop predictable models (see e.g. [17]). Qualitative and quantitative theories of fully developed turbulence elaborate on the original argument of Kolmogorov [2]. The cascade of energy from one scale to another is described in terms of local energy dissipation per unit mass within a box of linear size r. This quantity, ϵ_r, is given by:

$$\epsilon_r(\mathbf{x}) \propto \int_{|\mathbf{x}-\mathbf{x}'|<r} d\mathbf{x}' \sum_{ij} [\partial_i v_j(\mathbf{x}') + \partial_j v_i(\mathbf{x}')]^2 \tag{1}$$

where $v_i(\mathbf{x})$ is the ith component of the velocity at point $\mathbf{x}$. This variable has *Self-Similarity* (SS) properties that is, there is a range of scales r (called the inertial range) where:

$$< \epsilon_r^p > \propto r^{\tau_p}, \tag{2}$$

here $< \epsilon_r^p >$ denotes the pth moment of the energy dissipation marginal distribution. A more general scaling relation, called *Extended Self-Similarity* (ESS) has been found to be valid in a much larger scale domain. This relation reads

$$< \epsilon_r^p > \propto < \epsilon_r^q >^{\rho(p,q)} \tag{3}$$

where $\rho(p,q)$ is the ESS exponent of the pth moment with respect to the qth moment. Let us notice that if SS holds then $\tau_p = \tau_q \rho(p,q)$. In the following we will refer all the moments to $< \epsilon_r^2 >$.

2 The Local Edge Variance

For images the basic field is the contrast $c(\mathbf{x})$, that we define as the difference between the luminosity and its average. By analogy with the definition in eq. (1) we will consider a variable that accumulates the value of the variation of the contrast. We choose to study two variables, defined at position $\mathbf{x}$ and at scale r. The variable $\epsilon_{h,r}(\mathbf{x})$ takes contributions from edges transverse to a *horizontal* segment of size r:

$$\epsilon_{h,r}(\mathbf{x}) = \frac{1}{r} \int_{x_1}^{x_1+r} \left(\frac{\partial c(\mathbf{x}')}{\partial y} \right)^2 \Bigg|_{\mathbf{x}'=\{y,x_2\}} dy \tag{4}$$

A vertical variable $\epsilon_{v,r}(\mathbf{x})$ is defined similarly integrating along the vertical direction.

We will refer to the value of the derivative of the contrast along a given direction as an edge transverse to that direction. This is justified in the sense that in the presence of borders this derivative will take a great value, and it will almost vanish if evaluated inside an almost-uniformly illuminated surface. Sharp edges will be the maxima of this derivative. According to its definition, $\epsilon_{l,r}(\mathbf{x})$ ($l = h, v$) is the *local linear edge variance* along the direction l at scale r. Let us remark that edges are well known to be important in characterizing images. A recent numerical analysis suggests that natural images are composed of statistically independent edges [18].

We have analyzed the scaling properties of the local linear edge variances in a set of 45 images taken into a forest, of 256×256 pixels each (the images have been provided to us by D. Ruderman; see [16] for technical details concerning them). An analysis of the image resolution and of finite size effects indicates the existence of upper and lower cut-offs. These are approximately $r = 64$ and $r = 8$, respectively. First we show that SS holds in a range of scales r with exponents $\tau_{h,p}$ and $\tau_{v,p}$. This is illustrated in Fig. (1) where the logarithm of two moments of horizontal and vertical local edge variances are plotted as a function of $\ln r$; we see that SS holds, but not in the whole range.

ESS holds in the whole considered range; two representative graphs are shown in Fig. (2). The linear dependence of $\ln < \epsilon_{l,r}^p >$ vs $\ln < \epsilon_{l,r}^2 >$ is observed in both the horizontal ($l = h$) and the vertical ($l = v$) directions. This is similar to what is found in turbulence, where this property has been used to obtain a more accurate estimation of the exponents of the structure functions (see e.g. [17] and references therein). The exponents $\rho_h(p,2)$ and $\rho_v(p,2)$, estimated with a least squares regression, are shown in Fig. (3) as a function of p. The error bars refer to the statistical dispersion. From figs. (1-3) one sees that the horizontal and vertical directions have similar statistical properties. The SS exponents differ, as can be seen in Fig(1); but, surprisingly, ESS not only holds in both directions, but it does it with the *same* ESS exponents, i.e. $\rho_h(p,2) \sim \rho_v(p,2)$.

3   ESS and multiplicative processes

Let us now consider scaling models to predict the p-dependence of the ESS exponents $\rho_l(p,2)$. (Since ESS holds, the SS exponents $\tau_{l,p}$ can be obtained from the $\rho_l(p,2)'s$ by measuring $\tau_{l,2}$). The simplest scaling hypothesis is that, for a random variable $\epsilon_r(\mathbf{x})$ observed at the scale r (such as $\epsilon_{l,r}(\mathbf{x})$), its probability distribution $\bar{P}_r(\epsilon_r(\mathbf{x}) = \epsilon)$ can be obtained from any other scale L by

$$\bar{P}_r(\epsilon) = \frac{1}{\alpha(r,L)} \bar{P}_L\left(\frac{\epsilon}{\alpha(r,L)}\right) \tag{5}$$

From this one derives easily that $\alpha(r,L) = [\frac{<\epsilon_r^p>}{<\epsilon_L^p>}]^{1/p}$ (for any p) and $\rho(p,2) \propto p$; if SS holds, $\tau_p \propto p$: for turbulent flows this corresponds to the Kolmogorov prediction for the SS exponents [2]. Fig (3) shows that this naive scaling is violated.

This discrepancy becomes more dramatic if eq. (5) is expressed in terms of a normalized variable. Taking $\epsilon_r^\infty = \lim_{p\to\infty} < \epsilon_r^{p+1} > / < \epsilon_r^p >$ (that can be shown to be the maximum value of ϵ_r, which in fact is **finite**) the new variable is defined as $f_r = \epsilon_r/\epsilon_r^\infty; 0 < f_r < 1$. If $P_r(f)$ is the distribution of f_r, the scaling relation eq.(5) reads $P_r(f) = P_L(f)$; this identity does not hold as can be seen in Fig. (4). A way to generalize this scaling hypothesis is to say that α is no longer a constant as in eq. (5), but an stochastic variable. Thus, one has for $P_r(f)$:

$$P_r(f) = \int G_{rL}(\ln \alpha) \frac{1}{\alpha} P_L\left(\frac{f}{\alpha}\right) d\ln \alpha \tag{6}$$

This scaling relation has been first introduced in the context of turbulent flows [6, 19, 7]. Eq. (6) is an integral representation of ESS with general (not necessarily linear) exponents: once the kernel G_{rL} is chosen, the $\rho(p,2)$'s can be predicted. It can also be phrased in terms of multiplicative processes [20, 21] : now $f_r = \alpha f_L$, where the factor α itself becomes a stochastic variable determined by the kernel $G_{rL}(\ln \alpha)$. Since the scale L is arbitrary (scale r can be reached from any other scale L') the kernel must obey a composition law, $G_{rL'} \otimes G_{L'L} = G_{rL}$. Consequently f_r can be obtained through a cascade of infinitesimal processes $G_\delta \equiv G_{r,r+\delta r}$. Specific choices of G_δ define different models of ESS. The She-Leveque (SL) [6] model corresponds to a simple process such that α is 1 with probability $1 - s$ and is a constant β with probability s. One can see that $s = \frac{1}{1-\beta^2} \ln(\frac{<f^2_{r+\delta r}>}{<f^2_r>})$ and that this stochastic process yields a log-Poisson distribution for α [22]. It also gives ESS with exponents $\rho(p,q)$ that is expressed in terms of the parameter β as follows [6]:

$$\rho(p,q) = \frac{1 - \beta^p - (1-\beta)p}{1 - \beta^q - (1-\beta)q} \tag{7}$$

We can now test this models with the ESS exponents obtained with the image data set. The resulting fit for the SL model is shown in Fig. (3). Both the vertical and horizontal ESS exponents can be fitted with $\beta = 0.50 \pm 0.03$.

The integral representation of ESS can also be directly tested on the probability distributions evaluated from the data. In Fig. (4) we show the prediction for $P_r(f)$ obtained from $P_L(f)$ using eq. (6), compared with the actual $P_r(f)$.

The parameter β allows us to predict all the ESS exponents $\rho(p,2)$. To obtain the SS exponents τ_p we need another parameter. This can be chosen e.g. as τ_2 or as the asymptotic exponent Δ, given by $\epsilon_r^\infty \propto r^{-\Delta}$, $r \gg 1$; we prefer Δ. As $\tau_p = \tau_2 \rho(p,2)$, then from the definition of ϵ_r^∞ one can see that $\Delta = -\frac{\tau_2}{1-\beta}$. A least square fit of τ_p was used to determine Δ, obtaining $\Delta_h = 0.4 \pm 0.2$ for the horizontal variable and $\Delta_v = 0.5 \pm 0.2$. for the vertical one.

4   Multifractal analysis

Let us now partition the image in sets of pixels with the same singularity exponent h of the local edge variance: $\epsilon_r \propto r^h$. This defines a multifractal with dimensions $D(h)$ given by the Legendre transform of τ_p (see e.g. [17]): $D(h) = \inf_p \{ph+d-\tau_p\}$, where $d = 2$ is the dimension of the images. We are interested in the most singular of these manifolds; let us call D_∞ its dimension and h_{min} its singularity exponent. Since ϵ_r^∞ is the maximum value of the variable ϵ_r, the most singular manifold is given by the set of points where $\epsilon_r = \epsilon_r^\infty$, so $h_{min} = -\Delta$. Using again that $\tau_p = -\Delta(1-\beta)\rho(p,2)$ with $\rho(p,2)$ given by the SL model, one has $D_\infty = d - \frac{\Delta}{(1-\beta)}$. From our data we obtain $D_{\infty,h} = 1.3 \pm 0.3$ and $D_{\infty,v} = 1.1 \pm 0.3$. As a result we can say that $D_{\infty,h} \sim D_{\infty,v} \sim 1$: the most singular structures are almost one-dimensional. This reflects the fact that the most singular manifold consists of sharp edges.

5   Conclusions

We insist on the main result of this work, which is the existence of non trivial scaling properties for the local edge variances. This property appears very similar to the one observed in turbulence for the local energy dissipation. In fact, we have seen that the SL model predicts all the relevant exponents and that, in particular, it describes the scaling behaviour of the sharpest edges in the image ensemble. It would also be interesting to have a simple generative model of images which - apart from having the correct power spectrum as in [23] - would reproduce the self-similar properties found in this work.

Acknowledgements

We are grateful to Dan Ruderman for giving us his image data base. We warmly thank Bernard Castaing for very stimulating discussions and Zhen-Su She for a discussion on the link between the scaling exponents and the dimension of the most singular structure. We thank Roland Baddeley and Patrick Tabeling for fruitful discussions. We also acknowledge Nicolas Brunel for his collaboration during the early stages of this work. This work has been partly supported by the French-Spanish program "Picasso" and an E.U. grant CHRX-CT92-0063.

References

[1] Field D. J., *J. Opt. Soc. Am.* 4 2379-2394 (1987).

[2] Kolmogorov, *Dokl. Akad. Nauk. SSSR* 30, 301-305 (1941).

[3] Benzi R., Ciliberto S., Baudet C., Ruiz Chavarria G. and Tripiccione C., *Europhys. Lett.* 24 275-279 (1993)

[4] Benzi, Ciliberto, Tripiccione, Baudet, Massaioli, and Succi, *Phys. Rev. E* 48, R29 (1993)

[5] Benzi, Ciliberto, Baudet and Chavarria *Physica D* 80 385-398 (1995)

[6] She and Leveque, *Phys. Rev. Lett.* 72, 336-339 (1994).

[7] Castaing, *J. Physique II, France* 6, 105-114 (1996)

[8] Barlow H. B., in *Sensory Communication* (ed. Rosenblith W.) pp. 217. (M.I.T. Press, Cambridge MA, 1961).

[9] Laughlin S. B., *Z. Naturf.* 36 910-912 (1981).

[10] van Hateren J.H. *J. Comp. Physiology A* 171 157-170, 1992.

[11] Atick J. J. *Network* 3 213-251, 1992.

[12] Olshausen B.A. and Field D. J., *Nature* 381, 607-609 (1996).

[13] Baddeley R., *Cognitive Science*, in press (1997).

[14] Turiel A., Mato G., Parga N. and Nadal J.-P., to appear in *Phys. Rev. Lett.*, 1998.

[15] Ruderman D. and Bialek, *Phys. Rev. Lett.* 73, 814 (1994)

[16] Ruderman D., *Network* 5, 517-548 (1994)

[17] Frisch U., Turbulence, Cambridge Univ. Press (1995).

[18] Bell and Sejnowski, *Vision Research* 37 3327-3338 (1997).

[19] Dubrulle B., *Phys. Rev. Lett.* 73 959-962 (1994)

[20] Novikov, *Phys. Rev. E* 50, R3303 (1994)

[21] Benzi, Biferale, Crisanti, Paladin, Vergassola and Vulpiani, *Physica D* 65, 352-358 (1993).

[22] She and Waymire, *Phys. Rev. Lett.* 74, 262-265 (1995).

[23] Ruderman D., *Vision Research* 37 3385-3398 (1997).

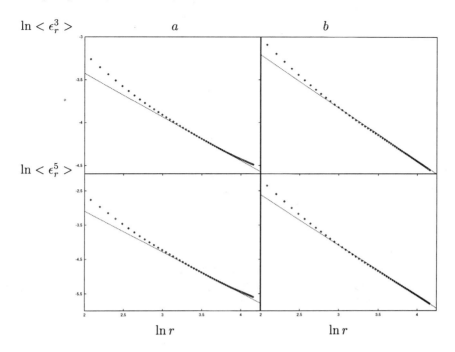

Figure 1: Test of SS. We plot $\ln < \epsilon^p_{l,r} >$ vs. $\ln r$ for $p = 3$ and 5; r from 8 to 64 pixels. a) horizontal direction, $l = h$. b) vertical direction, $l = v$.

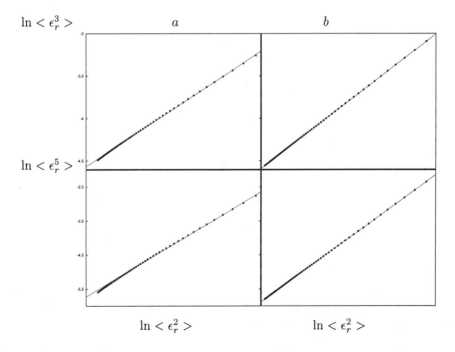

Figure 2: Test of ESS. We plot $\ln < \epsilon^p_{l,r} >$ vs. $\ln < \epsilon^2_{l,r} >$ for p=3, 5; r from 8 to $r = 64$ pixels. a) horizontal direction, $l = h$. b) vertical direction, $l = v$.

$\rho(p,2)$

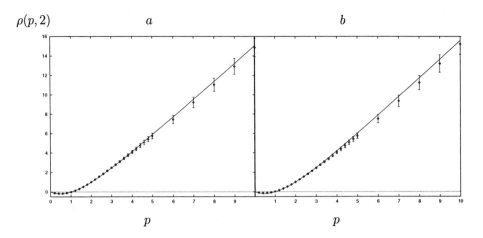

Figure 3: ESS exponents $\rho(p,2)$, for the vertical and horizontal variables. a) horizontal direction, $\rho_h(p,2)$. b) vertical direction, $\rho_v(p,2)$. The solid line represents the fit with the SL model. The best fit is obtained with $\beta_v \sim \beta_h \sim 0.50$.

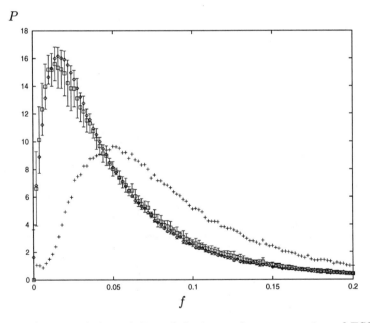

Figure 4: Verification of the validity of the integral representation of ESS, eq.(6) with a log-Poisson kernel, for horizontal local edge variance. The largest scale is $L = 64$. Starting from the histogram $P_L(f)$ (denoted with crosses), and using a log-Poisson distribution with parameter $\beta = 0.50$ for the kernel G_{rL}, eq.(6) gives a prediction for the distribution at the scale $r = 16$ (squares). This has to be compared with the direct evaluation of $P_r(f)$ (diamonds). Similar results hold for other pairs of scales. Although not shown in the figure, the test for vertical case is as good as for horizontal variable.

Multiresolution Tangent Distance for Affine-invariant Classification

Nuno Vasconcelos   **Andrew Lippman**
MIT Media Laboratory, 20 Ames St, E15-320M,
Cambridge, MA 02139, {nuno,lip}@media.mit.edu

Abstract

The ability to rely on similarity metrics invariant to image transformations is an important issue for image classification tasks such as face or character recognition. We analyze an invariant metric that has performed well for the latter - the *tangent distance* - and study its limitations when applied to regular images, showing that the most significant among these (convergence to local minima) can be drastically reduced by computing the distance in a multiresolution setting. This leads to the *multiresolution tangent distance*, which exhibits significantly higher invariance to image transformations, and can be easily combined with robust estimation procedures.

1   Introduction

Image classification algorithms often rely on distance metrics which are too sensitive to variations in the imaging environment or set up (e.g. the Euclidean and Hamming distances), or on metrics which, even though less sensitive to these variations, are application specific or too expensive from a computational point of view (e.g. deformable templates).

A solution to this problem, combining invariance to image transformations with computational simplicity and general purpose applicability was introduced by Simard et al in [7]. The key idea is that, when subject to spatial transformations, images describe manifolds in a high dimensional space, and an invariant metric should measure the distance between those manifolds instead of the distance between other properties of (or features extracted from) the images themselves. Because these manifolds are complex, minimizing the distance between them is a difficult optimization problem which can, nevertheless, be made tractable by considering the minimization of the distance between the tangents to the manifolds -the *tangent distance* (TD) - instead of that between the manifolds themselves. While it has led to impressive results for the problem of character recognition [8], the linear approximation inherent to the TD is too stringent for regular images, leading to invariance over only a very narrow range of transformations.

In this work we embed the distance computation in a multiresolution framework [3], leading to the *multiresolution tangent distance* (MRTD). Multiresolution decompositions are common in the vision literature and have been known to improve the performance of image registration algorithms by extending the range over which linear approximations hold [5, 1]. In particular, the MRTD has several appealing properties: 1) maintains the general purpose nature of the TD; 2) can be easily combined with robust estimation procedures, exhibiting invariance to moderate non-linear image variations (such as caused by slight variations in shape or occlusions); 3) is amenable to computationally efficient screening techniques where bad matches are discarded at low resolutions; and 4) can be combined with several types of classifiers. Face recognition experiments show that the MRTD exhibits a significantly extended invariance to image transformations, originating improvements in recognition accuracy as high as 38%, for the hardest problems considered.

2 The tangent distance

Consider the manifold described by all the possible linear transformations that a pattern $I(\mathbf{x})$ may be subject to

$$T_{\mathbf{p}}\left[I(\mathbf{x})\right] = I(\psi(\mathbf{x}, \mathbf{p})), \tag{1}$$

where $\mathbf{x}$ are the spatial coordinates over which the pattern is defined, $\mathbf{p}$ is the set of parameters which define the transformation, and ψ is a function typically linear on $\mathbf{p}$, but not necessarily linear on $\mathbf{x}$. Given two patterns $M(\mathbf{x})$ and $N(\mathbf{x})$, the distance between the associated manifolds - *manifold distance* (MD) - is

$$\mathcal{T}(M, N) = \min_{\mathbf{p}, \mathbf{q}} ||T_{\mathbf{q}}[M(\mathbf{x})] - T_{\mathbf{p}}[N(\mathbf{x})]||^2. \tag{2}$$

For simplicity, we consider a version of the distance in which only one of the patterns is subject to a transformation, i.e.

$$\mathcal{T}(M, N) = \min_{\mathbf{p}} ||M(\mathbf{x}) - T_{\mathbf{p}}[N(\mathbf{x})]||^2, \tag{3}$$

but all results can be extended to the two-sided distance. Using the fact that

$$\nabla_{\mathbf{p}} T_{\mathbf{p}}[N(\mathbf{x})] = \nabla_{\mathbf{p}} N(\psi(\mathbf{x}, \mathbf{p})) = \nabla_{\mathbf{p}} \psi(\mathbf{x}, \mathbf{p}) \nabla_{\mathbf{x}} N(\psi(\mathbf{x}, \mathbf{p})), \tag{4}$$

where $\nabla_{\mathbf{p}} T_{\mathbf{p}}$ is the gradient of $T_{\mathbf{p}}$ with respect to $\mathbf{p}$, $T_{\mathbf{p}}[N(\mathbf{x})]$ can, for small $\mathbf{p}$, be approximated by a first order Taylor expansion around the identity transformation

$$T_{\mathbf{p}}[N(\mathbf{x})] = N(\mathbf{x}) + (\mathbf{p} - \mathbf{I})^T \nabla_{\mathbf{p}} \psi(\mathbf{x}, \mathbf{p}) \nabla_{\mathbf{x}} N(\mathbf{x}).$$

This is equivalent to approximating the manifold by a tangent hyper-plane, and leads to the TD. Substituting this expression in equation 3, setting the gradient with respect to $\mathbf{p}$ to zero, and solving for $\mathbf{p}$ leads to

$$\mathbf{p} = \left[\sum_{\mathbf{x}} \nabla_{\mathbf{p}} \psi(\mathbf{x}, \mathbf{p}) \nabla_{\mathbf{x}} N(\mathbf{x}) \nabla_{\mathbf{x}}^T N(\mathbf{x}) \nabla_{\mathbf{p}}^T \psi(\mathbf{x}, \mathbf{p})\right]^{-1} \sum_{\mathbf{x}} D(\mathbf{x}) \nabla_{\mathbf{p}} \psi(\mathbf{x}, \mathbf{p}) \nabla_{\mathbf{x}} N(\mathbf{x}) + \mathbf{I}, \tag{5}$$

where $D(\mathbf{x}) = M(\mathbf{x}) - N(\mathbf{x})$. Given this optimal $\mathbf{p}$, the TD between the two patterns is computed using equations 1 and 3. The main limitation of this formulation is that it relies on a first-order Taylor series approximation, which is valid only over a small range of variation in the parameter vector $\mathbf{p}$.

2.1 Manifold distance via Newton's method

The minimization of the MD of equation 3 can also be performed through Newton's method, which consists of the iteration

$$\mathbf{p}^{n+1} = \mathbf{p}^n - \alpha \left[\nabla_{\mathbf{p}}^2 \mathcal{T}|_{\mathbf{p}=\mathbf{p}^n}\right]^{-1} \nabla_{\mathbf{p}} \mathcal{T}|_{\mathbf{p}=\mathbf{p}^n} \tag{6}$$

where $\nabla_{\mathbf{p}}\mathcal{T}$ and $\nabla_{\mathbf{p}}^2\mathcal{T}$ are, respectively, the gradient and Hessian of the cost function of equation 3 with respect to the parameter $\mathbf{p}$,

$$\nabla_{\mathbf{p}}\mathcal{T} = 2\sum_{\mathbf{x}} \left[M(\mathbf{x}) - T_{\mathbf{p}}[N(\mathbf{x})]\right] \nabla_{\mathbf{p}} T_{\mathbf{p}}[N(\mathbf{x})]$$

$$\nabla_{\mathbf{p}}^2\mathcal{T} = 2\sum_{\mathbf{x}} \left[-\nabla_{\mathbf{p}} T_{\mathbf{p}}[N(\mathbf{x})] \nabla_{\mathbf{p}}^T T_{\mathbf{p}}[N(\mathbf{x})] + [M(\mathbf{x}) - N(\mathbf{x})] \nabla_{\mathbf{p}}^2 T_{\mathbf{p}}[N(\mathbf{x})]\right].$$

Disregarding the term which contains second-order derivatives ($\nabla_{\mathbf{p}}^2 T_{\mathbf{p}}[N(\mathbf{x})]$), choosing $\mathbf{p}^0 = \mathbf{I}$ and $\alpha = 1$, using 4, and substituting in 6 leads to equation 5. I.e. the TD corresponds to a single iteration of the minimization of the MD by a simplified version of Newton's method, where second-order derivatives are disregarded. This reduces the rate of convergence of Newton's method, and a single iteration may not be enough to achieve the local minimum, even for simple functions. It is, therefore, possible to achieve improvement if the iteration described by equation 6 is repeated until convergence.

3   The multiresolution tangent distance

The iterative minimization of equation 6 suffers from two major drawbacks [2]: 1) it may require a significant number of iterations for convergence and 2), it can easily get trapped in local minima. Both these limitations can be, at least partially, avoided by embedding the computation of the MD in a multiresolution framework, leading to the *multiresolution manifold distance* (MRMD). For its computation, the patterns to classify are first subject to a multiresolution decomposition, and the MD is then iteratively computed for each layer, using the estimate obtained from the layer above as a starting point,

$$\mathbf{p}_l^{n+1} = \mathbf{p}_l^n + \alpha \left[\sum_{\mathbf{x}} \nabla_{\mathbf{p}} T_{\mathbf{p}_l^n}[N(\mathbf{x})] \nabla_{\mathbf{p}}^T T_{\mathbf{p}_l^n}[N(\mathbf{x})]\right]^{-1} \sum_{\mathbf{x}} D_l^n(\mathbf{x}) \nabla_{\mathbf{p}} T_{\mathbf{p}_l^n}[N(\mathbf{x})], \quad (7)$$

where, $D_l^n(\mathbf{x}) = M(\mathbf{x}) - T_{\mathbf{p}_l^n}[N(\mathbf{x})]$. If only one iteration is allowed at each image resolution, the MRMD becomes the multiresolution extension of the TD, i.e. the *multiresolution tangent distance* (MRTD).

To illustrate the benefits of minimization over different scales consider the signal $f(t) = \sum_{k=1}^K \sin(w_k t)$, and the manifold generated by all its possible translations $f'(t, d) = f(t + d)$. Figure 1 depicts the multiresolution Gaussian decomposition of $f(t)$, together with the Euclidean distance to the points on the manifold as a function of the translation associated with each of them (d). Notice that as the resolution increases, the distance function has more local minima, and the range of translations over which an initial guess is guaranteed to lead to convergence to the global minimum (at $d = 0$) is smaller. I.e., at higher resolutions, a better initial estimate is necessary to obtain the same performance from the minimization algorithm.

Notice also that, since the function to minimize is very smooth at the lowest resolutions, the minimization will require few iterations at these resolutions if a procedure such as Newton's method is employed. Furthermore, since the minimum at one resolution is a good guess for the minimum at the next resolution, the computational effort required to reach that minimum will also be small. Finally, since a minimum at low resolutions is based on coarse, or global, information about the function or patterns to be classified, it is likely to be the global minimum of at least a significant region of the parameter space, if not the true global minimum.

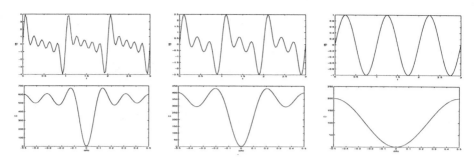

Figure 1: Top: Three scales of the multiresolution decomposition of $f(t)$. Bottom: Euclidean distance vs. translation for each scale. Resolution decreases from left to right.

4   Affine-invariant classification

There are many linear transformations which can be used in equation 1. In this work, we consider manifolds generated by affine transformations

$$\psi(\mathbf{x}, \mathbf{p}) = \left[\begin{array}{cccccc} x & y & 1 & 0 & 0 & 0 \\ 0 & 0 & 0 & x & y & 1 \end{array} \right] \mathbf{p} = \Phi(\mathbf{x})\mathbf{p}, \tag{8}$$

where $\mathbf{p}$ is the vector of parameters which characterize the transformation. Taking the gradient of equation 8 with respect to $\mathbf{p}$, $\nabla_{\mathbf{p}}\psi(\mathbf{x}, \mathbf{p}) = \Phi(\mathbf{x})^T$, using equation 4, and substituting in equation 7,

$$\mathbf{p}_l^{n+1} = \mathbf{p}_l^n + \alpha \left[\sum_{\mathbf{x}} \Phi(\mathbf{x})^T \nabla_{\mathbf{x}} N'(\mathbf{x}) \nabla_{\mathbf{x}}^T N'(\mathbf{x}) \Phi(\mathbf{x})^T \right]^{-1}$$
$$\sum_{\mathbf{x}} D'(\mathbf{x}) \Phi(\mathbf{x})^T \nabla_{\mathbf{x}} N'(\mathbf{x}), \tag{9}$$

where $N'(\mathbf{x}) = N(\psi(\mathbf{x}, \mathbf{p}_l^n))$, and $D'(\mathbf{x}) = M(\mathbf{x}) - N'(\mathbf{x})$. For a given level l of the multiresolution decomposition, the iterative process of equation 9 can be summarized as follows.

1. Compute $N'(\mathbf{x})$ by warping the pattern to classify $N(\mathbf{x})$ according to the best current estimate of $\mathbf{p}$, and compute its spatial gradient $\nabla_{\mathbf{x}} N'(\mathbf{x})$.

2. Update the estimate of $\mathbf{p}_l$ according to equation 9.

3. Stop if convergence, otherwise go to 1.

Once the final $\mathbf{p}_l$ is obtained, it is passed to the multiresolution level below (by doubling the translation parameters), where it is used as initial estimate. Given the values of $\mathbf{p}_i$ which minimize the MD between a pattern to classify and a set of prototypes in the database, a K-nearest neighbor classifier is used to find the pattern's class.

5   Robust classifiers

One issue of importance for pattern recognition systems is that of robustness to outliers, i.e errors which occur with low probability, but which can have large magnitude. Examples are errors due to variation of facial features (e.g. faces shot with or without glasses) in face recognition, errors due to undesired blobs of ink or uneven line thickness in character recognition, or errors due to partial occlusions (such as a hand in front of a face) or partially missing patterns (such as an undoted *i*). It is well known that a few (maybe even one) outliers of high leverage are sufficient to throw mean squared error estimators completely off-track [6].

Several robust estimators have been proposed in the statistics literature to avoid this problem. In this work we consider *M-estimators* [4] which can be very easily incorporated in the MD classification framework. M-estimators are an extension of least squares estimators where the square function is substituted by a functional $\rho(x)$ which weighs large errors less heavily. The robust-estimator version of the tangent distance then becomes to minimize the cost function

$$\mathcal{T}(M, N) = \min_{\mathbf{p}} \sum_{\mathbf{x}} \rho(M(\mathbf{x}) - T_{\mathbf{p}}[N(\mathbf{x})]), \tag{10}$$

and it is straightforward to show that the "robust" equivalent to equation 9 is

$$\mathbf{p}_l^{n+1} = \mathbf{p}_l^n + \alpha \left[\sum_{\mathbf{x}} \rho''[D(\mathbf{x})] \Phi(\mathbf{x})^T \nabla_{\mathbf{x}} N'(\mathbf{x}) \nabla_{\mathbf{x}}^T N'(\mathbf{x}) \Phi(\mathbf{x})^T \right]^{-1} \times$$

$$\left[\sum_{\mathbf{x}} \rho'[D(\mathbf{x})] \Phi(\mathbf{x})^T \nabla_{\mathbf{x}} N'(\mathbf{x}) \right], \tag{11}$$

where $D(\mathbf{x}) = M(\mathbf{x}) - N'(\mathbf{x})$ and $\rho'(x)$ and $\rho''(x)$ are, respectively, the first and second derivatives of the function $\rho(x)$ with respect to its argument.

6 Experimental results

In this section, we report on experiments carried out to evaluate the performance of the MD classifier. The first set of experiments was designed to test the invariance of the TD to affine transformations of the input. The second set was designed to evaluate the improvement obtained under the multiresolution framework.

6.1 Affine invariance of the tangent distance

Starting from a single view of a reference face, we created an artificial dataset composed by 441 affine transformations of it. These transformations consisted of combinations of all rotations in the range from -30 to 30 degrees with increments of 3 degrees, with all scaling transformations in the range from 70% to 130% with increments of 3%. The faces associated with the extremes of the scaling/rotation space are represented on the left portion of figure 2.

On the right of figure 2 are the distance surfaces obtained by measuring the distance associated with several metrics at each of the points in the scaling/rotation space. Five metrics were considered in this experiment: the Euclidean distance (ED), the TD, the MD computed through Newton's method, the MRMD, and the MRTD.

While the TD exhibits some invariance to rotation and scaling, this invariance is restricted to a small range of the parameter space and performance only slightly better than the obtained with the ED. The performance of the MD computed through Newton's method is dramatically superior, but still inferior to those achieved with the MRTD (which is very close to zero over the entire parameter space considered in this experiment), and the MRMD. The performance of the MRTD is in fact impressive given that it involves a computational increase of less than 50% with respect to the TD, while each iteration of Newton's method requires an increase of 100%, and several iterations are typically necessary to attain the minimum MD.

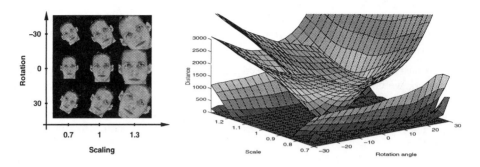

Figure 2: Invariance of the tangent distance. In the right, the surfaces shown correspond to ED, TD, MD through Newton's method, MRTD, and MRMD. This ordering corresponds to that of the nesting of the surfaces, i.e. the ED is the cup-shaped surface in the center, while the MRMD is the flat surface which is approximately zero everywhere.

6.2 Face recognition

To evaluate the performance of the multiresolution tangent distance on a real classification task, we conducted a series of face recognition experiments, using the Olivetti Research Laboratories (ORL) face database. This database is composed by 400 images of 40 subjects, 10 images per subject, and contains variations in pose, light conditions, expressions and facial features, but small variability in terms of scaling, rotation, or translation. To correct this limitation we created three artificial datasets by applying to each image three random affine transformations drawn from three multivariate normal distributions centered on the identity transformation with different covariances. A small sample of the faces in the database is presented in figure 3, together with its transformed version under the set of transformations of higher variability.

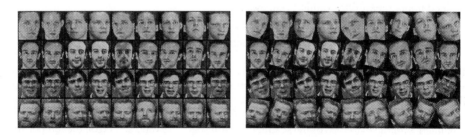

Figure 3: Left: sample of the ORL face database. Right: transformed version.

We next designed three experiments with increasing degree of difficulty. In the first, we selected the first view of each subject as the test set, using the remaining nine views as training data. In the second, the first five faces were used as test data while the remaining five were used for training. Finally, in the third experiment, we reverted the roles of the datasets used in the first. The recognition accuracy for each of these experiments and each of the datasets is reported on figure 4 for the ED, the TD, the MRTD, and a robust version of this distance (RMRTD) with $\rho(x) = \frac{1}{2}x^2$ if $x \leq \sigma T$ and $\rho(x) = \frac{T^2}{2}$ otherwise, where T is a threshold (set to 2.0 in our experiments), and σ a robust version of the error standard deviation defined as $\sigma = \text{median } |e_i - \text{median } (e_i)| / 0.6745$.

Several conclusions can be taken from this figure. First, it can be seen that the MRTD provides a significantly higher invariance to linear transformations than the ED or the TD, increasing the recognition accuracy by as much as 37.8% in the hardest datasets. In fact, for the easier tasks of experiments one and two, the performance of the multiresolution classifier is almost constant and always above the level of 90% accuracy. It is only for the harder experiment that the invariance of the MRTD classifier starts to break down. But even in this case, the degradation is graceful - the recognition accuracy only drops below 75% for considerable values of rotation and scaling (dataset D3).

On the other hand, the ED and the single resolution TD break down even for the easier tasks, and fail dramatically when the hardest task is performed on the more difficult datasets. Furthermore, their performance does not degrade gracefully, they seem to be more invariant when the training set has five views than when it is composed by nine faces of each subject in the database.

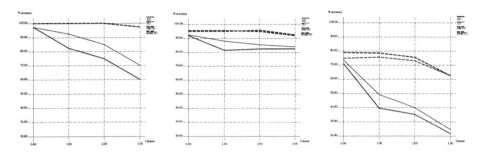

Figure 4: Recognition accuracy. From left to right: results from the first, second, and third experiments. Datasets are ordered by degree of variability: D0 is the ORL database D3 is subject to the affine transformations of greater amplitude.

Acknowledgments

We would like to thank Federico Girosi for first bringing the tangent distance to our attention, and for several stimulating discussions on the topic.

References

[1] P. Anandan, J. Bergen, K. Hanna, and R. Hingorani. Hierarchical Model-Based Motion Estimation. In M. Sezan and R. Lagendijk, editors, *Motion Analysis and Image Sequence Processing*, chapter 1. Kluwer Academic Press, 1993.

[2] D. Bertsekas. *Nonlinear Programming*. Athena Scientific, 1995.

[3] P. Burt and E. Adelson. The Laplacian Pyramid as a Compact Image Code. *IEEE Trans. on Communications*, Vol. 31:532–540, 1983.

[4] P. Huber. *Robust Statistics*. John Wiley, 1981.

[5] B. Lucas and T. Kanade. An Iterative Image Registration Technique with an Application to Stereo Vision. In *Proc. DARPA Image Understanding Workshop*, 1981.

[6] P. Rousseeuw and A. Leroy. *Robust Regression and Outlier Detection*. John Wiley, 1987.

[7] P. Simard, Y. Le Cun, and J. Denker. Efficient Pattern Recognition Using a New Transformation Distance. In *Proc. Neural Information Proc. Systems*, Denver, USA, 1994.

[8] P. Simard, Y. Le Cun, and J. Denker. Memory-based Character Recognition Using a Transformation Invariant Metric. In *Int. Conference on Pattern Recognition*, Jerusalem, Israel, 1994.

Phase transitions and the perceptual organization of video sequences

Yair Weiss
Dept. of Brain and Cognitive Sciences
Massachusetts Institute of Technology
E10-120, Cambridge, MA 02139
http://www-bcs.mit.edu/~yweiss

Abstract

Estimating motion in scenes containing multiple moving objects remains a difficult problem in computer vision. A promising approach to this problem involves using mixture models, where the motion of each object is a component in the mixture. However, existing methods typically require specifying in advance the number of components in the mixture, i.e. the number of objects in the scene.

Here we show that the number of objects can be estimated automatically in a maximum likelihood framework, given an assumption about the level of noise in the video sequence. We derive analytical results showing the number of models which maximize the likelihood for a given noise level in a given sequence. We illustrate these results on a real video sequence, showing how the phase transitions correspond to different perceptual organizations of the scene.

Figure 1a depicts a scene where motion estimation is difficult for many computer vision systems. A semi-transparent surface partially occludes a second surface, and the camera is translating horizontally. Figure 1b shows a slice through the horizontal component of the motion generated by the camera - points that are closer to the camera move faster than those further away. In practice, the local motion information would be noisy as shown in figure 1c and this imposes conflicting demands on a motion analysis system - reliable estimates require pooling together many measurements while avoiding mixing together measurements derived from the two different surfaces.

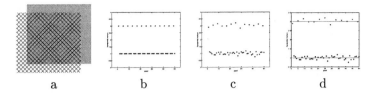

a   b   c   d

Figure 1: **a:** A simple scene that can cause problems for motion estimation. One surface partially occludes another surface. **b:** A cross section through the horizontal motion field generated when the camera translates horizontally. Points closer to the camera move faster. **c:** Noisy motion field. In practice each local measurement will be somewhat noisy and pooling of information is required. **d:** A cross section through the output of a multiple motion analysis system. Points are assigned to surfaces (denoted by different plot symbols) and the motion of each surface is estimated.

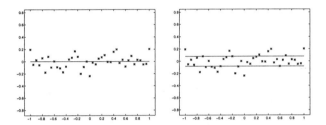

Figure 2: The "correct" number of surfaces in a given scene is often ambiguous. Was the motion here generated by one or two surfaces?

Significant progress in the analysis of such scenes has been achieved by multiple motion analyzers - systems that simultaneously segment the scene into surfaces and estimating the motion of each surface [9]. Mixture models are a commonly used framework for performing multiple motion estimation [5, 1, 10]. Figure 1d shows a slice through the output of a multiple motion analyzer on this scene - pixels are assigned to one of two surfaces and motion information is only combined for pixels belonging to the same surface.

The output shown in figure 1d was obtained by assuming the scene contains two surfaces. In general, of course, one does not know the number of surfaces in the scene in advance. Figure 2 shows the difficulty in estimating this number. It is not clear whether this is very noisy data generated by a single surface, or less noisy data generated by two surfaces. There seems no reason to prefer one description over another. Indeed, the description where there are as many surfaces as pixels is also a valid interpretation of this data.

Here we take the approach that there is no single "correct" number of surfaces for a given scene in the absence of any additional assumptions. However, given an assumption about the noise in the sequence, there are more likely and less likely interpretations. Intuitively, if we know that the data in figure 2a was taken with a very noisy camera, we would tend to prefer the one surface solution - adding additional surfaces would cause us to fit the noise rather than the data. However, if we know that there is little noise in the sequence, we would prefer solutions that use many surfaces, there is a lot less danger of "overfitting". In this paper[1] we show,

---

[1] A longer version of this paper is available on the author's web page.

following [6, 8] that this intuition regarding the dependence of number of surfaces to assumed noise level is captured in the maximum likelihood framework. We derive analytical results for the critical values of noise levels where the likelihood function undergoes a "phase transition" – from being maximized by a single model to being maximized by multiple models. We illustrate these transitions on synthetic and real video data.

1   Theory

1.1   Mixture Models for optical flow

In mixture models for optical flow (cf. [5, 1]) the scene is modeled as composed of K surfaces with the velocity of each vsurface at location (x, y) given by $(u^k(x, y), v^k(x, y)$. The velocity field is parameterized by a vector θ^k. A typical choice [9] is the affine representation:

$$u^k(x, y) = \theta_0^k + \theta_1^k x + \theta_2^k y \tag{1}$$
$$v^k(x, y) = \theta_4^k + \theta_5^k x + \theta_6^k y \tag{2}$$

The affine family of motions includes rotations, translations, scalings and shears. It corresponds to the 2D projection of a plane undergoing rigid motion in depth.

Corresponding pixels in subsequent frames are assumed to have identical intensity values, up to imaging noise which is modeled as a Gaussian with variance σ^2. The task of multiple motion estimation is to find the most likely motion parameter values given the image data. A standard derivation (see e.g. [1]) gives the following log likelihood function for the parameters Θ:

$$l(\Theta) = \sum_{x,y} \log(\sum_{k=1}^{K} e^{-R_k^2(x,y)/2\sigma^2}) \tag{3}$$

With $R_k(x, y)$ the residual intensity at pixel (x, y) for velocity k:

$$R_k(x, y) = I_x(x, y)u^k(x, y) + I_y(x, y)v^k(x, y) + I_t(x, y) \tag{4}$$

where I_x, I_y, I_t denote the spatial and temporal derivatives of the image sequence. Although our notation does not make it explicit, $R_k(x, y)$ is a function of θ_k through equations 1–2. As in most mixture estimation applications, equation 3 is not maximized directly, but rather an Expectation-Maximization (EM) algorithm is used to iteratively increase the likelihood [3].

1.2   Maximum Likelihood not necessarily with maximum number of models

It may seem that since K is fixed in the likelihood function (equation 3) there is no way that the number of surfaces can be found by maximizing the likelihood. However, maximizing over the likelihood may lead to a a solution in which some of the θ parameters are identical [6, 5, 8]. In this case, although the number of surfaces is still K, the number of *distinct* surfaces may be any number less than K.

Consider a very simple case where $K = 2$ and the motion of each surface is restricted to horizontal translation $u(x, y) = u, v(x, y) = 0$. The advantage of this simplified

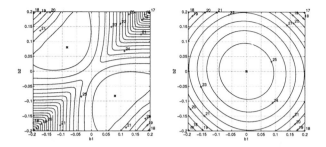

Figure 3: The log likelihood for the data in figure 2 undergoes a phase transition when σ is varied. For small values of σ the likelihood has two maxima, and at both these maxima the two motions are distinct. For large σ^2 the likelihood function has single maximum at the origin, corresponding to the solution where both velocities are equal to zero, or only one unique surface.

case is that the likelihood function is a function of two variables and can be easily visualized. Figure 3 shows the likelihood function for the data in figure 2 as σ is varied. Observe that for small values of σ^2 the likelihood has two maxima, and at both these maxima the two motions are distinct. For large σ^2 the likelihood function has single maximum at the origin, corresponding to the solution where both velocities are equal to zero, or only one unique surface. This is a simple example where the ML solution corresponds to a small number of unique surfaces.

Can we predict the range of values for σ for which the likelihood function has a maximum at the origin? This happens when the gradient of the likelihood at the origin is zero and the Hessian has two negative eigenvalues. It is easy to show that the if the data has zero mean, the gradient is zero regardless of σ. As for the Hessian, H, direct calculation gives:

$$H = c \begin{pmatrix} \frac{E}{2\sigma^2} - 1 & -\frac{E}{2\sigma^2} \\ -\frac{E}{2\sigma^2} & \frac{E}{2\sigma^2} - 1 \end{pmatrix} \tag{5}$$

where E is the mean squared residual of a single motion and c is a positive constant. The two eigenvalues are proportional to -1 and $E/\sigma^2 - 1$. So the likelihood function has a local maximum at the origin if and only if $E < \sigma^2$. (see [6, 4, 8] for a similar analysis in other contexts).

This result makes intuitive sense. Recall that σ^2 is the expected noise variance. Thus if the mean squared residual is less than σ^2 with a single surface, there is no need to add additional surfaces. The result on the Hessian shows that this intuition is captured in the likelihood function. There is no need to introduce additional "complexity costs" to avoid overfitting in this case.

More generally, if we assume the velocity fields are of general parametric form, the Hessian evaluated at the point where both surfaces are identical has the form:

$$H = c \begin{pmatrix} \frac{E}{2\sigma^2} - F & -\frac{E}{2\sigma^2} \\ -\frac{E}{2\sigma^2} & \frac{E}{2\sigma^2} - F \end{pmatrix} \tag{6}$$

where E and F are matrices:

$$E = \sum_{x,y} R^2(x,y) d(x,y) d(x,y)^t \tag{7}$$

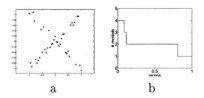

a   b

Figure 4: **a:** data generated by two lines. **b:** the predicted phase diagram for the likelihood of this dataset in a four component mixture. The phase transitions are at $\sigma = 0.084, 0.112, 0.8088$

$$F = \sum_{x,y} d(x,y)d(x,y)^t \tag{8}$$

with $d(x,y) = \frac{\partial R(x,y)}{\partial \theta}$, and $R(x,y)$ the residual as before.

A necessary and sufficient condition for the Hessian to have only negative eigenvalues is:

$$\|F^{-1}E\| < \sigma^2 \tag{9}$$

Thus when the maximal eigenvalue of $F^{-1}E$ is less than σ^2 the fit with a single model is a local maximum of the likelihood. Note that $F^{-1}E$ is very similar to a weighted mean squared error, with every residual weighted by a positive definite matrix (E sums all the residuals times their weight, and F sums all the weights, so $F^{-1}E$ is similar to a weighted average).

The above analysis predicts the phase transition of a two component mixture likelihood, i.e. the critical value of σ^2 such that above this critical value, the maximum likelihood solution will have identical motion parameters for both surfaces. This analysis can be straightforwardly generalized to finding the first phase transition of a K component mixture, although the subsequent transitions are harder to analyze.

2   Results

The fact that the likelihood function undergoes a phase transition as σ is varied predicts that a ML technique will converge to different number of distinct models as σ is varied. We first illustrate these phase transitions on a $1D$ line fitting problem which shares some of the structure of multiple motion analysis and is easily visualized.

Figure 4a shows data generated by two lines with additive noise, and figure 4b shows a phase diagram calculated using repeated application of equation 9; i.e. by solving equation 9 for all the data, taking the two line solution obtained after the transition, and repeating the calculation separately for points assigned to each of the two lines.

Figure 5 shows the output of an EM algorithm on this data set. Initial conditions are identical in all runs, and the algorithm converges to one, two, three or four distinct lines depending on σ.

We now illustrate the phase transitions on a real video sequence. Figures 6– 8 show the output of an EM motion segmentation algorithm with four components on the MPEG flower garden sequence (cf. [9, 10]). The camera is translating in

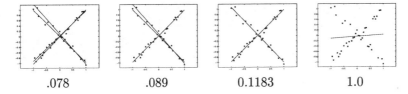

.078   .089   0.1183   1.0

Figure 5: The data in figure 1 are fit with one, two, three or four models depending on σ. The results of EM with identical initial conditions are shown, only σ is varied. The transitions are consistent with the theoretical predictions.

a   b

Figure 6: The first phase transition. The algorithm finds two segments corresponding to the tree and the rest of the scene. The critical value of σ^2 for which this transition happens is consistent with the theoretical prediction.

the scene, and objects move with different velocities due to parallax. The phase transitions correspond to different perceptual organizations of the scene - first the tree is segmented from the background, then branches are split from the tree, and finally the background splits into the flower bed and the house.

3   Discussion

Estimating the number of components in a Gaussian mixture is a well researched topic in statistics and data mining [7]. Most approaches involve some tradeoff parameter to balance the benefit of an additional component versus the added complexity [2]. Here we have shown how this tradeoff parameter can be implicitly specified by the assumed level of noise in the image sequence.

While making an assumption regarding σ may seem rather arbitrary in the abstract Gaussian mixture problem, we find it quite reasonable in the context of motion estimation, where the noise is often a property of the imaging system, not of the underlying surfaces. Furthermore, as the phase diagram in figure 4 shows, a wide range of assumed σ values will give similar answer, suggesting that an exact specification of σ is not needed. In current work we are exploring the use of weak priors on σ as well as comparing our method to those based on cross validation [7].

Figure 7: The second phase transition. The algorithm finds three segments - branches which are closer to the camera than the rest of the tree are segmented from it. Since the segmentation is based solely on motion, portions of the flower bed that move consistently with the branches are erroneously grouped with them.

Figure 8: The third phase transition. The algorithm finds four segments – the flower bed and the house are segregated.

Our analytical and simulation results show that an assumption of the noise level in the sequence enables automatic determination of the number of moving objects using well understood maximum likelihood techniques. Furthermore, for a given scene, varying the assumed noise level gives rise to different perceptually meaningful segmentations. Thus mixture models may be a first step towards a well founded probabilistic framework for perceptual organization.

Acknowledgments

I thank D. Fleet, E. Adelson, J. Tenenbaum and G. Hinton for stimulating discussions. Supported by a training grant from NIGMS.

References

[1] Serge Ayer and Harpreet S. Sawhney. Layered representation of motion video using robust maximum likelihood estimation of mixture models and MDL encoding. In *Proc. Int'l Conf. Comput. Vision*, pages 777–784, 1995.

[2] J. Buhmann. Data clustering and learning. In M. Arbib, editor, *Handbook of Brain Theory and Neural Networks*. MIT Press, 1995.

[3] A. P. Dempster, N. M. Laird, and D. B. Rubin. Maximum likelihood from incomplete data via the EM algorithm. *J. R. Statist. Soc. B*, 39:1–38, 1977.

[4] R. Durbin, R. Szeliski, and A. Yuille. An analysis of the elastic net approach to the travelling salesman problem. *Neural Computation*, 1(3):348–358, 1989.

[5] A. Jepson and M. J. Black. Mixture models for optical flow computation. In *Proc. IEEE Conf. Comput. Vision Pattern Recog.*, pages 760–761, New York, June 1993.

[6] K. Rose, F. Gurewitz, and G. Fox. Statistical mechanics and phase transitions in clustering. *Physical Review Letters*, 65:945–948, 1990.

[7] P. Smyth. Clustering using monte-carlo cross-validation. In *KDD-96*, pages 126–133, 1996.

[8] J. B. Tenenbaum and E. V. Todorov. Factorial learning by clustering features. In G. Tesauro, D.S. Touretzky, and K. Leen, editors, *Advances in Neural Information Processing Systems 7*, 1995.

[9] J. Y. A. Wang and E. H. Adelson. Representing moving images with layers. *IEEE Transactions on Image Processing Special Issue: Image Sequence Compression*, 3(5):625–638, September 1994.

[10] Y. Weiss and E. H. Adelson. A unified mixture framework for motion segmentation: incorporating spatial coherence and estimating the number of models. In *Proc. IEEE Conf. Comput. Vision Pattern Recog.*, pages 321–326, 1996.

PART VIII
APPLICATIONS

Using Expectation to Guide Processing:
A Study of Three Real-World Applications

Shumeet Baluja

Justsystem Pittsburgh Research Center &
School of Computer Science, Carnegie Mellon University
baluja@cs.cmu.edu

Abstract

In many real world tasks, only a small fraction of the available inputs are important at any particular time. This paper presents a method for ascertaining the relevance of inputs by exploiting temporal coherence and predictability. The method proposed in this paper dynamically allocates relevance to inputs by using expectations of their future values. As a model of the task is learned, the model is simultaneously extended to create task-specific predictions of the future values of inputs. Inputs which are either not relevant, and therefore not accounted for in the model, or those which contain noise, will not be predicted accurately. These inputs can be de-emphasized, and, in turn, a new, improved, model of the task created. The techniques presented in this paper have yielded significant improvements for the vision-based autonomous control of a land vehicle, vision-based hand tracking in cluttered scenes, and the detection of faults in the etching of semiconductor wafers.

1 Introduction

In many real-world tasks, the extraneous information in the input can be easily confused with the important features, making the specific task much more difficult. One of the methods in which humans function in the presence of many distracting features is to selectively attend to only portions of the input signal. A means by which humans select where to focus their attention is through the use of expectations. Once the important features in the current input are found, an expectation can be formed of what the important features in the next inputs will be, as well as where they will be. The importance of features must be determined in the context of a specific task; different tasks can require the processing of different subsets of the features in the same input.

There are two distinct uses of expectations. Consider Carnegie Mellon's Navlab autonomous navigation system. The road-following module [Pomerleau, 1993] is separate from the obstacle avoidance modules [Thorpe, 1991]. One role of expectation, in which unexpected features are de-emphasized, is appropriate for the road-following module in which the features to be tracked, such as lane-markings, appear in predictable locations. This use of expectation removes distractions from the input scene. The second role of expectation, to emphasize unexpected features, is appropriate for the obstacle avoidance modules. This use of expectation emphasizes unanticipated features of the input scene.

2 Architectures for Attention

In many studies of attention, saliency maps (maps which indicate input relevance) have been constructed in a bottom-up manner. For example, in [Koch & Ullman, 1985], a saliency map, which is not task-specific, is created by emphasizing inputs which are different from their neighbors. An alternate approach, presented in [Clark & Ferrier, 1992], places multiple different, weighted, task-specific feature detectors around the input image. The regions of the image which contain high weighted sums of the detected features are the portion of the scene which are focused upon. Top-down knowledge of which features are used and the weightings of the features is needed to make the procedure task-specific. In contrast, the goal of this study is to learn which task-specific features are relevant without requiring top-down knowledge.

In this study, we use a method based on *Input Reconstruction Reliability Estimation* (IRRE) [Pomerleau, 1993] to determine which portions of the input are important for the task. IRRE uses the hidden units of a neural network (NN) to perform the desired task and to reconstruct the inputs. In its original use, IRRE estimated how confident a network's outputs were by measuring the similarity between the reconstructed and current inputs. Figure 1(Left) provides a schematic of IRRE. Note that the weights between the input and hidden layers are trained to reduce both task and reconstruction error.

Because the weights between the input and hidden layers are trained to reduce both task and reconstruction error, a potential drawback of IRRE is the use of the hidden layer to encode all of the features in the image, rather than only the ones required for solving the particular task [Pomerleau, 1993]. This can be addressed by noting the following: if a strictly layered (connections are only between adjacent layers) feed-forward neural network can solve a given task, the activations of the hidden layer contain, in some form, the important information for this task from the input layer. One method of determining what is contained in the hidden layer is to attempt to reconstruct the original input image, *based solely upon the representation developed in the hidden layer.* Like IRRE, the input image is reconstructed from the activations of the units in the hidden layer. *Unlike IRRE, the hidden units are not trained to reduce reconstruction error, they are only trained to solve the particular task.* The network's allocation of its limited representation capacity at the hidden layer is an indicator of what it deems relevant to the task. *Information which is not relevant to the task will not be encoded in the hidden units.* Since the reconstruction of the inputs is based solely on the hidden units' activations, and the irrelevant portions of the input are not encoded in the hidden units' activations, the inputs which are irrelevant to the task *cannot* be reconstructed. See Figure 1(Right).

By measuring which inputs can be reconstructed accurately, we can ascertain which inputs the hidden units have encoded to solve the task. A synthetic task which demonstrates this idea is described here. Imagine being given a 10x10 input retina such as shown in Figure 2a&b. The task is to categorize many such examples into one of four classes. Because of the random noise in the examples, the simple underlying process, of a cross being present in one of four locations (see Figure 2c), is not easily discernible, although it is the feature on which the classifications are to be based. Given enough examples, the NN will be able to solve this task. However, even after the model of the task is learned, it is difficult to ascertain to which inputs the network is attending. To determine this, we can freeze the weights in the trained network and connect a input-reconstruction layer to the hidden units, as shown in Figure 1(Right). After training these connections, by measuring where the reconstruction matches the actual input, we can determine which inputs the network has encoded in its hidden units, and is therefore attending. See Figure 2d.

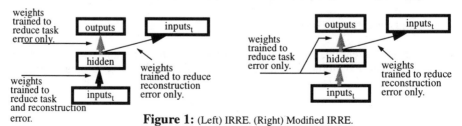

Figure 1: (Left) IRRE. (Right) Modified IRRE.

A: B: C: D: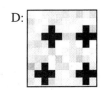

Figure 2: (A & B): Samples of training data (cross appears in position 4 & 1 respectively). Note the large amounts of noise. (C): The underlying process puts a cross in one of these four locations. (D): The black crosses are where the reconstruction matched the inputs; these correspond exactly to the underlying process.

IRRE and this modified IRRE are related to auto-encoding networks [Cottrell, 1990] and principal components analysis (PCA). The difference between auto-encoding networks and those employed in this study is that the hidden layers of the networks used here were trained to perform well on the specific task, not to reproduce the inputs accurately.

2.1 Creating Expectations

A notion of time is necessary in order to focus attention in future frames. Instead of reconstructing the current input, the network is trained to predict the *next* input; this corresponds to changing the subscript in the reconstruction layer of the network shown in Figure 1(Right) from t to $t+1$. The prediction is trained in a supervised manner, by using the next set of inputs in the time sequence as the target outputs. The next inputs may contain noise or extraneous features. However, since the hidden units only encode information to solve the task, the network will be unable to construct the noise or extraneous features in its prediction.

To this point, a method to create a task-specific expectation of what the next inputs will be has been described. As described in Section 1, there are two fundamentally different ways in which to interpret the difference between the expected next inputs and the actual next inputs. The first interpretation is that the difference between the expected and the actual inputs is a point of interest because it is a region which was not expected. This has applications in anomaly detection; it will be explored in Section 3.2. In the second interpretation, the difference between the expected and actual inputs is considered noise. Processing should be de-emphasized from the regions in which the difference is large. This makes the assumption that there is enough information in the previous inputs to specify what and where the important portions of the next image will be. As shown in the road-following and hand-tracking task, this method can remove spurious features and noise.

3 Real-World Applications

Three real-world tasks are discussed in this section. The first, vision-based road following, shows how the task-specific expectations developed in the previous section can be used to eliminate distractions from the input. The second, detection of anomalies in the plasma-etch step of wafer fabrication, shows how expectations can be used to emphasize the unexpected features in the input. The third, visual hand-tracking, demonstrates how to incorporate *a priori* domain knowledge about expectations into the NN.

3.1 Application 1: Vision-Based Autonomous Road Following

In the domain of autonomous road following, the goal is to control a robot vehicle by analyzing the image of the road ahead. The direction of travel should be chosen based on the location of important features like lane markings and road edges. On highways and dirt roads, simple techniques, such as feed-forward NNs, have worked well for mapping road images to steering commands [Pomerleau, 1993]. However, on city streets, where there are distractions like old lane-markings, pedestrians, and heavy traffic, these methods fail.

The purpose of using attention in this domain is to eliminate features of the road which the NN may mistake as lane markings. Approximately 1200 images were gathered from a

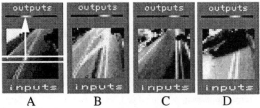

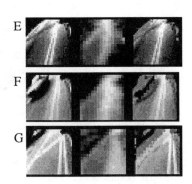

Figure 3: (Top): Four samples of training images. Left most shows the position of the lane-marking which was hand-marked. (Right): In each triplet: Left: raw input image$_t$. Middle: the network's prediction of the inputs at time t; this prediction was made by a network with input of image$_{t-1}$. Right: a pixel-by-pixel filtered image (see text). This image is used as the input to the NN.

camera mounted on the left side of the CMU-Navlab 5 test vehicle, pointed downwards and slightly ahead of the vehicle. The car was driven through city and residential neighborhoods around Pittsburgh, PA. The images were gathered at 4-5 hz. The images were subsampled to 30x32 pixels. In each of these images, the horizontal position of the lane marking in the 20th row of the input image was manually identified. The task is to produce a Gaussian of activation in the outputs centered on the horizontal position of the lane marking in the 20th row of the image, given the entire input image. Sample images and target outputs are shown in Figure 3. In this task, the ANN can be confused by road edges (Figure 3a), by extraneous lane markings (Figure 3b), and reflections on the car itself (since the camera was positioned on the side of the car), as shown in Figure 3c.

The network architecture shown in Figure 4 was used; this is the same architecture as in Figure 1(right) with the feedback shown. The feedback is used during both training and simulation. In each time-step, a steering direction and a prediction of the next inputs is produced. For each time-step, the magnitude of the difference between the input's expected value (computed in the previous time-step) and its actual value is computed. Each input pixel can be moved towards its *background value*[1] in proportion to this difference-value. The larger the difference value, the more weight is given to the background value. If the difference value is small, the actual inputs are used. This has the effect of de-emphasizing the unexpected inputs.

The results of using this method were very promising. The lane tracker removed distracting features from the images. In Figure 3G, a distracting lane-marking is removed: the lane marker on the right was correctly tracked in images before the distractor lane-marker appeared. In Figure 3F, a passing car is de-emphasized: the network does not have a model to predict the movement of passing cars, since these are not relevant for the lane-marker detection task. In Figure 3E, the side of the road appears brighter than expected; therefore it is de-emphasized. Note that the expectation-images (shown in the middle of each triplet

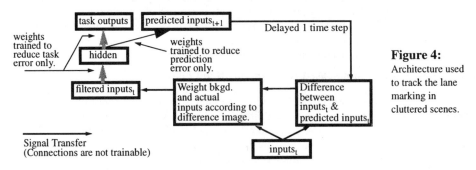

Figure 4: Architecture used to track the lane marking in cluttered scenes.

---

1. A simple estimate of the background value for each pixel is its average activation across the training set. For the road-following domain, it is possible to use a background activation of 0.0 (when the entire image is scaled to activations of +1.0 to -1.0) since the road often appears as intermediate grays.

in Figure 3) show that the expected lane-marker and road edge locations are not precisely defined. This is due to the training method, which attempts to model the many possible transitions from one time step to the next to account for inter- and intra-driver variability with a limited training set [Baluja, 1996].

In summary, by eliminating the distractions in the input images, the lane-tracker with the attention mechanisms improved performance by 20% over the standard lane-tracker, measured on the difference between the estimated and hand-marked position of the lane-marker in each image. This improvement was seen on multiple runs, with random initial weights in the NN and different random translations chosen for the training images.

3.2 Application 2: Fault Detection in the Plasma-Etch Wafer Fabrication

Plasma etch is one of the many steps in the fabrication of semiconductor wafers. In this study, the detection of four faults was attempted. Descriptions of the faults can be found in [Baluja, 1996][Maxion, 1996]. For the experiments conducted here, only a single sensor was used, which measured the intensity of light emitted from the plasma at the 520nm wavelength. Each etch was sampled once a second, providing approximately 140 samples per wafer waveform. The data-collection phase of this experiment began on October 25, 1994, and continued until April 4, 1995. The detection of faults is a difficult problem because the contamination of the etch chamber and the degradation parts keeps the sensor's outputs, even for fault-free wafers, changing over time. Accounting for machine state should help the detection process.

Expectation is used as follows: Given the waveform signature of wafer$_{T-1}$, an expectation of wafer$_T$ can be formed. The input to the prediction-NN is the waveform signature of wafer$_{T-1}$; the output is the prediction of the signature of wafer$_T$. The target output for each example is the signature of the next wafer in sequence (the full 140 parameters). Detection of the four faults is done with a separate network which used as input: the expectation of the wafer's waveform, the actual wafer's waveform, and the point-by-point difference of the two. In this task, the input is not filtered as in the driving domain described previously; the values of the point-by-point difference vector are used as extra inputs.

The performance of many methods and architectures were compared on this task, details can be found in [Baluja, 1996]. The results using the expectation based methods was a 98.7% detection rate, 100% classification rate on the detected faults (determining which of the four types of faults the detected fault was), and a 2.3% false detection rate. For comparison, a simple perceptron had an 80% detection rate, and a 40% false-detection rate. A fully-connected network which did not consider the state of the machine achieved a 100% detection rate, but a 53% false detection rate. A network which considered state by using the last-previous no-fault wafer for comparison with the current wafer (instead of an expectation for the current wafer) achieved an 87.9% detection rate, and a 1.5% false-detection rate. A variety of neural and non-neural methods which examined the differences between the expected and current wafer, as well those which examined the differences between the last no-fault wafer and the current wafer, performed poorly. In summary, methods which did not use expectations were unable to obtain the false-positives and detection rates of the expectation-based methods.

3.3 Application 3: Hand-Tracking in Cluttered Scenes

In the tasks described so far, the transition rules were *learned* by the NN. However, if the transition rules had been known *a priori*, processing could have been directed to only the relevant regions by explicitly manipulating the expectations. The ability to incorporate *a priori* rules is important in many vision-based tasks. Often the constraints about the environment in which the tracking is done can be used to limit the portions of the input scene which need to be processed. For example, consider visually tracking a person's hand. Given a fast camera sampling rate, the person's hand in the current frame will be close to

A. 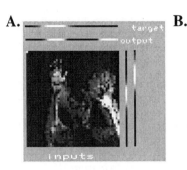 **B.**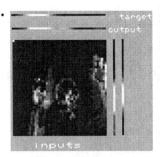

Figure 5:
Typical input images used for the hand-tracking experiments. The target is to track the subject's right hand. Without expectation, in (A) both hands were found in **X** outputs, and the wrong hand was found in the **Y** outputs. In (B) Subject's right hand and face found in the **X** outputs.

where it appeared in the previous frame. Although a network can learn this constraint by developing expectations of future inputs (as with the NN architecture shown in Figure 4), training the expectations can be avoided by incorporating this rule directly.

In this task, the input layer is a 48*48 image. There are two output layers of 48 units; the desired outputs are two gaussians centered on the (X,Y) position of the hand to be tracked. See Figure 5. Rather than creating a saliency map based upon the difference between the actual and predicted inputs, as was done with autonomous road following, the saliency map was explicitly created with the available domain knowledge. Given the sampling rate of the camera and the size of the hand in the image, the salient region for the next time-step was a circular region centered on the estimated location of the hand in the previous image. The activations of the inputs outside of the salient region were shifted towards the background image. The activations inside the salient region were not modified. After applying the saliency map to the inputs, the filtered inputs were fed into the NN.

This system was tested in very difficult situations; the testing set contained images of a person moving both of his hands and body throughout the sequence (see Figure 5). There-fore, both hands and body are clearly visible in the difference images used as input into the network. All training was done on much simpler training sets in which only a single hand was moving. To gauge the performance of an expectation-based system, it was com-pared to a system which used the following post-processing heuristics to account for tem-poral coherence. First, before a gaussian was fit to either of the output layers, the activation of the outputs was inversely scaled with the distance away from the location of the hand in the previous time step. This reduces the probability of detecting a hand in a location very different than the previous detection. This helps when both hands are detected, as shown in Figure 5. The second heuristic was that any predictions which differ from the previous prediction by more than half of the dimension of the output layer were ignored, and the previous prediction used instead. See Table I for the results. In summary, by using the expectation based methods, performance improved from 66% to 90% when tracking the left hand, and 52% to 91% when tracking the right hand.

Table I: Performance: Number of frames in which each hand was located (283 total images).

Method	Target: Find Left Hand				Target: Find Right Hand			
	Which Hand Was Found				Which Hand Was Found			
	% Correct	L	R	None	% Correct	L	R	None
No Heuristics, No Expect.	52%	146	44	93	16%	143	47	93
Heuristics	66%	187	22	74	52%	68	147	68
Expectation	91%	258	3	22	90%	3	255	25
Expectation + Heuristics	90%	256	3	24	91%	2	257	24

[Nowlan & Platt, 1995] presented a convolutional-NN based hand-tracker which used sep-arate NNs for intensity and differences images with a rule-based integration of the multi-ple network outputs. The integration of this expectation-based system should improve the performance of the difference-image NN.

4 Conclusions

A very closely related procedure to the one described in this paper is the use of Kalman Filters to predict the locations of objects of interest in the input retina. For example, Dickmanns uses the prediction of the future state to help guide attention by controlling the direction of a camera to acquire accurate position of landmarks [Dickmanns, 1992]. Strong models of the vehicle motion, the appearance of objects of interest (such as the road, road-signs, and other vehicles), and the motion of these objects are encoded in the system. The largest difference in their system and the one presented here is the amount of *a priori* knowledge that is used. Many approaches which use Kalman Filters require a large amount of problem specific information for creating the models. In the approach presented in this paper, the main object is to automatically learn this information from examples. First, the system must learn what the important features are, since no top-down information is assumed. Second, the system must automatically develop the control strategy from the detected features. Third, the system must also learn a model for the movements of all of the relevant features.

In deciding whether the approaches described in this paper are suitable to a new problem, two criteria must be considered. First, if expectation is to be used to remove distractions from the inputs, then given the current inputs, the activations of the relevant inputs in the next time step must be predictable while the irrelevant inputs are either unrelated to the task or are unpredictable. In many visual object tracking problems, the relevant inputs are often predictable while the distractions are not. In the cases in which the distractions are predictable, if they are unrelated to the main task, these methods can work. When using expectation to emphasize unexpected or potentially anomalous features, the activations of the relevant inputs should be unpredictable while the irrelevant ones are predictable. This is often the case for anomaly/fault detection tasks. Second, when expectations are used as a filter, it is necessary to explicitly define the role of the expected features. In particular, it is necessary to define whether the expected features should be considered relevant or irrelevant, and therefore, whether they should be emphasized or de-emphasized, respectively.

We have demonstrated the value of using task-specific expectations to guide processing in three real-world tasks. In complex, dynamic, environments, such as driving, expectations are used to quickly and accurately discriminate between the relevant and irrelevant features. For the detection of faults in the plasma-etch step of semiconductor fabrication, expectations are used to account for the underlying drift of the process. Finally, for vision-based hand-tracking, we have shown that *a priori* knowledge about expectations can be easily integrated with a hand-detection model to focus attention on small portions of the scene, so that distractions in the periphery can be ignored.

Acknowledgments

The author would like to thank Dean Pomerleau, Takeo Kanade, Tom Mitchell and Tomaso Poggio for their help in shaping this work.

References

Baluja, S. 1996, *Expectation-Based Selective Attention.* Ph.D. Thesis, School of Computer Science, CMU.

Clark, J. & Ferrier, N (1992), Attentive Visual Servoing, in: *Active Vision.* Blake & Yuille, (MIT Press) 137-154.

Cottrell, G.W., 1990, Extracting Features from Faces using Compression Network, *Connectionist Models,* Morgan Kaufmann 328-337.

Dickmanns, 1992, Expectation-based Dynamic Scene Understanding, in: *Active Vision.* A. Blake & A.Yuille, MIT Press.

Koch, C. & Ullman, S. (1985) "Shifts in Selective Visual Attention: Towards the Underlying Neural Circuitry", in: Human Neurobiology 4 (1985) 219-227.

Maxion, R. (1995) The Semiconductor Wafer Plasma-Etch Data Set.

Nowlan, S. & Platt, J., 1995, "A Convolutional Neural Network Hand Tracker". *NIPS 7.* MIT Press. 901-908.

Pomerleau, D.A., 1993. *Neural Network Perception for Mobile Robot Guidance,* Kluwer Academic.

Thorpe, C., 1991, Outdoor Visual Navigation for Autonomous Robots, in: *Robotics and Autonomous Systems* 7.

Structure Driven Image Database Retrieval

Jeremy S. De Bonet & Paul Viola
Artificial Intelligence Laboratory
Learning & Vision Group
545 Technology Square Massachusetts Institute of Technology
Cambridge, MA 02139

EMAIL: jsd@ai.mit.edu & viola@ai.mit.edu
HOMEPAGE: http://www.ai.mit.edu/projects/lv

Abstract

A new algorithm is presented which approximates the perceived visual similarity between images. The images are initially transformed into a feature space which captures visual structure, texture and color using a tree of filters. Similarity is the inverse of the distance in this *perceptual feature space*. Using this algorithm we have constructed an image database system which can perform example based retrieval on large image databases. Using carefully constructed target sets, which limit variation to only a single visual characteristic, retrieval rates are quantitatively compared to those of standard methods.

1 Introduction

Without supplementary information, there exists no way to directly measure the similarity between the content of images. In general, one cannot answer a question of the form: "is image A more like image B or image C?" without defining the criteria by which this comparison is to be made. People perform such tasks by inferring some criterion, based on their visual experience or by complex reasoning about the situations depicted in the images. Humans are very capable database searchers. They can perform simple searches like, "find me images of cars", or more complex or loosely defined searches like, "find me images that depict pride in America". In either case one must examine all, or a large portion, of the database. As the prevalence and size of multimedia databases increases, automated techniques will become critical in the successful retrieval of relevant information. Such techniques must be able to measure the similarity between the visual content of natural images.

Many algorithms have been proposed for image database retrieval. For the most part these techniques compute a feature vector from an image which is made up of a handful of image measurements. Visual or semantic distance is then equated with feature distance. Examples include color histograms, texture histograms, shape boundary descriptors, eigenimages, and hybrid schemes (QBIC, ; Niblack et al., 1993; Virage, ; Kelly, Cannon and Hush, 1995; Pentland, Picard and Sclaroff, 1995; Picard and Kabir, 1993; Santini and Jain, 1996). A query to such a system typically consists of specifying two types of parameters: the target values of each of the measurements; and a set of weights, which determine the relative importance of deviations from the target in each measurement dimension. The features used by these systems each capture some very general property of images. As a result of their lack of specificity however, many images which are actually very different in content generate the same feature responses.

In contrast our approach extracts thousands of very specific features. These features measure both local texture and global structure. The feature extraction algorithm computes color, edge orientation, and other local properties at many resolutions. This sort of multi-scale feature analysis is of critical importance in visual recognition and has been used successfully in the context of object recognition (von der Malsburg, 1988; Rao and Ballard, 1995; Viola, 1996)

Our system differs from others because it detects not only first order relationships, such as edges or color, but also measures how these first order relationships are related to one another. Thus by finding patterns between image regions with particular local properties, more complex – and therefore more discriminating – features can be extracted. This type of repeated, non-linear, feature detection bears a strong resemblance to the response properties of visual cortex cells (Desimone et al., 1984). While the mechanism for the responses of these cells is not yet clear, this work supports the conclusion that this type of representation is very useful in practical visual processing.

2 Computing the Characteristic Signature

The "texture-of-texture" measurements are based on the outputs of a tree of non-linear filtering operations. Each path through the tree creates a particular filter network, which responds to certain structural organization in the image. Measuring the appropriately weighted difference between the signatures of images in the database and the set of query-images, produces a similarity measure which can be used to rank and sort the images in the database.

The computation of the characteristic signature is straightforward. At the highest level of resolution the image is convolved with a set of 25 local linear features including oriented edges and bars. The results of these convolutions are 25 feature response images. These images are then rectified by squaring, which extracts the *texture energy* in the image, and then downsampled by a factor of two. At this point there are 25 half scale output images which each measure a local textural property of the input image. For example one image is sensitive to vertical edges, and responds strongly to both skyscrapers and picket fences.

Convolution, rectification and downsampling is then repeated on each of these 25 half resolution images producing 625 quarter scale "texture-of-texture" images. The second layer will respond strongly to regions where the texture specified in the first layer has a particular spatial arrangement. For example if horizontal alignments of vertical texture are detected, there will be a strong response to a picket fence and little response to a skyscraper. With additional layers additional specificity is achieved; repeating this procedure a third time yields 15,625 meta-texture images at eighth scale.

Each of the resulting meta-textures is then summed to compute a single value and provides one element in the characteristic signature. When three channels of color are included there are a total of 46,875 elements in the characteristic signature. Once computed, the signature elements are normalized to reduce the effects of contrast changes.

More formally the characteristic signature of an image is given by:

$$S_{i,j,k,c}(I) = \sum_{pixels} E_{i,j,k}(I_c) \tag{1}$$

where I is the image, i, j and k index over the different types of linear filters, and I_c are the different color channels of the image. The definition of E is:

$$E_i(I) = 2 \downarrow [(F_i \otimes I)^2] \tag{2}$$

$$E_{i,j}(I) = 2 \downarrow [(F_j \otimes E_i(I))^2] \tag{3}$$

$$E_{i,j,k}(I) = 2 \downarrow [(F_k \otimes E_{i,j}(I))^2] . \tag{4}$$

where F_i is the ith filter and $2 \downarrow$ is the downsampling operation.

3   Using Characteristic Signatures To Form Image Queries

In the "query by image" paradigm, we describe similarity in terms of the difference between an image and a group of example query images. This is done by comparing the characteristic signature of the image to the mean signature of the query images. The relative importance of each element of the characteristic signature in determining similarity is proportional to the inverse variance of that element across the example-image group:

$$L = -\sum_i \sum_j \sum_k \sum_c \frac{\left[\overline{S_{i,j,k,c}(I_q)} - S_{i,j,k,c}(I_{test})\right]^2}{Var\left[S_{i,j,k,c}(I_q)\right]} \tag{5}$$

where $\overline{S_{i,j,k,c}(I_q)}$ and $Var\left[S_{i,j,k,c}(I_q)\right]$ are the mean and variance of the characteristic signatures computed over the query set. This is a diagonal approximation of the Mahalanobis distance (Duda and Hart, 1973). It has the effect of normalizing the vector-space defined by the characteristic signatures, so that characteristic elements which are salient within the group of query images contribute more to the overall similarity of an image.

In Figure 1 three 2D projections of these 46,875 dimensional characteristic signature space are shown. The data points marked with circles are generated by the 10 images shown at the top of Figure 3. The remaining points are generated by 2900 distractor images. Comparing (a) and (b) we see that in some projections the images cluster tightly, while in others they are distributed. Given a sample of images from the target set we can observe the variation in each possible projection axis. Most of the time the axes shown in (a) will be strongly discounted by the algorithm because these features are not consistent across the query set. Similarly the axes from (b) will receive a large weight because the target images have very consistent values.

The axes along which target groups cluster, however, differ from target group to target group. As a result it is not possible to conclude that the axes in (b) are simply better than the axes in (a). In Figure 1 (c) the same projection is shown again this time with a different target set highlighted (with asterisks).

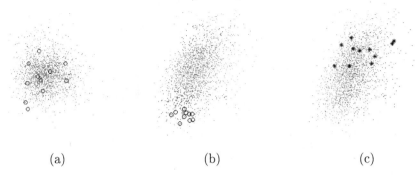

(a)   (b)   (c)

Figure 1: In some projections target groups do not cluster (a), and they do in others (b). However, different target groups will not necessarily cluster in the same projections (c).

4 Experiments

In the first set of experiments we use a database of 2900 images from 29 Corel Photo CD (collections 1000-2900.) Figure 2 shows the results of typical user query on this system. The top windows in each Figure contain the query-images submitted by the user. The bottom windows show the thirty images found to be most similar; similarity decreases from upper left (most similar) to lower right.

Though these examples provide an anecdotal indication that the system is generating similarity measures which roughly conform to human perception, it is difficult to fully characterize the performance of this image retrieval technique. This is a fundamental problem of the domain. Images vary from each other in an astronomical number of ways, and similarity is perceived by human observers based upon complex interactions between recognition, cognition, and assumption. It seems unlikely that an absolute criterion for image similarity can ever be determined, if one truly exists. However using sets of images which we believe are visually similar, we can establish a basis for comparing algorithms.

To better measure the performance of the system we added a set of 10 images to the 2900 image database and attempted to retrieve these new images. We compare the performance of the present system to ten other techniques. Though these techniques are not as sophisticated as those used in systems developed by other researchers, they are indicative of the types of methods which are prevalent in the literature.

In each experiment we measure the retrieval rates for a set of ten target images which we believe to be visually similar because they consist of images of a single scene. Images in the target set differ due to variation of a single visual characteristic. In some of the target sets the photographic conditions have been changed, either by moving the camera, the objects or the light. In other target sets post photograph image manipulation has been performed. Two example target sets are shown in Figure 3.

In each experiment we perform 45 database queries using every possible pair of images from the target set. The retrieval methods compared are: **ToT** The current textures-of-textures system; **RGB-216(or 512)C** R,G,B color histograms using 216 (or 512) bins by dividing each color dimension into 6 (or 8) regions. The target histogram is generated by combining the histograms from the two model images; **HSV-216(or 512)C** same using H,S,V color space; **RGB(or HSV)-216(or**

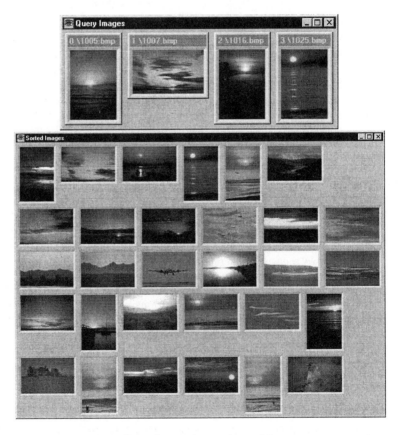

Figure 2: Sample queries and top 30 responses.

Figure 3: Two target sets used in the retrieval experiments. TOP: Variation of object location. BOTTOM: Variation of hard shadows.

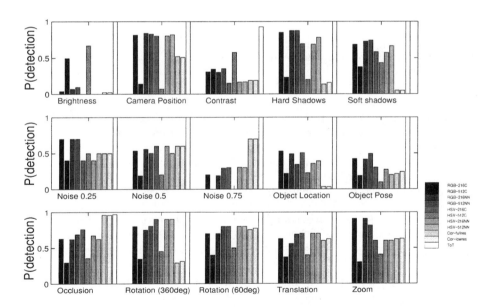

Figure 4: The percentage of target images ranked above all the distractor images, shown for 15 target sets such as those in Figure 3. The textures-of-textures model presented here achieves perfect performance in 13 of the 15 experiments.

512)NN histograms in which similarity is measured using a nearest neighbor metric; **COR-full(and low)res** full resolution (and 4× downsampled) image correlation.

Rankings for all 10 target images in each of the 45 queries are obtained for each variation. To get a comparative sense of the overall performance of each technique, we show the number of target images retrieved with a Neyman-Pearson criterion of zero, i.e. no false positives Figure 4. The textures-of-textures model substantially outperforms all of the other techniques, achieving perfect performance in 13 experiments.

5 Discussion

We have presented a technique for approximating perceived visual similarity, by measuring the structural content similarity between images. Using the high dimensional "characteristic signature" space representation, we directly compare database-images to a set of query-images. A world wide web interface to system has been created and is available via the URL:
        http://www.ai.mit.edu/~jsd/Research/ImageDatabase/Demo

Experiments indicate that the present system can retrieve images which share visual characteristics with the query-images, from a large non-homogeneous database. Further, it greatly outperforms many of the standard methods which form the basis of other systems.

Though the results presented here are encouraging, on real world queries, the retrieved images often contain many false alarms, such as those in Figure 2; however, we believe that with additional analysis performance can be improved.

References

Desimone, R., Albright, T. D., Gross, C. G., and Bruce, C. (1984). Stimulus selective properties of inferior temporal neurons in the macaque. *Journal of Neuroscience*, 4:2051–2062.

Duda, R. and Hart, P. (1973). *Pattern Classification and Scene Analysis*. John Wiley and Sons.

Kelly, M., Cannon, T. M., and Hush, D. R. (1995). Query by image example: the candid approach. *SPIE Vol. 2420 Storage and Retrieval for Image and Video Databases III*, pages 238–248.

Niblack, V., Barber, R., Equitz, W., Flickner, M., Glasman, E., Petkovic, D., Yanker, P., Faloutsos, C., and Taubin, G. (1993). The qbic project: querying images by content using color, texture, and shape. *IS&T/SPIE 1993 International Symposium on Electronic Imaging: Science & Technology*, 1908:173–187.

Pentland, A., Picard, R. W., and Sclaroff, S. (1995). Photobook: Content-based manipulation of image databases. Technical Report 255, MIT Media Lab.

Picard, R. W. and Kabir, T. (1993). Finding similar patterns in large image databases. *ICASSP*, V:161–164.

QBIC. The ibm qbic project. Web: http://wwwqbic.almaden.ibm.com/.

Rao, R. P. N. and Ballard, D. (1995). Object indexing using an iconic sparse distributed memory. Technical Report TR-559, University of Rochester.

Santini, S. and Jain, R. (1996). Gabor space and the development of preattentive similarity. In *Proceedings of ICPR 96*. International Conference on Pattern Recognition, Vienna.

Viola, P. (1996). Complex feature recognition: A bayesian approach for learning to recognize objects. Technical Report 1591, MIT AI Lab.

Virage. The virage project. Web: http://www.virage.com/.

von der Malsburg, C. (1988). Pattern recognition by labeled graph matching. *Neural Networks*, 1:141–148.

A General Purpose Image Processing Chip: Orientation Detection

Ralph Etienne-Cummings and Donghui Cai
Department of Electrical Engineering
Southern Illinois University
Carbondale, IL 62901-6603

Abstract

A 80 x 78 pixel general purpose vision chip for spatial focal plane processing is presented. The size and configuration of the processing receptive field are programmable. The chip's architecture allows the photoreceptor cells to be small and densely packed by performing all computation on the read-out, away from the array. In addition to the raw intensity image, the chip outputs four processed images in parallel. Also presented is an application of the chip to line segment orientation detection, as found in the retinal receptive fields of toads.

1 INTRODUCTION

The front-end of the biological vision system is the retina, which is a layered structure responsible for image acquisition and pre-processing. The early processing is used to extract spatiotemporal information which helps perception and survival. This is accomplished with cells having feature detecting receptive fields, such as the edge detecting center-surround spatial receptive fields of the primate and cat bipolar cells [Spillmann, 1990]. In toads, the receptive fields of the retinal cells are even more specialized for survival by detecting "prey" and "predator" (from size and orientation filters) at this very early stage [Spillmann, 1990].

The receptive of the retinal cells performs a convolution with the incident image in parallel and continuous time. This has inspired many engineers to develop retinomorphic vision systems which also imitate these parallel processing capabilities [Mead, 1989; Camp, 1994]. While this approach is ideal for fast early processing, it is not space efficient. That is, in realizing the receptive field within each pixel, considerable die area is required to implement the convolution kernel. In addition, should programmability be required, the complexity of each pixel increases drastically. The space constraints are eliminated if the processing is performed serially during read-out. The benefits of this approach are 1) each pixel can be as small as possible to allow high resolution imaging, 2) a single processor unit is used for the entire retina thus reducing mis-match problems, 3) programmability can be obtained with no impact on the density of imaging array, and

4) compact general purpose focal plane visual processing is realizable. The space constrains are then transformed into temporal restrictions since the scanning clock speed and response time of the processing circuits must scale with the size of the array. Dividing the array into sub-arrays which are scanned in parallel can help this problem. Clearly this approach departs from the architecture of its biological counterpart, however, this method capitalizes on the main advantage of silicon which is its speed. This is an example of mixed signal neuromorphic engineering, where biological ideas are mapped onto silicon not using direct imitation (which has been the preferred approach in the past) but rather by realizing their *essence* with the best silicon architecture and computational circuits.

This paper presents a general purpose vision chip for spatial focal plane processing. Its architecture allows the photoreceptor cells to be small and densely packed by performing all computation on the read-out, away from the array. Performing computation during read-out is ideal for silicon implementation since no additional temporal over-head is required, provided that the processing circuits are fast enough. The chip uses a single convolution kernel, per parallel sub-array, and the scanning bit pattern to realize various receptive fields. This is different from other focal plane image processors which and usually restricted to hardwired convolution kernels, such as oriented 2D Gabor filters [Camp, 1994]. In addition to the raw intensity image, the chip outputs four processed versions per sub-array. Also presented is an application of the chip to line segment orientation detection, as found in the retinal receptive fields of toads [Spillmann, 1990].

2 THE GENERAL PURPOSE IMAGE PROCESSING CHIP

2.1 System Overview

This chip has an 80 row by 78 column photocell array partitioned into four independent sub-arrays, which are scanned and output in parallel, (see figure 1). Each block is 40 row by 39 column, and has its own convolution kernel and output circuit. The scanning circuit includes three parts: virtual ground, control signal generator (CSG), and scanning output transformer. Each block has its own virtual ground and scanning output transformer in both x direction (horizontal) and y direction (vertical). The control signal generator is shared among blocks.

2.2 Hardware Implementation

The photocell is composed of phototransistor, photo current amplifier, and output control. The phototransistor performance light transduction, while the amplifier magnifies the photocurrent by three orders of magnitude. The output control provides multiple copies of the amplified photocurrent which is subsequently used for focal plane image processing.

The phototransistor is a parasitic PNP transistor in an Nwell CMOS process. The current amplifier uses a pair of diode connected pmosfets to obtain a logarithmic relationship between light intensity and output current. This circuit also amplifies the photocurrent from nanoamperes to microamperes. The photocell sends three copies of the output currents into three independent buses. The connections from the photocell to the buses are controlled by pass transistors, as shown in Fig. 2. The three current outputs allow the image to be processed using multiple receptive field organization (convolution kernels), while the raw image is also output. The row (column) buses provides currents for extracting horizontally (vertically) oriented image features, while the original bus provides the logarithmically compressed intensity image.

The scanning circuit addresses the photocell array by selecting groups of cells at one time. Since the output of the cells are currents, virtual ground circuits are used on each bus to mask the > 1pF capacitance of the buses. The CSG, implemented with shift registers

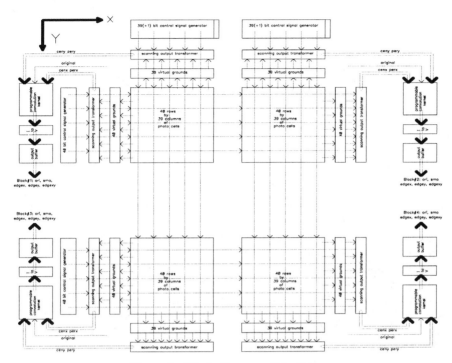

Figure 1: Block diagram of the chip.

produces signals which select photocells and control the scanning output transformer. The scanning output transformer converts currents from all row buses into I_{perx} and I_{cenx}, and converts currents from all row buses into I_{pery} and I_{ceny}. This transformation is required to implement the various convolution kernels discussed later.

The output transformer circuits are controlled by a central CSG and a peripheral CSG. These two generators have identical structures but different initial values. It consists of an n-bit shift register in x direction (horizontally) and an m-bit shift register in y direction (vertically). A feedback circuit is used to restore the scanning pattern into the x shift register after each row scan is completed. This is repeated until all the row in each block are scanned.

The control signals from the peripheral and central CSGs select all the cells covered by a 2D convolution mask (receptive field). The selected cells send I_{xy} to the original bus, I_{xp} to the row bus, and I_{yp} to the column bus. The function of the scanning output transformer is to identify which rows (columns) are considered as the center (I_{cenx} or I_{ceny}) or periphery (I_{perx} or I_{pery}) of the convolution kernel, respectively. Figure 3 shows how a 3x3 convolution kernel can be constructed.

Figure 4 shows how the output transformer works for a 3x3 mask. Only row bus transformation is shown in this example, but the same mechanism applies to the column bus as well. The photocell array is m row by n column, and the size is 3x3. The XC (x center) and YC (y center) come from the central CSG; while XP (x peripheral) and YP (y peripheral) come from the peripheral CSG. After loading the CSG, the initial values of XP and YP are both 00011...1. The initial values of XC and YC are both 10111...1. This identifies the central cell as location (2, 2). The currents from the central row (column) are summed to form I_{cenx} and I_{ceny}, while all the peripheral cells are summed to form I_{perx} and I_{pery}. This is achieved by activating the switches labeled XC, YC, XP and YP in figure 2. XP_i (YP_i) {i=1, 2, ..., n} controls whether the output current of one cell

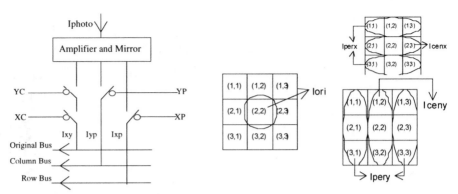

Figure 2: Connections between a photo-cell and the current buses.

Figure 3: Constructing a 3x3 receptive field.

goes to the row (column) bus. Since XP_i (YP_i) is connected to the gate of a pmos switch, a 0 in XP_i (YP_i) it turns on. YC_i (XC_i) {i=1, 2, ..., n} controls whether a row (column) bus connects to I_{cenx} bus in the same way. On the other hand, the connection from a row (column) bus to I_{perx} bus is controlled by an nmos and a pmos switch. The connection is made if and only if YC_i (XC_i), an nmos switch, is 1 and YP_i (XP_i), a pmos switches, is 0. The intensity image is obtained directly when XC_i and YC_i are both 0. Hence, $I_{ori} = I(2,2)$, $I_{cenx} = I_{row2} = I(2,1) + I(2,2) + I(2,3)$ and $I_{perx} = I_{row1} + I_{row3} = I(1,1) + I(1,2) + I(1,3) + I(3,1) + I(3,2) + I(3,3)$.

The convolution kernel can be programmed to perform many image processing tasks by loading the scanning circuit with the appropriate bit pattern. This is illustrated by configuring the chip to perform image smoothing and edge extraction (x edge, y edge, and 2D edge), which are all computed simultaneously on read-out. It receives five inputs (I_{ori}, I_{cenx}, I_{perx}, I_{ceny}, I_{pery}) from the scanning circuit and produces five outputs (I_{ori}, I_{edgex}, I_{edgey}, I_{smooth}, I_{edge2d}). The kernel (receptive field) size is programmable from 3x3, 5x5, 7x7, 9x9 and 11x11. Fig. 5 shows the 3x3 masks for this processing. Repeating the above steps for 5x5, 7x7, 9x9, and 11x11 masks, we can get similar results.

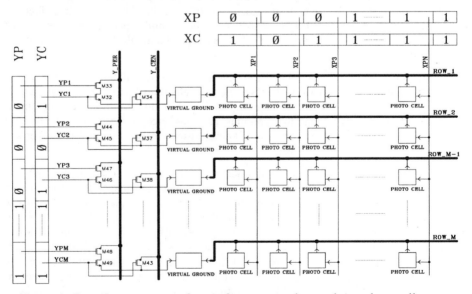

Figure 4: Scanning output transformer for an m row by n column photo cell array.

$I_{smooth}=I_{cenx}+I_{perx}$ $I_{edgex}=2*I_{cenx}-I_{perx}$ $I_{edgey}=2*I_{ceny}-I_{pery}$ $I_{edge2D}=6*I_{ori}-I_{cenx}-I_{ceny}$

1	1	1
1	1	1
1	1	1

-1	-1	-1
2	2	2
-1	-1	-1

-1	2	-1
-1	2	-1
-1	2	-1

0	-1	0
-1	4	-1
0	-1	0

(a) smooth (b) edge_x (c) edge_y (d) edge_2D

Figure 5: 3x3 convolution masks for various image processing.

In general, the convolution results under different mask sizes can be expressed as follows:

$I_{smooth}=I_{cenx}+I_{perx}$ $I_{edgex}=K_{1d}*I_{cenx}-I_{perx}$ $I_{edgey}=K_{1d}*I_{ceny}-I_{pery}$ $I_{edge2D}=K_{2d}*I_{ori}-I_{cenx}-I_{ceny}$

Where K_{1d} and K_{2d} are the programmable coefficients (from 2-6 and 6-14, respectively) for 1D edge extraction and 2D edge extraction, respectively. By varying the locations of the 0's in the scanning circuits, different types of receptive fields (convolution kernels) can be realized.

2.3 Results

The chip contains 65K transistors in a footprint of 4.6 mm x 4.7 mm. There are 80 x 78 photocells in the chip, each of which is 45.6 μm x 45 μm and a fill factor of 15%. The convolution kernel occupies 690.6 μm x 102.6 μm. The power consumption of the chip for a 3x3 (11x11) receptive field, indoor light, and 5V power supply is < 2 mW (8 mW).

To capitalize on the programmability of this chip, an A/D card in a Pentium 133MHz PC is used to load the scanning circuit and to collect data. The card, which has a maximum analog throughput of 100 KHz limits the frame rate of the chip to 12 frames per second. At this rate, five processed versions of the image is collected and displayed. The scanning and processing circuits can operate at 10 MHz (6250 fps), however, the phototransistors have much slower dynamics. Temporal smoothing (smear) can be observed on the scope when the frame rate exceeds 100 fps.

The chip displays a logarithmic relationship between light intensity and output current (unprocessed imaged) from 0.1 lux (100 nA) to 6000 lux (10 μA). The fixed pattern noise, defined as standard-deviation/mean, decreases abruptly from 25% in the dark to 2% at room light (800 lux). This behavior is expected since the variation of individual pixel current is large compared to the mean output when the mean is small. The logarithmic response of the photocell results in high sensitivity at low light, thus increasing the mean value sharply. Little variation is observed between chips.

The contrast sensitivity of the edge detection masks is also measured for the 3x3 and 5x5 receptive fields. Here contrast is defined as $(I_{max} - I_{min})/(I_{max} + I_{min})$ and sensitivity is given as a percentage of the maximum output. The measurements are performed for normal room and bright lighting conditions. Since the two conditions corresponded to the saturated part of the logarithmic transfer function of the photocells, then a linear relationship between output response and contrast is expected. Figure 6 shows contrast sensitivity plot. Figure 7 shows examples of chip's outputs. The top two images are the raw and smoothed (5x5) images. The bottom two are the 1D edge_x (left) and 2D edge (right) images. The pixels with positive values have been thresholded to white. The vertical black line in the image is not visible in the edge_x image, but can be clearly seen in the edge_2D image.

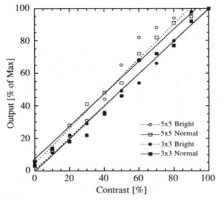

Figure 6: Contrast sensitivity function of the x edge detection mask.

Figure 7: (Clockwise) Raw image, 5x5 smoothed image, edge_2D and edge_x.

3 APPLICATION: ORIENTATION DETECTION

3.1 Algorithm Overview

This vision chip can be elegantly used to measure the orientation of line segments which fall across the receptive field of each pixel. The output of the 1D Laplacian operators, edge_x and edge_y, shown in figure 5, can be used to determine the orientation of edge segments. Consider a continuous line through the origin, represented by a delta function in 2D space by $\delta(y\text{-}x\tan\theta)$. If the origin is the center of the receptive field, the response of the edge_x kernel can be computed by evaluating the convolution equation (1), where $W(x) = u(x+m)\text{-}u(x\text{-}m)$ is the x window over which smoothing is performed, $2m+1$ is the width of the window and $2n+1$ is the number of coefficients realizing the discrete Laplacian operator. In our case, $n = m$. Evaluating this equation and substituting the origin for the pixel location yields equation (2), which indicates that the output of the 1D edge_x (edge_y) detectors have a discretized linear relationship to orientation from $0°$ to $45°$ ($45°$ to $90°$). At $0°$, the second term in equation (2) is zero. As θ increase, more terms are subtracted until all terms are subtracted at $45°$. Above $45°$ (below $45°$), the edge_x (edge_y) detectors output zero since equal numbers of positive and negative coefficients are summed. Provided that contrast can be normalized, the output of the detectors can be used to extract the orientation of the line. Clearly these responses are even about the x- and y-axis, respectively. Hence, a second pair of edge detectors, oriented at $45°$, is required to uniquely extract the angle of the line segment.

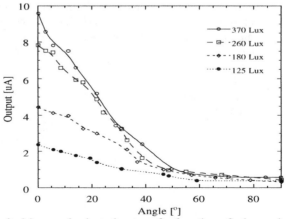

Figure 8: Measured orientation transfer function of edge_x detectors.

$$O_{edge\_x}(x,y) = [2nW(x \pm m)\delta(y) - \sum_{i=1}^{n} W(x \pm m)\delta(y \pm i)] * \delta(y - x\tan\theta) \qquad (1)$$

$$O_{edge\_x}(0,0) = 2n - [\sum_{i=1}^{n}(W(\frac{i}{\tan\theta}) + W(\frac{-i}{\tan\theta}))] \qquad (2)$$

3.2 Results

Figure 8 shows the measured output of the edge_x detectors for various lighting conditions as a line is rotated. The average positive outputs are plotted. As expected, the output is maximum for bright ambients when the line is horizontal. As the line is rotated, the output current decreases linearly and levels off at approximately 45°. On the other hand, the edge_y (not shown) begins its linear increase at 45° and maximizes at 90°. After normalizing for brightness, the four curves are very similar (not shown).

To further demonstrate orientation detection with this chip, a character consisting of a circle and some straight lines is presented. The intensity image of the character is shown in figure 9(a). Figures 9(b) and 9(c) show the outputs of the edge_x and edge_y detectors, respectively. Since a 7x7 receptive field is used in this experiment, some outer pixels of each block are lost. The orientation selectivity of the 1D edge detectors are clearly visible in the figures, where edge_x highlights horizontal edges and edge_y vertical edges. Figure 9(d) shows the reported angles. A program is written which takes the two 1D edge images, finds the location of the edges from the edge_2D image, the intensity at the edges (positive lobe) and then computes the angle of the edge segment. In figure 9(d), the black background is chosen for locations where no edges are detected, white is used for 0° and gray for 90°.

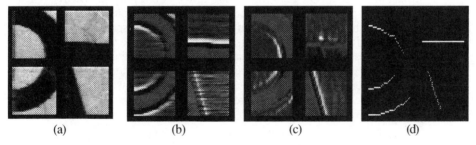

| (a) | (b) | (c) | (d) |

Figure 9: Orientation detection using 1D Laplacian Operators.

4 CONCLUSION

A 80x78 pixel general purpose vision chip for spatial focal plane processing has been presented. The size and configuration of the processing receptive field are programmable. In addition to the raw intensity image, the chip outputs four processed images in parallel. The chip has been successfully used for compact line segment orientation detection, which can be used in character recognition. The programmability and relatively low power consumption makes it ideal for many visual processing tasks.

References

Camp W. and J. Van der Spiegel, "A Silicon VLSI Optical Sensor for Pattern Recognition, " *Sensors and Actuators A*, Vol. 43, No. 1-3, pp. 188-195, 1994.

Mead C. and M. Ismail (Eds.), *Analog VLSI Implementation of Neural Networks*, Kluwer Academic Press, Newell, MA, 1989.

Spillmann L. and J. Werner (Eds.), *Visual Perception: The Neurophysiological Foundations*, Academic Press, San Diego, CA, 1990.

An Analog VLSI Model of the Fly Elementary Motion Detector

Reid R. Harrison and Christof Koch
Computation and Neural Systems Program, 139-74
California Institute of Technology
Pasadena, CA 91125
`[harrison,koch]@klab.caltech.edu`

Abstract

Flies are capable of rapidly detecting and integrating visual motion information in behaviorly-relevant ways. The first stage of visual motion processing in flies is a retinotopic array of functional units known as elementary motion detectors (EMDs). Several decades ago, Reichardt and colleagues developed a correlation-based model of motion detection that described the behavior of these neural circuits. We have implemented a variant of this model in a 2.0-μm analog CMOS VLSI process. The result is a low-power, continuous-time analog circuit with integrated photoreceptors that responds to motion in real time. The responses of the circuit to drifting sinusoidal gratings qualitatively resemble the temporal frequency response, spatial frequency response, and direction selectivity of motion-sensitive neurons observed in insects. In addition to its possible engineering applications, the circuit could potentially be used as a building block for constructing hardware models of higher-level insect motion integration.

1 INTRODUCTION

Flies rely heavily on visual motion information to survive. In the fly, motion information is known to underlie many important behaviors including stabilization during flight, orienting towards small, rapidly-moving objects (Egelhaaf and Borst 1993), and estimating time-to-contact for safe landings (Borst and Bahde 1988). Some motion-related tasks like extending the legs for landing can be excecuted less than 70 milliseconds after stimulus presentation. The computational machinery performing this sensory processing is fast, small, low-power, and robust.

There is good evidence that motion information is first extracted by local elementary motion detectors (see Egelhaaf *et al.* 1988 and references therein). These EMDs are ar-

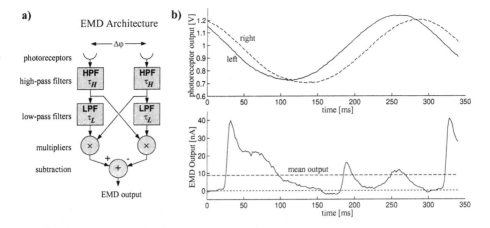

Figure 1: Elementary Motion Detector. a) A simplified version of our EMD circuit architecture. In the actual circuit implementation, there are separate ON and OFF channels that operate in parallel. These two channels are summed after the muliplication. b) The measured response of the EMD test circuit to a drifting sinusoidal grating. Notice that the output is phase dependent, but has a positive mean response. If the grating was drifting in the opposite direction, the circuit would give a negative mean response.

ranged retinotopically, and receive input from adjacent photoreceptors. The properties of these motion-sensitive units have been studied extensively during the past 30 years. Direct recording from individual EMDs is difficult due to the small size of the cells, but much work has been done recording from large tangential cells that integrate the outputs of many EMDs over large portions of the visual field. From these studies, the behavior of individual EMDs has been inferred.

If we wish to study models of motion integration in the fly, we first need a model of the EMD. Since many motion integration neurons in the fly are only a few synapses away from muscles, it may be possible in the near future to contruct models that complete the sensorimotor loop. If we wish to include the real world in the loop, we need a mobile system that works in real time. In the pursuit of such a system, we follow the neuromorphic engineering approach pioneered by Mead (Mead 1989) and implement a hardware model of the fly EMD in a commercially available 2.0-μm CMOS VLSI process. All data presented in this paper are from one such chip.

2 ALGORITHM AND ARCHITECTURE

Figure 1a shows a simplified version of the motion detector. This is an elaborated version of the correlation-based motion detector first proposed by Reichardt and colleagues (see Reichardt 1987 and references therein). The Reichardt motion detector works by correlating (by means of a multiplication) the response of one photoreceptor to the delayed response of an adjacent photoreceptor. Our model uses the phase lag inherent in a low-pass filter to supply the delay. The outputs from two mirror-symmetric correlators are subtracted to remove any response to full-field flicker ($\omega_s = 0$, $\omega_t > 0$).

Correlation-based EMDs are not pure velocity sensors. Their response is strongly affected by the contrast and the spatial frequency components of the stimulating pattern. They can best be described as direction-selective spatiotemporal filters. The mean steady-state response R of the motion detector shown in Figure 1a to a sinusoidal grating drifting in one direction can be expressed as a separable function of stimulus amplitude (ΔI), temporal

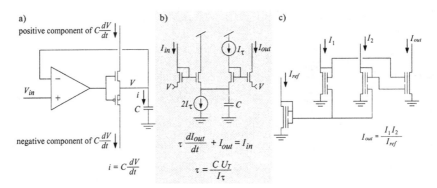

Figure 2: EMD Subcircuits. a) Temporal derivative circuit. In combination with the first-order low-pass filter inherent in the photoreceptor, this forms the high-pass filter with time constant τ_H. The feedback amplifier enforces $V = V_{in}$, and the output is the current needed for the nFET or pFET source follower to charge or discharge the capacitor C. b) Current-mode low-pass filter. The time constant τ_L is determined by the bias current I_τ (which is set by a bias voltage supplied from off-chip), the capacitance C, and the thermal voltage $U_T = kT/q$. c) Current-mode one-quadrant multiplier. The devices shown are floating-gate nFETs. Two control gates capacitively couple to the floating node, forming a capacitive divider.

frequency ($\omega_t = 2\pi f_t$), and spatial frequency ($\omega_s = 2\pi f_s$):

$$R(\Delta I, \omega_t, \omega_s) = R_I(\Delta I) \times R_t(\omega_t) \times R_s(\omega_s) \tag{1}$$

$$= \Delta I^2 \times \frac{\tau_L \omega_t}{(1 + 1/\tau_H^2 \omega_t^2)(1 + \tau_L^2 \omega_t^2)} \times \sin(\Delta\varphi\omega_s) \tag{2}$$

where $\Delta\varphi$ is the angular separation of the photoreceptors, τ_H is the time constant of the high-pass filter, and τ_L is the time constant of the low-pass filter (see Figure 1a). (Note that this holds only for motion in a particular direction. Motion detectors are not linearly separable overall, but the single-direction analysis is useful for making comparisons.)

3   CIRCUIT DESCRIPTION

In addition to the basic Reichardt model described above, we include a high-pass filter in series with the photoreceptor. This amplifies transient responses and removes the DC component of the photoreceptor signal. We primarily use the high-pass filter as a convenient circuit to switch from a voltage-mode to a current-mode representation (see Figure 2a).

For the photoreceptor, we use an adaptive circuit developed by Delbrück (Delbrück and Mead 1996) that produces an output voltage proportional to log intensity. We bias the photoreceptor very weakly to attenuate high temporal frequencies. This is directly followed by a temporal derivative circuit (Mead 1989) (see Figure 2a), the result being a high-pass filter with the dominant pole τ_H being set by the photoreceptor cutoff frequency. The outputs of the temporal derivative circuit are two unidirectional currents that represent the positive and negative components of a high-pass filtered version of the photoreceptor output. This resembles the ON and OFF channels found in many biological visual systems. Some studies suggest ON and OFF channels are present in the fly (Franceschini et al. 1989) but the evidence is mixed (Egelhaaf and Borst 1992). This two-channel representation is useful for current-mode circuits, since the following translinear circuits work only with unidirectional

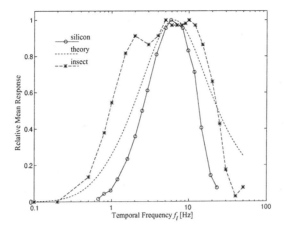

Figure 3: Temporal Frequency Response. Circuit data was taken with f_s = 0.05 cycles/deg and 86% contrast. Theory trace is $R_t(\omega_t)$ from Equation 2, where τ_H = 360 *ms* and τ_L = 25 *ms* were directly measured in separate experiments – these terms were not fit to the data. Insect data was taken from a wide-field motion neuron in the blowfly *Calliphora erythrocephala* (O'Carroll *et al.* 1996). All three curves were normalized by their peak response.

currents. It should be noted that the use of ON and OFF channels introduces nonlinearities into the circuit that are not accounted for in the simple model described by Equation 2.

The current-mode low-pass filter is shown in Figure 2b. The time constant τ_L is set by the bias current I_τ. This is a log-domain filter that takes advantage of the exponential behavior of field-effect transistors (FETs) in the subthreshold region of operation (Minch, personal communication).

The current-mode multiplier is shown in Figure 2c. This circuit is also translinear, using a diode-connected FET to convert the input currents into log-encoded voltages. A weighted sum of the voltages is computed with a capacitive divider, and the resulting voltage is exponentiated by the output FET into the output current. The capacitive divider creates a floating node, and the charge on all these nodes must be equalized to ensure matching across independent multipliers. This is easily accomplished by exposing the chip to UV light for several minutes. This circuit represents one of a family of floating-gate MOS translinear circuits developed by Minch that are capable of computing arbitrary power laws in current mode (Minch *et al.* 1996).

After the multiplication stage, the currents from the ON and OFF channels are summed, and the final subtraction of the left and right channels is done off-chip. There is a gain mismatch of approximately 2.5 between the left and right channels that is now compensated for manually. This mismatch must be lowered before large on-chip arrays of EMDs are practical. A new circuit designed to lessen this gain mismatch is currently being tested. It is interesting to note that there is no significant offset error in the output currents from each channel. This is a consequence of using translinear circuits which typically have gain errors due to transistor mismatch, but no fixed offset errors.

4 EXPERIMENTS

As we showed in Equation 2, the motion detector's response to a drifting sinusoidal grating of a particular direction should be a separable function of ΔI, temporal frequency, and

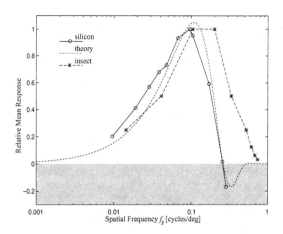

Figure 4: Spatial Frequency Response. Circuit data was taken with f_t = 4 Hz and 86%
contrast. Theory trace is $R_s(\omega_s)$ from Equation 2 multiplied by $\exp(-\omega_s{}^2/K^2)$ to account
for blurring in the optics. The photoreceptor spacing $\Delta\varphi = 1.9°$ was directly measured in
an separate experiment. Only K and the overall magnitude were varied to fit the data.
Insect data was taken from a wide-field motion neuron in the hoverfly *Volucella pelluscens*
(O'Carroll *et al.* 1996). Circuit and insect data were normalized by their peak response.

spatial frequency. We tested the circuit along these axes using printed sinusoidal gratings
mounted on a rotating drum. A lens with an 8-*mm* focal length was mounted over the chip.
Each stimulus pattern had a fixed contrast $\Delta I/2\bar{I}$ and spatial frequency f_s. The temporal
frequency was set by the pattern's angular velocity v as seen by the chip, where $f_t = f_s v$.

The response of the circuit to a drifting sine wave grating is phase dependent (see Figure 1b). In flies, this phase dependency is removed by integrating over large numbers of
EMDs (spatial integration). In order to evaluate the performance of our circuit, we measured the mean response over time.

Figure 3 shows the temporal frequency response of the circuit as compared to theory, and to
a wide-field motion neuron in the fly. The circuit exhibits temporal frequency tuning. The
point of peak response is largely determined by τ_L, and can be changed by altering the low-
pass filter bias current. The deviation of the circuit behavior from theory at low frequencies
is thought to be a consequence of crossover distortion in the temporal derivative circuit. At
high temporal frequencies, parasitic capacitances in current mirrors are a likely candidate
for the discrepancy. The temporal frequency response of the blowfly *Calliphora* is broader
than both the theory and circuit curves. This might be a result of time-constant adaptation
found in blowfly motion-sensitive neurons (de Ruyter van Steveninck *et al.* 1986).

Figure 4 shows the spatial frequency response of the circuit. The response goes toward zero
as ω_s approaches zero, indicating that the circuit greatly attenuates full-field flicker. The
circuit begins aliasing at $\omega_s = 1/2\Delta\varphi$, giving a response in the wrong direction. Spatial
aliasing has also been observed in flies (Götz 1965). The optics used in the experiment act
as an antialiasing filter, so aliasing could be avoided by defocusing the lens slightly.

Figure 5 shows the directional tuning of the circuit. It can be shown that as long as the
spatial wavelength is large compared to $\Delta\varphi$, the directional sensitivity of a correlation-
based motion detector should approximate a cosine function (Zanker 1990). The circuit's
performance matches this quite well. Motion sensitive neurons in the fly show cosine-like
direction selectivity.

Figure 6 shows the contrast response of the circuit. Insect EMDs show a saturating contrast

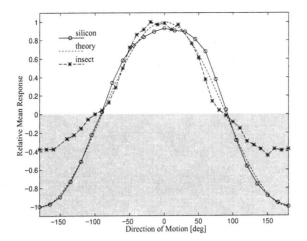

Figure 5: Directional Response. Circuit data was taken with $f_t = 6$ Hz, $f_s = 0.05$ cycles/deg and 86% contrast. Theory trace is $\cos \alpha$, where α is the direction of motion relative to the axis along the two photoreceptors. Insect data was taken from the H1 neuron in the blowfly *Calliphora erythrocephala* (van Hateren 1990). H1 is a spiking neuron with a low spontaneous firing rate. The flattened negative responses visible in the graph are a result of the cell's limited dynamic range in this region. All three curves were normalized by their peak response.

response curve, which can be accounted for by introducing saturating nonlinearities before the multiplication stage (Egelhaaf and Borst 1989). We did not attempt to model contrast saturation in our circuit, though it could be added in future versions.

5   CONCLUSIONS

We implemented and tested an analog VLSI model of the fly elementary motion detector. The circuit's spatiotemporal frequency response and directional selectivity is qualitatively similar to the responses of motion-sensitive neurons in the fly. This circuit could be a useful building block for constructing analog VLSI models of motion integration in flies. As an integrated, low-power, real-time sensory processor, the circuit may also have engineering applications.

Acknowledgements

This work was supported by the Center for Neuromorphic Systems Engineering as a part of NSF's Engineering Research Center program, and by ONR. Reid Harrison is supported by an NDSEG fellowship from ONR. We thank Bradley Minch, Holger Krapp, and Rainer Deutschmann for invaluable discussions.

References

A. Borst and S. Bahde (1988) Visual information processing in the fly's landing system. *J. Comp. Physiol. A* **163:** 167-173.

T. Delbrück and C. Mead (1996) Analog VLSI phototransduction by continuous-time, adaptive, logarithmic photoreceptor circuits. *CNS Memo No. 30*, Caltech.

M. Egelhaaf, K. Hausen, W. Reichardt, and C. Wehrhahn (1988) Visual course control in

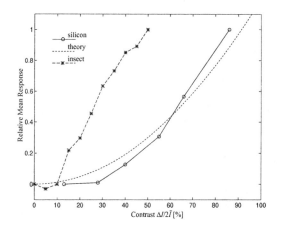

Figure 6: Contrast Response. Circuit data was taken with $f_t = 6$ Hz and $f_s = 0.1$ cycles/deg. Theory trace is $R_I(\Delta I)$ from Equation 2 with its magnitude scaled to fit the circuit data. Insect data was taken from the HS neuron in the blowfly *Calliphora erythrocephala* (Egelhaaf and Borst 1989). Circuit and insect data were normalized by their peak response.

flies relies on neuronal computation of object and background motion. *TINS* **11**: 351-358.

M. Egelhaaf and A. Borst (1989) Transient and steady-state response properties of movement detectors. *J. Opt. Soc. Am. A* **6**: 116-127.

M. Egelhaaf and A. Borst (1992) Are there separate ON and OFF channels in fly motion vision? *Visual Neuroscience* **8**: 151-164.

M. Egelhaaf and A. Borst (1993) A look into the cockpit of the fly: Visual orientation, algorithms, and identified neurons. *J. Neurosci.* **13**: 4563-4574.

N. Franceschini, A. Riehle, and A. le Nestour (1989) Directionally selective motion detection by insect neurons. In Stavenga/Hardie (eds.), *Facets of Vision,* Berlin: Springer-Verlag.

K.G. Götz (1965) Die optischen Übertragungseigenschaften der Komplexaugen von *Drosophila. Kybernetik* **2**: 215-221.

J.H. van Hateren (1990) Directional tuning curves, elementary movement detectors, and the estimation of the direction of visual movement. *Vision Res.* **30**: 603-614.

C. Mead (1989) *Analog VLSI and Neural Systems.* Reading, Mass.: Addison-Wesley.

B.A. Minch, C. Diorio, P. Hasler, and C. Mead (1996) Translinear circuits using subthreshold floating-gate MOS transistors. *Analog Int. Circuits and Signal Processing* **9**: 167-179.

D.C. O'Carroll, N.J. Bidwell, S.B. Laughlin, and E.J. Warrant (1996) Insect motion detectors matched to visual ecology. *Nature* **382**: 63-66.

W. Reichardt (1987) Evaluation of optical motion information by movement detectors. *J. Comp. Phys. A* **161**: 533-547.

R.R. de Ruyter van Steveninck, W.H. Zaagman, and H.A.K. Mastebroek (1986) Adaptation of transient responses of a movement-sensitive neuron in the visual system of the blowfly *Calliphora erythrocephala. Biol. Cybern.* **54**: 223-236.

J.M. Zanker (1990) On the directional sensitivity of motion detectors. *Biol. Cybern.* **62**: 177-183.

MELONET I: Neural Nets for Inventing Baroque-Style Chorale Variations

Dominik Hörnel
dominik@ira.uka.de
Institut für Logik, Komplexität und Deduktionssysteme
Universität Fridericiana Karlsruhe (TH)
Am Fasanengarten 5
D–76128 Karlsruhe, Germany

Abstract

MELONET I is a multi-scale neural network system producing baroque-style melodic variations. Given a melody, the system invents a four-part chorale harmonization and a variation of any chorale voice, after being trained on music pieces of composers like J. S. Bach and J. Pachelbel. Unlike earlier approaches to the learning of melodic structure, the system is able to learn and reproduce high-order structure like harmonic, motif and phrase structure in melodic sequences. This is achieved by using mutually interacting feedforward networks operating at different time scales, in combination with Kohonen networks to classify and recognize musical structure. The results are chorale partitas in the style of J. Pachelbel. Their quality has been judged by experts to be comparable to improvisations invented by an experienced human organist.

1   INTRODUCTION

The investigation of neural information structures in music is a rather new, exciting research area bringing together different disciplines such as computer science, mathematics, musicology and cognitive science. One of its aims is to find out what determines the personal style of a composer. It has been shown that neural network models – better than other AI approaches – are able to learn and reproduce style-dependent features from given examples, e.g., chorale harmonizations in the style of Johann Sebastian Bach (Hild et al., 1992). However when dealing with *melodic* sequences, e.g., folk-song style melodies, all of these models have considerable difficulties to learn even simple structures. The reason is that they are unable to capture high-order structure such as harmonies, motifs and phrases simultaneously occurring at multiple time scales. To overcome this problem, Mozer (Mozer, 1994) proposes context units that learn reduced descriptions of a sequence of individual notes. A similar approach in MELONET (Feulner et Hörnel, 1994) uses *delayed update units* that do not fire each time their input changes but rather at discrete time intervals. Although these models perform well on artificial sequences, they produce melodies that suffer from a lack of global coherence.

The art of melodic variation has a long tradition in Western music. Almost every great composer has written music pieces inventing variations of a given melody, e.g., Mozart's famous variations KV 265 on the melody "Ah! Vous dirai-je, Maman", also known as "Twinkle twinkle little star". At the beginning of this tradition there is the baroque type of chorale variations. These are organ or harpsichord variations of a chorale melody composed for use in the Protestant church. A prominent representative of this kind of composition is J. Pachelbel (1653 - 1706) who wrote about 50 chorale variations or partitas on various chorale melodies.

2   TASK DESCRIPTION

Given a chorale melody, the learning task is achieved in two steps:

1. A chorale harmonization of the melody is invented.
2. One of the voices of the resulting chorale is chosen and provided with melodic variations.

Both subtasks are directly learned from music examples composed by J. Pachelbel and performed in an interactive composition process which results in a chorale variation of the given melody. The first task is performed by HARMONET, a neural network system which is able to harmonize melodies in the style of various composers like J. S. Bach. The second task is performed by the neural network system MELONET I, presented in the following. For simplicity we have considered melodic variations consisting of 4 sixteenth notes for each melody quarter note. This is the most common variation type used by baroque composers and presents a good starting point for even more complex variation types, since there are enough music examples for training and testing the networks, and because it allows the representation of higher-scale elements in a rather straightforward way.

HARMONET is a system producing four-part chorales in various harmonization styles, given a one-part melody. It solves a musical real-world problem on a performance level appropriate for musical practice. Its power is based on a coding scheme capturing musically relevant information, and on the integration of neural networks and symbolic algorithms in a hierarchical system, combining the advantages of both. The details are not discussed in this paper. See (Hild et al., 1992) or (Hörnel et Ragg, 1996a) for a detailed account.

3   A MULTI-SCALE NEURAL NETWORK MODEL

The learning goal is twofold. On the one hand, the results produced by the system should conform to musical rules. These are melodic and harmonic constraints such as the correct resolving of dissonances or the appropriate use of successive interval leaps. On the other hand, the system should be able to capture stilistic features from the learning examples, e.g., melodic shapes preferred by J. Pachelbel. The observation of musical rules and the aesthetic conformance to the learning set can be achieved by a multi-scale neural network model. The complexity of the learning task is reduced by decomposition in three subtasks (see Figure 1):

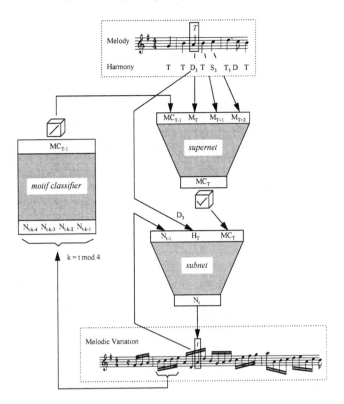

Figure 1: Structure of the system and process of composing a new melodic variation. A melody (previously harmonized by HARMONET) is passed to the supernet which predicts the current motif class MC_T from a local window given by melody notes M_T to M_{T+2} and preceding motif class MC_{T-1}. A similar procedure is performed at a lower time scale by the subnet which predicts the next motif note N_t based on MC_T, current harmony H_T and preceding motif note N_{t-1}. The result is then returned to the supernet through the motif classifier to be considered when computing the next motif class MC_{T+1}.

1. A melody variation is considered at a higher time scale as a sequence of melodic groups, so-called *motifs*. Each quarter note of the given melody is varied by one motif. Before training the networks, motifs are classified according to their similarity.

2. One neural network is used to learn the abstract sequence of motif classes. Motif classes are represented in a 1-of-n coding form where n is a fixed number of classes. The question it solves is: What kind of motif 'fits' a melody note depending on melodic context and the motif that has occurred before? No concrete notes are fixed by this network. It works at a higher scale and will therefore be called *supernet* in the following.

3. Another neural network learns the implementation of abstract motif classes into concrete notes depending on a given harmonic context. It produces a sequence of sixteenth notes – four notes per motif – that result in a melodic variation of the given melody. Because it works one scale below the supernet, it is called *subnet*.

4. The subnet sometimes invents a sequence of notes that does not coincide

with the motif class determined by the supernet. This motif will be considered when computing the next motif class, however, and should therefore match the notes previously formed by the subnet. It is therefore reclassified by the *motif classifier* before the supernet determines the next motif class.

The motivation of this separation into supernet and subnet arised from the following consideration: Having a neural network that learns sequences of sixteenth notes, it would be easier for this network to predict notes given a *contour* of each motif, i.e. a sequence of interval directions to be produced for each quarter note. Consider a human organist who improvises a melodic variation of a given melody in real time. Because he has to take his decisions in a fraction of a second, he must at least have some rough idea in mind about what kind of melodic variation should be applied to the next melody note to obtain a meaningful continuation of the variation. Therefore, a neural network was introduced at a higher time scale, the training of which really improved the overall behavior of the system and not just shifted the learning problem to another time scale.

4   MOTIF CLASSIFICATION AND RECOGNITION

In order to realize learning at different time scales as described above, we need a recognition component to find a suitable classification of motifs. This can be achieved using unsupervised learning, e.g., *agglomerative hierarchical clustering* or Kohonen's *topological feature maps* (Kohonen, 1990). The former has the disadvantage however that an appropriate distance measure is needed which determines the similarity between small sequences of notes respectively intervals, whereas the latter allows to obtain appropriate motif classes through self-organization within a two-dimensional surface. Figure 2 displays the motif representation and distribution of motif contours over a 10x10 Kohonen feature map. In MELONET I, the Kohonen algorithm is applied to all motifs contained in the training set. Afterwards a corresponding motif classification tree is recursively built from the Kohonen map. While cutting this classification tree at lower levels we can get more and more classes. One important problem remains to find an appropriate number of classes for the given learning task. This will be discussed in section 6.

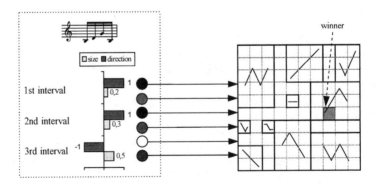

Figure 2: Motif representation example (left) and motif contour distribution (right) over a 10x10 Kohonen feature map developed from one Pachelbel chorale variation (initial update area 6x6, initial adaptation height 0.95, decrease factor 0.995). Each cell corresponds to one unit in the KFM. One can see the arrangement of regions responding to motifs having different motif contours.

5   REPRESENTATION

In general one can distinguish two groups of motifs: *Melodic motifs* prefer small intervals, mainly seconds, *harmonic motifs* prefer leaps and harmonizing notes (chord notes). Both motif groups heavily rely on harmonic information. In melodic motifs dissonances should be correctly resolved, in harmonic motifs notes must fit the given harmony. Small deviations may have a significant effect on the quality of musical results. Thus our idea was to integrate musical knowledge about interval and harmonic relationships into an appropriate *interval representation*. Each note is represented by its interval to the first motif note, the so-called *reference note*. This is an important element contributing to the success of MELONET I. A similar idea for Jazz improvisation was followed in (Baggi, 1992).

The interval coding shown in Table 1 considers several important relationships: *neighboring* intervals are realized by overlapping bits, *octave invariance* is represented using a special octave bit. The activation of the overlapping bit was reduced from 1 to 0.5 in order to allow a better distinction of the intervals. 3 bits are used to distinguish the direction of the interval, 7 bits represent interval size. Complementary intervals such as ascending thirds and descending sixths have similar representations because they lead to the same note and can therefore be regarded as *harmonically equivalent*. A simple rhythmic element was then added using a *tenuto* bit (not shown in Table 1) which is set when a note is tied to its predecessor. This final 3+1+7+1=12 bit coding gave the best results in our simulations.

Table 1: Complementary Interval Coding

		direction			octave	interval size						
ninth	↘	1	0	0	1	0	0	0	0	0	0.5	1
octave	↘	1	0	0	1	1	0	0	0	0	0	0.5
seventh	↘	1	0	0	0	0.5	1	0	0	0	0	0
sixth	↘	1	0	0	0	0	0.5	1	0	0	0	0
fifth	↘	1	0	0	0	0	0	0.5	1	0	0	0
fourth	↘	1	0	0	0	0	0	0	0.5	1	0	0
third	↘	1	0	0	0	0	0	0	0	0.5	1	0
second	↘	1	0	0	0	0	0	0	0	0	0.5	1
prime	→	0	1	0	0	1	0	0	0	0	0	0.5
second	↗	0	0	1	0	0.5	1	0	0	0	0	0
third	↗	0	0	1	0	0	0.5	1	0	0	0	0
fourth	↗	0	0	1	0	0	0	0.5	1	0	0	0
fifth	↗	0	0	1	0	0	0	0	0.5	1	0	0
sixth	↗	0	0	1	0	0	0	0	0	0.5	1	0
seventh	↗	0	0	1	0	0	0	0	0	0	0.5	1
octave	↗	0	0	1	1	1	0	0	0	0	0	0.5
ninth	↗	0	0	1	1	0.5	1	0	0	0	0	0

Now we still need a representation for harmony. It can be encoded as a *harmonic field* which is a vector of chord notes of the diatonic scale. The tonic T in C major for example contains 3 chord notes – C, E and G – which correspond to the first, third and fifth degree of the C major scale (1010100). This representation may be further improved. We have already mentioned that each note is represented by the interval to the *first* motif note (reference note). We can now encode the harmonic field starting with the first motif note instead of the first degree of the scale. This is equivalent to rotating the bits of the harmonic field vector. An example is displayed in Figure 3. The harmony of the motif is the dominant D, the first motif note is B which corresponds to the seventh degree of the C major scale. Therefore the harmonic field for D (0100101) is rotated by one position to the right resulting in (1010010). Starting with the first note B, the harmonic field indicates the intervals that lead to harmonizing notes B, D and G. In the right part of Figure 3 one can see a correspondance between bits activated in the harmonic field and bits set to 1 in the three interval codings. This kind of representation helps the neural network to directly establish a relationship between intervals and given harmony.

third up	0	0	1	0	0	0.5	1	0	0	0	0
sixth up	0	0	1	0	0	0	0	0	0.5	1	0
prime	0	1	0	0	1	0	0	0	0	0	0.5
harmonic field					1	0	1	0	0	1	0

Figure 3: Example illustrating the relationship between interval coding and rotated harmonic field. Each note is represented by its interval to the first note.

6   PERFORMANCE

We carried out several simulations to evaluate the performance of the system. Many improvements could be found however by just listening to the improvisations produced by the neural organist. One important problem was to find an appropriate number of classes for the given learning task. The following table lists the classification rate on the learning and validation set of the supernet and the subnet using 5, 12 and 20 motif classes. The learning set was automatically built from 12 Pachelbel chorale variations corresponding to 2220 patterns for the subnet and 555 for the supernet. The validation set includes 6 Pachelbel variations corresponding to 1396 patterns for the subnet and 349 for the supernet. Supernet and subnet were then trained independently with the RPROP learning algorithm.

	supernet			*subnet*		
	5 classes	12 classes	20 classes	5 classes	12 classes	20 classes
learning set	91.17%	86.85%	87.57%	86.31%	93.92%	95.68%
validation set	49.85%	40.69%	37.54%	79.15%	83.38%	86.96%

The classification rate of both networks strongly depends on the number of classes, esp. on the validation set of the supernet. The smaller the number of classes, the better is the classification of the supernet because there are less alternatives to choose from. We can also notice an opposite development of the classification behavior for the subnet. The bigger the number of classes, the easier the subnet will be able to determine concrete motif notes for a given motif class. One can imagine that the optimal number of classes lies somewhere in the middle. Another idea is to form a committee of networks each of which is trained with different number of classes.

We have also tested MELONET I on melodies that do not belong to the baroque era. Figure 4 shows a harmonization and variation of the melody "Twinkle twinkle little star" used by Mozart in his famous piano variations. It was produced by a network committee formed by 3*2=6 networks trained with 5, 12 and 20 classes.

7   CONCLUSION

We have presented a neural network system inventing baroque-style variations on given melodies whose qualities are similar to those of an experienced human organ-

Figure 4: Melodic variation on "Twinkle twinkle little star"

ist. The complex musical task could be learned introducing a multi-scale network model with two neural networks cooperating at different time scales, together with an unsupervised learning mechanism able to classify and recognize relevant musical structure.

We are about to test this multi-scale approach on learning examples of other epochs, e.g., on compositions of classical composers like Haydn and Mozart or on Jazz improvisations. First results confirm that the system is able to reproduce style-specific elements of other kinds of melodic variation as well. Another interesting question is whether the global coherence of the musical results may be further improved adding another network working at a higher level of abstraction, e.g., at a phrase level. In summary, we believe that this approach presents an important step towards the learning of complete melodies.

References

Denis L. Baggi. *NeurSwing: An Intelligent Workbench for the Investigation of Swing in Jazz.* In: Readings in Computer-Generated Music, IEEE Computer Society Press, pp. 79-94, 1992.

Johannes Feulner, Dominik Hörnel. *MELONET: Neural networks that learn harmony-based melodic variations.* In: Proceedings of the 1994 International Computer Music Conference. ICMA Arhus, pp. 121-124, 1994.

Hermann Hild, Johannes Feulner, Wolfram Menzel. *HARMONET: A Neural Net for Harmonizing Chorales in the Style of J. S. Bach.* In: Advances in Neural Information Processing 4 (NIPS 4), pp. 267-274. 1992.

Dominik Hörnel, Thomas Ragg. *Learning Musical Structure and Style by Recognition, Prediction and Evolution.* In: Proceedings of the 1996 International Computer Music Conference. ICMA Hong Kong, pp. 59-62, 1996.

Dominik Hörnel, Thomas Ragg. *A Connectionist Model for the Evolution of Styles of Harmonization.* In: Proceedings of the 1996 International Conference on Music Perception and Cognition. Montreal, 1996.

Teuvo Kohonen. *The Self-Organizing Map.* In: Proceedings of the IEEE, Vol. 78, no. 9, pp. 1464-1480, 1990.

Michael C. Mozer. *Neural Network music composition by prediction.* In: Connection Science 6(2,3), pp. 247-280, 1994.

Extended ICA Removes Artifacts from Electroencephalographic Recordings

**Tzyy-Ping Jung[1], Colin Humphries[1], Te-Won Lee[1], Scott Makeig[2,3],
Martin J. McKeown[1], Vicente Iragui[3], Terrence J. Sejnowski[1]**

[1]Howard Hughes Medical Institute and Computational Neurobiology Lab
The Salk Institute, P.O. Box 85800, San Diego, CA 92186-5800
{jung,colin,tewon,scott,martin,terry}@salk.edu
[2]Naval Health Research Center, P.O. Box 85122, San Diego, CA 92186-5122
[3]Department of Neurosciences, University of California San Diego, La Jolla, CA 92093

Abstract

Severe contamination of electroencephalographic (EEG) activity
by eye movements, blinks, muscle, heart and line noise is a serious
problem for EEG interpretation and analysis. Rejecting contaminated EEG segments results in a considerable loss of information
and may be impractical for clinical data. Many methods have been
proposed to remove eye movement and blink artifacts from EEG
recordings. Often regression in the time or frequency domain is
performed on simultaneous EEG and electrooculographic (EOG)
recordings to derive parameters characterizing the appearance and
spread of EOG artifacts in the EEG channels. However, EOG
records also contain brain signals [1, 2], so regressing out EOG activity inevitably involves subtracting a portion of the relevant EEG
signal from each recording as well. Regression cannot be used to
remove muscle noise or line noise, since these have no reference
channels. Here, we propose a new and generally applicable method
for removing a wide variety of artifacts from EEG records. The
method is based on an extended version of a previous Independent Component Analysis (ICA) algorithm [3, 4] for performing
blind source separation on linear mixtures of independent source
signals with either sub-Gaussian or super-Gaussian distributions.
Our results show that ICA can effectively detect, separate and remove activity in EEG records from a wide variety of artifactual
sources, with results comparing favorably to those obtained using
regression-based methods.

1 Introduction

Eye movements, muscle noise, heart signals, and line noise often produce large and distracting artifacts in EEG recordings. Rejecting EEG segments with artifacts larger than an arbitrarily preset value is the most commonly used method for eliminating artifacts. However, when limited data are available, or blinks and muscle movements occur too frequently, as in some patient groups, the amount of data lost to artifact rejection may be unacceptable. Methods are needed for removing artifacts while preserving the essential EEG signals.

Berg & Scherg [5] have proposed a spatio-temporal dipole model for eye-artifact removal that requires *a priori* assumptions about the number of dipoles for saccade, blink, and other eye-movements, and assumes they have a simple dipolar structure. Several other proposed methods for removing eye-movement artifacts are based on regression in the time domain [6, 7] or frequency domain [8, 9]. However, simple time-domain regression tends to overcompensate for blink artifacts and may introduce *new* artifacts into EEG records [10]. The cause of this overcompensation is the difference between the spatial EOG-to-EEG transfer functions for blinks and saccades. Saccade artifacts arise from changes in orientation of the retinocorneal dipole, while blink artifacts arise from alterations in ocular conductance produced by contact of the eyelid with the cornea [11]. The transfer of blink artifacts to the recording electrodes decreases rapidly with distance from the eyes, while the transfer of saccade artifacts decreases more slowly, so that at the vertex the effect of saccades on the EEG is about double that of blinks [11], while at frontal sites the two effects may be near-equal.

Regression in the frequency domain [8, 9] can account for frequency-dependent spatial transfer function differences from EOG to EEG, but is acausal and thus unsuitable for real-time applications. Both time and frequency domain regression methods depend on having a good regressor (e.g., an EOG), and share an inherent weakness that spread of excitation from eye movements and EEG signals is bidirectional. This means that whenever regression-based artifact removal is performed, a portion of relevant EEG signals also contained in the EOG data will be cancelled out along with the eye movement artifacts. Further, since the spatial transfer functions for various EEG phenomena present in the EOG differ from the regression transfer function, their spatial distributions after artifact removal may differ from the raw record. Similar problems complicate removal of other types of EEG artifacts. Relatively little work has been done on removing muscle activity, cardiac signals and electrode noise from EEG data. Regressing out muscle noise is impractical since regressing out signals from multiple muscle groups require multiple reference channels. Line noise is most commonly filtered out in the frequency domain. However, current interest in EEG in the 40-80 Hz gamma band phenomena may make this approach undesirable as well.

We present here a new and generally applicable method for isolating and removing a wide variety of EEG artifacts by linear decomposition using a new Independent Component Analysis (ICA) algorithm [4] related to a previous algorithm [3, 12]. The ICA method is based on spatial filtering and does not rely on having a "clean"reference channel. It effectively decomposes multiple-channel EEG data into spatially-fixed and temporally independent components. Clean EEG signals can then be derived by eliminating the contributions of artifactual sources, since their time courses are generally temporally independent from and differently distributed than sources of EEG activity.

2   Independent Component Analysis

Bell and Sejnowski [3] have proposed a simple neural network algorithm that blindly separates mixtures, $\mathbf{x}$, of independent sources, $\mathbf{s}$, using infomax. They show that maximizing the joint entropy, $H(\mathbf{y})$, of the output of a neural processor minimizes the mutual information among the output components, $y_i = g(u_i)$, where $g(u_i)$ is an invertible bounded nonlinearity and $\mathbf{u} = \mathbf{W}\mathbf{x}$. This implies that the distribution of the output y_i approximates a uniform density. Independence is achieved through the nonlinear squashing function which provides necessary higher-order statistics through its Taylor series expansion. The learning rule can be derived by maximizing output joint entropy, $H(\mathbf{y})$, with respect to $\mathbf{W}$ [3], giving,

$$\Delta \mathbf{W} \propto \frac{\partial H(\mathbf{y})}{\partial \mathbf{W}} \mathbf{W}^T \mathbf{W} = \left[\mathbf{I} + \hat{\mathbf{p}} \mathbf{u}^T \right] \mathbf{W} \tag{1}$$

where $\hat{p}_i = (\partial/\partial u_i) \ln(\partial y_i / \partial u_i)$. The 'natural gradient' $\mathbf{W}^T \mathbf{W}$ term [13] avoids matrix inversions and speeds convergence. The form of the nonlinearity $g(u)$ plays an essential role in the success of the algorithm. The ideal form for $g()$ is the cumulative density function (cdf) of the distributions of the independent sources. In practice, if we choose $g()$ to be a sigmoid function (as in [3]), the algorithm is then limited to separating sources with super-Gaussian distributions. An elegant way of generalizing the learning rule to sources with either sub- or super-Gaussian distributions is to approximate the estimated probability density function (pdf) in the form of a 4th-order Edgeworth approximation as derived by Girolami and Fyfe [14]. For sub-Gaussians, the following approximation is possible: $\hat{p}_i = + \tanh(u_i) - u_i$. For super-Gaussians, the same approximation becomes $\hat{p}_i = - \tanh(u_i) - u_i$. The sign can be chosen for each component using its normalized kurtosis, $k_4(u_i)$, giving,

$$\Delta \mathbf{W} \propto \frac{\partial H(\mathbf{y})}{\partial \mathbf{W}} \mathbf{W}^T \mathbf{W} = \left[\mathbf{I} - \text{sign}(k_4) \tanh(\mathbf{u}) \mathbf{u}^T - \mathbf{u} \mathbf{u}^T \right] \mathbf{W} \tag{2}$$

Intuitively, for super-Gaussians the $- \tanh(\mathbf{u})\mathbf{u}^T$ term is an anti-Hebbian rule that tends to minimize the variance of $\mathbf{u}$, whereas for sub-Gaussians the corresponding term is a Hebbian rule that tends to maximize its variance.

2.1   Applying ICA to artifact correction

The ICA algorithm is effective in performing source separation in domains where, (1) the mixing medium is linear and propagation delays are negligible, (2) the time courses of the sources are independent, and (3) the number of sources is the same as the number of sensors, meaning if we employ N sensors the ICA algorithm can separate N sources [3, 4, 12]. In the case of EEG signals [12], volume conduction is thought to be linear and instantaneous, hence assumption (1) is satisfied. Assumption (2) is also reasonable because the sources of eye and muscle activity, line noise, and cardiac signals are not generally time locked to the sources of EEG activity which is thought to reflect activity of cortical neurons. Assumption (3) is questionable since we do not know the effective number of statistically-independent signals contributing to the scalp EEG. However, numerical simulations have confirmed that the ICA algorithm can accurately identify the time courses of activation and the scalp topographies of relatively large and temporally-independent sources from simulated scalp recordings, even in the presence of a large number of low-level and temporally-independent source activities [16].

For EEG analysis, the rows of the input matrix $\mathbf{x}$ are the EEG signals recorded at different electrodes, the rows of the output data matrix $\mathbf{u} = \mathbf{W}\mathbf{x}$ are time courses of activation of the ICA components, and the columns of the inverse matrix, $\mathbf{W}^{-1}$, give the projection strengths of the respective components onto the scalp sensors. The scalp topographies of the components provide evidence for their biological origin (e.g., eye activity should project mainly to frontal sites). In general, and unlike PCA, the component time courses of activation will be nonorthogonal. 'Corrected' EEG signals can then be derived as $\mathbf{x}' = (\mathbf{W})^{-1}\mathbf{u}'$, where $\mathbf{u}'$ is the matrix of activation waveforms, $\mathbf{u}$, with rows representing artifactual sources set to zero.

3   Methods and Materials

One EEG data set used in the analysis was collected from 20 scalp electrodes placed according to the International 10-20 System and from 2 EOG placements, all referred to the left mastoid. A second EEG data set contained 19 EEG channels (no EOG channel). Data were recorded with a sampling rate of 256 Hz. ICA decomposition was performed on 10-sec EEG epochs from each data set using Matlab 4.2c on a DEC 2100A 5/300 processor. The learning batch size was 90, and initial learning rate was 0.001. Learning rate was gradually reduced to 5×10^{-6} during 80 training iterations requiring 6.6 min of computer time. To evaluate the relative effectiveness of ICA for artifact removal, the multiple-lag regression method of Kenemans et al. [17] was performed on the same data.

4   Results

4.1   Eye movement artifacts

Figure 1 shows a 3-sec portion of the recorded EEG time series and its ICA component activations, the scalp topographies of four selected components, and the 'corrected' EEG signals obtained by removing four selected EOG and muscle noise components from the data. The eye movement artifact at 1.8 sec in the EEG data (*left*) is isolated to ICA components 1 and 2 (*left middle*). The scalp maps (*right middle*) indicate that these two components account for the spread of EOG activity to frontal sites. After eliminating these two components and projecting the remaining components onto the scalp channels, the 'corrected' EEG data (*right*) are free of these artifacts.

Removing EOG activity from frontal channels reveals alpha activity near 8 Hz that occurred during the eye movement but was obscured by the eye movement artifact in the original EEG traces. Close inspection of the EEG records (Fig. 1b) confirms its presence in the raw data. ICA also reveals the EEG 'contamination' appearing in the EOG electrodes (*right*). By contrast, the 'corrected' EEG resulting from multiple-lag regression on this data shows no sign of 8 Hz activity at Fp1 (Fig. 1b). Here, regression was performed only when the artifact was detected (1-sec surrounding the EOG peak), since otherwise a large amount of EEG activity would also have been regressed out during periods without eye movements.

4.2   Muscle artifacts

Left and right temporal muscle activity in the data are concentrated in ICA components 14 and 15 (Fig. 1a, *right middle*). Removing them from the data (*right*) reveals underlying EEG activity at temporal sites T3 and T4 that had been masked by muscle activity in the raw data (*left*). The signal at T3 (Fig. 1c *left*) sums muscle activity from component 14 (*center*) and underlying EEG activity. Spectral analysis of the two records (*right*) shows a large amount of overlap between their power spectra, so bandpass filtering cannot separate them. ICA component 13 (Fig. 1a, *left middle*) reveals the presence of small periodic muscle spiking (in right frontal channels, map not shown) that is highly obscured in the original data (*left*).

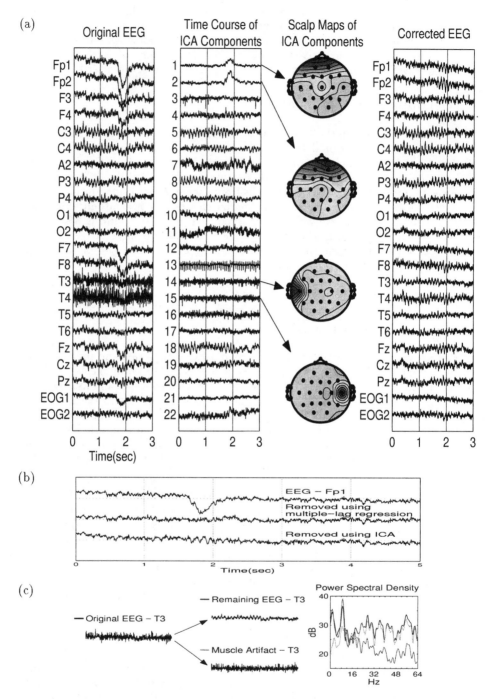

Figure 1: A 3-sec portion of an EEG time series (*left*), corresponding ICA components activations (*left middle*), scalp maps of four selected components (*right middle*), and EEG signals corrected for artifacts according to: (a) ICA with the four selected components removed (*right*), or (b) multiple-lag regression on the two EOG channels. ICA cancels multiple artifacts in all the EEG and EOG channels simultaneously. (c) The EEG record at T3 (*left*) is the sum of EEG activity recorded over the left temporal region and muscle activity occurring near the electrode (*center*). Below 20 Hz, the spectra of remaining EEG (dashed line) and muscle artifact (dotted line) overlap strongly, whereas ICA separates them by spatial filtering.

4.3   Cardiac contamination and line noise

Figure 2 shows a 5-sec portion of a second EEG time series, five ICA components that represent artifactual sources, and 'corrected' EEG signals obtained by removing these components. Eye blink artifacts at 0.5, 2.0 and 4.7 sec (*left*) are detected and isolated to ICA component 1 (*middle left*), even though the training data contains no EOG reference channel. The scalp map of the component captures the spread of EOG activity to frontal sites. Component 5 represents horizontal eye movements, while component 2 reveals the presence of small periodic muscle spiking in left frontal channels which is hard to see in the raw data. Line noise has a sub-Gaussian distribution and so could not be clearly isolated by earlier versions of the algorithm [3, 12]. By contrast, the new algorithm effectively concentrates the line noise present in nearly all the channels into ICA component 3. The widespread cardiac contamination in the EEG data (*left*) is concentrated in ICA component 4. After eliminating these five artifactual components, the 'corrected' EEG data (*right*) are largely free of these artifacts.

5   Discussion and Conclusions

ICA appears to be an effective and generally applicable method for removing known artifacts from EEG records. There are several advantages of the method: (1) ICA is computationally efficient. Although it requires more computation than the algorithm used in [15, 12], the extended ICA algorithm is effective even on large EEG data sets. (2) ICA is generally applicable to removal of a wide variety of EEG artifacts. (3) A simple analysis simultaneously separates both the EEG and its artifacts into independent components based on the statistics of the data, without relying on the availability of 'clean' reference channels. This avoids the problem of mutual contamination between regressing and regressed channels. (4) No arbitrary thresholds (variable across sessions) are needed to determine when regression should be performed. (5) Once the training is complete, artifact-free EEG records can then be derived by eliminating the contributions of the artifactual sources. However, the results of ICA are meaningful only when the amount of data and number of channels are large enough. Future work should determine the minimum data length and number of channels needed to remove artifacts of various types.

Acknowlegement

This report was supported in part by grants from the Office of Naval Research. The views expressed in this article are those of the authors and do not reflect the official policy or position of the Department of the Navy, Department of Defense, or the U.S. Government. Dr. McKeown is supported by a grant from the Heart & Stroke Foundation of Ontario.

References

[1] J.F. Peters (1967). Surface electrical fields generated by eye movement and eye blink potentials over the scalp, *J. EEG Technol.*, **7**:27-40.

[2] P.J. Oster & J.A. Stern (1980). Measurement of eye movement electrooculography, In: *Techniques in Psychophysiology*, Wiley, Chichester, 275-309.

[3] A.J. Bell & T.J. Sejnowski (1995). An information-maximization approach to blind separation and blind deconvolution, *Neural Computation* **7**:1129-1159.

[4] T.W. Lee and T. Sejnowski (1997). Independent Component Analysis for Sub-Gaussian and Super-Gaussian Mixtures, *Proc. 4th Joint Symp. Neural Computation* **7**:132-9.

[5] P. Berg & M. Scherg (1991) Dipole models of eye movements and blinks, *Electroencephalog. clin. Neurophysiolog.* **79**:36-44.

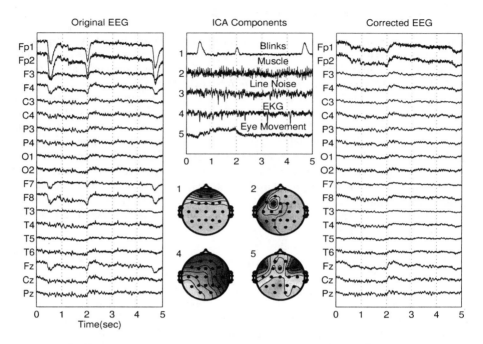

Figure 2: (*left*) A 5-sec portion of an EEG time series. (*center*) ICA components accounting for eye movements, cardiac signals, and line noise sources. (*right*) The same EEG signals 'corrected' for artifacts by removing the five selected components.

[6] S.A. Hillyard & R. Galambos (1970). Eye-movement artifact in the CNV, *Electroencephalog. clin. Neurophysiolog.* **28**:173-182.

[7] R. Verleger, T. Gasser & J. Möcks (1982). Correction of EOG artifacts in event-related potentials of EEG: Aspects of reliability and validity, *Psychoph.*, **19**(4):472-80.

[8] J.L. Whitton, F. Lue & H. Moldofsky (1978). A spectral method for removing eye-movement artifacts from the EEG. *Electroencephalog. clin. Neurophysiolog.* 44:735-41.

[9] J.C. Woestenburg, M.N. Verbaten & J.L. Slangen (1983). The removal of the eye-movement artifact from the EEG by regression analysis in the frequency domain, *Biological Psychology* **16**:127-47.

[10] T.C. Weerts & P.J. Lang (1973). The effects of eye fixation and stimulus and response location on the contingent negative variation (CNV), *Biological Psychology* 1(1):1-19.

[11] D.A. Overton & C. Shagass (1969). Distribution of eye movement and eye blink potentials over the scalp, *Electroencephalog. clin. Neurophysiolog.* 27:546.

[12] S. Makeig, A.J. Bell, T-P Jung, T.J. Sejnowski (1996) Independent Component Analysis of Electroencephalographic Data, In: *Advances in Neural Information Processing Systems* 8:145-51.

[13] S. Amari, A. Cichocki & H. Yang (1996) A new learning algorithm for blind signal separation, In: *Advances in Neural Information Processing Systems*, 8:757-63.

[14] M Girolami & C Fyfe (1997) Generalized Independent Component Analysis through Unsupervised Learning with Emergent Bussgang Properties, in *Proc. IEEE International Conference on Neural Networks*, 1788-91.

[15] A.J. Bell & T.J. Sejnowski (1995). Fast blind separation based on information theory, in *Proc. Intern. Symp. on Nonlinear Theory and Applications (NOLTA)* 1:43-7.

[16] S. Makeig, T-P Jung, D. Ghahremani & T.J. Sejnowski (1996). *Independent Component Analysis of Simulated ERP Data*, Tech. Rep. INC-9606, Institute for Neural Computation, San Diego, CA.

[17] J.L. Kenemans, P. Molenaar, M.N. Verbaten & J.L. Slangen (1991). Removal of the ocular artifact from the EEG: a comparison of time and frequency domain methods with simulated and real data, *Psychoph.*, **28**(1):114-21.

A Generic Approach for Identification of Event Related Brain Potentials via a Competitive Neural Network Structure

Daniel H. Lange
Department of Electrical Engineering
Technion - IIT
Haifa 32000
Israel
e-mail: lange@turbo.technion.ac.il

Hava T. Siegelmann
Department of Industrial Engineering
Technion - IIT
Haifa 32000
Israel
e-mail: iehava@ie.technion.ac.il

Hillel Pratt
Evoked Potential Laboratory
Technion - IIT
Haifa 32000
Israel
e-mail: hillel@tx.technion.ac.il

Gideon F. Inbar
Department of Electrical Engineering
Technion - IIT
Haifa 32000
Israel
e-mail: inbar@ee.technion.ac.il

Abstract

We present a novel generic approach to the problem of Event Related Potential identification and classification, based on a competitive Neural Net architecture. The network weights converge to the embedded signal patterns, resulting in the formation of a *matched filter* bank. The network performance is analyzed via a simulation study, exploring identification robustness under low SNR conditions and compared to the expected performance from an information theoretic perspective. The classifier is applied to real event-related potential data recorded during a classic *odd-ball* type paradigm; for the first time, within-session variable signal patterns are automatically identified, dismissing the strong and limiting requirement of *a-priori* stimulus-related selective grouping of the recorded data.

1   INTRODUCTION

1.1   EVENT RELATED POTENTIALS

Ever since Hans Berger's discovery that the electrical activity of the brain can be measured and recorded via surface electrodes mounted on the scalp, there has been major interest in the relationship between such recordings and brain function. The first recordings were concerned with the spontaneous electrical activity of the brain, appearing in the form of rhythmic voltage oscillations, which later received the term *electroencephalogram* or *EEG*. Subsequently, more recent research has concentrated on time-locked brain activity, related to specific events, external or internal to the subject. This time-locked activity, referred to also as Event Related Potentials (ERP's), is regarded as a manifestation of brain processes related to preparation for or in response to discrete events meaningful to the subject.

The ongoing electrical activity of the brain, the EEG, is comprised of relatively slow fluctuations, in the range of 0.1 - 100 Hz, with magnitudes of 10 - 100 uV. ERP's are characterized by overlapping spectra with the EEG, but with significantly lower magnitudes of 0.1 - 10 uV. The unfavorable Signal to Noise Ratio (SNR) requires filtering of the raw signals to enable analysis of the time-locked signals. The common method used for this purpose is signal averaging, synchronized to repeated occurrences of a specific event. Averaging-based techniques assume a deterministic signal within the averaged session, and thus signal variability can not be modeled unless *a-priori* stimulus- or response-based categorization is available; it is the purpose of this paper to provide an alternative working method to enhance conventional averaging techniques, and thus facilitating identification and analysis of variable brain responses.

1.2   COMPETITIVE LEARNING

Competitive learning is a well-known branch of the general unsupervised learning theme. The elementary principles of competitive learning are (Rumelhart & Zipser, 1985): (a) start with a set of units that are all the same except for some randomly distributed parameter which makes each of them respond slightly differently to a set of input patterns, (b) limit the strength of each unit, and (c) allow the units to compete in some way for the right to respond to a given subset of inputs. Applying these three principles yields a learning paradigm where individual units learn to specialize on sets of similar patterns and thus become *feature detectors*. Competitive learning is a mechanism well-suited for regularity detection (Haykin, 1994), where there is a population of input patterns each of which is presented with some probability. The detector is supposed to discover statistically salient features of the input population, without *a-priori* categorization into which the patterns are to be classified. Thus the detector needs to develop its own featural representation of the population of input patterns capturing its most salient features.

1.3   PROBLEM STATEMENT

The complicated, generally unknown relationships between the stimulus and its associated brain response, and the extremely low SNR of the brain responses which are practically *masked* by the background brain activity, make the choice of a self organizing structure for post-stimulus epoch analysis most appropriate. The competitive network, having the property that its weights converge to the actual embedded signal patterns while inherently averaging out the additive background EEG, is thus an evident choice.

2 THE COMPETITIVE NEURAL NETWORK

2.1 THEORY

The common architecture of a competitive learning system appears in Fig. 1. The system consists of a set of hierarchically layered neurons in which each layer is connected via excitatory connections with the following layer. Within a layer, the neurons are divided into sets of inhibitory clusters in which all neurons within a cluster inhibit all other neurons in the cluster, which results in a competition among the neurons to respond to the pattern appearing on the previous layer.

Let w_{ji} denote the synaptic weight connecting input node i to neuron j. A neuron learns by shifting synaptic weights from its inactive to active input nodes. If a neuron does not respond to some input pattern, no learning occurs in that neuron. When a single neuron wins the competition, each of its input nodes gives up some proportion of its synaptic weight, which is distributed equally among the active input nodes, fulfilling: $\sum_i w_{ji} = 1$. According to the standard competitive learning rule, for a winning neuron to an input vector x_i, the change Δw_{ji} is defined by: $\Delta w_{ji} = \eta(x_i - w_{ji})$, where η is a learning rate coefficient. The effect of this rule is that the synaptic weights of a winning neuron are shifted towards the input pattern; thus assuming zero-mean additive background EEG, once converged, the network operates as a *matched filter* bank classifier.

2.2 MATCHED FILTERING

From an information theoretic perspective, once the network has converged, our classification problem coincides with the general detection problem of known signals in additive noise. For simplicity, we shall limit the discussion to the binary decision problem of a known signal in additive white Gaussian noise, expandable to the M-ary detection in colored noise (Van Trees, 1968).

Adopting the common assumption of EEG and ERP additivity (Gevins, 1984), and distinct signal categories, the competitive NN weights inherently converge to the general signal patterns embedded within the background brain activity; therefore the converged network operates as a *matched filter* bank. Assuming the simplest binary decision problem, the received signal under one hypothesis consists of a completely known signal, $\sqrt{E}s(t)$, representing the EP, corrupted by an additive zero-mean Gaussian noise $w(t)$ with variance σ^2; the received signal under the other hypothesis consists of the noise $w(t)$ alone. Thus:

$$H_0 : \quad r(t) = w(t), \qquad\qquad 0 \le t \le T$$
$$H_1 : \quad r(t) = \sqrt{E}s(t) + w(t), \quad 0 \le t \le T$$

For convenience we assume that $\int_0^T s^2(t)dt = 1$, so that E represents the signal energy. The problem is to observe $r(t)$ over the interval $[0, T]$ and decide whether H_0 or H_1 is true. It can be shown that the *matched filter* is the optimal detector, its impulse response being simply the signal reversed in time and shifted:

$$h(\tau) = s(T - \tau) \tag{1}$$

Assuming that there is no *a-priori* knowledge of the probability of signal presence, the total probability of error depends only on the SNR and is given by (Van Trees, 1968):

$$Pe = \frac{1}{\sqrt{2\pi}} \int_{\sqrt{\frac{E}{\sigma^2}}}^{\infty} \exp(-\frac{x^2}{2})dx \tag{2}$$

Fig. 2 presents the probability of true detection: (a) as a function of SNR, for minimized error probability, and (b) as a function of the probability of false detection. These results are applicable to our detection problem assuming approximate Gaussian EEG characteristics (Gersch, 1970), or optimally by using a pre-whitening approach (Lange et. al., 1997).

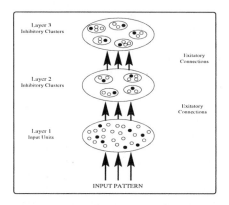

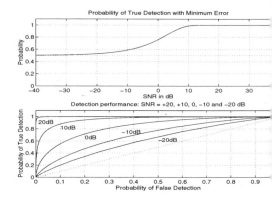

Figure 1: *The architecture of a compet-itive learning structure: learning takes place in hierarchically layered units, presented as filled (active) and empty (inactive) dots.*

Figure 2: *Detection performance. Top: probability of detection as a function of the SNR. Bottom: detection character-istics.*

2.3   NETWORK TRAINING AND CONVERGENCE

Our net includes a 300-node input layer and a competitive layer consisting of single-layered competing neurons. The network weights are initialized with random values and trained with the standard competitive learning rule, applied to the normalized input vectors:

$$\Delta w_{ji} = \eta \left(\frac{x_i}{\sum_i x_i} - w_{ji} \right) \tag{3}$$

The training is applied to the winning neuron of each epoch, while increasing the bias of the frequently winning neuron to gradually reduce its chance of winning consecutively (eliminating the *dead neuron* effect (Freeman & Skapura, 1992)). Symmetrically, its bias is reduced with the winnings of other neurons.

In order to evaluate the network performance, we explore its convergence by analyzing the learning process via the continuously adapting weights:

$$\rho_j(n) = \sqrt{\sum_i \Delta w_{ji}^2} \quad ; \quad j = 1, 2, ..., C \tag{4}$$

where C represents the pre-defined number of categories. We define a set of classifica-tion confidence coefficients of the converged network:

$$\Gamma_j = 1 - \frac{\rho_j(N)}{\max_j \{\rho_j(N)\}} \tag{5}$$

Assuming existence of a null category, in which the measurements include only back-ground noise (EEG), $\max_j\{\rho_j(N)\}$ corresponds to the noise variance. Thus the values of Γ_j, the confidence coefficients, ranging from 0 to 1 (random classification to com-pletely separated categories), indicate the reliability of classification, which breaks down with the fall of SNR. Finally, it should be noted that an explicit statistical evaluation of the network convergence properties can be found in (Lange, 1997).

2.4 SIMULATION STUDY

A simulation study was carried out to assess the performance of the competitive network classification system. A moving average (MA) process of order 8 (selected according to Akaike's condition applied to ongoing EEG (Gersch, 1970)), driven by a deterministic realization of a Gaussian white noise series, simulated the ongoing background activity $x(n)$. An average of 40 single-trials from a cognitive odd-ball type experiment (to be explained in the Experimental Study), was used as the signal $s(n)$. Then, five 100-trial ensembles were synthesized, to study the classification performance under variable SNR conditions. A sample realization and its constituents, at an SNR of 0 dB, is shown in Fig. 3. The simulation included embedding the signal $s(n)$ in the synthesized background activity $x(n)$ at five SNR levels (-20,-10,0,+10, and +20 dB), and training the network with 750 sweeps (per SNR level). Fig. 4 shows the convergence patterns and classification confidences of the two neurons, where it can be seen that for SNR's lower than $-10dB$ the classification confidence declines sharply.

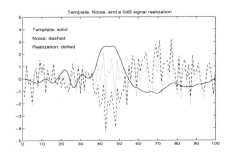

Figure 3: *A sample single realization (dotted) and its constituents (signal - solid, noise - dashed). SNR = 0 dB.*

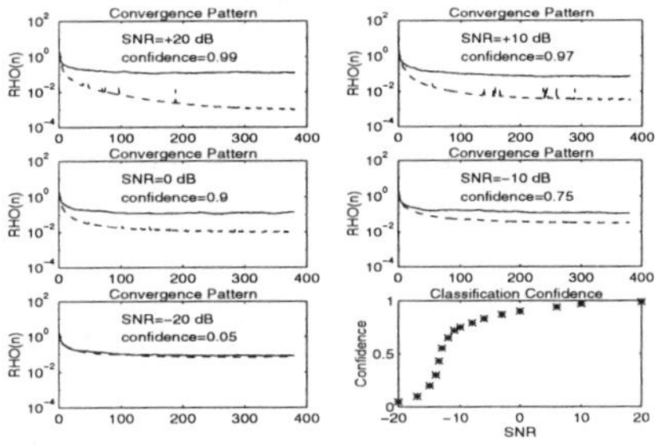

Figure 4: *Convergence patterns and classification confidence values for varying SNR levels.*

The classification results, tested on 100 input vectors, 50 of each category, for each SNR, are presented in the table below; due to the competitive scheme, Positives and False Negatives as well as Negatives and False Positives are complementary. These empirical results are in agreement with the analytical results presented in the above Matched Filtering section.

Table 1: Classification Results

	Pos	Neg	FP	FN
snr=+20dB	100%	100%	0%	0%
snr=+10dB	100%	100%	0%	0%
snr= 0dB	100%	100%	0%	0%
snr=-10dB	88%	92%	8%	12%
snr=-20dB	58%	54%	46%	42%

3 EXPERIMENTAL STUDY

3.1 MOTIVATION

An important task in ERP research is to identify effects related to cognitive processes triggered by meaningful versus non-relevant stimuli. A common procedure to study these effects is the classic *odd-ball* paradigm, where the subject is exposed to a random sequence of stimuli and is instructed to respond only to the task-relevant (Target) ones. Typically, the brain responses are extracted via selective averaging of the recorded data, ensembled according to the types of related stimuli. This method of analysis assumes that the brain responds equally to the members of each type of stimulus; however the validity of this assumption is unknown in this case where cognition itself is being studied. Using our proposed approach, *a-priori* grouping of the recorded data is not required, thus overcoming the above severe assumption on cognitive brain function. The results of applying our method are described below.

3.2   EXPERIMENTAL PARADIGM

Cognitive event-related potential data was acquired during an odd-ball type paradigm from Pz referenced to the mid-lower jaw, with a sample frequency of 250 Hz (Lange et. al., 1995). The subject was exposed to repeated visual stimuli, consisting of the digits '3' and '5', appearing on a PC screen. The subject was instructed to press a push-button upon the appearance of '5' – the *Target* stimulus, and ignore the appearances of the digit '3'.

With odd-ball type paradigms, the Target stimulus is known to elicit a prominent positive component in the ongoing brain activity, related to the identification of a meaningful stimulus. This component has been labeled P_{300}, indicating its polarity (positive) and timing of appearance (300 ms after stimulus presentation). The parameters of the P_{300} component (latency and amplitude) are used by neurophysiologists to assess effects related to the relevance of stimulus and level of attention (Lange et. al., 1995).

3.3   IDENTIFICATION RESULTS

The competitive network was trained with 80 input vectors, half of which were Target ERP's and the other half were Non Target. The network converged after approximately 300 iterations (per neuron), yielding a reasonable confidence coefficient of 0.7.

A sample of two single-trial post-stimulus sweeps, of the Target and Non-Target averaged ERP templates and of the NN identified signal categories, are presented in Fig. 5. The convergence pattern is shown in Fig. 6. The automatic identification procedure has provided two signal categories, with almost perfect matches to the stimulus-related selective averaged signals. The obtained categorization confirms the usage of averaging methods for this classic experiment, and thus presents an important result in itself.

4   DISCUSSION AND CONCLUSION

A generic system for identification and classification of single-trial ERP's was presented. The simulation study demonstrated the powerful capabilities of the competitive neural net in classifying the low amplitude signals embedded within the large background noise. The detection performance declined rapidly for SNR's lower than $-10dB$, which is in general agreement with the theoretical statistical results, where loss of significance in detection probability is evident for SNR's lower than $-20dB$. Empirically, high classification performance was maintained with SNR's of down to $-10dB$, yielding confidences in the order of 0.7 or higher.

The experimental study presented an unsupervised identification and classification of the raw data into Target and Non-Target responses, dismissing the requirement of stimulus-related selective data grouping. The presented results indicate that the noisy brain responses may be identified and classified objectively in cases where relevance of the stimuli is unknown or needs to be determined, e.g. in lie-detection scenarios (Lange & Inbar, 1996), and thus open new possibilities in ERP research.

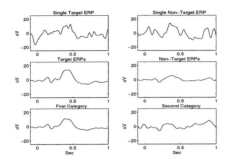

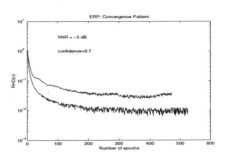

Figure 5: *Top row: sample raw Target and Non-Target sweeps. Middle row: Target and Non-Target ERP templates. Bottom row: the NN categorized patterns.*

Figure 6: *Convergence pattern of the ERP categorization process; convergence is achieved after 300 iterations per neuron.*

References

[1] Freeman J.A. and Skapura D.M. *Neural Networks: Algorithms, Applications, and Programming Techniques:* Addison-Wesley Publishing Company, USA, 1992.

[2] Gersch W., "Spectral Analysis of EEG's by Autoregressive Decomposition of Time Series," *Math. Biosc.,* vol. 7, pp. 205-222, 1970.

[3] Gevins A.S., "Analysis of the Electromagnetic Signals of the Human Brain: Milestones, Obstacles, and Goals," *IEEE Trans. Biomed. Eng.,* vol. BME-31, pp. 833-850, 1984.

[4] Haykin S. *Neural Networks: A Comprehensive Foundation.* Macmillan College Publishing Company, Inc., USA, 1994.

[5] Lange D. H. *Modeling and Estimation of Transient, Evoked Brain Potentials.* D.Sc. dissertation, Techion - Israel Institute of Technology, 1997.

[6] Lange D.H. and Inbar G.F., "Brain Wave Based Polygraphy," *Proceedings of the IEEE EMBS96 - the 18th Annual International Conference of the IEEE Engineering on Medicine and Biology Society,* Amsterdam, October 1996.

[7] Lange D.H., Pratt H. and Inbar G.F., "Modeling and Estimation of Single Evoked Brain Potential Components", *IEEE. Trans. Biomed. Eng.,* vol. BME-44, pp. 791-799, 1997.

[8] Lange D.H., Pratt H., and Inbar G.F., "Segmented Matched Filtering of Single Event Related Evoked Potentials," *IEEE. Trans. Biomed. Eng.,* vol. BME-42, pp. 317-321, 1995.

[9] Rumelhart D.E. and Zipser D., "Feature Discovery by Competitive Learning," *Cognitive Science,* vol. 9, pp. 75-112, 1985.

[10] Van Trees H.L. *Detection, Estimation, and Modulation Theory: Part 1:* John Wiley and Sons, Inc., USA, 1968.

A Neural Network Based Head Tracking System

D. D. Lee and H. S. Seung
Bell Laboratories, Lucent Technologies
700 Mountain Ave.
Murray Hill, NJ 07974
{ddlee|seung}@bell-labs.com

Abstract

We have constructed an inexpensive, video-based, motorized tracking system that learns to track a head. It uses real time graphical user inputs or an auxiliary infrared detector as supervisory signals to train a convolutional neural network. The inputs to the neural network consist of normalized luminance and chrominance images and motion information from frame differences. Subsampled images are also used to provide scale invariance. During the online training phase, the neural network rapidly adjusts the input weights depending upon the reliability of the different channels in the surrounding environment. This quick adaptation allows the system to robustly track a head even when other objects are moving within a cluttered background.

1 Introduction

With the proliferation of inexpensive multimedia computers and peripheral equipment, video conferencing finally appears ready to enter the mainstream. But personal video conferencing systems typically use a stationary camera, tying the user to a fixed location much as a corded telephone tethers one to the telephone jack. A simple solution to this problem is to use a motorized video camera that can track a specific person as he or she moves about. However, this presents the difficulty of having to continually control the movements of the camera while one is communicating. In this paper, we present a prototype, neural network based system that learns the characteristics of a person's head in real time and automatically tracks it around the room, thus alleviating the user of much of this burden.

The camera movements in this video conferencing system closely resemble the movements of human eyes. The task of the biological oculomotor system is to direct

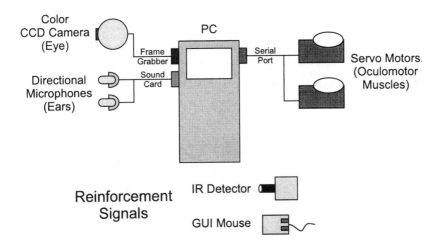

Figure 1: Schematic hardware diagram of Marvin, our head tracking system.

"interesting" parts of the visual world onto the small, high resolution areas of the retinas. For this task, complex neural circuits have evolved in order to control the eye movements. Some examples include the saccadic and smooth pursuit systems that allow the eyes to rapidly acquire and track moving objects [1, 2]. Similarly, an active video conferencing system also needs to determine the appropriate face or feature to follow in the video stream. Then the camera must track that person's movements over time and transmit the image to the other party.

In the past few years, the problem of face detection in images and video has attracted considerable attention [3, 4, 5]. Rule-based methods have concentrated on looking for generic characteristics of faces such as oval shapes or skin hue. Since these types of algorithms are fairly simple to implement, they are commonly found in real-time systems [6, 7]. But because other objects have similar shapes and colors as faces, these systems can also be easily fooled. A potentially more robust approach is to use a convolutional neural network to learn the appropriate features of a face [8, 9]. Because most such implementations learn in batch mode, they are beset by the difficulty of constructing a large enough training set of labelled images with and without faces. In this paper, we present a video based system that uses online supervisory signals to train a convolutional neural network. Fast online adaptation of the network's weights allows the neural network to learn how to discriminate an individual head at the beginning of a session. This enables the system to robustly track the head even in the presence of other moving objects.

2 Hardware Implementation

Figure 1 shows a schematic of the tracking system we have constructed and have named "Marvin" because of an early version's similarity to a cartoon character. Marvin's eye consists of a small CCD camera with a 65° field of view that is attached to a motorized platform. Two RC servo motors give Marvin the ability to rapidly pan and tilt over a wide range of viewing angles, with a typical maximum velocity of 300 deg/sec. The system also includes two microphones or ears that give Marvin the ability to locate auditory cues. Integrating auditory information with visual inputs allows the system to find salient objects better than with either sound or video alone. But these proceedings will focus exclusively on how a visual representation is learned.

RGB Images

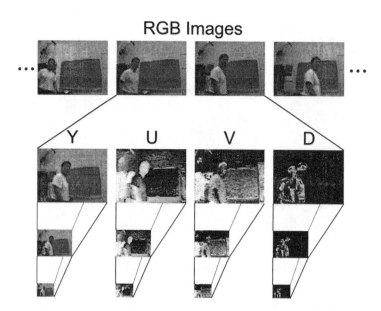

Figure 2: Preprocessing of the video stream. Luminance, chromatic and motion information are separately represented in the Y, U, V, D channels at multiple resolutions.

Marvin is able to learn to track a visual target using two different sources of supervisory signals. One method of training uses a small 38 KHz modulated infrared light emitter ($\lambda \approx 900\,\text{nm}$) attached to the object that needs to be tracked. A heat filter renders the infrared light invisible to Marvin's video camera so that the system does not merely learn to follow this signal. But mounted next to the CCD camera and moving with it is a small infrared detector with a collimating lens that signals when the object is located within a narrow angular cone in the direction that the camera is pointing. This reinforcement signal can then be used to train the weights of the neural network. Another more natural way for the system to learn occurs in an actual video conferencing scenario. In this situation, a user who is actively watching the video stream has manual override control of the camera using graphical user interface inputs. Whenever the user repositions the camera to a new location, the neural network would then adjust its weights to track whatever is in the center portion of the image.

Since Marvin was built from readily available commercial components, the cost of the system not including the PC was under $500. The input devices and motors are all controlled by the computer using custom-written Matlab drivers that are available for both Microsoft Windows and the Linux operating system. The image processing computations as well as the graphical user interface are then easily implemented as simple Matlab operations and function calls. The following section describes the head tracking neural network in more detail.

3 Neural Network Architecture

Marvin uses a convolutional neural network architecture to detect a head within its field of view. The video stream from the CCD camera is first digitized with a video capture board into a series of raw 120×160 RGB images as shown in Figure 2. Each RGB color image is then converted into its YUV representation, and a difference (D)

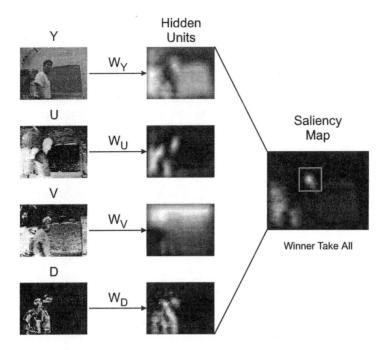

Figure 3: Neural network uses a convolutional architecture to integrate the different sources of information and determine the maximally salient object.

image is also computed as the absolute value of the difference from the preceding frame. Of the four resulting images, the Y component represents the luminance or grayscale information while the U and V channels contain the chromatic or color information. Motion information in the video stream is captured by the D image where moving objects appear highlighted.

The four YUVD channels are then subsampled successively to yield representations at lower and lower resolutions. The resulting "image pyramids" allow the network to achieve recognition invariance across many different scales without having to train separate neural networks for each resolution. Instead, a single neural network with the same set weights is run with the different resolutions as inputs, and the maximally active resolution and position is selected.

Marvin uses the convolutional neural network architecture shown in Figure 3 to locate salient objects at the different resolutions. The YUVD input images are filtered with separate 16×16 kernels, denoted by W_Y, W_U, W_V, and W_D respectively. This results in the filtered images $\bar{Y}^s$, $\bar{U}^s$, $\bar{V}^s$, $\bar{D}^s$:

$$\bar{A}^s(i,j) = W_A \circ A^s = \sum_{i',j'} W_A(i',j') A^s(i+i',j+j') \tag{1}$$

where s denotes the scale resolution of the inputs, and A is any of the Y, U, V, or D channels. These filtered images represent a single layer of hidden units in the neural network. These hidden units are then combined to form the saliency map X^s in the following manner:

$$X^s(i,j) = c_Y \, g[\bar{Y}^s(i,j)] + c_U \, g[\bar{U}^s(i,j)] + c_V \, g[\bar{V}^s(i,j)] + c_D \, g[\bar{D}^s(i,j)] + c_0. \tag{2}$$

Since $g(x) = \tanh(x)$ is sigmoidal, the saliency X^s is computed as a nonlinear, pixel-by-pixel combination of the hidden units. The scalar variables c_Y, c_U, c_V, and c_D represent the relative importance of the different luminance, chromatic, and motion channels in the overall saliency of an object.

With the bias term c_0, the function $g[X^s(i,j)]$ may then be thought of as the relative probability that a head exists at location (i,j) at input resolution s. The final output of the neural network is then determined in a competitive manner by finding the location (i_m, j_m) and scale s_m of the best possible match:

$$g[X_m] = g[X^{s_m}(i_m, j_m)] = \max_{i,j,s} g[X^s(i,j)]. \tag{3}$$

After processing the visual inputs in this manner, saccadic camera movements are generated in order to keep the maximally salient object located near the center of the field of view.

4   Training and Results

Either GUI user inputs or the infrared detector may be used as a supervisory signal to train the kernels W_A and scalar weights c_A of the neural network. The neural network is updated when the maximally salient location of the neural network (i_m, j_m) does not correspond to the desired object's true position (i_n, j_n) as identified by the external supervisory signal. A cost function proportional to the sum squared error terms at the maximal location and new desired location is used for training:

$$e_m^2 \;=\; |g_m - g[X^{s_m}(i_m, j_m)]|^2, \tag{4}$$

$$e_n^2 \;=\; \min_s |g_n - g[X^s(i_n, j_n)]|^2. \tag{5}$$

In the following examples, the constants $g_m = 0$ and $g_n = 1$ are used. The gradients to Eqs. 4–5 are then backpropagated through the convolutional network [8, 10], resulting in the following update rules:

$$\Delta c_A \;=\; \eta\, e_m g'(X_m) g[\bar{A}(i_m, j_m)] + \eta\, e_n g'(X_n) g[\bar{A}(i_n, j_n)], \tag{6}$$

$$\Delta W_A \;=\; \eta\, e_m g'(X_m) g'(\bar{A}_m) c_A A_m + \eta\, e_n g'(X_n) g'(\bar{A}_n) c_A A_n. \tag{7}$$

In typical batch learning applications of neural networks, the learning rate η is set to be some small positive number. However in this case, it is desirable for Marvin to learn to track a head in a new environment as quickly as possible. Thus, rapid adaptation of the weights during even a single training example is needed. A natural way of doing this is to use a fairly large learning rate ($\eta = 0.1$), and to repeatedly apply the update rules in Eqs. 6–7 until the calculated maximally salient location is very close to the actual desired position.

An example of how quickly Marvin is able to learn to track one of the authors as he moved around his office is given by the learning curve in Figure 4. The weights were first initialized to small random values, and Marvin was corrected in an online fashion using mouse inputs to look at the author's head. After only a few seconds of training with a processing time loop of around 200 ms, the system was able to locate the head to within four pixels of accuracy, as determined by hand labelling the video data afterwards. As saccadic eye movements were initiated at

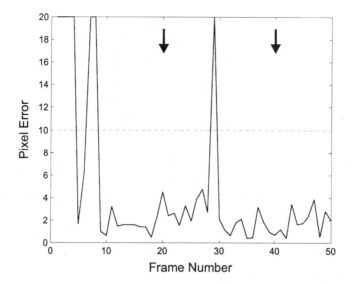

Figure 4: Fast online adaptation of the neural network. The head location error in pixels in a 120×160 image is plotted as a function of frame number (5 frames/sec).

the times indicated by the arrows in Fig. 4, new environments of the office were sampled and an occasional large error is seen. However, over time as these errors are corrected, the neural network learns to robustly discriminate the head from the office surroundings.

5 Discussion

Figure 5 shows the inputs and weights of the network after a minute of training as the author walked around his office. The kernels necessarily appear a little smeared because they are invariant to slight changes in head position, rotation, and scale. But they clearly depict the dark hair, facial features, and skin color of the head. The relative weighting $(c_Y, c_U, c_V > c_D)$ of the different input channels shows that the luminance and color information are the most reliable for tracking the head. This is probably because it is relatively difficult to distinguish in the frame difference images the head from other moving body parts.

We are currently considering more complicated neural network architectures for combining the different input streams to give better tracking performance. However, this example shows how a simple convolutional architecture can be used to automatically integrate different visual cues to robustly track a head. Moreover, by using fast online adaptation of the neural network weights, the system is able to learn without needing large hand-labelled training sets and is also able to rapidly accomodate changing environments. Future improvements in hardware and neural network architectures and algorithms are still necessary, however, in order to approach human speeds and performance in this type of sensory processing and recognition task.

We acknowledge the support of Bell Laboratories, Lucent Technologies. We also thank M. Fee, A. Jacquin, S. Levinson, E. Petajan, G. Pingali, and E. Rietman for helpful discussions.

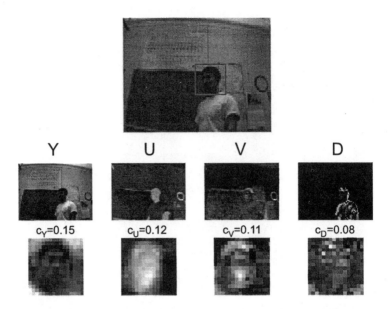

Figure 5: Example showing the inputs and weights used in tracking a head. The head position as calculated by the neural network is marked with a box.

References

[1] Horiuchi, TK, Bishofberger, B & Koch, C (1994). An analog VLSI saccadic eye movement system. *Advances in Neural Information Processing Systems 6*, 582–589.

[2] Rao, RPN, Zelinsky, GJ, Hayhoe, MM & Ballard, DH (1996). Modeling saccadic targeting in visual search. *Advances in Neural Information Processing Systems 8*, 830–836.

[3] Sung, KK & Poggio, T (1994). Example-based learning for view-based human face detection. *Proc. 23rd Image Understanding Workshop*, 843–850.

[4] Eleftheriadis, A & Jacquin, A (1995). Automatic face location detection and tracking for model-assisted coding of video teleconferencing sequences at low bit-rates. *Signal Processing: Image Communication* 7, 231.

[5] Petajan, E & Graf, HP (1996). Robust face feature analysis for automatic speechreading and character animation. *Proc. 2nd Int. Conf. Automatic Face and Gesture Recognition*, 357-362.

[6] Darrell, T, Maes, P, Blumberg, B, & Pentland, AP (1994). A novel environment for situated vision and behavior. *Proc. IEEE Workshop for Visual Behaviors*, 68–72.

[7] Yang, J & Waibel, A (1996). A real-time face tracker. *Proc. 3rd IEEE Workshop on Application of Computer Vision*, 142–147.

[8] Nowlan, SJ & Platt, JC (1995). A convolutional neural network hand tracker. *Advances in Neural Information Processing Systems 7*, 901–908.

[9] Rowley, HA, Baluja, S & Kanade, T (1996). Human face detection in visual scenes. *Advances in Neural Information Processing Systems 8*, 875–881.

[10] Le Cun, Y, et al. (1990). Handwritten digit recognition with a back propagation network. *Advances in Neural Information Processing Systems 2*, 396–404.

Wavelet Models for Video Time-Series

Sheng Ma and Chuanyi Ji
Department of Electrical, Computer, and Systems Engineering
Rensselaer Polytechnic Institute, Troy, NY 12180
e-mail: shengm@ecse.rpi.edu, chuanyi@ecse.rpi.edu

Abstract

In this work, we tackle the problem of time-series modeling of video traffic. Different from the existing methods which model the time-series in the time domain, we model the wavelet coefficients in the wavelet domain. The strength of the wavelet model includes (1) a unified approach to model both the long-range and the short-range dependence in the video traffic simultaneously, (2) a computationally efficient method on developing the model and generating high quality video traffic, and (3) feasibility of performance analysis using the model.

1 Introduction

As multi-media (compressed Variable Bit Rate (VBR) video, data and voice) traffic is expected to be the main loading component in future communication networks, accurate modeling of the multi-media traffic is crucial to many important applications such as video-conferencing and video-on-demand. From modeling standpoint, multi-media traffic can be regarded as a time-series, which can in principle be modeled by techniques in time-seres modeling. Modeling such a time-series, however, turns out to be difficult, since it has been found recently that real-time video and Ethernet traffic possesses the complicated temporal behavior which fails to be modeled by conventional methods[3][4]. One of the significant statistical properties found recently on VBR video traffic is the co-existence of the long-range (LRD) and the short-range (SRD) dependence (see for example [4][6] and references therein). Intuitively, this property results from scene changes, and suggests a complex behavior of video traffic in the time domain[7]. This complex temporal behavior makes accurate modeling of video traffic a challenging task. The goal of this work is to develop a unified and computationally efficient method to model both the long-range and the short-range dependence in real video sources.

Ideally, a good traffic model needs to be (*a*) accurate enough to characterize pertinent statistical properties in the traffic, (*b*) computationally efficient, and (*c*) feasible for the analysis needed for network design. The existing models developed to capture both the long-range and the short-range dependence include Fractional Auto-regressive Integrated Moving Average (FARIMA) models[4], a model based on Hosking's procedure[6], Transform-Expand-Sample (TES) model[9] and scene-based models[7]. All these methods model both LRD and SRD in the time domain. The scene-based modeling[7] provides a physically interpretable model feasible for analysis but difficult to be made very accurate. TES method is reasonably fast but too complex for the analysis. The rest of the methods suffer from computational complexity too high to be used to generate a large volume of synthesized video traffic.

To circumvent these problems, we will model the video traffic in the wavelet domain rather than in the time domain. Motivated by the previous work on wavelet representations of (the LRD alone) Fractional Gaussian Noise (FGN) process (see [2] and references therein), we will show in this paper simple wavelet models can simultaneously capture the short-range and the long-rage dependence through modeling two video traces. Intuitively, this is due to the fact that the (deterministic) similar structure of wavelets provides a natural match to the (statistical) self-similarity of the long-range dependence. Then wavelet coefficients at each time scale is modeled based on simple statistics. Since wavelet transforms and inverse transforms is in the order of $O(N)$, our approach will be able to attain the lowest computational complexity to generate wavelet models. Furthermore, through our theoretical analysis on the buffer loss rate, we will also demonstrate the feasibility of using wavelet models for theoretical analysis.

1.1 Wavelet Transforms

In $L^2(R)$ space, discrete wavelets $\phi_j^m(t)$'s are ortho-normal basis which can be represented as $\phi_j^m(t) = 2^{-j/2}\phi(2^{-j}t - m)$, for $t \in [0, 2^K - 1]$ with $K \geq 1$ being an integer. $\phi(t)$ is the so-called mother wavelet. $1 \leq j \leq K$ and $0 \leq m \leq 2^{K-j} - 1$ represent the time-scale and the time-shift, respectively. Since wavelets are the dilation and shift of a mother wavelet, they possess a deterministic similar structure at different time scales. For simplicity, the mother wavelet in this work is chosen to be the Haar wavelet, where $\phi(t)$ is 1 for $0 \leq t < 1/2$, -1 for $1/2 \leq t < 1$ and 0 otherwise.

Let d_j^m's be wavelet coefficients of a discrete-time process $x(t)$ ($t \in [0, 2^K - 1]$). Then d_j^m can be obtained through the wavelet transform $d_j^m = \sum_{t=0}^{2^K - 1} x(t)\phi_j^m(t)$. $x(t)$ can be represented through the inverse wavelet transform $x(t) = \sum_{j=1}^{K} \sum_{m=0}^{2^{K-j}-1} d_j^m \phi_j^m(t) + \phi_0$, where ϕ_0 is equal to the average of $x(t)$.

2   Wavelet Modeling of Video Traffic

2.1   The Video Sources

Two video sources are used to test our wavelet models: (1) "Star Wars"[4], where each frame is encoded by JPEG-like encoder, and (2) MPEG coded videos at Group of Pictures (GOP) level[7][11] called "MPEG GOP" in the rest of the paper. The modeling is done at either the frame level or the GOP level.

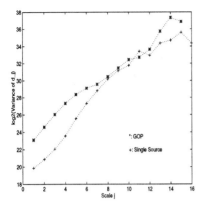

Figure 1: Log 2 of Variance of d_j versus the time scale j

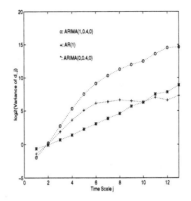

Figure 2: Log 2 of Variance of d_j versus the time scale j

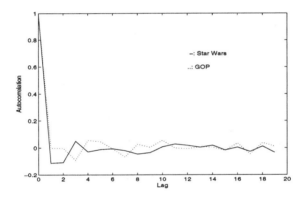

Figure 3: The sample autocorrelations of d_6^m.

2.2 The Variances and Auto-correlation of Wavelet Coefficients

As the first step to understand how wavelets capture the LRD and SRD, we plot in Figure (1) the variance of the wavelet coefficients d_j^m's at different time scales for both sources. To understand what the curves mean, we also plot in Figure (2) the variances of wavelet coefficients for three well-known processes: FARIMA$(0, 0.4, 0)$, FARIMA$(1, 0.4, 0)$, and AR(1). FARIMA$(0, 0.4, 0)$ is a long-range dependent process with Hurst parameter $H = 0.9$. AR(1) is a short-range dependent process, and FARIMA$(1, 0.4, 0)$ is a mixture of the long-range and the short-range dependent process.

As observed, for FARIMA$(0, 0.4, 0)$ process (LRD alone), the variance increases with j exponentially for all j. For AR(1) (SRD alone), the variance increases at an even faster rate than that of FARIMA$(0, 0.4, 0)$ when j is small but saturates when j is large. For FARIMA$(1, 0.4, 0)$, the variance shows the mixed properties from both AR(1) and FARIMA$(0, 0.4, 0)$. The variance of the video sources behaves similarly to that of FARIMA$(1, 0.4, 0)$, and thus demonstrate the co-existence of the SRD and LRD in the video sources in the wavelet domain.

Figure 3 gives the sample auto-correlation of d_6^m in terms of m's. The auto-correlation function of the wavelet coefficients approaches zero very rapidly, and

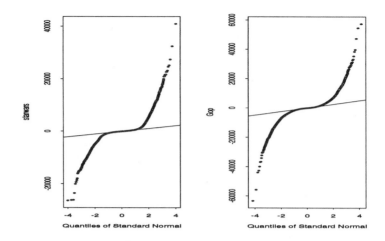

Figure 4: Quantile-Quantile of d_j^m for $j = 3$. Left: Star Wars. Right: GOP.

thus indicates the short-range dependence in the wavelet domain. This suggests that although the autocorrelation of the video traffic is complex in the time-domain, modeling wavelet coefficients may be done using simple statistics within each time scale. Similar auto-correlations have been observed for the other j's.

2.3   Marginal Probability Density Functions

Is variance sufficient for modeling wavelet coefficients? Figure (4) plots the $Q - Q$ plots for the wavelet coefficients of the two sources at $j = 3$[1]. The figure shows that the sample marginal density functions of wavelet coefficients for both the "Star Wars" and the MPEG GOP source at the given time scale have a much heavier tail than that of the normal distribution. Therefore, the variance alone is only sufficient when the marginal density function is normal, and in general a marginal density function should be considered as another pertinent statistical property.

It should be noted that correlation among wavelet coefficients at different time scales is neglected in this work for simplicity. We will show both empirically and theoretically that good performance in terms of sample auto-correlation and sample buffer loss probability can be obtained by a corresponding simple algorithm. More careful treatment can be found in [8].

2.4   An Algorithm for Generating Wavelet Models

The algorithm we derive include three main steps: (a) obtain sample variances of wavelet coefficients at each time scale, (b) generate wavelet coefficients independently from the normal marginal density function using the sample mean and variance [2], and (c) perform a transformation on the wavelet coefficients so that the

---

[1]Similar behaviors have been observed at the other time scales. A $Q - Q$ plot is a standard statistical tool to measure the deviation of a marginal density function from a normal density. The $Q - Q$ plots of a process with a normal marginal is a straight line. The deviation from the line indicates the deviation from the normal density. See [4] and references therein for more details.

[2]The mean of the wavelet coefficients can be shown to be zero for stationary processes.

resulting wavelet coefficients have a marginal density function required by the traffic. The obtained wavelet coefficients form a wavelet model from which synthesized video traffic can be generated. The algorithm can be summarized as follows.

Let $\hat{x}(t)$ be the video trace of length N.

Algorithm

1. Obtain wavelet coefficients from $\hat{x}(t)$ through the wavelet transform.

2. Compute the sample variance $\hat{\sigma}_j$ of wavelet coefficients at each time scale j.

3. Generate new wavelet coefficients d_j^m's for all j and m independently through Gaussian distributions with variances $\hat{\sigma}_j$'s obtained at the previous step.

4. Perform a transformation on the wavelet coefficients so that the marginal density function of wavelet coefficients is consistent with that determined by the video traffic(see [6] for details on the transformation).

5. Do inverse wavelet transform using the wavelet coefficients obtained at the previous step to get the synthesized video traffic in the time domain.

The computational complexity of both the wavelet transform (Step 1) and the inverse transform (Step 5) is $O(N)$. So is for Steps 2, 3 and 4. Then $O(N)$ is the computational cost of the algorithm, which is the lowest attainable for traffic models.

2.5 Experimental Results

Video traces of length $171,000$ for "Star Wars" and 66369 for "MPEG GOP" are used to obtain wavelet models. FARIMA models with 45 parameters are also obtained using the same data for comparison. The synthesized video traffic from both models are generated and used to obtain sample auto-correlation functions in the time-domain, and to estimate the buffer loss rate. The results[3] are given in Figure (6). Wavelet models have shown to outperform the FARIMA model.

For the computation time, it takes more than 5-hour CPU time[4] on a SunSPARC 5 workstation to develop the FARIMA model and to generate synthesized video traffic of length $171,000$[5]. It only takes 3 minutes on the same machine for our algorithm to complete the same tasks.

3 Theory

It has been demonstrated empirically in the previous section that the wavelet model, which ignores the correlation among wavelet coefficients of a video trace, can match well the sample auto-correlation function and the buffer loss probability. To further evaluate the feasibility of the wavelet model, the buffer overflow probability has been analyzed theoretically in [8]. Our result can be summarized in the following theorem.

---

[3] Due to page limit, we only provide plots for JPEG. GOP has similar results and was reported in [8].

[4] Computation time includes both parameter estimation and synthesized traffic generation.

[5] The computational complexity to generate synthesized video traffic of length N is $O(N^2)$ for an FARIMA model[5][4].

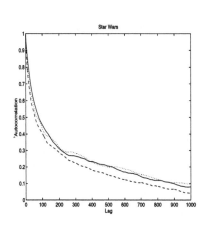

Figure 5: "-": Autocorrelation of "Star Wars"; "- -": ARIMA(25,d,20); "..": Our Algorithm

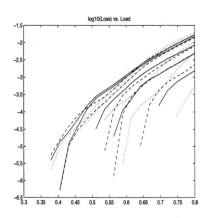

Figure 6: Loss rate attained via simulation. Vertical axis: $\log_{10}($Loss Rate); horizontal axis: work load. "-": the single video source; "..": FARIMA(25,d,20); "–" Our algorithm. The normalized buffer size: 0.1, 1, 10,30 and 100 from the top down.

Theorem *Let B_N and $\hat{B}_N$ be the buffer sizes at the Nth time slot due to the synthesized traffic by the our wavelet model, and by the FGN process, respectively. Let C and B represent the capacity, and the maximum allowable buffer size respectively. Then*

$$\ln Pr(B_N > B) \quad \sim \quad \ln Pr(\hat{B}_N > B)$$
$$\sim \quad -\frac{(C-\mu)^2(\frac{B}{C-\mu})^{2(1-H)}(\frac{1-H}{H})^{2H}}{2\sigma^2(1-H)^2}, \tag{1}$$

where $\frac{1}{2} < H < 1$ is the Hurst parameter. μ and σ^2 is the mean and the variance of the traffic, respectively. B is assume to be $(C-\mu)2^{k_0}$, where k_0 is a positive integer.

This result demonstrates that using our simple wavelet model which neglects the correlations among wavelet coefficients, buffer overflow probability obtained is similar to that of the original FGN process as given in[10]. In other words, it shows that the wavelet model for a FGN process can have good modeling performance in terms of the buffer overflow criterion.

We would like to point out that the above theorem is held for a FGN process. Further work are needed to account for more general processes.

4   Conclusions

In this work, we have described an important application on time-series modeling: modeling video traffic. We have developed a wavelet model for the time-series. Through analyzing statistical properties of the time-series and comparing the wavelet model with FARIMA models, we show that one of the key factors to successfully model a time-series is to choose an appropriate model which naturally fits the pertinant statistical properties of the time-series. We have shown wavelets are particularly feasible for modeling the self-similar time-series due to the video traffic.

We have developed a simple algorithm for the wavelet models, and shown that the models are accurate, computationally efficient and simple enough for analysis.

References

[1] I. Daubechies, *Ten Lectures on Wavelets.* Philadelphia: SIAM, 1992.

[2] Patrick Flandrin, "Wavelet Analysis and Synthesis of Fractional Brownian Motion", *IEEE transactions on Information Theory*, vol. 38, No.2, pp.910-917, 1992.

[3] W.E Leland, M.S. Taqqu, W. Willinger and D.V. Wilson, "On the Self-Similar Nature of Ethernet Traffic (Extended Version)", *IEEE/ACM Transactions on Networking*, vol.2, 1-14, 1994.

[4] Mark W. Garrett and Walter Willinger. "Analysis, Modeling and Generation of Self-Similar VBR Video Traffic.", in Proceedings of ACM SIGCOMM'94, London, U.K, Aug., 1994

[5] J.R.M. Hosking, "Modeling Persistence in Hydrological Time Series Using Fractional Differencing", *Water Resources Research*, 20, pp. 1898-1908, 1984.

[6] C. Huang, M. Devetsikiotis, I. Lambadaris and A.R. Kaye, "Modeling and Simulation of Self-Similar Variable Bit Rate Compressed Video: A Unified Approach", in Proceedings of ACM SIGCOMM'95, pp. 114-125.

[7] Predrag R. Jelenlnovic, Aurel A. Lazar, and Nemo Semret. The effect of multiple time scales and subexponentiality in mpeg video streams on queuing behavior. *IEEE Journal on Selected Area of Communications*, 15, to appear in May 1997.

[8] S. Ma and C. Ji, "Modeling Video Traffic in Wavelet Domain", to appear *IEEE INFOCOM*, 1998.

[9] B. Melamed, D. Raychaudhuri, B. Sengupta, and J. Zdepski. Tes-based video source modeling for performance evaluation of integrated networks. *IEEE Transactions on Communications*, 10, 1994.

[10] Ilkka Norros, "A storage model with self-similar input," *Queuing Systems*, vol.16, 387-396, 1994.

[11] O. Rose. "Statistical properties of mpeg video traffic and their impact on traffic modeling in atm traffic engineering", Technical Report 101, University of Wurzburg, 1995.

Reinforcement Learning for Call Admission Control and Routing in Integrated Service Networks

Peter Marbach[*]
LIDS
MIT
Cambridge, MA, 02139
email: marbach@mit.edu

Oliver Mihatsch
Siemens AG
Corporate Technology, ZT IK 4
D-81730 Munich, Germany
email: oliver.mihatsch@
mchp.siemens.de

Miriam Schulte
Zentrum Mathematik
Technische Universität München
D-80290 Munich
Germany

John N. Tsitsiklis
LIDS
MIT
Cambridge, MA, 02139
email: jnt@mit.edu

Abstract

In integrated service communication networks, an important problem is to exercise call admission control and routing so as to optimally use the network resources. This problem is naturally formulated as a dynamic programming problem, which, however, is too complex to be solved exactly. We use methods of reinforcement learning (RL), together with a decomposition approach, to find call admission control and routing policies. The performance of our policy for a network with approximately 10^{45} different feature configurations is compared with a commonly used heuristic policy.

1 Introduction

The call admission control and routing problem arises in the context where a telecommunication provider wants to sell its network resources to customers in order to maximize long term revenue. Customers are divided into different classes, called service types. Each service type is characterized by its bandwidth demand, its average call holding time and the immediate reward the network provider obtains, whenever a call of that service type is

---

[*]Author to whom correspondence should be addressed.

accepted. The control actions for maximizing the long term revenue are to accept or reject new calls (*Call Admission Control*) and, if a call is accepted, to route the call appropriately through the network (*Routing*). The problem is naturally formulated as a dynamic programming problem, which, however, is too complex to be solved exactly. We use the methodology of reinforcement learning (RL) to approximate the value function of dynamic programming. Furthermore, we pursue a decomposition approach, where the network is viewed as consisting of link processes, each having its own value function. This has the advantage, that it allows a decentralized implementation of the training methods of RL and a decentralized implementation of the call admission control and routing policies. Our method learns call admission control and routing policies which outperform the commonly used heuristic "Open-Shortest-Path-First" (OSPF) policy.

In some earlier related work, we applied RL to the call admission problem for a single communication link in an integrated service environment. We found that in this case, RL methods performed as well, but no better than, well-designed heuristics. Compared with the single link problem, the addition of routing decisions makes the network problem more complex and good heuristics are not easy to derive.

2 Call Admission Control and Routing

We are given a telecommunication network consisting of a set of nodes $\mathcal{N} = \{1, ..., N\}$ and a set of links $\mathcal{L} = \{1, ..., L\}$, where link l has a a total capacity of $B(l)$ units of bandwidth. We support a set $\mathcal{M} = \{1, ..., M\}$ of different service types, where a service type m is characterized by its bandwidth demand $b(m)$, its average call holding time $1/\nu(m)$ (here we assume that the call holding times are exponentially distributed) and the immediate reward $c(m)$ we obtain, whenever we accept a call of that service type. A link can carry simultaneously any combination of calls, as long as the bandwidth used by these calls does not exceed the total bandwidth of the link (*Capacity Constraint*). When a new call of service type m requests a connection between a node i and a node j, we can either reject or accept that request (*Call Admission Control*). If we accept the call, we choose a route out of a list of predefined routes (*Routing*). The call then uses $b(m)$ units of bandwidth on each link along that route for the duration of the call. We can, therefore, only choose a route, which does not violate the capacity constraints of its links, if the call is accepted. Furthermore, if we accept the call, we obtain an immediate reward $c(m)$. The objective is to exercise call admission control and routing in such a way that the long term revenue obtained by accepting calls is maximized.

We can formulate the call admission control and routing problem using dynamic programming (e. g. Bertsekas, 1995). Events ω which incur state transitions, are arrivals of new calls and call terminations. The state x_t at time t consists of a list for each route, indicating how many calls of each service type are currently using that route. The decision/control u_t applied at the time t of an arrival of a new call is to decide, whether to reject or accept the call, and, if the call is accepted, how to route it through the network. The objective is to learn a policy that assigns decisions to each state so as to

$$\text{maximize} \quad \left(J = E \left\{ \sum_{k=0}^{\infty} e^{-\beta t_k} g(x_{t_k}, \omega_k, u_{t_k}) \right\} \right)$$

where $E\{\cdot\}$ is the expectation operator, t_k is the time when the kth event happens, $g(x_{t_k}, \omega_k, u_{t_k})$ is the immediate reward associated with the kth event, and β is a discount factor that makes immediate rewards more valuable than future ones.

3 Reinforcement Learning Solution

RL methods solve optimal control (or dynamic programming) problems by learning good approximations to the optimal value function J^*, given by the solution to the Bellman optimality equation which takes the following form for the call admission control and routing problem

$$J^*(x) = E_\tau \left\{ e^{-\beta\tau} \right\} E_\omega \left\{ \max_{u \in U(x)} \left[g(x, \omega, u) + J^*(x') \right] \right\}$$

where $U(x)$ is the set of control actions available in the current state x, τ is the time when the first event ω occurs and x' is the successor state. Note that x' is a deterministic function of the current state x, the control u and the event ω.

RL uses a compact representation $\tilde{J}(\cdot, \theta)$ to learn and store an estimate of $J^*(\cdot)$. On each event, $\tilde{J}(\cdot, \theta)$ is both used to make decisions and to update the parameter vector θ. In the call admission control and routing problem, one has only to choose a control action when a new call requests a connection. In such a case, $\tilde{J}(\cdot, \theta)$ is used to choose a control action according to the formula

$$u = \arg \max_{u \in U(x)} \left[g(x, \omega, u) + \tilde{J}(x', \theta) \right] \tag{1}$$

This can be expressed in words as follows.

Decision Making: When a new call requests a connection, use $\tilde{J}(\cdot, \theta)$ to evaluate, for each permissible route, the successor state x' we transit to, when we choose that route, and pick a route which maximizes that value. If the sum of the immediate reward and the value associated with this route is higher than the value of the current state, route the call over that route; otherwise reject the call.

Usually, RL uses a global feature extractor $f(x)$ to form an approximate compact representation of the state of the system, which forms the input to a function approximator $\tilde{J}(\cdot, \theta)$. Sutton's temporal difference (TD(λ)) algorithms (Sutton, 1988) can then be used to train $\tilde{J}(\cdot, \theta)$ to learn an estimate of J^*. Using TD(0), the update at the kth event takes the following form

$$\theta_k = \theta_{k-1} + \gamma_k d_k \nabla_\theta \tilde{J}(f(x_{t_{k-1}}), \theta_{k-1})$$

where

$$\begin{aligned} d_k &= e^{-\beta(t_k - t_{k-1})} \left(g(x_{t_k}, \omega_k, u_{t_k}) + \tilde{J}(f(x_{t_k}), \theta_{k-1}) \right) \\ &\quad - \tilde{J}(f(x_{t_{k-1}}), \theta_{k-1}) \end{aligned}$$

and where γ_k is a small step size parameter and u_{t_k} is the control action chosen according to the decision making rule described above.

Here we pursue an approach where we view the network as being composed of link processes. Furthermore, we decompose immediate rewards $g(x_{t_k}, \omega_k, u_{t_k})$ associated with the kth event, into link rewards $g^{(l)}(x_{t_k}, \omega_k, u_{t_k})$ such that

$$g(x_{t_k}, \omega_k, u_{t_k}) = \sum_{l=1}^{L} g^{(l)}(x_{t_k}, \omega_k, u_{t_k})$$

We then define, for each link l, a value function $\tilde{J}^{(l)}(f^{(l)}(x), \theta^{(l)})$, which is interpreted as an estimate of the discounted long term revenue associated with that link. Here, $f^{(l)}$ defines a local feature, which forms the input to the value function associated with link l. To obtain an approximation of $J^*(x)$, the functions $\tilde{J}^{(l)}(f^{(l)}(x), \theta^{(l)})$ are combined as follows

$$\sum_{l=1}^{L} \tilde{J}^{(l)}(f^{(l)}(x), \theta^{(l)}).$$

At each event, we update the parameter vector $\theta^{(l)}$ of link l, only if the event is associated with the link. Events associated with a link l are arrivals of new calls which are potentially routed over link l and termination of calls which were routed over the link l. The update rule of the parameter vector $\theta^{(l)}$ is very similar to the TD(0) algorithm described above

$$\theta_k^{(l)} = \theta_{k-1}^{(l)} + \gamma_k^{(l)} d_k^{(l)} \nabla_{\theta^{(l)}} \tilde{J}^{(l)}(f^{(l)}(x_{t_{k-1}}), \theta_{k-1}^{(l)}) \tag{2}$$

where

$$\begin{aligned}
d_k^{(l)} &= e^{-\beta(t_k^{(l)} - t_{k-1}^{(l)})} \left(g^{(l)}(x_{t_k^{(l)}}, \omega_k^{(l)}, u_{t_k^{(l)}}) + \tilde{J}^{(l)}(f^{(l)}(x_{t_k^{(l)}}), \theta_{k-1}^{(l)}) \right) \\
&\quad - \tilde{J}^{(l)}(f^{(l)}(x_{t_{k-1}^{(l)}}), \theta_{k-1}^{(l)})
\end{aligned} \tag{3}$$

and where $\gamma_k^{(l)}$ is a small step size parameter and $t_k^{(l)}$ is the time when the kth event $\omega_k^{(l)}$ associated with link l occurs. Whenever a new call of a service of type m is routed over a route r which contains the link l, the immediate reward $g^{(l)}$ associated with the link l is equal to $c(m)/\#r$, where $\#r$ is the number of links along the route r. For all other events, the immediate reward associated with link l is equal to 0.

The advantage of this decomposition approach is that it allows decentralized training and decentralized decision making. Furthermore, we observed that this decomposition approach leads to much shorter training times for obtaining an approximation for J^* than the approach without decomposition. All these features become very important if one considers applying methods of RL to large integrated service networks supporting a fair number of different service types.

We use exploration to obtain the states at which we update the parameter vector θ. At each state, with probability $p = 0.5$, we apply a random action, instead of the action recommended by the current value function, to generate the next state in our training trajectory. However, the action $u_{t_k^{(l)}}$, that is used in the update rule (3), is still the one chosen according to the rule given in (1). Exploration during the training significantly improved the performance of the policy.

Table 1: Service Types.

SERVICE TYPE m	1	2	3
BANDWIDTH DEMAND $b(m)$	1	3	5
AVERAGE HOLDING TIME $1/\nu(m)$	10	10	2
IMMEDIATE REWARD $c(m)$	1	2	50

4 Experimental Results

In this section, we present experimental results obtained for the case of an integrated service network consisting of 4 nodes and 12 unidirectional links. There are two different classes of links with a total capacity of 60 and 120 units of bandwidth, respectively (indicated by thick and thin arrows in Figure 1). We assume a set $\mathcal{M} = \{1, 2, 3\}$ of three different service types. The corresponding bandwidth demands, average holding times and immediate

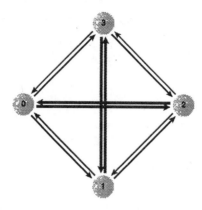

Figure 1: Telecommunication Network Consisting of 4 Nodes and 12 Unidirectional Links.

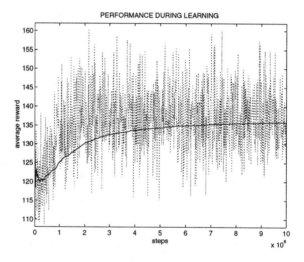

Figure 2: Average Reward per Time Unit During the Whole Training Phase of 10^7 Steps (Solid) and During Shorter Time Windows of 10^5 Steps (Dashed).

rewards are given in Table 1. Call arrivals are modeled as independent Poisson processes, with a separate mean for each pair of source and destination nodes and each service type. Furthermore, for each source and destination node pair, the list of possible routes consists of three entries: the direct path and the two alternative 2-hop-routes.

We compare the policy obtained through RL with the commonly used heuristic OSPF (Open Shortest Path First). For every pair of source and destination nodes, OSPF orders the list of predefined routes. When a new call arrives, it is routed along the first route in the corresponding list, that does not violate the capacity constraint; if no such a route exists, the call is rejected. We use the average reward per unit time as performance measure to compare the two policies.

For the RL approach, we use a quadratic approximator, which is linear with respect to the parameters $\theta^{(l)}$, as a compact representation of $\tilde{J}^{(l)}$. Other approximation architectures were tried, but we found that the quadratic gave the best results with respect to both the speed of convergence and the final performance. As inputs to the compact representation

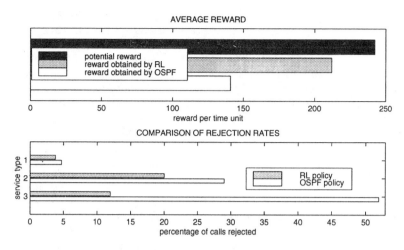

Figure 3: Comparison of the Average Rewards and Rejection Rates of the RL and OSPF Policies.

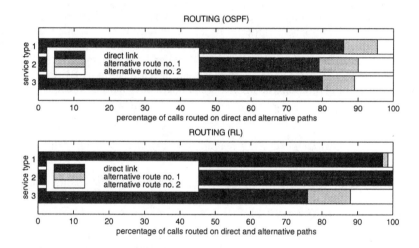

Figure 4: Comparison of the Routing Behaviour of the RL and OSPF Policies.

$\tilde{J}^{(l)}$, we use a set of local features, which we chose to be the number of ongoing calls of each service type on link l. For the 4-node network, there are approximately $1.6 \cdot 10^{45}$ different feature configurations. Note that the total number of possible states is even higher.

The results of the case studies are given in in Figure 2 (Training Phase), Figure 3 (Performance) and Figure 4 (Routing Behaviour). We give here a summary of the results.

Training Phase: Figure 2 shows the average reward of the RL policy as a function of the training steps. Although the average reward increases during the training, it does not exceed 141, the average reward of the heuristic OSPF. This is due to the high amount of exploration in the training phase.

Performance Comparison: The policy obtained through RL gives an average reward of 212, which as about 50% higher than the one of 141 achieved by OSPF. Furthermore, the RL policy reduces the number of rejected calls for all service types. The most significant reduction is achieved for calls of service type 3, the service type, which has the highest immediate reward. Figure 3 also shows that the average reward of the RL policy is close to the potential average reward of 242, which is the average reward we would obtain if all calls were accepted. This leaves us to believe that the RL policy is close to optimal. Figure 4 compares the routing behaviour of the RL control policy and OSPF. While OSPF routes about $15\% - 20\%$ of all calls along one of the alternative 2-hop-routes, the RL policy almost uses alternative routes for calls of type 3 (about 25%) and routes calls of the other two service types almost exclusively over the direct route. This indicates, that the RL policy uses a routing scheme, which avoids 2-hop-routes for calls of service type 1 and 2, and which allows us to use network resources more efficiently.

5   Conclusion

The call admission control and routing problem for integrated service networks is naturally formulated as a dynamic programming problem, albeit one with a very large state space. Traditional dynamic programming methods are computationally infeasible for such large scale problems. We use reinforcement learning, based on Sutton's (1988) $TD(0)$, combined with a decomposition approach, which views the network as consisting of link processes. This decomposition has the advantage that it allows decentralized decision making and decentralized training, which reduces significantly the time of the training phase. We presented a solution for an example network with about 10^{45} different feature configurations. Our RL policy clearly outperforms the commonly used heuristic OSPF. Besides the game of backgammon (Tesauro, 1992), the elevator scheduling (Crites & Barto, 1996), the jop-shop scheduling (Zhang & Dietterich, 1996) and the dynamic channel allocation (Singh & Bertsekas, 1997), this is another successful application of RL to a large-scale dynamic programming problem for which a good heuristic is hard to find.

References

Bertsekas, D. P. (1995) *Dynamic Programming and Optimal Control*. Athena Scientific, Belmont, MA.

Crites, R. H., Barto, A. G. (1996) Improving elevator performance using reinforcement learning. In D. S. Touretzky, M. C. Mozer and M. E. Hasselmo (eds.), *Advances in Neural Information Processing Systems 8*, pp. 1017–1023. Cambridge, MA: MIT Press.

Singh, S., Bertsekas, D. P. (1997) Reinforcement learning for dynamic channel allocation in cellular telephone systems. To appear in *Advances in Neural Information Processing Systems 9*, Cambridge, MA: MIT Press.

Sutton, R. S. (1988) Learning to predict by the method of temporal differences. *Machine Learning*, 3:9–44.

Tesauro, G. J. (1992) Practical issues in temporal difference learning. *Machine Learning*, 8(3/4):257–277.

Zhang, W., Dietterich, T. G. (1996) High performance job-shop scheduling with a time-delay $TD(\lambda)$ network. In D. S. Touretzky, M. C. Mozer and M. E. Hasselmo (eds.), *Advances in Neural Information Processing Systems 8*, pp. 1024–1030. Cambridge, MA: MIT Press.

Learning to Schedule Straight-Line Code

Eliot Moss, Paul Utgoff, John Cavazos
Doina Precup, Darko Stefanović
Dept. of Comp. Sci., Univ. of Mass.
Amherst, MA 01003

Carla Brodley, David Scheeff
Sch. of Elec. and Comp. Eng.
Purdue University
W. Lafayette, IN 47907

Abstract

Program execution speed on modern computers is sensitive, by a factor of two or more, to the order in which instructions are presented to the processor. To realize potential execution efficiency, an optimizing compiler must employ a heuristic algorithm for instruction scheduling. Such algorithms are painstakingly hand-crafted, which is expensive and time-consuming. We show how to cast the instruction scheduling problem as a learning task, obtaining the heuristic scheduling algorithm automatically. Our focus is the narrower problem of scheduling straight-line code (also called *basic blocks* of instructions). Our empirical results show that just a few features are adequate for quite good performance at this task for a real modern processor, and that any of several supervised learning methods perform nearly optimally with respect to the features used.

1 Introduction

Modern computer architectures provide semantics of execution equivalent to sequential execution of instructions one at a time. However, to achieve higher execution efficiency, they employ a high degree of internal parallelism. Because individual instruction execution times vary, depending on when an instruction's inputs are available, when its computing resources are available, and when it is presented, overall execution time can vary widely. Based on just the semantics of instructions, a sequence of instructions usually has many permutations that are easily shown to have equivalent meaning—but they may have considerably different execution time. Compiler writers therefore include algorithms to schedule instructions to achieve low execution time. Currently, such algorithms are hand-crafted for each compiler and target processor. We apply learning so that the scheduling algorithm is constructed automatically.

Our focus is *local instruction scheduling*, i.e., ordering instructions within a *basic block*. A basic block is a straight-line sequence of code, with a conditional or unconditional branch instruction at the end. The scheduler should find optimal, or good, orderings of the instructions prior to the branch. It is safe to assume that the compiler has produced a semantically correct sequence of instructions for each basic block. We consider only *reorderings* of each sequence (not more general rewritings), and only those reorderings that *cannot affect the semantics*. The semantics of interest are captured by *dependences* of pairs of instructions. Specifically, instruction I_j depends on (must follow) instruction I_i if: it follows I_i in the input block and has one or more of the following dependences on I_i: (a) I_j uses a register used by I_i and at least one of them writes the register (condition codes, if any, are treated as a register); (b) I_j accesses a memory location that may be the same as one accessed by I_i, and at least one of them writes the location. From the input total order of instructions, one can thus build a *dependence DAG*, usually a partial (not a total) order, that represents all the semantics essential for scheduling the instructions of a basic block. Figure 1 gives a sample basic block and its DAG. The task of scheduling is to find a least-cost total order of each block's DAG.

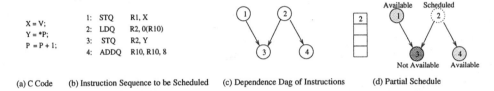

(a) C Code   (b) Instruction Sequence to be Scheduled   (c) Dependence Dag of Instructions   (d) Partial Schedule

Figure 1: Example basic block code, DAG, and partial schedule

2   Learning to Schedule

The learning task is to produce a scheduling procedure to use in the performance task of scheduling instructions of basic blocks. One needs to transform the partial order of instructions into a total order that will execute as efficiently as possible, assuming that all memory references "hit" in the caches. We consider the class of schedulers that repeatedly select the apparent best of those instructions that could be scheduled next, proceeding from the beginning of the block to the end; this *greedy* approach should be practical for everyday use.

Because the scheduler selects the apparent best from those instructions that could be selected next, the learning task consists of learning to make this selection well. Hence, the notion of 'apparent best instruction' needs to be acquired. The process of selecting the best of the alternatives is like finding the maximum of a list of numbers. One keeps in hand the current best, and proceeds with pairwise comparisons, always keeping the better of the two. One can view this as learning a relation over triples (P, I_i, I_j), where P is the partial schedule (the total order of what has been scheduled, and the partial order remaining), and I is the set of instructions from which the selection is to be made. Those triples that belong to the relation define pairwise preferences in which the first instruction is considered preferable to the second. Each triple that does not belong to the relation represents a pair in which the first instruction is not better than the second.

One must choose a representation in which to state the relation, create a process by which correct examples and counter-examples of the relation can be inferred, and modify the expression of the relation as needed. Let us consider these steps in greater detail.

2.1   Representation of Scheduling Preference

The representation used here takes the form of a logical relation, in which known examples and counter-examples of the relation are provided as triples. It is then a matter of constructing or revising an expression that evaluates to TRUE if (P, I_i, I_j) is a member of the relation, and FALSE if it is not. If (P, I_i, I_j) is considered to be a member of the relation, then it is safe to infer that (P, I_j, I_i) is not a member.

For any representation of preference, one needs to represent features of a candidate instruction and of the partial schedule. There is some art in picking useful features for a state. The method used here was to consider the features used in a scheduler (called DEC below) supplied by the processor vendor, and to think carefully about those and other features that should indicate predictive instruction characteristics or important aspects of the partial schedule.

2.2 Inferring Examples and Counter-Examples

One would like to produce a preference relation consistent with the examples and counter-examples that have been inferred, and that generalizes well to triples that have not been seen. A variety of methods exist for learning and generalizing from examples, several of which are tested in the experiments below. Of interest here is how to infer the examples and counter-examples needed to drive the generalization process.

The focus here is on supervised learning (reinforcement learning is mentioned later), in which one provides a process that produces correctly labeled examples and counter-examples of the preference relation. For the instruction-scheduling task, it is possible to search for an optimal schedule for blocks of ten or fewer instructions. From an optimal schedule, one can infer the correct preferences that would have been needed to produce that optimal schedule when selecting the best instruction from a set of candidates, as described above. It may well be that there is more than one optimal schedule, so it is important only to infer a preference for a pair of instructions when the first can produce some schedule better than any the second can.

One should be concerned whether training on preference pairs from optimally scheduled small blocks is effective, a question the experiments address. It is worth noting that for programs studied below, 92% of the basic blocks are of this small size, and the average block size is 4.9 instructions. On the other hand, larger blocks are executed more often, and thus have disproportionate impact on program execution time. One could learn from larger blocks by using a high quality scheduler that is not necessarily optimal. However, the objective is to be able to learn to schedule basic blocks well for new architectures, so a useful learning method should not depend on any pre-existing solution. Of course there may be some utility in trying to improve on an existing scheduler, but that is not the longer-term goal here. Instead, we would like to be able to construct a scheduler with high confidence that it produces good schedules.

2.3 Updating the Preference Relation

A variety of learning algorithms can be brought to bear on the task of updating the expression of the preference relation. We consider four methods here.

The first is the decision tree induction program ITI (Utgoff, Berkman & Clouse, in press). Each triple that is an example of the relation is translated into a vector of feature values, as described in more detail below. Some of the features pertain to the current partial schedule, and others pertain to the pair of candidate instructions. The vector is then labeled as an example of the relation. For the same pair of instructions, a second triple is inferred, with the two instructions reversed. The feature vector for the triple is constructed as before, and labeled as a counter-example of the relation. The decision tree induction program then constructs a tree that can be used to predict whether a candidate triple is a member of the relation.

The second method is table lookup (TLU), using a table indexed by the feature values of a triple. The table has one cell for every possible combination of feature values, with integer valued features suitably discretized. Each cell records the number of positive and negative instances from a training set that map to that cell. The table lookup function returns the most frequently seen value associated with the corresponding cell. It is useful to know that the data set used is large and generally covers all possible table cells with multiple instances. Thus, table lookup is "unbiased" and one would expect it to give the best predictions possible for the chosen features, assuming the statistics of the training and test sets are consistent.

The third method is the ELF function approximator (Utgoff & Precup, 1997), which constructs additional features (much like a hidden unit) as necessary while it updates its representation of the function that it is learning. The function is represented by two layers of mapping. The first layer maps the features of the triple, which must be boolean for ELF, to a set of boolean feature values. The second layer maps those features to a single scalar value by combining them linearly with a vector of real-valued coefficients called weights. Though the second layer is linear in the instruction features, the boolean features are nonlinear in the instruction features.

Finally, the fourth method considered is a feed-forward artificial neural network (NN) (Rumelhart, Hinton & Williams, 1986). Our particular network uses scaled conjugate gradient descent in its back-propagation, which gives results comparable to back-propagation with momentum, but converges much faster. Our configuration uses 10 hidden units.

3   Empirical Results

We aimed to answer the following questions: Can we schedule as well as hand-crafted algorithms in production compilers? Can we schedule as well as the best hand-crafted algorithms? How close can we come to optimal schedules? The first two questions we answer with comparisons of program execution times, as predicted from simulations of individual basic blocks (multiplied by the number of executions of the blocks as measured in sample program runs). This measure seems fair for local instruction scheduling, since it omits other execution time factors being ignored. Ultimately one would deal with these factors, but they would cloud the issues for the present enterprise. Answering the third question is harder, since it is infeasible to generate optimal schedules for long blocks. We offer a partial answer by measuring the number of optimal choices made within small blocks.

To proceed, we selected a computer architecture implementation and a standard suite of benchmark programs (SPEC95) compiled for that architecture. We extracted basic blocks from the compiled programs and used them for training, testing, and evaluation as described below.

3.1   Architecture and Benchmarks

We chose the Digital Alpha (Sites, 1992) as our architecture for the instruction scheduling problem. When introduced it was the fastest scalar processor available, and from a dependence analysis and scheduling standpoint its instruction set is simple. The 21064 *implementation* of the instruction set (DEC, 1992) is interestingly complex, having two dissimilar pipelines and the ability to issue two instructions per cycle (also called *dual issue*) if a complicated collection of conditions hold. Instructions take from one to many tens of cycles to execute.

SPEC95 is a standard benchmark commonly used to evaluate CPU execution time and the impact of compiler optimizations. It consists of 18 programs, 10 written in FORTRAN and tending to use floating point calculations heavily, and 8 written in C and focusing more on integers, character strings, and pointer manipulations. These were compiled with the vendor's compiler, set at the highest level of optimization offered, which includes compile- or link-time instruction scheduling. We call these the *Orig* schedules for the blocks. The resulting collection has 447,127 basic blocks, composed of 2,205,466 instructions.

3.2   Simulator, Schedulers, and Features

Researchers at Digital made publicly available a simulator for basic blocks for the 21064, which will indicate how many cycles a given block requires for execution, assuming all memory references hit in the caches and translation look-aside buffers, and no resources are busy when the basic block starts execution. When presenting a basic block one can also request that the simulator apply a heuristic greedy scheduling algorithm. We call this scheduler *DEC*.

By examining the DEC scheduler, applying intuition, and considering the results of various preliminary experiments, we settled on using the features of Table 1 for learning. The mapping from triples to feature vectors is: *odd:* a single boolean 0 or 1; *wcp*, *e*, and *d:* the sign ($-$, 0, or $+$) of the value for I_j minus the value for I_i; *ic:* both instruction's values, expressed as 1 of 20 categories. For ELF and NN the categorical values for *ic*, as well as the signs, are mapped to a 1-of-n vector of bits, n being the number of distinct values.

Table 1: Features for Instructions and Partial Schedule

Heuristic Name	Heuristic Description	Intuition for Use
Odd Partial (odd)	Is the current number of instructions scheduled odd or even?	If TRUE, we're interested in scheduling instructions that can dual-issue with the previous instruction.
Instruction Class (ic)	The Alpha's instructions can be divided into equivalence classes with respect to timing properties.	The instructions in each class can be executed only in certain execution pipelines, etc.
Weighted Critical Path (wcp)	The height of the instruction in the DAG (the length of the longest chain of instructions dependent on this one), with edges weighted by expected latency of the result produced by the instruction	Instructions on longer critical paths should be scheduled first, since they affect the lower bound of the schedule cost.
Actual Dual (d)	Can the instruction dual-issue with the previous scheduled instruction?	If Odd Partial is TRUE, it is important that we find an instruction, if there is one, that can issue in the same cycle with the previous scheduled instruction.
Max Delay (e)	The earliest cycle when the instruction can begin to execute, relative to the current cycle; this takes into account any wait for inputs for functional units to become available	We want to schedule instructions that will have their data and functional unit available earliest.

This mapping of triples to feature values loses information. This does not affect learning much (as shown by preliminary experiments omitted here), but it reduces the size of the input space, and tends to improve both speed and quality of learning for some learning algorithms.

3.3 Experimental Procedures

From the 18 SPEC95 programs we extracted all basic blocks, and also determined, for sample runs of each program, the number of times each basic block was executed. For blocks having no more than ten instructions, we used exhaustive search of all possible schedules to (a) find instruction decision points with pairs of choices where one choice is optimal and the other is not, and (b) determine the best schedule cost attainable for either decision. Schedule costs are *always* as judged by the DEC simulator. This procedure produced over 13,000,000 distinct choice pairs, resulting in over 26,000,000 triples (given that swapping I_i and I_j creates a counter-example from an example and vice versa). We selected 1% of the choice pairs at random (always insuring we had matched example/counter-example triples).

For each learning scheme we performed an 18-fold cross-validation, holding out one program's blocks for independent testing. We evaluated both how often the trained scheduler made optimal decisions, and the simulated execution time of the resulting schedules. The execution time was computed as the sum of simulated basic block costs, weighted by execution frequency as observed in sample program runs, as described above.

To summarize the data, we use geometric means across the 18 runs of each scheduler. The geometric mean $g(x_1,...,x_n)$ of $x_1,...,x_n$ is $(x_1 \cdot ... \cdot x_n)^{1/n}$. It has the nice property that $g(x_1/y_1,...,x_n/y_n) = g(x_1,...,x_n)/g(y_1,...,y_n)$, which makes it particularly meaningful for comparing performance measures via ratios. It can also be written as the anti-logarithm of the mean of the logarithms of the x_i; we use that to calculate confidence intervals using traditional measures over the logarithms of the values. In any case, geometric means are preferred for aggregating benchmark results across differing programs with varying execution times.

3.4 Results and Discussion

Our results appear in Table 2. For evaluations based on predicted program execution time, we compare with Orig. For evaluations based directly on the learning task, i.e., optimal choices, we compare with an optimal scheduler, but only over basic blocks no more than 10 instructions long. Other experiments indicate that the DEC scheduler almost always produces optimal schedules for such short blocks; we suspect it does well on longer blocks too.

Table 2: Experimental Results: Predicted Execution Time

Sche-duler	Relevant Blocks Only		All Blocks		Small Blocks
	cycles ($\times 10^9$)	ratio to Orig (95% conf. int.)	cycles ($\times 10^9$)	ratio to Orig (95% conf. int.)	% Optimal Choices
DEC	24.018	0.979 (0.969,0.989)	28.385	0.983 (0.975,0.992)	
TLU	24.338	0.992 (0.983,1.002)	28.710	0.995 (0.987,1.003)	98.1
ITI	24.395	0.995 (0.984,1.006)	28.758	0.996 (0.987,1.006)	98.2
NN	24.410	0.995 (0.983,1.007)	28.770	0.997 (0.986,1.008)	98.1
ELF	24.465	0.998 (0.985,1.010)	28.775	0.997 (0.988,1.006)	98.1
Orig	24.525	1.000 (1.000,1.000)	28.862	1.000 (1.000,1.000)	
Rand	31.292	1.276 (1.186,1.373)	36.207	1.254 (1.160,1.356)	

The results show that all supervised learning techniques produce schedules predicted to be better than the production compilers, but not as good as the DEC heuristic scheduler. This is a striking success, given the small number of features. As expected, table lookup performs the best of the learning techniques. Curiously, relative performance in terms of making optimal decisions does not correlate with relative performance in terms of producing good schedules. This appears to be because in each program a few blocks are executed very often, and thus contribute much to execution time, and large blocks are executed disproportionately often. Still, both measures of performance are quite good.

What about reinforcement learning? We ran experiments with temporal difference (TD) learning, some of which are described in (Scheeff, *et al.*, 1997) and the results are not as good. This problem appears to be tricky to cast in a form suitable for TD, because TD looks at candidate instructions in isolation, rather than in a preference setting. It is also hard to provide an adequate reward function and features predictive for the task at hand.

4   Related Work, Conclusions, and Outlook

Instruction scheduling is well-known and others have proposed many techniques. Also, optimal instruction scheduling for today's complex processors is NP-complete. We found two pieces of more closely related work. One is a patent (Tarsy & Woodard, 1994). From the patent's claims it appears that the inventors trained a simple perceptron by adjusting weights of some heuristics. They evaluate each weight setting by scheduling an entire benchmark suite, running the resulting programs, and using the resulting times to drive weight adjustments. This approach appears to us to be potentially very time-consuming. It has two advantages over our technique: in the learning process it uses measured execution times rather than predicted or simulated times, and it does not require a simulator. Being a patent, this work does not offer experimental results. The other related item is the application of genetic algorithms to tuning weights of heuristics used in a greedy scheduler (Beaty, S., Colcord, & Sweany, 1996). The authors showed that different hardware targets resulted in different learned weights, but they did not offer experimental evaluation of the quality of the resulting schedulers.

While the results here do not demonstrate it, it was not easy to cast this problem in a form suitable for machine learning. However, once that form was accomplished, supervised learning produced quite good results on this practical problem—better than two vendor production compilers, as shown on a standard benchmark suite used for evaluating such optimizations. Thus the outlook for using machine learning in this application appears promising.

On the other hand, significant work remains. The current experiments are for a particular processor; can they be generalized to other processors? After all, one of the goals is to improve and speed processor design by enabling more rapid construction of optimizing compilers for proposed architectures. While we obtained good performance *predictions*, we did not report performance on a real processor. (More recently we obtained those results (Moss, *et al.*, 1997); ELF tied Orig for the best scheme.) This raises issues not only of faithfulness of the simulator to reality, but also of *global instruction scheduling*, i.e., across basic blocks, and of somewhat more general rewritings that allow more reorderings of instructions. From the perspective of learning, the broader context may make supervised learning impossible, because the search space will explode and preclude making judgments of optimal vs. suboptimal. Thus we will have to find ways to make reinforcement learning work better for this problem. A related issue is the difference between learning to make optimal decisions (on small blocks) and learning to schedule (all) blocks well. Another relevant issue is the cost not of the schedules, but of the schedulers: are these schedulers fast enough to use in production compilers? Again, this demands further experimental work. We do conclude, though, that the approach is promising enough to warrant these additional investigations.

Acknowledgments: We thank various people of Digital Equipment Corporation, for the DEC scheduler and the ATOM program instrumentation tool (Srivastava & Eustace, 1994), essential to this work. We also thank Sun Microsystems and Hewlett-Packard for their support.

References

Beaty, S., Colcord, S., & Sweany, P. (1996). Using genetic algorithms to fine-tune instruction-scheduling heuristics. In *Proc. of the Int'l Conf. on Massively Parallel Computer Systems*.

Digital Equipment Corporation, (1992). *DECchip 21064-AA Microprocessor Hardware Reference Manual*, Maynard, MA, first edition, October 1992.

Haykin, S. (1994). *Neural networks: A comprehensive foundation*. New York, NY: Macmillan.

Moss, E., Cavazos, J., Stefanović, D., Utgoff, P., Precup, D., Scheeff, D., & Brodley, C. (1997). Learning Policies for Local Instruction Scheduling. Submitted for publication.

Rumelhart, D. E., Hinton, G. E., & Williams, R.J. (1986). Learning internal representations by error propagation. In Rumelhart & McClelland (Eds.), *Parallel distributed processing: Explorations in the microstructure of cognition*. Cambridge, MA: MIT Press.

Scheeff, D., Brodley, C., Moss, E., Cavazos, J., Stefanović, D. (1997). Applying Reinforcement Learning to Instruction Scheduling within Basic Blocks. Technical report.

Sites, R. (1992). *Alpha Architecture Reference Manual*. Digital Equip. Corp., Maynard, MA.

Srivastava, A. & Eustace, A. (1994). ATOM: A system for building customized program analysis tools. In *Proc. ACM SIGPLAN '94 Conf. on Prog. Lang. Design and Impl.*, 196–205.

Sutton, R. S. (1988). Learning to predict by the method of temporal differences. *Machine Learning, 3*, 9-44.

Tarsy, G. & Woodard, M. (1994). Method and apparatus for optimizing cost-based heuristic instruction schedulers. US Patent #5,367,687. Filed 7/7/93, granted 11/22/94.

Utgoff, P. E., Berkman, N. C., & Clouse, J. A. (in press). Decision tree induction based on efficient tree restructuring. *Machine Learning*.

Utgoff, P. E., & Precup, D. (1997). *Constructive function approximation*, (Technical Report 97-04), Amherst, MA: University of Massachusetts, Department of Computer Science.

Enhancing Q-Learning for Optimal Asset Allocation

Ralph Neuneier
Siemens AG, Corporate Technology
D-81730 München, Germany
Ralph.Neuneier@mchp.siemens.de

Abstract

This paper enhances the Q-learning algorithm for optimal asset allocation proposed in (Neuneier, 1996 [6]). The new formulation simplifies the approach by using only one value-function for many assets and allows model-free policy-iteration. After testing the new algorithm on real data, the possibility of risk management within the framework of Markov decision problems is analyzed. The proposed methods allows the construction of a multi-period portfolio management system which takes into account transaction costs, the risk preferences of the investor, and several constraints on the allocation.

1 Introduction

Asset allocation and portfolio management deal with the distribution of capital to various investment opportunities like stocks, bonds, foreign exchanges and others. The aim is to construct a portfolio with a maximal expected return for a given risk level and time horizon while simultaneously obeying institutional or legally required constraints. To find such an optimal portfolio the investor has to solve a difficult optimization problem consisting of two phases [4]. First, the expected yields together with a certainty measure has to be predicted. Second, based on these estimates, *mean-variance* techniques are typically applied to find an appropriate fund allocation. The problem is further complicated if the investor wants to revise her/his decision at every time step and if transaction costs for changing the allocations must be considered.

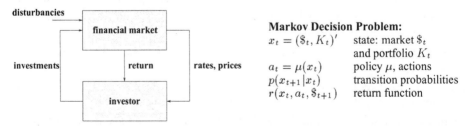

Markov Decision Problem:

$x_t = (\$_t, K_t)'$ state: market $\$_t$
                and portfolio K_t
$a_t = \mu(x_t)$ policy μ, actions
$p(x_{t+1}|x_t)$ transition probabilities
$r(x_t, a_t, \$_{t+1})$ return function

Within the framework of *Markov Decision Problems*, MDPs, the modeling phase and the search for an optimal portfolio can be combined (fig. above). Furthermore, transaction costs, constraints, and decision revision are naturally integrated. The theory of MDPs formalizes control problems within stochastic environments [1]. If the discrete state space is small and if an accurate model of the system is available, MDPs can be solved by conventional *Dynamic Programming*, DP. On the other extreme, reinforcement learning methods using function approximator and stochastic approximation for computing the relevant expectation values can be applied to problems with large (continuous) state spaces and without an appropriate model available [2, 10].

In [6], asset allocation is formalized as a MDP under the following assumptions which clarify the relationship between MDP and portfolio optimization:

1. The investor may trade at each time step for an infinite time horizon.
2. The investor is not able to influence the market by her/his trading.
3. There are only two possible assets for investing the capital.
4. The investor has no risk aversion and always invests the total amount.

The reinforcement algorithm *Q-Learning*, QL, has been tested on the task to invest liquid capital in the German stock market DAX, using neural networks as value function approximators for the Q-values $Q(x, a)$. The resulting allocation strategy generated more profit than a heuristic benchmark policy [6].

Here, a new formulation of the QL algorithm is proposed which allows to relax the third assumption. Furthermore, in section 3 the possibility of risk control within the MDP framework is analyzed which relaxes assumption four.

2 Q-Learning with uncontrollable state elements

This section explains how the QL algorithm can be simplified by the introduction of an artificial deterministic transition step. Using real data, the successful application of the new algorithm is demonstrated.

2.1 Q-Learning for asset allocation

The situation of an investor is formalized at time step t by the state vector $x_t = (\$_t, K_t)$, which consists of elements $\$_t$ describing the financial market (e. g. interest rates, stock indices), and of elements K_t describing the investor's current allocation of the capital (e. g. how much capital is invested in which asset). The investor's decision a_t for a new allocation and the dynamics on the financial market let the state switch to $x_{t+1} = (\$_{t+1}, K_{t+1})$ according to the transition probability $p(x_{t+1}|x_t, a_t)$. Each transition results in an immediate return $r_t = r(x_t, x_{t+1}, a_t)$ which incorporates possible transaction costs depending on the decision a_t and the change of the value of K_t due to the new values of the assets at time $t + 1$. The aim is to maximize the expected discounted sum of the returns, $V^*(x) = E(\sum_{t=0}^{\infty} \gamma^t r_t | x_0 = x)$, by following an optimal stationary policy $\mu^*(x_t) = a_t$. For a discrete finite state space the solution can be stated as the recursive Bellman equation:

$$V^*(x_t) = \max_a \left[\sum_{x_{t+1}} p(x_{t+1}|x_t, a)r_t + \gamma \sum_{x_{t+1}} p(x_{t+1}|x_t, a)V^*(x_{t+1}) \right]. \quad (1)$$

A more useful formulation defines a Q-function $Q^*(x, a)$ of state-action pairs (x_t, a_t),

$$Q^*(x_t, a_t) := \sum_{x_{t+1}} p(x_{t+1}|x_t, a_t)r_t + \gamma \sum_{x_{t+1}} p(x_{t+1}|x_t, a_t) \max_{a \in A}(Q^*(x_{t+1}, a)), \quad (2)$$

to allow the application of an iterative stochastic approximation scheme, called Q-Learning [11]. The Q-value $Q^*(x_t, a_t)$ quantifies the expected discounted sum of returns if one executes action a_t in state x_t and follows an optimal policy thereafter, i. e. $V^*(x_t) = \max_a Q^*(x_t, a)$. Observing the tuple (x_t, x_{t+1}, a_t, r_t), the tabulated Q-values are updated in the $k + 1$ iteration step with learning rate η_k according to:

$$\text{QL: } Q_{k+1}(x_t, a_t) = (1 - \eta_k)Q_k(x_t, a_t) + \eta_k(r_t + \gamma \max_{a \in A}(Q_k(x_{t+1}, a))) \,.$$

It can be shown, that the sequence of Q_k converges under certain assumptions to Q^*. If the Q-values $Q^*(x, a)$ are approximated by separate neural networks with weight vector w^a for different actions a, $Q^*(x, a) \approx Q(x; w^a)$, the adaptations (called NN-QL) are based on the temporal differences d_t:

$$d_t := r(x_t, a_t, x_{t+1}) + \gamma \max_{a \in A} Q(x_{t+1}; w_k^a) - Q(x_t; w_k^{a_t}) \,,$$

$$\text{NN-QL: } w_{k+1}^{a_t} = w_k^{a_t} + \eta_k d_t \nabla Q(x_t; w_k^{a_t}) \,.$$

Note, that although the market dependent part $\$_t$ of the state vector is independent of the investor's decisions, the future wealth K_{t+1} and the returns r_t are not. Therefore, asset allocation is a multi-stage decision problem and may not be reduced to pure prediction if transaction costs must be considered. On the other hand, the attractive feature that the decisions do not influence the market allows to approximate the Q-values using historical data of the financial market. We need not to invest real money during the training phase.

2.2 Introduction of an artificial deterministic transition

Now, the Q-values are reformulated in order to make them independent of the actions chosen at the time step t. Due to assumption 2, which states that the investor can not influence the market by the trading decisions, the stochastic process of the dynamics of $\$_t$ is an uncontrollable Markov chain. This allows the introduction of a deterministic intermediate step between the transition from x_t to x_{t+1} (see fig. below). After the investor has chosen an action a_t, the capital K_t changes to K_t' because he/she may have paid transaction costs $c_t = c(K_t, a_t)$ and K_t' reflects the new allocation whereas the state of the market, $\$_t$, remains the same. Because the costs c_t are known in advance, this transition is deterministic and controllable. Then, the market switches stochastically to $\$_{t+1}$ and generates the immediate return $r_t' = r'(\$_t, K_t', \$_{t+1})$ i.e., $r_t = c_t + r_t'$. The capital changes to $K_{t+1} = r_t' + K_t'$. This transition is uncontrollable by the investor. $V^*(\$, K) = V^*(x)$ is now computed using the costs c_t and returns r_t' (compare also eq. 1)

$$V^*(\$, K) = \max_{a_0, \dots} E\left[\sum_{t=0}^{\infty} \gamma^t (c(K_t, a_t) + r'(\$_t, K_t', \$_{t+1})) \,\middle|\, \begin{matrix} \$_0 = \$ \\ K_0 = K \end{matrix} \right] \,.$$

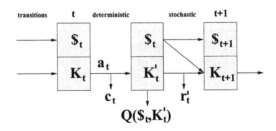

Defining $Q^*(\$_t, K_t')$ as the Q-values of the intermediate time step

$$Q^*(\$_t, K_t') := E\left[r'(\$_t, K_t', \$_{t+1}) + \gamma V^*(\$_{t+1}, K_{t+1}) \right] \,,$$

$$= E[r_t' + \gamma \max_{a_{t+1}}[c_{t+1} + Q^*(\$_{t+1}, K_{t+1}')]] \,,$$

gives rise to the optimal value function and policy (time indices are suppressed),

$$V^*(\$, K) = \max_a[c(K, a) + Q^*(\$, K')],$$

$$\mu^*(\$, K) = \arg\max_a[c(K, a) + Q^*(\$, K')].$$

Defining the temporal differences d_t for the approximation Q_k as

$$d_t := r'(\$_t, K'_t, \$_{t+1}) + \gamma \max_a[c(K_{t+1}, a) + Q^{(k)}(\$_{t+1}, K'_{t+1})] - Q^{(k)}(\$_t, K'_t)$$

leads to the update equations for the Q-values represented by tables or networks:

QLU: $\qquad Q^{(k+1)}(\$_t, K'_t) \;=\; Q^{(k)}(\$_t, K'_t) + \eta_k d_t \,,$

NN-QLU: $\qquad w^{(k+1)} \;=\; w^{(k)} + \eta_k d_t \nabla Q(\$, K'; w^{(k)}) \,.$

The simplification is now obvious, because (NN-)QLU only needs one table or neural network no matter how many assets are concerned. This may lead to a faster convergence and better results. The training algorithm boils down to the iteration of the following steps:

QLU for optimal investment decisions

1. draw randomly patterns $\$_t, \$_{t+1}$ from the data set, draw randomly an asset allocation K'_t

2. for all possible actions a: compute $r'_t, c(K_{t+1}, a), Q^{(k)}(\$_{t+1}, K'_{t+1})$

3. compute temporal difference d_t

4. compute new value $Q^{(k+1)}(\$_t, K'_t)$ resp. $Q(\$_t, K'_t; w^{(k+1)})$

5. stop, if Q-values have converged, otherwise go to 1

Since QLU is equivalent to Q-Learning, QLU converges to the optimal Q-values under the same conditions as QL (e. g [2]). The main advantage of (NN-)QLU is that this algorithm only needs one value function no matter how many assets are concerned and how fine the grid of actions are:

$$Q^*((\$, K), a) = c(K, a) + Q^*(\$, K') \,.$$

Interestingly, the convergence to an optimal policy of QLU does not rely on an explicit exploration strategy because the randomly chosen capital K'_t in step 1 simulates a random action which was responsible for the transition from K_t. In combination with the randomly chosen market state $\$_t$, a sufficient exploration of the action and state space is guaranteed.

2.3 Model-free policy-iteration

The reformulation also allows the design of a policy iteration algorithm by alternating a policy evaluation phase (PE) and a policy improvement (PI) step. Defining the temporal differences d_t for the approximation $Q_k^{\mu_l}$ of the policy μ_l in the k step of PE

$$d_t := r'(\$_t, K'_t, \$_{t+1}) + \gamma[c(K_{t+1}, \mu_l(\$_{t+1}, K_{t+1})) + Q^{(k)}(K'_{t+1}, \$_{t+1})] - Q^{(k)}(K'_t, \$_t)$$

leads to the following update equation for tabulated Q-values

$$Q_{\mu_l}^{(k+1)}(\$_t, K'_t) = Q_{\mu_l}^{(k)}(\$_t, K'_t) + \eta_k d_t \,.$$

After convergence, one can improve the policy μ_l to μ_{l+1} by

$$\mu_{l+1}(\$_t, K_t) = \arg \max_a [c(K_t, a) + Q^{\mu_l}(\$_t, K'_t)] .$$

By alternating the two steps PE and PI, the sequence of policies $[\mu_l(x)]_{l=0,...}$ converges under the typical assumptions to the optimal policy $\mu^*(x)$ [2].

Note, that policy iteration is normally not possible using classical QL, if one has not an appropriate model at hand. The introduction of the deterministic intermediate step allows to start with an initial strategy (e. g. given by a broker), which can be subsequently optimized by model-free policy iteration trained with historical data of the financial market. Generalization to parameterized value functions is straightforward.

2.4 Experiments on the German Stock Index DAX

The NN-QLU algorithm is now tested on a real world task: assume that an investor wishes to invest her/his capital into a portfolio of stocks which behaves like the German stock index DAX. Her/his alternative is to keep the capital in the certain asset cash, referred to as DM. We compare the resulting strategy with three benchmarks, namely Neuro-Fuzzy, Buy&Hold and the naive prediction. The Buy&Hold strategy invests at the first time step in the DAX and only sells at the end. The naive prediction invests if the past return of the DAX has been positive and v. v. The third is based on a Neuro-Fuzzy model which was optimized to predict the daily changes of the DAX [8]. The heuristic benchmark strategy is then constructed by taking the sign of the prediction as a trading signal, such that a positive prediction leads to an investment in stocks. The input vector of the Neuro-Fuzzy model, which consists of the DAX itself and 11 other influencing market variables, was carefully optimized for optimal prediction. These inputs also constitutes the $\$_t$ part of the state vector which describes the market within the NN-QLU algorithm. The data is split into a training (from 2. Jan. 1986 to 31. Dec. 1994) and a test set (from 2. Jan. 1993 to 1. Aug. 1996). The transaction costs (c_t) are 0.2% of the invested capital if K_t is changed from DM to DAX, which are realistic for financial institutions. Referring to an epoch as one loop over all training patterns, the training proceeds as outlined in the previous section for 10000 epochs with $\eta_k = \eta_0 \cdot 0.999^k$ with start value $\eta_0 = 0.05$.

Table 1: Comparison of the profitability of the strategies, the number of position changes and investments in DAX for the test (training) data.

strategy	profit	investments in DAX	position changes
NN-QLU	1.60 (3.74)	70 (73)%	30 (29)%
Neuro-Fuzzy	1.35 (1.98)	53 (53)%	50 (52)%
Naive Prediction	0.80 (1.06)	51 (51)%	51 (48)%
Buy&Hold	1.21 (1.46)	100 (100)%	0 (0)%

The strategy constructed with the NN-QLU algorithm, using a neural network with 8 hidden neurons and a linear output, clearly beats the benchmarks. The capital at the end of the test set (training set) exceeds the second best strategy Neuro-Fuzzy by about 18.5% (89%) (fig. 1). One reason for this success is, that QLU changes less often the position and thus, avoids expensive transaction costs. The Neuro-Fuzzy policy changes almost every second day whereas NN-QLU changes only every third day (see tab. 1).

It is interesting to analyze the learning behavior during training by evaluating the strategies of NN-QLU after each epoch. At the beginning, the policies suggest to change almost never or each time to invest in DAX. After some thousand epochs, these bang-bang strategies starts to differentiate. Simultaneously, the more complex the strategies become the more profit they generate (fig. 2).

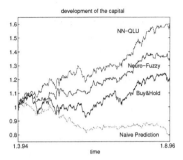

Figure 1: Comparison of the development of the capital for the test set (left) and the training set (right). The NN-QLU strategy clearly beats all the benchmarks.

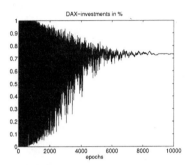
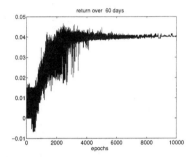

Figure 2: Training course: percentage of DAX investments (left), profitability measured as the average return over 60 days on the training set (right).

3 Controlling the Variance of the Investment Strategies

3.1 Risk-adjusted MDPs

People are not only interested in maximizing the return, but also in controlling the risk of their investments. This has been formalized in the Markowitz portfolio-selection, which aims for an allocation with the maximal expected return for a given risk level [4]. Given a stationary policy $\mu(x)$ with finite state space, the associated value function $V^\mu(x)$ and its variance $\sigma^2(V^\mu(x))$ can be defined as

$$V^\mu(x) = E\left[\sum_{t=0}^{\infty} \gamma^t r(x_t, \mu_t, x_{t+1}) \,\middle|\, x_0 = x\right],$$

$$\sigma^2(V^\mu(x)) = E\left[\left(\sum_{t=0}^{\infty} \gamma^t r(x_t, \mu_t, x_{t+1}) - V^\mu(x)\right)^2 \,\middle|\, x_0 = x\right].$$

Then, an optimal strategy $\mu^*(x; \lambda)$ for a *risk-adjusted MDP* (see [9], S. 410 for variance-penalized MDPs) is

$$\mu^*(x; \lambda) = \arg\max_\mu [V^\mu(x) - \lambda\,\sigma^2(V^\mu(x))] \quad \text{for } \lambda \geq 0 .$$

By variation of λ, one can construct so-called efficient portfolios which have minimal risk for each achievable level of expected return. But in comparison to classical portfolio theory, this approach manages multi-period portfolio management systems including transaction costs. Furthermore, typical min-max requirements on the trading volume and other allocation constraints can be easily implemented by constraining the action space.

3.2 Non-linear Utility Functions

In general, it is not possible to compute $\sigma^2(V^\mu(x))$ with (approximate) dynamic programming or reinforcement techniques, because $\sigma^2(V^\mu(x))$ can not be written in a recursive Bellman equation. One solution to this problem is the use of a return function r_t, which penalizes high variance. In financial analysis, the Sharpe-ratio, which relates the mean of the single returns to their variance i. e., $\bar{r}/\sigma(r)$, is often employed to describe the smoothness of an equity curve. For example, Moody has developed a Sharpe-ratio based error function and combines it with a recursive training procedure [5] (see also [3]). The limitation of the Sharpe-ratio is, that it penalizes also upside volatility. For this reason, the use of an utility function with a negative second derivative, typical for risk averse investors, seems to be more promising. For such return functions an additional unit increase is less valuable than the last unit increase [4]. An example is $r = log$(new portfolio value / old portfolio value) which also penalizes losses much stronger than gains. The Q-function $Q(x, a)$ may lead to intermediate values of a^* as shown in the figure below.

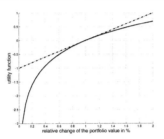
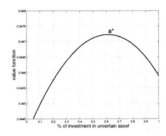

4 Conclusion and Future Work

Two improvements of Q-learning have been proposed to bridge the gap between classical portfolio management and asset allocation with adaptive dynamic programming. It is planned to apply these techniques within the framework of a European Community sponsored research project in order to design a decision support system for strategic asset allocation [7]. Future work includes approximations and variational methods to compute explicitly the risk $\sigma^2(V^\mu(x))$ of a policy.

References

[1] D. P. Bertsekas. *Dynamic Programming and Optimal Control*, vol. 1. Athena Scientific, 1995.

[2] D. P. Bertsekas and J. N. Tsitsiklis. *Neuro-Dynamic Programming*. Athena Scientific, 1996.

[3] M. Choey and A. S. Weigend. Nonlinear trading models through Sharpe Ratio maximization. In proc. of NNCM'96, 1997. World Scientific.

[4] E. J. Elton and M. J. Gruber. *Modern Portfolio Theory and Investment Analysis*. 1995.

[5] J. Moody, L. Whu, Y. Liao, and M. Saffell. Performance Functions and Reinforcement Learning for Trading Systems and Portfolios. *Journal of Forecasting*, 1998. forthcoming.

[6] R. Neuneier. Optimal asset allocation using adaptive dynamic programming. In proc. of *Advances in Neural Information Processing Systems*, vol. 8, 1996.

[7] R. Neuneier, H. G. Zimmermann, P. Hierve, and P. Naim. Advanced Adaptive Asset Allocation. *EU Neuro-Demonstrator*, 1997.

[8] R. Neuneier, H. G. Zimmermann, and S. Siekmann. Advanced Neuro-Fuzzy in Finance: Predicting the German Stock Index DAX, 1996. Invited presentation at ICONIP'96, Hong Kong, availabel by email from Ralph.Neuneier@mchp.siemens.de.

[9] M. L. Puterman. *Markov Decision Processes*. John Wiley & Sons, 1994.

[10] S. P. Singh. *Learning to Solve Markovian Decision Processes*. CMPSCI TR 93-77, University of Massachusetts, November 1993.

[11] C. J. C. H. Watkins and P. Dayan. Technical Note: Q-Learning. *Machine Learning: Special Issue on Reinforcement Learning*, 8, 3/4:279–292, May 1992.

Intrusion Detection with Neural Networks

Jake Ryan*
Department of Computer Sciences
The University of Texas at Austin
Austin, TX 78712
raven@cs.utexas.edu

Meng-Jang Lin
Department of Electrical and Computer Engineering
The University of Texas at Austin
Austin, TX 78712
mj@orac.ece.utexas.edu

Risto Miikkulainen
Department of Computer Sciences
The University of Texas at Austin
Austin, TX 78712
risto@cs.utexas.edu

Abstract

With the rapid expansion of computer networks during the past few years, security has become a crucial issue for modern computer systems. A good way to detect illegitimate use is through monitoring unusual user activity. Methods of intrusion detection based on hand-coded rule sets or predicting commands on-line are laborous to build or not very reliable. This paper proposes a new way of applying neural networks to detect intrusions. We believe that a user leaves a 'print' when using the system; a neural network can be used to learn this print and identify each user much like detectives use thumbprints to place people at crime scenes. If a user's behavior does not match his/her print, the system administrator can be alerted of a possible security breech. A backpropagation neural network called NNID (Neural Network Intrusion Detector) was trained in the identification task and tested experimentally on a system of 10 users. The system was 96% accurate in detecting unusual activity, with 7% false alarm rate. These results suggest that learning user profiles is an effective way for detecting intrusions.

1 INTRODUCTION

Intrusion detection schemes can be classified into two categories: misuse and anomaly intrusion detection. Misuse refers to known attacks that exploit the known vulnerabilities of the system. Anomaly means unusual activity in general that could indicate an intrusion.

---

*Currently: MCI Communications Corp., 9001 N. IH 35, Austin, TX 78753; jake.ryan@mci.com.

If the observed activity of a user deviates from the expected behavior, an anomaly is said to occur.

Misuse detection can be very powerful on those attacks that have been programmed in to the detection system. However, it is not possible to anticipate all the different attacks that could occur, and even the attempt is laborous. Some kind of anomaly detection is ultimately necessary. One problem with anomaly detection is that it is likely to raise many false alarms. Unusual but legitimate use may sometimes be considered anomalous. The challenge is to develop a model of legitimate behavior that would accept novel legitimate use.

It is difficult to build such a model for the same reason that it is hard to build a comprehensive misuse detection system: it is not possible to anticipate all possible variations of such behavior. The task can be made tractable in three ways: (1) Instead of general legitimate use, the behavior of individual users in a particular system can be modeled. The task of characterizing regular patterns in the behavior of an individual user is an easier task than trying to do it for all users simultaneously. (2) The patterns of behavior can be learned for examples of legitimate use, instead of having to describe them by hand-coding possible behaviors. (3) Detecting an intrusion real-time, as the user is typing commands, is very difficult because the order of commands can vary a lot. In many cases it is enough to recognize that the distribution of commands over the entire login session, or even the entire day, differs from the usual.

The system presented in this paper, NNID (Neural Network Intrusion Detector), is based on these three ideas. NNID is a backpropagation neural network trained to identify users based on what commands they use during a day. The system administrator runs NNID at the end of each day to see if the users' sessions match their normal pattern. If not, an investigation can be launched. The NNID model is implemented in a UNIX environment and consists of keeping logs of the commands executed, forming command histograms for each user, and learning the users' profiles from these histograms. NNID provides an elegant solution to off-line monitoring utilizing these user profiles. In a system of 10 users, NNID was 96% accurate in detecting anomalous behavior (i.e. random usage patterns), with a false alarm rate of 7%. These results show that a learning offline monitoring system such as NNID can achieve better performance than systems that attempt to detect anomalies on-line in the command sequences, and with computationally much less effort.

The rest of the paper outlines other approaches to intrusion detection and motivates the NNID approach in more detail (sections 2 and 3), presents the implementation and an evaluation on a real-world computer system (sections 4 and 5), and outlines some open issues and avenues for future work (section 6).

2 INTRUSION DETECTION SYSTEMS

Many misuse and anomaly intrusion detection systems (IDSs) are based on the general model proposed by Denning (1987). This model is independent of the platform, system vulnerability, and type of intrusion. It maintains a set of historical profiles for users, matches an audit record with the appropriate profile, updates the profile whenever necessary, and reports any anomalies detected. Another component, a rule set, is used for detecting misuse.

Actual systems implement the general model with different techniques (see Frank 1994; Mukherjee et al. 1994, for an overview). Often statistical methods are used to measure how anomalous the behavior is, that is, how different e.g. the commands used are from normal behavior. Such approaches require that the distribution of subjects' behavior is known. The behavior can be represented as a rule-based model (Garvey and Lunt 1991), in terms of predictive pattern generation (Teng et al. 1990), or using state transition analysis (Porras et al. 1995). Pattern matching techniques are then used to determine whether the sequence of events is part of normal behavior, constitutes an anomaly, or fits the description of a known attack.

IDSs also differ in whether they are on-line or off-line. Off-line IDSs are run periodically and they detect intrusions after-the-fact based on system logs. On-line systems are designed to detect intrusions while they are happening, thereby allowing for quicker intervention. On-line IDSs are computationally very expensive because they require continuous monitoring. Decisions need to be made quickly with less data and therefore they are not as reliable.

Several IDSs that employ neural networks for on-line intrusion detection have been proposed (Debar et al. 1992; Fox et al. 1990). These systems learn to predict the next command based on a sequence of previous commands by a specific user. Through a shifting window, the network receives the w most recent commands as its input. The network is recurrent, that is, part of the output is fed back as the input for the next step; thus, the network is constantly observing the new trend and "forgets" old behavior over time. The size of the window is an important parameter: If w is too small, there will be many false positives; if it is too big, the network may not generalize well to novel sequences. The most recent of such systems (Debar et al. 1992) can predict the next command correctly around 80% of the time, and accept a command as predictable (among the three most likely next commands) 90% of the time.

One problem with the on-line approach is that most of the effort goes into predicting the order of commands. In many cases, the order does not matter much, but the distribution of commands that are used is revealing. A possibly effective approach could therefore be to collect statistics about the users' command usage over a period of time, such as a day, and try to recognize the distribution of commands as legitimate or anomalous off-line. This is the idea behind the NNID system.

3 THE NNID SYSTEM

The NNID anomaly intrusion detection system is based on identifying a legitimate user based on the distribution of commands she or he executes. This is justifiable because different users tend to exhibit different behavior, depending on their needs of the system. Some use the system to send and receive e-mail only, and do not require services such as programming and compilation. Some engage in all kinds of activities including editing, programming, e-mail, Web browsing, and so on. However, even two users that do the same thing may not use the same application program. For example, some may prefer the "vi" editor to "emacs", favor "pine" over "elm" as their mail utility program, or use "gcc" more often than "cc" to compile C programs. Also, the frequency with which a command is used varies from user to user. The set of commands used and their frequency, therefore, constitutes a 'print' of the user, reflecting the task performed and the choice of application programs, and it should be possible to identify the user based on this information.

It should be noted that this approach works even if some users have aliases set up as shorthands for long commands they use frequently, because the audit log records the actual commands executed by the system. Users' privacy is not violated, since the arguments to a command do not need to be recorded. That is, we may know that a user sends e-mail five times a day, but we do not need to know to whom the mail is addressed.

Building NNID for a particular computer system consists of the following three phases:

1. Collecting training data: Obtain the audit logs for each user for a period of several days. For each day and user, form a vector that represents how often the user executed each command.

as	awk	bc	bibtex	calendar	cat	chmod	comsat	cp	cpp
cut	cvs	date	df	diff	du	dvips	egrep	elm	emacs
expr	fgrep	filter	find	finger	fmt	from	ftp	gcc	gdb
ghostview	gmake	grep	gs	gzip	hostname	id	ifconfig	ispell	last
ld	less	look	lpq	lpr	lprm	ls	machine	mail	make
man	mesg	metamail	mkdir	more	movemail	mpage	mt	mv	netscape
netstat	nm	objdump	perl	pgp	ping	ps	pwd	rcp	resize
rm	rsh	sed	sendmail	sh	sort	strip	stty	tail	tar
tcsh	tee	test	tgif	top	tput	tr	tty	uname	vacation
vi	virtex	w	wc	whereis	xbiff++	xcalc	xdvi	xhost	xterm

Table 1: **The 100 commands used to describe user behavior.** The number of times the user executed each of these commands during the day was recorded, mapped into a nonlinear scale of 11 intervals, and concatenated into a 100-dimensional input vector, representing the usage pattern for that user for that day.

2. Training: Train the neural network to identify the user based on these command distribution vectors.

3. Performance: Let the network identify the user for each new command distribution vector. If the network's suggestion is different from the actual user, or if the network does not have a clear suggestion, signal an anomaly.

The particular implementation of NNID and the environment where it was tested is described in the next section.

4 EXPERIMENTS

The NNID system was built and tested on a machine that serves a particular research group at the Department of Electrical and Computer Engineering at the University of Texas at Austin. This machine has 10 total users; some are regular users, with several other users logging in intermittently. This platform was chosen for three reasons:

1. The operating system (NetBSD) provides audit trail logging for accounting purposes and this option had been enabled on this system.

2. The number of users and the total number of commands executed per day are on an order of magnitude that is manageable. Thus, the feasibility of the approach could be tested with real-world data without getting into scalability issues.

3. The system is relatively unknown to outsiders and the users are all known to us, so that it is likely that the data collected on it consists of normal user behavior (free of intrusions).

Data was collected on this system for 12 days, resulting in 89 user-days. Instead of trying to optimize the selection of features (commands) for the input, we decided to simply use a set of 100 most common commands in the logs (listed in Table 1), and let the network figure out what information was important and what superfluous. Intelligent selection of features might improve the results some but the current approach is easy to implement and proves the point.

In order to introduce more overlap between input vectors, and therefore better generalization, the number of times a command was used was divided into intervals. There were 11 intervals, non-linearly spaced, so that the representation is more accurate at lower frequencies where it is most important. The first interval meant the command was never used; the second that it was used once or twice, and so on until the last interval where the command was used more than 500 times. The intervals were represented by values from 0.0 to 1.0 in 0.1 increments. These values, one for each command, were then concatenated into a 100-dimensional command distribution vector (also called user vector below) to be used as input to the neural network.

The standard three-layer backpropagation architecture was chosen for the neural network. The idea was to get results on the most standard and general architecture so that the feasibility of the approach could be demonstrated and the results would be easily replicable. More sophisticated architectures could be used and they would probably lead to slightly better results. The input layer consisted of 100 units, representing the user vector; the hidden layer had 30 units and the output layer 10 units, one for each user. The network was implemented in the PlaNet Neural Network simulator (Miyata 1991).

5 RESULTS

To avoid overtraining, several training sessions were run prior to the actual experiments to see how many training cycles would give the highest performance. The network was trained on 8 randomly chosen days of data (65 user vectors), and its performance was tested on the remaining 4 days (24 vectors) after epochs 30, 50, 100, 200, and 300, of which 100 gave the best performance. Four splits of the data into training and testing sets were created by randomly picking 8 days for training. The resulting four networks were tested in two tasks:

1. Identifying the user vectors of the remaining 4 days. If the activation of the output unit representing the correct user was higher than those of all other units, and also higher than 0.5, the identification was counted as correct. Otherwise, a false positive was counted.

2. Identifying 100 randomly-generated user vectors. If all output units had an activation less than 0.5, the network was taken to correctly identify the vector as an anomaly (i.e. not any of the known users in the system). Otherwise, the most highly active output unit identifies the network's suggestion. Since all intrusions occur under one of the 10 user accounts, there is a 1/10 chance that the suggestion would accidentally match the compromised user account and the intrusion would not be detected. Therefore, 1/10 of all such cases were counted as false negatives.

The second test is a suggestive measure of the accuracy of the system. It is not possible to come up with vectors that would represent a good sampling of actual intrusions; the idea here was to generate vectors where the values for each command were randomly drawn from the distribution of values for that command in the entire data set. In other words, the random test vectors had the same first-order statistics as the legitimate user vectors, but had no higher-order correlations. Therefore they constitute a neutral but realistic sample of unusual behavior.

All four splits led to similar results. On average, the networks rejected 63% of the random user vectors, leading to an anomaly detection rate of 96%. They correctly identified the legitimate user vectors 93% of the time, giving a false alarm rate of 7%.

Figure 1 shows the output of the network for one of the splits. Out of 24 legitimate user vectors, the network identified 22. Most of the time the correct output unit is very highly activated, indicating high certainty of identification. However, the activation of the highest unit was below 0.5 for two of the inputs, resulting in a false alarm.

Interestingly, in all false alarms in all splits, the falsely-accused user was always the same. A closer look at the data set revealed that there were only 3 days of data on this user. He used the system very infrequently, and the network could not learn a proper profile for him. While it would be easy to fix this problem by collecting more data in this case, we believe this is a problem that would be difficult to rule out in general. No matter how much data one collects, there may still not be enough for some extremely infrequent user. Therefore, we believe the results obtained in this rather small data set give a realistic picture of the performance of the NNID system.

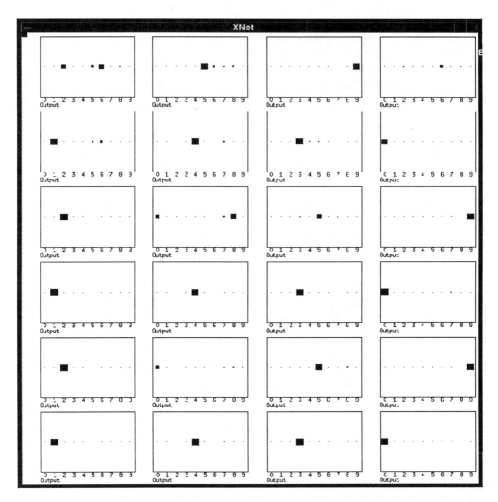

Figure 1: **User identification with the NNID Network.** The output layer of NNID is shown for each of the 24 test vectors in one of the 4 splits tested. The output units are lined up from left to right, and their activations are represented by the size of the squares. In this split there were two false alarms: one is displayed in the top right with activation 0.01, and one in the second row from the bottom, second column from the left with 0.35. All the other test vectors are identified correctly with activation higher than 0.5.

6   DISCUSSION AND FUTURE WORK

An important question is, how well does the performance of NNID scale with the number of users? Although there are many computer systems that have no more than a dozen users, most intrusions occur in larger systems with hundreds of users. With more users, the network would have to make finer distinctions, and it would be difficult to maintain the same low level of false alarms. However, the rate of detecting anomalies may not change much, as long as the network can learn the user patterns well. Any activity that differs from the user's normal behavior would still be detected as an anomaly.

Training the network to represent many more users may take longer and require a larger network, but it should be possible because the user profiles share a lot of common structure, and neural networks in general are good at learning such data. Optimizing the set of commands included in the user vector, and the size of the value intervals, might also have a large impact on performance. It would be interesting to determine the curve of performance versus the number of users, and also see how the size of the input vector and the granularity of the value intervals affect that curve. This is the most important direction of future work.

Another important issue is, how much does a user's behavior change over time? If behavior changes dramatically, NNID must be recalibrated often or the number of false positives would increase. Fortunately such retraining is easy to do. Since NNID parses daily activity of each user into a user-vector, the user profile can be updated daily. NNID could then be retrained periodically. In the current system it takes only about 90 seconds and would not be a great burden on the system.

7   CONCLUSION

Experimental evaluation on real-world data shows that NNID can learn to identify users simply by what commands they use and how often, and such an identification can be used to detect intrusions in a network computer system. The order of commands does not need to be taken into account. NNID is easy to train and inexpensive to run because it operates off-line on daily logs. As long as real-time detection is not required, NNID constitutes a promising, practical approach to anomaly intrusion detection.

Acknowledgements

Special thanks to Mike Dahlin and Tom Ziaja for feedback on an earlier version of this paper, and to Jim Bednar for help with the PlaNet simulator. This research was supported in part by DOD-ARPA contract F30602-96-1-0313, NSF grant IRI-9504317, and the Texas Higher Education Coordinating board grant ARP-444.

References

Debar, H., Becker, M., and Siboni, D. (1992). A neural network component for an intrusion detection system. In *Proceedings of the 1992 IEEE Computer Society Symposium on Research in Computer Security and Privacy*, 240–250.

Denning, D. E. (1987). An intrusion detection model. *IEEE Transactions on Software Engineering*, SE-13:222–232.

Fox, K. L., Henning, R. R., Reed, J. H., and Simonian, R. (1990). A neural network approach towards intrusion detection. In *Proceedings of the 13th National Computer Security Conference*, 125–134.

Frank, J. (1994). Artificial intelligence and intrusion detection: Current and future directions. In *Proceedings of the National 17th Computer Security Conference*.

Garvey, T. D., and Lunt, T. F. (1991). Model-based intrusion detection. In *Proceedings of the 14th National Computer Security Conference*.

Miyata, Y. (1991). *A User's Guide to PlaNet Version 5.6 – A Tool for Constructing, Running, and Looking in to a PDP Network*. Computer Science Department, University of Colorado, Boulder, Boulder, CO.

Mukherjee, B., Heberlein, L. T., and Levitt, K. N. (1994). Network intrusion detection. *IEEE Network*, 26–41.

Porras, P. A., Ilgun, K., and Kemmerer, R. A. (1995). State transition analysis: A rule-based intrusion detection approach. *IEEE Transactions on Software Engineering*, SE-21:181–199.

Teng, H. S., Chen, K., and Lu, S. C. (1990). Adaptive real-time anomaly detection using inductively generated sequential patterns. In *Proceedings of the 1990 IEEE Symposium on Research in Computer Security and Privacy*, 278–284.

Incorporating Contextual Information in White Blood Cell Identification

Xubo Song*
Department of Electrical Engineering
California Institute of Technology
Pasadena, CA 91125
xubosong@fire.work.caltech.edu

Yaser Abu-Mostafa
Dept. of Electrical Engineering
and Dept. of Computer Science
California Institute of Technology
Pasadena, CA 91125
Yaser@over.work.caltech.edu

Joseph Sill
Computation and Neural Systems Program
California Institute of Technology
Pasadena, CA 91125
joe@busy.work.caltech.edu

Harvey Kasdan
International Remote Imaging Systems
9162 Eton Ave.,
Chatsworth, CA 91311

Abstract

In this paper we propose a technique to incorporate contextual information into object classification. In the real world there are cases where the
identity of an object is ambiguous due to the noise in the measurements
based on which the classification should be made. It is helpful to reduce the ambiguity by utilizing extra information referred to as context,
which in our case is the identities of the accompanying objects. This
technique is applied to white blood cell classification. Comparisons are
made against "no context" approach, which demonstrates the superior
classification performance achieved by using context. In our particular
application, it significantly reduces false alarm rate and thus greatly reduces the cost due to expensive clinical tests.

*Author for correspondence.

1 INTRODUCTION

One of the most common assumptions made in the study of machine learning is that the examples are drawn *independently* from some joint input-output distribution. There are cases, however, where this assumption is not valid. One application where the independence assumption does not hold is the identification of white blood cell images. Abnormal cells are much more likely to appear in bunches than in isolation. Specifically, in a sample of several hundred cells, it is more likely to find either no abnormal cells or many abnormal cells than it is to find just a few.

In this paper, we present a framework for pattern classification in situations where the independence assumption is not satisfied. In our case, the identity of an object is dependent of the identities of the accompanying objects, which provides the contextual information. Our method takes into consideration the joint distribution of all the classes, and uses it to adjust the object-by-object classification.

In section 2, the framework for incorporating contextual information is presented, and an efficient algorithm is developed. In section 3 we discuss the application area of white blood cell classification, and address the importance of using context for this application. Empirical testing results are shown in Section 4, followed by conclusions in Section 5.

2 INCORPORATING CONTEXTUAL INFORMATION INTO CLASSIFICATION

2.1 THE FRAMEWORK

Let $\mathbf{x}_i$ be the feature vector of an object , and $c_i = c(\mathbf{x}_i)$ be the classification for $\mathbf{x}_i, i = 1, ...N$, where N is the total number of objects. $c_i \in \{1, ..., D\}$, where D is the number of total classes.

According to Bayes rule,

$$p(c|\mathbf{x}) = \frac{p(\mathbf{x}|c)p(c)}{p(\mathbf{x})}$$

It follows that the "with context" *a posteriori* probability of the class labels of all the objects assuming values $c_1, c_2, ..., c_N$, given all the feature vectors, is

$$p(c_1, c_2, ..., c_N | \mathbf{x}_1, \mathbf{x}_2, ..., \mathbf{x}_N) = \frac{p(\mathbf{x}_1, \mathbf{x}_2, ..., \mathbf{x}_N | c_1, c_2, ..., c_N) p(c_1, c_2, ..., c_N)}{p(\mathbf{x}_1, \mathbf{x}_2, ..., \mathbf{x}_N)} \quad (1)$$

It is reasonable to assume that the feature distribution given a class is independent of the feature distributions of other classes, *i.e.*,

$$p(\mathbf{x}_1, \mathbf{x}_2, ..., \mathbf{x}_N | c_1, c_2, ..., c_N) = p(\mathbf{x}_1 | c_1)...p(\mathbf{x}_N | c_N)$$

Then Equation (1) can be rewritten as

$$p(c_1, c_2, ..., c_N | \mathbf{x}_1, \mathbf{x}_2, ..., \mathbf{x}_N) = \frac{p(\mathbf{x}_1 | c_1)...p(\mathbf{x}_N | c_N) p(c_1, c_2, ..., c_N)}{p(\mathbf{x}_1, \mathbf{x}_2, ..., \mathbf{x}_N)} \quad (2)$$

$$= \frac{p(c_1 | \mathbf{x}_1)...p(c_N | \mathbf{x}_N) p(\mathbf{x}_1)...p(\mathbf{x}_N) p(c_1, c_2, ..., c_N)}{p(c_1)...p(c_N) p(\mathbf{x}_1, \mathbf{x}_2, ..., \mathbf{x}_N)}$$

where $p(c_i|\mathbf{x}_i)$ is the "no context" object-by-object Bayesian *a posteriori* probability, and $p(c_i)$ is the *a priori* probability of the classes, $p(\mathbf{x}_i)$ is the marginal probability of the features, and $p(\mathbf{x}_1, \mathbf{x}_2, ..., \mathbf{x}_N)$ is the joint distribution of all the feature vectors.

Since the features $(\mathbf{x}_1, \mathbf{x}_2, ..., \mathbf{x}_N)$ are given, $p(\mathbf{x}_1, \mathbf{x}_2, ..., \mathbf{x}_N)$ and $p(\mathbf{x}_i)$ are constant,

$$p(c_1, ..., c_N|\mathbf{x}_1, ..., \mathbf{x}_N) \propto p(c_1|\mathbf{x}_1)...p(c_N|\mathbf{x}_N) \frac{p(c_1, ..., c_N)}{p(c_1)...p(c_N)}$$

$$= p(c_1|\mathbf{x}_1)...p(c_N|\mathbf{x}_N)\rho(c_1, c_2, ..., c_N)$$

where

$$\rho(c_1, c_2, ..., c_N) \equiv \frac{p(c_1, c_2, ..., c_N)}{p(c_1)...p(c_N)} \tag{3}$$

The quantity $\rho(c_1, c_2, ..., c_N)$, which we call *context ratio* and through which the context plays its role, captures the dependence among the objects. In the case where all the objects are independent, $\rho(c_1, c_2, ..., c_N)$ equals one – there will be no context. In the dependent case, $\rho(c_1, c_2, ..., c_N)$ will not equal one, and the context has an effect on the classifications.

We deal with the application of object classification where it is the count in each class, rather than the particular ordering or numbering of the objects, that matters. As a result, $\rho(c_1, c_2, ..., c_N)$ is only a function of the count in each class. Let N_d be the count in class d, and $\nu_d = \frac{N_d}{N}, d = 1..., D$,

$$\rho(c_1, c_2, ..., c_N) = \frac{p(c_1, c_2, ..., c_N)}{p(c_1)...p(c_N)}$$

$$= \frac{N_1!...N_D!\, p(\nu_1, \nu_2, ..., \nu_D)}{N!\, P_1^{N\nu_1}...P_D^{N\nu_D}} \tag{4}$$

$$= \rho(\nu_1, ..., \nu_D)$$

where P_d is the prior distribution of class d, for $d = 1, ...D$. $\sum_{d=1}^{D} N_d = N$ and $\sum_{d=1}^{D} \nu_d = 1$.

The decision rule is to choose class labels $\hat{c}_1, \hat{c}_2, ..., \hat{c}_N$ such that

$$(\hat{c}_1, \hat{c}_2, ..., \hat{c}_N) = \underset{(c_1, c_2, ..., c_N)}{\text{argmax}}\ p(c_1, c_2, ..., c_N|\mathbf{x}_1, \mathbf{x}_2, ..., \mathbf{x}_N) \tag{5}$$

When implementing the decision rule, we need to compute and compare D^N cases for Equation 5. In the case of white blood cell recognition, $D = 14$ and N is typically around 600, which makes it virtually impossible to implement.

In many cases, additional constraints can be used to reduce computation, as is the case in white blood cell identification, which will be demonstrated in the following section.

3   WHITE BLOOD CELL RECOGNITION

Leukocyte analysis is one of the major routine laboratory examinations. The utility of leukocyte classification in clinical diagnosis relates to the fact that in various physiological and pathological conditions the relative percentage composition of the blood leukocytes changes. An estimate of the percentage of each class present in a blood sample conveys information which is pertinent to the hematological diagnosis. Typical commercial differential WBC counting systems are designed to identify five major mature cell types. But blood samples may also contain other types of cells, *i.e.* immature cells. These cells occur infrequently in normal specimen, and most commercial systems will simply indicate the presence of these cells because they can't be individually identified by the systems. But it is precisely these cell types that relate to the production rate and maturation of new cells and thus are important indicators of hematological disorders. Our system is designed to differentiate fourteen WBC types which includes the five major mature types: segmented neutrophils, lymphocytes, monocytes, eosinophils, and basophils; *and* the immature types: bands (unsegmented neutrophils), metamyelocytes, myelocytes, promyelocytes, blasts, and variant lymphocytes; as well as nucleated red blood cells and artifacts. Differential counts are made based on the cell classifications, which further leads to diagnosis or prognosis.

The data was provided by IRIS, Inc. Blood specimens are collected at Harbor UCLA Medical Center from local patients, then dyed with Basic Orange 21 metachromatic dye supravital stain. The specimen is then passed through a flow microscopic imaging and image processing instrument, where the blood cell images are captured. Each image contains a single cell with full color. There are typically 600 images from each specimen. The task of the cell recognition system is to categorize the cells based on the images.

3.1 PREPROCESSING AND FEATURE EXTRACTION

The size of cell images are automatically tailored according to the size of the cell in the images. Images containing larger cells have bigger sizes than those with small cells. The range varies from 20x20 to 40x40 pixels. The average size is around 25x25. See Figure 3.1. At the preprocessing stage, the images are segmented to set the cell interior apart from the background. Features based on the interior of the cells are extracted from the images. The features include size, shape, color [1] and texture. See Table 1 for the list of features. [2]

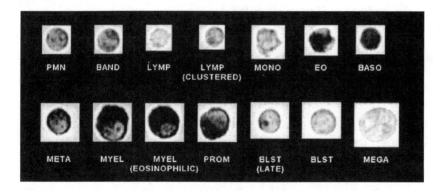

Figure 1: Example of some of the cell images.

3.2 CELL-BY-CELL CLASSIFICATION

The features are fed into a nonlinear feed-forward neural network with 20 inputs, 15 hidden units with sigmoid transfer functions, and 14 sigmoid output units. A cross-entropy error

---

[1] A color image is decomposed into three intensity images – red, green and blue respectively

[2] The red-blue distribution is the pixel-by-pixel log(red)- log(blue) distribution for pixels in cell interior. The red distribution is the distribution of the red intensity in cell interior.

feature number	feature description
1	cell area
2	number of pixels on cell edge
3	the 4th quantile of red-blue distribution
4	the 4th quantile of green-red distribution
5	the median of red-blue distribution
6	the median of green-red distribution
7	the median of blue-green distribution
8	the standard deviation of red-blue distribution
9	the standard deviation of green-red distribution
10	the standard deviation of blue-green distribution
11	the 4th quantile of red distribution
12	the 4th quantile of green distribution
13	the 4th quantile of blue distribution
14	the median of red distribution
15	the median of green distribution
16	the median of blue distribution
17	the standard deviation of red distribution
18	the standard deviation of green distribution
19	the standard deviation of blue distribution
20	the standard deviation of the distance from the edge to the mass center

function is used in order to give the output a probability interpretation. Denote the input feature vector as $\mathbf{x}$, the network outputs a D dimensional vector ($D = 14$ in our case) $\mathbf{p} = \{p(d|\mathbf{x})\}, d = 1, ..., D$, where $p(d|\mathbf{x})$ is

$$p(d|\mathbf{x}) = Prob(\text{ a cell belongs to class } d| \text{ feature } \mathbf{x})$$

The decision made at this stage is

$$d(\mathbf{x}) = \underset{d}{\mathrm{argmax}} \; p(d|\mathbf{x})$$

3.3 COMBINING CONTEXTUAL INFORMATION

The "no-context" cell-by-cell decision is only based on the features presented by a cell, without looking at any other cells. When human experts make decisions, they always look at the whole specimen, taking into consideration the identities of other cells and adjusting the cell-by-cell decision on a single cell according to the company it keeps. On top of the visual perception of the cell patterns, such as shape, color, size, texture, etc., comparisons and associations, either mental or visual, with other cells in the same specimen are made to infer the final decision. A cell is assigned a certain identity if the company it keeps supports that identity. For instance, the difference between lymphocyte and blast can be very subtle sometimes, especially when the cell is large. A large unusual mononuclear cell with the characteristics of both blast and lymphocyte is more likely to be a blast if surrounded by or accompanied by other abnormal cells or abnormal distribution of the cells.

This scenario fits in the framework we described in section 2. The Combining Contextual Information algorithm was used as the post-precessing of the cell-by-cell decisions.

3.4 OBSERVATIONS AND SIMPLIFICATIONS

Direct implementation of the proposed algorithm is difficult due to the computational complexity. In the application of WBC identification, simplification is possible. We observed the following: First, we are primarily concerned with one class blast, the presence of which has clinical significance. Secondly, we only confuse blast with another class lymphocyte. In other words, for a potential blast, $p(\text{blast}|\mathbf{x}) \gg 0$, $p(\text{lymphocyte}|\mathbf{x}) \gg 0$, $p(\text{any other class}|\mathbf{x}) \approx 0$. Finally, we are fairly certain about the classification of all other classes, *i.e.* $p(\text{a certain class}|\mathbf{x}) \approx 1$, $p(\text{any other class}|\mathbf{x}) \approx 0$. Based on the above observations, we can simplify the algorithm, instead of doing an exhaustive search.

Let $p_i^d = p(c_i = d|\mathbf{x}_i), i = 1, ..., N$. More specifically, let $p_i^B = p(\text{blast}|\mathbf{x}_i)$, $p_i^L = p(\text{lymphocyte}|\mathbf{x}_i)$ and $p_i^* = p(\text{class} * |\mathbf{x}_i)$ where $*$ is neither a blast nor a lymphocyte.

Suppose there are K potential blasts. Order the $p_1^B, p_2^B, ..., p_K^B$'s in a descending manner over i, such that

$$p_1^B \geq p_2^B \geq ... \geq p_K^B$$

then the probability that there are k blasts is

$$P_B(k) = p_1^B...p_k^B p_{k+1}^L...p_K^L \, p_{K+1}^*...p_N^* \, \rho(\nu_B = \tfrac{k}{N}, \nu_L = \nu_L' + \tfrac{K-k}{N}, \nu_3, ..., \nu_D)$$

where ν_L' is the proportion of unambiguous lymphocytes and $\nu_3, ..., \nu_D$ are the proportions of the other cell types.

We can compute the $P_B(k)$'s recursively.

$$P_B(0) = p_1^L...p_K^L \, p_{K+1}^*...p_N^* \, \rho(\nu_B = 0, \nu_L = \nu_L' + \frac{K}{N}, \nu_3, ..., \nu_D)$$

$$P_B(k+1) = P_B(k) \frac{p_{k+1}^B \, \rho(\nu_B = \frac{k+1}{N}, \nu_L = \nu_L' + \frac{K-k-1}{N}, \nu_3, ..., \nu_D)}{p_{k+1}^L \, \rho(\nu_B = \frac{k}{N}, \nu_L = \nu_L' + \frac{K-k}{N}, \nu_3, ..., \nu_D)}$$

for k = 1, ..., K-1, and

$$P_B(K) = p_1^B...p_K^B \, p_{K+1}^*...p_N^* \, \rho(\nu_B = \frac{K}{N}, \nu_L = \nu_L', \nu_3, ..., \nu_D)$$

This way we only need to compute K terms to get $P_B(k)$'s . Pick the optimal number of blasts k^* that maximizes $P_B(k), k = 1, ..., K$.

An important step is to calculate $\rho(\nu_1, ..., \nu_D)$ which can be estimated from the database.

3.5 THE ALGORITHM

Step 1 Estimate $\rho(\nu_1, ..., \nu_D)$ from the database, for $d = 1, ..., D$.

Step 2 Compute the object-by-object "no context" *a posteriori* probability $p(c_i|\mathbf{x}_i), i = 1, ..., N$, and $c_i \in \{1, ..., D\}$.

Step 3 Compute $P_B(k)$ and find k^* for $k = 1, ..., K$, and relabel the cells accordingly.

4 EMPIRICAL TESTING

The algorithm has been intensively tested at IRIS, Inc. on the specimens obtained at Harbor UCLA medical center. We compared the performances with or without using contextual information on blood samples from 220 specimens (consisting of 13,200 cells). In about 50% of the cases, a false alarm would have occurred had context not been used. Most cells are correctly classified, but a few are incorrectly labelled as immature cells, which raises a flag for the doctors. Change of the classification of the specimen to abnormal requires expert intervention before the false alarm is eliminated, and it may cause unnecessary worry. When context is applied, the false alarms for most of the specimens were eliminated, and no false negative was introduced.

methods	cell classification	normality identification	false positive	false negative
no context	88%	$\sim 50\%$	$\sim 50\%$	0%
with context	89%	$\sim 90\%$	$\sim 10\%$	0%

Table 2: Comparison of with and without using contextual information

5 CONCLUSIONS

In this paper we presented a novel framework for incorporating contextual information into object identification, developed an algorithm to implement it efficiently, and applied it to white blood cell recognition. Empirical tests showed that the "with context" approach is significantly superior than the "no context" approach. The technique described could be generalized to a number of domains where contextual information plays an essential role, such a speech recognition, character recognition and other medical diagnosis regimes.

Acknowledgments

The authors would like to thank the members of Learning Systems Group at Caltech for helpful suggestions and advice: Dr. Amir Atiya, Zehra Cataltepe, Malik Magdon-Ismail, and Alexander Nicholson.

References

Richard, M.D., & Lippmann, R.P., (1991) Neural network classifiers estimate Bayesian *a posteriori* probabilities. *Neural Computation* **3**. pp.461-483. Cambridge, MA: MIT Press.

Kasdan, H.K., Pelmulder, J.P., Spolter, L., Levitt, G.B., Lincir, M.R., Coward, G.N., Haiby, S. I., Lives, J., Sun, N.C.J., & Deindoerfer, F.H., (1994) The $WhiteIRIS^{TM}$ Leukocyte differential analyzer for rapid high-precision differentials based on images of cytoprobe-reacted cells. *Clinical Chemistry*. Vol. 40, No. 9, pp.1850-1861.

Haralick, R.M., & Shapiro, L.G.,(1992),*Computer and Robot Vision*, Vol.1, Addison-Welsley.

Aus, H. A., Harms, H., ter Meulen, V., & Gunzer, U. (1987) Statistical evaluation of computer extracted blood cell features for screening population to detect leukemias. In Pierre A. Devijver and Josef Kittler (eds.) *Pattern Recognition Theory and Applications*, pp. 509-518. Springer-Verlag.

Kittler, J., (1987) Relaxation labelling. In Pierre A. Devijver and Josef Kittler (eds.) *Pattern Recognition Theory and Applications*, pp. 99-108. Springer-Verlag.

Bach in a Box - Real-Time Harmony

Randall R. Spangler and Rodney M. Goodman[*]
Computation and Neural Systems
California Institute of Technology, 136-93
Pasadena, CA 91125

Jim Hawkins[†]
88B Milton Grove
Stoke Newington, London N16 8QY, UK

Abstract

We describe a system for learning J. S. Bach's rules of musical harmony. These rules are learned from examples and are expressed as rule-based neural networks. The rules are then applied in *real-time* to generate new accompanying harmony for a live performer. Real-time functionality imposes constraints on the learning and harmonizing processes, including limitations on the types of information the system can use as input and the amount of processing the system can perform. We demonstrate algorithms for generating and refining musical rules from examples which meet these constraints. We describe a method for including *a priori* knowledge into the rules which yields significant performance gains. We then describe techniques for applying these rules to generate new music in real-time. We conclude the paper with an analysis of experimental results.

1 Introduction

The goal of this research is the development of a system to learn musical rules from examples of J.S. Bach's music, and then to apply those rules in *real-time* to generate new music in a similar style. These algorithms would take as input a melody such

---

[*]rspangle@micro.caltech.edu, rogo@micro.caltech.edu
[†]jhawkins@cix.compulink.co.uk

Figure 1: Melody for Chorale #1 "Aus meines Herzens Grunde"

Figure 2: J. S. Bach's Harmony For Chorale #1

as Figure 1 and produce a complete harmony such as Figure 2. Performance of this harmonization in real-time is a challenging problem. It also provides insight into the nature of composing music.

We briefly review the representation of input data and the process of rulebase generation. Then we focus on methods of increasing the performance of rule-based systems. Finally we present our data on learning the style of Bach.

1.1 Constraints Imposed by Real-Time Functionality

A program which is to provide real-time harmony to accompany musicians at live performances faces two major constraints.

First, the algorithms must be fast enough to generate accompaniment without detectable delay between the musician playing the melody and the algorithm generating the corresponding harmony. For musical instrument sounds with sharp attacks (plucked and percussive instruments, such as the harp or piano), delays of even a few tens of milliseconds between the start of the melody note and the start of the harmony notes are noticeable and distracting. This limits the complexity of the algorithm and the amount of information it can process for each timestep.

Second, the algorithms must base their output only on information from previous timesteps. This differentiates our system from HARMONET (Hild, Feulnzer and Menzel, 1992) which required knowledge of the next note in the future before generating harmony for the current note.

1.2 Advantages of a Rule-Based Algorithm

A rule-based neural network algorithm was chosen over a recurrent network or a non-linear feed-forward network. Neural networks have been previously used for harmonizing music with some success (Mozer, 1991)(Todd, 1989). However, rule-based algorithms have several advantages when dealing with music. Almost all music has some sort of rhythm and is tonal, meaning both pitch and duration of individual notes are quantized. This presents problems in the use of continuous networks, which must be overtrained to reasonably approximate discrete behavior.

Rule-based systems are inherently discrete, and do not have this problem.

Furthermore it is very difficult to determine why a non-linear multi-layer network makes a given decision or to extract the knowledge contained in such a network. However, it is straightforward to determine why a rule-based network produced a given result by examining the rules which fired. This aids development of the algorithm, since it is easier to determine where mistakes are being made. It allows comparison of the results to existing knowledge of music theory as shown below, and may provide insight into the theory of musical composition beyond that currently available.

Rule-based neural networks can also be modified via segmentation to take advantage of additional *a priori* knowledge.

2   Background

2.1   Representation of Input Data

The choice of input representation greatly affects the ability of a learning algorithm to generate meaningful rules. The learning and inferencing algorithms presented here speak an extended form of the classical figured bass representation common in Bach's time. Paired with a melody, figured bass provides a sufficient amount of information to reconstruct the harmonic content of a piece of music.

Figured bass has several characteristics which make it well-disposed to learning rules. It is a symbolic format which uses a relatively small alphabet of symbols. It is also hierarchical - it specifies first the chord function that is to be played at the current note/timestep, then the scale step to be played by the bass voice, then additional information as needed to specify the alto and tenor scale steps. This allows our algorithm to fire sets of rules sequentially, to first determine the chord function which should be associated with a new melody note, and then to use that chord function as an input attribute to subsequent rulebases which determine the bass, alto, and tenor scale steps. In this way we can build up the final chord from simpler pieces, each governed by a specialized rulebase.

2.2   Generation of Rulebases

Our algorithm was trained on a set of 100 harmonized Bach chorales. These were translated from MIDI format into our figured bass format by a preprocessing program which segmented them into chords at points where any voice changed pitch. Chord function was determined by simple table lookup in a table of 120 common Bach chords based on the scale steps played by each voice in the chord. The algorithm was given information on the current timestep (Mel0-Te0), and the previous two timesteps (Mel1-Func2). This produced a set of 7630 training examples, a subset of which are shown below:

Mel0	Func0	So0	Ba0	Al0	Te0	Mel1	Func1	So1	Ba1	Al1	Te1	Mel2	Func2
D	V	S2	B1	A2	T0	E	I	S1	B0	A0	T2	C	I
E	I7	S1	B3	A0	T2	D	V	S2	B1	A2	T0	E	I
F	IV	S0	B1	A2	T1	E	I7	S1	B3	A0	T2	D	V
G	V	S0	B0	A1	T2	F	IV	S0	B1	A2	T1	E	I7

A rulebase is a collection of rules which predict the same right hand side (RHS) attribute (for example, Function0). All rules have the form **IF Y=y... THEN X=x.** A rule's order is the number of terms on its left hand side (LHS).

Rules are generated from examples using a modified version of the ITRULE algorithm. (Goodman et al., 1992) All possible rules are considered and ranked by a measure of the information contained in each rule defined as

$$J(\mathbf{X}; \mathbf{Y} = y) = p(y) \left[p(x|y) log \left(\frac{p(x|y)}{p(x)} \right) + (1 - p(x|y)) log \left(\frac{1 - p(x|y)}{1 - p(x)} \right) \right] \quad (1)$$

This measure trades off the amount of information a rule contains against the probability of being able to use the rule. Rules are less valuable if they contains little information. Thus, the J-measure is low when $p(x|y)$ is not much higher than $p(x)$. Rules are also less valuable if they fire only rarely ($p(y)$ is small) since those rules are unlikely to be useful in generalizing to new data.

A rulebase generated to predict the current chord's function might start with the following rules:

```
                                        p(corr) J-meas
1. IF  Melody0    E  THEN Function0   I   0.621   0.095

2. IF  Function1  V  THEN Function0  V7   0.624   0.051
   AND Melody1    D
   AND Melody0    D

3. IF  Function1  V  THEN Function0  V7   0.662   0.049
   AND Melody0    D
```

2.3   Inferencing Using Rulebases

Rule based nets are a form of probabilistic graph model. When a rulebase is used to infer a value, each rule in the rulebase is checked in order of decreasing rule J-measure. A rule can fire if it has not been inhibited and all the clauses on its LHS are true. When a rule fires, its weight is added to the weight of the value which it predicts, After all rules have had a chance to fire, the result is an array of weights for all predicted values.

2.4   Process of Harmonizing a Melody

Input is received a note at a time as a musician plays a melody on a MIDI keyboard. The algorithm initially knows the current melody note and the data for the last two timesteps. The system first uses a rulebase to determine the chord function which should be played for the current melody note. For example, given the melody note "C", it might play a chord function "IV", corresponding to an F-Major chord. The program then uses additional rulebases to specify how the chord will be voiced. In the example, the bass, alto, and tenor notes might be set to "B0", "A1", and "T2", corresponding to the notes "F", "A", and "C". The harmony notes are then converted to MIDI data and sent to a synthesizer, which plays them in real-time to accompany the melody.

3 Improvement of Rulebases

The J-measure is a good measure for determining the information-theoretic worth of rules. However, it is unable to take into account any additional *a priori* knowledge about the nature of the problem - for example, that harmony rules which use the current melody note as input are more desirable because they avoid dissonance between the melody and harmony.

3.1 Segmentation

A priori knowledge of this nature is incorporated by segmenting rulebases into more- and less-desirable rules based on the presence or absence of a desired LHS attribute such as the current melody note (Melody0). Rules lacking the attribute are removed from the primary set of rules and placed in a second "fallback" set. Only in the event that no primary rules are able to fire is the secondary set allowed to fire. This gives greater impact to the primary rules (since they are used first) without the loss of domain size (since the less desirable rules are not actually deleted).

Rulebase segmentation provides substantial improvements in the speed of the algorithm in addition to improving its inferencing ability. When an unsegmented rulebase is fired, the algorithm has to compare the current input data with the LHS of every rule in the rulebase. However, processing for a segmented rulebase stops after the first segment which fires a rule on the input data. The algorithm does not need to spend time examining rules in lower-priority segments of that rulebase. This increase in efficiency allows segmented rulebases to contain more rules without impacting performance. The greater number of rules provides a richer and more robust knowledge base for generating harmony.

3.2 Realtime Dependency Pruning

When rules are used to infer a value, the rules weights are summed to generate probabilities. This requires that all rules which are allowed to fire must be independent of one another. Otherwise, one good rule could be overwhelmed by the combined weight of twenty mediocre but virtually identical rules. To prevent this problem, each segment of a rulebase is analyzed to determine which rules are dependent with other rules in the same segment. Two rules are considered dependent if they fire together on more than half the training examples where either rule fires.

For each rule, the algorithm maintains a list of lower rank rules which are dependent with the rule. This list is used in real-time dependency pruning. Whenever a rule fires on a given input, all rules dependent on it are inhibited for the duration of the input. This ensures that all rules which are able to fire for an input are independent.

3.3 Conflict Resolution

When multiple rules fire and predict different values, an algorithm must be used to resolve the conflict. Simply picking the value with the highest weight, while most likely to be correct, leads to monotonous music since a given melody then always produces the same harmony.

To provide a more varied harmony, our system exponentiates the accumulated rule

Table 1: Rulebase Segments

RHS	REQUIRED LHS FOR SEGMENT	RULES
Function0	Melody0, Function1, Function2	110
	Melody0,Function1	380
	Melody0	346
Soprano0	Melody0, Function0	74
Bass0	Function0, Soprano0	125
	(none)	182
Alto0	Soprano0, Bass0	267
	(none)	533
Tenor0	Soprano0, Bass0, Alto0, Function0	52
	Soprano0, Bass0, Alto0	164
	(none)	115

Table 2: Rulebase Performance

RHS	RULEBASE	RULES	AVG EVAL	CORRECT
Function0	unsegmented	1825	1825	55%
	segmented	816	428	56%
	unsegmented #2	428	428	50%
Soprano0	unsegmented	74	74	95%
Bass0	unsegmented	307	307	70%
	segmented	307	162	70%
	unsegmented #2	162	162	65%
Alto0	unsegmented	800	800	63%
	segmented	800	275	63%
	unsegmented #2	275	275	59%
Tenor0	unsegmented	331	331	73%
	segmented	331	180	74%
	unsegmented #2	180	180	67%

weights for the possible outcomes to produce probabilities for each value, and the final outcome is chosen randomly based on those probabilities. It is because we use the accumulated rule weights to determine these probabilities that all rules which are allowed to fire must be independent of each other.

If no rules at all fire, the system uses a first-order Bayes classifier to determine the RHS value based on the current melody note. This ensures that the system will always return an outcome compatible with the melody.

4   Results

Rulebases were generated for each attribute. Up to 2048 rules were kept in each rulebase. Rules were retained if they were correct at least 30% of the time they fired, and had a J-measure greater than 0.001. The rulebases were then segmented.

These rulebases were tested on 742 examples derived from 27 chorales not used in the training set. The number of examples correctly inferenced is shown for each rulebase before and after segmentation. Also shown is the average number of rules evaluated per test example; the speed of inferencing is proportional to this number.

To determine whether segmentation was in effect only removing lower J-measure rules, we removed low-order rules from the unsegmented rulebases until they had the same average number of rules evaluated as the segmented rulebases.

In all cases, segmenting the rulebases reduced the average rules fired per example without lowering the accuracy of the rulebases (in some cases, segmentation even increased accuracy). Speed gains from segmentation ranged from 80% for Tenor0 up to 320% for Function0. In comparison, simply reducing the size of the unsegmented rulebase to match the speed of the segmented rulebase reduced the number of correctly inferred examples by 4% to 6%.

The generated rules for harmony have a great deal of similarity to accepted harmonic transitions (Ottman, 1989). For example, high-priority rules specify common chord transitions such as V-V7-I (a classic way to end a piece of music).

5 Remarks

The system described in this paper meets the basic objectives described in Section 1. It learns harmony rules from examples of the music of J.S. Bach. The system is then able to harmonize melodies in real-time. The generated harmonies are sometimes surprising (such as the diminished 7th chord near the end of "Happy Birthday"), yet are consistent with Bach harmony.

Figure 3: Algorithm's Bach-Like Harmony for "Happy Birthday"

Rulebase segmentation is an effective method for incorporating *a priori* knowledge into learned rulebases. It can provides significant speed increases over unsegmented rulebases with no loss of accuracy.

Acknowledgements

Randall R. Spangler is supported in part by an NSF fellowship.

References

J. Bach (Ed.: A. Riemenschneider) (1941) 371 Harmonized Chorales and 96 Chorale Melodies. Milwaukee, WI: G. Schirmer.

H. Hild, J. Feulner & W. Menzel. (1992) HARMONET: A Neural Net for Harmonizing Chorales in the Style of J. S. Bach. In J. Moody (ed.), *Advances in Neural Information Processing Systems 4*, 267-274. San Mateo, CA: Morgan Kaufmann.

M. Mozer, T. Soukup. (1991) Connectionist Music Composition Based on Melodic and Stylistic Constraints. In R. Lippmann (ed.), *Advances in Neural Information Processing Systems 3*. San Mateo, CA: Morgan Kaufmann.

P. Todd. (1989) A Connectionist Approach to Algorithmic Composition. *Computer Music Journal* **13**(4):27-43.

R. Goodman, P. Smyth, C. Higgins, J. Miller. (1992) Rule-Based Neural Networks for Classification and Probability Estimation. *Neural Computation* **4**(6):781-804.

R. Ottman. (1989) Elementary Harmony. Englewood Cliffs, NJ: Prentice Hall.

Experiences with Bayesian Learning in a Real World Application

Peter Sykacek, Georg Dorffner
Austrian Research Institute for Artificial Intelligence
Schottengasse 3, A-1010 Vienna Austria
peter, georg@ai.univie.ac.at

Peter Rappelsberger
Institute for Neurophysiology at the University Vienna
Währinger Straße 17, A-1090 Wien
Peter.Rappelsberger@univie.ac.at

Josef Zeitlhofer
Department of Neurology at the AKH Vienna
Währinger Gürtel 18-20, A–1090 Wien
Josef.Zeitlhofer@univie.ac.at

Abstract

This paper reports about an application of Bayes' inferred neural network classifiers in the field of automatic sleep staging. The reason for using Bayesian learning for this task is two-fold. First, Bayesian inference is known to embody regularization automatically. Second, a side effect of Bayesian learning leads to larger variance of network outputs in regions without training data. This results in well known moderation effects, which can be used to detect outliers. In a 5 fold cross-validation experiment the full Bayesian solution found with R. Neals hybrid Monte Carlo algorithm, was not better than a single maximum a-posteriori (MAP) solution found with D.J. MacKay's evidence approximation. In a second experiment we studied the properties of both solutions in rejecting classification of movement artefacts.

1 Introduction

Sleep staging is usually based on rules defined by Rechtschaffen and Kales (see [8]). Rechtschaffen and Kales rules define 4 sleep stages, stage one to four, as well as rapid eye movement (REM) and wakefulness. In [1] J. Bentrup and S. Ray report that every year nearly one million US citizens consulted their physicians concerning their sleep. Since sleep staging is a tedious task (one all night recording on average takes about 3 hours to score manually), much effort was spent in designing automatic sleep stagers.

Sleep staging is a classification problem which was solved using classical statistical techniques or techniques emerged from the field of artificial intelligence (AI). Among classical techniques especially the k nearest neighbor technique was used. In [1] J. Bentrup and S. Ray report that the classical technique outperformed their AI approaches. Among techniques from the field of AI, researchers used inductive learning to build tree based classifiers (e.g. ID3, C4.5) as reported by M. Kubat et. al. in [4]. Neural networks have also been used to build a classifier from training examples. Among those who used multi layer perceptron networks to build the classifier, the work of R. Schaltenbrand et. al. seems most interesting. In [10] they use a separate network to refuse classification of too distant input vectors. The performance usually reported is in the range of 75 to 85 percent.

Which enhancements to these approaches can be made to get a reliable system with hopefully better performance? According to S. Roberts et. al. in [9], outlier detection is important to get reliable results in a critical (e.g. medical) environment. To get reliable results one must refuse classification of dubious inputs. Those inputs are marked separately for further inspection by a human expert. To be able to detect such dubious inputs, we use Bayesian inference to calculate a distribution over the neural network weights. This approach automatically incorporates the calculation of confidence for each network estimate. Bayesian inference has the further advantage that regularization is part of the learning algorithm. Additional methods like weight decay penalty and cross validation for decay parameter tuning are no longer needed. Bayesian inference for neural networks was among others investigated by D.J. MacKay (see [5]), Thodberg (see [11]) and Buntine and Weigend (see [3]).

The aim of this paper is to study how Bayesian inference leads to probabilities for classes, which together with doubt levels allow to refuse classification of outliers. As we are interested in evaluating the resulting performance, we use a comparative method on the same data set and use a significance test, such that the effect of the method can easily be evaluated.

2 Methods

In this section we give a short description of the inference techniques used to perform the experiments. We have used two approaches using neural networks as classifiers and an instance based approach in order to make the performance estimates comparable to other methods.

2.1 Architecture for polychotomous classification

For polychotomous classification problems usually a 1-of-c target coding scheme is used. Usually it is sufficient to use a network architecture with one hidden layer. In [2] pp. 237–240, C. Bishop gives a general motivation for the softmax data model, which should be used if one wants the network outputs to be probabilities for classes.

If we assume that the class conditional densities, $p(\underline{z} \mid C_k)$, of the hidden unit activation vector, $\underline{z}$, are from the general family of exponential distributions, then using the transformation in (1), allows to interpret the network outputs as probabilities for classes. This transformation is known as normalized exponential or softmax activation function.

$$p(C_k \mid \underline{z}) = \frac{\exp(a_k)}{\sum_{k'} \exp(a_{k'})} \tag{1}$$

In (1) the value a_k is the value at output node k before applying softmax activation. Softmax transformation of the activations in the output layer is used for both network approaches used in this paper.

2.2 Bayesian Inference

In [6] D.J. MacKay uses Bayesian inference and marginalization to get moderated probabilities for classes in regions where the network is uncertain about the class label. In conjunction with doubt levels this allows to suppress a classification of such patterns. A closer investigation of this approach showed that marginalization leads to moderated probabilities, but the degree of moderation heavily depends on the direction in which we move away from the region with sufficient training data. Therefore one has to be careful about whether the moderation effect should be used for outliers detection.

A Bayesian solution for neural networks is a posterior distribution over weight space calculated via Bayes' theorem using a prior over weights.

$$p(\underline{w} \mid \mathcal{D}) = \frac{p(\mathcal{D} \mid \underline{w})p(\underline{w})}{p(\mathcal{D})} \tag{2}$$

In (2), $\underline{w}$ is the weight vector of the network and $\mathcal{D}$ represents the training data. Two different possibilities are known to calculate the posterior in (2). In [5] D.J. MacKay derives an analytical expression assuming a Gaussian distribution. In [7] R. Neal uses a hybrid Monte Carlo method to sample from the posterior. For one input pattern, the posterior over weight space will lead to a distribution of network outputs.

For a classification problem, following MacKay [6], the network estimate is calculated by marginalization over the output distribution.

$$P(C_1 \mid \underline{x}, \mathcal{D}) = \int P(C_1 \mid \underline{x}, \underline{w})p(\underline{w} \mid \mathcal{D})d\underline{w}$$
$$= \int y(\underline{x}, \underline{w})p(\underline{w} \mid \mathcal{D})d\underline{w} \tag{3}$$

In general, the distribution over output activations will have small variance in regions well represented in the training data and large variance everywhere else. The reason for that is the influence of the likelihood term $p(\mathcal{D} \mid \underline{w})$, which forces the network mapping to lie close to the desired one in regions with training data, but which has no influence on the network mapping in regions without training data. At least for for generalized linear models applied to regression, this property is quantifiable. In [12] C. Williams et.al. showed that the error bar is proportional to the inverse input data density $p(\underline{x})^{-1}$. A similar relation is also plausible for the output activation in classification problems.

Due to the nonlinearity of the softmax transformation, marginalization will moderate probabilities for classes. Moderation will be larger in regions with large variance of the output activation. Compared to a decision made with the most probable weight, the network guess for the class label will be less certain. This moderation effect allows to reject classification of outlying patterns.

Since upper integral can not be solved analytically for classification problems, there are two possibilities to solve it. In [6] D.J. MacKay uses an approximation. Using hybrid Monte Carlo sampling as an implementation of Bayesian inference (see R. Neal in [7]), there is no need to perform upper integration analytically. The hybrid Monte Carlo algorithm samples from the posterior and upper integral is calculated as a finite sum.

$$P(C_1 \mid \underline{x}, \mathcal{D}) \approx \frac{1}{L} \sum_{i=1}^{L} y(\underline{x}, \underline{w}_i) \tag{4}$$

Assuming, that the posterior over weights is represented exactly by the sampled weights, there is no need to limit the number of hidden units, if a correct (scaled) prior is used. Consequently in the experiments the network size was chosen to be large. We used 25 hidden units. Implementation details of the hybrid Monte Carlo algorithm may be found in [7].

2.3 The Competitor

The classifier, used to give performance estimates to compare to, is built as a two layer perceptron network with softmax transformation applied to the outputs. As an error function we use the cross entropy error including a consistent weight decay penalty, as it is e.g. proposed by C. Bishop in [2], pp. 338. The decay parameters are estimated with D.J. MacKay's evidence approximation (see [5] for details). Note that the restriction of D.J. MacKay's implementation of Bayesian learning, which has no solution to arrive at moderated probabilities in 1-of-c classification problems, do not apply here since we use only one MAP value. The key problem with this approach is the Gaussian approximation of the posterior over weights, which is used to derive the most probable decay parameters. This approximation is certainly only valid if the number of network parameters is small compared to the number of training samples. One consequence is, that the size of the network has to be restricted. Our model uses 6 hidden units.

To make the performance of the Bayes inferred classifier also comparable to other methods, we decided to include performance estimates of a k nearest neighbor algorithm. This algorithm is easy to implement and from [1] we have some evidence that its performance is good.

3 Experiments and Results

In this section we discuss the results of a sleep staging experiment based on the techniques described in the "Methods" section.

3.1 Data

All experiments are performed with spectral features calculated from a database of 5 different healthy subjects. All recordings were scored according to the Rechtschaffen & Kales rules. The data pool consisted from data calculated for all electrodes available, which were horizontal eye movement, vertical eye movement and 18 EEG electrodes placed with respect to the international 10-20 system.

The data were transformed into the frequency domain. We used power density values as well as coherency between different electrodes, which is a correlation coefficient expressed as a function of frequency as input features. All data were transformed to zero mean and unit variance. From the resulting feature space we selected 10 features, which were used as inputs for classification. Feature selection was done with a suboptimal search algorithm which used the performance of a k nearest neighbor classifier for evaluation. We used more than 2300 samples during training and about 580 for testing.

3.2   Analysis of Both Classifiers

The analysis of both classifiers described in the "Methods" section should reveal whether besides good classification performance the Bayes' inferred classifier is also capable of refusing outlying test patterns. Increasing the doubt level should lead to better results of the classifier trained by Bayesian Inference if the test data contains outlying patterns. We performed two experiments. During the first experiment we calculated results from a 5 fold cross validation, where training is done with 4 subjects and tests are performed with one independent test person. In a second test we examine the differences of both algorithms on patterns which are definitely outliers. We used the same classifiers as in the first experiment. Test patterns for this experiment were classified movement artefacts, which should not be classified as one of the sleep stages.

The classifier used in conjunction with Bayesian inference was a 2-layer neural network with 10 inputs, 25 hidden units with sigmoid activation and five output units with softmax activation. The large number of hidden units is motivated by the results reported from R. Neal in [7]. R. Neal studied the properties of neural networks in a Bayesian framework when using Gaussian priors over weights. He concluded that there is no need for limiting the complexity of the network when using a correct Bayesian approach. The standard deviation of the Gaussian prior is scaled by the number of hidden units.

For the comparative approach we used a neural network with 10 inputs, 6 hidden units and 5 outputs with softmax activation. Optimization was done via the BFGS algorithm (see C. Bishop in [2]) with automatic weight decay parameter tuning (D.J. MacKay's evidence approximation). As described in the methods section, the smaller network used here is motivated by the Gaussian approximation of the posterior over weights, which is used in the expression for the most probable decay parameters.

The third result is a result achieved with a k nearest neighbor classifier with k set to three.

All results are summaried in table 1. Each column summarizes the results achieved with one of the algorithms and a certain doubt level during the cross validation run. As the k nearest neighbor classifier gives only coarse probability estimates, we give only the performance estimate when all test patterns are classified.

An examination of table 1 shows that the differences between the MAP-solution and the Bayesian solution are extremely small. Consequently, using a t-test, the 0-hypothesis could not be rejected at any reasonable significance level. On the other hand compared to the Bayesian solution, the performance of the k nearest neighbor classifier is significantly lower (the significance level is 0.001).

Table 1: Classification Performance

MAP				
Doubt Cases	0	5%	10%	15%
Mean Perf.	78.6%	80.4%	81.6%	83.2%
Std. Dev.	9.1%	9.4%	9.4%	9.7%
Bayes				
Doubt Cases	0	5%	10%	15%
Mean Perf.	78.4%	80.2%	82.2%	83.6%
Std. Dev.	8.6%	9.0%	9.4%	9.7%
k nearest neighbor				
Doubt Cases	0	5%	10%	15%
Mean Perf.	74.6%	-	-	-
Std. Dev.	8.4%	-	-	-

Table 2: Rejection of Movement Periods

Method	MAP		Bayes	
recognized outliers	No.	%	No.	%
	0	0%	1	7.7%
	1	7.7%	6	46.1%
	2	15.4%	5	38.5%
	0	0%	5	38.5%
	1	7.7%	3	23.1%

The last experiment revealed that both training algorithms lead to comparable performance estimates, when clean data is used. When using the classifier in practice there is no guarantee that the data are clean. One common problem of all night recordings are the so called movement periods, which are periods with muscle activity due to movements of the sleeping subject. During a second experiment we tried to assess the robustness of both neural classifiers against such inputs. During this experiment we used a fixed doubt level, for which approximately 5% of the clean test data from the last experiment were rejected. With this doubt level we classified 13 movement periods, which should not be assigned to any of the other stages. The number of correctly refused outlying patterns are shown in table 2. Analysis of the results with a t-test showed a significant higher rate of removed outliers for the full Bayesian approach. Nevertheless as the number of misclassified outliers is large, one has to be careful in using this side-effect of Bayesian inference.

4 Conclusion

Using Bayesian Inference for neural network training is an approach which leads to better classification results compared with simpler training procedures. Comparing with the "one MAP" solution, we observed significantly larger reliability in detecting dubious patterns. The large amount of remaining misclassified patterns, which were obviously outlying, shows that we should not rely blindly on the moderating effect of marginalization. Despite the large amount of time which is required to calculate the solution, Bayesian inference has relevance for practical applications. On one hand the Bayesian solution shows good performance. But the main reason is the ability to encode a validity region of the model into the solution. Compared to all methods which do not aim at a predictive distribution, this is a clear advantage for Bayesian inference.

Acknowledgements

We want to acknowledge the work of R. R. Neal from the Departments of Statistics and Computer Science at the University of Toronto, who made his implementation of hybrid Monte-Carlo sampling for Bayesian inference available electronically. His software was used to calculate the full Bayes' inferred classification results. We also want to express gratitude to S. Roberts from Imperial College London, one of the partners in the ANNDEE project. His work and his consequence in insisting on confidence measures for network decisions had a large positive impact on our work.

This work was sponsored by the Austrian Federal Ministry of Science and Transport. It was done in the framework of the BIOMED 1 concerted action ANNDEE, financed by the European Commission, DG. XII.

References

[1] J.A. Bentrup and S.R. Ray. An examination of inductive learning algorithms for the classification of sleep signals. Technical Report UIUCDCS-R-93-1792, Dept of Computer Science, University of Illinois, Urbana-Champaign, 1993.

[2] C. M. Bishop. *Neural Networks for Pattern Recognition*. Clarendon Press, Oxford, 1995.

[3] W. L. Buntine and A. S. Weigend. Bayesian back-propagation. *Complex Systems*, 5:603–643, 1991.

[4] M. Kubat, G. Pfurtscheller, and D. Flotzinger. Discrimination and classification using both binary and continuous variables. *Biological Cybernetics*, 70:443–448, 1994.

[5] D. J. C. MacKay. Bayesian interpolation. *Neural Computation*, 4:415–447, 1992.

[6] D. J. C. MacKay. The evidence framework applied to classification networks. *Neural Computation*, 4:720–736, 1992.

[7] R. M. Neal. *Bayesian Learning for Neural Networks*. Springer, New York, 1996.

[8] A. Rechtschaffen and A. Kales. *A manual of standardized terminology, techniques and scoring system for sleep stages of human subjects*. NIH Publication No. 204, US Government Printing Office, Washington, DC., 1968.

[9] S. Roberts, L. Tarassenko, J. Pardey, and D. Siegwart. A confidence measure for artificial neural networks. In *International Conference Neural Networks and Expert Systems in Medicine and Healthcare*, pages 23–30, Plymouth, UK, 1994.

[10] N. Schaltenbrand, R. Lengelle, and J.P. Macher. Neural network model: application to automatic analysis of human sleep. *Computers and Biomedical Research*, 26:157–171, 1993.

[11] H. H. Thodberg. A review of bayesian neural networks with an application to near infrared spectroscopy. *IEEE Transactions on Neural Networks*, 7(1):56–72, January 1996.

[12] C. K. I. Williams, C. Quazaz, C. M. Bishop, and H. Zhu. On the relationship between bayesian error bars and the input data density. In *Fourth International Conference on Artificial Neural Networks, Churchill College, University of Cambridge, UK. IEE Conference Publication No. 409*, pages 160–165, 1995.

A Solution for Missing Data in Recurrent Neural Networks With an Application to Blood Glucose Prediction

Volker Tresp and Thomas Briegel *
Siemens AG
Corporate Technology
Otto-Hahn-Ring 6
81730 München, Germany

Abstract

We consider neural network models for stochastic nonlinear dynamical systems where measurements of the variable of interest are only available at irregular intervals i.e. most realizations are missing. Difficulties arise since the solutions for prediction and maximum likelihood learning with missing data lead to complex integrals, which even for simple cases cannot be solved analytically. In this paper we propose a specific combination of a nonlinear recurrent neural predictive model and a linear error model which leads to tractable prediction and maximum likelihood adaptation rules. In particular, the recurrent neural network can be trained using the real-time recurrent learning rule and the linear error model can be trained by an EM adaptation rule, implemented using forward-backward Kalman filter equations. The model is applied to predict the glucose/insulin metabolism of a diabetic patient where blood glucose measurements are only available a few times a day at irregular intervals. The new model shows considerable improvement with respect to both recurrent neural networks trained with teacher forcing or in a free running mode and various linear models.

1 INTRODUCTION

In many physiological dynamical systems measurements are acquired at irregular intervals. Consider the case of blood glucose measurements of a diabetic who only measures blood glucose levels a few times a day. At the same time physiological systems are typically highly nonlinear and stochastic such that recurrent neural networks are suitable models. Typically, such networks are either used purely free running in which the networks predictions are iterated, or in a teacher forcing mode in which actual measurements are substituted

---

* {volker.tresp, thomas.briegel}@mchp.siemens.de

if available. In Section 2 we show that both approaches are problematic for highly stochastic systems and if many realizations of the variable of interest are unknown. The traditional solution is to use a *stochastic* model such as a nonlinear state space model. The problem here is that prediction and training missing data lead to integrals which are usually considered intractable (Lewis, 1986). Alternatively, state dependent linearizations are used for prediction and training, the most popular example being the extended Kalman filter. In this paper we introduce a combination of a nonlinear recurrent neural predictive model and a linear error model which leads to tractable prediction and maximum likelihood adaptation rules. The recurrent neural network can be used in all generality to model the nonlinear dynamics of the system. The only limitation is that the error model is linear which is not a major constraint in many applications. The first advantage of the proposed model is that for single or multiple step *prediction* we obtain simple iteration rules which are a combination of the output of the iterated neural network and a linear Kalman filter which is used for updating the linear error model. The second advantage is that for maximum likelihood *learning* the recurrent neural network can be trained using the real-time recurrent learning rule RTRL and the linear error model can be trained by an EM adaptation rule, implemented using forward-backward Kalman filter equations. We apply our model to develop a model of the glucose/insulin metabolism of a diabetic patient in which blood glucose measurements are only available a few times a day at irregular intervals and compare results from our proposed model to recurrent neural networks trained and used in the free running mode or in the teacher forcing mode as well as to various linear models.

2   RECURRENT SYSTEMS WITH MISSING DATA

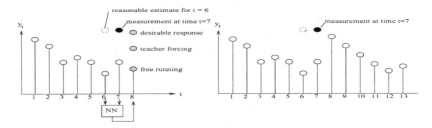

Figure 1: A neural network predicts the next value of a time-series based on the latest two previous measurements (left). As long as no measurements are available ($t = 1$ to $t = 6$), the neural network is iterated (unfilled circles). In a free-running mode, the neural network would ignore the measurement at time $t = 7$ to predict the time-series at time $t = 8$. In a teacher forcing mode, it would substitute the measured value for one of the inputs and use the iterated value for the other (unknown) input. This appears to be suboptimal since our knowledge about the time-series at time $t = 7$ also provides us with information about the time-series at time $t = 6$. For example the dotted circle might be a reasonable estimate. By using the iterated value for the unknown input, the prediction of the teacher forced system is not well defined and will in general lead to unsatisfactory results. A sensible response is shown on the right where the first few predictions after the measurement are close to the measurement. This can be achieved by including a proper error model (see text).

Consider a deterministic nonlinear dynamical model of the form

$$y_t = f_w(y_{t-1}, \ldots, y_{t-N}, u_t)$$

of order N, with input u_t and where $f_w(.)$ is a neural network model with parameter-vector w. Such a recurrent model is either used in a free running mode in which network predictions are used in the input of the neural network or in a teacher forcing mode where measurements are substituted in the input of the neural network whenever these are available.

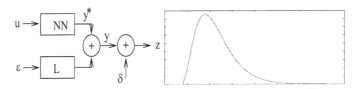

Figure 2: Left: The proposed architecture. Right: Linear impulse response.

Both can lead to undesirable results when many realizations are missing and when the system is highly stochastic. Figure 1 (left) shows that a free running model basically ignores the measurement for prediction and that the teacher forced model substitutes the measured value but leaves the unknown states at their predicted values which also might lead to undesirable responses. The traditional solution is to include a model of the error which leads to nonlinear stochastical models, the simplest being

$$y_t = f_w(y_{t-1}, \ldots, y_{t-N}, u_t) + \epsilon_t$$

where ϵ_t is assumed to be additive uncorrelated zero-mean noise with probability density $P_\epsilon(\epsilon)$ and represents unmodeled system dynamics. For prediction and learning with missing values we have to integrate over the unknowns which leads to complex integrals which, for nonlinear models, have to be approximated, for example, using Monte Carlo integration.[1] In general, those integrals are computationally too expensive to solve and, in practice, one relies on locally linearized approximations of the nonlinearities typically in form of the extended Kalman filter. The extended Kalman filter is suboptimal and summarizes past data by an estimate of the means and the covariances of the variables involved (Lewis, 1986).

In this paper we pursue an alternative approach. Consider the model with state updates

$$y_t^* = f_w(y_{t-1}^*, \ldots, y_{t-N}^*, u_t) \tag{1}$$

$$x_t = \sum_{i=1}^{K} \theta_i x_{t-i} + \epsilon_t \tag{2}$$

$$y_t = y_t^* + x_t = f_w(y_{t-1}^*, \ldots, y_{t-N}^*, u_t) + \sum_{i=1}^{K} \theta_i x_{t-i} + \epsilon_t \tag{3}$$

and with measurement equation

$$z_t = y_t + \delta_t. \tag{4}$$

where ϵ_t and δ_t denote additive noise. The variable of interest y_t is now the sum of the deterministic response of the recurrent neural network y_t^* and a linear system error model x_t (Figure 2). z_t is a noisy measurement of y_t. In particular we are interested in the special cases that y_t can be measured with certainty (variance of δ_t is zero) or that a measurement is missing (variance of δ_t is infinity). The nice feature is now that y_t^* can be considered a deterministic input to the state space model consisting of the equations (2)– (3). This means that for optimal one-step or multiple-step prediction, we can use the *linear* Kalman filter for equations (2)– (3) and measurement equation (4) by treating y_t^* as deterministic input. Similarly, to train the parameters in the linear part of the system (i.e. $\{\theta_i\}_{i=1}^{N}$) we can use an EM adaptation rule, implemented using forward-backward Kalman filter equations (see the Appendix). The deterministic recurrent neural network is adapted with the residual error which cannot be explained by the linear model, i.e. $target_t^{rnn} = y_t^m - \hat{y}_t^{linear}$

---

[1] For maximum likelihood learning of linear models we obtain EM equations which can be solved using forward-backward Kalman equations (see Appendix).

where y_t^m is a measurement of y_t at time t and where $\hat{y}_t^{linear}$ is the estimate of the linear model. After the recurrent neural network is adapted the linear model can be retrained using the residual error which cannot be explained by the neural network, then again the neural network is retrained and so on until no further improvement can be achieved.

The advantage of this approach is that all of the nonlinear interactions are modeled by a recurrent neural network which can be trained deterministically. The linear model is responsible for the noise model which can be trained using powerful learning algorithms for linear systems. The constraint is that the error model cannot be nonlinear which often might not be a major limitation.

3   BLOOD GLUCOSE PREDICTION OF A DIABETIC

The goal of this work is to develop a predictive model of the blood glucose of a person with type 1 Diabetes mellitus. Such a model can have several useful applications in therapy: it can be used to warn a person of dangerous metabolic states, it can be used to make recommendations to optimize the person's therapy and, finally, it can be used in the design of a stabilizing control system for blood glucose regulation, a so-called "artificial beta cell" (Tresp, Moody and Delong, 1994). We want the model to be able to adapt using patient data collected under normal every day conditions rather than the controlled conditions typical of a clinic. In a non-clinical setting, only a few blood glucose measurements per day are available.

Our data set consists of the protocol of a diabetic over a period of almost six months. During that time period, times and dosages of insulin injections (basal insulin u_t^1 and normal insulin u_t^2), the times and amounts of food intake (fast u_t^3, intermediate u_t^4 and slow u_t^5 carbohydrates), the times and durations of exercise (regular u_t^6 or intense u_t^7) and the blood glucose level y_t (measured a few times a day) were recorded. The $u_t^j, j = 1, \ldots, 7$ are equal to zero except if there is an event, such as food intake, insulin injection or exercise. For our data set, inputs u_t^j were recorded with 15 minute time resolution. We used the first 43 days for training the model (containing 312 measurements of the blood glucose) and the following 21 days for testing (containing 151 measurements of the blood glucose). This means that we have to deal with approximately 93% of missing data during training.

The effects on insulin, food and exercise on the blood glucose are delayed and are approximated by linear response functions. v_t^j describes the effect of input u_t^j on glucose. As an example, the response v_t^2 of normal insulin u_t^2 after injection is determined by the diffusion of the subcutaneously injected insulin into the blood stream and can be modeled by three first order compartments in series or, as we have done, by a response function of the form $v_t^2 = \sum_\tau g_2(t - \tau)u_\tau^2$ with $g_2(t) = a_2 t^2 e^{-b_2 t}$ (see figure 2 for a typical impulse response). The functional mappings $g_j(.)$ for the digestive tract and for exercise are less well known. In our experiments we followed other authors and used response functions of the above form.

The response functions $g_j(.)$ describe the delayed effect of the inputs on the blood glucose. We assume that the functional form of $g_j(.)$ is sufficient to capture the various delays of the inputs and can be tuned to the physiology of the patient by varying the parameters a_j, b_j. To be able to capture the highly nonlinear physiological interactions between the response functions v_t^j and the blood glucose level y_t, which is measured only a few times a day, we employ a neural network in combination with a linear error model as described in Section 2. In our experiments $f_w(.)$ is a feedforward multi-layer perceptron with three hidden units. The five inputs to the network were insulin ($in_t^1 = v_t^1 + v_t^2$), food ($in_t^2 = v_t^3 + v_t^4 + v_t^5$), exercise ($in_t^3 = v_t^6 + v_t^7$) and the current and previous estimate of the blood glucose. To be specific, the second order nonlinear neural network model is

$$y_t^* = y_{t-1}^* + f_w(y_{t-1}^*, y_{t-2}^*, in_t^1, in_t^2, in_t^3) \tag{5}$$

For the linear error model we also use a model of order 2

$$x_t = \theta_1 x_{t-1} + \theta_2 x_{t-2} + \epsilon_t \tag{6}$$

Table 1 shows the explained variance of the test set for different predictive models. [2]

In the first experiment (RNN-FR) we estimate the blood glucose at time t as the output of the neural network $\hat{y}_t = y_t^*$. The neural network is used in the free running mode for training and prediction. We use RTRL to both adapt the weights in the neural network as well as all parameters in the response functions $g_j(.)$. The RNN-FR model explains 14.1 percent of the variance. The RNN-TF model is identical to the previous experiment except that measurements are substituted whenever available. RNN-TF could explain more of the variance (18.8%). The reason for the better performance is, of course, that information about measurements of the blood glucose can be exploited.

The model RNN-LEM2 (error model with order 2) corresponds to the combination of the recurrent neural network and the linear error model as introduced in Section 2. Here, $y_t = x_t + y_t^*$ models the blood glucose and $z_t = y_t + \delta_t$ is the measurement equation where we set the variance of $\delta_t = 0$ for a measurement of the blood glucose at time t and the variance of $\delta_t = \infty$ for missing values. For ϵ_t we assume Gaussian independent noise. For prediction, equation (5) is iterated in the free running mode. The blood glucose at time t is estimated using a linear Kalman filter, treating y_t^* as deterministic input in the state space model $y_t = x_t + y_t^*$, $z_t = y_t + \delta_t$. We adapt the parameters in the linear error model (i.e. θ_1, θ_2, the variance of ϵ_t) using an EM adaptation rule, implemented using forward-backward Kalman filter equations (see Appendix). The parameters in the neural network are adapted using RTRL exactly the same way as in the RNN-FR model, except that the target is now $target_t^{rnn} = y_t^m - \hat{y}_t^{linear}$ where y_t^m is a measurement of y_t at time t and where $\hat{y}_t^{linear}$ is the estimate of the linear error model (based on the linear Kalman filter). The adaptation of the linear error model and the neural network are performed alternatively until no significant further improvement in performance can be achieved.

As indicated in Table 1, the RNN-LEM2 model achieves the best prediction performance with an explained variance of 44.9% (first order error model RNN-LEM1: 43.7%). As a comparison, we show the performance of just the linear error model LEM (this model ignores all inputs), a linear model (LM-FR) without an error model trained with RTRL and a linear model with an error model (LM-LEM). Interestingly, the linear error model which does not see any of the inputs can explain more variance (12.9%) than the LM-FR model (8.9%). The LM-LEM model, which can be considered a combination of both can explain more than the sum of the individual explained variances (31.5%) which indicates that the combined training gives better performance than training both submodels individually. Note also, that the nonlinear models (RNN-FR, RNN-TF, RNN-LEM) give considerably better results than their linear counterparts, confirming that the system is highly nonlinear.

Figure 3 (left) shows an example of the responses of some of the models. We see that the free running neural network (dotted line) has relatively small amplitudes and cannot predict the three measurements very well. The RNN-TF model (dashed line) shows a better response to the measurements than the free running network. The best prediction of all measurements is indeed achieved by the RNN-LEM model (continuous line).

Based on the linear iterated Kalman filter we can calculate the variance of the prediction. As shown in Figure 3 (right) the standard deviation is small right after a measurement is available and then converges to a constant value. Based on the prediction and the estimated variance, it will be possible to do a risk analysis for the diabetic (i.e a warning of dangerous metabolic states).

---

[2] MSPE($model$) is the mean squared prediction error on the test set of the model and MSPE($mean$) is the mean squared prediction error of predicting the mean.

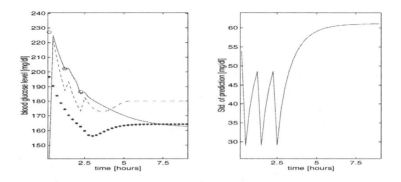

Figure 3: Left: Responses of some models to three measurements. Note, that the prediction of the first measurement is bad for all models but that the RNN-LEM model (continuous line) predicts the following measurements much better than both the RNN-FR (dotted) and the RNN-TF (dashed) model. Right: Standard deviation of prediction error of RNN-LEM.

Table 1: Explained variance on test set [in percent]: $100 \cdot \left(1 - \frac{\mathrm{MSPE}(model)}{\mathrm{MSPE}(mean)}\right)$

MODEL	%	MODEL	%
mean	0	RNN-TF	18.8
LM	8.9	LM-LEM	31.4
LEM	12.9	RNN-LEM1	43.7
RNN-FR	14.1	RNN-LEM2	44.9

4   CONCLUSIONS

We introduced a combination of a nonlinear recurrent neural network and a linear error model. Applied to blood glucose prediction it gave significantly better results than both recurrent neural networks alone and various linear models. Further work might lead to a predictive model which can be used by a diabetic on a daily bases. We believe that our results are very encouraging. We also expect that our specific model can find applications in other stochastical nonlinear systems in which measurements are only available at irregular intervals such that in wastewater treatment, chemical process control and various physiological systems. Further work will include error models for the input measurements (for example, the number of food calories are typically estimated with great uncertainty).

Appendix: EM Adaptation Rules for Training the Linear Error Model

Model and observation equations of a general model are[3]

$$x_t = \Theta x_{t-1} + \epsilon_t \qquad z_t = M_t x_t + \delta_t. \qquad (7)$$

where Θ is the $K \times K$ transition matrix of the K-order linear error model. The $K \times 1$ noise terms ϵ_t are zero-mean uncorrelated normal vectors with common covariance matrix Q. δ_t is m-dimensional [4] zero-mean uncorrelated normal noise vector with covariance matrix R_t. Recall that we consider certain measurements and missing values as special cases of

---

[3] Note, that any linear system of order K can be transformed into a first order linear system of dimension K.

[4] m indicates the dimension of the output of the time-series.

noisy measurements. The initial state of the system is assumed to be a normal vector with mean μ and covariance Σ.

We describe the EM equations for maximizing the likelihood of the model. Define the estimated parameters at the $(r+1)$st iterate of EM as the values μ, Σ, Θ, Q which maximize

$$G(\mu, \Sigma, \Theta, Q) = E_r(\log L | z_1, \ldots, z_n) \tag{8}$$

where $\log L$ is log-likelihood of the complete data $x_0, x_1, \ldots, x_n, z_1, \ldots, z_n$ and E_r denotes the conditional expectation relative to a density containing the rth iterate values $\mu(r), \Sigma(r), \Theta(r)$ and $Q(r)$. Recall that missing targets are modeled implicitly by the definition of M_t and R_t.

For calculating the conditional expectation defined in (8) the following set of recursions are used (using standard Kalman filtering results, see (Jazwinski, 1970)). First, we use the forward recursion

$$
\begin{aligned}
x_t^{t-1} &= \Theta x_{t-1}^{t-1} \\
P_t^{t-1} &= \Theta P_{t-1}^{t-1} \Theta^{\top} + Q \\
K_t &= P_t^{t-1} M_t^{\top} (M_t P_t^{t-1} M_t^{\top} + R_t)^{-1} \\
x_t^t &= x_t^{t-1} + K_t(y_t^* - M_t x_t^{t-1}) \\
P_t^t &= P_t^{t-1} - K_t M_t P_t^{t-1}
\end{aligned}
\tag{9}
$$

where we take $x_0^0 = \mu$ and $P_0^0 = \Sigma$. Next, we use the backward recursion

$$
\begin{aligned}
J_{t-1} &= P_{t-1}^{t-1} \Theta^{\top} (P_t^{t-1})^{-1} \\
x_{t-1}^n &= x_{t-1}^{t-1} + J_{t-1}(x_t^n - \Theta x_{t-1}^{t-1}) \\
P_{t-1}^n &= P_{t-1}^{t-1} + J_{t-1}(P_t^n - P_t^{t-1}) J_{t-1}^{\top} \\
P_{t-1,t-2}^n &= P_{t-1}^{t-1} J_{t-2}^{\top} + J_{t-1}(P_{t,t-1}^n - \Theta P_{t-1}^{t-1}) J_{t-2}^{\top}
\end{aligned}
\tag{10}
$$

with initialization $P_{n,n-1}^n = (I - K_n M_n)\Theta P_{n-1}^{n-1}$. One forward and one backward recursion completes the E-step of the EM algorithm.

To derive the M-step first realize that the conditional expectations in (8) yield to the following equation:

$$
\begin{aligned}
G = & -\tfrac{1}{2}\log|\Sigma| - \tfrac{1}{2}\text{tr}\{\Sigma^{-1}(P_0^n + (x_0^n - \mu)(x_0^n - \mu)^{\top})\} \\
& -\tfrac{n}{2}\log|Q| - \tfrac{1}{2}\text{tr}\{Q^{-1}(C - B\Theta^{\top} - \Theta B^{\top} - \Theta A\Theta^{\top})\} \\
& -\tfrac{n}{2}\log|R_t| - \tfrac{1}{2}\text{tr}\{R_t^{-1}\sum_{t=1}^n[(y_t^* - M_t x_t)(y_t^* - M_t x_t)^{\top} + M_t P_t^n M_t^{\top}]\}
\end{aligned}
\tag{11}
$$

where $\text{tr}\{.\}$ denotes the trace, $A = \sum_{t=1}^n(P_{t-1}^n + x_{t-1}^n x_{t-1}^{n\top})$,

$B = \sum_{t=1}^n(P_{t,t-1}^n + x_t^n x_{t-1}^{n\top})$ and $C = \sum_{t=1}^n(P_t^n + x_t^n x_t^{n\top})$.

$\Theta(r+1) = BA^{-1}$ and $Q(r+1) = n^{-1}(C - BA^{-1}B^{\top})$ maximize the log-likelihood equation (11). $\mu(r+1)$ is set to x_0^n and Σ may be fixed at some reasonable baseline level. The derivation of these equations can be found in (Shumway & Stoffer, 1981).

The E- (forward and backward Kalman filter equations) and M-steps are alternated repeatedly until convergence to obtain the EM solution.

References

Jazwinski, A. H. (1970) *Stochastic Processes and Filtering Theory*, Academic Press, N.Y.

Lewis, F. L. (1986) *Optimal Estimation*, John Wiley, N.Y.

Shumway, R. H. and Stoffer, D. S. (1981) *Time Series Smoothing and Forecasting Using the EM Algorithm*, Technical Report No. 27, Division of Statistics, UC Davis.

Tresp, V., Moody, J. and Delong, W.-R. (1994) *Neural Modeling of Physiological Processes*, in Comput. Learning Theory and Natural Learning Sys. 2, S. Hanson *et al.*, eds., MIT Press.

Use of a Multi-Layer Perceptron to Predict Malignancy in Ovarian Tumors

Herman Verrelst,
Yves Moreau and Joos Vandewalle
Dept. of Electrical Engineering
Katholieke Universiteit Leuven
Kard. Mercierlaan 94
B-3000 Leuven, Belgium

Dirk Timmerman

Dept. of Obst. and Gynaec.
University Hospitals Leuven
Herestraat 49
B-3000 Leuven, Belgium

Abstract

We discuss the development of a Multi-Layer Perceptron neural network classifier for use in preoperative differentiation between benign and malignant ovarian tumors. As the Mean Squared classification Error is not sufficient to make correct and objective assessments about the performance of the neural classifier, the concepts of sensitivity and specificity are introduced and combined in Receiver Operating Characteristic curves. Based on objective observations such as sonomorphologic criteria, color Doppler imaging and results from serum tumor markers, the neural network is able to make reliable predictions with a discriminating performance comparable to that of experienced gynecologists.

1 Introduction

A reliable test for preoperative discrimination between benign and malignant ovarian tumors would be of considerable help to clinicians. It would assist them to select patients for whom minimally invasive surgery or conservative management suffices versus those for whom urgent referral to a gynecologic oncologist is needed.

We discuss the development of a neural network classifier/diagnostic tool. The neural network was trained by supervised learning, based on data from 191 thoroughly examined patients presenting with ovarian tumors of which 140 were benign and 51 malignant. As inputs to the network we chose indicators that in recent studies have proven their high predictive value [1, 2, 3]. Moreover, we gave preference to those indicators that can be obtained in an objective way by any gynecologist. Some of these indicators have already been used in attempts to make one single protocol or decision algorithm [3, 4].

In order to make reliable assessments on the practical performance of the classifier, it is necessary to work with other concepts than Mean Squared classification Error (MSE), which is traditionally used as a measure of goodness in the training of a neural network. We will introduce notions as specificity and sensitivity and combine them into Receiver Operating Characteristic (ROC) curves. The use of ROC-curves is motivated by the fact that they are independent of the relative proportion of the various output classes in the sample population. This enables an objective validation of the performance of the classifier. We will also show how, in the training of the neural network, MSE optimization with gradient methods can be refined and/or replaced with the help of ROC-curves and simulated annealing techniques.

The paper is organized as follows. In Section 2 we give a brief description of the selected input features. In Section 3 we state some drawbacks to the MSE criterion and introduce the concepts of sensitivity, specificity and ROC-curves. Section 4 then deals with the technicalities of training the neural network. In Section 5 we show the results and compare them to human performance.

2 Data acquisition and feature selection

The data were derived from a study group of 191 consecutive patients who were referred to a single institution (University Hospitals Leuven, Belgium) from August 1994 to August 1996. Table 1 lists the different indicators which were considered, together with their mean value and standard deviations or together with the relative presence in cases of benign and malignant tumors.

Table 1	Indicator	Benign	Malignant
Demographic	Age	49.3 ± 16.0	58.3 ± 14.3
	Postmenopausal	40%	70.6%
Serum marker	CA 125 (log)	2.8 ± 1.1	5.2 ± 1.9
CDI	Blood flow present	72.9%	100%
Morphologic	Abdominal fluid	12.1%	52.9%
	Bilateral mass	11.4%	35.3%
	Unilocular cyst	42.1%	5.9%
	Multiloc/solid cyst	16.4%	49.0%
	Smooth wall	58.6%	2.0%
	Irregular wall	32.1%	76.5%
	Papillations	7.9%	74.5%

Table 1: Demographic, serum marker, color Doppler imaging and morphologic indicators. For the continuous valued features the mean and standard deviation for each class are reported. For binary valued indicators, the last two columns give the presence of the feature in both classes e.g. only 2% of malignant tumors had smooth walls.

First, all patients were scanned with ultrasonography to obtain detailed gray-scale images of the tumors. Every tumor was extensively examined for its morphologic characteristics. Table 1 lists the selected morphologic features: presence of abdominal fluid collection, papillary structures (> 3mm), smooth internal walls, wall irregularities, whether the cysts were unilocular, multilocular-solid and/or present on both pelvic sides. All outcomes are binary valued: every observation relates to the presence (1) or absence (0) of these characteristics.

Secondly, all tumors were entirely surveyed by color Doppler imaging to detect presence or absence of blood flow within the septa, cyst walls, solid tumor areas or ovarian tissue. The outcome is also binary valued (1/0).

Thirdly, in 173 out of the total of 191 patients, serum CA 125 levels were measured, using CA 125 II immunoradiometric assays (Centocor, Malvern, PA). The CA 125 antigen is a glycoprotein that is expressed by most epithelial ovarian cancers. The numerical value gives the concentration in U/ml. Because almost all values were situated in a small interval between 0 and 100, and because a small portion took values up to 30,000, this variable was rescaled by taking its logarithm.

Since age and menopausal status of the patient are considered to be highly relevant, these are also included. The menopausal score is -1 for premenopausal, $+1$ for postmenopausal. A third class of patients were assigned a 0 value. These patients had had an hysterectomy, so no menopausal status could be appointed to them.

It is beyond the scope of this paper to give a complete account of the meaning of the different features that are used or the way in which the data were acquired. We will limit ourselves to this short description and refer the reader to [2, 3] and gynecological textbooks for a more detailed explanation.

3 Receiver Operating Characteristics

3.1 Drawbacks to Mean Squared classification Error

Let us assume that we use a one-hidden-layer feed-forward NN with m inputs x_k^i, n_h hidden neurons with the tanh(.) as activation function, and one output $\hat{y}_k$,

$$y_k(\theta) = \sum_{j=1}^{n_h} w_j \tanh(\sum_{i=1}^{m} v_{ij} x_k^i + \beta_j), \tag{1}$$

parameterized by the vector θ consisting of the network's weights w_j and v_{ij} and bias terms β_j. The cost function is often chosen to be the squared difference between the desired d_k and the actual response y_k, averaged over all N samples [12],

$$J(\theta) = \frac{1}{N} \sum_{k=1}^{N} (d_k - y_k(\theta))^2. \tag{2}$$

This type of cost function is continuous and differentiable, so it can be used in gradient based optimization techniques such as steepest descent (back-propagation), quasi-Newton or Levenberg-Marquardt methods [8, 9, 11, 12]. However there are some drawbacks to the use of this type of cost function.

First of all, the MSE is heavily dependent on the relative proportion of the different output classes in the training set. In our dichotomic case this can easily be demonstrated by writing the cost function, with superscripts b and m respectively meaning benign and malignant, as

$$J(\theta) = \underbrace{\frac{N_b}{N_b + N_m}}_{\lambda} \frac{1}{N_b} \sum_{k=1}^{N_b} (d_k^b - y_k)^2 + \underbrace{\frac{N_m}{N_b + N_m}}_{(1-\lambda)} \frac{1}{N_m} \sum_{k=1}^{N_m} (d_k^m - y_k)^2 \tag{3}$$

If the relative proportion in the sample population is not representative for reality, the λ parameter should be adjusted accordingly. In practice this real proportion is often not known accurately or one simply ignores the meaning of λ and uses it as a design parameter in order to bias the accuracy towards one of the output classes.

A second drawback of the MSE cost function is that it is not very informative towards practical usage of the classification tool. A clinician is not interested in the averaged deviation from desired numbers, but thinks in terms of percentages found, missed or misclassified. In the next section we will introduce the concepts of sensitivity and specificity to express these more practical measures.

3.2 Sensitivity, specificity and ROC-curves

If we take the desired response to be 0 for benign and 1 for malignant cases, the way to make clearcut (dichotomic) decisions is to compare the numerical outcome of the neural network to a certain threshold value T between 0 and 1. When the outcome is above the threshold T, the prediction is said to be *positive*. Otherwise the prediction is said to be *negative*. With this convention, we say that the prediction was

True Positive (TP)   if the prediction was positive when the sample was malignant.
True Negative (TN)   if the prediction was negative when the sample was benign.
False Positive (FP)   if the prediction was positive when the sample was benign.
False Negative (FN)   if the prediction was negative when the sample was malignant.

To every of the just defined terms TP, TN, FP and FN, a certain subregion of the total sample space can be associated, as depicted in Figure 1. In the same sense, we can associate to them a certain number counting the samples in each subregion. We can then define sensitivity as $\frac{TP}{TP+FN}$, the proportion of malignant cases that

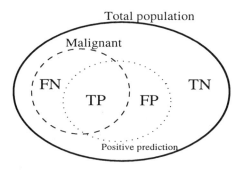

Figure 1: The concepts of true and false positive and negative illustrated. The dashed area indicates the malignant cases in the total sample population. The positive prediction of an imperfect classification (dotted area) does not fully coincide with this sub area.

are predicted to be malignant and specificity as $\frac{TN}{FP+TN}$, the proportion of benign cases that are predicted to be benign. The false positive rate is $1-$specificity.

When varying the threshold T, the values of TP, TN, FP, FN and therefore also sensitivity and specificity, will change. A low threshold will detect almost all malignant cases at the cost of many false positives. A high threshold will give less false positives, but will also detect less malignant cases. Receiver Operating Characteristic (ROC) curves are a way to visualize this relationship. The plot gives the sensitivity versus false positive rate for varying thresholds T (e.g. Figure 2).

The ROC-curve is useful and widely used device for assessing and comparing the value of tests [5, 7]. The proportion of the whole area of the graph which lies below the ROC-curve is a one-value measure of the accuracy of a test [6]. The higher this proportion, the better the test. Figure 2 shows the ROC-curves for two simple classifiers that use only one single indicator. (Which means that we classify a tumor being malignant when the value of the indicator rises above a certain value.) It is seen that the CA 125 level has high predictive power as its ROC-curve spans 87.5% of the total area (left Figure 2). For the age parameter, the ROC-curve spans only 65.6% (right Figure 2). As indicated by the horizontal line in the plot, a CA 125 level classification will only misclassify 15% of all benign cases to reach a 80% sensitivity, whereas using only age, one would then misclassify up to 50% of them.

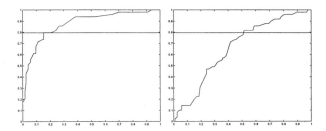

Figure 2: The Receiver Operating Characteristic (ROC) curve is the plot of the sensitivity versus the false positive rate of a classifier for varying thresholds used. Only single indicators (left: CA 125, right: age) are used for these ROC-curves. The horizontal line marks the 80% specificity level.

Since for every set of parameters of the neural network the area under the ROC-curve can be calculated numerically, this one-value measure can also be used for supervised training, as will be shown in the next Section.

4   Simulation results

4.1   Inputs and architecture

The continuous inputs were standardized by subtracting their mean and dividing by their standard deviation (both calculated over the entire population). Binary valued inputs were left unchanged. The desired outputs were labeled 0 for benign examples, 1 for malignant cases. The data set was split up: 2/3 of both benign and malignant samples were randomly selected to form the training set. The remaining examples formed the test set. The ratio of benign to all examples is $\lambda \approx \frac{2}{3}$.

Since the training set is not large, there is a risk of overtraining when too many parameters are used. We will limit the number of hidden neurons to $n_h = 3$ or 5. As the CA 125 level measurement is more expensive and time consuming, we will investigate two different classifiers: one which does use the CA 125 level and one which does not. The one-hidden-layer MLP architectures that are used, are 11-3-1 and 10-5-1. A tanh(.) is taken for the activation function in the hidden layer.

4.2   Training

A first way of training was MSE optimization using the cost function (3). By taking $\lambda = \frac{1}{3}$ in this expression, the role of malignant examples is more heavily weighted. The parameter vector θ was randomly initialized (zero mean Gaussian distribution, standard deviation $\sigma = 0.01$). Training was done using a quasi-Newton method with BFGS-update of the Hessian ($fminu$ in Matlab) [8, 9]. To prevent overtraining, the training was stopped before the MSE on the test set started to rise. Only few iterations (≈ 100) were needed.

A second way of training was through the use of the area spanned by the ROC-curve of the classifier and simulated annealing techniques [10]. The area-measure A^{ROC} was numerically calculated for every set of trial parameters: first the sensitivity and false positive rate were calculated for 1000 increasing values of the threshold T between 0 and 1, which gave the ROC-curve; secondly the area A^{ROC} under the curve was numerically calculated with the trapezoidal integration rule.

We used Boltzmann Simulated Annealing to maximize the ROC-area. At time k a trial parameter set of the neural network θ_{k+1} is randomly generated in the neighborhood of the present set θ_k (Gaussian distribution, $\sigma = 0.001$). The trial set θ_{k+1} is always accepted if the area $A_{k+1}^{ROC} \geq A_k^{ROC}$. If $A_{k+1}^{ROC} < A_k^{ROC}$, θ_{k+1} is accepted if

$$e^{(\frac{A_{k+1}^{ROC} - A_k^{ROC}}{A_k^{ROC}})/T_e} > \alpha$$

with α a uniformly distributed random variable $\in [0, 1]$ and T_e the temperature. As cooling schedule we took

$$T_e = 1/(100 + 10k),$$

so that the annealing was low-temperature and fast-cooling. The optimization was stopped before the ROC-area calculated for the test set started to decrease. Only a few hundred annealing epochs were allowed.

4.3 Results

Table 2 states the results for the different approaches. One can see that adding the CA 125 serum level clearly improves the classifier's performance. Without it, the ROC-curve spans about 96.5% of the total square area of the plot, whereas with the CA 125 indicator it spans almost 98%. Also, the two training methods are seen to give comparable results. Figure 3 shows the ROC-curve calculated for the total population for the 11-3-1 MLP case, trained with simulated annealing

Table 2	Training set	Test set	Total population
10-5-1 MLP, MSE	96.7%	96.4%	96.5%
10-5-1 MLP, SA	96.6%	96.2%	96.4%
11-3-1 MLP, MSE	97.9%	97.4%	97.7%
11-3-1 MLP, SA	97.9%	97.5%	97.8%

Table 2: For the two architectures (10-5-1 and 11-3-1) of the MLP and for the gradient (MSE) and the simulated annealing (SA) optimization techniques, this table gives the resulting areas under the ROC-curves.

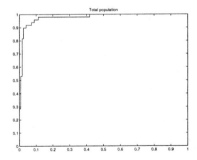

Figure 3: ROC-curves of 11-3-1 MLP (with CA 125 level indicator), trained with simulated annealing. The curve, calculated for the total population, spans 97.8% of the total region.

All patients were examined by two gynecologists, who gave their subjective impressions and also classified the ovarian tumors into (probably) benign and malignant. Histopathological examinations of the tumors afterwards showed these gynecologists to have a sensitivity up to 98% and a false positive rate of 13% and 12% respectively. As can be seen in Figure 3, the 11-3-1 MLP has a similar performance. For a sensitivity of 98%, its false positive rate is between 10% and 15%.

5 Conclusion

In this paper we have discussed the development of a Multi-Layer Perceptron neural network classifier for use in preoperative differentiation between benign and malignant ovarian tumors. To assess the performance and for training the classifiers, the concepts of sensitivity and specificity were introduced and combined in Receiver Operating Characteristic curves. Based on objective observations available to every gynecologist, the neural network is able to make reliable predictions with a discriminating performance comparable to that of experienced gynecologists.

Acknowledgments

This research work was carried out at the ESAT laboratory and the Interdisciplinary Center of Neural Networks ICNN of the Katholieke Universiteit Leuven, in the following frameworks: the Belgian Programme on Interuniversity Poles of Attraction, initiated by the Belgian State, Prime Minister's Office for Science, Technology and Culture (IUAP P4-02 and IUAP P4-24), a Concerted Action Project MIPS (Modelbased Information Processing Systems) of the Flemish Community and the FWO (Fund for Scientific Research - Flanders) project G.0262.97 : Learning and Optimization: an Interdisciplinary Approach. The scientific responsibility rests with its authors.

References

[1] Bast R. C., Jr., Klug T.L. St. John E., et al, "A radioimmunoassay using a monoclonal antibody to monitor the course of epithelial ovarian cancer," *N. Engl. J. Med.*, Vol. 309, pp. 883-888, 1983

[2] Timmerman D., Bourne T., Tailor A., Van Assche F.A., Vergote I., "Preoperative differentiation between benign and malignant adnexal masses," *submitted*

[3] Tailor A., Jurkovic D., Bourne T.H., Collins W.P., Campbell S., "Sonographic prediction of malignancy in adnexal masses using multivariate logistic regression analysis," *Ultrasound Obstet. Gynaecol.* in press, 1997

[4] Jacobs I., Oram D., Fairbanks J., et al., "A risk of malignancy index incorporating CA 125, ultrasound and menopausal status for the accurate preoperative diagnosis of ovarian cancer," *Br. J. Obstet. Gynaecol.*, Vol. 97, pp. 922-929, 1990

[5] Hanley J.A., McNeil B., "A method of comparing the areas under the receiver operating characteristics curves derived from the same cases," *Radiology*, Vol. 148, pp. 839-843, 1983

[6] Swets J.A., "Measuring the accuracy of diagnostic systems," *Science*, Vol. 240, pp. 1285-1293, 1988

[7] Galen R.S., Gambino S., *Beyond normality: the predictive value and efficiency of medical diagnosis*, John Wiley, New York, 1975.

[8] Gill P., Murray W., Wright M., *Practical Optimization*, Acad. Press, New York, 1981

[9] Fletcher R., *Practical methods of optimization*, 2nd ed., John Wiley, New York, 1987.

[10] Kirkpatrick S., Gelatt C.D., Vecchi M., "Optimization by simulated annealing," *Science*, Vol. 220, pp. 621-680, 1983.

[11] Rumelhart D.E., Hinton G.E., Williams R.J., "Learning representations by backpropagating errors," *Nature*, Vol. 323, pp. 533-536, 1986.

[12] Bishop C., *Artificial Neural Networks for Pattern Recognition*, OUP, Oxford, 1996

Modelling Seasonality and Trends in Daily Rainfall Data

Peter M Williams
School of Cognitive and Computing Sciences
University of Sussex
Falmer, Brighton BN1 9QH, UK
email: peterw@cogs.susx.ac.uk

Abstract

This paper presents a new approach to the problem of modelling daily rainfall using neural networks. We first model the conditional distributions of rainfall amounts, in such a way that the model itself determines the order of the process, and the time-dependent shape and scale of the conditional distributions. After integrating over particular weather patterns, we are able to extract seasonal variations and long-term trends.

1 Introduction

Analysis of rainfall data is important for many agricultural, ecological and engineering activities. Design of irrigation and drainage systems, for instance, needs to take account not only of mean expected rainfall, but also of rainfall volatility. In agricultural planning, changes in the annual cycle, e.g. advances in the onset of winter rain, are significant in determining the optimum time for planting crops. Estimates of crop yields also depend on the distribution of rainfall during the growing season, as well as on the overall amount. Such problems require the extrapolation of longer term trends as well as the provision of short or medium term forecasts.

2 Occurrence and amount processes

Models of daily precipitation commonly distinguish between the **occurrence** process, i.e. whether or not it rains, and the **amount** process, i.e. how much it rains, if it does. The occurrence process is often modelled as a two-state Markov chain of first or higher order. In discussion of [12], Katz traces this approach back to Quetelet in 1852. A first order chain has been considered adequate for some weather stations, but second or higher order models may be required for others, or at different times of year. Non-stationary Markov chains have been used by a number of investigators, and several approaches have been taken to the problem of seasonal variation, e.g. using Fourier series to model daily variation of parameters [16, 12, 15].

The amount of rain X on a given day, assuming it rains, normally has a roughly exponential distribution. Smaller amounts of rain are generally more likely than larger amounts. Several models have been used for the amount process. Katz & Parlange [9], for example, assume that $\sqrt[n]{X}$ has a normal distribution, where n is a positive integer empirically chosen to minimise the skewness of the resulting historical distribution. But use has more commonly been made of a gamma distribution [7, 8, 12] or a mixture of two exponentials [16, 15].

3   Stochastic model

The present approach is to deal with the occurrence and amount processes jointly, by assuming that the distribution of the amount of rain on a given day is a mixture of a discrete and continuous component. The discrete component relates to rainfall occurrence and the continuous component relates to rainfall amount on rainy days.

We use a gamma distribution for the continuous component.[1] This has density proportional to $x^{\nu-1}e^{-x}$ to within an adjustable scaling of the x-axis. The shape parameter $\nu > 0$ controls the ratio of standard deviation to mean. It also determines the location of the mode, which is strictly positive if $\nu > 1$. For certain patterns of past precipitation, larger amounts may be more likely on the following day than smaller amounts. Specifically the distribution of the amount X of rain on a given day is modelled by the three parameter family

$$P(X > x) = \begin{cases} 1 & \text{if } x < 0 \\ \alpha\Gamma\left(\nu, \dfrac{x}{\theta}\right) & \text{if } x \geq 0 \end{cases} \tag{1}$$

where $0 \leq \alpha \leq 1$ and $\nu, \theta > 0$ and

$$\Gamma(\nu, z) = \Gamma(\nu)^{-1} \int_z^\infty y^{\nu-1} e^{-y}\, dy$$

is the incomplete gamma function. For $\alpha < 1$, there is a discontinuity at $x = 0$ corresponding to the discrete component. Putting $x = 0$, it is seen that $\alpha = P(X > 0)$ is the probability of rain on the day in question. The mean daily rainfall amount is $\alpha\nu\theta$ and the variance is $\alpha\nu\{1 + \nu(1 - \alpha)\}\theta^2$.

4   Modelling time dependency

The parameters α, ν, θ determining the conditional distribution for a given day, are understood to depend on the preceding pattern of precipitation, the time of year etc. To model this dependency we use a neural network with inputs corresponding to the conditioning events, and three outputs corresponding to the distributional parameters.[2] Referring to the activations of the three output units as z^α, z^ν and z^θ, we relate these to the distributional parameters by

$$\alpha = \frac{1}{1 + \exp z^\alpha} \qquad \nu = \exp z^\nu \qquad \theta = \exp z^\theta \tag{2}$$

in order to ensure an unconstrained parametrization with $0 < \alpha < 1$ and $\nu, \theta > 0$ for any real values of $z^\alpha, z^\nu, z^\theta$.

---

[1]It would be straightforward to use a mixture of gammas, or exponentials, with time-dependent mixture components. A single gamma was chosen for simplicity to illustrate the approach.

[2]A similar approach to modelling conditional distributions, by having the network output distributional parameters, is used, for example, by Ghahramani & Jordan [6], Nix & Weigend [10], Bishop & Legleye [3], Williams [14], Baldi & Chauvin [2].

On the input side, we first need to make additional assumptions about the statistical properties of the process. Specifically it is assumed that the present is stochastically independent
of the distant past in the sense that

$$P(X_t > x \mid X_{t-1}, \ldots, X_0) = P(X_t > x \mid X_{t-1}, \ldots, X_{t-T}) \qquad (t > T) \qquad (3)$$

for a sufficiently large number of days T. In fact the stronger assumption will be made that

$$P(X_t > x \mid X_{t-1}, \ldots, X_0) = P(X_t > x \mid R_{t-1}, \ldots, R_{t-T}) \qquad (t > T) \qquad (4)$$

where $R_t = (X_t > 0)$ is the event of rain on day t. This assumes that today's rainfall
amount depends stochastically only on the occurrence or non-occurrence of rain in the
recent past, and not on the actual amounts. Such a simplification is in line with previous
approaches [8, 16, 12]. For the present study T was taken to be 10.

To assist in modelling seasonal variations, cyclic variables $\sin \tau$ and $\cos \tau$ were also provided as inputs, where $\tau = 2\pi t / D$ and $D = 365.2422$ is the length of the tropical year.
This corresponds to using Fourier series to model seasonality [16, 12] but with the number of harmonics adaptively determined by the model.[3] To allow for non-periodic nonstationarity, the current value of t was also provided as input.

5   Model fitting

Suppose we are given a sequence of daily rainfall data of length N. Equation (4) implies
that the likelihood of the full data sequence $(x_{N-1}, \ldots, x_0)$ factorises as

$$p(x_{N-1}, \ldots, x_0; \mathbf{w}) = p(x_{T-1}, \ldots, x_0) \prod_{t=T}^{N-1} p(x_t \mid r_{t-1}, \ldots, r_{t-T}; \mathbf{w}) \qquad (5)$$

where the likelihood $p(x_{T-1}, \ldots, x_0)$ of the initial sequence is not modelled and can be
considered as a constant (compare [14]). Our interest is in the likelihood (5) of the actual
sequence of observations, which is understood to depend on the variable weights $\mathbf{w}$ of the
neural network. Note that $p(x_t \mid r_{t-1}, \ldots, r_{t-T}; \mathbf{w})$ is computed by means of the neural
network outputs $z_t^\alpha, z_t^\nu, z_t^\theta$, using weights $\mathbf{w}$ and the inputs corresponding to time t.

The log likelihood of the data can therefore be written, to within a constant, as

$$\log p(x_{N-1}, \ldots, x_0; \mathbf{w}) = \sum_{t=T}^{N-1} \log p(x_t \mid r_{t-1}, \ldots, r_{t-T}; \mathbf{w})$$

or, more simply,

$$L(\mathbf{w}) = \sum_{t=T}^{N-1} L_t(\mathbf{w}) \qquad (6)$$

where from (1)

$$L_t(\mathbf{w}) = \begin{cases} \log(1 - \alpha_t) & \text{if } x_t = 0 \\ \log \alpha_t + (\nu_t - 1) \log x_t - \nu_t \log \theta_t - \log \Gamma(\nu_t) - x_t / \theta_t & \text{if } x_t > 0 \end{cases} \qquad (7)$$

where dependence of $\alpha_t, \nu_t, \theta_t$ on $\mathbf{w}$, and also on the data, is implicit.

To fit the model, it is useful to know the gradient $\nabla L(\mathbf{w})$. This can be computed using
backpropagation if we know the partial derivatives of $L(\mathbf{w})$ with respect to network outputs. In view of (6) we can concentrate on a single observation and perform a summation.

---

[3]Note that both $\sin n\tau$ and $\cos n\tau$ can be expressed as non-linear functions of $\sin \tau$ and $\cos \tau$,
which can be approximated by the network.

Omitting subscript references to t for simplicity, and recalling the links between network outputs and distributional parameters given by (2), we have

$$
\frac{\partial L}{\partial z^{\alpha}} = \begin{cases} -\alpha & \text{if } x = 0 \\ 1 - \alpha & \text{if } x > 0 \end{cases}
$$

$$
\frac{\partial L}{\partial z^{\nu}} = \begin{cases} 0 & \text{if } x = 0 \\ \nu \psi(\nu) - \nu \log \dfrac{x}{\theta} & \text{if } x > 0 \end{cases} \tag{8}
$$

$$
\frac{\partial L}{\partial z^{\theta}} = \begin{cases} 0 & \text{if } x = 0 \\ \nu - \dfrac{x}{\theta} & \text{if } x > 0 \end{cases}
$$

where

$$
\psi(\nu) = \frac{d}{d\nu} \log \Gamma(\nu) = \frac{\Gamma'(\nu)}{\Gamma(\nu)}
$$

is the digamma function of ν. Efficient algorithms for computing $\log \Gamma(\nu)$ in (7) and $\psi(\nu)$ in (8) can be found in Press et al. [11] and Amos [1].

6 Regularization

Since neural networks are universal approximators, some form of regularization is needed. As in all statistical modelling, it is important to strike the right balance between jumping to conclusions (overfitting) and refusing to learn from experience (underfitting). For this purpose, each model was fitted using the techniques of [13] which automatically adapt the complexity of the model to the information content of the data, though other comparable techniques might be used. The natural interpretation of the regularizer is as a Bayesian prior. The Bayesian analysis is completed by integration over weight space. In the present case, this was achieved by fitting several models and taking a suitable mixture as the solution. On account of the large datasets used, however, the results are not particularly sensitive to this aspect of the modelling process.

7 Results for conditional distributions

The process was applied to daily rainfall data from 5 stations in south east England and 5 stations in central Italy.[4] The data covered approximately 40 years providing some 15,000 observations for each station. A simple fully connected network was used with a single layer of 13 input units, 20 hidden units and 3 output units corresponding to the 3 parameters of the conditional distribution shown in (2). As a consequence of the pruning features of the regularizer, the models described here used an average of roughly 65 of the 343 available parameters.

To illustrate the general nature of the results, Figure 1 shows an example from the analysis of an early part of the Falmer series. It is worth observing the succession of 16 rainy days from day 39 to day 54. The lefthand figure shows that the conditional probability of rain increases rapidly at first, and then levels out after about 5–7 days.[5] Similar behaviour is observed for successive dry days, for example between days 13 and 23. This suggests that the choice of 10 time lags was sufficient. Previous studies have used mainly first or second order Markov chains [16, 12]. Figure 1 confirms that conditional dependence

---

[4]The English stations were at Cromptons, Falmer, Kemsing, Petworth, Rotherfield; the Italian stations were at Monte Oliveto, Pisticci, Pomarico, Siena, Taverno d'Arbia.

[5]In view of the number of lags used as inputs, the conditional probability would necessarily be constant after 10 days apart from seasonal effects. In fact this is the last quarter of 1951 and the incidence of rain is increasing here at that time of year.

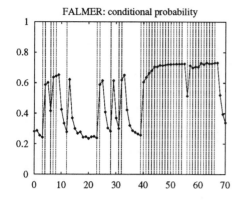
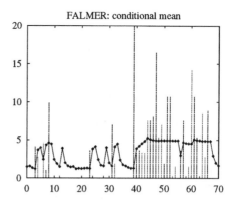

Figure 1: Results for the 10 weeks from 18 September to 27 November, 1951. The lefthand figure shows the conditional probability of rain for each day, with days on which rain occurred indicated by vertical lines. The righthand figure shows the conditional expected amount of rain in millimeters for the same period, together with the actual amount recorded.

decays rapidly at this station, at this time of year, but also indicates that it can persist for up to at least 5 days (compare [5, 4]).

8 Seasonality and trends

Conditional probabilities and expectations displayed in Figure 1 show considerable noise since they are realisations of random variables depending on the rainfall pattern for the last 10 days. For the purpose of analysing seasonal effects and longer term trends, it is more indicative to integrate out the noise resulting from individual weather patterns as follows.

Let R_t denote the event $(X_t > 0)$ and let $\overline{R}_t$ denote the complementary event $(X_t = 0)$. The expected value of X_t can then be expressed as

$$E(X_t) = \sum E(X_t \mid A_{t-1}, \dots, A_{t-T}) \, P(A_{t-1}, \dots, A_{t-T}) \qquad (9)$$

where each event A_t stands for either R_t or $\overline{R}_t$, and summation is over the 2^T possible combinations. Equation (9) takes the full modelled joint distribution over the variables $X_{N-1}, \dots, X_0$ and extracts the marginal distribution for X_t. This should be distinguished from an unconditional distribution which might be estimated by pooling the data over all 40 years. $E(X_t)$ relates to a specific day t. Note that (9) also holds if X_t is replaced by any integrable function of X_t, in particular by the indicator function of the event $(X_t > 0)$ in which case (9) expresses the probability of rain on that day.

Examining (9) we see that the conditional expectations in the first term on the right are known from the model, which supplies a conditional distribution not only for the sequence of events which actually occurred, but for any possible sequence over the previous T days. It therefore only remains to calculate the probabilities $P(A_{t-1}, \dots, A_{t-T})$ of T-day sequences preceding a given day t. Note that these are again time-dependent marginal probabilities, which can be calculated recursively from

$$P(A_t, \dots, A_{t-T+1}) =$$
$$P(A_t \mid A_{t-1}, \dots, A_{t-T+1} R_{t-T}) \, P(A_{t-1}, \dots, A_{t-T+1} R_{t-T}) \; +$$
$$P(A_t \mid A_{t-1}, \dots, A_{t-T+1} \overline{R}_{t-T}) \, P(A_{t-1}, \dots, A_{t-T+1} \overline{R}_{t-T})$$

provided we assume a prior distribution over the 2^T initial sequences $(A_{T-1}, \dots, A_0)$ as a base for the recursion. The conditional probabilities on the right are given by the model,

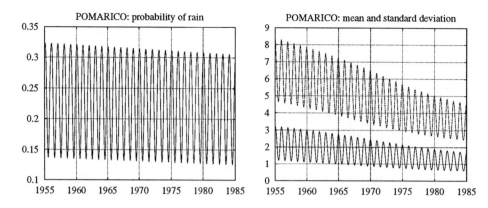

Figure 2: Integrated results for Pomarico from 1955–1985. The lefthand figure shows the daily probability of rain, indicating seasonal variation from a summer minimum to a winter maximum. The righthand figure shows the daily mean (above) and standard deviation (below) of rainfall amount in millimeters.

as before, and the unconditional probabilities are given by the recursion. It turns out that results are insensitive to the choice of initial distribution after about 50 iterations, verifying that the occurrence process, as modelled here, is in fact ergodic.

9   Integrated results

Results for the integrated distribution at one of the Italian stations are shown in Figure 2. By integrating out the random shocks we are left with a smooth representation of time dependency alone. The annual cycles are clear. Trends are also evident over the 30 year period. The mean rainfall amount is decreasing significantly, although the probability of rain on a given day of the year remains much the same. Rain is occurring no less frequently, but it is occurring in smaller amounts. Note also that the winter rainfall (the upper envelope of the mean) is decreasing more rapidly than the summer rainfall (the lower envelope of the mean) so that the difference between the two is narrowing.

10   Conclusions

This paper provides a new example of time series modelling using neural networks. The use of a mixture of a discrete distribution and a gamma distribution emphasises the general principle that the "error function" for a neural network depends on the particular statistical model used for the target data. The use of cyclic variables $\sin \tau$ and $\cos \tau$ as inputs shows how the problem of selecting the number of harmonics required for a Fourier series analysis of seasonality can be solved adaptively. Long term trends can also be modelled by the use of a linear time variable, although both this and the last feature require the presence of a suitable regularizer to avoid overfitting. Lastly we have seen how a suitable form of integration can be used to extract the underlying cycles and trends from noisy data. These techniques can be adapted to the analysis of time series drawn from other domains.

Acknowledgement

I am indebted to Professor Helen Rendell of the School of Chemistry, Physics and Environmental Sciences, University of Sussex, for kindly supplying the rainfall data and for valuable discussions.

References

[1] D. E. Amos. A portable fortran subroutine for derivatives of the psi function. *ACM Transactions on Mathematical Software*, 9:494–502, 1983.

[2] P. Baldi and Y. Chauvin. Hybrid modeling, HMM/NN architectures, and protein applications. *Neural Computation*, 8:1541–1565, 1996.

[3] C. M. Bishop and C. Legleye. Estimating conditional probability densities for periodic variables. In G. Tesauro, D. Touretzky, and T. Leen, editors, *Advances in Neural Information Processing Systems 7*, pages 641–648. The MIT Press, 1995.

[4] E. H. Chin. Modelling daily precipitation occurrence process with Markov chain. *Water Resources Research*, 13:949–956, 1977.

[5] P. Gates and H. Tong. On Markov chain modelling to some weather data. *Journal of Applied Meteorology*, 15:1145–1151, 1976.

[6] Z. Ghahramani and M. I. Jordan. Supervised learning from incomplete data via an EM approach. In Jack D. Cowan, Gerald Tesauro, and Joshua Alspector, editors, *Advances in Neural Information Processing Systems 6*, pages 120–127. Morgan Kaufmann, 1994.

[7] N. T. Ison, A. M. Feyerherm, and L. D. Bark. Wet period precipitation and the gamma distribution. *Journal of Applied Meteorology*, 10:658–665, 1971.

[8] R. W. Katz. Precipitation as a chain-dependent process. *Journal of Applied Meteorology*, 16:671–676, 1977.

[9] R. W. Katz and M. B. Parlange. Effects of an index of atmospheric circulation on stochastic properties of precipitation. *Water Resources Research*, 29:2335–2344, 1993.

[10] D. A. Nix and A. S. Weigend. Learning local error bars for nonlinear regression. In Gerald Tesauro, David S. Touretzky, and Todd K. Leen, editors, *Advances in Neural Information Processing Systems 7*, pages 489–496. MIT Press, 1995.

[11] W. H. Press, B. P. Flannery, S. A. Teukolsky, and W. T. Vetterling. *Numerical Recipes in C*. Cambridge University Press, 2nd edition, 1992.

[12] R. D. Stern and R. Coe. A model fitting analysis of daily rainfall data, with discussion. *Journal of the Royal Statistical Society A*, 147(Part 1):1–34, 1984.

[13] P. M. Williams. Bayesian regularization and pruning using a Laplace prior. *Neural Computation*, 7:117–143, 1995.

[14] P. M. Williams. Using neural networks to model conditional multivariate densities. *Neural Computation*, 8:843–854, 1996.

[15] D. A. Woolhiser. Modelling daily precipitation—progress and problems. In Andrew T. Walden and Peter Guttorp, editors, *Statistics in the Environmental and Earth Sciences*, chapter 5, pages 71–89. Edward Arnold, 1992.

[16] D. A. Woolhiser and G. G. S. Pegram. Maximum likelihood estimation of Fourier coefficients to describe seasonal variation of parameters in stochastic daily precipitation models. *Journal of Applied Meteorology*, 18:34–42, 1979.

The Observer-Observation Dilemma in Neuro-Forecasting

Hans Georg Zimmermann
Siemens AG
Corporate Technology
D-81730 München, Germany
Georg.Zimmermann@mchp.siemens.de

Ralph Neuneier
Siemens AG
Corporate Technology
D-81730 München, Germany
Ralph.Neuneier@mchp.siemens.de

Abstract

We explain how the training data can be separated into clean information and unexplainable noise. Analogous to the data, the neural network is separated into a time invariant structure used for forecasting, and a noisy part. We propose a unified theory connecting the optimization algorithms for cleaning and learning together with algorithms that control the data noise and the parameter noise. The combined algorithm allows a data-driven local control of the liability of the network parameters and therefore an improvement in generalization. The approach is proven to be very useful at the task of forecasting the German bond market.

1 Introduction: The Observer-Observation Dilemma

Human beings believe that they are able to solve a psychological version of the *Observer-Observation Dilemma*. On the one hand, they use their observations to constitute an understanding of the laws of the world, on the other hand, they use this understanding to evaluate the correctness of the incoming pieces of information. Of course, as everybody knows, human beings are not free from making mistakes in this psychological dilemma. We encounter a similar situation when we try to build a mathematical model using data. Learning relationships from the data is only one part of the model building process. Overrating this part often leads to the phenomenon of overfitting in many applications (especially in economic forecasting). In practice, evaluation of the data is often done by external knowledge, i. e. by optimizing the model under constraints of smoothness and regularization [7]. If we assume, that our model summerizes the best knowledge of the system to be identified, why should we not use the model itself to evaluate the correctness of the data? One approach to do this is called Clearning [11]. In this paper, we present a unified approach of the interaction between the data and a neural network (see also [8]). It includes a new symmetric view on the optimization algorithms, here learning and cleaning, and their control by parameter and data noise.

2 Learning

2.1 Learning reviewed

We are especially interested in using the output of a neural network $y(x, w)$, given the input pattern, x, and the weight vector, w, as a forecast of financial time series. In the context of neural networks learning normally means the minimization of an error function E by changing the weight vector w in order to achieve good generalization performance. Typical error functions can be written as a sum of individual terms over all T training patterns, $E = \frac{1}{T} \sum_{t=1}^{T} E_t$. For example, the maximum-likelihood principle leads to

$$E_t = 1/2 \left(y(x, w) - y_t^d \right)^2,\tag{1}$$

with y_t^d as the given target pattern. If the error function is a nonlinear function of the parameters, learning has to be done iteratively by a search through the weight space, changing the weights from step τ to $\tau + 1$ according to:

$$w^{(\tau+1)} = w^{(\tau)} + \Delta w^{(\tau)}.\tag{2}$$

There are several algorithms for choosing the weight increment $\Delta w^{(\tau)}$, the most easiest being *gradient descent*. After each presentation of an input pattern, the gradient $g_t := \nabla E_t|_w$ of the error function with respect to the weights is computed. In the batch version of gradient descent the increments are based on all training patterns

$$\Delta w^{(\tau)} = -\eta g = -\eta \frac{1}{T} \sum_{t=1}^{T} g_t,\tag{3}$$

whereas the pattern-by-pattern version changes the weights after each presentation of a pattern x_t (often randomly chosen from the training set):

$$\Delta w^{(\tau)} = -\eta g_t.\tag{4}$$

The learning rate η is typically held constant or follows an annealing procedure during training to assure convergence. Our experiments have shown that small batches are most useful, especially in combination with Vario-Eta, a stochastic approximation of a Quasi-Newton method [3]:

$$\Delta w^{(\tau)} = -\frac{\eta}{\sqrt{\frac{1}{T} \sum (g_t - g)^2}} \cdot \frac{1}{N} \sum_{t=1}^{N} g_t,\tag{5}$$

with and $N \leq 20$. Learning pattern-by-pattern or with small batches can be viewed as a stochastic search process because we can write the weight increments as:

$$\Delta w^{(\tau)} = -\eta \left[g + \left(\frac{1}{N} \sum_{t=1}^{N} g_t - g \right) \right].\tag{6}$$

These increments consist of the terms g with a drift to a local minimum and of noise terms $(\frac{1}{N} \sum_{t=1}^{N} g_t - g)$ disturbing this drift.

2.2 Parameter Noise as an Implicit Penalty Function

Consider the Taylor expansion of $E(w)$ around some point w in the weight space

$$E(w + \Delta w) = E(w) + \nabla E \, \Delta w + \frac{1}{2} \Delta w' H \Delta w\tag{7}$$

with H as the Hessian of the error function. Assume a given sequence of T disturbance vectors Δw_t, whose elements $\Delta w_t(i)$ are identically, independently distributed (i.i.d.) with zero mean and variance (row-)vector $\text{var}(\Delta w_i)$ to approximate the expectation $\langle E(w) \rangle$ by

$$\langle E(w) \rangle \approx \frac{1}{T} \sum_t E(w + \Delta w_t) = E(w) + \frac{1}{2} \sum_i \text{var}(\Delta w(i)) H_{ii}, \tag{8}$$

with H_{ii} as the diagonal elements of H. In eq. 8, noise on the weights acts implicitly as a penalty term to the error function given by the second derivatives H_{ii}. The noise variances $\text{var}(\Delta w(i))$ operate as penalty parameters. As a result of this flat minima solutions which may be important for achieving good generalization performance are favored [5].

Learning pattern-by-pattern introduces such noise in the training procedure i.e., $\Delta w_t = -\eta \cdot g_t$. Close to convergence, we can assume that g_t is i.i.d. with zero mean and variance vector $\text{var}(g_i)$ so that the expected value can be approximated by

$$\langle E(w) \rangle \approx E(w) + \frac{\eta^2}{2} \sum_i \text{var}(g_i) \frac{\partial^2 E}{\partial w_i^2}. \tag{9}$$

This type of learning introduces to a local penalty parameter $\text{var}(\Delta w(i))$, characterizing the stability of the weights $w = [w_i]_{i=1,\dots,k}$.

The noise effects due to Vario-Eta learning $\Delta w_t(i) = -\frac{\eta}{\sqrt{\sigma_i^2}} \cdot g_{ti}$ leads to

$$\langle E(w) \rangle \approx E(w) + \frac{\eta^2}{2} \sum_i \frac{\partial^2 E}{\partial w_i^2}. \tag{10}$$

By canceling the term $\text{var}(g_i)$ in eq. 9, Vario-Eta achieves a simplified uniform penalty parameter, which depends only on the learning rate η. Whereas pattern-by-pattern learning is a slow algorithm with a locally adjusted penalty control, Vario-Eta is fast only at the cost of a simplified uniform penalty term. We summarize this section by giving some advice on how to learn to flat minima solutions:

- Train the network to a minimal training error solution with Vario-Eta, which is a stochastic approximation of a Newton method and therefore very fast.

- Add a final phase of pattern-by-pattern learning with uniform learning rate to fine tune the local curvature structure by the local penalty parameters (eq. 9).

- Use a learning rate η as high as possible to keep the penalty effective. The training error may vary a bit, but the inclusion of the implicit penalty is more important.

3 Cleaning

3.1 Cleaning reviewed

When training neural networks, one typically assumes that the data is noise-free and one forces the network to fit the data exactly. Even the control procedures to minimize over-fitting effects (i.e., pruning) consider the inputs as exact values. However, this assumption is often violated, especially in the field of financial analysis, and we are taught by the phenomenon of overfitting not to follow the data exactly. Clearning, as a combination of cleaning and learning, has been introduced in the paper of [11]. The motivation was to minimize overfitting effects by considering the input data as corrupted by noise whose distribution has also to be learned. The Cleaning error function for the pattern t is given by the sum of two terms

$$E_t^{y,x} = \frac{1}{2} \left[\left(y_t - y_t^d \right)^2 + \left(x_t - x_t^d \right)^2 \right] = E_t^y + E_t^x \tag{11}$$

with x_t^d, y_t^d as the observed data point. In the pattern-by-pattern learning, the network output $y(x_t, w)$ determines the adaptation as usual,

$$w^{(\tau+1)} = w^{(\tau)} - \eta \frac{\partial E^y}{\partial w^{(\tau)}}. \tag{12}$$

We have also to memorize correction vectors Δx_t for all input data of the training set to present the cleaned input x_t to the network,

$$x_t = x_t^d + \Delta x_t \tag{13}$$

The update rule for the corrections, initialized with $\Delta x_t^{(0)} = 0$ can be described as

$$\Delta x_t^{(\tau+1)} = (1-\eta)\Delta x_t^{(\tau)} - \eta(y_t - y_t^d)\frac{\partial y}{\partial x} \tag{14}$$

All the necessary quantities, i. e. $(y_t - y_t^d)\frac{\partial y(x,w)}{\partial x}$ are computed by typical back-propagation algorithms, anyway. We experienced, that the algorithms work well, if the same learning rate η is used for both, the weight and cleaning updates. For regression, cleaning forces the acceptance of a small error in x, which can in turn decrease the error in y dramatically, especially in the case of outliers. Successful applications of Cleaning are reported in [11] and [9].

Although the network may learn an optimal model for the cleaned input data, there is no easy way to work with cleaned data on the test set. As a consequence, the model is evaluated on a test set with a different noise characteristic compared to the training set. We will later propose a combination of learning with noise and cleaning to work around this serious disadvantage.

3.2 Data Noise reviewed

Artificial noise on the input data is often used during training because it creates an infinite number of training examples and expands the data to empty parts of the input space. As a result, the tendency of learning by heart may be limited because smoother regression functions are produced.

Now, we are considering again the Taylor expansion, this time applied to $E(x)$ around some point x in the input space. The expected value $\langle E(x) \rangle$ is approximated by

$$\langle E(x) \rangle \approx \frac{1}{T}\sum_t E(x + \Delta x_t) = E(x) + \frac{1}{2}\sum_j \text{var}(\Delta x(j))H_{jj}, \tag{15}$$

with H_{jj} as the diagonal elements of the Hessian H_{xx} of the error function with respect to the inputs x. Again, in eq. 15, noise on the inputs acts implicitly as a penalty term to the error function with the noise variances $\text{var}(\Delta x(j))$ operating as penalty parameters. Noise on the input improve generalization behavior by favoring smooth models [1].

The noise levels can be set to a constant value, e. g. given by a priori knowledge, or adaptive as described now. We will concentrate on a uniform or normal noise distribution. Then, the adaptive noise level ξ_j is estimated for each input j individually. Suppressing pattern indices, we define the noise levels ξ_j or ξ_j^2 as the average residual errors:

$$\text{uniform residual error:} \quad \xi_j = \frac{1}{T}\sum_t \left|\frac{\partial E^y}{\partial x_j}\right|, \tag{16}$$

$$\text{Gaussian residual error:} \quad \xi_j^2 = \frac{1}{T}\sum_t \left(\frac{\partial E^y}{\partial x_j}\right)^2. \tag{17}$$

Actual implementations use stochastic approximation, e. g. for the uniform residual error

$$\xi_j^{(\tau+1)} = (1-\frac{1}{T})\xi_j^{(\tau)} + \frac{1}{T}\left|\frac{\partial E^y}{\partial x_j}\right|. \tag{18}$$

The different residual error levels can be interpreted as follows: A small level ξ_j may indicate an unimportant input j or a perfect fit of the network concerning this input j. In both cases, a small noise level is appropriate. On the other hand, a high value of ξ_j for an input j indicates an important but imperfectly fitted input. In this case high noise levels are advisable. High values of ξ_j lead to a stiffer regression model and may therefore increase the generalization performance of the network.

3.3 Cleaning with Noise

Typically, training with noisy inputs takes a data point and adds a random variable drawn from a fixed or adaptive distribution. This new data point x_t is used as an input to the network. If we assume, that the data is corrupted by outliers and other influences, it is preferable to add the noise term to the cleaned input. For the case of Gaussian noise the resulting new input is:

$$x_t = x_t^d + \Delta x_t + \xi\phi, \tag{19}$$

with ϕ drawn from the normal distribution. The cleaning of the data leads to a corrected mean of the data and therefore to a more symmetric noise distribution, which also covers the observed data x_t.

We propose a variant which allows more complicated noise distributions:

$$x_t = x_t^d + \Delta x_t - \Delta x_k, \tag{20}$$

with k as a random number drawn from the indices of the correction vectors $[\Delta x_t]_{t=1,...,T}$. In this way we use a possibly asymmetric and/or dependent noise distribution, which still covers the observed data x_t by definition of the algorithm.

One might wonder, why to disturb the cleaned input $x_t^d + \Delta x_t$ with an additional noisy term Δx_k. The reason for this is, that we want to benefit from representing the whole input distribution to the network instead of only using one particular realization.

4 A Unifying Approach

4.1 The Separation of Structure and Noise

In the previous sections we explained how the data can be separated into clean information and unexplainable noise. Analogous, the neural network is described as a time invariant structure (otherwise no forecasting is possible) and a noisy part.

> *data* → *cleaned data* + *time invariant data noise*
> *neural network* → *time invariant parameters* + *parameter noise*

We propose to use cleaning and adaptive noise to separate the data and to use learning and stochastic search to separate the structure of the neural network.

> *data* ← *cleaning(neural network)* + *adaptive noise (neural network)*
> *neural network* ← *learning (data)* + *stochastic search(data)*

The algorithms analyzing the data depend directly on the network whereas the methods searching for structure are directly related to the data. It should be clear that the model building process should combine both aspects in an alternate or simultaneous manner. The interaction of algorithms concerning data analysis and network structure enables the realization of the the concept of the Observer-Observation Dilemma.

The aim of the unified approach can be described, exemplary assuming here a Gaussian noise model, as the minimization of the error due to both, the structure and the data:

$$\frac{1}{2T} \sum_{t=1}^{T} \left[\left(y_t - y_t^d\right)^2 + \left(x_t - x_t^d\right)^2 \right] \to \min_{x_t, w} \tag{21}$$

Combining the algorithms and approximating the cumulative gradient g by $\tilde{g}$, we receive

$$
\begin{aligned}
\text{data} \\
\Delta x_t^{(\tau+1)} &= (1-\eta)\Delta x_t^{(\tau)} - \eta(y_t - y_t^d)\frac{\partial y}{\partial x} \\
x_t &= x_t^d + \underbrace{\Delta x_t^{(\tau)}}_{\text{cleaning}} - \underbrace{\Delta x_k^{(\tau)}}_{\text{noise}} \\[4pt]
\text{structure} \\
\tilde{g}^{(\tau+1)} &= (1-\alpha)\tilde{g}^{(\tau)} + \alpha(y_t - y_t^d)\frac{\partial y}{\partial w} \\
w^{(\tau+1)} &= w^{(\tau)} - \underbrace{\eta\tilde{g}^{(\tau)}}_{\text{learning}} - \underbrace{\eta(g_t - \tilde{g}^{(\tau)})}_{\text{noise}}
\end{aligned}
\tag{22}
$$

The cleaning of the data by the network computes an individual correction term for each training pattern. The adaptive noise procedure according to eq. 20 generates a potentially asymmetric and dependent noise distribution which also covers the observed data. The implied curvature penalty, whose strength depends on the individual liability of the input variables, can improve the generalization performance of the neural network.

The learning of the structure searches for time invariant parameters characterized by $\frac{1}{T}\sum g_t = 0$. The parameter noise supports this exploration as a stochastic search to find better "global" minima. Additionally, the generalization performance may be further improved by the implied curvature penalty depending on the local liability of the parameters. Note that, although the description of the weight updates collapses to the simple form of eq. 4, we preferred the formula above to emphasize the analogy between the mechanism which handles the data and the structure.

In searching for an optimal combination of data and parameters, the noise of both parts is not a disastrous failure to build a perfect model but it is an important element to control the interaction of data and structure.

4.2 Pruning

The neural network topology represents only a hypothesis of the true underlying class of functions. Due to possible misspecification, we may have defects of the parameter noise distribution. Pruning algorithms are not only a way to limit the memory of the network, but they also appear useful to correct the noise distribution in different ways.

Stochastic-Pruning [2] is basically a t-test on the weights w. Weights with low $test_w$ values constitute candidates for pruning to cancel weights with low liability measured by the size of the weight divided by the standard deviation of its fluctuations. By this, we get a stabilization of the learning against resampling of the training data. A further weight pruning method is EBD, *Early-Brain-Damage* [10], which is based on the often cited OBD pruning method of [6]. In contrast to OBD, EBD allows its application before the training has reached a local minimum. One of the advantages of EBD over OBD is the possibility to perform the testing while being slidely away from a local minimum. In our training procedure we propose to use noise even in the final part of learning and therefore we are only nearby a local minimum. Furthermore, EBD is also able to revive already pruned weights. Similar to Stochastic Pruning, EBD favors weights with a low rate of fluctuations. If a weight is pushed around by a high noise, the implicit curvature penalty would favor a flat minimum around this weight which leads to its elimination by EBD.

5   Experiments

In a research project sponsored by the European Community we are applying the proposed approach to estimate the returns of 3 financial markets for each of the G7 countries subsequently using these estimations in an asset allocation scheme to create a Markowitz-optimal portfolio [4]. This paper reports the 6 month forecasts of the German bond rate, which is one of the more difficult tasks due to the reunification of Germany and GDR. The inputs consist of 39 variables achieved by preprocessing 16 relevant financial time series. The training set covers the time from April, 1974 to December, 1991, the test set runs from January, 1992 to May, 1996. The network arcitecture consists of one hidden layer (20 neurons, tanh transfer function) and one linear output. First, we trained the neural network until convergence with pattern-by-pattern learning using a small batch size of 20 patterns (classical approach). Then, we trained the network using the unified approach as described in section 4.1 using pattern-by-pattern learning. We compare the resulting predictions of the networks on the basis of four performance measures (see table). First, the hit rate counts how often the sign of the return of the bond has been correctly predicted. As to the other measures, the step from the forecast model to a trading system is here kept very simple. If the output is positive, we buy shares of the bond, otherwise we sell them. The potential realized is the ratio of the return to the maximum possible return over the test (training) set. The annualized return is the average yearly profit of the trading systems. Our approach turns out to be superior: we almost doubled the annualized return from 4.5% to 8.5% on the test set. The figure compares the accumulated return of the two approaches on the test set. The unified approach not only shows a higher profitability, but also has by far a less maximal draw down.

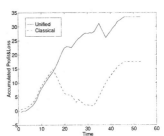

approach	our	classical
hit rate	81% (96%)	66% (93%)
realized potential	75% (100%)	44% (96%)
annualized return	8.5% (11.2%)	4.5% (10.1%)

References

[1]   Christopher M. Bishop. *Neural Networks for Pattern Recognition*. Clarendon Press, 1994.

[2]   W. Finnoff, F. Hergert, and H. G. Zimmermann. Improving generalization performance by nonconvergent model selection methods. In proc. of *ICANN-92*, 1992.

[3]   W. Finnoff, F. Hergert, and H. G. Zimmermann. Neuronale Lernverfahren mit variabler Schrittweite. 1993. Tech. report, Siemens AG.

[4]   P. Herve, P. Naim, and H. G. Zimmermann. Advanced Adaptive Architectures for Asset Allocation: A Trial Application. In *Forecasting Financial Markets*, 1996.

[5]   S. Hochreiter and J. Schmidhuber. Flat minima. *Neural Computation*, 9(1):1–42, 1997.

[6]   Y. le Cun, J. S. Denker, and S. A. Solla. Optimal brain damage. *NIPS*89*, 1990.

[7]   J. E. Moody and T. S. Rögnvaldsson. Smoothing regularizers for projective basis function networks. *NIPS 9*, 1997.

[8]   R. Neuneier and H. G. Zimmermann. How to Train Neural Networks. In *Tricks of the Trade: How to make algorithms really to work*. Springer Verlag, Berlin, 1998.

[9]   B. Tang, W. Hsieh, and F. Tangang. Clearning neural networks with continuity constraints for prediction of noisy time series. *ICONIP'96*, 1996.

[10] V. Tresp, R. Neuneier, and H. G. Zimmermann. Early brain damage. *NIPS 9*, 1997.

[11] A. S. Weigend, H. G. Zimmermann, and R. Neuneier. Clearning. *Neural Networks in Financial Engineering, (NNCM95)*, 1995.

PART IX
CONTROL, NAVIGATION AND PLANNING

Generalized Prioritized Sweeping

David Andre   Nir Friedman   Ronald Parr
Computer Science Division, 387 Soda Hall
University of California, Berkeley, CA 94720
{dandre,nir,parr}@cs.berkeley.edu

Abstract

Prioritized sweeping is a *model-based* reinforcement learning method that attempts to focus an agent's limited computational resources to achieve a good estimate of the value of environment states. To choose effectively where to spend a costly planning step, classic prioritized sweeping uses a simple heuristic to focus computation on the states that are likely to have the largest errors. In this paper, we introduce *generalized prioritized sweeping*, a principled method for generating such estimates in a representation-specific manner. This allows us to extend prioritized sweeping beyond an explicit, state-based representation to deal with compact representations that are necessary for dealing with large state spaces. We apply this method for generalized model approximators (such as Bayesian networks), and describe preliminary experiments that compare our approach with classical prioritized sweeping.

1 Introduction

In reinforcement learning, there is a tradeoff between spending time acting in the environment and spending time planning what actions are best. Model-free methods take one extreme on this question— the agent updates only the state most recently visited. On the other end of the spectrum lie classical dynamic programming methods that reevaluate the utility of every state in the environment after every experiment. Prioritized sweeping (PS) [6] provides a middle ground in that only the most "important" states are updated, according to a priority metric that attempts to measure the anticipated size of the update for each state. Roughly speaking, PS interleaves performing actions in the environment with propagating the values of states. After updating the value of state s, PS examines all states t from which the agent might reach s in one step and assigns them priority based on the expected size of the change in their value.

A crucial desideratum for reinforcement learning is the ability to scale-up to complex domains. For this, we need to use *compact* (or *generalizing*) representations of the model and the value function. While it is possible to apply PS in the presence of such representations (e.g., see [1]), we claim that classic PS is ill-suited in this case. With a generalizing model, a single experience may affect our estimation of the dynamics of many other states. Thus, we might want to update the value of states that are similar, in some appropriate sense, to s since we have a new estimate of the system dynamics at these states. Note that some of these states might never have been reached before and standard PS will not assign them a priority at all.

In this paper, we present *generalized prioritized sweeping* (GenPS), a method that utilizes a formal principle to understand and extend PS and extend it to deal with parametric representations for both the model and the value function. If GenPS is used with an explicit state-space model and value function representation, an algorithm similar to the original (classic) PS results. When a model approximator (such as a *dynamic Bayesian network* [2]) is used, the resulting algorithm prioritizes the states of the environment using the generalizations inherent in the model representation.

2   The Basic Principle

We assume the reader is familiar with the basic concepts of *Markov Decision Processes* (MDPs); see, for example, [5]. We use the following notation: A MDP is a 4-tuple, $(\mathcal{S}, \mathcal{A}, p, r)$ where $\mathcal{S}$ is a set of *states*, $\mathcal{A}$ is a set of *actions*, $p(t \mid s, a)$ is a *transition model* that captures the probability of reaching state t after we execute action a at state s, and $r(s)$ is a *reward function* mapping $\mathcal{S}$ into real-valued rewards. In this paper, we focus on infinite-horizon MDPs with a discount factor γ. The agent's aim is to maximize the expected discounted total reward it will receive. Reinforcement learning procedures attempt to achieve this objective when the agent *does not* know p and r.

A standard problem in *model-based* reinforcement learning is one of balancing between planning (i.e., choosing a policy) and execution. Ideally, the agent would compute the optimal value function for its model of the environment each time the model changes. This scheme is unrealistic since finding the optimal policy for a given model is computationally non-trivial. Fortunately, we can approximate this scheme if we notice that the approximate model changes only slightly at each step. Thus, we can assume that the value function from the previous model can be easily "repaired" to reflect these changes. This approach was pursued in the DYNA [7] framework, where after the execution of an action, the agent updates its model of the environment, and then performs some bounded number of value propagation steps to update its approximation of the value function. Each value-propagation step locally enforces the *Bellman equation* by setting $\hat{V}(s) \leftarrow \max_{a \in \mathcal{A}} \hat{Q}(s, a)$, where $\hat{Q}(s, a) = \hat{r}(s) + \gamma \sum_{s' \in \mathcal{S}} \hat{p}(s' \mid s, a)\hat{V}(s')$, $\hat{p}(s' \mid s, a)$ and $\hat{r}(s)$ are the agent's approximation of the MDP, and $\hat{V}$ is the agent's approximation of the value function.

This raises the question of which states should be updated. In this paper we propose the following general principle:

> **GenPS Principle:** Update states where the approximation of the value function will change the most. That is, update the states with the largest *Bellman error*, $E(s) = |\hat{V}(s) - \max_{a \in \mathcal{A}} \hat{Q}(s, a)|$.

The motivation for this principle is straightforward. The maximum Bellman error can be used to bound the maximum difference between the current value function, $\hat{V}(s)$ and the optimal value function, $V^*(s)$ [9]. This difference bounds the *policy loss*, the difference between the expected discounted reward received under the agent's current policy and the expected discounted reward received under the optimal policy.

To carry out this principle we have to recognize when the Bellman error at a state changes. This can happen at two different stages. First, after the agent updates its model of the world, new discrepancies between $\hat{V}(s)$ and $\max_a \hat{Q}(s, a)$ might be introduced, which can increase the Bellman error at s. Second, after the agent performs some value propagations, $\hat{V}$ is changed, which may introduce new discrepancies.

We assume that the agent maintains a value function and a model that are parameterized by θ_V and θ_M. (We will sometimes refer to the vector that concatenates these vectors together into a single, larger vector simply as θ.) When the agent observes a transition from state s to s' under action a, the agent updates its environment model by adjusting some of the parameters in θ_M. When performing value-propagations, the agent updates $\hat{V}$ by updating parameters in θ_V. A change in any of these parameters may change the Bellman error at other states in the model. We want to recognize these states without explicitly computing the Bellman error at each one. Formally, we wish to estimate the change in error, $|\Delta_{E(s)}|$, due to the most recent change Δ_θ in the parameters.

We propose approximating $|\Delta_{E(s)}|$ by using the gradient of the right hand side of the Bellman equation (i.e. $\max_a \hat{Q}(s,a)$). Thus, we have: $|\Delta_{E(s)}| \approx |\nabla \max_a \hat{Q}(s,a) \cdot \Delta_\theta|$ which estimates the change in the Bellman error at state s as a function of the change in $\hat{Q}(s,a)$. The above still requires us to differentiate over a max, which is not differentiable. In general, we want to to overestimate the change, to avoid "starving" states with non-negligible error. Thus, we use the following upper bound: $|\nabla(\max_a \hat{Q}(s,a)) \cdot \Delta_\theta| \leq \max_a |\nabla \hat{Q}(s,a) \cdot \Delta_\theta|$.

We now define the generalized prioritized sweeping procedure. The procedure maintains a priority queue that assigns to each state s a priority, $pri(s)$. After making some changes, we can reassign priorities by computing an approximation of the change in the value function.

Ideally, this is done using a procedure that implements the following steps:

> procedure update-priorities (Δ_θ)
>   for all $s \in S$ $pri(s) \leftarrow pri(s) + \max_a |\nabla \hat{Q}(s,a) \cdot \Delta_\theta|$.

Note that when the above procedure updates the priority for a state that has an existing priority, the priorities are added together. This ensures that the priority being kept is an overestimate of the priority of each state, and thus, the procedure will eventually visit all states that require updating.

Also, in practice we would not want to reconsider the priority of all states after an update (we return to this issue below).

Using this procedure, we can now state the general learning procedure:

> procedure GenPS ()
>   loop
>   perform an action in the environment
>   update the model; let Δ_θ be the change in θ
>   call update-priorities(Δ_θ)
>   while there is available computation time
>   let $s^{\max} = \arg\max_s pri(s)$
>   perform value-propagation for $\hat{V}(s^{\max})$; let Δ_θ be the change in θ
>   call update-priorities(Δ_θ)
> $pri(s^{\max}) \leftarrow |\hat{V}(s^{\max}) - \max_a \hat{Q}(s^{\max}, a)|$ [1]

Note that the GenPS procedure does not determine how actions are selected. This issue, which involves the problem of exploration, is orthogonal to the our main topic. Standard approaches, such as those described in [5, 6, 7], can be used with our procedure.

This abstract description specifies neither how to update the model, nor how to update the value function in the value-propagation steps. Both of these depend on the choices made in the corresponding representation of the model and the value function. Moreover, it is clear that in problems that involve a large state space, we cannot afford to recompute the priority of every state in update-priorities. However, we can simplify this computation by exploiting sparseness in the model and in the worst case we may resort to approximate methods for finding the states that receive high priority after each change.

3   Explicit, State-based Representation

In this section we briefly describe the instantiation of the generalized procedure when the rewards, values, and transition probabilities are explicitly modeled using lookup tables. In this representation, for each state s, we store the expected reward at s, denoted by $\theta_{\hat{r}(s)}$, the estimated value at s, denoted by $\theta_{\hat{V}(s)}$, and for each action a and state t the number of times the execution of a at s lead to state t, denoted $N_{s,a,t}$. From these transition counts we can

---

[1] In general, this will assign the state a new priority of 0, unless there is a self loop. In this case it will easy to compute the new Bellman error as a by-product of the value propagation step.

reconstruct the transition probabilities $\hat{p}(t \mid s, a) = \frac{N_{s,a,t} + N^0_{s,a,t}}{\sum_{t'} N_{s,a,t'} + N^0_{s,a,t'}}$, where $N^0_{s,a,t}$ are
fictional counts that capture our prior information about the system's dynamics.[2] After each
step in the world, these reward and probability parameters are updated in the straightforward
manner. Value propagation steps in this representation set $\theta_{\hat{V}(t)}$ to the right hand side of
the Bellman equation.

To apply the GenPS procedure we need to derive the gradient of the Bellman equation
for two situations: (a) after a single step in the environment, and (b) after a value update.

In case (a), the model changes after performing action $s \xrightarrow{a} t$. In this case, it is easy to
verify that $\nabla Q(s, a) \cdot \Delta_\theta = \Delta_{\theta_{\hat{r}(t)}} + \frac{\gamma}{\sum_t N_{s,a,t} + N^0_{s,a,t}} \left(V(t) - \sum_{t'} \hat{p}(t' \mid s, a) V(t') \right)$, and
that $\nabla Q(s', a') \cdot \Delta_\theta = 0$ if $s' \neq s$ or $a' \neq a$. Thus, s is the only state whose priority
changes.

In case (b), the value function changes after updating the value of a state t. In this case,
$\nabla Q(s, a) \cdot \Delta_\theta = \gamma \hat{p}(t \mid s, a) \Delta_{\theta_{\hat{V}(t)}}$. It is easy to see that this is nonzero only if t is reachable
from s. In both cases, it is straightforward to locate the states where the Bellman error
might have have changed, and the computation of the new priority is more efficient than
computing the Bellman-error.[3]

Now we can relate GenPS to standard prioritized sweeping. The PS procedure has the
general form of this application of GenPS with three minor differences. First, after performing a transition $s \xrightarrow{a} t$ in the environment, PS immediately performs a value propagation
for state s, while GenPS increments the priority of s. Second, after performing a value
propagation for state t, PS updates the priority of states s that can reach t with the value
$\max_a \hat{p}(t \mid s, a) \cdot \Delta_{\hat{V}(t)}$. The priority assigned by GenPS is the same quantity multiplied by
γ. Since PS does not introduce priorities after model changes, this multiplicative constant
does not change the order of states in the queue. Thirdly, GenPS uses addition to combine
the old priority of a state with a new one, which ensures that the priority is indeed an upper
bound. In contrast, PS uses max to combine priorities.

This discussion shows that PS can be thought of as a special case of GenPS when the
agent uses an explicit, state-based representation. As we show in the next section, when
the agent uses more compact representations, we get procedures where the prioritization
strategy is quite different from that used in PS. Thus, we claim that classic PS is desirable
primarily when explicit representations are used.

4 Factored Representation

We now examine a compact representation of $\hat{p}(s' \mid s, a)$ that is based on *dynamic Bayesian
networks* (DBNs) [2]. DBNs have been combined with reinforcement learning before in
[8], where they were used primarily as a means getting better generalization while learning.
We will show that they also can be used with prioritized sweeping to focus the agent's
attention on groups of states that are affected as the agent refines its environment model.

We start by assuming that the environment state is described by a set of *random variables*,
$X_1, \ldots, X_n$. For now, we assume that each variable can take values from a finite set
$Val(X_i)$. An *assignment* of values $x_1, \ldots, x_n$ to these variables describes a particular
environment state. Similarly, we assume that the agent's action is described by random
variables $A_1, \ldots, A_k$. To model the system dynamics, we have to represent the probability
of transitions $s \xrightarrow{a} t$, where s and t are two assignments to $X_1, \ldots, X_n$ and a is an assignment
to $A_1, \ldots, A_k$. To simplify the discussion, we denote by $Y_1, \ldots, Y_n$ the agent's state after

---

[2]Formally, we are using multinomial *Dirichlet* priors. See, for example, [4] for an introduction to
these Bayesian methods.

[3]Although $\frac{\partial \hat{Q}(s,a)}{\partial N_{s,a,t}}$ involves a summation over all states, it can be computed efficiently. To see
this, note that the summation is essentially the old value of $Q(s, a)$ (minus the immediate reward)
which can be retained in memory.

the action is executed (e.g., the state t). Thus, $p(t \mid s, a)$ is represented as a conditional probability $P(Y_1, \ldots, Y_n \mid X_1, \ldots, X_n, A_1, \ldots, A_k)$.

A DBN model for such a conditional distribution consists of two components. The first is a directed acyclic graph where each vertex is labeled by a random variable and in which the vertices labeled $X_1, \ldots, X_n$ and $A_1, \ldots, A_k$ are roots. This graph specifies the *factorization* of the conditional distribution:

$$P(Y_1, \ldots, Y_n \mid X_1, \ldots, X_n, A_1, \ldots, A_k) = \prod_{i=1}^{n} P(Y_i \mid Pa_i), \tag{1}$$

where Pa_i are the parents of Y_i in the graph. The second component of the DBN model is a description of the conditional probabilities $P(Y_i \mid Pa_i)$. Together, these two components describe a unique conditional distribution. The simplest representation of $P(Y_i \mid Pa_i)$ is a table that contains a parameter $\theta_{i,y,z} = P(Y_i = y \mid Pa_i = z)$ for each possible combination of $y \in Val(Y_i)$ and $z \in Val(Pa_i)$ (note that z is a joint assignment to several random variables). It is easy to see that the "density" of the DBN graph determines the number of parameters needed. In particular, a *complete* graph, to which we cannot add an arc without violating the constraints, is equivalent to a state-based representation in terms of the number of parameters needed. On the other hand, a sparse graph requires few parameters.

In this paper, we assume that the learner is supplied with the DBN structure and only has to learn the conditional probability entries. It is often easy to assess structure information from experts even when precise probabilities are not available. As in the state-based representation, we learn the parameters using Dirichlet priors for each multinomial distribution [4]. In this method, we assess the conditional probability $\theta_{i,y,z}$ using prior knowledge and the frequency of transitions observed in the past where $Y_i = y$ among those transitions where $Pa_i = z$. Learning amounts to keeping counts $N_{i,y,z}$ that record the number of transitions where $Y_i = y$ and $Pa_i = z$ for each variable Y_i and values $y \in Val(Y_i)$ and $z \in Val(Pa_i)$. Our prior knowledge is represented by fictional counts $N^0_{i,y,z}$. Then we estimate probabilities using the formula $\theta_{i,y,z} = \frac{N_{i,y,z} + N^0_{i,y,z}}{N_{i,\cdot,z}}$, where $N_{i,\cdot,z} = \sum_{y'} N_{i,y',z} + N^0_{i,y',z}$.

We now identify which states should be reconsidered after we update the DBN parameters. Recall that this requires estimating the term $\nabla Q(s, a) \cdot \Delta_\theta$. Since Δ_θ is sparse, after making the transition $s^* \overset{a^*}{\to} t^*$, we have that $\nabla Q(s, a) \cdot \Delta_\theta = \sum_i \frac{\partial Q(s,a)}{\partial N_{i,y_i^*,z_i^*}}$, where y_i^* and z_i^* are the assignments to Y_i and Pa_i, respectively, in $s^* \overset{a^*}{\to} t^*$. (Recall that s^*, a^* and t^* jointly assign values to all the variables in the DBN.)

We say that a transition $s \overset{a}{\to} t$ is *consistent* with an assignment $X = x$ for a vector of random variables X, denoted $(s, a, t) \models (X = x)$, if X is assigned the value x in $s \overset{a}{\to} t$. We also need a similar notion for a partial description of a transition. We say that s and a are consistent with $X = x$, denoted $(s, a, \cdot) \models (X = x)$, if there is a t such that $(s, a, t) \models (X = x)$.

Using this notation, we can show that if $(s, a, \cdot) \models (Pa_i = z_i^*)$, then

$$\frac{\partial Q(s,a)}{\partial N_{i,y_i^*,z_i^*}} = \frac{\gamma}{N_{i,\cdot,z_i^*}} \left[\frac{1}{\theta_{i,y_i^*,z_i^*}} \sum_{t:(s,a,t) \models y_i^*,z_i^*} \hat{p}(t \mid s, a) \hat{V}(t) - \sum_{t:(s,a,t) \models z_i^*} \hat{p}(t \mid s, a) \hat{V}(t) \right],$$

and if s, a are inconsistent with $Pa_i = z_i^*$, then $\frac{\partial Q(s,a)}{\partial N_{i,y_i^*,z_i^*}} = 0$.

This expression shows that if s is similar to s^* in that both agree on the values they assign to the parents of some Y_i (i.e., (s, a^*) is consistent with z_i^*), then the priority of s would change after we update the model. The magnitude of the priority change depends upon both the similarity of s and s^* (i.e. how many of the terms in $\nabla Q(s, a) \cdot \Delta_\theta$ will be non-zero), and the value of the states that can be reached from s.

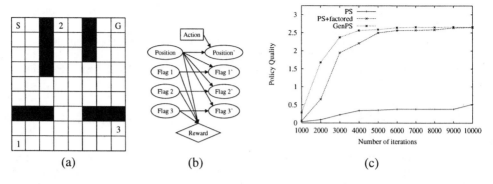

Figure 1: (a) The maze used in the experiment. S marks the start space, G the goal state, and 1, 2 and 3 are the three flags the agent has to set to receive the reward. (b) The DBN structure that captures the independencies in this domain. (c) A graph showing the performance of the three procedures on this example. PS is GenPS with a state-based model, PS+factored is the same procedure but with a factored model, and GenPS exploits the factored model in prioritization. Each curve is the average of 5 runs.

The evaluation of $\frac{\partial Q(s,a)}{\partial N_{i,y_i^*,z_i^*}}$ requires us to sum over a subset of the states –namely, those states t that are consistent with z_i^*. Unfortunately, in the worst case this will be a large fragment of the state space. If the number of environment states is not large, then this might be a reasonable cost to pay for the additional benefits of GenPS. However, this might be a burdensome when we have a large state space, which are the cases where we expect to gain the most benefit from using generalized representations such as DBN.

In these situations, we propose a heuristic approach for estimating $\nabla Q(s,a)\Delta_\theta$ without summing over large numbers of states for computing the change of priority for each possible state. This can be done by finding upper bounds on or estimates of $\frac{\partial Q(s,a)}{\partial N_{i,y_i^*,z_i^*}}$. Once we have computed these estimates, we can estimate the priority change for each state s. We use the notation $s \sim_i s^*$ if s and s^* both agree on the assignment to Pa_i. If C_i is an upper bound on (or an estimate of) $\left| \frac{\partial Q(s,a)}{\partial N_{i,y_i^*,z_i^*}} \right|$, we have that $|\nabla Q(s,a)\Delta_{\theta_M}| \leq \sum_{i:s\sim_i s^*} C_i$.

Thus, to evaluate the priority of state s, we simply find how "similar" it is to s^*. Note that it is relatively straightforward to use this equation to enumerate all the states where the priority change might be large. Finally, we note that the use of a DBN as a model does not change the way we update priorities after a value propagation step. If we use an explicit table of values, then we would update priorities as in the previous section. If we use a compact description of the value function, then we can apply GenPS to get the appropriate update rule.

5 An Experiment

We conducted an experiment to evaluate the effect of using GenPS with a generalizing model. We used a maze domain similar to the one described in [6]. The maze, shown in Figure 1(a), contains 59 cells, and 3 binary flags, resulting in $59 \times 2^3 = 472$ possible states. Initially the agent is at the start cell (marked by S) and the flags are reset. The agent has four possible actions, up, down, left, and right, that succeed 80% of the time, and 20% of the time the agent moves in an unintended perpendicular direction. The i'th flag is set when the agent leaves the cell marked by i. The agent receives a reward when it arrives at the goal cell (marked by G) and all of the flags are set. In this situation, any action resets the game. As noted in [6], this environment exhibits independencies. Namely, the probability of transition from one cell to another does not depend on the flag settings.

These independencies can be captured easily by the simple DBN shown in Figure 1(b) Our experiment is designed to test the extent to which GenPS exploits the knowledge of these independencies for faster learning.

We tested three procedures. The first is GenPS, which uses an explicit state-based model. As explained above, this variant is essentially PS. The second procedure uses a factored model of the environment for learning the model parameters, but uses the same prioritization strategy as the first one. The third procedure uses the GenPS prioritization strategy we describe in Section 4. All three procedures use the Boltzman exploration strategy (see for example [5]). Finally, in each iteration these procedures process at most 10 states from the priority queue.

The results are shown in Figure 1(c). As we can see, the GenPS procedure converged faster than the procedures that used classic PS. As we can see, by using the factored model we get two improvements. The first improvement is due to generalization in the model. This allows the agent to learn a good model of its environment after fewer iterations. This explains why PS+factored converges faster than PS. The second improvement is due to the better prioritization strategy. This explains the faster convergence of GenPS.

6 Discussion

We have presented a general method for approximating the optimal use of computational resources during reinforcement learning. Like classic prioritized sweeping, our method aims to perform only the most beneficial value propagations. By using the gradient of the Bellman equation our method generalizes the underlying principle in prioritized sweeping. The generalized procedure can then be applied not only in the explicit, state-based case, but in cases where approximators are used for the model. The generalized procedure also extends to cases where a function approximator (such as that discussed in [3]) is used for the value function, and future work will empirically test this application of GenPS. We are currently working on applying GenPS to other types of model and function approximators.

Acknowledgments

We are grateful to Geoff Gordon, Daishi Harada, Kevin Murphy, and Stuart Russell for discussions related to this work and comments on earlier versions of this paper. This research was supported in part by ARO under the MURI program "Integrated Approach to Intelligent Systems," grant number DAAH04-96-1-0341. The first author is supported by a National Defense Science and Engineering Graduate Fellowship.

References

[1] S. Davies. Multidimensional triangulation and interpolation for reinforcement learning. In *Advances in Neural Information Processing Systems 9*. 1996.

[2] T. Dean and K. Kanazawa. A model for reasoning about persistence and causation. *Computational Intelligence*, 5:142–150, 1989.

[3] G. J. Gordon. Stable function approximation in dynamic programming. In *Proc. 12th Int. Conf. on Machine Learning*, 1995.

[4] D. Heckerman. A tutorial on learning with Bayesian networks. Technical Report MSR-TR-95-06, Microsoft Research, 1995. Revised November 1996.

[5] L. P. Kaelbling, M. L. Littman and A. W. Moore. Reinforcement learning: A survey. *Journal of Artificial Intelligence Research*, 4:237–285, 1996.

[6] A. W. Moore and C. G. Atkeson. Prioritized sweeping—reinforcement learning with less data and less time. *Machine Learning*, 13:103–130, 1993.

[7] R. S. Sutton. Integrated architectures for learning, planning, and reacting based on approximating dynamic programming. In *Machine Learning: Proc. 7th Int. Conf.*, 1990.

[8] P. Tadepalli and D. Ok. Scaling up average reward reinforcement learning by approximating the domain models and the value function. In *Proc. 13th Int. Conf. on Machine Learning*, 1996.

[9] R. J. Williams and L. C. III Baird. Tight performance bounds on greedy policies based on imperfect value functions. Technical report, Computer Science, Northeastern University. 1993.

Nonparametric Model-Based Reinforcement Learning

Christopher G. Atkeson
College of Computing, Georgia Institute of Technology,
Atlanta, GA 30332-0280, USA
ATR Human Information Processing,
2-2 Hikaridai, Seiko-cho, Soraku-gun, 619-02 Kyoto, Japan
cga@cc.gatech.edu
http://www.cc.gatech.edu/fac/Chris.Atkeson/

Abstract

This paper describes some of the interactions of model learning algorithms and planning algorithms we have found in exploring model-based reinforcement learning. The paper focuses on how local trajectory optimizers can be used effectively with learned nonparametric models. We find that trajectory planners that are fully consistent with the learned model often have difficulty finding reasonable plans in the early stages of learning. Trajectory planners that balance obeying the learned model with minimizing cost (or maximizing reward) often do better, even if the plan is not fully consistent with the learned model.

1 INTRODUCTION

We are exploring the use of nonparametric models in robot learning (Atkeson et al., 1997b; Atkeson and Schaal, 1997). This paper describes the interaction of model learning algorithms and planning algorithms, focusing on how local trajectory optimization can be used effectively with nonparametric models in reinforcement learning. We find that trajectory optimizers that are fully consistent with the learned model often have difficulty finding reasonable plans in the early stages of learning. The message of this paper is that a planner should not be entirely consistent with the learned model during model-based reinforcement learning. Trajectory optimizers that balance obeying the learned model with minimizing cost (or maximizing reward) often do better, even if the plan is not fully consistent with the learned model.

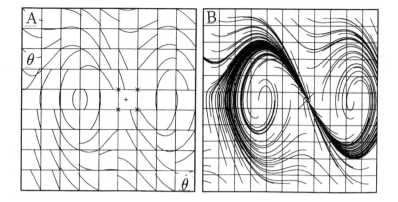

Figure 1: A: Planning in terms of trajectory segments. B: Planning in terms of trajectories all the way to a goal point.

Two kinds of reinforcement learning algorithms are direct (non-model-based) and indirect (model-based). Direct reinforcement learning algorithms learn a policy or value function without explicitly representing a model of the controlled system (Sutton et al., 1992). Model-based approaches learn an explicit model of the system simultaneously with a value function and policy (Sutton, 1990, 1991a,b; Barto et al., 1995; Kaelbling et al., 1996). We will focus on model-based reinforcement learning, in which the learner uses a planner to derive a policy from a learned model and an optimization criterion.

2   CONSISTENT LOCAL PLANNING

An efficient approach to dynamic programming, a form of global planning, is to use local trajectory optimizers (Atkeson, 1994). These local planners find a plan for each starting point in a grid in the state space. Figure 1 compares the output of a traditional cell based dynamic programming process with the output of a planner based on integrating local plans. Traditional dynamic programming generates trajectory segments from each cell to neighboring cells, while the planner we use generates entire trajectories. These locally optimal trajectories have local policies and local models of the value function along the trajectories (Dyer and McReynolds, 1970; Jacobson and Mayne, 1970). The locally optimal trajectories are made consistent with their neighbors by using the local value function to predict the value of a neighboring trajectory. If all the local value functions are consistent with their neighbors the aggregate value function is a unique solution to the Bellman equation and the corresponding trajectories and policy are globally optimal. We would like any local planning algorithm to produce a local model of the value function so we can perform this type of consistency checking. We would also like a local policy from the local planner, so we can respond to disturbances and modeling errors.

Differential dynamic programming is a local planner that has these characteristics (Dyer and McReynolds, 1970; Jacobson and Mayne, 1970). Differential dynamic programming maintains a local quadratic model of the value function along the current best trajectory $\mathbf{x}^*(t)$:

$$V(\mathbf{x}, t) = V_0(t) + V_x(t)(\mathbf{x} - \mathbf{x}^*(t))^\mathrm{T} + 0.5(\mathbf{x} - \mathbf{x}^*(t))^\mathrm{T} V_{xx}(t)(\mathbf{x} - \mathbf{x}^*(t)) \quad (1)$$

as well as a local linear model of the corresponding policy:

$$\mathbf{u}(\mathbf{x}, t) = \mathbf{u}^*(t) + \mathbf{K}(t)(\mathbf{x} - \mathbf{x}^*(t)) \tag{2}$$

$\mathbf{u}(\mathbf{x}, t)$ is the local policy at time t, the control signal $\mathbf{u}$ as a function of state $\mathbf{x}$. $\mathbf{u}^*(t)$ is the model's estimate of the control signal necessary to follow the current best trajectory $\mathbf{x}^*(t)$. $\mathbf{K}(t)$ are the feedback gains that alter the control signals in response to deviations from the current best trajectory. These gains are also the first derivative of the policy along the current best trajectory.

The first phase of each optimization iteration is to apply the current local policy to the learned model, integrating the modeled dynamics forward in time and seeing where the simulated trajectory goes. The second phase of the differential dynamic programming approach is to calculate the components of the local quadratic model of the value function at each point along the trajectory: the constant term $V_0(t)$, the gradient $V_x(t)$, and the Hessian $V_{xx}(t)$. These terms are constructed by integrating backwards in time along the trajectory. The value function is used to produce a new policy, which is represented using a new $\mathbf{x}^*(t)$, $\mathbf{u}^*(t)$, and $\mathbf{K}(t)$.

The availability of a local value function and policy is an attractive feature of differential dynamic programming. However, we have found several problems when applying this method to model-based reinforcement learning with nonparametric models:

1. Methods that enforce consistency with the learned model need an initial trajectory that obeys that model, which is often difficult to produce.

2. The integration of the learned model forward in time often blows up when the learned model is inaccurate or when the plant is unstable and the current policy fails to stabilize it.

3. The backward integration to produce the value function and a corresponding policy uses derivatives of the learned model, which are often quite inaccurate in the early stages of learning, producing inaccurate value function estimates and ineffective policies.

3   INCONSISTENT LOCAL PLANNING

To avoid the problems of consistent local planners, we developed a trajectory optimization approach that does not integrate the learned model and does not require full consistency with the learned model. Unfortunately, the price of these modifications is that the method does not produce a value function or a policy, just a trajectory $(\mathbf{x}(t), \mathbf{u}(t))$. To allow inconsistency with the learned model, we represent the state history $\mathbf{x}(t)$ and the control history $\mathbf{u}(t)$ separately, rather than calculate $\mathbf{x}(t)$ from the learned model and $\mathbf{u}(t)$. We also modify the original optimization criterion $C = \sum_k c(\mathbf{x}_k, \mathbf{u}_k)$ by changing the hard constraint that $\mathbf{x}_{k+1} = \mathbf{f}(\mathbf{x}_k, \mathbf{u}_k)$ on each time step into a soft constraint:

$$C_{new} = \sum_k \left[c(\mathbf{x}_k, \mathbf{u}_k) + \lambda |\mathbf{x}_{k+1} - \mathbf{f}(\mathbf{x}_k, \mathbf{u}_k)|^2 \right] \tag{3}$$

$c(\mathbf{x}_k, \mathbf{u}_k)$ is the one step cost in the original optimization criterion. λ is the penalty on the trajectory being inconsistent with the learned model $\widehat{\mathbf{x}}_{k+1} = \mathbf{f}(\mathbf{x}_k, \mathbf{u}_k)$. $|\mathbf{x}_{k+1} - \mathbf{f}(\mathbf{x}_k, \mathbf{u}_k)|$ is the magnitude of the mismatch of the trajectory and the model prediction at time step k in the trajectory. λ provides a way to control the amount of inconsistency. A small λ reflects lack of confidence in the model, and allows

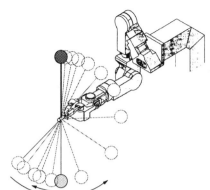

Figure 2: The SARCOS robot arm with a pendulum gripped in the hand. The pendulum axis is aligned with the fingers and with the forearm in this arm configuration.

the optimized trajectory to be inconsistent with the model in favor of reducing $c(\mathbf{x}_k, \mathbf{u}_k)$. A large λ reflects confidence in the model, and forces the optimized trajectory to be more consistent with the model. λ can increase with time or with the number of learning trials. If we use a model that estimates the confidence level of a prediction, we can vary λ for each lookup based on $\mathbf{x}_k$ and $\mathbf{u}_k$. Locally weighted learning techniques provide exactly this type of local confidence estimate (Atkeson et al., 1997a).

Now that we are not integrating the trajectory we can use more compact representations of the trajectory, such as splines (Cohen, 1992) or wavelets (Liu et al., 1994). We no longer require that $\mathbf{x}_{k+1} = \mathbf{f}(\mathbf{x}_k, \mathbf{u}_k)$, which is a condition difficult to fulfill without having $\mathbf{x}$ and $\mathbf{u}$ represented as independent values on each time step. We can now parameterize the trajectory using the spline knot points, for example. In this work we used B splines (Cohen, 1992) to represent the trajectory. Other choices for spline basis functions would probably work just as well. We can use any nonlinear programming or function optimization method to minimize the criterion in Eq. 3. In this work we used Powell's method (Press et al., 1988) to optimize the knot points, a method which is convenient to use but not particularly efficient.

4 IMPLEMENTATION ON AN ACTUAL ROBOT

Both local planning methods work well with learned parametric models. However, differential dynamic programming did not work at all with learned nonparametric models, for reasons already discussed. This section describes how the inconsistent local planning method was used in an application of model-based reinforcement learning: robot learning from demonstration using a pendulum swing up task (Atkeson and Schaal, 1997). The pendulum swing up task is a more complex version of the pole or broom balancing task (Spong, 1995). The hand holds the axis of the pendulum, and the pendulum rotates about this hinge in an angular movement (Figure 2). Instead of starting with the pendulum vertical and above its rotational joint, the pendulum is hanging down from the hand, and the goal of the swing up task is to move the hand so that the pendulum swings up and is then balanced in the inverted position. The swing up task was chosen for study because it is a difficult dynamic maneuver and requires practice for humans to learn, but it is easy to tell if the task is successfully executed (at the end of the task the pendulum is balanced upright and does not fall down).

We implemented learning from demonstration on a hydraulic seven degree of free-

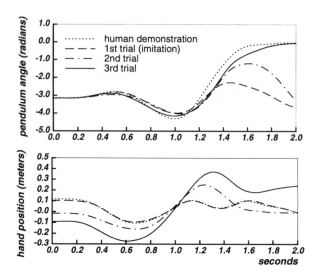

Figure 3: The hand and pendulum motion during robot learning from demonstration using a nonparametric model.

dom anthropomorphic robot arm (SARCOS Dextrous Arm located at ATR, Figure 2). The robot observed its own performance with the same stereo vision system that was used to observe the human demonstrations.

The robot observed a human swinging up a pendulum using a horizontal hand movement (dotted line in Figure 3). The most obvious approach to learning from demonstration is to have the robot imitate the human motion, by following the human hand trajectory. The dashed lines in Figures 3 show the robot hand motion as it attempts to follow the human demonstration of the swing up task, and the corresponding pendulum angles. Because of differences in the task dynamics for the human and for the robot, this direct imitation failed to swing the pendulum up, as the pendulum did not get even halfway up to the vertical position, and then oscillated about the hanging down position.

The approach we used was to apply a planner to finding a swing up trajectory that worked for the robot, based on learning both a model and a reward function and using the human demonstration to initialize the planning process. The data collected during the initial imitation trial and subsequent trials was used to build a model. Nonparametric models were constructed using locally weighted learning as described in (Atkeson et al., 1997a). These models did not use knowledge of the model structure but instead assumed a general relationship:

$$\dot{\theta}_{k+1} = model(\theta_k, \dot{\theta}_k, x_k, \dot{x}_k, \ddot{x}_k) \tag{4}$$

where θ is the pendulum angle and x is the hand position. Training data from the demonstrations was stored in a database, and a local model was constructed to answer each query. Meta-parameters such as distance metrics were tuned using cross validation on the training set. For example, cross validation was able to quickly establish that hand position and velocity (x and $\dot{x}$) played an insignificant role in predicting future pendulum angular velocities.

The planner used a cost function that penalizes deviations from the demonstration trajectory sampled at $60Hz$:

$$c(\mathbf{x}_k, \mathbf{u}_k) = (\mathbf{x}_k - \mathbf{x}_k^d)^T (\mathbf{x}_k - \mathbf{x}_k^d) + \mathbf{u}_k^T \mathbf{u}_k \tag{5}$$

where the state is $\mathbf{x} = (\theta, \dot{\theta}, x, \dot{x})$, $\mathbf{x}^{\text{d}}$ is the demonstrated motion, k is the sample index, and the control is $\mathbf{u} = (\ddot{x})$. Equation 3 was optimized using B splines to represent $\mathbf{x}$ and $\mathbf{u}$. The knot points for $\mathbf{x}$ and $\mathbf{u}$ were initially separately optimized to minimize

$$\left(\mathbf{x}_k - \mathbf{x}_k^{\text{d}}\right)^{\text{T}}\left(\mathbf{x}_k - \mathbf{x}_k^{\text{d}}\right) \tag{6}$$

and

$$\left(\mathbf{u}_k - \mathbf{u}_k^{\text{d}}\right)^{\text{T}}\left(\mathbf{u}_k - \mathbf{u}_k^{\text{d}}\right) \tag{7}$$

The tolerated inconsistency, λ was kept constant during a set of trials and set at values ranging from 100 to 100000. The exact value of λ did not make much difference. Learning failed when λ was set to zero, as there was no way for the learned model to affect the plan. The planning process failed when λ was set too high, enforcing the learned model too strongly.

The next attempt got the pendulum up a little more. Adding this new data to the database and replanning resulted in a movement that succeeded (trial 3 in Figure 3). The behavior shown in Figure 3 is quite repeatable. The balancing behavior at the end of the trial is learned separately and continues for several minutes, at which point the trial is automatically terminated (Schaal, 1997).

5 DISCUSSION AND CONCLUSION

We applied locally weighted regression (Atkeson et al., 1997a) in an attempt to avoid the structural modeling errors of idealized parametric models during model-based reinforcement learning, and also to see if a priori knowledge of the structure of the task dynamics was necessary. In an exploration of the swingup task, we found that these nonparametric models required a planner that ignored the learned model to some extent. The fundamental reason for this is that planners amplify modeling error. Mechanisms for this amplification include:

- The planners take advantage of any modeling error to reduce the cost of the planned trajectory, so the planning process seeks out modeling error that reduces apparent cost.
- Some planners use derivatives of the model, which amplifies any noise in the model.

Models that support fast learning will have errors and noise. For example, in order to learn a model of the complexity necessary to accurately model the full robot dynamics between the commanded and actual hand accelerations a large amount of data is required, independent of modeling technique. The input would be 21 dimensional (robot state and command) ignoring actuator dynamics. Because there are few robot trials during learning, there is not enough data to make such a model even just in the vicinity of a successful trajectory. If it was required that enough data is collected during learning to make an accurate model, robot learning would be greatly slowed down.

One solution to this error amplification is to bias the nonparametric modeling tools to oversmooth the data. This reduces the benefit of nonparametric modeling, and also ignores the true learned model to some degree. Our solution to this problem is to introduce a controlled amount of inconsistency with the learned model into the planning process. The control parameter λ is explicit and can be changed as a function of time, amount of data, or as a function of confidence in the model at the query point.

References

Atkeson, C. G. (1994). Using local trajectory optimizers to speed up global optimization in dynamic programming. In Cowan, J. D., Tesauro, G., and Alspector, J., editors, *Advances in Neural Information Processing Systems 6*, pages 663–670. Morgan Kaufmann, San Mateo, CA.

Atkeson, C. G., Moore, A. W., and Schaal, S. (1997a). Locally weighted learning. *Artificial Intelligence Review*, 11:11–73.

Atkeson, C. G., Moore, A. W., and Schaal, S. (1997b). Locally weighted learning for control. *Artificial Intelligence Review*, 11:75–113.

Atkeson, C. G. and Schaal, S. (1997). Robot learning from demonstration. In *Proceedings of the 1997 International Conference on Machine Learning*.

Barto, A. G., Bradtke, S. J., and Singh, S. P. (1995). Learning to act using real-time dynamic programming. *Artificial Intelligence*, 72(1):81–138.

Cohen, M. F. (1992). Interactive spacetime control for animation. *Computer Graphics*, 26(2):293–302.

Dyer, P. and McReynolds, S. (1970). *The Computational Theory of Optimal Control.* Academic, NY.

Jacobson, D. and Mayne, D. (1970). *Differential Dynamic Programming*. Elsevier, NY.

Kaelbling, L. P., Littman, M. L., and Moore, A. W. (1996). Reinforcement learning: A survey. *Journal of Artificial Intelligence Research*, 4:237–285.

Liu, Z., Gortler, S. J., and Cohen, M. F. (1994). Hierarchical spacetime control. *Computer Graphics (SIGGRAPH '94 Proceedings)*, pages 35–42.

Press, W. H., Teukolsky, S. A., Vetterling, W. T., and Flannery, B. P. (1988). *Numerical Recipes in C.* Cambridge University Press, New York, NY.

Schaal, S. (1997). Learning from demonstration. In Mozer, M. C., Jordan, M., and Petsche, T., editors, *Advances in Neural Information Processing Systems 9*, pages 1040–1046. MIT Press, Cambridge, MA.

Spong, M. W. (1995). The swing up control problem for the acrobot. *IEEE Control Systems Magazine*, 15(1):49–55.

Sutton, R. S. (1990). Integrated architectures for learning, planning, and reacting based on approximating dynamic programming. In *Seventh International Machine Learning Workshop*, pages 216–224. Morgan Kaufmann, San Mateo, CA. http://envy.cs.umass.edu/People/sutton/publications.html.

Sutton, R. S. (1991a). Dyna, an integrated architecture for learning, planning and reacting. http://envy.cs.umass.edu/People/sutton/publications.html, Working Notes of the 1991 AAAI Spring Symposium on Integrated Intelligent Architectures pp. 151–155 and SIGART Bulletin 2, pp. 160-163.

Sutton, R. S. (1991b). Planning by incremental dynamic programming. In *Eighth International Machine Learning Workshop*, pages 353–357. Morgan Kaufmann, San Mateo, CA. http://envy.cs.umass.edu/People/sutton/publications.html.

Sutton, R. S., Barto, A. G., and Williams, R. J. (1992). Reinforcement learning is direct adaptive optimal control. *IEEE Control Systems Magazine*, 12:19—22.

An Improved Policy Iteration Algorithm for Partially Observable MDPs

Eric A. Hansen
Computer Science Department
University of Massachusetts
Amherst, MA 01003
hansen@cs.umass.edu

Abstract

A new policy iteration algorithm for partially observable Markov decision processes is presented that is simpler and more efficient than an earlier policy iteration algorithm of Sondik (1971,1978). The key simplification is representation of a policy as a finite-state controller. This representation makes policy evaluation straightforward. The paper's contribution is to show that the dynamic-programming update used in the policy improvement step can be interpreted as the transformation of a finite-state controller into an improved finite-state controller. The new algorithm consistently outperforms value iteration as an approach to solving infinite-horizon problems.

1 Introduction

A partially observable Markov decision process (POMDP) is a generalization of the standard completely observable Markov decision process that allows imperfect information about the state of the system. First studied as a model of decision-making in operations research, it has recently been used as a framework for decision-theoretic planning and reinforcement learning with hidden state (Monahan, 1982; Cassandra, Kaelbling, & Littman, 1994; Jaakkola, Singh, & Jordan, 1995).

Value iteration and policy iteration algorithms for POMDPs were first developed by Sondik and rely on a piecewise linear and convex representation of the value function (Sondik, 1971; Smallwood & Sondik,1973; Sondik, 1978). Sondik's policy iteration algorithm has proved to be impractical, however, because its policy evaluation step is extremely complicated and difficult to implement. As a result, almost all subsequent work on dynamic programming for POMDPs has used value iteration. In this paper, we describe an improved policy iteration algorithm for POMDPs that avoids the difficulties of Sondik's algorithm. We show that these difficulties hinge on the choice of a policy representation and can be avoided by representing a policy as a finite-state controller. This representation makes the policy evaluation step easy to implement and efficient. We show that the policy improvement step can be interpreted in a natural way as the transformation of a finite-state controller into an improved finite-state controller. Although it is not always possible to represent an optimal policy for an infinite-horizon POMDP as a finite-state controller, it is always possible to do so when the optimal value function is piecewise linear and convex. Therefore representation of a policy as a finite-state controller is no more limiting than representation of the value function as piecewise linear and convex. In fact, it is the close relationship between representation of a policy as a finite-state controller and representation of a value function as piecewise linear and convex that the new algorithm successfully exploits.

The paper is organized as follows. Section 2 briefly reviews the POMDP model and Sondik's policy iteration algorithm. Section 3 describes an improved policy iteration algorithm. Section 4 illustrates the algorithm with a simple example and reports a comparison of its performance to value iteration. The paper concludes with a discussion of the significance of this work.

2 Background

Consider a discrete-time POMDP with a finite set of states S, a finite set of actions A, and a finite set of observations Θ. Each time period, the system is in some state $i \in S$, an agent chooses an action $a \in A$ for which it receives a reward with expected value r_i^a, the system makes a transition to state $j \in S$ with probability p_{ij}^a, and the agent observes $\theta \in \Theta$ with probability $q_{j\theta}^a$. We assume the performance objective is to maximize expected total discounted reward over an infinite horizon.

Although the state of the system cannot be directly observed, the probability that it is in a given state can be calculated. Let π denote a vector of state probabilities, called an *information state*, where π_i denotes the probability that the system is in state i. If action a is taken in information state π and θ is observed, the successor information state is determined by revising each state probability using Bayes' theorem: $\pi_j = \sum_{i \in S} \pi_i p_{ij}^a q_{j\theta}^a / \sum_{i,j \in S} \pi_i p_{ij}^a q_{j\theta}^a$. Geometrically, each information state π is a point in the $(|S| - 1)$-dimensional unit simplex, denoted Π.

It is well-known that an information state π is a sufficient statistic that summarizes all information about the history of a POMDP necessary for optimal action selection. Therefore a POMDP can be recast as a completely observable MDP with a continuous state space Π and it can be theoretically solved using dynamic programming. The key to practical implementation of a dynamic-programming algorithm is a piecewise-linear and convex representation of the value function. Smallwood and Sondik (1973) show that the dynamic-programming update for POMDPs preserves the piecewise linearity and convexity of the value function. They also show that an optimal value function for a finite-horizon POMDP is always piecewise linear and convex. For infinite-horizon POMDPs, Sondik (1978) shows that an optimal value function is sometimes piecewise linear and convex and can be aproximated arbitrarily closely by a piecewise linear and convex function otherwise.

A piecewise linear and convex value function V can be represented by a finite set of $|S|$-dimensional vectors, $\Gamma = \{\alpha^0, \alpha^1, \ldots\}$, such that $V(\pi) = \max_k \sum_{i \in S} \pi_i \alpha_i^k$. A dynamic-programming update transforms a value function V represented by a set Γ of α-vectors into an improved value function V' represented by a set Γ' of α-vectors. Each possible α-vector in Γ' corresponds to choice of an action, and for each possible observation, choice of a successor vector in Γ. Given the combinatorial number of choices that can be made, the maximum number of vectors in Γ' is $|A||\Gamma|^{|\Theta|}$. However most of these potential vectors are not needed to define the updated value function and can be pruned. Thus the dynamic-programming update problem is to find a minimal set of vectors Γ' that represents V', given a set of vectors Γ that represents V. Several algorithms for performing this dynamic-programming update have been developed but describing them is beyond the scope of this paper. Any algorithm for performing the dynamic-programming update can be used in the policy improvement step of policy iteration. The algorithm that is presently the fastest is described by (Cassandra, Littman, & Zhang, 1997).

For value iteration, it is sufficient to have a representation of the value function because a policy is defined implicitly by the value function, as follows,

$$\delta(\pi) = a(\arg\max_k \sum_{i \in S} \pi_i \alpha_i^k), \tag{1}$$

where $a(k)$ denotes the action associated with vector α^k. But for policy iteration, a policy must be represented independently of the value function because the policy evaluation step computes the value function of a given policy. Sondik's choice of a policy representation is influenced by Blackwell's proof that for a continuous-space infinite-horizon MDP, there is a stationary, deterministic Markov policy that is optimal (Blackwell, 1965). Based on this result, Sondik restricts policy space to stationary and deterministic Markov policies that map the continuum of information space Π into action space A. Because it is important for a policy to have a finite representation, Sondik defines an admissible policy as a mapping from a finite number of polyhedral regions of Π to A. Each region is represented by a set of linear inequalities, where each linear inequality corresponds to a boundary of the region.

This is Sondik's canonical representation of a policy, but his policy iteration algorithm makes use of two other representations. In the policy evaluation step, he converts a policy from this representation to an equivalent, or approximately equivalent, finite-state controller. Although no method is known for computing the value function of a policy represented as a mapping from Π to A, the value function of a finite-state controller can be computed in a straightforward way. In the policy improvement step, Sondik converts a policy represented implicitly by the updated value function and equation (1) back to his canonical representation. The complexity of translating between these different policy representations – especially in the policy evaluation step – makes Sondik's policy iteration algorithm difficult to implement and explains why it is not used in practice.

3 Algorithm

We now show that policy iteration for POMDPs can be simplified – both conceptually and computationally – by using a single representation of a policy as a finite-state controller.

3.1 Policy evaluation

As Sondik recognized, policy evaluation is straightforward when a policy is represented as a finite-state controller. An α-vector representation of the value function of a finite-state controller is computed by solving the system of linear equations,

$$\alpha_i^k = r_i^{a(k)} + \beta \sum_{j,\theta} p_{ij}^{a(k)} q_{j\theta}^{a(k)} \alpha_j^{s(k,\theta)}, \tag{2}$$

where k is an index of a state of the finite-state controller, $a(k)$ is the action associated with machine state k, and $s(k, \theta)$ is the index of the successor machine state if θ is observed. This value function is convex as well as piecewise linear because the expected value of an information state is determined by assuming the controller is started in the machine state that optimizes it.

---

1. Specify an initial finite-state controller, δ, and select ϵ for detecting convergence to an ϵ-optimal policy.

2. Policy evaluation: Calculate a set Γ of α-vectors that represents the value function for δ by solving the system of equations given by equation 2.

3. Policy improvement: Perform a dynamic-programming update and use the new set of vectors Γ' to transform δ into a new finite-state controller, δ', as follows:

    (a) For each vector α in Γ':
        i. If the action and successor links associated with α duplicate those of a machine state of δ, then *keep* that machine state unchanged in δ'.
        ii. Else if α pointwise dominates a vector associated with a machine state of δ, *change* the action and successor links of that machine state to those used to create α. (If it pointwise dominates the vectors of more than one machine state, they can be combined into a single machine state.)
        iii. Otherwise *add* a machine state to δ' that has the same action and successor links used to create α.

    (b) *Prune* any machine state for which there is no corresponding vector in Γ', as long as it is not reachable from a machine state to which a vector in Γ' does correspond.

4. Termination test. If the Bellman residual is less than or equal to $\epsilon(1 - \beta)/\beta$, exit with ϵ-optimal policy. Otherwise set δ to δ' and go to step 2.

Figure 1: Policy iteration algorithm.

3.2 Policy improvement

The policy improvement step uses the dynamic-programming update to transform a value function V represented by a set Γ of α-vectors into an improved value function V' represented by a set Γ' of α-vectors. We now show that the dynamic-programming update can also be interpreted as the transformation of a finite-state controller δ into an improved finite-state controller δ'. The transformation is made based on a simple comparison of Γ' and Γ.

First note that some of the α-vectors in Γ' are duplicates of α-vectors in Γ, that is, their action and successor links match (and their vector values are pointwise equal). Any machine state of δ for which there is a duplicate vector in Γ' is left unchanged. The vectors in Γ' that are not duplicates of vectors in Γ indicate how to change the finite-state controller. If a non-duplicate vector in Γ' pointwise dominates a vector in Γ, the machine state that corresponds to the pointwise dominated vector in Γ is changed so that its action and successor links match those of the dominating vector in Γ'. If a non-duplicate vector in Γ' does not pointwise dominate a vector in Γ, a machine state is added to the finite-state controller with the same action and successor links used to generate the vector. There may be some machine states for which there is no corresponding vector in Γ' and they can be pruned, but only if they are not reachable from a machine state that corresponds to a vector in Γ'. This last point is important because it preserves the integrity of the finite-state controller.

A policy iteration algorithm that uses these simple transformations to change a finite-state controller in the policy improvement step is summarized in Figure 1. An algorithm that performs this transformation is easy to implement and runs very efficiently because it simply compares the α-vectors in Γ' to the α-vectors in Γ and modifies the finite-state controller accordingly. The policy evaluation step is invoked to compute the value function of the transformed finite-state controller. (This is only necessary if a machine state has been changed, not if machine states have simply been added.) It is easy to show that the value function of the transformed finite-state controller δ' dominates the value function of the original finite-state controller, δ, and we omit the proof which appears in (Hansen, 1998).

Theorem 1 *If a finite-state controller is not optimal, policy improvement transforms it into a finite-state controller with a value function that is as good or better for every information state and better for some information state.*

3.3 Convergence

If a finite-state controller cannot be improved in the policy improvement step (i.e., all the vectors in Γ' are duplicates of vectors in Γ), it must be optimal because the value function satisfies the optimality equation. However policy iteration does not necessarily converge to an optimal finite-state controller after a finite number of iterations because there is not necessarily an optimal finite-state controller. Therefore we use the same stopping condition used by Sondik to detect ϵ-optimality: a finite-state controller is ϵ-optimal when the Bellman residual is less than or equal to $\epsilon(1-\beta)/\beta$, where β denotes the discount factor. Representation of a policy as a finite-state controller makes the following proof straightforward (Hansen, 1998).

Theorem 2 *Policy iteration converges to an ϵ-optimal finite-state controller after a finite number of iterations.*

4 Example and performance

We illustrate the algorithm using the same example used by Sondik: a simple two-state, two-action, two-observation POMDP that models the problem of finding an optimal marketing strategy given imperfect information about consumer preferences (Sondik,1971,1978). The two states of the problem represent consumer preference or lack of preference for the manufacturers brand; let B denote brand preference and $\neg B$ denote lack of brand preference. Although consumer preferences cannot be observed, they can be infered based on observed purchasing behavior; let P denote purchase of the product and let $\neg P$ denote no purchase. There are two marketing alternatives or actions; the company can market a luxury version of the product (L) or a standard version (S). The luxury version is more expensive to market but can bring greater profit. Marketing the luxury version also increases brand preference. However consumers are more likely to purchase the less expensive, standard product. The transition probabilities, observation probabilities, and reward function for this example are shown in Figure 2. The discount factor is 0.9.

Both Sondik's policy iteration algorithm and the new policy iteration algorithm converge in three iterations from a starting policy that is equivalent to the finite-state

Actions	Transition probabilities		Observation probabilities		Expected reward	
	B	~B	P	~P		
Market luxury product (L)	B 0.8	0.2	B 0.8	0.2	B	4
	~B 0.5	0.5	~B 0.6	0.4	~B	-4
	B	~B	P	~P		
Market standard product (S)	B 0.5	0.5	B 0.9	0.1	B	0
	~B 0.4	0.6	~B 0.4	0.6	~B	-3

Figure 2: Parameters for marketing example of Sondik (1971,1978).

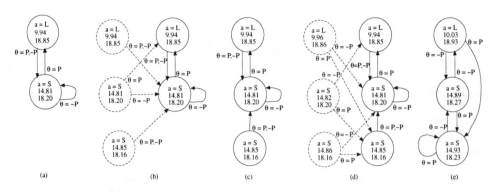

Figure 3: (a) shows the initial finite-state controller, (b) uses dashed circles to show the vectors in Γ' generated in the first policy improvement step and (c) shows the transformed finite-state controller, (d) uses dashed circles to show the vectors in Γ' generated in the second policy improvement step and (e) shows the transformed finite-state controller after policy evaluation. The optimality of this finite-state controller is detected on the third iteration, which is not shown. Arcs are labeled with one of two possible observations and machine states are labeled with one of two possible actions and a 2-dimensional vector that contains a value for each of the two possible system states.

controller shown in Figure 3a. Figure 3 shows how the initial finite-state controller is transformed into an optimal finite-state controller by the new algorithm. In the first iteration, the updated set of vectors Γ' (indicated by dashed circles in Figure 3b) includes two duplicate vectors and one non-duplicate that results in an added machine state. Figure 3c shows the improved finite-state controller after the first iteration. In the second iteration, each of the three vectors in the updated set of vectors Γ' (indicated by dashed circles in Figure 3d) pointwise dominates a vector that corresponds to a current machine state. Thus each of these machine states is changed. Figure 4e shows the improved finite-state controller after the second iteration. The optimality of this finite-state controller is detected in the third iteration.

This is the only example for which Sondik reports using policy iteration to find an optimal policy. For POMDPs with more than two states, Sondik's algorithm is especially difficult to implement. Sondik reports that his algorithm finds a suboptimal policy for an example described in (Smallwood & Sondik, 1973). No further computational experience with his algorithm has been reported.

The new policy iteration algorithm described in this paper easily finds an optimal finite-state controller for the example described in (Smallwood & Sondik, 1973) and has been used to solve many other POMDPs. In fact, it consistently outperforms value iteration. We compared its performance to the performance of value iteration on a suite of ten POMDPs that represent a range of problem sizes for which exact dynamic-programming updates are currently feasible. (Presently, exact dynamic-prorgramming updates are not feasible for POMDPs with more than about ten or fifteen states, actions, or observations.) Starting from the same point, we measured how soon each algorithm converged to ε-optimality for ε values of 10.0, 1.0, 0.1, and 0.01. Policy iteration was consistently faster than value iteration by a factor that ranged from a low of about 10 times faster to a high of over 120 times faster. On average, its rate of convergence was between 40 and 50 times faster than value iteration for this set of examples. The finite-state controllers it found had as many as several hundred machine states, although optimal finite-state controllers were sometimes found with just a few machine states.

5 Discussion

We have demonstrated that the dynamic-programming update for POMDPs can be interpreted as the improvement of a finite-state controller. This interpretation can be applied to both value iteration and policy iteration. It provides no computational speedup for value iteration, but for policy iteration it results in substantial speedup by making policy evaluation straightforward and easy to implement. This representation also has the advantage that it makes a policy easier to understand and execute than representation as a mapping from regions of information space to actions. In particular, a policy can be executed without maintaining an information state at run-time.

It is well-known that policy iteration converges to ϵ-optimality (or optimality) in fewer iterations than value iteration. For completely observable MDPs, this is not a clear advantage because the policy evaluation step is more computationally expensive than the dynamic-programming update. But for POMDPs, policy evaluation has low-order polynomial complexity compared to the worst-case exponential complexity of the dynamic-programming update (Littman et al., 1995). Therefore, policy iteration appears to have a clearer advantage over value iteration for POMDPs. Preliminary testing bears this out and suggests that policy iteration significantly outperforms value iteration as an approach to solving infinite-horizon POMDPs.

Acknowledgements

Thanks to Shlomo Zilberstein and especially Michael Littman for helpful discussions. Support for this work was provided in part by the National Science Foundation under grants IRI-9409827 and IRI-9624992.

References

Blackwell, D. (1965) Discounted dynamic programming. *Ann. Math. Stat.* 36:226-235.

Cassandra, A.; Kaelbling, L.P.; Littman, M.L. (1994) Acting optimally in partially observable stochastic domains. In *Proc. 13th National Conf. on AI*, 1023-1028.

Cassandra, A.; Littman, M.L.; & Zhang, N.L. (1997) Incremental pruning: A simple, fast, exact algorithm for partially observable Markov decision processes. In *Proc. 13th Annual Conf. on Uncertainty in AI*.

Hansen, E.A. (1998). *Finite-Memory Control of Partially Observable Systems*. PhD thesis, Department of Computer Science, University of Massachusetts at Amherst.

Jaakkola, T.; Singh, S.P.; & Jordan, M.I. (1995) Reinforcement learning algorithm for partially observable Markov decision problems. In NIPS-7.

Littman, M.L.; Cassandra, A.R.; & Kaelbling, L.P. (1995) Efficient dynamic-programming updates in partially observable Markov decision processes. Computer Science Technical Report CS-95-19, Brown University.

Monahan, G.E. (1982) A survey of partially observable Markov decision processes: Theory, models, and algorithms. *Management Science* 28:1-16.

Smallwood, R.D. & Sondik, E.J. (1973) The optimal control of partially observable Markov processes over a finite horizon. *Operations Research* 21:1071-1088.

Sondik, E.J. (1971) *The Optimal Control of Partially Observable Markov Processes*. PhD thesis, Department of Electrical Engineering, Stanford University.

Sondik, E.J. (1978) The optimal control of partially observable Markov processes over the infinite horizon: Discounted costs. *Operations Research* 26:282-304.

Automated Aircraft Recovery via Reinforcement Learning: Initial Experiments

Jeffrey F. Monaco
Barron Associates, Inc.
Jordan Building
1160 Pepsi Place, Suite 300
Charlottesville VA 22901
monaco@bainet.com

David G. Ward
Barron Associates, Inc.
Jordan Building
1160 Pepsi Place, Suite 300
Charlottesville VA 22901
ward@bainet.com

Andrew G. Barto
Department of Computer Science
University of Massachusetts
Amherst MA 01003
barto@cs.umass.edu

Abstract

Initial experiments described here were directed toward using reinforcement learning (RL) to develop an automated recovery system (ARS) for high-agility aircraft. An ARS is an outer-loop flight-control system designed to bring an aircraft from a range of out-of-control states to straight-and-level flight in minimum time while satisfying physical and physiological constraints. Here we report on results for a simple version of the problem involving only single-axis (pitch) simulated recoveries. Through simulated control experience using a medium-fidelity aircraft simulation, the RL system approximates an optimal policy for pitch-stick inputs to produce minimum-time transitions to straight-and-level flight in unconstrained cases while avoiding ground-strike. The RL system was also able to adhere to a pilot-station acceleration constraint while executing simulated recoveries.

1 INTRODUCTION

An emerging use of reinforcement learning (RL) is to approximate optimal policies for large-scale control problems through extensive simulated control experience. Described here are initial experiments directed toward the development of an automated recovery system (ARS) for high-agility aircraft. An ARS is an outer-loop flight control system designed to bring the aircraft from a range of initial states to straight, level, and non-inverted flight in minimum time while satisfying constraints such as maintaining altitude and accelerations within acceptable limits. Here we describe the problem and present initial results involving only single-axis (pitch) recoveries. Through extensive simulated control experience using a medium-fidelity simulation of an F-16, the RL system approximated an optimal policy for longitudinal-stick inputs to produce near-minimum-time transitions to straight and level flight in unconstrained cases, as well as while meeting a pilot-station acceleration constraint.

2 AIRCRAFT MODEL

The aircraft was modeled as a dynamical system with state vector $x = \{q, \alpha, p, r, \beta, V_t\}$, where q = body-axes pitch rate, α = angle of attack, p = body-axes roll rate, r = body-axes yaw rate, β = angle of sideslip, V_t = total airspeed, and control vector $\delta = \{\delta_{se}, \delta_{ae}, \delta_{af}, \delta_{rud}\}$ of effector and pseudo-effector displacements. The controls are defined as: δ_{se} = symmetric elevon, δ_{ae} = asymmetric elevon, δ_{af} = asymmetric flap, and δ_{rud} = rudder. (A pseudo-effector is a mathematically convenient combination of real effectors that, e.g., contributes to motion in a limited number of axes.) The following additional descriptive variables were used in the RL problem formulation: h = altitude, $\dot{h}$ = vertical component of velocity, Θ = pitch attitude, N_z = pilot-station normal acceleration.

For the initial pitch-axis experiment described here, five discrete actions were available to the learning agent in each state; these were longitudinal-stick commands selected from $\{-6, -3, 0, +3, +6\}$ lbf. The command chosen by the learning agent was converted into a desired normal-acceleration command through the standard F-16 longitudinal-stick command gradient with software breakout. This gradient maps pounds-of-force inputs into desired acceleration responses. We then produce an approximate relationship between normal acceleration and body-axes pitch rate to yield a pitch-rate flying-qualities model. Given this model, an inner-loop linear-quadratic (LQ) tracking control algorithm determined the actuator commands to result in optimal model-following of the desired pitch-rate response.

The aircraft model consisted of complete translational and rotational dynamics, including nonlinear terms owing to inertial cross-coupling and orientation-dependent gravitational effects. These were obtained from a modified linear F-16 model with dynamics of the form

$$\dot{x} = Ax + B\delta + b + \hat{N}$$

where A and B were the F-16 aero-inertial parameters (stability derivatives) and effector sensitivities (control derivatives). These stability and control derivatives and the bias vector, b, were obtained from linearizations of a high-fidelity nonlinear, six-degree-of-freedom model. Nonlinearities owing to inertial cross-coupling and orientation-dependent gravitational effects were accounted for through the term $\hat{N}$, which depended nonlinearly on the state. Nonlinear actuator dynamics were modeled via the incorporation of F-16 effector-rate and effector-position limits. See Ward et al. (1996) for additional details.

3 PROBLEM FORMULATION

The RL problem was to approximate a minimum-time control policy capable of bringing the aircraft from a range of initial states to straight, level, and non-inverted flight, while satisfying given constraints, e.g., maintaining the normal acceleration at the pilot station within an acceptable range. For the single-axis (pitch-axis) flight control problem considered here, recovered flight was defined by:

$$q = \dot{q} = \dot{\alpha} = \dot{h} = \dot{V_t} = 0. \tag{1}$$

Successful recovery was achieved when all conditions in Eq. 1 were satisfied simultaneously within pre-specified tolerances.

Because we wished to distinguish between recovery supplied by the LQ tracker and that learned by the RL system, special attention was given to formulating a meaningful test to avoid falsely attributing successes to the RL system. For example, if initial conditions were specified as off-trim perturbations in body-axes pitch rate, pitch acceleration, and true airspeed, the RL system may not have been required because the LQ controller would provide all the necessary recovery, i.e., zero longitudinal-stick input would result in a commanded body-axes pitch rate of zero $deg./sec.$ Because this controller is designed to be highly responsive, its tracking and integral-error penalties usually ensure that the aircraft responses attain the desired state in a relatively short time. The problem was therefore formulated to demand recovery from aircraft orientations where the RL system was primarily responsible for recovery, and the goal state was not readily achieved via the stabilizing action of the LQ control law.

A pitch-axis recovery problem of interest is one in which initial pitch attitude, Θ, is selected to equal $\Theta_{trim} + \mathcal{U}(\hat{\Theta}_{0_{min}}, \hat{\Theta}_{0_{max}})$, where $\Theta_{trim} \equiv \alpha_{trim}$ (by definition), $\mathcal{U}$ is a uniformly distributed random number, and $\Theta_{0_{min}}$ and $\Theta_{0_{max}}$ define the boundaries of the training region, and other variables are set so that when the aircraft is parallel to the earth ($\Theta_0 = 0$), it is "pancaking" toward the ground (with positive trim angle of attack). Other initial conditions correspond to purely-translational climb or descent of the aircraft. For initial conditions where $\Theta_0 < \alpha_{trim}$, the flight vehicle will descend, and in the absence of any corrective longitudinal-stick force, strike the ground or water. Because it imposes no constraints on altitude or pitch-angle variations, the stabilizing response of the LQ controller is inadequate for providing the necessary recovery.

4   REINFORCEMENT LEARNING ALGORITHM

Several candidate RL algorithms were evaluated for the ARS. Initial efforts focused primarily on (1) $\mathcal{Q}$-Learning, (2) alternative means for approximating the action-value function ($\mathcal{Q}$ function), and (3) use of discrete versus continuous-action controls. During subsequent investigations, an extension of $\mathcal{Q}$-Learning called Residual Advantage Learning (Baird, 1995; Harmon & Baird, 1996) was implemented and successfully applied to the pitch-axis ARS problem. As with action-values in $\mathcal{Q}$-Learning, the advantage function, $\mathcal{A}(x, u)$, may be represented by a function approximation system of the form

$$\mathcal{A}(x, u) = \phi(x, u)^T \theta, \tag{2}$$

where $\phi(x, u)$ is a vector of relevant features and θ are the corresponding weights. Here, the advantage function is linear in the weights, θ, and these weights are the modifiable, learned parameters.

For advantage functions of the form in Eq. 2, the update rule is:

$$\begin{aligned}
\theta_{k+1} &= \theta_k - \alpha \left(\left((r + \gamma^{\Delta t} \mathcal{A}(y, b^*)) \frac{1}{K\Delta t} + \left(1 - \frac{1}{K\Delta t}\right) \mathcal{A}(x, a^*) - \mathcal{A}(x, a) \right) \right. \\
&\quad \left. \bullet \left(\Phi \gamma^{\Delta t} \phi(y, b^*) \frac{1}{K\Delta t} + \Phi \left(1 - \frac{1}{K\Delta t}\right) \phi(x, a^*) - \phi(x, a) \right) \right),
\end{aligned}$$

where $a^* = argmin_a \mathcal{A}(x, a)$ and $b^* = argmin_b \mathcal{A}(y, b)$, Δt is the system rate (0.02 $sec.$ in the ARS), $\gamma^{\Delta t}$ is the discount factor, and K is an fixed scale factor. In the above notation,

y is the resultant state, i.e., the execution of action a results in a transition from state x to its successor y.

The Residual Advantage Learning update collapses to the Q-Learning update for the case $\Phi = 0$, $K = \frac{1}{\Delta t}$. The parameter Φ is a scalar that controls the trade-off between residual-gradient descent when $\Phi = 1$, and a faster, direct algorithm when $\Phi = 0$. Harmon & Baird (1996) address the choice of Φ, suggesting the following computation of Φ at each time step:

$$\Phi = \frac{\sum_\theta w_d w_{rg}}{\sum_\theta (w_d - w_{rg}) w_{rg}} + \mu$$

where w_d and w_{rg} are *traces* (one for each θ of the function approximation system) associated with the direct and residual gradient algorithms, respectively, and μ is a small, positive constant that dictates how rapidly the system forgets. The traces are updated during each cycle as follows

$$w_d \leftarrow (1-\mu)w_d - \mu \left[(r + \gamma^{\Delta t} \mathcal{A}(y, b^*)) \frac{1}{K\Delta t} + \left(1 - \frac{1}{K\Delta t}\right) \mathcal{A}(x, a^*) \right]$$
$$\bullet \left[-\frac{\partial}{\partial \theta} \mathcal{A}(x, a^*) \right]$$

$$w_{rg} \leftarrow (1-\mu)w_{rg} - \mu \left[(r + \gamma^{\Delta t} \mathcal{A}(y, b^*)) \frac{1}{K\Delta t} + (1 - \frac{1}{K\Delta t})\mathcal{A}(x, a^*) - \mathcal{A}(x, a) \right]$$
$$\bullet \left[\gamma^{\Delta t} \frac{\partial}{\partial \theta} \mathcal{A}(y, b^*) \frac{1}{K\Delta t} + (1 - \frac{1}{K\Delta t}) \frac{\partial}{\partial \theta} \mathcal{A}(x, a^*) - \frac{\partial}{\partial \theta} \mathcal{A}(x, a) \right].$$

Advantage Learning updates of the weights, including the calculation of an adaptive Φ as discussed above, were implemented and interfaced with the aircraft simulation. The Advantage Learning algorithm consistently outperformed its Q-Learning counterpart. For this reason, most of our efforts have focused on the application of Advantage Learning to the solution of the ARS. The feature vector $\phi(x, u)$ consisted of normalized (dimensionless) states and controls, and functions of these variables. Use of these nondimensionalized variables (obtained via the Buckingham π-theorem; e.g., Langharr, 1951) was found to enhance greatly the stability and robustness of the learning process. Furthermore, the RL system appeared to be less sensitive to changes in parameters such as the learning rate when these techniques were employed.

5 TRAINING

Training the RL system for arbitrary orientations was accomplished by choosing random initial conditions on Θ as outlined above. With the exception of $\dot{h}$, all other initial conditions corresponded to trim values for a Mach 0.6, 5 kft. flight condition. Rewards were -1 per-time-step until the goal state was reached. In preliminary experiments, the training region was restricted to $\pm 0.174 \, rad.$(10 $deg.$) from the trim pitch angle. For this range of initial conditions, the system was able to learn an appropriate policy given only a handful of features (approximately 30). The policy was significantly mature after 24 hours of learning on an HP-730 workstation and appeared to be able to achieve the goal for arbitrary initial conditions in the aforementioned domain.

We then expanded the training region and considered initial Θ values within $\pm 0.785 \, rad.$ (45 $deg.$) of trim. The policy previously learned for the more restricted training domain performed well here too, and learning to recover for these more drastic off-trim conditions was trivial. No boundary restrictions were imposed on the system, but a report of whether the aircraft would have struck the ground was maintained. It was noted that recovery from all possible initial conditions could not be achieved without hitting the ground. Episodes in which the ground would have been encountered were a result of inadequate control authority and not an inadequate RL policy. For example, when the initial pitch angle was at its maximum negative value, maximum-allowable positive stick (6 lbf.) was not sufficient to pull up the aircraft nose in time. To remedy this in subsequent experiments, the number of admissible actions was increased to include larger-magnitude commands: $\{-12, -9, -6, -3, 0, +3, +6, +9, +12\}$ lbf.

Early attempts at solving the pitch-axis recovery problem with the expanded initial conditions in conjunction with this augmented action set proved challenging. The policy that worked well in the two previous experiments was no longer able to attain the goal state; it was only able to come close and oscillate indefinitely about the goal region. The agent learned to pitch up and down appropriately, e.g., when h was negative it applied a corrective positive action, and *vice versa*. However, because of system and actuator dynamics modeled in the simulation, the transient response caused the aircraft to pass through the goal state. Once beyond the goal region, the agent applied an opposite action, causing it to approach the goal state again, repeating the process indefinitely (until the system was reset and a new trial was started). Thus, the availability of large-amplitude commands and the presence of actuator dynamics made it difficult for the agent to formulate a consistent policy that afforded all goal state criteria being satisfied simultaneously. One might remedy the problem by removing the actuator dynamics; however, we did not wish to compromise simulation fidelity, and chose to use an expanded feature set to improve RL performance. Using a larger collection of features with approximately 180 inputs, the RL agent was able to formulate a consistent recovery policy. The learning process required approximately 72 hours on an HP-730 workstation. (On this platform, the combined aircraft simulation and RL software execution rate was approximately twice that of real-time.) At this point performance was evaluated. The simulation was run in evaluation mode, i.e., learning rate was set to zero and random exploration was disabled. Performance is summarized below.

6   RESULTS

6.1   UNCONSTRAINED PITCH-AXIS RECOVERY

Fig. 1 shows the transition times from off-trim orientations to the goal state as a function of initial pitch (inclination) angle. Recovery times were approximately 11–12 sec. for the worst-case scenarios, i.e., $|\Theta_0| = 45$ deg. off-trim, and decrease (almost) monotonically for points closer to the unperturbed initial conditions. The occasional "blips" in the figure suggest that additional learning would have improved the global RL performance slightly. For $|\Theta_0| = 45$ deg. off-trim, maximum altitude loss and gain were each approximately 1667 ft. ($0.33 \times 5000 ft$.). These excursions may seem substantial, but when one looks at the time histories for these maneuvers, it is apparent that the RL-derived policy was performing well. The policy effectively minimizes any altitude variation; the magnitude of these changes are principally governed by available control authority and the severity of the flight condition from which the policy must recover.

Fig. 2 shows time histories of relevant variables for one of the limiting cases. The first column shows body-axes pitch rate (Qb) and commanded body-axes pitch rate ($Qbmodel$) in ($deg./sec.$), pilot station normal acceleration (Nz) in (g), angle of attack ($Alpha$) in ($deg.$), and pitch attitude ($Theta$) in ($deg.$), respectively. The second column shows the longitudinal stick action executed by the RL system (lbf.), the left and right elevator deflections ($deg.$), total airspeed ($ft./sec.$), and altitude ($ft.$). The majority of the 1600+ ft. altitude loss occurs between zero and five sec.; during this time, the RL system is applying maximum (allowable) positive stick. Thus, this altitude excursion is principally attributed to limited control authority as well as significant off-trim initial orientations.

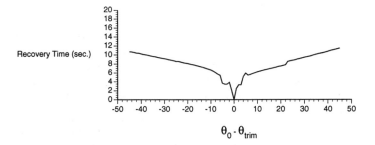

Figure 1: Simulated Aircraft Recovery Times for Unconstrained Pitch-Axis ARS

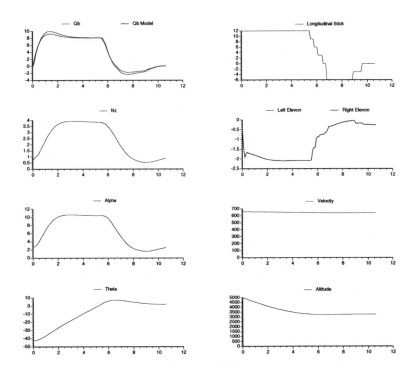

Figure 2: Time Histories During Unconstrained Pitch-Axis Recovery for $\Theta_0 = \Theta_{trim} - 45\ deg.$

6.2   CONSTRAINED PITCH-AXIS RECOVERY

The requirement to execute aircraft recoveries while adhering to pilot-safety constraints was a deciding factor in using RL to demonstrate the automated recovery system concept. The need to recover an aircraft while minimizing injury and, where possible, discomfort to the flight crew, requires that the controller incorporate constraints that can be difficult or impossible to express in forms suitable for linear and nonlinear programming methods.

In subsequent ARS investigations, allowable pilot-station normal acceleration was restricted to the range $-1.5\ g \leq N_z \leq 3.5\ g$. These values were selected because the unconstrained ARS was observed to exceed these limits. Several additional features (for a total of 189) were chosen, and the learning process was continued. Initial weights for the original 180 inputs corresponded to those from the previously learned policy; the new features were chosen to have zero weights initially. Here, the RL system learned to avoid the normal acceleration limits and consistently reach the goal state for initial pitch angles in the region $[-45 + \Theta_{trim}, 35 + \Theta_{trim}]\ deg$. Additional learning should result in improved recovery policies in this bounded acceleration domain for all initial conditions. Nonetheless, the results showed how an RL system can learn to satisfy these kinds of constraints.

7   CONCLUSION

In addition to the results reported here, we conducted extensive analysis of the degree to which the learned policy successfully generalized to a range of initial conditions not experienced in training. In all cases, aircraft responses to novel recovery scenarios were stable and qualitatively similar to those previously executed in the training region. We are also conducting experiments with a multi-axes ARS, in which longitudinal-stick and lateral-stick sequences must be coordinated to recover the aircraft. Initial results are promising, but substantially longer training times are required. In summary, we believe that the results presented here demonstrate the feasibility of using RL algorithms to develop robust recovery strategies for high-agility aircraft, although substantial further research is needed.

Acknowledgments

This work was supported by the Naval Air Warfare Center Aircraft Division (NAWCAD), Flight Controls/Aeromechanics Division under Contract N62269-96-C-0080. The authors thank Marc Steinberg, the Program Manager and Chief Technical Monitor. The authors also express appreciation to Rich Sutton and Mance Harmon for their valuable help, and to Lockheed Martin Tactical Aircraft Systems for authorization to use their *ATLAS* software, from which F-16 parameters were extracted.

References

Baird, L. C. (1995) Residual algorithms: reinforcement learning with function approximation. In A. Prieditis and S. Russell (eds.), *Machine Learning: Proceedings of the Twelfth International Conference*, pp. 30-37. San Francisco, CA: Morgan Kaufmann.

Harmon, M. E. & Baird, L. C. (1996) Multi-agent residual advantage learning with general function approximation. Wright Laboratory Technical Report, WPAFB, OH.

Langharr, H. L. (1951) *Dimensional Analysis and Theory of Models.* New York: Wiley and Sons.

Ward, D. G., Monaco, J. F., Barron, R. L., Bird, R.A., Virnig, J.C., & Landers, T.F. (1996) Self-designing controller. Final Tech. Rep. for Directorate of Mathematics and Computer Sciences, AFOSR, Contract F49620-94-C-0087. Barron Associates, Inc.

Reinforcement Learning for Continuous Stochastic Control Problems

Rémi Munos
CEMAGREF, LISC, Parc de Tourvoie,
BP 121, 92185 Antony Cedex, FRANCE.
Remi.Munos@cemagref.fr

Paul Bourgine
Ecole Polytechnique, CREA,
91128 Palaiseau Cedex, FRANCE.
Bourgine@poly.polytechnique.fr

Abstract

This paper is concerned with the problem of Reinforcement Learning (RL) for continuous state space and time stochastic control
problems. We state the Hamilton-Jacobi-Bellman equation satisfied by the value function and use a Finite-Difference method for
designing a convergent approximation scheme. Then we propose a
RL algorithm based on this scheme and prove its convergence to
the optimal solution.

1 Introduction to RL in the continuous, stochastic case

The objective of RL is to find -thanks to a reinforcement signal- an optimal strategy
for solving a dynamical control problem. Here we sudy the continuous time, continuous state-space stochastic case, which covers a wide variety of control problems
including target, viability, optimization problems (see [FS93], [KP95]) for which a
formalism is the following. The evolution of the *current state* $x(t) \in \bar{O}$ (the *state-
space*, with O open subset of $\mathbb{R}^d$), depends on the *control* $u(t) \in U$ (compact subset)
by a stochastic differential equation, called the *state dynamics*:

$$dx = f(x(t), u(t))dt + \sigma(x(t), u(t))dw \tag{1}$$

where f is the local drift and $\sigma.dw$ (with w a brownian motion of dimension r and
σ a $d \times r$-matrix) the stochastic part (which appears for several reasons such as lake
of precision, noisy influence, random fluctuations) of the diffusion process.

For initial state x and control $u(t)$, (1) leads to an infinity of possible trajectories
$x(t)$. For some trajectory $x(t)$ (see figure 1), let τ be its *exit time* from $\bar{O}$ (with
the convention that if $x(t)$ always stays in O, then $\tau = \infty$). Then, we define the
functional J of initial state x and control $u(.)$ as the expectation for all trajectories
of the discounted cumulative reinforcement :

$$J(x; u(.)) = E_{x,u(.)} \left\{ \int_0^\tau \gamma^t r(x(t), u(t))dt + \gamma^\tau R(x(\tau)) \right\}$$

where $r(x, u)$ is the *running reinforcement* and $R(x)$ the *boundary reinforcement*. γ is the *discount factor* ($0 \leq \gamma < 1$). In the following, we assume that f, σ are of class $\mathcal{C}^2$, r and R are Lipschitzian (with constants L_r and L_R) and the boundary ∂O is $\mathcal{C}^2$.

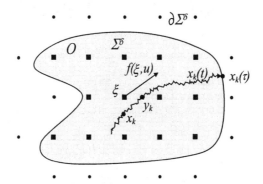

Figure 1: The state space, the discretized Σ^δ (the square dots) and its frontier $\partial \Sigma^\delta$ (the round ones). A trajectory $x_k(t)$ goes through the neighbourhood of state ξ.

RL uses the method of Dynamic Programming (DP) which generates an optimal (feed-back) control $u^*(x)$ by estimating the *value function* (VF), defined as the maximal value of the functional J as a function of initial state x :

$$V(x) = \sup_{u(.)} J(x; u(.)). \qquad (2)$$

In the RL approach, the state dynamics is unknown from the system ; the only available information for learning the optimal control is the reinforcement obtained at the current state. Here we propose a model-based algorithm, i.e. that learns on-line a model of the dynamics and approximates the value function by successive iterations.

Section 2 states the Hamilton-Jacobi-Bellman equation and use a Finite-Difference (FD) method derived from Kushner [Kus90] for generating a convergent approximation scheme. In *section 3*, we propose a RL algorithm based on this scheme and prove its convergence to the VF in *appendix A*.

2 A Finite Difference scheme

Here, we state a second-order nonlinear differential equation (obtained from the DP principle, see [FS93]) satisfied by the value function, called the *Hamilton-Jacobi-Bellman* equation.

Let the $d \times d$ matrix $a = \sigma.\sigma'$ (with $'$ the transpose of the matrix). We consider the *uniformly parabolic* case, i.e. we assume that there exists $c > 0$ such that $\forall x \in \overline{O}, \forall u \in U, \forall y \in \mathbb{R}^d, \sum_{i,j=1}^{d} a_{ij}(x, u) y_i y_j \geq c\|y\|^2$. Then V is $\mathcal{C}^2$ (see [Kry80]). Let V_x be the gradient of V and $V_{x_i x_j}$ its second-order partial derivatives.

Theorem 1 (Hamilton-Jacobi-Bellman) *The following HJB equation holds :*

$$V(x) \ln \gamma + \sup_{u \in U} \left[r(x, u) + V_x(x).f(x, u) + \tfrac{1}{2} \sum_{i,j=1}^{n} a_{ij} V_{x_i x_j}(x) \right] = 0 \text{ for } x \in O$$

Besides, V satisfies the following boundary condition : $V(x) = R(x)$ for $x \in \partial O$.

Remark 1 *The challenge of learning the VF is motivated by the fact that from V, we can deduce the following optimal feed-back control policy :*

$$u^*(x) \in \arg\sup_{u \in U} \left[r(x,u) + V_x(x).f(x,u) + \tfrac{1}{2} \sum_{i,j=1}^n a_{ij} V_{x_i x_j}(x) \right]$$

In the following, we assume that O is bounded. Let $e_1, ..., e_d$ be a basis for $\mathbb{R}^d$. Let the positive and negative parts of a function ϕ be : $\phi^+ = \max(\phi, 0)$ and $\phi^- = \max(-\phi, 0)$. For any *discretization step* δ, let us consider the lattices : $\delta \mathbb{Z}^d = \left\{ \delta. \sum_{i=1}^d j_i e_i \right\}$ where $j_1, ..., j_d$ are any integers, and $\Sigma^\delta = \delta \mathbb{Z}^d \cap O$. Let $\partial \Sigma^\delta$, the *frontier* of Σ^δ denote the set of points $\{\xi \in \delta \mathbb{Z}^d \setminus O$ such that at least one adjacent point $\xi \pm \delta e_i \in \Sigma^\delta\}$ (see figure 1).

Let $U^\delta \subset U$ be a finite control set that approximates U in the sense: $\delta \leq \delta' \Rightarrow U^{\delta'} \subset U^\delta$ and $\overline{\cup_\delta U^\delta} = U$. Besides, we assume that: $\forall i = 1..d$,

$$a_{ii}(x,u) - \sum_{j \neq i} |a_{ij}(x,u)| \geq 0. \tag{3}$$

By replacing the gradient $V_x(\xi)$ by the forward and backward first-order finite-difference quotients: $\Delta_{x_i}^{\pm} V(\xi) = \frac{1}{\delta} [V(\xi \pm \delta e_i) - V(\xi)]$ and $V_{x_i x_j}(\xi)$ by the second-order finite-difference quotients:

$$\Delta_{x_i x_i} V(\xi) = \frac{1}{\delta^2} [V(\xi + \delta e_i) + V(\xi - \delta e_i) - 2V(\xi)]$$

$$\Delta_{x_i x_j}^{\pm} V(\xi) = \frac{1}{2\delta^2} [V(\xi + \delta e_i \pm \delta e_j) + V(\xi - \delta e_i \mp \delta e_j)$$
$$- V(\xi + \delta e_i) - V(\xi - \delta e_i) - V(\xi + \delta e_j) - V(\xi - \delta e_j) + 2V(\xi)]$$

in the HJB equation, we obtain the following : for $\xi \in \Sigma^\delta$,

$$V^\delta(\xi) \ln \gamma + \sup_{u \in U^\delta} \left\{ r(\xi,u) + \sum_{i=1}^d \left[f_i^+(\xi,u).\Delta_{x_i}^+ V^\delta(\xi) - f_i^-(\xi,u).\Delta_{x_i}^- V^\delta(\xi) \right. \right.$$

$$\left. \left. + \frac{a_{ii}(\xi,u)}{2} \Delta_{x_i x_i} V(\xi) + \sum_{j \neq i} \left(\frac{a_{ij}^+(\xi,u)}{2} \Delta_{x_i x_j}^+ V(\xi) - \frac{a_{ij}^-(\xi,u)}{2} \Delta_{x_i x_j}^- V(\xi) \right) \right] \right\} = 0$$

Knowing that $(\Delta t \ln \gamma)$ is an approximation of $(\gamma^{\Delta t} - 1)$ as Δt tends to 0, we deduce:

$$V^\delta(\xi) = \sup_{u \in U^\delta} \left[\gamma^{\tau(\xi,u)} \sum_{\zeta \in \Sigma^\delta} p(\xi,u,\zeta) V^\delta(\zeta) + \tau(\xi,u) r(\xi,u) \right] \tag{4}$$

$$\text{with } \tau(\xi,u) = \frac{\delta^2}{\sum_{i=1}^d \left[\delta |f_i(\xi,u)| + a_{ii}(\xi,u) - \frac{1}{2} \sum_{j \neq i} |a_{ij}(\xi,u)| \right]} \tag{5}$$

which appears as a DP equation for some finite Markovian Decision Process (see [Ber87]) whose state space is Σ^δ and probabilities of transition :

$$p(\xi,u,\xi \pm \delta e_i) = \frac{\tau(\xi,u)}{2\delta^2} \left[2\delta |f_i^{\pm}(\xi,u)| + a_{ii}(\xi,u) - \sum_{j \neq i} |a_{ij}(\xi,u)| \right],$$

$$p(\xi,u,\xi + \delta e_i \pm \delta e_j) = \frac{\tau(\xi,u)}{2\delta^2} a_{ij}^{\pm}(\xi,u) \text{ for } i \neq j, \tag{6}$$

$$p(\xi,u,\xi - \delta e_i \pm \delta e_j) = \frac{\tau(\xi,u)}{2\delta^2} a_{ij}^{\mp}(\xi,u) \text{ for } i \neq j,$$

$$p(\xi,u,\zeta) = 0 \text{ otherwise.}$$

Thanks to a contraction property due to the discount factor γ, there exists a unique solution (the fixed-point) V^δ to equation (4) for $\xi \in \Sigma^\delta$ with the boundary condition $V^\delta(\xi) = R(\xi)$ for $\xi \in \partial \Sigma^\delta$. The following theorem (see [Kus90] or [FS93]) insures that V^δ is a convergent approximation scheme.

Theorem 2 (Convergence of the FD scheme) V^δ *converges to* V *as* $\delta \downarrow 0$:

$$\lim_{\substack{\delta \downarrow 0 \\ \xi \to x}} V^\delta(\xi) = V(x) \text{ uniformly on } \overline{O}$$

Remark 2 *Condition (3) insures that the* $p(\xi, u, \zeta)$ *are positive. If this condition does not hold, several possibilities to overcome this are described in [Kus90].*

3   The reinforcement learning algorithm

Here we assume that f is bounded from below. As the state dynamics (f and a) is unknown from the system, we approximate it by building a *model* $\widetilde{f}$ and $\widetilde{a}$ from samples of trajectories $x_k(t)$: we consider series of successive states $x_k = x_k(t_k)$ and $y_k = x_k(t_k + \tau_k)$ such that :

- $\forall t \in [t_k, t_k + \tau_k], \quad x(t) \in N(\xi)$ neighbourhood of ξ whose diameter is inferior to $k_N.\delta$ for some positive constant k_N,

- the control u is constant for $t \in [t_k, t_k + \tau_k]$,

- τ_k satisfies for some positive k_1 and k_2,

$$k_1\delta \le \tau_k \le k_2\delta. \tag{7}$$

Then incrementally update the model :

$$\begin{aligned}
\widetilde{f_n}(\xi, u) &= \frac{1}{n}\sum_{k=1}^{n} \frac{y_k - x_k}{\tau_k} \\
\widetilde{a_n}(\xi, u) &= \frac{1}{n}\sum_{k=1}^{n} \frac{\left(y_k - x_k - \tau_k.\widetilde{f_n}(\xi, u)\right)\left(y_k - x_k - \tau_k.\widetilde{f_n}(\xi, u)\right)'}{\tau_k} \\
\widetilde{r}(\xi, u) &= \frac{1}{n}\sum_{k=1}^{n} r(x_k, u)
\end{aligned} \tag{8}$$

and compute the approximated time $\widetilde{\tau}(x, u)$ and the approximated probabilities of transition $\widetilde{p}(\xi, u, \zeta)$ by replacing f and a by $\widetilde{f}$ and $\widetilde{a}$ in (5) and (6).

We obtain the following updating rule of the V^δ-value of state ξ :

$$V_{n+1}^\delta(\xi) = \sup_{u \in U^\delta}\left[\gamma^{\widetilde{\tau}(x,u)}\sum_{\zeta}\widetilde{p}(\xi, u, \zeta)V_n^\delta(\zeta) + \widetilde{\tau}(x, u)\widetilde{r}(\xi, u)\right] \tag{9}$$

which can be used as an off-line (synchronous, Gauss-Seidel, asynchronous) or on-time (for example by updating $V_n^\delta(\xi)$ as soon as a trajectory exits from the neighbourood of ξ) DP algorithm (see [BBS95]).

Besides, when a trajectory hits the boundary ∂O at some exit point $x_k(\tau)$ then update the closest state $\xi \in \partial\Sigma^\delta$ with :

$$V_n^\delta(\xi) = R(x_k(\tau)) \tag{10}$$

Theorem 3 (Convergence of the algorithm) *Suppose that the model as well as the* V^δ-*value of every state* $\xi \in \Sigma^\delta$ *and control* $u \in U^\delta$ *are regularly updated (respectively with (8) and (9)) and that every state* $\xi \in \partial\Sigma^\delta$ *are updated with (10) at least once. Then* $\forall\varepsilon > 0, \exists\Delta$ *such that* $\forall\delta \le \Delta, \exists N, \forall n \ge N$,

$$\sup_{\xi \in \Sigma^\delta} |V_n^\delta(\xi) - V(\xi)| \le \varepsilon \text{ with probability 1}$$

4 Conclusion

This paper presents a model-based RL algorithm for continuous stochastic control problems. A model of the dynamics is approximated by the mean and the covariance of successive states. Then, a RL updating rule based on a convergent FD scheme is deduced and in the hypothesis of an adequate exploration, the convergence to the optimal solution is proved as the discretization step δ tends to 0 and the number of iteration tends to infinity. This result is to be compared to the model-free RL algorithm for the deterministic case in [Mun97]. An interesting possible future work should be to consider model-free algorithms in the stochastic case for which a Q-learning rule (see [Wat89]) could be relevant.

A Appendix: proof of the convergence

Let M_f, M_a, M_{f_x} and M_{σ_x} be the upper bounds of f, a, f_x and σ_x and m_f the lower bound of f. Let $E^\delta = \sup_{\xi \in \Sigma^\delta} |V^\delta(\xi) - V(\xi)|$ and $E_n^\delta = \sup_{\xi \in \Sigma^\delta} |V_n^\delta(\xi) - V^\delta(\xi)|$.

A.1 Estimation error of the model $\widetilde{f_n}$ and $\widetilde{a_n}$ and the probabilities $\widetilde{p}_n$

Suppose that the trajectory $x_k(t)$ occured for some occurence $w_k(t)$ of the brownian motion: $x_k(t) = x_k + \int_{t_k}^t f(x_k(t), u)dt + \int_{t_k}^t \sigma(x_k(t), u)dw_k$. Then we consider a trajectory $z_k(t)$ starting from ξ at t_k and following the same brownian motion: $z_k(t) = \xi + \int_{t_k}^t f(z_k(t), u)dt + \int_{t_k}^t \sigma(z_k(t), u)dw_k$.

Let $z_k = z_k(t_k + \tau_k)$. Then $(y_k - x_k) - (z_k - \xi) = \int_{t_k} [f(x_k(t), u) - f(z_k(t), u)] dt + \int_{t_k}^{t_k + \tau_k} [\sigma(x_k(t), u) - \sigma(z_k(t), u)] dw_k$. Thus, from the C^1 property of f and σ,

$$\|(y_k - x_k) - (z_k - \xi)\| \le (M_{f_x} + M_{\sigma_x}).k_N.\tau_k.\delta. \tag{11}$$

The diffusion processes has the following property (see for example the Itô-Taylor majoration in [KP95]): $E_x[z_k] = \xi + \tau_k.f(\xi, u) + O(\tau_k^2)$ which, from (7), is equivalent to: $E_x\left[\frac{z_k - \xi}{\tau_k}\right] = f(\xi, u) + O(\delta)$. Thus from the law of large numbers and (11):

$$
\begin{aligned}
\limsup_{n \to \infty} \left\| \widetilde{f_n}(\xi, u) - f(\xi, u) \right\| &= \limsup_{n \to \infty} \left\| \frac{1}{n} \sum_{k=1}^n \left[\frac{y_k - x_k}{\tau_k} - \frac{z_k - \xi}{\tau_k} \right] \right\| + O(\delta) \\
&= (M_{f_x} + M_{\sigma_x}).k_N.\delta + O(\delta) = O(\delta) \text{ w.p. } 1 \tag{12}
\end{aligned}
$$

Besides, diffusion processes have the following property (again see [KP95]): $E_x\left[(z_k - \xi)(z_k - \xi)'\right] = a(\xi, u)\tau_k + f(\xi, u).f(\xi, u)'.\tau_k^2 + O(\tau_k^3)$ which, from (7), is equivalent to: $E_x\left[\frac{(z_k - \xi - \tau_k f(\xi, u))(z_k - \xi - \tau_k f(\xi, u))'}{\tau_k}\right] = a(\xi, u) + O(\delta^2)$. Let $r_k = z_k - \xi - \tau_k f(\xi, u)$ and $\widetilde{r}_k = y_k - x_k - \tau_k \widetilde{f_n}(\xi, u)$ which satisfy (from (11) and (12)):

$$\|r_k - \widetilde{r}_k\| = (M_{f_x} + M_{\sigma_x}).\tau_k.k_N.\delta + \tau_k.O(\delta) \tag{13}$$

From the definition of $\widetilde{a_n}(\xi, u)$, we have: $\widetilde{a_n}(\xi, u) - a(\xi, u) = \frac{1}{n}\sum_{k=1}^n \frac{\widetilde{r}_k.\widetilde{r}_k'}{\tau_k} - E_x\left[\frac{r_k.r_k'}{\tau_k}\right] + O(\delta^2)$ and from the law of large numbers, (12) and (13), we have:

$$
\begin{aligned}
\limsup_{n \to \infty} \quad & \|\widetilde{a_n}(\xi, u) - a(\xi, u)\| = \limsup_{n \to \infty} \left\| \frac{1}{n}\sum_{k=1}^n \frac{\widetilde{r}_k.\widetilde{r}_k'}{\tau_k} - \frac{r_k.r_k'}{\tau_k} \right\| + O(\delta^2) \\
= \quad & \|\widetilde{r}_k - r_k\| \limsup_{n \to \infty} \frac{1}{n} \sum_{k=1}^n \left(\left\|\frac{\widetilde{r}_k}{\tau_k}\right\| + \left\|\frac{r_k}{\tau_k}\right\| \right) + O(\delta^2) = O(\delta^2)
\end{aligned}
$$

with probability 1. Thus there exists k_f and k_a s.t. $\exists \Delta_1, \forall \delta \le \Delta_1, \exists N_1, n \ge N_1$,

$$\begin{aligned}
\left\| \widetilde{f_n}(\xi, u) - f(\xi, u) \right\| &\le k_f.\delta \text{ w.p. } 1 \\
\left\| \widetilde{a_n}(\xi, u) - a(\xi, u) \right\| &\le k_a.\delta^2 \text{ w.p. } 1
\end{aligned} \tag{14}$$

Besides, from (5) and (14), we have:

$$|\tau(\xi, u) - \widetilde{\tau}_n(\xi, u)| \le \frac{d.(k_f.\delta^2 + d.k_a\delta^2)}{(d.m_f.\delta)^2}\delta^2 \le k_\tau.\delta^2 \tag{15}$$

and from a property of exponential function,

$$\left| \gamma^{\tau(\xi, u)} - \gamma^{\widetilde{\tau}_n(\xi, u)} \right| = k_\tau.\ln\frac{1}{\gamma}.\delta^2. \tag{16}$$

We can deduce from (14) that:

$$\limsup_{n \to \infty} |p(\xi, u, \zeta) - \widetilde{p}_n(\xi, u, \zeta)| \le \frac{(2.\delta.M_f + d.M_a)(2.k_f + d.k_a)\delta^2}{\delta m_f - (2.k_f + d.k_a)\delta^2} \le k_p\delta \text{ w.p. } 1 \tag{17}$$

with $k_p = 4(d.M_a)(2.k_f + d.k_a)$ for $\delta \le \Delta_2 = \min\left\{ \frac{m_f}{2.k_f + d.k_a}, \frac{d.M_a}{2.\delta.M_f} \right\}$.

A.2   Estimation of $|V_{n+1}^\delta(\xi) - V^\delta(\xi)|$

After having updated $V_n^\delta(\xi)$ with rule (9), let Λ denote the difference $|V_{n+1}^\delta(\xi) - V^\delta(\xi)|$. From (4), (9) and (8),

$$\begin{aligned}
\Lambda \le\ & \gamma^{\tau(\xi, u)} \sum_\zeta [p(\xi, u, \zeta) - \widetilde{p}(\xi, u, \zeta)] V^\delta(\zeta) + \left(\gamma^{\tau(\xi, u)} - \gamma^{\widetilde{\tau}(\xi, u)} \right) \sum_\zeta \widetilde{p}(\xi, u, \zeta) V^\delta(\zeta) \\
& + \gamma^{\widetilde{\tau}(\xi, u)}.\sum_\zeta \widetilde{p}(\xi, u, \zeta) \left[V^\delta(\zeta) - V_n^\delta(\zeta) \right] + \sum_\zeta \widetilde{p}(\xi, u, \zeta).\widetilde{\tau}(\xi, u) \left[r(\xi, u) - \widetilde{r}(\xi, u) \right] \\
& + \sum_\zeta \widetilde{p}(\xi, u, \zeta) [\widetilde{\tau}(\xi, u) - \tau(\xi, u)] r(\xi, u) \text{ for all } u \in U^\delta
\end{aligned}$$

As V is differentiable we have : $V(\zeta) = V(\xi) + V_x.(\zeta - \xi) + o(\|\zeta - \xi\|)$. Let us define a linear function $\widetilde{V}$ such that: $\widetilde{V}(x) = V(\xi) + V_x.(x - \xi)$. Then we have: $[p(\xi, u, \zeta) - \widetilde{p}(\xi, u, \zeta)] V^\delta(\zeta) = [p(\xi, u, \zeta) - \widetilde{p}(\xi, u, \zeta)].[V^\delta(\zeta) - V(\zeta)] + [p(\xi, u, \zeta) - \widetilde{p}(\xi, u, \zeta)] V(\zeta)$, thus: $\sum_\zeta [p(\xi, u, \zeta) - \widetilde{p}(\xi, u, \zeta)] V^\delta(\zeta) = k_p.E^\delta.\delta + \sum_\zeta [p(\xi, u, \zeta) - \widetilde{p}(\xi, u, \zeta)] \left[\widetilde{V}(\zeta) + o(\delta) \right] = \left[\widetilde{V}(\eta) - \widetilde{V}(\widetilde{\eta}) \right] + k_p.E^\delta.\delta + o(\delta) = \left[\widetilde{V}(\eta) - \widetilde{V}(\widetilde{\eta}) \right] + o(\delta)$ with: $\eta = \sum_\zeta p(\xi, u, \zeta)(\zeta - \xi)$ and $\widetilde{\eta} = \sum_\zeta \widetilde{p}(\xi, u, \zeta)(\zeta - \xi)$. Besides, from the convergence of the scheme (theorem 2), we have $E^\delta.\delta = o(\delta)$. From the linearity of $\widetilde{V}$, $\left| \widetilde{V}(\zeta) - \widetilde{V}(\widetilde{\zeta}) \right| \le \left\| \zeta - \widetilde{\zeta} \right\|.M_{V_x} \le 2k_p\delta^2$. Thus $\left| \sum_\zeta [p(\xi, u, \zeta) - \widetilde{p}(\xi, u, \zeta)] V^\delta(\zeta) \right| = o(\delta)$ and from (15), (16) and the Lipschitz property of r,

$$\Lambda = \left| \gamma^{\widetilde{\tau}(\xi, u)}.\sum_\zeta \widetilde{p}(\xi, u, \zeta) \left[V^\delta(\zeta) - V_n^\delta(\zeta) \right] \right| + o(\delta).$$

As $\gamma^{\widetilde{\tau}(\xi, u)} \le 1 - \frac{\widetilde{\tau}(\xi, u)}{2} \ln\frac{1}{\gamma} \le 1 - \frac{\tau(\xi, u) - k_\tau\delta^2}{2} \ln\frac{1}{\gamma} \le 1 - \left(\frac{\delta}{2d(M_f + d.M_a)} - \frac{k_\tau}{2}\delta^2 \right) \ln\frac{1}{\gamma}$, we have :

$$\Lambda = (1 - k.\delta)E_n^\delta + o(\delta) \tag{18}$$

with $k = \frac{1}{2d(M_f + d.M_a)}$.

A.3 A sufficient condition for $\sup_{\xi \in \Sigma^\delta} |V_n^\delta(\xi) - V^\delta(\xi)| \leq \varepsilon_2$

Let us suppose that for all $\xi \in \Sigma^\delta$, the following conditions hold for some $\alpha > 0$

$$E_n^\delta > \varepsilon_2 \Rightarrow |V_{n+1}^\delta(\xi) - V^\delta(\xi)| \leq E_n^\delta - \alpha \tag{19}$$

$$E_n^\delta \leq \varepsilon_2 \Rightarrow |V_{n+1}^\delta(\xi) - V^\delta(\xi)| \leq \varepsilon_2 \tag{20}$$

From the hypothesis that all states $\xi \in \Sigma^\delta$ are regularly updated, there exists an integer m such that at stage $n + m$ all the $\xi \in \Sigma^\delta$ have been updated at least once since stage n. Besides, since all $\xi \in \partial G^\delta$ are updated at least once with rule (10), $\forall \xi \in \partial G^\delta, |V_n^\delta(\xi) - V^\delta(\xi)| = |R(x_k(\tau)) - R(\xi)| \leq 2.L_R.\delta \leq \varepsilon_2$ for any $\delta \leq \Delta_3 = \frac{\varepsilon_2}{2.L_R}$. Thus, from (19) and (20) we have:

$$E_n^\delta > \varepsilon_2 \Rightarrow E_{n+m}^\delta \leq E_n^\delta - \alpha$$

$$E_n^\delta \leq \varepsilon_2 \Rightarrow E_{n+m}^\delta \leq \varepsilon_2$$

Thus there exists N such that : $\forall n \geq N, E_n^\delta \leq \varepsilon_2$.

A.4 Convergence of the algorithm

Let us prove theorem 3. For any $\varepsilon > 0$, let us consider $\varepsilon_1 > 0$ and $\varepsilon_2 > 0$ such that $\varepsilon_1 + \varepsilon_2 = \varepsilon$. Assume $E_n^\delta > \varepsilon_2$, then from (18), $\Lambda = E_n^\delta - k.\delta.\varepsilon_2 + o(\delta) \leq E_n^\delta - k.\delta.\frac{\varepsilon_2}{2}$ for $\delta \leq \Delta_3$. Thus (19) holds for $\alpha = k.\delta.\frac{\varepsilon_2}{2}$. Suppose now that $E_n^\delta \leq \varepsilon_2$. From (18), $\Lambda \leq (1 - k.\delta)\varepsilon_2 + o(\delta) \leq \varepsilon_2$ for $\delta \leq \Delta_3$ and condition (20) is true.

Thus for $\delta \leq \min\{\Delta_1, \Delta_2, \Delta_3\}$, the sufficient conditions (19) and (20) are satisfied. So there exists N, for all $n \geq N$, $E_n^\delta \leq \varepsilon_2$. Besides, from the convergence of the scheme (theorem 2), there exists Δ_0 st. $\forall \delta \leq \Delta_0, \sup_{\xi \in \Sigma^\delta} |V^\delta(\xi) - V(\xi)| \leq \varepsilon_1$.

Thus for $\delta \leq \min\{\Delta_0, \Delta_1, \Delta_2, \Delta_3\}, \exists N, \forall n \geq N,$

$$\sup_{\xi \in \Sigma^\delta} |V_n^\delta(\xi) - V(\xi)| \leq \sup_{\xi \in \Sigma^\delta} |V_n^\delta(\xi) - V^\delta(\xi)| + \sup_{\xi \in \Sigma^\delta} |V^\delta(\xi) - V(\xi)| \leq \varepsilon_1 + \varepsilon_2 = \varepsilon.$$

References

[BBS95] Andrew G. Barto, Steven J. Bradtke, and Satinder P. Singh. Learning to act using real-time dynamic programming. *Artificial Intelligence*, (72):81–138, 1995.

[Ber87] Dimitri P. Bertsekas. *Dynamic Programming : Deterministic and Stochastic Models*. Prentice Hall, 1987.

[FS93] Wendell H. Fleming and H. Mete Soner. *Controlled Markov Processes and Viscosity Solutions*. Applications of Mathematics. Springer-Verlag, 1993.

[KP95] Peter E. Kloeden and Eckhard Platen. *Numerical Solutions of Stochastic Differential Equations*. Springer-Verlag, 1995.

[Kry80] N.V. Krylov. *Controlled Diffusion Processes*. Springer-Verlag, New York, 1980.

[Kus90] Harold J. Kushner. Numerical methods for stochastic control problems in continuous time. *SIAM J. Control and Optimization*, 28:999–1048, 1990.

[Mun97] Rémi Munos. A convergent reinforcement learning algorithm in the continuous case based on a finite difference method. *International Joint Conference on Artificial Intelligence*, 1997.

[Wat89] Christopher J.C.H. Watkins. *Learning from delayed reward*. PhD thesis, Cambridge University, 1989.

Adaptive choice of grid and time in reinforcement learning

Stephan Pareigis
stp@numerik.uni-kiel.de
Lehrstuhl Praktische Mathematik
Christian-Albrechts-Universität Kiel
Kiel, Germany

Abstract

We propose local error estimates together with algorithms for adaptive a-posteriori grid and time refinement in reinforcement learning. We consider a deterministic system with continuous state and time with infinite horizon discounted cost functional. For grid refinement we follow the procedure of numerical methods for the Bellman-equation. For time refinement we propose a new criterion, based on consistency estimates of discrete solutions of the Bellman-equation. We demonstrate, that an optimal ratio of time to space discretization is crucial for optimal learning rates and accuracy of the approximate optimal value function.

1 Introduction

Reinforcement learning can be performed for fully continuous problems by discretizing state space and time, and then performing a discrete algorithm like Q-learning or RTDP (e.g. [5]). Consistency problems arise if the discretization needs to be refined, e.g. for more accuracy, application of multi-grid iteration or better starting values for the iteration of the approximate optimal value function. In [7] it was shown, that for diffusion dominated problems, a state to time discretization ratio k/h of Ch^γ, $\gamma > 0$ has to hold, to achieve consistency (i.e. $k = o(h)$). It can be shown, that for deterministic problems, this ratio must only be $k/h = C$, C a constant, to get consistent approximations of the optimal value function. The choice of the constant C is crucial for fast learning rates, optimal use of computer memory resources and accuracy of the approximation.

We suggest a procedure involving local a-posteriori error estimation for grid refinement, similar to the one used in numerical schemes for the Bellman-equation (see [4]). For the adaptive time discretization we use a combination from step size control for ordinary differential equations and calculations for the rates of convergence of fully discrete solutions of the Bellman-equation (see [3]). We explain how both methods can be combined and applied to Q-learning. A simple numerical example shows the effects of suboptimal state space to time discretization ratio, and provides an insight in the problems of coupling both schemes.

2 Error estimation for adaptive choice of grid

We want to approximate the optimal value function $V : \Omega \to \mathbb{R}$ in a state space $\Omega \subset \mathbb{R}^d$ of the following problem: Minimize

$$J(x, u(.)) := \int_0^\infty e^{-\rho\tau} g(y_{x,u(.)}(\tau), u(\tau)) d\tau, \quad u(.) : \mathbb{R}_+ \to A \text{ measurable}, \quad (1)$$

where $g : \Omega \times A \to \mathbb{R}_+$ is the cost function, and $y_{x,u(.)}(.)$ is the solution of the differential equation

$$\dot{y}(t) = f(y(t), u(t)), \quad y(0) = x. \quad (2)$$

As a trial space for the approximation of the optimal value function (or Q-function) we use locally linear elements on simplices S_i, $i = 1, \ldots, N_S$ which form a triangulation of the state space, N_S the number of simplices. The vertices shall be called x_i, $i = 1, \ldots, N$, N the dimension of the trial space[1]. This approach has been used in numerical schemes for the Bellman-equation ([2], [4]). We will first assume, that the grid is fixed and has a discretization parameter

$$k = \max_i \text{diam}\{S_i\}.$$

Other than in the numerical case, where the updates are performed in the vertices of the triangulation, in reinforcement learning only observed information is available. We will assume, that in one time step of size $h > 0$, we obtain the following information:

- the current state $y_n \in \Omega$,

- an action $a_n \in A$,

- the subsequent state $y_{n+1} := y_{y_n,a_n}(h)$

- the local cost $r_n = r(y_n, a_n) = \int_0^h e^{-\rho\tau} g(y_{y_n,a_n}(\tau), a_n(\tau)) d\tau$.

The state y_n, in which an update is to be made, may be any state in Ω. A shall be finite, and a_n locally constant.

The new value of the fully discrete Q-function $Q_h^k(y_n, a_n)$ should be set to

$$Q_h^k(y_n, a_n) \qquad \text{shall be} \qquad r_n + e^{-\rho h} V_h^k(y_{n+1}),$$

where $V_h^k(y_{n+1}) = \min_a Q_h^k(y_{n+1}, a)$. We call the right side the update function

$$P_h(z, a, V_h^k) := r(z, a) + e^{-\rho h} V_h^k(y_{z,a}(h)), \quad z \in \Omega. \quad (3)$$

We will update Q_h^k in the vertices $\{x_i\}_{i=1}^N$ of the triangulation in one of the following two ways:

---

[1]When an adaptive grid is used, then N_S and N depend on the refinement.

Kaczmarz-update. Let $\lambda^T = (\lambda_1, \ldots, \lambda_N)$ be the vector of barycentric coordinates, such that

$$y_n = \sum_{i=1}^{N} \lambda_i x_i, \quad 0 \le \lambda_i \le 1, \text{ for all } i = 1, \ldots, N.$$

Then update

$$Q_h^k(x_i, a_n) := Q_h^k(x_i, a_n) + \frac{\lambda_i}{\lambda^T \lambda} \left[r_n + e^{-\rho h} V_h^k(y_{n+1}) - \sum_{i=1}^{N} \lambda_i Q_h^k(x_i, a_n) \right]. \quad (4)$$

Kronecker-update. Let $S \ni y_n$ and x be the vertex of S, closest to y_n (if there is a draw, then the update can be performed in all winners). Then update Q_h^k only in x according to

$$Q_h^k(x, a_n) := r_n + e^{-\rho h} V_h^k(y_{n+1}). \quad (5)$$

Each method has some assets and drawbacks. In our computer simulations the Kaczmarz-update seemed to be more stable over the Kronecker-update (see [6]). However, examples may be constructed where a (Hölder-)continuous bounded optimal value function V is to be approximated, and the Kaczmarz-update produces an approximation with arbitrarily high $||.||_{\sup}$-norm (place a vertex x of the triangulation in a point where $\frac{d}{dx}V$ is infinity, and use as update states the vertex x in turn with an arbitrarily close state $\bar{x}$).

Kronecker-update will provide a bounded approximation if V is bounded. Let $\bar{V}_h^k$ be the fully-discrete optimal value function

$$\bar{V}_h^k(x_i) = \min_a \{ r(x_i, a) + e^{-\rho h} V_h^k(y_{x_i, a}(h)), \quad i = 1, \ldots, N.$$

Then it can be shown, that an approximation performed by Kronecker-update will eventually be caught in an ε-neighborhood of $\bar{V}_h^k$ (with respect to the $||.||_{\sup}$-norm), if the data points $y_0, y_1, y_2, \ldots$ are sufficiently dense. Under regularity conditions on V, ε may be bounded by[2]

$$\varepsilon \le C(h + \frac{k}{h}). \quad (6)$$

As a criterion for grid refinement we choose a form of a *local a posteriori error estimate* as defined in [4]. Let $V_h^k(x) = \min_a Q_h^k(x, a)$ be the current iterate of the optimal value function. Let $a_x \in U$ be the minimizing control $a_x = \text{argmin}_a Q_h^k(x, a)$. Then we define

$$e_h(x) := |V_h^k(x) - P(x, a_x, V_h^k)|. \quad (7)$$

If V_h^k is in the ε-neighborhood of $\bar{V}_h^k$, then it can be shown, that (for every $x \in \Omega$ and simplex S_x with $x \in S_x$, a_x as above)

$$0 \le e(x) \le \sup_{z \in S_x} P(z, a_z, V_h^k) - \inf_{z \in S_x} P(z, a_z, V_h^k).$$

If $\bar{V}_h^k$ is Lipschitz-continuous, then an estimate using only Gronwall's inequality bounds the right side and therefore $e(x)$ by $C \frac{k}{\rho h}$, where C depends on the Lipschitz-constants of $\bar{V}_h^k$ and the cost g.

---

[2]With respect to the results in [3] we assume, that also $\varepsilon \le C(h + \frac{k}{\sqrt{h}})$ can be shown.

The value $e_j := \max_{x \in S_j} e_h(x)$ defines a function, which is locally constant on every simplex. We use e_j, $j = 1, \ldots, N$ as an indicator function for grid refinement. The (global) tolerance value $\mathtt{tol}_k$ for e_j shall be set to

$$\mathtt{tol}_k = C * (\sum_{i=1}^{N_S} e_i)/N_S,$$

where we have chosen $1 \le C \le 2$. We approximate the function e on the simplizes in the following way, starting in some $y_n \in S_j$:

---

1. apply a control $a \in U$ constantly on $[T, T + h]$
2. receive value r_n and subsequent state y_{n+1}
3. calculate the update value $P_h(x, a, V_h^k)$
4. if $(|P_h(x, a, V_h^k) - V_h^k(x)| \ge e_j)$ then $e_j := |P_h(x, a, V_h^k) - V_h^k(x)|$

It is advisable to make grid refinements in one sweep. We also store (different to the described algorithm) several past values of e_j in every simplex, to be able to distinguish between large e_j due to few visits in that simplex and the large e_j due to space discretization error. For grid refinement we use a method described in ([1]).

3 A local criterion for time refinement

Why not take the smallest possible sampling rate? There are two arguments for adaptive time discretization. First, a bigger time step h naturally improves (decreases) the contraction rate of the iteration, which is $e^{-\rho h}$. The new information is conveyed from a point further away (in the future) for big h, without the need to store intermediate states along the trajectory. It is therefore reasonable to start with a big h and refine where needed.

The second argument is, that the grid and time discretization k and h stand in a certain relation. In [3] the estimate

$$|V(x) - V_h^k(x)| \le C(h + \frac{k}{\sqrt{h}}), \quad \text{for all } x \in \Omega, \quad C \text{ a constant}$$

is proven (or similar estimates, depending on the regularity of V). For obvious reasons, it is desirable to start with a coarse grid (storage, speed), i.e. k large. Having a too small h in this case will make the approximation error large. Also here, it is reasonable to start with a big h and refine where needed.

What can serve as a refinement criterion for the time step h? In numerical schemes for ordinary differential equations, adaptive step size control is performed by estimating the local truncation error of the Taylor series by inserting intermediate points. In reinforcement learning, however, suppose the system has a large truncation error (i.e. it is difficult to control) in a certain region using large h and locally constant control functions. If the optimal value function is nearly constant in this region, we will not have to refine h. The criterion must be, that at an intermediate point, e.g. at time $h/2$, the optimal value function assumes a value considerably smaller (better) than at time h. However, if this better value is due to error in the state discretization, then do not refine the time step.

We define a function H on the simplices of the triangulation. $H(S) > 0$ holds the time-step which will be used when in simplex S. Starting at a state $y_n \in \Omega$, $y_n \in S_n$ at time $T > 0$, with the current iterate of the Q-function Q_h^k (V_h^k respectively) the following is performed:

---

1. apply a control $a \in U$ constantly on $[T, T+h]$
2. take a sample at the intermediate state $z = y_{y_n, a}(h/2)$
3. if $(H(S_n) < \mathtt{C} * \sqrt{\mathrm{diam}\{S_n\}})$ then end.
   else:
4. compute $V_h^k(z) = \min_b Q_h^k(z, b)$
5. compute $P_{h/2}(y_n, a, V_h^k) = r_{h/2}(y_n, a) + e^{-\rho h/2} V_h^k(z)$
6. compute $P_h(y_n, a, V_h^k) = r_h(y_n, a) + e^{-\rho h} V_h^k(y_{n+1})$
7. if $(P_{h/2}(y_n, a, V_h^k) \leq P_h(y_n, a, V_h^k) - \mathtt{tol})$ update $H(S_n) = H(S_n)/2$

The value $\mathtt{C}$ is currently set to

$$\mathtt{C} = C(y_n, a) = \frac{2}{\rho}|r_{h/2}(y_n, a) - r_h(y_n, a)|,$$

whereby a local value of $\frac{M_f L_g h^2}{\rho}$ is approximated, $M_f(x) = \max_a |f(x, a)|$, L_g an approximation of $|\nabla g(x, a)|$ (if g is sufficiently regular).

$\mathtt{tol}$ depends on the local value of V_h^k and is set to

$$\mathtt{tol}(x) = 0.1 * V_h^k(x).$$

How can a Q-function $Q_{h(x)}^{k(x)}(x, a)$, with state dependent time and space discretisation be approximated and stored? We have stored the time discretisation function H locally constant on every simplex. This implies (if H is not constant on Ω), that there will be vertices x_j, such that adjacent triangles hold different values of H. The Q-function, which is stored in the vertices, then has different choices of $H(x_j)$. We solved this problem, by updating a function $Q_H^k(x_j, a)$ with Kaczmarz-update and the update value $P_{H(y_n)}(y_n, a, V_h^k)$, y_n in an to x_j adjacent simplex, regardless of the different H-values in x_j. $Q_H^k(x_j, a)$ therefore has an ambiguous semantic: it is the value if a is applied for 'some time', and optimal from there on. 'some time' depends here on the value of H in the current simplex. It can be shown, that $|Q_{H(x_j)/2}^k(x_j, a) - Q_{H(x_j)}^k(x_j, a)|$ is less than the space discretization error.

4   A simple numerical example

We demonstrate the effects of suboptimal values for space and time discretisation with the following problem. Let the system equation be

$$\dot{y} = f(y, u) := \begin{pmatrix} u & 1 \\ -1 & u \end{pmatrix} (y - v), \quad v = \begin{pmatrix} .375 \\ .375 \end{pmatrix}, \quad y \in \Omega = [0, 1] \times [0, 1] \quad (8)$$

The stationary point of the uncontrolled system is v. The eigenvalues of the system are $\{u + i, u - i\}$, $u \in [-c, c]$. The system is reflected at the boundary.

The goal of the optimal control shall be steer the solution along a given trajectory in state space (see figure 1), minimizing the integral over the distance from the current state to the given trajectory. The reinforcement or cost function is therefore chosen to be

$$g(y) = \mathrm{dist}(L, y)^{\frac{1}{4}}, \tag{9}$$

where L denotes the set of points in the given trajectory. The cost functional takes the form

$$J_\rho(y, a(.)) = \int_0^\infty e^{-\rho \tau} g(y_{y, a}(\tau)) d\tau. \tag{10}$$

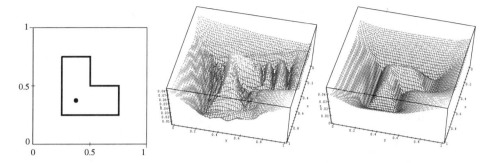

Figure 1: The left picture depicts the L-form of the given trajectory. The stationary point of the system is at $(.375, .375)$ (depicted as a big dot). The optimal value function computed by numerical schemes on a fine fixed grid is depicted with too large time discretization (middle) and small time discretization (right) (rotated by about 100 degrees for better viewing). The waves in the middle picture show the effect of too large time steps in regions where g varies considerably.

In the learning problem, the adaptive grid mechanism tries to resolve the waves (figure 1, middle picture) which come from the large time discretization. This is depicted in figure 2. We used only three different time step sizes ($h = 0.1$, 0.05 and 0.025) and started globally with the coarsest step size 0.1.

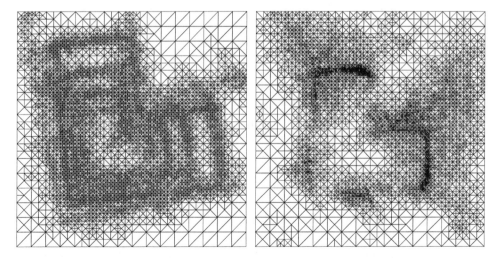

Figure 2: The adaptive grid mechanism refines correctly. However, in the left picture, unnecessary effort is spended in resolving regions, in which the time step should be refined urgently. The right picture shows the result, if adaptive time is also used. Regions outside the L-form are refined in the early stages of learning while h was still large. An additional coarsening should be considered in future work. We used a high rate of random jumps in the process and locally a certainty equivalence controller to produce these pictures.

5   Discussion of the methods and conclusions

We described a time and space adaptive method for reinforcement learning with discounted cost functional. The ultimate goal would be, to find a self tuning algorithm which locally adjusted the time and space discretization automatically to the optimal ratio. The methods worked fine in the problems we investigated, e.g. nonlinearities in the system showed no problems. Nevertheless, the results depended on the choice of the tolerance values C, tol and tol$_k$. We used only three time discretization steps to prevent adjacent triangles holding time discretization values too far apart. The smallest state space resolution in the example is therefore too fine for the finest time resolution. A solution can be, to eventually use controls that are of higher order (in terms of approximation of control functions) than constant (e.g. linear, polynomial, or locally constant on subintervals of the finest time interval). This corresponds to locally open loop controls.

The optimality of the discretization ratio time/space could not be proven. Some discontinuous value functions g gave problems, and we had problems handling stiff systems, too.

The learning period was considerably shorter (about factor 100 depending on the requested accuracy and initial data) in the adaptive cases as opposed to fixed grid and time with the same accuracy.

From our experience, it is difficult in numerical analysis to combine adaptive time and space discretization methods. To our knowledge this concept has not yet been applied to the Bellman-equation. Theoretical work is still to be done. We are aware, that triangulation of the state space yields difficulties in implementation in high dimensions. In future work we will be using rectangular grids. We will also make some comparisons with other algorithms like Parti-game ([5]). To us, a challenge is seen in handling discontinuous systems and cost functions as they appear in models with dry friction for example, as well as algebro-differential systems as they appear in robotics.

References

[1] E. Bänsch. Local mesh refinement in 2 and 3 dimensions. *IMPACT Comput. Sci. Engrg. 3, Vol. 3:181-191*, 1991.

[2] M. Falcone. A numerical approach to the infinite horizon problem of deterministic control theory. *Appl Math Optim 15:1-13*, 1987.

[3] R. Gonzalez and M. Tidball. On the rates of convergence of fully discrete solutions of Hamilton-Jacobi equations. *INRIA, Rapports de Recherche, No 1376, Programme 5*, 1991.

[4] L. Grüne. An adaptive grid scheme for the discrete Hamilton-Jacobi-Bellman equation. *Numerische Mathematik, Vol. 75, No. 3:319-337*, 1997.

[5] A. W. Moore and C. G. Atkeson. The parti-game algorithm for variable resolution reinforcement learning in multidimensional state-spaces. *Machine Learning, Volume 21*, 1995.

[6] S. Pareigis. *Lernen der Lösung der Bellman-Gleichung durch Beobachtung von kontinuierlichen Prozeßen*. PhD thesis, Universität Kiel, 1996.

[7] S. Pareigis. Multi-grid methods for reinforcement learning in controlled diffusion processes. In D. S. Touretzky, M. C. Mozer, and M. E. Hasselmo, editors, *Advances in Neural Information Processing Systems*, volume 9. The MIT Press, Cambridge, 1997.

Reinforcement Learning with Hierarchies of Machines *

Ronald Parr and Stuart Russell
Computer Science Division, UC Berkeley, CA 94720
{parr,russell}@cs.berkeley.edu

Abstract

We present a new approach to reinforcement learning in which the policies considered by the learning process are constrained by hierarchies of partially specified machines. This allows for the use of prior knowledge to reduce the search space and provides a framework in which knowledge can be transferred across problems and in which component solutions can be recombined to solve larger and more complicated problems. Our approach can be seen as providing a link between reinforcement learning and "behavior-based" or "teleo-reactive" approaches to control. We present provably convergent algorithms for problem-solving and learning with hierarchical machines and demonstrate their effectiveness on a problem with several thousand states.

1   Introduction

Optimal decision making in virtually all spheres of human activity is rendered intractable by the complexity of the task environment. Generally speaking, the only way around intractability has been to provide a hierarchical organization for complex activities. Although it can yield suboptimal policies, top-down hierarchical control often reduces the complexity of decision making from exponential to linear in the size of the problem. For example, hierarchical task network (HTN) planners can generate solutions containing tens of thousands of steps [5], whereas "flat" planners can manage only tens of steps.

HTN planners are successful because they use a plan library that describes the decomposition of high-level activities into lower-level activities. This paper describes an approach to learning and decision making in *uncertain* environments (Markov decision processes) that uses a roughly analogous form of prior knowledge. We use *hierarchical abstract machines* (HAMs), which impose constraints on the policies considered by our learning algorithms. HAMs consist of nondeterministic finite state machines whose transitions may invoke lower-level machines. Nondeterminism is represented by *choice states* where the optimal action is yet to be decided or learned. The language allows a variety of prior constraints to be expressed, ranging from no constraint all the way to a fully specified solution. One

---

*This research was supported in part by ARO under the MURI program "Integrated Approach to Intelligent Systems," grant number DAAH04-96-1-0341.

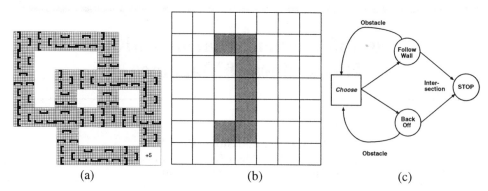

Figure 1: (a) An MDP with $\approx$ 3600 states. The initial state is in the top left. (b) Close-up showing a typical obstacle. (c) Nondeterministic finite-state controller for negotiating obstacles.

useful intermediate point is the specification of just the general organization of behavior into a layered hierarchy, leaving it up to the learning algorithm to discover exactly which lower-level activities should be invoked by higher levels at each point.

The paper begins with a brief review of Markov decision processes (MDPs) and a description of hierarchical abstract machines. We then present, in abbreviated form, the following results: **1)** Given any HAM and any MDP, there exists a new MDP such that the optimal policy in the new MDP is optimal in the original MDP among those policies that satisfy the constraints specified by the HAM. This means that even with complex machine specifications we can still apply standard decision-making and learning methods. **2)** An algorithm exists that determines this optimal policy, given an MDP and a HAM. **3)** On an illustrative problem with 3600 states, this algorithm yields dramatic performance improvements over standard algorithms applied to the original MDP. **4)** A reinforcement learning algorithm exists that converges to the optimal policy, subject to the HAM constraints, with no need to construct explicitly a new MDP. **5)** On the sample problem, this algorithm learns dramatically faster than standard RL algorithms. We conclude with a discussion of related approaches and ongoing work.

2   Markov Decision Processes

We assume the reader is familiar with the basic concepts of MDPs. To review, an MDP is a 4-tuple, (S, A, T, R) where S is a set of *states*, A is a set of *actions*, T is a *transition model* mapping $S \times A \times S$ into probabilities in $[0, 1]$, and R is a *reward function* mapping $S \times A \times S$ into real-valued rewards. Algorithms for solving MDPs can return a *policy* π that maps from S to A, a real-valued *value function* V on states, or a real-valued Q-function on state–action pairs. In this paper, we focus on infinite-horizon MDPs with a discount factor β. The aim is to find an optimal policy π^* (or, equivalently, V^* or Q^*) that maximizes the expected discounted total reward of the agent.

Throughout the paper, we will use as an example the MDP shown in Figure 1(a). Here A contains four primitive actions (up, down, left, right). The transition model, T, specifies that each action succeeds 80% of time, while 20% of the time the agent moves in an unintended perpendicular direction. The agent begins in a start state in the upper left corner. A reward of 5.0 is given for reaching the goal state and the discount factor β is 0.999.

3   Hierarchical abstract machines

A HAM is a program which, when executed by an agent in an environment, constrains the actions that the agent can take in each state. For example, a very simple machine might dictate, "repeatedly choose right or down," which would eliminate from consideration all policies that go up or left. HAMs extend this simple idea of constraining policies by providing a hierarchical means of expressing constraints at varying levels of detail and specificity. Machines for HAMs are defined by a set of states, a transition function, and a start function that determines the initial state of the machine. Machine states are of four types: **Action** states execute an action in the environment. **Call** states execute another machine as a subroutine. **Choice** states nondeterministically select a next machine state. **Stop** states halt execution of the machine and return control to the previous call state.

The transition function determines the next machine state after an action or call state as a stochastic function of the current machine state and some features of the resulting environment state. Machines will typically use a partial description of the environment to determine the next state. Although machines can function in partially observable domains, for the purposes of this paper we make the standard assumption that the agent has access to a complete description as well.

A HAM is defined by an initial machine in which execution begins and the closure of all machines reachable from the initial machine. Figure 1(c) shows a simplified version of one element of the HAM we used for the MDP in Figure 1. This element is used for traversing a hallway while negotiating obstacles of the kind shown in Figure 1(b). It runs until the end of the hallway or an intersection is reached. When it encounters an obstacle, a *choice point* is created to choose between two possible next machine states. One calls the backoff machine to back away from the obstacle and then move forward until the next one. The other calls the follow-wall machine to try to get around the obstacle. The follow-wall machine is very simple and will be tricked by obstacles that are concave in the direction of intended movement; the backoff machine, on the other hand, can move around any obstacle in this world but could waste time backing away from some obstacles unnecessarily and should be used sparingly.

Our complete "navigation HAM" involves a three-level hierarchy, somewhat reminiscent of a Brooks-style architecture but with hard-wired decisions replaced by choice states. The top level of the hierarchy is basically just a choice state for choosing a hallway navigation direction from the four coordinate directions. This machine has control initially and regains control at intersections or corners. The second level of the hierarchy contains four machines for moving along hallways, one for each direction. Each machine at this level has a choice state with four basic strategies for handling obstacles. Two back away from obstacles and two attempt to follow walls to get around obstacles. The third level of the hierarchy implements these strategies using the primitive actions.

The transition function for this HAM assumes that an agent executing the HAM has access to a short-range, low-directed sonar that detects obstacles in any of the four axis-parallel adjacent squares and a long-range, high-directed sonar that detects larger objects such as the intersections and the ends of hallways. The HAM uses these partial state descriptions to identify feasible choices. For example, the machine to traverse a hallway northwards would not be called from the start state because the high-directed sonar would detect a wall to the north.

Our navigation HAM represents an abstract plan to move about the environment by re-peatedly selecting a direction and pursuing this direction until an intersection is reached. Each machine for navigating in the chosen direction represents an abstract plan for moving in a particular direction while avoiding obstacles. The next section defines how a HAM interacts with a specific MDP and how to find an optimal policy that respects the HAM constraints.

4   Defining and solving the HAM-induced MDP

A policy for a model, M, that is *HAM-consistent* with HAM H is a scheme for making choices whenever an agent executing H in M, enters a choice state. To find the optimal HAM-consistent policy we *apply H to M* to yield an *induced* MDP, $H \circ M$. A somewhat simplified description of the construction of $H \circ M$ is as follows: **1)** The set of states in $H \circ M$ is the cross-product of the states of H with the states of M. **2)** For each state in $H \circ M$ where the machine component is an action state, the model and machine transition

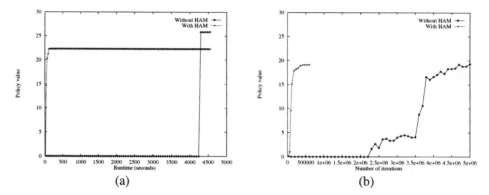

Figure 2: Experimental results showing policy value (at the initial state) as a function of runtime on the domain shown in Figure 1. (a) Policy iteration with and without the HAM. (b) Q-learning with and without the HAM (averaged over 10 runs).

functions are combined. **3)** For each state where the machine component is a choice state, actions that change only the machine component of the state are introduced. **4)** The reward is taken from M for primitive actions, otherwise it is zero. With this construction, we have the following (proof omitted):

Lemma 1 For any Markov decision process M and any[1] HAM H, the induced process $H \circ M$ is a Markov decision process.

Lemma 2 If π is an optimal policy for $H \circ M$, then the primitive actions specified by π constitute the optimal policy for M that is HAM-consistent with H.

Of course, $H \circ M$ may be quite large. Fortunately, there are two things that will make the problem much easier in most cases. The first is that not all pairs of HAM states and environment states will be possible, i.e., reachable from an initial state. The second is that the actual complexity of the induced MDP is determined by the number of choice points, i.e., states of $H \circ M$ in which the HAM component is a choice state. This leads to the following:

Theorem 1 For any MDP, M, and HAM, H, let $\mathcal{C}$ be the set of choice points in $H \circ M$. There exists a decision process, $reduce(H \circ M)$, with states $\mathcal{C}$ such that the optimal policy for $reduce(H \circ M)$ corresponds to the optimal policy for M that is HAM-consistent with H.

Proof sketch We begin by applying Lemma 1 and then observing that in states of $H \circ M$ where the HAM component is not a choice state, only one action is permitted. These states can be removed to produce an equivalent Semi-Markov decision process (SMDP). (SMDPs are a generalization of Markov decision processes that permit different discount rates for different transitions.) The optimal policy for this SMDP will be the same as the optimal policy for $H \circ M$ and by Lemma 2, this will be the optimal policy for M that is HAM-consistent with H. □

This theorem formally establishes the mechanism by which the constraints embodied in a HAM can be used to simplify an MDP. As an example of the power of this theorem, and to demonstrate that this transformation can be done efficiently, we applied our navigation HAM to the problem described in the previous section. Figure 2(a) shows the results of applying policy iteration to the original model and to the transformed model. Even when we add in the cost of transformation (which, with our rather underoptimized code, takes

---

[1]To preserve the Markov property, we require that if a machine has more than one possible caller in the hierarchy, that each appearance is treated as a distinct machine. This is equivalent to requiring that the call graph for the HAM is a tree. It follows from this that circular calling sequences are also forbidden.

866 seconds), the HAM method produces a good policy in less than a quarter of the time required to find the optimal policy in the original model. The actual solution time is 185 seconds versus 4544 seconds.

An important property of the HAM approach is that model transformation produces an MDP that is an accurate model of the application of the HAM to the original MDP. Unlike typical approximation methods for MDPs, the HAM method can give strict performance guarantees. The solution to the transformed model $reduce(H \circ M)$ is the optimal solution from within a well-defined class of policies and the value assigned to this solution is the true expected value of applying the concrete HAM policy to the original MDP.

5 Reinforcement learning with HAMs

HAMs can be of even greater advantage in a reinforcement learning context, where the effort required to obtain a solution typically scales very badly with the size of the problem. HAM contraints can focus exploration of the state space, reducing the "blind search" phase that reinforcement learning agents must endure while learning about a new environment. Learning will also be faster for the same reason policy iteration is faster in the HAM-induced model; the agent is effectively operating in a reduced state space.

We now introduce a variation of Q-learning called HAMQ-learning that learns directly in the reduced state space *without performing the model transformation* described in the previous section. This is significant because the the environment model is not usually known *a priori* in reinforcement learning contexts.

A HAMQ-learning agent keeps track of the following quantities: t, the current environment state; n, the current machine state; s_c and m_c, the environment state and machine state at the previous choice point; a, the choice made at the previous choice point; and r_c and β_c, the total accumulated reward and discount since the previous choice point. It also maintains an extended Q-table, $Q([s, m], a)$, which is indexed by an environment-state/machine-state pair and by an action taken at a choice point.

For every environment transition from state s to state t with observed reward r and discount β, the HAMQ-learning agent updates: $r_c \leftarrow r_c + \beta_c r$ and $\beta_c \leftarrow \beta \beta_c$. For each transition to a choice point, the agent does

$$Q([s_c, m_c], a) \leftarrow Q([s_c, m_c], a) + \alpha[r_c + \beta_c V([t, n]) - Q([s_c, m_c], a)],$$

and then $r_c \leftarrow 0$, $\beta_c \leftarrow 1$.

Theorem 2 For any finite-state MDP, M, and any HAM, H, HAMQ-learning will converge to the optimal choice for every choice point in $reduce(H \circ M)$ with probability 1.

Proof sketch We note that the expected reinforcement signal in HAMQ-learning is the same as the expected reinforcement signal that would be received if the agent were acting directly in the transformed model of Theorem 1 above. Thus, Theorem 1 of [11] can be applied to prove the convergence of the HAMQ-learning agent, provided that we enforce suitable constraints on the exploration strategy and the update parameter decay rate. □

We ran some experiments to measure the performance of HAMQ-learning on our sample problem. Exploration was achieved by selecting actions according to the Boltzman distribution with a temperature parameter for each state. We also used an inverse decay for the update parameter α. Figure 2(b) compares the learning curves for Q-learning and HAMQ-learning. HAMQ-learning appears to learn much faster: Q-learning required 9,000,000 iterations to reach the level achieved by HAMQ-learning after 270,000 iterations. Even after 20,000,000 iterations, Q-learning did not do as well as HAMQ-learning.[2]

---

[2]Speedup techniques such as eligibility traces could be applied to get better Q-learning results; such methods apply equally well to HAMQ-learning.

6   Related work

State aggregation (see, e.g., [18] and [7]) clusters "similar" states together and assigns them the same value, effectively reducing the state space. This is orthogonal to our approach and could be combined with HAMs. However, aggregation should be used with caution as it treats distinct states as a single state and can violate the Markov property leading to the loss of performance guarantees and oscillation or divergence in reinforcement learning. Moreover, state aggregation may be hard to apply effectively in many cases.

Dean and Lin [8] and Bertsekas and Tsitsiklis [2], showed that some MDPs are loosely coupled and hence amenable to divide-and-conquer algorithms. A machine-like language was used in [13] to partition an MDP into decoupled subproblems. In problems that are amenable to decoupling, this could approaches could be used in combinated with HAMs.

Dayan and Hinton [6] have proposed *feudal* RL which specifies an explicit subgoal structure, with fixed values for each subgoal achieved, in order to achieve a hierarchical decomposition of the state space. Dietterich extends and generalizes this approach in [9]. Singh has investigated a number of approaches to subgoal based decomposition in reinforcement learning (e.g. [17] and [16]). Subgoals seem natural in some domains, but they may require a significant amount of outside knowledge about the domain and establishing the relationship between the value of subgoals with respect to the overall problem can be difficult.

Bradtke and Duff [3] proposed an RL algorithm for SMDPs. Sutton [19] proposes *temporal abstractions*, which concatenate sequences of state transitions together to permit reasoning about temporally extended events, and which can thereby form a behavioral hierarchy as in [14] and [15]. Lin's somewhat informal scheme [12] also allows agents to treat entire policies as single actions. These approaches can be emcompassed within our framework by encoding the events or behaviors as machines.

The design of hierarchically organized, "layered" controllers was popularized by Brooks [4]. His designs use a somewhat different means of passing control, but our analysis and theorems apply equally well to his machine description language. The "teleo-reactive" agent designs of Benson and Nilsson [1] are even closer to our HAM language. Both of these approaches assume that the agent is completely specified, albeit self-modifiable. The idea of partial behavior descriptions can be traced at least to Hsu's *partial programs* [10], which were used with a deterministic logical planner.

7   Conclusions and future work

We have presented HAMs as a principled means of constraining the set of policies that are considered for a Markov decision process and we have demonstrated the efficacy of this approach in a simple example for both policy iteration and reinforcement learning. Our results show very significant speedup for decision-making and learning—but of course, this reflects the provision of knowledge in the form of the HAM. The HAM language provides a very general method of transferring knowledge to an agent and we only have scratched the surface of what can be done with this approach.

We believe that if desired, subgoal information can be incorporated into the HAM structure, unifying subgoal-based approaches with the HAM approach. Moreover, the HAM structure provides a natural decomposition of the HAM-induced model, making it amenable to the divide-and-conquer approaches of [8] and [2].

There are opportunities for generalization across all levels of the HAM paradigm. Value function approximation can be used for the HAM induced model and inductive learning methods can be used to produce HAMs or to generalize their effects upon different regions of the state space. Gradient-following methods also can be used to adjust the transition probabilities of a stochastic HAM.

HAMs also lend themselves naturally to partially observable domains. They can be applied directly when the choice points induced by the HAM are states where no confusion about the true state of the environment is possible. The application of HAMs to more general partially observable domains is more complicated and is a topic of ongoing research. We also believe that the HAM approach can be extended to cover the average-reward optimality criterion.

We expect that successful pursuit of these lines of research will provide a formal basis for understanding and unifying several seemingly disparate approaches to control, including behavior-based methods. It should also enable the use of the MDP framework in real-world applications of much greater complexity than hitherto attacked, much as HTN planning has extended the reach of classical planning methods.

References

[1] S. Benson and N. Nilsson. Reacting, planning and learning in an autonomous agent. In K. Furukawa, D. Michie, and S. Muggleton, editors, *Machine Intelligence 14*. Oxford University Press, Oxford, 1995.

[2] D. C. Bertsekas and J. N. Tsitsiklis. *Parallel and Distributed Computation: Numerical Methods*. Prentice-Hall, Englewood Cliffs, New Jersey, 1989.

[3] S. J. Bradtke and M. O. Duff. Reinforcement learning methods for continuous-time Markov decision problems. In *Advances in Neural Information Processing Systems 7: Proc. of the 1994 Conference*, Denver, Colorado, December 1995. MIT Press.

[4] R. A. Brooks. A robust layered control system for a mobile robot. *IEEE Journal of Robotics and Automation*, 2, 1986.

[5] K. W. Currie and A. Tate. O-Plan: the Open Planning Architecture. *Artificial Intelligence*, 52(1), November 1991.

[6] P. Dayan and G. E. Hinton. Feudal reinforcement learning. In Stephen Jose Hanson, Jack D. Cowan, and C. Lee Giles, editors, *Neural Information Processing Systems 5*, San Mateo, California, 1993. Morgan Kaufman.

[7] T. Dean, R. Givan, and S. Leach. Model reduction techniques for computing approximately optimal solutions for markov decision processes. In *Proc. of the Thirteenth Conference on Uncertainty in Artificial Intelligence*, Providence, Rhode Island, August 1997. Morgan Kaufmann.

[8] T. Dean and S.-H. Lin. Decomposition techniques for planning in stochastic domains. In *Proc. of the Fourteenth Int. Joint Conference on Artificial Intelligence*, Montreal, Canada, August 1995. Morgan Kaufmann.

[9] Thomas G. Dietterich. Hierarchical reinforcement learning with the MAXQ value function decomposition. Technical report, Department of Computer Science, Oregon State University, Corvallis, Oregon, 1997.

[10] Y.-J. Hsu. Synthesizing efficient agents from partial programs. In *Methodologies for Intelligent Systems: 6th Int. Symposium, ISMIS '91, Proc.*, Charlotte, North Carolina, October 1991. Springer-Verlag.

[11] T. Jaakkola, M.I. Jordan, and S.P. Singh. On the convergence of stochastic iterative dynamic programming algorithms. *Neural Computation*, 6(6), 1994.

[12] L.-J. Lin. *Reinforcement Learning for Robots Using Neural Networks*. PhD thesis, Computer Science Department, Carnegie-Mellon University, Pittsburgh, Pennsylvania, 1993.

[13] Shieu-Hong Lin. *Exploiting Structure for Planning and Control*. PhD thesis, Computer Science Department, Brown University, Providence, Rhode Island, 1997.

[14] A. McGovern, R. S. Sutton, and A. H. Fagg. Roles of macro-actions in accelerating reinforcement learning. In *1997 Grace Hopper Celebration of Women in Computing*, 1997.

[15] D. Precup and R. S. Sutton. Multi-time models for temporally abstract planning. In *This Volume*.

[16] S. P. Singh. Scaling reinforcement learning algorithms by learning variable temporal resolution models. In *Proceedings of the Ninth International Conference on Machine Learning*, Aberdeen, July 1992. Morgan Kaufmann.

[17] S. P. Singh. Transfer of learning by composing solutions of elemental sequential tasks. *Machine Learning*, 8(3), May 1992.

[18] S. P. Singh, T. Jaakola, and M. I. Jordan. Reinforcement learning with soft state aggregation. In G. Tesauro, D. S. Touretzky, and T. K. Leen, editors, *Neural Information Processing Systems 7*, Cambridge, Massachusetts, 1995. MIT Press.

[19] R. S. Sutton. Temporal abstraction in reinforcement learning. In *Proc. of the Twelfth Int. Conference on Machine Learning*, Tahoe City, CA, July 1995. Morgan Kaufmann.

Multi-time Models for Temporally Abstract Planning

Doina Precup, Richard S. Sutton
University of Massachusetts
Amherst, MA 01003
{dprecup|rich}@cs.umass.edu

Abstract

Planning and learning at multiple levels of temporal abstraction is a key problem for artificial intelligence. In this paper we summarize an approach to this problem based on the mathematical framework of Markov decision processes and reinforcement learning. Current model-based reinforcement learning is based on one-step models that cannot represent common-sense higher-level actions, such as going to lunch, grasping an object, or flying to Denver. This paper generalizes prior work on temporally abstract models [Sutton, 1995] and extends it from the prediction setting to include actions, control, and planning. We introduce a more general form of temporally abstract model, the *multi-time model*, and establish its suitability for planning and learning by virtue of its relationship to the Bellman equations. This paper summarizes the theoretical framework of multi-time models and illustrates their potential advantages in a gridworld planning task.

The need for hierarchical and abstract planning is a fundamental problem in AI (see, e.g., Sacerdoti, 1977; Laird et al., 1986; Korf, 1985; Kaelbling, 1993; Dayan & Hinton, 1993). Model-based reinforcement learning offers a possible solution to the problem of integrating planning with real-time learning and decision-making (Peng & Williams, 1993, Moore & Atkeson, 1993; Sutton and Barto, 1998). However, current model-based reinforcement learning is based on one-step models that cannot represent common-sense, higher-level actions. Modeling such actions requires the ability to handle different, interrelated levels of temporal abstraction.

A new approach to modeling at multiple time scales was introduced by Sutton (1995) based on prior work by Singh , Dayan , and Sutton and Pinette . This approach enables models of the environment at different temporal scales to be intermixed, producing temporally abstract models. However, that work was concerned only with predicting the environment. This paper summarizes an extension of the approach including actions and control of the environment [Precup & Sutton, 1997]. In particular, we generalize the usual notion of a primitive, one-step action to an *abstract action*, an arbitrary, closed-loop policy. Whereas prior work modeled the behavior of the agent-environment system under a single, given policy, here we learn different models for a set of different policies. For each possible way of behaving, the agent learns a separate model of what will happen. Then, in planning, it can choose between these overall policies as well as between primitive actions.

To illustrate the kind of advance we are trying to make, consider the example shown in Figure 1. This is a standard gridworld in which the primitive actions are to move from one grid cell to a neighboring cell. Imagine the learning agent is repeatedly given new tasks in the form of new goal locations to travel to as rapidly as possible. If the agent plans at the level of primitive actions, then its plans will be many actions long and take a relatively long time to compute. Planning could be much faster if abstract actions could be used to plan for moving from room to room rather than from cell to cell. For each room, the agent learns two models for two abstract actions, one for traveling efficiently to each adjacent room. We do not address in this paper the question of how such abstract actions could be discovered without help; instead we focus on the mathematical theory of abstract actions. In particular, we define a very general semantics for them—a property that seems to be required in order for them to be used in the general kind of planning typically used with Markov decision processes. At the end of this paper we illustrate the theory in this example problem, showing how room-to-room abstract actions can substantially speed planning.

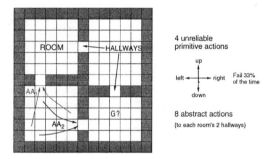

Figure 1: Example Task. The Natural abstract actions are to move from room to room.

1 Reinforcement Learning (MDP) Framework

In reinforcement learning, a learning *agent* interacts with an *environment* at some discrete, lowest-level time scale $t = 0, 1, 2, \ldots$ On each time step, the agent perceives the state of the environment, s_t, and on that basis chooses a primitive action, a_t. In response to each primitive action, a_t, the environment produces one step later a numerical reward, r_{t+1}, and a next state, s_{t+1}. The agent's objective is to learn a policy, a mapping from states to probabilities of taking each action, that maximizes the expected discounted future reward from each state s:

$$v^\pi(s) = E_\pi\Big\{\sum_{t=0}^{\infty} \gamma^t r_{t+1} \ \Big| \ s_0 = s\Big\},$$

where $\gamma \in [0, 1)$ is a *discount-rate* parameter, and $E_\pi\{\}$ denotes an expectation implicitly conditional on the policy π being followed. The quantity $v^\pi(s)$ is called the *value* of state s under policy π, and v^π is called the value function for policy π. The value under the optimal policy is denoted:

$$v^*(s) = \max_\pi v^\pi(s).$$

Planning in reinforcement learning refers to the use of models of the effects of actions to compute value functions, particularly v^*.

We assume that the states are discrete and form a finite set, $s_t \in \{1, 2, \ldots, m\}$. This is viewed as a temporary theoretical convenience; it is not a limitation of the ideas we present. This assumption allows us to alternatively denote the value functions, v^π and v^*, as column vectors, $\mathbf{v}^\pi$ and $\mathbf{v}^*$, each having m components that contain the values of the m states. In general, for any m-vector, $\mathbf{x}$, we will use the notation $x(s)$ to refer to its sth component.

The model of an action, a, whether primitive or abstract, has two components. One is an $m \times m$ matrix, P_a, predicting the state that will result from executing the action in each state. The other is a vector, $\mathbf{g}_a$, predicting the cumulative reward that will be received along the way. In the case of a primitive action, P_a is the matrix of 1-step transition probabilities of the environment, times γ:

$$P_a^T(s) = \gamma E \{\mathbf{s}_{t+1} \mid s_t = s, a_t = a\}, \qquad \forall s$$

where $P_a^T(s)$ denotes the sth column of P_a^T (these are the predictions corresponding to state s) and $\mathbf{s}_t$ denotes the unit basis m-vector corresponding to s_t. The reward prediction, $\mathbf{g}_a$, for a primitive action contains the expected immediate rewards:

$$g_a(s) = E \{r_{t+1} \mid s_t = s, a_t = a\}, \qquad \forall s$$

For any stochastic policy, π, we can similarly define its 1-step model, $\mathbf{g}_\pi, P_\pi$ as:

$$P_\pi^T(s) = \gamma E_\pi \left\{\mathbf{s}_{t+1} \mid s_t = s\right\} \qquad \text{and} \qquad g_\pi(s) = E_\pi \left\{r_{t+1} \mid s_t = s\right\} \qquad \forall s \qquad (1)$$

2   Suitability for Planning

In conventional planning, one-step models are used to compute value functions via the Bellman equations for prediction and control. In vector notation, the prediction and control Bellman equations are

$$\mathbf{v}^\pi = \mathbf{g}_\pi + P_\pi \mathbf{v}^\pi \qquad \text{and} \qquad \mathbf{v}^* = \max_a \{\mathbf{g}_a + P_a \mathbf{v}^*\}, \qquad (2)$$

respectively, where the max function is applied component-wise in the control equation. In planning, these equalities are turned into updates, e.g., $\mathbf{v}_{k+1}^\pi \leftarrow \mathbf{g}_\pi + P_\pi \mathbf{v}_k^\pi$, which converge to the value functions. Thus, the Bellman equations are usually used to define and compute value functions given models of actions. Following Sutton (1995), here we reverse the roles: we take the value functions as given and use the Bellman equations to define and compute models of new, abstract actions.

In particular, a model can be used in planning only if it is stable and consistent with the Bellman equations. It is useful to define special terms for consistency with each Bellman equation. Let $\mathbf{g}, P$ denote an arbitrary model (an m-vector and an $m \times m$ matrix). Then this model is said to be *valid* for policy π [Sutton, 1995] if and only if $\lim_{k \to \infty} P^k = 0$ and

$$\mathbf{v}^\pi = \mathbf{g} + P \mathbf{v}^\pi. \qquad (3)$$

Any valid model can be used to compute $\mathbf{v}^\pi$ via the iteration algorithm $\mathbf{v}_{k+1}^\pi \leftarrow \mathbf{g} + P \mathbf{v}_k^\pi$. This is a direct sense in which the validity of a model implies that it is suitable for planning. We introduce here a parallel definition that expresses consistency with the control Bellman equation. The model $\mathbf{g}, P$ is said to be *non-overpromising* (NOP) if and only if P has only positive elements, $\lim_{k \to \infty} P^k = 0$, and

$$\mathbf{v}^* \geq \mathbf{g} + P \mathbf{v}^*, \qquad (4)$$

where the $\geq$ relation holds component-wise. If a NOP model is added inside the max operator in the control Bellman equation (2), this condition ensures that the true value, $\mathbf{v}^*$, will not be exceeded for any state. Thus, any model that does not promise more than it is achievable (is not overpromising) can serve as an option for planning purposes. The one-step models of primitive actions are obviously NOP, due to (2). It is similarly straightforward to show that the one-step model of any policy is also NOP.

For some purposes, it is more convenient to write a model $\mathbf{g}, P$ as a single $(m+1) \times (m+1)$ matrix:

$$
M = \left[\begin{array}{c|c} 1 & - \; 0 \; - \\ \hline & \\ \mathbf{g} & P \\ & \end{array} \right].
$$

We say that the model M has been put in homogeneous coordinates. The vectors corresponding to the value functions can also be put into homogeneous coordinates, by adding an initial element that is always 1.

Using this notation, new models can be combined using two basic operations: composition and averaging. Two models M_1 and M_2 can be *composed* by matrix multiplication, yielding a new model $M = M_1 M_2$. A set of models M_i can be *averaged*, weighted by a set of diagonal matrices D_i, such that $\sum_i D_i = I$, to yield a new model $M = \sum_i D_i M_i$. Sutton (1995) showed that the set of models that are valid for a policy π is closed under composition and averaging. This enables models acting at different time scales to be mixed together, and the resulting model can still be used to compute $\mathbf{v}^\pi$. We have proven that the set of NOP models is also closed under composition and averaging [Precup & Sutton, 1997]. These operations permit a richer variety of combinations for NOP models than they do for valid models because the NOP models that are combined need not correspond to a particular policy.

3   Multi-time models

The validity and NOP-ness of a model do not imply each other [Precup & Sutton, 1997]. Nevertheless, we believe a good model should be both valid and NOP. We would like to describe a class of models that, in some sense, includes all the "interesting" models that are valid and non-overpromising, and which is expressive enough to include common-sense notions of abstract action. These goals have led us to the notion of a *multi-time model*.

The simplest example of multi-step model, called the *n-step model for policy* π, predicts the n-step truncated return and the state n steps into the future (times γ^n). If different n-step models of the same policy are averaged, the result is called a *mixture model*. Mixtures are valid and non-overpromising due to the closure properties established in the previous section. One kind of mixture suggested in [Sutton, 1995] allows an exponential decay of the weights over time, controlled by a parameter β.

Figure 2: Two hypothetical Markov environments

Are mixture models expressive enough for capturing the properties of the environment? In order to get some intuition about the expressive power that a model should have, let us consider the example in figure 2. If we are only interested if state G is attained, then the two environments presented should be characterized by significantly different models. However, n-step models, or any linear mixture of n-step models cannot achieve this goal. In order to remediate this problem, models should average differently over all the different trajectories that are possible through the state space. A full β-model [Sutton, 1995] can distinguish between these two situations. A β-model is a more general form of mixture model, in which a different β parameter is associated with each state. For a state i, β_i can be viewed as the probability that the trajectory through the state space ends in state i. Although β-models seem to have more expressive power, they cannot describe n-step models. We would like to have a more general form of model, that unifies both classes. This goal is achieved by accurate multi-time models.

Multi-time models are defined with respect to a policy. Just as the one-step model for a policy is defined by (1), we define $\mathbf{g}, P$ to be an accurate multi-time model if and only if

$$P^T(s) = E_\pi\left\{\sum_{t=1}^{\infty} w_t\, \gamma^t\, \mathbf{s}_t \,\Big|\, s_0 = s\right\},$$

$$g(s) = E_\pi\left\{\sum_{t=1}^{\infty} w_t\,(r_1 + \gamma r_2 + \cdots + \gamma^{t-1} r_t) \,\Big|\, s_0 = s\right\}$$

for some π, for all s, and for some sequence of random weights, $w_1, w_2, \ldots$ such that $w_t > 0$ and $\sum_{t=1}^{\infty} w_t = 1$. The weights are random variables chosen according to a distribution that depends only on states visited at or before time t. The weight w_t is a measure of the importance given to the t-th state of the trajectory. In particular, if $w_t = 0$, then state t has no weight associated with it. If $w_t = 1 - \sum_{i=0}^{t-1} w_i$, all the remaining weight along the trajectory is given to state t. The effect is that state $\dot{s}_t$ is the "outcome" state for the trajectory.

The random weights along each trajectory make this a very general form of model. The only necessary constraint is that the weights depend only on previously visited states. In particular, we can choose weighting sequences that generate the types of multi-step models described in [Sutton, 1995]. If the weighting variables are such that $w_n = 1$, and $w_t = 0, \forall t \neq n$, we obtain n-step models. A weighting sequence of the form $w_t = \Pi_{i=0}^{t-1} \beta_i\, \forall t$, where β_i is the parameter associated to the state visited on time step i, describes a full β-model.

The main result for multi-time models is that they satisfy the two criteria defined in the previous section. Any accurate multi-time model is also NOP and valid for π. The proofs of these results are too long to include here.

4 Illustrative Example

In order to illustrate the way in which multi-time models can be used in practice, let us return to the gridworld example (Figure 1). The cells of the grid correspond to the states of the environment. From any state the agent can perform one of four primitive actions, up, down, left or right. With probability 2/3, the actions cause the agent to move one cell in the corresponding direction (unless this would take the agent into a wall, in which case it stays in the same state). With probability 1/3, the agent instead moves in one of the other three directions (unless this takes it into a wall of course). There is no penalty for bumping into walls.

In each room, we also defined two abstract actions, for going to each of the adjacent hallways. Each abstract action has a set of input states (the states in the room) and two outcome states: the target hallway, which corresponds to a successful outcome, and the state adjacent to the other hallway, which corresponds to failure (the agent has wandered out of the room). Each abstract action is given by its complete model $\mathbf{g}_w^\pi, P_w^\pi$, where π is the optimal policy for getting into the target hallway, and the weighting variables w along any trajectory have the value 1 for the outcome states and 0 everywhere else.

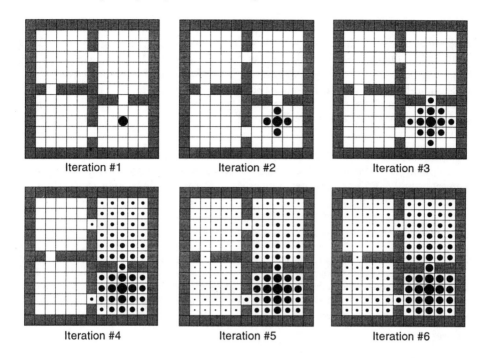

Figure 3: Value iteration using primitive and abstract actions

The goal state can have an arbitrary position in any of the rooms, but for this illustration let us suppose that the goal is two steps down from the right hallway. The value of the goal state is 1, there are no rewards along the way, and the discounting factor is $\gamma = 0.9$. We performed planning according to the standard value iteration method:

$$\mathbf{v}_{k+1} \leftarrow \max_a \mathbf{g}_a + P_a \mathbf{v}_k,$$

where $v_0(s) = 0$ for all the states except the goal state (which starts at 1). In one experiment, a ranged only over the primitive actions, in the other it ranged over the set including both the primitive and the abstract actions.

When using only primitive actions, the values are propagated one step away on each iteration. After six iterations, for instance, only the states that are at most six steps away from the goal will be attributed non-zero values. The models of abstract actions produce a significant speed-up in the propagation of values at each step. Figure 3 shows the value function after each iteration, using both primitive and abstract actions for planning. The area of the circle drawn in each state is proportional to the value attributed to the state. The first three iterations are identical with the case when only primitive actions are used. However, once the values are propagated to the first hallway, all the states in the rooms adjacent to that hallway will receive values as well. For the states in the room containing the goal, these values correspond to performing the abstract action of getting into the right hallway, and then following the optimal primitive actions to get to the goal. At this point, a path to the goal is known from each state in the right half of the environment, even if the path is not optimal for all states. After six iterations, an optimal policy is known for all the states in the environment.

The models of the abstract actions do not need to be given a priori, they can be learned from experience. In fact, the abstract models that were used in this experiment have been learned during a 1,000,000-step random walk in the environment. The starting point for learning was represented by the outcome states of each abstract action, along with the hypothetical utilities U associated with these states. We used Q-learning [Watkins, 1989] to learn the optimal state-action value function $Q^*_{U,B}$ associated with each abstract action. The greedy policy with respect to $Q^*_{U,B}$ is the policy associated with the abstract action. At the same time, we used the β-model learning algorithm presented in [Sutton, 1995] to compute the model corresponding to the policy. The learning algorithm is completely online and incremental, and its complexity is comparable to that of regular 1-step TD-learning.

Models of abstract actions can be built while an agent is acting in the environment without any additional effort. Such models can then be used in the planning process as if they would represent primitive actions, ensuring more efficient learning and planning, especially if the goal is changing over time.

Acknowledgments

The authors thank Amy McGovern and Andy Fagg for helpful discussions and comments contributing to this paper. This research was supported in part by NSF grant ECS-9511805 to Andrew G. Barto and Richard S. Sutton, and by AFOSR grant AFOSR-F49620-96-1-0254 to Andrew G. Barto and Richard S. Sutton. Doina Precup also acknowledges the support of the Fulbright foundation.

References

Dayan, P. (1993). Improving generalization for temporal difference learning: The successor representation. *Neural Computation, 5*, 613–624.

Dayan, P. & Hinton, G. E. (1993). Feudal reinforcement learning. In *Advances in Neural Information Processing Systems*, volume 5, (pp. 271–278)., San Mateo, CA. Morgan Kaufmann.

Kaelbling, L. P. (1993). Hierarchical learning in stochastic domains: Preliminary results. In *Proceedings of the Tenth International Conference on Machine Learning ICML'93*, (pp. 167–173)., San Mateo, CA. Morgan Kaufmann.

Korf, R. E. (1985). *Learning to Solve Problems by Searching for Macro-Operators*. London: Pitman Publishing Ltd.

Laird, J. E., Rosenbloom, P. S., & Newell, A. (1986). Chunking in SOAR: The anatomy of a general learning mechanism. *Machine Learning, 1*, 11–46.

Moore, A. W. & Atkeson, C. G. (1993). Prioritized sweeping: Reinforcement learning with less data and less real time. *Machine Learning, 13*, 103–130.

Peng, J. & Williams, J. (1993). Efficient learning and planning within the Dyna framework. *Adaptive Behavior, 4*, 323–334.

Precup, D. & Sutton, R. S. (1997). Multi-Time models for reinforcement learning. In *ICML'97 Workshop: The Role of Models in Reinforcement Learning*.

Sacerdoti, E. D. (1977). *A Structure for Plans and Behavior*. North-Holland, NY: Elsevier.

Singh, S. P. (1992). Scaling reinforcement learning by learning variable temporal resolution models. In *Proceedings of the Ninth International Conference on Machine Learning ICML'92*, (pp. 202–207)., San Mateo, CA. Morgan Kaufmann.

Sutton, R. S. (1995). TD models: Modeling the world as a mixture of time scales. In *Proceedings of the Twelfth International Conference on Machine Learning ICML'95*, (pp. 531–539)., San Mateo, CA. Morgan Kaufmann.

Sutton, R. S. & Barto, A. G. (1998). *Reinforcement Learning. An Introduction*. Cambridge, MA: MIT Press.

Sutton, R. S. & Pinette, B. (1985). The learning of world models by connectionist networks. In *Proceedings of the Seventh Annual Conference of the Cognitive Science Society*, (pp. 54–64).

Watkins, C. J. C. H. (1989). *Learning with Delayed Rewards*. PhD thesis, Cambridge University.

How to Dynamically Merge Markov Decision Processes

Satinder Singh
Department of Computer Science
University of Colorado
Boulder, CO 80309-0430
baveja@cs.colorado.edu

David Cohn
Adaptive Systems Group
Harlequin, Inc.
Menlo Park, CA 94025
cohn@harlequin.com

Abstract

We are frequently called upon to perform multiple tasks that compete for our attention and resource. Often we know the optimal solution to each task in isolation; in this paper, we describe how this knowledge can be exploited to efficiently find good solutions for doing the tasks in parallel. We formulate this problem as that of dynamically merging multiple Markov decision processes (MDPs) into a composite MDP, and present a new theoretically-sound dynamic programming algorithm for finding an optimal policy for the composite MDP. We analyze various aspects of our algorithm and illustrate its use on a simple merging problem.

Every day, we are faced with the problem of doing multiple tasks in parallel, each of which competes for our attention and resource. If we are running a job shop, we must decide which machines to allocate to which jobs, and in what order, so that no jobs miss their deadlines. If we are a mail delivery robot, we must find the intended recipients of the mail while simultaneously avoiding fixed obstacles (such as walls) and mobile obstacles (such as people), and still manage to keep ourselves sufficiently charged up.

Frequently we know how to perform each task in isolation; this paper considers how we can take the information we have about the individual tasks and combine it to efficiently find an optimal solution for doing the entire set of tasks in parallel. More importantly, we describe a theoretically-sound algorithm for doing this merging dynamically; new tasks (such as a new job arrival at a job shop) can be assimilated online into the solution being found for the ongoing set of simultaneous tasks.

1   The Merging Framework

Many decision-making tasks in control and operations research are naturally formulated as Markov decision processes (MDPs) (e.g., Bertsekas & Tsitsiklis, 1996). Here we define MDPs and then formulate what it means to have multiple simultanous MDPs.

1.1   Markov decision processes (MDPs)

An MDP is defined via its state set S, action set A, transition probability matrices P, and payoff matrices R. On executing action a in state s the probability of transiting to state s' is denoted $P^a(ss')$ and the expected payoff associated with that transition is denoted $R^a(ss')$. We assume throughout that the payoffs are non-negative for all transitions. A policy assigns an action to each state of the MDP. The value of a state under a policy is the expected value of the discounted sum of payoffs obtained when the policy is followed on starting in that state. The objective is to find an optimal policy, one that maximizes the value of every state. The optimal value of state s, $V^*(s)$, is its value under the optimal policy.

The optimal value function is the solution to the Bellman optimality equations: for all $s \in S$, $V(s) = \max_{a \in A}(\sum_{s'} P^a(ss')[R^a(ss') + \gamma V(s')])$, where the discount factor $0 \leq \gamma < 1$ makes future payoffs less valuable than more immediate payoffs (e.g., Bertsekas & Tsitsiklis, 1996). It is known that the optimal policy π^* can be determined from V^* as follows: $\pi^*(s) = \mathrm{argmax}_{a \in A}(\sum_{s'} P^a(ss')[R^a(ss') + \gamma V^*(s')])$. Therefore solving an MDP is tantamount to computing its optimal value function.

1.2   Solving MDPs via Value Iteration

Given a model (S, A, P, R) of an MDP value iteration (e.g., Bertsekas & Tsitsiklis, 1996) can be used to determine the optimal value function. Starting with an initial guess, V_0, iterate for all s $V_{k+1}(s) = \max_{a \in A}(\sum_{s' \in S} P^a(ss')[R^a(ss') + \gamma V_k(s')])$. It is known that $\max_{s \in S}|V_{k+1}(s) - V^*(s)| \leq \gamma \max_{s \in S}|V_k(s) - V^*(s)|$ and therefore V_k converges to V^* as k goes to infinity. Note that a Q-value (Watkins, 1989) based version of value iteration and our algorithm presented below is also easily defined.

1.3   Multiple Simultaneous MDPs

The notion of an optimal policy is well defined for a single task represented as an MDP. If, however, we have multiple tasks to do in parallel, each with its own state, action, transition probability, and payoff spaces, optimal behavior is not automatically defined. We will assume that payoffs sum across the MDPs, which means we want to select actions for each MDP at every time step so as to maximize the expected discounted value of this summed payoff over time. If actions can be chosen independently for each MDP, then the solution to this "composite" MDP is obvious — do what's optimal for each MDP. More typically, choosing an action for one MDP constrains what actions can be chosen for the others. In a job shop for example, actions correspond to assignment of resources, and the same physical resource may not be assigned to more than one job simultaneously.

Formally, we can define a composite MDP as a set of N MDPs $\{M^i\}_1^N$. We will use superscripts to distinguish the component MDPs, e.g., S^i, A^i, P^i, and R^i are the state, action, transition probability and payoff parameters of MDP M^i. The state space of the composite MDP, S, is the cross product of the state spaces of the component MDPs, i.e., $S = S^1 \times S^2 \times \ldots \times S^N$. The constraints on actions implies that the action set of the composite MDP, A, is some proper subset of the cross product of the N component action spaces. The transition probabilities and the payoffs of the composite MDP are *factorial* because the following decompositions hold: for all $s, s' \in S$ and $a \in A$, $P^a(ss') = \Pi_{i=1}^{N} P^{a^i}(s^i s^{i'})$ and $R^a(ss') = \sum_{i=1}^{N} R^{a^i}(s^i s^{i'})$. Singh (1997) has previously studied such factorial MDPs but only for the case of a fixed set of components.

The optimal value function of a composite MDP is well defined, and satisfies the following Bellman equation: for all $s \in S$,

$$V(s) \;=\; \max_{a \in A} \sum_{s' \in S} \left(\Pi_{i=1}^{N} P^{a^i}(s^i s^{i'}) \left[\sum_{i=1}^{N} R^{a^i}(s^i s^{i'}) + \gamma V(s') \right] \right). \tag{1}$$

Note that the Bellman equation for a composite MDP assumes an identical discount factor across component MDPs and is not defined otherwise.

1.4 The Dynamic Merging Problem

Given a composite MDP, and the optimal solution (e.g. the optimal value function) for each of its component MDPs, we would like to efficiently compute the optimal solution for the composite MDP. More generally, we would like to compute the optimal composite policy given only *bounds* on the value functions of the component MDPs (the motivation for this more general version will become clear in the next section). To the best of our knowledge, the dynamic merging question has not been studied before.

Note that the traditional treatment of problems such as job-shop scheduling would formulate them as nonstationary MDPs (however, see Zhang and Dietterich, 1995 for another learning approach). This normally requires augmenting the state space to include a "time" component which indexes all possible state spaces that could arise (e.g., Bertsekas, 1995). This is inefficient, and potentially infeasible unless we know in advance all combinations of possible tasks we will be required to solve. One contribution of this paper is the observation that this type of nonstationary problem can be reformulated as one of dynamically merging (individually) stationary MDPs.

1.4.1 The naive greedy policy is suboptimal

Given bounds on the value functions of the component MDPs, one heuristic composite policy is that of selecting actions according to a one-step greedy rule:

$$\pi(s) = \operatorname*{argmax}_{a} \left(\sum_{s'} \Pi_{i=1}^{N} P^{a^i}(s^i s^{i'}) \left[\sum_{i=1}^{N} (R^{a^i}(s^i, a^i) + \gamma X^i(s^{i'})) \right] \right),$$

where X^i is the upper or lower bound of the value function, or the mean of the bounds. It is fairly easy however, to demonstrate that these policies are substantially suboptimal in many common situations (see Section 3).

2 Dynamic Merging Algorithm

Consider merging N MDPs; job-shop scheduling presents a special case of merging a new single MDP with an old composite MDP consisting of several factor MDPs. One obvious approach to finding the optimal composite policy would be to directly perform value iteration in the composite state and action space. A more efficient approach would make use of the solutions (bounds on optimal value functions) of the existing components; below we describe an algorithm for doing this.

Our algorithm will assume that we know the optimal values, or more generally, upper and lower bounds to the optimal values of the states in each component MDP. We use the symbols L and U for the lower and upper bounds; if the optimal value function for the ith factor MDP is available then $L^i = U^i = V^{*,i}$.[1]

Our algorithm uses the bounds for the component MDPs to compute bounds on the values of composite states as needed and then incrementally updates and narrows these initial bounds using a form of value iteration that allows pruning of actions that are not *competitive*, that is, actions whose bounded values are strictly dominated by the bounded value of some other action.

Initial State: The initial composite state s_0 is composed from the start state of all the factor MDPs. In practice (e.g. in job-shop scheduling) the initial composite state is composed of the start state of the new job and whatever the current state of the set of old jobs is. Our algorithm exploits the initial state by only updating states that can occur from the initial state under competitive actions.

Initial Value Step: When we need the value of a composite state s for the first time, we compute upper and lower bounds to its optimal value as follows: $L(s) = \max_{i=1}^N L^i(s^i)$, and $U(s) = \sum_{i=1}^N U^i(s)$.

Initial Update Step: We dynamically allocate upper and lower bound storage space for composite states as we first update them. We also create the initial set of competitive actions for s when we first update its value as $A(s) = A$. As successive backups narrow the upper and lower bounds of successor states, some actions will no longer be competitive, and will be eliminated from further consideration.

Modified Value Iteration Algorithm:

At step t if the state to be updated is s_t:

$$L_{t+1}(s_t) = \max_{a \in A_t(s_t)} \left(\sum_{s'} P^a(s_t s')[R^a(s_t, s') + \gamma L_t(s')] \right)$$

$$U_{t+1}(s_t) = \max_{a \in A_t(s_t)} \left(\sum_{s'} P^a(s_t s')[R^a(s_t, s') + \gamma U_t(s')] \right)$$

$$A_{t+1}(s_t) = \bigcup a \in A_t(s_t) \text{ AND } \sum_{s'} P^a(s_t s')[R^a(s_t, s') + \gamma U_t(s')]$$

$$\geq \operatorname*{argmax}_{b \in A_t(s_t)} \sum_{s'} P^b(s_t s')[R^b(s_t, s') + \gamma L_t(s')]$$

$$s_{t+1} = \begin{cases} s_0 \text{ if } s^i \text{ is terminal for all } s^i \in s \\ s' \in S \text{ such that } \exists a \in A_{t+1}(s_t), P^a(s_t s') > 0 \text{ otherwise} \end{cases}$$

The algorithm terminates when only one competitive action remains for each state, or when the range of all competitive actions for any state are bounded by an indifference parameter ϵ.

To elaborate, the upper and lower bounds on the value of a composite state are backed up using a form of Equation 1. The set of actions that are considered competitive in that state are culled by eliminating any action whose bounded values is strictly dominated by the bounded value of some other action in $A_t(s_t)$. The next state to be updated is chosen randomly from all the states that have non-zero

---

[1]Recall that unsuperscripted quantities refer to the composite MDP while superscripted quantities refer to component MDPs. Also, A is the set of actions that are available to the composite MDP after taking into account the constraints on picking actions simultaneously for the factor MDPs.

probability of occuring from any action in $A_{t+1}(s_t)$ or, if s_t is the terminal state of all component MDPs, then s_{t+1} is the start state again.

A significant advantage of using these bounds is that we can prune actions whose upper bounds are worse than the best lower bound. Only states resulting from remaining competitive actions are backed up. When only one competitive action remains, the optimal policy for that state is known, regardless of whether its upper and lower bounds have converged.

Another important aspect of our algorithm is that it focuses the backups on states that are reachable on currently competitive actions from the start state. The combined effect of only updating states that are reachable from the start state and further only those that are reachable under currently competitive actions can lead to significant computational savings. This is particularly critical in scheduling, where jobs proceed in a more or less feedforward fashion and the composite start state when a new job comes in can eliminate a large portion of the composite state space. Ideas based on Kaelbling's (1990) interval-estimation algorithm and Moore & Atkeson's (1993) prioritized sweeping algorithm could also be combined into our algorithm.

The algorithm has a number of desirable "anytime" characteristics: if we have to pick an action in state s_0 before the algorithm has converged (while multiple competitive actions remain), we pick the action with the highest lower bound. If a new MDP arrives before the algorithm converges, it can be accommodated dynamically using whatever lower and upper bounds exist at the time it arrives.

2.1 Theoretical Analysis

In this section we analyze various aspects of our algorithm.

UpperBound Calculation: For any composite state, the sum of the optimal values of the component states is an upper bound to the optimal value of the composite state, i.e., $V^*(s = s^1, s^2, \ldots, s^N) \leq \sum_{i=1}^{N} V^{*,i}(s^i)$.

If there were no constraints among the actions of the factor MDPs then $V^*(s)$ would equal $\sum_{i=1}^{N} V^{*,i}(s^i)$ because of the additive payoffs across MDPs. The presence of constraints implies that the sum is an upper bound. Because $V^{*,i}(s^i) \leq U_t(s^i)$ the result follows.

LowerBound Calculation: For any composite state, the maximum of the optimal values of the component states is a lower bound to the optimal value of the composite states, i.e., $V^*(s = s^1, s^2, \ldots, s^N) \geq \max_{i=1}^{N} V^{*,i}(s^i)$.

To see this for an arbitrary composite state s, let the MDP that has the largest component optimal value for state s always choose its component-optimal action first and then assign actions to the other MDPs so as to respect the action constraints encoded in set A. This guarantees at least the value promised by that MDP because the payoffs are all non-negative. Because $V^{*,i}(s^i) \geq L_t(s^i)$ the result follows.

Pruning of Actions: For any composite state, if the upper bound for any composite action, a, is lower than the lower bound for some other composite action, then action a cannot be optimal — action a can then safely be discarded from the max in value iteration. Once discarded from the competitive set, an action never needs to be reconsidered.

Our algorithm maintains the upper and lower bound status of U and L as it updates them. The result follows.

Convergence: Given enough time our algorithm converges to the optimal policy and optimal value function for the set of composite states reachable from the start state under the optimal policy.

If every state were updated infinitely often, value iteration converges to the optimal solution for the composite problem independent of the intial guess V_0. The difference between standard value iteration and our algorithm is that we discard actions and do not update states not on the path from the start state under the continually pruned competitive actions. The actions we discard in a state are guaranteed not to be optimal and therefore cannot have any effect on the value of that state. Also states that are reachable only under discarded actions are automatically irrelevant to performing optimally from the start state.

3   An Example: Avoiding Predators and Eating Food

We illustrate the use of the merging algorithm on a simple avoid-predator-and-eat-food problem, depicted in Figure 1a. The component MDPs are the avoid-predator task and eat-food task; the composite MDP must solve these problems simultaneously. In isolation, the tasks avoid-predator and eat-food are fairly easy to learn. The state space of each task is of size n^4; 625 states in the case illustrated. Using value iteration, the optimal solutions to both component tasks can be learned in approximately 1000 backups. Directly solving the composite problem requires n^6 states (15625 in our case), and requires roughly 1 million backups to converge.

Figure 1b compares the performance of several solutions to the avoid-predator-and-eat-food task. The opt-predator and opt-food curves shows the performance of value iteration on the two component tasks in isolation; both converge quickly to their optima. While it requires no further backups, the greedy algorithm of Section 1.4.1 falls short of optimal performance. Our merging algorithm, when initialized with solutions for the component tasks (5000 backups each) converges quickly to the optimal solution. Value iteration directly on the composite state space also finds the optimal solutions, but requires 4-5 times as many backups. Note that value iteration in composite state space also updated states on trajectories (as in Barto etal.'s, 1995 RTDP algorithm) through the state space just as in our merging algorithm, only without the benefit of the value function bounds and the pruning of non-competitive actions.

4   Conclusion

The ability to perform multiple decision-making tasks simultaneously, and even to incorporate new tasks dynamically into ongoing previous tasks, is of obvious interest to both cognitive science and engineering. Using the framework of MDPs for individual decision-making tasks, we have reformulated the above problem as that of dynamically merging MDPs. We have presented a modified value iteration algorithm for dynamically merging MDPs, proved its convergence, and illustrated its use on a simple merging task.

As future work we intend to apply our merging algorithm to a real-world job-shop scheduling problem, extend the algorithm into the framework of semi-Markov decision processes, and explore the performance of the algorithm in the case where a model of the MDPs is not available.

a)

b)

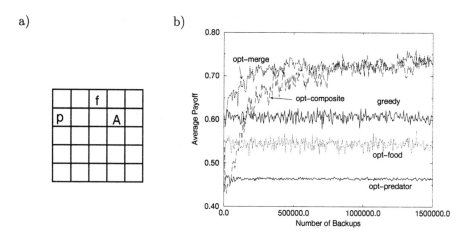

Figure 1: **a)** Our agent (A) roams an n by n grid. It gets a payoff of 0.5 for every time step it avoids predator (P), and earns a payoff of 1.0 for every piece of food (f) it finds. The agent moves two steps for every step P makes, and P always moves directly toward A. When food is found, it reappears at a random location on the next time step. On every time step, A has a 10% chance of ignoring its policy and making a random move. **b)** The mean payoff of different learning strategies vs. number of backups. The bottom two lines show that when trained on either task in isolation, a learner reaches the optimal payoff for that task in fewer than 5000 backups. The greedy approach makes no further backups, but performs well below optimal. The optimal composite solution, trained ab initio, requires requires nearly 1 million backups. Our algorithm begins with the 5000-backup solutions for the individual tasks, and converges to the optimum 4-5 times more quickly than the ab initio solution.

Acknowledgements

Satinder Singh was supported by NSF grant IIS-9711753.

References

Barto, A. G., Bradtke, S. J., & Singh, S. (1995). Learning to act using real-time dynamic programming. *Artificial Intelligence*, *72*, 81–138.

Bertsekas, D. P. (1995). *Dynamic Programming and Optimal Control*. Belmont, MA: Athena Scientific.

Bertsekas, D. P. & Tsitsiklis, J. N. (1996). *Neuro-Dynamic Programming*. Belmont, MA: Athena Scientific.

Kaelbling, L. P. (1990). *Learning in Embedded Systems*. PhD thesis, Stanford University, Department of Computer Science, Stanford, CA. Technical Report TR-90-04.

Moore, A. W. & Atkeson, C. G. (1993). Prioritized sweeping: Reinforcement learning with less data and less real time. *Machine Learning*, *13*(1).

Singh, S. (1997). Reinforcement learning in factorial environments. submitted.

Watkins, C. J. C. H. (1989). *Learning from Delayed Rewards*. PhD thesis, Cambridge Univ., Cambridge, England.

Zhang, W. & Dieterich, T. G. (1995). High-performance job-shop scheduling with a time delay TD(lambda) network. In *NIPSystems 8*. MIT Press.

The Asymptotic Convergence-Rate of Q-learning

Cs. Szepesvári*

Research Group on Artificial Intelligence, "József Attila" University,
Szeged, Aradi vrt. tere 1, Hungary, H-6720
szepes@math.u-szeged.hu

Abstract

In this paper we show that for discounted MDPs with discount factor $\gamma > 1/2$ the asymptotic rate of convergence of Q-learning is $O(1/t^{R(1-\gamma)})$ if $R(1-\gamma) < 1/2$ and $O(\sqrt{\log\log t / t})$ otherwise provided that the state-action pairs are sampled from a fixed probability distribution. Here $R = p_{\min}/p_{\max}$ is the ratio of the minimum and maximum state-action occupation frequencies. The results extend to convergent on-line learning provided that $p_{\min} > 0$, where $p_{\min}$ and $p_{\max}$ now become the minimum and maximum state-action occupation frequencies corresponding to the stationary distribution.

1 INTRODUCTION

Q-learning is a popular reinforcement learning (RL) algorithm whose convergence is well demonstrated in the literature (Jaakkola et al., 1994; Tsitsiklis, 1994; Littman and Szepesvári, 1996; Szepesvári and Littman, 1996). Our aim in this paper is to provide *an upper bound* for the convergence rate of (lookup-table based) Q-learning algorithms. Although, this upper bound is not strict, computer experiments (to be presented elsewhere) and the form of the lemma underlying the proof indicate that the obtained upper bound can be made strict by a slightly more complicated definition for R. Our results extend to learning on aggregated states (see (Singh et al., 1995)) and other related algorithms which admit a certain form of asynchronous stochastic approximation (see (Szepesvári and Littman, 1996)).

---

*Present address: Associative Computing, Inc., Budapest, Konkoly Thege M. u. 29–33, HUNGARY-1121

2   Q-LEARNING

Watkins introduced the following algorithm to estimate the value of state-action pairs in discounted Markovian Decision Processes (MDPs) (Watkins, 1990):

$$Q_{t+1}(x,a) = (1 - \alpha_t(x,a))Q_t(x,a) + \alpha_t(x,a)(r_t(x,a) + \gamma \max_{b \in A} Q_t(y_t,b)). \quad (1)$$

Here $x \in X$ and $a \in A$ are states and actions, respectively, X and A are finite. It is assumed that some random sampling mechanism (e.g. simulation or interaction with a real Markovian environment) generates random samples of form (x_t, a_t, y_t, r_t), where the probability of y_t given (x_t, a_t) is fixed and is denoted by $P(x_t, a_t, y_t)$, $E[r_t \,|\, x_t, a_t] = R(x,a)$ is the immediate average reward which is received when executing action a from state x, y_t and r_t are assumed to be independent given the history of the learning-process, and also it is assumed that $\mathrm{Var}[r_t \,|\, x_t, a_t] < C$ for some $C > 0$. The values $0 \leq \alpha_t(x,a) \leq 1$ are called the learning rate associated with the state-action pair (x, a) at time t. This value is assumed to be zero if $(x,a) \neq (x_t, a_t)$, i.e. only the value of the actual state and action is reestimated in each step. If

$$\sum_{t=1}^{\infty} \alpha_t(x,a) = \infty \quad (2)$$

and

$$\sum_{t=1}^{\infty} \alpha_t^2(x,a) < \infty \quad (3)$$

then Q-learning is guaranteed to converge to the only fixed point Q^* of the operator $T : \Re^{X \times A} \to \Re^{X \times A}$ defined by

$$(TQ)(x,a) = R(x,a) + \gamma \sum_{y \in X} P(x,a,y) \max_b Q(y,b)$$

(convergence proofs can be found in (Jaakkola et al., 1994; Tsitsiklis, 1994; Littman and Szepesvári, 1996; Szepesvári and Littman, 1996)). Once Q^* is identified the learning agent can act optimally in the underlying MDP simply by choosing the action which maximizes $Q^*(x,a)$ when the agent is in state x (Ross, 1970; Puterman, 1994).

3   THE MAIN RESULT

Condition (2) on the learning rate $\alpha_t(x,a)$ requires only that every state-action pair is visited infinitely often, which is a rather mild condition. In this article we take the stronger assumption that $\{(x_t, a_t)\}_t$ is a sequence of independent random variables with common underlying probability distribution. Although this assumption is not essential it simplifies the presentation of the proofs greatly. A relaxation will be discussed later. We further assume that the learning rates take the special form

$$\alpha_t(x,a) = \begin{cases} \frac{1}{S_t(x,a)}, & \text{if } (x,a) = (x_t, a_t); \\ 0, & \text{otherwise,} \end{cases}$$

where $S_t(x,a)$ is the number of times the state-action pair was visited by the process (x_s, a_s) before time step t plus one, i.e. $S_t(x,a) = 1 + \#\{\,(x_s, a_s) = (x,a), 1 \leq s \leq$

t }. This assumption could be relaxed too as it will be discussed later. For technical reasons we further assume that the absolute value of the random reinforcement signals r_t admit a common upper bound. Our main result is the following:

THEOREM 3.1 *Under the above conditions the following relations hold asymptotically and with probability one:*

$$|Q_t(x,a) - Q^*(x,a)| \leq \frac{B}{t^{R(1-\gamma)}} \tag{4}$$

and

$$|Q_t(x,a) - Q^*(x,a)| \leq B\sqrt{\frac{\log\log t}{t}}, \tag{5}$$

for some suitable constant $B > 0$. Here $R = p_{\min}/p_{\max}$, where $p_{\min} = \min_{(x,a)} p(x,a)$ and $p_{\max} = \max_{(x,a)} p(x,a)$, where $p(x,a)$ is the sampling probability of (x,a).

Note that if $\gamma \geq 1 - p_{\max}/2p_{\min}$ then (4) is the slower, while if $\gamma < 1 - p_{\max}/2p_{\min}$ then (5) is the slower. The proof will be presented in several steps.

Step 1. Just like in (Littman and Szepesvári, 1996) (see also the extended version (Szepesvári and Littman, 1996)) the main idea is to compare Q_t with the simpler process

$$\hat{Q}_{t+1}(x,a) = (1 - \alpha_t(x,a))\hat{Q}_t(x,a) + \alpha_t(x,a)(r_t(x,a) + \gamma \max_b Q^*(y_t,b)). \tag{6}$$

Note that the only (but rather essential) difference between the definition of $\hat{Q}_t$ and that of Q_t is the appearance of Q^* in the defining equation of $\hat{Q}_t$. Firstly, notice that as a consequence of this change the process $\hat{Q}_t$ clearly converges to Q^* and this convergence may be investigated along each component (x,a) separately using standard stochastic-approximation techniques (see e.g. (Wasan, 1969; Poljak and Tsypkin, 1973)).

Using simple devices one can show that the difference process $\Delta_t(x,a) = |Q_t(x,a) - \hat{Q}_t(x,a)|$ satisfies the following inequality:

$$\Delta_{t+1}(x,a) \leq (1 - \alpha_t(x,a))\Delta_t(x,a) + \gamma\alpha_t(x,a)(\|\Delta_t\| + \|\hat{Q}_t - Q^*\|). \tag{7}$$

Here $\|\cdot\|$ stands for the maximum norm. That is the task of showing the convergence rate of Q_t to Q^* is reduced to that of showing the convergence rate of Δ_t to zero.

Step 2. We simplify the notation by introducing the abstract process whose update equation is

$$x_{t+1}(i) = \left(1 - \frac{1}{S_t(i)}\right)x_t(i) + \frac{\gamma}{S_t(i)}\left(\|x_t\| + \epsilon_t\right), \tag{8}$$

where $i \in 1, 2, \ldots, n$ can be identified with the state-action pairs, x_t with Δ_t, ϵ_t with $\hat{Q}_t - Q^*$, etc. We analyze this process in two steps. First we consider processes when the "perturbation-term" ϵ_t is missing. For such processes we have the following lemma:

LEMMA 3.2 *Assume that $\eta_1, \eta_2, \ldots, \eta_t, \ldots$ are independent random variables with a common underlying distribution $P(\eta_t = i) = p_i > 0$. Then the process x_t defined* *by*

$$x_{t+1}(i) = \begin{cases} \left(1 - \frac{1}{S_t(i)}\right) x_t(i) + \frac{\gamma}{S_t(i)} \|x_t\|, & \text{if } \eta_t = i; \\ x_t(i), & \text{if } \eta_t \neq i, \end{cases} \qquad (9)$$

satisfies

$$\|x_t\| = O\left(\frac{1}{t^{R(1-\gamma)}}\right)$$

with probability one (w.p.1), where $R = \min_i p_i / \max_i p_i$.

Proof. (Outline) Let $T_0 = 0$ and

$$T_{k+1} = \min\{ t \geq T_k \,|\, \forall i = 1 \dots n, \, \exists s = s(i) : \eta_s = i \},$$

i.e. T_{k+1} is the smallest time after time T_k such that during the time interval $[T_k + 1, T_{k+1}]$ all the components of $x_t(\cdot)$ are "updated" in Equation (9) at least once. Then

$$x_{T_{k+1}+1}(i) \leq \left(1 - \frac{1-\gamma}{S_k}\right) \|x_{T_k+1}\|, \qquad (10)$$

where $S_k = \max_i S_k(i)$. This inequality holds because if $t_k(i)$ is the last time in $[T_k + 1, T_{k+1}]$ when the ith component is updated then

$$\begin{aligned} x_{T_{k+1}+1}(i) &= x_{t_k(i)+1}(i) = (1 - 1/S_{t_k(i)}) x_{t_k(i)}(i) + \gamma/S_{t_k(i)} \|x_{t_k(i)}(\cdot)\| \\ &\leq (1 - 1/S_{t_k(i)}) \|x_{t_k(i)}(\cdot)\| + \gamma/S_{t_k(i)} \|x_{t_k(i)}(\cdot)\| \\ &= \left(1 - \frac{1-\gamma}{S_{t_k(i)}}\right) \|x_{t_k(i)}(\cdot)\| \\ &\leq \left(1 - \frac{1-\gamma}{S_k}\right) \|x_{T_k+1}(\cdot)\|, \end{aligned}$$

where it was exploited that $\|x_t\|$ is decreasing. Now, iterating (10) backwards in time yields

$$x_{T_k+1}(\cdot) \leq \|x_0\| \prod_{j=0}^{k-1} \left(1 - \frac{1-\gamma}{S_j}\right).$$

Now, consider the following approximations: $T_k \approx Ck$, where $C \geq 1/p_{\min}$ (C can be computed explicitly from $\{p_i\}$), $S_k \approx p_{\max} T_{k+1} \approx p_{\max}/p_{\min}(k+1) \approx (k+1)/R_0$, where $R_0 = 1/C p_{\max}$. Then, using Large Deviation's Theory,

$$\prod_{j=0}^{k-1} \left(1 - \frac{1-\gamma}{S_j}\right) \approx \prod_{j=0}^{k-1} \left(1 - \frac{R_0(1-\gamma)}{j+1}\right) \approx \left(\frac{1}{k}\right)^{R_0(1-\gamma)} \qquad (11)$$

holds w.p.1. Now, by defining $s = T_k + 1$ so that $s/C \approx k$ we get

$$\|x_s\| = \|x_{T_k+1}\| \leq \|x_0\| \left(\frac{1}{k}\right)^{R_0(1-\gamma)} \approx \|x_0\| \left(\frac{C}{s}\right)^{R_0(1-\gamma)} \leq \|x_0\| \left(\frac{C}{s}\right)^{R(1-\gamma)},$$

which holds due to the monotonicity of x_t and $1/k^{R_0(1-\gamma)}$ and because $R = p_{\min}/p_{\max} \leq R_0$. $\qquad \square$

Step 3. Assume that $\gamma > 1/2$. Fortunately, we know by an extension of the Law of the Iterated Logarithm to stochastic approximation processes that the convergence

rate of $\|\hat{Q}_t - Q^*\|$ is $O\left(\sqrt{\log \log t / t}\right)$ (the uniform boundedness of the random rein-
forcement signals must be exploited in this step) (Major, 1973). Thus it is sufficient
to provide a convergence rate estimate for the perturbed process, x_t, defined by (8),
when $\epsilon_t = C\sqrt{\log \log t / t}$ for some $C > 0$. We state that the convergence rate of ϵ_t
is faster than that of x_t. Define the process

$$z_{t+1}(i) = \begin{cases} \left(1 - \frac{1-\gamma}{S_t(i)}\right) z_t(i), & \text{if } \eta_t = i; \\ z_t(i), & \text{if } \eta_t \neq i. \end{cases} \tag{12}$$

This process clearly lower bounds the perturbed process, x_t. Obviously, the convergence rate of z_t is $O(1/t^{1-\gamma})$ which is slower than the convergence rate of ϵ_t
provided that $\gamma > 1/2$, proving that ϵ_t must be faster than x_t. Thus, asymptoti-
cally $\epsilon_t \leq (1/\gamma - 1)x_t$, and so $\|x_t\|$ is decreasing for large enough t. Then, by an
argument similar to that of used in the derivation of (10), we get

$$x_{T_{k+1}+1}(i) \leq \left(1 - \frac{1-\gamma}{S_k}\right)\|x_{T_k+1}\| + \frac{\gamma}{s_k}\epsilon_{T_k}, \tag{13}$$

where $s_k = \min_i S_k(i)$. By some approximation arguments similar to that of Step 2,
together with the bound $(1/n^\eta)\sum_s^n s^{\eta-3/2}\sqrt{\log \log s} \leq s^{-1/2}\sqrt{\log \log s}$, $1 > \eta > 0$,
which follows from the mean-value theorem for integrals and the law of integration
by parts, we get that $x_t \approx O(1/t^{R(1-\gamma)})$. The case when $\gamma \leq 1/2$ can be treated
similarly.

Step 5. Putting the pieces together and applying them for $\Delta_t = \hat{Q}_t - Q_t$ yields
Theorem 3.1.

4   DISCUSSION AND CONCLUSIONS

The most restrictive of our conditions is the assumption concerning the sampling
of (x_t, a_t). However, note that under a fixed learning policy the process (x_t, a_t)
is a (non-stationary) Markovian process and if the learning policy converges in
the sense that $\lim_{t\to\infty} P(a_t \mid \mathcal{F}_t) = P(a_t \mid x_t)$ (here $\mathcal{F}_t$ stands for the history of the
learning process) then the process (x_t, a_t) becomes eventually stationary Markovian
and the sampling distribution could be replaced by the stationary distribution of
the underlying stationary Markovian process. If actions become asymptotically
optimal during the course of learning then the support of this stationary process
will exclude the state-action pairs whose action is sub-optimal, i.e. the conditions
of Theorem 3.1 will no longer be satisfied. Notice that the proof of convergence of
such processes still follows very similar lines to that of the proof presented here (see
the forthcoming paper (Singh et al., 1997)), so we expect that the same convergence
rates hold and can be proved using nearly identical techniques in this case as well.

A further step would be to find explicit expressions for the constant B of Theorem 3.1. Clearly, B depends heavily on the sampling of (x_t, a_t), as well as the
transition probabilities and rewards of the underlying MDP. Also the choice of harmonic learning rates is arbitrary. If a general sequence α_t were employed then the
artificial "time" $T_t(x, a) = 1/\Pi_{j=0}^t (1 - \alpha_t(x, a))$ should be used (note that for the
harmonic sequence $T_t(x, a) \approx t$). Note that although the developed bounds are
asymptotic in their present forms, the proper usage of Large Deviation's Theory
would enable us to develope non-asymptotic bounds.

Other possible ways to extend the results of this paper may include Q-learning when learning on aggregated states (Singh et al., 1995), Q-learning for alternating/simultaneous Markov games (Littman, 1994; Szepesvári and Littman, 1996) and any other algorithms whose corresponding difference process Δ_t satisfies an inequality similar to (7).

Yet another application of the convergence-rate estimate might be the convergence proof of some average reward reinforcement learning algorithms. The idea of those algorithms follows from a kind of Tauberian theorem, i.e. that discounted sums converge to the average value if the discount rate converges to one (see e.g. Lemma 1 of (Mahadevan, 1994; Mahadevan, 1996) or for a value-iteration scheme relying on this idea (Hordjik and Tijms, 1975)). Using the methods developed here the proof of convergence of the corresponding Q-learning algorithms seems quite possible. We would like to note here that related results were obtained by Bertsekas et al. et. al (see e.g. (Bertsekas and Tsitsiklis, 1996)).

Finally, note that as an application of this result we immediately get that the convergence rate of the model-based RL algorithm, where the transition probabilities and rewards are estimated by their respective averages, is clearly better than that of for Q-learning. Indeed, simple calculations show that the law of iterated logarithm holds for the learning process underlying model-based RL. Moreover, the exact expression for the convergence rate depends explicitly on how much computational effort we spend on obtaining the next estimate of the optimal value function, the more effort we spend the faster is the convergence. This bound thus provides a direct way to control the tradeoff between the computational effort and the convergence rate.

Acknowledgements

This research was supported by OTKA Grant No. F20132 and by a grant provided by the Hungarian Educational Ministry under contract no. FKFP 1354/1997. I would like to thank András Krámli and Michael L. Littman for numerous helpful and thought-provoking discussions.

References

Bertsekas, D. and Tsitsiklis, J. (1996). *Neuro-Dynamic Programming*. Athena Scientific, Belmont, MA.

Hordjik, A. and Tijms, H. (1975). A modified form of the iterative method of dynamic programming. *Annals of Statistics*, 3:203–208.

Jaakkola, T., Jordan, M., and Singh, S. (1994). On the convergence of stochastic iterative dynamic programming algorithms. *Neural Computation*, 6(6):1185–1201.

Littman, M. (1994). Markov games as a framework for multi-agent reinforcement learning. In *Proc. of the Eleventh International Conference on Machine Learning*, pages 157–163, San Francisco, CA. Morgan Kauffman.

Littman, M. and Szepesvári, C. (1996). A Generalized Reinforcement Learning Model: Convergence and applications. In *Int. Conf. on Machine Learning*. http://iserv.iki.kfki.hu/asl-publs.html.

Mahadevan, S. (1994). To discount or not to discount in reinforcement learning: A case study comparing R learning and Q learning. In *Proceedings of the Eleventh International Conference on Machine Learning*, pages 164–172, San Francisco, CA. Morgan Kaufmann.

Mahadevan, S. (1996). Average reward reinforcement learning: Foundations, algorithms, and empirical results. *Machine Learning*, 22(1,2,3):124–158.

Major, P. (1973). A law of the iterated logarithm for the Robbins-Monro method. *Studia Scientiarum Mathematicarum Hungarica*, 8:95–102.

Poljak, B. and Tsypkin, Y. (1973). Pseudogradient adaption and training algorithms. *Automation and Remote Control*, 12:83–94.

Puterman, M. L. (1994). *Markov Decision Processes — Discrete Stochastic Dynamic Programming*. John Wiley & Sons, Inc., New York, NY.

Ross, S. (1970). *Applied Probability Models with Optimization Applications*. Holden Day, San Francisco, California.

Singh, S., Jaakkola, T., and Jordan, M. (1995). Reinforcement learning with soft state aggregation. In *Proceedings of Neural Information Processing Systems*.

Singh, S., Jaakkola, T., Littman, M., and Csaba Szepesvá ri (1997). On the convergence of single-step on-policy reinforcement-learning al gorithms. *Machine Learning*. in preparation.

Szepesvári, C. and Littman, M. (1996). Generalized Markov Decision Processes: Dynamic programming and reinforcement learning algorithms. *Machine Learning*. in preparation, available as TR CS96-10, Brown Univ.

Tsitsiklis, J. (1994). Asynchronous stochastic approximation and q-learning. *Machine Learning*, 8(3–4):257–277.

Wasan, T. (1969). *Stochastic Approximation*. Cambridge University Press, London.

Watkins, C. (1990). *Learning from Delayed Rewards*. PhD thesis, King's College, Cambridge. QLEARNING.

Hybrid reinforcement learning and its application to biped robot control

Satoshi Yamada, Akira Watanabe, Michio Nakashima
{yamada, watanabe, naka}@bio.crl.melco.co.jp
Advanced Technology R&D Center
Mitsubishi Electric Corporation
Amagasaki, Hyogo 661-0001, Japan

Abstract

A learning system composed of linear control modules, reinforcement learning modules and selection modules (a hybrid reinforcement learning system) is proposed for the fast learning of real-world control problems. The selection modules choose one appropriate control module dependent on the state. This hybrid learning system was applied to the control of a stilt-type biped robot. It learned the control on a sloped floor more quickly than the usual reinforcement learning because it did not need to learn the control on a flat floor, where the linear control module can control the robot. When it was trained by a 2-step learning (during the first learning step, the selection module was trained by a training procedure controlled only by the linear controller), it learned the control more quickly. The average number of trials (about 50) is so small that the learning system is applicable to real robot control.

1 Introduction

Reinforcement learning has the ability to solve general control problems because it learns behavior through trial-and-error interactions with a dynamic environment. It has been applied to many problems, *e.g.*, pole-balance [1], back-gammon [2], manipulator [3], and biped robot [4]. However, reinforcement learning has rarely been applied to real robot control because it requires too many trials to learn the control even for simple problems.

For the fast learning of real-world control problems, we propose a new learning system which is a combination of a known controller and reinforcement learning. It is called the hybrid reinforcement learning system. One example of a known controller is a linear controller obtained by linear approximation. The hybrid learning system will learn the control more quickly than usual reinforcement learning because it does not need to learn the control in the state where the known controller can control the object.

A stilt-type biped walking robot was used to test the hybrid reinforcement learning system. A real robot walked stably on a flat floor when controlled by a linear controller [5]. Robot motions could be approximated by linear differential equations. In this study, we will describe hybrid reinforcement learning of the control of the biped robot model on a sloped floor, where the linear controller cannot control the robot.

2   Biped Robot

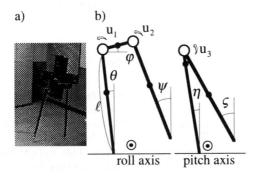

Figure 1: Stilt-type biped robot. **a)** a photograph of a real biped robot, **b)** a model structure of the biped robot. u_1, u_2, u_3 denote torques.

Figure 1-a shows a stilt-type biped robot [5]. It has no knee or ankle, has 1 m legs and weighs 33 kg. It is modeled by 3 rigid bodies as shown in Figure 1-b. By assuming that motions around a roll axis and those around a pitch axis are independent, 5-dimensional differential equations in a single supporting phase were obtained. Motions of the real biped robot were simulated by the combination of these equations and conditions at a leg exchange period. If angles are approximately zero, these equations can be approximated by linear equations. The following linear controller is obtained from the linear equations. The biped robot will walk if the angles of the free leg are controlled by a position-derivative (PD) controller whose desired angles are calculated as follows:

$$
\begin{aligned}
\bar{\varphi} &= \theta + \xi + \beta \\
\bar{\psi} &= \theta + 2\xi \\
\bar{\zeta} &= -A\dot{\eta} + \delta \\
A &= \sqrt{\frac{l}{g}},
\end{aligned}
\tag{1}
$$

where ξ, β, δ, and g are a desired angle between the body and the leg $(7°)$, a constant to make up a loss caused by a leg exchange $(1.3°)$, a constant corresponding to walking speed, and gravitational acceleration (9.8 ms^{-2}), respectively.

The linear controller controlled walking of the real biped robot on a flat floor [5]. However, it failed to control walking on a slope (Figure 2). In this study, the objective of the learning system was to control walking on the sloped floor shown in Figure 2-a.

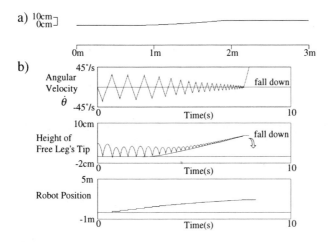

Figure 2: Biped robot motion on a sloped floor controlled by the linear controller. **a)** a shape of a floor, **b)** changes in angular velocity, height of free leg's tip, and robot position

3 Hybrid Reinforcement Learning

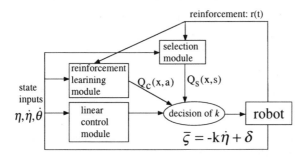

Figure 3: Hybrid reinforcement learning system.

We propose a hybrid reinforcement learning system to learn control quickly. The hybrid reinforcement learning system shown in Figure 3 is composed of a linear control module, a reinforcement learning module, and a selection module. The reinforcement learning module and the selection module select an action and a module dependent on their respective Q-values. This learning system is similar to the modular reinforcement learning system proposed by Tham [6] which was based on hierarchical mixtures of the experts (HME) [7]. In the hybrid learning system, the selection module is trained by Q-learning.

To combine the reinforcement learning with the linear controller described in (1), the output of the reinforcement learning module is set to k in the adaptable equation for $\bar{\zeta}$, $\bar{\zeta} = -k\dot{\eta} + \delta$. The angle and the angular velocity of the supporting leg at the leg exchange period $(\eta, \dot{\eta}, \dot{\theta})$ are used as inputs. The k values are kept constant until the next leg exchange. The reinforcement learning module is trained by "Q-sarsa" learning [8]. Q values are calculated by CMAC neural networks [9], [10].

The Q values for action k $(Q_c(x, k))$ and those for module s selection $(Q_s(x, s))$ are calculated as follows:

$$Q_c(x, k) = \sum_{m,i} w_c(k, m, i, t) y(m, i, t)$$

$$Q_s(x, s) = \sum_{m,i} w_s(s, m, i, t) y(m, i, t), \tag{2}$$

where $w_c(k, m, i, t)$ and $w_s(s, m, i, t)$ denote synaptic strengths and $y(m, i, t)$ represents neurons' outputs in CMAC networks at time t.

Modules were selected and actions performed according to the ε-greedy policy [8] with $\varepsilon = 0$.

The temporal difference (TD) error for the reinforcement learning module $(\hat{r}_c(t))$ is calculated by

$$\hat{r}_c(t) = \begin{cases} 0 & sel(t) = lin \\ r(t) + Q_c(x(t+1), per(t+1)) - Q_c(x(t), per(t)) & \begin{matrix} sel(t) = rein \\ sel(t+1) = rein \end{matrix} \\ r(t) + Q_s(x(t+1), sel(t+1)) - Q_c(x(t), per(t)), & \begin{matrix} sel(t) = rein \\ sel(t+1) = lin \end{matrix} \end{cases}$$
$$\tag{3}$$

where $r(t)$, $per(t)$, $sel(t)$, lin and $rein$ denote reinforcement signals ($r(t) = -1$ if the robot falls down, 0 otherwise), performed actions, selected modules, the linear control module and the reinforcement learning module, respectively.

TD error $(\hat{r}_t(t))$ calculated by $Q_s(x, s)$ is considered to be a sum of TD error caused by the reinforcement learning module and that by the selection module. TD error $(\hat{r}_s(t))$ used in the selection-module's learning is calculated as follows:

$$\hat{r}_s(t) = \hat{r}_t(t) - \hat{r}_c(t)$$
$$= r(t) + \gamma Q_s(x(t+1), sel(t+1)) - Q_s(x(t), sel(t)) - \hat{r}_c(t), \tag{4}$$

where γ denotes a discount factor.

The reinforcement learning module used replacing eligibility traces $(e_c(k, m, i, t))$ [11]. Synaptic strengths are updated as follows:

$$w_c(k, m, i, t+1) = w_c(k, m, i, t) + \alpha_c \hat{r}_c(t) e_c(k, m, i, t)/n_t$$

$$w_s(s, m, i, t+1) = \begin{cases} w_s(s, m, i, t) + \alpha_s \hat{r}_s(t) y(m, i, t)/n_t & s = sel(t) \\ w_s(s, m, i, t) & \text{otherwise} \end{cases}$$

$$e_c(k, m, i, t) = \begin{cases} 1 & k = per(t), y(m, i, t) = 1 \\ 0 & k \neq per(t), y(m, i, t) = 1 \\ \lambda e_c(k, m, i, t-1) & \text{otherwise} \end{cases} \tag{5}$$

where α_c, α_s, λ and n_t are a learning constant for the reinforcement learning module, that for the selection module, decay rates and the number of tilings, respectively.

In this study, the CMAC used 10 tilings. Each of the three dimensions was divided into 12 intervals. The reinforcement learning module had 5 actions ($k = 0, A/2, A, 3A/2, 2A$). The parameter values were $\alpha_s = 0.2$, $\alpha_c = 0.4$, $\lambda = 0.3$, $\gamma = 0.9$ and $\delta = 0.05$. Each run consisted of a sequence of trials, where each trial began with robot state of position=0, $-5° < \theta < -2.5°, 1.5° < \eta < 3°, \varphi = \theta + \xi, \psi = \varphi + \xi, \zeta = \eta + 2°, \dot{\theta} = \dot{\varphi} = \dot{\psi} = \dot{\eta} = \dot{\zeta} = 0$, and ended with a failure signals indicating robot's falling down. Runs were terminated if the number of walking steps of three consecutive trials exceeded 100. All results reported are an average of 50 runs.

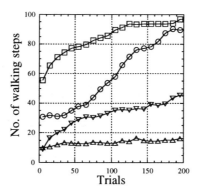

Figure 4: Learning profiles for control of walking on the sloped floor. (○) hybrid reinforcement learning, (□) 2-step hybrid reinforcement learning, (▽) reinforcement learning and (△) HME-type modular reinforcement learning

4 Results

Walking control on the sloped floor (Figure 2-a) was first trained by the usual reinforcement learning. The usual reinforcement learning system needed many trials for successful termination (about 800, see Figure 4(▽)). Because the usual reinforcement learning system must learn the control for each input, it requires many trials.

Figure 4(○) also shows the learning curve for the hybrid reinforcement learning. The hybrid system learned the control more quickly than the usual reinforcement learning (about 190 trials). Because it has a higher probability of succeeding on the flat floor, it learned the control quickly. On the other hand, HME-type modular reinforcement learning [6] required many trials to learn the control (Figure 4(△)).

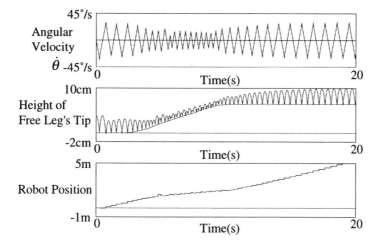

Figure 5: Biped robot motion controlled by the network trained by the 2-step hybrid reinforcement learning.

In order to improve the learning rate, a 2-step learning was examined. The 2-step learning is proposed to separate the selection-module learning from the reinforcement-learning-module learning. In the 2-step hybrid reinforcement learning, the selection module was first trained by a special training procedure in which the robot was controlled only by the linear control module. And then the network was trained by the hybrid reinforcement learning. The 2-step hybrid reinforcement learning learned the control more quickly than the 1-step hybrid reinforcement learning (Figure 4($\Box$)). The average number of trials were about 50. The hybrid learning system may be applicable to the real biped robot.

Figure 5 shows the biped robot motion controlled by the trained network. On the slope, the free leg's lifting was magnified irregularly (see changes in the height of the free leg's tip of Figure 5) in order to prevent the reduction of an amplitude of walking rhythm. On the upper flat floor, the robot was again controlled stably by the linear control module.

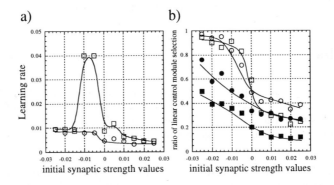

Figure 6: Dependence of (a) the learning rate and (b) the selection ratio of the linear control module on the initial synaptic strength values ($w_s(rein, m, i, 0)$). (a) learning rate of ($\bigcirc$) the hybrid reinforcement learning, and ($\Box$) the 2-step hybrid reinforcement learning. The learning rate is defined as the inverse of the number of trials where the average walking steps exceed 70. (b) the ratio of the linear-control-module selection. Circles represent the selection ratio of the linear control module when controlled by the network trained by the hybrid reinforcement learning, rectangles represent that by the 2-step hybrid reinforcement learning. Open symbols represent the selection ratio on the flat floor, closed symbols represent that on the slope.

The dependence of learning characteristics on initial synaptic strengths for the reinforcement-learning-module selection ($w_s(rein, m, i, 0)$) was considered (other initial synaptic strengths were 0). If initial values of $w_s(rein, m, i, t)$ ($w_s(rein, m, i, 0)$) are negative, the Q-values for the reinforcement-learning-module selection ($Q_s(x, rein)$) are smaller than $Q_s(x, lin)$ and then the linear control module is selected for all states at the beginning of the learning. In the case of the 2-step learning, if $w_s(rein, m, i, 0)$ are given appropriate negative values, the reinforcement learning module is selected only around failure states, where $Q_s(x, lin)$ is trained in the first learning step, and the linear control module is selected otherwise at the beginning of the second learning step. Because the reinforcement learning module only requires training around failure states in the above condition, the 2-

step hybrid system is expected to learn the control quickly. Figure 6-a shows the dependence of the learning rate on the initial synaptic strength values. The 2-step hybrid reinforcement learning had a higher learning rate when $w_s(rein, m, i, 0)$ were appropriate negative values (-0.01 ∼ -0.005). The trained system selected the linear control module on the flat floor (more than 80%), and selected both modules on the slope (see Figure 6-b), when $w_s(rein, m, i, 0)$ were negative.

Three trials were required in the first learning step of the 2-step hybrid reinforcement learning. In order to learn the Q-value function around failure states, the learning system requires 3 trials.

5 Conclusion

We proposed the hybrid reinforcement learning which learned the biped robot control quickly. The number of trials for successful termination in the 2-step hybrid reinforcement learning was so small that the hybrid system is applicable to the real biped robot. Although the control of real biped robot was not learned in this study, it is expected to be learned quickly by the 2-step hybrid reinforcement learning. The learning system for real robot control will be easily constructed and should be trained quickly by the hybrid reinforcement learning system.

References

[1] Barto, A. G., Sutton, R. S. and Anderson, C. W.: Neuron like adaptive elements that can solve difficult learning control problems, *IEEE Trans. Sys. Man Cybern.*, Vol. SMC-13, pp. 834–846 (1983).

[2] Tesauro, G.: TD-gammon, a self-teaching backgammon program, achieves master-level play, *Neural Computation*, Vol. 6, pp. 215–219 (1994).

[3] Gullapalli, V., Franklin, J. A. and Benbrahim, H.: Acquiring robot skills via reinforcement learning, *IEEE Control System*, Vol. 14, No. 1, pp. 13–24 (1994).

[4] Miller, W. T.: Real-time neural network control of a biped walking robot, *IEEE Control Systems*, Vol. 14, pp. 41–48 (1994).

[5] Watanabe, A., Inoue, M. and Yamada, S.: Development of a stilts type biped robot stabilized by inertial sensors (in Japanese), in *Proceedings of 14th Annual Conference of RSJ*, pp. 195–196 (1996).

[6] Tham, C. K.: Reinforcement learning of multiple tasks using a hierarchical CMAC architecture, *Robotics and Autonomous Systems*, Vol. 15, pp. 247–274 (1995).

[7] Jordan, M. I. and Jacobs, R. A.: Hierarchical mixtures of experts and the EM algorithm, *Neural Computation*, Vol. 6, pp. 181–214 (1994).

[8] Sutton, R. S.: Generalization in reinforcement learning: successful examples using sparse coarse coding, *Advances in NIPS*, Vol. 8, pp. 1038–1044 (1996).

[9] Albus, J. S.: A new approach to manipulator control: The cerebellar model articulation controller (CMAC), *Transaction on ASME J. Dynamical Systems, Measurement, and Controls*, pp. 220–227 (1975).

[10] Albus, J. S.: Data storage in the cerebellar articulation controller (CMAC), *Transaction on ASME J. Dynamical Systems, Measurement, and Controls*, pp. 228–233 (1975).

[11] Singh, S. P. and Sutton, R. S.: Reinforcement learning with replacing eligibility traces, *Machine Learning*, Vol. 22, pp. 123–158 (1996).

Index of Authors

Keyword Index

weight space structure, 378
weighted regression, 633
winner-take-all, 215
Winnow, 500
word/non-word recognition, 94